Zimbabwe, Botswana & Namibia

a Lonely Planet travel survival kit

Deanna Swaney

Zimbabwe, Botswana & Namibia

2nd edition

Published by
   Lonely Planet Publications
   Head Office: PO Box 617, Hawthorn, Vic 3122, Australia
   Branches: 155 Filbert St, Suite 251, Oakland, CA 94607, USA
                  10 Barley Mow Passage, Chiswick, London W4 4PH, UK
                  7 bis rue du Cardinal Lemoine, 75005 Paris, France

Printed by
   Colorcraft Ltd, Hong Kong

Photographs by
   Chris Barton   Peter Pschelinzew   David Wall
   Geoff Crowther   Mike Scott   Tony Wheeler
   Hugh Finlay   Deanna Swaney

   Front cover: Mekoro in the Okavango Delta, Botswana (Deanna Swaney)

First Published
   February 1992

This Edition
   November 1995

Although the authors and publisher have tried to make the information as accurate as possible, they accept no responsibility for any loss, injury or inconvenience sustained by any person using this book.

National Library of Australia Cataloguing in Publication Data

Swaney, Deanna.
   Zimbabwe, Botswana & Namibia.

   2nd ed.
   Includes index.
   ISBN 0 86442 313 6.

   1. Zimbabwe – Guidebooks. 2. Botswana – Guidebooks.
   3. Namibia – Guidebooks. I. Title. (Series: Lonely Planet travel survival kit).

916.8

text & maps © Lonely Planet 1995
photos © photographers as indicated 1995
climate charts compiled from information supplied by Patrick J Tyson, © Patrick J Tyson, 1995

Deanna Swaney

After completing university studies, Deanna Swaney made a shoestring tour of Europe and has been addicted to travel ever since. Despite an erstwhile career in computer programming, she managed intermittent forays away from encroaching yuppiedom in midtown Anchorage, Alaska, and at first opportunity, made a break for South America where she wrote Lonely Planet's *Bolivia – a travel survival kit*. Subsequent travels led through an erratic circuit of island paradises – Arctic and tropical – and resulted in three more travel survival kits: *Tonga*, *Samoa* and *Iceland, Greenland & the Faroe Islands*.

She returned to dry land for the first edition of this book and has since co-authored the second editions of the *Brazil* and *Mauritius, Réunion & Seychelles* travel survival kits, updated the second edition of *Madagascar & Comoros* and contributed to Shoestring guides to Africa, South America and Scandinavia.

Deanna now divides her time between travelling and her lakeside base in the English West Country.

From the Author

I'd especially like to thank Annemarie Grant of Bulawayo for her boundless hospitality and for providing me with a place to call home in Africa. Ernst & Norbert Schürer served as excellent companions for a fabulous circuit through Botswana and I also enjoyed the company of Jennifer, Bob, Claus and other punters on various stages of my recent update trip.

For his help and expertise in Namibia, thanks goes out to Aulden Harlech-Jones, who shared his limitless expertise on the Windhoek area. I'd also like to thank Ian Rodger & Petra Bosse, for making possible a wonderful time in the Naukluft and the Kaokoveld; and Marie Holstensen & Grant Burton, who shared the magic of Mudumu at Lianshulu Lodge in the Caprivi. Also helpful and hospitable were Marie & Brian Harlech-Jones of Windhoek. I'm especially grateful to Marisa Mowszowski of Melbourne, Australia, Paul Novitski of Dandemutande in

Seattle, and Norbert Schürer at Duke University, who contributed their expertise to the Zimbabwe music section. Virginia Luling of Survival International in the UK provided valuable information on the San and the Himba. Thanks also to David Else, UK, who provided useful information on Namibia, and George Monbiot, UK, for help with direction regarding conservation issues.

In Zimbabwe, I must also thank Arnold, Russ & Kirsten at Backpackers' Con-X-Shon, Rob Waters, Sue & Iain Jarvis, Lollie & Theo Nel, Lynn & Roslyn Rogers, Val Bell, Peter McIntyre, Bruce & Iris Brinson, Sandy Ramsey and Rudie & Kathie Van den Berg. Also, special love and thanks are in order for Hans and Val Van der Heiden, Mike & Anna Scott and Russell & Colleen Pumfrey. For their help and hospitality in Botswana, thanks also to Alec Campbell, Linda Halkon, Sue & Dave Adey, Nigel Ashby & Hanne Schoemann and Jan & Aileen Drotsky. Thanks also to Ms Gerda Senior for her considerable assistance in Windhoek.

Several readers wrote particularly helpful letters, some of which were extracted for use in the text. An especially entertaining one came in the form of a Low Life Guide to Zimbabwe from Andy Bollen of Australia, who must have had one amazing trip. I also appreciate the efforts of Joost Butenop & Astrid Pohl of Germany (yes, I remember you from Kazungula) for long and particularly useful letters on all three countries. Other useful information came from Stephen Millward, UK; Helen Crossan, Ireland; Philippa Woodward, UK; Mrs W Selles, Netherlands; Andrew Bryceson, UK; Catherine Webster, UK; Jordan Pollinger, USA; Marc van Doornewaard, Netherlands; Brad Posthumas, Netherlands; Luc Selleslagh, Belgium; Susan Loucks, USA; Andrew Phillips, UK; Shane Stoneman, New Zealand; Dan Bagatell, USA; Rachel, USA; Ann Shuttleworth, Australia; Rainer Feil, Germany; Sharon Freed, Australia and Wayne Lidlehoover, USA.

Finally, for their continuing tolerance and support, the best of my love and wishes go to Robert Strauss of Kyre Park, Earl Swaney of Fresno, and Dave Dault and Keith & Holly Hawkings back home in Anchorage.

This Book

The first edition of *Zimbabwe, Botswana & Namibia* was written by Deanna Swaney and Myra Shackley (Namibia). This second edition was updated and expanded by Deanna Swaney.

From the Publisher

This second edition of *Zimbabwe, Botswana & Namibia* was edited and proofed by Susan Noonan with assistance from Frith Pike, Rachel Scully and Kristin Odijk. Further proofing was done by Megan Fraser. Mapping and design were done by Indra Kilfoyle with mapping assistance from Andrew Smith, Chris Love, Greg Herriman and Sally Jacka. The illustrations were drawn by Indra Kilfoyle and Margaret Jung. Colour wraps were prepared by Greg Herriman. Simon Bracken designed the cover with assistance from Adam McCrow.

The Afrikaans language section was adapted from the language section in *South Africa, Lesotho & Swaziland* by Richard Everist and Jon Murray.

The Safari Guide was originally written by Hugh Finlay and Geoff Crowther; additional material was provided by Deanna Swaney and Myra Shackley. The Safari Guide was edited by David Meagher, proofed by Diana Saad and designed by Vicki Beale and Greg Herriman. Special thanks to Matt King for the Safari Guide illustrations. Thanks also to Sharon Wertheim for compiling the index and to Frith Pike, Sam Carew and Diana Saad for ongoing editorial support.

Finally, particular thanks to Books for Cooks, London, for all their assistance in locating African cookery books.

Thanks

Last but not least, a special thanks to those readers who found the time and energy to write to us from all over the world with suggestions and comments. Their names appear at the end of the book.

Warning & Request

Things change – prices go up, schedules change, good places go bad and bad places go bankrupt – nothing stays the same. So, if you find things better or worse, recently opened or long since closed, please write and tell us and help make the next edition better.

Your letters will be used to help update future editions and, where possible, important changes will also be included in a Stop Press section in reprints.

We greatly appreciate all information that is sent to us by travellers. Back at Lonely Planet we employ a hard-working readers' letters team to sort through the many letters we receive. The best ones will be rewarded with a free copy of the next edition or another Lonely Planet guide if you prefer. We give away lots of books, but, unfortunately, not every letter/postcard receives one.

Contents

NAMIBIA

Map Legend

BOUNDARIES

············· International Boundary
············· Regional Boundary

ROUTES

································· Freeway
································· Highway
································· Major Road
··········· Unsealed Road or Track
············· Four Wheel Drive Track
································· City Road
································· City Street
································· Railway
································· Bridge
················· Walking Track
················· Walking Tour
······················· Ferry Route
··········· Fence with Gate

AREA FEATURES

························· Park, Gardens
························· Built-Up Area
························· Pedestrian Mall
························· Market
························· Cemetery
························· Reef
··········· Beach, Desert or Dunes
························· Mountain Ranges

HYDROGRAPHIC FEATURES

························· Coastline
························· River, Creek
··········· Intermittent River or Creek
························· River Flow
··········· Lake, Intermittent Lake
························· Pan
························· Swamp

SYMBOLS

✪ CAPITAL ························· National Capital
◉ Capital ························· Regional Capital
⬤ CITY ························· Major City
● City ························· City
● Town ························· Town
● Village ························· Village
■ ························· Place to Stay
▼ ························· Place to Eat
························· Pub or Bar, Cafe
························· Post Office, Telephone
··········· Tourist Information, Bank
··········· Transport, Parking
··········· Museum, Youth Hostel
······ Caravan Park, Campground
························· Church, Cathedral
················· Mosque, Synagogue
Buddhist Temple, Hindu Temple

✚ ★ ················· Hospital, Police Station
✈ ✝ ················· Airport, Airfield
▬ ✿ ··········· Swimming Pool, Gardens
◆ 🐘 ··········· Shopping Centre, Zoo
⊗ ⚑ ··········· Embassy, Golf Course
← A25 One Way Street, Route Number
∴ ······ Archaeological Site or Ruins
🏛 ⚱ ············· Stately Home, Monument
⛽ ◙ ············· Petrol Station, Tomb
⌒ ⌂ ··········· Cave, Hut or Shelter
▲ ✳ ············· Mountain or Hill, Lookout
🔦 ⚓ ········· Lighthouse, Shipwreck
)(◎ ·········· Pass, Spring or Waterhole
························· Ancient or City Wall
··········· Rapids, Waterfalls
······ Cliff or Escarpment, Tunnel
························· Railway Station

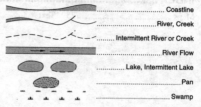

Note: not all symbols displayed above appear in this book

Introduction

Forming an east-west band across southern Africa, Zimbabwe, Botswana and Namibia are three distinctly different countries, each with its own unique topography, government and people. Many of today's visitors will have first known them as Rhodesia, Bechuanaland and South West Africa, but over the past three decades, all three have emerged as independent nations and in shedding their colonial governments, have also assumed new identities.

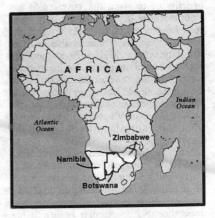

Zimbabwe is the most populated and perhaps best known of the three. The name is still associated with the violent war and subsequent uprisings that resulted in its break from the racially unethical Rhodesian regime and the establishment of majority government. Nevertheless, it has now been independent for over 15 years and has enjoyed a stable peace for nearly as long.

While it's not without problems, Zimbabwe is a beautiful and relatively safe country that caters to all budgets from shoestring to Sheraton. What's more, the Zimbabweans are generally a friendly and easy-going lot. They have accomplished wonders with their world-famous music, sculpture and traditional crafts. Their bright cities of Harare and Bulawayo, which boast a variety of museums, parks, markets, restaurants and nightclubs, provide well-organised urban breaks from the uncertainties of African travel.

In the hinterlands, one encounters a wealth of natural and cultural attractions. The greatest crowd puller is of course Victoria Falls, but Zimbabwe enjoys other equally appealing – but distinctly pristine and not overly touristed – destinations which include some of Africa's finest wildlife reserves, packed with the diverse creatures that represent the essence of the continent to much of the world. Then there are the lovely Eastern Highlands – more like Canada or England than anything you'd expect to find in Africa – and the ruins of Great Zimbabwe, sub-Saharan Africa's greatest ancient capital. In the south are the extraordinary hoodoo rocks and painted caves of Matobo National Park and beneath them, an encouragingly healthy population of black and white rhinos.

To the west of Zimbabwe is Botswana, truly an African success story. A long-neglected British protectorate, Botswana achieved its timely independence under democratic rule in 1966 and immediately thereafter, discovered in the Kalahari three of the world's richest diamond-bearing formations. Politically and ideologically, it enjoys enlightened nonracial policies and health, educational and economic standards which, apart from the new Republic of South Africa, are unequalled anywhere on the continent.

Beyond the narrow eastern corridor where the capital, Gaborone, and the majority of the population, transport and development are concentrated, Botswana is a country for the more intrepid traveller. A largely roadless wilderness of vast spaces – savannas, desert, wetlands and saltpans – and myriad traditional villages, it requires time and effort to enjoy to the fullest.

All its economic success has put Botswana, also rich in wildlife, artistic tradition, and natural appeal, in a unique situation. In response to the need to preserve the country's natural assets and still derive the benefits of tourism, the government has embraced a policy of courting only high-cost, low-impact tourism. As a result, the best of Botswana is inaccessible to shoe-string travellers. Mid-range budgets are accommodated in places by inexpensive camp sites, but there are no concessions to the impecunious. Having said that, you'll still find some reasonably priced options for visiting the country's primary tourist attraction, the anomalous wetlands of the Okavango Delta.

Namibia, which gained its independence in 1990, lies wedged between the Kalahari and the chilly South Atlantic, and is a country of practically unlimited potential and promise. Rich in natural resources and unquestionably spectacular beauty, it has also inherited a solid modern infrastructure and a diversity of cultures and national origins: Herero, San, Khoi-Khoi, Kavango,

Ovambo, Afrikaner, German, Asian and others.

It's also safe to say that Namibia's attractions are unparalleled anywhere. Well known only in southern Africa, its bushwalking opportunities, rugged seascapes, European and African cities and villages – and nearly unlimited elbow room – have only recently been discovered by outsiders. Along the coast stretches the Namib Desert with its brilliant red dunes and the surprising oasis of Sossusvlei. In the south is the immense Fish River Canyon, and in the north are the wild Skeleton Coast, the forests of the Caprivi, the mysterious rock paintings of the Brandberg and the colourful desert ranges and traditional cultures of Damaraland and Kaokoland.

Beyond Etosha, Africa's largest wildlife reserve, Namibia also hosts a whimsical array of floral and faunal oddities – where else will you find a 'dead' plant that has lived for 1200 years or beaches shared by antelopes, flamingoes, penguins, sea lions and ostriches!

Facts about the Region

HISTORY
Prehistory

Southern Africa's human history extends back through the millennia to the first rumblings of humanity on the planet; the countries covered in this book contain an archaeological record of the world's earliest inhabitants. In geologic time, the last two million years or so comprise the Pleistocene era – the last ice age – and although no ice reached southern Africa, its effects were manifested in a series of climatic shifts of varying length which formed the background for human evolution.

Continuing controversy amongst scholars makes it difficult to determine the latest opinion on who evolved into whom, but most accept that the earliest human-like creatures were a group of upright-walking 'hominids' who became established nearly four million years ago in the savannas of southern and eastern Africa. At least one advanced variety of these small creatures eventually developed rudimentary tool-making abilities around 1.3 million years ago, allowing people to hunt rather than just scavenge for food. This, combined with a series of climatic changes in the region (alternating wet or dry trends lasting thousands of years each) led to an increase in brain size, changes in body form and a growing population.

The next clearly identifiable stage is an early form of human called *homo erectus* or 'man who stands upright', whose camps and stone tools are found scattered throughout the region. One archaeological site in the Namib Desert provides evidence that these early people were hunting the ancestors of present-day elephants and butchering their remains with stone hand-axes as early as 750,000 years ago. The tools of the era were large and clumsy, but by 150,000 years ago, people were using lighter stone points, projectile heads, knives, saws and other finer tools useful for various hunting and gathering activities.

By the middle Stone Age, which lasted until 20,000 years ago, the Boskopoid people, the primary human group in southern Africa and presumed ancestry of the present-day San (traditionally known as Bushmen, although there is some controversy over the use of this name nowadays), had progressed into an organised hunting and gathering society. Use of fire was universal, tools – now made from wood and animal products as well as stone – had become more sophisticated, and natural pigments were being used for personal adornment. Artefacts from middle Stone Age sites in the Namib Desert suggest that certain nomadic groups hunted only particular species.

Between 20,000 and 30,000 years ago, southern Africans made sudden and significant progress in their standard of tool manufacture. Tools became smaller and better designed and this greatly increased hunting efficiency and allowed time for further innovation and artistic pursuits. This stage is known as the microlithic revolution because it was characterised by small-flake working of microliths, or small stones. These are accompanied by clear evidence of food gathering, consumption of shellfish and working of wood, bone and ostrich eggshell beads.

There are caves and rock shelters, particularly in Namibia's Brandberg mountains, where several metres of archaeological deposits from this period have been discovered. Not all these late Stone Age people used microliths, however, and although some believe they were ancestors of the modern Khoisan groups – San (Bushmen) and Khoi-Khoi (Hottentot or Nama) – this isn't conclusive. What is well substantiated is that from around 8000 BC, the hunting and gathering people of the late Stone Age began producing pottery and occupied rock shelters and caves all over southern Africa.

The artistic traditions and material crafts of these people are evidenced by their use of

REGIONAL HIGHLIGHTS

HIGHLIGHT	ACCESS	ACCOMMODATION
ZIMBABWE		
Victoria Falls	Air, train, bus & tarred highway	Camping, dormitories, hotels, lodges
Hwange National Park	Air, train, bus & tarred highway to the entrance, private vehicle inside, safari operator	Camping, National Parks' accommodation, safari lodges, hotels
Great Zimbabwe Ruins	Bus, tarred highway	Camping, hotels at site & in Masvingo
Chimanimani National Park	Buses to Chimanimani village, final 19 km private vehicle, private operator or on foot	Camping, mountain hut, hotel & back-packers' accommodation in Chimanimani Village
Matobo National Park	Private vehicle, safari operator	Camping, National Parks' accommodation, hotel guest house, safari lodges nearby
Mana Pools National Park	Private vehicle, road & canoe safari operators	Camping, National Parks' accommodation, safari lodges
Nyanga National Park	Bus, private vehicle	Camping, National Parks' accommodation, hotels
Lake Kariba	To Kariba town: bus & private vehicle. To Matusadona National Park: private 4WD, boat, safari lodge transfers	Kariba Town: camping & hotels. Matusadona National Park: camping, National Parks' accommodation, safari lodges
Vumba	Bus, private vehicle	Camping, backpackers' accommodation, guest houses, holiday cottages, hotels
Domboshawa & Ngomakurira	Bus, private vehicle	Wild camping only
Chizarira National Park	Private 4WD, safari operator	Camping safari lodge
BOTSWANA		
Okavango Delta	To Maun: air, bus, private vehicle. To the Delta: air (safari operators), 4WD, boat	Camping, safari lodges, hotels in nearby Maun
Chobe National Park	Air, private 4WD, safari operators from Kasane	Camping, safari lodges
Tsodilo Hills	Air with safari operators, private 4WD	Camping
Sua Pan	Private 4WD, safari operators	Camping & lodges nearby
Tuli Block	Safari operators, private 4WD	Safari lodges
Makgadikgadi & Nxai Pan National Park	Private 4WD, safari operators	Camping
Gcwihaba Caverns	Private 4WD	Wild camping
Serowe	Bus, private vehicle	Hotels
The Kalahari	Private 4WD, safari operators (to Deception Pan)	Wild camping, hotels in Ghanzi & Jwaneng
NAMIBIA		
Etosha National Park	Private vehicle, safari operators	Camping, National Parks' accommodation, safari lodges
The Namib	Private vehicle, safari operators	Camping, guest farms, hotel, safari lodges
Fish River Canyon	Private vehicle, safari operators	Camping, National Parks' accommodation
Lüderitz	Bus; private vehicle	Camping, hotels
Caprivi National Parks & Game Reserves	Bus; private 4WD	Camping, safari lodges (Mudumu only)
Waterberg Plateau Park	Private vehicle	Camping, National Parks' accommodation guest farms nearby
Khaudom Game Reserve	Private 4WD	Camping
Swakopmund	Air, bus, train, private vehicle	Camping, holiday cottages, guest houses; hotels
The Skeleton Coast & Damaraland	Private vehicle, safari operators	Camping, National Parks' accommodation, safari lodges
Windhoek	Air, bus, train, private vehicle	Camping, backpackers' accommodation guest houses, hotels, guest farms

DAYS	COMMENTS
3-5	Can get crowded but the falls remain lovely and unspoilt.
min 3	Great variety and concentration of wildlife, remains relatively uncrowded
1 (& night)	Sub-Saharan Africa's greatest archaeological site, also a serene place to relax for a few days of camping and exploring
min 3	Contains Zimbabwe's wildest and most rugged mountain wilderness, no roads in the park but lots of hiking tracks offer the best bushwalking country in Zimbabwe
min 2	Kopje-studded terrain and weird balancing rocks, hundreds of caves and rock paintings, best place in the world to see both white and black rhino
min 2	Visitors are permitted to strike out alone on foot
2	The 'civilised' mountain country of Nyanga and adjoining Mtarazi Falls National Park make a great highland escape
min 2	Good fishing, boating, wildlife-viewing, & camping
min 2	Good day-walking opportunites & far-ranging vistas across neaby Mozambique
1	Good hiking over beautiful lichen-covered domes, lots of rock paintings
2-5	Array of wildlife, remains a venue for adventure well off-the-beaten-track
min 3	A maze of channels and islands teeming with wildlife and inviting exploration
min 2	Wildlife-rich and elephant-ravaged river front and the inland marshes and savannas
min 2	Incredible gallery of ancient San paintings, one of the country's best hiking areas
2	Immortalised in 'The Gods Must Be Crazy'; Kubu Island is a highlight, and don't miss Nata Sanctuary
min 2	Private wildlife reserves and spectacular Old West scenery
min 2	Makgadikgadi offers a wilderness of grasslands and palms and Nxai Pan provides Botswana's best wet season wildlife-viewing
1	Entirely undeveloped underground experience, but only for the most adventurous.
1	Home of Sir Seretse Khama, museum, rhino sanctuary
min 10	Offers a spectacular solitude; don't miss a starry night camping in its wild expanses. The San maintian that at night in the Kalahari, 'you can hear the stars in song'.
Min 3	Vast salt pan which occasionally holds water and attracts flocks of flamingoes; vast bushveld with water holes for excellent wildlife-viewing
3	Brilliant and colourful dunes; surreal gravel plains and isolated massifs; the oasis of Sossusvlei, a desert pan surrounded by towering dunes
min 2	One of Africa's most spectacular natural wonders; hiking trips and relaxing Ai-Ais hot springs
1-2	Extraordinary desert pastel colours, the 'Little Bavaria' town of Lüderitz, and the diamond ghost town of Kolmanskop
min 3	Mudumu & Mamili National Parks and Mahango Game Reserve; ideal for experiencing a verdant side of Namibia's character and a range of wetland wildlife
min 2	A repository for endangered wildlife, with inspiring landscapes and far-ranging views
min 2	Packed with every sort of wildlife found in Namibia; you're likely to have the whole place to yourself
2	Holiday resort with a long beach, colonial architecture, continental restaurants, bakeries and beer gardens
2-5	The ethereal Skeleton Coast, with fog-bound coastal scenery, shipwrecks and Cape Cross Seal Reserve. In the vast spaces of Damaraland, don't miss the Spitzkoppe, Brandberg massif, Twyfelfontein, Petrified Forest and Burnt Mountain
2	Splendid colonial buildings dating from the turn of the century, lovely setting

pigments. Although they'd been used for bodily ornamentation for thousands of years, they have now found their way into rock paintings. Whether the San or some other group were directly responsible for the paintings, however, remains a matter of dispute. Although the artistic tradition in southern Africa chronologically and stylistically coincides with that of Europe, the spreading Sahara probably precluded any contact between the cultures and there's no substantial evidence supporting a theory of mutual influence.

Early Bantu Groups

The archaeological connection between the late Stone Age people and the first Khoisan arrivals isn't clear but it is generally accepted that the earliest inhabitants of Zimbabwe, Botswana and Namibia were San, a nomadic people organised into extended family groups who were able to adapt to the severe terrain. The San seem to have come under pressure from the Khoi-Khoi with whom they share a language group. The Khoi-Khoi were tribally organised people who raised stock rather than hunted and who were probably responsible for the region's first pottery production. They seem to have migrated from the south and gradually displaced and absorbed the San in Namibia and dominated the country until around 1500 AD. Their descendants still live in Namibia and Botswana, but few maintain a traditional lifestyle.

During the early Iron Age, between 2300 and 2400 years ago, rudimentary farming techniques appeared on the plateaux of south-central Africa. Whether the earliest farmers were Khoisan who'd settled into a stationary existence or migrants fleeing the advancing deserts of northern Africa remains in question but the latter is the favoured hypothesis. The arrival of these farmers in southern Africa marked the beginning of the tribal structure and the beginning of the group known as the Bantu. These people would more accurately be called 'Bantu-speaking' since the word actually refers to their language group. It has become a term of convenience for the Black African peoples and the grouping is as ill-defined as 'American' or 'Oriental'.

The first agriculturalists and iron workers of definite Bantu origin are known as the Gokomere culture. They settled the temperate savanna and cooler uplands of Zimbabwe and were the first occupants of the Great Zimbabwe site, the appeal of which as a natural fortification could not have been overlooked.

Between 500 and 1000 AD, the Gokomere and subsequent groups developed gold-mining techniques in the region and produced progressively finer quality ceramics, jewellery, soapstone carvings and textiles. Cattle ranching became the mainstay of the community and earlier San groups gradually disappeared from the scene, either retreating to the west or being enslaved and absorbed into Bantu society, a process which continues to the present day.

As early as the 11th century, some foundations and stonework were already in place at Great Zimbabwe and the settlement, generally regarded as the nascent Shona society, came into contact with Swahili traders who'd been plying the coast of what is now Mozambique for over four centuries. They traded African gold and ivory for glass, porcelain and cloth from Asia; Great Zimbabwe thereby became the capital of the wealthiest and most powerful society in south-eastern Africa. The hilltop acropolis at Great Zimbabwe came to serve not only as a fortress but as a shrine for the worship of Mwari, the pre-eminent Shona deity.

In about 1600, the Herero people, Bantu-speaking pastoralists, arrived in Namibia from the Zambezi Valley and occupied the north and west of the country, coming into conflict with the Khoi-Khoi with whom they competed for the best grazing lands and water sources.

Eventually all the indigenous groups submitted to the aggressive Herero, who displaced not only the San and Khoi-Khoi, but also the Damara people, whose origins are unclear.

It is thought that the Nama people of present-day Namibia are descended from the

PETER PTSCHELINZEW

PETER PTSCHELINZEW

PETER PTSCHELINZEW

DEANNA SWANEY

A	B
C	D

A: Brewing traditional beer, Zimbabwe
B: Chrome miner, Zimbabwe
C: Tobacco farmers, Zimbabwe
D: Bayei woodcarver, Botswana

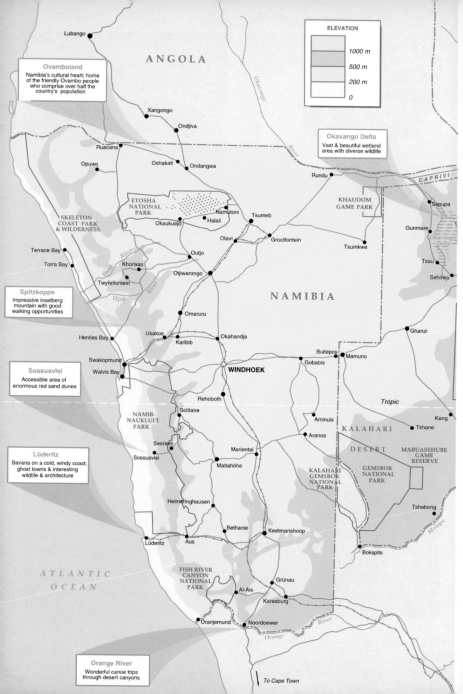

ELEVATION

1000 m
500 m
200 m
0

Lubango

ANGOLA

Ovamboland
Namibia's cultural heart; home of the friendly Ovambo people who comprise over half the country's population

Xangongo

Ondjiva

Okavango River

Ruacana

Okavango Delta
Vast & beautiful wetland area with diverse wildlife

Opuwo

Oshakati

Ondangwa

Rundu

CAPRIVI

SKELETON COAST PARK & WILDERNESS

ETOSHA NATIONAL PARK

Namutoni

Tsumeb

KHAUDOM GAME PARK

Sepupa

Gunmare

Okaukuejo

Halali

Otavi

Grootfontein

Tsumkwe

Okavango Delta

Terrace Bay

Hoanib River

Khorixas

Outjo

Tsau

Torra Bay

Twyfelfontein

Otjiwarongo

Sehitwa

Ugab River

Spitzkoppe
Impressive inselberg mountain with good walking opportunities

Omaruru

NAMIBIA

Henties Bay

Usakos

Karibib

Okahandja

Ghanzi

Swakopmund

Buitepos

Mamuno

Sossusvlei
Accessible area of enormous red sand dunes

Walvis Bay

Gobabis

WINDHOEK

Rehoboth

NAMIB-NAUKLUFT PARK

Solitaire

Tropic

Aminuis

Kang

KALAHARI

Tshane

Aranos

DESERT

MABUASEHUBE GAME RESERVE

Sesriem

Mariental

Lüderitz
Bavaria on a cold, windy coast; ghost towns & interesting wildlife & architecture

Sossusvlei

Maltahöhe

KALAHARI GEMSBOK NATIONAL PARK

GEMSBOK NATIONAL PARK

Helmeringhausen

Tshabong

Bethanie

Keetmanshoop

Lüderitz

Aus

Molopo River

Bokspits

ATLANTIC OCEAN

FISH RIVER CANYON NATIONAL PARK

Ai-Ais

Grünau

Karasburg

Oranjemund

Noordoewer

Orange River

Orange River
Wonderful canoe trips through desert canyons

To Cape Town

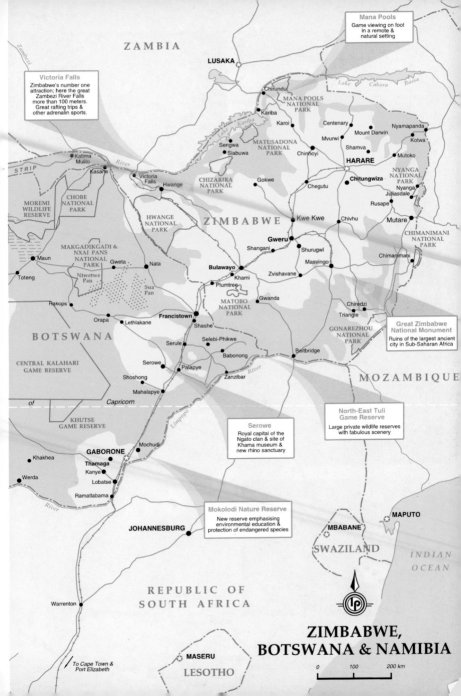

ZAMBIA

LUSAKA

Mana Pools
Game viewing on foot in a remote & natural setting

Victoria Falls
Zimbabwe's number one attraction; here the great Zambezi River Falls more than 100 meters. Great rafting trips & other adrenalin sports.

Chirundu

Lake Cabora Bassa

MANA POOLS NATIONAL PARK

Kariba

Lake Kariba

Karoi

Centenary

Mount Darwin

Nyamapanda

Mvurwi

Kotwa

Katima Mulilo

River

Sengwa

Siabuwa

MATUSADONA NATIONAL PARK

Chinhoyi

Shamva

Mutoko

STRIP

Kasane

Victoria Falls

Hwange

CHIZARIRA NATIONAL PARK

Gokwe

HARARE

Chitungwiza

NYANGA NATIONAL PARK

MOREMI WILDLIFE RESERVE

CHOBE NATIONAL PARK

Chegutu

Nyanga

Juliasdale

HWANGE NATIONAL PARK

ZIMBABWE

Kwe Kwe

Chivhu

Rusape

Mutare

Gweru

CHIMANIMANI NATIONAL PARK

Maun

MAKGADIKGADI & NXAI PANS NATIONAL PARK

Gweta

Nata

Shangani

Shurugwi

Chimanimani

Toteng

Ntwetwe Pan

Sua Pan

Bulawayo

Masvingo

Khami

Zvishavane

Rakops

Plumtree

Gwanda

Orapa

Lethlakane

Francistown

MATOBO NATIONAL PARK

Chiredzi

Triangle

BOTSWANA

Shashe

Serule

Selebi-Phikwe

Great Zimbabwe National Monument
Ruins of the largest ancient city in Sub-Saharan Africa

CENTRAL KALAHARI GAME RESERVE

Serowe

Babonong

Beitbridge

GONAREZHOU NATIONAL PARK

Shoshong

Palapye

Zanzibar

Mahalapye

River

MOZAMBIQUE

of

Capricorn

Limpopo

KHUTSE GAME RESERVE

North-East Tuli Game Reserve
Large private wildlife reserves with fabulous scenery

Serowe
Royal capital of the Ngato clan & site of Khama museum & new rhino sanctuary

GABORONE

Mochudi

Thamaga

Khakhea

Kanye

Lobatse

Werda

Ramatlabama

River

JOHANNESBURG

Mokolodi Nature Reserve
New reserve emphasising environmental education & protection of endangered species

MAPUTO

MBABANE

SWAZILAND

INDIAN OCEAN

REPUBLIC OF SOUTH AFRICA

Warrenton

MASERU

LESOTHO

To Cape Town & Port Elizabeth

0   100   200 km

ZIMBABWE, BOTSWANA & NAMIBIA

PETER PTSCHELINZEW

DEANNA SWANEY

PETER PTSCHELINZEW

DEANNA SWANEY

DEANNA SWANEY

PETER PTSCHELINZEW

A: Desert bloom, near Spitzkoppe, Namibia
B: Water Lily, Okavango Delta, Botswana
C: Adenium Obesum, Zimbabwe
D: Petrified wood, Zimbabwe
E: Welwitschia plant, Namibia
F: Social Weavers' nest, Namibia

early Khoi-Khoi groups who had held out against the Herero. There were violent clashes in the 1870s and '80s. A new Bantu group, the Ovambo, probably descended from people who had migrated from eastern Africa over 500 years earlier, had now settled in the north along the Okavango and Kunene rivers.

For the history of the colonial and postcolonial periods, see Facts about the Country – History for each country in this book.

FLORA & FAUNA

This section deals with flora, reptiles, birds, fish and insects native to Zimbabwe, Botswana and Namibia. Some larger animals are identified in the Safari Guide at the back of the book.

Flora

Zimbabwe Author TV Bulpin wrote of Zimbabwe 'there is not a more picturesque part than the wild garden of trees and aloes and flowering plants that lies between the Limpopo and Zambezi rivers...'

Despite Bulpin's assessment, Zimbabwe's vegetation cover is undeniably rather uniform throughout. Most of the central and western plateau country is covered in bushveld – thorny acacia savanna and *miombo* – or dry open woodland. The drier lowlands of the south and south-east are characterised by lower thorny scrub and baobabs.

Generalisations, however, fail to convey the richly colourful array of species that enlivens this plain canvas: towering cactus-like euphorbias resembling pipe-organs, 30 diverse species of aloe (which flower in the cool, sunny days of midwinter), spreading poinsettia shrubs as big as cottages, flowering jacarandas, hibiscus, citrus trees, jasmine, banana trees, flame trees, bougainvilleas and a host of other succulents, tropical flowers, palms and perennials.

The Eastern Highlands and their unique climatic conditions provide another botanical environment altogether. The higher slopes around Nyanga are draped with very un-African pine forests – some admittedly planted by the paper industry – and down the eastern slopes of the Vumba where Zimbabwe spills into Mozambique, one can find stands of tropical hardwood forest complete with ferns and lianas.

If you're after Africa's archetypal Tarzan jungles, however, you'll have to go to Zaïre or keep within 100 metres of Victoria Falls, where the constant misty spray has created a lush stand of tropical rainforest.

Botswana Most of Botswana is covered by savanna – either acacia or low thorn scrub – which rolls on across the flat and almost unchanging landscape. In the heart of the Kalahari the vegetation reaches through the sands to access underlying aquifers.

The country's only deciduous mopane forests are in the north-east. Here, six Chobe District forest reserves harbour stands of commercial timber for paper and construction, as well as both *mongonga* and *marula* trees, whose edible nuts once served as staple foods for the San. The soft wood of the marula is used in local crafts and its fruit goes into a local beer.

In the Okavango Delta, one encounters riparian environments dominated by marsh grasses, water lilies, reeds and papyrus, dotted with well-vegetated islands thick with palms, acacias, leadwood and sausage trees.

Namibia Much of Namibia is covered by scrub savanna grasses of the genera *Stipagrostis*, *Eragrostis* and *Aristida*, which are dotted with trees. In the south the grass is interrupted by stands of quivertrees *(kokerbooms)* and euphorbias, while ephemeral watercourses are lined with tamarisks, buffalo thorn and camelthorn.

In the sandy plains of south-eastern Namibia, raisin bushes *(Grewia)* and candlethorn grow among the scrubby trees, while hillsides are covered with the green-flowered *Aloe viridiflora* and camphor bush.

The eastern fringes of Namib-Naukluft Park are dominated by semisdesert scrub savanna vegetation, including some rare aloe species *(Aloe karasbergensis* and *Aloe sladeniana).* On the gravel plains east and north-east of Swakopmund grows the bizarre *Welwitschia mirabilis*, which is surely one of the world's most unusual plants.

In higher rainfall areas, the characteristic grass savanna gives way to acacia woodlands, and Etosha National Park enjoys two distinct environments: the wooded savanna in the east and thorn-scrub savanna in the west. The higher rainfall of Caprivi and Kavango sustains extensive mopane woodland and the riverine areas support scattered wetland vegetation, grasslands and stands of acacia. Around Katima Mulilo is a mixed sub-tropical woodland containing copalwood, Zambezi teak and leadwood, among other hardwood species.

Fauna

Reptiles Africa's reptile *extraordinaire* is the Nile crocodile. Female crocodiles lay up to 80 eggs at a time, depositing them in sandy areas above the high-water line. After three months' incubation in the hot sand, the young emerge. Newly hatched crocs are avocado green in colour and, like avocados, darken as they age to nearly black.

Other reptiles to watch for – but which shouldn't inspire bush paranoia – are snakes. Southern Africa has a complement of both venomous and harmless snakes, 76 varieties in all, but most fear humans (they fear anything larger than they are) and travellers will be lucky to even see one.

The largest snake – and one that is harmless to humans – is the python, which grows to over five metres in length. It is found mainly in eastern Zimbabwe from the lowveld north to Nyanga and subsists mainly on small mammals.

There are a host of other harmless snakes – the bush snake, the green water snake, the mole snake, and so on – and quite a few venomous sorts. The most sinister-looking – and for good reason – is the flat, fat and bloated gaboon viper. It has a massive triangular head and grows to over a metre in length. Although it's not common, watch for it on walking tracks in the eastern highlands

of Zimbabwe; its bite means bye-bye unless antivenin is administered quickly.

The related puff adder also enjoys sunning itself on mountain tracks. It reaches about one metre in length and although it isn't as hideous-looking as the gaboon viper, it's responsible for most snakebite poisoning in Zimbabwe. The puff adder isn't aggressive but because it's so lethargic, hikers should take care not to inadvertently kick one out of its sweet dreams.

Zimbabwe also boasts four species of cobra: the forest cobra, the rinkal, and the Egyptian cobra, all of which reach over two metres in length, and the metre-long Mozambique spitting cobra, which can spit a stream of venom up to three metres. It aims for the eyes.

Other venomous snakes include the common vine snake; both the green and black mamba; and the *boomslang* (Afrikaans for tree snake), a slender two-metre aquamarine affair with black-tipped scales.

The dry lands of Botswana and Namibia boast more than 70 species of snakes. These include three species of spitting cobra. It is actually the African puff adder which causes the most problems for humans, since it inhabits dry, sandy, and otherwise harmless-looking riverbeds. Boomslangs and vine snakes are common in the Okavango and Caprivi areas but they generally don't bother humans. Horned adders and sandsnakes inhabit the gravel plains of the Namib, and the sidewinder adder lives in the Namib dune sea.

Lizards are ubiquitous in southern Africa from Zimbabwe's eastern highlands to Namibia's Kaokoland and from the bathroom ceiling to the kitchen sink. The largest of these is the *leguaan* or water monitor; a docile creature that reaches over two metres in length, swims and spends a lot of time lying around water holes, perhaps dreaming of being a crocodile. A smaller version, the savanna leguaan, inhabits kopjes (small hills) and drier areas. Also present in large numbers are geckos, chameleons, legless snake lizards, rock-plated lizards and a host of others.

The Namib Desert supports a range of lizards, including a large vegetarian species, *Angolosaurus skoogi*. The sand-diving lizard, *Aprosaura achietae*, is known for its 'thermal dance'. In order to get some relief from the heat of the sand, it lifts its legs in turn as if following a dance routine. The unusual bug-eyed palmato gecko inhabits the high dunes and there's also a species of chameleon.

Birds Although southern Africa offers an adequate sampling of LBJ's ('little brown jobs'), it is also home to an array of colourful and exotic birdlife. The following are only a few of the most interesting and frequently encountered birds:

Bustard Also known as the great or kori bustard, the bustard is Africa's largest flying bird. It rarely flies, however, preferring to stride slowly and proudly across the savanna, making tself particularly vulnerable to attack by predators (including humans).

Cattle Egret These are those graceful white birds that like to go hitchhiking on the backs of cattle and antelopes.

Crowned Crane This dandified black and white crane, sporting a distinctive yellow crown of stiff feathers, primarily inhabits the higher plateau regions. Like the Japanese crane, its mating ritual includes a series of dances.

Dove Southern Africa has several species of dove including the African mourning dove and the emerald-spotted wood dove. Some visitors are enchanted, some haunted, and some perturbed by the endless cooing of doves in the bushveld, but nearly everyone agrees that if there's one sound evocative of Africa, this is it. The Cape Turtle Dove has the most distinctive call of all, but Zimbabweans and Batswana can't quite agree on what it's saying. In Zimbabwe, they hear it urging the world to 'work harder, work harder...', while in Botswana, it seems to chant a mantra to its native country, 'Botswana, Botswana...'.

Eagle Southern Africa boasts 17 species of eagle, including the bateleur, tawny, martial and several snake eagles. The best known, the African fish eagle, has a particularly haunting and memorable cry. It feeds almost exclusively on fish and can frequently be seen kamikaze diving for dinner in larger dams and along the Zambezi, Chobe and Okavango rivers.

Grey Lourie The grey lourie, the original sticky-beak, is an ordinary-looking grey bird with a notable crest. It is most often seen perched in an acacia tree surveying the scene. The lourie's distinctive 'Go-away' call, delivered in the whining tones of a spoilt child, is welcomed by the hunted but predators consider it rather inauspicious, hence its nickname, the 'warning bird'.

Guinea Fowl The roadrunners of Africa, guinea fowl are most often seen either rooting around in the dirt or retreating from following vehicles. Many African drivers take the challenge and try and run them down for a meal but the 'bush chickens' normally recognise imminent defeat and take to the air at the crucial moment.

Hornbill These noisy and awkwardly top-heavy birds are instantly recognisable by the shape of their bill which in some species is nearly as large as their bodies. They come in many colours and sizes and nearly every southern African habitat supports at least one variety. The most common is the yellow-billed hornbill, which is easily recognised by its drunken flight pattern.

Lilac-Breasted Roller This stunningly coloured aerobat is named for the colour on its chest and its unusual flight pattern when courting. When a male bird wants to attract the attentions of a female, its flight becomes erratic – complete with wingovers and side-slips – and early observers who lacked the benefits of slow-motion filming techniques thought it was actually rolling in flight. It's most often observed as a flash of turquoise blue in the bushveld. In Ndebele tradition, only the chief was permitted to wear its feathers in his headdress.

Marabou Stork Ominously resembling an undertaker in a long-tail coat, the lovably hideous marabou stork is a carrion eater that spends most of its time perched in dead straggly trees doing gangly vulture imitations. It's most easily observed in game parks where the best leftovers are found.

Secretary Bird

Secretary Bird The dour office hand of the feathered set is named not for its strong resemblance to a 19th-century British desk jockey, with a clutch of quill pens tucked behind the ear, but for its method of trouncing snakes. In its effort to pound them senseless, it hops up and down on them like a secretary banging on a typewriter. It's protected from bites by the armour plating on its legs. A relative of the eagle, this spindly character reaches 150 cm in length and subsists mainly on reptiles, rodents and insects. You'll most often see it strutting detachedly around grassland areas of western Zimbabwe and northern Botswana and Namibia.

Weaverbird Several species of these lively little birds are present in southern Africa. With their sharply pointed bills they construct and attach sac-like grass nests to branches and reeds. Placed on the western sides of trees due to prevailing weather patterns, these nests can serve as orientation devices for befuddled human wanderers. In Namibia, a variety known as the social weaver produces the avian equivalent of apartment blocks – huge multi-roomed nests which resemble immense hanging hay-stacks and can fill up entire trees.

Ostrich, Vulture, Flamingo and Penguin Information about these birds is included in asides which appear throughout the book.

The harbours and coastal wildfowl reserves of Namibia support an especially wide range of birdlife: white pelicans, grebes, herons, cormorants, ducks and hundreds of other wetland birds. The sheer numbers of birds there, which survive on the fish stocks nurtured by the cold Benguela Current, has contributed to Namibia's lucrative guano industry. Near Walvis Bay, artificial offshore islands have been constructed to stimulate production. Further south, around Lüderitz, flamingoes and jackass penguins share the same desert shoreline.

The canyons and riverbeds slicing across the central Namib are home to nine species of raptors, as well as the hoopoe, the unusual red-eyed bulbul and a small bird known as the familiar chat. Around the western edge of the Central Plateau you may see the colourful sunbirds or emerald cuckoos. Central Namibia also has bird species found nowhere else, such as the Namaqua sandgrouse and Grey's lark.

The well-watered areas of the far north support an entirely different range of birdlife, including such colourful species as lilac-breasted rollers and white-fronted, carmine and little bee-eaters.

Fish Zimbabwe, the wettest of the three countries covered in this book, has 117 species of fish. Not all are native to the country – many were introduced by anglers during the colonial period – but every aqua habitat in Zimbabwe has its own piscine community and angling remains a popular pastime and food source. Botswana's Okavango Delta and the Namib Coast also support fish species (and anglers). For more information, see Fishing under Activities in the Regional Facts for the Visitor chapter.

Insects & Spiders Although southern Africa doesn't enjoy the profusion of bug life found in countries further north, a few interesting specimens buzz, creep, and crawl around the place. Over 500 species of colourful butterflies – including the African monarch, the commodore, and the citrus swallowtail – are resident, as well as many fly-by-night moths.

Some of the more interesting buggy types include the large and rarely noticed stick insects, the also large (and frighteningly hairy) baboon spider and the leggy chongalolo, a millipede that reaches a foot in length.

Common garden variety insects like ants, stink bugs, grasshoppers and locusts sometimes find their way into frying pans and are served as snack and protein supplements.

Nuisance insects include malarial mosquitoes, which are profuse in the Zambezi Valley, the Zimbabwean lowveld and northeastern Namibia; and the tsetse fly, which carries sleeping sickness and is found in the lowveld and around Zimbabwe's Lake Kariba. There are also various stinging insects like the striped hornet, an evil-looking variety of house wasp.

The Namib Desert in particular has several wonderful species of spiders. The tarantula-like 'white lady of the dunes' is a white hairy affair which is attracted to light. It does a dance, of sorts, raising each of its eight hairy feet in turn. There is also a rare false spider known as a solifluge or sun spider. You can see its circulatory system through its light-coloured translucent outer skeleton. Much of the time, however, it remains buried in the sand.

The Namib dunes are known for their extraordinary variety of tenebrionid beetles, which come in all shapes and sizes. They've adapted well to their desert environment and most of their moisture is derived from fog. In the gravel plains, you'll also encounter such nuisance insects as ticks, which favour the shade of thorn trees and areas where there are lots of grazing animals.

CULTURE
Avoiding Offence

Short of public nudity or openly vocal criticism of the government, there aren't really any unforgivable (for foreigners, anyway) faux pas that must be avoided. A few straightforward courtesies, however, may greatly improve a foreigner's chances of acceptance by the local community, especially in rural areas.

In all three countries, pleasantries are taken quite seriously, and it's essential to greet or say goodbye to someone entering or leaving a room. Learn the local words for 'hello' and 'goodbye' and use them unsparingly. In rural Zimbabwe, verbal greetings are often accompanied by a clap of the hands. For those out of earshot, it is customary to offer a smile and a pleasant wave, even if you're just passing in a vehicle.

Emphasis is also placed on handshakes.

The Zimbabwean handshake consists of three parts: the normal Western handshake, followed by the linking of bent fingers while touching the ends of upward-pointing thumbs, then finishing off with a repeat of the conventional handshake. In Botswana, offer your right hand for a conventional handshake while holding your right elbow with your left hand. Often, people continue to hold hands right through their conversation.

As in most traditional societies, the achievement of old age is an accomplishment worthy of respect and elders are treated with deference – their word should not be questioned and they should be accorded utmost courtesy. Teachers, doctors, and other professionals often receive similar treatment.

Likewise, people holding positions of authority – immigration officers, government officials, police, village chiefs, and so on – should be dealt with pragmatically. Zimbabwe, Botswana, and Namibia are not as bad as most neighbouring countries – officials are normally refreshingly open and friendly – but if you do cross them or strike a nerve, all that may change. It is one thing to stand up for your rights but blowing a fuse or undermining an official's judgement or authority or insulting an ego may only serve to waste time, tie you up in red tape and inspire closer scrutiny of future travellers.

At the other end of the spectrum, children rate very low on the social scale. They are expected to do as they're told without complaint and defer to adults in all situations. It is considered rude for a child to occupy a seat in a bus, for example, if adults are standing. Foreigners are normally exempted. Similarly, southern Africa is largely still a man's country and a Black man will not normally give up his seat to a woman, never mind that she is carrying a baby and luggage and minding two toddlers. It makes one wonder what they must think of the local Whites and other Westerners who habitually do.

When visiting rural settlements, it is a good idea to request to see the chief to announce your presence and request permission before setting up camp or wandering through a village. You will rarely be refused permission. Women should dress and behave modestly, especially in the presence of chiefs or other highly esteemed persons.

Visitors should also ask permission before drawing water from community bore holes. If you do draw water at a community tap or bore hole, avoid letting it spill on the ground, especially in desert areas, where it's as precious as gold. If you wish to wash your body or your clothing, fill a container with water and carry it elsewhere.

Lone travellers may be looked upon with suspicion, women because they should be at home rearing families and men because in many areas, foreigners are potentially spies for right-wing factions. It may help to carry photographs of your family or evidence of a non-espionage-related profession.

Most travellers will have the opportunity to share an African meal sometime during their stay and will normally be given royal treatment and a seat of honour. Although concessions are sometimes made for foreigners, table manners are probably different

Africans & Foreigners

Despite the racial turmoil of the past, especially in Zimbabwe, travellers of European heritage needn't fear vindictive attitudes or vengeful violence. Most people have adopted an attitude of 'forgive and forget' in response to past misdeeds on the part of the Rhodesian and other former colonial governments.

A most disconcerting aspect of African/European relations for many travellers, is the deference light-skinned foreigners receive from most local people. After years of colonialism, many people have been conditioned to respond to Whites in a subservient manner; they frequently address men as 'Baas' (both pronounced and meaning 'Boss') and women as 'Madame'. Since these terms were once required signs of respect (and unfortunately still are under some circumstances) most people don't consider the implications of such words. You may choose to ignore them but it's probably better, in the interest of easing conversational tensions, to simply explain that you prefer to be addressed by your Christian name.

Foreigners of Black African descent may be faced with a different set of concerns. Among Black Africans, people of African heritage often aren't accorded as much cultural or linguistic slack as White travellers. To some, it may seem inconceivable that a Black person would speak English or French, for example, as a first language and have no knowledge of Setswana, Shona or whatever. Inability to communicate in the local language may be interpreted as conceit – a 'selling out' if you will – to the former colonial rulers. However, once you have explained yourself, you will normally be enthusiastically accepted by the local people. ■

from what you're accustomed to. The African staple, maize or sorghum meal, is the centre of nearly every meal. It is normally taken with the right hand from a communal pot, rolled into balls, dipped in some sort of relish – meat gravy or vegetables – and eaten. As in most societies, it is considered impolite to scoff food, or to hoard it or be stingy with it; if you do, your host may feel that he or she hasn't provided enough. Similarly, if you can't finish your food, don't worry; the host will be pleased that you have been satisfied. Often, containers of water or home-brew beer may be passed around from person to person. However, it is not customary to share coffee, tea or bottled soft drinks.

Finally, if you do visit a remote community, please tread lightly and leave as little lasting evidence of your visit as possible. In some African societies, it isn't considered impolite to ask others for items you may desire; if you're besieged with requests, it's perfectly acceptable to refuse without causing offence. If you start feeling guilty about your relative wealth and hand out all your earthly belongings, you may be regarded as very silly, indeed.

As for gift-giving, reciprocation of kindness is one thing but superficial altruism is another. Indiscriminate distribution of gifts from outside, however well intentioned, tends to create a taste for items not locally available, erodes well-established values, robs people of their pride and in extreme cases, creates villages of dependent beggars.

On the other hand, when you're offered a gift, don't feel guilty about accepting it; to refuse it would bring shame on the giver. To politely receive a gift, accept it with both hands and perhaps bow slightly. If you're receiving some minor thing you've asked for, such as a salt shaker or a pen, or getting back change at a shop, receive it with your right hand while touching your left hand to your right elbow; this is the equivalent of saying 'thanks'. Spoken thanks aren't common and local people tend to think Westerners say 'thank you' too often and too casually, so don't be upset if you aren't verbally thanked for a gift.

Facts for the Visitor

DOCUMENTS

All overseas visitors to Zimbabwe, Botswana and Namibia must carry a current passport from their country of citizenship, which must be produced when changing currency at banks or hotels. If you're entering directly from an infected area, you'll need proof of vaccination against yellow fever. For those intending to hire a vehicle, your home driving licence will suffice in all three countries covered in this book.

It's a good idea to make photocopies of all your important documents, especially your passport. This will help speed up replacement if they are lost or stolen. Other important items to photocopy would include airline tickets and credit cards. Keep these things (and a list of travellers' cheque numbers) separate from your other valuables.

MONEY

The best currency to carry in southern Africa is US dollars, in either cash or travellers' cheques. However, thanks to a recent rash of counterfeiting, the US$100 note has fallen from favour and isn't currently accepted anywhere in the region.

In major banks in all three countries, you can also exchange UK£ sterling, as well as South African rand, Botswana pula, French francs, Deutschmarks, Italian lira, Dutch guilders, Swiss francs and Australian or Canadian dollars.

Bargaining

In some areas, particularly at rural markets, bargaining for goods and services – including produce, clothing, lifts and especially, crafts and artwork – is a way of life. Such commodities are considered to be worth whatever their owners can get for them and the concept of fixed prices exists only where prices are actually marked.

In crafts stalls and markets, don't pay the first price asked. If you do – whether out of ignorance or guilt feelings about how much cash you have on hand relative to the local economy – you'll not only be considered silly, but you'll be doing fellow travellers a disservice by creating the impression that all foreigners are willing to pay any price named!

Visitors who voluntarily pay higher than market value in well-touristed areas actually cause market price increases. They thereby put some items and services out of reach of locals who generally have less disposable cash. And who can blame them – why sell an item to a local when foreigners will pay twice as much? (This is a serious problem in any place visited by overland trucks.)

Still, no matter how adept your bargaining skills, you probably won't get things as cheaply as the locals can. In Zimbabwe, even up-market establishments operate on a three-tier price system and to most traders, foreigners represent wealth. It's of little consequence whether it's a valid assessment in your case.

Bargaining is normally conducted in a friendly and spirited manner. The vendor's aim is to identify the highest price you're willing to pay. Your aim is to find the price below which the vendor will not sell. Some crafts vendors may initially ask a price four (or more) times higher than what they're prepared to accept, although it's usually lower than this. Decide what you want to pay or what others have told you *they've* paid; your first offer should be about half this. At this stage, the vendor may laugh or feign outrage, but the price will quickly drop from his or her original quote to a more realistic level. When it does, begin making better offers until you arrive at a mutually agreeable price.

There may be times when you cannot get a vendor to lower the price to anywhere near what you know the product should cost. This probably means that many tourists have passed through and if you refuse to pay the inflated prices, some other fool will.

There's no reason to lose your temper when bargaining. If you become fed up with an intransigent vendor or the effort seems a waste of time, politely take your leave. Sometimes vendors will change tack and call you back if they think their stubbornness may be losing a sale. If not, you can always look for another vendor or try again the following day.

WHEN TO GO

The three biggest factors in deciding when to visit Southern Africa will probably be the climate, crowds and opportunities for wildlife viewing. Although all three countries covered by this book lie within the tropics, a range of climatic conditions is represented. These vary from the cool, almost English, climate of Zimbabwe's Eastern Highlands to the dusty heat of the Namib Desert and the tropical humidity of the Zambezi valley.

Through most of the region, the year is divided into the dry winter season and the warmer and more humid wet season, with the former running approximately from May to October, and the latter from November to April. As a result of the moisture, the bushland takes on a lush green hue during the summer months, while through the winter, the prevailing colour is dry brown. In areas covered with mopane scrub, late autumn and winter are particularly colourful seasons.

Although quite a few winter-weary Europeans and North Americans venture southward between November and February, activities may be limited by heavy rains and other weather-related unpleasantness. Climatically, winter is generally the most comfortable season, especially in the Zambezi and Okavango valleys, the lowveld areas of Zimbabwe, and northern Namibia. Although night-time temperatures often drop below freezing, days are typically warm, sunny and very pleasant. The exception would be along the Namibian coast, where the winters are characterised by cold, damp and windy conditions.

Wildlife viewing is also generally more rewarding in the dry winter months, when animals gather around water holes in large numbers and are easy to observe. Only at Botswana's Nxai Pan National Park, which is a destination for migrating herds of animals, are the concentrations greater during the summer.

If you want to avoid the crowds, don't travel between mid-April and mid-May or from mid-July to mid-September, when residents of Zimbabwe, Botswana and Namibia and neighbouring countries – particularly South Africa – have winter school holidays (dates vary from country to country and province to province). Remember to book accommodation and National Parks facilities in advance or you may be out of luck.

June, on the other hand, is the coolest and quietest month of the year and many businesses close down because of lack of activity. Early July is still chilly, but things have begun to pick up in anticipation of the high season, which begins later in the month.

WHAT TO BRING

What items you'll need to be bring from home will depend on your intended budget, itinerary, mode of travel, time of visit and length of stay. While travelling as light as possible is always a good idea if you want to enjoy yourself, certain items will be indispensable if you can't splash out on hotel accommodation.

There are four items no budget traveller in southern Africa should be without: a tent, a sleeping bag, a torch (and plenty of batteries) or candle lantern, and a universal drain plug. The tent and sleeping bag will keep accommodation costs to a minimum, the light source will allow you to remain awake past 6 pm in the winter/dry season, and the drain plug will give you access to bathtubs in a region with few showers and even fewer drain plugs.

Backpacks are usually recommended as the most practical and useful carry-all. Internal-frame packs don't get battered around or broken quite as easily, but some walkers think that framed packs are more comfortable over long distances – cooler and better balanced. Carry the sturdiest and best-made pack you can afford, paying special attention to the strength of zippers, straps and tabs. A small padlock to secure the contents of your pack from opportunistic riflers is a good idea, though some contend that it may encourage thieves to take the whole bag! It's also wise to use plastic bags to protect the contents from moisture and dust. Generally, khaki or military-green bags aren't recommended. It's best not to resemble, however remotely, a soldier or mercenary, especially in border areas near Mozambique or Zambia.

If you're planning any hiking trips, you'll need track shoes or desert boots; sandals are entirely unsuitable. For walking in the bush, a pair of gaiters may also prove useful – firstly, to fend off thorns and annoying little seeds that cling to every passing thing, and secondly, to offer a thin line of protection against snakes.

For camping and bushwalking, it may be a good idea to carry a lightweight stove, preferably one which will run on petrol, since white gas (Shellite) isn't always readily available, especially in Zimbabwe. Note that you cannot carry stove fuel or butane cartridges on aeroplanes. There's little problem with obtaining batteries, stove fuel, butane cartridges or similar supplies in Windhoek, Harare and Gaborone, but smaller towns may have a more limited range. Butane cartridges, in Zimbabwe, come in two types and the availability of the notched variety for Bleuet stoves is very limited. Try Fereday & Son on Robert Mugabe Rd and the pet shop near the railway station, both in Harare.

If you're travelling in the dry period between May and August, you'll want to bring a range of clothing, especially if you plan to camp or spend any time in the Kalahari or Namib deserts, along the Namibian coast or in Zimbabwe's Eastern Highlands. You can expect T-shirt weather during the day across most of the region but overnight temperatures can dip below freezing and even at Hwange or Victoria Falls, mornings and evenings can be quite chilly. You won't need thermal underwear but a light jacket, a woolly jumper, a hat, a pair of gloves and some warm socks would be welcome.

During the rainy season – or for winter visits to Zimbabwe's Eastern Highlands or the Namibian coast – bring waterproofs and sturdy footwear. A bathing costume will also come in handy for swims in lakes and pools of the Eastern Highlands and in hot springs and public pools (elsewhere, intentions to swim are likely to be foiled by bilharzia – see Health). If you're travelling in the deserts, the Zambezi, Chobe or Okavango valleys, or during the summer wet season, bring some cool lightweight cottons (women should read the Women Travellers discussion later in this chapter).

People in the capital cities (Windhoek, Gaborone & Harare) tend to dress more formally than in other parts of the countries, so it's worth taking some respectable clothes for town living. In some rural areas with a high Afrikaner population, farmers tend to be conservative; and too-short shorts or swimwear won't normally be well received.

Additional items which will come in handy are a small travel alarm, a Swiss Army-style knife, a clothes line, a basic first-aid kit, a water bottle and water purification tablets, a towel, a sewing kit, a stack of passport-sized photos (for visa applications), photographic equipment and all the film you'll be needing; and, if you're visiting Zimbabwe, enough batteries to power all the gadgetry for the duration of your stay. Zimbabwe-made batteries will power a small torch for a minute or two but in a Walkman, they've been known to expire in less than 10 seconds!

USEFUL ORGANISATIONS
Cultural & Environmental Preservation

For further information on groups working towards general cultural preservation and/or environmental conservation, contact any of the following:

Australia
  Greenpeace Australia Ltd, 3/389 Lonsdale St, Melbourne 3000, Victoria (☎ (03) 9670 1633)
Botswana
  Kalahari Conservation Society, PO Box 859, Gaborone (☎ 314259; fax 374557)

Canada
> Wildlife Preservation Trust Canada, 17 Isabella St, Toronto, Ontario M4Y 1M7

Namibia
> Africat Foundation, Lise Hanssen, Okonjima, PO Box 793, Otjiwarongo (☎ (0658) 18212; fax (0658) 4382)
>
> Cheetah Conservation Fund, PO Box 247, Windhoek (☎ (0651) 4216)
>
> Save the Rhino Trust, PO Box 83, Khorixas (☎ (061) 222281)
>
> The Wildlife Society of Namibia, Namib Centre, PO Box 483, Swakopmund (☎ (0641) 5258)

South Africa
> Endangered Wildlife Trust, Private Bag X11, Parkview 2122 (☎ (011) 486 1102; fax (011) 486 1506)
>
> WWF South Africa, PO Box 456, Stellenbosch 7599
>
> Wilderness Trust of Southern Africa, PO Box 577, Bedfordview, 2008 (☎ (011) 453 7645)

Switzerland
> Worldwide Fund for Nature, Département de l'Information et de l'Education, Avenue de Mont Blanc, CH-1196 Gland

UK
> Earthwatch Europe, Belsyre Court, 57 Woodstock Rd, Oxford OX2 6HU (☎ (01865) 311600, fax (01865) 311383)
>
> Friends of the Earth, 26/28 Underwood St, London N17 JU
>
> Greenpeace, Canonbury Villas, London N1 2PN
>
> Jersey Wildlife Preservation Trust, Les Augrés Manor, Trinity, Jersey JE3 5BF
>
> Minority Rights Group, 29 Craven St, London WC2N 5NT (☎ (0171) 930 6659)
>
> Survival International, 310 Edgware Rd, London W2 1DY (☎ (0171) 723 5535)
>
> Worldwide Fund for Nature (WWF), Panda House, Weyside Park, Godalming, Surrey GU7 IXR (☎ (01483) 426444)

USA
> Earthwatch, 680 Mt Auburn St, Box 403, Watertown, MA 02272 (☎ (617) 926 8200)
>
> Conservation International, 1015 18th St, NW, Suite 1000, Washington, DC 20036 (☎ (202) 429-5660)
>
> The Ecotourism Society, 801 Devon Place, Alexandria, Virginia 22314
>
> Greenpeace, 1436 U St, NW, Washington, DC 20009 (☎ (202) 462 8817)
>
> The Nature Conservancy, 1815 N Lynn St, Arlington, VA 22209 (☎ (703) 841 5300)
>
> Survival International USA, 2121 Decatur Place, NW, Washington, DC 20006
>
> Wildlife Preservation Trust International, 3400 W Girard Ave, Philadelphia, PA 19104
>
> Worldwide Fund for Nature, 1250 24th St, NW, Washington, DC 20037

Zimbabwe
> The Zambezi Society, PO Box UA 334, Union Ave, Harare (☎ (14) 731596; fax (14) 63326)

Responsible Tourism Organisations

If you'd like more information or would like to help support the efforts of groups promoting responsible tourism in southern Africa and elsewhere, contact any of the following:

Germany
> Tourismus mit Einsicht, Arbeitsgemeinschaft Tourismus mit Einsicht, Herbert Hamele, Hadorferstr 9, D-8130 Starnberg, Germany

Spain
> World Tourism Organisation, Capitan Haya 42, 28020 Madrid

Thailand
> Ecumenical Coalition on Third World Tourism, PO Box 24, Chorakhebua, Bangkok 10230

UK
> Campaign for Environmentally Responsible Tourism, PO Box 4246, London SE23 2QB (☎ (0181) 291 0692)
>
> Centre for the Advancement of Responsible Travel, Dr Roger Millman, 70 Dry Hill Park Rd, Tonbridge, Kent TN10 3BX
>
> Tourism Concern, Froebel College, Roehampton Lane, London SW15 5PU (☎ (0181) 878 9053)

USA
> CAMPFIRE Association, 1401 16th St NW, Washington, DC 20036 (☎ (202) 939 9655)
>
> North America Coordinating Centre for Responsible Tourism, PO Box 827, San Anselmo, California
>
> Transitional Network for Appropriate Technologies, PO Box 567, Rangeley, Maine 04970

Zimbabwe
> CAMPFIRE Association, 15 Phillips Ave, Belgravia, PO Box 4027, Harare (☎ 790570)
>
> Nature Experiences Eco-Tourism Implementation, PO Box CH-69, Chisipite, Harare (☎ (14) 42858; fax (14) 792342)

TIME

During the summer months (October to April), Zimbabwe, Botswana and Namibia are two hours ahead of GMT/UTC. Therefore, when it's noon Saturday in southern Africa, it's 10 am Saturday in London, 5 am Saturday in New York, 2 am Saturday in Los Angeles and 8 pm Saturday in Sydney. In the winter (April to October), Namibia now turns its clocks back an hour, making it only one hour ahead of GMT/UTC and one hour behind Zimbabwe and Botswana.

ELECTRICITY

Electricity in southern Africa is generated at 220 V AC; both round and rectangular three-prong plug sockets (15-amp) are in use. Few Continental or North American plug adaptors will cope, and you may have to buy a plug locally and connect it yourself. A voltage adaptor is needed for US appliances.

WEIGHTS & MEASURES

All three countries covered in this book use the metric system. To convert between metric and imperial units, refer to the conversion chart at the back of the book.

BOOKS & MAPS

If there's one place that sparks writers' imaginations and emotions, it's Africa. Bibliophiles with a particular interest in southern African works – particularly literature and historical and political treatises – may want to look at the bi-monthly publication *Southern African Review of Books* (☎ (27-21) 462 2012; fax (27-21) 461 5407), Sir Lowry Rd, PO Box 13094, 7900 Cape Town, South Africa.

The following list outlines titles dealing with historical, social and conservation issues which are relevant throughout the region. Titles specific to individual countries are listed under Books in the Facts for the Visitor chapter for each country.

At the Hand of Man by Raymond Bonner (Alfred A Knopf, New York, 1993) is an interesting study of the decimation of African wildlife which promotes and sustains the idea that wildlife and habitat conservation will only work if Africans themselves realise benefits from it. He also rightly maintains that Western-style conservation measures involving laws, force, threats and lack of consideration for local cultures and traditions only create animosity and suspicion. In the end, it's the animals who suffer.

Banana Sunday – Datelines from Africa by Chris Munion (William Waterman Publi-

cations, 1993) contains a variety of humourous accounts based on dispatches by a journalist covering various African wars.

Dear Elephant, Sir by Clive Walker (Southern Book Publishers, Johannesburg, 1992) is an interestingly conceived book by a well-known southern African conservationist. It attempts to explain to elephants why humans have treated them so abominably (and to apologise for the treatment). It isn't quite as dizzy as it sounds and actually does a fairly good job of convincing humans that elephants deserve a bit more respect. But that's the whole point isn't it?

Fantastic Invasion – Dispatches from Africa by Patrick Marnham (Penguin, London, 1979) was written soon after many African states achieved independence. It reveals the shambles created when Western-style politics, government, boundaries, values and conservation efforts were superimposed upon established African cultures. For anyone distressed by today's problems on the continent, it's excellent and enlightening reading.

Like Chris Munion and Patrick Marnham, the author of *Fishing in Africa* (Pan-Picador, London, 1991), Andrew Buckoke, was also a newspaper correspondent in Africa, and this book exposes the staggering amount of chaos, corruption and violence he saw, from Sudan to Somalia and Kenya to Zimbabwe. It's a depressing read, enlightened only by moments when the author wanders away from the breaking stories and power games to seek out secret fishing holes – and real people – off the beaten track.

The History of Southern Africa by Kevin Shillington (Longman Group UK, Ltd, Essex, 1987) is a good overall historical discussion of Botswana, Namibia, South Africa, Lesotho and Swaziland in textbook form. It objectively and sensitively covers prehistory as well as African and colonial history.

The Last Elephant by Jeremy Gavron (HarperCollins Publishers, London, 1994) is a well-written account of a personal quest by an amateur elephant aficionado. It is a light and sympathetic introduction to debates about elephant poaching and culling in Africa. Particularly entertaining is the tale of the eponymous Last Elephant in Burundi, a solitary beast who has thus far managed to keep a step ahead of poachers and human development. The author also astutely covers the clash between the proponents and opponents of the resumption of a legal ivory trade.

To Save an Elephant by Allan Thornton & Dave Currey (Doubleday, London, 1991) is a gripping tale outlining the undercover work of two researchers for the Environmental Investigation Agency and their infiltration of the illicit ivory trade, from Kenya to Dubai to Hong Kong, and reveals the dark and disturbing facts about this ongoing slaughter. In Zimbabwe, they discovered a sinister trail of 'accidental' death, which seemed to befall those actively opposing the corruption that fuelled the trade in that country.

Finally, avid cooks may find the following of interest: *The African News Cookbook* (Penguin), *A Zimbabwean Cookery Book* (Mambo Press) and *A Taste of Africa* (A Channel Four Book).

Field Guides

In the UK, a good source for books on wildlife, vegetation and geology is the *Subbutteo Natural History Books, Ltd* (☎ (0352) 770581, fax (0352) 771590), Treuddyn, Mold, Clwyd CH7 4LN.

Birds of Botswana by Kenneth Newman (Southern Book Publishers, Johannesburg) is the most complete guide to the various bird species found in Botswana, and it includes full-colour plates.

Birds of Southern Africa, by SASOL (Baobab Books, 1993, Johannesburg) is a comprehensively illustrated book which is particularly easy to use, making it ideal for amateur birdwatchers.

Although the *Field Guide to the Butterflies of Southern Africa* by Igor Migdoll (New Holland Press, London) isn't totally comprehensive, but chances are you won't encounter a butterfly that isn't included in this volume.

Field Guide to the Mammals of Southern Africa by Chris & Tilde Stuart (New Holland Press, London, 1989) is a well-illustrated field guide to just about any furry thing you're likely to encounter in this part of the world.

Field Guide to Mammals of Africa Including Madagascar by Haltenorth & Diller (1988) is a good portable choice with lots of colour plates.

If you want to know what that is slithering underfoot – and whether or not it's dangerous – the *Field Guide to the Snakes and Other Reptiles of Southern Africa* by Bill Branch (New Holland Press, London) has the answer. It also covers lizards and turtles.

Flowers of Southern Africa by Auriol Batten (Southern Book Publishers, Johannesburg), a large-format volume, is less a field guide than a celebration of major flowering species, illustrated with superb and colourful paintings.

Illustrated Guide to the Birds of Southern Africa by Ian Sinclair (New Holland, UK) is mostly just an abridged version of Sinclair's Guide, listed later in this section. It includes only the most commonly observed species.

Land Mammals of Southern Africa by Reay Smithers (Southern Book Publishers, Johannesburg, 1992) is a rundown of the 200 most frequently observed mammal species. The author is one of South Africa's best known zoologists, and has been publishing books since 1992.

The comprehensive *Newman's Birds of Southern Africa* by Kenneth Newman (Macmillan, UK) is the standard work on the region's avifauna; all species are identified in colour or black and white illustrations.

Predators of Southern Africa by Hans Grobler (Southern Book Publishers, Johannesburg) contains in-depth coverage and an identification guide for all predatory mammal species.

Although *Robert's Birds of Southern Africa* by Gordon Lindsay (New Holland Press, London, 1988) is a requisite book for birdwatchers travelling through southern Africa, be warned that it's not a featherweight volume. The more luggable *Bundu*

Guide to the Birds of Zimbabwe published by Longmans, although not so comprehensive, is available at some Kingston's outlets in Zimbabwe.

Ian Sinclair's Field Guide to the Birds of Southern Africa by Ian Sinclair (Collins, UK) is a comprehensive field guide with colour photos depicting just about any avian species you may encounter in the region.

Southern, Central & East African Mammals by Chris & Tilde Stuart (New Holland Press, UK, 1992) is a handy pocket guide containing photos and descriptions of the most commonly seen mammal species in the southern half of the African continent.

Trees of Southern Africa by K Coates (New Holland, London) provides the most thorough coverage of the sub-continent's arboreal richness, illustrated with colour photos and paintings.

Maps

For an overall view of the region, the best map, at a scale of 1:4,000,000, is Michelin's *Sheet 955 – Africa Central & South, Madagascar*. Maps of individual countries are listed under Books & Maps for each country.

In the USA, a good source of maps, including topo sheets for all three countries, is Maplink (☎ (805) 965 4402), 25 E Mason St, Dept G, Santa Barbara, CA 93101. Stanfords (☎ (0171) 836 1321), 12-14 Long Acre, London WC2E 9L have a similarly extensive selection of mapping in the UK.

MEDIA

There are several magazines available by subscription and may be useful for those with an interest in the southern Africa region. Publications specific to each country are described in individual Media discussions.

Getaway is South Africa's largest and most popular travel magazine. Each month it contains at least one article on travel in Zimbabwe, Botswana or Namibia. To subscribe, contact Getaway (☎ (27-21) 531 0404; fax (27-21) 531 7303), PO Box 596, Howard Place 7450, South Africa. Foreign subscriptions cost the equivalent of R100 (around US$28) for 12 issues.

A more specialised magazine is *African Safari*, which is issued twice a year and contains articles about wildlife, safari trips and game reserves throughout the continent. For subscription information, contact African Safari Magazine, 2 Sidney Rd, Old Costessey, Norwich NR4 5DR, UK.

One of the best and most amazing wildlife magazines you'll ever encounter is *Africa Environment & Wildlife*, which is published six times a year. The original photography and writing are both of top quality, and the magazine examines issues all over the continent, with emphasis on southern Africa. Foreign subscriptions cost R105, US$32 or UK£21 annually; for information, contact Subscriptions, Africa Environment & Wildlife (☎ (27-21) 686 9001; fax (27-21) 686 4500), PO Box 44223, Claremont 7735, Cape Town, South Africa.

FILM & PHOTOGRAPHY

For photographers visiting southern Africa, especially Zimbabwe, it is best to bring all equipment from home. Where available, camera equipment can be prohibitively expensive. Thanks to loosening of economic controls, film is now available in most Zimbabwe towns, although Victoria Falls and Harare are best for quality film. In Botswana and Namibia, film is normally available in the cities, but is still expensive. Video tapes are available in Namibia, but aren't yet sold in Zimbabwe or Botswana.

If you're shooting transparencies, you'll probably get the best results with Fujichrome 100, Velvia or Kodachrome 64. The cost of the film sometimes includes processing and you can post the exposed film to the labs in the envelopes provided. If you don't trust your precious photos to the post (which is fairly reliable – if a bit slow – in all three countries), rewrap the package to disguise it and send it registered or recorded delivery.

Useful photographic accessories would include a small flash, a cable release, a polarising filter, a lens cleaning kit (fluid, tissue and aerosol), and silica-gel packs to protect against humidity. Also, remember to take spare batteries for cameras and flash units and make sure your equipment is insured. If you're using a video camera, you'll normally find 12-volt plugs in taxis (cigarette lighters) and hotels where you can recharge batteries.

General Hints

Factors worth remembering include heat, humidity, very fine sand, tropical sunlight and tropical shadows. Don't leave your camera for long in direct sunlight and don't store used film in humid conditions, or it could fade.

The best times to take photographs on sunny days are the first two hours after sunrise and the last two before sunset. This brings out the best colours and takes advantage of the colour-enhancing long red rays cast by a low sun. At other times, colours will be washed out by harsh sunlight and glare, although it's possible to counter this by using a polarising (UV) filter. If you're shooting on sand or near water, remember to adjust for glare; and remember to keep your photographic equipment well away from sand and salt water.

When photographing out of doors, be sure to take light readings on the subject and not the brilliant African background or your shots will turn out underexposed.

Photographing Animals

If you want to score some excellent wildlife shots effortlessly, a good lightweight 35-mm SLR camera, an ultraviolet filter and a 70 to 300-mm zoom or a 300-mm fixed-length telephoto lens should do the trick. If your subject is nothing but a speck in the distance, try to resist wasting film on it but keep the camera ready – anything can happen at any time. Unless you're an experienced photographer, you may want to consider carrying a 'point and shoot' automatic camera rather than a manual camera; once you've spent time adjusting the aperture, exposure and focus, your subject could be long gone.

Photographing People

As in most places, the quest for the perfect 'people shot' will prove a photographer's greatest challenge. While many Africans enjoy being photographed, others will be put off. They may be superstitious about your camera, suspicious of your motives, or simply interested in whatever economic advantage they can gain from your desire to photograph them. The main point is that you must respect the wishes of the locals, however photogenic or colourful, who may be camera-shy for whatever reason. Ask permission to photograph if a candid shot can't be made and don't insist or snap a picture anyway if permission is denied.

Often, people will allow you to photograph them provided you give them a photo for themselves, a real treasure in rural Africa. Understandably, people are sometimes disappointed not to see the photograph immediately materialise. If you don't carry a Polaroid camera, take their address and make it clear that you'll send the photo by post once it's processed.

Photographing people, particularly dark-skinned people, requires more skill than snapping landscapes. Make sure you take the light reading from the subject's face, not the background.

Taboo Subjects

Although officials in Zimbabwe, Botswana and Namibia aren't as paranoid about photography as their counterparts in many other African countries, photographing bridges, airports, military equipment, government buildings and anything that could be considered strategic or susceptible to sabotage is taboo.

HEALTH

Travel health depends largely on predeparture preparations, day to day attention to health-related matters, and the manner of handling medical emergencies should they arise. Although the following health section may seem like a who's who of unpleasant diseases, your chances of coming down with something serious in southern Africa are slight. You will, however, be exposed to different environmental factors, foods and sanitation standards, but if you take the recommended jabs, faithfully pop your antimalarials (especially if you're headed further north in Africa), and use common sense, there shouldn't be any problems.

This rundown of health risks includes some preventative measures, symptom descriptions and suggestions about what to do if there is a problem. It isn't meant to replace professional diagnosis or prescriptions and visitors should discuss with their physician the most up-to-date methods used to prevent and treat the threats to health which may be encountered.

Travel Health Guides

There are a number of books on travel health. *Staying Healthy in Asia, Africa & Latin America* (Moon Publications) is probably the best all-round guide to carry, as it's compact but very detailed and well organised.

Travellers' Health by Dr Richard Dawood (Oxford University Press) is comprehensive, easy to read, authoritative and also highly recommended, although it's rather large to lug around.

Where There is No Doctor by David Werner (Hesperian Foundation) is a very detailed guide intended for someone (like a Peace Corps worker) going to work in an undeveloped country, rather than for the average traveller.

Travel with Children, Maureen Wheeler (Lonely Planet Publications) includes basic advice on travel health for younger children.

Predeparture Preparations

Health Insurance A travel insurance policy to cover theft, loss and medical problems is a wise idea. There is a wide variety of policies and your travel agent will be able to make a recommendation. The international student travel policies handled by STA or other student travel organisations are usually good value. It's always important, however, to check the small print:

Some policies specifically exclude 'dangerous activities' which can include white-water rafting, motorbike riding or even trekking. If these activities

are on your agenda, such a policy would be of limited value.

You may prefer a policy which pays doctors or hospitals directly rather than requiring you to pay first and claim later. If you must claim after the fact, however, be sure you keep all documentation. Some policies ask you to phone (reverse charges) to a centre in your home country where an immediate assessment of the problem will be made.

Check on the policy's coverage of emergency transport or evacuation back to your home country. If you have to stretch out across several airline seats, someone has to pay for it!

Travel Health Information In the US you can contact the Overseas Citizens Emergency Center and request a health and safety information bulletin on African countries by writing to the Bureau of Consular Affairs Office, State Department, Washington, DC 20520. This office also has a special telephone number for emergencies while you're abroad, (202) 632-5525.

Read the Center for Disease Control's *Health Information for International Travel* supplement of the gruesomely titled *Morbidity & Mortality Weekly Report* or the World Health Organisation's *Vaccination Certificate Requirements for International Travel & Health Advice to Travellers*. Both of these sources (CDC and WHO) are superior to the Travel Information Manual published by the International Air Transport Association.

The International Association for Medical Assistance to Travelers (IAMAT) at 417 Center Street, Lewiston, New York, NY 14092 can provide you with a list of English-speaking physicians in southern Africa.

In the UK, contact the Medical Advisory Services for Travellers Abroad (MASTA), Keppel Street, London WC1E 7HT (☎ (0171) 631 4408). MASTA provides a wide range of services including a choice of concise or comprehensive 'Health Briefs' and a range of medical supplies. Another source of medical information and supplies is the British Airways Travel Clinic (☎ (0171) 831 5333). The Department of Health publishes leaflets SA40/41 on travellers' health requirements, and operates a phone service Freephone (0800) 555777.

In Australia, contact the Traveller's

Medical Kit

It's a good idea to carry a small, straightforward medical kit, which may include:

- Aspirin or paracetamol (called acetominophen in the USA) – for pain or fever
- Antihistamine (such as Benadryl) – useful as a decongestant for colds and allergies, to ease itching from insect bites, or to prevent motion sickness. (Note: antihistamines may cause sedation and interact with alcohol so care should be taken when using them.)
- Antibiotics – useful if you're travelling off the beaten track – most antibiotics are prescription medicines, so carry the prescription along with you. (Some individuals are allergic to commonly prescribed antibiotics such as penicillin or sulphur drugs. It would be sensible to always carry something identifying your allergy when travelling.)
- Kaolin and pectin preparation (such as Pepto-Bismol) for stomach upsets and Imodium or Lomotil to bung things up in case of emergencies during long-distance travel.
- Rehydration mixture – for treatment of severe diarrhoea. (This is particularly important when travelling with children.)
- Antiseptic liquid or cream and antibiotic powder – for minor injuries
- Calamine lotion – to ease irritation from bites and stings
- Bandages and band-aids
- Scissors, tweezers, and a thermometer – note that mercury thermometers are not permitted on airlines
- Insect repellent, 15+ sunblock (sunscreen), suntan lotion, chap stick and water purification tablets (or iodine)
- Sterile syringes, in case you need injections in countries with a high HIV/AIDS risk or where there may be medical hygiene problems (ask your doctor for a note explaining why they have been prescribed) and have at least one large enough for a blood test – those normally used for injections are too small

Ideally, antibiotics should be administered only under medical supervision and should never be taken indiscriminately. Overuse of antibiotics can weaken your immune system and can reduce the drug's efficacy in the future. Take only the recommended dosage at the prescribed intervals and continue using the antibiotic for the prescribed period, even if you're feeling better sooner. Antibiotics are quite specific to the infections they will react with so if you're in doubt about a drug's effects or suffer any unexpected reactions, discontinue use immediately. ■

Medical and Vaccination Centre in Sydney (☎ (02) 9221 7133) for general health information pertaining to Africa.

Health Preparations Make sure you're healthy before embarking on a long journey. Have your teeth checked and if you wear glasses or contacts, bring a spare pair and a copy of your optical prescription. Losing your glasses can be a real problem, but in southern Africa you can have a new pair made with little fuss.

At least one pair of good-quality sunglasses is essential, as the glare is terrific – and dust and blown sand can get into the corners of your eyes. A hat, sunscreen lotion and lip protection are also important.

If a particular medication is required, take an adequate supply as it may not be available locally. Take the prescription with the generic rather than brand name so it will be universally recognisable. Also, carry a copy of the prescription to prove you're using the medication legally – it's surprising how often over-the-counter drugs from one place are illegal without a prescription or even banned in another place. Customs and Immigration officers may get excited at the sight of syringes or mysterious powdery preparations. The organisations listed under Travel Health Information can provide medical supplies such as syringes, together with multilingual customs documentation.

Immunisations Vaccinations provide protection against diseases you may encounter along the way. It is important to understand the distinction between vaccines recommended for travel in certain areas and those required by law. Essentially the number of vaccines subject to international health regulations has been dramatically reduced over the last 10 years. Currently, yellow fever is the only vaccine subject to international health regulations. However, vaccination as an entry requirement is usually only enforced when you are coming from an infected area.

On the other hand a number of vaccines are recommended for different areas. These vaccines may not be required by law. However, they are recommended for your own personal protection.

All vaccinations should be recorded on an International Health Certificate, which is available from your physician or government health department.

Plan ahead for getting your vaccinations: some of them require an initial shot followed by a booster, while some should not be given together. You should seek medical advice at least six weeks prior to travel.

Most travellers from Western countries will have been immunised against various diseases during childhood but your doctor may still recommend booster shots against measles or polio, diseases still prevalent in many developing countries. The period of protection offered by vaccinations differs widely, and some vaccinations are contraindicated if you are pregnant.

In some countries immunisations are available from airport or government health centres. Travel agents or airline offices will tell you where.

For entry into Zimbabwe, Botswana and Namibia, a yellow-fever vaccination certificate will be required if you are coming from a more northerly African country. Most commonly recommended for travel to southern Africa are typhoid, tetanus DPT, polio and meningitis vaccines. Protection against hepatitis is also required. A cholera vaccine will also recommended by some physicians. However, as already stated, its effectiveness is minimal.

The possible list of vaccinations includes:

Cholera Although some border officials may ask to see evidence of this vaccine – often unofficially as a means of extracting bribes – it is of limited effectiveness, lasts only six months and is not recommended for pregnant women. There have been no recent reports of cholera vaccine requirements in Zimbabwe, Botswana or Namibia, but those travelling overland across Africa might want to have it anyway, to avoid delays at borders or excuses to solicit bribes.

Hepatitis A This is the most common travel-acquired illness which can be prevented by vaccination. Protection can be provided in two ways – either with the antibody gamma globulin or with a new vaccine called Havrix (currently unavailable in the USA). Gamma globulin is not a vaccination but a ready-made antibody which has proven very successful in reducing the chances of contracting hepatitis infection. Because it may interfere with the development of immunity, it should not be given until at least 10 days after administration of the last vaccine needed. It should also be given as near as possible to departure because of its relatively short-lived effectiveness, which tapers off gradually between three and six months. Havrix provides long-term immunity (up to 10 years or more) after an initial course of two injections and a booster at one year. It may be more expensive than gamma globulin but has many advantages, including length of protection and ease of administration. Since it is a vaccine, it will take about three weeks to provide satisfactory protection – hence the need for careful planning prior to travel. The long-term protection offered by this vaccine should prove particularly useful for regular or long-term travellers.

Smallpox Smallpox has now been wiped out worldwide, so immunisation is no longer necessary.

Tetanus DPT Boosters are necessary at least every 10 years and are highly recommended.

Typhoid Available either as an injection or oral capsules. Protection lasts from one to three years and is useful if you are travelling for long in rural, tropical areas. You may have side effects, such as pain at the injection site, fever, headache and a general unwell feeling. A new single-dose injectable vaccine, which appears to have few side effects, is now available but is more expensive. Side effects are unusual with the oral form but occasionally stomach cramps will occur.

Yellow Fever Protection lasts for 10 years and is recommended for all travel to Africa and Latin America. You usually need to visit a special yellow-fever vaccination centre. Vaccination is contraindicated during pregnancy; seek medical advice if you must travel to a high-risk area.

Basic Rules

Care in what you eat and drink is the most important health rule. Stomach upsets are the most common travel-health problem (30 to 50% of people travelling outside their home country for two weeks or less can expect to experience them) but the majority of these upsets will be minor. Don't be paranoid about sampling local foods – it's all part of the travel experience and shouldn't be missed.

Water & Drinks

In hot climates make sure you drink enough – don't rely on feeling thirsty to indicate when you should drink. Not needing to urinate or very dark yellow urine is a danger sign. Always carry a water bottle with you on long trips. Excessive sweating can lead to loss of salt and therefore muscle cramping. Salt tablets are not a good idea as a preventative, but in places where salt is not used much adding salt to food can help.

Although many African countries have problems with contaminated water, tap water is generally safe to drink in Zimbabwe, Botswana and Namibia. Care should be taken when drinking from rural bores, however, since many have been tested and the water is considered fit only for cattle. Except in the Okavango Delta and in a few areas of Zimbabwe's Eastern Highlands, surface water (ie from rivers, lakes and ponds) should not be drunk untreated due to the risk of contamination by giardia.

When it's hot, be sure to drink lots of liquids. Excessive sweating can lead to loss of salt and cause muscle cramping. Salt tablets are not a good idea as a preventative, but in places where salt is not used much, adding salt to food can help. Failure to urinate or dark yellow urine is a sign of dehydration. Always carry a bottle of water on long trips.

Reputable brands of bottled water or soft drinks are normally fine although sometimes water bottles are refilled and resold – check the seals before buying. In rural areas, take care with fruit juices since water may have been added. Milk should be treated with suspicion as it is often unpasteurised. Boiled milk is fine if it is kept hygienically and yoghurt is always good. Tea or coffee should also be okay since the water used was probably boiled.

Water Purification You may on occasion need to rely on surface water or rural bores which may be contaminated. The simplest way to purify suspect water is to boil it for eight to 10 minutes, but remember that at high altitude water boils at a lower temperature, so germs are less likely to be killed. Simple filtering won't remove all dangerous organisms so if you can't boil suspect water, it should be treated chemically. Chlorine tablets (Puritabs, Steritabs and other brand names) will kill many but not all pathogens. Iodine is very effective and is available in tablet form (such as Potable Aqua) but follow the directions carefully and remember that too much iodine is harmful.

If you can't find tablets, tincture of iodine (2%) or iodine crystals may be used. Add four drops of tincture of iodine per litre or quart of water and let it stand for 30 minutes. Iodine crystals can also be used to purify water but this is a more complicated and dangerous process since you first must prepare a saturated iodine solution. Iodine loses its effectiveness if it is exposed to air or damp so be sure to keep it in a tightly sealed container. Flavoured powder will disguise the foul taste of iodine-treated water and is an especially good idea for those travelling with children.

Food Salads and fruit should be washed with purified water or peeled where possible. Ice cream is usually okay but beware of ice cream that has melted and been refrozen. Thoroughly cooked food is safest but not if it has been left to cool or if it has been reheated. Take great care with shellfish or fish and avoid undercooked meat, particularly in the form of mince. Steaming does not make shellfish safe for eating. As common sense directs, if a place looks clean and well-run and the vendor also looks clean and healthy, then the food is probably all right.

In general, places that are packed with travellers or locals will be fine, while empty restaurants are questionable. Busy restaurants mean the food is being cooked and eaten quite quickly with little standing around, and is probably not being reheated.

Nutrition If your food is poor or limited in availability, if you're travelling hard and fast and therefore missing meals, or if you simply lose your appetite, you can soon start to lose weight and place your health at risk.

Make sure your diet is well balanced. Eggs, tofu, beans, lentils and nuts are all safe ways to get protein. Fruit which you can peel (bananas, oranges or mandarins for example) is always safe and a good source of vitamins. Try to eat plenty of grains (including rice) and bread. Remember that although food is generally safer if it is cooked well, overcooked food loses much of its nutritional value. If your diet isn't well balanced or if your food intake is insufficient, it's a good idea to take vitamin and/or iron pills.

Everyday Health A normal body temperature is 37°C (98.6°F); more than 2°C higher is a 'high' fever. A normal adult pulse rate is 60 to 80 beats per minute (children 80 to 100, babies 100 to 140). You should know how to take a temperature and a pulse rate. As a general rule the pulse increases about 20 beats per minute for each °C rise in fever.

An abnormal respiration rate is also an indicator of illness. Count the number of breaths per minute: between 12 and 20 is normal for adults and older children (up to 30 for younger children, 40 for babies). People with a high fever or serious respiratory illness (like pneumonia) breathe more quickly than normal. More than 40 shallow breaths a minute usually means pneumonia.

In Western countries with safe water and excellent human-waste disposal systems, people often take good health for granted. It is important for people travelling in areas of poor sanitation to be aware of local conditions and to take extra care with their own personal hygiene habits.

Clean your teeth with purified water rather than straight from the tap. Avoid climatic extremes: keep out of the sun when it's hot, dress warmly when it's cold. Avoid potential diseases by dressing sensibly. You can get worm infections through walking barefoot. You can avoid insect bites by covering bare skin when insects are around, by screening windows or beds and by using insect repellents. Seek local advice: if you're told the water is unsafe due to crocodiles or bilharzia, don't go in. In situations where there is no information, discretion is the better part of valour.

Medical Problems & Treatment

Potential medical problems can be broken down into several areas. First there are the climatic and geographical considerations – problems caused by extremes of temperature, altitude or motion. Then there are diseases and illnesses caused through poor environmental sanitation, insect bites or stings, and animal or human contact. Simple cuts, bites or scratches have also been known to cause problems.

Self-diagnosis and treatment can be risky, so wherever possible seek qualified help. Although we do give treatment dosages in this section, they are for emergency use only. Medical advice should be sought where possible before administering any drugs.

An embassy or consulate can usually recommend a good place to go for such advice. So can five-star hotels, although they often recommend doctors with five-star prices. (This is when that medical insurance really comes in handy.) In some places standards of medical attention are so low that for some ailments the best advice is to get on a plane and go somewhere else.

Pharmacies & Medications It's not necessary to take along every remedy for every illness you might conceivably contract during your trip. Just about everything available at home can also be found in local pharmacies, but most pharmaceutical drugs are available only with a prescription. Malaria treatments are the exception and most pharmacists will hand out treatment dosages of chloroquine or Fansidar based on a description of the symptoms. Some places are lax about storage of medicines, however, so be sure to check expiry dates and storage conditions before buying. Also, bear in mind that some drugs available in Africa may be no longer recommended or may even be banned in other countries.

It's also a good idea to take a sufficient supply of any prescriptions that you must take habitually, including contraceptive pills and vitamin tablets. Travellers should also be aware of any drug allergies they may have and avoid using those drugs or their derivatives while travelling in southern Africa. Since common names of prescription medicines may well be different from the ones you're used to, ask a pharmacist before taking anything you're not sure about.

Climatic & Geographical Considerations

Sunburn All three countries covered in this book lie mostly within the humid tropics where the sun's rays are more direct and concentrated than in temperate zones. Even in the cooler highland areas, everyone – particularly fair-skinned people – will be susceptible to hazardous UV rays.

You can be quickly sunburnt, even when it's cloudy. Don't be deceived on a foggy or windy day on the coast – you can be just as easily burnt through a layer of fog. Use a sunblock on any area of exposed skin, especially if you're near water, and take extra care to cover skin which rarely sees the sun. A hat will protect your face and scalp, and zinc oxide will prevent a burnt then peeling nose. Sunglasses will prevent eye irritation (especially if you wear contact lenses).

Prickly Heat Prickly heat is an itchy rash caused by excessive perspiration trapped under the skin. It usually strikes those newly arrived in a hot climate whose pores have not opened enough to accommodate profuse sweating. Taking frequent baths and applying plenty of talcum powder will help relieve the itch.

Heat Exhaustion Heat combined with humidity and exposure to the sun can be oppressive and leave you feeling lethargic, irritable and dazed. A cool swim or lazy afternoon in the shade will do wonders to your mood. You'll also need to drink lots of liquids and eat salty foods in order to replenish what's lost during sweating.

Dehydration or salt deficiency can lead to heat exhaustion. Take time to acclimatise to high temperature and be sure to drink sufficient liquids. Salt deficiency, which can be brought on by diarrhoea or nausea, is characterised by fatigue, lethargy, headaches, giddiness and muscle cramps. Salt tablets will probably solve the problem. Anhydrotic heat exhaustion, caused by an inability to sweat, is quite rare. Unlike the other forms of heat exhaustion it is likely to strike people who have been in a hot climate for some time, rather than newcomers.

Heat Stroke This serious, sometimes fatal, condition can occur if the body's thermostat breaks down and the body temperature rises to dangerous levels. Continuous exposure to high temperatures can leave you vulnerable to heatstroke. Alcohol intake and strenuous activity can increase chances of heatstroke, especially in those who've recently arrived in a hot climate.

Symptoms include minimal sweating, a high body temperature (39 to 41° C), and a general feeling of being unwell. The skin may become flushed and red. Severe throbbing headaches, decreased coordination, and aggressive or confused behaviour may be signs of heatstroke. Eventually, the sufferer will become delirious and go into convulsions. Hospitalisation is essential, but meanwhile get the victim out of the sun, remove their clothing, cover them with a wet sheet or towel and then fan continually.

Fungal Infections Hot-weather fungal infections are most likely to occur on the scalp, between the toes or fingers (athlete's foot), in the groin (jock itch or crotch rot) and on the body (ringworm). You get ringworm (which is a fungal infection, not a worm) from infected animals or by walking on damp areas, like shower floors.

To prevent fungal infections wear loose, comfortable clothes, avoid artificial fibres, wash frequently and dry carefully. If you do get an infection, wash the infected area daily with a disinfectant or medicated soap and water, and rinse and dry well. Apply an antifungal powder like the widely available Tinaderm. Try to expose the infected area to air or sunlight as much as possible and wash all towels and underwear in hot water as well as changing them often.

Hypothermia Hypothermia is a dangerous lowering of the body temperature. It is caused by exhaustion and exposure to cold, wet or windy weather, which can occur, for example, when hiking, trekking or hitching. Hypothermia is a threat whenever a person is exposed to the elements at temperatures below 10°C.

Symptoms of hypothermia are exhaustion, numb skin (particularly toes and fingers), shivering, slurred speech, irrational or violent behaviour, lethargy, stumbling, dizzy spells, muscle cramps and violent bursts of energy. Irrationality may take the form of sufferers claiming they are warm and trying to take off their clothes.

To treat mild hypothermia, first get the person out of the wind and/or rain, remove their clothing if it's wet and replace it with dry, warm clothing. Give them hot liquids – not alcohol – and some high-kilojoule, easily digestible food. Do not rub victims, instead allow them to slowly warm themselves. This should be enough to treat the early stages of hypothermia. The early recognition and treatment of mild hypothermia is the only way to prevent severe hypothermia, which is a critical condition.

Motion Sickness If you're susceptible to motion sickness even on short trips, you should be prepared; if Dramamine works for you, take some along. Eating very lightly

before and during a trip will reduce the chances of motion sickness. If you know you're susceptible, try to find a place in a moving vehicle that minimises disturbance – near the wing on aircraft or near the centre on buses. Fresh air almost always helps but reading or cigarette smoking (or even being around someone else's smoke) normally makes matters worse.

Commercial motion sickness preparations, which can cause drowsiness, have to be taken before the trip; after you've begun feeling ill, it's too late. Dramamine tablets should be taken three hours before departure and scopolamine patches (which are available only by prescription in most places) should be applied 10 to 12 hours before departure. Scopolamine will dilate the pupils if it accidentally comes in contact with the eyes and has been known to cause drowsiness, so caution should be exercised. Ginger can be used as a natural preventative and is available in capsule form.

Infectious Diseases

Diarrhoea Sooner or later – unless you're exceptional – you'll get diarrhoea so you may as well accept the inevitable. Travellers' diarrhoea is not caused by lack of sanitation or 'bad' food but primarily by a change in diet and a lack of resistance to local strains of bacteria. Your susceptibility will depend largely on how much you've been exposed to foreign bacteria and what your stomach is used to.

The first thing to remember is that every case of diarrhoea is not dysentery, so don't panic and start stuffing yourself with pills. If you've spent all your life living out of sterilised packets and tins from the local supermarket, you'll have a hard time until you adjust. A few rushed toilet trips with no other symptoms is not normally indicative of a serious problem. Moderate diarrhoea, involving half-a-dozen loose movements in a day, is more of a nuisance. Dehydration is the main danger with any diarrhoea, particularly for children where dehydration can occur quite quickly.

Fluid replacement remains the mainstay

of management. If and when you get a gut infection, avoid rushing off to the chemist and loading up on antibiotics. It's too harsh a treatment and you can build up a tolerance to them through overuse. If the bacteria in your body are able to build up immunity to them, the antibiotics may not work when you really need them.

Try to starve the bugs out first. Weak black tea with a little sugar, soda water, or soft drinks allowed to go flat and diluted 50% with water are all good. If you can't hack starvation, keep to a light diet of dry toast, biscuits and black tea. To keep up your liquids, drink bottled water or lemonade. Once you're headed towards recovery, try some yoghurt but stay away from sweets, fruit and any other dairy products.

With severe diarrhoea a rehydrating solution is necessary to replace minerals and salts. Commercially available oral rehydration salts (ORS) are very useful; add the contents of one sachet to a litre of boiled or bottled water. In an emergency you can make up a solution of eight teaspoons of sugar to a litre of boiled water and provide salted cracker biscuits at the same time. You should stick to a bland diet as you recover.

Lomotil or Imodium can be used to temporarily 'plug the system' but do not actually cure the problem. Only use these drugs if absolutely necessary. For children Imodium is preferable, but under all circumstances fluid replacement is the main message. Do not use these drugs if the person has a high fever or is severely dehydrated.

In certain situations antibiotics may be indicated:

- Watery diarrhoea with blood and mucous (gut-paralysing drugs like Imodium or Lomotil should be avoided in this situation)
- Watery diarrhoea with fever and lethargy
- Persistent diarrhoea for more than five days
- Severe diarrhoea, if it is logistically difficult to stay in one place

The recommended drugs (adults only) would be either norfloxacin 400 mg twice daily for three days or ciprofloxacin 500 mg twice daily for three days. The drug bismuth subsalicylate has also been used successfully (it is not available in Australia). The dosage for adults is two tablets or 30 ml and for children it is one tablet or 10 ml. This dose can be repeated every 30 minutes to one hour, with no more than eight doses in a 24-hour period.

The drug of choice in children would be co-trimoxazole (Bactrim, Septrin, Resprim) with dosage dependent on weight. A three-day course is also given. Ampicillin has been recommended in the past and may still be an alternative.

If you don't recover after a couple of days, it may be necessary to visit a doctor and be tested for other problems such as giardiasis, dysentery, cholera and so on.

Giardiasis Giardiasis is prevalent in tropical climates and is first characterised by a swelling of the stomach, pale-coloured faeces, diarrhoea, frequent gas, headache and later by nausea and depression. The symptoms may disappear for a few days and then return; this can go on for several weeks.

Tinidazole, known as Fasigyn, or metronidazole (Flagyl) are the recommended drugs for treatment. Either can be used in a single dose. Antibiotics are of no use.

Dysentery This serious illness is caused by contaminated food or water and is characterised by severe diarrhoea, often with blood or mucus in the stool, and painful gut cramps. There are two types: bacillary dysentery, which is uncomfortable but not enduring, and amoebic dysentery which, as its name suggests, is caused by amoebas. This variety is much more difficult to treat and is more persistent.

Bacillary dysentery is characterised by quite a high fever and rapid onset. Symptoms include headache, vomiting and stomach pains. It doesn't generally last more than a week, but it is highly contagious and because it's caused by bacteria, it responds well to antibiotics.

Amoebic dysentery, or amoebiasis, builds up more slowly and is more dangerous. It is caused by protozoans, or amoebic parasites, called *Entamoeba histolytica*, which are also transmitted through contaminated food or water. Once they've invaded, they live in the lower intestinal tract and cause heavy and often bloody diarrhoea, fever, tenderness in the liver area and intense abdominal pain. If left untreated, ulceration and inflammation of the colon and rectum can become very serious. If you see blood in your faeces over two or three days, seek medical attention.

A stool test is necessary to diagnose which kind of dysentery you have, so you should seek medical help urgently. In case of an emergency the drugs norfloxacin or ciprofloxacin can be used as presumptive treatment for bacillary dysentery, and metronidazole (Flagyl) for amoebic dysentery.

Bacillary dysentery hits quickly and because it's caused by bacteria, responds well to antibiotics. Often recommended is norfloxacin 400 mg, taken twice daily for seven days or ciprofloxacin 500 mg twice daily for seven days. If you're unable to find either of these drugs try co-trimoxazole 160/800 mg (Bactrim, Septrin, Resprim) twice daily for seven days. This is a sulphur drug (sulpha or sulphate) and must not be used in people with a sulphur allergy. In the case of children the drug co-trimoxazole is a reasonable first-line treatment.

On the other hand, since the symptoms themselves are actually the best treatment – diarrhoea and fever are both trying to rid the body of the infection – you may also just want to hole up for a few days and let it run its course. If activity or travel is absolutely necessary during the infection, you can take either Imodium or Lomotil to keep things under control until reaching a more convenient location to R & R (rest and run).

For amoebic dysentery, the recommended adult dosage of metronidazole (Flagyl) is one 750 mg to 800-mg capsule three times daily for five days. Children aged between eight and 12 years should have half the adult dose; the dosage for younger children is one-third the adult dose. An alternative to Flagyl is Tinaba, also called Fasigyn, taken as a two-gram daily dose for three days. Alcohol must be avoided during treatment and for 48 hours afterwards. These drugs should be used with caution during pregnancy.

Cholera The cholera vaccine is between 20 to 50% effective according to most authorities, and the vaccine can have some side effects. Vaccination is not usually recommended for (nor legally required by) the countries covered in this book, but some other African countries (eg Tanzania, Rwanda, Nigeria) may strongly recommend vaccination at borders. If you are travelling further north and want to avoid unplanned-for jabs, it may be worth having the shot before you leave home.

Over the past several years, there have been isolated cases of cholera in Zimbabwe's Eastern Highlands. Keep up to date with information about this and other diseases by contacting travellers' clinics or vaccination centres, and avoid areas where there are outbreaks.

Cholera is characterised by a sudden onset of acute diarrhoea with 'rice water' stools, vomiting, muscular cramps and extreme weakness. You will need medical attention but your first concern should be rehydration. Drink as much water as you can – if it refuses to stay down, keep drinking anyway. If there is likely to be an appreciable delay in reaching medical treatment, begin a course of tetracycline, administered in four 250-mg doses per day (adults). It is not recommended for children under eight years of age nor for pregnant women (be sure to check the expiry date since old tetracycline can become toxic). An alternative drug would be Ampicillin. Although antibiotics might kill the bacteria, remember that it is a toxin produced by the bacteria which causes the massive fluid loss. Also remember that fluid replacement is still by far the most important aspect of the treatment.

Viral Gastroenteritis This is not caused by bacteria but, as the name implies, a virus. It is characterised by stomach cramps, diarrhoea, vomiting and slight fever. All you can do is rest and keep drinking as much water as possible.

Hepatitis This incapacitating disease is caused by a virus which attacks the liver. Hepatitis A, which is the most common strain in southern Africa, is contracted through contact with contaminated food, water, cutlery, toilets or individuals. It is a very common problem amongst travellers visiting areas of poor sanitation. With good water and adequate sewage disposal in most industrialised countries since the 1940s, very few young adults now have any natural immunity and must be protected.

The symptoms are fever, chills, headache, fatigue, feelings of weakness and aches and pains, followed by loss of appetite, nausea, vomiting, abdominal pain, dark urine, light-coloured faeces, and jaundiced skin, and the whites of the eyes may turn a sickly yellow. In some cases you may feel tired and unwell, experience aches and pains, particularly tenderness in the right side of the abdomen. You should seek medical advice, but in general there is not much you can do except rest, drink lots of fluids, eat lightly and avoid fatty foods, keeping to a diet high in proteins and vitamins. Avoid alcohol and cigarettes completely. People who have had hepatitis must forego alcohol for six months after the illness, as hepatitis attacks the liver which needs this amount of time to recover.

If you contract hepatitis A during a short trip to Africa, you probably should make arrangements to go home. If you can afford the time, however, and have a reliable travelling companion who can bring you food and water, the best cure is to stay where you are, find a few good books and only leave bed to go to the toilet. After a month or so, you should feel like living again.

The best preventative measures available are either the recently introduced long-term hepatitis A vaccine; or a gamma globulin jab before departure from home and booster shots every three or four months thereafter while you're away (beware of unsanitary needles!). A jab is also in order if you come in contact with any infected person; and if

you come down with hepatitis, anyone who has been in recent contact with you should take the shot too.

Hepatitis B, formerly known as serum hepatitis, can only be caught by sexual contact with an infected person, unsterilised needles, blood transfusions or by skin penetration – such as tattooing, shaving or having your ears pierced.

The symptoms of type B are much the same as type A except that they are more severe and may lead to fatal liver failure, irreparable liver damage or even liver cancer. Although there is no treatment for hepatitis B, an effective prophylactic vaccine is readily available in most countries. The immunisation schedule requires two injections at least a month apart followed by a third dose five months after the second. Persons who should receive a hepatitis B vaccination include anyone who anticipates contact with blood or other bodily secretions, either as a health care worker or through sexual contact with the local population, particularly those who intend to stay in the country for a long period of time.

Hepatitis Non-A Non-B is a blanket term formerly used for several different strains of hepatitis, which have now been separately identified. Hepatitis C is similar to B but is less common. Hepatitis D (the 'delta particle') is also similar to B. Its occurrence is currently limited to IV drug users and it always occurs in concert with Hepatitis B, never on its own. Hepatitis E, however, is similar to A and is spread in the same manner, by water or food contamination.

Tests are available for these strains, but are very expensive. Travellers shouldn't be too paranoid about this apparent proliferation of hepatitis strains; they are fairly rare (so far) and following the same precautions as for A and B should be all that's necessary to avoid them.

Typhoid Contaminated food and water are responsible for typhoid fever, a gut infection that travels the faecal-oral route. Vaccination against typhoid isn't 100% effective.

Since typhoid can be very serious,

medical attention is necessary. Early symptoms are like those of many other travellers' illnesses – you may feel as though you have a bad cold or the flu combined with a headache, sore throat and a fever. The fever rises slowly until it is around 40°C or more while the pulse drops slowly, unlike a normal fever, in which the pulse increases. These symptoms may be accompanied by vomiting, diarrhoea or constipation.

In the second week, the fever and slow pulse continue and a few pink spots may appear on the body. Trembling, delirium, weakness, weight loss and dehydration set in. If there are no further complications, the fever and symptoms will slowly fade during the third week. Medical attention is essential, however, since typhoid is extremely infectious and possible complications include pneumonia, or peritonitis (perforated bowel).

When feverish, the victim should be kept cool. Watch for dehydration. The drug of choice is ciprofloxacin at a dose of one gram daily for 14 days. However, it is quite expensive and may not be available. The alternative, chloramphenicol, has been the mainstay of treatment for many years and in many countries it is still the recommended antibiotic. However, there are fewer side effects with the third alternative, Ampicillin. The adult dosage is two 250-mg capsules, four times a day. Children aged between eight and 12 years should have half the adult dose; younger children should have one-third the adult dose. People who are allergic to penicillin should not be given Ampicillin.

Tetanus This potentially fatal disease is found in underdeveloped tropical areas and is difficult to treat but is easily prevented by vaccination. Tetanus occurs when a wound becomes infected by the bacterium *clostridium* which can live in soil or in the intestines of humans or animals. Clean all cuts, punctures, and bites. Tetanus is also known as lockjaw and the first symptom may be difficulty in swallowing and a stiffening of the jaw and neck followed by painful convulsions of the jaw and whole body.

Rabies Rabies is found all over Africa and is caused by the bite or scratch of an infected animal. Avoid any animal that appears to be foaming at the mouth or behaving strangely (but naturally be cautious about approaching even apparently healthy animals). Dogs are particularly notable carriers. Any bite, scratch or even lick from a mammal should be cleaned immediately and thoroughly. Scrub with soap and running water and then clean with an alcohol solution. If there is any possibility that the animal is infected, help should be sought immediately. Even if the animal isn't rabid, all bites should be treated seriously as they can become infected or result in tetanus. A rabies vaccination is now available and should be considered if you spend a lot of time around animals.

If you do get bitten, try to capture (or, as a last option, kill) the offending animal so that it may be tested. If that's impossible, then you must assume the animal is rabid. The rabies virus incubates slowly in its victim, so while medical attention isn't urgent, it shouldn't be delayed.

Meningococcal Meningitis Sub-Saharan Africa is considered the 'meningitis belt'; in southern Africa, you're at greatest risk during the summer months, from November to April. The disease is spread by close contact with people who carry it in their throats and noses. They probably aren't aware they are carriers and pass it around through coughs and sneezes.

This very serious disease attacks the brain and can be fatal. A scattered blotchy rash, fever, severe headache, sensitivity to light and stiffness in the neck preventing nodding of the head are the first symptoms. Death can occur within a few hours so immediate treatment with large doses of penicillin is vital. If intravenous administration is impossible, it should be given intramuscularly. Vaccination offers reasonable protection for over a year but you should check for reports of recent outbreaks and try to avoid affected areas.

Tuberculosis (TB) Although this disease is widespread in many developing countries, it is not a serious risk to travellers. Young children are more susceptible than adults and vaccination is a sensible precaution for children under 12 years travelling in endemic areas. TB is commonly spread by coughing or by unpasteurised dairy products from infected cows. Milk that has been boiled is safe to drink; the souring of milk to make yoghurt or cheese also kills the bacilli.

Bilharzia Bilharzia, which is quite common in Africa, is caused by blood flukes, minute worms which live in the veins of the bladder or large intestine. The eggs produced by adult worms are discharged in urine or faeces. If they reach water, they hatch and enter the bodies of a certain species of freshwater snail where they multiply for four or more weeks and are then released into the snail's watery home. To survive, they must find and invade the body of a human being where they may develop, mate and reoccupy the veins of their choice. They lay eggs and the cycle starts over. The snail favours shallow water near the shores of lakes and streams and are most abundant in water polluted by human excrement. Generally speaking, moving water poses less risk than stagnant water but can still be a problem, and even deep water can be infected.

The worm enters through the skin, and the first symptoms may be a tingling and sometimes a light rash around the area where it entered. Weeks later, when the worm is busy producing eggs, a high fever may develop. A general feeling of being unwell may be the first symptom; once the disease is established, other signs include abdominal pain and blood in the urine.

To avoid contracting bilharzia, stay out of rivers, lakes and especially, dams – the streams of Zimbabwe's Eastern Highlands and Botswana's Okavango Delta are significant exceptions. Since the intermediate hosts – snails – live only in fresh water, there's no risk of catching bilharzia in the sea. If you do get wet, dry off quickly and dry your clothes as well. Seek medical attention if you have been exposed to the disease and tell the doctor your suspicions, as bilharzia in the early stages can be confused with malaria or typhoid.

Although locals maintain that it's impossible to contract bilharzia by drinking infected water, treat all surface water as suspect; refer to the discussion of water purification earlier in this section.

The disease is painful and causes persistent and cumulative damage by repeated deposits of eggs. If you suspect you have it, seek medical advice as soon as possible. If you cannot get medical help immediately, then praziquantel (Biltricide) is the recommended treatment. The recommended dosage is 40 mg per kg of body weight in divided doses over one day. Niridazole is an alternative drug.

Diptheria Diptheria can appear as a skin infection or a more serious throat infection. It is spread by contaminated dust coming in contact with the skin or being inhaled. About the only way to prevent the skin infection is to keep clean and dry. The throat infection is prevented by vaccination.

Sexually Transmitted Diseases

Sexual contact with an infected partner can spread a number of unpleasant diseases. While abstinence is the only guaranteed preventative measure, use of a condom will considerably lessen your risks. The most common of these diseases are gonorrhoea and syphilis which in men first appear as sores, blisters or rashes around the genitals and pain or discharge when urinating. Symptoms may be less marked or not evident at all in women. The symptoms of syphilis eventually disappear completely but the disease continues and may cause severe problems in later years. Antibiotics are used to treat both syphilis and gonorrhoea.

There are numerous other sexually transmitted diseases, for most of which effective treatment is available. However, there is no cure for herpes and there is also currently no cure for HIV/AIDS.

HIV/AIDS HIV/AIDS is another issue. HIV, the Human Immunodeficiency Virus, may develop into AIDS, Acquired Immune Deficiency Syndrome. It is a growing major problem around the world, but HIV/AIDS is prevalent in Africa to a degree unfamiliar to most Western travellers and should be a major concern to all visitors. Known colloquially as 'Slim' because it causes victims to appear emaciated, it is particularly rampant in East Africa – some areas of Uganda are already being depopulated by it – and it has spread southward, particularly along trucking routes and in areas where men migrate to work far from their families. Therefore, the most vulnerable segment of society are economically productive men and often, their wives as well.

Of the countries covered in this book, Zimbabwe has the most serious problem with this disease – currently, 90% of all deaths in Zimbabwe are AIDS-related – although it exists in all three countries. The statistics, especially for Zimbabwe, are both frightening and difficult to accept. Virtually ignored until the early 1990s, Zimbabwe's AIDS education programme is now gaining momentum. However, the cause isn't helped by the outspoken MP, Ruth Chinamano, who maintains the AIDS prevention campaign is a European plot designed to prevent Africans from reproducing.

A 1993 press release reported 25,300 reported cases of full-blown AIDS in Zimbabwe. Official estimates placed the total number – reported and unreported – at around 55,000, with over 700,000 people infected with HIV. An earlier report, however, estimated that in 1990, 60% of Zimbabwean soldiers, 30 to 50% of hospital patients and 20% of the general population were HIV positive. In addition, 5.18% of screened blood donations were found to be HIV positive.

Any exposure to blood, blood products or bodily fluids may put the individual at risk. Although in developed countries HIV/AIDS is most commonly spread through the sharing of contaminated needles by intravenous drug users and through contact between homosexual and bisexual males, in Africa it is transmitted primarily through heterosexual activity. Apart from abstinence, the most effective preventative is always to practise reasonably safe sex using condoms and to refrain from sharing needles. It is impossible to detect the HIV-positive status of an otherwise healthy-looking person without a blood test. Most people affected by the HIV virus are not aware they have it and hospitals are likely to diagnose their symptoms as something more mundane.

HIV/AIDS can also be spread through infected blood transfusions; Zimbabwe, Botswana and Namibia currently claim that all blood donations are screened for HIV. If you must have an emergency transfusion, private clinics are generally a better option than public hospitals but if you're able, you should still try to make absolutely certain that the blood in question is safe.

HIV is also spread by dirty needles – vaccinations, acupuncture, tattooing and ear or nose piercing are potentially as dangerous as intravenous drug use if the equipment isn't clean. If you do need an injection, it may be wise to buy a new syringe from a pharmacy and ask the doctor to use it. You may also want to carry a couple of syringes, in case of emergency.

Insect Borne Diseases

Malaria Malaria is caused by the blood parasite *plasmodium* which is transmitted by the nocturnal *anopheles* mosquito. There are four types of malaria: *Plasmodium falciparum*, the deadliest; *Plasmodium malariae* which is still universally sensitive to chloroquine; and finally *Plasmodium vivax* and *Plasmodium ovale* which are harboured outside the blood and can cause relapse. The drug-resistant status of different malarial strains in different parts of the world is constantly in flux.

Only the female mosquitoes spread the disease but you can contract it through a single bite from an insect carrying the parasite. Malaria sporozites enter the bloodstream and travel to the liver where they mature, infect the red blood cells and begin to multiply. This process takes between one and five weeks. Only when the infected cells re-enter the bloodstream and burst do the dramatic symptoms begin. For this reason, malaria can be extremely dangerous because the victim by this time has often left the malarial area, so the disease is not suspected and therefore is improperly treated.

Contrary to popular belief, once a person contracts malaria he/she does not have it for life. One of the parasites may lie dormant in the liver but this can also be eradicated using a specific medication. Malaria is therefore curable, as long as the traveller seeks medical help when symptoms occur, either at home or overseas.

Currently, the areas of greatest risk include the Zambezi and Chobe valleys, the lowveld of south-eastern Zimbabwe and Namibia's Caprivi Strip.

Prevention The most effective form of malaria prevention, of course, is to avoid being bitten. Since the mosquitoes bite at dusk, you can avoid bites by covering bare skin with long trousers and long-sleeved shirts and using an insect repellent. It helps if you use a repellent containing DEET (diethylmetatoluamide) on exposed areas of skin, wear light-coloured clothing, and avoid strongly scented perfumes or aftershave. An alternative would be the new eucalyptus-based product known as Mosi-Guard Natural, which matches the efficacy of DEET but isn't so harsh on the skin. It's available from MASTA (see Travel Health Information earlier in this chapter). It would also help to sleep under a mosquito net or at least light a mosquito coil.

Next best – but hardly 100% effective – is a course of antimalarials, which is normally taken two weeks before, during and several weeks after travelling in malarial areas. The malaria parasite mutates rapidly and although pharmacology manages to keep one step ahead of it, advice on which antimalarials you'll need to take goes out of date quickly. Your doctor or travellers' health clinic should have access to the latest information. Currently, chloroquine is the recommended prophylaxis for Zimbabwe, Botswana and Namibia, although local

strains are becoming resistant to it. As a result, more doctors are recommending newer drugs such as mefloquine (Lariam) and doxycycline (Vibramycin, Doryx). Regardless, expert advice should be sought regarding your choice of antimalarials.

Having said that, it must be pointed out that many local residents and expatriates working in southern Africa for long periods prefer not to take prophylactics, but to treat the disease if and when it strikes. The reasoning is that the drugs may cause serious side effects – specifically to the liver and eyes – if taken over long periods.

There's currently no vaccination against malaria and it has been alleged that development of the vaccine has been ignored by researchers and pharmaceutical companies because they haven't seen any profit in it. Although that might have been true 10 years ago – and is probably the reason medical science is so far behind on this score – with the current international travel explosion in Western countries and the economic blossoming in South-East Asia, it certainly would be profitable these days.

Diagnosis & Treatment If you are travelling in, or have recently left, a malaria area you must remain alert for any symptoms which might indicate you have become infected. The symptoms of malaria are very varied and may include gradual loss of appetite, fever and headache, chills, a flu-like illness, nausea, vomiting, diarrhoea and tiredness. If you have any symptoms, you must seek medical advice as soon as possible and have a malaria slide examination of your blood performed. Most deaths from malaria are due to delays in seeking medical attention. If you are not within reach of prompt medical treatment then self treatment is an emergency option. If self treatment is used the traveller must realise the treatment may not be complete and may mask the effects of other diseases. Always obtain medical care.

Malaria-prevention medicines are particular to the area of travel and the activities being undertaken and need to take into account the traveller's medical history. This is also the case for emergency self-treatment options and advice from your doctor or a specialised travel medicine centre should be obtained before travel. This is particularly vital when travelling with young children. The current emergency self-treatment medicines are Fansidar (for adults three tablets once only), mefloquine (for adults two tablets initially and two tablets every six hours – note: mefloquine must not be used as an emergency self treatment if it has been used as a preventative medicine), chloroquine (for adults four tablets = 600 mg initially, then four tablets again every eight hours followed by two tablets daily for two days) or quinine (for adults two tablets = 600 mg three times a day for seven days). Prevention medication should be continued after treatment for malaria and medical care must be obtained as soon as possible.

Myiasis This unpleasant affliction is caused by the larvae of the tumbu or putse fly which lays eggs on damp or sweaty clothing. The eggs hatch and the larvae burrow into the skin, producing an ugly boil as it develops. To kill the invader, place drops of hydrogen peroxide, alcohol or oil over the boil to cut off its air supply, then squeeze the boil to remove the bug. However revolting the process, at this stage the problem is solved.

Trypanosomiasis (Sleeping Sickness) This is another disease transmitted by biting insects, in this case the tsetse fly. Like malaria, it's caused by minute parasites which live in the blood. The risk of infection is very small and confined to only a fraction of the tsetse fly's total range, which includes western Zimbabwe and the Zambezi and Chobe valleys. The flies are responsible for the absence of cattle and horses from large tracts of central and southern Africa. The fly is about twice the size of a common house fly and recognisable from the scissor-like way it folds its wings at rest. Only a small proportion of tsetse flies carry the disease but it is best to try to avoid being bitten; there is no immunisation. The flies are attracted to large moving objects, like safari buses, to perfume or aftershave, and to colours like dark blue. The illness is serious but responds well to medical attention.

The first sign of infection is local oedema (swelling caused by excess water retention in body tissues), followed after two or three weeks by irregular fevers, abscesses, inflammation of the glands and physical and mental lethargy.

Dengue Fever There is no prophylactic available for this mosquito-spread disease; the main preventative measure is to avoid mosquito bites. A sudden onset of fever, headaches and severe joint and muscle pains are the first signs before a rash starts on the trunk of the body and spreads to the limbs and face. After a further few days, the fever will subside and recovery will begin.

Serious complications are not common, although the condition could develop into haemorrhagic fever; the first indication is normally a pinprick rash on the skin, which is due to capillary haemorrhaging. In this case, hospitalisation is essential.

Yellow Fever Yellow Fever is endemic in much of Africa but only the northern extremes of the area covered by this book – the Zambezi, Chobe and Okavango valleys and north-eastern Namibia are affected. This viral disease, which is transmitted to humans by mosquitoes, first manifests itself in fever, headache, abdominal pain and vomiting. There may appear to be a brief recovery before it progresses into its more severe stages when liver failure becomes a possibility. There is no treatment apart from keeping the fever down and avoiding dehydration. The yellow-fever vaccination, which is highly recommended for every traveller in Africa, offers good protection for 10 years.

Worms Worms are common in most humid tropical areas and a stool test when you return home isn't a bad idea if you think you may have contracted them. They can live on unwashed vegetables or in undercooked meat or you can pick them up through your skin by walking barefoot. Infestations may not be obvious for some time and although they are generally not serious, they can cause further health problems if left untreated. Once the problem is confirmed, over-the-counter medication is available to rid yourself of them.

The most common form you're likely to contract are hookworms. They are usually caught by walking barefoot on infected soil. They bore through the skin, attach themselves to the inner wall of the intestine and proceed to suck blood, resulting in abdominal pain and sometimes anaemia.

Threadworms, or *strongyloidiasis*, are also found in low lying areas and operate very much like hookworms, but symptoms are more visible and can include diarrhoea and vomiting.

Worms may be treated with thiabendazole or mabendazole taken orally twice daily for three or four days. As usual, however, it's best to get medical advice because the symptoms of worms so closely resemble those of other, more serious conditions.

Typhus Typhus is spread by ticks, mites or lice and begins as a severe cold followed by a fever, chills, headache, muscle pains, and rash. There is often a large and painful sore at the site of the bite and nearby lymph nodes become swollen and painful.

Trekkers in southern Africa may be at risk from cattle or wild game ticks. Seek local advice on areas where ticks pose a danger and always check your skin carefully for ticks after walking in a risk area, such as a forest. A strong insect repellent can help, and serious walkers in tick areas should consider having their boots and trousers impregnated with benzyl benzoate and dibutylphthalate.

Japanese Encephalitis This viral infection of the brain is transmitted by mosquitoes. Vaccination is recommended for those intending to spend more than a month in a rural risk area during the rainy season, for those making repeated trips into a risk area or who are planning to stay for a year or more

in a risk area, and for those visiting an area where there is an epidemic. The disease is not common in travellers and only 25 severe cases have been reported worldwide.

Cuts, Bites, & Stings

Cuts & Scratches The warm, moist conditions of the tropical lowlands invite and promote the growth of 'wee beasties' that would be thwarted in more temperate climates. Because of this, even a small cut or scratch can become painfully infected and lead to more serious problems.

Since bacterial immunity to certain antibiotics can build up, it's not wise to take these medicines indiscriminately or as a preventative measure. The best treatment for cuts is to cleanse the affected area with soap and water frequently and apply mercurachrome or an antiseptic cream. Where possible, avoid using bandages, which keep wounds moist and encourage the growth of bacteria. If, despite this, the wound becomes tender and inflamed then use of a mild, broad-spectrum antibiotic may be warranted.

Snakebite To minimise chances of being bitten, always wear boots, socks and long trousers when walking through undergrowth. A good pair of canvas gaiters will further protect your legs – or at least provide a measure of psychological peace of mind! Don't put your hands into holes and crevices and be careful when collecting firewood.

Puff adders are the most common cause of snake bite in southern Africa. They especially like the loose sand in dry river beds and it is a good idea always to wear stout footwear rather than sandals in such locations. Other dangerous species include green mambas, black mambas, gaboon vipers and spitting cobras.

Snakebites do not cause instantaneous death and antivenenes are usually available, but it is vital that you make a positive identification of the snake in question or at the very least, have a detailed description of it. Keep the victim calm and still, wrap the bitten limb as you would for a sprain and then attach a splint to immobilise it. Tourniquets and suction on the wound are now comprehensively discredited. Seek medical help immediately and if possible, bring the snake (if dead) along for identification (but don't attempt to catch it if there is a chance of being bitten again). Bushwalkers who are (wisely) concerned about snakebite should carry a field guide with photos and detailed descriptions of the possible perpetrators.

Insects Ants, gnats, mosquitoes, bees and flies are just as annoying in Africa as they are at home. Cover yourself well with clothing and use insect repellent on exposed skin. Burning incense and sleeping under mosquito nets in air-conditioned rooms or under fans also lowers the risk of being bitten. If you're going walking in humid or densely foliated areas, wear light cotton trousers and shoes, not shorts and sandals or thongs.

Unless you're allergic, bee and wasp stings are more painful than dangerous. Calamine lotion offers some relief and ice packs will reduce pain and swelling.

If you're camping in the bush, check your socks, shoes, hat and sleeping bag before inserting any part of your body. Scorpions and centipedes are particularly unpleasant and while their stings aren't normally fatal, the effects can be debilitating and quite painful. Also, large and hairy spiders – as well as several smaller black ones – will deliver a painful bite. The most dangerous is the button spider which lives in the Zambezi Valley, but fortunately it's rare.

Leeches & Ticks Leeches may be present in damp rainforest conditions; they attach themselves to your skin to suck your blood. Trekkers often get them on their legs or in their boots. Salt or a lighted cigarette end will make them fall off. Do not pull them off, as the bite is then more likely to become infected. An insect repellent may keep them away. Vaseline, alcohol or oil will persuade a tick to let go. You should always check your body if you have been walking through a tick-infested area, as they can spread typhus.

Women's Health
Gynaecological Problems Poor diet, lowered resistance due to use of antibiotics, and even contraceptive pills can lead to vaginal infections when travelling in hot climates. To prevent the worst of it, keep the genital area clean, wear cotton underwear and skirts or loose-fitting trousers.

Yeast infections, characterised by a rash, itch and discharge, can be treated with a vinegar or lemon-juice douche or with yoghurt. Nystatin suppositories are the usual medical prescription. Trichomoniasis is a more serious infection which causes a discharge and a burning sensation when urinating. If a vinegar and water douche is not effective, medical attention should be sought. Metronidazole (Flagyl) is the most frequently prescribed drug. Male sexual partners must also be treated.

Pregnancy Most miscarriages occur during the first trimester of pregnancy so this is the most risky time to be travelling. The last three months should also be spent within reasonable distance of good medical care since serious problems can develop at this stage as well. A baby born as early as 24 weeks stands a chance of survival, but only in a good modern hospital. Pregnant women should avoid all unnecessary medication but vaccinations and malarial prophylactics should still be taken where possible (seek medical advice). Extra care should be taken to prevent illness and particular attention to diet and proper nutrition will significantly lessen the chances of complications.

WOMEN TRAVELLERS
Southern Africa is one place in the developing world where it's possible for women to meet and communicate with local men – Black or White – without necessarily being misconstrued. That's not to say the 'loose foreigner' stigma that prevails in so many countries hasn't arrived to some degree but White Zimbabweans have done a lot to refute the image that women of European descent are willing to hop into bed with the first taker. Neither does it mean that you

won't get a lot of attention if you sally into a bar or a disco unaccompanied. Generally, however, sober men are polite and respectful and if it's obvious you're not interested, you won't have to fend off roving tentacles while conversing or dancing.

Keep in mind that some degree of modesty is expected of women; short sleeves are fine but hemlines shouldn't be much above knee-level. To avoid unwanted attention, prevent sunstroke and keep cool, it's probably best to cover as much as possible.

The threat of sexual assault isn't greater in southern Africa than it would be in Europe but women should do their best to avoid wandering alone through parks and back-streets, especially at night.

Although these countries are considerably safer than some other African countries, such as Kenya, hitching alone cannot really be recommended. In all three countries, you should be prepared to refuse a lift if the driver is visibly intoxicated (a sadly common condition) or the car is chock-a-block with men and there's not a female in sight. Similarly, if you must hitch alone, don't accept lifts from military transport vehicles – they'll almost always stop for you – unless you

don't mind an uncomfortable amount of male attention. It's best not to hitch at night and if possible, find a companion for trips through sparsely populated areas. Use common sense and things should go well.

ACTIVITIES
Safaris & Wildlife Viewing
If you're an average visitor to southern Africa, you're planning at least one foray into the bush to meet the endearing faces you've come to know over the years through National Geographic specials and nature programmes. Although the term 'safari' may conjure up the image of a single-file procession of adventurers stalking through the bush behind a very large elephant-gun, modern usage allows a broader spectrum of connotations. The word, which means 'we go' in Swahili, may refer to river rafting, bushwalking, horse-riding, even warming your seat in a train or aeroplane!

Most safaris are the wildlife-viewing sort, however. Because the majority of wildlife parks are off limits to those without vehicles, independent travellers can still appreciate wildlife-viewing activities without having to pay for car hire fees. Don't be put off by a

---

Poachers
Although few travellers wander far enough from the beaten routes to encounter poachers, a warning is still in order.

Each of the three countries covered in this book likes to blame the other two – as well as Zambia, Angola, Mozambique and South Africa – for their wildlife poaching problems. Wherever their place of origin, however, elephant and rhino poachers are ruthless businesspeople in pursuit of the high prices commanded for rapidly dwindling supplies of animal products such as ivory and especially rhino horn.

Rhino horn is highly sought after as a component in the sheaths of Yemeni dagger handles and is believed by some Oriental cultures to have medicinal properties. Both markets shell out big money for the commodity and as long as someone will pay (and the product isn't yet extinct), someone else is going to risk their neck to provide it.

Most African countries have a 'shoot to kill' policy with respect to poachers so the culprits are understandably jumpy about anyone seen travelling in the remote bush where they practice their heinous trade. Anything that stands between a poacher and their profits will be as endangered as the prey itself. ■

Large Animals

The threat of attack by wild animals in Africa is largely exaggerated and problems are extremely rare but compliance with a couple of rules will further diminish the chances of a close encounter.

The five animals most potentially dangerous to humans have been grouped into a sort of game hunter's checklist known as the 'Big Five' – lion, leopard, buffalo, elephant and rhino. Since they're normally abroad only at night, you'd have to be extremely fortunate to see a leopard, let alone have problems with one. Because rhinos are so rare these days, the threat of a rhino charge is negligible. If for some reason you are caught out, the advice normally given is to face the charge and step to one side at the last moment. The rhino can't really see you and will have too much forward momentum to turn quickly, anyway. If you're with other people, be sure the entire group steps to the same side.

Although buffaloes are docile while in a herd, individuals who've somehow become estranged from buffalo society can be more irritable. Avoid such animals. If you do encounter one in the bush, however, back quietly away without making any sudden moves until you're out of sight. If there is a charge, head for the nearest tree or dive into the bushes posthaste.

Lions, though rarely interested in humans, have been known to attack on occasion. If you're camping out in the bush, be sure to zip your tent up completely and if you hear a large animal outside, lie still even if it brushes against the tent. This is easier said than done, of course, but lions don't really know what to make of tents and normally leave them alone. If you encounter a lion (or especially a lioness) while walking in the bush, try to avoid an adrenalin rush (also easier said than done); whatever you do, don't turn and run. If you respond like a prey species, the lion could react accordingly.

Unless you're in a vehicle, elephants are best avoided; their size alone will probably put you off approaching them too closely anyway. Although elephants certainly aren't bloodthirsty creatures – they're vegetarian – it's been said that an elephant never forgets. An individual that's had trouble from humans previously may feel the need to take revenge. If an elephant is visibly holding its trunk erect and sniffing the air, it probably detects your presence and is worried; you should move away slowly. Cows with calves should also be avoided; similarly, do not approach any elephant with visible injuries, such as a damaged foot or trunk (an indication of having been caught in a snare). When camping, don't keep fresh fruit – especially oranges – in your tent, since it will attract elephants.

Other large animals which can be dangerous to humans are the crocodile and the hippo. It's often repeated that hippos kill more humans in Africa than any other animal. Like elephants, they aren't vicious but they are large. When boating or canoeing, watch for signs of hippos and steer well away from them. Never pitch a tent in an open area along an otherwise vegetated riverbank or shoreline; this will probably serve as a hippo run. Hippos spend most of their time underwater munching tender bottom-growing plants but when it's time to surface or to enter or leave the water, they don't much mind what's in their way.

Nile crocodiles have provided hours of hair-raising campfire tales and they can be worthy adversaries. Although not as large as their Australian counterparts, the crocs, which spend most of their time lying motionless around water holes or on riverbanks minding their own business, grow up to four metres in length and have been known to cause problems for the careless.

Visitors should take care not to swim in rivers or water holes where crocs (or hippos) are present – if local advice is not available, assume that there are crocs and don't swim (you may also be avoiding bilharzia) and use extreme caution when tramping along any river or shoreline. Crocodiles aren't readily recognisable as such; when they're snoozing in the sun, they look more like logs or branches.

Hyenas are also potentially dangerous, although they're normally just after your food. They aren't particularly fussy eaters, either; they'll eat boots, food and other equipment left outside a tent and they have been known to gnaw off headlamps and door handles from vehicles. One cheeky character at Zimbabwe's Mana Pools National Park spent several hours one night subduing – and flattening – one of my tyres! There are plenty of frightening tales of hyenas attacking people who are sleeping in the open or in an open tent – although this is rare, it's still wise to sleep inside and zip up your tent.

Smaller creatures such as hunting dogs and honey badgers can also be quite vicious but they are rarely seen. ■

glance at prices for overseas-booked safaris. Most of these are tailored for those who want all the comforts of home and are willing to pay dearly for them. There are numerous more affordable mid-range adventures including guided camping and bushwalking safaris which will be outlined in pertinent chapters.

Shoestring travellers, however, may be frustrated by the rules and regulations that appear to be designed specifically to keep them out. There is no public transport into the parks, hitching on park roads is forbidden, and individual walking tours and bush camping are prohibited in Zimbabwe, except at Mana Pools where the permit system makes access without a vehicle extremely awkward. Persistence, however, will normally pay off and I have never met anyone who really wanted to see the parks and has failed. Hitching may be prohibited in the parks, but hours spent waving your thumb outside the gates may result in a lift that takes you precisely where you want to go. I've even had lifts from park rangers who were more interested in chatting about my holiday than about the evils of hitching.

Canoeing & Rafting
The upper Zambezi River below Victoria Falls offers some world-class white water and below Lake Kariba, a more lethargic Zambezi accommodates those who prefer to take their thrills more slowly. Raft trips may be done either on the Zimbabwe or Zambia side. For further details, refer to the Victoria Falls section.

Lower Zambezi camping and canoe safaris run from three to nine days along the river between Kariba and Kanyemba on the Mozambique border, highlighted by overnight stops in Mana Pools National Park.

None of these trips are particularly inexpensive and nonresidents must pay in foreign currency or show bank receipts totalling at least the amount of the trip.

In Namibia, you won't find the sort of thrills inherent in the Zambezi trips, but rafts and canoes will provide access to unimaginable wilderness landscapes. The most popular canoeing and rafting venue is the Orange River, which flows through lovely desert country along the boundary between Namibia and South Africa. The water is tame by anyone's standards, but the trips aren't expensive and the scenery and sense of solitude and isolation provide all the motivation you'll need. For details, see the Southern Namibia chapter.

Alternatively, you can spend five days rafting the wild Kunene River, which forms the boundary between Namibia and Angola. There are a few decent whitewater stretches and the presence of crocodiles adds a measure of excitement. This exclusive wilderness foray carries a hefty price, but as with the Orange River, you'll be traversing territory that is otherwise practically inaccessible. For more information, see the North-Western Namibia chapter.

Hiking
Some of the best and most popular bushwalking areas – Nyanga, Vumba, and Chimanimani national parks – are in the Zimbabwe's Eastern Highlands. There you can spend an afternoon or a week walking, camping and enjoying the forests, streams and the country's highest peaks. Other excellent hiking areas include Matobo National Park near Bulawayo, Matusadona National Park near Kariba (but only with an armed guard) and the Mavuradonha Wilderness in northern Zimbabwe.

In Botswana, most trips through the Okavango Delta include some hiking on the palm islands, and the Tsodilo Hills are particularly attractive for bushwalkers.

In Namibia, bushwalking is permitted in some national parks without dangerous animals. Some, including Fish River Canyon and Waterberg Plateau Park, offer organised and accompanied hikes with rangers, which are good value but must be booked well in advance through the Ministry of Environment & Tourism (MET) in Windhoek. Thanks to its South African past, Namibia takes a particularly stringent 'nanny-state' approach towards hiking. Hikers in MET-administered parks must travel in groups of three to 10 people and each participant must present a doctor's certificate of fitness issued not more than 40 days prior to the hike. However ludicrous this may seem to most European, North American and Australasian hikers and trekkers, the policy is popularly defended in the region and you'll encounter it throughout Namibia and South Africa.

Hiking safaris are available through several companies but they are typically booked up well in advance, so it's wise to reserve early. For some suggestions, see Tours in the Zimbabwe Getting Around chapter. In some parks, guided walks are available with game scouts; Hwange is the most popular venue.

Minimum Impact Camping The following guidelines are recommended for hiking or camping in the wilderness or other fragile areas of southern Africa:

- Select a well-drained camp site and, especially if it's raining, use a plastic or other waterproof groundsheet to prevent having to dig trenches.
- Along popular routes, such as in Chimanimani National Park or Fish River Canyon, set up camp in established sites.
- Naturally, burn or carry out all rubbish, including cigarette butts. Bio-degradable items may be buried but anything with food residue should be either burned or carried out, lest it be dug up and scattered by animals.
- Use established toilet facilities if they are available. Otherwise, select a site at least 50 metres from water sources, and bury wastes at least several inches deep. If possible, burn the used toilet paper.
- Use only bio-degradable soap products (you'll probably have to carry them from home) and use natural temperature water where possible. When washing up dishes with hot water, avoid thermal pollution and damage to vegetation either by letting the water cool to outdoor temperature before pouring it out or dumping it in a gravelly, non-vegetated place away from natural water sources.
- Wash dishes and brush your teeth well away from watercourses.
- When building a fire, try to select an established site and keep fires as small as possible. Use only fallen dead wood and when you're finished, make sure ashes are cool and buried before leaving. Again, carry out cigarette butts.

Rail Safaris

For serious rail buffs with a lot of ready cash, Rail Safaris in Zimbabwe offers four-day and nine-day steam rail tours using 1st-class and luxury carriages. These expensive but informative tours will take you by rail from Victoria Falls to Mutare on the *Zambezi Special* and the *Eastern Highlander*.

They also organise connections with named trains in South Africa, and 'Runpast' and 'False Start' journeys for enthusiasts who specifically want to photograph the trains. In a runpast, the train stops at scenic spots, allowing photographers to get off and take photos of the train with the scenic backdrop; in a false start, the train chugs out of the station for photographs, then backs up to pick up the photographers. It's worth looking at their brochure *Rail Safaris Information*, which contains an excellent thumbnail history of rail in Zimbabwe.

For the tour from Victoria Falls to Mutare, prices range from US$1000 to US$1340 per person, including sightseeing along the way. For further information, contact Rail Safaris, Mr & Mrs G Cooke, 2c Prospect Ave, Raylton, Bulawayo (☎ 75575).

Namibia also has a special deal for rail buffs. Twice annually, on varying dates in the winter months, Consolidated Diamond Mines organises a six-day railway and diamond mining heritage tour which includes a special run of the steam-hauled Diamond Train between Keetmanshoop and Lüderitz. There's space for 200 passengers, who are feted by a live band in an imaginatively decorated and catered dining car. The return ticket costs US$192 per person and includes the return rail ticket, accommodation on board and tours of Kolmanskop and the Lüderitz Peninsula. Meals cost extra. For further details, contact Air Namibia Holidays (☎ (0181) 543 2122; fax (0181) 543 3398), 1 Approach Rd, Raynes Park, London SW1 A2BX, UK.

Horse-Riding

If you're acquainted with equine sports (or would like to be), you may want to try your hand in Zimbabwe's national parks and game reserves. Wild animals aren't generally frightened by horses and don't distinguish the horse from the rider so you'll be able to approach them without causing alarm. Several national parks and other game reserves run guided Horse Trails through wildlife reserves and other areas of interest. They normally charge around US$5 for a 1½-hour trip. Participating parks include Lake Chivero, Mutirikwe Recreational Park, Matobo National Park and Nyanga National Park, as well as the Tshabalala Wildlife Sanctuary near Bulawayo.

In addition to the national parks, a number of privately run safari companies organise horseback safaris in such diverse places as Zambezi National Park, the Save Valley (near Gonarezhou National Park) and the Mavuradonha Wilderness in Zimbabwe, and in Botswana's Okavango Delta.

Zimbabwe's increasing number of private wildlife ranches and private conservancies also provide ideal conditions for equine exploration. A favourite inexpensive option, for example, is the popular Mopani Park Farm, near Kwe Kwe in Zimbabwe, which keeps thoroughbred horses, runs backpackers' accommodation and conducts day rides and extended tours on horseback through the adjoining nature conservancy. They also provide riding lessons and stage polo matches. For details, see the Midlands & South-Eastern Zimbabwe chapter.

Fishing

The swift streams of Zimbabwe's Eastern Highlands abound with rainbow (Salmo gairdneri), brown (Salmo trutta) and brook (Salvelinus fontinalis) trout, and the area's dams are stocked by the trout hatchery at Nyanga National Park.

In Lake Kariba and the Zambezi Valley, the most sought after are several species of tilapia or bream – mozambiques (Tilapia mossambica), redbreasted bream (Tilapia rendalli) and greenheads (Tilapia macrochir). It's also popularly known for vundu (Heterobranchus lonigilis – also known as giant catfish), barbel (Clarias gariepinus),

chessa (Distichodus schenga), yellowbelly bream (Serranochromis robustus), bottlenose (Mormyrus longirostris), Nkupe (Distichodus mossambicus), Hunyani salmon (Labeo altivelis), yellowfish (Barbus mareuqensis and Barbus holubi) and 'fighting' tiger fish (Hydrocynus vittatus). Other main dams hold bream, yellowfish, barbel, black bass (Micropterus salmoides – introduced), bottlenose, Hunyani salmon and carp (Cyprinus carpio).

To learn more about licence fees and fishing seasons for individual dams and streams, anglers should try the Zimbabwe National Anglers' Union in Harare or one of the 70 or so angling societies throughout the country. Naturally, local tourist offices are the best sources of information.

In Namibia, the entire Namib desert coast from Swakopmund to the mouth of the Ugab River is a sea angler's paradise. No licence is required but there are restrictions on sizes and numbers of fish which can be taken. You need a licence for freshwater fishing in Namibia, which can be obtained from local tourist offices. The most popular species caught are black bass, carp, yellowfish, bream and barbel. The Lüderitz area is known for its crayfish.

Golf

Zimbabwe is one of the world's least expensive and least crowded golfing venues, and if you're interested in such novelties as warthogs rooting around on the fairways and crocodiles in the water hazards, it's ideal. There are over 70 courses dotted around the country, 14 of which lie within a 30-km radius of Harare. The two most renowned are the 18-hole Royal Harare golf club, three km from the city, and the lovely nine-hole Leopard Rock course in the Vumba region of the Eastern Highlands.

Having said that, everyone knows golf courses require a great deal of water. In drier areas and in times of drought, the maintenance of green grassy courses for tourists simply cannot be justified.

Getting There & Away

TRAVEL INSURANCE

In general, all travellers should consider buying a travel insurance policy, which will provide some sense of security in the case of a medical emergency or the loss or theft of money or belongings. It may seem an expensive luxury, but if you can't afford a travel-health insurance policy, you probably can't afford a medical emergency abroad, either. Travel-health insurance policies (described under Health in the Regional Facts for the Visitor chapter) can normally be extended to include baggage, flight-departure insurance and a range of other options.

Some policies are very good value, but to find them, you'll have to do a great deal of shopping around. Long-term or frequent travellers can generally find something for under US$200 per year, but these will normally be from a general business insurance company rather than one specialising in travel (which will normally charge higher rates). Note, however, that such inexpensive policies may exclude travel to the USA (where health care costs are very expensive) and may offer very limited baggage protection. Always read the fine print!

If you're taking an organised tour, the company will normally encourage you to purchase their own travel insurance policy, which may or may not be a good deal. Bear in mind that some unscrupulous companies – particularly in Europe – manage to keep their tour prices low and appealing by requiring overpriced travel insurance as part of the package.

AIR

Southern Africa isn't exactly a hub of international travel nor is it an obvious transit point along the major international routes – and air fares to or from Europe, North America and Australia certainly reflect that. The greatest hope for inexpensive transport to the region is the current tourism boom in South Africa. There are some bargain fares to Johannesburg (and increasingly, to Cape Town), from where you can easily travel overland or find decent short-haul flight deals to Harare, Gaborone or Windhoek.

You'll also get some relief from low-season fares – and fortunately, the low season partially coincides with the best times to visit the region. Low-season fares from Europe and North America are typically applicable from April to June while high season is between July and September. The rest of the year, with the exception of the several weeks around Christmas, which is considered high season, falls into the shoulder-season category.

Buying a Plane Ticket

Your plane ticket will probably be the single most expensive item in your budget, and buying it can be an intimidating business. There is likely to be a multitude of airlines and travel agents hoping to separate you from your money, and it is always worth putting aside a few hours to research the current state of the market. Start early: some of the cheapest tickets must be purchased months in advance, and some popular flights sell out early. Talk to other recent travellers. Look at the ads in newspapers and magazines (not forgetting the press of the ethnic group whose country you plan to visit), consult reference books and watch for special offers. Then phone around travel agents for bargains. (Airlines can supply information on routes and timetables; however, except at times of inter-airline price wars, they don't supply the cheapest tickets.) Find out the fare, the route, the duration of the journey and any restrictions on the ticket. Then sit back and decide which is best.

You may discover that those incredibly good deals are 'fully booked, but we have another one that costs a bit more...' Or the flight is on an airline notorious for its poor safety standards and leaves you in the

Air Travel Glossary

Apex Apex, or 'advance purchase excursion' is a discounted ticket which must be paid for in advance. There are penalties if you wish to change it.

Baggage Allowance This will be written on your ticket: usually one 20 kg item to go in the hold, plus one item of hand luggage.

Bucket Shop An unbonded travel agency specialising in discounted airline tickets.

Cancellation Penalties If you have to cancel or change an Apex ticket there are often heavy penalties involved, insurance can sometimes be taken out against these penalties. Some airlines impose penalties on regular tickets as well, particularly against 'no show' passengers.

Check In Airlines ask you to check in a certain time ahead of the flight departure (usually 1½ hours on international flights). If you fail to check in on time and the flight is overbooked the airline can cancel your booking and give your seat to somebody else.

Children's Fares Airlines will usually carry babies up to two years of age for 10% of the relevant adult fare, and some carry them free of charge. For children between two and 12 years of age, the fare on international flights is usually 50% of the regular fare or 67% of a discounted fare. These days, most fares are considered discounted.

Confirmation Having a ticket written out with the flight and date you want doesn't mean you have a seat until the agent has checked with the airline that your status is 'OK' or confirmed. Meanwhile you could just be 'on request'.

Discounted Tickets There are two types of discounted fares – officially discounted and unofficially discounted. The lowest prices often impose drawbacks like flying with unpopular airlines, inconvenient schedules, or unpleasant routes and connections. A discounted ticket can save you other things than money – you may be able to pay Apex prices without the associated Apex advance booking and other requirements. Discounted tickets only exist where there is fierce competition.

Economy-Class Tickets Economy-class tickets are usually not the cheapest way to go, although they do give you maximum flexibility and the tickets are valid for 12 months. Most are fully refundable if you don't use them, as are unused sectors of a multiple ticket.

Full Fares Airlines traditionally offer first class (coded F), business class (coded J) and economy class (coded Y) tickets. These days there are so many promotional and discounted fares available from the regular economy class that few passengers pay full economy fare.

Lost Tickets If you lose your airline ticket an airline will usually treat it like a travellers' cheque and, after inquiries, issue you with another one. Legally, however, an airline is entitled to treat it like cash and if you lose it then it's gone forever. Take good care of your tickets.

MCO MCO (Miscellaneous Charges Order) is a type of voucher (to the value of a given amount) which resembles a plane ticket and can be used to pay for a specific flight with any IATA (International Air Transport Association) airline. MCOs, which are more flexible than a regular ticket, may satisfy the irritating onward ticket requirement, but some countries are now reluctant to accept them. MCOs are fully refundable if unused.

No Shows No shows are passengers who fail to show up for their flight, sometimes due to unexpected delays or disasters, sometimes due to simply forgetting, sometimes because they

world's least favourite airport mid-journey for 14 hours. Or they may claim only to have the last two seats available for that country for the whole of July, which they will hold for a maximum of two hours. Don't panic – keep ringing around.

Use the fares quoted in this book as a guide only. They are approximate and based on the rates advertised by travel agents at the time of going to press. Note that quoted airfares don't necessarily constitute a recommendation for the carrier.

If you are travelling from the UK or the USA, you'll probably find the cheapest flights advertised by obscure bucket shops whose names haven't yet hit the telephone directory. Some such firms are honest and solvent, but there are a few rogues who'll take your money and disappear, only to reopen elsewhere a month or two later under a new name. If you're suspicious, don't hand over all the money at once – leave a deposit of 20% or so and pay the balance when you get the ticket. If they insist on cash in

made more than one booking and didn't bother to cancel the one they didn't want. Full fare passengers who fail to turn up are sometimes entitled to travel on a later flight. The rest of us are penalised (see Cancellation Penalties).

On Request An unconfirmed booking for a flight, see Confirmation.

Open Jaws A return ticket where you fly out to one place but return from another. If available this can save you backtracking to your arrival point.

Overbooking Airlines hate to fly empty seats and since every flight has some passengers who fail to show up (see No Shows) airlines often book more passengers than they have seats. Usually the excess passengers balance those who fail to show up but occasionally somebody gets bumped. If this happens guess who it is most likely to be? The passengers who check in late.

Reconfirmation At least 72 hours prior to departure time of an onward or return flight you must contact the airline and 'reconfirm' that you intend to be on the flight. If you don't do this the airline can delete your name from the passenger list and you could lose your seat. You don't have to reconfirm the first flight on your itinerary or if your stopover is less than 72 hours. It doesn't hurt to reconfirm more than once.

Restrictions Discounted tickets often have various restrictions on them – advance purchase is the most usual one (see Apex). Others are restrictions on the minimum and maximum period you must be away, such as a minimum of 14 days or a maximum of one year. See Cancellation Penalties.

Round-the-World Fares Round-the-World (RTW) tickets have become all the rage in the past few years. Basically, there are two types: airline tickets and agent tickets. An airline RTW ticket is issued by two or more airlines that have joined together to market a ticket which takes you around the world on their combined routes. It permits you to fly pretty well anywhere you choose using their combined routes as long as you don't backtrack, ie keep moving in approximately the same direction east or west. Other restrictions are that you (usually) must book the first sector in advance and cancellation penalties then apply. There may be restrictions on how many stops you are permitted. Usually, the RTW tickets are valid for 90 days up to a year. The other type of RTW ticket, the agent ticket, is a combination of cheap fares strung together by an enterprising travel agent. These may be cheaper than an airline RTW ticket but the choice of routes will be limited.

Standby A discounted ticket where you only fly if there is a seat free at the last moment. Standby fares are usually only available on domestic routes.

Student Discounts Some airlines offer student-card holders 15% to 25% discounts on their tickets. The same often applies to anyone under the age of 26. These discounts are generally only available on ordinary economy-class fares. You wouldn't get one, for instance, on an Apex or a RTW ticket, since these are already discounted.

Tickets Out An entry requirement for many countries is that you have an onward or return ticket, in other words, a ticket out of the country. If you're not sure what you intend to do next, the easiest solution is to buy the cheapest onward ticket to a neighbouring country or a ticket from a reliable airline which can later be refunded if you do not use it.

advance, go somewhere else. And once you have the ticket, ring the airline to confirm that your booking has actually been made.

You may opt to sacrifice the bargains and play it safe with a better known travel agent. Firms such as STA, who have offices worldwide, Council Travel in the USA or Travel CUTS in Canada offer good prices to most destinations and they aren't going to disappear overnight, leaving you clutching a receipt for a nonexistent ticket.

Once you have your ticket, copy down the

number, the flight number and other details, and keep the information safe and separate from the ticket. If the ticket is lost or stolen, this will help you get a replacement. It's sensible to buy travel insurance as early as possible. Travel insurance purchased the week before you fly may not cover flight delays caused by industrial action.

Air Travellers with Special Needs

If you have any special needs – you've broken a leg, you're vegetarian, travelling in a wheelchair, taking the baby, terrified of flying – let the airline know as soon as possible so that they can make appropriate arrangements. Then remind them when reconfirming your booking (at least 72 hours before departure) and again when checking in at the airport. It may also be worth ringing the airlines before making your booking to find out how they can handle your particular needs.

Airports and airlines can be surprisingly helpful, but they do need advance warning. Most international airports can provide escorts from the check-in desk to the plane where needed, and most have ramps, lifts, accessible toilets and phones within reach. Aircraft toilets, on the other hand, are likely to present problems; discuss this with the airline at an early stage and, if necessary, with the airline's doctor.

Guide dogs for the blind must normally travel in a specially pressurised baggage compartment with other animals, away from their owner, though smaller guide dogs may be admitted to the cabin. All guide dogs are subject to the same quarantine laws (six months in isolation etc) as any other animal when entering or returning to countries free of rabies such as the UK or Australia.

Deaf travellers can ask for airport and in-flight announcements to be written down for them.

Airlines will usually carry babies up to two years of age at 10% of the adult fare, and some carry them free of charge. Reputable international airlines usually provide nappies (diapers), tissues, talcum powder and all the other paraphernalia needed to keep babies clean, dry and half-happy. Airlines normally provide 'Skycots' for infants but need to be requested in advance; they'll hold a child weighing up to about 10 kg. Strollers (pushchairs) can often be taken as hand luggage.

To/From Europe
Bucket Shop Tickets There are bucket shops by the dozen in London, Paris, Amsterdam, Brussels, Frankfurt and other places. In London, several magazines with lots of bucket shop ads can put you on to the current deals. The best ones are:

Trailfinder A magazine put out quarterly by Trailfinders (☎ (0171) 603-1515 from 9 am to 6 pm Monday to Friday UK time or fax (0171) 938-3305 anytime), 42-48 Earls Court Rd, London W8 6EJ, UK. It's free if you pick it up in London but if you want it mailed, it costs UK£6 for four issues in the UK or Ireland and UK£10 or the equivalent for four issues in Europe or elsewhere (airmail). Trailfinders can fix you up with all your ticketing requirements, as well as jabs, visas and travel publications. They also have a library of information for prospective travellers. They've been in business for years and their staff are friendly.

Time Out (☎ (0171) 836-4411), Tower House, Southampton St, London WC2E 7HD, is London's weekly entertainment guide and contains travel information and advertising. It's available at bookshops, newsagents and newsstands. Subscription enquiries should be addressed to Time Out Subs, Unit 8, Grove Ash, Bletchley, Milton Keynes MK1 1BZ, UK.

TNT Magazine (☎ (0171) 937-3985), 52 Earls Court Rd, London W8, UK. This free magazine can be picked up at most London Underground stations and on street corners around Earls Court and Kensington. It caters to Australians and New Zealanders working in the UK and is therefore full of travel advertising. In these magazines, you'll find discounted fares to Harare and Johannesburg as well as other parts of Africa. Many of them use Aeroflot or Eastern European and Middle Eastern Airlines, but most of the best deals will land you in Nairobi.

You'll also find the latest deals listed in the travel sections of the weekend editions of London newspapers. A word of warning, however: don't take travel agency advertised fares as gospel truth. To comply with advertising laws in the UK, companies must be able to offer *some* tickets at their cheapest quoted price, but they may only have one or two of them per week. If you're not one of the lucky punters, you may be looking at higher fares. It's best to begin looking for deals well in advance so you can get a fair idea of what's available.

Discount Travel Agencies Especially in London, there is a growing number of travel agencies offering very good deals on long-haul travel. The following are good places to initiate your price comparisons:

Africa Travel Shop, 4 Madway Ct, Leigh St, London WC1H 9QX (☎ (0171) 387 1211)

Bridge the World, 52 Chalk Farm Rd, Camden Town, London NW1 8AN (☎ (0171) 911 0900; fax (0171) 916 1724)

Quest Worldwide, 29 Castle St, Kingston, Surrey KT1 1ST (☎ (0181) 547 3322)

STA Travel, 74 Old Brompton Rd, London SW7 (☎ (0171) 937 9962)
    117 Euston Rd, London NW1 2SX (☎ (0171) 465 0486)

Trailfinders, 42-48 Earls Court Rd, London W8 (☎ 0171) 938 3366)
    194 Kensington High St, London W8 (☎ (0171) 938 3939)

Travel Bug, 125A Gloucester Rd, London SW7 4SF (☎ (0171) 835 2000)
    597 Cheetham Hill Rd, Manchester M8 5EJ (☎ (0161) 721 4000)

Travel Mood, 246 Edgware Rd, London W2 1DS (☎ (0171) 258 0280)

Non-Discounted Tickets About the cheapest consistently available fare directly to southern Africa from Europe is the long and laborious London to Harare flight on Balkan Bulgarian Airlines, stopping in both Sofia (Bulgaria) and Lagos (Nigeria). The flight runs on Sunday and if there are no delays, it takes about 24 hours. Although service is improving, given their bare-bones equipment, typically severe overbooking and reluctance to change reservations or tickets, it may be worth paying more for something more reliable. Low-season return fares begin at around £500. High-season one-way fares start at £320.

Especially in the low and shoulder seasons, Air Zimbabwe offers some great deals between London and Harare, with return tickets costing anywhere from £480 to £550. Another inexpensive deal is on Zambia Airways from London to Harare, which flies via Lusaka and competes pricewise with Air Zimbabwe. To Gaborone or Windhoek, you'll pay approximately £200 more. British Airways, which flies on Monday and Friday between London and Harare, advertises low-season APEX fares starting at £550 but you must stay at least

three months. On Tuesday and Thursday, Air Botswana flies nonstop between London and Gaborone, but it's expensive and it would be considerably cheaper to fly to Johannesburg and travel overland from there.

Kenya Airways flies twice weekly from London and Frankfurt to Harare via Nairobi, and this leg forms part of some round-the-world itineraries. Egypt Air flies from Cairo to Harare on Thursday and returns on Friday. Ethiopian Airlines does one weekly run from London via Addis Ababa, Ethiopia and Mt Kilimanjaro, Tanzania. South African Airways has daily flights between London and Johannesburg with frequent connections to Harare, Gaborone and Windhoek.

Air Namibia operates a twice-weekly flight (Thursday and Saturday) direct to Windhoek International Airport from Frankfurt and London, which takes about 10 hours. This is an excellent deal at around £500 return from London. Similarly, LTU International offers low/high-season return fares between Munich or Düsseldorf and Windhoek for £500/600; to qualify, you must stay between one week and six months. En route to Windhoek, the flight stops in Mt Kilimanjaro, Tanzania. From Windhoek, it continues to Durban, South Africa.

If you're coming from the continent the most direct route is from Zürich to Harare with Swissair, which occasionally offers discounted deals. (For what it's worth, Swissair is probably the world's most ecologically conscious airline and should be applauded for its installation of ground-based power systems at Zürich airport. This has eliminated the need to use kerosene-fuelled power units while docked and saves up to 12 million litres of fuel annually.)

From other parts of Europe, it may be cheaper to find a scheduled flight to Johannesburg, Cape Town or Harare, then pick up a connecting flight to your destination.

To/From North America
In the USA, the best way to find cheap flights is by checking the Sunday travel sections in the major newspapers such as the *Los Angeles Times* or the *San Francisco Exam-*

iner or *Chronicle* on the west coast, and the *New York Times* on the east coast. The student travel bureaux – STA or Council Travel – are also worth a go but in the USA you must produce proof of student status and in some cases be under 26 years of age to qualify for their discounted fares.

North America is a relative newcomer to the bucket-shop traditions of Europe and Asia so ticket availability and the restrictions attached to them need to be weighed against what is offered on the standard APEX or full economy (coach class) tickets.

Do some homework before setting off. It may well be cheaper to fly first on an economy hop to London (you'll pay anywhere from US$225 one way), then buy a bucket shop or discount travel agency ticket from there to Africa. The magazines specialising in bucket-shop advertisements in London (see under To/From Europe) will post copies so you can study current pricing before you decide on a course of action.

Also recommended for North Americans is the newsletter *Travel Unlimited* (PO Box 1058, Allston, MA 02134) which publishes details of the cheapest airfares and courier possibilities for destinations all over the world from the USA.

As with US based travellers, Canadians will probably find the best deals travelling to Africa via London. Travel CUTS has offices in all major Canadian cities. The *Toronto Globe & Mail* carries travel agents' ads.

Discount Travel Agencies Although North Americans won't get the great deals that are available in London, there are a few discount agencies which keep a lookout for the best airfare bargains. To comply with regulations, these are sometimes associated with specific travel clubs.

CHA, 333 River Rd, Vanier, Ottawa, Ontario KIL 8H9
Canadian International Student Services, 80 Richmond St W #1202 Toronto, Ontario M5H 2A4 (☎ (416) 364-2738)
Council on International Educational Exchange, 205 East 42nd St, New York, NY 10017

STA Travel, 166 Geary St, Suite 702, San Francisco, CA 94108 (☎ (415) 391 8407)
  48 East 11th St, New York, NY 10017 (☎ (212) 486 0503)
  Suite 507, 2500 Wilshire Blvd, Los Angeles, CA 90057 (☎ (213) 380-2184)
Travel International, 114 Forrest Ave, Suite 205, Narbeth, PA 19072 (☎ (215) 668 2182)
Uni Travel, PO Box 12485, St Louis, MO 63132 (☎ (314) 569 2501)
Whole World Travel, Suite 400, 17 East 45th St, New York, NY 10017 (☎ (212) 986-9470)

Non-Discounted Tickets Due to excessive competition between carriers and a lot of governmental red tape in determining fare structures, flights originating in the USA are subject to numerous restrictions and regulations. This is especially true of bargain tickets; anything cheaper than the standard tourist or economy fare must be purchased at least 14 days, and sometimes as many as 30 days, prior to departure.

In addition, you'll have to book departure and return dates in advance and these tickets will be subject to minimum and maximum stay requirements: usually seven days and six months, respectively. It's often cheaper to purchase a return ticket and trash the return portion than to pay the one-way fare. From the USA, open tickets which allow an open return date within a 12-month period are generally not available, and penalties of up to 50% are imposed if you make changes to the return booking.

From the USA the major carrier gateway city to London (which is in turn the gateway to southern Africa) is New York, but there are also direct flights from nearly every other major city in the country, including Los Angeles, Houston, Miami and Boston. Economy fares often must be purchased two weeks in advance, with a requirement of a minimum stay of two weeks and a maximum stay of three months usually applied.

If you're a real masochist, it's also possible to fly Balkan Bulgarian Airlines to Sofia from New York on Sunday and from Toronto on Friday. These flights then connect with the Sunday flight from Sofia to Harare, via Lagos.

Otherwise, the only direct routing between North America and southern Africa – that is, one that doesn't require you to go via Europe – is American Airlines' direct flight from New York to Johannesburg, South Africa. From Johannesburg, you can make easy air connections to Harare, Windhoek or Gaborone. Johannesburg isn't far from the Zimbabwean border and overland travel is also possible. However, be warned that Johannesburg may not be the best place to introduce yourself to Africa, so think seriously about purchasing a connecting flight from there to Harare or elsewhere in southern Africa.

To/From Australia & New Zealand

Australians and New Zealanders are at a distinct disadvantage because there are few route options directly to Africa. On Monday and Thursday, Qantas and Air Zimbabwe fly a combined service to Harare direct from Sydney and Perth, Australia. They depart on the return trip to Sydney via Perth several hours after landing in Harare. These flights connect directly with a South African Airways flight to and from Johannesburg. There are no direct flights from New Zealand to southern Africa; New Zealanders must first get to Sydney.

Although the return flight between Australia and Harare is quite expensive – around A$2500 – one-way flights are available as part of a RTW package fare for substantial discounts. If you prefer a one-way ticket, for around A$1500 you can fly from Sydney to Singapore on British Airways (stopping over in Singapore), then Singapore to Mauritius with Air Mauritius (for another stopover), and finally, with Air Mauritius to Harare.

For those not pressed for time, it makes sense for Australasians to think in terms of a RTW ticket or a return ticket to Europe with a stopover in Nairobi. RTW tickets with various stopovers may still be found for as little as A$2100. The best publications for finding good deals are the Saturday editions of the daily newspapers such as the *Sydney Morning Herald* and the Melbourne *Age*. Also, try the student travel agencies (STA

Travel), with branches at universities and in the state capitals.

Your cheapest option may well be to work out a routing via Singapore, from where you'll find several ways of reaching Africa including via Mauritius in the Indian Ocean. The cheapest routing will probably land you in Nairobi, from where you can find your way overland or fly on another airline to southern Africa. Discuss your options with several travel agents before buying. Few have had much experience with inexpensive routings to Africa.

Discount Travel Agencies

In Australia and New Zealand, inexpensive travel is available mainly from STA, with branches in all capital cities and on most university campuses.

- 1A Lee St, Railway Square, Sydney, NSW (☎ (02) 9212-1255)
- 25 Rundle St, Adelaide, SA (☎ (08) 223 2426)
- 111-117 Adelaide St, Brisbane, Qld (☎ (07) 9221 3722)
- 224 Faraday St, Carlton, Victoria, 3056 (☎ (03) 9347 6911)
- 53 Market St, Fremantle, WA (☎ (09) 4305553)
- 10 High St, Auckland (☎ (9) 390458)

To/From Asia

The only reasonable way to travel between India or Pakistan and Africa is to fly. There are marginal bucket shops in New Delhi, Bombay and Calcutta. In New Delhi, Tripsout Travel, 72/7 Tolstoy Lane, behind the Government of India Tourist Office, Janpath, is recommended. It's very popular with travellers and has been in business for many years. If you're taking this route, you'll have to resign yourself to flying into Nairobi on Air India and continuing from there on another carrier or overland to southern Africa.

In addition, during low season (November to March) the Russian airline Aeroflot runs a series of special flights between Moscow and Harare, via Bombay. They're cheap, but dates are very limited and they're likely to book up early.

For travel from South-East Asia, your best

bet is Bangkok, where you'll find bucket shops galore. There, you should have little difficulty finding an inexpensive flight from Singapore to Harare, which may be routed through Mauritius and/or Nairobi.

To/From Elsewhere in Africa

Since Harare is the major hub between Nairobi and Johannesburg, many intra-Africa flights to Zimbabwe, Botswana and Namibia are routed through there. Unfortunately, there aren't really any bargain fares – you may get a break for advance purchase but that's about it – so it won't be worth too much shopping around.

Kenya Airways and Air Zimbabwe fly between Harare and Nairobi two and three times weekly for around US$300 each way. Air Mauritius has one direct weekly flight from Mauritius to Harare and three more with connections through Johannesburg. To fly between Harare and Antananarivo, Madagascar, must connections in Mauritius.

Both Air Zimbabwe and Air Tanzania fly between Harare and Dar es Salaam, Tanzania. Air Zimbabwe and Air Malawi fly to/from Lilongwe six times weekly for around US$150 each way. Linhas Aéreas de Moçambique (LAM) flies to/from Maputo and Beira in Mozambique. Zambia Airways and Air Zimbabwe each do three weekly trips between Harare and Lusaka. Egypt Air flies between Harare and Cairo once weekly and South African Airways and Air Zimbabwe have daily flights between Harare and Johannesburg, with connections to Cape Town and Durban. To continue to Botswana, Air Botswana and Air Zimbabwe each have two weekly flights between Harare and Gaborone. Air Zimbabwe also flies on Friday between Harare and Windhoek, and Air Namibia has flights daily from Tuesday to Saturday between Harare and Windhoek, as well as numerous flights to South Africa. For more information, see the Getting There & Away chapters for each country.

LAND

With the exception of the Israel-Egypt connection, all overland travel to Africa must begin in Europe and even that will involve a ferry crossing at some point.

Whether you're hitching or travelling by bus or train across Europe, you should decide which of the two routes south through Africa you want to take – through the Sahara from Morocco and Mauritania to West Africa (the traditional route through Algeria is currently blocked by Muslim fundamentalists with a habit of shooting foreigners) or up the Nile from Egypt to Uganda and Kenya. It's very difficult to travel overland between the two routes in North Africa due to the roadblock imposed by Libya (which, incidentally, may open up in the near future) so travellers between Morocco, Algeria or Tunisia, and Egypt will probably have to fly. Also bear in mind that even the fortunate travellers who can somehow wangle a Sudanese visa may have problems south of Khartoum, so the Nile route would be greatly facilitated by a flight from Cairo – or at best from Khartoum – to Kampala or Nairobi.

From Nairobi, there are several options for reaching Zimbabwe, Botswana and Namibia. The most popular route seems to be the TAZARA Railway between Dar es Salaam, Tanzania, (accessible by bus or plane from Nairobi) and Kapiri Mposhi, Zambia, from where you can pick up an onward train to Lusaka and Livingstone. It's extremely inexpensive for the distance travelled – around US$50 at the time of writing – but be prepared for a slow pace and frequently uncomfortable conditions.

Another option takes you across Tanzania to Kigoma on Lake Tanganyika, then by steamer to Mpulungu, Zambia, and overland to Chitipa, Malawi, or Lusaka, Zambia. It's also possible to enter Zambia at Nakonde or Malawi between Mbeya and Karonda. There's no public transport along the latter route so you'll have to hitch.

Other possibilities from Nairobi include travelling through Uganda, Zaïre, Rwanda and Burundi, catching the Lake Tanganyika steamer from Bujumbura, Burundi, and connecting up with the previously outlined route at Mpulungu, Zambia. However, Rwanda has recently suffered a horrific civil war and the resulting refugee crisis is ongoing. At present, because of serious shortages of food and supplies, travellers would be wise not to venture in and compound the problems.

The other option – which could require months – is a very long and tedious route through Uganda or Burundi and Zaïre to north-western Zambia. Once you've completed it, however, you may not feel like travelling any further!

Once in Zambia, it's fairly straightforward reaching Lusaka or Livingstone and entering Zimbabwe at Chirundu, Kariba or Victoria Falls, or crossing into Botswana at Kazungula. For information on these routes, see the Zimbabwe Getting There & Away chapter. You'll also find details on the route between Malawi and Zimbabwe via Mozambique.

Driving

Explaining how to bring your own vehicle to southern Africa is beyond the scope of this book, but the good news for drivers is that you don't need a carnet de passage to travel through and around most of the southern African region.

Thanks to the Southern African Customs Union, you can drive through Botswana, Lesotho, Namibia, South Africa and Swaziland with a minimum of ado, and with the proper paperwork – a Blue Book sheet detailing the vehicle's particulars and proof of insurance and current registration – you can secure temporary import permits to visit Malawi, Mozambique, Zimbabwe and Zambia. To travel further north, however, will require a carnet de passage, which can amount to heavy expenditure, and more serious consideration.

TOURS

Literally hundreds of tour and safari companies are adding Zimbabwe, Botswana and Namibia to their list of offerings, and as South Africa continues to grow as a major holiday destination, so will the spillover to neighbouring countries.

There are basically two types of tour com-

panies: the overseas agents who do the booking and cobble together a range of itineraries in conjunction with the locally based operators, and those locally based operators, who actually provide the tours. Within southern Africa, there is a large number of these tour companies; most of them run their trips in small coaches, safari vehicles or minibuses. However, some overseas packagers merely provide self-guided itineraries, including prebooked flights, accommodation and vehicle hire.

If you're thinking of taking a package, it always pays to shop around for deals. Especially in Europe, it's becoming increasingly popular to look for late bookings, which are available at a fraction of the normal price. The best place to begin looking is in the travel sections of weekend newspapers. In some cases, there are special late bookings counters at international airports.

If you prefer not to pre-book everything, you can pre-book your flights and hotels for the first few nights, then take your chances on joining a tour locally (lists of local operators are provided under Tours in the Getting Around chapters for individual countries in this book).

While it would be impractical – and almost impossible – to provide a comprehensive rundown of everyone selling packages, the following list will provide some idea of the range available, and includes some of the more creative and offbeat offerings of package deals. Any of these packages may be booked through your travel agent:

Japan
    Springbok Corporation, Ishinkuru Bldg, 2F 214-3 Taishido, Setagayo-ku, Tokyo 154 (☎ (03) 5486 8185; fax (03) 5486 5696) Guided tours including the northern and southern circuits through the major sites in Namibia.
Netherlands
    Footprints, Singelstraat 27, 3513 BM Utrecht (☎ (030) 300038; fax (030) 343213) Highly recommended camping tours through little-visited areas of Namibia, with emphasis on contact with local cultures (particularly in Kaokoland, Ovamboland and Bushmanland) and wilderness adventure. Tours are conducted in English.

New Zealand

Adrift, PO Box 354, Ngongotaha (☎ (07) 347 2345; fax (07) 346 3167) As its name would suggest, this company specialises in liquid experiences, and in the case of Zimbabwe, that means rafting on the Zambezi below Victoria Falls.

South Africa

African Routes, 164 Northway, Durban North 4051 (☎ (031) 833348; fax (031) 837234) This friendly and very reasonably priced company offers overland tours and hiking trips through Namibia and Zimbabwe, as well as all around Africa.

Afro Ventures, PO Box 2339, Randburg 2125 (☎ (011) 886 1524; fax (011) 886 2349) Of primary interest are Afro Ventures trips through the Central Kalahari Game Reserve and their camping, canoeing and bushwalking safaris in Zimbabwe and Namibia. The tours aren't cheap, but low accommodation costs mean reasonably accessible prices.

Clive Walker Trails, PO Box 645, Bedfordview 2008 (☎ (011) 453 7645; fax (011) 453 7649) Emphasis is on walking trips and the study of wilderness ecology, mainly in the Okavango Delta and Tuli Block areas of Botswana. These trips aren't luxurious, but they are among the cheapest ways to see the Okavango Delta in comfort – and do offer a different perspective on the bush.

Penduka Safaris, PO Box 55413, Northlands 2116 (☎ /fax (011) 883 4303) This company deals mainly with Botswana and South Africa. Of particular interest are Penduka Safaris trips through the Kalahari, including Kubu Island, Deception Pan, Nxai Pan, Mabuasehube, Tsodilo Hills and the Makgadikgadi Pans. Their prices are mid-range.

Wayfarer Adventures, 4 Norwich Ave, Observatory, Cape Town 7925 (☎ (021) 470792; fax (021) 474675) Wilderness adventures travel throughout southern Africa, including Land Rover tours around Namibia.

Wilderness Safaris, PO Box 651171, Benmore 2010 (☎ (011) 884 1458; fax (011) 883 6255) This company offers a range of tours in Zimbabwe, Botswana, Namibia and other African countries. In addition to the standard lodge-based tours, Wilderness Safaris offer bushwalking, birdwatching, canoeing, photography and other activity-based trips. However, they are quite expensive and their tours seem a bit rushed.

Wild Frontiers, PO Box 844, Halfway House 1685 (☎ (011) 315 4838; fax (011) 315 4850) Middle price range canoeing and walking trips in Zimbabwe.

Spain

Expediciones César Cañareras, Roberto Franco, Plaza de la Concordia, 3 41002, Sevilla, Spain (☎ (95) 421 4737, (91) 319 6214; fax (95) 456 4009); specialises in tours through Etosha National Park and around northern Namibia.

UK

Abercrombie & Kent, Sloane Square House, Holbein Place, London SW1 (☎ (0171) 730 9600) This well-heeled company organises up-market luxury safaris in southern Africa, with particular emphasis on the Okavango Delta.

Adrift, Hyde Park House, Manfred Rd, London SW15 2RS (☎ (0181) 874 4969; fax (0181) 875 9236) This UK subisidiary of the New Zealand company of the same name specialises in rafting trips on the Zambezi River.

Africa Exclusive, Ltd, Hamilton House, 66 Palmerston Rd, Northhampton NN1 5EX (☎ (01604) 28979; fax (01604) 31628) Custom itineraries which will take you pleasantly off the beaten track. They concentrate on Zimbabwe, but also cover Namibia.

Discover the World, The Flatt Lodge, Bewcastle near Carlisle, Cumbria CA6 6PH (☎ (016977) 48361; fax (016977) 48327) They do exclusive wildlife tours to various sites worldwide, including a two-week excursion through Namibia.

Explore Worldwide Ltd, 1 Frederick St, Aldershot, Hampshire GU11 1LQ (☎ (01242) 344161; fax (01252) 343170) Organised group tours through Zimbabwe, Botswana and Namibia, focusing on adventure and hands-on activities.

Hartley's Safaris, 12 Queensberry Mews West, London SW7 2DU (☎ (0171) 584 5005; fax (0171) 584 5054) Up-market, tailor-made, lodge-based safaris in Botswana's Okavango Delta and Chobe National Park.

Okavango Tours & Safaris, 28 Bisham Gardens, London N6 6DD (☎ (0181) 341 9442; fax (0181) 348 9983) This company combines their forté, the Okavango Delta, with tours through Chobe National Park as well as Zimbabwe and Namibia.

Peregrine Holidays, 40/41 South Parade, Summertown, Oxford OX2 7JP (☎ (01865) 511642; fax (01865) 512583) Up-market wildlife and botanical safaris, including Botswana's Okavango Delta and Chobe National Park.

Tusk Tours, Hawksfield, Uplands Rd, Totland Bay, Isle of Wight PO39 0DZ (☎ (01983) 756748/9; fax (01983) 756758) This friendly and down-to-earth company runs their own tours which take in the major sights as well as some of Zimbabwe's more ignored destinations.

United Touring Company (UTC), Paramount House, 71/75 Uxbridge Rd, Ealing Broadway, London W5 5SL (☎ (0181) 566 1660; fax (0181) 566 1348) This large company has tentacles all over Africa and offers everything from day tours around the capital cities, to multi-week trips through several countries.

Voyages Jules Verne, 21 Dorset Square, London NW1 6QG (☎ (0171) 723 5066; fax (0171) 723 8629) This company specialised in luxury-tinted tours around the highlights of Zimbabwe and Botswana. They offer some particularly reasonable off-season prices. They also organise expensive 14-day rail safaris from Victoria Falls to Cape Town on the *Zambezi Express* and the *Pride of Africa*.

Wild Africa Safaris, Castlebank House, Oak Rd, Leatherhead KT22 7PG (☎ (01372) 362288; fax (01372) 360147) Two-week to three-week up-market tours taking in Zimbabwe highlights. They also use local operators to organise speciality safaris, including tiger fishing, canoeing, walking safaris in the national parks (including tracking rhinos), rail safaris and even (very expensive) trips by Catalina flying boat.

Wildlife Worldwide, Naturetrek, Chautara, Bighton Airesford, Hampshire SO24 9RB (☎ (01962) 733051; fax (01962) 733368) As the name reveals, this company's speciality is wildlife and its aim is to get you to where the animals are. They offer specialised wildlife-viewing itineraries in Zimbabwe, Botswana and Namibia, as well as other areas of southern Africa.

Wildwings, International House, Bank Rd, Bristol BS15 2LX (☎ (0117) 984 8040; fax (0117) 967 4444) If you've always wanted to spend 22 days in search of birds in Namibia, here's your opportunity. Wildwings is interested in birds and if you see larger animals as well, they're frosting on the cake.

USA

Abercrombie & Kent, 1420 Kensington Rd, Oak Brook, IL 60521 (☎ (708) 954 2944) Pricey organised tours around the Zimbabwe and Botswana highlights, with particular emphasis on luxury.

Adventure Center, 1311 63rd St, Emeryville, CA 91608 (☎ (510) 654 1879) This isn't actually a tour operator, but rather a travel agency specialising in adventure tours worldwide.

Africa Adventure Company, 1620 S Federal Hwy, Suite 900, Pompano Beach, FL 33062 (☎ (305) 781 3933) This company offers a wide range of safari options all over Africa. They have a particularly large choice of safaris in Zimbabwe.

Africa Travel Centre, 23830 Route 99, Suite 112, Edmonds, WA 98026 (☎ (206) 672 3697; fax (206) 672 9678) This is a travel and resource centre for prospective visitors to Africa. Chances are, they have information on exactly the trip you're looking for.

Desert & Delta Safaris, 16179 E Whittier Blvd, Whittier, CA 90603 (☎ (213) 947 5100) Focuses on lodge-based tours in the Okavango, but also

offers connecting packages around southern Africa.

Journeys, 1536 NW 23rd Ave, Portland, OR 97210 (☎ (503) 226 7200) Specialises in trekking and camping trips through the more remote areas of Zimbabwe and Botswana.

Ker & Downey, Inc, 13201 Northwest Freeway Suite 850, Houston, TX 77040 (☎ (713) 744 5260; fax (713) 895 8753) This is far and away the most exclusive company operating in Botswana. They focus on lodge-based tours in Chobe National Park and the Okavango Delta, including a frighteningly expensive elephant-back safari in the Delta.

Safariplan, 673 E California Blvd, Pasadena, CA 91106 (☎ (818) 578 0510; fax (818) 796 6365) Luxury, lodge-based tours through the highlights of Zimbabwe.

Spector Travel of Boston, 31 St James Ave, Boston, MA 02116 (☎ (617) 338 0111) This company puts together budget tours all over Africa, and combines them with discounted airfares.

United Touring Company (UTC), 400 Market St, Suite 260, Philadelphia, PA 19106 (☎ (215) 923 8700; fax (215) 985 1008) One of the largest tour operators in Africa, UTC does everything from day tours to longer itineraries.

Voyagers, PO Box 915, Ithaca, NY (☎ (800) 633 0299) Photographic and wildlife-viewing safaris.

Wilderness Travel, 801 Alston Way, Berkeley, CA 94710 (☎ (800) 368 2794, ext 114) This company offers guided, small group tours around the world, including southern Africa. The emphasis is on down-to-earth touring, including hikes, treks and other hands-on pursuits.

Overland Companies

Although for practical purposes, the days of overlanding along the Cairo-to-the-Cape are quite difficult due to unrest in Sudan, some overland operators have taken up the trans-Sahara route through Morocco, Mauritania and West Africa, across the Central African Republic, Zaïre and Uganda to Kenya and on to Zimbabwe, Botswana and South Africa.

While these trips are popular, they're designed primarily for inexperienced travellers who feel uncomfortable striking out on their own or to those who prefer guaranteed social interaction to the uncertainties of the road. If you have the slightest inclination towards independence or would feel confined travelling with the same group of 25 or so people for most of the trip (although quite a few normally drop out along the way), think twice before booking an overland trip.

Increasingly, many overland companies are opting for shorter hauls and some also provide transport – a sort of backpackers' bus and transfer service. Independent travellers may join overland trucks for around US$15 per day, plus food kitty contributions. Just visit an overland truck stop and ask the driver if there's space available. This is a particularly useful way to transfer quickly between Harare and Malawi or Nairobi, Victoria Falls and Maun, or even Harare and Windhoek.

For more information or a list of agents selling overland packages in your home country, contact one of the following Africa overland operators, all of which are based in the UK (Dragoman, Exodus and Encounter Overland also have offices in Australia, New Zealand, the USA and Canada):

Dragoman, Camp Green, Kenton Rd, Debenham, Stowmarket, Suffolk IP14 6LA (☎ (01728) 861133, fax (01728) 861127)

Encounter Overland, 267 Old Brompton Rd, London SW5 9JA (☎ (0171) 3706845)

Exodus Overland Expeditions, 9 Weir Rd, London SW12 0LT (☎ (0181) 673-0859, fax (0181) 6757996)

Guerba Expeditions, 101 Eden Vale Rd, Westbury, Wiltshire BA13 3QX (☎ (01373) 826689, fax (01373) 838351)

Hann Overland, 201/203 Vauxhall Bridge Rd, London SW1V 1ER (☎ (0171) 834-7337, fax (0171) 828-7745)

Kumuka Expeditions, 40 Earls Court Rd, London W8 6EJ (☎ (0171) 937 8855; fax (0171) 937 6664)

Top Deck, Top Deck House, 131/135 Earls Court Rd, London SW5 9RH (☎ (0171) 244-8641, fax (0171) 373-6201)

World Tracks Ltd, 12 Abingdon Rd, London W8 6AF (☎ (0171) 9373028; fax (0171) 937 3176)

WARNING

This chapter is particularly vulnerable to change – prices for international travel are volatile, routes are introduced and cancelled, schedules change, special deals come and go, rules and visa requirements are amended. Airlines and governments seem to take a perverse pleasure in making price structures and regulations as complicated as possible. You should check directly with the airline or travel agent to make sure you understand how a fare (and ticket you may buy) works. In addition, the travel industry is highly competitive, and there are many schemes, deals and bonuses. The upshot of this is that you should get opinions, quotes and advice from as many airlines and travel agents as possible before you part with your hard-earned cash. The details given in this chapter should be regarded as pointers and are not a substitute for careful, up-to-date research.

Safari Guide

PRIMATES

Baboons
Papio ursinus (Chacma Baboon)
Papio cynocephalus (Yellow Baboon)

DAVID WALL

Chacma Baboon

The Chacma baboon, just one of at least five species of baboon, is the one most commonly sighted in southern Africa. The dog-like snouts of baboons give them a more aggressive appearance than most other primates, which have much more human-like facial features. Having said that, when you watch them playing or merely sitting around contemplating their surroundings, it's difficult not to make anthropomorphic comparisons.

Baboons live in large troops of up to 150 animals, each of which has its own two to 30 sq km area and is headed by one dominant male. Individuals spend much of their time searching for insects, spiders and birds' eggs. They've also discovered that lodges, camp sites and picnic areas provide easy pickings, especially those occupied by idiotic tourists who throw food and leave their tents unzipped. In the camp site at Victoria Falls, a troop of baboon thugs makes daily rounds, tipping over rubbish barrels and wreaking general mayhem. Often baboons become such a nuisance that they have to be dealt with harshly by park officials, so please resist the temptation to feed them!

Baboons' greatest natural enemy is the leopard, for whom they're a favourite meal, but young baboons are also taken by lions and hunting dogs.

Bushbabies
Otolemur crassicaudatus (Greater or Giant Bushbaby)
Galago senegalensis (Lesser Bushbaby)

The greater bushbaby, which resembles an Australian possum, is in fact a small pro-simian (lemur-like) creature about the size of a rabbit. It inhabits dense, moist forest areas, mainly in north-eastern Zimbabwe and points north-east, but it's nocturnal and is therefore rarely observed. The bushbaby has a small head, large rounded ears, dark brown fur, a thick bushy tail and the enormous eyes that are typical of nocturnal primates. On average, adults weigh under two kg and measure 80 cm in length, but 45 cm of this is tail.

The lesser bushbaby is about half the size of the greater bushbaby. It is a very light grey and has yellowish colouring on the legs.

Greater or Giant Bushbaby

Samango Monkey (White-throated Guenon)
Cercopithecus mitis

Also known as the white-throated guenon or diademed monkey, the Samango monkey inhabits much of eastern Africa, from Kenya south to Natal in South Africa. In Zimbabwe it occurs only in the eastern highlands, concentrated on the Chirinda Forest Reserve and the densely forested regions along the Mozambique border.

The face is grey to black, but most of the back and the flanks and upper limbs have a greenish cast. The rump is yellow and the lower limbs are black. Mature males make coughing sounds; females and young of both sexes make chirping and chattering sounds.

The Samango monkey feeds in the early morning and late afternoon in the higher treetops, descending into shady areas during the day. They normally live in social groups of four to 12 and eat mainly shoots, leaves, young birds, insects, moss, fungi, fruit, berries and eggs. They occasionally even raid plantations, taking chickens. Enemies include leopards, pythons and eagles.

Samango Monkey (White-throated Guenon)

Vervet Monkey (Savanna Monkey)
Cercopithecus aethiops

The playful vervet monkey is southern Africa's most common monkey, inhabiting nearly all parks and reserves (and camp sites and picnic areas!) in all three countries. It's easily recognisable by its black face fringed with white hair. The hair is yellowish-grey hair elsewhere, except on the underparts, which are whitish. The male has an extraordinary bright blue scrotum.

Vervet monkeys usually live in woodland and savanna, running in groups of up to 30. They're extremely cheeky and inquisitive, as you may well find when camping in the game reserves. Many have become habituated to humans and will stop at nothing to steal food or secure handouts, including making themselves welcome at dining tables or inside tents or cars.

DAVID WALL
Vervet Monkey (Savanna Monkey)

CARNIVORES

In East African parks, carnivores are the animals most seriously affected by tourism, and often find themselves trailing dozens of white minibuses while trying to hunt. In southern African parks, however, tourism is better regulated, so natural patterns are little altered by human onlookers.

Safari companies are bound by strict rules and are threatened with loss of their operator's licence if they drive off the roads or knowingly disturb wildlife, but independent tourists in their own vehicles – particularly the local school holiday crowds – still manage to cause a fair amount of disruption.

Just remember to keep as low a profile as possible; if an animal is obviously hunting, try to control your excitement and avoid the temptation to move in too close, lest you distract the predator or spook the intended prey.

Banded Mongoose
Mungos mungo

Southern Africa has at least eight species of mongoose, but the most common is the banded (or Zebra) mongoose, which is present in all game parks. This brown or grey mongoose, which measures about 40 cm in length and weighs 1.3 to 2.3 kg, is easily identified by the dark bands which stretch from the shoulder to the tail.

Mongooses are very sociable animals, living in packs of 30 to 50 individuals. They emit a range of sounds which they use for communication within the pack. When threatened they make growling and spitting noises, much like a domestic cat.

Being diurnal animals they enjoy sunning themselves by day, but at night, they retire to warrens in rock crevices, hollow trees and abandoned anthills. Each pack generally has several warrens within its territory.

A mongoose's favourite foods are insects, grubs and larvae, but they'll also eat amphibians, reptiles, birds, eggs, fruit and berries. Its main predators are birds of prey, though they are also taken by lions, leopards and wild dogs.

Banded Mongoose

Bat-Eared Fox
Otocyon megalotis

True to its name, the bat-eared fox is basically a long-legged fox with enormous ears. As you'd expect, its sense of hearing is exceptional. Its tail is very bushy and the body is brown with white markings and black-tipped ears. The bat-eared fox eats mainly insects, small animals, fruits and berries, and while foraging for subterranean insects it can hear even faint sounds coming from below ground. By lowering its head towards the soil, ears parallel, it can use a sort of triangulation to get an exact fix on potential food. This is followed by a burst of frantic digging to capture the prey.

The bat-eared fox normally inhabits multi-roomed burrows with several entrances, which it either digs or takes over. It's active at night, especially just after sunset. Its only enemies are large birds of prey and hyenas.

In Zimbabwe bat-eared foxes are found only in Hwange National Park, but are more readily observed in Botswana and Namibia, particularly in Chobe, Etosha and the Namib Desert.

Bat-Eared Fox

Black-Backed Jackal
Canis mesomelas

Black-backed jackals are a common sight in most southern African parks and reserves. Its back, which is actually more grizzled than black, is wide at the neck and tapers to the tail. Although jackals are dogs, their bushy tails and large ears cause them to more closely resemble foxes.

Jackals are mostly scavengers, and commonly hang around kills awaiting morsels. If nothing is forthcoming they'll often hunt insects, birds, rodents and even the occasional small antelope. They also hang about outside human settlements and often go for sheep, poultry and young calves or foals.

Each jackal pair looks after a home territory of around 250 hectares. Pups are born in litters of five to seven. Although they don't reach maturity until they're almost a year old, most jackal pups are on their own at the age of just two months, and are especially vulnerable to enemies, such as leopards, cheetahs and eagles.

DAVID WALL

Black-Backed Jackal

Cape Clawless Otter
Aonyx capensis

The Cape (or African) clawless otter, a river otter, is common in the Chobe and Okavango rivers of northern Botswana as well as near the Namibian coast. It has a light greyish brown back, the snout, face and throat are white or cream-coloured and each cheek has a large rectangular spot. Unlike most otters, Cape clawless otters don't have webbed feet, and although some are truly clawless, others have short pointed claws on the third and fourth toes.

The otters are normally active by day, and with a bit of luck may be seen playing, swimming and diving throughout the afternoon. In areas where they're hunted by humans, however, otters have adopted a nocturnal schedule.

Their main foods include fish, crabs, frogs, and both bird and crocodile eggs. Their only known natural enemy is the crocodile.

Cape Clawless Otter

Caracal (African Lynx)
Felis caracal

Once considered to be a true lynx, the caracal is now placed in the small-cat genus *Felis*. The caracal is certainly very cat-like, and despite its sometimes sleepy appearance is the fastest cat of its size.

It is distinguished by its height (about 50 cm at the shoulder), relatively small head, long, narrow ears densely tufted with long hairs at the tips, lack of whiskers on the face, and long, stout legs. The colour of the coat ranges from reddish-brown to yellow-grey, with a white underside and a black line joining the nose and eye.

Caracals are 80 to 120 cm long (including a tail of 20 to 30 cm), and weigh between 13 and 23 kg. They live in porcupine burrows, rocky crevices or dense vegetation. They inhabit many areas, but prefer dry country (woodland, savanna and scrub) and avoid sandy deserts.

Their favourite prey are birds, rodents and other small mammals, including young deer. They stalk their prey until a quick dash or leap can capture it. They are usually active at twilight, but they may hunt by night in hot weather and by day in cold weather. They are generally solitary animals, but might sometimes be seen in pairs with their young. They are believed to be territorial, marking the territory with urine sprays. The calls are typical of cats – miaows, growls, hisses and coughing noises.

Litters of one to four kittens (usually three) can be born at any time of the year. The kittens open their eyes after 10 days, are weaned at 10 to 25 weeks, and can breed from as young as six months.

Caracal (African Lynx)

Cheetah
Acinonyx jubatus

The cheetah is one of nature's most magnificent accomplishments; this sleek, streamlined and graceful creature exists in limited numbers in all major southern African reserves: Hwange, Zambezi, Gonarezhou, Kazuma Pan, Mana Pools, Chobe, Moremi, Etosha, and so on.

Although it superficially resembles a leopard, the cheetah is longer and lighter, and has a slightly bowed back and a much smaller and rounder face. It stands around 80 cm at the shoulder, measures around 210 cm in length, including the tail, and weighs from 40 to 60 kg. Occasionally, a beautiful genetic mutation produces what's known as a king cheetah; instead of spots, it has a marbled coat and striped legs. King cheetahs are most common around Gonarezhou National Park in Zimbabwe and neighbouring Kruger National Park in South Africa.

Normally cheetahs hunt in early morning or late evening. While hunting, a cheetah stalks its prey as closely as possible. When the time is ripe, it launches into an incredible 100-metre sprint in which it can reach a speed of up to 110 km/h. However, this phenomenal speed can only be sustained for a short distance. If it fails to bring down its intended victim, it gives up and tries elsewhere. The prey, often a small antelope, may be brought to the ground with a flick of the paw to trip it up. Other favourite meals include hares, jackals and young warthogs.

The main breeding period is between March and December, when mature females produce litters of two to four cubs. The cubs reach maturity at around one year, but stay with the mother much longer to learn hunting and survival skills. Cheetahs rarely fight, but do suffer from predation by lions, leopards and hyenas; most victims are cubs.

HUGH FINLAY

Cheetah

Civet (African Civet)
Viverra (Civetticus) civetta

The civet is a medium-sized omnivore around 40 cm high at the shoulder and 90 cm long, excluding the tail, with some canine features and short, partially retractile claws. Its long, coarse and mainly grey coat is specked with a varying pattern of black spots, with one set of black bands stretching from the ears to the lower neck and another around the upper hind legs. When the animal is moving, the black tail, which is bushy at the grey-banded base and thinner towards the tip, is held out straight. The head is mostly greyish white and the small, rounded ears are tipped with white hairs. Another conspicuous feature is a set of musk glands in the anal region which produce a foul-smelling oily substance used to mark territory. This musk is used in manufacturing perfumes, though in Western countries it's collected from captive animals.

Civets are solitary, nocturnal animals; by day they nestle in thickets, tall grass or abandoned burrows. Your best chance of seeing one will be by torchlight in the early morning or late evening at Hwange or other parks in western Zimbabwe. The rare tree civet is found only in Zimbabwe's Eastern Highlands.

Civets have a very varied diet consisting of rodents, birds, eggs, reptiles, amphibians, snails, insects (especially ants and termites), berries, young shoots and fruit.

Litters consist of up to four cubs, which have a similar but slightly darker colour compared to the adults.

Civet (African Civet)

Genets
Genetta genetta (felina) (Small-spotted Genet)
Genetta tigrina (Large-Spotted Genet)

More than the civet, the genet resembles the domestic cat, although the body is considerably longer, the long, coarse coat has a prominent crest along the spine and the tail is longer and bushier. The basic colour varies from grey to fawn, patterned from the neck to the tail with dark brown to black spots. The tail, which has a white tip, is banded with nine or 10 similarly coloured rings.

Genets live singly or in pairs in riverine forests and dry scrub savanna and open country. They're agile climbers, but are seldom sighted because they're only active nocturnally. By day they sleep in abandoned burrows, rock crevices or hollow trees, or up on high branches, apparently returning to the same spot each day.

Genets may climb trees to seek out nesting birds and their eggs, but normally hunt on the ground. Like the domestic cat, they stalk prey by crouching flat on the ground. Their diet consists of small rodents, birds, reptiles, insects and fruits. They're well known for being a wasteful killer, often eating only small bits of the animals they catch. Like domestic cats, genets spit and growl when angered. Litters typically consist of two or three kittens.

Genet

Honey Badger (Ratel)
Mellivora ratel

The honey badger is of a similar size and shape to the European badger and is every bit as ferocious. They've even been known to attack creatures as large as Cape buffalo! They're present throughout Zimbabwe, northern Botswana and Namibia, but are normally only active between dusk and dawn. There's a good population around Sinamatella Camp in Zimbabwe's Hwange National Park, where they're almost tame, and anyone camping there will almost certainly see them. They're also frequently seen at the camp sites in Namibia's Brandberg mountains.

Honey badgers subsist on fish, frogs, scorpions, spiders, and reptiles, including poisonous snakes; at times they'll even take young antelopes. They also eat a variety of roots, honey, berries and eggs, and are adept at raiding rubbish bins.

Honey Badger (Ratel)

Hunting Dog
Lycaon pictus

The hunting dog, which is roughly the size of a large domestic dog, is found in areas with a high concentration of game animals, and is therefore resident in all Zimbabwe and Botswana reserves, as well as in Etosha and the Caprivi Strip in Namibia.

Constant characteristics include the large rounded ears and white-tipped tail, but colouration is different in every animal, and is made up of variable-sized splotches of black, yellow and every hue in between.

Litters of seven to 15 pups are born in grass-lined burrows; by six months of age they're competent hunters and have abandoned the burrow. The hunting dog has no common predators, although unguarded pups may fall prey to hyenas and eagles.

Hunting dogs rarely scavenge, preferring to kill their own prey. They move in packs of four to 40 and work well together. Once the prey has been selected and the chase is on, two lead dogs will chase hard while the rest pace themselves; once the first two tire another pair steps in, and so on until the quarry is exhausted. Favoured prey include springbok, impala and other mid-sized antelope.

Hunting Dog

MIKE SCOTT

Hyena

Hyenas
Crocuta crocuta (Spotted Hyena)
Hyena brunnea (Brown or African Laughing Hyena)

The spotted hyena is fairly common throughout most of Zimbabwe, Botswana and Namibia, especially where game is plentiful, while the rarer brown hyena is found only in limited areas of the Kalahari and Namib deserts. This shy and secretive animal was the focus of the study recounted in Mark & Delia Owens' book *Cry of the Kalahari*. Good places to observe spotted hyenas are Robins Camp in Hwange National Park and around Savuti Camp in Chobe National Park, where they tend to make a real nuisance of themselves.

Hyenas appear distinctly canine, but are generally larger and more powerfully built than your average dog, and have a broad head, large eyes, weak hindquarters and a sloping back that gives them a characteristic loping gait when running. Its short coat is dull grey to buff-coloured and patterned with black spots except on the throat. Its powerful jaws and teeth enable it to crush and swallow bones, which give its scat a characteristic calcium whitewash.

Although they're mainly nocturnal, hyenas are often seen during the day, especially around lion or cheetah kills, impatiently squabbling with the vultures for a turn at the carcass. Otherwise, a hyena's days are spent in long grass, abandoned aardvark holes or large burrows, which they excavate up to a metre below the surface. They're noisy animals; when camping out in the bush at night you'll frequently hear the hyena's spine-chilling yelp, which rises in a crescendo to a high-pitched scream. On other occasions, particularly when it's successful at finding food or mating, it's also known to 'laugh' with what might only be described as glee.

Hyenas have highly developed senses of smell, sight and hearing, which are all important in locating carrion or live prey and for mutual recognition among pack members and mating pairs. They're also well known as scavengers and often follow lions and hunting dogs – usually at a respectable distance – though they occasionally do force larger animals to abandon a kill. Carrion does form an important part of their diet, but hyenas are also true predators. Running hyenas can reach speeds of up to 60 km/h and a pack of them will often bring down small antelope, wildebeest and zebras. They also stalk pregnant antelope to snatch and kill the newly born calf – and occasionally the mother as well. They also prey on domestic stock.

During the mating season – especially on moonlit nights – hyenas assemble in large numbers for a bit of night-time chorus, which sounds like hell has broken loose. In their burrow, females produce a litter of up to four pups after a gestation period of about 110 days. The pups are weaned at around six weeks old and are on their own shortly.

Humans are the hyena's main enemies, but wild dogs will occasionally kill or mutilate a hyena that approaches a kill.

Leopard (Panther)
Panthera pardus

Although leopards are among the most widespread of African carnivores and are present all over Zimbabwe, Botswana and Namibia, they're mainly nocturnal and are therefore rarely observed. Leopards are agile and climb as well as domestic cats, and normally spend their days resting in trees up to five metres above the ground. They also protect their kills by dragging them up trees, where they're out of reach of scavengers and other would-be freeloaders.

The leopard's short orange coat is densely covered with mostly hollow black spots, although some individuals – often called panthers – are black all over. The underparts are white with fewer spots. Coats of savanna-dwelling leopards are generally lighter than those of forest dwellers. Leopards are heard more often than seen; their cry sounds very much like a hacksaw cutting through metal.

This powerfully built animal uses cunning to catch its prey, which consists mainly of birds, reptiles and mammals including large rodents, dassies, warthogs, small antelope, monkeys and baboons (a particular favourite). Occasionally, they also take domestic animals such as goats, sheep, poultry and dogs, and often enjoy a very poor reputation among the human population. This flexibility explains why they can survive even in areas of dense human settlement long after other large predators have disappeared. It also explains why they can inhabit so many different environments, ranging from semidesert to dense forest, and even the heights of Zimbabwe's Chimanimani Mountains.

Leopards are solitary animals, except during the mating season when the male and female cohabit. A litter of up to three cubs is produced after a gestation period of three months.

DAVID WALL

Leopard (Panther)

DAVID WALL

TONY WHEELER

Lions

Lion
Panthera leo

Lions are big attractions in the national parks and game reserves, but are most easily seen in the dry season (May to September) when they congregate near waterholes. Lions are most active in the late afternoon, but spend much of the day lying under bushes or in other attractive places.

Unlike Kenyan lions, which are generally quite docile and allow vehicles to approach to close range, lions in southern Africa are less accustomed to people and will avoid them whenever possible. They're hardly the human-eaters their reputation would have you believe, but older or irritable individuals do occasionally attack people. The most dangerous lions are those which can no longer bring down more fleet-footed animals. More often than not, however, they're off like a shot at the first unusual noise or sudden movement.

Lions are territorial beasts. A pride of up to three males and 15 accompanying females and young will defend an area of anything from 20 to 400 sq km, depending on the type of terrain and the amount of game food available. Lions generally hunt in prides; males drive the prey toward the concealed females, who do the actual killing. Although they cooperate well together, lions aren't the most efficient hunters and as many as four out of five attempts are unsuccessful.

Cubs are born in litters of two or three and become sexually mature by 1½ years. Males are driven from the family group shortly after, but don't reach full maturity until around six years of age. Unguarded cubs are preyed on by hyenas, leopards, pythons and hunting dogs.

Serval
Felis (Lepitailurus) serval

The serval, a type of wild cat, is about the size of a domestic cat but has much longer legs. It inhabits thick bush and tall grass around streams in central and eastern Zimbabwe.

Servals stand about 50 cm high and measure 130 cm long, including the tail. Their dirty yellow coat is dotted with large black spots which follow lines along the length of the body. Other prominent features include large upright ears, a long neck and a relatively short tail. It's an adept hunter, favouring birds, hares and rodents, and can catch birds in mid-flight by leaping into the air. Owing to its nocturnal nature, the serval is usually observed only in the early morning or late evening.

Kittens are born in litters of up to four. Although they leave their mother after one year, they don't reach sexual maturity until two years of age.

Serval

UNGULATES

Antelope
Bushbuck
Tragelaphus scriptus

Although the bushbuck exists in fairly large numbers in wooded areas of many southern African game parks, it's a shy solitary animal and is rarely sighted. The easiest place to see them is Zimbabwe's Victoria Falls rainforest park, which is home to several semi-tame individuals.

Standing about 80 cm at the shoulder, the bushbuck is chestnut to dark brown in colour. It has a variable number of white vertical stripes on the body between the neck and rump, and usually two horizontal white stripes lower down which give the animal a harnessed appearance, as well as a number of white spots on the upper thigh and a white splash on the neck. Normally only the males grow horns, but females have been known to grow them on rare occasions. The horns are straight with gentle spirals and average about 30 cm long.

Bushbuck are rarely found in groups of more than two, and prefer to stick to areas with heavy brush cover. When startled they bolt and crash loudly through the undergrowth. They're nocturnal browsers, yet rarely move far from their home turf. Though shy and elusive they can be aggressive and dangerous when cornered. Their main predators are leopards and pythons.

MIKE SCOTT

Bushbuck

Common or Grey Duiker
Silvicapra grimmia

As the name would suggest, the common duiker is the most common of the 16 duiker species in Africa (the other 15 being forest-dwellers). Even so, it's largely nocturnal and is sighted only infrequently. Duikers usually live in pairs, and prefer areas with good scrub cover.

Only 60 cm high at the shoulder, the common duiker is greyish light-brown in colour, with a white belly and a dark brown vertical stripe on the face. Only the males have horns, which are straight and pointed, and grow to only 20 cm in length.

Common duikers are almost exclusively browsers and only rarely eat grasses, though they appear to supplement their diet with insects and guinea fowl chicks. They're capable of going without water for long periods but will drink whenever water is available.

Duikers are widely distributed through a range of habitats from open bush to semidesert, but they prefer low open scrub and even occupy cultivated areas where other herbivores have been exterminated. You'll find them throughout Zimbabwe and much of Botswana. The rare blue duiker *(Cephalophus monticola)* lives only in the forests of Zimbabwe's Eastern Highlands.

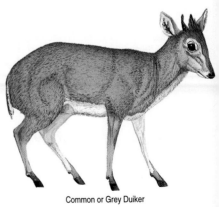

Common or Grey Duiker

Damara Dik-Dik

Damara Dik-Dik
Madoqua (Rhynchotragus) kirkii damarensis

There are seven subspecies of Kirk's dik-dik, but only the Damara dik-dik is found in south-western Africa. This tiny mostly reddish-brown antelope has a white underside and stands only around 35 cm at the shoulder. Dik-diks are best identified by their small size, but other tell-tale marks include the negligible tail and the tuft of dark hair on the forehead. Only the males have horns, but they're short – around six cm – and are often lost in the hair tuft. The males weigh no more than six kg; females are slightly larger.

Dik-diks usually move singly or in pairs, and can live in extremely dry places – they seem to derive most of their necessary moisture from their food. They're also territorial, and each individual male lays claim to around five hectares. They are mainly nocturnal and rest through the heat of the day, but are often seen grazing in the early morning and late afternoon.

The females bear a single fawn twice a year. After six months young dik-diks reach sexual maturity and are driven from their home territory.

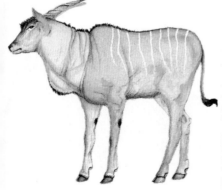

Eland

Eland
Taurotragus oryx

The eland is the largest antelope species, standing about 170 cm at the shoulder; a mature bull can weigh up to 1000 kg. Oddly enough, eland resemble some varieties of cattle native to the Indian subcontinent. Although rare, it's widespread, and is found in all the Zimbabwean parks as well as in Moremi and Chobe in Botswana and around Namutoni in Namibia's Etosha National Park.

Eland have light brown coats with up to 15 vertical white stripes on the body, although they're often almost indistinguishable. Both sexes have horns about 65 cm long, which spiral at the base and sweep straight back. Males have a much hairier head than the females, and their horns are stouter and shorter.

Eland prefer savanna scrub to open spaces, but they avoid thick forest. They feed on grass and tree foliage in the early morning and late afternoon, and are also active on moonlit nights. They normally drink daily, but can go for a month or more without water.

Eland usually live in groups of around six to 12, but herds can contain as many as 50 individuals. A small herd normally consists of several females and one male, but in larger herds there may be several males, which is made possible by a strict hierarchy. Females reach sexual maturity at around two years and can bear up to 12 calves in a lifetime. The young are born in October or November.

Gemsbok (South African Oryx)
Oryx gazella

The gemsbok, a large grey antelope standing around 120 cm at the shoulder, is frequently observed in all the Botswanan wildlife parks and reserves, and is also common in the Namib Desert, Damaraland and around Etosha National Park. There are also a few in the southernmost parts of Hwange National Park in Zimbabwe.

There are two types of gemsbok in southern Africa: the Namibian subspecies has a pale grey upper body and a white abdomen, with black and white markings on the face and a band of black on each flank. These animals have a specially adapted cooling system which allows them to cope with temperature extremes, especially along the Namib Desert coast.

The other subspecies is sandy fawn in colour, with a black stripe along the spine down to the tip of the tail. The underparts are white and separated from the lower flanks by another black stripe. There are also two black rings just above the knee of each foreleg. Both males and females of both subspecies have long, rapier-like horns, which are used for defence.

Gemsbok are principally grazers, but will also browse on thorny shrubs. They can survive for long periods without water.

Herds vary from five to 40 individuals, but the bulls normally prefer a solitary existence.

Gemsbok (South African Oryx)

Greater Kudu
Tragelaphus strepsiceros

The beautiful greater kudu, one of the largest antelope, is found all over Zimbabwe, Namibia and northern and eastern Botswana, preferring hilly country with fairly dense bush cover.

Kudu stand around 1.5 metres at the shoulder, with a long neck and broad ears, and weigh up to 250 kg, yet they're very regal in appearance. Their bodies are light grey in colour with six to 10 vertical white stripes along the sides and a white chevron between the eyes. The horns, carried only by males, form large spirals; an old buck can have up to three complete twists.

Kudu live in small herds of up to five females and their young, but during rainy periods, the herds often split. The normally solitary males occasionally band into small herds.

Kudu are mainly browsers and can eat a variety of leaves which would be poisonous to other animals. On occasion, they also eat grasses.

Although they're somewhat clumsy when on the move, kudu can easily clear obstacles of over two metres and are known for their unhealthy habit of leaping in front of oncoming vehicles.

Greater Kudu

Hartebeest

Hartebeest
Alcelaphus buselaphus (Red Hartebeest)
Sigmoceros lichtensteinii (Lichtenstein's Hartebeest)

The hartebeest is a medium-size antelope found in small numbers in the wildlife reserves of Zimbabwe and Botswana and in Namibia's Etosha National Park. Both Lichtenstein's and red hartebeest are found in Zimbabwe and Botswana, while Namibia has only red hartebeest.

Hartebeest are easily recognised by their long, narrow face and short horns, which are distinctively angular and heavily ridged. In both sexes, the horns form a heart shape, hence their name, which means 'heart beast' in Afrikaans). The back slopes away from the humped shoulders and is light brown, becoming lighter towards the rear and underside.

Hartebeest prefer grassy plains for grazing but are also found in sparsely forested savanna or hills. They feed exclusively on grass and usually drink twice daily, although they can go for months without water if necessary.

They're social beasts and often mingle with animals such as zebra and wildebeest. Sexual maturity is reached at around two years, and hartebeest can calve at any time of year, although activity peaks in February and August. Predators are mainly the large cats, hyenas and hunting dogs.

Impala
Aepyceros melampus

The graceful impala is one of the most common antelope and is found in large numbers in all the national
parks and reserves in Zimbabwe, northern Botswana
and far northern Namibia. Further south in Namibia,
however, its place is filled by the springbok. There is
an Etosha subspecies of impala, called the black-
faced impala *(Aepyceros melampus petersi)*, with a
darker coat than its relative and a pronounced purple-
black blaze on the forehead.

Individuals weigh from 50 to 60 kg and stand about
80 cm at the shoulder. The coat is a glossy rufous
colour, though more pale on the flanks, and the underparts, rump, throat and chin are white. A narrow black
band runs from the middle of the rump to about
halfway down the tail and there's also a vertical black
stripe on the back of the thighs. Males have long,
lyre-shaped horns averaging 75 cm in length.

Impala are both browsers and grazers, and are
active day and night. They're very dependent on water
but are capable of existing on dew for fairly long
periods.

Impala are gregarious animals, and males have
harems of up to 100 females, although 15 to 20 are
more common. Single males form bachelor groups,
and there is fierce competition and fighting between
them during the rutting season. The normal gestation
period is six to seven months, but that can be prolonged if low rainfall has produced insufficient grass to
nourish the young. Males usually leave the herd
before they reach breeding age.

Impala are known for their speed and ability to leap;
they can spring as much as 10 metres in a single
bound or three metres off the ground – and frequently
do – even when there's nothing to jump over! And it's
lucky they can; impala are the rabbits of Africa, and
make a tasty meal for all large predators, including
lions, leopards, cheetahs, wild dogs and even hyenas.

HUGH FINLAY

Impala

Klipspringer
Oreotragus oreotragus

The delicate little klipspringer, which stands about 50 cm at the shoulder, is shy and easily disturbed. It's easily recognised by its curious tip-toe stance – the hooves are adapted for balance and grip on rocky surfaces – and the greenish tinge of its coarse speckled hair. The widely-spaced 10-cm-long horns are present only on the male.

Klipspringers normally inhabit rocky outcrops in Hwange and Matobo national parks in Zimbabwe, and in Namibia are most often seen on the western slopes of the Central Plateau, including Kuiseb Canyon, the Brandberg and the Naukluft. They also venture into adjacent grasslands, but when alarmed they retreat into the rocks for safety. These amazingly agile and sure-footed creatures are capable of bounding up impossibly rough rock faces. They get all the water they need from their diet of greenery and go for long periods without drinking. They're most active around midday, and single males often keep watch from a good vantage point.

Each male has a clearly defined territory and lives with one or two females. They reach sexual maturity at around one year, and females bear one calf twice annually. Calves may stay with their parents for up to a year, but young males normally establish their own territory even sooner.

Main predators are leopards, crowned eagles, jackals and baboons.

Klipspringer

Lechwe

Lechwe
Kobus leche

The red (or Zambezi) lechwe is a yellowish-brown mid-size antelope which inhabits marshes, rivers, swamps and lakes up to 50 cm deep. It feeds on riverine grasses mainly along Botswana's Chobe riverfront and Okavango Delta, and Namibia's Linyanti Marshes. Both sexes have a pronounced rump and males have lyre-shaped horns, each with an average of 200 rings.

Lechwe live in herds of up to hundreds of males, females and young. Females reach sexual maturity at about 1½ years, after which they can mate and give birth at any time of year.

Hunted by lions, cheetahs, leopards, hunting dogs, hyenas, pythons, and even humans and crocodiles, the apparently tasty lechwes have good reason to be paranoid. They're mainly active around dawn and dusk, but in areas where they're hunted by humans, lechwe are only out and about at night.

Nyala
Tragelaphus angasii (Common Nyala)
Tragelaphus buxtoni (Mountain Nyala)

The medium-size nyala is one of Africa's rarest and most beautiful antelope. Males are grey with a mane and long hair under the throat and hind legs. They also have vertical stripes down the back and long, lyre-shaped horns with white tips. Females are a ruddy colour with vertical white stripes, but have no horns.

Although nyalas are found in small numbers throughout south-eastern Africa, their only Zimbabwean populations are in Gonarezhou and Mana Pools national parks. Their main foods are shoots, buds, bark, fruit and leaves of trees and bushes. During the dry season they're active only in the morning and evening, while during the rains, they more often feed at night.

Female nyala and their young live in small groups, with one older dominant male to guard and defend them from young males, which organise their own social groups. Nyala defend themselves bravely against humans and enemies – mainly leopards and lions. The young may even be taken by baboons and birds of prey.

Nyala

Oribi
Ourebia ourebi

Similar to the duiker in appearance, the small oribi is relatively difficult to see; your best chance of spotting one is in Zimbabwe's Kazuma Pan National Park or around Nogatsaa in Botswana's Chobe National Park.

Oribi are a uniform golden brown with white on the belly and the insides of the legs. The males have short straight horns about 10 cm long. The oribi's most distinguishing mark – although you'll need binoculars to spot it – is a circular patch of naked black skin below the ear, which is actually a scent gland. Another identifying characteristic is the tuft of black hair on the tip of the short tail.

Being quite small, the oribi has many predators, including the larger cats. They usually graze on high grass savanna plains, where they're well sheltered from predators. They can go without water entirely, but if it's available, they'll drink. When alarmed they bolt, making erratic bounces with all four legs held rigidly straight. It's thought this helps them with orientation in high grasses. After 100 metres or so, they stop to assess the danger.

Oribi are territorial and usually live in pairs. They reach sexual maturity at around one year, and the females bear one calf twice annually.

Oribi

Puku

Puku
Kobus vardonii

Also known as the kob, the extremely rare and endangered puku is limited to about 100 individuals along the Chobe River in Botswana, the Linyanti Marshes in Namibia and a few in Zambia. They never stray far from permanent water sources, eating mainly foliage and riverine grasses. Although puku are similar to the lechwe in shape and colour, they're a bit larger and have thicker horns (males only) and slightly different markings.

There's no set mating season; females normally bear two single offspring each year. Young males, mature males and females with young generally divide into separate herds. They rarely range more than one km from home base. Within that area, they designate a rutting ground to be used only for mating.

Puku are normally active at dawn and from late afternoon to dusk, with sporadic activity during the day. They're hunted by lions, leopards, hyenas and hunting dogs.

Reedbuck

Reedbuck
Redunca redunca (Bohar Reedbuck)
Redunca arundinum (Common Reedbuck)
Redunca fulvorufula (Mountain Reedbuck)

The dusky brown reedbuck is found throughout southern African wetlands or riverine areas, and never strays more than a few km from a permanent water source. The rare mountain reedbuck is protected in Mokolodi Nature Reserve, near Gaborone, Botswana.

These medium-size antelope stand around 80 cm at the shoulder and males have distinctive forward-curving horns. The underbelly, inside of the thighs, throat and underside of the bushy tail are white.

Reedbuck are territorial and live in small groups of up to 10 animals. Groups usually consist of an older male and accompanying females and young. Their diet consists almost exclusively of grass and some foliage.

At mating time, competing males fight with spirit. After sexual maturity at 1½ years, females bear one calf at a time. Predators include big cats, hyenas and hunting dogs.

Ringed (Common) Waterbuck
Kobus ellipsiprymnus

The ringed waterbuck, so called because of the bulls-eye ring around its rump, has white markings on the face and throat. It's a solid animal with a thick, shaggy, dark brown coat, white inner thighs and proportionally long neck and short legs. It's commonly seen in all the Zimbabwean parks, Chobe and Moremi in Botswana, and the northern Namibian parks.

Only the males have horns, which curve gradually outward before shooting straight up to a length of about 75 cm. Waterbuck are good swimmers and readily enter the water to escape predators. They never stray far from water, and a male's territory will always include a water source. Herds are small and consist of cows, calves and one mature bull, while younger bulls live in small groups apart from the herd.

The bulk of the waterbuck's diet consists mainly of grass, but it also eats some foliage. Sexual maturity is reached at just over one year, although a male will not become dominant in the herd until around five years of age. Females and younger males are permitted to wander at will through territories of breeding males.

Predators such as lions, leopards and hunting dogs go for the young calves and females, but mature waterbucks are not a favoured prey species because of their tough flesh and the distinct odour of the meat.

Ringed (Common) Waterbuck

Roan Antelope
Hippotragus equinus

The roan is one of southern Africa's rarest antelope species, but still exists in some numbers in Hwange, Kazuma Pan and Chobe national parks. To increase numbers, they've also been introduced into Etosha and Waterberg in Namibia. As grazers, they prefer tall grasses and sites with ample shade and fresh water.

Roan are the third largest antelope species, after eland and kudu, reaching up to 150 cm at the shoulder. They bear a striking resemblance to a horse, hence the English and Latin names. Bulls can weigh up to 270 kg.

The coat varies from reddish fawn to dark rufous, with white underparts and a conspicuous mane of stiff, black-tipped hairs stretching from the nape to the shoulders. There's another mane of sorts on the underside of the neck, consisting of long dark hairs. The ears are long, narrow and pointed, with a brown tassel at the tip. The face has a distinctive black and white pattern. Both sexes have curving, back-swept horns up to 70 cm long.

Roan have an extremely aggressive nature and fight from an early age, thus deterring predators. For most of the year they're arranged in small herds of normally less than 20 individuals, led by a master bull. However, in the mating season, bulls become solitary and take a female from the herd. The pair remain together until the calf is born, after which the females and calves form a separate herd; when the dry season comes, the females and calves rejoin the original herd.

Roan Antelope

Sable Antelope

Sable Antelope
Hippotragus niger

In Zimbabwe, the sable is present in Matobo, Hwange and Zambezi national parks, and is occasionally seen in Chobe in Botswana and Waterberg Plateau in Namibia. Sable are slightly smaller than roan, but are more solidly built. The colouring is dark brown to black, with a white belly and face markings. Both sexes carry 80-cm sweeping horns, but those of the male are longer and more curved. Sable feed mainly on grass, but foliage accounts for around 10% of their diet.

Sable live in territorial herds of up to 25 – sometimes more in the dry season – and are active mainly in the early morning and late afternoon. Each herd occupies its own area, within which each individual male has his own territory of up to 30 hectares.

Females start bearing calves at around three years of age; most are borne in January and September. Like the roan, the sable is a fierce fighter and has been known to kill lions when attacked. Other predators include leopards, hyenas and hunting dogs.

Sharpe's Grysbok

Sharpe's Grysbok
Raphiceros sharpei

This small, stocky antelope is reddish-brown with a pale red underside. The back and sides are speckled with individual white hairs from the nape of the neck to the rump, hence the Afrikaans name grysbok, or 'grey buck'. Sharpe's grysbok stand only about 50 cm high and weigh no more than nine kg. Only the males have horns, which are small, sharp and straight.

Grysbok inhabit both bushy and woodland savanna country and rocky kopjes throughout Zimbabwe and northern Botswana, feeding primarily on shoots and leaves. They also like to munch the reeds which grow in wetlands.

Grysbok are solitary, and you'll rarely see more than two together. They're most active from morning to late afternoon, spending the night resting in bushy thickets and stony outcrops.

Sitatunga
Tragelaphus spekii

The sitatunga is a swamp antelope with unusual elongated hooves, allowing it to walk on marshy ground without sinking. It's restricted mainly to Botswana's Moremi Reserve and the Linyanti Marshes along the Botswana-Namibia border. Sitatunga feed largely on papyrus and other reeds. Animals normally live singly or in pairs, but have been observed in herds of up to 15 individuals.

Sitatunga, which stand a little over a metre at the shoulder, are vaguely similar to bushbuck in appearance, but the male's coat is much darker and the hair of both sexes is longer and shaggier. Males have twisted horns up to 90 cm long.

The normally shy sitatunga are good swimmers. When alarmed, they often submerge, leaving only their nostrils exposed. They're also hunted by humans for food and their numbers are dwindling. Although there's evidence that they're normally diurnal, in areas of high human predation, some individuals have adopted nocturnal habits. Sightings, therefore, are rare.

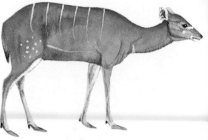

Sitatunga

Springbok
Antidorcas marsupialis

The springbok, the only gazelle in southern Africa, is the most common antelope in Namibia and exists in large numbers in Etosha and Namib-Naukluft national parks as well as unprotected areas of Damaraland and Kaokoland.

Springbok are easily recognised by their white head, with a black stripe connecting the nose and eye. The fawn-coloured back and white belly are separated by a ruddy brown stripe along the animal's side. Both male and female springbok have ribbed, lyre-shaped horns of medium length. It's one of several species of antelope known for its pronking (leaping vertically in the air).

They generally move in herds of 20 to 100 animals; sometimes herds of several hundred can be seen. Male springbok are only territorial during the rutting season, when they collect harems of females and defend them against other potential suitors. At other times, herds consist of mixed groups of males and females, although groups made up entirely of bachelors are often observed.

Springbok are active early in the morning and from late afternoon to dusk. They also emerge on nights with strong moonlight. They eat grass and the leaves of low bushes, and occasionally dig out roots and tubers. Females calve from December to January.

They drink often, but can survive for long periods without water. Occasionally, in conditions of severe drought, huge herds migrate in search of water; in the great migration of 1896, the surface area covered by millions of springbok was 220 km long and 25 km wide. In the past in Namibia, great herds, driven mad by thirst or hunger, flocked to the coast, drank seawater and died, leaving the shoreline littered with carcasses.

DEANNA SWANEY

Springbok herd

Steenbok
Raphiceros campestris

The steenbok, sometimes spelt 'steinbock', bears a resemblance to both the duiker and the grysbok, with a short tail and proportionally long and slender legs. The back and hindquarters range from light reddish brown to dark brown, and on the upper edge of the nose is a black, wedge-shaped spot. Males have small, straight and widely separated horns.

Steenbok live mainly on open plains, but are also seen in level areas of the Kalahari in western Botswana and eastern Namibia. They're solitary animals, and only have contact with others during the mating season.

Normally, steenbok are active in the morning and evening, but may stay out late when there's a bright moon. At other times, they seek out high grass or ant bear holes which offer some protection from enemies, which include leopards, eagles, pythons, monitor lizards, jackals and hyenas.

DEANNA SWANEY

Steenbok

Tsessebi (Topi)
Damaliscus lunatus

The tsessebi is not unlike the hartebeest in appearance but is darker – in some cases appearing almost violet – with black patches on the rear thighs, front legs and face. Its horns, carried by both sexes, curve gently up, out and back. The tsessebi is found in all Zimbabwean national parks, in Mudumu and Mamili national parks in Namibia, and in both Chobe and Moremi in northern Botswana.

A highly gregarious antelope, it lives in herds of at least 15 and frequently mingles with wildebeest, hartebeest and zebras. During the mating season, bulls select a well-defined patch which they defend against all rivals, while females wander from one patch to another. After mating, herds divide into separate male and female groups.

Tsessebi are exclusively grazers. Although they can live on dry grasses spurned by other antelope, they prefer floodplains and moist areas which support lush pasture. When water is available they drink frequently, but they are also capable of surviving long periods without water as long as sufficient grass is available. Lions are their main predators.

Tsessebi (Topi)

Wildebeest (Gnu)
Connochaetes taurinus (Blue Wildebeest or Brindled Gnu)
Connochaetes gnou (Black Wildebeest or White-tailed Gnu)

The wildebeest, also called the gnu after its low and languid grunt, is to the African savanna what the bison once was to the American prairies. Wildebeest are gregarious, to say the least, and sometimes move about in herds up to tens of thousands strong, normally in association with zebras and other herbivores, accompanied by a cacophony of amusing snorts and low grunts. In southern Africa, populations peak in central Botswana and in Hwange, Chobe and Etosha national parks.

The wildebeest's ungainly appearance makes it unmistakable; it's heavily built and has a massive head and wild, frayed mane. It has been described as having the forequarters of an ox, the hind parts of an antelope and the tail of a horse. It's also known for its rather eccentric behaviour, which includes snorting, cavorting, frantically shaking the head, bucking, running around in circles and rolling in the dust. This is thought to be a reaction to the botfly larva which finds its way up the nostrils and into the brain.

Wildebeest are almost exclusively grazers, and move constantly in search of good pasture and water. Their annual migration between Botswana's Makgadikgadi Pans and Nxai Pan (and vice versa) is an amazing sight. However, many succumb to thirst or mere exhaustion while trying to get around the Kuke buffalo fence, which extends from east to west across central Botswana.

During the mating season, groups of up to 150 females and their young are gathered by up to three bulls, which defend a defined territory against rivals, even when on the move. There's apparently no hierarchy amongst the bulls and, at the end of the mating season, breeding herds are reabsorbed into the main herds.

Because they prefer to drink daily and can survive only five days without water, wildebeest will migrate up to 50 km to find it. During the rainy season they graze haphazardly, without any apparent social organisation, but in the dry season they coalesce around waterholes.

Major predators include lions, cheetahs and wild dogs, and hyenas are also partial to young wildebeest calves.

TONY WHEELER

Wildebeest (Gnu)

Other Ungulates

Cape Buffalo
Syncerus caffer

TONY WHEELER

Cape Buffalo

Cape (or African) buffalo occur in great numbers in all major parks in Zimbabwe and Botswana, but in Namibia they exist only in Waterberg Plateau Park. Both sexes have the distinctive curving horns which broaden and almost meet over the forehead, but those of the female are usually smaller. Their colouration varies from ruddy brown to black.

Buffalo have a penetrating gaze, and one safari operator has noted that 'buffalo always look at you as if you owe them a lot of money'. Although for the most part they're docile and stay out of humans' way, these 800-kg creatures can be very dangerous and should be treated with caution. Solitary rogue bulls and females protecting young are the most aggressive.

Cape buffalo are territorial, but when food and water are plentiful the herds, which normally consist of 100 or more individuals, may disperse over an area 100 km in diameter. However, they never stray far from water, especially in dry periods.

Giraffe
Giraffa camelopardalis

DAVID WALL

Giraffe

Giraffes are found in all the major game parks of Zimbabwe, Botswana and Namibia. The two most common subspecies are the Masai giraffe *(G.c. tippelskirchii)* and the reticulated giraffe *(G.c. reticulata)*.

The name giraffe is derived from the Arabic *zarafah* ('the one who walks quickly'). The main distinguishing feature of the Masai giraffe is its irregular, star-like spots, compared with the more regular pattern of the reticulated giraffe. The reticulated giraffe is a deeper brown and its body has a more intricate tortoise-shell pattern.

The average male is around 5½ metres tall. Females are mere midgets at 4½ metres and are normally lighter in colour and have less well-defined markings. Both sexes have 'horns', actually just short projections of skin-covered bone and probably a remnant of what might once have been antlers. Despite the giraffe's incredibly long neck, it still has only seven cervical vertebrae – the same number as all mammals, including humans.

Giraffes are out and about in the early morning and afternoon, browsing on acacia. You may be surprised to see them chewing bones, a practice known as *pica*, which indicates a shortage of minerals in their diet. When the sun is high and hot, they relax in a cool, shady spot. At night they also rest for several hours.

Giraffes most often drink in the late afternoon or early evening, but they must go through all sorts of contortions to reach water level. They're at their most vulnerable at waterholes and always appear hesitant and visibly nervous when drinking. In fact, if they feel the slightest uncertainty about the safety of the situation, they'll often forgo their drink altogether.

Hippopotamus
Hippopotamus amphibius

In southern Africa the hippo is found in greatest numbers in the Okavango Delta, the Zambezi and Chobe rivers, waterholes in all the parks, and some popular recreational dams in Zimbabwe. In Namibia, the falls at Andara are a good place to see them.

Hippos, as you probably already know, are huge, fat animals with enormous heads and short legs. When fully grown they weigh in at 1350 kg to 2600 kg. Their ears, eyes and nostrils are so placed that they can remain inconspicuously above water even when the animal is submerged.

Hippos spend most of the day submerged, feeding on bottom vegetation and surfacing only occasionally to grab a breath of air before plunging again. Only at night do they emerge from the water, often wandering up to several km from their aquatic haunts to graze. They're voracious feeders and can consume up to 60 kg of vegetable matter, mostly a variety of grasses, each night. They urinate and defecate in well-defined areas – often in the water – dispersing the excreta with their tails.

They're very gregarious animals and live in schools of 15 to 30 or more. Each school generally contains an equal number of bulls and cows (with their calves) and hippo society operates under an established hierarchy. They may appear placid, but the males do frequently fight among themselves for dominance and some of the resulting wounds can be quite horrific. Virtually every male hippo bears the scars of such conflicts.

To humans, hippos are statistically Africa's most dangerous animal. Most accidents occur when hippos surface beneath boats and canoes or when someone sets up camp on a riverside hippo run or blocks a hippo's retreat route to the water. They may look sluggish but they do manage considerable speeds and don't much care what stands in their way.

Hippos breed year-round. Cows give birth to a single calf after a gestation period of 230 days and suckle it both in the water and on land for four to six months. At this time it begins to graze on its own. Hippos live for about 30 years and sexual maturity is reached at about four years.

The hippo's only natural predators are lions and crocodiles, which prey on the young. Though they occasionally tangle fishing nets, they're considered beneficial because their wallowing stirs up the bottom mud and their excreta is a valuable fertiliser which encourages the growth of aquatic organisms.

GEOFF CROWTHER

Hippopotamus

DAVID WALL
White or Square-lipped Rhinoceros

DAVID WALL
Black or Hook-lipped Rhinoceros

Rhinoceros

Diceros bicornis (Black or Hook-lipped Rhinoceros)
Ceratotherium simum (White or Square-lipped Rhinoceros)

Currently, rhinos are Africa's most endangered large animals, thanks mainly to the mistaken Asian belief that rhino horn has medicinal and aphrodisiac properties, and the Yemeni notion that all real men need a dagger made of rhino horn. Poaching has caused dramatic declines in rhino numbers in recent years, and in many countries they've been completely exterminated.

Conservation efforts in Zimbabwe, Botswana and Namibia have not kept pace with the losses, and most programmes are failing badly. Many translocated animals die of stress, radio collaring only reveals the location of dead animals, and parks' patrols realise that poachers will stop at nothing to shoot rhinos.

It was once thought that dehorning programmes would render the animals commercially worthless, but they've had only limited success (mainly in Namibia and South Africa, where poaching is still limited). First, poachers will kill a rhino for the smallest stump of horn. Second, after a poacher has spent five days tracking a hornless rhino, it's shot so it won't have to be tracked again. Third, Far Eastern dealers realise the rhino's extinction will render their stockpiles of horn priceless. To that end they've ordered poachers to shoot every rhino they encounter, whether it has a horn or not.

Given these circumstances, visitors who see rhinos can count themselves lucky. The best place in Zimbabwe is Matobo National Park, where rhinos are guarded day and night. There are also several left in Hwange National Park. Zimbabwe's Chizarira National Park now has one or two individuals at most. In Botswana, try the Khama Sanctuary near Serowe or the Mokolodi Nature Reserve near Gaborone. In Namibia, you'll have the most luck seeing black rhinos around Okaukuejo in Etosha National Park. White rhinos can be seen in Waterberg Plateau Park.

Black rhinos are browsers, living in scrubby country and eating mainly leaves, shoots and buds, while white rhinos are grazers and prefer open plains. Both species feed in the cooler hours of the morning or late afternoon.

While white rhinos are generally docile, black rhinos are prone to charging when alarmed, but their eyesight is extremely poor and chances are they'll miss their target anyway. They've even been known to charge trains or elephant carcasses! A black rhino's territory can range from two to 50 sq km, depending on the terrain and availability of food, but only white rhino males actively defend these territories.

Rhinos reach sexual maturity by five years but females first breed at around seven years of age. Calves average 40 kg at birth and grow to 140 kg at three months of age. Adult black rhinos weigh from 800 to 1100 kg but the much larger white rhinos tip the scales at 1200 to 1600 kg. Both species are solitary, only socialising during the mating season. Calves stay with the mother for up to three years, although they're weaned after one year.

Warthog
Phacochoerus aethiopicus

Warthogs are found in all the major parks in Zimbabwe, Botswana and Namibia but are most profuse in Hwange. They take their name from the rather unusual wart-like growths on the face. They usually live in family groups, known as 'sounders', which include a boar, a sow and three or four young. Their most endearing habit is the way they trot away with their thin tufted tail stuck straight up in the air like antennae.

Males are usually larger than females, measuring up to one metre long and weighing around 100 kg. They grow two sets of tusks; the upper ones curve outwards and upwards and grow as long as 60 cm; the lower ones are usually less than 15 cm long.

Warthogs feed mainly on grass, but also eat fruit and bark. In hard times they'll burrow with their snout for roots and bulbs. They also rest and give birth in abandoned burrows, or sometimes excavate cavities in abandoned termite mounds. Piglets are born in litters of two to eight.

TONY WHEELER
Warthog

Zebras
Equus burchelli (Common or Burchell's Zebra)
Equus zebra (Hartmann's Mountain Zebra)

Zebras are widely distributed, and are observed in large numbers in all the national parks and reserves, especially Hwange, Chobe, Etosha, Mana Pools, Zambezi and Moremi. Zebras often mingle with other animals, such as wildebeest, elephants and impala.

Southern Africa has two species, the more common of which is Burchell's zebra. Some taxonomists classify several Burchell's subspecies, but this is a contentious issue since no two zebras have exactly the same markings. The other species is Hartmann's Mountain Zebra, which lives mainly in mountain areas of Namibia – the Erongo, the Khomas Hochland and the Naukluft. It may initially be difficult to distinguish between them, but Hartmann's zebras don't have shadow lines between the black stripes. They also have a gridiron pattern of black stripes just above the tail and a dewlap below the chin.

Zebras are grazers but occasionally browse on leaves and scrub. They need water daily and rarely wander far from a waterhole. During the breeding season, stallions engage in fierce battles for control over a herd of mares. A single foal is born after a gestation period of 12 months. Lions are the zebra's worst enemy, but they're also taken by hyenas and wild dogs.

DAVID WALL
Zebra

OTHER ANIMALS

Aardvark (Antbear)
Orycteropus afer

The porcine-looking aardvark has thick and wrinkled pink-grey skin with very sparse and stiff greyish hair. Its has an elongated tubular snout and a round, sticky, pink tongue, which are used to lap up ants and termites dug from nests and rotting wood with the long claws of its front feet.

Aardvarks dig metre-long holes which are also used as burrows by many other species, including hares, hyenas, jackals, warthogs, owls and rodents. They normally emerge only at night, but in the morning after a cold night they may bask in the sun awhile before retiring underground. When aardvark holes are occupied, the entrances are sealed except for small ventilation holes. When confronted by an enemy, aardvarks somersault and bleat loudly or if there's time, quickly excavate a refuge. When cornered, it resists attack with the foreclaws, shoulders and tail.

Aardvarks are normally solitary animals; only mother and offspring live together.

Aardvark (Antbear)

African Elephant
Loxodonta africana

African elephants are much larger than their Asian counterparts and their ears are wider and flatter. A fully grown bull can weigh more than 6½ tonnes.

Elephants are present in all the major wildlife parks in all three countries, with the exception of Matobo and Waterberg Plateau Park (where the environment is too fragile to handle elephant destruction) and the parks of central and southern Botswana, where there is insufficient water. The greatest concentrations of elephants are in Hwange, Matusadona, Chobe, Moremi and Etosha national parks.

Both males and females grow tusks, although the female's are usually smaller. The tusks on an old bull can weigh as much as 50 kg each, and those of one big guy shot in Zimbabwe's Gonarezhou National Park weighed in at 110 kg – but 15 kg to 25 kg is more usual.

Elephants are gregarious animals, and usually live in herds of 10 to 20. These herds will consist of one mature bull and a couple of younger bulls, cows and calves, but herds may incorporate up to 50 individuals. Old bulls appear to lose the herding instinct and eventually leave to pursue a solitary existence, rejoining the herd only for mating. Because elephants communicate using a range of sounds, herds often make a great deal of noise: snorting, bellowing, rumbling and belching produced by the trunk or mouth. The best-known elephant call, however, is the high-pitched trumpeting which they produce when they're frightened or want to appear threatening.

Herds are on the move night and day in pursuit of water and fodder, both of which they consume in vast quantities. An adult's average daily food intake is

DAVID WALL

African Elephant

about 250 kg. Elephants are both grazers and browsers and feed on a wide variety of vegetable matter, including grasses, leaves, twigs, bark, roots and fruits, and they frequently knock down quite large trees to get at the leaves. Especially in drought years, they're capable of turning dense woodland into open grassland in a relatively short time. Because of this destructive capacity they're often perceived as a serious threat to a fragile environment, but some schools of thought maintain that elephant damage is necessary in the natural cycle of the bushveld.

Elephants do, however, come into conflict with Africa's rapidly increasing human population. More and more elephant habitat is being given over to cultivated land and there's nothing more tasty to an elephant than bananas, maize and sugar cane. Once an elephant has tasted these goodies, it will always come back for more; farmers don't generally tolerate nuisance elephants longer than it takes to grab a rifle, although in Zimbabwe the CAMPFIRE programme has a fund to compensate rural farmers for elephant damage.

Mineral salts obtained from 'salt licks' are also essential in an elephant's diet. Salt is dug out of the earth with the tusks and devoured in large quantities.

Elephants breed year-round and have a gestation period of 22 to 24 months. Expectant mothers leave the herd along with one or two other females and select a secluded spot to give birth, then rejoin the herd a few days later. Calves weigh around 130 kg at birth and stand just under a metre high. They're very playful and are guarded carefully and fondly by their mothers until weaned at two years of age. They continue to grow for the next 20 years, reaching puberty at around 10 to 12 years. On average, an elephant's life span is 60 to 70 years, though some individuals reach the ripe old age of 100 or more.

DAVID WALL

African Elephant

Cape Pangolin
Manis temminckii

The Cape pangolin (also called Temminck's Ground Pangolin) is one of four species of African pangolins, but it is the only species in southern Africa. Pangolins are sometimes known as scaly anteaters because they're covered with large rounded scales over the back and tail, with hair only around the eyes, ears, cheeks and belly. Their primary foods include ants and termites dug from termite mounds, rotting wood and dung heaps. They walk on the outside edges of their hands, with claws pointed inward. They rarely excavate their own holes, however, and prefer to live in abandoned aardvark holes.

Cape pangolins are present all over Zimbabwe, Botswana and northern Namibia, normally keeping to dry scrubby country, especially areas with light sandy soil such as the Kalahari. They're mainly nocturnal but are most active between midnight and dawn and are therefore rarely seen.

Cape Pangolin

Short-Tailed Porcupine
Hystrix africaeaustralis

The prickly porcupine, the largest rodent native to southern Africa, can weigh as much as 24 kg and measure up to a metre in length. Although it ranges throughout the region, it prefers wild, rugged and forested habitats, and is found mainly around the reserves of western Zimbabwe, northern Botswana and north-eastern Namibia. Because porcupines are nocturnal they're quite difficult to observe, although on cooler days, they occasionally emerge during daylight hours.

Porcupines are covered with a spread of long black and white banded quills from the shoulders to the tail. Along the ridge from the head to the shoulders runs a crest of long coarse hair, which stands on end when the animal is alarmed.

For shelter, they either occupy rock caves or excavate their own burrows. Their diet consists mainly of bark, tubers, seeds and a variety of plants and ground-level foliage. The young are born during the hot summer months, normally in litters of one or two.

DEANNA SWANEY
Short-Tailed Porcupine

Rock Hyraxes
Procavia capensis (Dassie or Cape Hyrax)
Procavia welwitschii (Kaokoveld Hyrax)

Southern Africa's most common hyrax species is the dassie, or rock hyrax. (The Kaokoveld hyrax is restricted to northern Namibia and southern Angola.) This small but robust animal is about the size of a rabbit, with a short and pointed snout, large ears and thick fur. The tail is either absent or reduced to a stump.

Hyraxes are sociable animals and live in colonies of up to 60 individuals, usually in rocky, scrub-covered locales, such as rock kopjes. They feed in the morning and evening on grass, bulbs, roots, grasshoppers and locusts. During the rest of the day hyraxes sun themselves on rocks or chase each other in play. Where they're habituated to humans, they're often quite tame, but otherwise they dash into rock crevices when alarmed, uttering shrill screams. They have excellent hearing and eyesight.

Hyraxes breed all year and have a gestation of around seven months, which is a remarkably long period for an animal of this size. Up to six young are born at a time, and are cared for by the entire colony. Predators include leopards, wild dogs, eagles, mongooses and pythons.

Despite its small size, the hyrax is thought to be more closely related to the elephant than any other living creature, but the exact relationship is unclear. It's most often observed in Matobo, Hwange and Chizarira national parks and anyplace with the low rocky kopjes that it loves.

Rock Hyraxes

Zimbabwe

Facts about the Country

HISTORY

For history prior to the Great Zimbabwe era, turn to the History section in the Facts about the Region chapter at the beginning of this book.

The Shona Kingdoms & the Portuguese

By the 15th century, Great Zimbabwe's influence had crested and begun to decline. Although reasons for its ultimate desertion in the 1500s remain something of a mystery, those most often cited are overpopulation, overgrazing by cattle, popular insubordination, and fragmentation of the realm.

During Great Zimbabwe's twilight period, several scattered Shona dynasties began to drift away from the ruling dynasties and form autonomous states. The most prominent of these was the Mutapa dynasty which occupied the land of the Karanga people. After a series of raids on Zambezi Valley tribes, it took in most of northern and eastern Zimbabwe and much of Mozambique. Their powerful *mambo* or king, Mutota, came to be known as Mwene Mutapa or 'the great raider', and his Mutapa Empire grew quite wealthy by policing and taxing the trade routes between Zimbabwe and the coast.

Upon Mutota's death in 1450, his son and successor, Motope, moved the seat of empire to Fura Mountain just 50 km or so north of present-day Harare. Motope's successor, a weaker character called Nyahuma, lost the southern two-thirds of Mutapa territory (and his life) to Motope's son, Changa later founded the Changamire dynasty which would spawn the Rozwi dynasty in the late 1600s.

Another Shona kingdom, the Torwa, emerged in 1480 in south-western Zimbabwe, with its capital at Khami. It is generally considered the successor to the Great Zimbabwe state and its ruling class amassed considerable wealth from cattle and the ongoing gold trade.

In 1502, the Portuguese voyager Vasco da

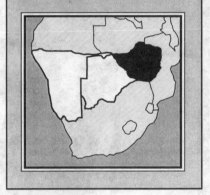

ZIMBABWE
Area: 390,580 sq km
Population: 11,215,000
Population Growth Rate: 3.5%
Capital: Harare
Head of State: Robert Gabriel Mugabe
Official Language: English
Currency: Zimbabwean dollar
Exchange Rate: Z$8.48 = US$1
Per Capita GNP: US$748
Time: GMT/UTC + 2

Gama landed at Sofala on the Mozambique coast. Shortly thereafter, Portuguese traders arrived on the scene. From the Swahili, they learned typically exaggerated tales of unlimited wealth and golden cities on the African plateau, and of the vast empire of Mwene Mutapa (Monomatapa to European tongues), custodian of King Solomon's mines and the long-sought land of Ophir. In 1512, the Portuguese government sent the exiled Antonio Fernandez to ascertain the validity of the rumours.

Over the next century, both Portuguese and Swahili traders exploited squabbles among the Africans to their own ends: the collection of as much gold as could be carted off. In 1565 when the mambo of Manyika (a

state in the Eastern Highlands) challenged the incumbent Mwene Mutapa, Portuguese forces under the command of Francisco Barreto, governor of loosely defined Portuguese East Africa, attempted to help the Mwene Mutapa seize Manyika. However when this failed the Portuguese had to resort to bribery and manipulation of African ruling classes in order to gain influence over the interior.

In 1629, Mwene Mutapa Kapararidze tried and failed to muster sufficient support to drive the Portuguese out for good. He was summarily replaced by Mwene Mutapa Mavura, a Catholicised Portuguese vassal. Iberian interests were not only preserved but given free reign. Their grip was broken, however, by the southern state of Guruhuswa and the Changamire dynasty which attacked Mutapa and deposed the puppet leader. The new Mwene Mutapa formed an alliance with the Changamire and forced the Portuguese to retreat to Mozambique and stay out of African politics for a while.

Meanwhile, in 1684 the Torwa dynasty in the south-west was forcefully absorbed by the Changamire (the clan which started by conquering southern Mutapa in the late

Zimbabwe Itinerary

Low-Budget Tour This option includes low-cost options which can be reached on public transport or inexpensive tours, with budget accommodation available. Some of these are accessible by overnight train, allowing you to avoid additional days spent travelling between attractions.

1. Harare (two days)
2. Hippo Pools (three days)
3. Drifters, near Mutare (two days)
4. Vumba Botanical Reserve (two days)
5. Great Zimbabwe (one day)
5. Mopane Park Farm in Kwe Kwe (two days)
7. Bulawayo, with day tour to Matobo National Park (two days)
8. Hwange National Park, with two game drives (two days)
9. Victoria Falls (three days)

Hikers' Tour This option is for those who love walking. Most of these places are accessible on public transport, but may require adding extra days to accommodate uncertainties. Alternatively, contact one of the companies listed under Tours in the Zimbabwe Getting Around chapter and book a walking expedition through one or several of the country's wildlife reserves.

1. Harare, with a day trip to Domboshawa & Ngomakurira (two days)
2. Mavuradonha Wilderness – access is by private vehicle only (three days)
3. Mana Pools – access is by private vehicle only (three days)
3. Nyanga National Park – climb Mt Nyangani (one day) or walk from Mt Nyangani to Honde Valley (four days)
4. Vumba Botanical Reserve (one day)
5. Chimanimani National Park (three days)
6. Matobo National Park (two days)
7. Victoria Falls (two days)

Activities Tour There are an increasing number of activities, particularly around Victoria Falls.

1. Harare (two days)
2. Hippo Pools – wildlife walks and excursions (two days)

1400s). The result was the creation of the Rozwi state, which took in over half of present-day Zimbabwe and had its capital at Danangombe (Dhlo-Dhlo). Its power and influence continued until 1834 when Nguni forces under Soshangane and Zwangendaba invaded from the south, stormed the Shona fortifications and assassinated the Rozwi leader.

The Ndebele

After Portuguese influence withered, various Shona groups remained in control of most of present-day Zimbabwe. South of the Limpopo River, however, several loosely associated Sotho-speaking Bantu tribes, the Nguni, competed for territory and power.

In 1780, in a bid to command a larger and more respectable force, the chief of the Mtetwe clan, Dingiswayo, set about forcibly confederating them. In 1818, however, an ambitious youngster called Shaka, from a minor clan, engineered the commander's death and took control of the (by now) ruling Mtetwe. He renamed it 'Zulu' after his own humble clan and launched into a campaign of military despotism and expansionism that would reverberate through all of southern Africa.

As the Zulu plundered and conquered their way across Natal, some Nguni tribes fled northward on the *mfecane*, an African version of the Exodus. These tribes ploughed their way through existing political entities and by the 1820s, one contingent, the Soshangane, had reached southern Mozambique and eastern Manyika. It established the Gaza state, installed a ruthless and oppressive military government, and more or less enslaved the local population. Gaza was

3. Canoe trip on the middle Zambezi (trips run from two to 10 days)
4. Horse-riding on Mopane Park Farm near Kwe Kwe (two days)
5. Matobo National Park – day tour from Bulawayo (one or two days)
6. Camping safari in Hwange National Park (three days)
7. Victoria Falls – rafting, kayaking, microlighting, wildlife-viewing, bungee jumping, fishing, etc (five days)

Historical & Cultural Tour This option takes in both cultural and historical highlights, in addition to Zimbabwe's most popular attractions. Although most of these historical and cultural sites of interest can be reached on public transport, you will need to have a car to make the most of this particular option.

1. Harare (three days) – Chapungu Kraal, National Gallery, Mbare, Domboshawa & Ngomakurira
2. Tengenenge Farm or Nyanga National Park (two days)
3. Masvingo (three days) – Great Zimbabwe National Monument, Serima Mission
4. Bulawayo (three days) – Natural History Museum, Mzilikazi Arts & Crafts Centre, Khami Ruins, Cyrene Mission, Nalatale & Danangombe Ruins
5. Matobo National Park (two days)
6. Hwange National Park (two days)
7. Victoria Falls (two days)

Wildlife Tour If you are coming to Africa to see the wildlife, you will have plenty of opportunities. Most of these places will either require a private vehicle (4WD in some cases) or a booking with one of the safari operators. See the Tours information in the Zimbabwe Getting Around chapter in this book.

1. Harare, visit Mukuvisi Woodlands or Lake Chivero (one day)
2. Mana Pools National Park (three days)
3. Matusadona National Park (three days)
4. Bulawayo – Natural History Museum, Tshabalala Wildlife Reserve & Chipangali Wildlife Orphanage (two days)
5. Matobo National Park day tour (one day)
6. Hwange National Park by camping safari (four days)
7. Victoria Falls, with wildlife tours to Zambezi National Park (three days)

finally reined in by Portuguese forces in the late 1800s after official international recognition of Portuguese control in Mozambique.

In the 1830s, further west, Rozwi was mown down and its government dismantled by the forces of Zwangendaba, who was headed for greener pastures in present-day Zambia, Malawi and points north. Rozwi's final chapter, however, was written by the Ndebele ('those who carry long shields') under command of Mzilikazi, who was chief of the Xumalo clan. (The initial 'x' in 'Xumalo' is pronounced as a click against the front teeth; this word is sometimes spelt 'Kumalo'.) Mzilikazi and a band of his followers had fled northward after his father was executed for failing to hand over to Shaka the spoils of a cattle raid.

Along the way, Mzilikazi peacefully encountered the missionary Robert Moffat, who'd posted himself to what is now South Africa, and took a beating in several scrapes with northbound Boer trekking parties. Upon reaching the Matobo (Matopos) Hills near present-day Bulawayo, Mzilikazi established a settlement and adopted a policy of total confederation of all Nguni tribes within his sphere of influence before continuing northward, perhaps to assess the potential of the country beyond the Zambezi River. Upon his return, he found the *indunas* (captains or councillors) had elected a new chief – Mzilikazi's son. Legend has it that those involved were promptly executed for treason on the hill called Thabas Indunas north-east of Bulawayo, effectively cementing consolidation of the Ndebele state.

Mzilikazi ultimately set up his capital at Inyati, 60 km north of Bulawayo. In 1859 he allowed Robert Moffat and his son John

Smith Moffat to establish a London Missionary Society mission nearby. Although Mzilikazi never was much taken with Christianity and refused to convert, he initially afforded the foreigners the full measure of Ndebele hospitality. He took exception, however, to the Moffats' preaching that even the lowliest of the Ndebele had access to God's personal attention, and relations began to break down. Moffat left Inyati in 1864, and Ndebele interest in Christianity remained lukewarm.

During the 1850s, missionary and geographer David Livingstone passed through Ndebele territory and briefly made his home there with his wife, Mary Moffat, the daughter of Robert Moffat. But Livingstone couldn't help gazing dreamily northward towards the Congo Basin and the source of the Nile; whether it was a case of religious fervour or simply wanderlust remains a matter of dispute. Leaving his family in the care of the London Missionary Society, he set off towards his 'presumptuous' meeting with Stanley in Ujiji, Tanzania.

When Mzilikazi died in 1868, he was mourned with the words *Uku dilika kwe ntaba*: 'a mountain has fallen'. Soon after, his son Lobengula ascended to the throne and the Ndebele capital was relocated to Bulawayo. Meanwhile, European opportunists – gold seekers and ivory hunters – from the Cape were already making forays into Shona and Ndebele territory. Frederick Courteney Selous' reports of gold workings (albeit abandoned ones), artist Thomas Baines' gold find in Mashonaland and Adam Renders' 1868 'discovery' of Great Zimbabwe launched a wholesale European grab for the region's presumed wealth.

Enter the British

Perhaps the best known opportunist of them all was Cecil John Rhodes, who had made his fortune in South Africa's Kimberley diamond fields and was keen to take the Queen's interests – and his own enterprise – into the potentially rich and exploitable country north of the Limpopo. From there, it is likely he envisioned a broad corridor of

British territory stretching north to south across Africa and a railway from Cairo to the Cape, providing elbow-room, access and appeal for wholesale colonisation and the eventual British-style 'civilisation' of the African continent.

In 1888, Rhodes managed to wangle the Rudd Concession with the Ndebele leader Lobengula. (Lobengula heard a deliberately mistranslated version of the concession – he would never have agreed to it otherwise.) This agreement permitted British mining and colonisation of lands between the Limpopo and the Zambezi rivers while at the same time prohibiting any Boer activity in Matabeleland. In exchange, the king would receive £100 monthly, 1000 rifles, 10,000 rounds of ammunition, and a riverboat. Lobengula had apparently hoped the concession to Rhodes would also eliminate European competition for minerals and thereby limit the number of prospectors and

David Livingstone
(La Trobe collection, State Library of Victoria)

other itinerants entering his territory. In fact, it had just the opposite effect.

In 1889, Rhodes formed the British South Africa Company (BSAC) and applied for and received a royal charter allocating the power to 'make treaties, promulgate laws, maintain a police force...make land grants and carry on any lawful trade', installing on his board such heavyweights as the dukes of Abercorn, Fife, and Earl Grey (a trio who would later be temporarily memorialised in the names of major Bulawayo streets).

The following year, Rhodes mustered an army of 500, the 'Pioneer Column', and a contingency of settlers who marched northward into Mashonaland. On 27 June, they hoisted the Union Jack over Fort Victoria (Masvingo), and on 12 September established Fort Salisbury. Their next target was Manyika, still occupied by the Portuguese, but they were able to coerce Africans to join their efforts, and after a skirmish resulting in a border shift, the BSAC established Umtali (Mutare) as an eastern headquarters on the new frontier.

Although no great quantities of gold had been discovered, the colonists recognised the potential of the Mashonaland plateau and appropriated vast tracts of farmland. In 1893, Lobengula, who still hadn't realised he'd been duped by the British, sent Ndebele raiders to Masvingo to put down a band of Shona attempting to drive a wedge between the Ndebele and the British by sabotaging colonial telegraph lines. Leander Starr Jameson, commander of Fort Victoria (Masvingo), mistook this action as an offence against the British and prepared to invade Matabeleland.

For the Ndebele, it was an unequal contest against superior arms, and anticipating a humiliating defeat, Lobengula burned his capital at Bulawayo and fled. He died of smallpox shortly after the Ndebele thrashed enemy forces at the Battle of Shangani River 150 km north-west of Bulawayo. Although the Ndebele continued to resist the BSAC forces, which by this time were striking from all directions, the death of Lobengula produced a marked drop in morale and their

effectiveness waned and eventually foundered. By 1895, the spoils had been divided among White settlers, and Africans had been relegated to marginal scrubby and tsetse fly-infested lands. Not surprisingly, this provided incentive to remain on White lands as indentured workers. Those who failed to work for the landowner at least four months per year were required to pay a substantial 'hut tax' to be allowed to remain.

By 1895, the new country was known as 'Rhodesia' after its heavy handed founder. Shortly thereafter, Mark Twain wrote in *More Tramps Abroad*: 'Rhodesia is the right name for that land of piracy and pillage, and puts the right stain upon it'.

The First Chimurenga

As would be expected, the government of Rhodesia was set up 'for, by, and of' the Whites. Although the Ndebele had effectively been squashed and their bovine wealth commandeered by the victors, trade continued between the Shona and the Europeans until it became apparent the British were there to stay and intended to control both African and Rhodesian interests.

Recognising the weakness of the BSAC army after an abortive raid against Kruger's Boers in the Transvaal in March 1896, the Ndebele came back with a vengeance, gathering forces and single-mindedly aiming to drive the enemy from their land forever. This warlike spirit proved contagious; by June, the Shona, traditional enemies of the Ndebele, had joined in, calling it Chimurenga, the War for Liberation.

This jihad-like crusade was led by two African *mhondoro* (spiritualists), Nehanda Charwe Nyakasikana (a female incarnation of the oracle spirit Nehanda) and Sekuru Kaguvi, who preached solidarity and cooperation among both the Shona and Ndebele. Although the revolt gained some momentum, it was effectively stalled in 1897 when the leaders were captured and hanged. Nehanda's parting words, 'my bones will rise again', prophesied the Second Chimurenga which culminated in Zimbabwean independence.

The Ndebele indunas conferred with the BSAC and came to an agreement of sorts but the fragmented Shona groups were only quelled after violent BSAC persuasion. In 1899, an all-White Legislative Council was installed to govern the colony.

At this point, lasting European control of the region seemed ensured, and White immigration then began in earnest. By 1904 there were some 12,000 European settlers in the country and double that number by 1911. In 1922, a referendum was held in which Whites voted to become a self-governing colony under 'Responsible Government', rather than a province in the Union of South Africa (the Cape and Natal combined with the conquered Boer Republics of Transvaal and Orange Free State). The following year the BSAC, realising that Rhodesian profits were not meeting expectations, happily handed Southern Rhodesia over to the British crown.

Although the colony's constitution was in theory nonracial, suffrage was based on British citizenship and annual income and only a few Blacks qualified. Taxation was introduced, and the wholesale exploitation of African labour kept the mines and farms humming the White government's tune. In the 1930s, White supremacy was legislated by the Land Apportionment Act which excluded Africans from ownership of the best farming land, and by a labour law in 1934 which called for separate development of the races (Zimbabweans also refer to this by the Afrikaans term *apartheid*). It prohibited Blacks entering into skilled trades and professions or settling in White areas (including all towns and cities), thereby leaving them dependent on the whims of White landowners and commercial bosses for their livelihood.

Rumbles of Nationalism

The first Black resistance to their unequal status surfaced in the 1920s and 30s with the formation of the Rhodesia Bantu Voters' Association, the Southern Rhodesia Native Association and the Southern Rhodesia African National Congress. These repre-

sented only middle-class Africans (as the name of the first implies – only the middle class could vote), and sought to reform the system rather than dismantle it. They were effectual only in that they raised Black consciousness of the realities of inequality.

Abysmally poor wages and conditions led to the gradual radicalisation of the African labour force. During the 1940s, active resistance surfaced in the form of the African Voice Association, headed by Benjamin Burombo. Nationalistic fervour was fanned with the passage of the Native Land Husbandry Act of 1951 in which common pasture land on Native reserves was divided into smallholdings and allocated to individual families, some of whom were recent evictees from White lands. Herd sizes were necessarily reduced to the number that could be grazed on the tiny individual plots.

By 1953, when Southern Rhodesia, Northern Rhodesia and Nyasaland were politically joined into the Federation of Rhodesia and Nyasaland, mining and industrial concerns favoured a more racially mixed middle class as a counterweight to the increasingly dissatisfied labour force. Pressure from the British government eliminated several of the economic segregation policies and allowed Blacks to enter skilled professions and work in city centres, but no concessions were made to the sort of one-man-one-vote system the nationalist movements envisioned.

Meanwhile, White farmers, skilled workers and business people perceived that growing nationalistic sentiments posed a threat to their privileged status. When Garfield Todd, the Federation's prime minister, attempted to satisfy some of the more moderate African demands, he was thrown out. The same thing happened to his successor in 1962, following his approval of a new constitution which envisaged a vague African-European parity sometime in the distant future, an unacceptable position as far as most Whites were concerned.

In Salisbury in 1955, the City Youth League was formed by the most adamant nationalist leaders, and two years later

ZIMBABWE

The Worst Drought in Living Memory

In the early 1990s, southern Africa in general and Zimbabwe in particular suffered a devastating drought which crippled agriculture, inflicted hardship and water rationing on city folk and caused even greater suffering among poorer rural people.

In 1991, the government was slow to react to warnings of drought and sold off the surplus maize crop to Zambia and Mozambique, only to be faced with shortages in 1992. In fact, in 1992, southern Africa had lost a greater proportion of its crops than Ethiopia and Sudan in the catastropic drought of 1985. Zimbabwe was able to produce only 20% of its normal annual yield of its staple, maize. By the middle of the year, 500,000 rural Zimbabweans were at risk of starvation. Thousands of poor people abandoned their land and their emaciated animals and set off in search of food because in rural areas, even people with money were unable to find commodities to buy.

Some people sought help from relatives or larger ranches, while others migrated to cities looking for work. Due to lack of water and grazing, 30% of communal livestock succumbed or were slaughtered and even large ranches were forced to slaughter most of their herds. A November 1992 letter from a Zimbabwean friend describes the situation that year:

The drought which has affected southern Africa has been termed the worst in living memory and coupled with the new economic programme being implemented by the leaders, it has meant extreme hardship for the peoples of Zimbabwe. Efforts are being made to relieve the suffering with a massive mobilisation to ferry food to worst hit areas. Maize is being imported, amounting to 2.5 million tonnes, as well as cooking oil and wheat. Electricity cuts are planned due to low water in Lake Kariba.

Gonarezhou National Park has been devastated with only three mm of rain this year. This has resulted in most of the grazing species being written off. Translocation of the more endangered species (sable, roan and Lichtenstein's hartebeest) is underway. Other species are also being captured and placed in feed lots in hopes of not losing the gene pool. These include the waterbuck, eland, nyala and giraffe species. The animal now hogging the limelight is the hippo. Sponsorship of groups or individuals has focused attention on their plight and there is an infant called Hippy who travels to various events around the country to raise awareness of the plight of the hippo community.

Beat Accorsi, Zimbabwe

Matabeleland was the hardest hit area and in Bulawayo, even city officials took to petitioning the rainmaking shrines of the Matobo Hills. The following article from *Time* magazine describes a surprising source of high-level string-pulling:

Thousands of Zimbabweans in the parched south-west of the country pleaded with Britain's Queen Elizabeth II to stay longer after rain coincided with her visit to Bulawayo. People cheered the queen when a torrential downpour suddenly started at the onset of her visit. The first rain of the season on the parched Matabeleland plains interrupted her speech in the country's second largest city, which had only enough water in its reservoirs to last a few more weeks. As the queen proclaimed: 'I pray that the drought may end soon, and that you have ample rain in the coming year' the showers began.

To add a footnote: Queen Elizabeth again demonstrated her rainmaking skills on her March 1995 visit to South Africa, where her arrival in drought-stricken Natal and Transvaal coincided with copious rainfall which revived dessicated vegetation and crops. She thereby earned the African name *Motlalepula*, 'she who brings rain'. ∎

merged with the Southern Rhodesian African National Congress to form a new ANC under the leadership of labour activist Joshua Nkomo. Although the organisation was banned in 1959, it continued for a short time under the guise of the National Democratic Party (NDP). During this period the resistance turned to violent uprising in the form of *zhii* (vengeful annihilation of the enemy) in response to the State of Emergency declared on 26 February 1959. Protests, labour strikes and sabotage punctuated this violent period of organised unrest. The government responded by banning the party and, tragically, taking violent and deadly action at one Bulawayo rally. Unfazed, the NDP re-emerged on 17 December 1961 as the Zimbabwe African People's Union (ZAPU) with Joshua Nkomo again at the helm.

Predictably, ZAPU was banned after a few months, accused of sponsoring rural vandalism and sabotage. In 1962 the newly elected ultra-right-wing government (Winston Field's Rhodesian Front Party) countered by banning Black assemblies and political debates and instituting a mandatory death sentence for arson.

Nkomo bandied about the possibility of setting up a government in exile, but internal disputes caused a rift in ZAPU and the dissident members, including Robert Mugabe, Ndabaningi Sithole and Leopold Takawira, were ousted and shortly thereafter formed the Zimbabwe African National Union (ZANU). After squabbles between the two groups in the aftermath of the Federation's 1963 breakup – which later resulted in the independence of Northern Rhodesia (Zambia) and Nyasaland (Malawi) – both ZAPU and ZANU were banned and most of the leadership imprisoned.

Ian Smith & UDI

In April 1964, Ian Smith took over both the Rhodesian Front and the presidency and began actively pressing for Rhodesian independence. British prime minister Harold Wilson countered by outlining a series of requisite conditions which had to be met before Britain would even consider cutting the tether. These conditions included guarantees of internal racial equality, evidence of a charted course towards majority rule, and majority sanction of the prospect of independence. In 1965, realising he had as much chance as a snowball in hell of securing such concessions from the White constituency, Smith pressed for a Unilateral Declaration of Independence from Britain (UDI). In the election of May 1965, Smith's party picked up all 50 seats in government and UDI was declared in December.

Britain reacted by declaring Smith's action illegal and imposing economic sanc-

tions in an attempt to bring him to heel. The UN eventually (1968) voted to make these sanctions mandatory, but with South Africa openly assisting Smith and Mozambique still under colonial rule, the loopholes were enormous. The sanctions were ignored by most Western countries and even by some British companies (including British Petroleum), and action that was intended to force Smith to the negotiating table failed miserably. The Rhodesian economy actually prospered; sanctions provided the incentive to increase and diversify domestic production. In fact, laws were passed to restrict export of profits and to impose import controls. Smith staunchly refused to even countenance any concessions, and considered the revocation of the UDI and especially acceptance of majority rule entirely out of the question. 'Never in a thousand years,' he declared, would Black Africans rule Rhodesia.

Given such intransigence, both ZANU and ZAPU decided that only by armed conflict could power be wrested from Smith and his Rhodesian Front. On 28 April 1966 (now known as Chimurenga Day), the Second Chimurenga began when ZANU guerrillas launched an attack on Rhodesian forces at Chinhoyi, north-west of the capital. This, and subsequent guerrilla actions failed due to lack of cohesion and the vulnerability of training facilities within the country. However, after Frelimo liberated substantial areas of neighbouring Mozambique, ZANU nationalists were able to establish bases there and escalate the conflict. Following suit, ZAPU (combined with South Africa's ANC) set up its own Zimbabwe Peoples' Revolutionary Army (ZIPRA) bases in Zambia and training camps were organised in Tanzania.

The increasingly organised nationalist movements didn't faze Smith nearly as much as Britain's refusal to budge on the issue of independence. His response was to submit a new constitution guaranteeing Blacks eight out of 66 seats in parliament but Britain, intent upon hearing the will of the people, organised the Pearce Commission to solicit Black African opinion before it would consider taking any action. Despite the

Rhodesian Front's massive and costly campaign to secure Black acceptance of the new constitution, the Smith government – which had apparently been on holiday from reality for some time – was surprised to find its scheme summarily and forcefully thrown back in its face.

As the liberation movement gained momentum, Josiah Tongogara, commander of ZANLA (Zimbabwe African National Liberation Army), ZANU's military forces, went to China for Maoist tactical training. As a result, the civilian public was drafted into cooperation; young men operated as scouts and messengers, and women assisted and cooked for guerrilla troops. When the government got wind of all this, it set up 'protected villages' and, to shield them from 'intimidation', forcibly relocated those suspected of helping or harbouring guerrillas and terrorists.

Nationalist forces struck with ever-increasing ferocity throughout the country: ZANLA from Samora Machel's Mozambique and ZIPRA from Kaunda's Zambia, and Whites, most of whom had been born in Africa and knew no country but Rhodesia, gradually realised the gravity of their situation. Many abandoned their homes and farms, particularly in the Eastern Highlands, and emigrated to South Africa or the Commonwealth countries. It finally dawned on Ian Smith that all was not well in Rhodesia.

The Lisbon Coup and subsequent overthrow of the fascist regime in Portugal in April 1974, which brought independence, pseudo-Marxism and eventual chaos to both Angola and Mozambique, completely altered the balance of power in the area. It forced such powers as the USA and South Africa to reappraise their positions in southern Africa and surprisingly, both advised Smith to accommodate the nationalists.

On 8 December 1974, at Lusaka, Zambia, the various nationalist groups were united under Abel Muzorewa's African National Congress. On 11 December on the Zambezi Bridge at Victoria Falls, the unlikely duo of South Africa's John Vorster and Zambia's Kenneth Kaunda persuaded Smith to call a

Robert Mugabe

ceasefire and release from detention the highest ranking members of the nationalist movement – Nkomo, Sithole, and Mugabe among them – to allow peace negotiations to begin.

The talks, however, were hardly peaceful and broke down in an atmosphere of recrimination between Smith and the nationalists on one hand and between nationalist leaders on the other. ZANU split, Joshua Nkomo had differences with ANC leader Muzorewa and was expelled from the organisation, and Robert Mugabe, a highly respected former teacher and 10-year detainee under Smith, made his way to Mozambique where he replaced Sithole as the leader of ZANU. The following year, ZANU chairman Herbert Chitepo was assassinated in Lusaka by Rhodesian intelligence.

Nationalist groups continued to fragment and reform in an alphabet soup of 'Z' acronyms. In January, 1976, at Geneva, the ZANU and the ZAPU were induced to form an alliance known as the Patriotic Front, with Sithole and Muzorewa leading separate delegations. Although the hoped for spirit of cooperation between the two was never realised, the Patriotic Front survived in name. Similarly, ZIPRA and ZANLA combined to form ZIPU (Zimbabwe People's Army) under Rex Nhongo.

At this stage, Ian Smith, faced with wholesale White emigration and a collapsing economy, was forced to change his strategy to one of internal settlement. Both Sithole and Muzorewa were persuaded to join a so-called transitional government in which the Whites were to be guaranteed 28 out of 100 parliamentary seats as well as a veto over all legislation for the next 10 years. In addition, White property would be guaranteed and White control of the armed forces, police, judiciary and civil service would continue. In exchange, Patriotic Front guerrillas would be granted amnesty. The effort was a dismal failure, as might have been expected, and indeed only resulted in escalation of violence. To salvage the settlement, Smith entered into clandestine negotiations with Nkomo, offering to ditch both Sithole and Muzorewa, but Nkomo wouldn't be swayed.

Finally, with support for Smith waning among the White population and the country's largest fuel depot sabotaged by Patriotic Front guerrillas, Smith opted to call a general election by both Blacks and Whites. On 1 May 1979, he handed the office of prime minister over to Muzorewa, who was effectively a puppet, and opened up 50% of European-designated lands to people of any race. Government structure was, however, much the same as that proposed under the 'internal settlement'. The changes weren't taken very seriously; no one was cheering and international diplomatic recognition of Zimbabwe-Rhodesia, as it was now called, wasn't forthcoming. At best, a few countries regarded Zimbabwe-Rhodesia as simply a passable transitional government.

Independence

In Britain, the Conservatives won the 1979 election and Margaret Thatcher immediately began pressing for a solution to the Rhodesian problem. It was finally decided that any new constitution would have to be satisfactory to Britain and be ratified in free and well-monitored elections. On 10 September 1979, the delegations met at Lancaster House in London to draw up a constitution satisfactory to both the Patriotic Front represented by Nkomo and Mugabe and the Zimbabwe-Rhodesia government, represented by Muzorewa and Smith. Also attending were Kenneth Kaunda and Julius Nyerere, to encourage the Patriotic Front towards a settlement, and Margaret Thatcher, who would pressure Smith to compromise. For several months, the talks accomplished nothing; Mugabe, who wanted ultimate power in the new government, refused to make any concessions whatsoever.

After 14 weeks of talks and some heavy-handed coercion by the British, the racially imbalanced Lancaster House Agreement, which guaranteed Whites (3% of the population) 20 of the 100 seats in the new parliament, was reached. The agreement also stipulated that private land-holdings could not be nationalised or appropriated without adequate compensation, a more logical 'concession' to Whites than the race-dictated imbalance in parliamentary representation. Despite the agreement's failings, the way for independence was paved and the various factions got down to the business of jostling for a position in the queue for power.

In the carefully monitored election of 4 March 1980, Mugabe and ZANU won 57 of the 80 seats available to Blacks, Nkomo's ZAPU party won 20, and Muzorewa's UANC won only three. Zimbabwe joined the ranks of Africa's independent nations from this date, under an internationally recognised majority government headed by Robert Mugabe. In Salisbury (Harare) on 16 April 1980, the Reverend Canaan Banana was officially sworn in as first president of independent Zimbabwe and Robert Mugabe took the helm as prime minister.

Despite the long and bitter struggle, Mugabe displayed restraint and kept vengeful tendencies at bay in the new society. (Interestingly, Ian Smith himself stayed on and still lives quietly in Harare, beside the Cuban embassy.) The remaining Whites were a nuisance but Mugabe wasn't keen to throw out the baby with the bath-water and lose their wealth, technical expertise and access to foreign investment – all necessary to the fulfilment of the dream he, as a committed Marxist, had of creating a one-party socialist state. He appointed White ministers of Agriculture and Commerce & Industry, made assurances that 'there is a place for everyone in this country...the winners and the losers', and that he aimed not to bring about a new Mozambique or a new Kenya, but a new Zimbabwe. The economy soared, wages increased and basic social programmes – notably education and health care – were re-formed or established.

It was a promising start, but the euphoria and the optimistic sense of national unity brought on by independence quickly faded. There was a resurgence of the rivalry between ZANU and ZAPU which escalated into armed conflicts between supporters of the two parties. Mugabe ordered five prominent Nkomo supporters arrested in 1980 and ousted Nkomo from his cabinet position in 1981. Tensions were further inflamed by the arrest of the Minister of Manpower Planning, Edgar Tekere, for the alleged murder of a White farmer. Although Tekere was found not guilty, the arrest marked the end of his political career.

More recently, Nkomo was accused of plotting to overthrow the government and there was a resurgence of guerrilla activity in Matabeleland, the area from which ZAPU drew the bulk of its support. In early 1983, Mugabe sent in the North Korean-trained Fifth Brigade to quell the disturbances, but they launched into an assault in which several thousand civilians fell victim. Villagers were gunned down and prominent members of ZAPU were systematically eliminated in order to rout out dissidents. Bodies are still being uncovered in rural Matabeleland. Essentially, the conflict was a tribal one between the majority Shona (largely ZANU supporters) and the minority Ndebele (largely ZAPU supporters).

Nkomo meanwhile fled to England and was to remain there until Mugabe, realising Zimbabwe's enemies were watching with interest as internal strife threatened to escalate into civil war, publicly relented and guaranteed his safe return. At this point, the two began the talks which would result in the combining of ZANU and ZAPU. An amnesty was offered to the dissidents and the entire affair, but not the underlying discontent, was thereby masterfully swept under the rug.

Recent Developments

Despite the tragic examples of Kaunda's Zambia, Nyerere's Tanzania, and the violent and oppressive revolutionary government in Mozambique, Mugabe still harboured dreams of transforming Zimbabwe into a one-party state. The long overdue abolition in mid-1988 of the law guaranteeing 20 parliamentary seats to Whites, the imposition of strict and strangling controls on currency, foreign exchange and trade and, in April 1990, a review of White land ownership guarantees (after the British-brokered constitution expired on the 10th anniversary of independence) all seemed to indicate steps in this direction.

The late 1980s were characterised by scandal and government corruption. Some MPs and cabinet ministers were loudly professing socialism, a few sincerely, but many of the same group were privately greasing their own palms. In 1988, the government was linked with shady practices at the Willowvale automobile assembly plant near Harare. The corruption was exposed by the press, and students at the University of Zimbabwe launched a protest against Mugabe for having allowed crooked government to exist in Zimbabwe when he'd pledged it would never happen. Mugabe felt threatened by the uprising, and cut off some areas of university funding, refusing to restore them until the students admitted their mistake. Late 1990 saw further student unrest when riot police resorted to using tear gas to break up a demonstration against a proposed increase in government control over University of Zimbabwe policy.

Some particularly dirty business surrounding the March 1990 elections revealed similar facets of the president. The newly formed ZUM (Zimbabwe Unity Movement) party under the leadership of Edgar Tekere, which promoted a free-enterprise economy and a multiparty democratic state, played mouse to the elephant and challenged ZANU in several electorates. Like the elephant, Mugabe overreacted and engineered some last minute gerrymandering to waylay any possible ZUM victories. Shortly following the election (a ZANU landslide all around) the ZUM candidate who'd shown promise in the Gweru North electoral district, Patrick Kombayi, was wounded in an apparent assassination attempt and anyone having ties with ZUM quickly sought a low profile.

The latest development in the one-party state issue came in August 1990, when, at a Central Committee meeting 22 of 26 members voted against continuation of the idea. They argued that introducing a one-party state at a time when the worldwide trend was in the opposite direction could be interpreted as a step backward and severely affect Zimbabwe's credibility in the eyes of potential investors.

With Mugabe's popularity waning and elections coming up the following month, in February 1995, the president revealed vote-catching plans for a US$160 million 'anti-poverty programme' aimed at training workers, developing rural areas and providing a safety net for the poor. He also paid lip service to nationalisation of White land and

---

The Land Issue & ESAP

At Independence in 1980, 270,000 Whites lived in Zimbabwe. There are now only 90,000 and they make up less than 1% of the population, but they still own one third of the country's arable land and produce 42% of the nation's annual export income. When Mugabe came to power in 1980, he promised to resettle 162,000 Black families on the White-owned lands. However, under the British-brokered peace agreement of 1980, the government could not force farmers to sell their land. This issue has been the bugbear of the Mugabe government.

During the first decade after independence, only four million acres had been purchased and 55,000 families resettled, far short of the original goal. The government sought another six million hectares for the resettlement of 110,000 more families, leaving six million hectares for commercial farming ventures.

Under the 'willing buyer, willing seller' scheme, which operated through the 1980s, the government had the power to set land prices – although the government itself was the buyer. Farmers could each sell only one farm; absentee landlords would automatically lose their claims; land could not be sold to foreigners; and farmers would be compensated in Zimbabwe dollars, effectively preventing their leaving the country after selling out. The proposed methods of land takeover, however, were protested against by the Commercial Farmers Union (which not surprisingly is comprised mostly of White farmers).

Over subsequent years, in order to hold on to voter confidence, Mugabe publically paid lip service to his resettlement scheme. At the same time, he tried to remain pragmatic. One official, recognising commercial farmers' gripes, admitted the government didn't want to 'kill the goose that lays the golden eggs' or frighten away foreign investors. Eventually, the land reformers had no choice but to return to the drawing board.

In 1990, the 'willing buyer, willing seller' clause expired. The National Farmers Association and the Zimbabwe National Farmers Union (both mainly non-White organisations) wisely suggested that resettlement continue to be handled on a mutually willing buyer and seller basis, but that the government offer easy-terms loans to allow small or peasant farmers to purchase their own land.

The government however, ignored this advice, and in late 1990 and early 1991, decided to redistribute 50% of lands held by White commercial farmers to Black subsistence farmers. This meant risking nearly half Zimbabwe's foreign exchange earnings, turning the country into a food importer, inviting international criticism and thwarting foreign investment.

Then in late 1991, in an about-turn aimed at courting foreign investment and aid, the Zimbabwe government revealed the Economic Structural Adjustment Programme (ESAP) which was formulated by the International Monetary Fund and the World Bank. The goal was economic

promised to reduce unemployment, which would inevitably mean an increase in the size of the public service sector.

The election, however, was characterised by general apathy and was boycotted by the growing opposition groups, who voiced concerns that both the cards and the constitution were stacked against everyone but the ruling party. The voters, feeling powerless to change the situation, stayed away en masse.

To end on a positive note, Zimbabwe is gradually recovering from the initial shocks brought on by the ESAP (see boxed story) and by the catastrophic drought of the early 1990s. However, despite the relatively good rainfall in 1993, there was a serious shortfall in both 1994 and 1995, and it's possible the drought will carry on for several years yet.

GEOGRAPHY

Zimbabwe is a landlocked country in south-central Africa shaped roughly like a water droplet falling from the Caprivi Strip. It's situated entirely within the tropics – between 15°S and 22°S latitude – but most of Zimbabwe consists of highveld and midleveld plateau lying between 900 and 1700 metres above sea level. The country enjoys a remarkably temperate climate. It is bound on the north-west by Zambia, on the east and north-east by Mozambique, on the south-west by Botswana, and on the south by the Republic of South Africa. Four countries – Zambia, Zimbabwe, Botswana and Namibia – meet at a single point at the country's westernmost extreme.

Zimbabwe's maximum width is 725 km,

ZIMBABWE

---

liberalisation, which required a realistic official exchange rate, lifting of price controls and competition from imports, in order to bring about long-term economic vitality and usher Zimbabwe into the international community.

Naturally, these drastic measures inspired immediate price increases, which were accompanied by hardship among the poorer classes. Some suggested the acronym ESAP really stood for 'Ever-Struggling African Peoples'. These hardships were worsened by the severe drought which struck in the early 1990s and caused widespread crop failure. The result was a rash of migration to urban areas, along with increased unemployment and crime.

With these compounding problems, popular disenchantment with the Mugabe government reached an all-time high. It was under these conditions that the land issue again showed its face. In March 1992, the Land Acquisition Act was unanimously approved in Parliament. The new goal was to seize five million hectares of mostly White-owned commercial farmland for the resettlement of one million Black subsistence farmers. The former landowners would be compensated in government bonds (which were nigh unto worthless at that stage).

The underlying intent of the Land Acquisition Act was to send a message to the common people that the government hadn't forgotten them. In international aid and investment circles, however, it set off alarm bells and the new law was criticised as being irreconcilably at odds with ESAP. In hopes of rekindling some international goodwill, Mugabe inserted palatability clauses in the legislation providing for fair cash compensation for farmers and landowners' right to judicial appeal. There was, however, little he could do about the major international concern, which was the credit worthiness of a country which had disenfranchised the source of half its export income.

Thus far, most White farms taken over have been abandoned or second farms. However, some of these are being reallocated to government officials, in blatant defiance of the spirit of the plan. One well-publicised farm takeover was that of 260-hectare Churu Farm, which was owned by Ndabaningi Sithole, the hot-headed Black leader of the small opposition party, ZANU-Ndonga. Mr Sithole described the move as 'politically motivated theft' (and given the circumstances, one could hardly disagree with him). Immediately thereafter, 4000 families illegally settled on the farm and refused to leave, despite government intentions to evict them on health grounds. Unfortunately for Mr Sithole, a last minute court order allowed them to stay.

As yet, there are no solutions to the land quandary. Perhaps the most interesting proposal put forth comes from Diana Mitchell, writing in the Zimbabwean tourist paper, *Travellers' News* in mid-1994. In a nutshell, she suggested that the government approximate traditional African custom and convert all private and communal lands to leasehold land, granting leases to those who use it. ■

while north to south it stretches 835 km. The total area is 390,580 sq km, roughly half the size of Australia's New South Wales or the same size as the British Isles with an extra Scotland thrown in.

A low ridge across the country from the Mvurwi Range in the north-east to the Matobo Hills in the south-west marks the divide between two of Africa's great river systems, the Zambezi in the north-west and the Limpopo-Save in the south-east. The former consists mostly of plateau, sloping gently away from the ridge before dropping dramatically to the broad Zambezi plain in the north-east and into the tangled hills and valleys around Lake Kariba in the north-west. This plateau landscape is characterised by bushveld dotted with small rocky outcrops called *kopjes* and bald knob-like domes of slickrock known as *dwalas*.

The hot, dry lowveld of southern Zimbabwe is comprised mostly of the relatively flat savanna lands of the Save Basin, sloping almost imperceptibly towards the Limpopo River.

The only significant mountainous region is the Eastern Highlands, which straddles the Zimbabwe-Mozambique border from the Nyanga region in the north to the Chimanimani Mountains in the south. Zimbabwe's highest peak, Nyangani, rises 2592 metres near the northern end of the range.

CLIMATE

What surprises people about Zimbabwe's climate is that it's not as hot as the latitude would suggest. Although it lies entirely within the tropics, the country stretches over a high plateau averaging 900 metres above sea level and, during the dry season, it enjoys a pleasantly temperate climate.

Winters (May to October) are like luscious Mediterranean summers with warm, sunny days and cool, clear nights. It never snows, not even in the Eastern Highlands, but overnight frosts and freezing temperatures aren't uncommon on the plateau. Winter is also the best time for wildlife viewing since animals tend to gather around pans and never stray far from water sources.

The lowveld and the Zambezi valley experience hotter and more humid temperatures but in the winter months, there's still a minimum of rainfall. Although spring and autumn aren't really obvious as seasons, the highveld mopane trees change colours throughout the winter and provide touches of orange, yellow and red reminiscent of a European or North American autumn.

Most of Zimbabwe's rain falls in brief afternoon deluges and electrical storms in the summer months (November to April) and brings only fleeting relief from the typically stifling humidity. Although temperatures are rarely over 30°C, the air can feel oppressive.

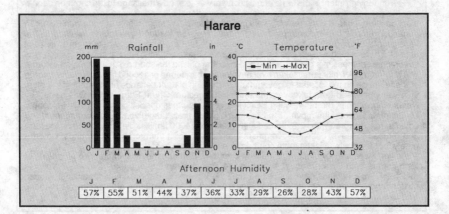

Afternoon Humidity											
J	F	M	A	M	J	J	A	S	O	N	D
57%	55%	51%	44%	37%	36%	33%	29%	26%	28%	43%	57%

NATIONAL PARKS & WILDLIFE RESERVES

Warning Zimbabwe National Park fees for foreigners rose dramatically on 1 November 1996. This means non-residents of Zimbabwe must now pay US$20 admission to most parks, including Victoria Falls. There are also indications that many Zimbabwean national parks may soon be closed between November and May, but deliberations are ongoing and at the time of writing no conclusive decisions had been made.

If your ideal African adventure would include rambling through forest and savanna bushlands, and pursuing and photographing the menagerie that symbolises wild Africa to armchair dreamers worldwide, Zimbabwe is for you. Without the commercial assembly-line feeling of Kenya; the expense of Botswana or Tanzania; the cushy development of South Africa; or the political uncertainties of most other countries, Zimbabwe's wilderness wildlife reserves offer pristine natural habitats, large animal populations and as much variety of species as any place on the continent.

In addition to the national parks, there are several recreational parks, most of which focus on recreational dams; these include Lake Chivero, Lake Mutirikwe, Sebakwe Dam, Ngezi Dam, Lake Manyame, Lake Manjirenji and Lake Cunningham.

The following list outlines the parks. Relevant chapters are given in brackets:

Chimanimani (Eastern Highlands) This roadless park along the Mozambique border takes in the country's most dramatic range of mountains – and its best bushwalking country.

Chinhoyi Caves (Northern Zimbabwe) This tiny 'roadside' national park protects Chinhoyi Caves, a series of limestones inkholes and underground pools in northern Zimbabwe.

Chizarira (Western Zimbabwe) Chizarira, Zimbabwe's wildest national park, blends stunning scenery and relatively little-disturbed wildlife habitat.

Gonarezhou (Midlands & South-eastern Zimbabwe) Until the wildlife populations of Gonarezhou ('abode of elephants') were destroyed by poachers and Mozambican soldiers, this park was home to some of the largest elephants in Africa. It was closed to foreigners for many years, but has now been reopened and is recovering fairly well. Gonarezhou is also known for its herds of nyala antelopes.

Great Zimbabwe (Midlands & South-eastern Zimbabwe) This small national monument protects the ruins complex of sub-Saharan Africa's greatest ancient city. It sits amid a lovely, haunting landscape and is a country highlight.

Hwange (Western Zimbabwe) Hwange is Zimbabwe's largest and most wildlife-packed national park. Thanks to its relative accessibility, it's a favourite with visitors.

Kazuma Pan (Western Zimbabwe) The centrepiece of this wild and little-visited park in the extreme western corner of Zimbabwe is a large grassy pan surrounded by teak and mopane forest. It contains Zimbabwe's only gemsboks and is also home to a few oribis.

Mana Pools (Northern Zimbabwe) Mana Pools National Park takes in lovely riverine landscapes along the Zambezi and is popular for canoe trips and walking safaris. It's the only wildlife park in which visitors are free to walk wherever they please and without a guide.

Matobo (Bulawayo) The hills and balancing rock kopjes of Matobo form Zimbabwe's most bizarre landscape and the attached wildlife park is the best place in the world to see white and black rhinos.

Matusadona (Northern Zimbabwe) Along the shores of Lake Kariba, Matusadona National Park contrasts a watery shoreline with high and wild mountain country. It's well known for its elephants and large buffalo herds, and also serves as a dubious relocation site for black rhinos.

Mtarazi Falls (Eastern Highlands) Little more than an appendage tacked onto Nyanga National Park, this small park focuses on 762m Mtarazi Falls, which plunges over the dramatic Honde Escarpment.

Nyanga (Eastern Highlands) Long established as a weekend getaway for Harare people, this former estate of Cecil Rhodes has some lovely highlands, picturesque waterfalls, great fishing and Mt Nyangani, which is Zimbabwe's highest mountain.

Vumba (Eastern Highlands) This high and misty forest and botanical garden in the Eastern Highlands is a popular retreat for city dwellers and homesick British.

Zambezi/Victoria Falls (Western Zimbabwe) This beautiful national park encompasses 40 km of Zambezi River frontage as well as a vast area of wildlife-rich mopane forest and savanna. The small extension known as Victoria Falls National Park contains the falls of the same name and the forestland around the Victoria Falls town.

Visiting the Parks For foreigners, day entry to the parks is US$20; weekly permits are also available. Unfortunately, revenue collected in

---

The Sausage Tree

It would be difficult to mistake the sausage tree *(Kigelia africana)*, which is native to most of central and southern Africa, and has been introduced to other tropical areas worldwide. The tree takes its name from its immense sausage-shaped brown fruits, which weigh up to 10 kg and grow up to one metre in length and 18 cm in diameter.

From September to late February, the tree erupts with unusual and striking maroon-coloured flowers. When they fall, they're a favourite snack for antelopes. The fruit is poisonous when unripe and essentially insipid at other times, but when roasted, it can be dried into a powder and added to local beer to speed up the fermentation process. The seeds are edible when roasted and although they're not particularly tasty, they do fine in an emergency.

The Batonka people of the Zambezi Valley have long used powdered sausages as an ointment for tropical ulcers, but sausage-tree cream is also gaining international recognition as a cure for basal-cell carcinoma, a form of skin cancer associated with aging and prolonged exposure to the sun. The cream is available in Zimbabwean pharmacies and although it isn't yet accredited by Western drug administrations, many who have used it will swear by its efficacy. ∎

---

the parks (of which 30.6% is derived from hunting) goes straight into the central treasury and very little is returned to the parks. As a result, the parks face constant budget problems; artificially pumped water holes are going dry, facilities are becoming increasingly shabby and the reservations system is a shambles.

Organised activities are limited, but in some parks, you can go horse riding or hire a game scout for a walk in the bush. Horse-riding tours cost US$5 per person for 1½ hours and must be booked in advance. Walks led by game scouts cost US$15.50 per hour for up to six people (except at Hwange Main Camp, where a two-hour walk is US$5 per person); two/three/four-day walks are US$154/205/257. For information on parks accommodation – and the hopeless booking system – see Accommodation in the Zimbabwe Facts for the Visitor chapter.

Note that hitching is technically forbidden in parks, so the only legitimate economical way of visiting them is to muster a group, hire a vehicle and organise everything yourself. Note that in the wildlife-oriented parks, such as Hwange and Mana Pools, you must be back in camp prior to dusk. There's a US$5 fine if you're not back before the gates close.

In Zimbabwean national parks, as well as most private campgrounds and caravan parks and some general stores, pre-cut firewood is sold in bundles for very reasonable

prices, eliminating the need for car campers to decimate the surrounding bush to stoke their braai pits. Wilderness campers, however, are advised to carry a fuel stove for cooking and avoid building fires if at all possible.

GOVERNMENT

The legislative body of the Republic of Zimbabwe consists of the executive president, and a parliament made up of the Senate and the House of Assembly. The president, who serves a six-year term, is elected by members of Parliament and is the official head of state and commander-in-chief of the armed forces. Currently, executive president Robert Mugabe's ZANU party is in undisputed control of the national government.

The Senate consists of 40 senators; 36 of these are chosen by the electoral college and four are appointed by the president. A Senate Legal Committee has power to investigate legislative goings-on. The House of Assembly consists of 100 representatives or members of parliament, who are elected by the constituency of the district being represented every five years.

The judicial branch of government is made up of a tribunal consisting of both General and Appellate Divisions, with power in both civil and criminal matters. The chief justice is appointed by the president in council with the prime minister. Appellate

Zimbabwe Hunting & Conservation Practices

Although it may seem inappropriate to mention both hunting and conservation in the same breath, Zimbabwe's official policy is one of 'sustained yield use'; that is, limiting hunting to the level of natural growth in the game population. The government needs foreign exchange and sees in its wildlife resources an abundant and relatively painless (for them, anyway) method of acquiring it. Safari areas allow game hunting and the government cites their annual net of millions of dollars in foreign exchange as justification for their existence and therefore, for the conservation of wildlife.

Revenues from hunting on communal lands, where wildlife can become a nuisance to subsistence farmers, is channelled back into the affected communities in the form of schools, hospitals and other infrastructure.

In addition to the national parks and reserves, an increasing number of private ranches are being converted into hunting and game reserves. Some are open to big game hunting in order to both finance the operation and turn a profit.

Despite all the rhetoric about the benefits of sustained yield and the resulting windfalls for government coffers, for many people it would be difficult to fathom anyone deriving more pleasure from hunting animals than simply watching and photographing them. Those determined to go hunting should direct enquiries to the Provincial Warden – Hunting Division (☎ 707624), Department of National Parks & Wildlife Management, PO Box 8365, Causeway, Harare or to The Registration Office (☎ 706511), PO Box 8052, Causeway, Harare.

On a positive note, the Zimbabwean government does seem to realise the value of wild lands and preservation of habitat for their aesthetic as well as their economic values. Since the turn of the century, the human population has grown from 500,000 to 12 million. As increasing population pressures to develop and farm wild lands increase, so too does the need for retreat from all the chaos.

In an effort to foster an appreciation for wildlife and wilderness in school children, particularly urban dwellers, several amateur conservation groups have purchased small protected reserves in urban areas, primarily for the purpose of education. These include Mukuvisi Woodlands near Harare, Cecil Kop near Mutare and Tshabalala near Bulawayo. ■

justices are appointed by the president in concordance with the Judicial Commission.

Zimbabwe is divided into eight provinces, each of which has its own local government headed by a state-appointed governor.

ECONOMY

Zimbabwe's economic potential is considerable; its temperate climate, ample natural resources and increasingly skilled workforce are all factors. Despite the deceleration and economic stagnation experienced during the Second Chimurenga (or 'bush war'), the effects of Rhodesia's necessary industrial diversification during UDI-related international sanctions are still being felt, and the country does have a reasonably sound industrial base. However, during the first decade of independence, the economy suffered serious setbacks under strict isolationist policies: an artificially valued Zimbabwe dollar, strict currency controls and crippling import duties.

In late 1991, however, the government conspired with the World Bank and the International Monetary Fund to implement the Economic Structural Adjustment Programme (ESAP), which was intended to liberalise the Zimbabwean economy. It brought the official exchange rate more or less into parity with the parallel rate, and lifted price controls and stifling import restrictions with the aim of stimulating competitive trade and turning the country into an international player.

ESAP also brought about changes in the restrictive currency laws for residents. Zimbabwe citizens and residents were suddenly permitted to hold foreign bank accounts and were also given a 'holiday allowance', which permitted them to export up to US$2000 annually. Few could manage this, however, and indeed, the price increases brought about by ESAP were initially devastating, particularly for the country's poorest people.

The structural changes notwithstanding, a major roadblock to international trade and

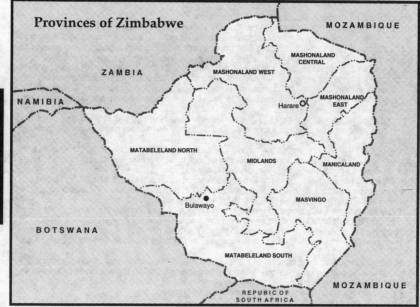

Provinces of Zimbabwe

MOZAMBIQUE

ZAMBIA

MASHONALAND CENTRAL

MASHONALAND WEST

NAMIBIA

MASHONALAND EAST

Harare ✪

MATABELELAND NORTH

MIDLANDS

MANICALAND

Bulawayo ●

MASVINGO

BOTSWANA

MATABELELAND SOUTH

MOZAMBIQUE

REPUBIC OF SOUTH AFRICA

ZIMBABWE

economic prosperity is transport. Land-locked Zimbabwe is dependent upon its neighbours for access to port facilities. The Zambezi River route is blocked by Mozambique's moribund Cabora Bossa hydro project, and the crippling war in that country left the Mutare-Beira rail link in dubious condition. Currently, the country relies mainly on South Africa for access to the sea.

Although about 80% of Zimbabwe's population is dependent upon agriculture, it accounts for only 20% of the GNP because the majority of farmers and pastoralists operate on the subsistence level while many larger, commercially viable farms are being purchased by the government for resettlement. Currently, less than 15% of arable land is under cultivation.

The staple food crop is maize, while cotton, coffee, tea, both burley and Virginia tobacco (tobacco is the largest export earner in the economy), wine grapes (Zimbabwe's white wines are palatable but the reds still

have a way to go) and sugar cane are the primary cash crops. The country also supplies small quantities of fresh flowers, citrus fruits and vegetables for the European market.

The sugar cane, which is grown in the lowveld, is turned into table sugar, molasses and 40 million litres of ethanol annually. When it's available, sugar-cane ethanol is blended with petrol and used as fuel to supplement the imported petrol entering the country via the carefully guarded but vulnerable pipeline through the Beira corridor.

Livestock, the major indication of wealth in precolonial Zimbabwe, remains a major commodity. The country is nearly self-sufficient in milk, beef, poultry, pork and mutton. In addition, more than a million goats roam the communal lands (grazing them into wastelands) and provide subsistence-level protein. Game ranching, particularly of antelopes, is also currently on the increase.

Mining interests account for around 40%

of exports; gold is the major earner. Coal, chromite, nickel, asbestos, copper, iron ore and tin are also exported in significant quantities. Currently, oil exploration by Mobil is going on in the Zambezi Valley east of Mana Pools. Nothing has been found, but thanks to pressure from the Zambezi Society, a private conservation group, environmental impact is being considered.

Forestry is an up-and-coming venture, especially in the Eastern Highlands, where vast tracts of softwood forests have been planted and are being harvested for pulp, and in the south-west where mahogany and teak provide raw materials for railway construction and a growing furniture industry.

Manufacturing comprises only a small sector of the economy and is dominated by textiles, including spinning, weaving and dyeing enterprises. Other manufacturing concerns include hardwood furniture, leathergoods, food processing, and tobacco products. Perhaps Zimbabwe's most controversial foreign exchange earner is the new export arms industry. It revolves around two Harare factories which employ 300 people making ammunition and filling grenades, shells and mortar bombs with high explosives. Currently, the major markets are trouble spots in Africa.

As with most places, tourism in Zimbabwe is on the increase, and the setbacks faced by the tourist industry during the war are now behind it. Hordes of package tours descend on Hwange and Victoria Falls, and the country is figuring in more and more African itineraries. The tourism industry has already become a major player in the foreign exchange arena and visitors can now expect frequent encounters with other travellers. There are growing concerns about security problems, but they're out of proportion to the real dangers – Zimbabwe is still more secure than Kenya, for example.

Currently, South Africa sends the greatest numbers of tourists, but most of Zimbabwe's tourism revenue comes from British and US tourists. Interestingly, hunting brings in more money than any other sector of the tourist industry.

For information on investment in Zimbabwe, contact the Zimbabwe Investment Centre (☎ (14) 790991), PO Box 5950, Harare or the national export promotion organisation, ZimTrade (☎ (14) 731020; fax (14) 707531), PO Box 2738, Harare.

POPULATION & PEOPLE

Zimbabwe has an estimated population of 11,215,000, with a growth rate of 3.5% annually since 1985. Of these, 65% live permanently in rural areas and 40% are under 18 years of age. The average life expectancy at birth is nearly 60 years.

Most Zimbabweans are of Bantu origin; 76% belong to various Shona groups (Ndau, Rozwi, Korekore, Karanga, Manyika and Zezuru) occupying the eastern two-thirds of the country, 18% are of Ndebele stock (including the Kalanga) living primarily in south-western Zimbabwe, and the remainder are divided between Batonka (2%) of the upper Kariba area, Shangaan or Hlengwe (1%) of the lowveld, Venda (1%) of the far south and European and Asian (2%), scattered around the country.

After independence, the European population declined steadily, and in the early 1980s, White emigration averaged 17,000 people annually. The European population has now stabilised at around 100,000. In addition, there are about 25,000 people of mixed European and African descent and 10,000 Asians, primarily of Indian origin.

EDUCATION

Prior to independence in 1980, education was only free and compulsory for students of European background. Schools were segregated, and Black African children were required to pay tuition fees. Despite the staggering odds against them, over 40% managed to attend at least one term. It's not surprising then that the overall literacy rate stayed at around 50% until the new majority government established a universal, integrated and compulsory educational system. Between 1979 and 1992, the number of schools increased from 177 to 1517 and

ZIMBABWE

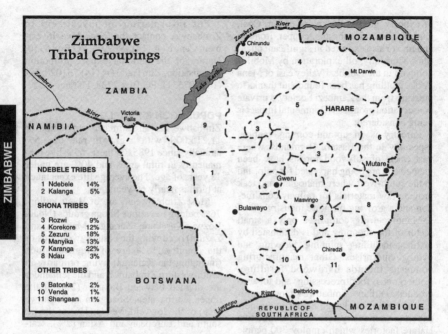

Zimbabwe Tribal Groupings

NDEBELE TRIBES

| 1 | Ndebele | 14% |
| 2 | Kalanga | 5% |

SHONA TRIBES

3	Rozwi	9%
4	Korekore	12%
5	Zezuru	18%
6	Manyika	13%
7	Karanga	22%
8	Ndau	3%

OTHER TRIBES

9	Batonka	2%
10	Venda	1%
11	Shangaan	1%

school enrolment increased by over 1000%, from 66,200 to 687,742.

Although education remains under funded – texts, materials and qualified teachers are in short supply – 93% of Zimbabwean children receive at least some education and nearly 100% of those who complete primary school go on to secondary school. Although both a primary and secondary education were initially free and compulsory for everyone, school fees were reintroduced in conjunction with the ESAP in the early 1990s. In general, however, children attending rural primary schools are still exempt from school fees. Most Whites and affluent Blacks pay to send their children to private schools.

Classes are held from mid-January to mid-April, mid-May to early August and mid-September to early December.

The national examination authorities still use the Cambridge System of assessing academic achievement. Continuing education is offered at the University of Zimbabwe in Harare and at technical, vocational and agricultural schools in Harare, Bulawayo, Kwe Kwe and Mutare.

ARTS

Visitors to Zimbabwe are normally surprised by the scope and degree of artistic talent Zimbabweans seem to take for granted. From even the humblest practical ceramic pot or basket created in a remote village emerges evidence of artistic sensitivity and attention to detail.

Artists are held in high esteem in Zimbabwean society and a greater percentage of artists are making a viable living at their trade than in most other countries. In Harare and Bulawayo arts centres seek out those with the greatest talents for special training. One problem for the artists is the abundance of talent and therefore, of competition. This means that pieces that would fetch huge sums elsewhere are scarcely noticed. As a result, however, quality pieces are therefore affordable for most visitors and the work thereby gains international exposure.

Shona Sculpture

Although it's a relatively recent addition to Zimbabwe's cultural arts – it has no functional or ceremonial value and therefore wasn't significant in traditional society – Shona sculpture has garnered most of the laurels as far as international recognition is concerned. It isn't simply considered great *African* art but great art in the broadest sense.

Although the movement is known as Shona sculpture, the Shona tribe has no exclusive rights to the genre and smaller tribal groups are participating as well. Today's sculpture has been evolving over the past 30 years or so, a product of welding African themes and ideas with European artistic training.

African folklore provides themes for a majority of the work and pieces are populated by stylised animals, gods, spirits, ancestors and totems as well as deeply emotional humans heavily involved in life. One recurring theme is the metamorphosis of man into beast, the prescribed punishment for violation of certain social interdictions – such as making a meal of one's totem animal. Most of the work is superb.

Four of the major practitioners these days are considered to be among the world's greatest living sculptors. The late John Takawira, highly acclaimed in Europe, was best known for his facility with a number of forms, sizes and themes. Minimalist Nicholas Mukomberanwa, on the other hand, tends to utilise consistently bulky masses while striving to simplify the designs into only their essential components. The third, Henry Munyaradzi, learned his art at the Tengenenge colony in northern Zimbabwe. Although his pleasant and instantly recognisable works seem reminiscent of the cubist tradition and he's been highly successful, he risks becoming repetitious. Bernard Matemera, Tengenenge's best known artist,

experiments with deliberately surreal dimensions and forms, testing responses. In 1986, he won a major international award in India. Other acclaimed sculptors include Joram Mariga, Sylvester Mubayi and Joseph Ndandarika.

In addition to these, Zimbabwe has hundreds of exceptionally talented sculptors, many at schools, art centres, and sculpture communities around the country.

Traditional Crafts

Traditional African crafts, though utilitarian, display a degree of art that reflects and reveals ancient traditional values and the spiritual attitude of the culture. Tools and implements are consciously designed to be both functional and aesthetically pleasing. Women in particular have perpetuated characteristically African themes and shapes by integrating them into everyday items – pottery, basketry, textiles, and jewellery – while men have focused on woodcarving, iron sculpture and architecture in the context of tool-making and home construction.

Textiles & Basketry Even before Arab traders brought cloth from India, Zimbabweans were spinning and weaving garments from wild cotton that grew on the plateau, and making blankets, mats and clothing from strands of the soft and pliable tree bark known as *gudza*. This art is still practised.

The quality of woven baskets in Zimbabwe is phenomenal and the patterns well thought out and beautifully symmetrical. As in many cultures, baskets are used for a variety of purposes, from trapping fish underwater to storing food and belongings. They are even used as table service.

A number of materials – *imizi* grass, reeds, *ilala* palm, and sisal – are utilised, and the characteristic earth-tone dyes are derived from a variety of tree barks. The largest baskets, which typically contain well over a cubic metre, are a favourite with tourists who take them home to use as laundry baskets.

More recently, Zimbabwean women have proven highly skilful at crocheting, batik,

Ancient Rock Art

Many visitors to southern Africa have the privilege to see examples of ancient rock paintings. There's a great deal of speculation about the origins of these paintings, and there is no way of dating them reliably without destroying them. Thanks to deposits left in painted caves and scenes depicted in the paintings themselves, it's surmised that the artists were nomadic hunter-gatherers without knowledge of agriculture or pottery. For that reason, it's thought that these wilderness art galleries are the work of early San people.

As would be expected, most rock painting reflected the people's interaction with the natural element. Some were stylised representations but the majority faithfully and skilfully portray the people and animals of the region: hunters, giraffes, elephants, rhinos, lions, antelopes and so on in red, yellow, brown and ochre.

Most of the human figures reflect the nomadic hunting and gathering society of the San. Common themes include the roles of men and women, hunting scenes and natural medicine. This last includes examples of trance dancing and spiritual healing using the San life force, known as *nxum*, which was invoked to control aspects of the natural world, including climate and disease. All these things still feature in San tradition.

It has been considered that, as with similar cave art found in Europe, perhaps the animal paintings were intended to magically ensure an abundance of those particular animals. However, this concept hasn't been noted in any present-day African culture, and there's no evidence of ancient ties with Europe. Furthermore, few of the animals portrayed served as food for the ancient San.

Although the earliest works have long faded, flaked and eroded into oblivion, the dry climate and their normal location in sheltered granite overhangs has preserved many of the more recent ones. No reliable method of dating these paintings has yet been devised but anthropological studies have used the content, skill level and superposition of the paintings to identify three distinct stages.

The earliest paintings seem to reflect a period of gentle nomadism during which people were occupied primarily with the hunt. Later works suggest peaceful incursions by outside groups, perhaps Bantu or Khoisan (from whom the San and Khoi-Khoi/Nama are descended). During this stage, many significant paintings were produced, revealing great artistic improvement.

The final stage indicates a decline in the standard of the paintings; either a loss of interest in and facility with the genre or imitation of earlier works by subsequently arriving peoples. For the archaeologist, there are considerable difficulties in relating the paintings to the cultural sequences preserved in soil layers of caves and rock shelters but recent advances in radiocarbon dating are beginning to shed some light.

The red pigments were ground mainly from iron oxides, which were powdered and mixed with animal fat to form an adhesive paste. The whites came from silica, powdered quartz and white clays and were by nature less adhesive than the red pigments. For that reason, white paintings survive only in sheltered locations, such as well-protected caves. Both pigments were applied to the rock using animal hair brushes, sticks and the artist's fingers.

The most poignant thing about rock art is that it remains in the spot where it was created. Unlike in a museum, sensitive viewers may catch a glimpse of the inspiration that went into the paintings. The best place to see rock art in Zimbabwe is undoubtedly Matobo National Park. Almost as good are Domboshawa and Ngomakurira, both north of Harare. There are also several sites around Mutoko, Lake Mutirikwe and Lake Chivero, as well as scattered in rock overhangs all around the country. Botswana also has numerous examples, the most renowned of which are found at the Tsodilo Hills. ■

tie-dyeing and clothing design. Although these aren't traditional Zimbabwean arts, these inexpensive creations are typically of optimum quality.

Pottery Ceramics, another traditionally female activity in Zimbabwe, has played an essential role in the development of its cul-

tures. Pots were used for storage, cooking, serving, carrying, preparing curdled milk and even the brewing of yeast beer. While their various shapes have always been undoubtedly practical, the typically understated colours and intricate but unpretentious designs make Zimbabwean pottery an enduring art form.

Carving Although souvenir hunters will be tempted by row upon row of identical soapstone elephants and hippos and rough-hewn wooden giraffes and lions in kitsch gift shops and public squares, there's much more to Zimbabwe's carving heritage than such assembly-line productions would suggest. Traditionally, such tools as hoes, axe handles, ladles, bowls, and penis sheaths *(umncwado)* were all carved from wood in simplistic and practical designs. Spear, knobkerrie and dagger handles were decoratively rendered and shields were mounted on a carved wooden frame. Even small canoes were typically hewn out of a single bit of wood.

Carved *mutsago* or *umqamelo* (Shona and Ndebele words for 'headrest') were considered emblematic of family responsibility, and headrests of distant ancestors were passed down male lines and called upon to evoke ceremonially the spirits of earlier owners. Various theories have arisen about the extent of their early use – whether for afternoon rests, protection of elaborate coiffures, or as concessions to the comfort of the elderly. Now, their worth lies primarily in their antique or heirloom value.

Wooden stools, whose expertly intricate decorations reach their highest level in the Batonka culture of western Lake Kariba, are carved from a single piece of wood. Historically, only men were allowed to sit on them and male heads of household used them as a 'throne' from which to oversee family affairs.

Divining devices or *hakata* are carved from bone, wood or ivory and are used to forecast future events, determine guilt and communicate with ancestors in traditional rural areas. There are four tablets in a set: *chirume* which has a male value, *kwami* with a female value, *nhokwara* with 35 triangular cuts representing good luck, and *chitokwadzima* which represents bad luck and bears the image of a crocodile. Interpretations are made by a reader based on the tablets' configuration after being thrown.

Music

Traditional Music Music has always been a given in traditional Zimbabwean culture. The melody and rhythm of repetitive chanting becomes a mesmerising declaration of unity between the singers, while individuality is sustained by harmonisation of the various parts. Shared song has served as an evocation and confirmation of solidarity in common struggles, whether battle with a neighbouring tribe, cooperation on a successful harvest, or confrontation with natural disaster. Moreover, African stories and legends are punctuated by musical choruses in which the audience participates, and social events – weddings, funerals, and religious ceremonies, harvests, and births – are each accompanied by unique songs.

Only over the past decade has the rest of the world begun to take notice of African music – especially since the release of Paul Simon's *Graceland* album – and most modern Zimbabwean artists use traditional music as a base for new musical direction.

Zimbabwe's traditional musical instruments, though fashioned from natural materials on hand, produce an array of effects. The best known is the *marimba*, a wooden xylophone which creates tones similar to those in Western music and is often used for pieces with strong European influences. The keys of the best marimbas are made from the hard wood of the *mwenje* tree

Ukhamba – a pottery vessel, usually used for holding beer

of northern Mozambique, which produces optimum resonance. Sound boxes are normally made of dried gourds.

Another instrument which enjoys popularity among souvenir hunters as well as musicians is the *mbira* or thumb piano. It was originally used to accompany historical epics set to music. Although there are several variations, most mbira consist of 22 to 24 narrow iron keys mounted in rows on a wooden sound board. The player plucks the ends of the keys with the thumbs or specially grown thumbnails. An accomplished mbira player is known as a *gwenyambira*.

Percussion instruments include an array of rattles and drums. Rattles can be made of seeds, gourds and even bottle caps. *Hosho* (maracas) rattles are held in the hands while *magagada*, *majaka*, *madare* (bells), and Ndebele *mahlwayi* rattles are attached to the legs and ankles of dancers. The *ngoma*, a tapered cylindrical drum made from the *mutiti* or 'lucky bean' tree, comes in all sizes. Although the standard skin covering these days is cowhide, the optimum skins are considered to be zebra and *leguaan* (a water-loving lizard). To achieve maximum resonance, drums are treated with beeswax and dried over a flame before a performance.

Probably the oddest percussion instrument ever used in Zimbabwe was the *mujejeje*, the 'stone bells'. Many stones in granite kopjes around the country have exfoliated in such a way that when struck, they'll resound with a lovely bell-like tone (Zimbabwe's first rock music?). Historically, special occasions were held around these stones in order to take advantage of this novel musical opportunity. The most famous of these can be seen today at the Khami Ruins near Bulawayo.

The woodwind group is represented by several types of flutes, including pan pipes and the *nyanga* or 'horn' which is, logically, fashioned from the horn of an animal. Although traditional string instruments (mostly bow-shaped like the Shangaan *makweyana*) have been used historically in Zimbabwe, they are rarely played these days. Kwanongoma College in Bulawayo was

established to promote the revival of these traditional instruments, particularly the marimba and mbira. It focuses on training musicians and makers of musical instruments, and fosters popular appreciation for age-old Zimbabwean tones and rhythms.

Popular Music In Shona culture, as in so many African cultures, music is incorporated into almost every aspect of life. Through traditional songs, stories are told, games are played and important lessons passed from generation to generation. These songs use the traditional rhythmic structures of Zimbabwean music and are often accompanied by various percussion instruments (such as dried gourd rattles and skin drums), the mbira, marimbas and the nyanga.

In the period between WWII and the start of Zimbabwe's war of independence in the early 1970s, little attention or interest was afforded by the music industry to these traditional musical forms. Musically, Zimbabwe was inundated with foreign material – from Swing in the 1940s through to South African pennywhistle in the 1950s to Otis Redding and other US soul music in the 1960s. Many local groups, including some of today's famous names such as Thomas Mapfumo and Oliver Mtukudzi, began their careers doing Beatles and Elvis covers.

To the great benefit of Zimbabwean music lovers, the war of independence inspired musicians to write, perform and record original protest songs, which were based on traditional Shona sounds, transposed onto Western instruments. These songs, known as Chimurenga, form the musical basis for much of Zimbabwean popular music today. Particularly in Harare, there is no shortage of excellent groups performing their own variations on this essentially Zimbabwean style, mostly with lyrics sung in Shona. Some of the best musicians have been snapped up by overseas audiences, but the majority are still in Harare, which is very fortunate indeed for the traveller. The recordings of Thomas Mapfumo, Zimbabwe's best known musician, are sold around the world. The Bhundu Boys with their fast *jit* dance music went

African A Cappella: Black Umfolosi

Zimbabwe's most internationally famous singing group is probably Black Umfolosi, an a cappella ensemble from Bulawayo. The name is derived from the Umfolosi River in South Africa, and the group added 'Black' to emphasise their identity. The eight male members of the group, who hail from Matabeleland, have been singing together since 1982.

Black Umfolosi sing their a cappella pieces in both Ndebele and English, in a style known as *imbube*. Their songs address general human concerns – love, family, God – as well as contemporary problems – wars, apartheid, the environment and AIDS. Their music is fresh and surprising not only for the interesting texts and lyrics, but also for the typically intricate rhythms, unusual harmonies and interspersed clicking, clapping and shouting, which combine to produce a natural, funky and rugged aura.

Black Umfolosi consider their music not just as entertainment or a route to renown, but as a means of reviving Zimbabwean – particularly Ndebele – culture and introducing it abroad. They achieve this not just by singing their songs, but also by performing traditional dances on stage – including such modern additions as the miners' gumboot dance, which usually closes their performances. For several years now, Black Umfolosi have been collecting funds to build a cultural centre in Bulawayo, to be called the Enkundleni Cultural Centre. This centre will serve not only as a performance venue, but also as a training centre for new groups, a children's educational centre, a community events facility and a site for the documentation of African music and dance.

Currently, Black Umfolosi has two CDs on the World Circuit label: *Unity* and *Festival-Umdalo*. A portion of the proceeds from record sales go to the Enkundleni Cultural Centre. Black Umfolosi also offers their services to tourist groups through the Black Umfolosi Performing Arts Project. Their office (☎(19) 77409; fax (19) 65016) is on the corner of George Silundika Ave and 3rd Ave in Bulawayo. For further information, write to the Chairperson, Black Umfolosi Project, ZIMFEP, PO Box 673, Bulawayo (fax (19) 65016).

Norbert Schürer, USA

---

international in 1987. Sadly, the group has been plagued by AIDS and since its inception the band has lost some of its members.

Zimbabwe has also over the past decade become a kind of asylum for South African exiles – there are quite a number of musicians hanging around there until the time is right to return to their homeland. This, and the fact that so many foreign bands include Zimbabwe on their tours combine to make Harare one of Africa's great musical centres. One way to tap into what's current and popular is to take your own radio and tune in to one of the Shona stations which play great local and not-so-local music.

As well as popular Shona and Shangaan styles, there is a strong market for Zaïrois kwasa kwasa music, which tends to be based on the rhumba beat. In fact, so admired is the rhumba that Zimbabwean record shops have four categories for African music: local, South African, reggae and rhumba. The general rule is: if it's not obviously local, South African or reggae, you'll find it under

rhumba! There's also some great West African music around (under rhumba, of course).

For any sort of African music, try the Pop Shop on the corner of First St and Baker Ave in Harare – the staff are as helpful and enthusiastic as they can be and if you ask them to play something local, they may even dance to it as you listen!

Groups & Musicians Some of Zimbabwe's better-known music names include the following: Thomas Mapfumo and the Blacks Unlimited, Oliver Mtukudzi, The Four Brothers, New Black Montana (in the Mapfumo genre), Robson Banda and the Black Eagles, Joseph Mutero, Steve Dyer, The Real Sounds of Africa, the Khiami Boys, the Ngwenya Brothers, Leonard Dembo, Black Umfolosi, John Chibudura and the Tembo Brothers.

Bands, however, are constantly breaking up, changing members and changing names, so don't be discouraged if you can't find a group you know of – those people in the record shop can be a useful source of information. Or just keep your eye out for the posters to get an idea of who's around.

National Anthem Until recently, Zimbabwe – like much of Africa – used as its national anthem the hymn of African nationalism *Nkosi Sikilele Africa* ('God Bless Africa'). In 1987, however, a competition was launched to find a unique anthem for the country. It attracted over 1600 entries and it took nine years to select a winner. That turned out to be *Ngaikomborerwe Nyika Yezimbabwe* ('Blessed be the Land of Zimbabwe'), which was introduced at the April 1994 Independence Day celebrations.

Further Information If you're a fan of Zimbabwean music, a good information source is *Dandemutande Magazine & Calendar* published by Paul Novitski (☎ (206) 323 6592; fax (206) 329 9355), 1711 East Spruce St, Seattle, WA 98122-5728, USA. The name means 'spiderweb', 'network' or 'complex arrangement', with reference to the intricate weaving of melodic lines in Shona music and 'a nod in passing to the spider-egg casings used as buzzers in Zimbabwean music.' It's self-described as 'A web connecting lovers of Zimbabwean marimba and mbira music and related arts – throughout the world.'

The publications are a great resource for anyone interested in the Zimbabwean music scene. There's a calendar of events worldwide and a quarterly magazine with articles on trends, personalities and hints on making and playing traditional Zimbabwean instruments. Annual subscriptions currently cost US$15/25 inside/outside the USA for both the calendar and magazine.

Other useful contacts for music fans include:

International Library of African Music, Andrew Tracy, Rhodes University, Grahamstown 6140, South Africa (☎ (461) 318557; fax (461) 24411) This is the world's largest and most comprehensive collection of African ethnomusicological recordings and academic writings, including music from numerous Zimbabwean cultural groups.

Kunzwana Trust, Keith Goddard, 3 Maxwell Rd, Groombridge, Harare, Zimbabwe (☎ /fax (14) 301519) The aim of this organisation is to help Zimbabwean musicians and instrument makers become commercially self-sufficient. They also sponsor the fabulous annual Houses of Stone music festival, in Harare. Write for advance information and specific dates.

The Kutsinhira Center, Joel Lindstrom, PO Box 26111, Eugene, OR 97402, USA (☎ (503) 461 3442) – This is a school for Zimbabwean musical arts, focusing on mbira and marimba.

Mother Earth, Stella Chiwashe, PO Box 66513, Kopje, Harare, Zimbabwe (☎ /fax (14) 301519) An organisation of female performing artists which sponsors performances and educational workshops, such as the Pasirisangana International Women's Voices Workshop, held in May 1995.

Ozema Studio, Joseph Oze Matare, Breisacherstr 60, Basel, CH-4057, Switzerland (☎ /fax (61) 692 5705) This school of Zimbabwean musical arts focuses on song and percussion.

The Rufaro School of Marimba, Michael & Osha Breez, 161 Dougherty Lane, Friday Harbor, WA 98250, USA (☎ (360) 378 6649) A school for Zimbabwean musical arts, also focusing on mbira and marimba.

Literature

Prior to the 1960s, most of Zimbabwe's written literature was produced by the White sector of the population. Popular novelists like Cynthia Stockley and Gertrude Page wrote simplistic but well-received novels during the early part of the century. The first work to express scepticism of Rhodesia's social structure was *The Bay Tree Country* penned by Arthur Cripps, a British-born poet and missionary, published in 1913. In the same vein, in 1950, Doris Lessing produced the very successful *The Grass is Singing*.

Although both Shona and Ndebele oral tradition had perpetuated a large body of stories, legends, songs and poetry, the first written works by Black authors didn't appear in print until the publication (in Shona) of *Feso* by S Mutswairo in 1956. The first published Ndebele novel was *Umthawakazi* by P S Mahlangu, which appeared in 1957.

Subsequent works by both groups fall mainly into two categories: those dealing with pre-colonial traditions, myths and folk tales and those focusing on the social and political experiences of Black Africans under a White regime. Although numerous protest pieces were written during the following 10 years, the first serious treatise of the topic was Stanlake Samkange's *On Trial for my Country* published in 1966.

Zimbabwean independence in 1980 brought an end to oppression-inspired literature, however. Although some axe-grinding still goes on, most independence-era literature has focused on the liberation effort and the struggles to build a new society. In 1992, the Commonwealth Prize for Literature went to Zimbabwean writer Shimmer Chinodya for *Harvest of Thorns*, his epic novel of the Second Chimurenga.

Thanks to increasing literacy rates, better education and higher wages over the past decade, Zimbabwean literature is enjoying a boom. New novels, nonfiction and poetry titles in English, Shona and Ndebele are appearing frequently and are being studied as serious literature, as evidenced by the University of Zimbabwe's offering a university degree in Shona literature.

For information on other titles and players, see the Books discussion in the Zimbabwe Facts for the Visitor chapter.

RELIGION
Christianity
Between 40% and 50% of Zimbabweans belong to Christian churches, but their belief system is characterised more by a hybrid of Christian and traditional beliefs than by dogmatic Christianity.

In 1859, Reverend Robert Moffat of the London Missionary Society established Zimbabwe's first Christian mission at Inyati near Bulawayo. He was followed by Black African representatives of the Dutch Reformed Church from South Africa and the Jesuits who set up their headquarters at Lobengula's Kraal in Matabeleland in 1880. Anglicans and Methodists came later. All the Protestant groups set up schools, medical facilities, and agricultural assistance.

Many Zimbabwean Christians identify with some Protestant sect (the result of numerous early missions zealously competing for converts) but the Roman Catholic church, with 800,000 members in Zimbabwe, claims more adherents than any of the Protestant denominations which include Methodist, Salvation Army, Seventh-Day Adventist, Dutch Reformed, Presbyterian, Congregational, Episcopalian, North American fundamentalist groups and a number of African splinter organisations.

Although the Portuguese first brought Catholicism to Zimbabwe in 1561, it wasn't a recognised presence until 1890 and only became a significant force in the 1950s. In 1972, the Church established the Catholic Commission for Justice & Peace to monitor human rights violations within the country and promote peace and justice. Although it was most active during the Second Chimurenga, it has continued its work to the present day. Another organisation, the Catholic Development Commission, is working to upgrade socioeconomic conditions in rural areas. The church also operates a number of private schools in Namibia.

Mwari Cult
The majority of Zimbabweans profess traditional religious beliefs as well as those introduced by Europeans. The Mwari Cult, a monotheistic animist belief system which entails ancestor worship and spiritual proxy and intercession, has predominated at least since the height of Great Zimbabwe. Because of its rather clandestine nature, however, little is actually known about the scope of the cult's current influence. Of the numerous Mwari cave shrines in Zimbabwe, only the Matonjeni grouping near Bulawayo – Njelele and Wirarani in the Matobo and Dula near Esigodini – are thought to be still active. These shrines remain officially off limits to outsiders.

The original concept of Mwari, the supreme deity, was probably brought by southward migrating Bantu groups who arrived in Zimbabwe during the 1300s. The new religion spread quickly across southern Africa and took a firm hold. In fact, it was one of the few elements of the Rozwi Empire that survived the Nguni invasions of the early 1800s, and the conquering Ndebele were themselves absorbed into the Rozwi religion. Even Christianity could not displace it and converts to European sects took it that Mwari and the Christian God were one and the same. In Shona, the Christian God is still known as Mwari.

Mwari theology is quite simple. Occasionally referred to as Musiki (Creator), Musikavanhu (Origin of Man), or Nyadenga (Father of the Skies), Mwari is the unknowable supreme being. He speaks to his human subjects (or victims) through The Voice of Mwari, a cave-dwelling oracle who is most often female. The oracle is not only responsible to serve as a vehicle for divine will, but also to serve as intercessionary between the spirits, the god and the people, especially in cases of natural disaster or outside aggression, both considered deserved punishments for religious infractions. It was the oracle, in fact, who received the go-ahead to begin the First Chimurenga in 1896.

Midzimu, Mhondoro & Mambo

Although Mwari is the head honcho, followers also believe that spirits of their ancestors or *midzimu*, all the way back to the *tateguru* (the common ancestors who lived at some hazy point in the distant past and ultimately deliver messages to Mwari), continue to inhabit the human world. These spirits, whose afterlife status is determined by the length of time since their deaths, retain a great deal of influence over the physical world. A person with happy midzimu will be kept out of harm's way while those whose forbears are dissatisfied may meet with all sorts of misfortune.

When that happens, a medium is contacted and the disgruntled ancestor is identified. Normally, a *bira* or family gathering is held in which the unhappy mudzimu (singular form of midzimu) is invited to enter the victim's body, state the complaint and make suggestions for remedying the problem. If all goes well, the victim becomes the family *svikiro* or medium for the now appeased mudzimu.

The mhondoro ('lions' in Shona) operate under much the same principle as the midzimu but rather than confining attentions to their descendants, the mhondoro are often territorial spirits and can affect entire communities of people. When a problem such as a plague or drought strikes, these are the spirits who must be consulted.

Svikiros of individual mhondoro spirits may appear erratically through many generations. Due to their ferocity and fearlessness, they are normally associated with a lion character, hence their name, and the svikiro of a mhondoro effects the aspect of a lion. Prior to the fall of Rozwi, it was most often the Rozwi mambo or king who served as the svikiro. Although his ravings were normally indecipherable to the lay populace, they were easily interpreted by the Mwari priesthood.

In the early 1800s, one mambo managed to fall afoul of Mwari himself, a particularly serious infraction for someone in his position. It wasn't long before the offended made known to the priests that Rozwi was doomed and would soon fall at the hands of outsiders. Soon thereafter, the Nguni invasions began.

LANGUAGE

The official language of Zimbabwe – that used in government, legal and business proceedings – is English, but it is a first language for only about 2% of the population. The rest of the people are native speakers of some Bantu language, the two most prominent of which are Shona, spoken by 76% of the population, and Ndebele, spoken by 18%.

Shona, which is actually a collection of numerous Bantu dialects, is spoken in the central and eastern parts of the country. The 'high' dialect and the one used in broadcasts and other media is Zezuru which is indigenous to the Harare area.

Ndebele is spoken primarily in Matabeleland in the western and south-western parts of Zimbabwe. It is derived from the Zulu group of languages and is not mutually intelligible with Shona.

Another dialect, Chilapalapa, is actually a pidgin version of Ndebele, English, Shona, and Afrikaans, among other things, and is used primarily as a lingua franca for communication between employers and employees. It isn't overly laden with niceties and it's a safe bet that Zimbabweans would prefer to hear straight English than this aberration.

Pronunciation
Since both Shona and Ndebele were first written down by phonetic English transliteration, most letters are pronounced as they would be in English. The major exception are the Ndebele 'clicks', drawing of the tongue away from the front teeth (dental), slapping it on the roof of the mouth (palatal) or drawing it quickly sideways from the right upper gum (lateral). Each of these come in four different varieties: voiced, aspirated, nasal, and aspirated nasal. For interest only – non-native speakers rarely get the hang of this – the following table outlines standard transliterations of each of these sounds:

	voiced	aspirated	nasal	aspirated/nasal
dental	gc	ch	nc	ngc
palatal	gq	hn	qn	ngq
lateral	gx	xh	nx	ngx

Other Ndebele differences of note include:

b	pronounced implosively
th	is aspirated like the t in 'tarmac'
o	is like aw in 'law'
m	when placed before a consonant at the beginning of a word is pronounced as a little hum
n	when placed before a consonant at the beginning of a word, it's a hum with an 'n' sound

Shona differences of note:

dya	pronounced 'jga', as near to one syllable as possible
tya	this one is 'chka', also said quickly
sv	similar to the Chinese (Pinyin) x. If that's not familiar, say 's' with your tongue touching the roof of your mouth
zv	similar to sv but say 'z' instead of 's'
m, n	same as in Ndebele when placed before a consonant at the beginning of a word

Although most urban Zimbabweans have at least a little knowledge of English, many rural dwellers' English vocabulary is very limited, so it may help to know a few pleasantries in the local lingo. Even those Zimbabweans who speak English well will normally be pleasantly surprised to hear a foreigner make an attempt to speak a few words of Shona or Ndebele.

For a list of words in Shona or Ndebele, see the table on page 128. If two translations are given for the same word or expression, the first is used when speaking to one person, the second with more than one.

Zimbabwean English
In addition to the indigenous languages, Zimbabweans have some unique ways of expressing themselves in English. Some words have been adopted from Afrikaans, Shona or Ndebele, some are common words adapted to local usage, and others are entirely new. The following is a rundown of several you can expect to encounter:

ablutions block – a building which contains a loo, bath, washing up area and sometimes a shower. It's also known as an 'amenities block'.

baas – boss, subservient address reserved mainly for White males

babalass – a hangover; those who indulge in *chibuku* are particularly vulnerable

bakkie – utility or pick-up truck

bashas – thatched A-frame chalets

bazaar – inexpensive department store

bhundu – in Australia this would be called 'the bush'. Elsewhere, it's known as 'the tules', 'the sticks', the 'boonies', etc.

biltong – dried and salted jerked meat that can be made from just about anything from eland or ostrich to mutton or beef

blair toilet – high-tech dunny developed in Zimbabwe and used in rural areas. It has an odd spiral long-drop with a black-painted interior to drive flies up air vents toward daylight where they are trapped in a mesh just short of freedom.

bioscope – a cinema

boerewors – a spicy Afrikaner sausage which

ZIMBABWE

	Shona	Ndebele
Greetings & Civilities		
Hello. (initial)	Mhoro/Mhoroi.	Sawubona/Salibonani.
Hello. (reply)	Ahoi.	Yebo.
How are you?	Makadii/Makadi-ni?	Linjani/Kunjani?
I am well.	Ndiripo.	Sikona.
Thank you.	Ndatenda/Masvita.	Siyabonga kakulu.
Welcome.	Titambire.	Siyalemukela.
Good morning.	Mangwanani.	Livukenjani.
Good afternoon.	Masikati.	Litshonile.
Good evening.	Manheru.	Litshone njani.
Please.	Ndapota.	Uxolo.
Goodbye.(person staying)	Chisarai zvakanaka.	Lisalekuhle.
Goodbye. (person leaving)	Fambai zvakanaka.	Uhambe kuhle.
Useful Words & Phrases		
What is your name?	Unonzi ani zita rako?	Ibizo lakho ngubani?
My name is...	Ndini...	Elami igama ngingu...
I would like...	Ndinoda...	Ngicela...
How much?	I marii?	Yimalini?
I am from...	Ndinobva ku...	Ngivela e...
Where is the station?	Chiteshi chiri kupi?	Singapi isiteshi?
When does the...leave?	...richaynda rihni?	Izawuhamba nini ...?
bus	Ehazi	bhasi
train	Chitima	isitimela
car?	Motokari	imoto
yesterday	nezuro	izolo
tomorrow	mangwana	kusasa
today	nhas	lamhla
What time is it?	Dzavanguvai?	Yisikhati bani?
men/women	varume/vakadz	amadoda/abafazi
Yes/No.	Ehe/Aiw.	Yebo/Hayi.
friend	shamwari	mngane
small/large	diki/guru	okuncane/ncinyane
sir/madam	changamire/mudzimai	umnimzana/inkosikazi
boy/girl	mukomana/musikana	umfana/inkazana
market/shop	musika/chitoro	imakethe/isitolo
Food & Drink		
bread	chingwa	isinkwa
meat	nyama	inyama
fish	hove	ininhlanzi
beef	mombe	nkomo
chicken	huku	nkukhu
potatoes	mbatatisi	amagwili
vegetables	muriwo	imbhida
ground nuts	nzungu	amazambane
butter	bhat	ibatha
salt	muny	isaudo
sugar	shuga	ushukela

	Shona	**Ndebele**
eggs	*mazai*	*amaqanda*
maize	*chibage*	*umbila*
maize porridge (grits)	*sadza*	*sadza*
fruit	*michero*	*izithelo*
beer	*doro/whawha*	*utshwala*
coffee	*kofi*	*ikofi*
tea	*ti*	*itiye*
milk	*mukaka*	*ucago*
water	*mvura*	*amanzi*

Animals

giraffe	*twiza*	*ntundla*
dog	*imbwa*	*nja*
buffalo	*nyati*	*nyathi*
impala	*mhara*	*mpala*
hippopotamus	*mvuu*	*mvubu*
horse	*bhiza*	*ibhiza*
goat	*mbudzi*	*mbuzi*
rabbit	*tsuro*	*mvundla*
baboon	*gudo*	*ndwangu*
zebra	*mbiz*	*ndube*
leopard	*mbada*	*ngwe*
rhinoceros	*chipembere*	*ubhejane*
monkey	*bveni*	*nkawu*
elephant	*nzou*	*ndhlovu*
lion	*shumbai*	*silwane*
hyaena	*bere*	*mpisi*
warthog	*njiri*	*ungulube yeganga*

Days of the Week

Sunday	*svondo*	*ngesonto*
Monday	*muvhuro*	*umbulo*
Tuesday	*chipiri*	*olwesibili*
Wednesday	*chitatu*	*ngolwesithathu*
Thursday	*china*	*ngolwesine*
Friday	*chishanu*	*ngolwesihlanu*
Saturday	*mugovera*	*ngesabatha*

Numbers

1	*potsi*	*okukodwa*
2	*piri*	*okubili*
3	*tatu*	*okutathu*
4	*ina*	*okune*
5	*shanu*	*okuyisihlanu*
6	*tanhatu*	*okuyisithupha*
7	*nomwe*	*okuyisikhombisa*
8	*tsere*	*okuyisitshiyangalo mbila*
9	*pfumbamwe*	*okuyisitshiyangalo lunye*
10	*gumi*	*okuli tshumi*

ranges from the consistency of mince meat to solid and bricklike. No braai could happen without it.

braai – a barbecue which normally includes several varieties of meat grilled on a braai stand or pit. It is an southern African institution, particularly among Whites.

buppies – Black yuppies

chibuku – the 'beer of good cheer'. Both inexpensive and revolting, this grain and yeast concoction is stored in large vats at beer halls and is served up in buckets. It's good for a quick euphoria and a debilitating babalass.

Club Special shandy – a nonalcoholic drink made from lemonade, gingerbeer and Mazoe orange

Comrade (or Cde) – a Marxist title used primarily by the media when referring to Black Zimbabwean citizens, especially government officials

dam – in Zimbabwe, a dam is what other English speakers would call a reservoir

dam wall – what other English speakers would call a dam

daga hut – a traditional African round house consisting of a wooden frame covered with mud and manure walls reinforced with straw, also known as 'pole and daga hut'

donkey boiler – it may sound cruel but it has nothing to do with donkeys. It's an elevated watertank positioned over a wood fire and used to heat water for baths and showers. It's also known as a 'Rhodesian boiler', which may also seem a bit cruel.

drift – a river ford; most are normally dry

Dutchman – a White Zimbabwean or South African of Afrikaner descent. It's always used in a derogatory manner and offence is always taken, so be forewarned.

flotty – a hat for canoe safaris, with a chinstrap and a bit of cork in a zippered pocket to ensure that it floats in case of a capsize

gap it – to 'split' in the sense of making a quick exit

guti – dank and drizzly weather that can afflict the Eastern Highlands in the winter.

Izzit? – rhetorical question which most closely translates as 'Really?' and is used without regard to gender, person, or number of the subject. Therefore, it could mean 'Is it?', 'Are you?', 'Is he?', 'Are they?', 'Is she?', 'Are we?', etc.

just now – reference to some time in the future but intended to imply some degree of imminence. It could be half an hour from now or two days from now.

kaffir – derogatory reference to a Black person

kloof – a ravine or small valley

kopje – pronounced 'coppie', this translates from Afrikaans as 'little hill'. In Zimbabwe, any old heap of rocks qualifies.

kraal – Afrikaans version of the Portuguese *curral*. It can refer to an enclosure for livestock or fortified village of daga huts.

koeksesters – small doughnuts dripping in honey – very gooey and figure-enhancing

lekker – very good or tasty

location – another word for township, but used more in Namibia and South Africa than Zimbabwe

make a plan – this can refer to anything from working out a complicated procedure to circumventing bureaucracy

Malawi shandy – non-alcoholic drink made from ginger beer, Angostura bitters, orange or lemon slices, soda and ice

Mazoe orange – sweet orange cordial made from citrus grown in the Mazoe area. It's a Zimbabwe staple.

mielie pap or *mealie meal* – maize porridge

mopane worms – the caterpillar of the moth *Gonimbrasiabelina*; these lovely larval delicacies are available in mopane trees and some Zimbabwe markets

murunge – this is actually a Shona word referring to a White European. For White travellers visiting rural areas, it may seem to reside on every lip.

não faz mal – Portuguese expression meaning, literally, 'it doesn't make bad', used in Zimbabwe as 'no problem'

now now – definitely not now but sometime sooner than 'just now'

peg – milepost

peri peri – ultra-hot pepper-based sauce that usurps the flavour of your *sadza ne nyama*

PK – the WC, the toilet

pronking – gleeful leaping by several species of antelope, apparently for sheer fun

Rhodey – a normally derogatory term for a White Zimbabwean. It's roughly the equivalent of 'ocker' or 'redneck' in Aussie and the US.

robot – no, not R2-D2. It's just a traffic light.

rock shandy – a wonderful nonalcoholic concoction made of lemonade, soda water and angostura bitters

rondavel – a round, African-style hut

rusks – solid bits of bread that North Americans would save for the Thanksgiving turkey or throw out long before they reached such a state. They're often flavoured with cinnamon or raisins and made edible by immersion in coffee or tea.

scuds – two-litre plastic bottles of chibuku

Shake-shake – Chibuku sold in waxed cardboard cartons

Shame! – used half-heartedly as an expression of commiseration

shebeen – an illegal drinking establishment cum brothel, nonregulars are unwelcome without an invitation

sjambok – whip

Snice! – equivalent of 'Wow!'

spruit – a little streambed, which rarely contains any water

Sus! – the opposite of 'snice', roughly the equivalent of 'yuck'

tackies – trainers, tennisshoes, gym shoes

TAB – 'That's Africa, baby.' Standard utterance when things are AFU, that is, not going according to plan.

TIZ – 'This is Zimbabwe', same connotation as TAB

Tonkies – Rhodey word for members of the Batonka tribe

township – high-density black residential area outside a central city or town

tsotsis – thieves

TWOGs – acronym for 'Third World groupies', used by White Zimbabweans in reference to foreigners who travel to underdeveloped countries and consciously sink to the lowest level of local society

Van der Merwe – archetypal Boer country bumpkin who is the butt of jokes throughout southern Africa

veld – open grassland, normally in plateau regions. One variation, 'bushveld', has the grassland replaced with thorn scrub.

veldskoens – comfortable bush shoes made of soft leather, similar to moccasins

vlei – any low open landscape, sometimes marshy

Ziko ndaba – Zimbabwean version of the Swahili *Hakuna matata*, has the same meaning as 'Não faz mal'(see earlier)

ZIMBABWE

Facts for the Visitor

VISAS & EMBASSIES

Visas are not required by nationals of Commonwealth countries, members of the European Union, Japan, Norway, Switzerland or the USA, but everyone needs a valid passport. Citizens of the Republic of South Africa can pick up a visa at the port of entry. Visa requirements occasionally change, so if you're not sure whether you need one, direct enquiries to the Zimbabwe embassy or high commission in your home country or the Chief Immigration Officer, Private Bag 7717, Causeway, Harare, Zimbabwe.

Immigration officials are normally immovable about onward tickets – although a ticket out of a neighbouring country or even Kenya will usually suffice – and they rarely ask to see your money or credit card unless you cannot produce a ticket. If you're entering by bus or rail, a return ticket via the same route will sometimes work but it's best not to count on it; they'll normally want a ticket back to your home country. Miscellaneous Charge Orders are not acceptable.

If you front up at the border without an onward ticket or at least a major credit card, you may be refused entry or carefully scrutinised for 'sufficient funds'. Some people may even be required to pay a refundable deposit in cash or travellers' cheques which can run to as much as US$1000. The biggest concern will be getting it back when you leave. There's no worry about the officials absconding with the money – things thank-

---

Zimbabwe Diplomatic Missions

Zimbabwe is diplomatically represented abroad at the following missions (telephone numbers include country codes and area codes in brackets):

Botswana
High Commission of Zimbabwe, 1st floor, IGI Building PO Box 1232, Gaborone (☎ (267) 314495; fax (267) 305862)

Canada
High Commission of Zimbabwe, 112 Kent St, Suite 915, Place de Ville, Tower B, Ottawa, Ontario K1P 5P2 (☎ (1-613) 237 4388; fax (1-613) 563 8269)

France
Ambassador of Zimbabwe, 5 rue de Tilsit, Paris 75008 (☎ (33-1) 47 63 48 31; fax (33-1) 44 09 05 36)

Germany
Ambassador of Zimbabwe, Villichgasse 7, 5300 Bonn 2 (☎ (49-228) 356071; fax (49-228) 356309)

Japan
Ambassador of Zimbabwe, 11-23 Minami, Ababu, 2 Chome, Minatoku, Tokyo 106 (☎ (813) 4730 266)

Kenya
High Commission of Zimbabwe, 6th floor ICDC Building, Mamlaka Rd, PO Box 30806, Nairobi (☎ (254-2) 721071)

Mozambique
Consulate of Zimbabwe, Don Carlos Hotel, PO Box 649, Beira (☎(258-3) 325 1191)

Namibia
High Commission of Zimbabwe, Gamsberg Building, PO Box 23056, Windhoek (☎(264-61) 228134; fax (264-61) 226859)

South Africa
Bank of Lisbon Building, 37 Sauer St, Johannesburg (☎(27-11) 838 2156; fax (27-11) 838 5620)

Sweden
Ambassador of Zimbabwe, Oxtorget 5, 10290 Stockholm (☎(46-8) 304355)

UK
High Commission of Zimbabwe, Zimbabwe House, 429 The Strand, London WC2R 0SA (☎(44-171) 836 7744; fax (44-171) 379 1167)

USA
Ambassador of Zimbabwe, 2852 McGill Terrace NW, Washington, DC 20008 (☎(1-202) 332 7100; fax (1-202) 438 9326)

Zambia
High Commission of Zimbabwe, 4th floor, Ulendo House, Cairo Rd, Lusaka (☎(260-1) 229382; fax (260-1) 227474)

fully don't work that way in Zimbabwe – but they may possibly return it in Zimbabwe dollars just before you're due to leave and you may carry only Z$500 out of the country.

On the immigration form, you'll be asked for the name of a hotel or address in Zimbabwe. In the interest of minimising hassles, don't write 'camping' or 'don't know'. It would be better to select the name of a mid-range hotel in Harare or the next city you'll be visiting, whether you've booked it or not. If you state an intention to visit friends in Zimbabwe, you'll be expected to provide names, addresses, telephone numbers and any other details the officer may want.

To further avoid red tape – especially if you're just on holiday – don't cite your occupation as 'journalist' on the immigration form. Otherwise, you could be issued a 24-hour visa and required to apply for a temporary employment permit from the Ministry of Home Affairs. On the other hand, this could be useful (especially if you are on assignment). The 14-day work permit requires only about two hours' effort to secure and you're issued with a press card. The office is on the 7th floor, Liquenda House, Baker Ave, in Harare. Unlike some immigration offices elsewhere, this is normally an efficient and pleasant operation.

Visa Extensions
The average maximum length of stay granted is 90 days, although this can be readily extended to a maximum of six months at any immigration office. The catch is that you can extend for only one month at a time. The procedure is normally hassle-free, and you'll only have to fill in a form and demonstrate that you have enough money for the longer length of stay. If possible, avoid the Harare office, where queues may be long and service slow.

Visas for Other Countries
Harare is probably the best place in southern Africa to pick up visas for other African countries. Requirements are constantly changing but nearly all require a fee – some must be paid in US dollars – and multiple

passport-sized photos. If you plan to do a lot of border hopping, carry a stack of them.

Kenya The Kenya High Commission (☎ 792901) at 95 Park Lane issues single-entry visas for US$10. They require two photos and are issued in 24 hours. Multiple-entry visas are slower to obtain, so you're better off getting a single-entry visa and changing it in Nairobi.

Mozambique The Mozambique Embassy (☎ 790387) is at 152 Herbert Chitepo Ave, Harare. A transit visa allowing travel through the Tête corridor to Malawi costs US$9 (Z$66 – this is certain to increase in the near future), requires three photos and is issued in 24 hours with little fuss. A double-entry transit visa, good for a return trip to Malawi, costs US$22 (Z$170). Tourist visas cost US$17 (Z$126 – also sure to increase) and take eight days to issue. The embassy is open Monday to Friday from 8 am to noon.

Some travellers have had problems here; when you receive your visa, immediately ascertain that it won't expire on the following day – or that it hasn't already expired!

Namibia The Namibian High Commission (☎ 722113/47930) has now opened at Lintas House on Union St, Harare. Visas are free and require two photos. They're issued in 24 hours. Both Australians and New Zealanders require visas for Namibia.

West Africa The French Embassy in Harare issues visas for the Cote d'Ivoire, Senegal, Burkina Faso, the Central African Republic and Gabon. Check with them for information on visas for other former French West African countries. Note that the Nigerian High Commission won't issue visas if you could have obtained them in your home country prior to your journey – no matter what excuse you have.

Zaïre The Zaïre Embassy (☎ 730893), at 24 Van Praagh Ave, Milton Park, off Prince Edward St, is open Monday to Friday 8 am to 3 pm. Visa applications are accepted in the

Foreign Embassies & High Commissions in Zimbabwe
Countries with diplomatic representation in Zimbabwe include the following (all addresses are in Harare):

Australia
   Karigamombe Centre, 53 Samora Machel Ave (☎ 750352)
Austria
   Room 216, New Shell House, 30 Samora Machel Ave (☎ 702921)
Botswana
   10Bedford Rd, Avondale (☎ 729553)
Canada
   45 Baines Ave, on the corner of Moffat St, PO Box 1430 (☎ 733881)
Denmark
   UDC Centre, on the corner of Union Ave and First St (☎ 790398)
France
   Renelagh Rd near Orange Grove Dr, PO Box 1378, Highlands (☎ 48096)
Germany
   14 Samora Machel Ave, PO Box 2168 (☎ 731955)
Italy
   7 Bartholomew Close, PO Box 1062, Greendale (☎ 47279)
Japan
   Karigamombe Centre (☎ 727500)
Kenya
   95 Park Lane (☎ 792901)
Malawi
   Malawi House, 42/44 Harare St, PO Box 321 (☎ 705611)
Mozambique
   152 Herbert Chitepo Ave (☎ 790387)

Namibia
   Lintas House, Union St (☎ 722113)
Netherlands
   47 Enterprise Rd, Highlands (☎ 731428)
New Zealand
   6th floor, Batanai Gardens, 57 Jason Moyo Ave, PO Box 5448 (☎ 728681)
South Africa
   Temple Bar House, Baker Ave (☎ 707901)
Spain
   16 Phillips Ave, PO Box 3300, Belgravia (☎ 738681)
Sweden
   Pegasus House, Samora Machel Ave (☎ 790651)
Switzerland
   9 Lanark Rd, Belgravia (☎ 703997)
Tanzania
   23 Baines Ave, PO Box 4841 (☎ 724173)
UK
   6th floor, Stanley House, on the corner of Jason Moyo Ave and First St (☎ 793781)
USA
   Arax House, 172 Herbert Chitepo Ave, PO Box 3340 (☎ 794521)
Zaïre
   24 Van Praagh Ave, Milton Park (☎ 730893)
Zambia
   6th floor, Zambia House, Union Ave, PO Box 4698(☎ 790851)

morning and visas are issued at 4 pm the same afternoon. Three-month visas cost (sit down please) US$195 single entry and US$255 multiple entry (they're considerably cheaper in Nairobi and elsewhere).

Zambia The Zambian High Commission (☎ 790851) is on the 6th floor, Zambia House, Union Ave, Harare. Visas are required by all except nationals of Commonwealth countries, the Irish Republic, Romania, Sweden and the former Yugoslavia. Citizens of Commonwealth countries don't need a visa for Zambia unless they've been resident in East Africa and are of Bangladeshi, Indian, Chinese, or Pakistani descent.

The price of Zambian visas varies according to nationality. A double-entry tourist visa for US citizens in Harare costs US$10 and is issued the same day. Seven-day transit visas are available at the Victoria Falls border (and possibly elsewhere) for US$10.

Day-trippers to Zambia at Victoria Falls are subject to the same visa requirements, but their visa will be issued only for the day of travel unless otherwise requested, in which case it is valid for 21 days. Visa extensions are readily arranged at immigration on Cairo Rd, next to the post office in Lusaka.

DOCUMENTS
Yellow fever vaccination certificates are required of anyone entering Zimbabwe from

African countries to the north where the disease is endemic. Cholera vaccines are required only if you're entering Zimbabwe from an infected area.

A driving licence from your home country is sufficient to drive in Zimbabwe provided it's written in English. Otherwise, you'll need an authenticated translation plus a photograph. Driving licences from Zambia, Malawi, Namibia, South Africa, Botswana and Swaziland are valid until their expiry dates and other foreign licences are valid for 90 days.

CUSTOMS

Visitors may import a maximum of Z$1000 in non-trade items, excluding personal effects. Travellers over 18 years of age can also import up to five litres of alcohol, including two litres of spirits. Firearms must be declared at the border.

Motor vehicles may be imported temporarily as long as they bear current number plates and are licensed, registered and titled in the home country. For more information, see under Car & Motorbike in the Zimbabwe Getting Around chapter.

If you're travelling with a pet or a guide dog (unless you reside inside the Southern African customs union), you'll need a permit issued by the Director of Veterinary Services; apply to the Director of Veterinary Services, PO Box 8012, Causeway, Harare, Zimbabwe. This procedure takes a minimum of three months, so apply well in advance of your visit. There are no quarantine laws regarding pets, but in order to get the permit, all animals require vaccination certificates and a clean bill of health from a government veterinary office in their home country.

Animals belonging to residents of Botswana, Lesotho, Namibia, South Africa and Swaziland need only a clean bill of health from their nearest government veterinary office.

MONEY

Banks are open Monday, Tuesday, Thursday, and Friday between 8.30 am and 2 pm. On Wednesday, they close at noon and on Saturday they're open from 8.30 to 11 am. The exchange desk at Harare airport is open whenever there's an incoming flight, but often limits transactions to US$100. Hotel reception desks will sometimes exchange currency but the service is normally reserved for hotel guests and includes a substantial commission.

All brands of travellers' cheques in US dollars or UK pounds may be easily exchanged for Zimbabwe dollars at any bank. Major international currencies are also welcomed, but due to rampant counterfeiting, no one in Zimbabwe is currently accepting US$100 notes. If you have Visa travellers' cheques, the best exchange rates are available at Barclays Bank.

You can also purchase foreign currency travellers' cheques but never at a good rate since the transaction is converted from foreign currency into Zimbabwe dollars and then back to foreign currency, and each step yields a commission for the bank. Funds transferred from outside the country can only be received in Zimbabwe dollars or foreign-currency travellers' cheques – at the same loss ratio as when buying travellers' cheques outright.

Currency

The unit of currency is the Zimbabwe dollar (Z$1=100 cents). Notes come in denominations of two, five, 10 and 20 dollars. Coins are valued at one, five, 10, 20 and 50 cents, and Z$1.

Although it's no longer necessary to declare currency and travellers' cheques on arrival, immigration forms still ask for this information to ascertain whether you have enough for your intended length of stay. Customs officers occasionally want to see bank receipts as you leave the country, as proof you've exchanged your foreign currency at the official rate, so don't throw them away.

Bear in mind that import or export of Zimbabwean banknotes is limited to Z$500 per person per visit. However, now that local residents may hold overseas bank accounts, Zimbabweans have a US$2000 annual

ZIMBABWE

ZIMBABWE

holiday allowance, and exporters can retain up to 50% of their foreign earnings. This rule is likely to be relaxed in the near future.

For hotels and organised activities such as rafting or canoeing, non-residents must pay in foreign currency.

Exchange Rates

A$1	=	Z$6.07
UK£1	=	Z$13.55
US$1	=	Z$8.48
¥100	=	Z$1.78
DM1	=	Z$6.04
SFr1	=	Z$7.35
FFr1	=	Z$1.72
NZ$1	=	Z$5.66
C$1	=	Z$6.16
SAfR1	=	Z$2.31
BotP1	=	Z$3.13

Costs

Although hotels, national parks and tour operators employ a two-tier (or three-tier) pricing system, in which foreigners pay considerably more for goods and services than Zimbabwe residents, Zimbabwe is still not an expensive country for foreigners unless they're using the international-class hotels, safari lodges, fine dining establishments and package safaris that support the bulk of the country's tourist industry.

Fortunately for budget travellers, inexpensive accommodation alternatives, such as backpackers' hostels, are springing up around the country, and although prices for foreigners have risen phenomenally in recent years, national parks are still generally good value. In addition, you'll find comfortable and inexpensive campgrounds and caravan parks in and around most cities, towns and places of interest.

Food is very reasonably priced and those eating at small local establishments or self-catering will be able to eat heartily on a very tight budget. A meal of the Zimbabwean staple, *sadza ne nyama* (mealies with meat relish), in a local eatery will set you back around US$0.75. Big hotels offer all-you-can-eat buffet meals, and if you're really hungry, they're good value at US$5 to US$8.

Any item that must be imported – and therefore purchased with foreign exchange – is expensive. With the new economic restructuring, this is becoming less of a headache, but Zimbabweans must still save for years to buy, for example, a television, which may set them back thousands of Zimbabwe dollars. Even cheap digital watches are incredibly expensive and would make well-appreciated gifts for local friends. Consumer goods produced in Zimbabwe on the other hand, although rarely of optimum quality, are quite affordable.

Consumer taxes, which are almost invariably included in the price of the item, are fairly substantial: 16% on retail items, excluding food, and 19% on such 'luxury' items as electronic equipment, airline tickets, furniture and automobiles. There is also a 15% tax on hotel rooms, safaris and other tourist services. Up-market travellers can avoid this expense by booking and paying for all such items before leaving home, although you'll then be subjected to agents' commissions, which work out to roughly the same percentage.

Credit Cards

Credit cards – American Express, Diner's Club, MasterCard and Visa, as well as Eurocheques – are accepted by establishments catering to tourists and business people. Petrol credit cards – even those issued by oil companies represented in Zimbabwe – aren't accepted at all.

When purchasing currency with a credit card, you're limited to Z$20 (about US$2.50!) in foreign currency per transaction, although you can buy as many official-rate Zimbabwe dollars as you like. With a Visa card, you can draw instant cash at Barclays Bank automatic teller machines. Otherwise, prepare to wait a while for authorisation, especially in smaller towns. In Victoria Falls recently, authorisation was taking up to three days.

Tipping

Tips of approximately 10% are expected by taxi drivers and in tourist-class hotels and restaurants. Some establishments automatically add a 10% service charge to the bill, however, which replaces the gratuity.

Black Market

Although in the late 1980s strict currency controls created a thriving black market in Zimbabwe, the recently adopted Economic Structural Adjustment Programme and the relaxation of import regulations have put an end to any advantage a currency black market may once have afforded. Informal currency exchange remains illegal in Zimbabwe and, at most, unofficial rates are only a few cents higher than bank rates and aren't worth the considerable risks required to obtain them.

If you do encounter street money changers offering considerably higher than official rates, you can be 100% certain that it's an attempt at scamming. If you bite, they'll either turn you into the police or attempt to separate you and your money; many people wind up with a wad of clipped newspaper sandwiched between two Z$20 notes. This practice is particularly rife in Victoria Falls, which attracts large numbers of wealthy and inexperienced tourists. Don't let greed get the better of you!

WHEN TO GO

Although Zimbabwe is a tropical country, most of it lies on a plateau, and therefore enjoys a more temperate climate than its latitude would otherwise suggest. Climatic conditions range from the cool and moist conditions of the Eastern Highlands to the temperate Midlands and the sticky heat of the lowveld and the Zambezi Valley.

Generally, the dry winter months are the most comfortable for travelling around, but you'll miss the lovely green landscapes that characterise the hotter and wetter summer season. In the winter, daytime temperatures are optimum, but at night they can fall below freezing. Summer daytime temperatures can climb into the mid-30s Celsius, but are normally tempered by afternoon thunderstorms.

Winter is also the best season for wildlife viewing because the animals tend to concentrate close to water holes and are easily observed. During the summer, the presence of water allows them to spread out over a wider area, making viewing a hit or miss operation.

National parks and tourist sites are most crowded during South African school holidays, so if you want to avoid the throngs and find accommodation, avoid travelling between mid-April and mid-May or from mid-July to mid-September. There's a secondary rush around Namibian school holidays in December and early January. For these months, national parks accommodation – particularly lodges, chalets and cottages – must be booked well in advance.

If you don't want to trip over too many other tourists, a good month to visit is June, which is the coolest and quietest month in Zimbabwe. Bear in mind, however, that during this period, many tourist-related businesses close up shop and the owners head off on holidays of their own.

TOURIST OFFICES
Local Tourist Offices

Several publicity associations around the country distribute brochures, maps and pamphlets about their respective areas. Although some are considerably more helpful and better organised than others, they can at least provide up-to-date information on any new developments in their area.

Bulawayo
    Bulawayo Publicity Association, City Hall, Fife St, PO Box 861, Bulawayo (☎ 60867)
Gweru
    Gweru Publicity Association, City Hall, Livingstone Ave, PO Box 295, Gweru (☎ 2226)
Harare
    Harare Publicity Association, African Unity Square, 95 Jason Moyo Ave, PO Box 1483, Harare (☎ 705085)
Kariba
    Kariba Publicity Association, PO Box 86, Kariba (☎ 2328)
Masvingo
    Masvingo Publicity Association, Robert Mugabe St, PO Box 340, Masvingo (☎ 2643)

ZIMBABWE

Mutare
    Manicaland Publicity Association, Market Square, Milner Ave, PO Box 69, Mutare (☎ 64711)
Victoria Falls
    VictoriaFalls Publicity Association, Stand 412, Parkway/Livingstone Rd, PO Box 97, Victoria Falls (☎ 4202)

Representatives Abroad
Australia
    Zimbabwe Travel Bureau, Level 7, 75 Miller St, North Sydney, NSW (☎ (02) 959 4922)
Germany
    Zimbabwe Fremdenverkehrsamt, Wienerstrasse 40, 6000 Frankfurt am Main 1 (☎ (069) 653204)
Republic of South Africa
    Zimbabwe Tourist Board, Tower Mall, Upper Shopping Level, Carlton Centre, Commissioner St, PO Box 9398, Johannesburg 2001 (☎ (011) 331 6970)
    Zimbabwe Tourist Board, 2 President Place, Jan Smuts Ave, Rosebank, Johannesburg 2196 (☎ (011) 788 1748)
UK
    Zimbabwe Tourist Board, Zimbabwe House, 429 The Strand, London WC2R OSA (☎ (0171) 836 7755; fax (0171) 379 1167)
USA
    Zimbabwe Tourist Board, 525 5th Ave, New York, NY 10017 (☎ (212) 307 6565)

USEFUL ORGANISATIONS
The Automobile Association of Zimbabwe (☎ 707021), which dates back to 1923, offers a wide range of member services, including technical and legal advice, maps and touring assistance, emergency breakdown services and access to services of other similar organisations worldwide. Members also receive discounts on a variety of automobile-related services. For information, contact them at Fanum House, 7th floor, Samora Machel Ave, PO Box 585, Harare.

In the UK, those with a particular interest in Zimbabwe may want to contact the British Zimbabwe Society, Marieke Clark, 5a Cricke Rd, Oxford OX2 6QJ, UK (☎ (01865) 57807). This organisation publishes a newsletter and organises Zimbabwe-related events.

BUSINESS HOURS & HOLIDAYS
Shops are generally open between 8 am and 5 pm Monday to Friday, with early closing on Wednesday in some places and lunch closing from 1 to 2 pm. Saturday hours are from 8 am to 12 noon. Petrol stations open up at 6 am and the majority close at 6 pm, although several in Harare and Bulawayo keep later hours. Banks are open between 8.30 am and 2 pm Monday to Friday, except Wednesday when they close at noon, and from 8.30 to 11 am on Saturday. Postal services are available from 8.30 am to 4 pm Monday to Friday and from 8.30 to 11.30 am on Saturday.

Public Holidays
Zimbabwe observes the following public holidays:

1 January
    New Year's Day
March or April
    Good Friday, Easter Sunday, Easter Monday
18 April
    Independence Day
1 May
    Workers' Day
25 & 26 May
    Africa Days
11 & 12 August
    Heroes' Days & Defence Forces Day
25 December
    Christmas Day
26 December
    Boxing Day

CULTURAL EVENTS
In Zimbabwe, the most pleasant cultural events you're likely to experience will be those you run across incidentally: a rural agricultural fair, a primary school theatre production, a traditional wedding or a town anniversary (Bulawayo's Centenary celebrations in 1994 carried on for months). Zimbabweans are usually pleased and proud to find that strangers are interested in their special events, and you'll almost certainly be welcomed to share in the festivities. This sort of thing is one of the greatest joys of travel, but if you want to fully appreciate such opportunities, you will need to keep your itinerary flexible.

For those with more restrictive schedules,

there are also several fixed events. On 18 April, Independence Day festivities are celebrated around the country with various cultural events, and in late May, Africa Day commemorates past independence struggles all around the continent. On 11 and 12 August, the Zimbabwean military forces are fêted and national heroes – particularly those who were instrumental in the independence movement – are remembered and honoured.

If you're interested in literature and publishing in Zimbabwe and the rest of Africa, don't miss the annual Zimbabwe International Book Fair, which is held in Harare in late July or early August. For further information, see under Books later in this chapter.

Music lovers should try to attend the annual Houses of Stone Music Festival in Harare, which is a celebration of traditional Zimbabwean music. The date moves around every year, but the organisers, Kunzwana Trust, can provide specific information. For contact details, see Music in the Arts section of the Zimbabwe Facts about the Country chapter.

Farmers and agriculture students will want to attend the enormous Zimbabwe Agricultural Society Show, which is held at the showgrounds in Harare around the end of August. In Bulawayo, the big event is the Zimbabwe International Trade Fair held the last week in April or first week in May. It draws at least 1000 exhibitors and 200,000 visitors from around the country and worldwide.

POST & TELECOMMUNICATIONS
Post
In spite of long queues at service windows, the Zimbabwean postal system is generally quite good, especially in larger cities and towns. There are direct flights to and from Australia and Europe and although delays do occur, the system is relatively efficient. Still, it's wise to register anything of value; registration costs only US$0.15 for anything valued under Z$50 and is worth it for the peace of mind. At the time of writing, international postal services were relatively inexpensive; to post a 10-gram airmail letter

to Europe, North America or Australia cost around US$0.25. Domestic letters went for US$0.05. Sending air or surface-mail parcels weighing under two kg is relatively inexpensive if you send them as letters. They go for US$2 each and in fact, it works out cheaper to send five two-kg parcels than one 10 kg parcel. Figure that one out!

When joining a long queue at a post office, check the notice over the window in question. It normally lists services available at that window and also advises when the attendant is scheduled to go to lunch.

Poste restante services are available in all major cities and towns but Harare is probably the best and most efficient. Have mail sent to you c/o Poste Restante, GPO, Inez Terrace, Harare, Zimbabwe. The address for American Express Customer Mail is PO Box 3141, Harare.

For shipping handicraft and artwork, the least expensive air-freight option is Affretair (Zimbabwe's national cargo airline) at Harare International Airport. You must box it up yourself, but they charge just US$3.20 per kg to Europe, North America or Australasia. Another more expensive company, which does the boxing for you, is AirLink (☎ 736783), on the corner of Boshoff Dr and Conald Rd in Graniteside, Harare. For really large items or bulk freight, the best deals are from the consolidators, TNT Express Worldwide (☎ 722129; fax 796689), Caprivi Carriers, Ltd, 100 Central Ave, Harare.

Telephone
The Zimbabwean telephone system may be the butt of jokes but it is improving – or so they say. Local calls are the most notorious. Although there are lots of public telephone boxes, the frequent foul-ups in local services combined with staggeringly crowded party lines generally mean long queues for the phones, especially in Bulawayo and Harare. Local calls cost just a few cents.

Overseas services are considerably better but there are no card phones and no telephone offices where you can book and pay for calls without plugging coins into the box.

ZIMBABWE

Trunk Dialling Codes

The following is a list of commonly-used internal trunk dialling codes (a dash indicates that you'll hear a second dialling tone). Naturally, these codes are unnecessary when making local calls. If you're dialling from outside the country, omit the leading (1).

Arcturus (174)
Beitbridge (186)
Binga & Mlibizi (115)
Bulawayo (19)
Chimanimani (126)
Chinhoyi (167)
Chipinge (127)
Chiredzi (131 or 133–8)
Chirundu (163–7)
Dete & Gwaai River (118)
Figtree (183)
Gweru (154)
Harare (14)
Hwange (181)
Juliasdale & Nyanga (129)
Kadoma (168)
Kariba (161)
Kwe Kwe (155)
Lupane (135)
Makuti (163)
Marondera (122)
Masvingo (139)
Matobo (183)
Mutare & Vumba (120)
Norton & Lake Chivero (162)
Odzi (130)
Plumtree (180)
Ruwa (173)
Shangani (150)
Shurugwi (152)
Victoria Falls (113)

To make an overseas call, you'll either have to phone from a private telephone (be warned that posh hotels charge double or triple the official rates) or carry a large stack of Z$1 coins. Oddly enough, overseas telephone calls are considerably cheaper from rural areas than from cities and towns. Reverse-charge calling is available to a few countries but only from private lines.

The international access code is (110). Calls to Australia, most of Western Europe and North America cost around US$9 for the first three minutes and US$2 for each minute thereafter. To other places, including New Zealand, you'll pay around US$11 for the first three minutes and US$2.50 for each additional minute.

Zimbabwe's country code is (263); if you're calling from outside the country, drop the leading (1) from the internal trunk code. If you're phoning the USA from Zimbabwe, you can get an AT&T USA Direct operator by dialling 110-899.

Fax

Public fax services are available at post offices in larger towns. Within southern Africa, you can send a fax for US$2.50 per A4 sheet. To other countries, you'll pay US$6 for each A4 sheet.

In Harare, the public fax number is (263-4) 731901 and the office is open from 8.30 am to 5 pm Monday to Friday and from 8 to 11.30 am on Saturday. If you wish to receive faxes at this number, advise correspondents to clearly mark your name, contact address and telephone number at the top of the fax. Other public fax numbers include Bulawayo (19) 78053; Gweru (154) 51638; Kadoma (168) 2893; Kwe Kwe (155) 2169; Masvingo (139) 63897; and Mutare (120) 64238.

ELECTRICITY

Electricity is generated at 220V AC, so for use of US appliances you'll need an adaptor. Both round and rectangular three-prong plugs and sockets are in use.

LAUNDRY

All mid-range hotels in Zimbabwe offer laundry services to their guests for very reasonable prices while up-market hotels tend to charge significantly more. If you're camping or staying in hostels, there's a coin-operated laundrette in Harare and commercial laundries/drycleaners in Harare and Bulawayo. Nearly all National Parks' and private campgrounds are equipped with laundry sinks, but you'll need your own universal drain plug.

BOOKS

Compared with most African countries, Zimbabwe offers a range of reading materials and has well-stocked bookshops, but there's nothing like what you'd find even in neighbouring Botswana. Most of the books available are published locally, and foreign imports are expensive. If you need pulpy paperbacks to while away long nights in a tent, bring a few from home or trade with other travellers or at book swaps in Harare and Bulawayo.

Otherwise, you can get acquainted with the local literature, much of which is very good. Quite a few foreign writers and researchers have heard the call of Africa and set about committing it to ink, but recently the Africans themselves are beginning to realise their unique perspective also needs to be heard.

The country's largest popular bookshop chain is government-owned Kingston's, which has outlets of varying quality in most cities and towns. For the largest selection of Zimbabwe-related topics, try the Grass Roots Bookshop in Harare. It's a bit odd – there's an entire wall devoted to Marxism and Leninism – but you'll also find a variety of African literature and many African-perspective works on history, economy, politics, music, languages and the natural history of both Zimbabwe and the entire continent.

If you're interested in the publishing scene in Zimbabwe in particular and Africa in general, try to attend the annual Zimbabwe International Book Fair, which is held in Harare in late July or early August. In Europe, the information address is Zimbabwe International Book Fair, Ltd (☎ (0181) 348 8463; fax (0181) 348 4403), 25 Endymion Rd, London N4 1EE, UK. In Zimbabwe and elsewhere, contact the Zimbabwe International Book Fair Trust (☎ (14) 750282; fax (14) 751202), New Book House, PO Box CY-1179, Causeway, Harare.

History

The word 'introduction' in the title of *An Introduction to the History of Central Africa – Zambia, Malawi, and Zimbabwe* by A J Wills (Oxford University Press, 4th Edition, 1985) is misleading. Although it's a bit disorganised, this 500-page work, generally considered the best work on the history of the region, will probably tell you more than you wanted to know on the subject.

Great Zimbabwe Described & Explained by Peter Garlake (Zimbabwe Publishing House, Harare, 1982) is an attempt at sorting out the history, purpose and architecture of the ancient ruins at Great Zimbabwe.

Mapondera 1840-1904 by D N Beach (Mambo Press, Gweru, 1989) is a biography of Kadungure Mapondera, a descendent of the Changamire and Mutapa dynasties, who resisted settler encroachment into northeastern Zimbabwe.

Mugabe by Colin Simpson & David Smith (Pioneer Head, Salisbury, UK, 1981) is a biography of Robert Mugabe tracing his rise to the office of executive president of Zimbabwe.

The Struggle for Zimbabwe: the Chimurenga War by David Martin & Phyllis Johnson (Faber, London, 1981) is a popular history of the Second Chimurenga which describes in detail the Zimbabwean perspective of the tragic war that led to the country's independence. It is also available in Zimbabwe in an edition published by Zimbabwe Publishing House.

If you're interested in the colonial history of Zimbabwe in particular or Africa in general, look for the biographies and diaries of such figures as Robert Moffat, David Livingstone, Cecil John Rhodes, Frederick Courteney Selous, Leander Starr Jameson, and so on, which should be available at libraries.

Two other titles which may be of interest include *Mapondera: Soldier of Zimbabwe* by Solomon Mutswairo (3 Continents Press, 1978) and *Robert Mugabe of Zimbabwe* by Richard Worth (Messner Julian, 1990).

Literature

There are currently several established and emerging names in Zimbabwean literature whose works are available in the Heinemann African Writers Series, Longman African

Classics and a couple of locally published series. My favourite – and one which shouldn't be missed by any visitor to Zimbabwe – is Tsitsi Dangarembga's *Nervous Conditions*, first published by the Women's Press, London, 1988, and subsequently by the Zimbabwe Publishing House, Harare. Set in eastern Zimbabwe, it's the tale of a young Black woman attending a mission school in 1960s Rhodesia. It's available in the bookshop at the Harare Sheraton.

Also worthwhile are the works of Charles Mungoshi, one of Zimbabwe's first internationally recognised Black writers, who captures the despair and hopelessness of Black Africans in pre-independence Rhodesia masterfully . His most highly acclaimed work is *Coming of the Dry Season*, originally published by the Oxford University Press in 1972 and again by the Zimbabwe Publishing House, Harare, after independence. If you like this one, look for his other works which are published in the Heinemann African Writers' Series. They are available at most Zimbabwe bookshops.

Other Black writers to watch for include Dambudzo Marechera, John Munoye, Ngugi and John Nagenda. The late Stanlake Samkange, whose 1967 book *On Trial for my Country* raised the ghosts of both Lobengula and Cecil John Rhodes, is a favourite. Also, *Bones* by Chenjerai Hove is a highly acclaimed account of a soldier in the Liberation war; it's worthwhile but at times gets a bit cliched.

Doris Lessing, the most widely known serious writer to examine the Rhodesian experience and expose its inequalities, sensitively portrays the country and its people in *The Grass is Singing*, published in the Heinemann African Writers Series in 1973. She's also done two anthologies of African stories, *Sun Between Their Feet* and *This was the Old Chief's Country*, both published in 1979 by Panther Books. During the 1980s and early 1990s, she returned to the country (after being banned for opposition to the Rhodesian government) four times; these trips resulted in *African Laughter* (Harper-Collins, London, 1992), a treatise on the changes observed since independence. She also has a large number of other works to choose from.

Most visitors to Zimbabwe will probably have read at least one novel by Wilbur Smith, who was born in what was Northern Rhodesia (now Zambia) and has written over a score of adventure novels set in southern Africa, past and present. Although they aren't exactly great literature, they are page-turners and great for diversion. Those which take place at least partially in Zimbabwe include *A Falcon Flies*, *Men of Men*, *The Angels Weep*, *Power of the Sword*, *Elephant Song*, *The Leopard Hunts in Darkness* and *A Time to Die*. The last two are currently banned in Zimbabwe mainly because they side with Ndebele factions, expose gruesome realities of the war in Mozambique and speculate in some detail about corruption in the Zimbabwe government.

Travel Guides

Africa Calls Handbook of Zimbabwe by Mark & Hazel Igoe (Roblaw, Harare) is more like an expanded tourist brochure than a guidebook, but it contains some useful information and lots of advertising for tourism-related services. Several spinoffs are also available, including titles on Victoria Falls, Kariba, Manicaland and the Zambezi River. However, some of these haven't been updated for 10 years or more.

Backpacker's Africa – East and Southern edited by Hilary Bradt (Bradt Publications, Chalfont St Peter, 1989) contains a rundown of hiking possibilities in Zimbabwe (and every country from the Sudan to South Africa). Much of the information is dated, but an update should be forthcoming.

Although *Discovery Guide to Zimbabwe* by Melissa Shales (Michael Haag Ltd, London, 1989) is necessarily sparse with information – nearly half of each page is blank – but it's a good general guide to Zimbabwe and includes great coverage of all major attractions. However, it desperately needs an update.

Globetrotter's Zimbabwe by Paul Tingay

(New Holland, London, 1994) is a pocket-sized mini-guide containing lots of great photos and essential information. It would be excellent for package tour or fly/drive travellers who may want concise background reading or an extra 'information edge'

As its name would imply, *Guide to Southern African Safari Lodges*, by Peter Joyce (Struik Publishers, Cape Town, 1991), provides a detailed rundown of most National Parks' camps and private safari lodges in Zimbabwe, as well as the Republic of South Africa, Namibia, Botswana and Zambia.

A good general background and a rundown of sights is contained in *Spectrum Guide to Zimbabwe* by Camerapix (Moorland Publishing, UK 1993) and it is packed with enticing colour photos. It's especially useful for planning your trip, but beware – some of the prose is excruciating and occasionally lapses into flights of fancy.

If you read German, the worthwhile volume *Zimbabwe* by Astrid & Marcus Cornaro (DuMont Büchverlag, Köln, Germany, 1991), is full of background information on the history, arts, culture, sights, wildlife and landscape of Zimbabwe. Because the series emphasises background information, practical treatment is thin.

Zimbabwe & Botswana – the Rough Guide by Barbara McRae & Tony Pinchuck (Penguin, London, 1990) is quite solidly researched, but it certainly could lighten up a bit politically.

Language

Several English-Shona and English-Ndebele dictionaries are sold in Zimbabwe bookshops. If you want to pick up a bit of Shona, the pamphlet-sized book *Fambai Zvakanaka mu Zimbabwe – Have a Nice Trip in Zimbabwe* offers some basic grammar and vocabulary. It's available only in Zimbabwe.

Art & Music

Images of Power – Understanding Bushman Rock Art by David Lewis-Williams (Thomas Dawson, 1987) is a comprehensive examination of rock art sites in southern Africa and educated speculation about their history and meaning.

Life in Stone by Oliver Sultan (Baobab Books, Harare, 1992) outlines the 15 top-rated Zimbabwean sculptors, with a short biography of each, and brilliant black and white photos.

Making Music – Musical Instruments in Zimbabwe Past & Present by Claire Jones – outlines teaching, playing and construction of indigenous Zimbabwean musical instruments. It's available from *Dandemutande* in the USA; see under Music in the Zimbabwe Facts about the Country chapter.

The Material Culture of Zimbabwe by H Ellert (Longman Zimbabwe, Harare, 1984) is the most complete coverage of all aspects of Zimbabwe's material crafts cultures, both ancient and modern, including weapons, musical instruments, tools, pottery, jewellery, basketry and so on.

The Painted Caves – An Introduction to the Prehistoric Art of Zimbabwe by Peter Garlake (Modus Publications, Harare, 1987) contains explanations and locations of major prehistoric rock art sites in Zimbabwe. This is an essential companion for anyone searching out Zimbabwe's prehistoric art works.

Roots Rocking in Zimbabwe by Fred Zindi (Mambo Press, Gweru, 1985) provides good coverage of Zimbabwe's pop-music scene including background information on the music itself and data on all the major players.

Serima by Albert B Plangger (Mambo Press, Gweru, 1974) is a history and outline of the beautiful Serima Mission near Masvingo and its modern sculpture and woodcarving traditions.

Although the photographs in *Shona Sculpture* by F Mor (Jongwe, Harare, 1987) are superb, the text seems utterly inaccessible, and particularly heavy on artsy hyperbole. Maybe I'm just out of touch.

The Soul of Mbira – Music & Traditions of the Shona People of Zimbabwe by Paul F Berliner is a scholarly treatise on the mbira and marimba musicians of Zimbabwe and includes an appendix with instructions on how to build and play an mbira (thumb piano). The book is available through *Dan-*

demutande (see under Music in the Zimbabwe Facts about the Country chapter).

Other Books

A Concise Encyclopaedia of Zimbabwe edited by Denis Berens (Mambo Press, Harare, 1988) isn't exactly comprehensive, but any historical event that may be of interest is covered in this collection of information snippets. It also includes entries on government, politics, religion, climate, wildlife etc. It's occasionally sold at Kingston's.

MAPS

City plans of larger towns are available at Publicity Associations (municipal tourist offices), but maps of other towns are more difficult to come by. Some Publicity Associations sell photocopied national parks maps (most of which were produced by Shell Oil in the 1960s). If you're spending time in Harare, you may want to look for the detailed *Greater Harare Street Guide*, an atlas of large-scale maps of all the suburbs. It was once sold by the Harare Publicity Association, but now appears to be out of print. You may be able to scare up a copy somewhere. A similar Bulawayo atlas remains in print and is sold by the Bulawayo Publicity Association.

The colourful national map which was once distributed by publicity associations is now available only sporadically. In any case, it doesn't contain much detail, especially on minor routes, but would probably include enough for most visitors.

The best available national map is *Zimbabwe Relief, 1:1,000,000*, published by the Surveyor General (☎ 794545) in Electra House on Samora Machel Ave, Harare and sold for US$5. It depicts relief using colour and includes thorough coverage of railroads, mines, rural missions, hydrography and roads, right down to very minor country tracks.

The Surveyor General also sells 1:50,000 ordnance survey topographic maps, covering the entire country, for US$2.50 per sheet, and a range of thematic maps. These include

---

City & Town Name Changes

Since independence in 1980, the Zimbabwe government has attempted to rid the country of the nomenclature bestowed upon it by the colonial power. City names were the first to change and in 1990, they really got down to business and began changing names of streets, dams, parks, rivers, military installations and anything else with a colonial-sounding name. Ironically Rhodes-like, Robert Mugabe's name crops up on street signposts with some frequency. The following is a list of city name changes. Street name changes are included under the individual cities.

Old Name	New Name
Balla Balla	Mbalabala
Belingwe	Mberengwa
Bulalima-Mangwe	Bulilima-Mangwe
Chipinga	Chipinge
Dett	Dete
Enkeldoorn	Chivhu
Essexvale	Esigodini
Fort Victoria	Masvingo
Gatooma	Kadoma
Gwelo	Gweru
Hartley	Chegutu
Ingezi	Ngezi
Inyanga	Nyanga
Inyazura	Nyazura
Mangula	Mhangura
Marandellas	Marondera
Mashaba	Mashava
Matepatepa	Mutepatepa
Mazoe	Mazowe
Melsetter	Chimanimani
Miami	Wami
Mrewa	Murewa
Mtok	Mutoko
Nkai	Nkayi
Nuanetsi	Mwenezi
Que Que	KweKwe
Salisbury	Harare
Selukwe	Shurugwi
Shabani	Zvishavane
Sinoia	Chinhoyi
Sipolilo	Guruve
Somabula	Somabhula
Tjolotjo	Tsholotsho
Umniati	Munyati
Umtali	Mutare
Umvukwes	Mvurwi
Umvuma	Mvuma
Urungue	Hurungwe
Vila Salazar	Sango
Wankie	Hwange

Facts for the Visitor 145

some national parks maps ranging from US$2 to US$4 and a large-scale Harare street plan at 1:15,000 for US$2.50. The salesperson may ask to check your ID when purchasing maps but usually they only want your name and home address on the chit. For a catalogue, write to PO Box 8099, Causeway, Harare, Zimbabwe.

Occasionally, you'll find the updated version (ie with town-name changes) of the old Shell Oil maps. On one side is a fairly good road map of the country. The reverse side includes larger scale insets of areas of tourist interest. An even better map (which nevertheless does contain a few printing oddities) is the Automobile Association's *AA Tourist Map of Zimbabwe* at a scale of 1:1,800,000. The reverse side has insets of the most popular national parks. It's available at tourist shops or directly through the AA (see under Useful Organisations in this chapter) for less than US$2.

Finally, there's the *Mini-map of Zimbabwe* published in South Africa by Map Studio. This compact little map depicts the country at a scale of 1:2,000,000, and also includes inset maps of national parks and street plans of Harare and Bulawayo. It costs around US$4, but is unfortunately hard to find in Zimbabwe itself. To order, contact the publisher directly: Map Studio, PO Box 624, Wynberg 2012, the Republic of South Africa (☎ (11) 444 9473)

A decent road map covering the entire region is *Michelin #955 Central and Southern Africa*. It's available internationally.

MEDIA
Newspapers & Magazines
The two daily papers published in Zimbabwe – the Bulawayo *Chronicle* and the Harare *Herald* – are both long on local, national and especially sports news; international events get short shrift. The Friday *Financial Gazette* offers a modicum of outside news but the best source of information about world events will probably be *Time* and *Newsweek*, both of which are available from street vendors (check the dates before buying) and bookshops in Harare and Bulawayo. Hotel gift shops often stock international newspapers as well.

The Catholic monthly magazine *Moto*, published by Mambo Press, is probably the most interesting of Zimbabwe's periodicals and covers national, cultural and political issues. It was first published in 1959 and became a weekly newspaper in 1971. *Moto* was banned by the Smith government in 1974 but resurfaced to become one of the most influential pre-independence influences on the Black population.

Africa Calls Worldwide, a travel and general-interest magazine published in Harare, offers some light reading about sights, arts, dining, wildlife and other tourism-related issues. It's published bimonthly and is available internationally by subscription. For further information, contact Africa Calls Worldwide (☎ (14) 704715), 6th floor, Islip House, on the corner of Samora Machel Ave and Park St, PO Box 2677, Harare.

Another interesting publication – at least for the travel industry – is *Zimbabwe Travel News* (☎ (14) 752125; fax (14) 751802), 6th floor, Memorial Building, Samora Machel Ave, PO Box 4128, Harare. The alternative address is Tourism in Print, 4th floor, Grosvenor Crescent, London SW1X 7EE, UK. It's good for keeping up with the latest tourism developments, but is expensive (US$57 per year in Europe) and makes a rather corporate meal of things.

The excellent tourist newspaper *The Travellers Times* (☎ (14) 729505) is published monthly and distributed free via hotels, lodges, travel agents and tour operators. The annual subscription rate of US$3.50 for 12 issues covers the cost of overseas postage only. For information, contact Travellers Times (☎ (14) 794737); fax (14) 727080), 148 Baker Ave (near 7th St) Private Bag 7402, Chisipite, Harare.

Radio & TV
Radio and television broadcasting are overseen by ZBC, the Zimbabwe Broadcasting Corporation. There are currently two television stations and four radio stations in

ZIMBABWE

Zimbabwe. TV 2 and Radio 4 are funded by the government; both are commercial-free and education-oriented. Radio 1 broadcasts interviews in English and emphasises classical music. Radio 2 focuses on African music and broadcasts primarily in Shona but also in Ndebele. Radio 3 broadcasts mainly in English and plays popular top 40-style music.

BBC World Service broadcasts four times daily. For specific times and frequencies, contact the BBC African Service bureau (☎ 793961) on the 4th floor of Frankel House, 2nd St, Harare. The Voice of America is also broadcast twice daily. With ideal atmospheric conditions and a good receiver, you can also pick up Radio Australia's South East & North Asian service.

HEALTH

This section includes information on health services specific to Zimbabwe. For a general rundown on keeping healthy in southern Africa, refer to the Health section in the regional Facts for the Visitor chapter at the beginning of the book.

Medical services in Zimbabwe are generally quite good, and both Harare and Bulawayo have excellent general hospitals. However, for potentially serious problems or complications, it's probably best to arrange to go home, or at least get to Johannesburg, which offers a full range of medical services.

In hospitals and private clinics, medical equipment is well sterilised and blood products are carefully screened, so despite the proliferation of HIV/AIDS in Zimbabwe, there's little chance of infections from needles or transfusions. However, bush clinics operate on much stricter budgets and proper equipment may not always be available, especially in emergency situations. To ease any concerns, you may want to carry a couple of sterile syringes; see Predeparture Preparations in the Health section at the beginning of the book.

The emergency telephone number around the country is (☎ 99). If a medical emergency arises while you're on safari in the bush, you're likely to be treated or evacuated by the very efficient Medical Air Rescue Service (☎ 734513; fax 735517) on Elcombe Ave in the Belgravia suburb of Harare. Ascertain whether your safari operator subscribes to this service, and if you have a specific medical condition which may present problems – diabetes, epilepsy, a heart condition, bee-sting allergy etc – be sure to advise the operator at the time of booking. Independent travellers can purchase insurance against evacuation costs directly from the Medical Air Rescue Service for a nominal fee. However, remember that if something does go wrong, you'll have to get to a phone or radio to alert them of the problem.

Pharmacies and chemists are found in all major towns, but unlike those in many African countries, they will not dispense medicines and drugs without a doctor's prescription. Zimbabwe is also blessed with an outstanding natural pharmacopoeia and to take advantage of it, a homoeopathic medicine shop, The Herbalist, has opened in First Street Mall in Harare, near the corner of Jason Moyo Ave. Here you'll find everything from sausage tree (*Kigelia africana*) cream, which is used as a remedy for skin cancer, to natural sunblocks made from extracts of sausage tree cream, Zimbabwean aloes (*Aloe excelsa*) and lavendar trees (*Heteropyxis dehniae*).

DANGERS & ANNOYANCES
Con Artists & Scams

Operating mainly in Harare and to a lesser extent in Bulawayo and Victoria Falls, adept con artists take tourists for staggering amounts of money and often the victims don't even realise they've been conned. There are countless fabricated sob stories, all tailored to separate you from some of your cash. But there's no call for paranoia; just remain alert and you'll avoid the worst of it.

Scams are often fairly innocuous. If someone approaches you claiming to be hungry (they know this one is difficult to ignore), rather than giving money, perhaps offer to buy them some inexpensive food item or direct them to one of the church missions that dispense free meals to anyone in need.

There are also characters running around with notes, ostensibly from the Ministry of Health, stating that the bearer is mentally indigent (or some such thing) and therefore dependent upon public generosity for support. This is all rubbish, of course, and only foreigners are approached.

Also rife are 'sponsorship scams', and some Zimbabweans are becoming expert and inventive. Someone will approach you requesting donations for one good cause or another – anything from their school building fund to a kidney transplant for their grandmother. There's a one-armed fellow in Harare who appears 100% legit, but in fact, he's been soliciting funds for a new arm for at least 17 years (this comes from a traveller who'd met him on two occasions, 17 years apart). Contributors sign an official-looking sponsorship form and fill in the amount donated. They are lavished with smiles and effusive thanks, then they stroll away wishing they'd been able to donate more. This guy has collected so much money that he should resemble a tantric deity by now!

The advice is simple: don't fall for ridiculous stories, don't add your name to the bottom of a list of Z$100 donations and never reach for your money when there are several people crowding around you. Many thieves simply want to see where your money is kept so they can grab it.

Other people approach total strangers – always foreigners – and ask them to loan their watch, camera etc for one reason or another, arranging a date and time to meet for the return of the loaned goods. Anyone who falls for this one probably deserves to lose their belongings.

Another scam involves betting. Foreigners are invited for an informal game of cards, or billiards or whatever. One instigator suggests a 'friendly bet' and teams up with the foreigner who is then entrusted to hold winnings and temporarily make good the losses for their team so the game can progress smoothly. There seem to be a lot of losses for the befuddled foreigner's team – but the

foreigner chalks that up to being unfamiliar with the rules. At some point, the foreigner's team mate will count up wins and losses, ostensibly to pay the team's fair share of the debt. Once the cash is in hand, all the instigators split, leaving the foreigner feeling very stupid indeed.

More sinister scams are thankfully not so common. Sometimes, someone may claim to have seen you smoking dope or changing money illegally or whatever and threaten to report the incident to the police. Don't panic. Sometimes, this ploy is merely used to distract you from your belongings momentarily. At other times, especially if you are guilty of whatever infractions they're alleging, it's simply attempted extortion.

Theft

In addition to the previously mentioned scams, which give the alert victim a fighting chance, theft and mugging are also concerns. As a result of the recent drought in Zimbabwe, many subsistence farmers migrated to the cities in search of employment. However, most lacked marketable skills and few were successful. Some took to hawking fruit and other goods in the city centres, but many were recruited into crime gangs organised by a particularly insidious Nigerian mafia, which moved in when they saw an exploitable opportunity. The resulting crime wave has left Harare streets much less secure than they were just a few years ago. When the country's reputation began to slide in tourism circles, extra police were hired to patrol city centres by day. At night, however, they're still dangerous.

The warning should be obvious: don't walk around at night in the cities. Even by day, avoid small groups of youths loitering outside hotels; they're invariably pickpockets, and foreigners are prime targets. When you're out and about, have loose change handy for small purchases, but never pull out a stash of cash in the streets.

Places which warrant special caution, particularly at night, are bus terminals, crowded discos and the big parks in Harare and Bulawayo. Campgrounds and caravan parks have guards posted to watch over campers' belongings but occasionally things do go missing, so it's not a good idea to leave valuables in your tent. If you have a car, don't leave tempting items anywhere in sight while you're away from it.

Another problem in Harare involves taxi drivers who drop clients far enough from their door to allow accomplices to attack with knives. The drivers then receive a share of the booty. Before you climb into a taxi, always note the number plate and, especially at night, insist on being dropped right at your door.

The following letter is from an older woman traveller from New Zealand, who had problems in a notorious part of Harare:

I travel lightly, with a medium-sized pack and sand shoes, believing it's best not to appear ostentatious and not too affluent. As it was, I was mugged in Harare (but not harmed), and they got away with my valuables. I want to warn all travellers to be on the lookout for such attacks in Harare. Practically every tourist I spoke to afterwards had some story of a successful bag-snatching or of being brushed by a pickpocket.

Men, with their more obvious breast and hip pockets are most at risk from the latter. I strongly advise people not to wear those conspicuous belly pouches on which every eye focuses, but to use the flat money belts which are hidden by clothing.

My attack happened as I was crossing the city at 6 pm on a Sunday, from the bus station to the Selous Hotel. I know everyone is warned not to walk around at night; later, I tried to be off the streets by 5 pm, but at that time, I didn't really consider 6 pm to be night, although it was dusk and dark falls suddenly.

Only a few doors from the hotel, two men came up swiftly behind me, put me out of action with an arm around the neck, grabbed my money belt and ran off. Although I yelled, none of the many bystanders did anything but make sympathetic clucking noises. Thankfully it happened very quickly and at no time did I have to fear they were interested in anything but my valuables.

I reported it to the local police immediately, but they took a long time to arrive and I didn't feel they could have done anything helpful. Most importantly, I got a statement of what had been lost, which was confirmed by a trip to the central police station the following day – an important point to remember.

Thankfully, Harare is a small city, because the next day, I had to foot it around, trying to replace my lost passport, travellers' cheques, cash dollars and air tickets. After I replaced my passport, the New Zealand

High Commission phoned and said my old passport had been found abandoned and handed in. True to their advertised word, American Express replaced all my travellers' cheques because I had the serial numbers safely stored away in my pack, and British Airways wrote me another ticket, although there was a charge of Z$149. This and the US$200 stolen were later replaced through the budget travellers' insurance I had taken out, so apart from the shock and inconvenience, the experience wasn't that bad.

But, from the numbers of reports of problems in Harare, I learned several things. Don't think Sunday is a safe day, watch for groups of young men who may try to surround you, carry only necessary cash and documents and leave the rest in the hotel security safe – not locked in your room.

A traveller, New Zealand

Beware especially when you're climbing into a bus or emergency taxi. Thieves often work in teams. Two pretend to be getting into the vehicle but are really just blocking the way for anyone else trying to get in. Meanwhile, the pickpocket is in the crowd, going through your pockets or bags. There are also people who will start a conversation with you, perhaps attempting to sell you something, and suddenly, there's one on either side of you. This is when you must be most alert.

Mrs W Selles, Netherlands

Racism

Although Zimbabwe has been independent for some time now, visitors will notice that racism based on skin colour and tribal origin still exists, and the fact that the country is governed by the Shona majority has had little effect on old habits. It is tempting to sweep the issue under the rug and present Zimbabwe in the image its tourist industry would most appreciate – that it's a free country where all races and tribes are treated equally – but that's simply not the case.

The situation is not, as many foreigners are conditioned to believe by the Western media, merely an issue of Black and White. Although the economic disparity between those of European and African origin is more obvious and exploitation of inexpensive labour is still a problem, the long-standing animosity between the majority Shona and the minority Ndebele is just as serious and has caused untold grief.

In this Zimbabwe section, efforts will be made to present things as they are, or at least as they appear to be. No offence is intended towards anyone.

Police & Military

Compared to most African countries, Zimbabwe's police and military presence is neither obvious nor intimidating. Drivers may be asked for food or money at routine roadblocks. If you offer something, you'll get a smile and thanks; if not, the officers normally tell you to have a nice day and wave you on.

The Zimbabwe military wear green soldierly uniforms and are easily recognisable – they'll often be carrying an automatic weapon. The police normally wear khaki – long trousers in the winter and shorts in the summer – with peaked caps. Traffic police wear all-grey uniforms. Other units wear grey shirts and blue trousers or all-blue uniforms with white caps.

Most police are both friendly and courteous and problems are very rare; should you encounter an officer behaving in an unprofessional manner, note their name and ID number. If the offence is serious, it should be reported to the Public Relations Officer at the Central Police Station in Harare.

Land Mines

Those intending to travel in the eastern highlands of Zimbabwe, particularly around Mutare and Chimanimani National Park, should note that there is danger of encountering land mines and unexploded ordnance in the area.

The mines were planted along the border both by Renamo rebels from Mozambique and by the Zimbabwe military in the hope of discouraging cross-border forays during the height of guerrilla activity in Mozambique. Some ordnance may even date back to the Second Chimurenga. Despite efforts by the Zimbabwe authorities to remove the devices, it is generally believed that mines still exist in considerable numbers, since they are regularly detonated by wild animals. The well-publicised 1989 fatality near Skeleton Pass in Chimanimani National Park should

provide sufficient warning to hikers tempted to wander off marked tracks.

If you do find yourself away from well-trodden areas, be wary of earth that appears to have been disturbed, don't touch anything vaguely resembling weaponry, and tread as lightly as possible.

WORK

Although it isn't impossible to secure permission to work in Zimbabwe, neither is it easy and officials definitely prefer that intending workers organise the permit in their home country. If you've simply run out of money, however, and have a skill that is in demand, you may be able to convince them that your case warrants hardship considerations (however, bear in mind that advising them of such a situation will also qualify you for deportation). At this stage, your best bet is to seek out an employer, secure a solid job offer, and then set about arranging a permit with the prospective employer's help.

Upper or A-level teachers, especially science teachers, engineers, computer experts and medical personnel, will have the most luck. Professions for which there are sufficient qualified Zimbabwean citizens such as nurses or primary teachers will have less chance of being granted a permit.

Currently, teachers in Zimbabwe are permitted to teach up to the level they have completed. A university degree and/or education certificate are not necessary to teach A level courses, but those so qualified will command a higher starting salary than those who've completed only A levels. If you're really committed to teaching in Zimbabwe and are prepared for a challenge, you can improve your chances of success by requesting a posting in a rural area.

Wages in Zimbabwe are very low by European, North American or Australasian standards and salaries are paid only in Zimbabwe dollars. With special permission, some people are allowed to export up to one-third of their salaries. Otherwise you're subject to the same currency controls as Zimbabwean citizens (see Money). Also, be

ZIMBABWE

aware that the system doesn't work as smoothly as it could; government employees, including teachers, sometimes wait months for a pay cheque. The normal teaching contracts are negotiated for an extendible two years.

Private colleges pay better than government schools (usually about twice the salary), but require teachers to hold at least a four-year degree. The two best colleges in Harare are Speciss College on Herbert Chitepo Ave and ILSA Independent College on Fife Ave. Paid leave at both government and private schools amounts to about four months annually.

Applications for permanent residence or work permits must be accompanied by a doctor's certificate stating the applicant has had a recent chest x-ray and shows no evidence of tuberculosis or other serious illnesses.

HIGHLIGHTS

Zimbabwe has a lot to offer and to enjoy it thoroughly will require more time than most travellers allow. If you're in a real hurry, visits to a few outstanding places and experiences can provide a sampling of the best Zimbabwe has to offer. If you must keep to a rigid itinerary, you may want to include some of the following:

Victoria Falls Zimbabwe's number one attraction, Victoria Falls is included on most whirlwind Africa tours so the tourist district can get crowded, but the falls themselves remain lovely and unspoilt.

Hwange National Park Hwange is the most accessible of Zimbabwe's wildlife parks and offers the greatest variety and concentration of wildlife. It nevertheless remains relatively uncrowded and offers accommodation for all budgets.

Great Zimbabwe Ruins The former capital of Great Zimbabwe is sub-Saharan Africa's greatest archaeological site. It's also a serene place to relax for a few days of camping and exploring.

Chimanimani National Park Chimanimani contains Zimbabwe's wildest and most rugged mountain wilderness. There are no roads in the park but lots of hiking tracks offer the best bushwalking country in Zimbabwe.

Matobo National Park The kopje-studded terrain and weird balancing rocks of the Matobo Hills near Bulawayo shelter hundreds of caves and rock paintings. The park is also the best place in the world to see white rhinos.

Mana Pools National Park More remote than Hwange, Mana Pools is one park where visitors are permitted to strike out alone on foot. Since access is awkward, most travellers arrive by canoe safari along the Zambezi River.

Nyanga National Park The 'civilised' mountain country of Nyanga and the wilderness of adjoining Mtarazi Falls National Park make this area *the* highland escape for affluent Harare dwellers.

Lake Kariba Few visitors are overwhelmed by Kariba but Zimbabweans seem to believe it's paradise on earth so who can argue? Around the lake there's good fishing, boating, game viewing and camping.

Vumba The forests and botanical gardens of Vumba offer good day-walking opportunities and far-ranging vistas across nearby Mozambique.

Domboshawa & Ngomakurira Both these sites, just 30 km from Harare, offer good hiking over beautiful lichen-covered domes as well as the opportunity to see lots of rock paintings.

Bulawayo Museum of Natural History If you have an interest in geology, palaeontology, anthropology, zoology or history, don't miss this, by far the best of Zimbabwe's museums. It's worth an all-day ramble through and the surrounding gardens are good for lounging and allowing the information to filter in.

Mzilikazi Arts & Crafts Centre This practical art centre just outside Bulawayo reveals the scope and amount of artistic talent to be found in Zimbabwe. Some of their pieces are repetitious, although much of the work is positively inspired.

ACCOMMODATION

In Zimbabwe, the pace of life is considerably more casual than in Europe or North America – perhaps that's why it's so appealing – but unless you're prepared to pay for five stars, a holiday will be most enjoyable if you take a *laissez-faire* attitude towards accommodation and service. Most visitors to Zimbabwe are pleasantly surprised at the juxtaposition of pleasant standards and reasonable prices.

Happily, the country is also becoming more accommodation-friendly for budget travellers. In addition to all the National Parks' facilities and municipal caravan parks, there is a growing number of backpackers' hostels and B&B places, so those without tents are no longer relegated to the quirky youth hostels and back street brothel hotels.

In all cases – except at the budget hostels and B&B – foreigners are required to pay in foreign currency. Travellers have found that when making their calculations, some hotels offer very poor deals.

On several occasions, we found that the rates offered by hotels were lower than those in the banks. When we enquired about this, it was often explained away as a mistake and a rate closer to (although not the same as) the bank rate would be suggested. Always double check hotel arithmetic!

Andrew Bryceson, UK

Camping

All larger cities and towns have well-maintained caravan parks with space for both caravans and tent camping. Most are exceptionally clean, and all offer toilet and bath facilities. Some even have showers, and at the most popular ones there's an attendant on duty 24 hours a day, so your belongings are reasonably secure when left inside your tent.

At National Parks' and Recreation Area campgrounds, you'll find braai pits, hot showers and sometimes specially planted grassy areas for tent camping. At Hwange Main Camp, however, they seem to have got it backwards – caravans are allotted the big grassy lawn areas while tents may only be erected in cement-like earth. Bring tent pegs that are up to the challenge. Even when it's disguised by grass, the typically cast-iron terra firma tends to resist the wimpy aluminium or fibreglass sorts.

For foreigners, National Parks' camp sites with toilets and baths cost US$2.50 per person for tent campers and US$4 per person in caravans. Large exclusive camp sites, accommodating parties of up to 12 people, exist in all wildlife-oriented parks and cost US$62 per night. Fishing camps in Gonarezhou and Zambezi National Parks cost US$21 for up to 12 people. Most of these are equipped with braai pits and long-drop toilets, although some have running water, flush toilets and showers. For infor-

mation on booking camp sites and on National Parks' cottages, chalets and lodges, see National Parks' Accommodation later in this section.

Camping in rural areas or communal lands is often prohibited and generally discouraged. However, if you are caught without accommodation, you should secure permission from property owners or villagers before setting up camp.

Hostels

Harare and Bulawayo each have a youth hostel but they're somewhat dilapidated and are characterised by distinctly Rhodesian attitudes. Alternative budget accommodation includes private homes which have been converted into dormitory-style accommodation. If they're full, you'll often be given the option to sleep on the floor or wherever until space becomes available. Although such establishments are completely above board, the police like to keep an eye on them.

B&Bs

Although it's just getting off the ground, Zimbabwe has started an association of home and farm-stay B&Bs. For the latest listings and information, phone or visit Bed & Breakfast (☎ 724331), 161 2nd St Extension, Harare.

Hotels

If you want a quiet place to crash, the cheapest hotels are probably best avoided. Their regular patrons are normally more interested in sex and swill than in sleep, so the noise level remains fairly constant. Not only could snoozing prove difficult, you may experience misunderstandings with the personal services squads, so be warned.

Middle-range accommodation is comfortable, adequate and in most cases, reasonably priced. Middle to upper-range hotels are rated on a zero to five-star scale based on an elaborate points system for service, cleanliness and amenities. Most mid-range hotels have either one or two stars and will average US$15 to US$30 for a double room. Three-star hotels will range from US$25 to US$50

ZIMBABWE

The Three-Tier Pricing System

In the days when the government controlled hotel rates, hoteliers' applications for price increases were often rejected and hotel owners were faced with increasing overheads but limited income. The solution, which was approved by the government, was to charge overseas guests in hard foreign currency. Somehow, this evolved into a three-tier pricing system in which overseas guests pay European-level rates.

Although price controls are no longer in place, most safari lodges and some four and five-star hotels (Zimbabwe Sun Hotels, Rainbow Hotels, Meikles, Sheraton and Holiday Inn, among others) cling to this system. Foreign rates can be up to two or three times those paid by Zimbabwe residents. 'Regional' guests (including South Africans) get marginal discounts off the foreign rates. The Cresta Hotels group, however, has abandoned this practice; for this standard of accommodation, they offer foreigners the best value for money in the region and they should be heartily applauded.

Over the past couple of years, this issue has been a matter of heated contention and debate. Although some travellers may feel guilty about their relatively high incomes and happily pay the higher rates, you may want to consider several things. First, many companies charging multi-tier rates are owned by foreign corporations, so most of the profits are soaked out of the country.

Second, you can be certain that the Zimbabwean resident rates are not below the cost value of the accommodation; that is, no one is making a loss on the local rates.

Third, no tax dollars are contributed towards the support of these businesses, which might entitle local taxpayers to a discount (in theory, that's the rationale behind the two-tier National Parks' fees, although it's not quite that simple since the fees don't actually go towards National Parks' maintenance).

Fourth, foreigners don't inherently consume more goods or services than locals do, necessitating a higher tariff (although in the case of some safari lodges, the higher rates do include activities not available on the local rate, such as game drives).

Lastly – and perhaps most importantly – overhead costs in Zimbabwe are commensurate with the local economy, and the staff are paid the same typically low wages (by European standards, anyway), whether they're serving foreigners or locals. Unless staff salaries are brought into line with those of their European counterparts, there's little justification for charging European-level rates. ∎

for a double. In some four and five-star hotels, foreigners pay a higher rate – as much as 120% more – than Zimbabwe residents.

Game Ranches

The most rapidly growing accommodation sector in Zimbabwe comprises private game ranches. Most are owned by White Zimbabweans, and they represent a large and prospering business. Former commercial farms and cattle ranches are being given over to bushland, and are being stocked with wildlife. Some of this is for the enjoyment of visitors and some is to breed and sell on to other game ranches.

Many of these ranches are also used as hunting reserves and the accommodation is incidental to the hunting trip. In others, the emphasis is on wildlife viewing and photography, and the quality of accommodation and

catering are likely to be drawing cards. The pro-hunting crowd maintains that the income derived from their activities demonstrates to local people that there is money in wildlife conservation. At any rate, if you have any problems with hunting, before you book a visit to a game ranch, be sure to ascertain its orientation.

Pricewise, game ranches are not generally budget options, although several have recognised the budget market and opened up camping areas or basic inexpensive cottages. For further information or bookings, contact Zimbabwe Safari Farms (☎ 733573), PO Box 592, Harare.

National Parks Accommodation

Zimbabwe's National Parks are relatively well organised, with over 250 chalets, cottages and lodges as well as well-appointed camp sites. Chalets, the most basic accommodation option, provide furniture, fridges, cooking implements (but no crockery or cutlery), bedding, towels and lighting. Cooking is done outside the main unit and amenities are communal. Cottages add both kitchens and private baths. The lodges are fully self-contained and serviced by National Parks staff. All three types offer one or two-bedroom units with two beds per room. Hwange, Matusadona, Mana Pools and other parks also offer exclusive camps which accommodate varying numbers of people.

Bookings are essential for National Parks accommodation and camp sites, but the current reservation system isn't exactly a well-oiled machine, so book early and hang onto your receipt. If they tell you everything is full, don't despair; the reservation system accepts bookings without payment and there are lots of no-shows. The catch is that you must wait until 5.30 pm on the day you wish to stay, so have an alternative plan in case you are turned away. The following letter, which outlines a typical experience with the system, well illustrates what you can expect:

The National Parks Central Reservations booking system for the parks lodges is the most disastrous booking system I've ever come across. Both Hwange Main Camp and Sinamatella, and also Zambezi National Park were practically deserted in May/early June, yet I saw people being told they were full, both in Harare and on site...

You can only book centrally in Harare (or Bulawayo). I tried to book but everything in Hwange and Zambezi National Parks was fully reserved months in advance. People can book and not pay, or they can book and pay and not turn up (it's so cheap). The camps themselves don't know until 5.30 pm whether a chalet/cottage/lodge will be taken or available, so no booking means you have to hang around till then. If you want to stay more than one night, you must check out every day and wait. Unless you ring Harare, of course. One Australian couple we met spent 2½ hours at Hwange Main Camp reception trying to phone Harare – and failed.

On three occasions at Zambezi, we were told all accommodation was full – that all 19 lodges were paid for and everyone had turned up. Each time I checked the registration book and there were only two or three signatures. Each time, after 10 to 15 minutes of persistence we were given a lodge. Persistence sometimes pays off.

Catherine Webster, UK

Bookings for National Parks accommodation are most reliably made through the Central Booking Office (☎ 706077), National Botanical Gardens, on the corner of Borrowdale Rd and Sandringham Dr, PO Box 8151, Harare, or the Bulawayo Booking Agency (☎ 63646), 140A Fife St, PO Box 2283, Bulawayo. Both offices are open Monday to Friday 7.45 am to 4.15 pm. Bookings are available up to six months in advance.

Fees for admission, camp sites and cottages are standardised, and foreigners must pay double the advertised rates (all rates given in this section are those for foreigners). Day entry costs US$1.30 (except Victoria Falls, which costs US$3) and seven-day entry permits cost US$5. Tent sites are US$2.50 per person and caravan sites, US$4 per person; exclusive camps accommodating up to 12 people cost US$62 and basic fishing camps are US$21. Lukosi hunting camp in Hwange National Park is US$129.

Basic one/two-bedroom chalets with shared facilities cost US$10/20.50; one/two-bedroom cottages with en suite bathrooms cost US$13/26 and fully-equipped one/two bedroom lodges cost US$15.50/31 (except those at Mana Pools, which are double this rate). The ridiculously overpriced hut at Chimanimani National Park is US$8 per person.

If you've paid for accommodation and can't arrive before 5.30 pm, phone and inform the attendant or you'll forfeit the booking and the money.

FOOD

Zimbabwean cuisine, the legacy of bland British fare combined with normally stodgy African dishes, makes for some pretty ordinary eating. The dietary staple is sadza – the white maize meal porridge upon which nearly all meals are built. The second component is meat (or nyama – sadza with meat gravy is known as sadza ne nyama) which is both plentiful and inexpensive.

Fruits and vegetables are limited but what's available is quite good. Gem squash, a type of marrow, is delicious and popular.

Tomatoes, cucumbers, maize, pumpkins, courgettes (zucchini), and tropical fruits such as papayas, mangoes and bananas are also inexpensive and plentiful.

Zimbabwe is one of the world's great producers of beef, which is available nearly everywhere. Chicken is also a staple and on occasion, game meat, including kudu, crocodile and impala, is available. In the rural communal lands, people eat lots of goat and mutton.

The most popular domestic fish include bream from Lake Kariba, which is available only occasionally, and the anchovy-like dried *kapenta (Limnothrissa mioda)*, also from Kariba. Trout is a speciality in the eastern highlands and is superb. Until just a couple of years ago, heavy import restrictions meant that it was practically impossible to find any other sort of fish or seafood in Zimbabwe, apart from some very expensive – and smuggled – Mozambican prawns. Now, the market has opened right up and you'll find seafood from all over southern Africa.

Normally anonymous dried meat or *biltong*, which can be anything from beef to kudu or ostrich, is usually delicious and makes a great snack. It can be deceptively salty so don't eat too much unless you have lots of water handy.

Buffets
For those with hearty appetites who aren't on the strictest of budgets, nothing can beat the hotel buffets for value. For breakfast, you can get unlimited fresh and tinned fruit, cereals, breads, porridge, bacon, sausages, eggs, cheese, yoghurt, coffee, and so on for an average of US$5.

Lunch buffets normally include salads, several meat dishes, casseroles and desserts for a similar price although in some places, vegetarians can opt out of the meat for a significant reduction. At the Holiday Inn in Harare, for example, a vegetarian lunch costs only US$3 compared to nearly twice that for the full board.

Although all-you-can-eat dinners are rare, the buffet braai at the Victoria Falls Hotel shouldn't be missed if you can at all swing it. This is the original pig-out with table after table of wonderful European and African dishes, meats, salads, casseroles, breads and myriad sweets. The three or four hours you'll spend gorging and socialising are worth every bit of the US$8.50.

Self-Catering
If you insist on shopping at supermarkets, self-catering will be easier in Botswana than in Zimbabwe. That's not to say that Zimbabwe doesn't offer some variety and quality, but there are production problems and shortages are not uncommon. Normally, no amount of running around town will turn up an ingredient in short supply. If one shop doesn't have it, chances are none of them do.

Township markets/bus terminals, although limited in their variety of fruits and vegetables, are good for picking up inexpensive fresh produce.

Vegetarian Food
Vegetarians find it particularly difficult to travel in Africa since most of the inexpensive fare is based upon meat. Vegetable dishes politely concocted for vegetarian foreigners are often bland or stodgy. Eggs and groundnuts, both good sources of protein, are readily available in southern Africa and fresh breads and vegetables can be found nearly everywhere, but to form an interesting meal from them, you'll probably have to resort to self-catering.

Fast Food
Bus terminals also brim with cheap and greasy snack stalls where you can pick up groundnuts, corn on the cob, eggs, sweets, and even deep-fried beetles. Basic cooked meals are available in a central eating area of the markets but aren't really recommended for those who have a weak stomach or functional olfactory receptors.

One step up are the Mum & Pop style takeaways which serve chips, sausages, meat pies, sandwiches, burgers and so on. Some offer a wider variety of fare and are excellent value. Next up the scale (although not necessarily better) are the fast-food chains, the most prominent of which are Wimpy and Chicken Inn, found all around the country.

Restaurants

In the major cities, especially around transportation terminals, you will find lots of small eating halls which serve up plain but filling fare – usually some form of sadza ne nyama – for just a dollar or two. These places are normally happy to try their hand at vegetarian fare as well, but it doesn't always work out well. The best they wil probably manage for you is sadza overlain with tinned baked beans, boiled cabbage and onions, or a boiled green known as *rabe* (which is the best of the lot).

Near the central business districts are a variety of pleasant little coffee houses. International cuisine – Italian, Chinese, Greek, Indian and so on – is available primarily in Harare and Bulawayo. All the big tourist hotels harbour expensive restaurants serving European dishes – mostly the meat, potatoes and two vegies variety – and a couple of elegant places around the two major cities admirably attempt gourmet cuisine with the limited available ingredients.

There are normally dress restrictions in bars and restaurants after about 4 pm but the definition of the standard 'smart casual dress' will vary from place to place. At the very least, it excludes anyone wearing shorts, jeans, T-shirts or thongs (flip-flops).

DRINKS
Nonalcoholic Drinks

Southern Africa's refreshing contribution to liquid enjoyment is the shandy, which comes in three varieties. The Malawi shandy is comprised of ginger beer, angostura bitters and soda water with ice and lemon. The delicious rock shandy is a smoother alternative, made with lemonade, soda water and angostura bitters. The Club Special shandy is a mixture of lemonade, ginger beer and Mazoe orange, a ubiquitous orange cordial which fills the noncarbonated drink niche. Some travellers love it; others find it too sticky sweet.

If you just want a glass of water, which is safe to drink straight from the tap in Zimbabwe, order a Zambezi cocktail. If someone offers you one, a good comeback to this tired little joke, which gets a lot of mileage in Zimbabwe whenever there are dumb tourists around, would be 'Yeah, but hold the crocs (or the bilharzia, or whatever...groan!)'.

Hot Drinks

Coffee addicts who want to kick the habit should think about a holiday in Zimbabwe. Although both tea and coffee are grown on plantations in the Eastern Highlands, the best of it is for export and not readily available in

---

Glass vs Aluminium

The first thing to remember about soft drink consumption in Zimbabwe is that the bottle is worth more than the drink inside. Bottles represent money and aren't taken lightly. A Coke drunk on the spot costs a mere 30 cents, but if you want to take it away in the bottle, you'll pay at least a 50 cent deposit – that is if the establishment will let the bottle out of sight.

Normally, to take a bottle one must exchange an empty. Everyone must obey the laws of bottle conservation; unless they pay for new bottles, merchants can only sell as many bottles of soft drink as they can supply empties to the distributor. The major plusses are the employment created by manufacturing and cleaning bottles and the limited amount of unsightly litter in Zimbabwe.

In 1994, both glass-bottle manufacturers and environmentalists were up in arms when the government debated allowing import of beverages in aluminium cans. If you want to see what can happen when aluminium cans are introduced to replace glass, just visit Botswana, where mountains of empty cans roll and scatter about the streets and fields of every village and town. Clearly, the benefits of using returnable glass more than compensate for the inconvenience of returning bottles; Western countries take note! ■

the country. A few restaurants, which will be identified in the regional chapters, serve real local or imported coffee but what you'll normally get, including in most of the big hotels, is a revolting blend of instant coffee and chicory, with the emphasis on the latter.

Although it isn't the optimum-quality stuff, Nyanga tea is quite good and it is available throughout the country.

Alcohol

The alcoholic tipple of the Zimbabwean masses is *chibuku*, which is, as its advertising asserts, 'the beer of good cheer'. Chibuku is not at all tasty. Served up in buckets which are passed between partakers, it has the appearance of hot cocoa, the consistency of thin gruel and a deceptively mellow build up to the knockout punch. The whole idea is to mess one's self up as cheaply as possible and at that, it succeeds.

Since chibuku is brewed from indigenous ingredients – yeast, millet, sorghum and mealie meal – it can also be used for ceremonial purposes. For the mass market, it was once sold in paper cartons, but is now marketed in large plastic bottles which, after the Gulf War, came to be known as *scuds*.

You probably wouldn't go into a pub and order chibuku – it just isn't done. Chibuku is drunk mainly in high-density township beer halls – an overwhelmingly male social scene – or in shebeens, those not-quite-legal drinking establishments to which admission is reserved for invited guests. Unescorted women will feel uncomfortable in either sort of place.

One step below chibuku is *skokiaan*, a dangerous and illegal grain-based swill spiked with whatever's lying around. It was common 50 years ago but is fortunately no longer popular.

The beer you're probably more used to is also available in the form of lager, which is always served cold – or at least as cold as they can get it. The most popular brand is Castle, which is excellent, followed by Lion and the misnamed Black Label. You can also now buy the excellent Zambezi Lager, which until recently was only for export. The very

agreeable label bears a painting of Victoria Falls. Some beer bottles in Zimbabwe are unlabelled and the brand name is only printed on the bottle cap. There seems to be some debate about whether this anonymity is due to cost-cutting measures or just the inferior glue used to affix labels.

Although Zimbabwe's climate isn't ideal for grapes, it does sustain a limited wine industry centred on the area east and southeast of Harare. The largest and best winery, Mukuyu, is near Marondera. Although there are some palatable white wines, the reds range from mediocre to disastrous and the main reason to drink them at all is the price. Imported wines all carry steep duties.

Spirits are also available in varying qualities and imports are relatively expensive. The local produce is cheaper and in most cases bearable, but Zimbabwean ouzo, whisky and brandy all taste a bit odd.

ENTERTAINMENT

Like most countries, Zimbabwe enjoys a range of pubs, discos, nightclubs, cinemas and sporting events, but of most interest to visitors will be the unique style of music that has become a national trademark (see Culture in the Zimbabwe Facts about the Country chapter). Many travellers make a point of attending a live African music performance sometime during their visit. Although some visitors are put off by the potential hassles and uncomfortable attention strangers receive in Black clubs, the only alternative will be to stick with comparatively bland hotel music and dancing extravaganzas.

Music Venues The easiest way to find out who's playing where is to look in the entertainment section of the newspaper. The lesser known but often equally exciting bands usually advertise through posters around the outskirts of town and by the railways. Most hotels have a band playing there on a regular basis and ask Z$10 (US$1.50) to Z$15 (US$2) cover charge. Popular venues in Harare are the Mushandira Pamwe Hotel in Nyandoro Rd, Highfields, the

Queens Hotel on the corner of Robert Mugabe Rd and Kaguvi St and the Playboy Night Club in Union Ave (a little more expensive than the others). In Bulawayo, try the Bulawayo Sun Hotel or 'Z' International in the Show Grounds.

Pungwes The exact origin of the commonly used word *pungwe* is unknown but is believed to be derived from the word *ngwe* which means 'from darkness to light'. It was first used in the 1960s and referred to all-night urban discos. During the Second Chimurenga (1972-80), however, all-night celebrations of nationalistic unity between villagers and guerrillas, accompanied by morale-inspiring song and dance, came to be known as pungwes. Nowadays, any sort of event, ordinarily a disco or musical performance, may be advertised as a pungwe, meaning it begins in the evening and carries on through the night.

Warnings Bear in mind that up-market pubs and hotel bars require 'smart casual' dress, which normally means sporty dress for men, skirts or suits for women, and no trainers (joggers, sandshoes), thongs (flip-flops), denims or T-shirts. Although this is interpreted less rigidly than in the past, unless you're prepared to be turned away, it's wise to err on the side of conservatism.

Foreigners are welcomed in Black bars, discos and nightclubs, but you should be prepared to attract a great deal of attention. Much of it is the product of friendly curiosity, but an equal share is mercenary. To many Zimbabweans, foreigners represent wealth and your presence may inspire requests for money and drinks. Also, remember that while dancing at a crowded performance or disco, leave your cash with a member of your group back at your table. Even better, leave all your money and valuables at your hotel and carry only enough to cover the evening's expenses, including a taxi home.

Unfortunately, unaccompanied women often encounter uncomfortable situations at discos, drinking establishments and live music venues. Unless you're prepared to face them head on, you'd probably be happier with a male companion. You can avoid some hassles by gravitating towards the local women, who will usually be happy to teach you some African dance steps.

THINGS TO BUY
Curio shops in Zimbabwe dispense a remarkable amount of tourist kitsch. Notwithstanding the numerous soapstone and wooden carvings lining roadsides and city footpaths, serious sculpture is a new and well-received form of expression in Zimbabwe. The big-name sculptors will naturally command high prices, but there are sculpture gardens, arts centres and gallery shops in Harare and Bulawayo where you can pick up some competent work by budding artists for very competitive prices. When looking for Shona sculpture, beware of scampsters attempting to pass off second-rate tourist carvings for work by the big names. Before investing, get a good feel for the real thing by visiting a reputable art gallery, or the National Gallery, Chapungu Kraal or Gallery 2000 in Harare.

Precious and semiprecious stones such as malachite, verdite, serpentine and low-grade emeralds are carved or set into jewellery and make pleasant mementos. If you're intrigued by unusually beautiful natural patterns and 'meditation' pieces, some of the most interesting stone specimens are polished into egg-shaped chunks and sold for around US$4.50.

Another recent artistic manifestation is crochet, and magnificently intricate lace table coverings and bedspreads are hawked for very low prices – as little as Z$20 ($US10). Competition and therefore the lowest prices seem to be concentrated in the Kariba area but it's hard to avoid guilt pangs paying so little for the considerable time and expertise involved in their creation.

Baskets also display a rare level of skill and facility with design and are excellent value. They are sold along roadsides and in shops nationwide. Around Binga and the upper Zambezi Valley you'll find Batonka stool seats with their roughly carved wooden

ZIMBABWE

bases. These are a speciality item and not easy to come by but if you're looking for something unusual to take home, they're a great choice. They're more readily available in Victoria Falls than in the area of origin.

Along the roadsides and in craft markets and curio shops around the country, you'll see row upon row of appealing – and often lovely and well-executed – African faces, hippos, rhinos and gracefully elegant giraffes carved from stone or wood. These can be very good value when purchased directly from the producer, and bargaining is expected. Plan on paying around 40% of the initial asking price. One caveat: when purchasing wooden carvings, be aware that carvings and creations made of low-grade wood are often stained in hot tar and passed off as mahogany, mukwa, ebony or other prestigious and expensive woods. Some are quite skilfully done, but sometimes, just a whiff will reveal the deception.

If you prefer something more unusual, you may want to take home a toilet seat made of *mukwa* wood, which is a Zimbabwean speciality. They're available in Harare at ironmongers (hardware) shops, such as PG

Timbers. In Bulawayo, try J&F on the corner of Herbert Chitepo St and 4th Ave or UBM on Fife St between 5th and 6th Aves.

On the issue of ivory, carvings sold in tourist shops around Zimbabwe will come with a certificate stating it's 100% culled ivory, which may or may not be legitimate. It is illegal to import non-certified ivory products into countries who are signatories to the CITES agreement – which include virtually all Western countries. Therefore, certainly don't buy anything without such certification or it won't be allowed back into your home country. Potential buyers should also consider the environmental impact of their purchase. Tourists who buy ivory and other wildlife products – even certified items – bolster the market for these products and indirectly support the illicit trade in endangered wildlife.

As a matter of interest, Harare is scheduled to host the next international meeting of CITES, which will take place in 1997. Zimbabwe sees its selection as venue for the meeting as a positive step toward international recognition of its efforts to achieve sustainable use of its wildlife resources.

Getting There & Away

This chapter covers access into Zimbabwe only from neighbouring countries. Information about reaching southern Africa from elsewhere on the African continent and from other continents is outlined in the regional Getting There & Away chapter at the beginning of the book.

AIR

Air Zimbabwe and Air Botswana, respectively, have two and three nonstop flights weekly between Harare and Gaborone. Air Zimbabwe also flies on Friday between Harare and Windhoek. Air Namibia flies on Tuesday and Friday between Harare and Windhoek.

Although Harare is the obvious hub for travel between Zimbabwe and neighbouring countries, there are also international services to and from Bulawayo and Victoria Falls. South African Airways, for example, has three nonstop flights weekly between Bulawayo and Johannesburg. SAA also flies on Tuesday and Saturday between Johannesburg and Victoria Falls, with package discounts available occasionally. Air Botswana covers the safari market with three weekly flights between Maun and Victoria Falls, via Kasane. Air Namibia's Monday and Wednesday service between Windhoek and Victoria Falls is a real milk run, stopping en route in Tsumeb, Rundu and Katima Mulilo (Mpacha). The Friday service runs via Maun and Katima Mulilo.

LAND
Border Crossings

All land border crossings are open between 6 am and 6 pm daily except Beitbridge (South Africa) which stays open until 10 pm and the Plumtree rail border with Botswana, which opens whenever a train passes.

There are three land crossings into Zambia at Chirundu, Kariba and Victoria Falls. The Kazungula ferry crossing between Zambia and Botswana is just two km or so from the Zimbabwe-Botswana border post at Kazungula, and 55 km west of there (also in Botswana) is the Namibian border post at Ngoma Bridge. There are crossings to or from Mozambique at Mutare and Nyamapanda. The only crossing into South Africa is at Beitbridge. To Botswana, you can cross at Plumtree (by road or rail) or on the Kazungula road, west of Victoria Falls.

For temporary entry to Zimbabwe with a hired vehicle, you'll need a sheet known as a Blue Book, detailing the vehicle's particulars, as well as proof of insurance in the vehicle's country of registration. At the border, you must procure a temporary import permit, which must be presented when you depart.

Before you accept a lift into Zimbabwe on a truck from a neighbouring country, ascertain what's in the back. Travellers have reported that drivers sometimes try to force passengers to pay fines on goods they've attempted to smuggle across borders.

Overland Trucks

An increasingly popular option for A-to-B travel is on overland trucks. Although they were once known for exhausting long-haul routes across Africa, some companies also run shorter itineraries. If there's space, you can ride along for around US$15 per day plus a food kitty contribution. Just speak with the drivers at overland stops (such as The Rocks in Harare or the Town Council Caravan Park in Victoria Falls). Currently, the most popular routes are from Harare to Nairobi (via Zambia, Malawi and Tanzania) or between Harare and Windhoek, Namibia. Most routes run via Victoria Falls, as well as Chobe and the Okavango Delta in Botswana and the Caprivi Strip and Etosha National Park in Namibia.

To/From Botswana

There are two major border crossings between Botswana and Zimbabwe – one at

Kazungula-Kasane and the other at Plumtree-Ramokgwebana. The latter has both road and rail crossings. There's also a secondary crossing at Pandamatenga, west of Hwange National Park.

Bus By bus, the Plumtree-Francistown route is served by a twice-weekly Chitanda & Sons express bus from Harare to Gaborone via Bulawayo and Francistown, departing from the Holiday Inn in Harare and the President Hotel in Gaborone. Book through Manica Travel Services (☎ 793421, Harare; ☎ 62521, Bulawayo).

On Thursday and Sunday at 6 am, Express Motorways (☎ 720392, Harare; ☎ 61402, Bulawayo) runs from Harare (the corner of Baker Ave and Rezende St) to Gaborone – via Bulawayo – and costs US$35. In the opposite direction, buses depart from the African Mall and the Gaborone Sun Hotel in Gaborone on Tuesday and Saturday at 6 am. For information in Gaborone, call ☎ 304470.

There's also a daily (except Sunday) no-frills coach service between Bulawayo and Francistown, departing early from the Lobengula St terminus in Bulawayo. Book through the Zimbabwe Omnibus Company (☎ 67291) on Lobengula St, Bulawayo. Mach Coach Lines (☎ 60499) has a similar service daily at 4 pm.

To cross between Victoria Falls and Kazungula, the only option apart from hitching is the UTC bus from Victoria Falls to Kasane, Botswana. It costs US$20 each way.

Train There's a daily train between Bulawayo and Gaborone which departs from Bulawayo in the afternoon and arrives the following morning. The fares from Bulawayo and Gaborone are US$30/45/10 in 1st/2nd/economy class. This train doesn't always carry a buffet car (despite reassurances to the contrary) so it would be wise to bring along snacks and drinks, just in case.

Sexes are separated in 1st and 2nd-class sleepers unless you book a whole compartment or a two-person coupé. If there is a

buffet car, you must pay in the currency of the country you are travelling through. Customs and immigration formalities are handled on the train.

Note that this service no longer runs through to Johannesburg and Capetown.

Station	Departs	Station	Departs
Bulawayo	1.30 pm	Gaborone	9.00 pm
Plumtree	5.35 pm	Mahalapye	1.15 am
Francistown	9.00 pm	Palapye	3.00 am
Palapye	12.20 am	Francistown	6.45 am
Mahalapye	2.25 am	Plumtree	8.30 am
Gaborone	6.40 am	Bulawayo	1.00 pm

The rail crossing between Plumtree and Francistown is probably the most relaxed for entering and leaving Zimbabwe. Fortunately for travellers, there are so many people to process through immigration that searches, questions and hassles are usually kept to a minimum. Arrivals entering Zimbabwe on the train will be processed into the country at the Plumtree border, but they must then clear customs at the station in Bulawayo. Foreign travellers will normally get by saying 'nothing to declare' and marching past the sinuous and stagnant queue of hapless Zimbabwe residents awaiting scrutiny for contraband.

If you're travelling by rail from Zimbabwe to either Botswana or on to South Africa, you'll have to show your passport when booking the ticket. Bear in mind that your Zimbabwe dollars are worthless on the international train so be sure to have some Botswana pula (or other hard currency) before setting out.

Hitching Hitching between Francistown and Bulawayo via the Plumtree border crossing is fairly easy. Mornings are best for hitching into Botswana, while most afternoon traffic is headed towards Bulawayo. For lifts between Victoria Falls and Kazungula-Kasane, wait at the Kazungula Rd turn-off about one km south-east of town.

To/From Mozambique & Malawi

The most direct route between Malawi and Zimbabwe is across the formerly infamous

Tête Corridor between Zobue, Malawi, and Nyamapanda, Zimbabwe. Many travellers these days are opting to avoid Zambia's high crime rate and paranoid officials and take their chances with Mozambique.

Everyone needs a visa for Mozambique, even if they're only passing through the Tête Corridor to Malawi. The route is from Harare to Blantyre via the Nyamapanda and Mwanza border crossings. Coming from Malawi, pick up a Mozambique transit visa in Lilongwe, Malawi.

Bus It's relatively easy to hitch all the way, but you'll also find minibuses between Nyamapanda and Tête and between Tête and Zobue on the Malawi border. If you're headed for Beira, they run from Harare to Chimoio (via Mutare) for US$12. For information phone ☎ 727231 or 721658 in Harare.

Alternatively, you can take the Stagecoach Malawi (four times weekly) or Tauya (daily) buses which travel direct from Nyamapanda to Blantyre. The trip takes from nine to 14 hours – depending on the delay at the border – and costs around US$13. Mach Coach Lines (☎ (14) 60499) travels from Harare to Blantyre via Tête on Friday at 8 am and to Lilongwe via Lusaka on Wednesday and Saturday at 6 am. The one-way fare is US$14.

At both Nyamapanda and Mutare, there's an informal 'border tax' of US$5 or Rand10 or 30 Malawi kwacha, payable only in hard currency – a nice little money spinner for the border guards. When travelling between Zimbabwe and Mozambique, you're only permitted to import or export Z$250 in Zimbabwe dollars.

Alternatively, coming from Blantyre, you can go to the border at Mwanza and arrange a lift or take a bus or minibus. The K9 Express bus leaves Blantyre at 2.30 pm and takes two hours. Either stay the night in Mwanza and find a lift in the morning, or continue the four km to the border post and find something there. The informal border tax applies in this direction as well.

Via Zambia Heading for Malawi from Zimbabwe, the easiest route across Zambia is via Lusaka (for details, see under To/From Zambia). From there, you'll find direct buses to Lilongwe on Sunday, Tuesday and Friday which depart at 6 am and are scheduled to arrive at 8.30 pm, though you can expect delays at the border. In Lusaka, the buses leave from the terminal in Dedan Kimathi Rd. Tickets should be booked a day in advance. The fare from Lusaka to Lilongwe is US$15.

If you're coming from Malawi, it's easy to find a bus from Lilongwe to the Zambian border. From there, you catch a minibus to Chipata, Zambia, and then another bus into Lusaka. There are three daily buses between Lusaka and Harare (US$7) which all depart at 6 am and arrive in Harare at around 4 pm. There's no advance booking, so you need to get to the Inter-City bus station at around 5.30 am – from there the touts will rope you in.

The alternative is the twice-weekly Giraffe bus service. Bookings can be made at their office on Cairo Rd opposite Mr Rooster. The fare is US$7. Alternatively, you can catch a bus from Lusaka to Livingstone and cross into Zimbabwe at Victoria Falls; from Livingstone there are taxis to the border for US$3 and a twice daily rail service for US$1.50 each way.

In Harare, check Backpackers & Overlanders (☎ (14) 5074115); the new management may still operate the Backpackers' Bus between Harare and Blantyre, Malawi, every Thursday at 6.30 am (US$20 per person each way).

To/From South Africa

The only direct crossing between Zimbabwe and the Republic of South Africa is by road or by the Trans-Limpopo rail link, both of which run via Beitbridge. Fortunately, economic reforms in Zimbabwe and the new government in the Republic of South Africa have inspired a considerable lightening up of customs procedures. Zimbabwean officials are still keen to catch travellers trying to smuggle in South African goods without paying duty, but foreign travellers will have few problems. If you're crossing into Zimbabwe and intend to return to the Republic of South Africa, it's still wise to declare photo equipment, radios etc on the form provided, including serial numbers.

Bus Express Motorways (☎ 720392, Harare; or 61402, Bulawayo), Rezende St, Harare, has daily buses from Harare to Johannesburg, via Bulawayo. They depart from the corner of Leopold Takawira St and Baker St in Harare at 6 pm daily, stop at the City Hall car park in Bulawayo at around 1 am, and arrive in Johannesburg around midday the following day. Fares are US$50 from Harare to Johannesburg and US$37 from Bulawayo. Advance bookings are essential.

Mach Coach Lines runs from Mbare to Beitbridge daily at 8 am, connecting with the Transtate City to City Coach, which leaves Beitbridge for Johannesburg at 4 pm.

Quicker and more comfortable are the Mini-Zim Luxury Mini-Coaches (☎ 76644), Budget Tours, on the corner of Fife St and 10th Ave, Bulawayo. They run from the Holiday Inn in Bulawayo to Johannesburg's Rotunda bus terminal on Wednesday and Sunday at 6.30 am and arrive at 5.15 pm the same day. The fare is US$45.

The Silverbird Coach Lines (☎ 729771, ext 109) in Harare departs from the Harare Sheraton Monday and Friday at 1 pm and arrives in Johannesburg at 6.30 am the next day. From Johannesburg, it departs from the Rotunda terminal at 1 pm Wednesday and 6.30 am Sunday and arrives in Harare at 7 am Thursday and 9.50 pm Sunday. The fare between Harare and Johannesburg is US$76 each way.

A more luxurious option between Harare, Bulawayo and Johannesburg is UTC's Blue Arrow Coach Lines (☎ 791305, Harare and (69763, Bulawayo). Coaches have TVs, videos, reclining seats, air conditioning, toilets and amazingly, first-aid trained attendants who also serve drinks. There are services daily except Saturday. The route is shared with the South African company, Greyhound, which takes over south of the border.

There are also daily minibuses running from Harare and Bulawayo to Johannesburg. They depart when full from the Monomatapa Hotel in Harare (US$26) and the City Hall Car Park in Bulawayo (US$23) and operate to no fixed schedule. As one reader put it, 'you can wait 30 minutes or six hours'.

Train The rail connection between Harare and Johannesburg now passes through Beitbridge; there's no longer rail service via Botswana. The Trans-Limpopo Express to Johannesburg leaves Harare at 7 am Sunday (and Bulawayo at 9 am Sunday) and arrives in Johannesburg at 8.02 am Monday. Advance bookings are essential. Connections between the Harare-Johannesburg train and Bulawayo are made at Somabhula.

The 1st/2nd/economy class fares are US$76/55/35. There's also a daily run from Beitbridge to Johannesburg, departing at 1 pm and arriving at 5.30 am the next day. The fares in 1st/2nd/economy class are US$41/28/17. Departure times are as follows:

Station	Time	Day
Johannesburg	8.30 am	Friday
Pretoria	9.42 am	Friday
Louis Trichardt	5.57 pm	Friday
Messina	8.20 pm	Friday
Beitbridge	9.10 pm	Friday
Rutenga	10.53 pm	Friday
Somabhula	2.48 am	Saturday
Gweru	4.39 am	Saturday
Kwe Kwe	5.40 am	Saturday
Harare	9.25 am	Saturday

Station	Time	Day
Harare	7.00 am	Sunday
Kwe Kwe	10.47 am	Sunday
Gweru	12.15 pm	Sunday
Somabhula	2.48 pm	Sunday
Rutenga	4.55 pm	Sunday
Beitbridge	7.05 pm	Sunday
Messina	8.19 pm	Sunday
Louis Trichardt	10.41 pm	Sunday
Pretoria	6.49 am	Monday
Johannesburg	8.02 am	Monday

The train to/from Harare connects with the train to/from Johannesburg at Somabhula. From Harare the train departs Bulawayo at 9 am, and from Johannesburg it arrives at Bulawayo at 7.25 am

Hitching Hitching into South Africa via Beitbridge is relatively easy, but expect waits. The main problem is with South African immigration officials, who seem to regard hitchhikers as a lower form of humanity. If there's a best time to cross the border, it's around 12.30 pm when the shift is changing or after 9.45 pm, just before the border closes, when everyone is ready to go home without delay.

An alternative for finding lifts between the Republic of South Africa and Zimbabwe (and other countries) is to use the South African Dial-a-Lift system, which helps bring lifts and riders together. There's a small fee for the service, but beyond that, you'll probably only have to help with petrol. In Johannesburg, they're at Bizarre Cut, Shop 9, on the corner of Rockey and Raymond Sts, Yeoville 2198 (☎ (011) 648 8136 or (011) 648 8602).

To/From Namibia
There's no direct overland connection between Zimbabwe and Namibia. The most straightforward route is between Victoria Falls and the Caprivi Strip via Botswana, which entails driving or hitching first to Kazungula (across the Botswana border from Victoria Falls) and thence across the free transit route through Chobe National Park (you won't be subject to the preposterous park fees unless you turn off onto the tourist route) to the Namibian border crossing at Ngoma Bridge. From there, it's a short and relatively easy hitch to Katima Mulilo in the Caprivi Strip. For information on the Victoria Falls/Kazungula border crossing, refer to the To/From Botswana section, earlier in this chapter.

There's now a bus service between Harare and Windhoek, leaving Mbare on Tuesday at around 7 am and Victoria Falls at 7 am on Wednesday. From Harare to Windhoek costs US$92 and from Victoria Falls, US$75.

To/From Zambia
Between Zambia and Zimbabwe, there are three border crossings: Chirundu, Kariba and Victoria Falls. The first two are open from 6 am to 6 pm daily; the Victoria Falls crossing stays open until 8 pm.

Most travellers cross at Victoria Falls/Livingstone; this is the most relaxed of the three crossings. The Zimbabwean border post lies one km from Victoria Falls town. Between Livingstone and the border post, you can take an overpriced minibus or opt for a taxi, which costs just US$3 or the twice daily rail service for US$1.50. It's a one-km walk between the Zambian and Zimbabwean border posts, but you're rewarded with great views of the falls from the Zambezi bridge. Alternatively, you can hire a taxi between the two border posts for a couple of US dollars, but that isn't good value.

You can also cross at Kariba or Chirundu. The latter lies on the main Harare-Lusaka route, but the road is in poor repair between the border and Lusaka. There are three daily buses – operated by UBZ, ZUPCO and Giraffe – from Harare's Mbare bus terminal to Lusaka; the first leaves at 6 am but the buses get crowded so arrive early. The trip takes nine hours and costs US$7. For a bit more comfort, there's the Power Coach Express (☎ 60466), 10 Williams Ave, Ardbennie, Harare, with daily service between Mbare and Lusaka. They leave Mbare at 8 am, and Lusaka at 7 am (their motto is 'We jump around for you'). The one-way fare is US$8.

There are also United Bus Company of Zambia (UBZ) buses running from Lusaka to Bulawayo (US$15) on Thursday at 6 am which are scheduled to arrive at 12.25 am the next day. Tickets should be booked in advance at the Kamwala (Inter-City) bus terminal in Lusaka.

Day Trips From Victoria Falls If you're only going over for the day to see the Zambia side of Victoria Falls, Zambian officials normally aren't fussed about onward tickets or sufficient funds. Visas are available at the border for US$10 which can be validated for

21 days' stay if you request it (some travellers have reported being refused more than a single-day visa at the border post, so if you need more time, you may want to play it safe and secure your visa in Harare). If you're only crossing for the day, you're meant to leave Zimbabwe currency in excess of Z$500 with customs officials, to be picked up on your return.

If you're in Zambia wanting to cross for the day to visit the Zimbabwe shore of Victoria Falls, you'll have to go through standard Zimbabwe customs and immigration procedures. You'll probably be asked for an onward ticket as well. This may be waived if it's obvious all your gear is sitting in Zambia, but don't count on it.

LEAVING ZIMBABWE

For nonresidents over 12 years of age, the airport departure tax is US$20 per person (residents pay Z$20). At the airport, it must be paid in US currency. You can pre-pay the departure tax in Zimbabwe dollars at any commercial bank at the official rate but you may have to produce bank receipts proving the money has been exchanged legitimately.

Getting Around

At independence, Zimbabwe inherited good rail links between all major centres and a superb network of tarred roads which, although they've deteriorated considerably over the past few years, are still among the best on the African continent.

What Zimbabwe lacks, however, is sufficient foreign exchange to purchase and maintain public transport commensurate with the quality of its infrastructure. Although things are improving with the new Economic Structural Adjustment Plan and Export Retention Scheme, spares are frequently difficult to find. And while Zimbabweans are adept at gerry-rigging repairs, there remains a shortage of equipment. As a result, if you're relying on public transport, avoid formulating tight schedules.

One corollary of the transport shortage is that buses will run only where there is sufficient demand to justify running them. If you wish to strike out into the country's wilder areas – national parks, for instance – you'll have to find alternative means. The masses aren't going that way; most locals visiting the national parks have their own vehicles, and the bulk of the tourists are on prearranged tours which include transport.

AIR

Air Zimbabwe, the national carrier, flies domestic routes between Harare, Bulawayo, Kariba, Victoria Falls, Hwange National Park and Gweru. Services to Masvingo and Buffalo Range (Triangle/Chiredzi) have now been handed over to United Air Charters. Foreigners may purchase Air

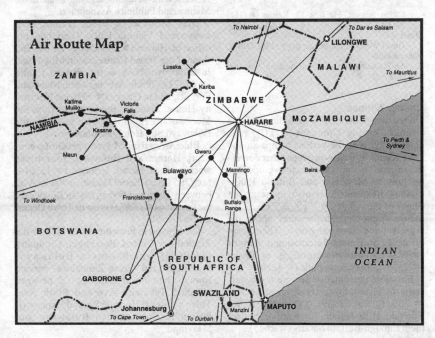

Air Route Map

Zimbabwe domestic (but not international) flight tickets with Zimbabwe dollars.

Air Zimbabwe Offices
You'll find Air Zimbabwe offices at the following addresses:

Bulawayo
    Treger House, Jason Moyo St, PO Box 1000, Bulawayo (☎ (19) 72051)
Chiredzi
    Lowveld Travel, Mutual House, 77 Knobthorne Rd, Chiredzi (☎ (131) 2295)
Gweru
    Manica Travel Services, on the corner of Robert Mugabe St and Fifth Ave, PO Box 1347, Gweru (☎ (154) 3316)
Harare
    City Air Terminal, on the corner of 3rd St and Speke Ave, PO Box 1319, Harare (☎ (14) 794481; reservations (14) 575021)
Hwange National Park
    United Touring Company, Hwange Safari Lodge, PO Box DT-5792, Dete (☎ (118) 393)
Kariba
    Kariba Airport, PO Box 13, Kariba (☎ (161) 2913)
Masvingo
    Travel World, Allan Wilson St (☎ (139) 62131)
Victoria Falls
    Air Zimbabwe Terminal, Livingstone Way, Victoria Falls (☎ (113) 4316)

Charter Airlines
United Air Charters, a subsidiary of the United Touring Company (UTC), runs charter flights to the various camps around Lake Kariba as well as between other domestic airports. It's now the exclusive operator on runs to Masvingo and Buffalo Range (Triangle/Chiredzi). It also operates the Flight of the Angels at Victoria Falls, a 10-minute flight through the spray above the falls and the Zambezi gorge. Their main office is at Harare International Airport (☎ 731713), with branch offices in Kariba (☎ 2305) and Victoria Falls (☎ 4220).

For more personalised service to any airstrip in Zimbabwe, try Executive Air (☎ 33941; fax 32949), PO Box EH 96, Emerald Hill, Harare. In Kariba, contact them through Buffalo Safaris (☎ 2645).

BUS
There are two types of buses operating in Zimbabwe – express and local buses (also known as African buses). A third option is with overland trucks, which are often available as a travellers' no-frills bus service; for more information, see the Zimbabwe Getting There & Away chapter.

Express Buses
Express buses are relatively efficient, operating according to published timetables and making scheduled snack and toilet stops along the way. They are operated mostly by Express Motorways, Ajay Motorways and Blue Arrow/United Transport Group, and run scheduled services between major cities.

Express Motorways services Harare, Bulawayo, Gweru, Victoria Falls, Mutare, Masvingo and Kariba. In Harare, their booking office (☎ 720392) is at the Rezende St station. In Bulawayo, book at Musgrove & Watson travel agents, and in Mutare at the Manicaland Publicity Association.

Ajay Motorways serves Harare, Bulawayo and Victoria Falls. Their booking office in Harare (☎ 703421) is on the 2nd floor of the Travel Centre, Jason Moyo Ave. In Bulawayo, book at the Federal Centre (☎ 62521), Tenth Ave between Main and Fort Sts, and in Gweru (☎ 3316) at Electricity House, Sixth St. Buses depart from the Monomatapa Hotel in Harare and from the Bulawayo Sun Hotel in Bulawayo.

Blue Arrow/United Transport Group connects Harare and Bulawayo four times weekly. Their Harare terminal (☎ 729514; fax 729572) is Chester House, on Speke Ave, between Third and Fourth Sts. In Bulawayo, the terminal (☎ 69673) is Swift Town Depot, at 73a Fife St.

Other express bus companies include the Zimbabwe United Passenger Company (ZUPCO) which runs a Bulawayo-Masvingo (and Great Zimbabwe) service from the terminus in Lobengula St between Leopold Takawira Ave and Sixth Ave. There's also the Hwange Special Express (F Pullen & Co) between Bulawayo and Masvingo.

Local (African) Buses

Local buses, on the other hand, go just about everywhere. Fares are very good value and between the main centres, there's usually a bus leaving at least hourly. Some of the best companies are Tenda, Phumulani, Tauya, Shu-Shine, Zimbabwe Omnibus and the ominously named Tombs Motorways. The level of service and reliability varies, but they're often just as quick as express buses.

These buses are also fairly crowded (although not by Asian or Latin American standards) but are ultra cheap – for instance, only Z$30 (US$4) between Harare and Bulawayo. The novelty of having a foreigner aboard will scarcely be containable for most people so you're more likely to meet Zimbabweans than on the express buses, which cater mainly to foreign travellers. Two readers had the following to say:

We travelled mostly on African buses overland and felt safe. It was a good way of coming into contact with locals and we were the only Whites on the bus. Mainly, children wanted to try their English and asked us about Germany. Always the first question asked is what the weather is like at home. Some were keen to know what snow is like. I found this a particularly difficult task because I never thought about how to describe something so normal to people who've never seen it. Most of the pupils we talked to in the buses thought that where we came from, the skin colour is also mainly black, and were very astonished to find out that this isn't the case.

Perhaps we were lucky, but everywhere we went, we felt welcome and were sometimes an object of curiosity rather than unwelcome foreigners. However, it was essential to state at the beginning that we weren't White South Africans. Part of our trip fell during South African school holidays and it was clear to see why some of them aren't so popular.

Joost Butenop & Astrid Pohl, Germany

Zimbabwe has had several horrendous and well-publicised bus accidents in recent years; one in 1990 killed 79 people and in another in 1991, 89 died. Despite that, local buses aren't inherently unsafe, but poor tyre maintenance means frequent blow-outs which can cause accidents. There are also problems with driver sobriety – or lack of it.

The main drawback, however, is that most local buses depart from the *musika* or *renkini*, township markets which are outside the town centre. Theft and robbery are rife around local bus terminals so be extremely careful with your luggage. If you must put luggage on the roof rack, keep an eye on it, especially at stops. Note that the person hoisting the bag onto the roof will ask an enormous tip for their services – anything up to Z$10 if you're a foreigner! Watch what other people are paying, which shouldn't be more than about Z$0.50.

Larger cities and towns also have an 'in-town bus terminus', where you can be picked up or dropped in the city centre. The problem with catching the bus in town will be the lack of available seats – or even standing spaces – once it has left the *musika*.

Your chances of reaching a given destination on a given day will be largely determined by the hour of your arrival at the terminal. If you turn up at 6 am, you'll have a good chance of catching the first – and often the only – bus of the day going in your direction. This is less of an issue between major population centres, however, since buses depart when full throughout the day, usually until mid-afternoon.

Don't get flustered if local people can't help you with schedules or frequency of buses. Although you'll hear vague murmurings about average numbers of buses per day, the buses follow no real timetables and locals have the same problems finding buses as foreigners do.

Along the way, local buses make roadside stops where passengers can pick up snacks and soft drinks. For the latter, carry an empty soft drink bottle to exchange – bottles are in short supply in rural areas and few merchants will accept cash deposits on bottles. Journeys are often long and hot, so it's also advisable to carry drinking water with you.

As enjoyable and interesting as the local buses can be, finding the right bus can strain otherwise mellow natures. Especially at Harare's Mbare *musika*, travellers and locals alike are often assailed by touts who will cluster around and create confusion, some physically grabbing and dragging people in several directions at once to get them on one

ZIMBABWE

bus or another, others hoping to separate travellers from their luggage. To avoid the worst of it, try not to get rattled; if someone is behaving aggressively, don't reveal your destination and hold tightly to your luggage. If things do become uncomfortable, sit down long enough to regain your composure before continuing. If you need help finding a particular bus, it may be best to ask a woman or an older man.

One last word of advice – avoid travelling on weekends after pay day or at the beginning and ending of school holidays, when pandemonium reigns at every bus station in the country. People spend up to two nights queuing for transport and tourists aren't accorded any special treatment

TRAIN

Zimbabwe has a good network of railways connecting the major centres – Harare, Bulawayo, Victoria Falls and Mutare. Trains are very cheap, especially in third or economy class, which is available on all but express runs.

The majority of trains in Zimbabwe run at night, and because of the relatively short distances, move very slowly in order to arrive at a convenient hour of the morning. Sleeping compartments and bedding are inexpensive and good for a comfortable night, especially if you've been camping and sleeping on the hard earth for a while.

Sexes are separated at night unless you reserve a family compartment or a coupé (two-person compartment) in advance for an additional charge. Second-class compartments hold six adults but, since children are not counted and most Zimbabwean women have at least one child with them, single women are advised to book a coupé if they want any sleep.

Although the romantic scheduled steam service between Bulawayo and Victoria Falls was discontinued in 1993, there are still expensive steam 'rail safaris' which operate along this route, and steam locomotives are still used for shunting duties in the Bulawayo rail yard. Travellers report the occasional use of steam on some runs (perhaps when the

diesel engines are being serviced). The rolling stock includes 1920s passenger cars, complete with beautiful brass and wood-trimmed interiors, even in 2nd class.

Only some trains pull buffet cars, so be prepared with food and drink. On international trains, you must pay for food and drink in the currency of the country you are travelling through. Theft is becoming a problem on trains; unless you have a private coupé (which can be locked by the conductor), leave someone to watch your gear or take it with you when you leave the compartment.

For domestic trains, bookings open 30 days ahead. For international trains to Johannesburg, you can book 90 days ahead. You're advised to book as early as possible. Let them know if you're bringing your own bedding so you won't be charged for it.

Questions about fares or schedules may be directed to the enquiries desks at the stations in Harare (☎ 700011, after hours 700033), Bulawayo (☎ 363111, after hours 322284) and Victoria Falls (☎ 391).

Generally, train travel is straightforward, although hitches can occur:

Our journey to Harare began with the night train from Victoria Falls to Bulawayo. Unfortunately, the train collided with an elephant at three in the morning and derailed. After an eight-hour delay during which the train was re-railed and the heavy obstruction somehow removed, we continued to Bulawayo.
Jordan Pollinger, USA

Timetables

This section includes only domestic timetables. For information on international connections to Botswana and South Africa, see the Zimbabwe Getting There & Away chapter.

Harare to Mutare The 1st/2nd/economy-class fares between Harare and Mutare are US$6/4/3. Trains run daily:

Station	Departs	Station	Departs
Harare	9.30 pm	Mutare	9.00 pm
Marondera	11.50 pm	Nyazura	11.15 pm
Rusape	3.23 am	Rusape	12.20 am
Nyazura	4.01 am	Marondera	4.00 am
Mutare	6.00 am	Harare	6.00 am

Bulawayo to Harare There is a nightly run in both directions, with all classes available, from Monday to Thursday and on Saturday. Between Bulawayo and Harare, the 1st/2nd/economy-class fares are US$9/6/4.

Station	Departs	Station	Departs
Bulawayo	9.00 pm	Harare	9.00 pm
Gweru	1.10 am	Kadoma	12.01 am
Kwe Kwe	2.28 am	Kwe Kwe	1.21 am
Kadoma	4.00 am	Gweru	3.00 am
Harare	6.55 am	Bulawayo	6.40 am

Bulawayo to Victoria Falls Between Bulawayo and Victoria Falls, the fares for 1st/2nd/economy classes are US$9/6/4. Also, note that there is no longer a scheduled steam locomotive service along this route.

Station	Departs	Station	Departs
Bulawayo	7.00 pm	Victoria Falls	6.30 pm
Dete*	1.30 am	Hwange	10.22 pm
Hwange	3.09 am	Dete*	12.45 am
Victoria Falls	7.00 am	Bulawayo	7.05 am

* Dete is the station for Hwange Park

CAR & MOTORBIKE

The easiest way to travel around Zimbabwe is in a private vehicle; you can stop where you like, visit national parks at leisure and reach places not served by public transport. Motorbikes also perform well on Zimbabwe's open highways but they aren't permitted in national parks. Even in a car, you can't drive in wildlife-oriented national parks after sunset.

Foreign-registered vehicles can be imported temporarily free of charge, and third-party insurance – albeit expensive – is available at the border if you're not already covered. Hire cars from Botswana, Namibia or South Africa may be brought into Zimbabwe with permission from the car-hire company, but at the border you'll need to secure a temporary export permit from the vehicle's home country and a temporary import permit for Zimbabwe. Ask the hire company to provide the relevant paperwork.

A driving licence from your home country is sufficient to drive in Zimbabwe (for visits of up to 90 days), provided it's written in English. Otherwise, you'll need an authenticated translation plus a photograph. In Zimbabwe, as in the rest of southern Africa, traffic keeps to the left. Use of seat belts is technically compulsory in the front seat and motorists are required to use headlights between 5.30 pm and 5.30 am every day of the year. If you see the presidential motorcade, identifiable by the accompanying police motorbikes with sirens and blue flashing lights, you're required to pull over and wait for it to pass before proceeding.

Naturally, you'll also need to be on the lookout for wildlife on the roads – elephants will saunter onto the pavement without warning and a collision would be fatal for the car. Similarly, antelopes and other large animals can jump onto the road from seemingly nowhere. On communal lands the highways become footpaths for people and their domestic animals. If you run down a suicidal goat or sheep with a vehicle, you will be expected to financially compensate the owner.

At the time of writing, petrol or 'blend' (which is fossil fuel blended with sugar cane ethanol) cost around Z$3.25 (US$0.50) per litre.

Car Hire

Hiring a vehicle in Zimbabwe can be expensive, so if you're on a tight budget, you'll need to be part of a group to make it worthwhile. On the other hand, it's really the most feasible way of touring the national parks unless you have plenty of time to wait around for lifts. Rental vehicles are in short supply, however, so make bookings well in advance.

Insurance & Restrictions Naturally, all drivers must have a valid driving licence from their home country. Minimum driving age varies from agency to agency, but it's usually between 23 and 25 years. The maximum age is usually 65 years.

The larger companies will probably insist on a credit card as a collateral deposit; smaller companies will most often accept a cash deposit of Z$1000 to Z$5000.

With all rental agencies, CDW (collision

damage waiver) insurance (normally, with an excess of between Z$2000/US$260 and Z$3500/US$450) is charged on top of the hire rate and if you opt not to take it, you'll be responsible for all damage; if you're making a cash deposit, you'll probably be required to increase it by the amount of the excess. Having said that, no CDW policy covers 2WD vehicles in Mana Pools or on remote gravel roads in the Eastern Highlands and elsewhere. For that, you'll have to hire a 4WD, which will be extremely expensive.

Rental Agencies The three major companies – Avis, Hertz, and Europcar/Inter-rent – accept their own credit cards as well as Visa, MasterCard, American Express and Diners Club. Although several inexpensive car-hire companies have emerged in recent years, the vehicles are generally not well maintained, and in the case of a breakdown, few provide rescue service or replacement vehicles. They may even try to charge renters for even routine repairs. Read the fine print carefully!

At present, for the cheapest Group A car (normally a Mazda 323 or similar), the big companies charge around US$28 per day plus US$0.30 per km. If you hire the vehicle for a longer period – normally more than five days – you'll pay US$55 per day but without the km charge up to 250 or 300 km. Smaller firms charge considerably less, averaging US$20 per day plus US$0.20 per km, or US$45 per day with unlimited km.

The following list includes most car hire firms in Zimbabwe:

Avis
5 Samora Machel Ave, Harare (☎ 720351; fax 750526)
99 Robert Mugabe Way, Bulawayo (☎ 68571)
Livingstone Way/Mallet Dr, Victoria Falls (☎ 4532)
Ceefax Car Hire
30 Charter Rd, Private Bag 7211, Highlands, Harare (☎ 796665)
Compass Car Hire
Shop 2, Parkade Centre, on the corner of Ninth Ave and Fife St, PO Box 9287, Hillside, Bulawayo (☎ /fax 78576)
Efficient Car Hire
103 Harare St, Harare (☎ 752444)

Europcar/Inter-rent
19 Samora Machel Ave, PO Box 3430, Harare (☎ 752559; fax 752083)
Sheraton Hotel, PO Box 3033, Harare (☎ 729771; fax 728450)
9a Africa House, Fife St, PO Box 2320, Bulawayo (☎ 67925)
Fairmile Motel, Bulawayo Rd, PO Box 1232, Gweru (☎ 4144; fax 3189)
Cutty Sark Hotel, PO Box 80, Kariba (☎ 2321; fax 2575)
Grants Service Station, 1 Crawford Rd, PO Box 897, Mutare (☎ 62304; fax 62367)
Sprayview Hotel, PO Box 70, Victoria Falls (☎ 4344; fax 4713)
ERB Car Hire
113 Fife St, on the corner of Third St, PO Box 6390, Harare (☎; fax 721023)
Glory Car
Shop 4, BB House, Leopold Takawira St, Harare (☎ 737867; fax 7327972)
Hertz
4 Park St, Harare (☎ 792791; fax 792794)
on the corner of George Silundika St and Fourteenth Ave, Bulawayo (☎ 74701)
Hwange Safari Lodge, Dete (☎ 393)
Lake View Hotel, Kariba (☎ 2411; fax 2632)
43 Hughes St, Masvingo (☎ 2131)
Manicaland Publicity Bureau, Mutare (☎ 64784)
Zimbank bldg, Victoria Falls (☎ 4267;fax 4225)
Late Model Car Hire
No 1 Union Ave, PO Box 8394, Causeway, Harare (☎ 751618; fax 751619)
No 7 Belmont House, PO Box 1031, Mutare (☎ 63938)
Sky's Car Hire
136 Samora Machel Ave, PO Box 6390, Harare (☎ 738460)
Transit Car & Truck Hire
On the corner Twelfth Ave and Fife St, PO Box FM 260, Bulawayo (☎ 76495)
Triple M Car Hire
124 Baker Ave, Oasis Hotel, Suite 7, PO Box 6748, Harare (☎ 790861; fax 790865)

Vehicle Purchase
Unless you're loaded with cash and staying for an extended period, buying a vehicle in Zimbabwe will be an unreasonable option. Not only are vehicles generally expensive and in less-than-optimum condition, they're also in short supply.

If you're intent upon purchasing a vehicle to drive around Zimbabwe, you'll find it considerably easier and less expensive to buy a car in South Africa, especially in

Johannesburg, but be sure to secure the paperwork necessary to take it to Zimbabwe temporarily. When you're finished with the vehicle, you'll have to return to South Africa to sell it – you won't be permitted to sell a vehicle in Zimbabwe without officially importing it and paying a substantial duty.

BICYCLE

Most major routes in Zimbabwe are surfaced and in excellent repair, and road shoulders are often sealed and separated from the mainstream of vehicular traffic by painted yellow lines, so they may be used as bicycle lanes. Although there are certainly rough hilly sections, the relatively level landscape over much of the country (particularly along major roads) further facilitates long-distance cycling. However, it is important to take note of the fact that bicycles are not permitted in game parks.

The predictable climate helps cyclists considerably. Winter weather is especially ideal, with cool, clear days and the generally easterly winds are only rarely strong enough to hinder cycling. Although distances between towns and points of interest are long by European standards, there are plenty of small stores between towns where you can stop for a drink and a chat.

If you're riding a lightweight bicycle, bear in mind that next to nothing is available in terms of spares, not even in Harare. Local cycles take 26 or 28-inch tyres, so you can sometimes find these, but 27-inchers or 700C tyres are almost impossible to obtain. Bring with you all the tools and spares you think may be necessary. The best cycle shops in Harare are Zacks, on Kenneth Kaunda Ave opposite the railway station, and nearby Manica Cycles on Second Ave. Bicycles may be hired in Harare, Bulawayo and Victoria Falls.

HITCHING

Hitching is never entirely safe in any country in the world, and we don't recommend it. Travellers who do decide to hitch a ride should understand that they are taking a small but potentially serious risk. However, many people do choose to hitch, and the advice that follows should help to make their journeys as fast and safe as possible.

Hitching is easy in Zimbabwe and is many locals' standard means of transport. It offers a good opportunity to meet Zimbabweans, and many travellers consider hitching easier and more reliable than taking the local buses. Many drivers accept passengers in order to help pay for their journey, so ask about charges before you climb in; the rate will never exceed the local bus fare.

It's probably not wise to hitch in the afternoon or evening on weekends or public holidays, when a large proportion of drivers are under the influence of alcohol.

Although it's better to hitch in pairs, it is possible for women to hitch alone if there are women and/or children in the car. Obviously it is not worth the risk of accepting a lift from a car full of men. It is also best to ascertain what the driver's degree of sobriety is before climbing in to the car; drunken driving is a serious problem in Zimbabwe. Hitching at night is not advisable, nor is it permitted in national parks.

It's important to note that away from the main road system vehicles are few and far between, so if you're headed for the hinterlands, plan on walking and waiting. Even on some major highways – the approaches to Beitbridge from Masvingo or Bulawayo, or the long haul from Bulawayo to Victoria Falls – there isn't an abundance of traffic. Vehicles that do pass, however, are more than likely to offer a lift.

In cities or towns, the best place to solicit lifts is at petrol pumps, especially at the last station before the open road where everyone heading in your direction will stop to top up the tank. Don't feel uncomfortable about asking; locals do it too, and it's a straightforward way to select the right lift and determine prices.

You must remember that there are inherent dangers associated with hitching anywhere in the world. At its best, however, hitching does provide opportunities to meet interesting people. Readers have sent the following stories:

Remember that a car is never full, even if you think it is. Two of us and our backpacks had a ride in an ancient Peugeot 404 together with 12 other people.
Marc van Doornewaard, Netherlands

I could not believe how easy hitching was, despite foolishly deciding to hitch around the eastern part of the country in a group of four. We always managed to get a lift within 20 minutes of setting up camp beside the road. One such lift managed to cram all of us plus our packs into his car, drove 77 km out of his way to drop us off, and then three days later came to collect us and take us to his farm to stay for as long as we wished. It is occurrences like this which made travelling worthwhile.
Stephen Millward, UK

I was lucky enough to be offered transport to Mlibizi in response to a message I left on the campground notice board in Victoria Falls. It was with a lovely South African couple who, despite my offers to pay my way, said all they wanted was company and conversation. Although they wanted to leave at 4 am to catch the ferry the next day, we cracked open some student plonk red wine that night to celebrate our meeting. I staggered back to my cabin at midnight thinking how lucky I was. The 300-km drive the next morning went smoothly and for me, the bonus was meeting a couple of socially conscious and environmentally committed South Africans.
A traveller, New Zealand

I hitched everywhere – a lone White female – and I never felt uncomfortable with the people who picked me up. In fact, I met some of the most fascinating types – a fellow who'd just discovered gold in his yard, an entrepreneur refurbishing an historic hotel, etc. I hitched in rural areas as well, with the same experiences. I always asked if they charged, but almost never had to pay. I really felt hitching was a part of seeing Zimbabwe!
Susan Loucks, USA

WALKING
For the majority of Zimbabweans, recreational walking is unheard of, but since walking is the cheapest method of transport, people often resign themselves to foot travel, particularly in rural areas where hitching is difficult. It's not uncommon to meet someone without luggage who's strolling off to visit friends or relatives, or to visit a market, in a village 30 km away.

Off the main bus routes, where visitors – particularly hitchhikers – may find themselves in a similar situation, time allowances should be made for this sort of thing.

BOAT
Since Zimbabwe is a landlocked country, the only boats of any consequence are two ferry systems that operate on Lake Kariba between Kariba town and Binga or Mlibizi near the western end of the lake. They're handy especially if you want to do a circular tour of Zimbabwe without retracing your steps between Victoria Falls and Bulawayo.

The more popular and comfortable option is with Kariba Ferries, whose two car ferries, the *Seahorse* and *Sea Lion*, each sail twice weekly between Kariba and Mlibizi. The more basic DDF ferry connects National Parks Harbour in Kariba with Binga and Gache Gache. The Binga ferry departs fortnightly, with overnights in Chalala and Sengwa. There are also weekly runs to Tashinga and Gache Gache. For further details about both ferries, see Kariba in the Northern Zimbabwe chapter.

Transport to Binga and Mlibizi can be difficult; without a vehicle, you'll have to rely on lifts from fellow passengers. There are local buses from Bulawayo to Binga via Dete Crossroads, but they only pass within 15 km of Mlibizi.

LOCAL TRANSPORT
To/From the Airport
For the 15-km trip from Harare's international airport to the centre, taxis cost approximately US$6.50. There's also an express bus which costs US$2 per person and stops at most hotels and guesthouses in the centre. In the other direction, it departs from Meikles Hotel. Phone (☎ 720392) for schedules. The Meikles Hotel, the Sheraton and the Monomatapa offer free airport shuttles for guests.

There are no hotel-booking facilities at the airport but currency exchange is available whenever international flights arrive.

Bus

Both Harare and Bulawayo have city bus services connecting the centre with suburban areas. In both cities, try to board the bus at the terminus if at all possible, otherwise, it will be packed to overflowing. Once people are hanging out the windows and doors, the driver won't bother to stop to pick up more. Local bus fares are currently Z$1 to Z$2 per ride, or less than US$0.25.

Emergency Taxi

Emergency taxis are easily recognised – look for clunky stripped-down Peugeot station wagons with 'emergency taxi' painted across one door. The name has nothing to imply about the urgency of their condition; most just keep plugging along against all odds. They're licensed to operate only within city limits along set routes and charge a standard nationwide rate of Z$1.50 to anywhere they're going. Their routes aren't advertised, so you'll have to ask for help from the driver or one of the numerous locals certain to be milling around the terminals.

Taxi

By Western standards, city and suburban taxis are inexpensive in Zimbabwe – generally less than US$2 anywhere in the city centres and US$4 to US$5 into the Harare or Bulawayo suburban areas.

Most legal taxis are metered, but if you're boarding at a railway station or bus terminal, especially if you're headed for a hotel, drivers will often forego the meter and offer competitive fixed prices. If you think you're being taken for a ride, however, insist on using the meter.

Unlicensed taxis aren't actually any cheaper than licensed taxis (they're constantly having to pay fines and bribes) and there are plenty of horror tales about high-speed chases involving unlicensed taxis and pursuing police vehicles.

A problem in Harare involves unscrupulous taxi drivers who drop clients far enough from their door to allow accomplices to attack with knives. The drivers then get a share of the booty. Before you climb into a taxi, always note the number plate and, especially at night, insist on being dropped right at your door. In Harare, Rixi Taxi and Cream Line are recommended as the most reliable companies. Unlicensed taxis often take similar sounding names, such as Pixi or Dream Line, so be aware.

TOURS

Tours of all sorts – bushwalking, rail tours, canoe and raft trips, sightseeing, wildlife viewing, birdwatching and even all-inclusive lounging around – are available throughout Zimbabwe from local operators and agencies.

In many cases, it's advisable to book these tours on the spot rather than in advance through an overseas agent, where you'll often pay up to four times more for the same tour. The following is a list of local tour operators who accept individual and on-the-spot bookings. Specific tours are described in more detail in relevant chapters, but addresses are listed only in this section.

Africa Dawn Safaris, PO Box 128, Bulawayo (☎ /fax 46696). This company focuses on Matabeleland, with day tours around Bulawayo and Matobo National Park. They also go further afield, with frequent wildlife-viewing trips around Hwange National Park and longer tailor-made safaris all over the country.

Backpackers' Africa, PO Box 44, Victoria Falls (☎ /fax 4510). This operation leads half-day to 12-day walking safaris in Western Zimbabwe's four national parks: Chizarira, Kazuma Pan, Hwange and Zambezi, including one trip which takes in all four. You can choose between straight backpacking, hiking with porters or a combination of driving and hiking, with vehicle back up. They also have trainee guides for hire.

Birds of a Feather Tours, PO Box BW 594, Borrowdale, Harare (☎ 882478; fax 728744). This company offers ornithological tours in the Eastern Highlands, along the middle Zambezi and around Hwange and Victoria Falls, and also, a raptor tour in Matobo National Park.

Black Rhino Safaris, PO Box FM 89, Famona, Bulawayo (☎ /fax 41662). This is one of Zimbabwe's best and most enthusiastic companies. They specialise day trips to Matobo National Park, which they know better than anyone else, and also run superb trips from Bulawayo to Mana Pools and Hwange national parks.

Buffalo Safaris PO Box 113, Kariba (☎ 2645; fax 2827). This recommended company incorporates Zambezi Canoeing and Lake Wilderness Safaris. They offer middle Zambezi and Lake Kariba canoe trips and walking safaris in Mana Pools and Matusadona. They also run Lake Wilderness Lodge and Nyakasanga Lodge on Lake Kariba, and are well disposed to backpackers.

Bukima Africa, The Rocks, 18 Seke Rd, Hatfield, Harare (☎ 796226; fax 753199). They offer good value overland transits between Harare and Victoria Falls starting at US$20, and longer circuits around Zimbabwe and Botswana, including Matobo and the Okavango Delta, for US$270 per person, plus food and sightseeing.

Carew/Wild Side Safaris, 18th floor, Livingstone House, Samora Machel Ave, PO Box 295A, Harare (☎ 796978; fax 795301). They offer expensive but fabulous horse tours through the wild and beautiful Tingwa Valley in the Mavuradonha range. Special backpackers' deals (see Northern Zimbabwe chapter) are available off-season or when there are last minute vacancies.

Chikwenya Safaris, PO Box 292, Kariba (☎ 2525). This company operates Chikwenya Camp at Mana Pools National Park and Fothergill Island Lodge in Lake Kariba. They offer wildlife viewing by vehicle, boat, and on foot from these two lodges.

Chipembere (Wild Frontiers) Safaris, PO Box 9, Kariba (☎ 2946). This South African-based company runs canoe trips on the middle Zambezi from Mana Pools to Kanyemba, as well as highly recommended and reasonably priced four-day walking and backpacking trips through Mana Pools National Park. In South Africa, contact them at Wild Frontiers (☎ (011) 314 5838; fax (011) 4850), PO Box 844, Halfway House 1685.

Club Wununda Safaris, PO Box 9084, Hillside, Bulawayo (☎ /fax 42379). This original company brings together the unlikely combination of golfing and photographic holidays. Tours range from a circuit of Zimbabwe's major golf venues to a countrywide photographic study.

Dabula Safaris, PO Box 210, Victoria Falls (☎ /fax 4453). This company organises game drives, walking safaris, booze cruises, fishing trips, bush dinners and transfers in and around Victoria Falls.

Eddie's Tours, 114 Gayview Mansions, George Silundika St, Bulawayo (☎ 66660; fax 65016). This company is ideal if you're after a glimpse of traditional African culture. The Ndebele owner organises trips to local villages and communal lands, as well as the main sites around Bulawayo. He also offers longer tours around the country, including a two-day tour from Bulawayo to Victoria Falls tracing Ndebele history.

Far & Wide Zimbabwe, PO Box 14, Juliasdale (☎ 26329). The speciality is white-water rafting trips on the Pungwe River in the Eastern Highlands. This company also runs a small safari camp near Mtarazi Falls.

Footprint Safaris, Trish Reynolds, PO Box BW-276, Borrowdale, Harare (☎ 882883). This small, enthusiastic company offers cheap personalised guided tours in Harare and around Zimbabwe.

Frontiers, Shop 1, Parkway, PO Box 35, Victoria Falls (☎ 4772). Frontiers specialises in white-water rafting on the Zambezi below Victoria Falls. They also run overnight and longer rafting trips right through Batoka Gorge.

Goliath Safaris, Suite 336, Brontë Hotel, PO Box CH 294 Chisipite, Harare (☎ 708843). This small and personable company is also recommended. They operate routes between Chirundu and Kanyemba. They tend to be the least 'routine' of the operators and are gaining popularity.

Gwaai Valley Safaris, PO Box 17, Gwaai River (☎ 3401; fax 375). Gwaai Valley specialises in game drives and custom safaris through Hwange National Park, and also runs the budget-oriented Nyati Lodge near Gwaai River outside the park.

Ivory Safaris, PO Box 9127, Hillside, Bulawayo (☎ 61079). Ivory runs safaris through Hwange National Park based at their own camp, Ivory Lodge, just outside the park boundaries.

Kandahar Safaris, Sopers Arcade Shop 9, Parkway, PO Box 233, Victoria Falls (☎ 4502; fax 4556). Kandahar specialises in canoe day trips above Victoria Falls and camping trips along the Upper Zambezi between Kazungula and Victoria Falls.

Kasambabezi Safaris, PO Box 279, Kariba (☎ 2641). This company offers canoeing trips between Kariba and Chirundu. It's good and cheap for canoeing, especially if you're short on time.

Kalambeza Safaris, VFR Tours, 6th floor, 35 Samora Machel Ave, PO Box 4128, Harare (☎ 793996; fax 791188) or PO Box 121, Victoria Falls (☎ 4480; fax 4644). Kalambeza concentrates on day tours near Harare and Victoria Falls, and wildlife-viewing safaris through Hwange and Kazuma Pan National Parks.

Khangela Safaris, PO Box FM 296, Famona, Bulawayo (☎ /fax 49733). This highly recommended operation is run by professional guide Mike Scott, who leads walking, camping and wilderness backpacking trips through Chizarira, Hwange, Zambezi and Gonarezhou National Parks, and with good advance notice, you can also organise walking trips through Matusadona National Park. You can either take day walks from semi-permanent base camps or put a pack on your back and trek through the wilderness. Either way, you'll have a whole new perspective of the African bush.

Khatshana Tours & Travel, 1 Colray House, Ninth Ave, PO Box 8253, Belmont, Bulawayo (☎ 66538; fax 77310). Khatshana organises custom tours around Zimbabwe; the basic charge is US$0.60 per km, including transport and guide only.

Kuteza Tours, Harare (☎ 64338, after hours ☎ 729008). This operator runs day tours to Lake Chivero, including a variety of watersports, fishing, birdwatching and wildlife viewing.

Landela Safaris PO Box 66293, Kopje, Harare (☎ 702634). Landela owns and operates Chokamella Camp near Hwange National Park.

Londa Mela Safaris, PO Box 130, Queens Park, Bulawayo (☎ 41286; fax 78319). This up-market organiser specialises in tours around Bulawayo and further afield. Although they work mainly with overseas operators, you may be able to make late bookings for good rates.

Muvimi Photographic Safaris, PO Box 2233, Harare (☎ 793107). This outfit does photographic theme tours to Matusadona National Park, as well as four-night backpacking safaris through the park with professional guides.

Mzingeli Tours, 16A Third Ave, Bulawayo (☎ 77244; fax 68214). This company operates cultural tours in and around Bulawayo, offering unique opportunities to visit communal lands, villages and rural self-help projects – as well as the well-known sites.

Nemba Safaris, PO Box 4, Gwaai River (☎ 33, Lupane). This company, owned by Chris and Val van Wyk, organises walking tours in the remote Mzola Wilderness area and operates Linkwasha Wilderness Lodge inside Hwange National Park.

N'taba Trails, 102 Pioneer House, Fife St, Bulawayo (☎ 79563; fax 76658). N'taba offers budget day tours to the Matobo Hills, including a visit to an African village.

Peter Ginn Birding Safaris, PO Box 44, Marondera (☎ 430017; fax 3340). Peter Ginn organises birdwatching trips around Marondera, including courses in bird identification. His company also organises trips around Zimbabwe for clients who 'want to spend more time on birds than on big game'.

Rail Safaris, Mr & Mrs G Cooke, 2c Prospect Ave, Raylton, Bulawayo (☎ 75575). For rail buffs, this company runs expensive but informative tours from Victoria Falls to Mutare on the *Zambezi Special* and the *Eastern Highlander*. They also organise connections with named trains in South Africa. If you just want a high-season steam trip from Bulawayo to Victoria Falls, you'll pay US$398/518 in Ivory/Emerald (posh/posher) class. If you splash out on Emerald Class, you'll even have the chance to take a memorable bath on a moving train!

Ruwezi Canoe Trails Bushlife Zimbabwe, PO Box GD 305, Greendale, Harare (☎ 48548;fax 48265). Ruwezi runs leisurely three-day canoe safaris along the 64-km stretch of shoreline through Mana Pools National Park.

Sabre Adventures & Expeditions, Private Bag A6106, Avondale, Harare (☎ 733711; fax 733718). If you want to go far beyond the end of the tourist track, here's your opportunity. How about joining the rhino-protection squads in the remote bush or learning navigation, tracking and bush survival on a foot expedition through the Zambezi Valley?

Safari Par Excellence, 3rd floor, Travel Centre, Jasom Moyo Ave, Harare (☎ 720527; fax 722872). This multi-faceted company is known for its rafting trips below Victoria Falls and canoeing on Zambia side of the middle Zambezi. They also organise walking and backpacking trips through Matusadona National Park, and offer luxury accommodation. Their *Kayila Lodge* on the Zambian shore of the Zambezi near Mana Pools is characterised by appealing rock-bound architecture. There's even a toilet inside a baobab tree.

Shamwari Safaris, PO Box 53, Dete (☎ 248). This operator organises highly recommended safaris and game drives through Hwange National Park. The owner, Roberto 'Beat' Accorsi is one of the best photographic guides and naturalists around. You can choose between tailor-made itineraries or standard packages.

Shearwater, Edward Building, on the corner of 1st St and Baker Ave, PO Box 3961, Harare (☎ 735712; fax 735716). This safari operator is Zimbabwe's largest organiser of rafting trips at Victoria Falls and Middle Zambezi canoeing trips from Kariba all the way to Kanyemba. They also operate backpacking safaris in Mana Pools National Park.

Sunbird Safaris, Great Zimbabwe Hotel, PO Box 644, Masvingo (☎ 62718). Sunbird runs day tours from Masvingo, including Great Zimbabwe and the Mutirikwe Game Park, birdwatching, horseback riding trips, and cruises on Lake Mutirikwe.

Tchechenini Trails, Mhangura (☎ 727080, Harare). This small operator, based on a working tobacco farm, runs horse-riding trips through wilderness areas of the Zambezi Escarpment in north-eastern Zimbabwe. A small thatched lodge serves as a base for all trips.

Touch the Wild, Private Bag 6, Hillside, Bulawayo (☎ 74589; fax 44696). This up-market company, informally known as Touch the Wallet, runs a variety of tours and game drives around the country. They work mainly with overseas operators and are well out of range for budget-conscious travellers. Their saving grace is the lovely Matobo Hills Lodge in Matobo National Park, which is worth even the top-tier rates charged to foreigners.

ZIMBABWE

ZIMBABWE

United Touring Company, United House, 4 Park St, PO Box 2914, Harare (☎ 793701; fax 792794). With tentacles all over Africa, UTC runs a range of day trips in Harare, Kariba, Bulawayo, Hwange National Park and Victoria Falls.

Wilderness Safaris, PO Box 18, Victoria Falls (☎ 4637; fax 4417). One of several affiliated companies in southern Africa, Wilderness Safaris specialises in up-market safaris in northern and western Zimbabwe. They also offer a sort of 'northern tier' trail, which begins at Victoria Falls and roughly follows the Zambezi all the way to Kariba and beyond, and run Chizarira Wilderness Lodge and Water Wilderness Houseboats at Matusadona.

Wild Horizons, PO Box 159, Victoria Falls (☎ 4219). Wild Horizons organises half-day and full-day game walks through Zambezi National Park, runs Imbabala Camp and Hwange's Jijim Safari camp.

Wildlife Adventures, PO Box A88, Avondale, Harare (☎ 751331; fax 751333). This budget safari company specialises in mobile safaris to get you from point A to point B with the maximum possible interest along the way. For US$675, they'll take you from Harare to Victoria Falls via Botswana and Namibia, allowing time to visit Bulawayo, the Okavango Delta, Etosha, Swakopmund,

Walvis Bay, Sossusvlei, Popa Falls and Katima Mulilo. The price includes transport only; meals and sightseeing are extra.

Zambezi Canoe Company, Shop 14, Sopers Arcade, Parkway, Victoria Falls (☎ 4298; fax 4683). This appealing company operates day trips and camping trips by inflatable canoe, along the Upper Zambezi between Kazungula and Victoria Falls. Pick up a copy of their brochure, which contains a great map of the river above the falls.

Zambezi Hippo Trails, Dalmatia House, Speke Ave, PO Box 3158, Harare (☎ 702148). This operator offers middle Zambezi canoeing from Mana Pools to Kanyemba, but also continuing downstream to Cabora Bassa Dam in Mozambique.

Zimbabwe Eastern Border Adventure Company (ZEBAC) PO Box 18, Chimanimani (☎ /fax 450). This imaginative company runs backpacking and sightseeing trips in and around Chimanimani National Park, rafting on the Haroni River and horseback tours, as well as trips to such remote locations as Corner, Rusitu Valley, and the Haroni Forest Reserve.

Zindele Safaris, Private Bag 232A, Harare (☎ 721696; fax 702006). Zindele Safaris organises custom trips to all sites of interest around Zimbabwe, and also have their own guest farm north of Harare.

Harare

Harare, with a metropolitan population of over 1.6 million, is the capital and heart of the nation in nearly every respect. The city was bequeathed a distinctly European flavour by its colonisers, and it continues as Zimbabwe's showpiece city and centre of commerce, with high-rise buildings, traffic and all their attendant bustle. Whatever action Harare lacks, you can safely assume Zimbabwe doesn't provide it.

Most visitors flying into Zimbabwe will make the country's acquaintance in Harare. If it's not the Africa you expected – and chances are it isn't – don't be discouraged, what you're looking for isn't far away. The bustle of the African marketplace hums only a few km from the city centre at Mbare musika, and giraffes and zebras roam at Lake Chivero, half an hour away by car.

History

The first Shona inhabitants of the marshy flats near the kopje, where Harare stands today, called themselves Ne-Harawa after the regional chief, whose name meant The One Who Does Not Sleep. The Mbare, under rule of the lower Chief Mbare, controlled the kopje itself. Later, another small clan led by Chief Gutsa settled in what is now Hillside, south-east of the city centre. When the inevitable clash between the two groups came, latecomer Gutsa emerged victorious, killing his rival Mbare and sending the Mbare people packing off into the rugged north-western plateau, above the Zambezi Valley.

However successful at small-scale combat, Chief Gutsa and his people had little chance of ousting the subsequent intruder. On 11 September 1890, the British South Africa Company's Pioneer Column, led by Major Frank Johnson, discovered Chief Gutsa's kopje and decided the site was favourable for agriculture and ripe for expropriation by the colonists. He even suggested to Leander Starr Jameson that the little kopje was destined to become the modern capital of the country they were founding.

On 13 September 1890, the Union Jack was raised at the present site of African Unity Square and the anticipated settlement was named Fort Salisbury after British prime minister Robert Cecil, the Marquis of Salisbury. A fort was built but things got off to a rocky start; the subsequent rainy season brought lean times and an unusually high incidence of malaria. The next winter brought the first influx of White settlers from the south, arriving to collect on promises of fertile farm lands and lucrative gold claims along the Zambezi.

Over the following seasons, more White settlers and merchants arrived and began developing the low-lying lands immediately east of the kopje. At this stage, the government decided the higher ground to the north-east was eminently more suitable and attempted to relocate the entire settlement. Those entrenched at the kopje refused to budge, however, and the two areas developed separately, hence the distinct clash in street grids between the main area of town and Kopje. Even so, they inevitably merged into one city. Black African workers were

ZIMBABWE

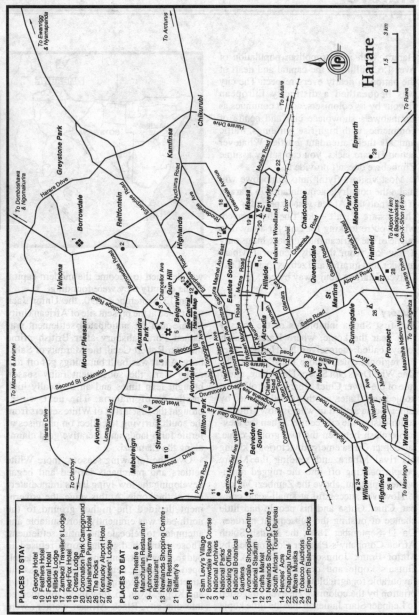

Harare

To Ewanrig & Nyamapanda

To Arcturus

To Mutare

To Ruwa

To Domboshawa & Ngomakuria

To Mazowe & Mvurwi

To Chinhoyi

To Bulawayo

To Masvingo

To Chitungwiza

To Airport (4 km) & Backpackers Con-X-Shon (6 km)

Harare Drive

Greystone Park

Borrowdale

Chikurubi

Kamfinsa

Relfontein

Valnona

Highlands

Masasa

Beverley

Chadcombe

Mount Pleasant

Alexandra Park

Gun Hill

Belgravia

See Central Harare Map

Eastlea South

Hillside

St Martins

Queensdale

Meadowlands Park

Hatfield

Avonlea

Avondale

Milton Park

Belvedere South

Arcadia

Sunningdale

Prospect

Ardbennie

Waterfalls

Mbare

Willowvale

Highfield

Mabelreign

Strathaven

Second St Extension

Chancellor Ave

College Road

Enterprise Road

Borrowdale Road

Rhodesville Ave

Greendale Ave

Mutare Road

Arcturus Road

Samora Machel Ave East

Samora Machel Ave Central

Robert Mugabe Road

Herbert Chitepo Ave

Josiah Tongogara Ave

Seke Road

Glenara

Namwi

George Road

Airport Road

Harare Drive

Masotsha Ndlovu Way

Simon Mazorodze Road

Highfield Road

Coventry Road

Lytton Road

Chartel Road

Tanganda Ave

Harare St

Hanyani Ave

Bishop Gaul Ave

Samora Machel Ave West

Princes Road

Second St

West Road

Lomagundi Road

Harare Drive

Sherwood Drive

Makuvisi Woodland

Mukuvisi River

Chiremba Road

Mbare Road

Waterfalls Ave

Mukuvisi River

Epworth

3 km

	PLACES TO STAY
8	George Hotel
10	Feathers Hotel
15	Federal Hotel
16	Hillside Lodge
17	Zambezi Traveller's Lodge
18	Red Fox Hotel
19	Cresta Lodge
20	Coronation Park Campground
25	Mushandira Pamwe Hotel
26	The Rocks
27	Kentucky Airport Hotel
28	Wayfarers' Lodge

	PLACES TO EAT
6	Reps Theatre & Manchurian Restaurant
9	Aphrodite Taverna Restaurant
13	Newlands Shopping Centre - Sitar Restaurant
21	Raffely's

	OTHER
1	Sam Levy's Village
2	Borrowdale Race Course
3	National Archives
4	National Parks' Booking Office
5	National Botanical Gardens
7	Avondale Shopping Centre
11	National Stadium
12	Crafts Market
13	Newlands Shopping Centre - South African Tourist Bureau
14	Heroes' Acre
22	Chapungu Kraal
23	Mbare Musika
24	Tobacco Auctions
29	Epworth Balancing Rocks

forced to remain outside the settlement proper around present-day Mbare, which remains the heart of the high-density working-class suburbs.

Salisbury was officially proclaimed a municipality in 1897 and was recognised as the colony's capital in 1923. In 1935, it was granted city status. Through WWII and the Federation of Rhodesia and Nyasaland, business and industry boomed. The city grew until 1965, when Ian Smith and his UDI cast a tarpaulin of uncertainty over the country's biggest construction site.

Salisbury languished through the war but at independence in 1980, things began to pick up. The city summarily became the capital of the new Republic of Zimbabwe and was renamed Harare, a mis-transliteration of Ne-Harawa, the name of the early regional chief, which had been in use among local Blacks for some years.

Orientation

Since central Harare is formed by the collision of two grids, the street pattern isn't entirely straightforward. On the main grid, streets run roughly north and south whilst avenues run east and west. On the Kopje grid, streets run in both directions except where they are extensions of avenues from the main grid.

Central Harare is quite compact, making it a breeze to get around on foot. The trendy central shopping area, which is on the main grid, focuses on 1st St Mall and is bounded by Samora Machel Ave, Robert Mugabe Rd, 4th St and Julius Nyerere Way. The peripheral business district, known as Kopje, lies south and west of the core area, and contains more crowded streets and smaller, cheaper shops and businesses.

Jason Moyo Ave is the heart of the central booking-office scene and to organise a trip into the provinces, you should try around here first. Here you'll also find the Air Zimbabwe office, the Zimbabwe Tourist Bureau and the Harare Publicity Association (conveniently placed on African Unity Square).

The big hotels are spaced around the edges of the core area, while most mid-range hotels are quietly interspersed between the private homes and apartment blocks of the avenues. This neighbourhood, characterised by tidy and lovely acacia and jacaranda-lined streets, is bounded by Herbert Chitepo Ave, Princes Rd/North Ave, Prince Edward St and 10th St.

Cheap hotels and much of central Harare's night life are concentrated on the bustling south-western area of town between Julius Nyerere Way, the Civic Centre and the railway line. This is also the heart of the disco and live African-music scene as well as the playground for nocturnal life wanting to drink or carouse the night away in a local tavern or brothel.

The rest of Harare sprawls outward into both high-and low-density suburbs which house the wealthy, middle and working classes. The city's industrial heart is centred on Workington, Southerton and Willowvale (between the city core and Mbare) Highfield and other high-density south-western suburbs. The most densely packed dormitory community is sprawling Chitungwiza, south of Harare, which is actually a separate city. Most of the park lands and suburban shopping centres are in the north and east, where the wealthier professional people live.

Information

The best source of information about daily events is the booklet *What's on in Harare*, published monthly and distributed by the Harare Publicity Association. Sports, cinema, and cultural events are also outlined in the local daily, the *Harare Herald*. To find out the time of day, phone (☎ 93).

Tourist Offices The Harare Publicity Association (☎ 705085), PO Box 1483, Causeway, Harare, has its office at the south-west corner of African Unity Square. It's open weekdays from 8 am to 5 pm and on Saturday until noon. It's Zimbabwe's least helpful tourist office but it is worth stopping by to pick up their monthly publication, *What's on in Harare*, as well as pamphlets and advertising about local attractions.

Nationwide information is more reliably

ZIMBABWE

obtained from the Zimbabwe Tourist Bureau (☎ 793666) on the corner of Jason Moyo Ave and 4th St. It's open from 8 am to 1 pm and 2 to 4.30 pm, and is generally more helpful than the Publicity Association. It sells a lovely set of posters portraying the ruins at Great Zimbabwe, the Eastern Highlands, a hippopotamus, a saddle-bill stork and the magnificent Victoria Falls for just US$0.80 each. If you ask, staff will pack the posters in a mailing tube.

For national parks' information and bookings, go to the National Parks' Central Booking Office (☎ 706077), on Sandringham Dr near the northern end of the Botanic Gardens.

A useful operation is Travelquip (☎ 721567) on the corner of Julius Nyerere Way and Baker Ave. It provides fax and telephone facilities, travel advice and bookings; and mail, freight and left-luggage services. Both these places also hire camping gear (for details, see Camping Equipment later in this section).

If you're travelling onward to South Africa, you may want to stop by the South African Tourist Bureau in the Newlands shopping centre which is located on Enterprise Rd.

Money All banks change US dollars and pounds sterling, both in cash and travellers' cheques. As in all of Zimbabwe, they're open Monday, Tuesday, Thursday and Friday from 8.30 am to 2 pm. On Wednesday they close at noon and on Saturday at 11 am. The exchange desk at Harare airport opens for international arrivals. Hotels will sometimes exchange currency for a commission.

For details about credit cards and travellers' cheques, see the Money section in the earlier Zimbabwe Facts for the Visitor chapter.

Post & Telecommunications The GPO is on Inez Terrace. You'll find stamp sales and poste restante upstairs in the arcade, while

post boxes and the parcel office are in a separate corridor just above street level. The philatelic bureau, where you will find colourful and historical stamps, is on the 2nd floor.

The poste restante (only available at the GPO) and stamp sales counters are open between 8.30 am and 4 pm weekdays and until 11.30 am on Saturday.

Other central post offices are found on the corner of 3rd St and Julius Nyerere Crescent and near the corner of 2nd St and Union Ave. Each of the suburbs has a local post office as well.

The central telecommunications office upstairs in the GPO is little more than a chronically busy block of public telephone boxes; you'll still have to plug money into the phone. If you're phoning overseas, don't waste your time in the queue without a sack full of Z$1 coins – the phones run through them very quickly.

The easiest way to make long distance calls would be to either find a private telephone or use a hotel phone. Directory assistance is available by dialling ☎ 92. For fax information, see the Post & Telecommunications section in the Zimbabwe Facts for the Visitor chapter.

There are several clean and functional telephone boxes in the 1st St Mall, and it's more pleasant to queue here than at the GPO – and you can pass the time watching the people go by.

Immigration For visa and length-of-stay extensions, the relatively amenable Department of Immigration Control office (☎ 791913) can be found on the 1st floor of Liquenda House, Baker Ave between 1st and 2nd Sts.

Travel Agencies American Express is represented in Harare by Manica Travel (☎ 703421) in the Travel Centre on Jason Moyo Ave. The Thomas Cook office (☎ 728961) is in the Pearl Assurances building on 1st St. A recommended budget and overland travel agency is World Wide

Adventure Travel (☎ /fax 721901) on the 1st floor of BB House on the corner of Samora Machel Ave and Leopold Takawira St.

For information on tour companies operating in Zimbabwe, see Tours in the Zimbabwe Getting Around chapter.

National Parks' Bookings Bookings for national parks accommodation are most reliably made at the Central Booking Office (☎ 706077), National Botanical Gardens, on the corner of Borrowdale Rd and Sandringham Dr, PO Box 8151, Harare.

Film & Photography The novel Strachan's Photo Chemist at 66 Baker Ave near 2nd St does one-hour photo processing and sells camping equipment – as well as pharmaceuticals. While you wait, you can enjoy real Zimbabwean coffee and a range of cakes, snacks and light meals. Another decent – but less original – place for processing print film is Goldprint at 7 George Silundika Ave, between 1 and Angwa Sts. Both slides and print film are sold at Photo Inn on the corner of 1st St and Baker Ave.

Bookshops The largest selection of popular books and magazines in Zimbabwe, including foreign paperbacks, local literature and school texts as well as an array of gift and coffee-table books is available at Kingston's (government-owned by the Media Trust). Kingston's has two major outlets in Harare: one in the Parkade Centre on 1st St between Samora Machel and Union Aves, and on the corner of 2nd St and Jason Moyo Ave opposite the Publicity Association. Textbooks are available at the campus bookshop on the university campus.

Speciality publications, Marxist-oriented treatises on African historical, political and social issues, art books and a few items on natural history can be found at Grass Roots Bookshop on Jason Moyo Ave opposite the National Parks' office. For souvenir books and guides, have a look in the new tourist shopping complex on Jason Moyo Ave between 2nd and 3rd Sts.

If you just need some pulp reading material, there are two book exchanges: Booklover's Paradise at 48 Angwa St and the Treasure Trove at 26C 2nd St, on the corner of Jason Moyo Ave. As its name would suggest, the latter is a real Ali Baba's cave, with stacks of second-hand books as well as used clothing, knives, and sports and camping equipment.

Maps The useful *Greater Harare Street Guide*, a gazetteer of large-scale maps, which include the city centre and all the suburbs, was once sold for US$2.50 from the Harare Publicity Association. It now appears to be between printings, but may be available again in the future.

You may want to pick up a copy of the *Central Harare* map from the Surveyor General (☎ 794545), also for US$2.50. The office is on the ground floor of Electra House, Samora Machel Ave; it's open weekdays from 8 am to 1 pm and 2 to 4 pm.

Left Luggage You can deposit luggage at the Air Zimbabwe office on Jason Moyo Ave for Z$10 per piece per day or at the railway station for Z$3 per day. The railway station left-luggage deposit is open Monday to Friday from 6 am to 1 pm and 2 to 9.30 pm. On Saturday, it's open from 6 am to 10 pm and on Sunday from 5.30 to 9.30 pm. Alternatively, there's Travelquip (see Camping Equipment in this section), which charges US$0.15/1/5 per piece per hour/day/week.

Although all the backpackers' lodges offer safe luggage storage, it's not currently advisable to leave things at the youth hostel or the cheaper hotels, locked up or otherwise.

Laundry Harare's only coin-operated laundry is the Fife Avenue Laundrette, in the Fife Ave shopping centre near the corner of Fife Ave and 5th St. It's open from 7 am to 7 pm every day, and costs US$2 to wash and US$1.20 to dry.

If you're staying in a mid-range hotel, you can utilise their laundry services, which should cost around US$1 for a T-shirt and US$1.20 to US$2 for trousers. The big hotels charge considerably more. The Coronation

Street Name Changes

Remember that many of the major street names changed in early 1990, so older maps will be outdated.

Old Name	New Name
Beatrice	Simon Mazorodze
Watt	Simon Mazorodze
Stuart Chandler	Simon Mazorodze
Forbes	Robson Manyika
Golden Stairs	2nd St Extension
Gordon	George Silundika
Harare	Masvingo
Beatrice	Masvingo
Harari	North Harare
Harari	South Mbare
Hatfield	Seke
Prince Edward Dam	Seke
Kings Crescent	Julius Nyerere
Mackenzie	Julius Nyerere
Mainway	Julius Nyerere
Mcneilage	Masotsha Ndlovu
Manica	Robert Mugabe
Umtali	Robert Mugabe
Moffat	Leopold Takawira
Montagu	Josiah Chinamano
Mazoe	Mazowe
Mtoko	Mutoko
North	Josiah Tongogara
Pioneer	Kaguvi
Queensway	Airport
Queensway	Airport
Queensway beyond Mazorodze	Chitungwiza
Rhodes	Herbert Chitepo
Salisbury	Harare
Harare	Harare
Salisbury	Harare
Sinoia	Chinhoyi
Sir James McDonald	Rekayi Tangwena
Stanley	Jason Moyo
Victoria	Mbuya Nehanda
Widdecombe	Chiremba

Park caravan park has a laundry sink where you can scrub away at will, but you'll need a universal drain plug to use it.

Camping Equipment Limited camping equipment, including butane Camping Gaz canisters for Bleuet stoves, is available at Fereday & Sons on Robert Mugabe Rd between 1st and Angwa Sts. You can hire camping equipment at Rooney's Hire Service (☎ 792724), located at 144 Seke Rd, south of the city centre. However, they only have older and heavier tents and sleeping bags, and other items suitable for mobile safaris, such as propane lamps and cookers, cool boxes, camp tables and chairs.

Travelquip (☎ 721567), on the corner of Julius Nyerere Way and Baker Ave, hires two/four-person tents for Z$80/90 per week, plus a deposit of Z$100. It also hires sleeping bags, hurricane lamps and cooking equipment.

Dangers & Annoyances During the drought period of the early 1990s, Harare was swamped with desperate rural farmers seeking work. Few, however, had any marketable skills and predictably, many wound up unemployed and living in very marginal conditions. Seeing an opportunity, several unscrupulous factions – including an insidious Nigerian syndicate – moved in and began organising these people into criminal gangs and teaching them the ropes. Between 1990 and early 1994, the city saw an alarming increase in mugging and other violent crime, and tourists were prime targets.

When word began to spread through the tourist industry that the city was unsafe (a majority of readers' letters I received during this period reported problems), the city countered by drastically increasing its police force and posting officers on virtually every street corner.

Although there are still problems – especially in quieter areas around the avenues – things have vastly improved. By day, you're at little risk if you use common sense and watch out for pickpockets. After dark, however, everything changes; never walk around the city at night and only use official taxis!

You should also be aware that Chancellor Ave, a short stretch of the street known in the city as 7th St and further out as Borrowdale Rd, is the site of both the Executive

President's residence and the State House. It's off limits and normally barricaded between 6 pm and 6 am. The trigger-happy guards are under official orders to fire without question upon any person or vehicle entering this area between those hours – even when the guards themselves have inadvertently failed to lower the booms.

Emergency Services Police, fire and ambulance services are available by dialling the emergency number ☎ 99. For non-emergency police calls, phone ☎ 733033.

Parking Multi-storey parking garages, known as parkades, are found on Julius Nyerere Crescent near the GPO and between Union and Samora Machel Aves on 1st St. They're open from 6 am to 11 pm. Metered parking is available all over the city and you'll normally find a spot after only a brief search.

National Archives

Founded in 1935 by the Rhodesian government, the National Archives are the repository for the history of both Rhodesia and modern Zimbabwe. It's on Ruth Taylor Rd, just off Borrowdale Rd about three km north of the city centre.

In the upstairs foyer is some striking artwork done by Zimbabwean children, and the Beit Trust Gallery displays colonial historical artefacts and photos as well as original early opportunists' and explorers' accounts. The downstairs foyer contains revolving exhibits and a biographical display of Zimbabwean war heroes. In separate rondavels are old photos and newspaper clippings from the Second Chimurenga, one containing general war information and the other saluting the exploits of ZANU. As one reader put it, 'You get to know the people you read on street signs all over the country'.

If you're conducting any sort of research on Zimbabwe (or Rhodesia), the ground-floor reading room is the place to go. There you'll find a pleasant atmosphere and the largest available collection of Zimbabwean records and literature to be found anywhere.

You can also buy prints of old African maps and paintings by Thomas Baines, including a wonderful painting of Victoria Falls, for US$2.50 each.

The archives are open from 7.45 am to 4.30 pm Monday to Friday and from 8 am to noon on Saturday, and admission is free. The aloe gardens alone are worth the trip out there. To get there, take the Borrowdale or Domboshawa bus from the market square terminal. The archives are well signposted on Borrowdale Rd as you head north out of town.

Queen Victoria Museum

The best part about this small and easily digestible rundown on the history of life and rocks in Zimbabwe are the appealing concrete creatures standing guard out front – a chameleon, a praying mantis, a pangolin and a snail. Although the museum isn't as good as its Bulawayo counterpart, the fossils and the dioramas of various Zimbabwe wildlife habitats are quite good, and the other exhibits are pleasant for an hour or so. Zimbabwe residents pay Z$2 and foreigners pay US$2.

The museum is in the Civic Centre complex between Pennefather Ave and Rotten Row. It's open from 9 am to 5 pm daily, including weekends.

National Gallery of Zimbabwe

This museum is the final word on African art and material culture from around the continent. It was founded in 1957 around a core of works by European artists and was augmented several years later by the fruits of an African sculptors' workshop established by Frank McEwen, who was the museum's first director. (He died aged 86 in January 1994.) Although the sculpture movement was off to an uncertain start – early Zimbabwean artists often chose to cater more to European taste rather than raise a uniquely African voice – it is today the recognised force in the national art movement. Both the gallery's small indoor sculpture exhibit and crowded outdoor sculpture garden exemplify some of the genre's best work.

On the ground floor are drawings and

ZIMBABWE

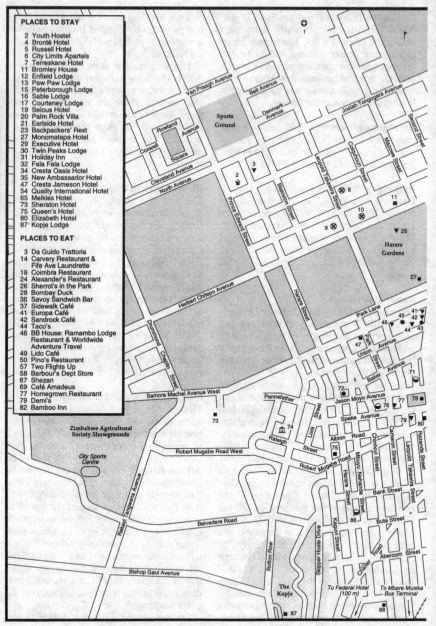

PLACES TO STAY

2 Youth Hostel
4 Brontë Hotel
5 Russell Hotel
6 City Limits Apartels
7 Terreskane Hotel
11 Bromley House
12 Enfield Lodge
13 Paw Paw Lodge
15 Peterborough Lodge
16 Sable Lodge
17 Courteney Lodge
19 Selous Hotel
20 Palm Rock Villa
21 Earlside Hotel
23 Backpackers' Rest
27 Monomatapa Hotel
29 Executive Hotel
30 Twin Peaks Lodge
31 Holiday Inn
32 Fala Fala Lodge
34 Cresta Oasis Hotel
35 New Ambassador Hotel
47 Cresta Jameson Hotel
54 Quality International Hotel
65 Meikles Hotel
73 Sheraton Hotel
75 Queen's Hotel
80 Elizabeth Hotel
87 Kopje Lodge

PLACES TO EAT

3 Da Guido Trattoria
14 Carvery Restaurant &
    Fife Ave Laundrette
18 Coimbra Restaurant
24 Alexander's Restaurant
26 Sherrol's in the Park
28 Bombay Duck
36 Savoy Sandwich Bar
37 Sidewalk Café
41 Europa Café
42 Sandrock Café
44 Taco's
46 BB House: Ramambo Lodge
    Restaurant & Worldwide
    Adventure Travel
49 Lido Café
50 Pino's Restaurant
57 Two Flights Up
58 Barbour's Dept Store
67 Shezan
69 Café Amadeus
77 Homegrown Restaurant
79 Demi's
82 Bamboo Inn

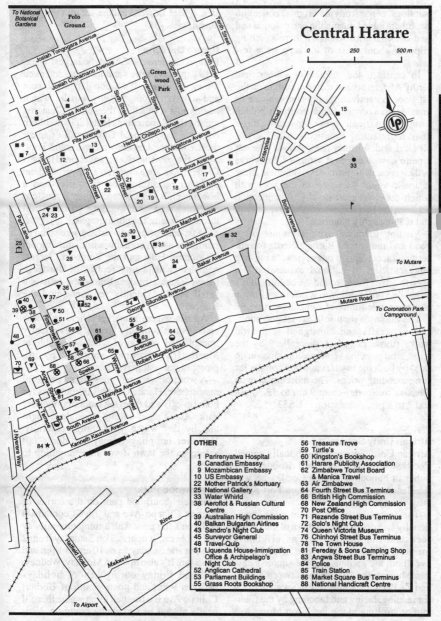

Central Harare

0   250   500 m

To National Botanical Gardens

Polo Ground

Josiah Tongogara Avenue

Josiah Chinamano Avenue

Green wood Park

Baines Avenue

File Avenue

Herbert Chitepo Avenue

Livingstone Avenue

Selous Avenue

Central Avenue

Samora Machel Avenue

Union Avenue

Baker Avenue

George Silundika Avenue

Robert Mugabe Road

Speke Avenue

R. Manyika Avenue

South Avenue

Kenneth Kaunda Avenue

Josiah Tongogara Avenue

Tenth Street

Ninth Street

Eighth Street

Seventh Street

Sixth Street

Fifth Street

Fourth Street

Third Street

Prim Street

Park Lane

Enterprise Road

Boss Avenue

First Street Mall

Angwa Street

Wynne Street

Inez Terrace

J Nyerere Way

Mukuvisi

Harare Road

To Mutare

Mutare Road

To Coronation Park Campground

To Airport

OTHER	
1 Parirenyatwa Hospital	56 Treasure Trove
8 Canadian Embassy	59 Turtle's
9 Mozambican Embassy	60 Kingston's Bookshop
10 US Embassy	61 Harare Publicity Association
22 Mother Patrick's Mortuary	62 Zimbabwe Tourist Board
25 National Gallery	& Manica Travel
33 Water Whirld	63 Air Zimbabwe
38 Aeroflot & Russian Cultural	64 Fourth Street Bus Terminus
Centre	66 British High Commission
39 Australian High Commission	68 New Zealand High Commission
40 Balkan Bulgarian Airlines	70 Post Office
43 Sandro's Night Club	71 Rezende Street Bus Terminus
45 Surveyor General	72 Solo's Night Club
48 Travel-Quip	74 Queen Victoria Museum
51 Liquenda House-Immigration	76 Chinhoyi Street Bus Terminus
Office & Archipelago's	78 The Town House
Night Club	81 Fereday & Sons Camping Shop
52 Anglican Cathedral	83 Angwa Street Bus Terminus
53 Parliament Buildings	84 Police
55 Grass Roots Bookshop	85 Train Station
	86 Market Square Bus Terminus
	88 National Handicraft Centre

paintings, some from the original collection and others added during the late colonial and post-colonial eras. Although there's nothing gripping about most of it, there are a few gems.

In contrast, the display of vibrant and earthy African art and material culture on the 1st floor is captivating. It's a storehouse of insight into a private Africa normally hidden from non-African eyes, especially those items representing a particular tribe's mythological and spiritual rites. Allow yourself time to absorb the dual nature of the works – their practical purposes and their clear aesthetic value – as well as the skill with which they were created. The connection between the two was intentional, even ritual, and is thoroughly haunting.

Visiting thematic exhibitions are often good and the annual Baringa/Nedlaw competition (according to one review, 'a rag-bag representation of national expression') is open to artists from around the country. If it's on while you're in town, it offers a glimpse at the possible future of Zimbabwean art.

The museum shop sells art-related publications, crafts and consigned sculptural works (those placed in the gallery by the artist, who pays the vendor a commission on sale) by both the masters and newcomers for corresponding prices. The museum is open Tuesday to Sunday from 9 am to 12.30 pm and 2 to 5 pm. Admission is US$2.

African Unity Square

African Unity Square was originally named Cecil Square, not for Cecil Rhodes, but rather in honour of Robert Cecil, who was the British prime minister when Fort Salisbury was founded in 1890.

The footpaths in the square were intentionally laid down in the pattern of the Union Jack and the flower gardens originally memorialised colonial settlers. Now, however, both the gardens and the square's new name honour the 1988 unity between ZANU and ZAPU. On a sunny day, it's a great place for reading, lazing and lunching by the fountain or strolling along the Jason Moyo Ave

side, where flower vendors set up their colourful stalls.

Harare Gardens

Harare Gardens is the city's largest park, with expansive lawns and gardens, and even a mini rainforest. It's a popular picnic spot and a haven from the city bustle, which begins just a block to the south. Clustered around the Monomatapa Hotel at its southern edge are the National Gallery, an open-air theatre and the Les Brown Swimming Pool. Near the northern entrance on Herbert Chitepo Ave are a children's playground, an open-air restaurant and teahouse, and a bowling club. On weekends, there's music at the bandstand and wedding parties stroll through, posing for photographs.

Most interesting is the island-like stand of rainforest which contains a miniature model of Victoria Falls and the Zambezi Gorges, complete with a tiny replica of the Zimbabwe-Zambia bridge. Below the falls is a small pond, evidently representing Lake Kariba.

An arts and crafts market is held on weekends, but it's mostly just a conveniently transplanted version of what's available at Mbare. It's sometimes improved by impromptu musical performances.

A word of warning – despite its peaceful atmosphere, Harare Gardens is notorious for both rip-offs and rape, the latter mainly after dark. Avoid short-cutting through at night and by day watch your things carefully. However tempting it may be, don't fall asleep on the lawn if you have anything to lose.

Greenwood Park

This neighbourhood park on the corner of Herbert Chitepo Ave and 7th St contains a children's fun park with a miniature railway and cable car. It operates on Saturday from 2 to 5 pm and Sunday from 10 am to 1 pm and 2 to 5 pm. It's also open on Monday, Wednesday and Friday during school holidays between 9 am and noon. South of Herbert Chitepo Ave is a football pitch where there'll nearly always be something going on. Visitors are normally welcome to watch or even join the game.

The Kopje

Rising above the south-west corner of the central Harare is the Kopje. This granite hill once served as Chief Mbare's capital, and at its foot the White pioneers first set up their shops and businesses. Access to the summit, where the Eternal Flame of Independence was lit on 18 April 1980, is from Bank St and Rotten Row. Points of interest below are indicated by small scopes fixed at the lookout.

National Botanic Gardens

The 58-hectare Botanic Gardens between Belgravia and Alexandra Park contain examples of the diverse flowers and greenery that thrive in Harare's pleasant climate. Most of the botanical species found in Zimbabwe are represented as are specimens from around Africa and elsewhere, and it's a great place for relaxing, birdwatching and spending a day getting lost.

The National Herbarium (☎ 303211) at Downie Rd and Sandringham Dr is a botanical research centre, and dispenses advice and information to gardeners and plant enthusiasts by appointment. There's a map of the gardens at the parking area off Sandringham Dr, south of the herbarium.

The gardens are open daily between sunrise and sunset, and admission is free. To get there, walk for 25 minutes north of Herbert Chitepo Ave along 5th St or the 2nd St Extension. Alternatively, take a northbound bus along 2nd St Extension and get off at Downie Ave, where there's a signpost pointing the way to the gardens. Then walk two blocks east to the herbarium.

Historic Buildings

If you're interested in Harare's colonial architecture, look for a copy of the book *Historical Buildings of Harare* by Peter Jackson, published by Quest Publishing, Harare, 1986. It can be hard to find, so if it's not in the shops, contact the publisher (☎ 704076) at Makomva House, 107 Leopold Takawira St.

For a glimpse of colonial Harare, stroll down Robert Mugabe Rd, where many of the older buildings remain.

Market Hall The old market hall, built in 1893, is at the Market Square bus terminus near the corner of Bank and Mbuya Nehanda Sts. It still serves as a market and has been recently renovated.

Mother Patrick's Mortuary This tiny place, in front of the Mukwati building on Livingstone Ave between 4th and 5th Sts, is one of Harare's oldest buildings. Built in 1895, it was used to store the deceased until their relatives could be contacted and brought in from the countryside. Mother Patrick, born Mary Patrick Cosgrave, was an Irish missionary who organised hospitals around Zimbabwe in the late 1800s. Today, there's a small display about Mother Patrick and her work.

Parliament Buildings The Parliament buildings, on the corner of Baker Ave and 3rd St, were originally conceived as a hotel in 1895 by two South African politicians Daniel Mitchell and Robert Snodgrass. Although it was only partially completed, the building – by this time known as the Cecil building – was commandeered the following year by the Rhodesian army as a barracks. In 1896 Mitchell and Snodgrass had failed to repay their loan on the building and the government repossessed it, intending to turn it into a post office. However, the new Legislative Assembly took a liking to it almost immediately and on 15 May 1899, it was taken over as the Parliament building. The building has undergone several renovations – in 1969 it grew to six storeys – but is still used by the Senate and Legislative Assembly for official proceedings. The current plan is to construct new Parliament buildings on the Kopje, but that is still a few years off by all present indicators.

To attend a weekly guided tour and an explanation of government operations, or sit in the gallery seats during sessions, apply to the Chief Information Officer (☎ 700181), Parliament of Zimbabwe, PO Box 8055, Causeway, Harare.

Anglican Cathedral The first church in Harare was constructed African style of mud and pales by Canon Balfour in 1890 on the corner of 2nd St and Baker Ave. On the same site today is the Anglican Cathedral of St Mary & All Saints, a not particularly inspiring granite-block structure designed by South African architect Sir Herbert Baker.

The church was begun in 1913 but wasn't completed until 1964. Part of the delay has been attributed to a dispute over the shape of the bell tower (which wasn't finished until 1961). The architect originally proposed a Great Zimbabwe-like conical tower but the idea was turned down in favour of the square dungeon-like thing that now chimes daily at 6 pm. The tower holds 10 bells cast in London by Whitechapel Foundry.

The cloisters were finished in the late 1940s. Have a look at the only remaining artefact from the Balfour Church – an altar cross fashioned from cigar boxes, which is housed in St George's chapel of the main cathedral.

If you're interested in attending an African church service, reader Joost Butenop recommends the Baptist church on the corner of 2nd St and Fife Ave, near the Terreskane Hotel.

Town House The Town House, on Julius Nyerere Way near the GPO, dates back to 1933 and serves as Harare's town hall. This primarily Italian Renaissance-style structure houses the mayoral, City Council and town clerk's offices. The centrepiece of the gardens is a colourful floral clock. If you'd like a look around the interior, phone ☎ 706536 for an appointment.

ZANU Headquarters When you're out and about, don't miss seeing the modern ZANU headquarters near the Sheraton Hotel, topped by the Mugabe government's cockerel crest. The building, shaped like a local Chibuku beer carton, is appropriately known as the Shake-shake building.

Mukuvisi Woodlands
The nearest thing to a zoo in Harare is Mukuvisi Woodlands (☎ 731596), a 265-hectare woodland reserve seven km east of the city. Of the total area, 156 hectares are natural *msasa* parkland for picnics, walking and birdwatching. The remaining area has been set aside as a game park where zebras, sables, wildebeests, steenboks, bushbucks, duikers, giraffes, warthogs and impalas roam free. There used to be a rhino but it has now been removed for its own safety.

The park is open from 6 am to 6 pm every day. Guided two-hour foot safaris are conducted on Wednesday and Saturday at 2.30 pm and on Sunday at 8.30 am and 2.30 pm, and cost US$3 per person. Guided one-hour horse rides are conducted from Tuesday to Sunday at 8.30 am and 4 pm. If you're there at any other time, there's a game-viewing platform overlooking the waterhole, where you can while away an hour or two watching the animals. Admission to the platform is US$0.75 (Z$5). Proceeds go to Mukuvisi Woodlands trust for the upkeep of the park.

Mukuvisi Woodlands is a 20-minute walk from Coronation Park along Glenara Ave South; caravan park attendants can explain the quickest route over the railway line. From the city centre, take the Msasa bus from Market Square or from the corner of 4th St and Robert Mugabe Rd, or the Greendale bus from the Rezende St terminus, and ask the driver to drop you as near to Mukuvisi as possible.

Chapungu Kraal
Chapungu Kraal and Shona village is an attempt to create a sort of cultural theme park for tourists. Okay, Gallery Delta may call itself the 'artistic heartbeat of Harare', but this place is the lifeblood for the entire continent – 'The Pulse of Africa'. You can't get much more vital than that! Admission is just US$0.50 (unless you're with a group and get a guided tour, in which case it's US$2.50) and the sculpture garden and weekend

African dance performances (Saturday at 3 pm and Sunday at 11 am and 3 pm) are worth seeing.

The name Chapungu is the Shona word for the bateleur eagle, the spirit messenger for the Shona people. The sculptural displays are accessible in a half-hour guided tour which leads you through the motivation behind the granite, jasper, verdite etc works of Zimbabwe's most renowned artists. Quite a few, you'll notice, deal with the hazards of social failure – drinking too much beer, for example, or (horror of horrors) eating your totem animal. The latter can yield some very unpleasant results, as you will see.

Chapungu Kraal (☎ 786648) is open daily from 8 am to 6 pm at Doon Estate, 1 Harrow Rd, Beverley East, Msasa. It's within reasonably easy walking distance of Coronation Park, but about eight km from the Harare centre. Take the Greendale bus to the caravan park from the Rezende St terminus and walk from there or hitch east on Mutare Rd past the Beverley shopping centre and Chicken Inn. Turn right into the industrial area and after a sharp right turn, pass through the security gate at the Sorbaire sign.

Epworth Balancing Rocks

Although there are better examples of balancing rocks all over Zimbabwe, the ones at Epworth, a mission and former squatter camp 13 km south-east of Harare, are probably the most famous. The big attraction is the group known as the Bank Notes, catapulted to rock stardom when they were featured on Zimbabwe paper currency. If you're not interested in paying the US$1 admission, there are plenty of balanced rocks across the road which cost nothing to visit and are just as interesting.

To get there, take the Epworth bus from the 4th St and Jason Moyo Ave terminus and get off at either Munyuki shopping centre or the turn-off to Epworth Primary School. From the latter, it's 500 metres further along the road to the park entrance. You'll be surrounded by the balancing boulders – and Epworth kids – for the entire walk. You may want to hire one as a guide to the site, but try

to ignore all the demands for gifts and cash you'll probably encounter along the way. By car, follow Robert Mugabe Rd east and turn right on Chiremba Rd, which will take you directly to Epworth.

Heroes' Acre

On a hill overlooking Harare, the dominating obelisk of Heroes' Acre serves as a monument to the ZIPRA and ZANLA dead during the struggle for liberation from the Rhodesian oppressor. It holds the tombs of the war heroes (as well as several who died in car accidents) and is the future site of a war museum. This North Korean-designed canonisation of the dead heroes – as well as the Leninisation of Robert Mugabe – is quite an impressive production. However, the liberators' just cause is mocked by a preoccupation with military violence and 'raised fist' lip service to socialism. The designers even left empty headstones in anticipation of future war heroes!

The most recent inductee into Heroes' Acres is Ms Sarah 'Sally' Mugabe, the Ghanaian wife of Zimbabwean president Robert Mugabe, who died of kidney failure in 1994 at the age of 60.

If you can avoid being swept away by the propaganda, Heroes' Acre is worth a visit. You must first apply for a visitor's permit from the Ministry of Information, (Room 514 of Liquenda House on Baker Ave) which, if you're a foreigner, will normally be issued immediately. Zimbabwean citizens have considerably more difficulty getting visitors' permits.

To reach Heroes' Acre, which is five km from the city centre out on the Bulawayo Rd, catch the Warren Park bus from the terminus just west of Chinhoyi St along Samora Machel Ave. Admission and guided tours of the site are free.

Tobacco Auctions

Zimbabwe is one of the world's largest producers of tobacco, currently the country's largest single foreign-exchange earner, and Harare serves as the tobacco-trading centre of southern Africa.

ZIMBABWE

The world's largest tobacco auction floor on Gleneagles Rd in Willowvale, eight km from Harare, was constructed in 1986. Auctions are held daily between April and October (exact dates will vary from year to year depending on the harvest) from 8 am to noon. During a single day an average of 16,000 bales will change hands, one every six seconds. Visitors are welcome to watch proceedings and guided tours of the floor as well as the lowdown on the complex tobacco industry are available at the site. Take the Highfields bus from the corner of 4th St and Robert Mugabe Rd.

For further information and confirmation of trading activity, contact the Tobacco Sales floor (☎ 68921) or the Tobacco Marketing Board (☎ 66311).

Zimbabwe Agricultural Society Show

The Zimbabwe Agricultural Society Show is held at the showgrounds, near the Sheraton Hotel, around the end of August. It's a national showcase for agricultural, commercial and manufacturing industries – a bit like a state fair in the midwestern USA. It was first held in 1897 as a cattle and produce show, and has grown into an annual event attracting over 150,000 spectators and 150 commercial exhibitions along with traditional dance performances, live music and military demonstrations. Check with the Publicity Association for dates and scheduled events.

Sports

The Olympic-sized Les Brown Swimming Pool between Harare Gardens and the Monomatapa Hotel is open daily from 10 am to 6.30 pm from late August to early May. The rest of the year, hours are from 11 am to 4 pm. It costs US$0.10 (Z$0.90) for a swim. Another variation on swimming is available at Waterwhirld, with water slides and an artificial beach less than two km east of the centre along Samora Machel Ave.

Golf is also popular in Zimbabwe and green fees are some of the world's least expensive – 18 holes for around Z$30 on weekdays and Z$50 on weekends. Golf

clubs may be hired at clubhouses for around Z$20 per day and caddies will cost about Z$15 per game. There are seven courses in the Harare area alone, including the internationally acclaimed Royal Harare Golf Club on Josiah Tongogara Ave, just a 20-minute walk north of the city centre. Those who prefer miniature golf will find a course at Waterwhirld.

For climbing, trekking, birdwatching and bushwalking information, contact the Mountain Club of Zimbabwe. The phone numbers of members conducting monthly climbing and bushwalking outings are listed in *What's on in Harare*, published by the Harare Publicity Association. Visitors are always welcome to participate.

For information on tennis and squash, contact the Harare Sports Club (☎ 791151). Squash court bookings can be made by phoning ☎ 722234; for tennis court bookings, call ☎ 724424. Harare's Hash House Harriers meet weekly on Monday; for information, phone ☎ 79130.

Spectator sporting events are announced in the *Herald* and held regularly at the Chinese-constructed National Stadium, a few km west of the city centre along the Bulawayo road (take Samora Machel Ave).

On weekends, you can see – and bet on – horse racing at the track in the 'mink and manure' suburb of Borrowdale. It's one of the most popular sports in Harare and interested visitors have a good chance of catching one of Mashonaland Turf Club's 41 annual meets at the Borrowdale Park track. The Harare area boasts 600 active thoroughbred horses. Alternatively, trotting races are held every Sunday at the National Trotting Club's Waterfalls Stadium on Hatfield Rd.

If you've always wanted to learn skydiving – or just give it a try – courses are available for just US$90 per person. For further information, phone Bruce (☎ 787404).

For budding survivalists, even paintball (mock war using balls of watercolour paint instead of bullets) has sprung up in Zimbabwe and there are currently two places in Harare. The nearest to town is Predator

Paintball Games, between the Lewisam Garage and Lewisam Shops on Enterprise Rd. The other is ZAP Paintball Games (☎ 791013), which is 20 km outside Harare. For one/two/three hours of flying colours, you'll pay Z$40/78/120 per person.

Organised Tours

Two main companies operate day tours around the Harare area. Departures are guaranteed with two or more participants.

One is *Kalambeza Safaris*, which is booked through VFR Africa (☎ 793996; fax 791188), 6th floor Memorial building, 35 Samora Machel Ave, PO Box 4128, Harare. Tours to Chapungu Kraal and the Epworth Balancing Rocks cost US$11.50 and to Mbare musika, the Kopje and Mukuvisi Woodlands (or the Queen Victoria Museum) cost US$10. Tours to the tobacco-auction floors run Monday to Friday from April to September and cost $10.

UTC departs from Meikles Hotel and should be booked through UTC (☎ 793701; fax 792794), United House, 4 Park St on the corner of Jason Moyo Ave, PO Box 2914, Harare. They run a Scenic City Tour for US$11 per person, which takes in historical buildings, the Kopje and the National Archives (or the Queen Victoria Museum). On weekdays from April to September, it visits the tobacco-auction floors; at other times, it stops at the Epworth Balancing Rocks instead.

Both companies also run day tours to Ewanrigg National Park, Larvon Bird Gardens, the Lion & Cheetah Park, the Snake Park and Lake Chivero, as well as trips further afield which are detailed in the relevant sections of the book.

Places to Stay – bottom end

Camping Price-wise, the bottom of the accommodation scale is the campground in Coronation Park (☎ 46282), seven km east of the centre along Mutare Rd (which merges with Samora Machel Ave just outside the centre). Camp sites, including use of showers, baths and public phones, cost just US$0.90 per person.

The Menara and Greendale buses from Rezende St terminus pass the entrance and the Msasa bus from Market Square terminus stops a few minutes' walk away. Otherwise, hitching isn't difficult.

An alternative is *The Rocks* (☎ 796226; fax 753199), an overland truck stop run by Wayne and Sparky at 18 Seke Rd. It's set in 2.5 hectares of natural bushland, protected by huge boulders. Camping costs US$1.50 and basic dorm beds are US$3.50. This is a good place to connect with overland trucks for transits to Nairobi or elsewhere. Laundry facilities are available, mainly for the benefit of arrivals caked in overland dust. The immense outdoor bar is good fun and sets the mood of the place.

To get there, either take an emergency taxi labelled Hatfield from the Mobil petrol station on the corner of Robson Manyika Ave and Julius Nyerere Way; or take the Zengeza or St Mary's bus from the Angwa St bus terminus. It's a five-minute walk from Seke Rd.

Several backpackers' lodges also allow camping.

Hostels & Backpackers Lodges Rock bottom quality-wise is *Fala Fala Lodge* (☎ 796606), 101 Union Ave. They charge US$3.50 for dorm beds, US$6.50 for a double room or caravan and US$2.50 for camping in the dust and dirt.

Just as bad is the *Youth Hostel* (☎ 796436) at 6 Josiah Chinamano Ave. Separate dormitory accommodation for men and women costs US$1.30/2 for IYHF members/nonmembers. It's a bit of a hovel and security isn't very good but it does have cooking facilities (which can be very dirty). Guests are locked out from 10 am to 5 pm and the kitchen closes at the 10 pm curfew – and these times are strictly enforced. At least there are no chores to do. For men only, an alternative is the basic *Toc-H (YMCA) Hostel* (☎ 721777) at 163 Union Ave.

More amenable is the recently upgraded *Sable Lodge* (☎ 726017) at 95 Selous Ave between 8th and 9th Sts, which is run by Ralph Mardon. The atmosphere is friendly

ZIMBABWE

and laid-back, and they sell soft drinks and snacks out the back. All guests have access to cooking facilities, but they also have a cook who'll prepare meals for you – and he's good at vegetarian dishes. If you like lazing around the pool and meeting other travellers, this is the place to go. Dorm beds cost US$3.50, double rooms are US$10.25 and a mattress on the floor is US$2.50.

At 33 Fort Rd near Rotten Row, opposite the power plant, is the friendly and highly recommended *Kopje Lodge* (☎ 790637), with dorm beds for US$2.50 and floor space, camping or a space on the roof for just US$2. Double rooms cost US$7.70. In addition to a bar, kitchen and laundry facilities, they do bread and pizzas in the evening and braais on Sunday. Most travellers love the laid-back atmosphere; the only drawback is the dodgy location.

At 39 Selous Ave is the clean and cosy *Palm Rock Villa* (☎ 724550), run by Henry, a friendly South African who's already planning to expand the operation into the building next door. He's done up the rooms in safari décor, and the result is quite homely. Dorm beds cost US$4 and doubles are US$9, including use of kitchen facilities. There's also a self-contained family room for US$13.

The popular but scruffy *Paw Paw Lodge* (☎ 724337), at 262 Herbert Chitepo Ave, charges US$4 for beds (if you have a sleeping bag). A Mattress on the floor are US$3.50 and camping costs US$2.50 per person. They have a lounge and cooking facilities for guests, but they're often filled with friends of the owner. There's no curfew and drugs and alcohol are prohibited inside.

Twin Peaks Lodge (☎ 730537), opposite the Holiday Inn at 130 Samora Machel Ave, is a bit nicer. It has 18 dorm beds at US$4.50, and camping in the front or back garden costs US$2 per person. There's a television and laundry and cooking facilities, but the kitchen is very small.

Peterborough Lodge (☎ 796735 or 738459), 11 Peterborough St, near Water Whirld, is used mainly by volunteer organisations. It's ideal for those who relish peace and quiet, so don't expect a raucous backpackers' scene. It's most accurately described as a 'home away from home'. Dorm beds cost US$3.20.

Even more secluded is the quiet and quirky *Hillside Lodge* at 71 Hillside Rd, an old colonial home surrounded by jacaranda trees. Singles/doubles cost US$6.40/7.70, dorm beds are US$2.50 and camping in a lovely, tree-studded site costs US$2.20. The extraordinary décor of the place, particularly in the bathroom, may leave you feeling dizzy, but you won't see anything else like it in Zimbabwe. It's a long trek from the centre; to get within striking distance, take the Msasa, Tafara or Mabvuku bus and get off at the Children's Home.

At 6 Wavell Close in Highlands is the *Zambezi Travellers' Lodge* (☎ /fax 46178). It's a large house with several amenities, including cooking facilities, a bar, snooker table and sculpture garden. Transfers to and from the centre are free .

The *Wayfarer Lodge* (☎ 572125) at 47 Jesmond Rd in Hatfield is out of town, but offers free pickup from the centre. Camping costs US$2.80, dorm beds are US$4.50 and double-thatched chalets cost US$5.80. All prices include use of cooking facilities, TV/video and swimming pool.

Near the airport at 932 Delport Rd is the friendly and highly recommended *Backpackers' Con-X-Shon* (☎ 5074115), which charges US$4.50 for dorm beds, US$3 for camping and US$10 for a double room. It's best described as a backpackers' resort, with a bar, swimming pool, billiards table, tennis courts, TV/video room, and walls plastered with travel information. Meals are available and they offer free airport pickup and four daily runs to the Lido Restaurant in Harare centre. What's more, it's a long way from the bustle, and you can be fairly confident that your belongings are safe.

An alternative backpackers' option is *Backpackers' Rest*, formerly a block of bachelor flats on the corner of 3rd St and Livingstone Ave. Private rooms with toilets will cost US$7.70/10.25 a single/double. The main drawback is the lack of cooking facilities.

Women may like spotless *Bromley House* (☎ 724072) at 182 Herbert Chitepo Ave, opposite Harare Gardens, which is a hostel for female students and office workers. Rooms are available only between school terms, but it's a bargain at US$5 a single with tea and dinner and it's an excellent place to meet local women.

Hotels Many bottom-end hotels in Harare are noisy and double as brothels so lone women who don't want to risk being misconstrued may want to look for accommodation elsewhere.

The most popular and central of these is the *Elizabeth Hotel* (☎ 708591) on the corner of Julius Nyerere Way and Robert Mugabe Rd. Singles/doubles with shared facilities cost US$12/US$19.50. Ask for a room over the street. Although these rooms are noisy, those in the back are dark and rather prison-like. There's a disco nightly until 11.30 pm and local bands are sometimes featured.

Similar is the *Queens Hotel* (☎ 738977) on Kaguvi St near the corner of Robert Mugabe Rd, which has a restaurant and features live bands and a disco until 11.30 pm on Friday, Saturday and Sunday nights. On Friday and Saturday night, they also stage occasional pungwe performances in the garden, featuring well-known bands. Singles/doubles cost US$12/19.50.

At 9 Harare St near the southern end of the Kopje between the centre and Mbare is the *Federal Hotel* (☎ 706118). It's the most distinctly African of all the inexpensive places. Prices are the same as those at the Queens Hotel. The friendly *Elmfield Lodge* (☎ 724014) at 111 Fife Ave is reasonably cheap at US$9 per person, but it's in a dangerous area (at night, anyway), the kitchen is dirty, the toilets don't lock and some rooms lack windows.

The *Earlside Hotel* (☎ 721101) on the corner of 5th St and Selous Ave is quiet and centrally located. The outside looks seedier than it really is, but there are serious security problems and it's best avoided – as are the unsavouries who like to hang out around the

entrance. Rooms cost US$13/17 for a single/double.

More respectable are the *Russell Hotel* (☎ 791894) at 116 Baines Ave and its annexe, the *City Limits Apartels* on the corner of 2nd St and Baines Ave. In the main hotel, you'll pay US$17/22 a single/double on the ground floor and US$23/26 upstairs. In the apartels, you'll pay US$13/21. All rooms include bed and breakfast and have private baths, radio and a telephone. At the Russell, there's a pool which may be used by guests of both places. For the apartels, register in the Russell itself.

At 102 Fife Ave, between 2nd and 3rd Sts, the one-star *Terreskane Hotel* (☎ 707031) offers singles/doubles with bath for US$9/10.50; without bath, they're US$10.50/18. Family rooms with bath go for US$27. There's a restaurant, bar and swimming pool, as well as a television lounge and a beer garden out the front where you can relax in the sun. If you're not in a partying mood on Friday or Saturday night, you'll be happier with a room at the back, away from the raucous disco which blares until 4 am.

Further from the centre, the *Mushandira Pamwe Hotel* (☎ 64355) at Nyandoro Rd, Stand 4806 in Highfields sits between a couple of local music venues. Rooms are rock bottom price-wise but it's an expensive taxi ride from the centre of town. Similarly, the one-star *Nyagonzera Skyline Motel* (☎ 67588), on the Masvingo road about 19 km from Harare, offers excellent live music performances but transport can be problematic or expensive for those without their own vehicles.

Places to Stay – middle

For the most part, mid-range hotels in Harare are quite acceptable and comfortable, though not luxurious. Non-Zimbabwean guests are now required to pay their bill in foreign currency; they no longer accept Zimbabwe dollars backed up by exchange receipts. In most mid-range hotels, everyone pays the same rates, but foreigners must settle up in foreign currency.

The *Executive Hotel* (☎ 792803), on the

corner of 4th St and Samora Machel Ave, formerly a block of flats, offers private baths, telephones and TV in every room. There's no pool but they do have a sundeck. Singles/doubles cost US$23/27. The restaurant is open for lunch and dinner.

The *Selous Hotel* (☎ 727940), on the corner of Selous Ave and 6th St, costs US$20 a single/double, including breakfast. However, the place has little to recommend it.

Another option is the recently upgraded *Quality International Hotel* (☎ 700333), in the centre near the corner of Baker Ave and 4th St. It's well located but doesn't have a pool or television. Bed and breakfast in singles/doubles with shared bath cost US$36/48 for foreigners and US$28/37 for locals.

A fairly friendly alternative – although we have had complaints about theft and poor service – is the *Courteney Hotel* (☎ 706411) on the corner of Selous Ave and 8th St. It has a secluded and relaxing pool area; the bar known as the Old Crow; a coffee shop; and an excellent but expensive restaurant, *L'Escargot*. Single/double rooms with private baths cost US$38/49.

The *New Ambassador* (☎ 708121; fax 708126), at 88 Union Ave, is now affiliated with the Rainbow Group and is quite acceptable. It sits on a relatively quiet street, right at the far edge of the action in Harare. In the foyer of Ambassador House, next door, are African sculpture and painting exhibits. For single/double rooms with breakfast, telephones, TV and private, foreigners pay US$35/50 and locals pay US$29/39.

You can't beat the delightfully olde worlde *Brontë Hotel* (☎ 796631) at 132 Baines Ave for a splash-out. It's clean and set back from the street in its own quiet gardens. For relaxation, they have a pool and a bar and there's even a special monthly rate anyone who can't tear themselves away. The downside is that it's booked out at least a month in advance so, unless you get lucky, you can't just turn up and expect to find a room. Rooms cost US$38/49 for a single/ double, with breakfast.

For something less central, but still good value there's the *George Hotel* (☎ 36677; fax

723230) on King George Rd near Avondale shopping centre. Single/double rooms with en suite facilities cost US$22/29.

Also recommended is the new and comfortable *Cresta Lodge* (☎ 787006; fax 787009), which is away from the centre at the junction of Samora Machel Ave and Robert Mugabe Rd. Single/double rooms with en suite facilities and colour TV cost US$26/32. It's considerably nicer than its prices would suggest.

On the corner of Greendale Ave and Stewart Rd, five km from the centre, is the two-star *Red Fox Hotel* (☎ 45466), done up as a black and white English cottage. Rooms with private facilities cost US$20/25; they also have family rooms and suites. The restaurant, The Huntsman, specialises in fish and beef and, emphasising the English theme, there are also two pubs.

The *Feathers Hotel* (☎ 28472), on the corner of Sherwood Dr and Notley Rd in Mabelreign, is more of a suburban motel. Rooms are reasonably priced at US$16/21 a single/double, and there's a swimming pool, grill, three bars, a conference centre – and even an adjoining 18-hole golf course.

The *Kentucky Airport Hotel* (☎ 506550) on St Patrick's Rd, Hatfield, not far from the airport, isn't bad if you're flying in late or flying out early. It costs US$16/23 for a single/double room, including breakfast. Airport transfers are free for guests.

Places to Stay – top end

Bear in mind that in Harare, hotel prices and quality are not always proportional, so if you're looking for high standards, don't be put off by low rates. Hotels which employ a three-tier pricing scheme are considerably more pricey for foreigners than those in which everyone pays the same rate, yet standards are largely the same. For example, the Cresta Jameson offers international standards for a fraction of the rate you'll pay for similar accommodation at the Holiday Inn.

Straddling the mid-range and top-end categories, the three-star *Cresta Oasis* (☎ 704217, fax 794655) at 124 Baker Ave (the entrance is on Union Ave between 5th and 6th Sts) offers high standards and a quiet location. Prices are US$31/44 for a standard room and US$33/47 for deluxe; all rooms include bed and breakfast.

The Oasis' relative, the four-star *Cresta Jameson* (☎ 794641; fax 794655), on Samora Machel Ave at Park St, is quite nice and sits right in the heart of high-rise Harare. Standard rooms cost US$40/54 a single/double; all rooms have private facilities, and rates include breakfast.

On Samora Machel Ave between 5th and 6th Sts is the *Holiday Inn* (☎ 795611; fax 735695), which is pretty much like Holiday Inns everywhere. For foreigners, standard single/double rooms cost US$109/158 and deluxe rooms are US$125/182. Locals pay US$37/54 for a standard room and US$43/62 for a deluxe.

The recently refurbished *Meikles Hotel* (☎ 795655; fax 707754), on Jason Moyo Ave, served as the foreign correspondents' watering hole during Zimbabwe's liberation war. It claims five stars and caters to high standards, but the attitude may be too stuffy for some tastes. Unless you're a hotel snob, you'd probably be happier at the Sheraton or Monomatapa. For standard rooms, foreigners pay US$150/175 a single/double and locals pay US$48/57.

The Yugoslavian-designed *Harare Sheraton* (☎ 729771; fax 796678) and conference centre, between Samora Machel Ave and the end of Pennefather Ave, is Harare's most luxurious and expensive digs. In Chicago or Singapore, no one would give it a passing glance, but in Harare, it stands out as a monument to modernity. The shiny opulence extends to the interior, as well, resulting in an international-class retreat from the uncertainties of the city outside. It boasts all the regular amenities; shops, hairdressers, snack bars, gourmet restaurants and pubs. For a standard single/double room, foreigners pay US$172/200 and locals pay US$58/64; all rooms include breakfast.

Size-wise, however, the Daddy of 'em All is the immense, wave-like *Monomatapa* (☎ 704501; fax 791920) on Park Lane, overlooking Harare Gardens. For standard rooms

with breakfast, foreigners pay US$123/178 and locals pay US$41/60.

Out-of-Town Lodges In Ruwa, 40 minutes out along the Mutare road south-east of Harare, is *Landela Lodge* (☎ 702634; fax 702546), PO Box 66293, Kopje, Harare. This colonial country farmhouse, which is reminiscent of the set used in the film *Out of Africa*, has a small attached wildlife park, and offers plenty of opportunity for relaxation. Prices are quite reasonable, starting at US$90 per person with accommodation and meals. Ad-vance bookings are essential, and they're happy to fetch you from the airport.

Also in Ruwa is the lodge known rather unimaginatively as *Dinner, Bed & Breakfast Accommodation* (☎ 2381), which offers horse-riding and wildlife viewing on a 100-hectare farm. Rates are quite reasonable at US$23/36 for a single/double room with breakfast. Despite the name, the price doesn't include dinner, although meals are available. To get there, follow the Mutare road to the 25.5-km peg and turn right into the driveway after the greenhouses, beside a vegetable kiosk.

Another pleasant farmhouse is *Mwanga Lodge* (☎ 22721; fax 430), 44 km north-east of Harare off the Shamva road (in the Arcturus exchange). Accommodation is in A-frame thatched cottages set amid the low granite hills of Bally Vaughan Game Farm. The price is US$48 per person, including excellent meals and wildlife-viewing trips by canoe. If you prefer just a day trip, contact Sun Link International (☎ 729025; fax 728744) in Harare; plan on spending around US$50 per person, including lunch.

Harare's best-known wild retreat is the *Cresta Pamuzinda Safari Lodge* (☎ 703131; fax 794655), which sits on a game farm near Selous, 80 km south-west of Harare on the Bulawayo road. Standard lodges cost US$76/152 a single/double and luxury or 'royal' lodges are US$82/165. Prices include all meals, guided walks and game drives – not bad considering the standard of accommodation. Note, however, that they do not allow children under the age of 12.

ZIMBABWE

Off the Masvingo road, 39 km south of Harare, is *Carolina Wilderness* (☎ /fax 736772 Harare or ☎ 29565 Norton), PO Box W83, Waterfalls. Owners Dave and Pauline Tomlinson offer comfortable safari lodges, as well as safari drives, canoeing, fishing, birdwatching and photo walks on a private wildlife reserve. You can choose between self-catering or a full meal plan. Again, no children are allowed and advance booking is essential. To get there from Harare, head south towards Masvingo past the Manyame River bridge, then turn right and continue for 9.5 km, where you should turn right towards Norton. From there, it's 8.5 km to Carolina Wilderness.

Nearer in – off Delport Rd about seven km south-east of the airport – is the *Airport Game Park* (☎ 572886; fax 700812), which offers fishing, birdwatching, an 11-km canoe route along the Manyame (sometimes called the Hunyani) River and limited wildlife viewing (small antelope only). It's not the best organised of places, but it's very convenient to town and the landscape is dotted with balanced-rocks and ancient rock paintings.

Places to Eat

Breakfast A full breakfast of cereal, juice, eggs, bacon, sausage, toast, and (not recommended) coffee or tea at *The Cottage Pie* in the Courteney Hotel is especially convenient if you're staying at Sable Lodge, and costs only US$1.30. In the centre, *Le Paris*, Samora Machel Ave near 2nd Ave, serves great full breakfasts for US$2. Also highly recommended is *Lido Café* (☎ 726316), at 51 Union Ave, which serves well-prepared full breakfasts for around US$2. *Cafe Europa* is recommended for its coffee.

Perhaps the best choice, however, is *Café Amadeus* in the Ximex Mall near Angwa St and George Silundika Ave, where you can enjoy US$3.50 English breakfasts or delicious spinach omelettes while listening to 18th-century classical music. Don't miss their amazing home-baked brown bread or fresh fruit juices.

Zimbabwe's extravagant buffet breakfasts and lunches at the four and five-star hotels

will satisfy you for most of the day. For details, see Buffets later in this section.

Snacks & Lunches The *Lido Café* at 51 Union Ave is highly recommended for burgers, which start at US$1.20. More creative concoctions, which are equally good, average from US$2.50 to US$4. Their emphasis on quality is reflected in their delicious sandwiches, curry, grills, goulash and a range of sweets: shakes, apple pie and lemon pancakes. It's also open for dinner.

For inexpensive lunches, you can't beat the praiseworthy *Sidewalk Cafe* on 1st St, with burgers, chicken, salads, sweets and vegetarian dishes, as well as a mean apple pie. The music is good and the atmosphere is pleasant and loud. Also trendy and popular is the sidewalk seating at the *Sandrock Café* on Julius Nyerere Way.

Café Amadeus, which was recommended for breakfast, also serves light and tasty lunches and full dinners. It's open Monday to Saturday from 7.30 am to midnight. You'll find great sandwiches and pies at the *Savoy Sandwich Bar* on the corner of Samora Machel Ave and 2nd St.

If you're in the Coronation Park area, don't miss the fabulous *Rafferty's Bakery*, on the Mutare road 200 metres east of the campground turn-off. Their delicious and healthy lunches are unbeatable – and more readers have recommended this place than any other restaurant in Harare!

If you want to sit in the sun, drink coffee and spend two hours writing postcards, go to the laid-back *Terrace Restaurant* on the third level of Barbour's Department Store. The lunches are also decent and they're enhanced by a fresh-air view. The small and dank coffee shop in the basement is also OK for snacks and coffee, but you miss out on the light, sunny atmosphere. Nearby, also on 1st St Mall, is *Two Flights Up*, which serves coffee and light lunches, and boasts an excellent and popular salad bar.

Try *Dagwood's* in the 1st St Parkade for sandwiches and sadza ne nyama (mealies with meat gravy). For excellent peri-peri chicken, trek out to *Nando's* in the Avondale shopping centre. The restaurant and tea garden at the *National Handicraft Centre* (☎ 721816), on Chinhoyi St south of Kenneth Kaunda Ave, serves Zimbabwean dishes and other traditional African fare.

Around the centre you'll find takeaway places selling chips, burgers, 'samoosas', soft drinks and other fast fare. If you're after cheap and filling fast food or African fare, the takeaways in the Kopje grid are good value.

More institutionalised fast food is available from Chicken Inn, and there are several in central Harare. Beside the Chicken Inn on 1st St Mall is the affiliated *Bakers Inn* where you can buy sticky pastries and doughnuts and *Creamy Inn*, which sells mainly ice cream. There's another Chicken Inn at the Beverley shopping centre near Coronation Park. Wimpy is also an option, but isn't really recommended.

Real filtered coffee is available at *Brazita's* in the 1st St Parkade but they don't like you lingering over a slow cuppa. The nearby *Le Paris* on the Samora Machel Ave side of the Parkade also has good coffee and is better for a chat. They also do light meals and sandwiches, as well as coffee and snacks.

On sunny afternoons, try the reasonably priced *Sherrol's in the Park* in Harare Gardens, which emphasises Mediterranean dishes, but also serves excellent salads, toasted sandwiches and steak and kidney pie. It's open daily from noon to 3 pm.

Buffets The big hotels – the Sheraton, Monomatapa, Meikles and the Holiday Inn – put on extravagant (for Zimbabwe) buffet meals which could easily become a budget travellers' mainstay. In the morning you can try the large English or continental breakfast fare or wait until midday for the lunch version. One or the other could satisfy an appetite for most of the day.

For breakfast, the best deals are at the *Monomatapa Hotel* and *Holiday Inn* where all you can eat will cost around US$3.50; less for a continental breakfast. The Sheraton and Meikles both charge US$5. Lunch buffets

include salads, meat dishes, vegetables, casseroles and desserts for around US$6. Vegetarians can opt for the cheaper salad bars at US$3. If you prefer to just pig out at the dessert table, you'll pay only around US$2.50. For dinners, you'll pay around US$9. However, don't turn up at any of these hotels looking like you've just crawled out of a sleeping bag or you may be asked to leave.

Dinners Although there isn't much for the gourmet in Harare, there is a surprising number of very good and relatively inexpensive restaurants.

Very popular with travellers is *Da Guido Trattoria* (☎ 723349) in the Montagu shopping centre on the corner of Harare St and Josiah Chinamano Ave. Each evening they have pasta specials for around US$3.50 and a meat dish for US$5, as well as pizza and other Italian standbys. And don't miss their salads, espresso and cappuccino. You'd be hard-pressed to find a better inexpensive restaurant in Harare. They're open for lunch from noon to 2 pm; dinner starts at 6.30 pm.

Spago's (☎ 791894) in the Russell Hotel on Baines Ave comes highly recommended for its Italian cuisine and reasonable prices. Their salads and garlic bread are made all the tastier by real filtered coffee and they serve some of the nicer Zimbabwean wines, as well. In addition to Italian meals, you'll also find seafood and a range of beef and chicken dishes. At lunchtime, you can enhance the nice Mediterranean atmosphere by eating in their shady outdoor garden.

There are also more unusual ethnic options which are fine for a leisurely lunch of dinner. One is *Coimbra*, 61 Selous Ave, with delicious Portuguese-style seafood and legendary peri peri chicken. *Taco's Restaurant*, in Lintas House at 46 Union Ave, serves the nearest thing to Mexican food you'll find in Zimbabwe.

Even better is *Demi's* (☎ 723308), near the corner of Speke Ave and Leopold Takawira St, with a large Greek menu. The Greek salad is particularly good and you can have a filling meal, including a delicious Greek starter, main course and alcohol for around

US$8. It's open for lunch and takeaways between 10 am and 2.30 pm weekdays and for dinners Monday to Saturday from 6.30 to 10.30 pm. Harare's other Cypriot/Greek restaurants are the *Acropolis* (☎ 39181) in Avondale, which serves reportedly great Greek meals for under US$7 and the *Aphrodite Taverna* (☎ 35500) at Strathaven Plaza, Strathaven.

Shezan, at 88 Robert Mugabe Rd, specialises in Pakistani cuisine. For Indian fare, try the *Bombay Duck* at 7 Central Ave. It's an Indian curry house open for dinner nightly, except Sunday. The adjoining takeaway serves curry and rice for US$1.50. If you have a vehicle or don't mind a taxi ride into the suburbs, another Indian option is the *Sitar* (☎ 729132) in Newlands shopping centre on Enterprise Rd.

The best Chinese option is the *Bamboo Inn* (☎ 705457) on Robert Mugabe Rd near 1st St. A different Oriental twist, especially for hard-core carnivores, is on offer at the *Manchurian* (☎ 36166), beside the Reps Theatre on 2nd St Extension in Avondale, which serves a Mongolian barbecue. *Alexander's* (☎ 700340) at 7 Livingstone Ave serves fairly high-priced (but arguably the best) meals in town.

You'll find excellent vegetarian fare, as well as steaks and seafood dishes, at *The Homegrown* (☎ 703545), on the corner of Speke Ave and Leopold Takawira St. Meals average around US$5, but an all-you-can-eat salad bar costs just US$2. It's open Monday to Friday from noon to 2 pm and 6.30 to 10 pm, and on Saturday from 6.30 to 10 pm. Dinner is occasionally accompanied by live music performances.

For fish and seafood, a good choice is *Pino's* (☎ 792303) at 73 Union Ave. The fresh kingclip from South Africa and the paella valencia are particularly good, and they often serve crab, crayfish, vegetarian dishes and other treats, all at medium prices. Plan on spending around US$10 per person, without drinks.

Perhaps in emulation of Nairobi's renowned Carnivore restaurant, *Ramambo Lodge* (☎ 792029) serves a spread of wild game dishes, from impala and warthog to ostrich steak, eland stroganoff and crocodile in cheese sauce. If that's not your bag, they also do traditional cuisine, beef, vegetarian meals and seafood. As you'd expect, the décor reflects the 'safari lodge' theme, and you can almost forget that Harare's widest street bustles just below. Lunches are backed up by a marimba band and in the evening, they stage a 'traditional dance cabaret'. You'll find it upstairs in BB House, on the corner of Samora Machel Ave and Leopold Takawira St. It's closed on Sunday.

All the big hotels and most smaller ones offer both fine dining and mid-range restaurants. In the Sheraton are *La Chandelle*, for gourmet fare, and *Harvest Garden*, serving more down-to-earth meals. On Thursday nights, the Harvest Garden puts on an African buffet, complete with traditional dancing. *L'Escargot* (☎ 706411) at the Courteney Hotel is also touted as one of Harare's finest and most highly acclaimed restaurants.

In the *Quality International Hotel Restaurant*, you can opt for a three-course meal featuring an obscenely sized steak for just US$8. Another option for large chunks of beef is the mid-range *Carvery Restaurant* in the Fife Ave shopping centre.

Self-Catering There's a TM supermarket on Baker Ave between 1st and 2nd Sts and a Woolworth's on the 1st St pedestrian mall. The supermarket at the Fife Ave shopping centre, on the corner of Fife Ave and 5th St, is open Monday to Saturday until 6.30 pm and on Sunday from 8 to 11.30 am.

Entertainment
Harare is a great place to hear African music – both live and disco. A good place to find information on upcoming events is the monthly tourist office booklet *What's on in Harare*, which lists cultural, sports and musical events which they deem of interest to tourists. More obscure venues and cinema schedules are normally listed in the daily *Herald*.

Most pubs, hotel bars and nightclubs are

conservative and 'smart casual' dress rules apply. And remember – don't walk to or from any of these late-night spots after dark; take a taxi right to your front door!

Cinema Harare has no shortage of cinemas, with 11 movie houses and two drive-ins. In the afternoon and evening, most cinemas run three or four screenings of US films. Cinemas include the Rainbow on Park Lane, Cinemas 1, 2, 3 and 4 near the GPO on Baker Ave and the Liberty Theatre on Cameron St. Admission averages US$1.50. Check the daily *Herald* for listings.

Theatre Harare doesn't have much in the way of theatre; for information on the current month's activities, either phone or check *What's on in Harare*.

Gallery Delta (☎ 792135) at 110 Livingstone Ave likes to bill itself as the 'artistic heartbeat of Harare', but on my last visit, it seemed to be suffering from cardiac arrest. Nevertheless, it does occasionally host quality theatrical, artistic and musical productions and performances, and visiting exhibitions.

Harare Reps, which stage some entertaining albeit middle-of-the-road productions, have their auditorium 40 minutes' walk from the centre in the Belgravia shopping centre on the corner of Thurston Lane and 2nd St Extension, Avondale. Advance booking for Reps productions is through Spotlight (☎ 724754) in Chancellor House, Samora Machel Ave. Occasionally Harare also stages performances by visiting theatre groups which normally use the Seven Arts Theatre, a large auditorium also in Avondale.

Live Music Most travellers interested in the local music scene come to Harare looking for a pungwe, an all-night drinking and dancing musical performance by one of Zimbabwe's top musicians. Unfortunately, the Publicity Association doesn't normally keep up with such things. Your best bet is to cruise the streets of the Kopje area; coming events are normally advertised on walls, lampposts and shop windows. All venues impose a cover

charge for live events and some even charge for disco music. For some guidelines, see Entertainment in the Zimbabwe Facts for the Visitor chapter.

The best places to catch local bands are the Federal, Queen's or Elizabeth hotels on Friday and Saturday nights. There's not much quality control so you do get the occasional dud, but once in a while, a well-known name may drop by for a session. Both the Elizabeth and Queen's have African and Western disco music nightly until 11.30 pm. They can be good places to meet and party with locals, but the sound systems appear to date back several decades. Another place which occasionally brings big names is the New Yorkish Playboy Night Club at 40 Union Ave.

The garden of the Nyagonzera Skyline Motel (☎ 67588) at Km 19 of the Beatrice-Masvingo road also attracts superb talent, but it's a long and expensive taxi ride from town and there's no cheaper public transport running at the hours you'd be needing it. Anyway, phone in advance to ascertain whether the trip is worth the effort.

For a better chance of hearing such greats as the Bhundu Boys, Thomas Mapfumo & the Blacks Unlimited or Ilanga, try weekend gigs at Job's Night Spot, owned by Job Kadengu, in the Wonder shopping centre on Julius Nyerere Way between Kenneth Kaunda and Robson Manyika Aves. For the more intrepid, the three nightclubs in Highfields – Machipisa, Club Saratoga and the Mushandira Pamwe Hotel – have live bands on weekends and at least one should be offering something of interest.

Marimba bands, including the renowned Jairos Jiri Marimba Band, give free performances in the bandstand at Harare Gardens. Local bands also play at the drinking halls at Mbare market on Saturday afternoons. Men will find them interesting cultural scenes but lone women should steer clear.

Bigger musical events such as national celebrations or concerts by foreign stars normally take place in the National Stadium. For the latter, half of Zimbabwe seems to descend upon Harare so it will be vital to book tickets well in advance – an option not available to most travellers.

Pubs, Discos & Night Clubs The popular watering hole at the Terreskane Hotel is always thronged with a lively clientele from late afternoon until closing. Other hotel bars are unpredictable: some nights they're entertaining, sometimes less animated. The Bird & Bottle in the Ambassador Hotel on Union Ave has been recommended. For a more sedate drinking experience, try the Old Crow Bar at the Courteney Hotel on the corner of 8th St and Selous Ave or the pubs at one of the four or five-star hotels.

Currently, the most popular places with White Zimbabweans are The Tube (with a London tube station theme), on Mbuya Nehanda St, and Archipelago's in Liquenda House on Baker Ave; both get lively from around 11 pm and rock until 4 am most days. Also up and coming is the glitzy but recommended Solo's on the corner of Jason Moyo Ave and Harare St. It's open daily for lunch and nightly for disco and live performances. Another new and popular place is Turtles, in a basement on Jason Moyo Ave, between 1st and 2nd Sts. It features disco on Friday and Saturday nights, and live music on Sunday.

If you prefer a more mixed clientele, there's Tacos on Union Ave near Julius Nyerere Way, where the emphasis is on reggae music. The Elizabeth Hotel and Queen's Hotel offer African and Western disco music nightly until 11.30 and both are great places to meet and party with locals, but the sound systems are less than optimum.

One reader recommends the bar at the Meikles Hotel for 'relaxed bibbling with the emergent entrepreneurial classes and strange Whites' and the Quality International Hotel, on the corner of 4th St and Baker Ave, 'a low-life drinking hole that's good fun'. For the young and mode-conscious White set, try Rosalind's in Avondale shopping centre. Trendy dress and hairstyle are obligatory.

'Mall rats' may want to visit Sam Levy's Village shopping mall in the suburb of Borrowdale, with more than 70 shops, cinemas, restaurants, delis and other estab-lishments. On weekends, Aguila's Pub/Club, which is popular with the local White community, features live European pop music performances and on Sunday, there's a flea market. The self-contained building is patrolled by a force of English-style Bobbies.

Things to Buy
All the big hotel gift shops and the plethora of souvenir and curio shops around the centre dispense locally made crafts and souvenirs of varying quality. While they're convenient, they're not the cheapest way to go and normally, similar or superior items may be found at informal markets and lower-overhead outlets around town. For real works of art, particularly the Shona sculpture for which Zimbabwe is famous, the National Gallery and several commercial galleries offer a variety of names and prices.

Although Zimbabwe has signed the Convention of International Trade in Endangered Species (CITES) Agreement, which prohibits trade in elephant ivory, several Harare shops continue to deal in ivory products. They'll provide certification that their ivory has been taken in accordance with CITES, but this system is rather leaky and tourists are generally advised not to buy ivory products. Shops selling ivory include Solo Arts & Crafts in the Samora Machel Parkade; Moore's Trophies on the corner of 1st St and Jason Moyo Ave and Space Age Products, 54 Edison Crescent in Graniteside, among others. See also Things to Buy in the Zimbabwe Facts for the Visitor chapter.

Commercial Sculpture Galleries & Art Dealers In addition to the shop at the National Gallery, several galleries and crafts shops sell original African art and skilled craft work. Those inspired by Shona sculpture can find original creations at several commercial galleries around town. The four major ones deal primarily in works by known sculptors.

Stone Dynamics at 56 Samora Machel Ave specialises in serpentine and verdite works by older well-known and established artists. Vhikutiwa Gallery, north of town on the corner of Harvey Brown Ave and Blakiston St, is in a pleasant old suburban home. Besides sculptural works by well-knowns and newcomers, it also deals in handicrafts, including Batonka material arts. At 114 Leopold Takawira St is Matombo Gallery which also emphasises big names but also devotes space to emerging talents.

The Ramambo Lodge restaurant also has an attached gallery, with a selection of Shona sculpture. Gallery 42, at 42a Enterprise Rd in Newlands, concentrates more on metal sculpture and original paintings than stone sculpture; they also deal in curios. Other places to look for sculpture include the Nyati Gallery, on Spitzkop Rd, 18 km out of town in the direction of Bulawayo; and Similitudes, at 1 Bodle Ave in Eastlea, just off Robert Mugabe Rd beyond Enterprise Rd. If money is no object and you're looking for antique, traditional, esoteric or ritual items, visit Dendera Gallery on the corner of Robert Mugabe Rd and 2nd St.

In the eastern suburbs at Doon Estate, 1 Harrow Rd, Msasa, is The Gallery of Shona Sculpture at Chapungu Kraal. The sculptures are spread around a large, grassy lawn beside a scenic lake – and the sales people are easy-going. The only drawback is the admission charge, but it does buy you a guided tour of the gardens and a spoon-fed appreciation for the inspiration behind some of the works. It's open daily from 8 am to 4.30 pm. For more information, see the discussion of Chapungu Kraal earlier in this chapter.

One of the most renowned – and most tasteful – galleries is Gallery Delta, which refers to itself as 'The artistic heartbeat of Harare'. It's in the former home of Zimbabwean artist Robert Paul (110 Livingstone Ave). The building dates back to 1894 and is probably the oldest house in the city.

Crafts & Material Arts Plenty of reasonably priced crafts outlets exist around Harare. The best and cheapest are found at the large outdoor crafts market on Enterprise Rd and at Mbare musika, where stall upon stall of carvings and practical items – as well as kitsch souvenirs – may be purchased at negotiable prices. You'll also find crafts pedlars set up in Harare Gardens and along Jason Moyo Ave in the centre. A reader writes:

You'll be hassled by street vendors trying to sell ridiculously cheap Shona sculptures – the cops move them on but they keep coming back. I retaliated by selling them *my* cheap Walkman. One eventually hustled it from me for a ridiculously low price. I was no match.

Andy Bollen, Australia

If you're prepared to pay more for something a bit more inspired, visit the National Handicraft Centre, on the corner of Grant and Chinhoyi Sts in Kopje. You'll find musical instruments, mats, carvings, handmade toys, baskets, pottery, leatherwork, weavings, crocheted and knitted items, and handprinted textiles. It's open daily from 9.30 am to 5 pm. They also have a restaurant and tea garden where you can sample local and traditional foods.

For something really beautiful and unusual, traipse out to the amazing Kudhinda Fabrics at The Shop, Doon Estate, on Harrow Rd near Chapungu Kraal. Here you'll find wall-hangings, bags, clothing, cushions, tablecloths and other items made from fabric which has been block-printed by hand in local designs. In the same complex, you can also buy hand-decorated Ros Byrne pottery and wickerwork items from Malawi. It's open from 8 am to 5 pm Monday to Friday and 9 am to 4 pm on Saturday.

The Jairos Jiri Crafts Shop, which benefits disabled Zimbabweans, is in the Park Lane building on Julius Nyerere Crescent opposite the National Gallery. At the Danhiko Project School on the Mutare road opposite the Nite-Star Drive in Cinema, you'll find a variety of locally made clothing and carpentry items for sale at well below shop prices. The colourful fabrics are produced by disabled and low-income Zimbabweans, with Scandinavian aid. Otherwise, check out the shop selling inexpensive African-print clothing between South and Kenneth Kaunda Aves, near the railway station. The cheapest T-shirts in the centre are at Zimcraft Co-operative Shop in the 1st St Parkade where you'll pay at least 30% less than at Rado Arts, a trendy but expensive designer clothing shop on the 1st St Mall.

For more crafts options, see Mbare and Cold Comfort Farm Society, both in the Around Harare section.

Getting There & Away

Air Harare International Airport lies 15 km south-east of the city, and handles all international and Air Zimbabwe domestic traffic. Charter flights and light aircraft operate out of Charles Prince Airport 18 km north-west of Harare.

There are direct domestic Air Zimbabwe flights between Harare and Bulawayo, Buffalo Range, Kariba, Victoria Falls, Gweru, Masvingo and Hwange National Park. For more information, refer to the Zimbabwe Getting Around chapter. Information about getting to Harare from other countries is found in the Getting There & Away chapters.

Airline offices in Harare include:

Aeroflot Karigamombe Centre, Samora Machel Ave (☎ 731971)
Air Botswana suite 501, Jameson Hotel, on the corner of Samora Machel and Union Aves(☎ 703132)
Air India Batanai Gardens, on the corner of 1st St and Jason Moyo Ave (☎ 700318)
Air Malawi Throgmorton House, on the corner of Samora Machel Ave and Julius Nyerere Way (☎ 706497)
Air Mauritius 13th floor, Old Mutual Centre, on the corner of 3rd St and Jason Moyo Ave (☎ 735738)
Air Tanzania Lintas House, Union Ave (☎ 706444)
Air Zimbabwe City Air Terminal, on the corner of 3rd St and Speke Ave (☎ 575111; fax 575068), reservations (☎ 575021)
American Airlines Leopard Rock Hotel Group (☎ 733073; fax 791484)
Balkan Bulgarian Airlines Trustee House, 55 Samora Machel Ave (☎ 759271; fax 757684)
British Airways Batanai Gardens, on the corner of 1st St and Jason Moyo Ave (☎ 759173; fax 756670)
Egypt Air ConstructionHouse, 110 Leopold Takawira St(☎ 728860)
Ethiopian Airlines Central African Building Society Centre, Jason Moyo Ave (☎ 790705)
Kenya Airways, Stanley House, Jason Moyo Ave (☎ 792181)
KLM 1st floor, Harvest House, Baker Ave (☎ 731042; fax 736021)

Linhas Aéreas de Moçambique Chancellor House, 69 Samora Machel Ave (☎ 703338)
Lufthansa Mercury House, 24 George Silundika Ave (☎ 707606)
Qantas 5th floor, Karigamombe Centre, 54 Union Ave (☎ 794676)
Royal Swazi Airlines 6 Chancellor House, 69 Samora Machel Ave(☎ 730170)
South African Airways 2nd floor, Takura House, 69-71 Union Ave (☎ 738922)
TAP Air Portugal 5th floor, Prudential House, on the corner of Angwa St and Speke Ave(☎ 706231)
Zambia Airways Pearl Assurance Building, 1st St (☎ 793235)

Bus Express Motorways (☎ 720392; fax 737438) has daily departures to Mutare (US$6.40), Bulawayo (US$13), Beitbridge (US$11) and Johannesburg (US$38). The Johannesburg run is in conjunction with the South African company, Trans-Lux. Express Motorways also goes to Masvingo/Great Zimbabwe (US$8.50) and Kariba (US$11) on Friday only and to Gaborone (US$35) on Thursday and Sunday. To Victoria Falls (US$26), you must change buses in Bulawayo, entailing at least an overnight stop. Their booking office is on the corner of Baker Ave and Rezende St.

For its terminal, Ajay's Motorways uses the Monomatapa Hotel. They have services from Harare to Bulawayo daily except Friday, and from Bulawayo to Harare daily except Thursday. The one-way fare is US$11. Book through Manica Travel (☎ 703421), on the 2nd floor of the Travel Centre on Jason Moyo Ave.

For more luxury, the Blue Arrow/United Transport Group (☎ 729514; fax 729572) coaches also connect Harare and Bulawayo. They leave Harare on Tuesday, Thursday and Sunday at 1.45 pm (arriving at 8 pm); and on Friday at 3.45 pm (arriving at 10 pm). From Bulawayo to Harare, they depart on Monday, Wednesday, Friday and Saturday at 7 am. One-way costs US$16. In Harare, the office is Chester House, on Speke Ave between 3rd and 4th Sts. In Bulawayo, they use the Swift Town Depot (☎ 69673) at 73a Fife Ave. These coaches also offer services to Johannesburg, operated by South Africa's Greyhound line.

Long-distance local or African buses depart from the extensive Mbare musika in Mbare township, five km from the centre. To smaller villages, there may only be one bus daily and chances are, it will depart at or shortly after 6 am. Buses to Bulawayo depart from early morning into the afternoon, but especially for Masvingo, Kariba or Mutare, the closer to 6 am you arrive, the better your chances of getting a seat.

There are signs at the terminal indicating the buses' destinations. They're grouped according to which road they'll be taking out of the city: the Mutare, Beatrice or Bulawayo roads. The buses aren't normally as crowded as one may expect, but on weekends and holidays, they're packed to overflowing.

For Mutare (US$2.50), Tenda buses depart every half hour and you can catch them either from Mbare or from Msasa along the Mutare road. Numerous buses depart from Mbare for Bulawayo (US$4) between 6 am and 1 pm; you shouldn't have to wait more than a few minutes. From Mbare to Kariba (US$3.50), take the Mucheche or ZUPCO buses. To Masvingo (US$3), the recommended company is Mhunga, departing from Mbare in the early morning.

For information on international buses from Harare, see the Zimbabwe Getting There & Away chapter.

Train The railway station is on the corner of Kenneth Kaunda Ave and 2nd St. Trains run daily to and from Bulawayo and Mutare. Timetables are detailed in the Zimbabwe Getting Around chapter.

The reservations office is open from 8 am to 1 pm and 2 to 4 pm Monday to Friday and from 8 to 11.30 am Saturday. The ticket office opens Monday to Friday between 8 am and 1 pm, 2 to 4 pm, and 7 to 9.30 pm. On Saturday, you can buy tickets from 8 to 11.30 am and 7 to 9.30 pm. On Sunday, it's only open between 7 and 9.30 pm.

Getting Around
To/From the Airport The Express Motorways airport bus (☎ 720392) runs between the centre and the airport to connect with

arriving or departing flights (more or less hourly, on the hour) from Speke Ave and 2nd St, near Meikles Hotel. It will also pick up booked passengers staying in the central area. The fare is US$2 each way. On the return trip, it will drop you at any central hotel or guesthouse. Phone for schedules or bookings.

Taxis to or from the airport cost US$6.50. The larger hotels – Meikles, Sheraton, Monomatapa and so on – send courtesy vehicles for their guests.

Bus Harare city buses, which exist mainly to connect the city centre with the suburban areas, are very crowded. If want to use them heading away from the centre, catch them at one of the five central city bus termini. Otherwise, your chances of squeezing on – or even inspiring a driver to stop for you – are inversely proportional to the number of stops you are from the terminus. If your destination isn't near the end of the line, the return trip could be problematic. Fares are just Z$1 to Z$1.50 – less than US$0.25. Alternatively, you can use the new commuter buses, which are 15-seater vans.

The five central termini are the Market Square terminus, between Harare and Mbuya Nehanda Sts; the 4th St terminus, on Robert Mugabe Rd between 4th and 5th Sts; the Angwa St terminus, on the corner of Angwa St and Robson Manyika; the Rezende St terminus, on Rezende St between Jason Moyo and Baker Aves; and the Chinhoyi St terminus, on Speke Ave between Cameron and Chinhoyi. Buses to Mbare intercity bus terminal depart from the Angwa St and Robson Manyika terminus. There's also a string of bus stops along Jason Moyo Ave, near the corner of 4th St.

Taxi Taxi stands are found in front of all hotels; on the corner of 1st St and Baker Ave; on Samora Machel Ave near 1st St; and on Union Ave between Angwa St and Julius Nyerere Way. Although there are hundreds of maverick taxis, they are not controlled and using them can be risky. Official services include Rixi Taxi (☎ 707707 or 724222), the economically priced Cream Line Taxis (☎ 703333), and A1 Taxi (☎ 706996).

To or from anywhere in the city centre costs from US$0.60 to US$0.90 (Z$5 to Z$7). Trips into the suburbs run between US$2 and US$2.25 (Z$15 and Z$18) and to the airport, about US$2.50 (Z$20). Taxi meters all run at different speeds and controls are nonexistent but Rixi, based on the corner of Samora Machel Ave and Harare St, seems to be reliable.

If you don't mind a bit of research to work out their routes, look for emergency taxis around the corner of George Silundika Ave and 4th St, or on Rezende St between Jason Moyo and Baker Aves. Emergency taxis cost Z$1.50 (less than US$0.20) from anywhere to anywhere along their fixed routes.

Bicycle Harare is compact and mostly flat, and lends itself well to bicycle exploration, even for those unused to cycling. However, whenever you're stopped, watch your equipment closely.

Bikes may be hired at Bushtrackers at the Brontë Hotel, corner of 4th St and Baines Ave. They're open from 9 am to 2 pm.

Around Harare

MBARE
Just five km from the centre, Mbare is probably the only Harare suburb worth visiting in its own right. Before independence, when Harare was called Salisbury, Mbare was known as Harare Township. The name now honours the Shona chief Mbare, who was headquartered on the Kopje in what is now Central Harare.

All Mbare's activity is centred on the musika, Zimbabwe's largest market and busiest bus terminal. Between 6 am and 6 pm, it hums constantly, crowded with shoppers, travellers, and sales and business people. Shoppers can find everything from second-hand clothing and appliances to herbal remedies, African crafts and

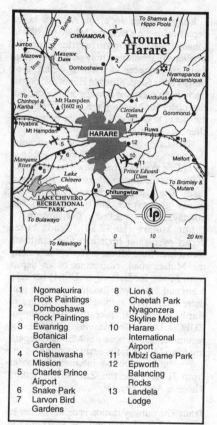

1	Ngomakurira Rock Paintings	8	Lion & Cheetah Park
2	Domboshawa Rock Paintings	9	Nyagonzera Skyline Motel
3	Ewanrigg Botanical Garden	10	Harare International Airport
4	Chishawasha Mission	11	Mbizi Game Park
5	Charles Prince Airport	12	Epworth Balancing Rocks
6	Snake Park	13	Landela Lodge
7	Larvon Bird Gardens		

jewellery. Fresh fruit and vegetables can be bought in the local produce stalls at a fraction of supermarket prices. A particularly good time to visit is Sunday afternoon; while the rest of Harare shuts down, Mbare keeps buzzing.

Also of interest is the Canon Paterson Art Centre on Chaminuka Rd, which was founded by the Bulawayo reverend Canon Paterson in the 1940s. Here you can watch artists carving soapstone, verdite, wood and serpentine into souvenirs which are sold around the country. You can also purchase the items at the centre for substantial savings over what you'd pay elsewhere.

Getting There & Away

To reach Mbare from the centre, take the municipal bus from the terminus on the corner of Angwa and Robson Manyika Sts. Official taxis for up to five passengers cost around US$2 each way; if you take an unlicensed taxi (not really a good idea), the price will depend on your bargaining skills.

For information on tours to Mbare, see Harare, Organised Tours. For more about the inter-city bus terminal at Mbare musika, see Getting There & Away for Harare.

CHITUNGWIZA

In the face of unchecked rural immigration since Zimbabwean independence, Harare was bursting at the seams and city planners realised something had to give. The result was the creation of the massive 'satellite' of Chitungwiza south of the airport, which is effectively a city in its own right. It's now home to nearly one million people and in fact, when counted as separate from Harare (which it certainly is – at least physically), Chitungwiza is Zimbabwe's third largest city, after Harare and Bulawayo. When it's included in statistics for metropolitan Harare, the capital's population practically doubles.

Chitungwiza is divided into several units. Unit B is the wealthiest, while units C and D are considerably poorer. A visit to this sprawling high-density community may prove to be an interesting social experience, but in reality, it's much like Mbare – although it is, admittedly, much bigger.

Getting There & Away

To get there, catch a bus from in front of the London Bakery on Rezende St in Harare. You can also hitch along Hatfield Road.

EWANRIGG NATIONAL PARK

This small and loosely defined national park 40 km north-east of Harare consists of an elaborate 40 hectare botanical garden and 200 hectares of woodland. The garden is characterised by an array of prehistoric-looking aloes, cacti and palm-like cycads and during the winter, the slopes glow with the brilliant red and yellow blooms of the succulents and the variegated hues of tropical flowers. Along with the flowering plants, there's a stand of bamboo, a herb garden, a water garden and an arboretum.

Originally, Ewanrigg was the farm and personal hobby garden of botanist Harold Basil Christian, who set up housekeeping on the site in 1891. It was named *Ewanrigg* (Manx for Ewan's Ridge) after the family holdings on the Isle of Man. Upon Christian's death on 12 May 1950, his holdings were bequeathed to the state.

Ewanrigg is a popular picnic site with the Harare crowd and sunny weekends bring them out in droves for braais, cricket, football and strolling along the many footpaths. During the rest of the week it's a serenely inspiring alternative to Harare's version of civilisation. Facilities include picnic tables, braai pits, water taps, toilet blocks and firewood. However, there are no camp sites. Admission is US$1.20 per person.

Mermaid's Pool

This nice vegetated spot six km from the Ewanrigg turn-off was once a small resort, organised around its stone water slide and eponymous pool. However, it has now been converted into a private residence and is no longer open to the public.

Getting There & Away

To reach Ewanrigg on public transport, take the Shamva bus from Mbare as early in the morning as possible and ask to be dropped at the Ewanrigg turn-off. From there, it's a three-km walk to the gardens. You can also hitch from the city to the Shamva turn-off (route A15) about 20 km north-east along the Mutoko Highway (Enterprise Rd). From there, it's 20 km to the Ewanrigg turn-off.

If you prefer an easier route, Kalambeza Safaris runs daily tours costing US$12 per person.

HARARE TO LAKE CHIVERO
Snake Park

The Snake Park, 11 km from Harare on the Bulawayo road, is a kitsch collection of serpentine sorts owned by the same folks as the Lion & Cheetah Park. On display are some harmless varieties as well as such renowned baddies as spitting cobras, gaboon vipers, puff adders, boomslangs and mambas. However, unless you're passing by anyway or have a particular fascination with that ilk, it's not worth a special trip. It's open daily from 8.30 am to 5 pm and admission costs US$2.50. All Bulawayo-bound buses pass the Snake Park; for information on tours, see the Lion & Cheetah Park and Lake Chivero sections.

Larvon Bird Gardens
Larvon Bird Gardens, with over 400 species on display, is especially worthwhile for birdwatchers hoping to familiarise themselves with southern African species. They operate a bird orphanage as well as a conservation reserve, and it's a sensitive set-up. The larger birds are allowed room to roam while waterfowl enjoy a pleasant natural lake. It's open weekdays except Thursday from 10 am to 5 pm and on weekends from 9 am to 5 pm. Admission is US$1.50. On weekends, a tea garden beside the lake serves light snacks and drinks.

Larvon lies 18 km south-west of Harare just off the Bulawayo road. To get there, drive out along the Bulawayo road or take any Bulawayo-bound bus from Harare and ask to be dropped at the Oatlands Rd turnoff. From the intersection, it's just one km to the entrance. Larvon Bird Gardens is also included in a UTC tour, described under Lion & Cheetah Park later in this section.

Cold Comfort Farm Society
The well-established Cold Comfort Farm Society (☎ 703372) is an artists' cooperative on Cowie Rd, two km off the Bulawayo road 13 km from Harare. They produce African tapestries from local wool and natural dyes, which are sold for very reasonable prices, and also support cooperative agricultural, carpentry and metalworking ventures. At the recently established Amon Shonge Gallery, which is housed in one of the farm's former barns, you'll find a variety of original work

produced by village women around the country. However, things are a bit pricey.

In addition to material arts, you can also buy agricultural products grown on the farm. It's open to visitors Monday to Friday from 10 am to 5 pm and on weekends from 10 am to 4 pm.

Lion & Cheetah Park
The Lion & Cheetah Park (☎ 6437 Norton), 24 km from Harare just off the Bulawayo road, is the only place in the area to see big cats. It's on a large private estate which also boasts a population of baboons and crocodiles. Admission is US$5 per vehicle and US$2.50 for each adult. It's open daily from 8.30 am to 5 pm.

Since walking and hitching aren't permitted, you must arrive in a private vehicle or take a UTC or Kalambeza tour from Harare. With UTC, a three-hour tour of the Lion & Cheetah Park combined with Lake Chivero departs daily except Thursday at 9.30 am and costs US$25. Kalambeza operates daily (except Sunday) tours to the Lion & Cheetah Park and the Snake Park for US$15.

LAKE CHIVERO RECREATIONAL PARK
Although few travellers are set alight by Lake Chivero (formerly Lake McIlwaine), it's all the rage with Harare day-trippers, who love to spend sunny weekends fishing, boating, partying and organising braais on the lakeshore.

The 5500-hectare national recreational park 32 km south-west of Harare focuses on 57-sq-km Lake Chivero, a reservoir created by the 1952 damming of the Manyame (also known as the Hunyani) River. It was originally named for Sir Robert McIlwaine, first chairman of the board of National Resources. The water level has been quite low for several years now and the shore is becoming choked with rapidly spreading water hyacinth.

The North Shore
The commercialised California-esque northern shore of Lake Chivero is lined with private boat harbours and special-interest

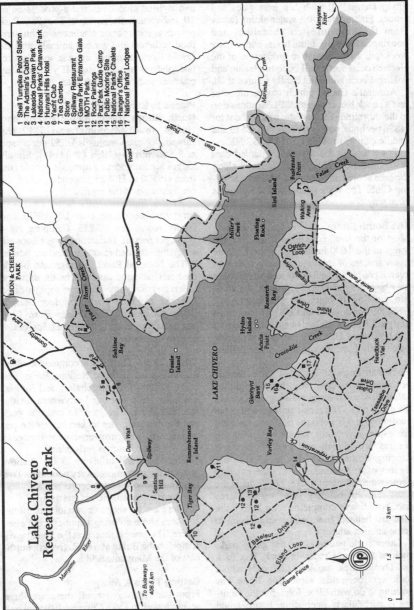

Lake Chivero Recreational Park

1 Shell Turnpike Petrol Station
2 The Admiral's Cabin
3 Lakeside Caravan Park
4 National Parks' Caravan Park
5 Hunyani Hills Hotel
6 Yacht Club
7 Tea Garden
8 Store
9 Spillway Restaurant
10 Game Park Entrance Gate
11 MOTH Park
12 Rock Paintings
13 Pax Park Guide Camp
14 Public Mooring Site
15 National Parks' Chalets
16 Ranger's Office
17 National Parks' Lodges

ZIMBABWE

group camps, all with big iron gates and fences. Fishing, boating, water-skiing (away from the croc-infested shoreline) and boozing are the big attractions, and on any weekend, a representative proportion of the Harare social scene will be found lazing and dazing. Peace and quiet hardly figures at all.

Admiral's Cabin, which has picnic sites and a snack bar, charges US$1.30 admission to the shoreline. You can hire a motorboat for US$8 per hour, pontoon boats for US$13 and paddle canoes for US$1.50 to US$2.50.

For a look at the zealously guarded dam wall, stroll from Hunyani Hills Hotel along the lake shore and through the Mazowe Sailing Club. The walk takes about 25 minutes each way.

The South Shore

Most of the southern shore of the lake belongs to the 1600-hectare game park where many species of antelope, zebra, giraffe, and even a couple of well-protected white rhino may be observed. Overall, though, the wildlife viewing is marginal. Foreigners pay US$2.50 for day use and US$5 for a multi-day pass. Ranger-guided horse safaris lasting 1½ hours cost US$5 per person and operate twice daily from the camp reception office.

Rock Paintings Bushman's Point at the end of the southern shore drive has been designated a picnic site and walking area within the game park. The rock paintings above the lake shore just beyond the traffic turnaround are especially worth a look. Most of the figures are human and include hunters, dancing women and a row of 13 kneeling figures of undetermined sex. One painting depicts the felling of a tree, but perhaps the most relevant painting is of several large fish, which was completed long before the lake just beneath them was even a gleam in some ancient angler's eye.

Other rock paintings in the game park, such as those at Crocodile Rock, Pax Park and Ovoid Rock, are accessible only with a park service guide. Crocodile Rock has nothing to do with Elton John, but the painting is particularly interesting: two detailed

and stylised crocodiles and a procession of 10 individualistic hunters. The Pax Park paintings incorporate renditions of hunters, food gatherers and various animals, and the Ovoid Rock paintings include some as yet unexplained ovoid shapes. If you're interested, enquire at the park gate.

Places to Stay & Eat

North Shore Basic double rooms cost US$10, four-bed rooms are US$12 and camping or caravanning is US$2 per person at the *Admiral's Cabin* (☎ 27144). Simple lodges accommodating up to six people cost from US$20 to US$25, depending upon the configuration of the rooms.

At the *Hunyani Hills Hotel* (☎ 2236), single/double rooms cost US$19/25 and family rooms are US$35. Camping costs US$2 per person. The setting is nice enough, as are the attached restaurant and tea house.

The National Parks' campground beside the hotel has camp sites with baths, showers, toilets and braai pits. The more sophisticated *Lakeside Caravan Park* next door charges US$3 per person. The *Trader Horn Club* camp site further east is for the exclusive use of club members.

South Shore The only accommodation on the southern shore is the National Parks' rest camp, which has both chalets and lodges. Camping isn't permitted anywhere on the southern shore. The gates to both the park and the rest camp are locked between 6 pm and 6 am, and non-emergency access between those hours is forbidden.

Crocodiles and bilharzia in the shallow water make swimming a very poor idea. Two swimming pools, tennis courts and a volleyball court are available for guests' use.

There are no shops or restaurants on the southern shore so bring supplies from elsewhere. The nearest shop is at the Shell petrol station on the Bulawayo road, five km northeast of the Manyame bridge.

Getting There & Away

From the Bulawayo road, there are three access routes to Lake Chivero. Especially at weekends, hitchhikers will have the most success with the northern access, Oatlands Rd, which passes Larvon Bird Gardens and winds up at the north shore. The middle access route, which is nearest the lake, turns off at the Shell Turnpike petrol station and convenience store, five km north of the Manyame bridge. From there, it's just three km over the ridge to the Hunyani Hills Hotel on the northern shore.

Hitchers should remember that the southern access, which turns off immediately south-west of the Manyame bridge, isn't connected by road to the northern shore. To get in or out of the National Parks' rest camp or Bushman's Point, you must pass through the game park where walking and hitching are prohibited. If you can reach the game park gate, however, the friendly wardens can normally help you find a lift in or out.

Sometime after 8 am daily, there's a bus from Mbare to the northern shore. Otherwise, wait at the bus stop just down from the Cresta Jameson Hotel on Samora Machel Ave. Buses run frequently out the Bulawayo road and can get you within striking distance of the lake. Alternatively, go to Mbare, hop on any Bulawayo-bound bus and get off at one of the three access routes to the lake.

Alternatively, you can take a tour. UTC runs four-hour tours from Harare to Lake Chivero and the Lion & Cheetah Park at 9 am and 2 pm daily for US$25. Kalambeza does full day tours – and includes the Snake Park – for US$32. If you wish to spend more time than the tours allow, you can normally rejoin the tour on another day, but make arrangements before setting out.

Another option is with Kuteza Tours (☎ 64338; after hours 729008), which offers a choice of parasailing, water-skiing, sailboarding, fishing, canoeing, birdwatching and game-viewing activities. Day trips from Harare cost US$25 including lunch.

DOMBOSHAWA & NGOMAKURIRA

Even without its ancient rock paintings, the Chinamora Communal lands are worthy of a visit for their scenic value alone. There are lots of opportunities for walking and rock scrambling and the stark and colourful lichen-covered domes that characterise the region are unusually intriguing.

In addition to the two popular sites, Domboshawa and Ngomakurira, the Chinamora area is packed with numerous other paintings. For further information and directions to the more obscure sites, refer to *The Painted Caves* by Peter Garlake, which is available at Kingston's in Harare.

Domboshawa

Because it is nearer to Harare, Domboshawa is the more frequently visited of the two painted cave sites, but unless you go on a weekend, you're still likely to have the place to yourself. A small museum at the car park has information on rock painting in general and speculation about these Chinamora sites. From there, a well-marked 15-minute walk takes you to Domboshawa Caves, where the rock paintings are concentrated.

The main cave contains a dense concentration of figures, the most visible of which are several kudu. Elephants, zebras, buffaloes, human figures and four outlined rhinos randomly decorate the interior walls. In a fracture to the left of the main cave, seven San-like stick figures attack an irritable elephant. A very faded panel about 30 metres to the right of the cave depicts a troupe of dancing, long-waisted beings known colloquially as 'the rainmakers'.

Once you've seen the paintings, allow time to wander over the peaceful and colourful domes and rock formations surrounding the cave. The site is open until 5 pm. Foreigners pay US$2.60 admission.

Ngomakurira

Due to the glare caused by direct sunlight on the paintings, Ngomakurira is best seen in the afternoon. Its romantic name means 'the mountain of drums' after the acoustic effect created by the natural form of the stone. It's believed that the reverberations one hears there are the beating drums of festive spirits. It's generally agreed that Ngomakurira offers the finest easily accessible rock paintings in Zimbabwe.

ZIMBABWE

Once you've reached the rock, follow the green painted arrows over the rock to the best paintings on the eastern side. Alternatively, from the base of the hill, walk around the northern end to a small valley containing a stream bed. Follow it up to the foot of the orange lichen-stained cliff that rises to the dome's eastern summit. The paintings are found at its base. The main panel is centred around a procession of four very large elephants flanked by various human figures: women, couples, sleeping children and hunters. On the head of the third elephant is depicted a violent confrontation between a man with a club and his terrified unarmed victim. Other human figures dance across the rock or perform daily tasks while various anonymous animals meet their doom at the hands of hunters.

Don't forget to coax a performance out of the spirit drummers – they'll always comply if you start pounding first.

Getting There & Away

To reach Domboshawa, you can take the Bindura via Chinamora bus from Mbare musika, get off at the turn-off four km north of Domboshawa village (30 km north of Harare), and walk the remaining one km to the base of the rock. The same bus continues on to the Sasa road turn-off. Ngomakurira lies just two km east of there. Alternatively, you can reach Domboshawa by taking the Domboshawa bus from Mbare to Domboshawa village and walking the km from there to the site. From Harare, you can also catch the buses on 7th St – known further out as Chancellor Ave and Borrowdale Rd. Hitching is difficult north of Domboshawa village.

CHISHAWASHA

The Chishawasha Catholic Mission, 21 km north-east of Harare, lies on a little-travelled road midway between the Shamva turn-off on the Mutoko road and the Arcturus road. It was founded on 31 July 1892 by the German priest, Francis Richartz. After the First Chimurenga, it became a profitable farming, printing and teaching centre. The interior murals and nearby cemetery have both historical and aesthetic value.

Northern Zimbabwe

With the exception of eastern Kariba and Mana Pools National Park, the country north of Harare geographically draws a blank from many Zimbabweans and visitors alike. This beautiful rolling landscape supports numerous small villages and such little-visited gems as the Mavuradonha Wilderness, the Umfurudzi Safari Area, the wilderness of the middle Zambezi Valley and the sculptors' community at Tengenenge Farm.

History

If the high incidence of prehistoric rock paintings around the present town of Mutoko is any indication, north-eastern Zimbabwe has been inhabited for millennia. In the mid-1500s, the name of the small mountain Fura, now known as Mt Darwin, was taken by early Portuguese arrivals to be a corruption of 'Ophir' and for several centuries, Europeans wildly speculated that the 'Empire of Monomatapa' guarded the biblical land of Ophir and the elusive mines of King Solomon. The British who arrived in the late 19th century settled the Harare area because they believed the country immediately south of the Zambezi to be as rich in minerals and precious metals as the Kimberley and Witwatersrand regions of South Africa.

Later, this wild country attracted the exiled and dispossessed of other regions, including the people of the defeated chief Mbare who had ruled from the Kopje at present-day Harare, and the charismatic 19th-century Shona outlaw, Mapondera, who died in prison on a hunger strike after admitting defeat in his attempts to resist encroaching colonial rule.

The North-East

NYAMAPANDA

The only reason anyone goes to Nyamapanda is to connect with the run across Mozambique's Tête Corridor to Malawi. For details on this trip, refer to the discussion of Malawi in the Zimbabwe Getting There & Away chapter.

MAZOWE

Mazowe, the heart of Zimbabwe's citrus production zone, lies in a fertile agricultural area 40 km north of Harare. The idea of planting orange, lemon and lime groves at Mazoe stemmed from the early discovery of wild Indian lemon trees, which had apparently been imported by 15th-century Swahili and Portuguese traders. The first commercial citrus crop was harvested on Mazoe Citrus Estates, a subsidiary of the British South Africa Company, in 1913. Today, the area boasts 200,000 citrus trees, which occupy 700 hectares.

Nearby, the lovely blue Mazowe Dam draws weekend visitors from Harare for boating and braais.

Places to Stay

The only place in town is the *Mazoe Hotel* (☎ 2243), a colonial country-style building dating from 1895. It has a bar and licensed restaurant. *Zindele Guest Farm* (☎ 721696;

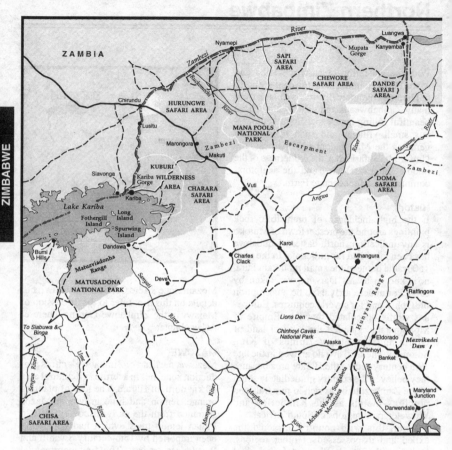

fax 702006, Harare), 30 km north of Mazowe, is both a working tobacco farm and game ranch. Day trips cost US$70, and overnight stays, US$125 per person.

TENGENENGE FARM

Although it's well off the trampled route, Tengenenge Farm, the remote sculptors' community at the foot of the Great Dyke near Guruve, makes a worthwhile visit. The farm is supported by the sale of artists' works as well as outside sponsorships and it is always on the lookout for new talent. Some of the original artists remain and maintain farms at the community while others have established studios nearer their market.

Regrettably, Tengenenge is becoming more of a commercial operation, so don't envision any sort of bohemian utopia in the wilderness. Although the patrons have tried to prevent a mass-production mentality from creeping into the work, many of the artists are now being tempted to surrender to market forces. Still, travellers seeking an appreciation of Shona sculpture will certainly enjoy the place. Visiting foreign sculptors are welcome, but they're required to pay the hefty tourist rates like anyone else.

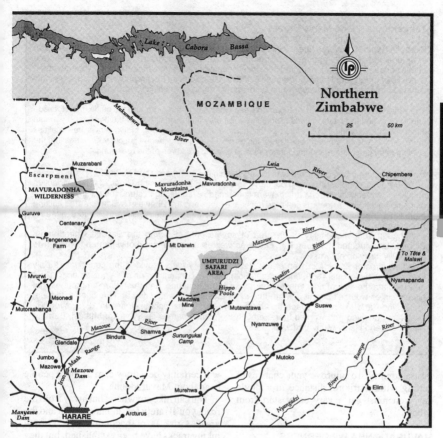

Visitors are welcomed and are invited to stroll through the extensive sculpture gardens. Room and board is expensive at the farm, but you can bring your own food and there should be little problem finding a camp site in the bush. For further information contact Tengenenge Farm (☎ 1223, Guruve), PO Box 169, Mvurwi.

Getting There & Away

If you're driving from Harare, follow the Mazowe road to Mazowe Dam, where you should turn left. After 56 km, turn left again, towards Mvurwi, at a big dome rock. On the road out of town, turn right and continue towards Guruve. After 34.5 km, 12 km south of Guruve, take the right turning, which is signposted for Tengenenge. After 11 km, you'll run out of tar. Continue for two km on the gravel and turn left; it's then five km to Tengenenge.

There is no public transport directly to Tengenenge. From Mbare, take the Guruve bus – or you can go to Mvurwi and change buses. Get off at the Tengenenge turn-off 12 km south of Guruve. Unless you are lucky with a lift, you will have to walk the remaining 19 km through grasslands and upland

Tengenenge – One Man's Dream

The sculptors' community at Tengenenge Farm is the realised vision of tobacco farmer Tom Blomefield who discovered Great Dyke chrome on his land during the UDI (Unilateral Declaration of Independence) days and from it earned enough money to abandon farming and concentrate on his consuming interest in art. In 1966, local soapstone sculptor Crispen Chakenyoka revealed deposits of magnificent black serpentine in the hills surrounding the property; fate had seemingly dictated that Blomefield's focus would be on sculpture. In Blomefield's words:

The world is like a cattle kraal; you can only see what is in it, the earth and the cattle, the stockade and the sky and the passing birds. Sometimes you may find a small hole in the back...and you can escape from this world into the mists of the invisible universal field. You may discover new realities there, and dare to dream and desire great things and – visualising them – put out your hands into the swirling mist, grasp them and bring them back to become creatures of the real world.

Malawian sculptor Lemon Moses was the first to join the community and before long, artists were arriving from around southern Africa, carrying with them the artistic traditions of their respective cultures. Zimbabwean Shona artists were consumed with defining in stone the mystical aspects of their own folklore. Angolans sculpted mask-like faces and the Chewa of Malawi created hulking monolithic pieces, while their compatriots, the Yao, infused their beliefs in a more abstract iconography.

Although Tengenenge lay in an area of severe conflict during the Second Chimurenga, Blomefield respected the guerrillas' cause as well as their spiritual motivation and was left to peacefully carry on his work.

When director Frank McEwen of the National Gallery (who provided the community's only Harare sales outlet until 1969) encouraged Bolmefield to concentrate on a few outstanding artists and regulate the flow of new talent into and out of Tengenenge, he refused on the grounds that his principles wouldn't permit it. More and more artists were welcomed and provided with food, tools, stone and exhibition space and by the time the formal school closed in 1979, over 500 sculptors had lived and worked there, among them such names as Sylvester Mubayi, Bernard Matemera and Henry Munyaradzi. ■

msasa country. To improve your chances of getting within striking distance in a single day, you must get a very early start from Mbare.

MAVURADONHA WILDERNESS

In 1988, the Zimbabwe government set aside a 500-sq-km chunk of the Mavuradonha Range above the Zambezi Escarpment as a wilderness area and game reserve. Characterised by rugged, mountainous uplands, the wild landscape is simultaneously beautiful and daunting. Although the area was a main theatre of operations during the bush war and was largely hunted out, its new protected status has lured back several species of antelope, as well as baboons and even a few elephants, and there's talk of importing stocks from elsewhere. Leopards have always been present and even lions are occasionally seen. Bird life is profuse and

will certainly be a draw card as more people hear about Mavuradonha.

You can hike anywhere, but away from the road, you'll rarely see another person and the greatest risk is of becoming lost. Formal hiking tracks have been established, but they aren't always easy to follow and there's no trail map available (apart from the one in this book). Prospective hikers may get some use out of the Banirembezi A3 topo sheet, which is sold at the surveyor general's office in Harare. A recommended short walk is down the Musengedzi Trail to Kemavanga Falls.

Organised Tours

To penetrate even further into the wilderness you can ride with Carew/Wild Side Safaris on a week-long horseback trip through the remote mountain-acacia dotted ridges and depths of the Tingwa Valley area. For up to eight people, they charge US$2400, includ-

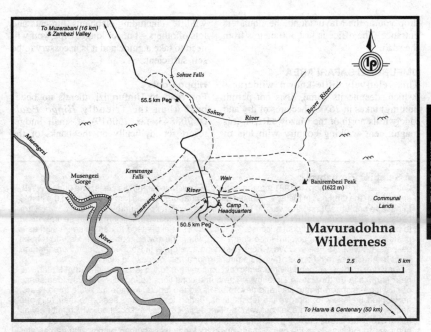

ZIMBABWE

To Muzerabani (16 km) & Zambezi Valley

Sohwe Falls

55.5 km Peg

Sohwe River

Boore River

Musengezi

Musengezi Gorge

Kemavanga Falls

Kemavanga River

Weir

River

Camp Headquarters

50.5 km Peg

River

Banirembezi Peak (1622 m)

Communal Lands

Mavuradohna Wilderness

0   2.5   5 km

To Harare & Centenary (50 km)

ing everything except transport from Harare, which costs an additional US$60 per person. Enquire about special backpackers' rates, which may be available off-season or when there are last minute vacancies.

The Zimbabwe Travel Board, in conjunction with villagers in the Mavuradonha area, has organised a novel rural-tourism programme for Murota village. For US$63, tourists can enjoy a quiet weekend in a small Harare, basic accommodation, meals, drinks and information on village life. The trips leave Harare at 7 am and return on Sunday afternoon. For further information, contact the Zimbabwe Travel Bureau (☎ 702941), PO Box UA 534, Harare. Bookings should be made by Thursday prior to the weekend you want to go.

Places to Stay & Eat

As part of the highly lauded Campfire Programme, the camp at the Mavuradonha Wilderness headquarters is maintained by the local community, which also benefits from the income it generates. Accommodation is in tent-like thatched A-frames, which sleep two people and cost US$2.60. It gets cold up here, and there's no bedding – you sleep on a mattress of straw – so you'll need a sleeping bag. Basic toilets and showers are available, and the staff sell small bundles of firewood for US$1.20.

For supplies – and an excursion into a totally different world – head down to the country supermarket in Muzerabani, 12 km from the foot of the Zambezi Escarpment.

Getting There & Away

The Mavuradonha headquarters lies at the 50.5-km peg on the Muzerabani road north of Centenary. By car from Harare, it's about a two-hour journey. Fuel is available at Muzerabani from Monday to Saturday; on Sunday, get it from Mvurwi (115 km away).

From Mbare, buses run occasionally to Centenary and Muzerabani. Ask the driver to drop you at the Mavuradonha headquarters entrance. The office is just 300 metres from the road.

UMFURUDZI SAFARI AREA

This relatively little-known wilderness (which, despite its name, does not permit hunting) takes in 76,000 hectares of dry and lonely hills north of the Mazowe River. It is magnificent walking country with lots of wildlife – including elephants, big cats and lots of others – but for longer trips, you will need to take a guide and it is necessary to be self-sufficient.

Hippo Pools

For visits to Umfurudzi, there's no better base than the friendly *Hippo Pools* (☎ 708843; fax 750619), a small budget resort set idyllically on the banks of the

---

A Saint for Zimbabwe?

John Bradburne was born in 1921 into the Anglican English upper middle class, and during WWII, served with the Gurkhas in Malaya. After the fall of Singapore, he was forced to flee into the jungle to escape capture. During the war, he became friends with fellow Gurkha John Dove, who later became a Jesuit priest. In 1947, Bradburne converted to Roman Catholicism and three times tried to become a monk, but without success. After a penniless pilgrimage to Jerusalem, a stint as a busker in England and a sojourn in southern Italy, where he vowed to the virgin Mary to remain celibate, he wrote to Father Dove, who was serving as a priest in Rhodesia. Soon thereafter, he went to Africa where he spent 10 years searching for a holy purpose in his life.

One day in 1969, a friend invited him to accompany her to the leper settlement at Mutemwa, near Mutoko in north-eastern Zimbabwe. The horrid conditions he found – and a sudden sense of mission – inspired him to stay and devote his life to the lepers. For the following three years, he worked tirelessly to improve the lepers' lives, caring for them and seeing to their religious needs. In 1972, however, he fell out with the Rhodesia Leprosy Association, which felt he was being overly generous providing one loaf of bread per person per week. He'd also refused to affix numbers to individuals in the camp, maintaining that they were human beings with names and not simply statistics.

As a result, he was kicked out of the compound, but he didn't go away. For the next six years, he lived outside the fence, entering the camp at night to minister to the lepers. By day, he became a hermit without interest in money or possessions, praying, writing religious verse, scarcely eating, and wearing the habit of a third order Franciscan, which had been permitted by the order.

Throughout this period, the bush war for Zimbabwean independence heated up, and the north-eastern part of the country saw the worst of the fighting. On midnight of 2 September 1978, John Bradburne was visited by about 10 youths – *mujibhas* – who weren't actually guerrillas, but rather messengers and 'intelligence officers' for the ZANU fighters. They were probably acting on a tip-off from a disgruntled local who had been reprimanded by Bradburne for stealing the lepers' rations. They took him away to a meeting, where he was taunted, and then to a cave known as Gwaze, which was used for ceremonies invoking tribal ancestors.

He was put on trial there by the guerrillas. They were sure he was a good man – and were angry with the mujibhas for kidnapping him – but thought he'd seen too much of their operation and offered him asylum in China or Mozambique, which he refused. Late in the day, he was taken to a pungwe. In the small hours of the morning, after the crowd had dispersed, he was ordered onto the main road by about 50 guerrillas, and one of them shot him dead.

John Bradburne had confided in a priest his three wishes: to minister to the lepers of Mutemwa, to die a martyr and be buried with his Franciscan habit. Father Dove saw to it that his third request was granted. During the funeral services, the officiating Jesuit priest, Michael O'Halloran, saw three drops of fresh blood fall from the coffin. (When the coffin was later opened, there was no sign of a leak.)

The mission at Mutemwa has now become a minor pilgrimage site and in 1986, John Bradburne's case was presented to the Vatican for possible canonisation. They've determined it's too soon to know one way or another, but at some time in the future, Zimbabwe may have its first saint. Meanwhile, the work with the lepers at Mutemwa continues. For information, contact the John Bradburne Memorial Society, c/o John Reid, 11 Kilmarsh Rd, London W6 0PL, UK. ∎

Mazowe River. It's ideal for a few days of hiking, canoeing, fishing and relaxing at camp, and the area is rich in wildlife.

You can either explore on your own or join arranged activities. Owners Sue and Iain Jarvis organise guided walks and drives for wildlife-viewing, as well as excursions around the Umfurudzi Safari Area. Worthwhile sites include ancient rock paintings, a basic gold-mining operation, old Shona and Portuguese forts and the communal lands across the river – the source of all that drumming at night! A wonderful day-long game drive will take you to the picnic spot and swimming hole at Fantasy Pools – the name says it all! During high water from January to April, they run two-night rafting trips on the Mazowe River, and they're currently trying to set up organised mountain-bike tours.

Camping costs US$3.50 per person and accommodation in rustic open chalets is US$8 per person, but special backpackers' rates are available. For home-cooked lunches and dinners, you'll pay US$4, but self-catering facilities are also available. A special seven-day budget safari, including transfers, accommodation, half-board and activities, will cost just US$77 per person.

Getting There & Away Transfers from Harare (US$8 return) run on Monday and Friday at 2.30 pm from the Brontë Hotel. Book by telephone or write to Hippo Pools, PO Box 90, Shamva.

In the winter, Hippo Pools is accessible

ZIMBABWE

The CAMPFIRE Programme

Almost everyone agrees that tourism holds vast potential as a source of income for Zimbabwe. However, over the past years, much tourism development has been made at the expense of subsistence farmers on communal lands, and the maintenance of national parks and wildlife reserves has placed strain on people inhabiting surrounding areas. As a result, local people have seen these large tracts of usable land placed off limits to their ever-increasing numbers, and have been forced to suffer the ravages of their wild neighbours on their crops and families.

Historically, a major part of the problem lay in the fact that the government held all formal authority over national parks, and attempted to manage wildlife areas from the central National Parks' Department. All revenue from hunting and tourism in the parks was shunted straight into the National Treasury – or to the private owners of tour companies and safari lodge operators. Few locals realised any of the economic benefits which were being touted as justification for conservation and tourism development. The inevitable result was an increase in poaching, domestic encroachment onto protected land and a general resentment of the parks and wildlife by people in surrounding areas.

In response to this dilemma, in 1987, the Zimbabwe government set up the Communal Area Management Programme for Indigenous Resources. The idea was to encourage active popular participation in conservation by providing a means for local people to benefit from tourism ventures on their lands. It hoped to vest in local people proprietary rights to wildlife resources and was intended to help them see wildlife and protected lands as assets rather than liabilities.

Three years after it was created, CAMPFIRE had already been extended to 12 districts surrounding wildlife-rich national parks and reserves. Here's how it works: proceeds from big game hunting on these lands are divided equally between district councils and private safari operators. Councils are permitted to take 15% of the proceeds for their general funds, while 35% goes to wildlife management (for example, to build electric fences to keep elephants out of the corn!). The remaining 50% is passed on to surrounding communities to spend as they wish. In 1994, the programme earned a total of US$1.2 million.

Although CAMPFIRE's emphasis is on revenue from hunting, some communities have carried the concept a step further and set up their own tourist facilities. Among these are the Mavuradonha Wilderness Camp and the Sunungukai Camp, both in north-eastern Zimbabwe. The former maintains basic accommodation in a magnificent wilderness hiking area, while the latter provides tourists with a glimpse at traditional village life in Zimbabwe. Revenue generated by Sunungukai has been channelled into a community grist mill and the construction of a local primary school. ■

without 4WD. From Harare, take Enterprise Rd out of town and turn left towards Shamva. Beyond the river crossing past Shamva, take the right turn towards Madziwa Mine. After 33 km, turn right into Madziwa village. Just beyond the village shop (which sells basic supplies), turn right down a hill and follow the road to the T-junction, then turn left. You'll have six km of tarred road to Amms Mine; don't turn towards the mine, but keep heading straight, past the National Parks sign. After six km, you'll reach the National Parks office turn-off, but unless you want to speak with the rangers, continue straight on. From this point, it's 12 km, mostly downhill, to Hippo Pools.

Sunungukai Camp

The Campfire Programme camp Sunungukai ('welcome and be free'), on the banks of the Mazowe River, sits at the edge of the Umfurudzi Safari Area near the village of Nyagande. It's quite basic, but is an honest effort by local villagers to bring tourism to this lovely and quiet corner of Zimbabwe and in 1994, it won the British Airways Tourism for Tomorrow Award.

The area is good for fishing, birdwatching and hiking, and one nearby mountain has ancient rock paintings. Revenue from the project is being ploughed into such community development projects as a local school, a clinic and a grist mill.

Simple four-bed rondavels at the camp Sunungukai cost US$3.50 per person (minimum charge US$6.50) and camp sites are US$1.50 (maximum two people per site). For bookings, contact the Campfire Association (☎ 790570), 15 Phillips Ave, Belgravia, Harare.

Getting There & Away From Harare, take one of the two daily Kukura Kurerwa buses. The first, marked 'Nyava via Shamva & Mazoe Bridge', leaves Mbare musika at around noon and the second, 'Nhakiwa via Bindura & Glendale', departs around 4 pm.

To get there by car from Harare, take the Mutoko road to Murewa and turn left onto the tarred road leading into the Uzumba

Maramba Pfungwe communal lands. After 55 km, turn left at the Sunungukai signpost and continue for three km to the Nyagande General Dealer shop, where you should turn right. After 1.5 km, you'll see the camp on your right. You can also take the scenic route via Shamva, but the road along the Mazowe River is in poor condition and may not be passable after rains.

Harare to Chirundu

The tarred road between Harare and Chirundu is well travelled. Hitchers should have few problems (especially at weekends).

If you want to fish for bream (tilapia) and tiger fish at Kariba, pick up fishing worms around Chinhoyi town, where salespeople hang sacks of worms from small roadside tripod structures.

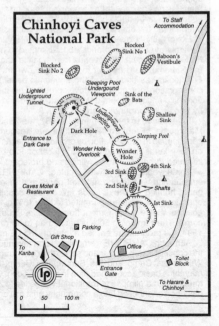

Chinhoyi Caves National Park

The Great Dyke
The Great Dyke is a spine of low rocky hills 530 km in length, stretching from north to south down Zimbabwe from the Zambezi Escarpment near Guruve all the way to Mberengwa and Shurugwi in the Midlands. Its northern anchor is the jumbled Mvurwi Range, which rises to nearly 1700 metres at the western end of the Mavuradonha Mountains. At its southern end, it rears up beneath the Chironde Range, near Shurugwi.

The ridge is of volcanic origin, an exposed extrusion of erosion-resistant igneous material which is 70% serpentine and is extremely rich in platinum, chromite, asbestos and magnesium. The easiest places to view it from the road are at Great Dyke Pass, which offers long-ranging views across the surrounding maize and tobacco farmlands, on Wolfshall Pass in the Chironde Range east of Shurugwi. ■

CHINHOYI

The town of Chinhoyi, 120 km north-west of Harare, serves as the administrative centre for the surrounding rich tobacco, maize and cattle-farming region. Alaska Mine, 20 km north-west of town, began producing export quantities of copper in 1959.

Chinhoyi's place in history was secured on 28 April 1966, when ZANLA forces, led by Bernard Mutuma, and well-armed Rhodesian Security Forces met in the 12-hour clash now known as the Battle of Chinhoyi. The skirmish resulted in the loss of seven ZANLA guerrillas and effectively launched the Second Chimurenga which eventually led to Zimbabwean independence. In Zimbabwe, 28 April is now commemorated as Chimurenga Day.

Places to Stay

The clean and comfortable *Orange Grove Motel* (☎ 2785; fax 3095) is the only place to stay in the town itself. Standard rooms cost US$23/33 a single/double; with TV, they're US$28/37. Ask about special backpackers' rates. Campers, who have use of the swimming pool, pay US$1.60 per tent or US$2 per caravan.

Another option is the small *Mazvikadei*

Dam Lodge (☎ 573766, Harare), beside the dam of the same name north-east of Chinhoyi. It's reasonably priced at US$13 per person, including bed and breakfast and transport from Harare or Chinhoyi. Meals are also available and there are opportunities for walking and birdwatching around the dam. To book, either phone or visit Shane Maurel, 11 Manondo Rd, Hatfield, Harare.

See also under Chinhoyi Caves National Park.

CHINHOYI CAVES NATIONAL PARK

Although small, this 'roadside' national park, 1½ hours north-west of Harare is worthwhile visiting. It is riddled with limestone and dolomite caves and sinkholes which have been used for storage and refuge by local people for nearly 1500 years. Although the largest caves were once well-decorated with stalactites and stalagmites, most of those in accessible passages have long since been broken off.

The main pool is called Sleeping Pool or Chirorodzira ('Pool of the Fallen'), which inaccurately suggests commemoration of an accident or a battle. In fact, the 'fallen' were local people intentionally cast into the formidable hole by the invading Nguni tribes in the early 19th century. In 1887, colonial hunter Frederick Courteney Selous found the area occupied by the subjects of Chief Chinhoyi. He took the Swiss-cheese-like landscape, which resembled that around the modern Alaska copper mines (a few km away), to be result of ancient mine workings.

Chirorodzira maintains a constant temperature of 22°. From the park entrance, a footpath descends 46 metres to water level, with good views into the dark recesses of the cave, its 91-metre-deep aquamarine pool and its resident plants and fish. From Dark Cave, the rear entrance to Chirorodzira, one can look through the sombre shadows to the sunlit waters far below. The effect is magical; the clear water so perfectly admits light that the water line disappears and the pool takes on the appearance of a smoky blue underworld. Also, divers have discovered a submarine passage leading from the Bat

ZIMBABWE

The Zambezi Valley

In ancient geologic history, the Zambezi flowed from what is now southern Angola to join the Limpopo on its trip to the Indian Ocean. Subsequent igneous upheavals, however, diverted the northern headwaters into the Kalahari, where it disappeared into the sands and formed the vast swamplands of the Okavango Delta and the Linyanti Marshes. Another branch of the river spilled into the Luangwa Valley, which was a tributary fault of Africa's remarkable Great Rift Valley.

The pools for which Mana Pools National Park is named are leftovers from the gradual northward migration of the main Zambezi River channel. Elsewhere, they'd be called billabongs, bayous or oxbows – puddles occupying the low-lying patches of the former riverbed. On the northern bank of the Zambezi, the rugged green mountains of Zambia abut the flood-plain, but as the river pushes further northward, they're doomed to the same erosion that flattened out the broad series of river terraces to the south.

The abrupt and dramatic escarpment delineating the southern edge of the Zambezi Valley extends from the Mozambique border in the east, through Mana Pools National Park to Kariba in the west. Above it are the cooler, undulating highlands of the Mavuradonha Range and below, an expansive mopane-covered plain stretching away to the river itself. The best views are to be had on the Chirundu Rd between Marongora and the Mana Pools National Park entrance, and from near Centenary, where the view extends all the way to Mozambique's Cabora Bassa Dam. ∎

Cave, a sub-chamber of Dark Cave, to another room known as Blind Cave.

The park is open during daylight hours year round and admission is US$1.20 per person. The hotel sells petrol.

Places to Stay & Eat

The *Caves Motel* (☎ 2340) at the park entrance charges US$21/27 a single/double, including a set breakfast. They also have a restaurant. The adjacent National Parks' campground charges US$1.30 per person for tent camping and US$2 in a caravan. Use of picnic facilities costs US$1.20 and firewood is available for US$2 per bundle.

Getting There & Away

The park entrance is right on the Harare-Chirundu road, eight km north-west of Chinhoyi town. From Harare, take any Kariba or Chirundu bus and get off at the Caves Motel.

KAROI

Karoi ('little witch'), the centre of the commercial tobacco-growing Makonde district, may serve as a break for travellers between Harare and Kariba or Chirundu. It lies near the eastern end of the Siabuwa road (less commonly known as the Hostes Highway), the rough gravel route to Matusadona,

Siabuwa and the western end of Lake Kariba. There's an unreliable daily bus service between Karoi and Binga via Siabuwa. Enquire locally for further information, especially since the westbound bus leaves Karoi at varying small hours of the morning.

Places to Stay & Eat

You can stay at the *Karoi Hotel* (☎ 6317), which has an attached restaurant and bar, for US$23/34 a single/double. There's also a caravan park at the dam, which lies beyond the industrial area. To get there, take the side street turning off at the Mobil petrol station. The *As You Like It* restaurant and takeaway on the main street offers simple meals.

MAKUTI

Makuti sits on the edge of the Zambezi Escarpment, where the land gently spills down jumbled forested hills towards Lake Kariba, 66 km away. The tiny settlement is little more than a motel, a road junction and the last petrol station before Kariba. This is also the last petrol available if you're driving into Mana Pools National Park.

Places to Stay & Eat

Apart from the run-down pub beside the petrol station, most of Makuti's activity centres on the *Cloud's End Hotel* (☎ 526).

Surrounded by pleasant if somewhat un-kempt gardens and backed by a far-ranging view, it's a favourite of Harare-dwellers heading for Kariba after work on Friday. There's a dilapidated swimming pool and a nice dining room which serves up a mean buffet breakfast. Singles/doubles cost US$23/32 with bed and breakfast.

MARONGORA
In the beautifully subtle hills near the lip of the Zambezi Escarpment, Marongora is the administrative centre for Mana Pools National Park. Visitors without private vehicles – who may not pre-book Mana Pools accommodation in Harare – will probably find Marongora their best prospect for both transport and accommodation in the park.

Visitors bound for Mana Pools must secure a park-entry permit at the Marongora office *before 3.30 pm* on the day of entry into the park. You'll need both accommodation reservations and transport before permits will be issued. If you haven't pre-booked park accommodation in Harare and lodges or camp sites are still available – and you have secured a guaranteed lift – the rangers here can sort it out for you. Otherwise, you can opt for a day entry permit and hope that accommodation comes available. For further information, see Permits under Mana Pools National Park later in this chapter.

Places to Stay
If you must wait a day or two to get into the park, you can either stay in Makuti, 10 km south of Marongora, or camp behind the office, where there's a small camp site with braai pits, cold showers and toilets. There's no shop so bring your own food.

CHIRUNDU
This uninspiring little border town on the Zambezi is one of several put-in points for Zambezi canoe safaris. It's also a respite for travellers coming from the rigours of Zambia or a place to contemplate a headlong plunge into that country. The two countries are joined by the impressive Otto Beit Bridge.

Its name honours Alfred Beit, the philanthropist who established the Beit Trust and financed the bridge's construction. The border is open from 6 am to 6 pm.

Chirundu is known for its abundance of wildlife close at hand. One correspondent has written: 'Do *not* go walking, even down to the river, or you are liable to be eaten. Just sitting by the side of the road you see plenty of big game and every day elephants come to drink from the swimming pool'. Although the thirsty elephants have been avoiding the swimming pool of late, the sign still reads 'Swim at your own risk – elephants drink here'. Having said that, elephants, buffaloes and other larger animals are still seen chug-a-lugging at the camp site water hole.

Activities
Canoe safaris should be booked in Harare or Kariba, but you can take a speedboat fishing trip on the Zambezi with Willy Reed of Tiger Safaris in Chirundu. He charges US$37 per day for three people, plus driver and fuel. Contact him at the Tiger Safaris camp one km downstream from the bridge.

Places to Stay & Eat
The floodlit riverside camp site downstream of the bridge offers basic amenities for US$2 per site, but the facilities are run-down and it's not really recommended. Because wildlife is profuse, campers should exercise caution – zip your tent at night, avoid hippos and, if possible, don't venture outside after dark.

The *Chirundu Valley Motel* (☎ 618) is good value at US$14/24 for single/double units with bath, including a full buffet breakfast.

There's also the *Tiger Safaris Lodge*, one km downstream of the bridge, where self-catering chalets for four people cost US$45. Each chalet has two double bedrooms, bath, kitchen, veranda and car port.

Getting There & Away
As you'd expect, there a lot of commercial traffic along the main route between Harare and Lusaka (Zambia), so hitching isn't too

ZIMBABWE

difficult. If you prefer the bus, daily services run between Harare and Chirundu from Mbare musika. Alternatively, take the more frequent Kariba buses to Makuti and hitch from there.

Also, buses between Harare and Lusaka stop at Chirundu. Daily services are run by UBZ, ZUPCO and Giraffe; the first leaves Mbare at 6 am but arrive early to get a seat. For more comfort, go with Power Coach Express (☎ 60466, Harare), with service from Mbare at 8 am daily. The fare to Chirundu is US$4.

The Middle Zambezi

Although the stretch of the Zambezi below Kariba and above Kanyemba is known locally as the Lower Zambezi, apparently relative to Kariba (the centre of some Zimbabweans' universe!), it is more accurately called the Middle Zambezi since an awful lot of the river lies further downstream in Mozambique territory.

Apart from Chirundu and Mana Pools National Park, this stretch of river is inaccessible from the Zimbabwe highway system by ordinary vehicle. In fact, for many locals, the river *is* the highway system. To take advantage of its appeal as a wilderness route, several canoe safari companies run two to nine-day river trips between Kariba and Kanyemba on the Mozambique border.

MANA POOLS NATIONAL PARK

Mana Pools is magnificent, but allow it more than a quick glance, or it may disappoint. Away from the river's edge, the landscapes are less than overwhelming and as far as wildlife density is concerned, the park pales in comparison to Hwange. The Mana magic stems from a pervading sense of the wild and unaltered, aspects which visitors miss at the artificial dams and petrol-generated water holes of Hwange. It also lies in the park's relative remoteness, as well as the license granted to wander on foot according to the dictates of individual courage.

The word 'Mana' means four, in reference to the four pools around park headquarters: Main, Chine, Long and Chisambik. This magnificent wilderness barely escaped inundation in 1982, when successful lobbying by the Zambezi Society convinced the government to abandon plans for a dam at Mutapa Gorge. In recognition of its ecological significance, UNESCO has designated both Mana Pools and neighbouring Chewore Safari Area a World Heritage Site.

Mana Pools is open to motor vehicles only during the dry season, from 1 May to 31 October. The National Parks lodges remain open during the rest of the year, but may be accessed only by boat or on foot.

Information
Permits All visitors to Mana Pools National Park must first secure an entry permit. First, you'll need to book accommodation through the National Parks Central Booking Office in Harare (or through the alternative method outlined in the discussion of Marongora earlier in this chapter). In order to book accommodation, you'll have to demonstrate that you have transport into the park. They'll probably ask how you intend to travel into the park. Don't say you're hitching, because it isn't permitted in the park. And don't say you're hiring a vehicle, because car-hire agencies don't allow their vehicles into Mana Pools on the grounds that the road is too rough.

For hitchhikers, one option will be to convince them that a local friend has loaned you a vehicle – then somehow get to the park on the day you've booked. Alternatively, you can hitch to Marongora and hope there's a lift and a camp site available when you arrive. Hitchhikers can't be added to their driver's permit, so it's wise to buy a permit which is valid beyond your intended stay, thus allowing time to find a lift out of the park.

If you reach Marongora and the camps are fully booked, you can get a day entry permit for US$2.50 per person. Unfortunately, it's very difficult to extend a day permit into a multi-day permit at the Nyamepi office

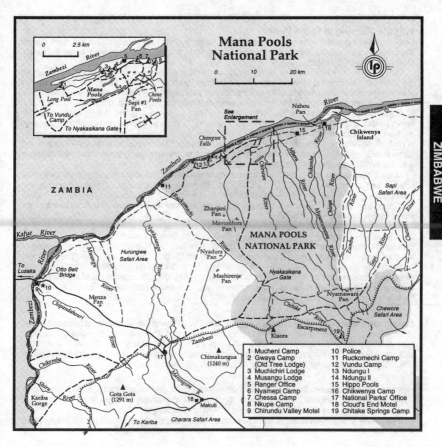

Mana Pools National Park

ZIMBABWE

1 Mucheni Camp
2 Gwaya Camp (Old Tree Lodge)
3 Muchichiri Lodge
4 Musangu Lodge
5 Ranger Office
6 Nyamepi Camp
7 Chessa Camp
8 Nkupe Camp
9 Chirundu Valley Motel
10 Police
11 Ruckomechi Camp
12 Vundu Camp
13 Ndungu I
14 Ndungu II
15 Hippo Pools
16 Chikwenya Camp
17 National Parks' Office
18 Cloud's End Motel
19 Chitake Springs Camp

because no-shows can't be confirmed until 5.30 pm. Should nothing become available, you wouldn't have time to exit the park before the gate closes.

To get the permit, you must arrive at the Marongora office before 3.30 pm on the day you plan to enter Mana Pools. Once the permit is issued, get to the ranger's office near Nyamepi camp later that day or a search may be mounted! En route, the permit will be scrutinised no less than four times before you reach the Zambezi – at Marongora, at the park turn-off, at the park boundary and at Nyamepi – so don't even consider trying to sneak past without one. And once you've arrived, don't lose it; you'll have to produce it three more times to get out of the park.

Game Viewing on Foot Perhaps Mana Pools' greatest appeal lies in its concession to those who want to walk in the African bush. Some people won't be able to get enough bushwalking while others, especially after a tense night of unsettling noises, may be put off by the prospect. If you can't muster the nerve to strike out on foot, no points will be tallied against you; walking at Mana Pools is meant to be an enjoyable

Wildlife Viewing at Mana Pools

Only in the rainy season do any of Mana Pools' larger animals venture far from the river; during the drier months, wildlife is concentrated on the several km wide alluvial terraces along the park's riverine northern boundary.

Since the heat of the Zambezi Valley days sends most of the creatures under cover of shade, the best wildlife viewing is done early in the morning and just before dusk. The most popular viewing areas are along the Mana River terraces and at Long Pool, where crocodiles and hundreds of hippos share the water hole with anyone else who may come to quench a thirst.

Common antelopes include the kudu, eland and nyalas, as well as the ubiquitous impala that seem to mill and pronk around everywhere. Baboons, buffaloes, zebras and elephants are also present, sometimes in staggering numbers. Birdlife at Mana Pools, as in most of southern Africa, is both diverse and abundant, augmented by the meeting of several avian habitats – mopani and jesse scrub, savanna, open woodlands, the riparian environment along the newest river terraces and the fish-filled waters of the Zambezi itself.

Mana Pools is also one of the final strongholds of the black rhino, but its numbers are dwindling fast. At last count, fewer than 1000 individuals remained in Africa and despite dehorning and transplanting schemes – and the wardens' ruthless treatment of suspected poachers – rhinos continue to be gunned down at a staggering and sadly uncontrollable rate. If you do see a black rhino, count yourself very fortunate.

For campers, the most memorable moments will come at night, while lying sleeplessly (and breathlessly?) listening to the surrounding evidence of timeless nocturnal activity. Elephants splash and trumpet beside the river while hippos grunt nearby. The almost incessant roaring of lions reverberates through camp (remember, hungry lions don't roar lest they send prey species scattering to all quarters; roaring lions are normally fat and satisfied lions!) and hyena yelp with their odd characteristic crescendoes. Anonymously stealthy footfalls approach and retreat outside the tent and unidentified raucous cacophonies erupt and subside in the bush. For many – at least for the first night – sleep is fitful if it comes at all!

Safety on Foot While the risks are very real and the (often sensationalised) stories reiterated in travellers' haunts Africa-wide can get pretty gory, the reality is that humans have safely coexisted with African wildlife for aeons and generations of bush wisdom are at the disposal of modern visitors. Although caution is warranted, paranoia is not and following time-honoured (and some relatively new) guidelines will practically ensure only pleasant encounters:

- It has been discovered that oranges and other fresh fruits, particularly citrus, attract elephants. Although park rangers make a point of confiscating oranges brought into the park, all sweet-smelling fruit should be kept safely locked up in a vehicle.
- If you want to observe wildlife at a visible distance, don't dazzle it with shocking pink, fluorescent

experience. You're permitted to walk only between 6 am and 6 pm. For more information and safety tips, see the box Wildlife Viewing at Mana Pools.

If you prefer more structured exploration, several companies offer four to six-day walking safaris.

Long Pool

Except in the heat of midday, Long Pool is a busy spot. You're almost guaranteed to see hippos and crocodiles in the water and basking on the shore, and chances are there'll also be zebras, antelopes and elephants. The entire human population of the park seems to descend upon the Long Pool car park at dusk so those without vehicles may find this the best time to look for a lift from Nyamepi Camp.

Fishing & Canoeing

Visitors are permitted to take a maximum of six fish per day from the Zambezi River without a licence. National Parks used to rent three-person canoes for US$11 per day from the park office near Nyamepi Camp. However, you'll need a vehicle to transport the canoes from the office to the river. Alternatively, ask a canoe operator to transport them on their trailer for a small fee. For

yellow or even (unlikely once you've arrived at Mana!) freshly scrubbed white. It's best to wear natural earthy colours the animals are accustomed to seeing.

- Try to stay out of heavy bush or high grass where you can't observe what may be lurking ahead. If you must pass through such areas, climb a tree every so often and have a good look around before proceeding. Watch for ripples in the grass and listen carefully.
- Keep a close watch for larger animals and scan tree lines for felines. Keep an eye on what's happening behind you. If you do encounter elephants, lions, buffaloes or rhinos, try to pass quietly downwind of them, especially if they're with young ones. Furthermore, don't block their escape route to the water or bush. If they're moving in your direction, move quietly away but never run, especially in the case of large cats. Your retreat may trigger their reflex to give chase.
- While avoiding the big guys, don't forget to watch where you're putting your feet. Black mambas also thrive along the middle Zambezi as do such other nasties as centipedes and scorpions. Carefully check your shoes in the morning and your sleeping bag at night!
- When walking along river banks, beware of logs that could turn out to be crocodiles and steer away from hippo runs. Before drawing water from any source, make a slow and careful assessment of what's occupying the water in question.
- Don't even think about swimming in the Zambezi. Although the risk of bilharzia may be minimal; crocodiles, hippos and the strong, fast current are all deadly hazards.
- Keep a good distance from all animals and don't be seduced into carelessness by what may appear to be the ultimate photo opportunity. On foot, you're lucky to approach within even telephoto range.
- Although the Milky Way or the full moon of the Zambezi nights will tempt you to try sleeping in the open, it's not a good idea. Lions, elephants and hyena are all known to prowl around camp sites at night, so zip up your tent and stay quietly inside. The obvious corollaries to this are to drink liquids in moderation before bedtime and use the toilet before crawling into the sack.

For further animal-related advice, refer to the discussion of Dangers & Annoyances in the Facts for the Visitor chapter at the beginning of the book. ■

information on organised canoe safaris, see later in this section.

Places to Stay

Most visitors wind up at *Nyamepi Camp* near park headquarters. Although advance booking is advised – and essential during Zimbabwean and South African school holidays – cancellations and low periods sometimes expedite last-minute bookings from Marongora.

The Nyamepi campground has showers, baths, toilets and sinks. Firewood is sold at the office, but due to environmental concerns, National Parks' requests that campers

bring their own stoves or fuel. Individual collection of firewood is prohibited.

In addition, there are several smaller camp sites. *Mucheni*, eight km west of Nyamepi, has four camp sites. *Chessa Camp*, just east of Nyamepi; *Nkupe Camp*, just east of Mana Mouth; and *Gwaya Camp* or 'Old Tree Lodge', near the national park lodges, each accommodate groups of up to 12 people. *Ndungu Camp*, 11 km west of Nyamepi, has two group camp sites, accommodating 12 people each.

Vundu Camp, 13 km upstream from Nyamepi, has sleeping huts, a cooking area, a living area and an ablutions block with hot water and showers. It accommodates up to 12 people and is rented out in six-day blocks.

Just west of the Nyamepi office are two National Parks' lodges, *Musangu* and *Muchichiri*, with eight beds each. They cost twice as much as other Zimbabwe park lodges but are still very popular, so book well in advance – up to six months prior to your visit. Even then, the reservations office often resorts to a lottery allocation system.

In addition to the riverfront camps, there's the recently established *Chitake Springs Camp*, 20 km inland near the Zambezi Escarpment, but it's very remote and is only accessible by 4WD.

There are no shops or restaurants in the park so hikers and campers are required to be self-sufficient.

Luxury Camps For more comfort, there are two luxury lodges which occupy private concessions within the park. Both employ professional guides to accompany guests on forays into the bush. They remain open only from early April to mid-November.

Ruckomechi Camp, near the western boundary of Mana Pools, offers well-appointed chalets and full-board for US$270 per person. It's accessible by vehicle, plane, boat and canoe; and return transfers cost US$180 per person by plane and US$100 by boat from Chirundu. Shearwater uses it as a scheduled stop for their canoe safaris, and also organises three-day canoe trips through Mana Pools, using Rukomechi as a base camp. Book through Shearwater in Harare. Children under 16 years are not permitted, but in December and January, they do run children's bush orientation courses for participants from eight to 16 years of age.

Also comfortable but not as expensive is *Chikwenya Camp*, at the confluence of the Sapi and Zambezi rivers. It's set on the riverbank in a grove of Natal mahogany and accommodates up to 16 people. All-inclusive packages cost US$250 per person per day and air transfers are US$200 per person return. Book through Acacia Hotels (☎ 707438, Harare), which has headquarters at the George Hotel in Harare, or through Chikwenya Safaris (☎ 2525, Kariba).

Getting There & Away

To reach the vicinity of Mana Pools by bus, follow the instructions outlined in the Chirundu section; get off at Marongora to find a lift into the park and pick up your permit. From Marongora, the Chirundu road continues northward to the lip of the Zambezi Escarpment then steeply descends 900 metres into the broad Zambezi Valley. The Mana Pools turn-off lies just below the escarpment.

Once past the turn-off gate, it's a long, corrugated, low-visibility route, primarily through dense and thorny *jesse* scrub, to the Nyakasikana park entrance at the Ruckomechi River. Once across the bridge, sign in at the boom gate and then turn left. Everyone has to check in at the ranger office before proceeding to their lodge or camp site.

Alternatively, Buffalo Safaris (☎ 2645) in Kariba organises transport into Mana Pools from Kariba or Makuti for reasonable prices. You can also arrange to be picked up from the park at a pre-specified time.

If you have a vehicle and would like to share petrol and expenses to Mana Pools from Harare, post notices at Harare backpackers' hostels or check the hostels regularly for travellers interested in doing the trip. You'll be enthusiastically received by those who might have given up hope of ever getting there!

The alternative access to Mana Pools is by canoe from Chirundu.

MIDDLE ZAMBEZI CANOE SAFARIS

For tourists seeking a little soft adventure, a growing number of operators is organising multi-day canoe safaris on the middle Zambezi. The entire route extends from Kariba Gorge to Kanyemba on the Mozambique border, but is normally done in stages: Kariba to Chirundu, Chirundu to Mana Pools and Mana Pools to Kanyemba. If your pockets are deep enough, any west to east combination is possible.

To get into the river's rhythm, become

familiar with its moods and reach a comfortably relaxed state, a single three-day stage won't be enough for most people. If you can do only one stage, I'd recommend the Chirundu-Mana Pools segment, which offers a diversity of wildlife and superb scenery. If you have more time and money, add Mana-Kanyemba. The very motivated can go for the entire 10-day whole-hog shebang from Kariba to Kanyemba, and watch the slow metamorphosis of the Zambezi from its newly liberated frolic below Kariba Dam to its self-assured amble into Mozambique territory.

The biggest attraction, however, remains the solitude and the opportunity to silently pass through the wild domain while having only minimal impact upon it. Hippos and crocs will seem almost constant – and at times formidable – companions, but the guides know where the big guys lurk and steer clear accordingly.

All the companies make camp on the river banks, but you may not wander more than 50 metres from the river unless you're lucky enough to have a guide who is trained and licensed to lead foot safaris, a real plus if you can manage it. July to October are peak months for wildlife viewing along the banks.

Kariba to Chirundu

Since Kariba and Chirundu are both easily accessible on public transport, this stage is convenient if you're satisfied with just an introduction to the Zambezi. The lovely and dramatic Kariba Gorge is quickly left behind and you're issued abruptly into the plains. The contrast between the dark recesses of the gorge and the openness of the plains, with small African villages dotted along the Zambian shore, is astounding. Between the mouth of the gorge and Chirundu, there's a good chance of seeing elephants and perhaps even lions.

Chirundu to Mana Pools

The most popular and, wildlife-wise, most interesting stage is the three-day paddle from Chirundu through Mana Pools National Park. After leaving Chirundu, you'll notice the transition as the village life along the river, especially on the Zambian shore, gives way to wildlife-rich game reserves on both sides of the river. On this stretch, the Zambezi is broad and flat and allows canoeists to safely paddle within close range of the abundant wildlife. Overnight stops in the national park normally include Vundu, Nyamepi and Nyamatusi camps.

Mana Pools to Kanyemba

This stage is the wildest and most thrilling of the three options. Leaving Mana Pools, the river slides along between Zimbabwe's Chewore Safari Area and Zambia's Lower Zambezi National Park. It then passes through a region of low and nondescript hill country before picking up a bit and slotting between the high walls of 30-km-long Mupata Gorge, a dramatic slice in the Chewore Mountains. With no villages and little wildlife, it's a profoundly silent place.

Beyond Mupata, things liven up a bit, with occasional villages, fishing canoes and traditional life in evidence along the shoreline. This is the territory of the Va Dema, also known as the Two-Toed Tribe, which is Zimbabwe's only nonagricultural society. (The moniker is derived from a genetic mutation affecting a small percentage of families.) Although many have been resettled in communal lands, some retiring and independent Va Dema, who have been somewhat successful at eluding tenacious Western anthropologists, still manage a living by hunting and gathering wild foods.

If your safari doesn't include transport out, there's an inexpensive African bus which operates occasionally between Harare and Kanyemba.

Canoe Safaris

Shop around when arranging your Zambezi canoe trip. The various operators use different camps and employ different approaches. All their canoe guides are licensed and most are knowledgeable and experienced in the bush. Buffalo Safaris and Goliath Safaris are

ZIMBABWE

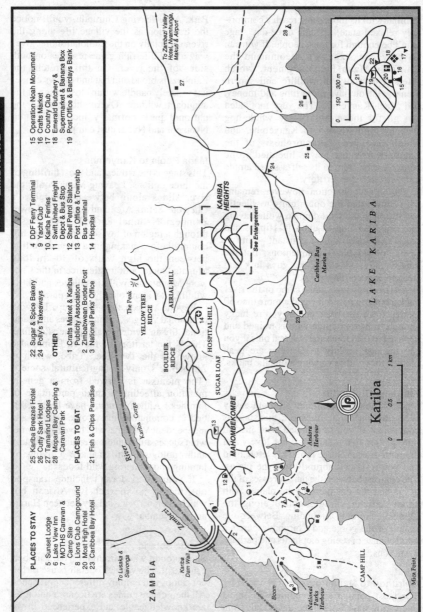

PLACES TO STAY

5 Sunset Lodge
6 Lake View Inn
7 MOTHS Caravan &
 Camp Site
8 Lions Club Campground
20 Most High Hotel
23 Caribbea Bay Hotel
25 Kariba Breezes Hotel
26 Cutty Sark Hotel
27 Tamarind Lodges
28 Mopani Bay Camping &
 Caravan Park

PLACES TO EAT

21 Fish & Chips Paradise
22 Sugar & Spice Bakery
24 Polly's Takeaways

OTHER

1 Crafts Market & Kariba
 Publicity Association
2 Zimbabwean Border Post
3 National Parks' Office
4 DDF Ferry Terminal
9 Yacht Club
10 Kariba Ferries
11 Swift United Freight
 Depot & Bus Stop
12 Shell Petrol Station
13 Post Office & Township
 Bus Terminal
14 Hospital
15 Operation Noah Monument
16 Crafts Market
17 Country Club
18 Emerald Butchery &
 Supermarket & Banana Box
19 Post Office & Barclays Bank

To Lusaka &
Siavonga

ZAMBIA

Kariba Dam Wall

National Parks
Harbour

Boom

CAMP HILL

Mica Point

Andora Harbour

Kariba Gorge

Zambezi River

MAHOMBEKOMBE

SUGAR LOAF

BOULDER RIDGE

YELLOW TREE RIDGE

HOSPITAL HILL

AERIAL HILL

The Peak

KARIBA HEIGHTS

See Enlargement

Kariba

LAKE KARIBA

Caribbea Bay Marina

To Zambezi Valley
Hotel, Nyamhunga,
Makuti & Airport

0   150   300 m

highly recommended for independent travellers. Up-market patrons tend more towards the Shearwater approach which offers the soft option of Ruckomechi Camp in Mana Pools rather than National Parks' camp sites.

All operators use 5.7-metre Canadian-design fibreglass canoes. Most companies operate from April-May to October-November. However, since demand is great and participation limited, some operate year-round. Since Zimbabwe limits the number of operators allowed on each of the three segments – and restricts their days of operation, some Zimbabwe companies have set up operations from the unrestricted Zambian side of the river. Unfortunately, Zambian authorities place few restrictions on environmental impact. If you travel with such an operator, please encourage them to avoid lighting wood fires and carry out all your rubbish!

Single travellers can often find places on the spot, but if you have several people, one to three months advance booking is advised, especially if you're travelling during peak months or school holidays. Some companies, such as Buffalo Safaris, offer reduced rates in June, November, the first half of December, the last half of January and from February to April. They also offer discounts for groups of four or more people.

Most operators include transport between Harare or Kariba and the put-in and take-out points, but you can also arrange your own transport. Foreigners must normally pay in foreign currency. Use the following table as a general guide to prices; remember some operators offer discounts for groups or off-season travel:

Stage	Day	Nights	Average Price
Kariba-Chirundu	3	2	US$300
Chirundu-Mana Pools	4	3	US$365
Mana Pools-Kanyemba	5	4	US$550
Kariba-Mana Pools	5	5	US$600
Chirundu-Kanyemba	6	6	US$700

Trips along the Zambian shore range from US$765 to US$1095, plus transfer fees.

Eastern Lake Kariba

KARIBA

The name of this impromptu-looking town of 13,000 people is derived from *Kariwa*, the Shona word for trap. It was originally applied to Kariba Gorge, into which the Zambezi waters were sucked as if into a drainpipe. Now that they're trapped by the dam wall, the metaphor continues to apply and may be extrapolated even further – Kariba has also become a trap for tourists!

It's only natural that ocean-starved upper-class Zimbabweans take to Kariba like – well – fish take to water. While foreigners flock to Victoria Falls, Zimbabweans who can afford the luxury of a holiday – mostly Whites and professional Blacks – spend their leisure time and Zimbabwe dollars fishing, relaxing and puttering around the lake.

Budget travellers, on the other hand, may not find Kariba too appealing. The most interesting sights are dispersed about the lake; transport is expensive and accommodation mostly exclusive. Kariba town itself, an unconsolidated two-level jumble with no definable character, is of little interest and the filthy Mahombekombe township beside the lake could well be the country's least appealing. If you can't afford to join the 'beautiful people' you may not want to burden yourself with too much time here.

Orientation

Kariba's lack of an overall plan leaves it with a distinctly disjointed geography. In fact, no one knows exactly where Kariba is; the town stretches for over 10 km along the lakeshore between the airport and the Zambian border. There's no central area devoted to tourism and all the up-market hotels seem to intentionally keep their distance from competitors. The MOTHS camp site and Andora boat harbour are separated from the main highway by Mahombekombe, the African township containing the post office, shops and bus terminal. The bank, shopping centre, cinema, country club, bakery and

ZIMBABWE

The Trials of Kariba Dam

The history of Kariba is the history of Kariba Dam. The town of Kariba, with a current population of approximately 13,000, sprang up in 1955 as an Impresit (the Italian firm responsible for the dam building) work camp to house engineers and labourers during the trouble-fraught construction of the dam wall.

In desperation, the Batonka people of the upper Zambezi Valley, who would be threatened with inundation or displacement by the proposed lake, called upon the fish-headed and serpent-tailed Zambezi River god, Nyaminyami. They asked him to intervene in order to preserve his own environment, and also to do something about the predicament of his faithful neighbours, the Batonka.

Edward Abbey's *Monkey Wrench Gang* would have been proud of Nyaminyami, who either complied with his charges' request or simply went into a raging fit over the whole matter. On Christmas Eve 1955, the river rose dramatically, swept away the workers' pontoon bridge and swamped the foundations of the unfinished coffer dam. The next setback came in the form of scorching temperatures which stifled work on the project and slowed progress to a crawl. In July (the dry season) 1957, a torrential storm on the upper Zambezi sent floodwaters roaring through the work site, damaging the main coffer dam.

The following March, yet another climatic anomaly – a 1000-year flood – unleashed 16,000 cubic metres of water per second, again destroying the coffer dam and also collapsing the highway suspension bridge across the Zambezi. In all, 86 project workers were killed during construction, including 18 who were buried in wet concrete. Several of these men are still honoured by what must be the world's largest tombstone.

After weathering the suspicious climatic setbacks and fatal tragedies, the 10,000-strong Impresit crew completed the main dam wall in December 1958 and the waters began to rise and fill in the valleys and branches of the middle Zambezi. In 1959, stranded animals were rescued in the public-inspired Operation Noah (see under Operation Noah Monument in this chapter), and the 50,000 displaced – and justifiably disgruntled – Batonka people were resettled on higher ground. The river god, apparently having spoken his piece, cooled his wrath – at least for the time being.

No sooner had the lake begun to fill, however, than a pesky and destructive weed, the appropriately named *Salvinia molesta* or Kariba weed, began creeping across its surface. By 1962, it covered 20% of the lake and was spreading rapidly, transported by the wind. It became so thick that it created an underwater shadow which prevented sunlight from nourishing the plankton and aquatic plants which sustain fish and other lake dwellers. To combat it, the deadly chemical paraquat was sprayed across the lake. Several biological solutions were also considered, and in 1970, amphibious South American grasshoppers were imported to devour the green scourge.

The little nibblers succeeded, but a new problem surfaced. Salvinia mats cut loose by grasshoppers were dying and washing up around the lake shoreline, and ecologists were concerned about possible negative effects on wildlife. In the end, however, it decomposed nicely into a mulch that stimulated the prolific growth of *Panicum repens* or torpedo grass, which in turn provided shoreline grazing for large mammals whenever fodder was scarce further inland. Although the creation of such a large artificial lake severely altered the Zambezi ecosystem, it seems that a new ecology has arisen and has apparently stabilised satisfactorily.

In the early 1990s, however, tragedy again threatened. This time it came in the form of a drought which caused water levels to drop to crisis lows. There wasn't enough water passing through the dam's turbines to generate sufficient power for both Zimbabwe and Zambia. As a result, Zimbabwe suffered frequent power cuts and was forced to purchase electricity from South Africa to make up the slack.

Meanwhile, the still-agitated Batonka people maintain Nyaminyami isn't yet through with the nuisance dam – and that he won't be satisfied until Kariba's monumental obstruction has been flushed away. Although the rains thankfully returned to southern Africa in 1993, the lake level remains extremely low. Furthermore, there are now tenuous plans for a second large dam in Batoka Gorge (or alternatively, Devil's Gorge) farther upstream, to supply the country's growing electricity needs (see the Western Zimbabwe chapter). Given Nyaminyami's penchant for havoc, however, officials may be playing with fire. ■

supermarket are all in Kariba Heights, a cooler and more prestigious neighbourhood disappearing into the clouds 600 metres above the rest of town.

Information
The Kariba Publicity Association (☎ 2814) at Kariba Dam Observation Point building isn't terribly helpful, but it is friendly.

Another source of information is the Central Booking Office (☎ 2255; fax 2777) at the supermarket in Kariba Heights. The agency can book accommodation and set you off on safaris and lake activities. They do take a commission, however, so it's cheaper to make your own arrangements.

Climate Kariba is hot. During the summer months, you can anticipate average temperatures of 40° to 42°C accompanied by stifling humidity and frequent rain. During the winter – June to August – expect daytime temperatures of around 25°C.

Dangers & Annoyances Lake Kariba is home to around 25,000 crocodiles, which kill an average of 20 to 30 people per year. Around the lakeshore, the risk is considerable so swimming isn't an option.

Other dangers are from elephants which march into town, especially during dry periods. They drink from the town swimming pool, trample flower gardens and uproot trees. Both Kariba campgrounds are favourite elephant habitats; the best advice is to simply steer clear. Although some elephants are quite tolerant of humans, several people who've stood in their way have been killed by overly enthusiastic elephants.

Kariba Dam Wall
On 17 May 1960, with the Queen Mother officiating, the switch was flipped on the first Kariba generator. Until Egypt's Aswan High Dam was completed in 1971, Kariba was Africa's largest hydroelectric project. With the rising waters – which eventually covered 5200 sq km and held a capacity of 186 billion cubic metres of water – Kariba also rose and

metamorphosed into the holiday and service centre it is today.

You can visit the dam wall, which is a sort of no-go area between Zimbabwe and Zambia. Leave your passport at Zimbabwe immigration and walk down onto the hulking concrete mass, which vibrates unsettlingly to the rhythm of the 700-megawatt generators that power most of Zimbabwe and Zambia. The arching 579-metre-wide dam wall rises 128 metres above the Zambezi River, newly spilled into Kariba Gorge below. The structure contains nearly one million cubic metres of concrete which, at the base, is 24 metres thick. At maximum capacity, it can handle 9000 cubic metres of water per second. At the foot of the spillway, the drainage has eroded a 60-metre-deep hole in the riverbed.

The best all round view of the dam is available from the observation point which is less than one km uphill from the Shell petrol station. From the lake, boaters are not permitted past the nets and floating markers at the gorge entrance. The vulnerability of the dam wall is of grave concern to both Zimbabwe and Zambia and the military guards of both these countries take the boundary very seriously.

Church of Santa Barbara
The circular Church of Santa Barbara in Kariba Heights is dedicated to the patron saint of engineers as well as the Virgin Mary and St Joseph, the patron saint of carpenters. Workers from Impresit (the Italian company which built Kariba Dam) built it in memory of their 86 colleagues who died during construction. A stone plaque lists their names.

The open circular shape of the building represents a coffer dam; the open walls are a concession to the climate. Inside are two sculptures of Carrara marble, one of St Catherine and the other of St George, the latter a copy of the renowned original by Donatello.

Operation Noah Monument
The rising lake waters caused problems not only for the Batonka people but also for animals trapped on intermediate islands

ZIMBABWE

threatened with inundation by the rising Kariba waters.

Word of the crisis got around and the resulting public outcry prompted the Rhodesian government to assign Rupert Fothergill and a team of 57 wildlife personnel to effect a rescue project. They worked throughout the dry season – from March to December, 1959 – tracking, trapping and relocating over 5000 creatures of at least 35 species, including reptiles (even black mambas!) and small

mammals, as well as lions and rhinos. It was all orchestrated to the tune of much pomp and ceremony in the world media. The project, dubbed Operation Noah after a similar operation quite a few years earlier, resulted in artificially dense concentrations of game on the southern shore, particularly in Matusadona National Park.

A monument commemorating the efforts behind Operation Noah has been erected at the lake viewpoint in Kariba Heights.

Canoe Safari Operators

Buffalo Safaris/Zambezi Canoeing, PO Box 113, Kariba (☎ 2645; fax 2827) Buffalo offers three to 10-day trips on various stages between Kariba and Kanyemba. This company is highly recommended for its friendliness and professionalism. They operate canoe trips throughout the year.

Bushlife Zimbabwe, PO Box GD 305, Greendale, Harare (☎ 48548; fax 48265) This company runs the up-market Ruwesi Canoe Trail, a three-night trip through the Mana Pools section of the river, from just west of the Ruckomechi River to Waterbuck camp, east of Chikwenya.

Chipembere (Wild Frontiers) Safaris, PO Box 9, Kariba (☎ 2946) Chipembere ('black rhino') does a five-day run from Chirundu to Mana Pools on Sunday and the six-day trip from Mana Pools to Kanyemba on Tuesday. They also operate fabulous four-day walking safaris based at Chitake Springs or the riverfront in Mana Pools (US$340), and backpacking safaris around the park (US$265), in which you carry your own food and camping equipment.

Goliath Safaris, Suite 336, Brontë Hotel, PO Box CH 294 Chisipite, Harare (☎ 708843). This small and personable company is also recommended. They operate routes between Chirundu and Kanyemba. They tend to be the least 'routine' of the operators and are gaining popularity among travellers.

Kasambabezi Safaris, PO Box CY 420, Causeway, Harare (☎/fax 787012) This company does the 60-km run from Kariba to Chirundu. Since access to both the start and finish are relatively easy, it's a good, inexpensive option. Kasambabezi also has an office in Kariba (☎ 2641).

Kingdom Safaris, PO Box 255, Kariba (☎/fax 2777) Kingdom Safaris does only the run from Kariba to Chirundu.

Ruwezi Canoe Trails, Bushlife Zimbabwe, PO Box GD 305, Greendale, Harare (☎ 48548; fax 48265) Runs leisurely three-day canoe safaris along the 64-km stretch of shoreline through Mana Pools National Park.

Safari Par Excellence, Third Floor, Travel Centre, Jason Moyo Ave, PO Box 5920, Harare (☎ 700911; fax 722872) Safari Par Excellence runs three to five-day luxury canoe safaris between Chirundu and the Mupata Gorge, on the Zambian side of the river. It visits fully equipped tented camps. Alternatively, there's a more basic – and considerably less expensive – four-day camping safari which runs between Chirundu and Chongwe Falls. They also run a five-day combination walking and canoeing package through Mana Pools National Park, which costs US$250 per day.

Shearwater , Edward Building, on the corner of 1st St and Baker Ave, PO Box 3961, Harare (☎ 735712, fax 735716 Harare) Shearwater offers a wide range of itineraries and accommodation options, covering the entire route 10-day from Kariba to Kanyemba. At Mana Pools, they stay in the plush Ruckomechi Camp. They also offer a soft option four-day canoe trip through Mana Pools.

Sobek, PO Box 30263, Lusaka, Zambia (☎ (260-1) 224248; fax (260-1) 224265) For a different twist, this company begins its tours in Siavonga, on the Zambian side of Kariba Dam for three-day trips to Chirundu or beyond into Lower Zambezi National Park and the Mozambique border. Along the way, armed guides lead walking tours through this little-visited area.

Zambezi Hippo Trails, Dalmatia House, Speke Ave, PO Box 3158, Harare (☎/fax 702148) This company does the section from Mana Pools to Kanyemba, but with an unusual twist: the option to continue downstream to Cabora Bassa Dam in Mozambique. The entire trip from Mana Pools to Cabora Bassa takes nine days. ■

Crocodile Farm

Kariba's crocodile park lies 20 km from town, on the lakeshore beyond the airport, so it isn't convenient for anyone without a vehicle. Admission is a Z$10. It's open from 8 am to noon and 2 to 5 pm daily except Monday.

Activities

Organised Tours A popular day trip from Kariba is the misnamed Matusadona Picnic Cruise (it doesn't go to Matusadona at all), which leaves Cutty Sark jetty at 9.30 am and returns in the afternoon in time for the airport transfer to the Harare flight. Fishing is possible, but bring your own tackle. The trip costs US$9 per person, including a picnic lunch aboard; bring extra cash for the bar. Book through Tamarind Lodges or the Cutty Sark Hotel.

UTC (☎ 2453), PO Box 100, Kariba, offers a Kariba town tour for US$9, departing at 10.30 am from the Cutty Sark Hotel, followed by pickups at the Caribbea Bay and Lake View. Morning or evening game drives in the Charara Safari Area cost US$14 per person.

In addition, UTC and Cruise Kariba (☎ 2697), PO Box 1, Kariba, do two daily booze cruises: the Siesta Cruise which costs US$3 and departs from Cutty Sark jetty at 2 pm (returning in time for the airport transfer) and the Sunset Cruise, which costs US$4 and leaves at 4.30 pm.

If you're unable to do a longer canoe trip on the middle Zambezi, Kingdom Safaris (☎ 2255) runs one-day canoe excursions through Kariba Gorge for a very steep US$200 per person. The price includes transport, breakfast, lunch and a game drive. Trips are available daily except Sunday from the Cutty Sark Hotel.

Another way to see the lake is to buzz it from the air. Trips aloft for up to five people cost US$43 for 15 minutes, US$86 for 30 minutes and US$172 for one hour. Contact Chris Worden at Tropic Air (☎ 2321).

Water Sports Crocodiles and bilharzia in Lake Kariba put a damper on many water activities in the lake, and even the well-protected beach at Caribbea Bay has now banned swimming. However, the hotel still hires sailboards, canoes, paddleboats, dinghies and rowing boats. To launch your own boat from their yacht harbour costs US$8. Moorings and vehicle parking each cost US$2 per day.

Powerboats may be hired through UTC (☎ 2662). They charge US$39 for a half-day (6 am to noon or noon to 5 pm) not including petrol. All-day hire is US$52. Fishing tackle and bait are available for an extra charge. If a canoe is more your pace, you can hire one from Kingdom Safaris for US$8 per half-day; contact the Central Booking Office (☎ 2255) in Kariba Heights.

Parasailing and waterskiing (away from the bilharzia and crocodile-infested shoreline) are available for US$20/10 respectively. For information, phone Tobin Langbrenner on ☎ 2475 or 2771.

Boat Charter & Rental The easiest, least expensive and most straightforward way of cruising on the lake is with Rex Taylor, at the Kariba Breezes Hotel marina. There are special rates for backpackers: US$85 per eight-hour day for up to six people, including fuel, plus an additional US$5 per person for lunch. Overnight trips cost US$99 per 24 hours, plus US$9 per person for lunch and dinner. Book through the MOTHS campground.

Yachts accommodating up to four adults may be hired for individual lake cruising from Kariba Yachts (☎ 2983, Kariba, or 736789, Harare) at the Cutty Sark Hotel Marina. You have a choice of self-catering or fully inclusive options. Their postal address is Cutty Sark Hotel Marina, PO Box 80, Kariba; the main office is at 6 Fairfield Rd, Hatfield, Harare.

Another charter company is Simpson's Cruises (☎ 2308) run by Robin and Barry Simpson. For lake trips aboard the *Queen II*, including pilot, fuel, meals and wildlife viewing, it costs US$180 per night for up to eight people.

For longer trips, you can hire the pontoon

houseboat *What a Pleasure*. They charge US$385 per day for up to 10 people, including meals and pilot. For information contact Pleasure Cruises & Safaris (☎ 2785; fax 3095, Chinhoyi), PO Box 16, Kariba.

If you prefer five days cruising the length of Kariba in the floating hotel, a few days on a luxury catamaran motor cruiser or a week of fishing from a houseboat on the lake, there's also a boat charter for you.

For the first option, contact MV *Manica* Touring Services (☎ 736091), PO Box 429, Harare. During high season, they charge US$775 per day, with pilot, meals, booze and all fishing gear. The low-season rate is just US$625 per day. The boat will take up to 10 people and will cruise as far as Masana on the upper Zambezi, right through magnificent Devil's Gorge.

For the motor cruiser, contact *Catalina* (☎ /fax 79627), PO Box 9099, Hillside, Bulawayo. If the houseboat is more your speed, talk to Bambazonke Charters (☎ 35486), PO Box ST 172, Southerton, Harare. Self-catering trips aboard the *Belinda* houseboat cost US$320 per day for up to eight people. Alternatively, there's Kaluga Safaris (☎ 75749; fax 74058), at 118 Josiah Tongogara, on the corner of 12th Ave and Josiah Tongogara St in Bulawayo, which charges US$490 per day for up to 10 people, including meals and petrol.

Places to Stay – bottom end

The bottom end at Kariba is primarily camping. The most popular with travellers is the friendly and convenient *MOTHS Caravan & Camp site* (☎ 2809), 20 minutes' walk from Mahombekombe township. The problem of theft has been assuaged by employing guards and installing other security measures. Camping costs US$1.50 per person in your own tent, or US$3 in pre-erected tents. Furnished six-person chalets with cooking facilities – and a particular attention to detail – cost US$4.50 per person, with a minimum of three people; double rooms are US$6.50.

They also sell braai packs and firewood, and have laundry services and a small reading library. For tents and chalets, bookings are essential during weekends and school holidays. The postal address is PO Box 67, Kariba. Advise them if you'll be arriving after 6.30 pm (when the office closes), so they can alert the security guard. Elephants also make themselves welcome here; an electric fence was installed to keep them out, but they weren't fazed, so now the gate is left open. A reader wrote:

At night, elephants came through the fence to eat the trees. That was just wonderful. We heard a lion roaring, just about 50 metres away, and hippos bellowing through the night from the lakeshore, just behind the hut. There are elephants everywhere, and buffaloes, which can be dangerous. Don't walk around in the evening – and watch your step at all times. In the township, they get annoyed with the elephants; whenever they try to grow anything, the elephants knock down their fences, and eat it.

Andy Bollen, Australia

You can also camp at the *Lion's Club Campground* just uphill for the same prices, but there's no gate, it's not always attended and security is a problem.

If you prefer more peace, quiet and the occasional exciting wildlife encounter, head for *Mopani Bay Camping & Caravan Park* (☎ 2485) on the lakeshore about two km from the Cutty Sark Hotel. Tents and other equipment for use on the site may be hired for reasonable rates. All sites cost US$0.75, plus the following rates per person: with power and braai pits, US$3; without power, US$1.50; undeveloped, US$1.30. The attendants are cagey about undeveloped sites, so you must specifically request one. Since the property is unfenced, elephant visits are common and on my last visit, one angry fellow stomped through and proceeded to bulldoze some fairly substantial trees. Grounds maintenance is handled by hippos, who keep the grass closely chopped.

For a relatively inexpensive backpackers' option on the lake, see Lake Wilderness & Nyakasanga under Lake Kariba Resorts later in this chapter. See also Kuburi Wilderness Area for other possibilities.

Places to Stay – middle

The pleasant, clean, friendly and inexpensive *Kariba Breezes Hotel* (☎ 2433; fax 2767) is the best mid-range choice in Kariba, and it's constantly being upgraded. Single/double rooms cost US$25/42, with breakfast. Because locals and foreigners pay the same rate, the standards are far better than the price would imply.

The *Cutty Sark Hotel* (☎ 2321) at Mopani Bay affords a good view of distant hills. It's a way out of town but quieter for it. Standard singles/doubles cost US$40/59, with bed and breakfast. Until renovations are complete, older rooms cost US$22/32.

Just off the main road, en route to the Cutty Sark, are *Tamarind Lodges* (☎ 2697), a self-catering complex with cooking facilities and fridges. The cool stone and thatch open-air construction is especially appealing during the warmer months. For anglers, a fish freezer is available at the reception desk. Four/six-bed lodges cost US$24/36 and are very good value, especially if you have a group. Guests have access to the Cutty Sark's swimming pool and tennis courts.

In a quiet location, high above the lakeshore is the spacious *Sunset Lodge* (☎ 2645; fax 2827), a beautiful self-catering unit which comfortably accommodates 10 people in four bedrooms. All kitchen facilities are included, but meals or a private chef are available on request. The entire building costs US$100 per night for up to 10 people, and an additional US$12 for each extra person. Breakfast costs US$2 per person.

Then there's the *Most High Hotel* (☎/fax 2965). It does sit at the highest altitude in town, but the name of this Christian mission hotel on the peak at Kariba Heights actually has more religious connotations. It's clean, quiet and friendly and the view is excellent. Alcohol is forbidden, however, and smoking is only permitted in the gardens outside. Also, unmarried couples (of opposite sexes) may not share the same room. Foreigners pay US$30 per person, including bed and an amazing breakfast (which is available to non-guests for US$3.50). Incredible seven-course table d'hôte dinners are on offer for just US$7; and on the terrace and in the tea garden, they serve homemade cakes and tasty, inexpensive ice cream.

The *Zambezi Valley Hotel* (☎ 2926), in Nyamhunga township near the airport, is the opposite of quiet. If you're looking for African-style boozing and all-night disco music, this should be your haunt. They charge US$25/35 for singles/doubles. Women travelling alone may want to try somewhere else.

Places to Stay – top end

The up-market hotel is *Caribbea Bay* (☎ 2453; fax 2765), which can get nearly as noisy as the Zambezi Valley Hotel but the boozing here is Rhodie-style. This sparkling monument to pseudo-Mexican stucco architecture could have been the inspiration for the Eagles' *Hotel California*. With its beach, palm trees, tennis courts and casino, it aims to fulfil holiday fantasies by transporting patrons away from Africa to an imaginary tropical paradise Somewhere Else. Nonresidents pay US$94/138 a single/double, with bed and breakfast.

For many, Caribbea Bay's main attraction is the casino (non-guests pay US$1.50 admission). Monte Carlo or Las Vegas it's not, but die-hards and amateurs alike can either become absorbed with roulette and blackjack or just relax while feeding hungry one-armed bandits. Smart casual dress is strictly enforced.

The well located *Lake View Inn* (☎ 2411; fax 2413) offers average accommodation and, as its name would imply, a glorious view of the lake. Nonresident rates for singles/doubles, with breakfast are US$82/120. Locals pay US$32/47.

Places to Stay – Zambian shore

Although the Zimbabwean side is more popular, it's also possible to stay on the Zambian side of Kariba but if you're planning a lot of activities on the Zimbabwean side, the border post and visa requirements could make international commuting inordinately awkward. Still, if you pay in Zambian kwacha, accommodation works out cheaper than comparable pickings in Zimbabwe.

The self-catering *Eagle's Rest Chalets* (☎ 52 Siavonga or ☎ 250981 Lusaka) in Siavonga East comes highly recommended. The chalets, which rent for US$5 a double, are equipped with bedding, electricity, a fridge and a shower and toilet block with hot water but cooking implements are not provided. Although Eagle's Rest was once a popular camp site, camping is no longer permitted. To get to the chalets, take the Siavonga turn-off and follow the signs. They're about four km from the main road.

Also in Siavonga is the government *rest house* – it has a bar and meals are served but the place lacks the views and tranquillity of the chalets. There's also a bar and restaurant at the *Lakeside Lodge* in Siavonga West, though rooms are expensive. The bus to Lusaka departs from here at 5 am daily, so guests have a chance of getting a seat.

Places to Eat

One of the best places for cheap eats is the *Country Club* in the Heights where a hearty, traditionally English spread costs about US$2.50. People have been ignoring the 'members only' sign for years, but non-members may be asked to pay a 10% surcharge. Also in the Heights is the basic *Fish & Chips Paradise*, which may not be as heavenly as the name would imply.

A very good bet is *Polly's Takeaways*, at the turn-off to Kariba Breezes Hotel. The emphasis is on takeaways – burgers, pasties, chips, chicken and ice cream – but you're welcome to eat on the shady lakeview terrace out the side.

If you're staying in the lower town, the most convenient and cheapest snacks, groceries and sadza ne nyama are available in Mahombekombe township. The beer hall sometimes features live music – you don't even have to be close to hear it. The self-catering option in Mahombekombe is the Spar market; nearby are an inexpensive bakery and butchery. In the Heights is the more up-market *Emerald Butchery & Supermarket*, as well as the *Banana Box* green

grocery, and the excellent *Sugar & Spice* bakery.

The prices of the hotel dining rooms are pretty much proportional to their room rates. The *Cutty Sark* does a good buffet breakfast for US$3.50. *Lake View Inn* offers a magnificent view from their patio and it's just a quick uphill jaunt from the MOTHS camp site.

Pedro's (☎ 2453, bookings essential) at Caribbea Bay, with sittings at 7 and 9 pm nightly, once made brave attempts at Mexican cuisine but failed miserably and returned to beef, chicken and other standards. If you need a big home-cooked meal, see the folks at the *Most High Hotel* in Kariba Heights. They also offer big buffet breakfasts for US$3.50 and set menu dinners – typically enormous home-cooked-USA-country-style – for US$7 per person.

Things to Buy

At the Kariba Publicity Association in the Kariba Dam Observation Point Building, you'll find the famous (and fabulous) Nyaminyami walking sticks carved by master carver, Rainos Tawonameso. In fact, both the Queen Mother and Pope John Paul II own examples of these original creations. The Publicity Association shop also sells assorted kitsch souvenirs. Also worthwhile are the beautiful crocheted tablecloths and bedcovers sold by local women at the observation point (for very low prices). One feels guilty purchasing so much time and creativity for the low prices they're asking.

Getting There & Away

Air Air Zimbabwe has daily 45-minute flights between Harare and Kariba, departing Harare at 9 am and Kariba at 4.50 pm. They also fly from Victoria Falls, at 2.50 pm, arriving at 4.30 pm. From Kariba to Hwange and Victoria Falls, flights depart at 10.05 am, arriving at Hwange at 10.55 am and the Falls at 11.45 am.

Warning: especially on Kariba flights, Air Zimbabwe seems to have rules of its own. Although the Harare flight officially leaves at 4.50 pm, don't check in any later than 3.45 pm if you can help it. If the pilot gets antsy to go, waiting passengers are boarded, the plane is filled with standbys and they're off, sometimes as early as 4 or 4.15 pm. Confirmed passengers arriving later are out of luck.

Bus Several daily buses link Kariba with Mbare and once or twice weekly, African buses also connect Kariba with Binga via the Siabuwa road, with an occasional branch service south to Gokwe. The Kariba bus terminal is in Mahombekombe township.

The only express service is with Express Motorways (☎ 2662), which leaves Harare at 1 pm on Friday and arrives in Kariba at 6.55 pm. In the opposite direction, it leaves Kariba at 2 pm Sunday and arrives in Harare at 7.25 pm. The fare is US$10.

Hitching The road between Harare and Kariba is fairly well travelled, but weekends are the best time for hitching. Coming from Harare, hitching is easiest on late Friday or early Saturday. Naturally, the optimum time to return to Harare is Sunday afternoon or evening.

Ferry There are two ferry services linking the eastern and western ends of Lake Kariba: Kariba Ferries, which connects Kariba with Mlibizi, and DDF, which runs from Kariba to Binga.

The more plush and popular option is with Kariba Ferries. There are no cabins, but passengers do have comfortable seats which recline into full-length beds, and meals are included in the fare. The *Sea Lion*, with room for 16 cars, sails at 9 am Monday and Thursday from Kariba and on Tuesday and Friday from Mlibizi. The *Seahorse* carries eight cars and sails at 9 am on Tuesday and Friday from Kariba and Wednesday and Saturday from Mlibizi. During busy times, they occasionally put on unscheduled sailings. When the weather is fine, the boat may stop for passengers to take a 10-minute swim.

Foot passengers (non-residents pay US$70 one way) are advised to pre-book, but for vehicles, booking is essential; and it's best to reserve from two to 12 months in advance. To transport an ordinary car, they charge US$45. A motorbike costs US$35 and a 4WD vehicle, US$60. For bookings and current scheduling information, contact Kariba Ferries Ltd (☎ 65476 Harare, ☎ 2475 Kariba), PO Box 578, Harare.

Without a vehicle, reaching Mlibizi to catch the ferry can be tricky. It will entail catching the more or less daily Binga bus (some days there are two buses) from Dete Crossroads near Hwange on the Bulawayo-Victoria Falls road. Ask to be dropped at the turn-off to Binga and then begin the hot, dry 15-km slog down to Mlibizi; carry plenty of water. You may get lucky and catch a lift if your visit is synchronous with the ferry departure but don't count on it. Going the other way, hitching will undoubtedly be easier since most ferry passengers will have vehicles.

There's also the more basic DDF ferry (☎ 2694) which connects Kariba's National Parks Harbour with Binga and Gache Gache. For the more popular Binga trip, the ferry *Chaminuka* departs from Kariba fortnightly on Thursday at 9 am. The trip takes 2½ days, with stops in Chalala, Sabilobilo, Mackenzie, Sengwe, Chibuyu, Sinamwenda and Chete (which has a small game park). At Sengwe, there's a hunting and fishing lodge, which may be booked through Sunshine Tours (☎ 67791; fax 74832) in Bulawayo.

No food is available on board, although they do have a cooker to boil water for sadza. There are no cabins, so passengers either sleep on the boat and cope with swarms of mosquitoes or stay on shore. At night, watch for boats fishing for kapenta (*Limnothrissa miodom*), a type of salty small fry which was introduced to Kariba in 1966 and is now a favourite with locals. Kapenta are caught in nets suspended beneath a light to attract the fish.

Overnights are in Chalala, where you can stay at the *Brooke-mee Chalets* for US$20 per person, and Sinamwenda, a navigation-control post with only camping and private local accommodation. The village is mainly a crocodile-breeding centre.

Binga itself is a budding resort town, with

ZIMBABWE

hot springs, a rest camp and the DDF offices (see Western Zimbabwe chapter). There are one or two buses daily between Binga and Dete Crossroads, on the Bulawayo-Victoria Falls road. The route is now asphalted, so the trip is straightforward.

Every Monday, the *Nyaminyami* runs to Chalala via Kings Camp, Tashinga (Matusadona National Park), Musamba, Musango and Bumi Hills, arriving in Chalala at 5 pm the same day. On Wednesday at 10 am, the ferry *Mbuya Nehanda* leaves Kariba for Gache Gache, returning the same afternoon. From Kariba to Binga costs US$9; to Kings Camp, US$2.50; to Tashinga, US$3; and to Chalala US$4.50.

Getting Around
To/From the Airport UTC does transfers between the airport and the Lake View, Caribbea Bay and Cutty Sark hotels in town for US$3 per person. They meet all incoming flights.

Bus & Taxi A viable but less convenient alternative is the bus which connects the Swift United Freight Depot with Nyamhunga suburb near the airport, following a circuit through Mahombekombe and Kariba Heights. It appears about every 30 to 60 minutes.

Taxi services (☎ 2454) operate from the Caribbea Bay Hotel.

Bicycle Mountain bikes may be hired for US$9 per day from the Mopani Bay and MOTHS campgrounds, or any of the hotels except Zambezi Valley. You'll have to leave your passport as a deposit.

Hitching Without a vehicle, you're at a major disadvantage in sprawling, up-and-down Kariba, and walking makes for a hot, tiring and time-consuming experience. Fortunately – or unfortunately, depending on your perspective – most locals are in the same boat, so hitching has become the standard city transport system. Normally, you shouldn't wait more than a few minutes for a lift from one area of town to another. The

downside is that even these areas sprawl, and the road and street patterns are convoluted, so you're still guaranteed a fair amount of exercise.

KUBURI WILDERNESS AREA
Carved from part of the Charara and Hurungwe safari areas, this recently designated wilderness area has actually been leased from the Ministry of Natural Resources & Tourism by the Zimbabwe Wildlife Society. Bounded on the south by Lake Kariba, the west by Kariba Gorge and the north by a series of minor gorges, this rugged landscape of peaks and watersheds takes in 37,700 hectares and harbours a variety of wildlife, including 67 species of birds and even a few elusive black rhinos.

As a condition of the lease, the reserve is divided into several usage areas, intended variously for educational tours, game drives, wild camping, game hides, game walks, hiking, picnics, administration and organised camping. Proceeds must be cycled back into the reserve.

Places to Stay
At the confluence of the Nyamanzura and Zambezi rivers in Kariba Gorge, about 30 km downstream from Kariba, is *Nyamasowa Camp* (☎ 2777). This is the least expensive semi-luxury resort in the area, charging US$75 per person for accommodation and half-board. Lunch and transfers from Kariba each cost an additional US$20.

A basic option is to spend a night or two in the *Kuburi Platform*, which consists only of a game hide and a longdrop toilet. Use of the platform costs US$4 for the whole group, plus US$1.30 per person.

In the interior of the park, on the upper Nyanyana River, is *Tracker's Camp*, a basic bush camp designed specifically for budget travellers. For one night's stay, including transport from Kariba, you'll pay US$10. With bed and breakfast, transfers and one game walk, it's US$32. Add a game drive and a picnic lunch, and the price is US$45 per day. The camp has a cash bar and sells braai packs for making your own barbecue.

ZIMBABWE

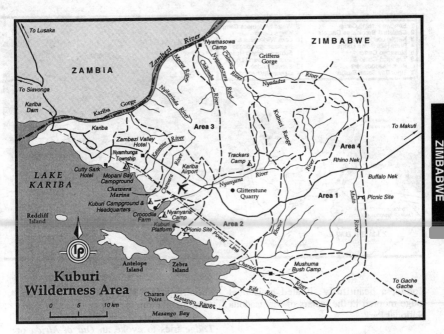

Kuburi Wilderness Area

Map labels:
To Lusaka, Zambezi River, ZIMBABWE, Nyamasowa Camp, Griffens Gorge, Chuzu River, Mburi River, ZAMBIA, Nyamazura River, Chitomba River, Nyadadza, River, Nyilunerua River, To Siavonga, Kariba Gorge, Kariba Dam, Kariba, Area 3, Kuburi Range, To Makuti, Zambezi Valley Hotel, Kanese River, Trackers Camp, Area 4, Rhino Nek, Cutty Sark Hotel, Nyamhunga Township, Kariba Airport, River, Buffalo Nek, LAKE KARIBA, Mopani Bay Campground, Clavura River, Nyanyana River, Glitterstune Quarry, Area 1, Picnic Site, Chawara Marina, Kuburi Campground & Headquarters, Crocodile Farm, Nyanyana Camp, Area 2, Rhunu River, Muto River, Redcliff Island, Kuburi Platform, Picnic Site Power Line, Antelope Island, Zebra Island, Chararu, Mushuma Bush Camp, To Gache Gache, Charara Point, Masango Range, Rifa River, River, Masango Bay

0 5 10 km

Pickups from in-town hotels and camp sites leave daily at 3.30 pm daily; for information, see the Central Booking Office in Kariba Heights.

Kuburi Platform, Tracker's Camp and Nyamasowa camp bookings are organised by the reserve concessionaire, Kingdom Safaris (☎ 2255; fax 2777), in Kariba.

A bit more up-market is Safari Par Excellence's *Mushuma Bush Camp*, with six twin-bedded safari tents with en suite facilities. The main appeal is the profuse wildlife in the area. In the high season (from 16 June to 15 January), you'll pay US$215/290 for a single/double, including meals, drinks, two game drives daily and walks with armed guides. Book through Safari Par Excellence in Harare.

As yet, bush camping isn't permitted, so if you prefer to organise things on your own, you'll have to resort to National Parks' *Nyanyana Camp* (☎ 2337), at the mouth of the Nyanyana River. It's five km down a dirt

track from the main Makuti-Kariba road, about 30 km from town. All camp sites have braai pits and access to baths, showers and toilets. For weekends and holidays, pre-bookings are strongly advised.

Getting There & Away
Kuburi lies on the main road between Kariba and Mukuti, so access is easy. If you're staying at any of the Kingdom Safaris concessions, transport from Kariba is included in the price of accommodation. Nyanyana camp is accessible in private vehicles.

LAKE KARIBA RESORTS
The shores of Lake Kariba, especially around Matusadona National Park, support a growing number of resorts. The 'biggies' cater only to higher budgets, trying to maintain a sense of isolated luxury where guests can experience the bush and its residents and still enjoy the comforts of home. The only concession to budget travellers is Nyakasanga

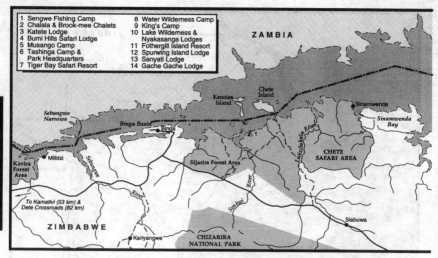

1 Sengwe Fishing Camp
2 Chalala & Brook-mee Chalets
3 Katete Lodge
4 Bumi Hills Safari Lodge
5 Musango Camp
6 Tashinga Camp &
   Park Headquarters
7 Tiger Bay Safari Resort
8 Water Wilderness Camp
9 King's Camp
10 Lake Wilderness &
   Nyakasanga Lodges
11 Fothergill Island Resort
12 Spurwing Island Lodge
13 Sanyati Lodge
14 Gache Gache Lodge

Lodge, a beautifully situated houseboat lodge moored in the waters of Matusadona National Park.

Bumi Hills

Bumi Hills Safari Lodge (☎ 2353; fax 2354), PO Box 41, Kariba, which belongs to the Zimbabwe Sun hotels group, is a beautiful but pricey three-star wilderness resort west of Matusadona National Park. It caters mainly to an up-market crowd looking for low-key adventure: organised fishing, wildlife viewing, water sports, bushwalking and other activities.

Bumi Hills charges around US$275 per person per day, including accommodation, meals and wildlife viewing. Book through Zimbabwe Sun central reservations (☎ 736644; fax 736646), Travel Centre, Jason Moyo Ave, PO Box 8221, Harare.

To escape even further into high finance, visit their *Water Wilderness Camp*, which features accommodation on houseboats in the Ume estuary. This should be booked through Caribbea Bay Hotel (☎ 2353; fax 2354) in Kariba. For singles/doubles on the Water Wilderness option, foreigners pay a

shocking US$338/552. For the same accommodation, locals pay US$130/212.

The new and even more luxurious *Katete Lodge* tries to evoke an *Out of Africa* or *White Mischief* ambience, with huge rooms, candlelit meals and silver service. Bookings can be made through Bumi Hills.

Return air transfers from Kariba to Bumi Hills cost US$75. The resort is also accessible by 4WD vehicle over a long, poor track from the Siabuwa road. A weekly DDF ferry connects Bumi Hills with National Parks Harbour in Kariba but if you're in need of the luxury level afforded by Bumi Hills, it's a safe bet you won't enjoy this ferry!

Fothergill Island

Fothergill Island Resort (☎ 2253), PO Box 2081, Kariba, is in a bushy area on Fothergill Island, just offshore from Matusadona National Park. (Since the lake level is now so low, both Fothergill and Spurwing islands are actually peninsulas.) Canoes and fishing tackle are available to guests, and they run organised fishing trips, game walks and game drives. It's one of the few luxury camps that allow children. Accommodation, meals

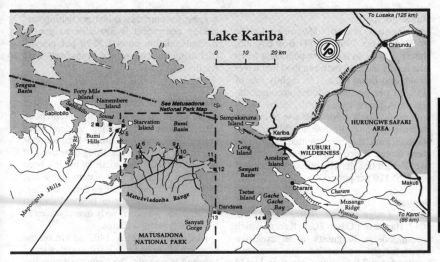

and activities cost US$160 per person. Return transfers from Kariba cost US$70

Gache Gache Lodge

On the banks of the Gache Gache estuary, directly across the lake from Kariba town, is *Gache Gache Lodge* (☎ 732091; fax 739879), PO Box 293, Kopje, Harare , run by Landela Safaris. It lies well east of Mausadona National Park, but there's still a fair bit of wildlife. The nightly rate of US$200 per person includes accommodation, meals, game walks, game drives and use of canoes. The lodge is outside the park, so night wildlife viewing is possible.

Lake Wilderness & Nyakasanga Lodges

Lake Wilderness Lodge (☎ 2645; fax 2827), Lake Wilderness Safaris, PO Box 113, Kariba consists of a large houseboat and two floating lodges. They lie moored in Matusadona National Park, surrounded by Kariba's archetypal drowned tree landscape. It's run by professional game guide Hans van der Heiden and his wife, Valerie. For the price, you get three hefty meals plus two excursions daily: canoe trips, pontoon trips and guided game walks in Matusadona National Park. You may even meet Curiosity, the semi-tame hippo who spends his days lounging beneath the boat. Single/double rates are US$270 and US$470 respectively, including accommodation, three meals, game walks, pontoon trips, use of canoes and transfers from Kariba.

Nyakasanga Lodge (the same address as Lake Wilderness) is a wonderful concession to budget travellers. If you're feeling that Kariba was made only for the wealthy, here's your chance to enjoy what most people come to see – without the expense. The lodge is actually a small houseboat moored alongside Lake Wilderness Lodge in Matusadona National Park waters. It costs US$25 per person including accommodation, meals, use of canoes for exploring the lake and canoe transfers from Kings Camp (accessible on the DDF ferry – see Kariba – Getting There & Away). Fishing tackle is also available; bring your own hooks and bait. Alternatively, you can self-cater for a discounted rate. It's especially nice to sleep out on the roof of the boat. Game walks in the national park and pontoon trips cost extra. Bookings are essential.

Musango

The tented camp, *Musango Lodge* (☎ 796821; fax 796822), PO Box UA 306, Harare, sits on an island (or peninsula when lake levels are low) between the Ume River mouth and Bumi Hills. The nightly rate of US$220 per person includes accommodation in A-frame tents, meals, game walks with professional guides and use of canoes. Because Musango lies outside Matusadona National Park, they're permitted to run night game drives, which allow a unique perspective. Return transfers by plane and boat and cost US$120 per person.

Sanyati

Sanyati Lodge (☎ /fax 703000), PO Box 4047, Harare or PO Box 2008, Kariba, which accommodates 16 guests, is an exclusive venue for the well-heeled. The area isn't known for wildlife, but Sanyati is highly acclaimed for its fabulous food, and enjoys a superb hillside setting at the mouth of Sanyati Gorge. All-inclusive accommodation in thatch and stone chalets costs US$270 per person; transfers are extra. A notable treat is the 'moonlight' supper, served on a small island in the lake.

Spurwing Island

Nearby *Spurwing Island Lodge* (☎ 2466; fax 2301), PO Box 101, Kariba, overlooking Buffalo Creek and Agate Bay, is a bit smaller and less expensive than Fothergill but offers similar amenities. Its biggest advantage over Fothergill is its sparser vegetation, which results in better wildlife viewing. Tented accommodation, including meals, is US$130 per person, plus US$40 for activities. Boat transfers from Kariba are US$70. The resort also organises three-day backpacking trips into the Matuzviadonha Range.

Tiger Bay

The name of *Tiger Bay Safari Resort* (☎ 2569), PO Box 102, Kariba, refers to Kariba's fighting tiger fish and not stray Asian cats. Its thatched A-frame chalets sit beside the Ume River just outside Matusadona National Park. As the name would

suggest, the emphasis is on tiger fishing, and fishing equipment is available to guests. Accommodation costs US$96 per person, including meals; return transfers from Kariba are US$57.

MATUSADONA NATIONAL PARK

If you're intrigued by those photos and postcards of fish eagles sitting in dead trees before a mountain backdrop, Matusadona is where you'll find the real thing. The trees, of course, are drowning victims, having been inundated by rising lake waters in the late 1950s. The eagles have been there all along. The mountain backdrop is the Zambezi Escarpment, which cleverly masquerades as the Matuzviadonha Range.

Matusadona takes in 1407 sq km on the southern shore of Lake Kariba, sandwiched between two rivers: the Sanyati, which lies in a pronounced gash between rumpled peaks; and the Ume, a broad islet-studded watercourse. Much of the wildlife displaced

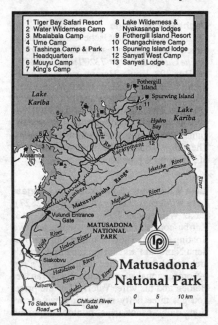

1 Tiger Bay Safari Resort
2 Water Wilderness Camp
3 Mbalabala Camp
4 Ume Camp
5 Tashinga Camp & Park Headquarters
6 Muuyu Camp
7 King's Camp
8 Lake Wilderness & Nyakasanga lodges
9 Fothergill Island Resort
10 Changachirere Camp
11 Spurwing Island lodge
12 Sanyati West Camp
13 Sanyati Lodge

Matusadona National Park

0   5   10 km

by Lake Kariba eventually settled down in the Matusadona area. So wildlife populations are predictably dense, especially on the plains which provide a good crop of torpedo grass *(Panicum repens)* for grazing animals such as buffaloes, zebras and antelopes.

Although tourists come for the wildlife, the most popular Matusadona activity is fishing and each October, the Kariba International Tiger Fishing Tournament is held in the lake's eastern basin. The tiger fish *(Hydrocynus vittatus)* is a predatory fish which can weigh up to 15 kg. It's a worthy adversary for anglers and is also quite beautiful, with silvery black sides and a yellow, orange and black tail.

You'll also find lots of walking opportunities along rivers and gorges and near the shore along 4WD tracks, but you'll need an armed guide or game scout: there's a profusion of large and intimidating animals hereabouts.

Organised Tours

From Tashinga, guided walks with armed game scouts cost US$8 per person per hour. Most of the safari lodges discussed under Lake Kariba Resorts earlier in this chapter also organise walking trips and game drives in the park.

For longer trips, you'll have to go with a safari company. Currently, the two major companies operating in Matusadona are Safari Par Excellence (in conjunction with Graeme Lemon Safaris) and Muvimi Safaris. Both of these run four-day wilderness backpacking and camping trips through the park. These trips aren't cheap – you'll pay US$115 per person per day – but they're good value and if you can manage it, they're the best way to see Matusadona.

Places to Stay

National Parks operates three camp sites near the lakeshore, all with showers, baths, toilets and laundry sinks – Changachirere, on the shore near Spurwing Island; Sanyati West Camp near the mouth of the Sanyati River; and Tashinga Camp, which is the park headquarters with the airstrip and a large campground. You can hire camping equipment at Sanyati and Tashinga, but the latter offers the greater selection of gear.

In addition to the two main sites, there are three exclusive camps accommodating up to 12 people. *Ume* and *Mbalabala* are both on the estuary of the Ume River, and *Muuyu* is near Elephant Point, not far from Tashinga. Each camp consists of two two-bedroom units with three beds in each room, a bathroom and toilet, kitchen, dining room, and storeroom. A refrigerator, stove, cooking implements, linen and lighting are all provided.

For other options, see under Lake Kariba Resorts earlier in this chapter.

Getting There & Away

Access to Matusadona is tricky no matter how you look at it. The buses between Kariba/Karoi and Binga only skirt the southern park boundary and won't get you any closer than 82 km from the Tashinga park headquarters. Even with your own vehicle, for most of the year you'll need 4WD for the final bit into Tashinga – and for wildlife viewing on park roads. The Matusadona access road turns off the Siabuwa road 150 km west of Karoi, from where it's about 10 km to the Chifudze River gate into the park. Those entering by road pay US$5 per person for a week permit.

Another possibility is to hitch a lift on a boat from Kariba to Tashinga. Of course, once you've reached the park, you're faced with the logistics of arranging a lift back, much easier if you're staying at Tashinga rather than Sanyati. Take extra food in case the wait proves longer than anticipated.

The final option is to connect with the crowded DDF ferry *Nyaminyami*, which goes to Chalala via Tashinga every Monday. Since you are not permitted to walk on your own in the park, the problem will then be what to do with yourself for the next week until the ferry returns; take a few good books!

Eastern Highlands

Few first-time travellers to Zimbabwe expect to find anything like the Eastern Highlands, but once they've been discovered, fewer still can get enough of them. The narrow strip of mountain country that makes up Manicaland, Zimbabwe's easternmost province, isn't the Africa that normally crops up in armchair travellers' fantasies. Homesick colonists in the Eastern Highlands have been reminded of Ireland, Scotland and the English Lake District. Whatever your vision, these uplands serve as pleasantly cool retreats from the heat of lowland summers, and optimum hiking country during the brisk dry winter season.

Public transport is fairly sparse in the Eastern Highlands, so without a vehicle, a rapid tour of the region would require lots of luck hitching or connecting with infrequent buses. In most cases, the transport system exists mainly to connect the region with Harare and provide access to communal lands in western Manicaland. The areas of interest to most travellers aren't always well-served.

MARONDERA

Although it isn't actually in Manicaland, during the dry winter season, you'll catch your first whiffs of high-country pine amidst the eucalyptus at Marondera (population 22,000), just 72 km east of Harare. Marondera has the highest altitude of any town in Zimbabwe and its temperate climate is ideal for maize, sheep, European garden vegetables and deciduous orchards.

Wineries

Marondera's biggest agricultural development is viticulture. Okay, the climate isn't optimum, but it's the nearest Zimbabwe has and it allows Zimbabweans to enjoy wine without having to pay prohibitive excise duties on imported products. The white wines aren't bad and even the reds are improving. Marondera wines are produced by the Mukuyu division of Monis wineries, which has an outlet in town where you can taste the product. The main winery lies a half-hour drive along the Ruzawe road and offers both tours and tastings, but it's difficult to reach without a vehicle. Winery tours cost less than US$1 per person.

Malwatte Farm House

The friendly and recommended Malwatte Farm House & Tea Room (☎ 3239), 10 km east of Marondera, makes a pleasant stop for tea, coffee, snacks or meals while travelling between Harare and the Eastern Highlands. They also sell delicious homemade goat cheese. It's open daily from 8 am to 5 pm Monday to Friday and evenings on weekends. The setting is lovely, and both overnight accommodation (☎ 344112) and camping are sometimes available.

Gosho Park

At the girls' school on the Mutare road is an excellent little wildlife reserve known as Gosho Park. You can either drive or walk around and you're guaranteed to see antelopes. Admission is just US$0.75 per person

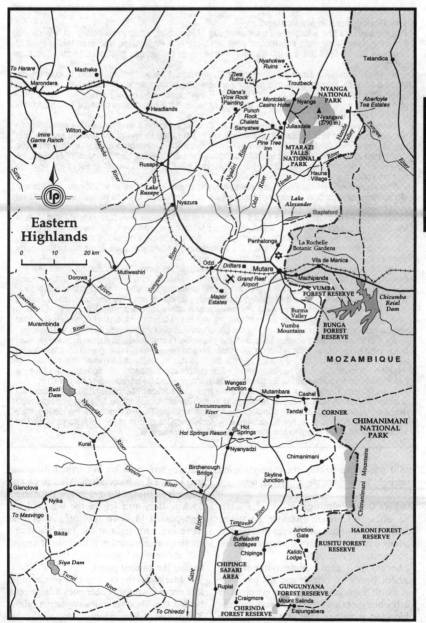

Eastern Highlands

0   10   20 km

The Portuguese in Manicaland

The Portuguese first established themselves in Manicaland, albeit superficially, in the 1560s. Although King Sebastiano entertained grand designs of a Portuguese dominion taking in all of southern Africa, their primary interest in the area lay in the access it afforded to the goldfields further north.

In 1569, Francisco Barreto, governor of Portuguese East Africa, attempted to contact the Mwene Mutapa to negotiate gold-mining concessions in the interior. An outbreak of sickness among the men was blamed on Arab traders who were accused of poisoning the water supply (the problem was, in fact, brought on by early rains) and the two groups became embroiled in a bloody skirmish.

Several years earlier, the Manyika *Mutasa* Chikanga *(mutasa* was a Manyika dynastic title established in the 16th century) had made a bid to usurp the throne of the Mwene Mutapa, but the incumbent naturally hadn't looked favourably upon the attempted mutiny. By the time the decimated and somewhat bedraggled Portuguese expedition reached the Mwene Mutapa, he agreed to open the territory to Portuguese mining if the Europeans would assist in the revenge he was scheming against Mutasa Chikanga.

The showdown, which took place near Nyanga, ended in stalemate. In the end, the Mwene Mutapa's goldfields proved less productive than rumoured and Barreto himself was killed in a subsequent skirmish north of the Zambezi. However, the Europeans' indefatigable gold lust lured a successor, Fernandes Homem, who discovered that the Manyika were mining gold in the Vumba Mountains. Observation of the arduous mining techniques, however, dampened Portuguese enthusiasm for the project; they weren't a great enough force to enslave the locals, so they returned to the coast. Nevertheless, a 1629 treaty with the Mwene Mutapa and Mutasa Chikanga granted the Portuguese a feeble grip on Manicaland.

By the time the British South Africa Company arrived, Mutasa Chifambausiku controlled the province from his capital on a hilltop near present-day Mutare. The highland areas further south were effectively controlled by the aggressive bandit Gungunyana, who was based in Mozambique but whose sphere of havoc had spread considerably further. Cecil Rhodes immediately sought diplomatic relations with both chiefs. His several objectives included annulling any Portuguese claims to the region, as well as securing mining rights in Manicaland, encircling the Boer states with British influence and guaranteeing the BSAC safe access to the Indian Ocean at Beira.

An 1890 agreement between Lord Salisbury and the Portuguese government, however, had placed the Mozambique border along the Masheke and Save rivers, leaving eastern Manicaland within Portuguese territory. Rhodes' demands that the agreement be rescinded resulted in mounting disputes over the region. Leander Starr Jameson stepped in and coerced the Mutasa into guaranteeing protection of British interests in Manicaland for annual payments of £100.

The unhappy Portuguese countered by sending a slave-trader, Manoel de Souza, to forcefully encourage the Mutasa to break relations with the British. In response to such underhanded dealing, the British launched an attack on the Mutasa's village. The Portuguese were ousted, their leaders arrested and a treaty was drawn up by Archibald Colquhoun of the BSAC and signed by the Mutasa, thereby bringing Manicaland under British control. ∎

---

and if you'd like to stay, the price includes overnight accommodation in small huts.

Markwe Cave Paintings

The difficult-to-reach Markwe paintings portray a host of human figures involved in various unidentified tasks interspersed with a menagerie of animal forms.

Access will prove almost impossible without your own vehicle and it's probably not worth the considerable time required to hitch when there are other more easily accessible cave paintings around. Coming from

Harare, turn right on Watershed Rd about two km west of Marondera. After three km, turn left on Bridge Rd and follow it for about 35 km, then turn left at the unpaved but sign-posted Markwe turn-off. After four more km, turn right at the farmhouse and continue nearly one km to the base of a small hill, above which you'll find the cave containing the painted panel.

If Markwe is too far afield for you, another less impressive panel decorates a large rock behind the Macheke railway station, about 35 km east of Marondera.

Imire Game Park

Imire Game Park (☎/fax 354), PO Box 3750, Marondera, began as a 4500-hectare tobacco farm but was transformed into a game park in 1972 when the owners rescued some impala – potential culling victims – from Mana Pools National Park. Later, other species such as elephant, buffalo, giraffe, zebra and other antelope were added to the 2000-hectare fenced area. Lions and leopards are confined to a separate enclosure as is a small herd of black rhinos. One rock kopje shelters ancient paintings.

A novel offering here is wildlife-viewing from elephant-back. Imire is also a venue for Peter Ginn's Birding Breakaway tours. All visits, accommodation and meals at the park must be pre-booked. Very up-market with an all-inclusive night costing around US$250 per person and day safaris around US$50.

Places to Stay

Given its atmosphere and setting, it's surprising Marondera doesn't have a colonial wonder of a hotel. Never mind – the *Hotel Marondera* (☎ 4005) is okay – but unless you're really stuck, it's better to continue on to Harare or Rusape for the night.

Things to Buy

On the main road through town, you can buy inexpensive handmade textiles and carpets at the Gatehouse Training Centre, a cooperative organisation which provides training for unskilled unwed mothers.

RUSAPE

This small town of 9000 people between Marondera and Mutare lies at the junction of the Harare, Mutare and Nyanga roads, in a prime tobacco-growing region, amid scenic dwala domes and kopjes. However, apart from the unusual Diana's Vow rock painting, there's nothing specific to see.

Diana's Vow Rock Paintings

There are several imaginative explanations behind the intriguing rock painting at Diana's Vow, which is Zimbabwe's answer to Namibia's White Lady of the Brandberg, but most of them are entirely incompatible with the artists' likely perspective.

The central figure is a leisurely reclining man with an elongated torso and stretched dangling penis, and he's holding an object above his head as a waiter would hold a tray. His face is painted with the characteristic markings of a sable antelope. A large semi-circular appendage is attached to the small of his back and beneath him, a large group of men – with their entire bodies painted with sable-antelope markings – appear to be dancing, some trance-like, towards the left side of the panel. Onlookers, who are scattered about, include women, children and animals – and even a dog made up to resemble a sable antelope.

Some flights of fancy have seen a reclining white king. Others construe a dead king wrapped mummy-like, with his funeral procession dancing him into the world beyond. The most accepted interpretation postulates that the scene is indeed connected with the sable antelope and the dancers have entered their trance-like state in order to generate potency in the central figure, which is represented by the large object on his back.

To get there, you'll either need a private vehicle or a lot of time (and luck) with lifts. The paintings are sheltered beneath a rock overhang a couple of hundred metres from the gate of Diana's Vow Farm. Coming from Rusape, turn east off the Harare-Mutare road towards Juliasdale onto route A14. After 29 km, turn left on Constance Rd and follow it for 13 km to the intersection of Silver Bow Rd, where you turn left again. After 200 metres, turn left again through a gate; this track leads about one km to a small clearing where you can leave your vehicle. The painting is 100 metres away on foot.

Places to Stay

The colonial-style hotel *Balfour* (☎ 2945) is more pleasant than the hotel in Marondera, and is relatively inexpensive. It serves as the rest stop for express buses between Harare and Mutare. The one-star *Crocodile Motel* (☎ 2404) on the main road west of Rusape is a more modern alternative, charging US$32/

ZIMBABWE

39 for a single/double. You can camp at *Rusape Dam Caravan Park*, 10 km south of town.

ODZI

Odzi is mainly a tobacco-growing, tungsten-mining and wine-producing village 35 km west of Mutare. *Mapor Estates* (☎ 13), 16 km south of the village, is a working tobacco farm and in the right season you can observe the harvesting, drying or curing processes. Mapor receives rave reviews for its hospitality, camping facilities, and swimming pool. Guests can try bouldering and rock climbing, or explore on foot or horseback in the hills, which harbour caves and rock paintings. There's a basic shop, a petrol pump, braai pits and cooking facilities, but no meals are available. Day visits cost US$0.50 per person and overnight camping is US$1.30 per person. Accommodation in the farmhouse must be pre-booked.

Getting There & Away

Coming from Harare, turn south at the bridge immediately west of the Odzi River, 32 km west of Mutare. Follow this road for six km to Odzi post office and turn left at the sign marked 'Maranke-Mapembe'. After 10.5 km, turn left at the Mapor Estate signpost. Continue 2.5 km along this road to another signposted left turn and follow the signs into the farmhouse.

If you lack transport, phone Mapor Estates and arrange a time to be picked up (for a minimal charge) from the Odzi River bridge (accessible on any Harare-Mutare bus) or get off at the bridge, walk six km to Odzi post office and phone from there.

MUTARE

Mutare, Zimbabwe's fourth-largest city, is beautifully situated in a bowl-like valley surrounded by mountains. It has an odd cold-country feel and indeed, some of the surrounding hills are cloaked in pine woods and the main route into town is called Christmas Pass. Oh well, Mutare's palm-lined main street should quickly sort out the delusions of any high-latitude romantics.

History

The first Umtali, as Mutare was known until Zimbabwean independence in 1980, was a White gold-mining settlement near present-day Penhalonga. When Fort Umtali was built further down Penhalonga Valley in 1891 (thanks to an 1890 border dispute between the British and Portuguese), the name was commandeered. In 1896, the town was shifted again, this time over the mountain to its present location 16 km south of the old fort, to accommodate the railway line to Beira. Today, Mutare remains a garrison town.

Street Name Changes

Even more than the larger cities of Harare and Bulawayo, Mutare has made a point of purging itself of any and all British or 'colonial' sounding street names. Even 'Love Rd' was changed!

Old Name	New Name
Aerodrome/Victory	Aerodrome
Allan Wilson	Leopold Takawira
Cecil	Independence
Churchill	Robert Mugabe
Milner	Robert Mugabe
Coghlan	Robson Manyika
Cowley	Simon Mazorodze
Crawford	Josiah Tongogara
Devonshire	Makoni
Earl Grey	Gukurahundi
Eickoff	Chimoio
Evans	Nyadzonya
Guide	Eighth
Jan Smuts	Magamba
Kingsley Fairbridge	George Silundika
Kingsway	Chamunika
Kitchener	Takunda
Love	Batanai
Lundi	Runde
Macintosh	Tatonga
Main	Herbert Chitepo
Meikle	Simon Mazorodze
Melsetter	Chimanimani
Moffat Ave/Circular	Rekayi Tangwena
Rhodes	Jason Moyo
Rudland	Jongwe
Salisbury	Harare
Selous	Mutasa
Turner	Tembwe
Vumba	Bvumba
Vumba	Bvumba

Orientation & Information

Mutare lies at or near the intersection of several roads, so travellers to the Eastern Highlands will probably pass through at least once.

Tourist Office The well-organised Manicaland Publicity Association (☎ 64711) on Market Square, near the corner of Herbert Chitepo St and Robert Mugabe Ave, is Zimbabwe's most helpful tourist office. They also publish the rather entertaining monthly, *Mountain Digest*, which they like to point out has a readership as far away as Tunisia. It's open Monday to Friday from 8.30 am to 12.45 pm and 2 to 4 pm.

Travel Agencies Transport bookings and American Express matters are handled by Manica Travel (☎ 64112) at 92 Herbert Chitepo St, near 2nd Ave.

Bookshops If you're heading for the mountains and need reading material, try the Book Centre in the Norwich Union Centre on Herbert Chitepo St. Book Centre stocks a selection of light-reading foreign novels and Zimbabwean publications. There's also a book exchange beside Manica Travel on Herbert Chitepo St.

Mutare Museum

The Mutare Museum has a well-mounted agglomeration of exhibits – geology, history, anthropology, technology, zoology and the arts. There's even a collection of lethargic snakes which have been granted amnesty for the time being, but the Manicaland wildlife habitat dioramas are populated by pitiable creatures who made the ultimate sacrifice to bring you this production.

You may also want to check out the collection of 16th to 19th-century armaments; the stone, iron and agricultural age exhibits; and the transportation museum (which contains what must be the world's most unusual flightless aeroplane). Out the back is an active beehive, with a cross section cut for easy viewing, and a walk-in aviary where you may see a bird or two.

The museum is within easy walking distance of the centre. It's open from 9 am to 5 pm daily; foreigners pay US$2 admission.

Main Park & Aloe Garden

Mutare's Main Park and Aloe Garden are

The Beira Corridor

Mutare serves as the Zimbabwe terminus of the Beira corridor, a 32-km-wide swathe along the Mutare-Beira railway line to the Indian Ocean. In 1974, the Portuguese colonial government in Mozambique was overthrown and replaced by the rebel *FRELIMO* government. Skilled labour and technical expertise fled for Portugal, leaving in its wake a trail of sabotaged buildings and equipment. The new government, professing a Marxist ideology, took up where the Portuguese had left off and proceeded to dismantle what remained of the country's economy, infrastructure and educational system. The railway line to Beira was closed and the enemy, Rhodesia, was left cloistered.

The reaction of the Smith government was to clandestinely establish an insidious counter-revolutionary destabilisation force called RENAMO *(Resistência Nacional de Moçambique* or MNR). Their engagement of FRELIMO's defence forces launched Mozambique into a devastating civil war which continued until the early 1990s. The railway line (which had re-opened for freight transport after independence in FRELIMO-friendly Zimbabwe) was repeatedly being shut down by South African-backed RENAMO saboteurs.

In 1990, FRELIMO ditched its Marxist idology and announced that the country would switch to a market economy, thereby pulling the carpet out from under RENAMO. Following two rounds of peace talks in Rome in 1990, a cease-fire was arranged.

Miraculously, the situation in Mozambique now appears to have calmed. The widespread droughts of the early 1990s didn't help matters any, but in 1994, democratic elections were held and presently, investors are cautiously returning and the economy is slowly rebounding from what once seemed to be a hopeless collapse. As a result, the Beira corridor is now open for trade and a growing trickle of tourists is reaching the Beira coast. ■

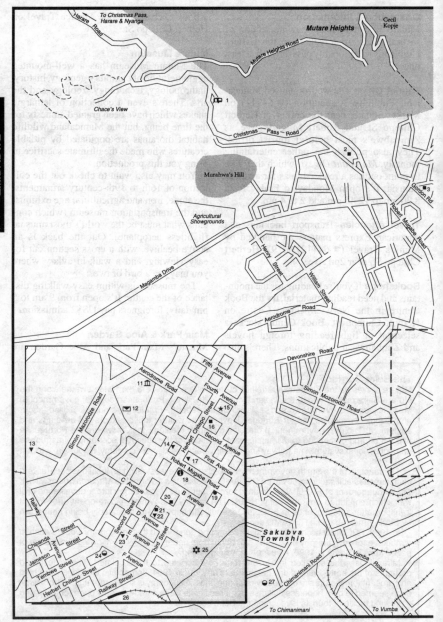

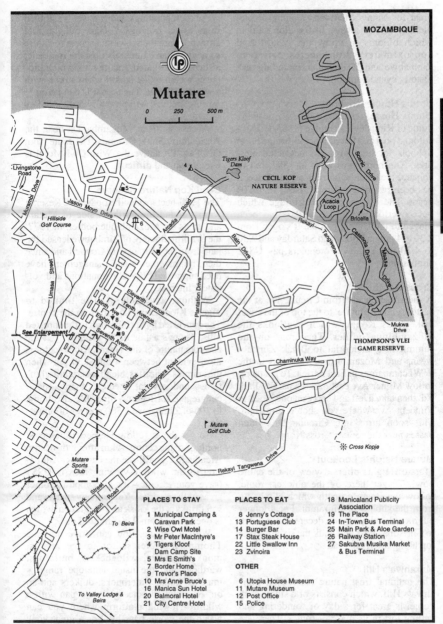

ZIMBABWE

Mutare

0   250   500 m

MOZAMBIQUE

Tigers Kloof Dam

CECIL KOP NATURE RESERVE

Livingstone Road

Murambi Drive

Jason Moyo Drive

Hillside Golf Course

Umasa Street

Arcadia Road

Bain Drive

Plantation Drive

Scenic Drive

Acacia Loop

Brioella

Rekayi Tangwena Drive

Cassonia Drive

Misasa Drive

Mukwa Drive

THOMPSON'S VLEI GAME RESERVE

Eleventh Avenue

Tenth Avenue

Ninth Ave

Eighth Ave

Seventh Avenue

See Enlargement

Sabinha

Josiah Tongogara Road

River

Chaminuka Way

Mutare Golf Club

Cross Kopje

Rekayi Tangwena Drive

Mutare Sports Club

Park Street

Carrington Road

To Beira

To Valley Lodge & Beira

PLACES TO STAY

1 Municipal Camping & Caravan Park
2 Wise Owl Motel
3 Mr Peter MacIntyre's
4 Tigers Kloof Dam Camp Site
5 Mrs E Smith's
7 Border Home
9 Trevor's Place
10 Mrs Anne Bruce's
16 Manica Sun Hotel
20 Balmoral Hotel
21 City Centre Hotel

PLACES TO EAT

8 Jenny's Cottage
13 Portuguese Club
14 Burger Bar
17 Stax Steak House
22 Little Swallow Inn
23 Zvinoira

OTHER

6 Utopia House Museum
11 Mutare Museum
12 Post Office
15 Police
18 Manicaland Publicity Association
19 The Place
24 In-Town Bus Terminal
25 Main Park & Aloe Garden
26 Railway Station
27 Sakubva Musika Market & Bus Terminal

great for sunny afternoons reading or picnicking on the lawns. In the aloe garden, which blooms in midwinter, you'll find approximately 250 species native to Zimbabwe and Madagascar, including prehistoric cycad palms.

Utopia House Museum

Utopia House, on Jason Moyo Dr, was the home of Kingsley Fairbridge (1885-1924), a colonial poet and founder of Fairbridge Farm Schools for homeless and neglected children. The home was built in 1897, but to enhance the colonial homestead ambience, it has been restored and refurnished in 1920s décor. The statue of Mr Fairbridge which once overlooked Christmas Pass has been moved to the Utopia garden. It's open from 2.30 to 4 pm on Friday and Saturday and 2.30 to 4.30 pm Sunday. Foreigners pay US$2 admission.

Cross Kopje

A short track leads from Circular Dr, at the eastern end of Mutare, to the top of the small hill, Cross Kopje, which overlooks the Mozambique border. The cross on the summit is a memorial to Black Zimbabweans and Mozambicans who died in the WWI campaigns in East Africa. To get there, follow Milner Ave east past the park to Park Rd, then take a left and carry on one block to Vintcent Ave where you should turn right. This soon turns into Circular Dr, which passes near the foot of Cross Kopje.

Mutare Heights Lookout

Mutare Heights offers a view of the entire bowl. To get there by the quickest route, follow the steep footpath which climbs up from the suburb of Murambi. For a longer but more level hike with decent views, hitch to Christmas Pass and walk the six km to the top along the ridge road.

Murahwa's Hill

The national trust nature reserve on Murahwa's Hill, which consists of a single rock kopje, is great for a day of wandering and getting lost in its maze of routes. There are

some rock paintings and the well-crumbled ruins of an iron-age village, but the real attractions are the views and access to nature so near Mutare. Look also for the mujejeje, a slice of exfoliated granite rock which produces a chime-like sound when struck with a wooden mallet. The leopards can be quite retiring, but you will probably see a monkey or two.

Access is from Magamba Dr near the Agricultural Show Grounds. The route from Old Pass Rd above the Wise Owl Motel is overgrown and difficult.

Cecil Kop Nature Reserve

The 1700-hectare Cecil Kop Nature Reserve wraps around the northern side of Mutare and abuts the Mozambique border. In 1977, the Wildlife Society of Zimbabwe leased the land from the Mutare City Council and since then, improvements and management have been supported by public donations and volunteer interest.

Without a vehicle, you're limited to Tiger's Kloof Dam 3.5 km from the centre. The dam is fed by springs high in the forested hills. There's a fair bit of wildlife, but the zoo-like nature of the Tiger's Kloof sector is most evident between 4 and 4.30 pm when the animals – giraffes, elephants, zebras, buffaloes and several species of antelope – congregate for feeding time. It's also home to 200 of Zimbabwe's 500 species of butterfly.

To get there, follow Herbert Chitepo St north from the centre. A km after it turns into Arcadia Rd, you'll see the car park. Admission to the wildlife-viewing area is US$1 (save your receipt – it's also good for other areas of the reserve). You can buy snacks and soft drinks at the kiosk and tea garden, which is open daily from 9.30 am until dusk.

With a vehicle, you can drive into the Thompson's Vlei sector to see zebras, monkeys, nyala, wildebeests, buffaloes, warthogs and the usual antelope range – impalas, kudu, waterbucks, duikers and so on. Near the entrance gate is a pan with a wildlife-viewing platform where you can watch the world pass by. For a great view over the city, the Vumba Mountains and Mozambique, drive up the winding road to the peak at the reserve's north-eastern corner.

The third region, the Wilderness, takes in the western half of the reserve. It's characterised mostly by mountainous terrain and hiking trails are currently being laid out.

One ticket admits you to all three sectors of the reserve. Don't wander anywhere near the fence along the eastern boundary – this is the Mozambique border and the boundary swathe is riddled with land mines.

Organised Tours

If you want a day tour to the Vumba, Burma and Essex valleys, Penhalonga, La Rochelle, Nyanga or Honde Valley, the cheapest option is with Pickup Tours (☎ 63061), run by a Mutare man and his open bed pickup truck. The transport isn't terribly comfortable, but the tours are cheap and lots of fun. If you have eight people, an all-day tour of the Vumba Mountains, including Burma and Essex valleys, costs just US$8 per person. With only four people, they're US$11 and with two, US$16. Day tours to Nyanga, including a peek into Honde Valley, will cost US$15 per person with eight people, US$21 with four and US$31 with two. Book directly or through Mutare backpackers' lodges: Peter McIntyre, Anne Bruce, Trevor's Place or Border Home.

If riding in a pickup truck is more adventure than you need, there's always UTC (☎ 64784). For a Mutare city tour they charge US$8; day tours of the Vumba Mountains cost US$20 per person; a run around the Burma and Essex Valley loop is US$16; and a leisurely visit to a Vumba coffee plantation and the Leopard Rock Hotel costs US$22. Half-day trips to Odzi, including the winery and Mapor Estates, cost US$14 and day trips to Nyanga are US$45. A circuit taking in Nyanyadzi Hot Springs and Birchenough Bridge is US$35. All UTC tours, except Odzi, include lunch.

Places to Stay – bottom end

The pleasantly landscaped *Municipal Camping & Caravan Park*, is unfortunately

placed just metres from the noisy Harare-Mutare highway, six km from town (US$2.50 by taxi) near Christmas Pass. If you're arriving from Harare by bus, get off at the summit of Christmas Pass – drivers won't stop on the slopes of the hill – and walk the two km downhill to the caravan park. Sites cost just US$1.60 per person. More convenient is the new camp site at Tiger's Kloof Dam, which is 3.5 km from the centre. Sites cost US$2.50 per person.

Mutare also has a clutch of backpackers' hostels. A well-known and recommended choice is run by *Mrs Anne Bruce* (☎ 63569) at 99 4th St (on the corner of 6th Ave). Beds cost US$2.50 and meals are available for very reasonable rates, but it's not for anyone who's allergic to cats.

Mr Peter McIntyre (☎ 63968) runs a similar, highly recommended place at 5 Livingstone Rd in Murambi. He charges US$3.50 per person for rooms, US$2 for dorm beds and US$7 for a caravan that sleeps four people. Every morning, he offers free lifts to the centre; at other times, transfers to the centre or to Sakubva musika to meet the Chimanimani bus cost US$0.80. To the Mozambique border post costs US$2.

A new inexpensive option is the friendly *Trevor's Place* (no phone) run by Mr Trevor Parry at 119 4th St, on the corner of 8th Ave. It's central, and has cooking, laundry and braai facilities, as well as bicycle hire. Dorm beds cost US$4 and camping is US$2.50 per person.

Also, the clean *Border Home* (☎ 63346), 3A Jason Moyo Dr, costs US$3.20 in the dorms and US$4.50 per person in family rooms. They offer both laundry facilities and bicycle hire, and if you phone in advance, they will collect you from anywhere in Mutare.

The cheapest hotel is the seedy but adequate *Balmoral Hotel* (☎ 61435) on C Ave, which charges US$8 for a double room with breakfast. Next up the price scale – but down the quality scale – is the *City Centre Hotel* (☎ 62441) on the corner of Herbert Chitepo St and D Ave. Singles and doubles will cost you US$10/16 respectively. This place is a

ZIMBABWE

real dump but it's a good place to meet the local drinking crowd.

If you don't have to stay in town, however, your best choice is *Drifters* (☎ 62964), a friendly new backpackers' lodge 25 km west of Mutare on the Harare road. Comfortable dorm beds cost US$4.50; double rondavels are US$9.60 and camping is US$2 per person. Best of all, transfers are free to and from town or the Nyanga turn-off. Upstairs, there's a large bar and restaurant (meals US$2) and on Friday nights, they hold a pizza bake in the outdoor oven; or you can buy your own braai pack for US$1.60.

You needn't worry about being so far from town; you'll find plenty to do. There are lots of walks on the surrounding property, which is actually a small game reserve, and game drives are available on a larger ranch nearby for a small charge. If you have more energy, you can climb to the ruins, rock paintings and ancient smelting operations on Chikanga mountain over the road; guides are available for this challenging four-hour walk.

La Rochelle (☎ 250), at the botanic gardens in the Imbeza Valley, 15 km from Mutare, has six quiet cottages for around US$8 for a single and US$ 2.50 for each additional person, or you can camp for a nominal fee.

Places to Stay – middle

On the far side of Christmas Pass, 10 km from town, is the colonial-style *Christmas Pass Hotel* (☎ 63818; fax 63875). There's a garden and a swimming pool in a quiet setting for out-of-town relaxation. Singles/doubles cost US$27/43 with breakfast.

The *Wise Owl Motel* (☎ 64643) is a way out from the centre on Robert Mugabe Rd (Christmas Pass Rd). Single/double rooms with breakfast cost US$27/40. It's clean and if you have a vehicle, it isn't bad. However, check your bill carefully and insist on a fair exchange rate; it seems they've been adding 10% to bills on the ruse that the bank charges that much on deposits; in fact, the banks charge just 0.5%!

For bed and breakfast accommodation, contact *Mrs E Smith* (☎ 61003 or 60712) at

8 Chace Ave, in the Murambi suburb. On the Penhalonga road across Christmas Pass are two B&Bs: *Dandaro Lodge* (☎ 22267) and *Mrs H Heyns'* (☎ 62661).

Six km from Mutare, along the Beira road, is the relatively new and nicely situated *Valley Lodge* (☎ 62868). Accommodation is in individual lodges, all with lounges and private facilities. Single/double lodges cost US$29/40 with bed and breakfast. They don't accept children under 12 years of age.

Places to Stay – top end

The only top-end accommodation is the *Manica Sun* (☎ 64431; fax 64466), one of those cast-in-a-mould expense-account hotels, on the corner of Herbert Chitepo St and Aerodrome Rd. Foreigners pay US$77/113 for single/double rooms and residents pay US$31/45.

Places to Stay – Vumba

Other bottom-end, mid-range and top-end accommodation is available in the Vumba Mountains east of Mutare. For specifics, see the Vumba Mountains section, later in this chapter.

Places to Eat

If you're hungry in the morning, hit the breakfast buffet at the *Manica Sun* hotel. It's one of Zimbabwe's best breakfast buffets; and for US$2.50, the continental version includes fresh fruit, breads, pastries, cereals and cheeses. For US$3.50, you get a full English breakfast, with all the above, plus sausage, bacon, kidneys, eggs and fried potatoes. They also serve lunches and dinners.

Colonial tradition lives on at the *Meikles Department Store*, also on Herbert Chitepo St, where you'll find snacks and lunches in their terrace bistro. It's a favourite of the 'old school' and a real Mutare institution, but it's not open for dinner. The slightly pretentious crafts shop, *Jenny's Cottage*, at 130 Herbert Chitepo St, does light lunches, salads and afternoon teas. The *Portuguese Club* does pub meals in the evening and lunches on the weekends.

For life-sustaining sadza ne nyama, go to the *Little Swallow Inn*, near the City Centre Hotel, where it costs less than US$0.50. Alternatively, there's *Zvinoira* on E Ave near Herbert Chitepo St.

The nicest mid-range place (and the only one that's open in the evenings) is the friendly *Stax Steak House* in the Norwich Union Centre Arcade. Try the Belgian waffles piled with cream and berries. The *Dairy Den* isn't bad for takeaway lunches, ice cream and greasy fare but it's only open until 8 pm. There's also a *Wimpy* on Herbert Chitepo St.

The *Wise Owl Motel* restaurant has also been recommended for great continental dinners; meals start at US$4 and the substantial Sunday braai costs US$5. The *Fantails Restaurant* (☎ 62868) at the Valley Lodge, six km out the Beira road, serves table d'hôte dinners for US$6.50. Advance bookings are requisite.

If you just want to pick up basics, there's a large fruit and vegetable market at Sakubva musika.

Entertainment

If it's evening, you're not tired and everything seems to be closed – which is normal in Mutare – check out The Place, a sane boozing joint and a mildly entertaining night spot, with live music at weekends. Two other popular spots are the Portuguese Club and the Motoring Club. The former has served as the watering hole of choice for the European players in all recent conflicts in Zimbabwe and Mozambique. They also do meals in the evenings and lunches on weekends. For something more local and lively, the City Centre Hotel sees riotous drinking nightly, with live performances in the beer garden on weekend afternoons.

Mutare also has a cinema showing mostly rubbishy North American films and the Courtauld Theatre provides a venue for conservative local theatrical productions. You'll find both near the Civic Centre Complex on Robert Mugabe Ave.

The Olympic-sized swimming pool, near the Civic Centre complex on Robert Mugabe

Rd, opens daily except Mondays from 6 to 7 am and 10 am to 5 pm, between late August and mid-May. Admission is US$0.30 for as long as you'd like to swim.

Getting There & Away

Air There is no scheduled air service to or from Mutare. Charter and commuter flights use the military airport over the hill at Grand Reef.

Bus The in-town bus terminal is between Herbert Chitepo and Tembwe Sts, near F Ave. If you're coming from Harare or other points over Christmas Pass, be sure to get off here unless you're heading for Sakubva musika several km away in Sakubva township. Buses entering Mutare from the south will probably be swamped upon arrival at Sakubva and won't continue to the in-town bus terminus, although some do. Never mind – there are plenty of local buses from Sakubva into the centre and taxis charge only US$1.50 or so – bargain or try to find one with a functional meter.

For the seven-hour trip to Harare, buses leave hourly from the in-town terminus. From Sakubva musika and the in-town terminal, ZUPCO, Zvinoira and Masara buses leave for Nyanga between 6 am and 1 pm daily (except Saturday) and cost US$1; arrive as early as possible. An Express Motorways (☎ 63343) bus runs once or twice daily between Harare and the Manica Sun hotel in Mutare, taking four to five hours. The fare is US$4.

There is also at least one daily bus to Birchenough Bridge, Honde Valley, Cashel Valley, Chipinge and Masvingo, and periodic service to Chiredzi, Triangle and Beitbridge. Tenda runs a daily video bus to Bulawayo (US$8), via Masvingo, but if you want a seat, be at Sakubva by 5 am.

Many travellers, however, are trying to reach Chimanimani, and fortunately, service is now more reliable than in past years. There are daily ZUPCO and Msabaeka buses to Chimanimani at around 7 am and 10.30 am from Sakubva (they don't stop at the in-town terminal). If you miss them – or they aren't running for some reason – a scenic but time-consuming alternative route to Chimanimani is on the Chipinge bus; get off the bus at the intersection seven km north of Chipinge, and try hitching to Skyline Junction and thence Chimanimani Village. Alternatively, take any bus passing through Birchenough Bridge, get off at Wengezi, 67 km south of Mutare, hitch to Skyline Junction and then down to Chimanimani. Allow a very long day for either of these options. From Chimanimani, the daily bus for Mutare departs between 5 and 6 am.

Most daily buses leave Sakubva between 6 and 7 am and it's a long nine-km slog from the caravan park to the musika. If you're departing early and staying at the caravan park, it' wise to prearrange a morning taxi.

Train The easiest way to travel between Harare and Mutare is by overnight train. The service departs from Harare nightly at 9.30, arriving in Mutare at 6 am. From Mutare, it leaves at 9 pm and arrives at 6 am in Harare. The 1st-class fare is US$5, 2nd class is US$3.50 and economy is US$2.30. The reservations and ticket office are open from 8 am to 12.30 pm and 2 to 4 pm weekdays.

Getting Around

There are taxi stands at Sakubva musika, the in-town bus terminus, the Manica Sun Hotel and the Manicaland Publicity Association. You can phone for a taxi on (☎ 63344 or 63166). Urban buses run between Sakubva musika and the centre.

You can hire a vehicle from Hertz Rent-a-Car (☎ 64784) at the Manicaland Publicity Association.

AROUND MUTARE
La Rochelle Botanical Gardens

Over the mountain in Imbeza Valley is La Rochelle, the former estate Sir Stephan and Lady Virginia Courtauld, with gardens containing plants and trees imported from around the world. It was bequeathed to the nation upon Lady Courtauld's death in 1972. After several years of deterioration in the late

1980s, La Rochelle became less a botanical garden than a trampled and weed-ridden back-to-nature experience, but it has now been cleaned up considerably and is again worth a visit.

The gardens are open daily from 8 am to 5 pm, and the tearoom serves snacks, light lunches and teas from 9.30 am to 4.30 pm; you'll pay around US$2.50 for a meal. Foreigners' admission is US$1 per person. For accommodation, see Places to Stay – bottom end, under Mutare.

Getting There & Away To get there from Mutare, cross Christmas Pass to the Christmas Pass service station and turn right on the Penhalonga road. After six km, turn right and continue three km to the entrance. Otherwise, take any Penhalonga bus from the in-town bus terminus, get off at the intersection six km up the Penhalonga road and walk the remaining three km.

Penhalonga

The secluded gold mining village of Penhalonga (from the Portuguese for 'long rocky cliff'). The mines were first worked by the Manyika people in the 16th century. In the late 1800s, A R Colquhoun arrived with a contingent from the Pioneer Column, built a fort, ostensibly against Portuguese aggression from the east, and founded the first Umtali. The mines were reactivated by gold-crazed colonial prospectors and settlers in the 1920s. By the 1960s, the ore had begun to play out, but in 1968, the discovery of a new lode revitalised the operations. Forestry also contributes to the economy; the first pines were planted by John Meikle in 1905 and by the 1930s, local tree plantations were booming.

Not much remains of Penhalonga's colourful history, but like so many mining towns, it's full of character and scenically set in a bowl of hills. The turn-of-the-century Anglican Church of St Michael & All Angels, constructed in 1906 from corrugated iron, is worth a look. Further afield you can visit Lake Alexander/Odzani Dam, about 20

ZIMBABWE
Drowned tree in the sunset, Matusadona National Park

DEANNA SWANEY

PETER PTSCHELINZEW

ZIMBABWE
A: Chimanimani National Park, Chimanimani Mountains
B: Nalatale Ruins

km north of Penhalonga, which provides a watery playground for Mutare residents.

Getting There & Away Buses to Penhalonga depart several times daily from Mutare's in-town bus terminus. Overnight visitors can either stay at La Rochelle (see Places to Stay under Mutare) or at the pleasant little caravan park in the village.

VUMBA MOUNTAINS

Just a 28-km hop south-east of Mutare, the Vumba Mountains are characterised by cool, forested highlands alternating with deep, almost jungled valleys. In Manyika, the name Vumba (or Bvumba as it's often spelt) means 'mist' and you'll probably have the opportunity to determine the name's validity. If you're English and prone to homesickness, stay away – when the mist settles over the forests and meadows, apple orchards and country gardens, it'll be too late!

Altar Site Ruins

A few km south-east of Mutare just north off the Vumba road is a small archaeological site amid a thick stand of msasa trees. In 1905, archaeologist E M Andrews uncovered 134 human and animal effigies in soapstone near the hilltop platform now presumed to have been an 'altar', hence the ruin's name. The information plaque at the site indicates that the structure probably served a ritual purpose similar to the Shona *chikuva*, small platforms placed behind huts for offerings to ancestral spirits. Other speculation suggests that the altar was actually a high throne.

Indications are that this was a large settlement and remains of many hut platforms have been uncovered in the surrounding district. An 80-metre length of paving runs through the site from two monoliths on the south-east corner and smaller strips of pavement connect other prominent structures. Although you can't make much of a meal of what's left at Altar Site, excavators speculate that it may have served as a provincial capital of the Great Zimbabwe state sometime around 1450. A map at the site details the presumed layout.

Vumba & Bunga National Botanical Reserves

The Vumba and Bunga Botanical reserves are two small protected enclaves just over 30 km from Mutare in the Vumba Mountains. The tiny Bunga Botanical Reserve, which has no facilities, encompasses 39 hectares straddling the Vumba road.

Until the 1950s, the Vumba section was the very English private estate of former Mutare mayor Fred Taylor, and was known as Manchester Gardens. It consists of 200 hectares of sloping ground, 30 beautifully manicured hectares of which make up the Botanical Gardens. Unspoilt indigenous bushland characterises the remaining 170 hectares, comprising the Vumba Botanical Reserve.

In the gardens, one finds an international sampling of botanical wonders as well as wide lawns and the obligatory teahouse. The fine views stretch past several ranges of hills to the tropical lowlands of Mozambique, 1000 metres below. The wilder section of the park is criss-crossed with footpaths through natural bush. They can all be hiked in a couple of hours, but a more leisurely pace is recommended to fully appreciate the unique semi-tropical vegetation.

Wildlife in the forests includes samango monkeys, unique to the Eastern Highlands, as well as elands, duikers, bushbucks, sables and flashy tropical birds. Watch the forest floor for the odd little elephant shrew, a tiny but ferocious beast that hops like a kangaroo and has long ears and an elongated, trunk-like nose.

The gardens are open to day visitors from 9 am to 5 pm daily; and the teahouse from 10 am to 4 pm daily except Monday. Foreigners pay US$2.60 admission.

Chinyakwaremba (Leopard Rock)

The Chinyakwaremba ('sitting down hill') monolith, also known as Leopard Rock, may be easily climbed via a signposted track from Vumba Rd about two km east of the Botanical Reserve turn-off. The views from the top are naturally excellent. For information on the imposing hotel, see Places to Stay below.

ZIMBABWE

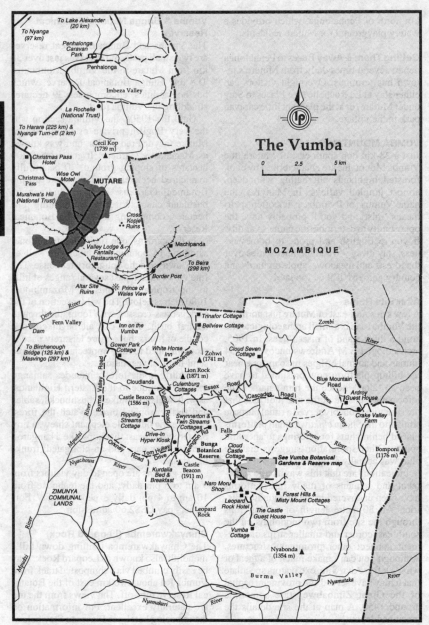

The Vumba

0   2.5   5 km

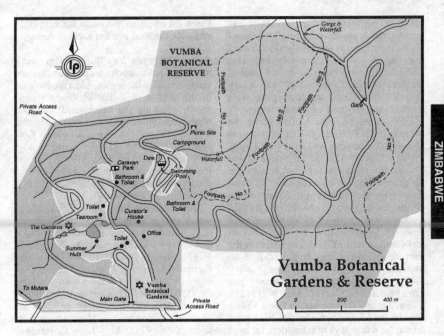

Vumba Botanical
Gardens & Reserve

0   200   400 m

Burma & Essex Valleys

These two lush and densely populated lowland valleys, nearly 900 metres lower than Vumba, are accessed by a 70-km scenic loop road. The Burma Valley side turns off 12 km from Mutare while Essex Valley is accessed by continuing past the Vumba turn-off at Cloudlands, 23 km from Mutare. Along the partially tarred route you pass through coffee, banana, tobacco and cotton plantations and over beautiful forest-laden mountains with frequent views into Mozambique. Essex Valley in particular is a taste of Africa as it is further north, reminiscent in places of Uganda and the Kenyan highlands.

A favourite stop is the Crake Valley Farm at Km 20 of the Essex Valley road. The famous soft, ripe Vumba cheese, as well as such other varieties as Pepperoni Cheese, made with green peppercorns from Chipinge; the solid and mild Dutch cheese; Zonwe cheddar cheese; and soft Alpine cheese are produced here. What is the secret

of their success? According to the Mountain Digest, the cheesemakers 'give most of the credit to the cows that set the ball rolling'. (That's credit where credit is due!) Tours and samples are available for US$1.50, Monday to Saturday from 10 am to 3 pm.

Places to Stay

Camping & Hostels The idyllic campground and caravan park in the heart of the Botanical Gardens have all the standard National Parks' amenities: braai pits and ablutions facilities – including hot baths and showers – as well as a swimming pool. It's a lovely place to disappear and spend a few days ambling around the forests.

Cloud Castle Cottage (☎ 217620), run by Peter and Tracy Hancock, would be worthwhile even if it weren't in the heart of the misty mountains, with a super view into Mozambique, and just 20 minutes' walk from Vumba Botanical Reserve. Cooking facilities are provided; wholemeal bread is baked on request and both breakfast and evening meals are served. There's a menu of eight dinner choices – everyone who's eating must agree on one. Dormitory beds cost US$4.50; try to get one on the top floor of the main house. It's topped off with a cosy fireplace, quiet garden and sunny patio. A tea room is currently in the planning stages.

Free transfers from Mutare leave the Manicaland Publicity Association on Monday, Wednesday and Friday at 11 am. Trips back to town leave on the same days at 7 am, although special trips may be arranged for groups. For self-caterers, there's a small shop on the premises, or you can buy staples at the local shop, *Naro Moru* (perhaps someone was reminded of Mt Kenya?), 2.5 km away. Head east from the Vumba Botanical Gardens turn-off and take a right at the next opportunity. The shop is closed on Monday.

If you prefer something more remote, you can't beat *Ardroy Guest House* (☎ 217121), a lovely colonial farmhouse in Essex Valley, hard by the Mozambique border. It's a great retreat for a few days of relaxation, far from the beaten track. As well as the views over the Mozambique plains, there are opportunities for walking and birdwatching, and the tennis and squash courts at the neighbouring sports club (temporary membership US$0.80). Bed and breakfast costs US$5.20 per person, or you can camp for US$3. Light lunches and home-cooked dinners are also available for reasonable prices.

For US$1.50 per person (a minimum of two people), booked guests will be picked up in Mutare. Otherwise, take the 6-am Mapofu bus from the in-town bus terminus in Mutare; get off at the Mapofu stop and continue along the road for another km to Blue Mountain road, where you should turn left. From there, it's one km north to the guesthouse. Otherwise, it's a long winding drive or a slow hitch; don't get lost in the convoluted tracks through the wattle plantation on Essex Rd. You can also take the 11-am Burma Valley bus, which travels counterclockwise around the Burma-Essex Valley loop; in this case, get off on the corner of Essex Rd and Blue Mountain Rd, turn right and walk the final one km north to Ardroy.

Guest Cottages You'll find a growing number of holiday cottages and guesthouses scattered across the region. Most are covered in this section, but the list changes constantly. Pick up the latest rundown from Manicaland Publicity Association in Mutare.

The two self-catering *Culemburg Cottages* (☎ 212327 or 62108), owned by Mrs Vermeulen, lie 18 km from Mutare near the Essex Rd turn-off. They accommodate four people each and rent for US$20, with a minimum stay of two days.

Other self-catering possibilities, all of which charge from US$25 to US$35 per night for four to six people, include *Trinafor Cottage* (☎ 64522) owned by Mrs Tebb; *Vumba Cottage* (☎ 210310 or 81354), Mrs Campbell-Morrison; *Rippling Streams Cottage* (☎ 210320); *Cloud Seven Cottage* (☎ 219617 or 64711), Jenny and Sandy Robertson; *Bellview Cottage* (☎ 64522), Mr Mattison; *Forest Hills & Misty Mount Cottages* (☎ 62911), Mrs Joan Coleridge; *Gower Park Cottage* (☎ 62911), Mrs Wilde; *Swynnerton & Twin Streams Cottages* (☎ 81273), Mrs Manson. For locations, see the Vumba map.

Another fine place is *Kurdalia*, a B&B owned by Mrs Hayter. She has one double and one single and charges Z$40 per person. Book through Manicaland Publicity Bureau in Mutare.

For more up-market tastes, there's *The Castle* (☎ 210320), a secluded, medieval-looking mountain-top hideaway near Leopard Rock. The management spares nothing to provide a cosy and luxurious stay and all meals (home-cooked), are included. There are three rooms with single/double occupancy rates at US$59/102. The catch is that you must have at least three people for a minimum charge of US$161.

The Castle is popular, so book well in advance – over a year in advance if you want to stay on a weekend. They accept groups of up to six and bathroom facilities are shared. If you're conjuring up visions of Transylvania, note the warning on their brochure: 'During the rainy season (November to March), it is recommended that groups should not exceed four in number, to avoid use of the tower bedroom, access to which can be daunting on a stormy night'.

Hotels Hotels in the Vumba area seem to be struggling to out-do each other in the charm competition, yet each fills a different niche. Nearest Mutare is the *Inn on the Vumba* (☎ /fax 60722). Unlike many places in the area, families are encouraged and there's a swimming pool and playground for the kids. Standard rooms, all with a mountain view, cost Z$29/48 for singles/doubles. Otherwise, you can opt for a self-catering cottage, which accommodates up to four people, for US$52 a double, plus US$13 for each extra adult and half that for each child. The pub is a local favourite. Transport from Mutare is provided on request.

A more exclusive place is the *White Horse Inn* (☎ 60325), beautifully situated on Laurenceville Rd, in a deep valley amid trees and gardens. It's known for its elegant dining room and French menu; in the evening, guests must dress for dinner – no jeans or T-shirts. Each room is pleasantly (if a bit ostentatiously) trimmed in a different floral theme, reminiscent of an English country B&B. Singles/doubles cost US$39/54, with breakfast. Carrying the Anglo thread even further, there's also a garden cottage, which affords more privacy, for US$54 plus US$13 per adult.

Eden Lodge (☎ 62000; fax 62001) on Freshwater Rd is perhaps more like a transplanted safari lodge than an Old Country estate. Its immense lounge and dining room, with high ceilings and hardwood floors, overlook perhaps the best view in the Vumba. For a lovely cottage in the trees, you'll pay US$37/48 for single/double occupancy, including vouchers allowing you to use the facilities at the Leopard Rock Hotel. Try for one of the two cosy wooden cottages which hang over the precipice. Unless the proprietors are going to town anyhow, transfers from Mutare cost US$6 per party.

Below the flanks of Chinyakwaremba (Leopard Rock) is the immense palace-like *Leopard Rock Hotel* (☎ 60115; fax 61165), with its vast lawns and lavish gardens. It was built entirely of stone by Italian prisoners of war during WWII. Its mark in history was made when the British Queen Mother, Elizabeth, stayed there on a royal visit in 1953. In 1978, during the Second Chimurenga, the building suffered devastation, but it has now been renovated and houses Zimbabwe's fourth casino and one of its poshest hotels. Since the three-tier pricing system is in force, foreigners who pre-book overseas pay excruciating prices, which range from US$165/220 (local rate US$45/84) a single/double for a room by the casino to US$350 (local rate US$95) for a suite in the turret. Rack rates are about 30% lower.

For a round of golf on the surrounding 18-hole course, hotel guests pay US$8 and outsiders, US$11. Clubs, carts and caddies are also available for hire. Other leisure facilities include a croquet pitch, bowling green, billiards, tennis courts and a swimming pool, sauna and gym. Horse-riding on the nearby Campbell-Morisson farm costs US$5 per hour and organised 2½-hour birdwatching tours through the montane forest on Seldomseen Ornithalogical Study Centre cost US$11 per group.

Things to Buy

If you're craving such Vumba specialities as pickles, honey, Vumba cheese, biltong, coffee from the Zimbabwean highlands and locally grown protea flowers, visit the oddly named Vumba Dawn Hyper-Kiosk at the 21-km peg of the Vumba road. See also Crake Valley Farm under Burma & Essex valleys earlier in this section.

Getting There & Away

Without a vehicle, access to the Vumba area is quite limited. From the in-town bus terminal in Mutare, there's a bus to Leopard Rock at 8 am and 3 pm on Friday, Saturday and Sunday, returning to Mutare just over an hour later. There's also a bus departing from

ZIMBABWE

Mutare at 6 am for Essex Valley; a Burma Valley bus leaves Mutare at 11 am.

Nyanga Area

The tame highlands around Nyanga have long been the summer holiday spot for heat-weary Harare dwellers. Well, at least for those who could afford the luxury of a few days fishing and vegetating in the mountain country.

Nyanga National Park, the scenic wonderland around which the region revolves, is more a popular and developed resort area than a real wilderness, although there's scope for some remote bushwalking around the perimeter, especially in the park's southern extremes. Adjoining Mtarazi Falls National Park, which is little more than an appendage of Nyanga, is completely undeveloped – there's not even a camp site – and the only vehicle access is a steep, rutted track leading to the park's namesake attraction. Just east of the park lie the tropical agricultural lowlands and tea estates of the Honde Valley.

JULIASDALE

Piney Juliasdale, it seems, is little more than a holiday cottage settlement and a repository for scattered hotels and private holiday cottages in need of a town name in their address. From the centre, inasmuch as Juliasdale has one, there are good westward views across the farm lands, intermittent forests and granite domes. It boasts a petrol station, a post office, and a couple of small shops.

Places to Stay & Eat

To fill the budget niche in Juliasdale, Frank van Rensburg has opened *Juliasdale Camp & Cabin* (☎ 202), a comfortable alternative to camping (with great hot showers) in Nyanga National Park. Garden camp sites cost US$2 per person and simple cabins accommodating up to four people cost US$3.50 per person. Horse-riding trips cost US$2.50 per hour and mountain bikes, which are ideal for exploring the region, may

be hired for US$5 per day. They also conduct guided walks and arrange transport to sites of interest around the park.

The three-star *Brondesbury Park Hotel* (☎ 341), 30 km west of Juliasdale on the Rusape road, charges US$41/66 for singles/doubles, with dinner and breakfast, and use of the swimming pool, tennis courts and bowling green. A golf course adjoins the hotel grounds.

Nearer town, the recommended *Pine Tree Inn* (☎ /fax 388) is especially known for its excellent meals. Standard single/double rooms cost US$29/48 with dinner and breakfast. Luxury suites cost US$57.

The four-star *Montclair Casino Hotel* (☎ 441; fax 447), which boasts one of Zimbabwe's four casinos, attracts wealthy tourists and Zimbabwe's elegant crowd with its luxurious trappings: tennis courts, a swimming pool, croquet, horse-riding, golf and so on. (However, if I had the money to spend on such digs, I'd opt instead for Troutbeck near the national park.) As one of the Sun Hotels, it still has a three-tier pricing system, so it's not good value for foreigners, who pay US$126/196 a single/double, compared with the local rate of US$42/66.

There is also the *Silver Rocks Holiday Farm* (☎ 394), with self-catering holiday cottages with a swimming pool, 10 km off the Rusape road.

On the highway between Juliasdale and Nyanga Park, stop at Claremont Orchard Shop (the sign announces 'exciting biting') for fresh Nyanga trout and locally grown apples.

Getting There & Away

From Harare, the Masara bus line runs a service to Juliasdale and Nyanga (Nyamhuka township) daily except Saturday at 7 am. In Harare, catch the bus marked Nyanga/Nyamaropa from the corner of Glenara Rd and Robert Mugabe St, or flag it down from opposite the Chicken Inn in Msasa, on the Mutare road. The fare is around US$4. Alternatively, take a bus to Rusape and connect there with the hourly services to Juliasdale and Nyanga.

From the in-town bus terminal in Mutare, ZUPCO, Zvinoira and Masara buses depart for Juliasdale and Nyanga hourly until midday and cost US$1.50.

NYANGA NATIONAL PARK

Although it can hardly be described as pristine – nearly all the naturally occurring vegetation in easily accessible areas was cleared for farming long ago – 33,000-hectare Nyanga National Park is a scenically distinct enclave in the Eastern Highlands. Cecil Rhodes fell in love with it and, as only he could have done, bought it for his own residence. Not surprisingly, the park, like the entire country, acquired his name; it's still sometimes referred to as Rhodes Inyanga. The African name, Nyanga, means 'the shaman's horn'.

Around Nyanga Dam

The Nyanga National Park service centre focuses on Nyanga Dam, which was the site of the Rhodes' estate homestead. Indeed, Rhodes' stone cottage residence stands surrounded by English gardens and imported European hardwoods beside the small artificial lake that once bore his name. Near the lodges is the National Parks' office (☎ 274), open 7 am to 6 pm daily.

Rhodes Museum The Rhodes Museum, which occupies Cecil Rhodes' old stables, is worth a good peruse. One would expect devotion to the coloniser himself, but the museum also dedicates space to positive facets of Black African history; the struggles of the Second Chimurenga and its spirit-inspired elements; and the good works of Zimbabwean war hero and philanthropist Rekayi Tangwena. Then of course there are the obligatory Rhodes relics! The museum is open daily except Monday from 9 am to 1 pm and 2.30 to 5.30 pm.

Brighton Beach Between the Nyanga Dam complex and the Nyangombe camping area is a natural wide spot below a cascade in the Nyangombe River. There's a sandy beach,

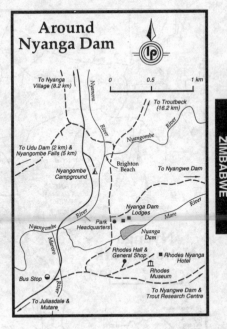

unofficially known as Brighton Beach, a green lawn, changing rooms and bilharzia-free swimming – if you're prepared to brave the chilly mountain water.

Pit Structures Although there are unrestored pit structures strewn haphazardly around the Nyanga landscape, the reconstructed pit structure near Nyanga Dam may help put the architecture into perspective. For comparison, take a look at the similar but unrestored one in a grove of trees behind the main pit. These particular sites have been dated to the 1500s.

The most plausible explanation is that these dry stone-walled pits were used as corrals for small livestock: goats, sheep, pigs or small cattle. They were entered through dark, narrow tunnels; the animals were kept in (and protected) by pales extending through the floor of the family hut, which was built on a level stone platform above the tunnel. Smaller stone platforms surrounding

ZIMBABWE

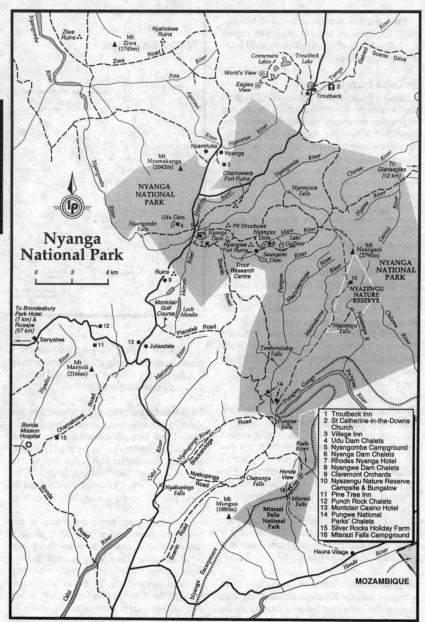

Nyanga National Park

0   3   6 km

1 Troubeck Inn
2 St Catherine-in-the-Downs Church
3 Village Inn
4 Udu Dam Chalets
5 Nyangombe Campground
6 Nyanga Dam Chalets
7 Rhodes Nyanga Hotel
8 Nyangwe Dam Chalets
9 Claremont Orchards
10 Nyazengu Nature Reserve Campsite & Bungalow
11 Pine Tree Inn
12 Punch Rock Chalets
13 Montclair Casino Hotel
14 Pungwe National Parks' Chalets
15 Silver Rocks Holiday Farm
16 Mtarazi Falls Campground

the pit were probably used as foundations for grain-storage huts.

Chawomera Fort A pleasant morning hike from Nyanga Dam is to Chawomera Fort, six km up the Nyangombe River; follow the well-defined path along the north bank. With a vehicle, however, the fort is more easily accessed from the Troutbeck road. Like Nyangwe Fort, Chawomera Fort is one of a series of similar structures stretching across the Nyanga region. Although they resemble defence structures, it's more likely they served as simple lookouts. Local sources have suggested that sentries posted in these hilltop structures, which are mutually visible on clear days, communicated by blowing on the spiral kudu horn.

Udu Dam Udu Dam, two km west of Nyanga Dam, lies at the bottom of a grassy parabolic valley sloping up towards the hills. The quiet lodges at Udu Dam are A-frame basha huts. Visitors can swim in a convenient pool of the Udu River, but if you're not a camp guest, you may attract suspicion if you wander through. Rowing boats may be hired for US$1 per hour.

Because the low vegetation allows good visibility, both the Udu Valley and surrounding hills are easy to explore on foot and hikers are rewarded with a high incidence of unexcavated ancient ruins. There aren't any tracks per se, but park personnel can direct you to the most interesting sites.

Nyangombe Falls Just outside the park boundary, the Nyangombe River tumbles white over terraced stacks of cuboid boulders and plunges into a steep but shallow gorge. The whole thing may remind you more of an abstractly sculpted fountain than a work of nature.

The falls are a five-km walk from Nyangombe campground and three km from Udu Dam, with good mountain scenery all around. Wear strong shoes with a good tread because the descent from the car park, although short, is steep and slippery. For the best views, follow one of the several well-worn tracks to the right as you approach the river. Once you've seen the upper falls, which are depicted on all the brochures and postcards, have a look just downstream, where there's a higher and louder single drop into a nice deep river pool. Stay off the rocks near the falls; the flowing water fosters the growth of moss which can be hazardously slick.

Nyangwe (Mare) Dam Trout Research Centre At the Trout Research Centre near Nyangwe Dam, pisciphiles can learn from the experts about breeding and hatching rainbow *(Salmo gairdneri)* and brown trout *(Salmo trutta)* to stock Zimbabwe rivers. The staff conduct free 15-minute tours of the site whenever there's interest. It's open daily except Saturday from 2 to 3 pm and 4.30 to 5 pm.

Nyangwe Fort Nyangwe Fort and other hilltop enclosures have traditionally been ascribed to defence but, as with Chamowera Fort, it was more likely used as a lookout. However, closer scrutiny has revealed that implicit features in their structures would have precluded their use for that purpose. Although the hilltop sites might have been favourable, the placement of the structures away from water sources would prevent resistance under longer periods of siege. Despite rock loopholes, which resemble gun sights, their small size and odd positioning would command no field of fire. Furthermore, the enclosures are so broad that the occupants would been subjected to fire by assailants.

Whatever its purpose, Nyangwe is the best preserved of the Nyanga fort structures. The main enclosure, full of storage-hut platforms and partially overgrown with aloes and msasa trees, is surrounded by five smaller fort-like enclosures. Nyangwe is just a two-km walk from Nyangwe Dam along a motorable road.

Mt Nyangani
Rising to 2593 metres, flat-topped and myth-shrouded Mt Nyangani is Zimbabwe's

ZIMBABWE

Nyanga Vegetation & Wildlife

The Nyanga landscape ranges from subtle to spectacular. Much of the upland regions, typically 2000 to 2300 metres above sea level, are comprised of gentle granite mountains and heath-covered moors. The Nyanga highlands are also a stronghold of Zimbabwe's national flower, the flame lily, whose colour ranges from red to orange. Many of Nyanga's stone ruins have been overcome by red aloes and protea trees, whose pink blooms come straight out of a Dr Seuss fantasy. Lower areas, like the steep-walled gash of Pungwe Gorge and the precipitious Nyanga escarpment, offer some indigenous semi-tropical vegetation and views down into entirely separate, rather jungly ecosystems, where ferns, orchids and tropical hardwoods replace the heath and grasslands of the higher regions.

Although you won't find vast herds of African beasts at Nyanga, the park isn't completely lacking in wildlife. The Eastern Highlands are the sole Zimbabwe range of the samango monkey, which is blue-grey in colour with yellow highlights, black legs and a brown face. Another inhabitant native only to this region is the blue duiker, Zimbabwe's smallest antelope. These rarely observed forest-dwellers are grey-brown in colour except for a white throat and a dark line from the nose to between the short ringed horns. Other animals to watch for include baboons, hyena, klipspringers, kudu and reedbucks. There are also leopards around but they're as elusive as leopards are everywhere. Occasionally, someone even finds evidence of lions or buffaloes, but such animals are rarely seen. ∎

---

highest mountain. Viewed from the park, it's not dramatic by any description, and its loftiness only becomes apparent from the context of Honde Valley, over 1000 metres lower than the high moors west of the mountain. Nearly every visitor with a bit of stamina makes the obligatory climb to the summit. This can take anywhere from 1½ to three hours from the car park 14 km east of Nyanga Dam.

While there are plenty of reasons to climb Nyangani, there are also plenty of reasons not to. The weather can change abruptly; wind-driven rain can render the trip very unpleasant and when the *guti* mists drop around the marshy peak, the view becomes irrelevant. Local inhabitants, however, believe there are more implicit reasons for avoiding Nyangani. There aren't many Black Africans interested in climbing it (although on my last climb, I encountered quite a few of them); this hallowed mountain has earned a reputation for devouring hikers.

Park regulations ask prospective walkers to register at park headquarters before setting off, and to check back in once the trip is completed. At the base, you're met with an intimidating warning sign which outlines the climatic uncertainties and forbids hiking with children. If you remain undaunted, set out as early as possible to increase your chances of decent weather. Hitchhikers will have the best chances of finding a lift from the Nyanga Dam area. Otherwise, it's a 15-km walk each way.

Mt Nyangani to Honde Valley Walk

For a fairly easy – but not entirely straightforward – three or four-day walk, consider the increasingly popular route from Mt Nyangani into the Honde Valley.

From the car park at the base of Mt Nyangani, a southbound track skirts the base of the mountain. Once you've reached the summit of Mt Nyangani, either return to the car park the way you came, then follow the track southward; or descend along the southwestern slope of the mountain, where you'll strike the track four km south of the car park (this option is for experienced hikers only).

South of the car park, a motorable 4WD track winds for 12 km over grass-covered hills, then widens into a more amenable road. Part of this stretch passes through the recently created Nyazengu Private Nature Reserve (with a small admission charge), which is an ideal place to be delayed for a couple of days. It has two camp sites – one of which is an undeveloped site beside dramatic Nyazengu Falls – and a six-person bungalow, known as *Stonechat Cottage*, which rents for US$30. For bookings contact

Nyangani Farms (☎ 303518), 128 East Rd, Mt Pleasant, Harare.

Heading south from Nyazengu, you have 10 km of excellent views along the lip of the escarpment before descending into the upper reaches of Pungwe Gorge at Pungwe Drift.

At Pungwe Drift are some National Parks' chalets, which were destroyed during the Second Chimurenga but have since been rebuilt and are available for rent. From the chalets, a one-hour return side trip will take you to the top of 240-metre Pungwe Falls. The chilly, bilharzia-free eddies above the falls make for refreshing, tooth-chattering swimming. Between Pungwe Drift and the falls are several possible camp sites with plenty of fresh water available from the hell-bound Pungwe River. The most favoured site is the prominent sand bar near Pungwe Drift.

From Pungwe Drift, follow the little-travelled road back onto the escarpment and on to the car park at Mtarazi Falls. Along the way, don't miss Pungwe View, where a magnificent vista of the gorge, the falls and the now-distant Mt Nyangani opens up along a short detour from the main road. About four km beyond the Mtarazi Falls turn-off is Honde View, which reveals an enticing panorama of Honde Valley, nearly 1000 metres below, and the Mozambique frontier.

After three more downhill km, you'll arrive at the Mtarazi Falls National Parks' campground. There, a footpath leads 700 metres to a view of 762-metre Mtarazi Falls (Africa's second or third highest waterfall, depending upon your source) as it plunges over the escarpment.

The steep nine-km farm workers' track (actually a tangle of tracks) over the escarpment and into Honde Valley begins several hundred metres from the Mtarazi Falls campground. It's a bit tricky to find – it starts about 500 metres back up the road from the campground – but the isolated car park attendant would probably welcome the opportunity to offer direction. The track branches on the way down; take the right fork and you'll emerge on the Honde Valley road about one km above Hauna, from where you can connect with a Mutare bus. Inciden-

tally, the Honde Valley is well known as a favourite haunt of black mambas, so be especially cautious where you step.

Nyamziwa Falls

Nyamziwa Falls lies one km north of the northern loop road between Nyanga Dam and Mt Nyangani. The upper part of the falls resembles an immense slippery slide (but don't be tempted into trying it!) falling way to a 30-metre drop off into the gorge below. It's ideal for a couple of hours relaxation on a sunny day, especially after a morning climb of Mt Nyangani, which is an easily walkable five km away.

Troutbeck

The lovely *Troutbeck Inn* (☎ 305; fax 474), founded by Irishman Major Robert McIlwaine, sits at an altitude of 2000 metres. The food is 100% typically English – cream teas, Yorkshire puddings and game pies – with an atmosphere and the weather to match. Tradition has it that the log fire roaring in the main hall has been burning since the hotel was founded in 1950! Typical of the country-estate atmosphere, there's tennis, swimming, shooting, squash courts, a golf course, a private lake for trout fishing, lawn bowls, and stables. Unfortunately, it has recently been taken over by Sun Hotels, so that three-tier pricing system rears its ugly head and puts this beautiful place out of reach for most foreigners. Non-residents pay US$126/196 for a single/double room with a lake view, including dinner and breakfast. Locals get a much better deal, paying US$42/66.

Even if you're not staying in Troutbeck, stop for a look at the pretty and immaculately maintained Church of St Catherine-in-the-Downs in Troutbeck village. In the tiny churchyard is the grave of Colonel Robert McIlwaine, who created Troutbeck and Connemara lakes. He died in 1983.

Connemara Lakes

These stunning lakes, surrounded by lovely pine forests, were created and named by the same homesick Irishman who founded Troutbeck Inn. Unfortunately, they're sadly

ZIMBABWE

Forestry in Zimbabwe

Due south of Nyanga National Park are the rolling, forested hillsides, striped with logging roads and occasional clearcuts, which are the source of most of that characteristically pulpy Zimbabwe paper.

The slopes around Nyanga were originally covered with hard-wood forests, but they were cleared by early inhabitants for agricultural purposes. The vast stands of conifers, eucalyptus and wattle that replace them are little more than tree farms. Zimbabwe's first modern tree-planting scheme was started in 1905 by John Meikle in the Penhalonga area, and 25 years later, when the government became involved, the plantations began spreading northward. In the Eastern Highlands, these forests now cover nearly 1000 sq km, and that area is increasing all the time.

To many tourists, the large-scale logging activities may seem an affront to the aesthetics of an otherwise superb countryside. However, the logging of non-indigenous forests conserves foreign exchange capital. The pine forests, which account for 700 sq km, are used for lumber and paper production. Over 300 sq km are covered in eucalyptus, which is used for firewood and lumber. The newest and (it seems) most rapidly growing forestry endeavour in Zimbabwe is growing the fernlike black wattle for tanbark. These vast plantations lend the Eastern Highlands landscape a distinctly North American feel. ∎

---

inaccessible to the public. In fact, it's scarcely possible to even catch a glimpse of them with all the fences, gates, dogs, security systems and 'Keep Out' signs!

World's View

World's View, atop the Troutbeck Massif, sits perched on a precipice, 11 winding km up the mountain road from Troutbeck. As its name implies, this National Trust site affords a broad view across northern Zimbabwe. Visitors pay a fee of US$0.25 for upkeep of the landscaped lawns and picnic facilities.

The most interesting access is on foot; follow the steep four-km footpath which leads up the scarp from six km north of Nyanga village. Alternatively, you can hitch from Troutbeck. World's View is on most Nyanga itineraries, so finding lift won't be a problem except perhaps in June, when much of the park seems to close down. Even if you don't find a lift, it's a pleasant and straightforward walk up from Troutbeck. However, Troutbeck buses run infrequently and your chances of making a connection are slim.

Nyanga

Separated from the Nyamhuka township by a km of highway, Nyanga conspires to unsettle visitors with its beautifully manicured gardens and well-tended hedges. Its village common, tiny library and little stone church, all beneath the towering Troutbeck Massif.

Brits will probably be reminded of home, which is apparently intentional. Don't miss the winning hedge near the hotel, which is certainly unequalled in this quarter of the world.

A surprising highlight is the excellent Zuwa Weaving Cooperative (the name means either 'day' or 'sun'), behind the village post office. You'll find a range of sturdy and well-executed wool and cotton blankets and rugs, and mohair scarves. The creations are some of the most original available in Zimbabwe, and this place is well worth a look. It's open Monday to Friday from 8 am to 4 pm and on Saturday from 8 am to 2 pm. Another crafts outlet is Dilly's Craft Shop, which sells handmade knives with ebony handles, among other interesting items.

Other services in Nyanga include a petrol station, a small grocery store and a bottle store. Fresh vegetables are available from the gardener living behind the hotel. The Zimbank is open for currency exchange on Monday, Tuesday, Thursday and Friday from 8 am to 1 pm; on Wednesday from 8 am to noon; and on Saturday from 8 am to 4 pm. The nearby Rochdale Store also changes money, including travellers' cheques.

Nyamhuka township, with an entirely separate character, is the terminal for buses to and from Mutare, Rusape and Harare. When you've had enough nostalgia and are again longing for Africa, a visit to Nyamhuka should do the trick! There are a couple of shops and stalls selling inexpensive food, a shabby 'crafts village' – and a generally more relaxed atmosphere than anywhere else in the Nyanga highlands. At the entrance to Nyamhuka is an exhibition of Shona sculpture, with some pieces for sale.

Pungwe View & Pungwe Gorge

If you're travelling along the back roads between Nyanga and Mtarazi Falls, pull into the Pungwe View turn-off for a look down dramatic Pungwe Gorge, just inside the southern boundary of Nyanga National Park. The slopes of the truncated Mt Nyangani rise in the distance and below, the ground drops away to the Pungwe River. From the viewpoint, you can just see the top of 240-metre Pungwe Falls, where the river is swallowed up in the lush vegetation that fills the gorge.

About four km along Scenic Rd north of Pungwe View is the turning down to Pungwe Drift. From there, it's a pleasant half-hour walk downstream to the swimming holes immediately above the falls. Alternatively, follow the walking track down to the Drift from Pungwe View.

North-east of Pungwe Drift, the track climbs back onto the heath. After 10 km or so, it deteriorates, passes through the Nyazengu Private Nature Reserve and, 12 km later, emerges at the Mt Nyangani car park. The hiking route from Mt Nyangani to Honde Valley crosses the Pungwe River at Pungwe Drift.

To see the Pungwe River from a different angle, contact Far & Wide Zimbabwe (☎ 26329), PO Box 14, Juliasdale, which conducts raft and kayak trips down the white waters between December and April, water levels permitting. Offerings range from half-day paddles to seven-day camping expeditions. The popular five-hour whitewater trip, which costs US$50, departs from km six on the Brackenridge Rd.

Unfortunately, the Zimbabwean cabinet has recently approved the controversial Pungwe Water Supply Project, which is intended to provide Mutare with a reliable water supply. The project involves blasting a four-km tunnel through the rocks and building a pipeline to carry the water to the Odzani water works.

No environmental impact assessment has been done, but it's clear the effects will be far reaching. The Pungwe River's decreased flow will diminish Pungwe Falls and decrease water availability in the agricultural Honde Valley. Furthermore, less water will also mean saline intrusion into the Pungwe Flats wetlands in Mozambique, and will almost certainly affect Beira's water supply. The less damaging alternative, a water pipeline from the Odzi River, would cost about US$30 million less, but it has been shelved. Fortunately, the World Bank has said that financing will go ahead only once proper feasibility studies and environmental impact assessments have been completed.

Activities

Nyanga streams and lakes are stocked with rainbow, brook and brown trout and trout fishing licences cost US$1/7/13 per day/week/season at all sites except Gulliver and Saunyami (Purdon) dams, which cost US$2.50 per day. Fishing is permitted between the hours of 5 am and 6.30 pm. Seasons for the various venues are as follows: Mare Dam (December to August); Nyanga Dam (August to April); Udu Dam (April to December); Gulliver and Saunyami (Purdon) dams (October to July); and all rivers (October to May).

Guided 1½ hour/six-hour horseback tours around the Nyanga Dam area archaeological sites cost US$5/16 per person. Book through the National Parks' office (☎ 274) near Nyanga Dam.

Places to Stay

Camping The National Parks' *Nyangombe Camping & Caravan Site* lies between the Nyangombe River and the highway. It's full of big piney woods, reminiscent of a US national park, and has nice hot showers, baths, braai pits and toilets.

Camping in other areas of the park is officially prohibited and unofficially tolerated, but if you do camp in these areas, be discreet about it. The park administration can't fathom why anyone would enjoy an overnight hiking trip, but they don't organise sting operations to reel in violators. Just use your own discretion. Mt Nyangani is a special case; hikers are technically expected to register at headquarters before making the trip, but they must also sign out the same day. If you're climbing Nyangani en route to Pungwe Gorge, you'll have to forego the registration process. If you're continuing on to the southern part of the park, you're unlikely to encounter problems.

Lodges & Cottages You'll find cosy National Parks' lodges at Udu Dam, Nyanga Dam and Nyangwe Dam, all within a few km of the main park service area. At Pungwe Drift near the southern extreme of the park are two remote lodges which are also booked through National Parks.

If you prefer a self-catering holiday cottage, your options include rudimentary *Brackenridge Cottage* (☎ 26321), which enjoys an ideal location three km from Pungwe Falls and *Nyanga Mountain Haven* (☎ 721696, Harare), beside the Connemara Lakes. There's also the relaxing *Ezulwini Cottages* (☎ 61121), north of Troutbeck on the slopes of Mt Rukotso. It lies on the borders of Nyangui Forest Reserve and overlooks an idyllic stream broken by pools and waterfalls. There are no shops or services within walking distance of any of these places; when booking, enquire about what you'll need to bring.

Hotels The small, basic and friendly *Village Inn* (☎ 336; fax 335), at the end of the road through Nyanga village, is a good alternative to camping. The restaurant serves very nice set meals and when it's cold outside, you can curl up beside the log fire in the lounge. The hotel even grows its own vegetables, for use in the restaurant and there's a piano for anyone feeling musically inspired. For dinner, bed and breakfast, single/double rooms with bath cost US$25/41. For budget

singles without private facilities, they charge US$18 and cottages are US$23 per person.

The one-star *Rhodes Nyanga Hotel* (☎ 377; fax 477) near Nyanga Dam, with its tropical verandah and well-kept gardens, isn't a bad option either. Now more relaxed than in years past, it's quite friendly and no longer such a suitable tribute to its heavy-handed namesake, who once lived on the site. Rooms with shared baths (including dinner, bed and breakfast) cost US$22/36 a single/double. With private facilities, you'll pay US$26/43. Single/double rondavels are US$19/29.

For information on *Troutbeck Inn*, which deserves separate treatment, see under Troutbeck earlier in this section.

Places to Eat
Apart from the hotel dining rooms, there isn't much available in way of prepared food. The Rochdale shop in Nyanga village sells groceries and the market food stalls in Nyamhuka township provide another option. For fresh dairy products and local produce, go to *Nyamoro Farm* at Troutbeck. It's open daily except Saturday from 8.30 am to noon and 3 to 5.30 pm. Take the road north of Troutbeck and turn left at the top of the hill past the 'jersey cow' sign, then turn left again at the signposted gate.

Getting There & Away
Between 7 and 8 am, buses leave Nyamhuka for Harare, Mutare, Masvingo and Bulawayo. For specifics, see Getting There & Away under Juliasdale; all buses passing through Juliasdale either originate or terminate in Nyamhuka township. In the national park, the bus stop is right in front of Nyangombe campground.

NORTH OF NYANGA
The highland areas north of Nyanga, which hold the greatest concentration of pre-colonial ruins in Zimbabwe, are for the most part accessible only by private vehicle. Since some of the best ruins lie only about 22 km from Nyanga village, walking is straightforward. The area was formerly used as a

Frelimo guerrilla-training zone, but visitors no longer require military permission to enter.

Ziwa & Nyahokwe Ruins

As you drive north from Nyanga village, you'll constantly see examples of the ancient terraces that characterise the region. The most extensive expanse of ruins in the Nyanga area is the Ziwa complex, sprawling over 80 sq km. They were formerly known as Van Niekerk's Ruins, after the Boer who showed them to archaeologist Donald Randall McIver in 1905, but have now been renamed Ziwa after 1745-metre mountain which rises in their midst (which was itself named Sa Ziwa, after a 19th-century Karanga chief).

The parallel walls, housing platforms, agricultural terraces, circular enclosures, pit corrals and disjointed rubble that litters the intermediate ground are thought to be evidence of a Karanga agricultural community, everyday farmers closely associated for defence purposes. With the exception of some excavation for artefacts, these post-Great Zimbabwe ruins have remained much as their inhabitants left them. Stone seats and built-in grinding niches are also in evidence. A small interpretive display outlines what little is known about the complex.

Although it's thought to be the work of earlier stonemasons, Nyahokwe, named for the Karanga chief Hokwe from the same era as Sa Ziwa, is more of a consolidated village than the extensive Ziwa. Although it was inhabited as recently as the 19th century, this hilltop site is attributed to the migrating tribes who are also credited with constructing Great Zimbabwe. The inhabitants were probably involved in iron smelting and the ruin is believed to be the remains of a rudimentary ore-crushing operation. For novelty value, don't miss the lonely juniper tree (*Juniperus procura*) which, as far as anyone knows, is the only one in Zimbabwe.

Getting There & Away

The shortest route to Ziwa Ruins turns west from the main road about one km south of Nyanga village; after 11 km, turn right and continue another 10 km to the site. A better alternative is via Nyahokwe; the road turns west 14 km north of Nyanga village. After five km, you'll come to the turn-off for Nyahokwe Ruins, which are one km away. If, instead of turning, you continue straight on for eight km, you'll arrive at Ziwa. Without a private vehicle, your only option is to walk, which is pleasant, or attempt hitching, which is nigh hopeless. You can camp anywhere in the area.

MTARAZI FALLS NATIONAL PARK

Tiny Mtarazi Falls National Park lies just south of Nyanga National Park and is, for practical purposes, a part of the same entity. The central attraction, 762-metre Mtarazi Falls, is little more than a trickle of water that reaches the lip of the escarpment and nonchalantly plummets over the edge, passing out of sight in long cascades through the forest below.

According to Mark and Hazel Igoe, authors of the booklet, *The Manicaland Guide*, the pool at the bottom is inhabited by water spirits who drag the unwary down into its watery depths. Perhaps it's fortunate that access to this pool is quite difficult.

Honde View

Drivers on Mtarazi Falls road aren't normally aware of the sharp escarpment dropping off to their left. Then they pull off at Honde View, scramble over the rocks to the edge and receive a dramatic awakening when they behold a patchwork of agricultural patterns in the broad Honde Valley below.

Places to Stay

A new National Parks' campground has been opened beside the falls parking area.

Getting There & Away

From the main Mutare-Nyanga route, take the Honde Valley turn-off, bearing left onto Scenic Rd after two km or so. The right turning to the falls will be 16 (occasionally rough) km from there. Follow that road for

ZIMBABWE

seven km to the car park, from which it's a one km or so walk down through intermittent forest and grass to the most spectacular vantage points.

Although hitching isn't impossible, plan on long waits and remember that most drivers visit Mtarazi Falls as an obligatory stop on their Nyanga tour. For more information, see the description of the Mt Nyangani to Honde Valley walk in the Nyanga National Park section.

HONDE VALLEY

A former haunt of Mozambican MNR raiders, the picturesque Honde Valley sits vulnerably estranged from the rest of Zimbabwe by the Nyanga Mountains. This low-lying and well-watered basin, a world apart from the cool highlands immediately west, contains some of Zimbabwe's richest communal lands. It's ideal for growing coffee, tea and tropical fruit and the views up to the brooding Nyanga Escarpment are awesome, especially when dark clouds gather over the peaks.

With a car, you can visit the lovely Aberfoyle Tea Estates at the end of the road, which date back to the 1940s. Here, most of Zimbabwe's export tea is grown and in the summer, the idyllic rolling landscape turns as green as Ireland. Have a look around the tea estates, take a tour of the factory and take a stroll to the series of cascades about five km away.

From near Hauna village, there's foot access to the forest pool beneath Mtarazi Falls. The footpath to the top of the falls, which is used mainly by Hauna people working up on the escarpment, turns off the main road about one km south of the village.

Places to Stay & Eat

On the Aberfoyle Tea Estates, you'll find accommodation at the *Aberfoyle Country Club* (☎ 213, Nyanga or 708239, Harare), 30 km north of Hauna. The comfortable rooms are enhanced by gardens, a golf course, squash and tennis courts and a swimming pool – as well as a stunning setting. Camping is normally permitted, but you may have to

get out of sight of the lodge. A small workers' shop sells food staples, but if you can manage it, don't miss the memorable three-course meals at the Country Club restaurant.

Getting There & Away

From Sakubva musika in Mutare, buses depart for Hauna daily, early in the morning, but they don't go as far as the tea estates. Get off at the end of the line and look for a local bus continuing to Aberfoyle. Hitching is possible, but not great.

If you're coming from Nyanga, a good road turns off 27 km south of Juliasdale, passing through pine forests until it drops steeply off the escarpment and descends, winding and twisting, into the valley. There's also a steep and tedious 4WD road descending from Troutbeck to the northern end of Honde Valley.

Chimanimani Area

CASHEL VALLEY

The Cashel Valley was named for Colonel R Cashel of the British South Africa Police, who retired there after WWI. It's the origin of the brand name on all those tinned fruits and veggies you see on supermarket shelves, although few things are grown here these days. In the 1970s, Cashel Valley was the site of a successful agricultural scheme, but after Zimbabwean independence, it was run into the ground by corruption and inexperience. The valley lies amidst some lovely mountain scenery and it's worth a quick side trip from the Wengezi-Chimanimani road.

CHIMANIMANI

Chimanimani may like to call itself 'the best kept secret in Zimbabwe', but the secret is now out. Enclosed by green hills on three sides and open on the fourth side to the dramatically abrupt wall of the Chimanimani Range, its appeal is undeniable.

The first European visitor to be taken with Chimanimani was George Benjamin Dunbar Moodie of Melsetter ('floury uplands'), on

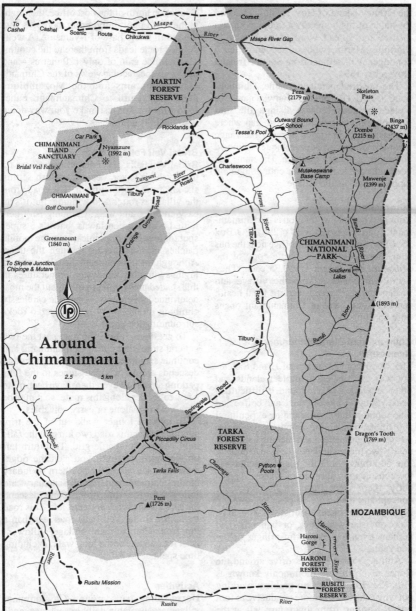

Around Chimanimani

0   2.5   5 km

To Cashel
Cashel Scenic Route
Chikukwa
Msapa River
Corner
Msapa River Gap
Peza (2179 m)
Skeleton Pass
Binga (2437 m)
MARTIN FOREST RESERVE
Outward Bound School
Dombe (2215 m)
Rocklands
Tessa's Pool
Car Park
CHIMANIMANI ELAND SANCTUARY
Nyamzure (1992 m)
Bridal Veil Falls
Charleswood
Mutekeswane Base Camp
Mawenje (2399 m)
Zunguni River
Orange Grove Road
CHIMANIMANI
Tilbury
Golf Course
Haroni River
CHIMANIMANI NATIONAL PARK
Greenmount (1840 m)
Southern Lakes
To Skyline Junction, Chipinge & Mutare
Tilbury Road
Bundi River
(1893 m)
Tilbury
Springvale Road
Nyahodi River
Piccadilly Circus
TARKA FOREST RESERVE
Dragon's Tooth (1769 m)
Tarka Falls
Chisengu River
Python Pools
Peni (1726 m)
MOZAMBIQUE
Haroni River
Haroni Gorge
HARONI FOREST RESERVE
Rusitu Mission
RUSITU FOREST RESERVE
Rusitu River

the Orkney island of Hoy. He duly attached the name of his home town to the mountain district and spread word of its beauty to Martinus Martin, who subsequently led a contingency of settlers from South Africa in November 1894.

The post-independence name, Chimanimani, is derived from the Manyika name for a place that must be passed single file, presumably referring to the narrow gap where the Msapa River flows through the range from Zimbabwe to Mozambique, followed closely by a narrow footpath. The name has been enlarged to include the entire mountain range, as well as the village.

Information
Your best bet for information is the Chimanimani Tourist Association (☎ 294), PO Box 75, Chimanimani, with its office near the bus stop. Here you can pick up a copy of the *Milkmaps Guides* for US$0.75 each. They detail hill walks around the village and further afield. Proceeds benefit local health services. The bank in Chimanimani opens only on Thursday.

Chimanimani Eland Sanctuary & Nyamzure
The 18-sq km Chimanimani Eland Sanctuary was established to protect elands and other antelopes which found it difficult to resist young shoots of maize and coffee and pine saplings in the surrounding agricultural and timber lands. Tan-coloured elands are Africa's largest antelope, reaching heights of nearly two metres and weighing in at 600 kg. The odd thing about the Eland Sanctuary is the conspicuous absence of elands. Apparently, there were flaws in the sanctuary concept and they were all poached, ostensibly by Mozambican insurgents. You may, however, see waterbuck or baboons, and perhaps even a duiker, klipspringer or the odd zebra.

Although most visitors drive around the slopes of Nyamzure (commonly known as Pork Pie Hill, and it's no problem working out why), the track is more conducive to foot travel. Coming from town, turn left at the

T-junction north of the post office, then right at the first opportunity. From there, it's five km uphill to the base of Nyamzure. A well-defined route leads from there to the summit – an altitude gain of only 120 metres – and opens up spectacular views of the Chimanimani Mountains and the Mozambique plains. To return to Chimanimani, either follow the road or just make your way down over the hills and ridges.

Bridal Veil Falls
Bridal Veil Falls, a slender 50-metre drop on the Nyahodi River, occupies a lush setting six km from Chimanimani. The road from the village is rough and winding, but it's an easy and pleasant walk. Camping isn't permitted on the green lawns, but it's a super spot for lounging or picnicking in the mobile patches of sun filtering through the trees. Although the pool beneath the falls seems to invite swimming, the water temperatures in this shaded niche will put off all but the most determined swimmers (or anyone carelessly climbing on the slimy moss-covered rocks surrounding the pool).

To get there, follow the road past the two general stores and out of Chimanimani, and continue six more km as it twists, climbs and descends around wooded slopes to the falls parking area. However, there have been quite a few robberies along this route, so it may be wise not to go alone or carry valuables.

To make a longer walk out of the trip, continue along this road two km past the falls until you reach a cattle grid. Then turn left up the fence line until you gain the ridge; there, turn left along the southern boundary of the Chimanimani Eland Sanctuary and follow it for four km. At this point, descend the ridge to the road, and turn left. This road meets the Bridal Veil Falls road less than a km from Chimanimani Village. Allow at least four hours for the loop walk, excluding time spent at the falls.

Activities
Horse-riding trips around Chimanimani village are available daily except weekends

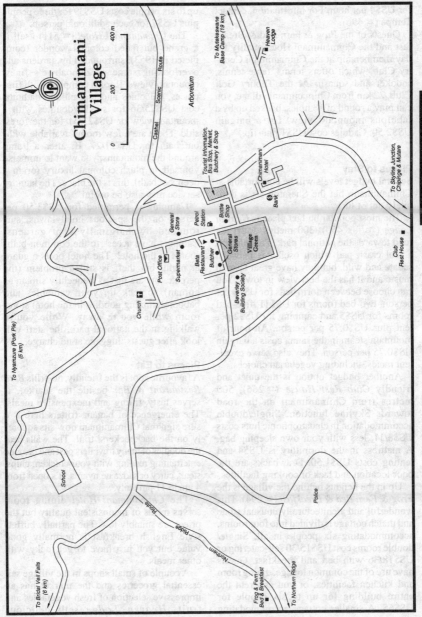

Chimanimani Village

To Mutekeswane Base Camp (19 km)

Heaven Lodge

Cashel Scenic Route

Arboretum

Tourist Information, Bus Stop, Market, Butchery & Shop

Chimanimani Hotel

To Skyline Junction, Chipinge & Mutare

Bank

General Store

Petrol Station

Bottle Shop

General Stores

Post Office

Supermarket

Beta Restaurant

Butcher

Village Green

Church

Beverley Building Society

Club Rest House

To Nyamzure (Pork Pie) (5 km)

School

Ridge Route

Northern Ridge Route

Police

To Bridal Veil Falls (6 km)

Frog & Fern Bed & Breakfast

To Northern Ridge

0   200   400 m

ZIMBABWE

for US$4 per hour. For information, contact Tempé (☎ 496).

Guests of the Frog & Fern Bed & Breakfast and the Chimanimani Hotel qualify for day membership at the Chimanimani Country Club, which offers tennis, table tennis, snooker and squash. At the Tilbury Golf Club, 22 km from Chimanimani village, you can play a round of 18 holes, backed up by a fabulous mountain view, for a bargain US$2.50. Caddies cost US$1 plus tip.

Places to Stay

Several budget levels will be comfortable at Chimanimani, but the Sheraton set is definitely out of luck.

The most popular budget place is *Heaven Lodge* (☎ /fax 450), 300 metres down the road towards the national park. This place is a real crash pad which oscillates between sedate and wild, but they have great taste in music and it has the best view in town. You can choose between dorm beds for US$4 per person, two-bed rooms for US$11, five-bed rooms for US$5 and camping for US$2 per tent plus US$0.75 per person. An hour of mountain steam in the sauna costs a bargain US$0.75 per person. They also serve excellent meals, including vegetarian choices.

Another budget option is the quiet and friendly *Club Rest House* (☎ 266), 500 metres from Chimanimani on the road towards Skyline Junction. Single/double accommodation in claustrophobic huts costs US$8/11; less with your own sleeping bag. A mattress in the dormitory is US$4 and tenting costs US$1.50. Drawbacks are the poor location and lack of cooking facilities.

Up in the heights behind the village is the *Frog & Fern Bed & Breakfast* (☎ 294). This wonderful and architecturally unusual stone and thatch cottage is divided into four rooms, accommodating six people in all. Single/double rooms cost US$15/30 self-catering or US$18/36 with bed and breakfast. Guests have use of the common lounge, dining room and kitchen facilities; or you can rent the entire building for up to six people for US$65. A smaller cottage accommodating

up to six people costs US$39 for three people plus US$7 for each additional person.

The *Chimanimani Hotel* (☎ 511) itself is a grand but faded colonial wonder (completed in 1953), surrounded by gardens and overlooking some of Zimbabwe's finest mountain views. Rooms complete with fireplaces, balconies and big antique bathtubs cost US$25/36 for singles/doubles with a mountain view or US$23/31 for the forest side. There are a few rooms available without bath for US$21/27. If, after a tramp around the mountains, you want to immerse yourself in plush colonial luxury (or in a deep, hot bath), this is the place. The laundry service may also be useful.

Camping is permitted for US$3.50 per person on the spacious hotel lawns, surrounded by marginally kept gardens. Campers have access to the common bathrooms in the hotel. The hotel posts a guard at night, but theft is still a problem (the perpetrators are just as frequently simian as human) so lock up your valuables and baboon-tempting goodies in the hotel storeroom while you're away. While you're walking in the national park, the staff will look after guests' luggage at no charge.

Places to Eat

A favourite spot is the friendly, no-frills *Beta Restaurant & Bar* beside the market. It serves tasty, filling and inexpensive meals. The emergence of banana fritters here is a sure sign that Chimanimani now sits squarely on the backpackers' trail. The walls bear the doodles of many travellers past and provide entertaining reading with your chicken, chips, steak, curry or sadza ne nyama. It's open from 4 am to 11 pm daily.

The *Chimanimani Hotel* dining room serves meals of inconsistent quality but the prices are suitably low. The partially buffet-style English breakfast is normally good value but you just have to get lucky with other meals.

A couple of small shops in the village sell essential groceries and the market has an impressive selection of fresh vegetables and fruit. *Heaven Lodge* sells delicious

Chimanimani cheese, which goes well on mountain hikes.

Things to Buy
Near the market in the village is a small cooperative shop selling local handicrafts, particularly *gudza* (chewed bark) dolls and bags.

Another local speciality is the delicious garlic and peppercorn Chimanimani cheese. It's produced by a local woman and distributed only through Heaven Lodge in Chimanimani and Hot Springs resort in Nyanyadzi. Don't miss it!

Getting There & Away
There are two daily buses from Mutare, departing from Sakubva at around 7 am and 10.30 am. The bus from Chimanimani departs sometime between 5 and 6 am. There are also two weekly Ajay's Motorways buses between Chimanimani and Masvingo.

Hitching is not great, and will probably result in a series of short lifts rather than one all the way to or from Mutare. The route in from Chipinge is normally easier than from Wengezi Junction (between Mutare and Birchenough Bridge). Once you reach Skyline Junction, it's 18 winding km downhill to the road's dead end at Chimanimani village. Don't consider hitching the 'scenic' back road to or from Cashel Valley unless you want to walk or be stuck a good long time.

CHIMANIMANI NATIONAL PARK
The formidable mountain wall that faces Chimanimani village is the heart of Chimanimani National Park, a wilderness wonderland of steep sandstone peaks and towers, clear rivers, savanna valleys and hoodoo-like stone forests. The water is good to drink and the pools safe for swimming. Orchids and hibiscus grow on the tangled slopes; and lobelia, heather, aloes and many species of meadow wildflowers carpet the intermittent savanna plains.

Chimanimani isn't a game park, however, so don't expect a range of African wildlife. There are quite alot of baboons to be heard screeching throughout the night and some retiring antelopes – including blue duikers, klipspringers and waterbucks – but not much else. Rangers report that leopards are common (although rarely observed) and that lions and buffaloes are occasional visitors, but they remain mostly in the park's remote southern reaches.

Tessa's Pool
At the end of a marked track leading off from the Outward Bound approach road is inviting Tessa's Pool, where you'll find a classic swimming hole and a rope swing, as well as a barbecue shelter with braai pits. It's actually one of series of three levels of pools located on government land outside the national park. Many visitors stop on their way up to the mountains, but this spot is even more welcome at the end of a long hike, especially after descending the Hadange River track.

The nearby Outward Bound school (☎ 5440), which leases the land, uses the pool for some of its courses, so you may want to phone in advance to see if it's available. They prohibit climbing above the pool or picnicking around it (there's a barbecue shelter provided at the parking area), and restrict visits to between 9 am and 4 pm. Visitor numbers are limited to groups of 10.

Incidentally, Outward Bound has written to inform us that travellers or tourists aren't welcome on their courses, so don't pester them with queries.

Mutekeswane Base Camp
Mutekeswane Base Camp, 19 km from Chimanimani village, is for most hikers the entry point to Chimanimani National Park. There's a ranger station and a campground with hot showers and elaborate braai pits. If you're driving, it's also the car park at the end of the road.

In the summer, the ranger office is open Monday to Friday from 6 am to noon and 2 to 5 pm, and Saturday from 6 am to 12.30 pm. In the winter, it's open 7 am to noon and 2 to 4 pm Monday to Friday, and 8 am to 12.30 pm Saturday. Visitors must report

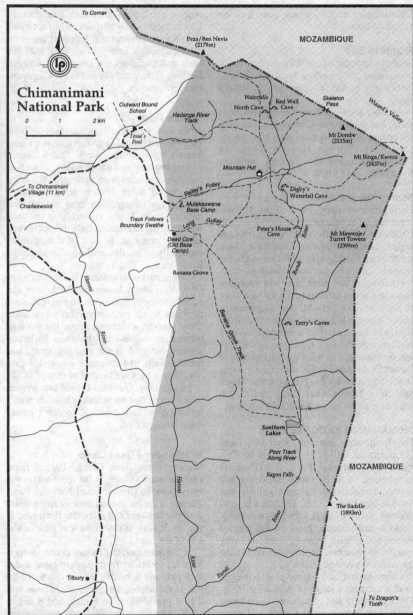

ZIMBABWE

To Comer

Peza/Ben Nevis
(2179m)

MOZAMBIQUE

Chimanimani
National Park

0   1   2 km

Outward Bound
School

Hadange River
Track

Waterfalls
North Cave

Red Wall
Cave

Skeleton
Pass

Wizard's Valley

Mt Dombe
(2215m)

Tessa's
Pool

Mt Binga/Kweza
(2437m)

Mountain Hut

To Chimanimani
Village (11 km)

Charleswood

Balley's Folley

Digby's
Waterfall Cave

Mutekeswane
Base Camp

Track Follows
Boundary Swathe

Long   Gulley

Peter's House
Cave

Mt Mawenje/
Turret Towers
(2399m)

Dead Cow
(Old Base
Camp)

Banana Grove

Harmi
River

Bundi
River

Banana Grove Track

Terry's Caves

Southern
Lakes

Poor Track
Along River

Ragon Falls

MOZAMBIQUE

Harmi
River

The Saddle
(1893m)

Bundi
River

Tilbury

To Dragon's
Tooth

here, sign in and pay fees before proceeding into the park.

Corner

This recent addition to the national park is a salient which juts into Mozambique, detached from the rest of the park by the Martin Forest Reserve and the communal lands along the international boundary. Well, that's not quite true; the two sections are actually connected by a 10-km-long and approximately 300-metre-wide swathe along the international boundary.

For some time, National Parks' has had plans to construct lodges in Corner, but the area still remains undeveloped, wild and inviting. The highlight is probably the narrow 'chimanimani' through the constricted Msapa River Gap, which gave its name to the entire region. You can camp anywhere in the Corner area, but firewood collection is prohibited.

Corner is accessible by vehicle from Chimanimani along the Cashel Scenic Route via Martin Forest Reserve to the village of Chikukwa. You can reach Chikukwa on a daily bus which leaves Chimanimani in the early evening (and returns early the next morning), but from there, you have a good 10-km walk into Corner.

Walking in Chimanimani

Chimanimani National Park is a paradise for hikers, and is accessible only to foot traffic. Whether you're doing a day hike from Mutekeswane Base Camp or a five-day camping trip through the back country, this place is bound to get a grip on you.

Chimanimani walking tracks are mostly well defined, so if you lose the way, don't wander off along a trail of flattened grass; this is probably the trail of someone else who was lost. When walking through heavy bush or casually strolling along sunny tracks, keep an eye out for several species of poisonous snakes which may be either hiding or sunning themselves in these places. You may even see a python lounging along the track.

All moving surface water in Chimanimani National Park is potable (quick-flowing streams are the cleanest), but it's still wise to follow the water-purification procedures outlined under Health in the general Facts for the Visitor chapter. Walking in the sun is hot and dry work; carry at least one litre of water per person and, unless you are following the Bundi River, make sure you top up the bottle at every opportunity.

Unfortunately, photocopied walking maps are available only sporadically (try at Heaven Lodge in the village rather than Mutekeswane), but the map in this book should be sufficient for most trips. The Ordnance Survey mapping dates back to the early 1930s (the park is covered in the Melsetter 1:50,000 quadrangle, sheets C1, C3 and D4) and doesn't depict walking tracks, but is essential for any cross-country exploration.

Warning Hikers, especially those climbing the higher peaks or bushwhacking through the back country, must remain aware of the Mozambique border. It's marked only at Skeleton Pass and the Saddle but the possibility of encountering unexploded mines makes it especially relevant. Naturally, keeping to the Zimbabwe side won't guarantee your safety but your chances will be better. The safest option would be to stick only to well-travelled tracks and not venture too far afield.

The only track leading to Chimanimani National Park's southern extremes leaves Zimbabwe at the Saddle and passes through eight km of Mozambique territory before re-entering Zimbabwe at Dragon's Tooth. This route should be avoided. To reach the remote south, either drive the long way around through Rusitu Forest or attempt the long slog through deep grass and bush along the Bundi and Haroni rivers. While the popular Mt Binga climb also loops briefly into Mozambique (in fact, Mt Binga is Mozambique's highest peak), it's sufficiently well travelled not to present more risks than other hiking routes in the park.

Bailey's Folly Bailey's Folly is the shortest and most popular route between Mutekeswane and the mountain hut. It's a straightforward track which leads up through groves of msasa trees, then levels off a couple of times before passing through a magnificent forest of standing rocks. After crossing a meadow, it winds down to the mountain hut above Bundi Valley. The walk takes two to three hours, depending on how may times you and your camera are distracted by the scenery.

Hadange River Track This alternative route to the mountain hut begins near the Outward Bound school and follows the Hadange River up a shadowy ravine to eventually connect with the Bundi River track just below North Cave. If it has recently rained or the track is wet, the passage may be muddy, slippery and generally difficult, so you may prefer to opt for the easier Bailey's Folly route.

However, lots of hikers descend by this route, thanks to the incentive provided by Tessa's Pool at the bottom. The track tends to be quite muddy and slippery, so take it easy.

Skeleton Pass Skeleton Pass, once notorious as a guerrilla route between Zimbabwe and Mozambique, is now a major trade route between the two countries. At the top is a sign denoting the frontier, an easy 40-minute walk from the mountain hut, and beyond the path winds down into the Wizards Valley.

Many people rush up to Skeleton Pass in the morning, yawn and retreat from the singularly unspectacular affront of a bright glaring sun and hazy hills fading into a nondescript horizon. In the late afternoon, however – provided the sun is shining – you'll be treated to an unsurpassed view into Wizards Valley and range after range of green fluted Mozambican mountains divided by plunging valleys. On a clear day, the distant blue line of the Indian Ocean meets the horizon.

Mt Binga The highest point in the Chimanimani Range, 2437-metre Mt Binga on the Mozambique border (again, it's also the highest point in Mozambique) is a stiff two to three-hour climb from the mountain hut. If you have fine weather, don't miss it. The view from the top encompasses a vast amount of territory and you can sometimes see right across Mozambique to the Indian Ocean.

Carry at least one litre of water per person. The last stream is less than halfway between the hut and the summit, so drink deeply and fill your water bottle for the steep, hot climb to the peak. There's a reasonably level camp site 150 to 200 metres below the peak, but no water is available.

Southern Lakes Little more than wide spots in a U-turn bend of the Bundi River, the vegetation-murky pools known as Southern Lakes provide a nice lunch spot or, if you have a tent, a passable camp site. The obvious mountain rising to the east is Mt Mawenje, also known as Turret Towers.

From Southern Lakes, another track heads south-east towards the Saddle. Four km south along the river on a not-so-clear track, you'll reach Ragon Falls. They're not terribly exciting, but make a pleasant day trip from Southern Lakes.

The Saddle The Saddle, at 1893 metres, is another pass into Mozambique. To get there, cross the Bundi River between the first and second Southern Lakes and walk north along the river until you reach a steep track heading up the slope. From there, it's about an hour to the top.

Banana Grove & Long Gully These two routes up to the first level of peaks begin south of Mutekeswane. The Banana Grove Track, named for the grove of strelitzia trees growing alongside it, is a gentler ascent than the more popular Bailey's Folly. It also is a considerably longer route to the caves and mountain hut, but provides access to Southern Lakes. The lush, rocky ravine known as Long Gully is a bit steeper, but provides ready access to Digby's Waterfall Cave.

Both routes begin at Mutekeswane. Descend steeply from the south side of the road, about 250 metres west of the ranger's office. At the bottom, slop your way through the small and disagreeable swamp, then follow the up-and-down fire swathe to the old base camp, enigmatically known as Dead Cow. Here, the track turns sharply to the left and winds upward. At the fork above Dead Cow, you must choose your route; the left one ascends Long Gully and the right one climbs to Banana Grove. At the top of the ridge, those headed for Southern Lakes should follow the downward-trending track, which hits the Bundi River at the northernmost Southern Lake. Allow four to five hours for this hike.

The Banana Grove route is most often used by hikers returning from the northern part of the park to Mutekeswane via Southern Lakes. Coming from the mountain hut, head south along the Bundi River, watching carefully on your right as you approach the first Southern Lake. There you'll see the red-earth track, which climbs steeply about 30 metres above the main river route before levelling off. Allow seven to nine hours to walk from the mountain hut to Mutekeswane via Southern Lakes and Banana Grove.

Places to Stay
Unless you have a vehicle or get lucky with lifts, you may spend the first night at Mutekeswane Base Camp, where steep slopes mean that camp sites must occupy stonewalled terraces. From there you'll have broad vistas of nearby forested hills and the red-earth coffee plantations beyond. Amazingly, hot baths and showers are available, but there's no electricity in the ablutions block so bring a torch!

Overlooking the Bundi Valley, across the first range of peaks, two to three-hours from Mutekeswane, is a classic stone mountain hut, complete with wooden bed bases, propane cooking rings (but no cutlery or cooking implements) and cold showers. It comfortably sleeps from 20 to 30 people but foreigners must pay US$8 per person to stay there – an absurdly high price by Zimbabwe standards – and it remains empty most of the time. If you're not staying, use of the burners for cooking costs US$1 per meal.

Your best bet is to camp. The Bundi Valley is riddled with small caves and rock overhangs which make ideal sites, so you don't necessarily need a tent. The nicest and most accessible caves lie near the valley's northern end. North Cave, a 30-minute walk from the mountain hut, overlooks a waterfall and opens onto views of the highest peaks. Above the waterfall is a pool, good for a cold swim, and Red Wall Cave lies 10 minutes further along. These are the first caves to be occupied, so if you hope to find space, get an early start from base camp.

A similar distance down the valley from the hut is Digby's Waterfall Cave, where the river provides a swimming hole, and beyond that is Peter's House Cave. Still further along, one km north of Southern Lakes and two hours from the hut, is Terry's Cave, which is divided into two rooms by an artificial stone wall. It's on the eastern bank of the river and not easily found, but there's a faint track leading from the river.

However, don't leave anything edible in the caves while you're out and about – baboons will plunder anything and ravenous rodents will happily gnaw through your pack to get at whatever's inside.

Getting There & Away
The most reliable access to the national park is with Eastern Tours, which provides a transfer service to Mutekeswane for US$2.50 per person, for a minimum of three people. They can be booked through the Chimanimani Publicity Association, Frog & Fern Bed & Breakfast or Heaven Lodge.

Some people get lucky with hitching. Ask at Heaven Lodge and the Chimanimani Hotel for someone heading your direction. The road sees very little other traffic – just army, National Parks' and agricultural school vehicles, and tractors used by local farmers.

Otherwise, you can walk the 19-km road walk to Mutekeswane. It's not an unpleasant prospect but will take four hours in either direction. From Chimanimani village, set out along the Tilbury road for nine km to Charleswood. There, turn left at the coffee

ZIMBABWE

plantation and immediately take the right fork. After five km, you'll reach the Outward Bound/Tessa's Pool turn-off. From there, it's a further five km to Mutekeswane Base Camp.

There's an occasional bus going as far as Charleswood, but it leaves in the evening and is therefore of limited use for travellers heading for the national park.

HARONI & RUSITU FOREST RESERVES
These two remote reserves actually take in parts of the Haroni and Rusitu valleys, at the southernmost extremes of Chimanimani National Park. They represent the only lowland rainforests in Zimbabwe, harbouring wild orchids, ferns and such rare trees as wild coffee *(Coffea salvatrix)* and large-fruited rinorea *(Rinorea arborea)*. The reserves are best known, however, for their incredible variety of unique bird species, such as the chestnut-fronted helmet shrike, the eastern honeyguide, the slender bulbul, Pel's fishing owl, blackheaded apalis, blue-spotted dove, green coucal, Angola pitta and the Vanga flycatcher, among others. Unusual wildlife species present include the Argus tree frog, the tree civet and Grant's lesser bushbaby.

The Wildlife Society of Zimbabwe is currently planning to mark and fence the legislated reserve boundaries, then establish a hardwood nursery and interpretive centre at nearby Vimba School. The school children would be involved in tending the seedlings, providing both an educational experience and financial support for the school. If you'd like to make a donation or want more information, contact the Secretary, Wildlife Society of Zimbabwe – Chipinge Branch, PO Box 382, Chipinge.

Organised Tours
If you don't have a suitable 4WD vehicle, Zimbabwe Eastern Border Adventure Company or ZEBAC (☎ 450) in Chimanimani runs a range of adventure tours through the Haroni and Rusitu reserves. Offerings including walks in the Haroni rainforest; hiking in the southern area of Chimanimani

National Park; horse tours; botanical and birdwatching tours; and whitewater rafting and kayaking on the class IV Haroni River and the easier Rusitu River.

Getting There & Away
These remote reserves lie on the Mozambique border, 35 km down a rugged 4WD track from the junction of the roads between Chimanimani, Chipinge and Birchenough Bridge. There's no public transport and precious little chance of finding a lift to this remote corner of the country. Perhaps ask around Chimanimani for Rory Duncan, who occasionally runs transfers to the reserves.

CHIPINGE
Named for a local chief, Chipinge lies in the heart of a rich agricultural district. Much of its wealth derives from the coffee and tea plantations spread across the rolling landscape towards the Mozambique border. There's a coffee research institute just off Mt Selinda road, and logging and wattle extraction operations on the surrounding hillsides. Chipinge is also a dairying centre.

Most commercial farmers in Chipinge are descended from the Boers who arrived with the Moodie Trek and created a rather unique cultural enclave. This boozey little town, with its corrugated iron roofs, jacaranda-lined streets and bougainvillea gardens, may remind you of a town somewhere in rural Australia.

Places to Stay & Eat
The *Chipinge Hotel* (☎ 2226) has certainly seen better times but unless you're set up for camping, it's your only option. Singles/doubles with attached bath cost US$20/32, without bath, and US$18/30. The hotel restaurant is only average but there isn't much choice apart from the market snacks, the supermarkets or the *Busi-Grill* snack bar and take-away.

The secluded riverside *campground* and *caravan park* lies about 500 metres west of town, away from the confusion of the centre. They charge US$1.30 per tent, plus US$0.75

per person. For caravans, they charge around US$3/4 without/with electric hook-ups.

If you prefer a quiet place out of town, stay at the self-catering *Kiledo Lodge* (☎ 2944), on a tea and coffee estate 18 km along the Eastern Border road, north-east of Chipinge. The area is quite unique, with stocked dams for fishing and its own small botanical reserve. The area is home to unique samango monkeys and it's a good base for exploring the Rusitu Valley and Haroni Forest Reserve.

Along the road to Birchenough Bridge, beside the Tanganda River, is *Buffelsdrift Guest Cottages* (☎ 226220). The two self-catering cottages accommodate up to 12 adults and cost US$14 for two people and US$3.50 for each additional person. The farm produces tobacco, coffee, wheat and tropical fruits, and is home to a wealth of birdlife.

Getting There & Away

Chipinge is the gateway to Mt Selinda, but otherwise, it's nothing to go out of your way for. Hitchers to or from Chimanimani are often stuck there. The bus terminal at market square (three blocks east of the main street) serves adjoining communal lands, Birchenough Bridge, the lowveld and, occasionally, Chimanimani. There are also three or four buses daily to both Mutare and Masvingo and frequent services to nearby Mt Selinda.

MT SELINDA

The village of Mt Selinda sits in a hilltop hollow above the Chipinge district coffee plantations. It revolves around a health mission founded by the American Board of Commissioners in 1893 and developed over the years into a vocational and agricultural training centre. In fact, the Mt Selinda mission was responsible for the first irrigation scheme in the dry scrubland around Nyanyadzi Hot Springs. The village, which abuts the Mozambique border, also served as a refugee camp during that country's recent civil war.

Monument buffs may want to hunt up Swynnerton's Memorial, just north of the road into the village. This long-untended slab commemorates the work of the 19th-century British naturalist and entomologist who settled in Chimanimani to catalogue local bugs and flora. His accomplishments include extensive studies on tsetse flies and, after WWI, service as the first game warden in Britain's newly acquired territory of Tanganyika (Tanzania).

Chirinda Forest Botanical Reserve

The Chirinda Forest Botanical Reserve, a 949-hectare slice of tropical hardwood forest, may be similar to the Vumba, but it's further from the trodden track. Its dark and dank depths are criss-crossed with paths, but lovers of superlatives will gravitate towards the Big Tree route. This obvious track turns off the Mt Selinda road, just up the 'tree tunnel' from the mission hospital. And it leads to – you guessed it – Zimbabwe's biggest tree (or so it's claimed). This 1000-year-old, 66-metre-high and 15-metre round behemoth belongs to the species *Khaya nasica* (red mahogany).

The red mahogany is relatively common on the eastern slopes of Zimbabwe's Eastern Highlands, and normally reaches heights of 20 to 30 metres. Its small, white and fragrant flowers bloom in early spring and the red wood polishes brilliantly. Africans use the seeds of its brownish fruit to make natural remedies and aromatic oils.

Several other species of mahogany are present at Chirinda. the most common is the *Trichilia dregeana* (forest mahogany) which has pinkish fine-grained wood. Stands of both red and forest mahogany, ironwood and other large trees grow throughout the forest reserve, particularly along the walking route known as Valley of the Giants. Chirinda is also one of the only habitats of the Swynnerton's robin.

Places to Stay

There are no amenities or camping facilities at the forest reserve but at a pinch, campers could easily melt into the big trees without detection; remember to take water.

Getting There & Away

Frequent but unscheduled buses do the 30-km run between Chipinge and Mt Selinda, but hitching is a better option. The road may be sparsely travelled, but since Mt Selinda sits at the end of the line (the road continues into Mozambique but the border is closed), everyone will know where you're going.

BIRCHENOUGH BRIDGE

Above the braided Save River, Birchenough Bridge rises mirage-like from the ruddy cactus, thorn and baobab scrub. This strategic structure appears on Zimbabwe's 20 cent coin and is guarded day and night against terrorist attacks. Photography is prohibited from the span itself.

If it appears that someone plucked up the Sydney Harbour Bridge and plopped it down in a most unlikely place, that's not far off the mark. This 378-metre-long span was designed by Ralph Freeman, who was also responsible for Sydney's 'Coat Hanger' (the Sydney Harbour Bridge, that is). It was named for Sir Henry Birchenough, chairman of the Beit Trust which financed its construction in 1935. His ashes now rest in one tower of the bridge.

Apart from the stark beauty of the surrounding Save Communal Lands, Birchenough Bridge village boasts a vibrant rural market out of all proportion to the size of the population.

Places to Stay

Birchenough Bridge has a single hotel, the rather seedy but friendly *Birchenough Bridge Hotel* (☎ 225819), where single/double rooms cost US$18/25. There's a nice little dining room but don't expect *haute cuisine*; try the sadza. They allow campers to set up on the lawn, from where there's a front-row view of the bridge itself.

Getting There & Away

At the bus terminal, you can make connections to Harare, Mutare, Chimanimani, Chipinge, Masvingo and even Chiredzi and Beitbridge. On Friday, most buses to Masvingo leave after 6 pm.

NYANADZI HOT SPRINGS

The Hot Springs resort at Nyanyadzi, 32 km north of Birchenough Bridge, was reduced to a heap of rubble during the war, but it has now been rebuilt and is going strong. The large swimming pool is filled by a piping hot natural spring, which reputedly has magical powers and curative properties. The peaceful setting, on communal lands between the dry highlands and the Odzi River, enhances its relaxing spell.

For comfortable lodges, they charge US$40/60 a single/double, with bed and breakfast. There's also a small backpackers' section on the corner, where camping costs US$4 per person (including use of the hot springs) but there's a limit of five tents at any given time. Caravan campers pay US$5 per caravan plus US$4 per person for the first night and just US$4 per person per night thereafter. Day use costs US$2.50 per person.

There's a small shop, an open-air video lounge and a fabulous dam-view restaurant serving imaginative buffet lunches and dinners. There's always a vegetarian option – this is a health resort after all – and a variety of delicious breads and cheeses. In fact, Hot Springs is one of only two places which distribute the famous garlic and peppercorn Chimanimani cheese.

Sometime during your visit, be sure to make the acquaintance of Rocky the Rock Hyrax, who likes to make his presence felt every morning around breakfast time.

Getting There & Away

Transfers from Mutare are available for US$2.50 per person each way. Alternatively, take any bus between Mutare and Birchenough Bridge. The resort lies 100 metres from the highway.

Just north of Nyanyadzi, towards Mutare, the road crosses a river with the enchantingly curious name of Umvumvumvu. This is an onomatopoeic reference to the sound made by the water splashing over rocks.

The Midlands & South-Eastern Zimbabwe

The sort of traveller who seeks out areas regarded by the tourist industry as dull and uninteresting will find plenty of joy in the Midlands and south-eastern Zimbabwe and, except at Great Zimbabwe, you won't encounter a lot of other tourists. However, anyone on a rushed tour may not want to linger.

Geographically, the cooler, higher Midlands are known as the highveld, while low-lying south-eastern Zimbabwe is referred to as the lowveld. At the transition between the uplands and the south-east lies the town of Masvingo and nearby, the fabulous Great Zimbabwe, the 'stone houses' which gave their name to the entire country.

The highveld, sliced neatly through by the metal and mineral-rich Great Dyke, has historically been the heart of Zimbabwean mining activity. Several thousand mines were already working when the European colonists arrived and the veins still produce enough gold, nickel, chromium and asbestos to keep the Midlands humming.

The route between Chegutu, the first town south-west of Harare, and Bulawayo came to be known as the 'Hunters Road' after the late 19th-century ivory hunters who travelled through this once elephant-infested district. The only elephants that survive today occupy the empty hill country west of Kadoma, around the remote town of Gokwe.

The scrubby lowveld, on the other hand, is mainly ranching and agricultural country. With the eradication of the tsetse fly, large cattle holdings were established and ranchers managed a meagre living on the dry, unproductive and theretofore uninhabited land. More recently, exotic streams like the Save, Chiredzi and Limpopo have been tapped and have transformed parts of the lowveld into green and productive agricultural areas. Wheat, sugar cane and cotton fields drape the former thorn scrub, produc-

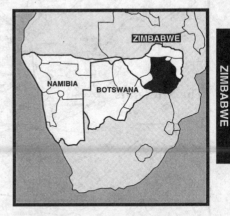

ing food staples and supplying the nation's sugar, ethanol and textile industries.

The lowveld's greatest potential attraction is the wildly beautiful and – as yet – little-visited Gonarezhou National Park. During the Civil War in Mozambique, the park was used as a bush larder by cross-border insurgents, and it remained closed to foreigners until 1994.

The Midlands

Perhaps inspired by their own thrilling Midlands, early British colonists passed the moniker on to the heart of Zimbabwe. The region covers most of the open and largely level territory from Harare south-west to Bulawayo and south to Masvingo.

MANYAME RECREATIONAL PARK

The nine sq km Manyame Recreational Park (formerly known as Darwendale – Lake Robertson), just 40 km west of Harare, brims with tiger fish, Hunyani Salmon, five species of bream and more, and offers diverse and

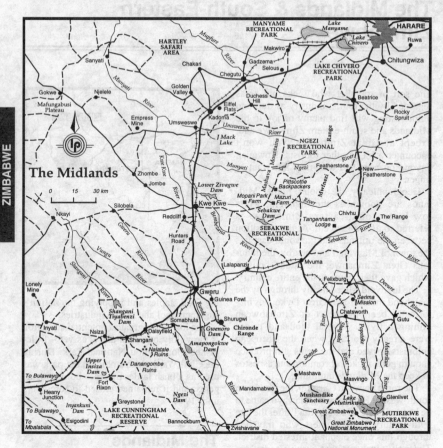

The Midlands

productive fishing. The dam was constructed in 1976 to supply water to the capital.

There are National Parks picnic areas and camp sites with braai pits, hot water and all facilities. Fishing permits are available from National Parks in Harare. From Harare, public buses only go as far as Darwendale and Norton; naturally, weekends are the best time for hitching.

CHEGUTU
Formerly known as Hartley, this soporific town of 22,000 began life as an 18th-century Portuguese trading post. At the crossroads of

the cotton and maize farming, cattle ranching and gold and nickel mining districts, it tries to be an administrative and commercial centre. The fact is, anything that could potentially liven the place up seems to pass through town quickly without looking back. As a result, Chegutu is a strong contender for Zimbabwe's least happening town. In fact, the hotel burned down in the late 1980s and no one has missed it enough to rebuild it.

KADOMA
Although its name means 'silent', Kadoma is louder, more interesting and nicer to look

at than neighbouring Chegutu. It was founded by an enterprising trader in 1906 as a service centre for the surrounding gold mines. The area proved to be so rich in gold ore – as well as magnesite, nickel and copper – that the region came to be called Africa's Klondike.

Although mining continues around nearby Eiffel Flats and along the tangle of roads threading between the settlements of aptly named Golden Valley, the present emphasis is on the cotton textile industry. With a population of 50,000, Kadoma now boasts weaving, spinning and dyeing mills, as well as a cotton research institute and a textiles training facility.

There isn't much to divert tourists, but if you're in town anyway, the colonial architecture is worth a look. Also, note the several steam engines, the Mozambican coach and the steam roller languishing behind barbed wire along the Harare road.

Places to Stay

Kadoma is proud of its three-star *Kadoma Ranch Motel* (☎ 2321, fax 2325), situated 'in the heart of Zimbabwe' on the Harare-Bulawayo road. Single/double rooms with breakfast cost US$40/46.

On Union St in the centre is the cheaper *Speck's Hotel* (☎ 3302). Apart from its retro façade, the *Grand Hotel* (☎ 4035) on Herbert Chitepo St at the square is not very grand – unless you're in the market for a bit of boozing followed by a very brief romantic liaison.

SEBAKWE & NEGEZI NATIONAL RECREATION AREAS

These twin dams in the never-never lands between the Masvingo and Bulawayo roads, are mostly of interest to the fishing crowd. Unlike the more popular dams nearer Harare, however, they see few visitors and the natural elements come into better focus. If you like things relaxed – or even deserted – consider visiting one of these forgotten parks. Be warned, however, that both dams are bilharzia breeding grounds so swimming is out.

The height of the dam wall at the 27-sq-km Sebakwe park was increased by seven metres in the late 1980s. Were it not for the recent drought, Sebakwe Dam, which is pinched in the middle by two fingers of the Great Dyke, would be Zimbabwe's fourth largest lake.

Ngezi, the larger of the two parks at 63 sq km, is quite a long way from anywhere. It has both camp sites and lodges, which should be booked through National Parks. For further information, contact the senior ranger (☎ 2405 Munyati), Ngezi Recreational Park, PO Box 8046, Kwe Kwe.

Getting There & Away

Sebakwe lies 10 km from the Kwe Kwe-Mvuma road (the turn-off is 18 km east of Kwe Kwe) and Ngezi lies about 90 km by road west of Chivhu and 93 km east of Kwe Kwe. There's no public transport to either park and an attempt at hitching will probably prove a waste of time.

KWE KWE

The unusual name of this midlands town of 60,000 is derived from the sound made by croaking frogs along the river banks, but the frogs have now been drowned out by the sounds of progress. In the publicity association's promotional hand-out, you'll learn that Kwe Kwe is, in fact, 'Where Industry Leads the Nation'. Inside are enticing photos of 'rolled barbed wire awaiting transport', an 'automatic mixer and bagging of castable material', and 'a view of the water pumping station at Dutchman's Pool'. If that isn't enough, it goes on to boast that 'Kwe Kwe could fill 1500 swimming pools with water every day'. Perhaps the frogs would be happy to hear that, but one wonders why we're not all packing our bags and rushing off to Kwe Kwe.

If you're passing through, however, take time to look around the town centre, which is crowded with beautiful colonial buildings. Kwe Kwe also has one of Zimbabwe's finest museums.

ZIMBABWE

History

Despite its faded present, Kwe Kwe has enjoyed a rich past and has the tailings dumps to prove it. The region's gold-producing value has been known for at least a thousand years and there are signs of ancient workings throughout the district. When the English South African fortune-seekers arrived in the late 1800s, rumours of an African El Dorado had reached fever pitch. Although the pickings never reached the levels they did in the fabulously rich goldfields further south, Kwe Kwe has produced enough booty to justify its existence.

The first modern gold-mining operation, one of Zimbabwe's oldest, was the Globe & Phoenix on the edge of town. In later years, iron smelting and steel production arrived in Kwe Kwe and similar operations were set up by ZISCO (Zimbabwe Iron & Steel Company) at nearby Redcliff. The gold veins are almost exhausted but the area produces significant quantities of chromium, silica and copper, and mining remains the town's major source of income.

Mosque

Most visitors to Kwe Kwe are surprised to career through the roundabout in the centre and find a dominating and colourfully painted mosque. The town is the unlikely headquarters of Zimbabwe's Islamic Mission.

National Museum of Gold Mining

This friendly and worthwhile stop will provide a fascinating introduction to commercial gold mining in Zimbabwe, past and present. You're greeted by a working scale model of the Globe & Phoenix mine which bears a startling resemblance to the real thing which can be heard grinding away just off the museum grounds.

Another interesting feature is the Paper House, Zimbabwe's first prefabricated building. Imported in 1894, it is really made of paper. The outer walls are constructed of wire mesh-reinforced papier mache while the inner panels are of cardboard, all mounted on a wooden frame. It was brought from Great Britain in 1894 as the residence of the Globe & Phoenix mine's general manager but was later converted into the mine office.

Scattered around the lawns you'll see the mechanical detritus of 100 years of gold mining in southern Africa – pumps and crushers, graders and compressors – and the museum attendant will be happy to explain the function of every piece. There are tentative plans to construct an artificial mine shaft on the grounds, allowing visitors to go subterranean. It's open from 9 am to 5 pm daily; foreigners pay US$2 for admission and a guided tour.

Lower Zivagwe Dam (Dutchman's Pool)

Lower Zivagwe Dam, previously known as Dutchman's Pool, was constructed in 1954 to provide water for Kwe Kwe. It's a small but very pretty dam set in a peaceful wooded area about six km north of town. Birdlife includes ducks, herons, hornbills, African jacanas, cormorants, francolins and even fish eagles.

Use of the Angling Society picnic site and campground costs US$1 per person, and fishing is permitted. From town, travel two km north towards Harare to the signposted turning, then continue about four more km to the dam.

Sable Park Game Park & Snake Farm

Just 300 metres from Lower Zivagwe Dam is a small but scenic game park with sable, tsessebes, kudu, impalas, steenboks, elands, duikers, wildebeests, dassies, zebras and warthogs. It's open only on weekends and public holidays, and you must have a vehicle. Outside the game park gate is a snake enclosure with various serpentine specimens – pythons, gaboon vipers and so on – as well as a few crocodiles. Admission to both the game park and the snake enclosure is US$1.

Places to Stay

Kwe Kwe's caravan park is dirty, ill-kept and occupied by full-time tenants working in local industry. There's no guard so don't leave anything of value around. It's behind the cemetery on Ely Dr, just south of town.

CHRIS BARTON

TONY WHEELER

CHRIS BARTON

ZIMBABWE
A: View of the Great Enclosure, Great Zimbabwe
B: Central Parallel Passage, Great Enclosure, Great Zimbabwe
C: Mother & Baby Balancing Rocks, Matobo National Park

CHRIS BARTON

DEANNA SWANEY

DEANNA SWANEY

A	B
C	

ZIMBABWE
A: Aerial view of Victoria Falls in the dry season
B: Autumn colours, Chizarira National Park
C: Zambezi River from Deka Drum Resort

Among Kwe Kwe's several hotels, there aren't any of outstanding value but they'll do at a pinch. The friendly three-star *Golden Mile Motel* (☎ 3711; fax 3120) is the most popular one; singles/doubles cost US$30/49, and there's a nice pool-side bar.

Alternatively, the decent one-star *Shamwari Hotel* (☎ 2387), on the main road through town, costs US$25/40. Next down the scale is the no-star *Sebakwe Machipisa Hotel* (☎ 2981), a cheap but clean digs that functions mainly as a boozing joint. Rooms cost US$20 a double. The *Phoenix Hotel* (☎ 3748) on 2nd St is the local bottom end in just about every way. The dilapidated *Sumba Hotel* on Nelson Mandela Way near 2nd Ave is actually just a local bar.

Out of Town Kwe Kwe is now emerging as a travellers' destination thanks to several remote farms which have opened their doors to budget travellers.

Most people head for the popular *Mopani Park Farm* (☎ 247822), deep in the bush 49 km from Kwe Kwe. Owners Kathie and Rudy have combined their original property with seven other farms to create one large private nature reserve, where they've set up a mecca for riding enthusiasts. There are 55 horses in residence and both experienced riders and beginners are welcome.

Accommodation with dinner, bed and breakfast costs just US$10 and you can ride around the game reserve to your heart's content for US$2.50 per hour. For novices, riding lessons are provided for US$5 per hour. Advanced equestrians can even attempt polo, jumping and cross-country courses. Once you return from a long day on the trail, it's a great spot to sit around the bar chatting with fellow travellers. Three-day horseback trips to Sebakwe Dam cost US$33 per person per day, including three meals and accommodation in tented camps. Transfers from town cost US$3; if you arrive in Kwe Kwe during business hours, phone Arthur (☎ 2625), their in-town liaison.

Even more remote (60 km from Kwe Kwe) in the black rhino conservancy beside the Munyati River, is *Pitscottie Backpackers*

(☎ 2475; fax 4361). It's run by Roy Small, who offers wildlife viewing, fishing, canoeing and walking trails. He charges US$10 per day, with dinner, bed and breakfast. Phone from Kwe Kwe for information on transfers.

The more up-market 5600-hectare *Mazuri Farm* (☎ 247523 or 4039), run by Eleanor, Rob and Debbie Lowe, charges US$100 per person for lodges, but they also cater to backpackers with camping for US$5 and dormitories for US$10. All prices include meals and return transfers from Kwe Kwe. Horse-trekking is US$2.50 per hour, and two-hour game drives or guided game walks cost US$2 each. Backpackers may be picked up from the Odds & Ends shop on 3rd St in Kwe Kwe daily between 12.30 and 1.30 pm. It's wise to phone and confirm.

Places to Eat

For meals, the *Que Que Grill* at the Shamwari Hotel is Kwe Kwe's best eating spot. There's also a *Wimpy* just opposite the mosque. For inexpensive African fare, try either the *Africa Centre Restaurant* or the *Siyapambili Restaurant*.

Getting There & Away

The Ajay's and Express Motorways terminals are at the Golden Mile Motel, two km south of town on the Bulawayo road. Local bus services operate from the market. Trains between Harare and Bulawayo call in at Kwe Kwe in the small hours of the morning.

GWERU

Gweru, Zimbabwe's third-largest city with 105,000 residents, isn't a travellers' destination by any means, but most overland travellers pass through it at some stage and comment on its friendly small-town feel – a bit like 1950s Hill Valley in the film *Back to the Future*.

History

The city's backdrop, Senga Hill, has been worked by agriculturalists almost continuously since the stone age, but modern Gweru was founded quite recently (1894) by Leander Starr Jameson, who thought the site

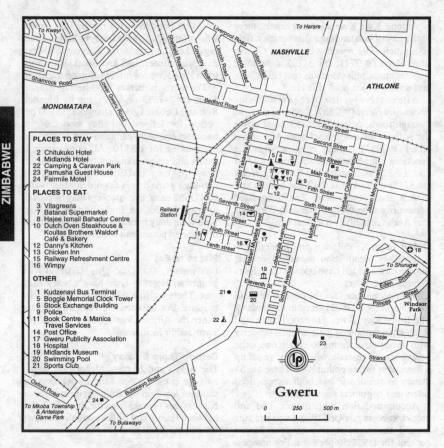

ZIMBABWE

PLACES TO STAY
2 Chitukuko Hotel
4 Midlands Hotel
22 Camping & Caravan Park
23 Pamusha Guest House
24 Fairmile Motel

PLACES TO EAT
3 Vitagreens
7 Batanai Supermarket
8 Hajee Ismail Bahadur Centre
10 Dutch Oven Steakhouse &
    Koullas Brothers Waldorf
    Café & Bakery
12 Danny's Kitchen
13 Chicken Inn
15 Railway Refreshment Centre
16 Wimpy

OTHER
1 Kudzenayi Bus Terminal
5 Boggie Memorial Clock Tower
6 Stock Exchange Building
9 Police
11 Book Centre & Manica
    Travel Services
14 Post Office
17 Gweru Publicity Association
18 Hospital
19 Midlands Museum
20 Swimming Pool
21 Sports Club

Gweru

would be ideal for a service centre for the Midlands goldfields. The original name, Gwelo, was believed to mean 'steep' in the local vernacular, possibly in reference to the sloping banks of the Gweru River. Growth began in earnest in 1902 with the arrival of the Harare-Bulawayo railway line. On 18 June 1914, the settlement gained municipal status but Gweru didn't become an official city until October 1971.

Information
The helpful Gweru Publicity Association (☎ 226) in the City Hall on the corner of 8th St and Robert Mugabe Way is open from 8 am to 4.30 pm Monday to Friday.

American Express' agent is Manica Travel Services (☎ 3316) at Meikles on the corner of Robert Mugabe Way and 5th St.

Midlands Museum
The Midlands Museum, near the corner of 11th St and Lobengula Ave, is devoted to the evolution of Zimbabwe's military and police history and technology, from the earliest tribal wars through the Rhodesian years to modern Zimbabwe. Given only that description, few travellers would be inclined to visit,

but as museums go, it's well done and quite informative. Of particular interest are the descriptions of pre-colonial weapons and warfare, and the military and police uniforms from way back. The aviation exhibits are being expanded into a national aviation museum.

It's open daily (except Christmas and Good Friday) from 9 am to 5 pm. Foreigners pay US$2 admission.

Interesting Buildings

In the municipal gardens near the City Hall, the 315-seat Gweru Theatre is a 'civic pride and joy'. Take a look at the lovely carved wooden mural entitled *Theatre Through the Ages*. On Main St between Robert Mugabe Way and Leopold Takawira Ave is the colonial-style Stock Exchange. Constructed in 1898, it is Gweru's oldest building.

Boggie Memorial Clock Tower

While you're in the neighbourhood, take a look at the Boggie Memorial Clock Tower, which can't be missed since it blocks Gweru's two main streets. This non-attraction was erected by Mrs Jeannie Boggie in 1937, as a memorial to her husband, Major W J Boggie (who had died nine years earlier), as well as to 'all colonial pioneers and their beasts of burden'. Mr Boggie's remains were interred in the tower, but one post-Independence morning in 1981, they were removed and the clock ceased functioning. Until they were repaired 10 years later, the hands on all four faces remained frozen at 10.50 am.

Antelope Game Park

The zoo-like antelope game park nine km from Gweru is a small enclave containing most of the antelope species present in Zimbabwe as well as giraffes, zebras and other wildlife. Large cats are kept in a separate enclosure.

To get there with a vehicle, head out on the Bulawayo road (Robert Mugabe Way) and turn right onto Tratford Rd at the Fairmile Motel, then left on Bristol Rd and follow it out of town through Mkoba township. The park is open from 10 am to 5 pm daily, with feeding at 3 pm. Admission costs US$1 per person.

Places to Stay

Gweru's green Caravan Park (☎ 2929) fronts up to the sports club about 500 metres from the centre on the Bulawayo road. You will pay US$1.30 for a car or caravan, US$4.50 for a large family tent and US$1 to camp in a small tent. Check in at the cocktail bar in the sports club.

The amorphous *Midlands Hotel* (☎ 2581) is mainly frequented by business travellers. It's one of the Sun Hotel chain, and the three-tier pricing system makes it especially poor value for foreigners, who pay US$82/120 a single/double. Zimbabweans pay just US$28/41.

Non-residents and other highway travellers caught by darkness may prefer the *Fairmile Motel* (☎ 4144) on the Bulawayo road. It enjoys the same three-star rating as the Midlands but manages to avoid the bland pretences to luxury. Standard single/double rooms cost US$31/45; rooms in the new wing are US$42/65. All prices include breakfast. Another good choice is the *Pamusha Guest House* (☎ 3535), at 75 Kopje Rd, one km from the caravan park.

The local arm-benders' venue – with two lively bars – is the *Chitukuko Hotel* (☎ 2862; fax 4212) on the corner of 3rd and Moffat Sts. It more closely resembles a hospital clinic than a hotel (and there's no sign out the front), but the resident band does provide decent African-style entertainment nightly. Single/double rooms cost US$22/30. A reader has this to say:

We recommend the Chitukuko Hotel – just ask the locals for 'Gunsmoke'. The receptionist was at first fazed by our request for a room for the entire evening, but eventually worked out a reasonable price. The room was covered in cheap scarlet velvet and lacked only a mirrored ceiling to complete the country bordello effect. Out the back in the beer hall, Africans were drinking Chibuku from white plastic buckets and listening to very bad reggae music.

Andy Bollen, Australia

ZIMBABWE

Places to Eat

A diner catering to passing travellers is the *The Dutch Oven Steakhouse* on 5th St, which proudly announces 'Food American Style'. As the name would imply, their speciality is steak, which isn't surprising here in cattle country. You can neutralise the saturated fats on the next block at *Vitagreens*, which sells fresh produce.

In the Hajee Ismail Bahadur Centre, off 5th St, you'll find *Nommy's Chinese Kitchen*, the *Sno-Flake Ice Cream Parlour* and the *Quick-Bake Bakery*. *Danny's Kitchen*, a Muslim-run takeaway on 5th St is great for quick snacks, but don't look for pork sausage rolls. *Koullas Brothers Waldorf Café* serves below average African and greasy fare, but their attached bakery is OK.

The *Chicken Inn*, on the corner of 6th St and Robert Mugabe Way, is like all Chicken Inns with billiards, deep-fried chicken and chips. For Chinese takeaway, go to the *Railway Refreshment Centre* which, not surprisingly, is opposite the railway station. It's open late.

Entertainment

Apart from the cinema and Gweru's flashy theatre, which infrequently stages visiting performances, the Midlands Hotel's Dandaro Bar and disco, with occasional live bands at weekends, provides the only up-market entertainment.

The Chitukuko Hotel offers live African music and boozing and the Msopero Midnight Club at 62 7th St serves meals by day and cranks up their 'Jungle Mix Disco' from 9 pm to 5 am.

If none of that excites you, head for the swimming pool near the Midlands Museum. It's open (summer only) Tuesday to Friday from 10 am to 2 pm and 3 to 6 pm, and on weekends from 10 am to 12.30 pm and 2.30 to 6 pm.

Getting There & Away

All buses between Harare and Bulawayo stop in Gweru. African buses use the Kudzenayi terminal near the market on Robert Mugabe Way between 2nd and 3rd Sts.

Express Motorways and Ajay's buses stop at the Fairmile Motel on the Bulawayo road. Book express services through Manica Travel Services (☎ 3316) at Electricity House on 6th St. Rail services between Bulawayo and Harare stop at Gweru in the early morning hours.

AROUND GWERU

Lost in the back roads between Shangani and Nsiza, south-west of Gweru, are some little-visited but nevertheless fascinating ancient ruins. They're attributed to the Torwa state prior to its conquest by the Rozwi.

The Torwa state is thought to have risen from the declining Great Zimbabwe culture further east, improving upon its architecture and material culture. Nalatale, Danangombe, Bila and Zinjanja are all grouped within a 40-km radius. The other Torwa centre, Khami, lies near Bulawayo and is discussed in that chapter.

Villages are sparse in this region, so access is limited to private vehicles; hitching will almost certainly require long waits. During busy periods, such as August and September, three or four vehicles may visit the sites in a day. In June, a week may pass with no activity at all. If you're coming from Bulawayo, speak with the inspector of monuments (at the museum). He or his crew inspect the sites periodically and may know about lifts.

Nalatale Ruins

Although it's small and less elaborate than Great Zimbabwe, Nalatale rates among the nicest of Zimbabwe's 150 walled ruins. A simple structure on a remote granite hilltop, it enjoys a commanding view across the hills, plains and kopjes of Somabhula Flats. (On one hill, Wadai, which is visible across the Flats, is a large colony of nesting Cape vultures. It's the most northerly colony of this protected species.)

The main feature, a decorated wall, exhibits in one go all the primary decorative wall patterns found in Zimbabwe: chevron, chequer, cord, herringbone and ironstone. The original wall was topped by nine plinths, but only seven haphazardly reconstructed

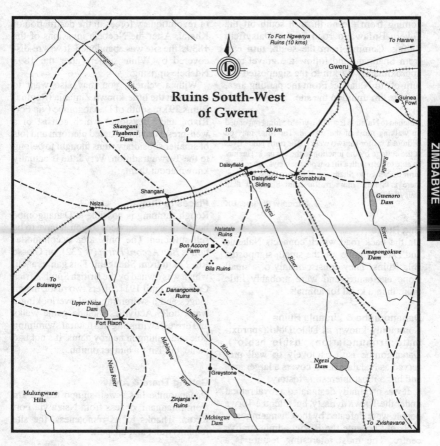

Ruins South-West of Gweru

ones remain. The plaster along the top of the wall was added in 1937 to prevent deterioration of the best preserved section.

Archaeologist Donald Randall McIver dug into the site in 1905-06, but found little – just two iron spearheads, a pair of elephant tusks, copper tools and a couple of soapstone pipes. From the scant evidence that has been unearthed, credit for building Nalatale has gone to the Torwa dynasty and it probably served as the Torwa capital during the early 17th century. It's thought to have fallen to the Rozwi state sometime in the 1680s.

In the centre of the roughly elliptical complex are the remains of the principal hut, presumed to have belonged to the Torwa king. Its walls radiate from the main complex like spokes of a wheel. All other huts are at least two metres lower.

Places to Stay There are no facilities or services at Nalatale. Visitors can rough camp outside the enclosure, but must carry all their own food and water.

Getting There & Away Fortunately, Nalatale ruins (alternatively spelt Nalatela or Nalatele) are well signposted. If you're coming from the north, turn south off the Gweru-Bulawayo road at the Daisyfield Siding. Coming from the south, turn east from Shangani and follow the gravel road approximately 27 km to the signposted left turn-off to Nalatale. From the parking area, it's one km uphill to the site.

I hitched to Nalatale from Daisyfield Siding but ended up walking most of the way in. The ruins may go without a visitor for two weeks. The ruins guide lives at the cottage by the junction to the car park. He may be able to help with a lift out on weekdays, when local farm trucks go to Shangani. If anyone must hitch in, there is a little more traffic from Shangani than Daisyfield.

Andrew Phillips, UK

Bila Ruins

On the back road which connects Nalatale and Danangombe are the small, signposted Bila Ruins. They consist mainly of a small stone enclosure, and were probably little more than a kraal for animals.

Danangombe & Zinjanja Ruins

Commonly known as Dhlo Dhlo (approximate pronunciation: 'hshlo hshlo'), Danangombe isn't as lovely or well-preserved as Nalatale but it covers a larger area and has a most interesting history.

It was originally designated a royal retreat under the Torwa dynasty, but after the Torwa people were defeated by the Changamires, it probably became the Rozwi administrative centre. The most interesting feature is a crumbling enclosure formed partially by natural boulders. The whole thing is overgrown by wandering tree roots and sheltered by large trees. Some amazing cactus-like euphorbias (*Euphorbia ingens*) have also pushed their way up through the ruins.

Relics of Portuguese origin have been uncovered at Danangombe by ruthless amateur treasure hunters – a priest's ring, a silver chalice, a slave's leg-iron, a bell, a cannon, gold jewellery and part of a candlestick – but Danangombe's past remains a mystery. It has been postulated that Portuguese traders were held captive there by the ruling mambo, possibly for their assistance

of revolutionary forces in the destruction of Khami. After the Ndebele invasions of the 1830s, the site was abandoned. It was re-discovered by White settlers after the 1893 Ndebele uprising.

With a vehicle, you may also want to check out the little-known Zinjanja (Regina) Ruins 29 km south of Danangombe (via Fort Rixon and Greystone) which consist of a well-preserved three-tiered platform and lots of smaller subsidiary ruins thought to belong to the Torwa tradition. Very little is actually known about them.

Places to Stay

Rough camping is possible at Danangombe but there are no services so you'll have to be self-sufficient. The only area accommodation is *Bon Accord Farm* (☎ 232), on Glasse Rd, 27 km from Shangani. This game ranch, which was owned by the British South Africa Company until 1911, offers two rustic thatch lodges and a swimming pool overlooking a water hole. Activities include game walks and drives, swimming in a natural swimming hole and fishing in nearby dams. It's not bad value, but isn't a budget option.

Getting There & Away

Danangombe lies a well-signposted 22 km from Shangani, or less from Nsiza via Fort Rixon. Thanks to its remoteness, the site remains quiet and unspoilt.

SHURUGWI

It's nice to think that not all Midlands towns are cast in the mould of Gweru and Chegutu. Shurugwi, the 'highlands of the Midlands', is actually a wonderful place. Now dependent upon chromium mining, this country town is lodged in a time-warped bowl created by a steep escarpment in the Sebakwe Hills. Were it in North America, Shurugwi would be either a bohemian art colony or a retreat for the rich and famous; in Europe, it would be a favoured holiday destination. In Zimbabwe, however, it sits lonely and forgotten.

ZIMBABWE

On the loose

The truck was driven by an old drunk called Dr Love and his side-kick, Thank-on Turnover (I swear it) from Zambia. This was great fun. Dr Love sang us Shona freedom songs and told dirty jokes in broken English, played Dolly Parton on the tape Machine (I worked out why Dolly is so popular with truckies – her voice has a built-in tape wobble). We stopped at the Chinhoyi Hotel for more beers – this is where it all happens in Chinhoyi on a Friday Night. We met the local intelligence who kept asking guarded questions and staring quizzically at my 'Worker's of the world, unite. Mayday is ours!' T-shirt. They were friends with Dr Love (this is something I like about Zimbabwe – there seemed to be no real class barriers, socially, anyway). We also met a friendly young prostitute who kept asking my companion if she could have a few minutes alone with me, or alternatively, whether she had a spare condom for a commercial transaction with Thank-on.

We spent a day or two in Harare recovering from tummy bugs. The last stage of our trip was to the ruins at Great Zimbabwe. This started off well enough with a lift with a rich Indian couple, but they put us on the road to Gweru rather than Masvingo and we didn't immediately realise the mistake. By the time we did, it was too late, and it wound up taking us two days to get there. A Chinese couple picked us up; they were charming, polite and friendly, but they insisted that we be dropped off at Lake Chivero to have lunch. Not that they wanted to have lunch with us; they just thought it would be a good idea. 'Just drop us at the service station...' we said. 'Yes, lunch at Lake Chivero' they replied, and we wound up a further 20 km out of our way. Lunch at Lake Chivero was foul.

Eventually, we got a lift with a crazed young South African special-effects guy, his wife and their new baby. His speciality was blowing things up for movies, and we rode in the back of his Hino with a load of explosives and fuses. He was drunk and stoned and became more so as the trip progressed. So did we.

He was very good value, talking nonstop about absolutely everything, but was probably the most dangerous driver I've ever travelled with. We passed three major accidents on the way to Gweru – cars overturned and people staggering and bleeding. This only seemed to fuel his death wish. His wife, by contrast, was totally silent, except to shout obscenities at people jumping out of our way as we swerved over the median strip and the verges. Getting to Gweru alive was a relief.

Andy Bollen, Australia

Things to See

The entire central area of Shurugwi is effectively a tumble-down historical district, specked with remnants of bygone days. The town is also renowned for its flowering trees and msasa, both of which are at their most colourful in the late winter and spring.

In days past, a Disneyland-like narrow gauge railway carried tourists on a scenic circuit though the hills. The tracks remain and perhaps the operation will one day be resurrected. The Shurugwi Peak Scenic Drive crosses the narrow-gauge railway and climbs for eight km to the town's eponymous peak for a great view. If you prefer your own steam, follow the Hospital Hill Scenic Walk just east of town, which also renders a view.

Historically, the fabulously scenic Wolfshall Pass approach was used by teams of oxen pulling heavy wagon-loads of asbestos up to the plateau from the mines in Zvishavane. From a lay-by on the pass, three km outside Shurugwi, a toilet-paper lined walking track leads down to perennial Dunraven's Falls, deep in a forested valley.

Places to Stay & Eat

The *Ferny Creek Caravan Park* (☎ 220) lies 2.5 km from town, past the sun-baked golf course and down a red dirt road into a wooded valley. It has apparently seen better days, evidenced by descriptions of it in long outdated tourist literature. You can choose between camping or staying in extremely basic chalets.

The pleasant *Garden Motel* (☎ 6548), which actually does occupy a garden, lies 1.5 km off the main road near the western entrance to town. It's quite good value at US$15/24 for singles/doubles; or US$2 extra if you want TV. Unfortunately, the swimming pool has a few problems. On

Friday and Saturday nights, the place rocks to Shurugwi's only disco.

For meals, Shurugwi's best nosh is served at the friendly hotel dining room. For something more informal, there's a fish & chips takeaway place in the centre. You will also find basic meals at the pathetically faded local booze hall, the *Grand Hotel*, just a block away.

CHIVHU

Chivhu, originally called Enkeldoorn or 'lone thorn' (the Dutch would maintain it's 'ankle thorn'), was first established in the late 1890s by Afrikaners from the Orange Free State. Today, it's mainly a cattle ranching area and there's little else to say about this rather unmemorable town.

The item of most tourist interest around Chivhu is probably *Tangenhamo Lodge* (☎ 796821; fax 796822, both in Harare), on Tangenhamo Game Ranch, south of town on the road towards Masvingo. This secluded stone and thatch safari lodge is integrated into a lovely landscape of trees and boulders. It's not cheap, but it caters for only eight guests at a time. Activities include game walks and drives, fishing and horse-riding.

MVUMA

The name of Mvuma, a gold-mining and railway community, was taken from the Mvuma River which means 'place of magic singing' after a river pool where mysterious singing, drumming and lowing of cattle were once heard. This small community is the site of the historic Falcon Mine, abandoned in 1925, which pioneered Zimbabwe's oil flotation smelting process. Today, only the Athens Mine is still worked.

The town's landmark is the crumbling Falcon Mine Stack, a 40-metre-high remnant dating from 1913. Town residents are waiting for the thing's collapse which, given its current condition, appears imminent.

SERIMA MISSION

Serima Mission is a treasure house of African art based on the traditions of West and Central Africa where the genre reached its peak. Although the church exterior is now a bit worn, the spacious interior and all its artistic enhancements remain intact and are certainly worth the effort of visiting. For further information, look for *Serima* by Albert Plangger, Mambo Press, Gweru, 1974, which details its history, art and architecture in words and photos. It's sold at the National Gallery in Harare.

History

Serima was founded in 1948 by Swiss Catholic priest and art instructor Father John Gröber who had earned a degree in architecture before coming to teach on rural missions in southern Africa in 1939. At Serima, he was impressed by the level of artistic talent in young Shona people. Beginning with sketch drawings of masks, he helped students progress to clay models and finally to carvings and sculpture, encouraging them to express themselves without pandering to European sensitivities.

The students' first projects were to decorate the school building with carved pillars and patterns. The priest then invoked his ultimate purpose, the promotion of Christian belief, and familiarised the students with the spiritual rather than dogmatic elements of Christian tradition. He then admonished them to infuse those scenes and the feelings they inspired into their work. The resulting potpourri of carvings, shot through with African expression, grace the church today.

Church

The Serima Mission church, which was designed by Father Gröber, encloses an open, airy and magically lighted space. Like a museum, the room and its simple furnishings emphasise the dense and diverse frescoes, sculptures and carved pillars and reliefs, yet seem to relate well to the altar, which is the focus of the room. In his book *A Tourist in Africa*, Evelyn Waugh predicted that Africans would one day see it with the same reverence as Europeans behold the medieval cathedrals of Europe.

On shelves above the church entrance, shepherds and wise men make their way laboriously towards a nativity scene in the centre. The bell tower is a circle of African angels gripping musical instruments. Events from the Bible are depicted in a series of frescoes above the arcaded interior walls, and the Last Supper scene above the main altar is masterful. Except for the reed-matted ceiling beams, not a single piece of wood in the building remains uncarved.

Places to Stay
Serima lacks formal accommodation, but the Catholic sisters will normally allow travellers to camp on the grounds.

Getting There & Away
From Mucheke musika in Masvingo, there's a Bream Express bus which runs to Serima several times weekly in the early morning. It first passes Great Zimbabwe, then continues to Serima, where it stays overnight before returning to Masvingo early the next morning. The Felixburg bus from Masvingo will drop you at the turn-off 10 km from Serima. Alternatively, take a bus from Masvingo towards Harare, and get off at Fairfield Siding, where the railway crosses the road south of Mvuma. From there, three buses run to Serima daily.

If you're driving, from the Harare-Masvingo road, turn east onto the Felixburg road 60 km north of Masvingo. After six km, you'll cross the railway; continue four more km and turn right again. From there, it's about 10 km to the mission, which is on the right side of the road past a small dam.

MASVINGO
Masvingo, with a population of 40,000, is characterised by the schizophrenic tendencies that afflict most Zimbabwean towns. In this case, the personalities are neatly demarcated by the Mucheke River. While the centre emits a clean and routine small-town laziness, Mucheke township, two km away, is vibrant Africa, with as lively a market as you can imagine.

The name Masvingo, which was adopted after Zimbabwean independence, is derived from *rusvingo*, the Shona word for walled-in

enclosures, in reference to the nearby Great Zimbabwe ruins.

History
Historically, Masvingo prided itself on being the first White settlement in Zimbabwe (a fact which few people cared about one way or another). The pioneer column of the British South Africa Company, under Frederick Courteney Selous, moved through Lobengula's stronghold in Matabeleland and across the dry lowveld to the cooler plateaux. In August 1890, they paused at a spot now known as Clipsham Farm a few km south of present-day Masvingo to establish Fort Victoria and construct a rude mud fortification.

After just a few days, the main contingency moved northward to found Fort Salisbury, the next in their line of defence installations. A drought two years later forced the removal of the settlement to a more amenable location between the Shagashe and Mucheke Rivers, where a new, more permanent fort was built.

During its early years, Masvingo served as a jumping-off point to the mines of central Mashonaland and at one stage was Rhodesia's largest town. However, the Ndebele uprisings of the First Chimurenga and the subsequent defeat of Lobengula in Matabeleland opened up the Bulawayo area for White settlement and lured many Fort Victoria settlers towards the scent of more promising pickings. Bulawayo grew to be

Street Name Changes

Recent street name changes in Masvingo include:

Old Name	New Name
Allan Wilson	Robert Mugabe
Brown	Rekayi Tangwena
Colquhoun	Herbert Chitepo
Dillon	Leopold Takawira
Fitzgerald	Josiah Tongogara
McLeod	George Silundika
Thompson	Simon Mazorodze
Unnamed road to Bus Terminus	Jairos Jiri Rd
Welby Ave	Jason Moyo Ave

the country's second largest city while Masvingo has now dropped to eighth place.

Orientation & Information

The Masvingo Publicity Association (☎ 62643), with a prominent miniature replica of the Great Zimbabwe conical tower out the front, is helpful with specific questions and distributes maps, hand-outs and local advertising. Their monthly *Masvingo Diary*, which outlines upcoming happenings, is marginally useful but the map omits Mucheke township. It's open from 8 am to 1 pm and 2 to 4.30 pm Monday to Friday.

The public fax number in Masvingo is 64238.

Interesting Buildings

Masvingo isn't bad for an hour or so strolling around the centre. Have a look at the old steam engine languishing in the railway station and the nearby modern civic centre, which beckons to conventioneers. Next door are the green Queen Elizabeth Gardens, which have seen better days. The tower near the post office was one of the look-out turrets from the second Fort Victoria.

As a matter of interest, don't miss the toilets at Riley's Shell Station, which are accurately self-described as the cleanest in Zimbabwe. They even have a guest book beside the sink for users to sign in and register their comments.

Church of St Francis of Assisi

The Italian-style Church of St Francis of Assisi was constructed between 1942 and 1946 by Italian POWs; the interior holds the remains of 71 of their compatriots who died in Zimbabwe between 1942 and 1947. The simulated mosaics in the apse were the work of an Italian engineer while the wall murals were completed 10 years later by Masvingo artists.

To get there, go three km east towards Mutare, take the left turn and then turn immediately left again. Just in front of the military barracks, turn left yet again; you'll see the church 100 metres away.

Ecological Designs

If you're interested in Zimbabwe's contribution to global energy-saving efforts, visit Ecological Designs (☎ 63503), 'Your Appropriate Technology Workshop' at 697 Industria Rd, just north of town. They'll show you around and explain environmental problems and solutions pertinent in this part of the world. Notice the odd collection of machinery in the permanent display.

Shagashe Game Park

The Shagashe Game Park has been in the development stages for some time now, but it still isn't open. It lies 10 km from Masvingo, out along the Harare road, and may open soon. The Masvingo Publicity Association should have details.

Organised Tours

Sunbird Safaris (☎ 62718) operates tours of Masvingo and its environs. Since Sunbird is based in Masvingo, it's probably the best option for impromptu bookings. Day tours to the Great Zimbabwe ruins or the Mutirikwe Game Park cost US$12 per person. They can also organise horse rides, birdwatching trips, cruises on Mutirikwe Dam and trips to Shona villages.

Zimtours (☎ 793666 Harare) offers daily tours of Great Zimbabwe commencing at 9.30 am from the Chevron and Flamboyant hotels. After a couple of hours at Great Zimbabwe, you get lunch and watch traditional dancing at Mutirikwe Lakeshore Lodges before visiting the Mutirikwe Dam wall and the Mutirikwe Game Park.

Places to Stay – bottom end

Masvingo's *Caravan Park* (☎ 62431), with great lawns and a riverside setting, is just a short walk from the centre. Tent sites cost US$2 per person and it's open to 'bona fide tourists only', whatever they are. Day use of the park-like grounds costs US$0.15 per person, and showers are US$0.25 for non-guests.

The favourite travellers' spot is the friendly and homely *Clovelly Lodge* (☎ 64751), run by Bruce and Iris Brinson. It

ZIMBABWE

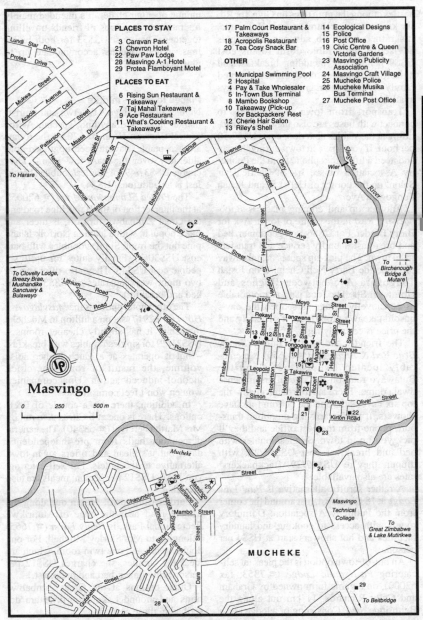

PLACES TO STAY

3 Caravan Park
21 Chevron Hotel
22 Paw Paw Lodge
28 Masvingo A-1 Hotel
29 Protea Flamboyant Motel

PLACES TO EAT

6 Rising Sun Restaurant &
   Takeaway
7 Taj Mahal Takeaways
9 Ace Restaurant
11 What's Cooking Restaurant &
   Takeaways

17 Palm Court Restaurant &
   Takeaways
18 Acropolis Restaurant
20 Tea Cosy Snack Bar

OTHER

1 Municipal Swimming Pool
2 Hospital
4 Pay & Take Wholesaler
5 In-Town Bus Terminal
8 Mambo Bookshop
10 Takeaway (Pick-up
   for Backpackers' Rest
12 Cherie Hair Salon
13 Riley's Shell

14 Ecological Designs
15 Police
16 Post Office
19 Civic Centre & Queen
   Victoria Gardens
23 Masvingo Publicity
   Association
24 Masvingo Craft Village
25 Mucheke Police
26 Mucheke Musika
   Bus Terminal
27 Mucheke Post Office

Masvingo

0   250   500 m

MUCHEKE

nestles among the gum trees on Glyn Tor Rd, six km from the centre towards Bulawayo. It's rather small, so advance booking is advised. Comfortable dorm rooms cost US$9 per person, including breakfast and delicious home-cooked dinners served family-style (vegetarian choices are always available).

Transport from town and transfers to connect with buses are also included. Horse-riding at the stables next door costs US$3.50 per hour. If you arrive in town during the day and need a lift, either phone from the Publicity Association or see Iris at Cherie Hair Salon, on the corner of Hellet St and Josiah Tongogara Ave.

Another up and coming place is *Backpackers' Rest* in the centre of town. Ask for Barry Binder. For US$6, you get dinner, bed and breakfast, laundry service and transfers from town. The pick-up spot is the takeaway place beside Barry Nell Chemist, on Josiah Tongogara Ave between Hughes and Hofmeyer Sts. The food isn't as memorable as at Clovelly Lodge (it's often the day's unsold takeaway food), but it's friendly and the price is certainly right.

The friendly and slightly quirky *Breezy Brae Bed & Breakfast* (☎ 64650) is memorably located five km out along the Bulawayo road on the side of an immense dwala dome. There are 10 rooms in all – the top six have baths and the bottom four have showers. If you're arriving on public transport, phone from the post office and they'll pick you up in town. Singles/doubles with bed and breakfast cost US$13/22; with dinner, they're US$17/29. Backpackers' rates are also available.

A rather scruffy alternative is *Paw Paw Lodge* at 18 Kirton Rd, just around the corner from the Publicity Association. Dormitory rooms with access to cooking and laundry facilities and hot showers start at US$4 per person.

An out-of-town option is the pleasant self-catering *Pa-Nyanda Lodge* (☎ 7353; fax 62000), on a game farm owned by Graham and Cally Richards, 11 km out along the Beitbridge road. Consisting of a lodge and a unique open-air chalet, it's intended mainly for families or groups of friends travelling together. They cost US$33 for both buildings, which together accommodate up to nine people.

Places to Stay – middle

Neither of Masvingo's two two-star tourist-market hotels are anything special. At the central *Chevron Hotel* (☎ 62054) the rooms are acceptable, having been upgraded considerably over the past few years. They charge US$37/49 for singles/doubles; breakfast is an additional US$4.

The *Protea Flamboyant Motel* (☎ 62005), at the intersection of the Beitbridge road and the Great Zimbabwe turn-off, is nicer and more popular, with a leaning Norfolk Island pine out the front. Singles/doubles with bath cost US$30/36. Family suites for up to six people cost US$43. They also offer special two-night weekend rates of US$39/52 for bed and breakfast.

The other hotel option is the *Masvingo A-1 Hotel* (☎ 62917) set on a hilltop in Mucheke township. It has slightly cheaper rooms – US$21/29 for singles/doubles with breakfast – but it operates at a much higher noise volume, the result of round-the-clock alcohol-induced action. Unaccompanied women won't feel comfortable.

In addition, there are a couple of B&B options. There is one at 6 Citrus Ave run by Mrs Martha Percival (☎ 63340). The general demeanour hails from pre-independence days, but it's clean and offers an in-town alternative to the hotels. For self-catering, you'll pay US$12 per person; meals are also available.

Further from town, 16 km out along the Mutare road near the edge of Mutirikwe Recreational Park, is *Beuly Farm* (☎ 7665) belonging to Mrs Shirley Mitchell. For one double room and one twin room, which are ideal for families, she charges US$12 per person with dinner, bed and breakfast.

Other options at the Great Zimbabwe ruins and around Lake Mutirikwe are described in those sections.

Places to Eat

Petrol stations in Masvingo cater to hungry travellers in a rush to eat and depart quickly for somewhere else. *Riley's Shell* (famous for its toilets) and the *Ace Restaurant* at the BP station are best for snacks. At the Caltex station, half a block from the BP, is the *Breadbasket Bakery*. A snack bar at the *Meikles* store serves tea, cakes and pastries. Lots of produce, junk food and snacks are available in and around the Mucheke musika bus station. Ever had the urge to try deep-fried stink bugs? Here's your chance.

Although you won't have a memorable meal at the *Acropolis Restaurant* on Herbert Chitepo St, it's still the best choice in the town centre. The town centre also has several other combined restaurants and takeaway places, a couple of which are ethnically named, but don't expect any of them to stray far from the usual chicken, burgers, chips and deep-fried snacks themes. They include *Taj Mahal*, *Rising Sun*, *Palm Court* and *What's Cooking*. For lights snacks and teas, there's the *Tea Cosy Snack Bar* on Robert Mugabe St.

The terrace in front of the *Chevron Hotel* is great for a snack and drink on a sunny day, and their dining room has been vastly improved in recent years. The *Protea Flamboyant Motel* is even better. They do breakfast buffets, à la carte lunches and snacks, and on weekend evenings, they lay on a buffet braai.

The big wholesaler *Pay & Take*, on the Mutare side of town, offers excellent deals on groceries, but you must buy in bulk.

Things to Buy

The Masvingo Craft Village lies just uphill from the Publicity Association, near the Mucheke turn-off. They have a good range of carvings, baskets, sculpture and other items, some of them pleasantly original.

Strung out along the Beitbridge road south of Masvingo is at least a score of impromptu craft markets, some of which display good work. The fierce competition also means competitive prices.

Getting There & Away

Buses between Harare and Masvingo depart frequently from both Mbare and the Mucheke terminal, and there are several daily services to both Bulawayo and Mutare. The recommended long-haul company is Masara Transport Ltd.

At least one early bus leaves daily for Beitbridge, although it may be delayed until 11 am. The surrounding communal lands are well served and the high population density of Masvingo province makes it relatively easy to reach smaller destinations.

Long-distance buses use the Mucheke musika terminal, less than two km from the town centre. Although emergency taxis are available and there are hourly buses between the town centre and Mucheke, it's not a difficult walk unless you're carrying lots of luggage. All Mucheke-bound long-distance buses stop in the centre, so get off at the first Masvingo stop unless you're specifically going to Mucheke.

For information on getting to Great Zimbabwe, refer to the discussion of Great Zimbabwe below.

GREAT ZIMBABWE NATIONAL MONUMENT

Great Zimbabwe, the greatest medieval city in sub-Saharan Africa, provides evidence that ancient Africa reached a level of civilisation not suspected by earlier scholars. As a religious and temporal capital, this city of 10,000 to 20,000 people dominated a realm which stretched across eastern Zimbabwe and into Botswana, Mozambique and South Africa. Archaeologists have attributed over 150 tributary zimbabwes to the Great Zimbabwe society, which was actually an amalgamation of smaller groups gathered under a central political system.

The name *Zimbabwe* is believed to be derived from one of two possible Shona origins; either *dzimba dza mabwe* (great stone houses) or *dzimba woye* (esteemed houses). The grand setting and history-filled walls certainly qualify as highlights of southern Africa. The site is open from 6 am to 6 pm daily; foreigners pay US$5 admission,

ZIMBABWE

Great Zimbabwe
National Monument

0   150   300 m

including a visit to the attached reconstructed Karanga village, which is open 8 am to 5 pm. Three-hour guided tours are available six times daily for US$1.50 per person.

History
Several volumes have been written about Great Zimbabwe and speculations over its purposes and origins have been hashed over for centuries now. If you're keen to learn more, the most comprehensive and scholarly work on the subject is *Great Zimbabwe Described and Explained* by Peter Garlake, Zimbabwe Publishing House, Harare, 1982.

It's available at Kingston's bookshops. Failing that, contact the publisher: Zimbabwe Publishing House (☎ 790416), 144 Union Ave, PO Box 350, Harare.

Despite nearly 100 years of effort by colonial governments to ascribe the origins of Great Zimbabwe to someone else – anyone else – conclusive proof of its Bantu origins was already in place in 1932, after British archaeologist Gertrude Caton-Thompson spent three years examining the ruins and their artefacts.

One can almost forgive the scepticism of early colonists – the African peoples they

ZIMBABWE

Visiting Great Zimbabwe

Great Zimbabwe merits at least a full day of exploration. If you're staying overnight at the ruins, either at the hotel or camping, try at least once to witness morning light on the ruined walls. The gates open at 8 am and the effects of a low sun and its long red rays add a beguiling dimension.

The following is just a suggested itinerary which moves chronologically through the site. Other possible routes are outlined in the pamphlet *A Trail Guide to the Great Zimbabwe National Monument*, available from the museum for US$1, and in *Trails of Discovery*, a photocopied brochure which may be purchased at the hotel for the same price.

To see the site in the order it was constructed, begin with the Hill Complex, which probably first served as the earliest royal enclave and later became a religious centre. From the curio shop, climb the Ancient Ascent, the oldest of the four summit routes. The rambling walls and intermittent boulders covering the hilltop are good for a couple of hours exploring. West of the Hill Complex, three other routes (the Modern, Terrace and Watergate Routes) connect the level ground with the summit and also merit exploration.

Next, continue along to the remains of the inner perimeter wall and return to the curio shop, where you'll connect with a track leading to the easternmost ruins and the reconstructed Karanga Village. This slightly tacky compound (note the plaster of paris inhabitants) will provide some idea of how common folk lived at Great Zimbabwe. While nobility occupied the stone buildings, more than 10,000 other people occupied huts scattered around the city perimeter.

From the village, continue to the Valley Enclosures, perhaps the most intriguing structures on the site, where heaps of overgrown rubble and crumbling walls suggest that wealthier commoners made their homes. One can almost imagine an inhabited version of the reconstructed Karanga village spread over the raised platforms. For the tour de force, climb the aloe-decked Sunken Passageway to the crowning achievement of the Rozwi Culture, the fabulous Great Enclosure and its instantly recognisable conical tower.

En route to the museum, notice the Ridge Enclosures, which were rough additions to the original structure by post-Great Zimbabwe occupants, possibly Karanga. In the museum, you can peruse some of the material residue discovered around the site. The highlight is the lineup of the world-famous Zimbabwe birds, probably totems of the ruling dynasty, which now serve as the national emblem. Once armed with the new perspective offered by the museum, it may be tempting to repeat the entire circuit and have a look at each site from a new angle. ■

---

encountered seemed to have no tradition of building in stone and none of the stone cities were inhabited at the time of colonisation. However, even up to the time of Zimbabwe's independence, the Rhodesian government ignored the evidence and supported far-fetched fantasies of foreign influence and habitation. Despite results based on radiocarbon dating of materials found at the site, many Rhodesian officials perpetuated the nonsense that Great Zimbabwe dated from the pre-Christian era. Not a scrap of proof for Phoenician, Jewish, Greek, Egyptian, Arabic or any other origins has surfaced.

Other outside influences did, however, play a role in the *development* of Great Zimbabwe. Swahili traders were present along the Mozambique coast from the 10th century through the height of Rozwi influence in the 14th and 15th centuries. Trade goods – porcelain from China, crockery

from Persia and beads and other trinkets from India – have been unearthed on the site and the Africans undoubtedly adopted and adapted some of the outsiders' ways.

In the 11th century came the first society to occupy the Great Zimbabwe site. It was probably comprised of several scattered groups which recognised the safety of numbers. Construction of their first project, the royal enclosures on the Hill Complex, commenced sometime during the 13th century, while the remainder of the city was completed over the next 100 or so years.

Apparently, Great Zimbabwe was primarily a blue-collar project. Despite the beauty of the ruins, the remains do not provide evidence of superior architectural skills and it seems that only a sketchy overall plan was devised before work began. Construction was a labour-intensive venture requiring thousands of hands to hew out millions of granite blocks for the extensive walls. Since the main walls and platforms weren't intended to support roofs, precise measurements and straight lines were unnecessary. The structure's wonderfully haphazard curving and twisting lines either circumvented or incorporated natural features into the buildings, resulting in an impressive harmony with the landscape.

Fuelled by Swahili gold trade, the city grew into a powerful and prestigious religious and political capital; in every way it was the heart of the Rozwi culture whose influence extended through eastern Zimbabwe, much of Mozambique and Botswana and even bits of South Africa. Royal herds increased and coffers overflowed with gold and precious trade goods. At its height, Great Zimbabwe was a thriving city of at least 10,000 inhabitants.

In the end, however, Great Zimbabwe probably became a victim its own success. By the 15th century, the growing human and bovine populations and their environmental pressures had depleted local resources, necessitating emigration to more productive lands. One contingency under the Mwene Mutapa relocated its capital to Fura Moun-

tain in northern Zimbabwe. Another group migrated westwards to Khami, the new capital, and later to Danangombe and Nalatale. Great Zimbabwe declined rapidly and when the Portuguese arrived in the 1500s, the city was nearly deserted.

At this point, the site was taken over by a dynasty called Nemanwa, which endured until the late 1700s, when it was overthrown by the Mugabe dynasty. The Mugabe were in turn toppled by a contingent of Nguni under Zwangendaba in 1834, throwing the conquered leaders from the cliffs and ruthlessly seizing power. By the time German-US hunter, Adam Renders, stumbled upon Great Zimbabwe in 1868, only ruins remained.

Hill Complex

Once known as the Acropolis, the Hill Structure was probably the first of the Great Zimbabwe complexes to be constructed. This clearly wasn't a fortress, but rather a series of royal and ritual enclosures. Instead of ripping out the boulders to install the chambers, builders followed the path of least resistance, integrating them into the structures as best they could. Evidence indicates

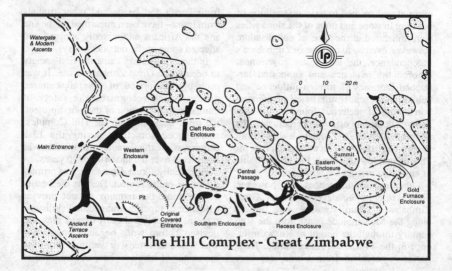

The Hill Complex - Great Zimbabwe

that the Hill Complex was occupied for at least 300 years.

The most salient feature of the Hill Complex is the Western Enclosure, where the Ancient and Terrace ascent routes converge. On the eight-metre-high western wall, note the small upright towers for which no purpose has yet been determined. The pit in its centre is a recent excavation, clearly revealing the layered floors of the consecutive huts that have stood on the site. When the site was inhabited, collapsing huts were razed and their floors smoothed over with wall material to provide floors for subsequent structures.

Leading through the eastern wall of the Western Enclosure is the Covered Entrance, which conducts you into a passageway through to the Southern Enclosures. Beyond them you'll see the small three-sided Recess Enclosure, from which a series of steps leads into the wall. This is the entrance to the Eastern or Ritual Enclosure, where artificial and natural elements combine to form a well-protected site, possibly for ritual purposes. Zimbabwe birds once stood atop six of the pillars around its periphery. On a lower level east of the Eastern Enclosure, traces of gold-smelting operations have been found, hence the name, Gold Furnace Enclosure.

Entering from the Watergate or Modern ascents, you skirt the northern wall of the Western Enclosure and pass through a collapsed entrance into the Cleft Rock Enclosure, a large area contained by boulders, where it's believed the female spirit mediums once performed their rites. A passage through from its eastern end leads to the Eastern Enclosure.

Valley Enclosures
The Valley Enclosures, a series of 13th-century enclosures, *daga* hut platforms and even a small conical tower, stretch from the Sunken Passageway, below the Great Enclosure, towards the Karanga village reconstruction. They have yielded some of the site's finest archaeological finds, including metal tools and the odd Great Zimbabwe

birds, with their mammal-like feet, that became the national symbol.

Great Enclosure
The elliptical Great Enclosure is the structure normally conjured up by the words 'Great Zimbabwe'. It's the most oft-photographed and perhaps the most photogenic of all the ruins. Nearly 100 metres across and 255 metres in circumference, it is the largest ancient structure in sub-Saharan Africa. The mortarless walls reach heights of 11 metres and in places are five metres thick.

The outer wall appears to have been built in a counter-clockwise progression. Builders began with the roughly constructed north-west entrance, honing their techniques as they moved around to the north-eastern side, where the walls are highest and most skilfully completed. This is a another indication that no pre-determined plan had been formulated.

The most commonly accepted theory is that the Great Enclosure was used as a royal compound and a sort of cloister for the king's mother and senior wives. The object of greatest speculation is, of course, the 10-metre-high, convex Conical Tower, tucked away beneath overhanging trees at the south-western end. This solid and apparently ceremonial structure is almost certainly of phallic significance, but no conclusive evidence has yet been uncovered. Treasure hunters of yore believed the tower sheltered the royal treasury (it now contains only rocks and dirt) while current speculation is that it represented the king's grain store. The tower was originally capped with three rows of chevron designs.

In the reconstructed version, the Great Enclosure has three entrances, all of which in the original were probably lintelled and covered, opening through rounded buttresses. The North Entrance, probably the main gate, is met outside by the Sunken Passageway which connects it to the Valley Enclosures.

Leading away north-east from the Conical Tower is the narrow 70-metre-long Parallel Passage. It may have been a means of

ZIMBABWE

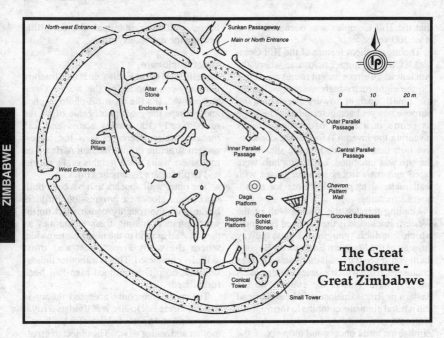

Labels in figure: North-west Entrance, Sunken Passageway, Main or North Entrance, Altar Stone, Enclosure 1, Stone Pillars, Inner Parallel Passage, Outer Parallel Passage, Central Parallel Passage, West Entrance, Chevron Pattern Wall, Daga Platform, Stepped Platform, Green Schist Stones, Grooved Buttresses, Conical Tower, Small Tower

The Great Enclosure - Great Zimbabwe

0   10   20 m

moving from the North Entrance to the Conical Tower without being detected by those in the living area of the Enclosure. It's also possible that the Parallel Passage's inner wall was intended to be an outer wall but by the time the builders had completed that far around, their construction methods had improved so dramatically that they decided to rebuild all of the wall in the superior manner. The outside wall of the Parallel Passage, perhaps the most architecturally advanced structure in Great Zimbabwe, is six metres thick at the base and four metres thick at the top, with each course of stone tapering fractionally to add stability to the 11-metre-high wall. This stretch is capped by three rings of decorative chevron patterns.

Museum

The site museum, open daily from 8 am to 4.30 pm, houses most of the Great Zimbabwe archaeological finds not dispersed to far corners of the earth by amateur treasure hunters. The seven-and-a-bit soapstone Zimbabwe birds, which were probably Rozwi dynasty totems, are what most visitors want to see. The two taken away to South Africa in the late 1890s were returned in 1985 – exchanged for a collection of butterflies – and have taken their place beside the rest. Described variously as falcons, fish eagles and mythological creatures, the 40-cm-high avians have come to represent Zimbabwe on its flag, stamps and official seal.

Other exhibits of interest include porcelain and glass-trade goods brought by Swahili traders. These artefacts are generally considered proof of foreign contact during Great Zimbabwe's heyday. Iron relics are prominently displayed along with gold, bronze and copper items, soapstone dishes and clay pottery. Some of the iron pieces were ritual objects and owned by the king, while others were practical items treasured by common folk.

Places to Stay & Eat

Campers have the best deal at Great Zimbabwe – the opportunity to set up house-keeping in a lovely field within sight of the Hill Complex, just over a rise from the other ruins. This *National Museums & Monuments Campground* (☎ 7052) is an experience not to be missed. Camping costs US$2 per person. Cold showers are available and security guards are posted to keep an eye on your belongings while you're off exploring. Don't leave anything outside your tent – baboons and vervet monkeys aren't picky and will abscond with anything from cooking utensils to underwear left out to dry.

The only formal accommodation at the site is the *Great Zimbabwe Hotel* (☎ 2449) which belongs to the Sun Hotels group. It's not great value for foreigners, who pay US$86/126 for single/double rooms, but that does include a fabulous buffet breakfast with African, English and continental options. Zimbabwe residents pay just US$29/43 for the same deal. The breakfast is available to campers for US$4. Non-guests can use the pool for US$3 per person. The hotel will also change travellers' cheques for the same rate as the banks.

The hotel's terrace restaurant is good for drinks, coffee and snacks although you'll be constantly pestered by hordes of cheeky vervet monkeys who stroll up to diners' plates and help themselves the moment someone is distracted. When they're not thieving, they're sitting in the trees overhead planning the next heist. Sugar sachets seem to be their favourite spoil.

If you prefer bed and breakfast, try the *farm guesthouse* of Mrs Sharon Knowles (☎ 7105, ext 109), which lies 16 km from Masvingo on the Great Zimbabwe road, then eight km south. She has one double room and one twin room and charges US$12 per person for dinner, bed and breakfast. Transport from Masvingo is available.

Getting There & Away

Public transport access to Great Zimbabwe is straightforward. The Morgenster Mission bus runs from Mucheke musika in Masvingo at 8 am, noon and 3.30 pm daily. It's normally crowded, so you'll have to be quick. Get off at the turn-off to the Great Zimbabwe Hotel (the driver will know where you're going) and walk the final km to the Great Zimbabwe Hotel. On the return trip, it passes the Great Zimbabwe turn-off at 9.20 am and 1.20 and 4.50 pm. You can also ride the bus on to Morgenster Mission, where you can see Finger Rock, an interesting rock pillar, before the bus returns to the Great Zimbabwe turn-off.

Taxis to Great Zimbabwe are currently running at about US$10 for up to five passengers. Tours are available from Sunbird; see Organised Tours under Masvingo. Alternatively, you can hire a vehicle from Hertz (☎ 2131) at Founders House on Robert Mugabe St in Masvingo.

MUTIRIKWE (KYLE) RECREATIONAL PARK

A decade of drought has caused the waters of Mutirikwe Dam (still commonly called Lake Kyle) to fall to record low levels and the lake has shrunk to $1/100$ of its capacity. Although the summer rains picked up a bit in 1993, lowveld irrigation projects continue to suffer. Therefore, the dam itself is currently of limited recreational value, but the surrounding scenic area is worthwhile and combines nicely with a visit to Great Zimbabwe.

Popoteke Gap

The signposted access road to Popoteke Gap actually leads to the steep-walled water gap where the Popoteke River flows through the Beza Range on its way to Mutirikwe Dam. It lies 2.5 km south of the Masvingo-Mutare road, 20 km east of Masvingo. It's a scenic stop and ideal for picnicking but camping is prohibited.

Mutirikwe Dam Wall

The 305-metre-wide Mutirikwe (Kyle) Dam wall blocks the impressive Mutirikwe Gorge, forming Lake Mutirikwe. It was completed in 1961 as part of a scheme to irrigate the parched lowveld and allow culti-

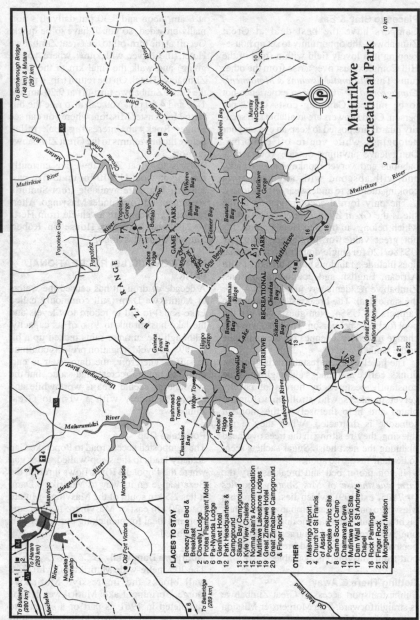

Mutirikwe Recreational Park

PLACES TO STAY

1 Breezy Brae Bed & Breakfast
2 Clovelly Lodge
5 Protea Flamboyant Motel
6 Pa-Nyanda Lodge
9 Glenlivet Hotel
12 Park Headquarters & Campground
13 Sikato Bay Campground
14 Kyle View Chalets
15 Norma Jean's Accommodation
16 Mutirikwe Lakeshore Lodges
19 Great Zimbabwe Hotel
20 Great Zimbabwe Campground & Finger Rock

OTHER

3 Masvingo Airport
4 Church of St Francis of Assisi
8 Game Scout Camp
10 Popoteke Picnic Site
11 Chamavara Cave
17 Mutirikwe Picnic Site
17 Dam Wall & St Andrew's Chapel
18 Rock Paintings
21 Finger Rock
22 Morgenster Mission

vation of such thirsty crops as cotton and sugar cane.

Rock Paintings

Two relatively accessible rock painting sites can be seen near the lakeshore. The easier to reach is a small unnamed one about two km south-west of the dam wall and 100 metres from the road. It's well signposted.

The better known Chamavara paintings at Chamavara Cave lie 18 km north-west of the dam wall on Murray McDougall Dr, then five km east on the signposted turn-off. You'll probably have to walk much of the way, because of boulders blocking the road. Most of the painted human and animal figures are confusingly dense on the cave wall and are at times hard to discern.

Because many figures have white faces, there has been speculation about connections with Middle Eastern and European peoples. The cave's main figure, known as the Giant Man of Chamavara, who is surrounded by several elegantly painted kudus, is unique in Zimbabwe.

Mutirikwe (Kyle) Game Park

Although it seems a bit artificial, the marginally maintained Mutirikwe Game Park offers the possibility of seeing white rhinos and hosts more species of antelope than any other national park in Zimbabwe. Easily observed along the 64 km of dirt roads are warthogs, impalas, kudu, tsessebes, wildebeests, waterbucks, giraffes, zebras, buffaloes and baboons. Oribis and elands are seen occasionally, but there are no elephants or big cats. Game park gates close at 6 pm.

Walking is permitted only around Mushagashe Arm near the National Parks' lodges and camp site. It's outside the game fence, so you won't observe much wildlife, but hippos and crocodiles are often seen in and around the water. The area north of the dwala, around the parks' lodges, is an arboretum, with over 150 species of indigenous trees. However, access is difficult – the way hasn't been cleared for some time.

Activities

National Parks' guided horseback trips through the game park allow wildlife viewing from closer range than a vehicle would permit. They depart at 7.45 am from park headquarters and return at 10.30 am. Advance bookings are essential.

Places to Stay

Southern Shore Most Mutirikwe accommodation is along the lake's southern shore. Camping is available at the beautiful National Parks' Sikato Bay camp site, six easily walkable km from Great Zimbabwe National Monument.

East of the camp site, the laid-back *Kyle View Chalets* (☎ 7202) has one, two and three-bedroom self-catering chalets with en suite facilities for US$16 per person; camping costs US$3. Amenities include a swimming pool, tennis courts and a relaxed restaurant and pub.

Further east are the *Mutirikwe Lakeshore Lodges* (☎ 7151). These two-storey self-catering rondavels with en suite facilities accommodate up to six people. They're good value at US$9/16 single/double occupancy, plus US$7 for each additional person. There's a swimming pool, as well as a shop and pub.

Norma Jean's Accommodation (☎ 7206) on Dunollie Estate, 42 km down Mutirikwe Rd, is recommended for its friendly, homely atmosphere. Go 200 metres east of Kyle View Chalets and look to the right; it's on the hillside, facing the lake. Self-catering rooms cost US$12 per person. Meals are available on request.

Northern Shore On the northern shore, the only accommodation is the *National Parks' camp*, with two and three-bedroom lodges. The attached campground has all the standard features – showers, baths and braai pits. As always, book in advance through the National Parks' booking office in Harare.

In the hills at the eastern end of the lake is the secluded *Glenlivet Hotel* (☎ 7611; fax 62846), which dates back to the 1940s. For relaxation, there's a sauna, as well as tennis courts and a swimming pool. In the surrounding hills, you'll find plenty of walks, including a steep climb up to a mountain-top shelter and a pleasant stroll to the spring which supplies the hotel's water. Rooms are great value at US$22 per person, including bed and breakfast and a table d'hôte dinner.

Places to Eat

Apart from the dining room at the nearby *Great Zimbabwe Hotel*, the only restaurant is at *Kyle View Chalets*. Both Mutirikwe Lakeshore Lodges and Kyle View Chalets sell basic supplies and beer (considered by some a basic supply) so campers should bring food from elsewhere.

The game park has two picnic sites, the Mutirikwe site, on the point at the end of Ostrich Loop, and the Popoteke Gorge site, where the river of the same name issues into Mutirikwe Dam.

Getting There & Away

Once you're at Great Zimbabwe, it's an easy matter to walk or hitch the six km to the Mutirikwe southern shore. The main sites of interest are further along, however, and the only public transport is the infrequent Glenlivet bus.

Along the barely travelled Murray McDougall Scenic Drive and Circular Drive between Great Zimbabwe and the Masvingo-Mutare road, hitching is not good at all.

To reach the game park, it's probably easier to go the other way round, from Great Zimbabwe via Masvingo. The northern shore is best accessed from the turning from the Mutare road, 13 km east of Masvingo.

When there's sufficient water in the lake, from Mutirikwe Lakeshore Lodges, it may be possible to hitch a boat ride to the game park with one of the rangers. Phone the warden or the senior ranger (☎ 2913) during office hours (7 am to 6 pm daily) and arrange to be picked up at a specified time.

Tours of the game park are also available, see Organised Tours under Masvingo.

MUSHANDIKE SANCTUARY

A well-kept secret, the 13,360-hectare Mushandike Sanctuary lies 11 km south of the Masvingo-Bulawayo road; the turn-off is 25 km west of Masvingo. Its focus is Mushandike Dam, a blue jewel filling valleys between serene wooded hills.

Visiting in winter is great when the air is clear and cold and the mopane forest puts on brilliant golds, reds and oranges. For solitude, it's superb. Look for sables, kudu, tsessebes, klipspringers, steenboks, grysboks, duikers, waterbucks, impalas and wildebeests, as well as zebras, leopards and warthogs.

The scenic drives through the eastern two-thirds of the sanctuary are quite rough and the bit between the dam and the southern boundary is steep and rough. Note that the gates on the boundary are locked and there's no access to the Beitbridge road.

For much of the year, you're likely to have the National Parks' campground to yourself, but there's still an attendant on hand to tend the boiler and chop firewood as necessary. Some sites provide a small patch of grassy lawn suitable for tent camping, and it's well worth the price.

Water and hot showers are available but the nearest shops are at Mashava and Masvingo. The friendly information office can help with enquiries. Also, have a look at the eland research institute.

Zebra

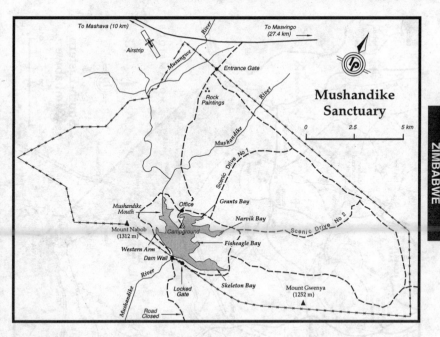

Getting There & Away

Without a vehicle, access will probably entail an 11 km walk from the Masvingo-Bulawayo road. Lifts from the turn-off are hard to come by (on my most recent visit, the last private car had been through 11 days earlier) unless you connect with a ranger vehicle. To reach the entrance, either hitch or take any Masvingo-Bulawayo bus.

South-Eastern Zimbabwe

Much of south-eastern Zimbabwe is comprised of the hot, low-lying lowveld, which is characterised mainly by low scrub. Add water, however, and the desert blossoms, as it has around the well-irrigated sugar cane-growing area of Triangle. For tourists, the main draw to this region is the newly re-

opened – and as yet, little-visited – Gonarezhou National Park.

MANJIRENJI DAM

In the beautiful transition zone between the highveld and lowveld, Manjirenji Dam Recreational Park lies lost in communal lands, 12 km off MacDougall Rd (the untarred back route between Chiredzi and Masvingo). You'll find pleasant hiking tracks, ample picnic sites, and free camping in the basic shelters, but it's not a wilderness area and is heavily used by local people. There's no public transport into this area.

RUNDE RIVER

This village on the Beitbridge-Masvingo road beside the slow and shallow Runde River enjoys a lovely setting. It may remind you of a Chinese painting, with big, rounded monolithic hills, dwala domes and lush vegetation. There's a crafts centre in the village and lots of rock-climbing potential, but no

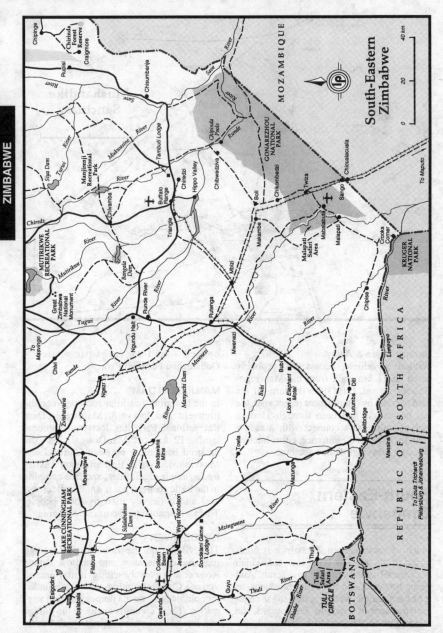

South-Eastern Zimbabwe

amenities. If 'the road less taken' appeals to you, be sure to bring a tent.

TRIANGLE

It isn't hard to deduce that Triangle is a company town. Neat and square cornered (despite its name), Triangle appears to have been erected somewhere else and transplanted wholesale to the lowveld sea of waving sugar cane. Workers and company seem to melt into one entity; in this beehive of bland cooperation, everyone and everything is stamped with the Triangle logo.

The success of Triangle – and it is successful – may be attributed to the persistence of one man, an unconventional Scot by the name of Thomas Murray McDougall, who was single-handedly responsible for introducing lowveld irrigation and converting the country into a productive agricultural area.

McDougall Museum

Housed in McDougall's home, the McDougall museum sits on a hill about 1.5 km off the highway. Here you get the lowdown on the events that led to the foundation of Triangle Sugar Estates and its takeover by the Sugar Industry Board, as well as its resourceful founder and the sugar industry in general. The building is now designated a National Monument. It's open

daily except Monday from 8.30 to 9.30 am and 3.30 to 4.30 pm. Admission is less than US$0.03, even for foreigners.

Places to Stay & Eat

The only accommodation is at the Country Club (☎ 6492) which costs US$10 per person. It also serves cheap basic meals.

Getting There & Away

There are daily buses between Harare, Masvingo and Chiredzi, which pass through Triangle.

CHIREDZI

Hot and malaria-infested Chiredzi sprang up with the lowveld irrigation schemes of the mid-1960s. It's mainly a sugar town these days, but isn't as anomalous or interesting as nearby Triangle.

Places to Stay & Eat

The one-star *Planter's Inn* (☎ 2281) which sits on a hill in the centre, isn't too bad. It has a raucous pub and a reasonable dining room. Single/double rooms including bed and breakfast cost US$27/39. Chalets accommodating four people cost US$54, excluding breakfast.

The alternative is two-star *Tambuti Lodge* (☎ 2575; fax 3187), 12 km from town on the

ZIMBABWE

Thomas Murray McDougall

Thomas Murray McDougall ran away from Scotland to the British Guiana (now known as Guyana) sugar plantations at the age of 14, but by 1908, he found himself in lowveld Rhodesia. The purchase of a herd of cattle – all bearing a triangle brand – from a bankrupt rancher led to his first attempt at enterprise in the lowveld but at that stage, the vast, flat and dry territory was far from productive.

When his ranch failed, McDougall hatched a new scheme; he saw the exotic waters of the Mutirikwe and other lowveld rivers as the key to agriculture in the otherwise desert country. The following seven years saw him digging and blasting two 425-metre irrigation tunnels through solid granite to divert the river waters onto his property.

By 1931, McDougall was growing cotton, vegetables, tobacco and cereal grains and tending orchards, but before long, his efforts were decimated by swarms of locusts. At last-ditch pinch, he remembered his early days in South America and opted to turn to sugar cane. Although the government was less than enthusiastic, it allowed him to import three stalks of cane from Natal in South Africa. The rest he had to smuggle in, merely a formality for this determined character. The events that led to the foundation of Triangle Sugar Estates and its takeover by the Sugar Industry Board are detailed in the museum on the site, which has now been designated a national monument. ■

Birchenough Bridge road. The staff take a disinterested attitude towards the hotel's ongoing decline, but its riverside setting is nice enough. Singles/doubles without baths cost US$24/34 with breakfast. Add a TV and rooms cost US$1.30 more.

For meals, your best option is the friendly *Continental Restaurant* in the town centre, with a surprising variety of dishes and an odd mirrored décor on the walls. A lesser option is the dining room at the Planter's Inn. In the Black township, two km from the town centre, you'll find a plethora of inexpensive snack stalls and takeaways. Next door to the Continental Restaurant is the raucous La Bamba Night Club, with a bar and nightly entertainment.

The nearest camping is at Gonarezhou National Park; see later in this chapter.

Getting There & Away

Chiredzi's airport, serving mainly agricultural business traffic, is at Buffalo Range, 15 km west of town. United Air Charters has three flights weekly between Buffalo Range and Bulawayo, and flies daily except Saturday between Harare via Masvingo.

Bus services connect Chiredzi's township bus terminal with Harare, Masvingo, Mutare, Bulawayo and Beitbridge, as well as the nearby communities of Triangle, Hippo Valley and Buffalo Range.

GONAREZHOU NATIONAL PARK

When largescale agriculture began encroaching on wildlife habitat in the late 1960s, tsetse-fly control measures (both largescale bush-burning and shooting) claimed the lives of 55,000 large animals. In response, Nuanetsi District Commissioner Alan Wright encouraged the government to establish a refuge for wildlife and a poaching control corridor along the border. The result was the designation of a scenic 5000-sq-km chunk of south-eastern Zimbabwe – virtually an extension of South Africa's Kruger National Park – as the Gonarezhou Game Reserve. In 1975, the reserve became a national park. If you'd like to read more about the park's history, perhaps you can scare up copies of the books *Valley of the Ironwoods* and *Grey Ghosts of Buffalo Bend*, written by Alan Wright about his 10 years in the area.

The park landscapes are impressive. Through the parched scrublands wind the broad Mwenezi, Save and Runde rivers, which form ribbon-like oases providing food and water for wildlife. It is speculated that during wetter times, when Great Zimbabwe was flourishing, traders were able to navigate upstream along the Save River as far as Chivilila Falls. The falls still serve as an impediment to fish, resulting in the evolution of such unique species as freshwater goby *(Chonophorus aeneofusucus)* and black bream *(Oreochromis placida)*. In addition, the falls block upstream movement of such saltwater species as Zambezi sharks, sawfish and tarpon. When poking around pans in the Mwenezi area, look for the bright turquoise killifish *(Nothobranchius furzeri)* which inhabits only these tiny desert pools.

In Shona, *gona-re-zhou* means 'abode of elephants', and some of Africa's largest tuskers have lived there. It's also one of only two Zimbabwe habitats of the nyala antelope (the other is Mana Pools). Tiny suni antelopes reach their highest concentrations at Gonarezhou and rare and reclusive king cheetahs, marbled or racing-striped models of the world's fastest animal, inhabit the park's furthest reaches. It's estimated that no more than 25 remain.

Tragically, poaching has been a serious problem; in the 1920s, one of Africa's most notorious poachers, Stephanus Barnard, shot his way through some of the continent's largest tuskers. His kills included the famous Dhulamithi, a jumbo pachyderm reckoned to have been the largest elephant ever taken in southern Africa – his tusks reportedly weighed in at over 110 kg.

More recently, during the Mozambican civil war, guerrillas regularly crossed the border to escape pursuers and use the park as a bush larder. During the worst of the fighting, in the late 1980s and early 1990s, the park remained closed to non-Africans. The drought of the early 1990s also took its toll,

ZIMBABWE

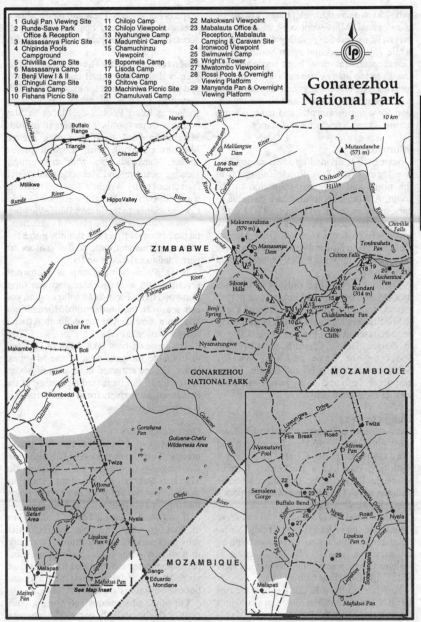

Gonarezhou National Park

1 Guluji Pan Viewing Site	11 Chilojo Camp	22 Makokwani Viewpoint
2 Runde-Save Park Office & Reception	12 Chilojo Viewpoint	23 Mabalauta Office & Reception, Mabalauta Camping & Caravan Site
3 Massasanya Picnic Site	13 Nyahungwe Camp	24 Ironwood Viewpoint
4 Chipinda Pools Campground	14 Madumbini Camp	25 Swimuwini Camp
5 Chivililla Camp Site	15 Chamuchinzu Viewpoint	26 Wright's Tower
6 Massasanya Camp	16 Bopomela Camp	27 Mwatombo Viewpoint
7 Benji View I & II	17 Lisoda Camp	28 Rossi Pools & Overnight Viewing Platform
8 Chinguli Camp Site	18 Gota Camp	29 Manyanda Pan & Overnight Viewing Platform
9 Fishans Camp	19 Chitove Camp	
10 Fishans Picnic Site	20 Machiniwa Picnic Site	
	21 Chamuluvati Camp	

and 750 Gonarezhou elephants had to be translocated. Most went only as far as the privately owned Save Valley Conservancy, while 150 or so wound up in South Africa. Gonarezhou has now been reopened but thanks to too many close calls with elephant guns and AK47s, Gonarezhou elephants bear a grudge against humans and have a reputation for a temperamental and cantankerous nature – keep a respectable distance.

Information

Gonarezhou is divided into two administrative regions: the Save-Runde subregion in the north and Mwenezi subregion in the south. Although some roads are passable to cars, most are rough and require 4WD, especially in the south. The park is open to day visitors from 6 am to 6 pm from May to October. From November to April, access is restricted to Chipinda Pools, Mabalauta and Swimuwini.

Fishing is permitted only at camp sites unless you have a special limited-bag permit issued by the Department of National Parks & Wildlife Management. These permits may be purchased at the Chipinda Pools office or in Harare. Below Chivilila (or Chivirira) Falls on the Save and Chitove (or Selawondoma) Falls on the Runde, bream and tiger fish and even some saltwater species have been caught.

Things to See

Save-Runde Subregion The park's foremost photographic fodder, the rugged red sandstone Chilojo Cliffs (also spelt Tjolotjo), rise like a Rajasthani fortress above the Runde River, near its confluence with the Save. The area also offers the park's best wildlife viewing.

With a good 4WD vehicle, you can drive right to the top of the cliffs at Chilojo Viewpoint and Chamuchinzu Viewpoint. With an ordinary car, you'll only get as close as Fishans Camp, where you'll have good view of the cliff face from below.

Another worthwhile side trip is to the two Benji View viewpoints; although you won't see a lot of wildlife, the stark, silent landscape is impressive. There are picnic sites at Massasanya Dam and Fishans Camp, both accessible by ordinary cars in the dry season.

Mwenezi Subregion The Mwenezi Subregion is dotted with small and scenic pools and pans, which make for excellent wildlife viewing. There's an overnight viewing shelter at Rossi Pools (see Places to Stay below); other pools of interest include Mwatomba Pool, deep in a rock shelter; Mukokwani Pool, with a small picnic shelter; Manyanda Pan, with an overnight viewing platform; and Makonde Pool, which is overlooked by Wright's Tower. The tower was built by Alan Wright, a former District Commissioner, to facilitate wildlife viewing.

Samalena Gorge ('the place of execution') on the Mwenezi River is a shallow gorge full of semi-permanent rock pools. Visitors are permitted to explore it on foot.

Near Swimuwini Camp is Ironwood Overlook, on a sharp ridge between large ironwood trees. From this vantage point, you can see over the border into Mozambique and, on a clear day, as far as South Africa's Kruger National Park.

The large ox-bow lake, Majinji Pan, lies just outside the park west of the Mwenezi River. It once attracted thousands of water-loving birds, but increased siphoning of the Runde and Save rivers for lowveld irrigation is causing it to dry up.

Organised Tours

From May to October at the full moon, groups of six or fewer people can join four-day ranger-guided game walks through the Mwenezi Subregion. Overnight camps are made within sight of permanent water holes, making for excellent wildlife viewing.

If you want to see the best of Gonarezhou on foot, go with Khangela Safaris, which runs backpacking safaris through the park, as well as a series of daywalks from semi-permanent camps. Scheduled trips last from six to 10 days and run at least once a month, but custom safaris are also available.

For other adventurous activities, a company with the unlikely name of Mungwezi

Ranching Company (☎ 2640; fax 3026), PO Box 297, Chiredzi, offers a variety of options. Three to five-day 4WD trips cost US$75 per person per day for up to four people, including meals. Four-day backpacking safaris through the Chilojo Cliffs area cost US$175 per group per day, with a maximum of five people. This includes meals and the final night spent at the natural stone, wood and thatch Makwekwete Lodge, outside the park. Horseback trips through the park cost US$150 per group per day, with a maximum of four people. Riding in the nearby Chiredzi River Conservancy, costs US$75 per person per day or US$200 per group of up to seven people.

Places to Stay

The most accessible camp site in the Save-Runde subregion is idyllic Chipinda Pools, which lies 63 km from Chiredzi along a badly corrugated but easily passable gravel road. Camp sites all have shelters and braai areas, and overlook the vegetation-lined pools, which teem with hippos. Further upstream is Chinguli Camp. These camps have showers and flush toilets and, in the dry season, both are accessible without 4WD.

More primitive camps are strung along Runde River between Chipinda Pools and its confluence with the Save River. They're limited to one party at a time, with a maximum of 12 people. With the exception of Fishans Camp, you can reach them only with 4WD.

In the Mwenezi Subregion, the nicest camp is *Swimuwini Camp*, (the 'place of baobabs'), which overlooks Buffalo Bend in the Mwenezi River. It's accessible in an ordinary car and offers both camping and chalets. It's also a haunt of both elephants and lions, and the small pond frequently attracts thirsty nyalas. The more basic *Mbalauta Camping & Caravan Site* has five camp sites and an ablutions block. Two wildlife-viewing hides, Rossi Pools and Manyanda Platform, may be occupied overnight by individual parties.

Formal accommodation is limited to three safari lodges outside the national park. Two of these lie on the 30,000-hectare Lone Star

game ranch. The emphasis here is on conservation and the owner, Malilangwe Conservation Trust, claims that all profits from tourism are cycled back into the reserve. The reservations number is ☎ 703131; fax 794655, both in Harare.

The less expensive of the two camps is the family oriented *Kwali Camp*, with thatched wooden bungalows and communal ablutions facilities accommodating up to 18 people. Activities include fishing and wildlife viewing. Rates are US$75 per person, including meals. *Induna Lodge*, which caters mainly to adults, charges US$130 per person for accommodation in six sandstone and thatch bungalows, all with en suite facilities. The architecture accommodates the surrounding landscape, with favourable effects. Game walks, fishing and hides for wildlife viewing are all near at hand. Day trips into Gonarezhou are available at extra cost.

The third option is the new *Mahenye Wilderness Lodge* (☎ 736644; fax 736646, both in Harare), magically situated on the island at the confluence of the Runde and Save rivers. Accommodation is in natural material chalets, which were inspired by the local Shangaan architecture. They cost a very reasonable US$40 per person, including meals. Air taxis from Chiredzi cost US$150 for up to three people.

The nearest groceries and other supplies are at Rutenga and Chiredzi.

BEITBRIDGE

Beitbridge was named for the Limpopo River bridge, of course, which was in turn named for Alfred Beit of the Beit Trust which financed it. Exciting in name only is the 'great grey-green greasy Limpopo', an unimpressive green channel sliding through a dry scrubby flood-plain. Unless you're crossing the border, however, you won't catch even a glimpse of the river.

Even if they're just stopping for petrol (Beitbridge must have more petrol stations per capita than anywhere else in Zimbabwe), travellers generally spend more time here than they'd like to. This is Zimbabwe's only border crossing with South Africa, and hot,

ZIMBABWE

tedious waits are possible. To avoid hassles, hitchers recommend crossing 15 minutes before the 10 pm closing, when officials want nothing more than to go home.

Places to Stay

If you're caught out after the border closes, try *Peter's Hotel* (☎ 309), which charges US$24/33 for a single/double room. The other possibility is the more up-market but not so friendly *Beitbridge Inn* (☎ 214; fax 413), where single/double cottages cost US$27/32. Single/double rooms in the main building are US$24/29 without bath and US$25/30 with bath.

If you're heading north, try to reach the pleasant *Lion & Elephant Motel* (☎ 701502 in Harare) at Bubi River, 78 km north of Beitbridge. They allow camping in a beautiful spot beside the river for US$3 per person, including use of all facilities. Singles/doubles with dinner, bed and breakfast cost US$32/42 without bath; rooms with bath are US$7 more. For campers, the buffet breakfast costs US$3.

At West Nicholson, 125 km north-west of Beitbridge on the Bulawayo road, is the lovely *Sondelani Game Lodge* (☎ 68739; fax 64997, both in Bulawayo). At this private game ranch, US$220 per person includes accommodation, three meals, walking safaris, games drives (including night drives) and transfers from Beitbridge or Bulawayo.

Places to Eat

The *Bird Cage Restaurant & Snack Bar* at the Beitbridge Inn is the only real eating establishment. If you prefer to pick up supplies and press on, *Sunrise Takeaways* serves snacks and there's also a small supermarket. The South African side offers a wider range of goods, but prices are considerably higher.

Getting There & Away

For information on buses to and through Beitbridge, see To/From South Africa in the Zimbabwe Getting There & Away chapter.

GWANDA

Gwanda, a railway cattle-loading station 127 km south-east of Bulawayo on the Beitbridge road, began as a goldfields service centre and there is still considerable low-key mining activity in the region.

The former gold mine at Colleen Bawn, 25 km south-east of Gwanda, was first claimed in 1895 by Irish prospector Sam Daly, who named it for his girlfriend back in Dublin. He didn't have any luck with it, but in 1905, a marginal vein was discovered. The gold long ago ceased to be profitable and today, the mountain behind Colleen Bawn is literally being removed and converted into cement.

Places to Stay

Although I can think of absolutely no reason to visit Gwanda, if you're caught out for the night, there's a caravan park 200 metres south of the highway, just east of town. On the main (and essentially, the only) street is run-down *Hardy's Motel*.

TULI CIRCLE

The Tuli Circle is the odd semi-circular Zimbabwean bridgehead on the western bank of the Shashe River. This geographical anomaly is the result of an 1891 definition of magisterial jurisdiction over a 10-mile radius of Thuli village, east of the Shashe River. The appropriate name is derived from the Shona word *uthuli*, meaning 'dust'.

The Tuli Circle contains the 416-sq-km Tuli Safari Area, created in 1963, which takes in some stunning riverine scenery. Within this hunting area are three small botanical reserves which are characterised by mopane woodland and riverine forest.

History

This was the site of Fort Tuli, built in 1890 by the Rhodesian Pioneer Column. Trivia buffs may wish to note that in the same year, Fort Tuli hosted Zimbabwe's first rugby match; it was played in the Shashe riverbed between the Pioneers and the soldiers posted there. The following year, a contingent of

Lobengula's army arrived for a visit (probably to assess the feasibility of attack), and were fêted with an impressive demonstration of British firepower. No confrontation ever materialised.

During the Boer Wars, Fort Tuli served as a supply and training depot, and even attracted a Catholic nursing mission led by Mother Patrick, of Harare fame. In 1897, however, the railway from South Africa arrived in Bulawayo, bypassing the Tuli Circle, and by the turn of the century, the colonists had all but abandoned the area. All that remains is a monument, a flag marking the site of the fort and a European cemetery.

Getting There & Away

Access is for ground-breakers only – you can approach along the rough track following the Limpopo from north of Beitbridge or the equally rough track turning south from the Beitbridge-Bulawayo road, midway between Gwanda and Beitbridge. A daily Bulawayo-Beitbridge bus runs via Thuli (across the Shashe River from the Tuli Circle) but it's a slow, rough trip.

ZIMBABWE

Bulawayo

Originally called Gu-Bulawayo or 'the killing place', Bulawayo (population 900,000) is Zimbabwe's bright and historically intriguing second city. The name presumably resulted from Mzilikazi's Thabas Indunas (Hill of Chiefs) executions that accompanied the development of the Ndebele state. However, because relative latecomer Harare managed to usurp the seat of government during the colonial era, Bulawayo has lately avoided most of the cares associated with politics.

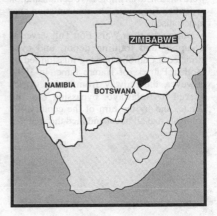

History

In early 19th-century Transvaal, newly unified Zululand suffered a series of distinctly disunifying political disturbances. After the overthrow of Zulu leader Dingiswayo by an ambitious young captain called Shaka, the realm was brought to its knees by the ruthless new king's reign of terror. Many subordinate groups, now known as Nguni, who had experienced or feared his wrath, fled northward on the *mfecane*, the 'forced migration'. One such refugee, Mzilikazi, who'd had a collateral dispute with King Shaka, arrived in south-western Zimbabwe with his Kumalo clan in the 1830s. The Kumalo prevailed over the incumbent Rozwi and established themselves at Inyati, 60 km north-west of Bulawayo under the name Ndebele or 'those who carry long shields'.

Upon Mzilikazi's death in 1870, his son Lobengula ascended to the throne and moved his capital to Bulawayo, soon finding himself face to face with the British South Africa Company. In 1888, Cecil John Rhodes met with Lobengula and duped him into accepting the Rudd Concession, which granted the foreigners mineral rights in exchange for money and weapons.

A series of misunderstandings followed. Lobengula sent a contingent of Ndebele raiders to Fort Victoria (Masvingo) to prevent Shona interference between the British and the Ndebele. The British mistook

this as aggression against them and launched an attack on Matabeleland, which was rumoured to harbour vast mineral deposits. As a result, Lobengula's kraals were destroyed, Bulawayo was burned and the king fled northward to escape the pursuing BSAC troops. A peace offering of gold sent by Lobengula to the BSAC was commandeered by company employees and never reached Rhodes. The vengeful British instead sent the Shangani Patrol to track down the missing king and finish him off. In the end, it was the patrol that was finished off – and in spectacular fashion (see Matobo National Park later in this chapter). Shortly after, Lobengula died in exile of smallpox.

Without their king, the Ndebele continued to resist the BSAC and foreign rule. In the early 1890s, the tribe allied itself with its traditional enemy, the Shona, in the spirit of Chimurenga, and what remained of Lobengula's army became embroiled in a guerrilla war in the Matobo Hills. When Rhodes suggested a negotiated settlement, the Ndebele, with their depleted numbers and weakened state, couldn't really refuse. An uneasy peace was effected, the foreigners moved into Bulawayo and the BSAC

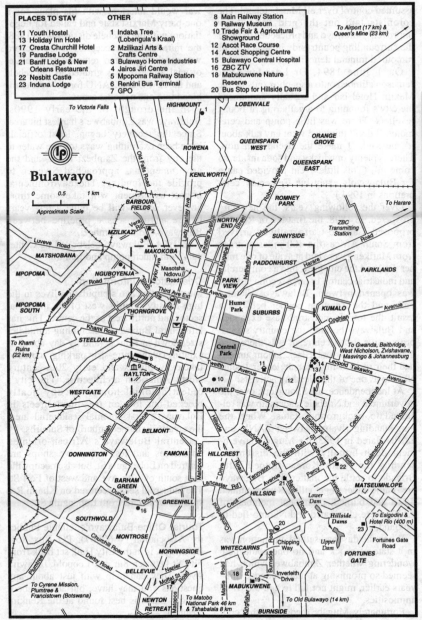

PLACES TO STAY
11 Youth Hostel
13 Holiday Inn Hotel
17 Cresta Churchill Hotel
21 Banff Lodge & New Orleans Restaurant
22 Nesbitt Castle
23 Induna Lodge

OTHER
1 Indaba Tree (Lobengula's Kraal)
2 Mzilikazi Arts & Crafts Centre
3 Bulawayo Home Industries
4 Jairos Jiri Centre
5 Mpopoma Railway Station
6 Renkini Bus Terminal
7 GPO

8 Main Railway Station
9 Railway Museum
10 Trade Fair & Agricultural Showground
12 Ascot Race Course
14 Ascot Shopping Centre
15 Bulawayo Central Hospital
16 ZBC ZTV
18 Mabukuwene Nature Reserve
20 Bus Stop for Hillside Dams

Bulawayo

0   0.5   1 km
Approximate Scale

To Victoria Falls

HIGHMOUNT

LOBENVALE

ROWENA

QUEENSPARK WEST

ORANGE GROVE

KENILWORTH

QUEENSPARK EAST

To Harare

BARBOUR FIELDS

ROMNEY PARK

ZBC Transmitting Station

MZILIKAZI

NORTH END

SUNNYSIDE

Luveve Road

MAKOKOBA

PARK VIEW

PADDONHURST

PARKLANDS

MATSHOBANA

NGUBOYENJA

Masotsha Ndlovu Road

MPOPOMA

Road

First Avenue

Hume Park

SUBURBS

KUMALO

Coghlan Avenue

MPOPOMA SOUTH

THORNGROVE

Khami Road

Central Park

To Khami Ruins (22 km)

STEELDALE

Main Street

Twelfth Avenue

To Gwanda, Beitbridge, West Nicholson, Zvishavane, Masvingo & Johannesburg

Leopold Takawira Avenue

WESTGATE

RAYLTON

BRADFIELD

BELMONT

Fairbridge Way

MATSEUMHLOPE

DONNINGTON

FAMONA

HILLCREST

Sarah Bain St

Percy Ave

Cecil Avenue

BARHAM GREEN

Lancaster Rd

HILLSIDE

Lower Dam

To Esigodini & Hotel Rio (400 m)

SOUTHWOLD

GREENHILL

Hillside Dams

Fortunes Gate Road

MONTROSE

Chipping Way

Upper Dam

FORTUNES GATE

Churchill Road

MORNINGSIDE

WHITECAIRNS

BELLEVUE

Inverleith Drive

To Cyrene Mission, Plumtree & Francistown (Botswana)

NEWTON RETREAT

To Matobo National Park 46 km & Tshabalala 8 km

MABUKUWENE

To Old Bulawayo (14 km)

BURNSIDE

To Airport (17 km) & Queen's Mine (23 km)

Robert Mugabe Street

Old Falls Road

Lobengula Street

Khami Road

Matopos Road

Burnside Road

Kingfisher

assumed control over all Matabeleland. The colonists laid out the grid for a 'new improved' Bulawayo and proceeded to scour the surrounding countryside in search of its rumoured mineral deposits.

On 1 June 1894, Dr Leander Starr Jameson climbed onto a soapbox outside the Maxim Hotel bar and casually announced the city's founding to a gathering of boozy revellers. There was little pomp and ceremony: 'I don't think we want any talk about it', he said. 'I make the declaration now. There is plenty of whisky and soda inside, so come in'. (This little event provided cause for Bulawayo's extensive Centenary celebrations in 1994.)

Over the following years, the new city prospered. In 1898, the first leg of Rhodes' proposed Cape-to-Cairo railway arrived from South Africa (the 400 miles of track from Mafikeng were laid at a rate of one mile per day) and the city grew into a commercial and industrial centre. Later, a second railway was opened between Bulawayo, Victoria Falls and the Zambian copper belt. As a result, the town's industrial base expanded and Bulawayo became the country's most progressive urban centre. It was there also that the nation's first Black labour unions had their roots, with Ndebele leader Joshua Nkomo as one of their leading activists.

At Independence, the Shona took over the government and Ndebele leadership was relegated to background status. When the long-standing rivalry between ZANU and ZAPU flared in 1983, the Mugabe government dealt brutally with the dissenters, sending the North Korean-trained Fifth Brigade to settle the matter. The Bulawayo area came under siege; villages were gunned down and burned, prominent members of ZAPU were eliminated and Nkomo fled to England.

When the dust had settled, the nation was in a state of shock and no one could help wondering whether Zimbabwe, which had seemed so promising at independence three years earlier, might not fall to age-old tribal animosities.

Fortunately, Mugabe recognised that civil war would interfere with his plans for a one-party Marxist state and called for negotiations with the Ndebele dissidents. In 1988, the miraculously successful Unity Accord was reached; Nkomo returned from exile, official amnesty was granted to the rebels and the ZAPU and ZANU forces were combined into one national army.

In the drought of the early 1990s, Bulawayo was Zimbabwe's hardest hit area. Since the recovery began, local officials have been examining ways to pipe water to the city from the Zambezi River, and the government has approached Sweden to provide the funding. The environmental impact assessment will take some time, however, and it will be quite a few years before anyone sees a pipeline between Bulawayo and the Zambezi.

In 1994, Bulawayo celebrated its Centenary with much pomp and fanfare.

Orientation & Information

Most of Bulawayo's population lives in the high-density suburbs west of the industrial sector and north-west of the centre. This has left central Bulawayo resembling a middle-sized town in Kansas (and by day about as exciting) with centre-strip parking, scores of takeaway places and early 20th-century North American architecture. The city's oldest colonial homes occupy neatly blocked-out lots on tree-lined streets in Bulawayo's first colonial residential area, the creatively named suburb of Suburbs.

Central Bulawayo's African-oriented businesses and less expensive shops are centred on Lobengula St, but also occupy the area south of 12th Ave and west of Fort St. The industrial sector, centred on Khami Rd, sprawls westward from Lobengula St.

Tourist Office Bulawayo's reliable Publicity Association (☎ 60867), PO Box 861, Bulawayo, is in the City Hall, set back from Fife St between 8th and Leopold Takawira Aves. They can help with just about any questions you may have, but advice about African buses is best found at the Renkini terminal.

Street Name Changes

In March 1990, Bulawayo, like a number of other cities in Zimbabwe, changed its street names.

Old Name	New Name
Abercorn	Jason Moyo
Borrow	Samuel Parirenyat
Grey	Robert Mugabe
Birchenough	Robert Mugabe
Queens	Robert Mugabe
Kings	Masotsha Ndlovu
Jameson	Herbert Chitepo
Johannesburg	Gwanda
London	Josiah Chinamano
Mafikeng	Plumtree
Rhodes	George Silundika
Salisbury	Harare
Selborne	Leopold Takawira
Wilson	Josiah Tongogara

The Publicity Association distributes a free tourist publication, *Bulawayo This Month*, with a city plan (some copies may be difficult to read because of poor printing) and a rundown of cultural events, club meetings and even a horoscope. In addition, they distribute advertising and photocopied maps of other areas around Zimbabwe for US$0.15 each.

Visa Extensions The Dept of Immigration Control (☎ 65621) is on the 1st floor of the Central Africa Building Society building, on the corner of Jason Moyo St and Leopold Takawira Ave.

Post & Telecommunications The GPO, on the corner of 8th Ave and Main St, is an efficient poste restante address. It's open during normal post office hours: 8.30 am to 5 pm weekdays except Wednesday (poste restante closes at 4 pm), 8 am to 1 pm Wednesday and 8 to 11.30 am on Saturday. On public holidays, it's open from 9 to 10.30 am. The parcel office entrance is around the other side of the building on Fort St.

You'll find the public telephone kiosks and their obligatory queues inside the GPO. To send or receive faxes, use either the public fax number (fax 78053) at the GPO or the friendly and reasonably priced Copy Centre (fax 65016) on Fife St between 9th and 10th Aves.

Travel Agencies The American Express Representative is Manica Travel (☎ 62521) on 10th Ave between Main and Fort Sts. Unfortunately, they're not authorised to handle foreign cash transactions so all currency exchanges must be done at the bank. It's also the booking agent for Ajay's Motorways. If you're going to Hwange or Victoria Falls, advance booking is essential.

For general travel information and bookings try the recommended Sunshine Tours (☎ 67791) in the Old Mutual Arcade near the corner of Jason Moyo St and 8th Ave. Also recommended is Budget Travel.

Bookshops The main Kingston's outlet, with a wider selection than its Harare counterpart, is on Jason Moyo St between 8th and 9th Aves. Book Centre, on 8th Ave between Main and Jason Moyo Sts, has a more sophisticated selection, including a range of Africa-theme books and pulp novels. One block west on Fort St is the Matopos Book Centre, a primarily Christian and school textbook shop which sells the cheapest postcards in Bulawayo.

You'll also find a couple of book exchanges. The best is probably Book Mart at 103 George Silundika St, which has a good selection of books and is slightly cheaper than its main rival, Page One, on Main St. Both these places also buy used books at decent prices, but the third option, Bookworm, pays much less.

For maps, go to the Surveyor General in the Tredgold Building on the corner of Fort St and Leopold Takawira Ave. You can't miss this place; just look for the passport queue winding around the block.

Camping Equipment Eezee Kamping, near the corner of 10th Ave and George Silundika St, is probably the best outdoors shop in Zimbabwe, which isn't really saying a lot. If you prefer to hire camping equipment, try Iverson's (☎ 61644) on the Khami road west of town, which hires everything from tents and stoves to warm clothing.

Left Luggage You can leave luggage at the railway station indefinitely for just US$0.15 per piece per day.

Emergency Services The emergency services number in Bulawayo is (☎ 99). The best equipped and most accessible hospital is Bulawayo Central (☎ 72111) on St Lukes Ave, Kumalo suburb, near the Ascot Race Course.

Dangers & Annoyances More laid-back than Harare, Bulawayo is also more amenable security-wise. Still, there are a couple of potential trouble spots. Lone women should avoid remote parts of Centenary and Central parks at any time of day, and no one should walk alone between the city centre and the Municipal Caravan Park & Campsite after dark. Caution should be exercised if you must walk there during the day.

Centenary & Central Parks
The vast spreads of Central and Centenary parks, separating Bulawayo's commercial centre from the up-market suburbs, provide a lunchtime green fix for harried city office workers, a nap spot for idle hours and spacious playing fields for children. Centenary Park further caters to the younger set with a playground, a miniature railway and a model boating pond. It also contains an aviary and well-tended botanical gardens, as well as the Museum of Natural History and the Bulawayo Theatre. Central Park, on the other hand, offers some areas of true bushland as well as shady lawns, benches and a few small garden areas. The Municipal Caravan Park & Campsite is in a fenced enclosure in Central Park.

City Hall Square
Along the Fife St footpath at City Hall Square, street souvenir hawkers, needleworkers, artists and flower vendors display their wares. The city hall building itself houses the Bulawayo Publicity Association

as well as city council chambers and the Bulawayo archives.

Museum of Natural History
Bulawayo's famous Museum of Natural History in Centenary Park probably merits an entire day of exploration. Every sort of wildlife indigenous to Zimbabwe and southern Africa – birds, antelopes, predators, fish, reptiles (a few of which are still alive) and even (they claim) the world's second largest stuffed elephant – is represented in well-realised displays and dioramas. One room is dedicated entirely to bugs. In all, 75,000 animal specimens are on display.

Historical displays include facets of both African and European cultures, arts and artefacts. One section is dedicated to prehistoric humanity, and others to weaponry ancient and modern, mining and geology. In one corner, an artificial mine emphasises Zimbabwe's considerable mineral wealth and explains extraction methods through the ages. There's also an extensive collection of rock and mineral specimens, with geological explanations of Zimbabwe's most prominent features.

The museum is open from 9 am to 5 pm daily except Christmas and Good Friday. Foreigners pay US$2 admission.

Railway Museum
To tell the story of rail in Zimbabwe, the Railway Museum houses a collection of historic steam locomotives, old railway offices and buildings, passenger carriages and a model of a historic railway station with period furnishings. Don't miss Cecil Rhodes' opulent private carriage, which dates to the 1890s, or the £2556 'Service Coach' number 0831. Then there's the especially beautiful 9B Class Locomotive number 115, built at the North British Loco Co in 1912 and sold for £8124.

Although it's within walking distance of the centre, the Railway Museum is lost in the railroad tracks and roughly defined streets of the Raylton suburb. The quickest route is the roundabout circuit through the railway station and across myriad tracks. Ask directions at every opportunity.

The museum is open from 9.30 am to noon and 2 to 4 pm Tuesday to Friday, and weekends from 3 to 5 pm. This museum has managed to resist multi-tier pricing; admission is still just US$0.15.

Die-hard rail buffs can join the engineers in the steam locomotives that chug around Bulawayo. Pick up a photography permit and make arrangements with the National Railways of Zimbabwe publicity officer, on the 6th floor of the National Railways Headquarters on Fife St.

Douslin House & the Bulawayo Art Gallery

The imposing Douslin House, on the corner of Main St and Leopold Takawira Ave, is one of Bulawayo's finest buildings. Originally known as the Willoughby Building, this beautiful colonial structure was completed in 1900 and first occupied the following year by the Willoughby Consolidated Co, a mining and ranching firm. Thanks to the cost of cement at the time of construction, the foundations extend only 15 cm below the surface.

In 1956, the building was taken over by the African Associated Mines and was given the riveting name of Asbestos House. In 1980, it was purchased by the Bulawayo Art Gallery and the name was changed again, this time to Douslin House in honour of William Douslin, its original architect.

The building now contains the Bulawayo Art Gallery, with a permanent collection which includes some excellent modern African art and Matabeleland material crafts. Many paintings are the work of Bulawayo artists. The gallery is open from 10 am to 5 pm Tuesday to Friday and Sunday, and on Saturday from 10 am to noon. Admission is US$0.15 and believe it or not, students get a discount.

Mzilikazi Arts & Crafts Centre & Bulawayo Home Industries

The Mzilikazi Arts & Crafts Centre is a Bulawayo highlight. It was originally established by the city of Bulawayo in 1963 to provide art training for otherwise latent talent. You'll be amazed at the concentration of artistic ability in this one institution, which in places seems more like a museum than a school (indeed, there is a small museum, where the best of recent students' work is displayed). The current full-time enrolment stands at about 150 with nearly 500 school-age children attending part-time classes. Proceeds from sales are ploughed back into the school.

Free guided tours are conducted Monday to Friday from 10 am to 12.30 pm and 2 to 5 pm, except during school holidays. The school is divided into ceramics and stoneware, painting, iron and stone sculpting and carving classrooms, and you can watch the work emerge almost effortlessly. Pottery and stoneware seconds are available for pleasantly low prices from the office shop.

Across the lawn beside the library is Bulawayo Home Industries, where you can watch artesans weaving rugs and producing sweaters, needlecraft, batik, crochet, tapestries and other home arts. The centre was originally set up for widows, divorcees and abandoned and elderly women with no other means of support, and was subsidised by the city council. It now pays for itself, selling choice items for less than curio shop prices. It's open 9 am to 4 pm weekdays.

Mzilikazi and Bulawayo Home Industries are three km from the town centre. Take the Mpilo or Barbour Fields (marked BF) bus from the Lobengula St terminus and get off at either Bulawayo Home Industries or the Mzilikazi Primary School.

Hillside Dams

The two Hillside Dams, five km from the centre on Hillside Rd, are now dry for much of the year. They were once popular for picnics and braais in the surrounding rock kopjes and gardens, and the aloe gardens were great for strolling in. Unfortunately, there has been a high incidence of crime, including muggings; maintenance has slackened off and few people bother going there now. If you'd still like a look at them, take

ZIMBABWE

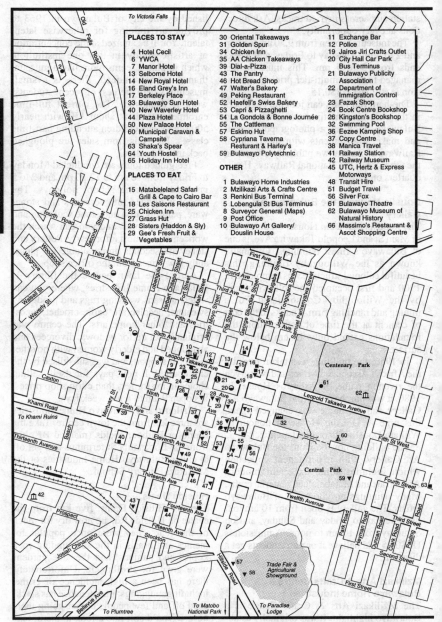

PLACES TO STAY

4 Hotel Cecil
6 YWCA
7 Manor Hotel
13 Selborne Hotel
14 New Royal Hotel
16 Eland Grey's Inn
17 Berkeley Place
33 Bulawayo Sun Hotel
40 New Waverley Hotel
44 Plaza Hotel
50 New Palace Hotel
60 Municipal Caravan &
   Campsite
63 Shaka's Spear
64 Youth Hostel
65 Holiday Inn Hotel

PLACES TO EAT

15 Matabeleland Safari
   Grill & Cape to Cairo Bar
18 Les Saisons Restaurant
25 Chicken Inn
27 Grass Hut
28 Sisters (Haddon & Sly)
29 Gee's Fresh Fruit &
   Vegetables

30 Oriental Takeaways
31 Golden Spur
34 Chicken Inn
35 AA Chicken Takeaways
39 Dial-a-Pizza
43 The Pantry
46 Hot Bread Shop
47 Walter's Bakery
49 Peking Restaurant
52 Haefeli's Swiss Bakery
53 Capri & Pizzaghetti
54 La Gondola & Bonne Journée
55 The Cattleman
57 Eskimo Hut
58 Cypriana Taverna
   Resturant & Harley's
59 Bulawayo Polytechnic

OTHER

1 Bulawayo Home Industries
2 Mzilikazi Arts & Crafts Centre
3 Renkini Bus Terminal
5 Lobengula St Bus Terminus
8 Surveyor General (Maps)
9 Post Office
10 Bulawayo Art Gallery/
   Douslin House

11 Exchange Bar
12 Police
19 Jairos Jiri Crafts Outlet
20 City Hall Car Park
   Bus Terminus
21 Bulawayo Publicity
   Association
22 Department of
   Immigration Control
23 Fazak Shop
24 Book Centre Bookshop
26 Kingston's Bookshop
32 Swimming Pool
36 Eezee Kamping Shop
37 Copy Centre
38 Manica Travel
41 Railway Station
42 Railway Museum
45 UTC, Hertz & Express
   Motorways
48 Transit Hire
51 Budget Travel
56 Silver Fox
61 Bulawayo Theatre
62 Bulawayo Museum of
   Natural History
66 Massimo's Restaurant &
   Ascot Shopping Centre

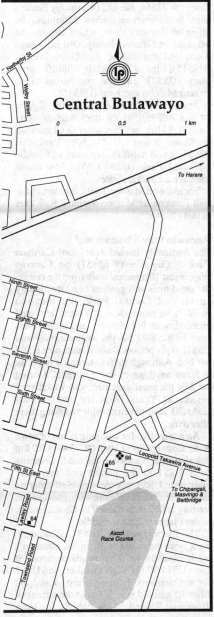

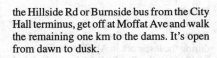

Central Bulawayo

0   0.5   1 km

To Harare

To Chipangali,
Masvingo &
Beitbridge

Leopold Takawira Avenue

65   66

Fifth St East

64

Ascot
Race Course

the Hillside Rd or Burnside bus from the City Hall terminus, get off at Moffat Ave and walk the remaining one km to the dams. It's open from dawn to dusk.

Mabukuwene Nature Reserve

This 12-hectare park in Burnside provides a bit of bushland within city limits. In addition to a range of indigenous trees, plants and bird life, there's a wild aloe garden and a gazebo with a view across the entire city. It lies one km west of Burnside Rd, via Chipping Way.

Old Bulawayo

Currently in progress is a project to develop a historic theme park around the ruins of Old Bulawayo and the nearby Jesuit Mission, 18 km south of town along Hillside/Burnside Rd. This was the site of the first town constructed by Ndebele king Lobengula, which was occupied until 1881. You can still see the walls of the old Jesuit mission, the remains of several hut floors and the stone walls of Lobengula's wagon garage. The plan is to restore the settlement to its former appearance. It's scheduled for completion in 1996, so if you prefer your ruins in ruins, go soon.

Lobengula's Kraal

The original Bulawayo was established by Lobengula in 1881, at the site of the present-day State House. In 1886, however, it was burned as the chief fled the approaching BSAC forces. All that remains of his kraal is the Indaba tree, which oddly escaped the fire. It was here that he met with his tribal council to conduct official business. There's now a small museum in a rondavel constructed for Cecil Rhodes on one of his official visits.

The kraal is in the Highmount suburb north of town. Take any bus headed out on Lady Stanley Ave (the new Vic Falls road) and get off at State House drive. On foot, it's a good 40-minute walk from the centre. Before traipsing out there, check current opening times with the Bulawayo Publicity Association.

ZIMBABWE

Events
Bulawayo's main annual event is the Zimbabwe International Trade Fair, held during the last week in April or the first week in May at the Trade Fair & Agricultural Society Show Ground where Samuel Parirenyatwa and Robert Mugabe Sts become Hillside Rd. This well-attended event draws at least 200,000 visitors and 1000 exhibitors from around Zimbabwe and worldwide, with displays and booths on technology and commercial ventures. A number of peripheral events provide further entertainment.

Organised Tours
An increasing number of companies are offering day tours in and around Bulawayo. UTC (☎ 61402), on the corner of 14th Ave and George Silundika St, operates half-day city tours for US$11, which take in the Museum of Natural History, Centenary Park, the Mzilikazi Art & Craft Centre and Bulawayo Home Industries, or just the Museum of Natural History and the Railway Museum for US$7. Other excursions include Khami Ruins (US$13); Chipangali (US$11); and half/full-day tours of Matobo National Park.

Black Rhino Safaris (☎ 41662) runs tours to Khami Ruins for US$16 and to Chipangali for US$11. Although lots of companies have started Matobo tours in recent years, Black Rhino's (US$22) is still the best and most enthusiastic.

A unique option for culture-oriented tours is Eddie's Tours (☎ 66660; fax 65016), which does two half-day city tours: architecturally interesting buildings (US$10), and the Museum of Natural History and the Railway museum (US$10). Other offerings include trips to Old Bulawayo Kraal (US$12); Bulawayo's high-density suburbs (US$10); Khami Ruins (US$12); Chipangali and nearby communal lands (US$20); Cyrene Mission and nearby communal lands (US$20); and a tour of cultural self-help programmes (US$20). Half/full-day tours of Matobo National Park with a historical and cultural emphasis are US$15/20.

Similar tours are available from Mzingeli Tours (☎ 77244; fax 68214), run by Eddie's aunt. In addition to Eddies' offerings, she offers all-day city tours, which include the Museum of Natural History, Old Bulawayo Kraal and the unique Amakhosi Theatre (US$15); trips to Tshabalala Wildlife Sanctuary (US$7); and the communal lands around Matobo and Kezi (US$15).

Another option is *Africa Dawn Safaris* (☎ /fax 46696), which does half-day city tours (US$10); half-day tours to Chipangali or Khami Ruins: (US$12.50); Tshabalala (US$13); and half/full-day tours of Matobo National Park (US$15/25). Ask about special backpackers' rates.

For more on Matobo Tours, turn to Organised Tours under Matobo National Park later in this chapter.

Places to Stay – bottom end
The frequently lauded *Municipal Caravan Park & Campsite* (☎ 63851), on Caravan Way, is just 10 minutes' walk from the centre. Set amid trees and gardens in a large grassy enclave of Central Park, the location couldn't be more ideal. It's clean and well guarded, with hot showers and baths. Sites cost US$2.50/3.50 per tent/caravan and US$1.70 per person. Basic chalets cost US$7 per bed. Although theft is rare, it's not wise to leave anything of value in tents. During the day, the guards are happy to watch your rucksack. Taxis from the centre cost US$1.30. Don't even consider walking there after dark.

An alternative for camping is out of town at the *Country Rest Camp* (☎ 73491), 19 km out along the Victoria Falls road. Camping costs US$1.50 per person and dormitory beds cost US$4 per person. Self-catering chalets for four people are very good value, starting at US$9. See also The Coach House, under Places to Stay – middle.

The *Youth Hostel* (☎ 76488), 20 minutes' walk from the centre, is in an old house in a predominantly wealthy neighbourhood. It costs US$1.30 for YHA members and US$2 for nonmembers, but guests are locked out from 10 am to 5 pm. It's near the corner of Townsend Rd and 3rd St (which, for some unfathomable reason, is an extension of 12th Ave). The 10.30 pm curfew is strictly enforced. You can choose between dorms and family rooms. There's a TV lounge, cooking facilities and hot showers. With luggage, it's a long walk from the railway station, but taxis are inexpensive and there's an infrequent Waterford bus from City Hall.

The rollicking *Shaka's Spear* (☎ 61385), at Leopold Takawira 232, is Bulawayo's most popular backpackers' haunt, thanks mainly to its enthusiastic proprietors, Karen and Henry Meinie. The atmosphere of this amazing place is a bit like a return to Kathmandu in the early 1970s–without the noxious weeds, of course. Dorm beds cost US$4.50, including access to cooking and laundry facilities, and the bar, pool table, dart board, juke box, library, luggage storage and TV. Breakfasts and dinners cost an additional US$2.50 each; a total package, with dinner, bed and breakfast is US$7.

At 11 Inverleith Dr in Burnside (4.5 km from the centre) is the friendly, secure and quiet *Paradise Lodge* (☎ 46481) run by Allan Burke. Dorm beds cost US$6.50 per person including use of the pool, sun deck, barbecue, videos and laundry and cooking facilities. In addition, there are two private 'honeymoon suites' with their own facilities. Basic groceries are sold at the lodge and barbecues are held regularly. Allan makes several trips into town daily and is happy to pick you up from the centre, but special trips cost US$2.50. The entrance is only 200 metres from Mabukuwene Park.

A bit more expensive is the *YWCA* (☎ 60185), on Lobengula St, which accepts men and women. They charge US$8 for bed and breakfast in a private room and US$1.30 for dinner. Monthly rates are US$70/74 for singles/doubles.

With the exception of Berkely Place, bottom-end hotels aren't really an option for women travelling alone. The cheapest hotel is the *New Waverley Hotel* (☎ 60033), on the corner of Lobengula St and 12th Ave, charging US$8/11 single/double. This place is noisy, but the bar is one of the Bulawayo's liveliest night spots – and if you need a break,

you can take advantage of their openly advertised two-hour 'resting rooms' for US$3.50.

Next up is the *New Palace Hotel* (☎ 64294) on Jason Moyo St, starting at US$9/12 without/with bath, for a single or double. All rooms include breakfast. Just a touch more plush is the *Plaza Hotel* (☎ 64280), at 14th Ave and Jason Moyo St, with basic singles/doubles without bath for US$14/15.50; with bath they will cost you US$16.50/18.

The basic *Manor Hotel* (☎ 61001) on Lobengula St has single/double rooms with bath for US$15/16 and without bath for US$14/17; all rates include breakfast. Another good bet, with only favourable reports, is the friendly and secure *Berkeley Place* (☎ 67701). Singles or doubles without/with shower and sink cost US$10/13. No alcohol is served on the premises, and it's hassle-free and safe for women travelling alone.

If you have a car, you may enjoy the basic new 'bush camp' accommodation at *Chipangali Wildlife Orphanage* (☎ 70764). Single/double bungalows with cooking facilities cost US$5/6. For access, see Around Bulawayo.

Places to Stay – middle

The *Hotel Cecil* (☎ 60295), on the corner of Fife St and 3rd Ave, straddles the middle and lower ranges, charging US$15/17 for singles/doubles with private bath, including bed and breakfast. There's also a good restaurant with a noisy disco attached. It's comfortable enough and fairly clean, and is one of Bulawayo's best deals. However, the doors don't always lock well and security can be a problem. The two-star *New Royal Hotel* (☎ 65764) near the corner of George Silundika St and 6th Ave charges US$25/29 for singles/doubles.

The popular *Eland Grey's Inn* (☎ 60121) on Robert Mugabe St near Leopold Takawira Ave charges US$22/26 for singles or doubles without/with bath. Unfortunately, when this research was done their exchange rates weren't favourable, their meals were not of

Baobab Tree

a high standard and some of the clientele were intoxicated much of the time.

The *Selborne Hotel* (☎ 65471), an old favourite on the corner of Leopold Takawira Ave and George Silundika St, has gone downhill is recent years. Single/double rooms cost US$26/34, including breakfast. Ask for a room with a veranda facing the street; the smaller rooms in the back are within earshot of the clunky kitchen fans.

South-east of the centre, at 16 Fortunes Gate Rd in Matsheumhlope is *Induna Lodge* (☎ 45684; fax 45627). Single/double rooms cost US$32/48 with bed and breakfast. Add an elaborate dinner and the price climbs to US$54/83.

Although it's better known for its restaurant, the New Orleans, *Banff Lodge* (☎ 43176; fax 43177), in a quiet residential area of Bulawayo, is also a guest house. Single/double rooms cost US$23/30 with bed and breakfast.

For a peaceful break, *The Coach House* (☎ 26009), in a beautiful setting 27 km out on the Airport road, is recommended. The name should be taken literally; it's a repository for a collection of coaches and horse-drawn vehicles which have been used

in several Zimbabwean films. It's run by a friendly local couple, Bill and Elizabeth MacKinney. Camping with use of braai pits and cooking facilities costs an additional US$4 per tent or caravan plus US$4 per person. You can also hire tents or on-site caravans for US$4 per person. Double guest rooms cost US$17 with breakfast. Horse-riding is also available.

Another out-of-town option is the two-star *Hotel Rio* (☎ 41384; fax 49407), 11 km from the centre on the Old Esigodini road. When it was built in 1933, the location of this pleasant hotel was determined by early Bulawayo liquor laws, which permitted only out-of-town 'travellers' inns to serve alcohol on Sunday. Singles/doubles are US$28/33, plus US$2 for colour television.

Places to Stay – top end

Bulawayo's most imposing hotel, the *Bulawayo Sun* (☎ 60101; fax 61739), is a centrally located tower that serves as Bulawayo's business and package-tour hotel. However, the three-tier pricing system makes it inordinately expensive for foreigners, who pay US$102/150 for a single/double room (as opposed to the local rate of US$35/50). Note that identical standards are available at the Cresta Churchill for a fraction of the price.

The imitation Tudor *Cresta Churchill* (☎ 41016; fax 44247), five km out on Matopos Rd, is probably the best deal in town, but its location necessitates the use of taxis to and from the centre. Both locals and foreigners pay US$34/47 for single/double rooms.

The third up-market hotel, which is convenient to Ascot Shopping Centre is the *Holiday Inn* (☎ 72464; fax 44247). It's well out of town – a half-hour walk from City Hall – so it's probably not practical unless you have a vehicle or are prepared to use taxis. For single/double rooms, foreigners pay US$110/162 while Zimbabwe residents pay US$38/54.

For a foray into decadence, consider the luxurious *Nesbitt Castle* (☎ 42726; fax

41864), a cross between a medieval castle and an English country estate, at 6 Percy Ave in Hillside. It was constructed at the turn of the century by a former mayor of Bulawayo. Amenities include a sauna, gymnasium, library, gardens, swimming pool and billiards room. Breakfasts are served with champagne and each of the nine rooms has suite-like proportions. Foreigners pay US$185 per person for dinner, bed and breakfast. Zimbabwe residents pay US$84 per person. Only advance bookings are accepted.

If you prefer a safari-lodge atmosphere, there's *Chief's Lodge* (☎ 26110; fax 78784), formerly known as N'tabazinduna Lodge, 16 km outside Bulawayo on the Harare road, then east on N'tabazinduna Rd for five km to the lodge. The name means 'hill of chiefs' and it was here that Bulawayo got its reputation as 'the killing place'. Before they started the project, the owners consulted with the local *nganga* (witch doctor), to learn about the implications of building on a sacred site. Apparently, the chiefs were pleased to be commemorated in that way.

Don't be put off by the directions in their brochure ('go past the MacDonald Works...the United Portland Cement factory...the Oka Enterprises garage...the Imbizio barracks...'); it's not on an industrial site. Solar-powered bush lodges cost US$100 per person, including meals, transfers, game drives, guided walks and tours to Khami Ruins, Matobo National Park and other area sites. With just full board and game drives, the price is US$60; with dinner, bed and breakfast, it's US$40. Transfers from town cost US$15 each way. Locals and South Africans do get substantial discounts.

Places to Eat
Breakfast If you're after coffee, try the friendly and interestingly decorated *Grass Hut* on Fife St between 8th and 9th Aves. Their breakfast menu is also good value and includes eggs, omelettes, bacon, sausages and several toast concoctions.

Bonne Journée, on Robert Mugabe St between 10th and 11th Aves, serves up an impressive English breakfast for US$2.50 per person. If you're really hungry, however, visit the *Homestead Restaurant*'s breakfast buffet in the Bulawayo Sun Hotel between 7 and 10 am. All you can eat of their ample spread costs US$5. The continental breakfast is just US$3. Note that they serve real, unadulterated coffee.

Pizzaghetti near the corner of 11th Ave and George Silundika St serves set English breakfasts from 7 to 10 am for US$3. If your head and disposition are suffering from too much Saturday night action, *Oasis* on the corner of 9th Ave and Josiah Tongogara St puts on a therapeutic 'Babalazi Breakfast' for US$3.

Lunch & Snacks Bulawayo has a range of takeaway places, but naturally, some are better than others. *AA Chicken Takeaways*, on Robert Mugabe St between 9th and 10th Aves, isn't bad for chicken, samosas, soft drinks and (rather greasy) chips. *Oriental Takeaways*, near the corner of George Silundika St and 8th Ave, is one of the best. Herbivores will welcome the opportunity to fill up on vegetarian burgers, samosas and other excellent vegetarian and curry options. Near the corner of 12th Ave and Fife St, the *Hot Bread Shop* serves ordinary takeaway meals as well as more creative concoctions. It's good for something different and one reader has written: 'I returned three times in a single afternoon – proof of its excellence'. Chinese standards are the speciality at the frankly named *Tunku's Chop Suey Centre* in the City Building, on 8th Ave between Robert Mugabe St and George Silundika St. For traditional Zimbabwean fare, try *The Pantry*, open from 5 am to 3 pm on 15th Ave between Main and Fort Sts. Another local possibility is the patio bar at the *New Palace Hotel*, which serves basic African meals and lots of beer.

The ultimate trendy – albeit expensive – takeaway is *Eskimo Hut* on Hillside Rd near the Trade Fair & Agricultural Showground.

For a pizza to take away, go for the recommended *Dial-a-Pizza* (☎ 66847 or 76803) at 101 Lobengula St opposite the Manor Hotel.

It's open daily from 10 am to 9 pm and they deliver anywhere in Bulawayo.

If you don't mind playing guinea pig for cooking students, try the *Bulawayo Polytechnic School* around the corner from the caravan park, which serves inexpensive and potentially great three-course lunches for US$2, including a starter, main course and a sweet. It's closed for school holidays in May and August.

The Portuguese-owned *Bonne Journée*, on Robert Mugabe St between 10th and 11th Aves, opposite the cinemas, serves impressive ice cream confections – thick shakes, banana splits, iced coffee – as well as meals, which include steaks, burgers, chicken, omelettes and standard snacks like chips and hot dogs. Unless you're after a steak, you can fill up here for US$2 to US$4.

Another place for sweet treats is *Collectible's Coffee Shop* on Josiah Tongogara St between 11th and 12th Aves. They're great for the goodies – chocolate cake, quiche, biscuits and muffins – but not so hot with the more mainstream items like ploughman's lunches. The friendly *Golden Teapot* in the One-Stop Co-op, on the corner of 11th Ave and Main St, serves snacks, refreshments, light meals and hot drinks.

Although it was once a great lunch venue, *Pizzaghetti*, near the corner of 11th Ave and George Silundika St, has now declined. At the time of this research, their selection of pasta was small and their salad platters had increased in price but decreased in volume. The décor is still worth a look, however – sort of a cross between provincial bathroom and contemporary industrial – and the chairs are certainly industrial strength. They're open 7 am to 11 pm, with 24-hour takeaway service.

For English-style teas and excellent light lunches, including small but well-conceived buffets for under US$2, you can't beat *Sisters*, on the second floor of Haddon & Sly department store. Not to be outdone, *Meikles*, on the corner of Jason Moyo St and Leopold Takawira Ave, does a similar set-up. Light pub meals are also available at the *Old Vic Pub* at the Bulawayo Sun Hotel.

The clean *YWCA* on Lobengula St is open to nonresidents for lunch between 12.30 and 3 pm. For around US$1, you'll get a filling plate of sadza ladled over with the relish of the day, normally some sort of beef stew.

Chicken Inn, with branches on the corner of 9th Ave and Robert Mugabe St, and on the corner of 8th Ave and Jason Moyo St, is mainly a hang-out for local teens. Along with the video games and billiard tables, they do cover the chicken and chips market fairly well. The other fast-food chain is *Wimpy*, which serves greasy burgers at two Bulawayo outlets.

Dinner One of the city's nicest restaurants is the *Capri* (☎ 68639), on the corner of 11th Ave and George Silundika St. They make Italian dishes, and serve free garlic bread and vegetable starters while you're waiting. The wine list includes expensive South African wines as well as the best Zimbabwean vintages at more reasonable prices. It's open at 6.30 pm nightly for dinner. It may appear closed – the door is locked for security purposes – but if you knock through the grating, they'll open it up.

Another recommended Italian place is *La Gondola* (☎ 62986), on Robert Mugabe St between 10th and 11th Aves. Their fare and prices are comparable to those at the Capri, and their service is particularly good. A third Italian option, which is recommended by locals, is *Massimo's* in the Ascot Shopping Centre. A Mediterranean alternative is *Cypriana Taverna* (☎ 62081), on the Trade Fair grounds, with Cypriot and Greek cuisine. The best meals must be ordered 24 hours in advance. For Spanish food, there's *Granada* (☎ 70716) on the 1st floor of the Parkade Centre, on the corner of 9th Ave and Fife St. They're open Tuesday to Friday for lunch and dinner, Monday for lunch only and Saturday for dinner only.

An increasingly popular restaurant and night spot is the *Matabeleland Safari Grill* (☎ 72387) – also known as the *Cape-to-Cairo*, after its popular bar. This very tasteful colonial-theme bar and restaurant specialises in game dishes but they also do super steaks and laudable seafood and peri peri chicken. While you're in the bar, give your regards to Bishop, who has informally been proclaimed the 'best barman in Bulawayo'.

For Chinese food, the best choice is the *Peking* (☎ 60646) on Jason Moyo St, with tasty renditions of Sichuan and Cantonese fare. Plan on US$4 for a meat and rice dish or set-lunch specials with more food than most people require.

The *Homestead Restaurant* (☎ 60101) in the Bulawayo Sun Hotel is open from 12.30 to 2.30 pm for lunch and 6 to 10 pm for dinner. For steak and other meals heavy on Zimbabwean beef, try *The Cattleman* (☎ 76086) opposite the Bulawayo Sun Hotel on the corner of Josiah Tongogara St and 10th Ave, or the *Golden Spur* (☎ 70318) on Robert Mugabe St between 8th and 9th Aves.

The Highwayman (☎ 60121), at the Eland Grey's Inn, serves simple but recommended cuisine. Their inexpensive speciality seems to be Chicken Kiev with salad and chips, but the beef choices aren't bad either. *Buffalo Bill's* (a pizzeria and steak house) in the Selborne Hotel serves steaks for US$4, pizza for around US$2.50 and has a salad or dessert bar for US$1.50 each. It's popular with travellers.

Haute cuisine in Bulawayo comes in three forms – à la *Les Saisons* (☎ 77292) on Josiah Tongogara St between 6th and Leopold Takawira Aves, *Maison Nic* (☎ 61884) on Main St near 4th Ave, or *New Orleans* (☎ 43176) on Banff Rd in Hillside. The best is Les Saisons, a newish place run by the former owner of Maison Nic (which, under his tutelage, took Zimbabwe's Best Restaurant Award year after year). Despite the exclusive atmosphere, prices aren't prohibitive. Try the antelope venison or the nicely prepared vegetarian options and fish dishes, including Malawi *chambo*, Kariba bream and whitebait. The new *Maison Nic* is still acceptable, however, and a bit cheaper. The New Orleans serves continental and Cajun cuisine (inasmuch as it can be reproduced in Zimbabwe). Advance bookings are recommended for all these places.

Self-Catering For cheap fruit and vegetables the best place is Makokoba market beyond Renkini bus terminal. The best selection of produce is at *Gee's* on 8th Ave between George Silundika and Fife Sts.

General groceries are available on the ground floor of *Haddon & Sly* on the corner of 8th Ave and Fife St, or try one of the numerous small family owned shops scattered throughout the city centre. For refined tastes, the supermarket at Ascot Centre is probably the best stocked in town.

Wholemeal bread, doughnuts, European-style cakes, pies and pastries are found at *Haefeli's Swiss Bakery* on Fife St between 10th and 11th Aves. Get there early, however, since they're sometimes sold out by mid-morning.

Also highly recommended is *Walter's Bakery* at 124 Robert Mugabe St. A reader writes, 'Definitely try Walter's. The bread comes in many varieties (including good Portugese) and it has a lot of characters.'

My budget didn't allow for much eating out, and so I was particularly happy to discover Chunks (vegetable protein). Any self-catering traveller, and especially vegetarians, would do well to take a bag of these along – they're lightweight, cheap, rich in protein and easy to prepare, even though they look something like dog food when you buy them. Basically, you just add hot water and salt and let them soak, and they taste very much like ground beef. They're good with noodles and in an emergency, you can even eat them dry. In Bulawayo, you'll find 500-gram bags at ABC, the Seventh-Day Adventist store on Herbert Chitepo St between 9th and 10th Aves.

Really dedicated health-food people can stock up at a place appropriately called Industrial Mining Supplies, on the corner of 12th Ave and Fife St. They also stock Chunks, as well as soy milk, fructose, wholewheat noodles and vegetarian seasoning in 'environmentally friendly packaging', which the uninitiated might call a plastic bag.

Susan Loucks, USA

Entertainment
Nightspots Compared to their Harare counterparts, Bulawayo pubs and clubs are more sticky about 'smart casual dress' requirements. That means (after 4.30 pm) no open-top shoes, no trainers, no denim and

nothing that could remotely be construed as grubby. If you're not equipped with a neat, clean and tidy wardrobe – and few backpackers are – resign yourself to drinking and dancing at the seedier places where you'll get a more representative taste of Bulawayo nightlife anyway.

The Alabama, around the side of the Bulawayo Sun Hotel, is a pleasant and normally crowded bar with live jazz music almost every evening. Fortunately, the smart-casual dress code is very loosely enforced. The Top of the Sun offers live music nightly and a more up-market atmosphere than the Alabama.

A popular place with local people is the Exchange Bar near the corner of Leopold Takawira Ave and Jason Moyo St, with separate bars for men and women. Another good evening drinking venue is the bar at the Palace Hotel.

The Italian restaurants, Capri and La Gondola, have music and dancing on weekends, but they cater mainly for senior crowds. When you tire of dancing, the satellite television at the pool hall beside the Capri constantly plays sports broadcasts.

The Silver Fox, on the corner of 10th Ave and Robert Mugabe St, has a reputation as a sleaze lounge. It's open for disco dancing until 3 am Monday to Saturday, and until midnight on Sunday. Foreign visitors are a real novelty. The more lively New Waverley Hotel has frequent live performances, but it's definitely not for unaccompanied women (even accompanied women may receive a measure of hassle).

For Saturday-night disco dancing, a respectable option is Talk of the Town in the Monte Carlo Building on the corner of Fife St and 12th Ave; no jeans or trainers are allowed. For a glimpse of the Rhodie teen scene, check out Harley's (formerly Catch 22) at the International Trade Fair Grounds. Unaccompanied women shouldn't walk to or from this place after dark.

The hotels all have bars and/or cocktail lounges. For Anglo-Zimbabwean atmosphere, try the Old Vic Pub in the Bulawayo Sun Hotel or the Knight's Arms in the Holiday Inn. Picasso's in the Granada Restaurant, on the 1st floor of the Parkade Centre on the corner of Fife St and 9th Ave is also reputedly atmospheric.

For a very enjoyable local scene, go to the public bar at the Cresta Churchill on a Friday night. There's live music and if they're featuring a well-known name, it can be fabulous. This is one of Zimbabwe's most integrated bars and is popular with locals of all walks of life.

Cinemas Bulawayo offers a relatively good choice of quality cinema. The best are the Kine 600 and Elite 400 on Robert Mugabe St between 10th and 11th Aves, the Rainbow Vistarama on Fife St between 11th and 12th Aves and the Seven-Arts on Jason Moyo St between 10th and 11th Aves. The Bulawayo Art Gallery occasionally sponsors lunchtime films – enquire at the gallery or the Publicity Association.

Alliance Française de Bulawayo (☎ 30814 after 5 pm) at 60 Josiah Tongogara St screens French films with English subtitles several times a month. They also have a lending library open on Saturday from 11.15 am to noon and offer French evening classes for adults.

Theatre The Bulawayo Theatre (☎ 65393) in Centenary Park stages dramatic productions and occasionally hosts visiting troupes. Phone for information on current productions or consult the *Daily Chronicle* or *Bulawayo This Month.*

Sport Every imaginable sport has some sort of following in Bulawayo and they've set up a club to accommodate it. *Bulawayo This Month* lists all the clubs; for further information on their activities, contact numbers and meeting times, check with the Publicity Association.

Golf is available at the Bulawayo Country Club, the Bulawayo Golf Club and the Harry Allen Golf Club, all within a few km of the city centre.

On the corner of 9th Ave and Fort St is a gymnasium (with a weights room, aerobics classes, a sauna and squash courts) charging very reasonable daily, weekly and monthly rates for use of all equipment.

The municipal swimming pool in Central Park on Samuel Parirenyatwa St is open from late August to late May between 10 am and 2 pm and from 3 to 6 pm. They charge US$0.25 for as long as you'd like to swim.

Catch horseracing at Ascot on alternating Sunday afternoons.

Things to Buy

The Jairos Jiri Crafts outlet, at the eastern end of City Hall Car Park, sells the work of disabled Zimbabwean artists and offers good value on Ndebele pottery and basketry. You'll also find unique and surprisingly inexpensive Batonka stools from western Kariba, as well as all the standard curios.

The largest curio shop in town is Fazak on Main St, opposite the post office, but they mostly sell T-shirts, mass-produced kitsch and curios that usually you can buy for a fraction of the price along the road near Victoria Falls. For an interesting selection of African beadwork, go to Buhlaluse, in the Tshabalala suburb about six km from the centre near the Khami road.

Two readers have the following suggestion:

There's a fantastic tape available in Bulawayo called *Blue Skies Bulawayo*. It's a *Centenary Compilation*, a 'delightful and spirited collection of archives, revivals and contemporary music from Bulawayo between 1948 and 1994'. It's most readily available for US$4 (Z$30) at the new National Gallery in Douslin House. Alternatively, you can order it from the producer, Phaphama Promotions (☎ 78159; fax 78053), PO Box 2792, Bulawayo.

Joost Butenop & Astrid Pohl, Germany

Getting There & Away

Air Air Zimbabwe connects Bulawayo to all major airports in the country, with two or three flights daily to and from Harare; daily flights except on Monday to Hwange National Park, with connections to Victoria Falls, and twice weekly to Johannesburg. From Harare, there are easy connections to Kariba and Lusaka, Zambia.

Bus The long-distance private bus terminal is Renkini musika on the 6th Ave Extension, opposite the Mzilikazi police station. Domestic buses to Harare, Masvingo, Beitbridge and Victoria Falls depart daily between 6 and 7 am or when full. Try to arrive at least an hour earlier than you want to leave, and two hours earlier on holidays and weekends when everyone in town, it seems, is trying to squeeze onto the few conveyances.

Each morning, three Hwange Special Express buses depart from Renkini when full for Gwaai River, Safari Crossroads (for Hwange National Park) and Victoria Falls. The fare to Safari Crossroads is US$6, to Victoria Falls, US$8.

For its terminal, Ajay's Motorways uses the Bulawayo Sun Hotel. Their service to Victoria Falls (US$7) via Gwaai River and Hwange Safari Lodge departs on Monday, Wednesday and Friday at 7 am. To Harare (US$11), they leave each day except Tuesday and Thursday at 8 am, arriving in Harare at 2 pm. On Tuesday, the Harare service departs at midday and arrives at 6 pm. Book Ajay's services through Manica Travel (☎ 62521) on 10th Ave between Main and Fort Sts.

Between Bulawayo and Harare, Express Motorways (☎ 61402) has one or two services daily, departing from City Hall Car Park. The trip takes seven hours and costs US$13. Make bookings at the UTC/Hertz office (☎ 61402) on the corner of 14th Ave and George Silundika St.

To Masvingo, ZUPCO leaves daily except Sunday from the Lobengula St terminus at 1 pm. From Masvingo, it continues to the Great Zimbabwe turn-off (about one km from Great Zimbabwe), arriving at around 7 pm. The fare is US$4. Shu-Shine leaves Renkini at 6 am for the same price.

To Francistown and Gaborone (Botswana), Chitanda & Sons runs twice weekly; book through Manica Travel Services (☎ 62521). On Thursday and Sunday, Express Motorways (☎ 61402) runs from the City Hall Car Park to Gaborone for US$35. In the opposite direction, they depart from

ZIMBABWE

the African Mall and the Gaborone Sun Hotel on Tuesday and Saturday at 6 am.

The Zimbabwe Omnibus Company (☎ 67291) at Lobengula St also has a daily (except Sunday) service from Bulawayo to Francistown, departing from the Lobengula St terminus between 8 and 10 am. Mach Coach Lines (☎ 60499) has a similar service daily at 4 pm.

To Johannesburg, Express Motorways (☎ 61402) has daily buses, leaving from City Hall Car Park at around 1 am and arriving around midday the following day. The fare is US$37 and advance bookings are essential. More comfortable are the Mini-Zim Luxury Mini-Coaches (☎ 76644), bookable through Budget Tours on the corner of Fife St and 10th Ave. They depart from the Holiday Inn on Wednesday and Sunday at 6.30 am and arrive at 5.15 pm the same day. The fare is US$45. There are also informal minibuses leaving for Johannesburg when full from City Hall Car Park; the fare is US$23.

Train Especially if you're bound for Johannesburg, book rail tickets well in advance and purchase them at least a week before travel or your reservations may be cancelled. At the railway station, bookings and ticket sales are handled at separate windows and if there's a queue, it will move slowly, so take something to read.

The daily trains between Bulawayo and Harare depart at 9 pm in both directions, arriving before 7 am the following day. To Hwange and Victoria Falls, the service departs at 7 pm, arriving at Dete (Hwange National Park) at 1.30 am and Victoria Falls at 7 am. From Victoria Falls, the train departs daily at 6.30 pm, passes Dete at 12.45 am and arrives in Bulawayo at 7.05 am. The 1st/2nd class one-way fares to Harare or Victoria Falls are US$9/6.

The daily train to Gaborone departs from Bulawayo in the afternoon and arrives the following morning. The fares to Gaborone are US$45/30/10 in 1st/2nd/economy class. The rail connection between Bulawayo and Johannesburg now passes through Beitbridge rather than Botswana. The service departs from Bulawayo at 9 am Sunday and arrives in Johannesburg at 8.02 am Monday. Only 1st and 2nd classes are available and advance bookings are essential. The 1st/2nd/economy class fares are US$76/55/35. For more information on both these routes, turn to the Zimbabwe Getting There & Away chapter earlier in the book. You must show your passport when making international bookings.

For information on schedules and bookings phone rail service enquiries (☎ 363111 day; ☎ 322284 after hours).

Getting Around

To/From the Airport The Air Zimbabwe bus runs between the Bulawayo Sun Hotel and the airport north of town for US$2 per person. Taxis cost at least US$5 each way.

Bus Bulawayo has two suburban bus termini. The City Hall Terminal on 8th Ave, between Robert Mugabe St and George Silundika Sts, serves the more affluent northern, eastern and southern suburbs. The published timetable is often inaccurate.

The other terminus is on the corner of Lobengula St and 6th Ave, and serves the high-density suburbs west and south-west of the centre. Buses can get extremely crowded and if you're in a hurry, it would probably be worth going by taxi.

City buses cost US$0.15 per ride. Emergency taxis ply set routes around the city but cannot operate outside city limits. They cost a set US$0.20 per ride, regardless of the destination.

Taxi Quite a few taxi services operate in Bulawayo. Most are metered, but on popular runs, you can normally bargain for a lower price. For example, expect to pay around US$1.50 from the railway station to the Municipal Caravan & Campsite. For bookings, phone Rixi Taxi (☎ 60666, 61933/4/5). Other companies are available on ☎ 72454, 60154 and 60704.

Bicycle The level countryside in and around Bulawayo is ideal for amateur cyclists. Hire mountain bikes from Transit Car & Truck Hire (☎ 76495), on the corner of 12th Ave and Robert Mugabe St, for US$3.60 per day. There's usually a US$13 returnable deposit and a US$0.65 insurance fee. Take a spin around the car park to check your bike before accepting it. If you pay by credit card, the deposit is waived.

Around Bulawayo

Bulawayo's surroundings contain some scenic and unusual landscapes, with balancing rocks and several ancient ruins and rock paintings. The highlight, of course, is Matobo National Park with its ample outdoor opportunities and rhino-rich game park. This impressive region once served as the spiritual capital of the Mwari-worshipping Rozwi Empire. Later, it so impressed Cecil John Rhodes, that he requested to be buried there.

TSHABALALA WILDLIFE SANCTUARY
Tshabalala, eight km from Bulawayo, is a small wildlife reserve. It was established on the former land holding of Fairburn Usher, a British sailor who arrived in 1883, and his Ndebele wife, who was one of the daughters of Lobengula. It's perfect for a relaxing day of close encounters with the more docile side of Zimbabwe wildlife. There are no large or dangerous predators – only antelopes, zebras, giraffes, warthogs and similar sorts – and both walking and horse-riding are permitted and encouraged. With a bit of imagination, the savanna scrub landscape will carry you far from the rigours of the city. Carry a picnic lunch – there are lots of picnic sites and braai pits – and plan on spending a full day.

Tshabalala is open from 6 am to 6 pm in the summer and 8 am to 5 pm in winter. Foreigners pay US$2.50 admission and horse hire costs US$2.50 per person per hour for groups of up to 11 people. You may cycle,

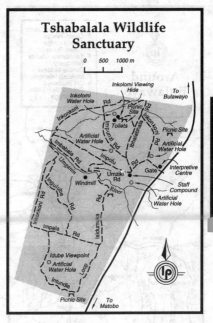

walk, or drive on the sanctuary roads, but no motorbikes are allowed.

Getting There & Away
To get there, hitching isn't bad but you'll have to get away from the congested area. The Kezi bus from Renkini Bus Terminal passes Tshabalala, and the Matobo Rd bus from City Hall Terminal can drop you at Retreat, just three km or so from Tshabalala.

CHIPANGALI WILDLIFE ORPHANAGE
Chipangali, 24 km from Bulawayo, was founded in 1973 by Viv Wilson and her son Kevin. It is intended to be a centre for the rearing of orphaned animals, primarily the offspring of poaching victims, and caring for injured, illegally captured or sick animals. The idea is to release them into the wild when they're able to cope. Unfortunately, it now feels more like a zoo than the Wilsons intended and it seems that many inmates may be there for good. The large walk-through

ZIMBABWE

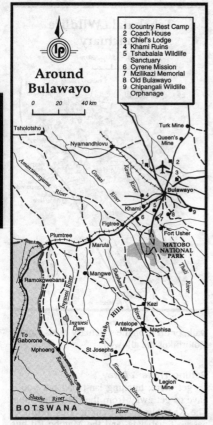

Around Bulawayo

0   20   40 km

1 Country Rest Camp
2 Coach House
3 Chief's Lodge
4 Khami Ruins
5 Tshabalala Wildlife
  Sanctuary
6 Cyrene Mission
7 Mzilikazi Memorial
8 Old Bulawayo
9 Chipangali Wildlife
  Orphanage

Tsholotsho
Turk Mine
Nyamandhlovu
Queen's Mine
Umzingwane River
Gwaai River
Kame River
Bulawayo
Khami
Figtree
Fort Usher
MATOBO NATIONAL PARK
Plumtree
Marula
Ramokgwebana
Mangwe
Kezi
Ingwesi River
Shashani River
Matobo Hills
Thuli River
To Gaborone
Ingwesi Dam
Antelope Mine
Maphisa
Mphoeng
St Josephs
Ramokgwebana River
Simukwe River
Legion Mine
Shashe River
BOTSWANA
River

aviaries are quite nice, and house both large raptors and smaller birds.

It's open daily, except Monday and at Christmas, from 10 am to 5 pm but the gates close at 4.30 pm. They feed the animals at 3.30 pm. Admission is US$1.50.

Getting There & Away

To hitch, walk out past the Ascot Shopping Centre and wait for a lift out of town. Chipangali lies two hundred metres from the Masvingo road, 24 km east of Bulawayo. Alternatively, take an Esigodini bus from the Renkini Bus Terminal and ask to be dropped at Chipangali.

Several tour companies run day tours to Chipangali; see Organised Tours in the Bulawayo section.

KHAMI RUINS

The peaceful and deserted ruins of Khami (also spelt Kame or Khame) aren't as expansive as those of Great Zimbabwe, but here, visitors can wander through the crumbled 40-hectare city and see more or less what remained after its former inhabitants fled the fire that destroyed it.

A small museum on the site attempts to piece together an explanation of Khami's history. Before exploring the ruins, pick up the pamphlet *A Trail Guide to the Khami National Monument* which is sold at the museum. The site is open from 8 am to 5 pm daily; for foreigners, admission is US$3. There are currently no facilities but National Museums & Monuments is planning a campground, which would be a welcome addition.

History

The Khami area was inhabited by Stone Age people for perhaps 100 millennia before the construction of the now-ruined city. By about 1000 AD, southern Africa was well into the Iron Age and formerly subsistence cultures had already settled down to agriculture and trade. North of the Khami River, the Leopard's Kopje culture had established itself in a village of daga huts, raising cattle and trading with the Swahilis from the Indian Ocean coast. Trade with the Portuguese continued through the 16th and 17th centuries.

By the late 1400s, the Leopard's Kopje culture had been absorbed, along with scattered groups throughout the region, into a political entity called the Torwa state. Torwa was probably a unification brought about – or at least influenced – by refugees from the collapsing Great Zimbabwe state 250 km away.

Khami became the Torwa capital. Its mambo occupied the highest enclave in the city, a well-protected court surrounded by the dwellings of the aristocracy. Commoners lived outside the core of the settlement, probably around the eastern side of the main hill.

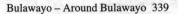

ZIMBABWE

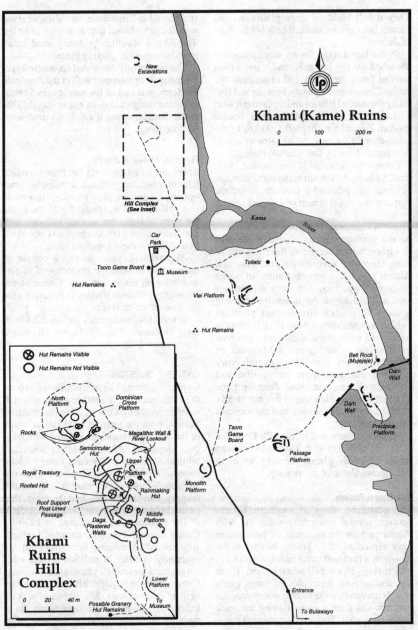

Khami (Kame) Ruins

0   100   200 m

Hill Complex
(See Inset)

Kame   *River*

New
Excavations

Car
Park

P

Tsoro Game Board

🏛 Museum

Toilets

Hut Remains

Vlei Platform

Hut Remains

Bell Rock
(Mujejeje)

Dam
Wall

Dam
Wall

Precipice
Platform

Tsoro
Game Board

Passage
Platform

Monolith
Platform

Entrance

To Bulawayo

Khami Ruins Hill Complex

0   20   40 m

⊗ Hut Remains Visible

◯ Hut Remains Not Visible

North
Platform

Dominican
Cross
Platform

Rocks

Megalithic Wall &
River Lookout

Semicircular
Hut

Upper
Platform

Royal Treasury

Roofed Hut

Rainmaking
Hut

Roof Support
Post Lined Passage

Middle
Platform

Daga
Plastered Walls

Lower
Platform

To Museum

Possible Granary
Hut Remains

They didn't build on stone platforms, and former hut sites are marked only by deposits of daga.

In the late 1600s, Torwa was apparently absorbed by the larger Rozwi state, which arrived from the north and conquered the ruling Changamire dynasty, burning and levelling the capital Khami and replacing it with Danangombe (see the Midlands & South-Eastern Zimbabwe chapter), 100 km to the north-east. In the early 1830s, Rozwi was in turn snuffed out by the Ndebele raiders.

Europeans first saw Khami around 1893. Until Lobengula's death in the same year, the Ndebele had guarded it from the colonists, perhaps as a royal retreat or a sacred site.

The Hill Complex

At the northern end of Khami is the Hill Complex, which served as the royal enclosure. Here are several hut platforms and Khami's greatest concentration of stone walling. A small royal treasury was uncovered at the foot of the three-step stairway leading to a semi-circular hut platform (which was probably a ritual site). Here were uncovered most of the Khami artefacts now on display in Bulawayo's Museum of Natural History including several ivory divining pieces, copper items, iron and bronze weapons, and ritual drinking pots. The main passage leading to this hut clearly once supported a daga roof, and the supports are still standing.

At the northern end of the Hill Complex is an odd platform with a stone Dominican cross, reputedly placed there by an early Portuguese Catholic missionary.

Southern Ruins

The scattered ruins of southern Khami contain several interesting sites; the Vlei Platforms near the museum are believed to have served as cattle kraals. Nearby is the *mujejeje*, a resonant stone near the dam wall, which rings like a bell when struck. There are also several examples of tsoro game boards carved into the stones; one is near the car park and there's another along the track to the dam wall. Tsoro, a complicated game

still played in Zimbabwe, now uses a carved wooden game board with four rows of holes. The Khami dwellers probably used small rounded stones as playing pieces.

The beautifully decorated six-metre-high, 68-metre-long retaining wall of the Precipice Platform, just east of the dam, bears a chequerboard design along its entire length. Due to the dam, however, it's difficult to observe at close range.

Getting There & Away

There are no buses along the little-travelled Khami road, so without a vehicle, your options are limited. Most travellers hire bicycles in Bulawayo and pedal the 22 flat km to the ruins, making for an easy half-day trip. Just head out on 11th Ave beyond Lobengula St and follow the signposted route.

Alternatively, you can pay a couple of dollars to ride with the inspector of monuments on an inspection tour. Check at the Museum of Natural History in Bulawayo for the time of the next trip.

Several tour companies include Khami in their itineraries. For details, see Organised Tours under Bulawayo.

CYRENE MISSION

Cyrene Mission, 32 km from Bulawayo on the Plumtree road, is another artistically rich mission. Although not as overwhelming as Serima, both the internal and external walls of the thatched chapel are painted with frescoes depicting African interpretations of biblical accounts and scenes from African history. The mission was named after the African Simon, 'a Cyreneian...out of the country, and on him they laid the cross, that he might bear it after Jesus'. (St Luke 23:26).

The mission was established in 1939 by Canon Edward Paterson, an artist himself, who served as mission principal until his retirement in 1953. In addition to basic education and practical vocational training, Canon Paterson required his students to participate in art classes. His emphasis was on individual creativity in several media – drawing, sculpture, wood carving and painting – and no European examples were provided.

The paintings and carvings that cover the chapel today are almost entirely the work of students (Paterson himself is responsible for a couple of the works). All of them depict African characters, animals, homes and backdrops. Some are brilliant, others merely competent, but the variety of styles employed is worth examining.

Getting There & Away

From the Renkini Bus Terminal in Bulawayo, take the Figtree or Plumtree bus (or the Francistown bus from the Lobengula St Terminus) and get off at Cyrene Rd, eight km short of Figtree. From there, it's a 2.5 km walk to the mission. Alternatively, hitch out the Plumtree road to Cyrene Rd and walk the remaining distance.

Coming from Matobo National Park, Cyrene lies 10 km along infrequently travelled Cyrene Rd from Cecil Rhodes' old rail terminus, just outside the park near the Arboretum gate. Hitching will be tough so plan on walking the entire distance; it's a hot, dry area so carry lots of water.

MATOBO NATIONAL PARK

You need not be in tune with any alternative wavelength to sense that the Matobo Hills are one of the world's power places. These otherworldly formations appear as though some very young deity has been playing with thousand-tonne building blocks, stacking them precariously into fanciful castles and towering imaginary cities, then populating them with stone-faced human figures – women in billowing dresses, men working and socialising and children following or looking on. It's no wonder that the Rozwi regarded the Matobo as their spiritual capital; its latent and pervasive power cannot be denied.

Dotted around the modern park are numerous signs of former habitation. In addition to the wealth of ancient San paintings, which decorate the rock, and bits of pottery scattered around the hills, there are examples of old grain bins, where

Lobengula's warriors once stored their provisions. Some hidden niches still shelter clay ovens which were used as iron smelters in making the infamous *assegais*, or spears, to be used against the growing colonial hordes. Hidden in a rock cleft is the Ndebele's sacred rain shrine, Njelele, where people still pray to Mwali and petition for rain. During the recent devastating drought, even government officials came to pull some strings here.

With the history comes a superb array of wildlife. You may have the chance to see the African hawk eagle *(Hieraaetus spilogaster)* or the rare Cape eagle owl *(Bubo capensis mackinderi)*. Matobo is also home to the world's greatest concentration of nesting sites of the black eagle *(Aquila verreauxi)* – the park is actually shaped like an eagle – and you may well observe these birds soaring above their kopje-bound nests. The bad news is that the eagles are coming under pressure from poachers, who lift both chicks and eggs from nests to supply illicit overseas pet markets.

The Whovi Game Park portion of Matobo offers a variety of wildlife, but is best known for its zealously guarded population of both white and black rhinos.

An encouraging story is told of two Zambians who arrived at the Bulawayo railway station carrying long – and ominously rifle-shaped – canvas bags and asking directions to Matobo National Park (they might as well have worn flashing neon signs reading 'We are rhino poachers'). One local woman immediately became suspicious and took the story to the police. A massive sting operation was organised and the would-be poachers were thwarted.

History

As many as 100,000 years ago, the first hunting and gathering societies appeared around the Matobo Hills. Evidence of their inhabitation and apparent fascinations are preserved in hundreds of rock paintings which decorate castle kopje caves, shelters and overhangs throughout the region, both inside and outside the park. From this work, we've learned that the Matobo was indeed a natural haunt of the white rhino, justifying its reintroduction there, as well as the

ZIMBABWE

The Matobo Hills – a Geologic Perspective

Geologic analyses tell us that the Matobo Hills are the final remnants of a granite batholith, a vast igneous intrusion which worked its way up from the earth's molten core and thrust up the crustal material around Matobo into a high dome of peaks. As erosion took its toll and slowly dragged off the softer overlying material, the mountains diminished in size. The resistant rock that remained – now exposed to the weather – heated, cooled, cracked and crumbled along weaker fissures and left dwala domes as well as piles and crenellated pinnacles of the strongest rock. The domes exfoliated or peeled off in sheets that sloughed away into the valleys. Steeper features eroded more slowly along cracks and fissures. (Interestingly, the builders of Great Zimbabwe used fire and water to artificially simulate the exfoliation process in the rock they used for construction.)

In short, the balancing boulders of Matobo weren't stacked that way, as one would be inclined to believe (and wonder who hefted them up there), but rather, were eroded *in situ* and separated from each other by the forces of natural weathering. By all indications, they will continue to do so and eventually crumble into an entirely new – if perhaps not quite so interesting – landscape. ■

quagga, the giant zebra-like wild horse, for which it's now too late for reintroduction.

It would be difficult to imagine such a place escaping religious attention. In the late 1600s, the Torwa state, whose capital was at nearby Khami, was conquered by the Rozwi, who invaded from the north and absorbed rather than wiped out the incumbent dynasty.

After Khami was burned and razed by the invaders, a new political centre was established at Danangombe, while the enigmatic Matobo Hills became a ritual capital and religious retreat. Here, the cult of Mwari took hold and it dominated Rozwi thinking until the Ndebele swept in from the south and finished them off. Interestingly, the Ndebele were so taken by the Mwari religion – or they were afraid not to be – that they adopted it for their own purposes. King Mzilikazi

Buffalo Thorn

Conventional wisdom has it that buffalo thorn (*Ziziphus mucronata*) or 'wait-a-bit' (*blinkblaar wag 'n bietjie* in Afrikaans) trees grow only over subsurface streams and therefore make an excellent indicator of underground water supplies. The small edible fruit is also quite tasty, but this tree isn't to be taken lightly. The sinister back-pointing thorns can rip flesh and clothing at the slightest brush and legend has it that this tree was used to make the crown of thorns when Jesus was crucified. ■

himself bestowed the name *Amatobo*, which means 'bald heads'.

Even the next wave of conquerors, the White Matabeleland farmers, hedged their climatic bets by petitioning Mwari for rain during the prolonged post WWII drought. It is believed that Mwari and his mediums, priests and other subsidiaries still thrive at several shrines in the communal lands around Matobo today. (For details on the Mwari belief system, turn to Religion in the Zimbabwe Facts about the Country Chapter.)

Once heavily farmed, the Matobo area was subject to considerable controversy in the mid-1900s between Whites and Blacks over the fate of the land. While Whites struggled to protect the area as a natural preserve and national shrine to C J Rhodes, Blacks argued that the farmland was needed by subsistence farmers to feed their families. Whites countered that unnatural erosion caused by domestic animals and outdated farming techniques would render the land useless anyway. Blacks reminded them that the Matobo country held religious significance as the headquarters of Mwari, a figure at least as important as the Whites' revered Rhodes.

In 1962, the White government won out, moving Matobo resident farmers to communal lands outside the proposed park boundaries, which now contain an area of 43,200 hectares. Resistance raged but the

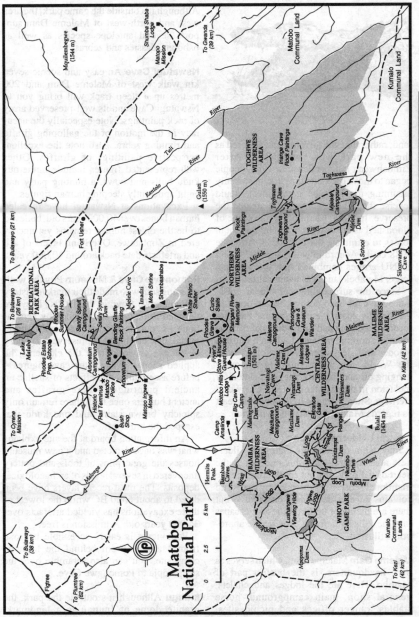

Matobo National Park

Crocodile

ZIMBABWE

land, rather than the government, suffered as the new park was vandalised. After Zimbabwean independence in 1980, people began to move back into the park, mistakenly assuming the Mugabe government would reverse the White decision that created the preserve. In 1983, Matobo was the scene of bloodshed as the powers from Harare sent in forces to eliminate the dissidents. After the 1988 Unity Accord in which the ZAPU and ZANU armies combined into one national force, Matabeleland was again calm.

Since the surrounding communal grasslands have all been cut or chewed down to the roots by goats, Matobo National Park has recently been opened to residents of the surrounding communal lands for thatch-cutting. Rhodes still sleeps peacefully atop View of the World, the white rhino is tenuously hanging on and the park has been slated for inclusion in the register of UNESCO World Heritage Sites. Perhaps in the end – at least as regards Matobo – everyone will win.

Central Wilderness Area
It may seem oxymoronic calling a wilderness area 'central', but this one lies at the heart of the park. It's not a wilderness in the traditional sense – it's threaded by roads and contains several developed enclaves – but there are plenty of opportunities for escapes into the hills, which can provide the appropriate illusion.

Maleme Dam Maleme Dam, which serves as park headquarters, is the busiest part of Matobo. Here are the lodges and chalets, general shop, main campground, horse stables, ranger offices and picnic sites.

Although it's outside the game park, the area west and north-west of Maleme Dam supports several antelope species as well as baboons, dassies and zebras.

Nswatugi Cave An easy and scenic seven km walk west of Maleme Dam and 200 metres up a steep track will bring you to Nswatugi Cave and its well-preserved array of rock paintings. Note especially the accuracy in the motion of the galloping giraffe and running zebra. Also note the excellent perspective paintings of giraffes. Other well-represented figures include numerous kudu bulls and cows, a hunting party and eight apparently sleeping human figures.

Excavations at Nswatugi have revealed human bones over 40,000 years old, believed to be the oldest human remains yet uncovered in Zimbabwe. Overlying layers of ash and artefacts date back around 10,000 years.

Pomongwe Cave & Museum Pity the well-meaning soul who made their mark in history at Pomongwe Cave in the 1920s. They are destined to be forever maligned by generations of tourists for an undeniably stupid mistake: in an attempt to preserve the gallery of ancient artwork from the elements, he applied shellac over all the cave figures – before ascertaining the effects of shellac on ancient paintings. Where giraffes and ancient hunters once trod, there remain only splotchy brown stains and one kudu that escaped the brush-off.

An information board at the site explains what was once depicted and a new museum houses the great piles of tools and pottery uncovered in several levels of archaeological deposits. The most recent layers have been dated to about 6500 BC while the lowest of these excavations has yielded artefacts over 35,000 years old. Admission is free.

Pomongwe is easily accessible by road from Maleme. From behind the Maleme camp site, you can also scramble over the steep kopje to Pomongwe Cave.

Inungu Although it's outside the park, the granite dome of Inungu is a landmark, topped by a large and obtrusive cross. It's a half-day return walk and climb from the Maleme camp site.

Northern Wilderness Area

Near the park's north-eastern entrance, you'll have a nice view down the Mjelele Valley. Surprisingly, it's not unusual to see rhinos *outside the game park*, grazing on the dry grasses of the valley floor.

Mjelele Cave

Just outside national park boundaries, the Mjelele Cave paintings are on the northern faces of two very large boulders a few hundred metres east of the road eight km north of White Rhino Shelter. They contain a human-crocodile figure and some detailed ancient paintings blotted out by the amateurish work of later imitators.

Arboretum & Rhodes' Rail Terminus

Not much remains of Cecil Rhodes' rail terminus two km outside the park's north-west entrance. The line was originally built so that turn-of-the-century Bulawayo socialites could have easy Sunday afternoon access to the rocky wonders of Matobo Park.

The nearby arboretum is just inside the park boundary from the rail terminus. If you're after greenness, the camp site will prove pleasant.

White Rhino Shelter

White Rhino Shelter lies several hundred metres along a clearly marked path from the signposted car park about five km north of the View of the World turn-off. These are paintings with a difference: outline drawings rather than the polychrome paintings more commonly found in Matobo and indeed, all over Zimbabwe. Most prominent are the finely executed outlines of five white rhinos and the head of a black rhino, with human figures visible behind them, and five well-observed and exquisitely drawn wildebeests. Peripheral figures include a procession of human hunters and a prominent polychrome lion, which are believed to postdate the other paintings by many millennia.

Malindidzimu

The lichen-streaked boulders that surround Cecil John Rhodes' grave atop the mountain which Rhodes called View of the World, seem to have been placed there deliberately to mark the spot, but the old boy wasn't quite so influential. Still, it seems odd that he unknowingly chose this particular mountain, which the Ndebele knew as Malindidzimu, or 'Dwelling place of Benevolent Spirits' (see the aside).

While some of the more traditional Rhodies still make an annual pilgrimage to the site on the anniversary of his death (26 March) most visitors just appreciate the solitude and the view that so strongly gripped CJ nearly a century ago.

Just down from Rhodes' grave is that of Dr Leander Starr Jameson, a good friend of Rhodes, who commanded Fort Victoria (Masvingo) after its 1890 founding. He died in England on 26 November 1917, but because of WWI, was not brought to View of the World until 1920. Also interred at View of the World is Charles Patrick John Coghlan, the first premier of Southern Rhodesia, buried there on 14 August 1930.

The Shangani River (Allan Wilson) Memorial, an imposing structure just downhill from Rhodes' Grave, was erected in 1904 to the memory of Allan Wilson and the 33 soldiers of his Shangani River Patrol. The entire troupe was wiped out by the forces of General Mtjaan and his 30,000 Ndebele warriors, of whom more than 400 were slain by the patrol's superior firepower. Mistakenly believing that Lobengula's impis (spear-carrying 'soldiers') had committed acts of war against the British at Fort Victoria, the patrol had been sent in pursuit of the fleeing king. Lobengula himself conceded that their battle was bravely fought, a moving human reaction from a singularly intriguing individual.

The bodies were brought at Rhodes' request from Great Zimbabwe, where they had previously been interred. The inscription reads simply: 'Erected in the enduring memory of Allan Wilson and his men who fell in a fight against the Matabele on the Shangani River, December 4th, 1898. There was no survivor.'

ZIMBABWE

ZIMBABWE

Cecil Rhodes & Malindidzimu

The Ndebele name of the hill Malindidzimu means 'Dwelling Place of the Benevolent Spirits', where they believe the more saintly of their ancestors dwell on in peaceful bliss. Ironically, they now share their lovely mountain top haunt with a sort of colonial Heroes' Acre.

Cecil John Rhodes, the source of everything Rhodesian, didn't spend much time at his estate near Rhodes Dam just outside Matobo Park, but was taken with the surrounding country and its spell. After one foray into the hills with Lord Grey, he returned home to exclaim 'We have found a hill from the top of which a marvellous view is to be seen...'. The same day he returned to the site with friends and, apparently seized with catharsis, declared 'I shall be buried here, looking towards the north, and the remains of Allan Wilson and his party must be brought from Fort Victoria and placed inside the memorial I shall put up to their memory...I call this one View of the World'.

When Rhodes died of heart failure in South Africa on 26 March 1902, at the age of 49, his body was carried to the spot and buried in the way he'd requested. The funeral party included a band of Ndebele who requested that no saluting volley be fired lest the benevolent spirits of the place be disturbed. Instead, they offered the respectful salute *Hayate*, the only time the honour has ever been accorded to a European. ■

Another Malindidzimu attraction is its population of lizards – the females are grey-green and the males, rainbow-coloured – skittering around the equally rainbow-coloured lichen-encrusted rocks. Several times daily, one long-time park attendant proffers a lump of mealies and forces them to jump for a share of the meal – the original leaping lizards.

Although the easiest access to the summit is via a road leading up the from the eastern side of the hill, an alternative and more scenic walking route ascends from the picnic area directly south of it. A display at the bottom of the hill outlines highlights of Rhodes' life and career.

Whovi Game Park

The well-guarded white rhino population at Whovi (pronounced Hoo-vee) is relatively healthy (at last count, there were around 35) and lucky visitors may even spot the more elusive black rhino, which is also present, but in much smaller numbers (at last count, nine). What's more, the scenery, with

Matobo's most precarious and imaginative pinnacles and boulder stacks, is as good as the wildlife.

The relatively dense wildlife population provides opportunities to observe klipspringers, kudu, reedbucks, sables, impalas, wildebeests, dassies, warthogs, giraffes, zebras, ostriches and even tiny elephant shrews. Leopards are also happily at home in the rambling rock ramparts – Matobo is reputed to have Africa's densest concentration of these cats – but you'd still be lucky to catch a glimpse of one.

As at Maleme, guided 1½ hour horseback trips are available at White Waters (near the game park entrance). If you don't have a vehicle and aren't lucky with hitching, this will be your only access to this area of the park.

Gates open at 8 am and close at dusk.

Bambata Cave

Bambata Cave is in the tiny Bambata Wilderness Area, west of the main body of Matobo Park. This well-painted cave is best known for its rendition of a cheetah, a clearly individual cat which appears to have striped legs. Elephants and eland figure prominently in other sections of the work. Extensive excavations in the cave have uncovered tools and pottery from the first few centuries BC and have given the name Bambata to similar finds from the same period elsewhere in Zimbabwe. The cave is a 40-minute walk off the Whovi-Bulawayo road. The road isn't really suited to low-clearance vehicles.

Toghwe Wilderness Area

The remote eastern third of Matobo lies in the Toghwe Wilderness Area, the wildest of all the park's wilderness areas. It contains parts of the scenic Mjelele and Toghwana valleys, as well as Inange Cave and its fine collection of rock paintings. Roads are rough with some very steep bits and vehicles are infrequent; low-slung cars may encounter problems. After rains, low-lying stretches of the rough roads may become impassable without 4WD.

Mjelele Dam This long, narrow and nearly empty dam at the park's south-eastern corner is becoming choked with vegetation. It's little-visited at the moment but the road has been improved and the camp site upgraded. It's a long walk from anywhere, so without a car, access is nearly impossible. The road between Mjelele and Toghwana is horrid, requiring a lion-hearted and preferably high-clearance 4WD vehicle.

Togwhana Dam Toghwana Dam is a remote and lovely spot set amid tightly packed peaks. It has a wonderful camp site, and you could make a good three-day, 45-km return walk from Maleme Dam to the Inange Cave paintings, which are seven km on foot from Toghwana. If you return via Mjelele Dam, it's a 60-km return walk. Alternatively, walk one-way via the 27-km route through communal lands to or from Sandy Spruit at Matobo's north entrance.

The access roads have some very steep

sections and although 4WD isn't essential, you'll need a strong vehicle.

Inange Cave Inange Cave (sometimes spelt Inanke), which sits atop a high whaleback dwala, is a four to six-hour return walk from the Toghwana Dam camp site. In this remote site, you'll encounter one of the most complex and well executed of Zimbabwe's cave paintings. Mixed herds of well-observed African animals march in confused profusion across the walls, interspersed with hunters, and geometric and stylised designs. The greatest of these is a puzzle, a series of 16 rectangles overlying layers of egg-like ovals. Across and around the whole thing strut parades of giraffes. Large and bizarre human figures also make appearances around the panel.

Inange is a rough – and often steep – seven-km walk from Toghwana Dam. It's a good idea to get an early start, which will be facilitated if you stay at Toghwana Dam. Most of the route is marked by green-painted arrows and small rock cairns and although the way may become confusing as it passes over a series of nearly identical ridges and valleys, you shouldn't have problems.

Silozwane Cave Silozwane, a little-visited cave in the communal lands south of the park, is more easily reached than Inange. Although not overwhelming, it is appealing. The panel is a dense mishmash of delicately executed figures, a wall full of doodles bearing little apparent relationship to each other. Particularly interesting are the rows of intricate human figures involved in various easily identified domestic tasks.

From Maleme, go six km east to the Mjelele and Toghwana Dam turn-off. Turn right and follow that road for 12 km, then take the signposted right fork onto a very rough road and follow it for nearly two km to the car park. This section of the road is in very poor condition, so you'll probably have to walk it (if you have a vehicle, don't leave anything of value inside it). From there, it's a short, steep walk over the dome to the cave

ZIMBABWE

hollow, with beautiful views along the way. Hitching prospects are remote.

Organised Tours

Quite a few Bulawayo operators offer day tours of Matobo National Park. The day tour with Black Rhino (☎ /fax 41662) can't be recommended highly enough. It's apparent that the work is a labour of love: the guides and owners, Russell and Colleen, have probably spent more time at Matobo than most people, yet their enthusiasm for the place remains infectious and they'll accompany you on walks and climbs and visit remote areas overlooked by other companies – some of these places were rediscovered by Russell himself. Tours fill up quickly, so advance booking is recommended. If you want more time in the park, they'll drop you at Maleme Dam when the tour is finished and return you to Bulawayo on another day. Nine-hour day tours cost US$22 per person, including lunch and a visit to Whovi Game Park. No two tours are identical, so you can actually go more than once.

Our trip to Matobo with Black Rhino Safaris was one of the highlights of our three months in Africa. We went off the beaten track, it included a walking trip and anything our guide didn't know about the park or its animals probably isn't worth knowing.
Shane Stoneman, New Zealand

UTC is also an option, especially if you're arriving late in Bulawayo, because they have a guaranteed departure for the following morning. The full-day tour costs US$14/23 and includes Whovi Game Park.

As described in the Bulawayo section, both Eddie's Tours (☎ 66660; fax 65016) and Mzingeli Tours (☎ 77244; fax 68214) are recommended if you specifically want a cultural experience of the Matobo area. They visit cultural sites within the hills, as well as communal lands outside the park. However, some tours include visits to sacred sites, such as Mzilikazi's Grave at Nthumbane and the Njelele cave shrine, where people still come to petition the god Mwari. Out of respect for local traditions that outsiders not be admitted

to these sacred sites, no other company includes them in their itineraries.

Finally, N'taba Tours (☎ 79563; fax 76658) does Matobo tours daily except Sunday for US$17. This includes the main sites as well as a trip through the game park, a stop in an African village and an 'authentic Zim meal' which, according to their pamphlet, is 'hygienically prepared from chicken or beef – no unknown food stuff'. You can't beat that.

Places to Stay

All telephone numbers are on the Bulawayo exchange, unless otherwise indicated.

National Parks' Accommodation Since most overnight visitors wind up at Maleme Dam chalets and campground, the place can be packed on weekends and holidays – these are naturally the best times to be hitching in but not always the most pleasant to actually *be* there. In the winter and during the week, however, you'll share Maleme only with the odd traveller and the baboons, dassies and klipspringer which inhabit surrounding bouldery hills.

Maleme has National Parks' campgrounds, chalets and lodges, including two luxury lodges, the *Black Eagle* and *Fish Eagle*, which afford a boulder-studded hilltop vista of Maleme and surroundings. They're well worth the price, especially if you can muster four people to share the costs. Advance bookings are essential.

Maleme is the most popular campground, but there are several others around the park. At the northern entrance is Sandy Spruit Dam, an ordinary campground too close to the highway, but it's conveniently located if you're arriving late. Toghwana Dam in the Toghwe Wilderness Area is exceptionally nice, but access is difficult, while the equally remote Mjelele Dam, eight km south of Toghwana Dam has recently been improved. Near the Arboretum entrance is a very civilised site and there's also a small but beautiful tent site at Mezilume Dam.

Water at all camp sites but Maleme should be boiled or purified before drinking. No toilet paper is supplied at any of the camping areas and all park waters are infected with bilharzia.

Hotels & Lodges Adjacent to Fryer's Store, 10 km from Maleme, is *Inungu Guest House*, which accommodates only one party of up to six people. The setting is stunning and it's an inexpensive place to get away from it all in the Matobo. They charge US$29 for up to four adults and two kids. Book through Sunshine Tours (☎ 67791) on the corner of 8th Ave and Jason Moyo St, Bulawayo.

Another basic option is the friendly and adequate *Matopo Ingwe Motel* (☎ 8217, Figtree), on Gladstone Farm just outside the Matobo park boundary. Comfortable rondavels cost US$15 per person, with bed and breakfast.

If I could cast a vote for Zimbabwe's most appealing lodge, it would be *Matobo Hills Lodge* (☎ 74589; fax 44696), lost amid the magnificent natural rock gardens west of the Northern Wilderness Area outside the park boundary. Best of all, the simple stone-and-thatch architecture blends assiduously with the magical setting, and has impeccable feng shui. The swimming pool is hewn from natural rock and the spacious and airy bar overlooks a sublime landscape of standing rocks. All that detracts is the three-tier pricing, which places it out of reach for most foreigners (including myself). The all-inclusive international rate is US$170 per person; locals pay US$54. Table d'hôte meals, served family style, are included, as are two game drives. If you opt out of the game drives, the rate is US$100/34 for foreigners/residents.

More novel is Londa Mela Safaris' *Camp Amalinda* (☎ 41286; fax 78319), on private land just north of Bambata Wilderness Area. It boasts such original features as a dining table made from sleepers from Cecil Rhodes' Matopos rail line and a cave bar inside the Matobo rock, as are some of the rooms.

A London *Daily Mail* reviewer called it 'a little corner of the cartoon town of Bedrock'. There's also a tiny swimming pool and a cosy fire circle for cold evenings which, in this setting, emulates a camp site somewhere on a long cattle drive. In high season (1 May to 1 November), foreigners pay US$170 per person, including meals; off-season, it's US$112. Transfers from Bulawayo cost an extra US$18 per person. Zimbabweans pay US$33 per person any time, plus US$13 for transfers. Camp Amalinda also organises Matobo tours, game drives, game walks and horseback trips.

Another option is *Big Cave Camp* (☎ /fax 77176), which sits atop a rock dwala about five km off the Whovi-Bulawayo road. The surrounding wilderness area supports a variety of wildlife, including antelopes and leopards, and birdwatchers will be pleased to hear that over 110 species have been observed. Foreigners pay US$150 per person including accommodation in thatched A-frame chalets, meals, game drives and most drinks. Transfers from Bulawayo cost US$20 per person. Locals pay US$37 per person and US$10 for transfers from Bulawayo.

East of the park just off the Gwanda road is Zindele Safaris' *Shumba Shaba Lodge* (☎ /fax 64128). It's further from the park, but the surroundings are great and it's cheaper than the other up-market lodges. The name means 'red lion', after the dwala on which it's perched. For chalets, foreigners pay US$68 per person sharing, with meals; transfers from Bulawayo cost US$20.

Further afield, on the Stone Hills Game Sanctuary south of the Plumtree road, is the luxurious and highly acclaimed *Malalangwe Lodge* (☎ 74693; fax 76917). The name means 'place where the leopard sleeps' and the décor revolves around *mukwa* (African mahogany) furnishings and trim. The area offers good hiking and birdwatching. A unique claim to fame is an example of the rare Transvaal red balloon tree. From the main road, 70 km west of Bulawayo, the turn-off is marked by a big green sign which reads 'Richard Peek'. Bungalows cost US$125 per person. This price includes meals, drinks, game drives, game walks and day tours. Return transfers to Bulawayo are an additional US$30 per person.

Also near the Plumtree road, just west of

ZIMBABWE

Figtree, is the new *Izintaba Safari Lodge*
(☎ /fax 256, Figtree), which caters especially for photographers with its attached
6000-hectare game ranch in the Matobo
Hills. In Bulawayo, contact Intaba Safaris
(☎ 60137; fax 63120), 4 Elgar Building,
which you'll find on the corner of 12th Ave
and Robert Mugabe St.

Places to Eat
Apart from the hotels and lodges, there are
no restaurants in the Matobo Hills. The only
supplies are at the basic shop at Maleme and
at Fryer's Store, just outside the boundary of
the park.

Fryer's is six km upstream from Maleme
Dam or 10 km along the road.

Getting There & Away
Without a vehicle, budget access to Matobo
isn't easy, but most travellers manage
somehow. Hitching is slow, but hitchers
always arrive eventually and since there are
several campgrounds around the park perimeter, one need only reach the proximity to be
within striking distance on foot.

Alternatively, you can take the Kezi bus
from Renkini Bus Terminal in Bulawayo and
get off at one of the three Matobo turn-offs.
Your best bet is to hire bicycles at Transit
Hire in Bulawayo and carry them on the bus
into the park (however, cyclists aren't permitted in the game park).

If you get off at the first turn-off, you can
cycle, walk or hitch the six km to Sandy
Spruit camp site. From the second turn-off at
Rhodes' rail terminus, it's five km into the
Arboretum camp site.

To reach Maleme, get off at the Whovi
access road and take the new six-km shortcut
or the 12-km circuit past Mezilume,
Nswatugi and Madingizulu dams, and
Nswatugi Cave.

PLUMTREE
This tiny settlement in the heart of cattle
country on the Botswana border is the
customs and immigration post for the
highway and rail line between Bulawayo and
Francistown.

If you're entering Zimbabwe, don't get
stuck behind a bus or you may have a long
wait, otherwise things normally go quite
smoothly for non-Zimbabweans.

Western Zimbabwe

With Zimbabwe's major attractions – Victoria Falls and Hwange National Park – and a few minor ones, Western Zimbabwe looms big on most travellers' southern African itineraries. Naturally Hwange and The Falls, as they're known with local familiarity, are the main draws, but there are also other wonderful places. Western Lake Kariba, a wild shadow of its eastern counterpart, offers leisurely stays at the casual Mlibizi Resort; Binga with its unique Batonka culture; and rugged and remote Chizarira, Zimbabwe's wildest – and arguably most beautiful – national park.

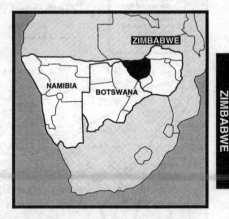

GWAAI RIVER

Gwaai River, also called Dahlia Siding, is an obligatory stop for all highway travellers between Bulawayo and Hwange or Victoria Falls. Most travellers just stop for petrol and a snack or drink at the hotel, but the area also offers pleasant day walks and fishing streams. You can also visit Gwaai Valley Pottery, the local pottery-making cooperative which still use traditional techniques. Visitors are welcome to have a go at making something.

Mzola Forest Reserve

Nemba Safaris (☎ 33, Lupane) runs an appealing option known as Mzola Wilderness Safaris – walking trips through the remote Mzola Forest Reserve between the Karna, Shangani and Mzola rivers. These trips aren't terribly strenuous; luggage is carried by oxcart and the distance between each of the camps – Carmine, Mzola and Figtree – is only seven km. For information, contact Chris or Val van Wyk, Nemba Safaris, PO Box 4, Gwaai River. You'll pay around US$250 per day, including meals, accommodation, transfers and an armed guide.

Places to Stay & Eat

The focus of Gwaai River is the charming *Gwaai River Hotel* (☎ 3400), where you can settle in for the night or just stop for tea and a snack in the sunny garden. One appeal is its exceptional owners, Harold and Sylvia Broomberg, who seem to be on first-name terms with half of Zimbabwe and treat travellers like long-lost friends. Standard family units with bed and breakfast cost US$13 per person; with half-board, they're US$16 per person. Plusher options at the hotel include Syringa Suites or Jacaranda Square (US$32/40), Acacia Lodge (US$38/45), all with half-board. Although camping isn't advertised, if you're short of cash, they may permit you to camp in the grounds for a night for a good rate. The indoor pub is the hub of nightlife (and daylife) in Gwaai River.

For other options, see Hotels, Camps & Lodges in the Hwange National Park section.

DETE

Dete, which is little more than a village, serves as the rail terminal for Hwange National Park. Unfortunately, rail access to the park is fraught with problems; the trains between Bulawayo and Victoria Falls, in both directions, arrive at a red-eye hour of

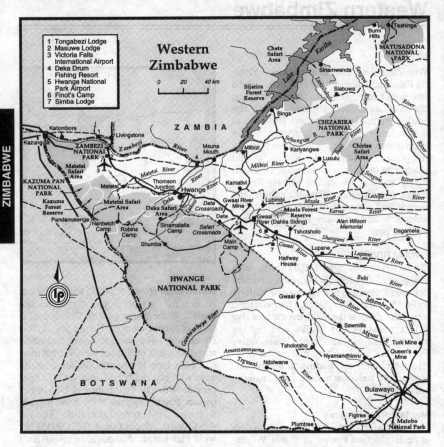

Western Zimbabwe

1 Tongabezi Lodge
2 Masuwe Lodge
3 Victoria Falls International Airport
4 Deka Drum Fishing Resort
5 Hwange National Park Airport
6 Finot's Camp
7 Simba Lodge

0   20   40 km

the morning. Once you've arrived, you're still faced with a 12-km walk or hitch to the park entrance – and another seven km to Hwange National Park Main Camp (along a road where walking and hitching are not allowed).

Places to Stay

The dilapidated but friendly *Game Reserve Hotel* (☎ 366) has a screechy mega-decibel disco that can be enjoyed by all Dete citizens from the comfort of their own homes. When the disco isn't blaring, the hotel restaurant serves cheap and bearable meals; but order

sadza ne nyama and avoid anything resembling chicken.

If you're arriving on the train, book in advance or the hotel will be locked up when you arrive. Rooms cost about US$11/15 for singles/doubles. At a pinch, you can crash on the concrete floor of the '1st-class' lounge at the railway station. It gets cold at night, so bring a sleeping bag.

HWANGE

Hwange town, like the national park, was named after an early Ndebele chief. For many years, it was spelt Wankie and this mispronunciation has endured to the present day (much to the amusement of international visitors), although some Black Zimbabweans pronounce it 'HWAN-gay'.

Hwange owes its existence to the discovery of coal. The proposed Copper Belt railway line was originally intended to cross the Zambezi River at Chirundu and proceed from there into Zambia, but construction was held up by the Boer Wars and the route was diverted westward to provide transport to and from the coalfields. The town today is nestled between mountains of mine tailings.

Unless you're interested in the seven German Henschel steam locomotives which serve the colliery, there's little reason to visit the town and most people hurry through. If you want to break up a trip, however, the two-star *Baobab Hotel* (☎ 323) on the hill offers agreeable accommodation for about Z\$50/70 for singles/doubles, including breakfast. Buses and trains between Bulawayo and Victoria Falls pass through Hwange.

HWANGE NATIONAL PARK
Although Hwange National Park is Zimbabwe's most accessible and most wildlife-packed national parks by Kenyan standards it would rank as scarcely visited. It's normally uncrowded and most safari vehicles concentrate along the short loop drives within 10 km of Main Camp. The best time to visit is the dry season (September and October) when the animals congregate around water holes (most of which are artificially engineered with petrol-powered compressors). When the rains come and rivers are flowing, successful wildlife viewing requires more diligence because animals spread out across the park's 14,650 sq km for a bit of trunk and antler room.

Hwange National Park sits at the ragged edge of the Kalahari sands and although the area was once home to nomadic families of San people, it was considered by other groups to be too hot, dry and sandy for permanent habitation. It wasn't originally thickly populated with wildlife, either. Although animals spread across the region

during the rainy season, they retreated to the perennial rivers of the Zambezi Valley during the dry. Over the past centuries, however, as human pressure increased in favourable lands to the east, north and west, animals were driven permanently into marginal areas. By default, then, Hwange became a wildlife reserve because the land was considered unsuitable for the habitation of humans.

Much of the credit for recent conservation efforts should go to Mr Mike Edwards of the Hwange Conservation Society in Hwange town, a group which has established its own anti-poaching unit and oversees the drilling, pumping and maintenance of bore holes.

History
During the 19th century, the area now known as Hwange National Park served as a hunting reserve for the Ndebele kings. When Europeans arrived on the scene, they couldn't help identifying the area's richness in wildlife and set about overhunting it.

Because its poor soils and lack of surface water made it unsuitable for farming, Hwange was accorded national park status in 1929. The idea was to provide a wildlife-viewing venue for tourists en route to nearby Victoria Falls. Settlers created 60 artificial water holes fed by underground water and by the 1970s, Hwange had one of the densest concentrations of wildlife in Africa.

Since Zimbabwe's independence in 1980, wildlife management has become a relatively low priority and park budgets have dropped off. Due to funding shortfalls, artificial water holes have dried up, pumps have broken down, poaching has become rampant and the park's rhino population has all but disappeared. At one stage in 1994, the British army was called in to provide expertise and repair 25 water pumps. In spite of all that, Hwange still provides some of the continent's best wildlife-viewing opportunities.

Orientation
Travellers using the Hwange Special Express bus arrive at Safari Crossroads; Ajay's Motorways passengers are set down

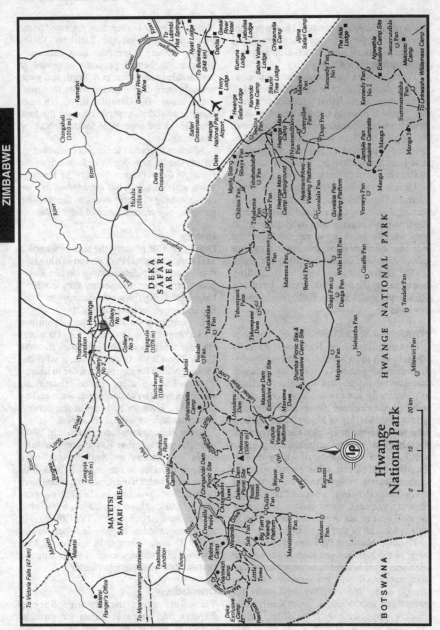

at Hwange Safari Lodge; those on Air Zimbabwe arrive at Hwange National Park Airport; and railway passengers arrive at Dete railway station. From Safari Crossroads, it's seven km to the airport turn-off and 11.5 km to the Hwange Safari Lodge. From there, it's another five km to the railway tracks marking the park entrance and seven km further to Main Camp. Railway travellers coming from Dete should follow the road for 12 km south-east along the railway line and turn right at the T-junction. From there, the Safari Lodge is seven km along the road to the left and Main Camp, seven km down the road to the right.

The Main Camp area is characterised by savanna and thorny acacia scrub while just south-east around Ngwethla are broad grassy *vleis*, acacia-dotted plains and wildlife concentrations reminiscent of the great parks of Kenya – but without the crowds and the striped white safari minibuses. Here you'll find some of the largest herds of antelopes, zebras, buffaloes and elephants in Zimbabwe as well as staggering numbers of baboons.

As you travel west from Main Camp, around Shumba Picnic Site, the savanna dissolves into rolling thorn and mopane-covered hills, where heavy bush tends to obscure visibility. Although you won't see the staggering numbers of individual animals, there's a good chance of observing such predators as lions, leopards, cheetahs, hyena, jackals and wild dogs.

Information

Park information and sketchy photocopied maps are available at the Main, Sinamatella and Robins Camp ranger offices.

Organised Tours

Game Drives & Mobile Safaris Geared especially for backpackers, Shamwari Safaris (☎ /fax 248) is warmly recommended as a friendly and inexpensive option for game drives and longer camping safaris in the national park. The owner, Roberto 'Beat' Accorsi, is one of the best photographic guides and naturalists around.

I highly recommend Shamwari Safaris in Hwange National Park. The guide on our half-day drive was extremely knowledgeable and his fascination with the land and its flora and fauna really shone through. When we spotted a rare animal, you could tell it made *his* day. You can't pay less for a game drive in Hwange and you can't find a better guide. Driving yourself isn't worth it for the price you pay Shamwari.

Dan Bagatell, USA

Two-hour game drives cost US$11.50; a half-day trip is US$20.50 and a 12-hour return trip from Main Camp to Sinamatella costs US$40. He also offers tailored safaris for groups of up to six people for US$75 per person per day from Hwange Main Camp, including transfers, meals, camping equipment and camping fees (or he can arrange National Parks' accommodation at extra cost). Budget travellers with their own camping gear (equipment is available for hire) can do similar trips, but without transfers, meals or set-up camps, starting at US$40 per day. Shamwari does transfers for up to seven people between Hwange Main Camp and Dete railway station (US$4), Hwange Safari Lodge (US$5.50), Hwange Aerodrome (US$6.50), Safari Crossroads (US$9), Gwaai River Hotel (US$15.50) and the Mlibizi ferry landing (US$77). These safaris are popular, so booking is strongly advised.

Gwaai Valley Safaris (☎ 3401; fax 375), PO Box 17, Gwaai River, is a laid-back operation run by Mr Harry Bennie. If you're staying inside the park, half/full-day game drives cost US$17/33 per person; the full-day option includes lunch. Longer mobile safaris are also available for reasonable prices, and are tailor-made to your plans. You can be picked up from Hwange Main Camp, Gwaai River village or the Dete railway station (provided you wait until dawn). There are also three and four-day Backpacker Special Safaris which operate around the Ajay's Motorways bus schedule.

A third major player is Africa Dawn Safaris, based in Bulawayo, which operates multiple day camping safaris, mainly to the Ngwethla area. For transport, accommodation, meals and two game drives, they charge

ZIMBABWE

Elephant Control

One practice which remains highly controversial is the Zimbabwe National Parks Department's culling of elephants. Although an average of 16 to 20 elephants are poached every week, the country now has over 70,000 elephants, and that, officials claim, is twice Zimbabwe's carrying capacity. For evidence of the destruction that results from elephant overpopulation, say culling proponents, one need only look at Botswana's Chobe National Park which has four times the ideal elephant population. It's true – in places, the bush appears to have experienced nuclear holocaust. Although the culling is done relatively humanely – entire herds are destroyed rather than individuals to prevent emotional stress on the survivors – many argue that nature should simply be allowed to take its course. Others favour translocation as an alternative to culling.

The flaw in this argument, according to officials, is that humans have interfered so drastically with lands outside game reserves – setting up farms and veterinary control fences; grazing domestic stock; and clearing the tasty bushland trees that elephants bulldoze, uproot and devour in staggering quantities – the herds haven't the ability to spread out as they'd be inclined to if there had been no human interference.

When elephants do decide to spread out, they create problems for local farmers, who get no benefit from the huge parcels of land set aside as national parks. Historically, culling has provided a sort of compensation for local people in the form of meat. The recent drought has also compounded the problem. Instead of controlling the elephant population, it has forced record numbers of elephants into urban areas, especially Kariba, where they've taken to drinking from swimming pools, and destroying trees and gardens. This has produced a dangerous situation for local people, their property, their crops and their animals.

Even the large number of elephants in wild and wonderful Hwange National Park is a feat of human-engineering. Because the park's dams and artificially pumped water holes are unnatural creations, many ecologists agree that Hwange's wildlife must be carefully managed. Otherwise, they say, the park will face an irreconcilable conflict between conservation and tourism. Tourists come to see wildlife, so new water holes are created to attract more animals to visitor areas. Thanks to the presence of water, wildlife populations increase in these areas. Because of this wildlife density, tourist numbers increase and so does pressure on the environment, exerted by both wildlife and increased demand for tourist facilities. The environment begins to degrade and at this stage, it becomes clear something has to give. In the past, park managers have opted for culling.

The opposite camp argues very convincingly that elephants and their destruction play a vital

US$100 per person per day. To base yourself at Sinamatella Camp, the price is US$187 per person. Three-hour/full-day game drives cost US$20/32.

If you prefer straight game drives, United Touring Company offers two hour-game cruises around the 10-Mile Drive several times daily from Hwange Safari Lodge or Hwange Main Camp for US$20 per person. Full-day drives with lunch are US$45. UTC is based at Main Camp but also maintains an office at Hwange Safari Lodge. Touch the Wild also runs two-hour/full-day game drives for US$48/154 but, as the prices would indicate, they cater mainly for pre-booked package tours.

Walking Trips For walking, camping and backpacking trips through Hwange National Park, you can't beat Khangela Safaris, run by professional guide Mike Scott. He leads two-day to eight-day trips through the park's backcountry, either backpacking from camp to camp or doing day walks from a base camp. There's a good chance of seeing lions and leopards – you may even have the unique opportunity to track a black rhino through the thick bush. Best of all, the trips are very reasonably priced at just US$120 per day, including meals.

Backpackers Africa runs three to eight-day walking safaris through the park, including occasional trips to the remote Shakwankie Wilderness area, where buffaloes and elephants gather in large numbers to drink from natural springs rising from the Kalahari sands. They also run 12-day walking trips through the four national parks in Western Zimbabwe, including Hwange.

role in complicated bush ecosystems and that culling interferes with these natural processes. The mopane tree *(Colophospermum mopane)*, for example, covers much of the elephant's habitat in southern Africa and is a favoured food for the pachyderms. The fact that they strip leaves and turn tall mopane trees into stunted hedge shrubbery means that the trees begin to grow tender new leaves before their taller counterparts, providing food for impalas, kudu, eland and other browsers to see them through the end of the dry season. The young leaves also contain more energy, protein and nitrogen – and less indigestible tannin – than mature leaves.

Elephants also strip the bark from the mopane trees. While this may look unsightly, it opens the tree up to colonisation by termites, which hollow out the centre of the tree and make way for helpful cocktail ants. When an animal begins to browse on the tree, they're attacked by these ants, who rush to the tree's defence.

Thus, the elephants are actually part of a larger and less obvious cycle than simple observation would indicate.

What's more, the culling of elephants clearly isn't popular with typically sentimental Western tourists. They not only lament the killing, they also want to imagine they've stumbled upon a bit of wild Africa and rankle at the thought of complex management plans. On the other hand, few tourists relish the sight of decimated bush and starving elephants. As an alternative, the wildlife managers have experimented with translocating elephants out of overcrowded areas, but such operations are very expensive and park budgets don't stretch that far. To help handle these problems, there are currently plans to allocate to the parks a larger share of the revenues they earn, but that's still a long way off. ■

These trips aren't cheap – they are fully catered by a camp staff – but are still quite popular.

Hwange Main Camp

Although the rewarding scenery and possibility of spectacular chance encounters with wildlife lure people into the park's outer limits, for sheer density and variety of animals visitors need not wander far beyond Main Camp.

The 10-Mile Drive All that many visitors experience of Hwange is the 10-Mile Drive, a convenient loop around the most wildlife-packed part of the park, which can be easily completed in a two-hour game drive. The route takes in several popular water holes including Dom Pan (an apocryphal story explains that the name was derived from the sound made by its artificial pumping system – dom-dom-dom...); Balla-Balla Pan; and the highlight, Nyamandhlovu Pan. This pan, 10 km from Main Camp, features the high-rise Nyamandhlovu Viewing Platform. From this commanding perch, you'll have a view over Nyamandhlovu Pan where large numbers of animals come to drink.

The platform once provided a concession to visitors without vehicles, who would ride out on the morning UTC game drive, spend the day watching the comings and goings at the water hole, and ride back on the afternoon game drive. The whole system was derailed when two tourists grew bored of watching and tried to walk back to Main Camp. They were caught by National Parks staff who overreacted to this breach of the rules by banning the day trips for everyone.

Activities From Main Camp office, two hour ranger-guided walks to the wildlife-viewing hide at Sedina Pan depart at 6.30 and 10 am and 4 pm. No one should miss this safe and easy opportunity to strike into the bush on foot and see the herds of antelopes, zebras and giraffes that congregate around Main Camp. Occasionally, elephants, buffaloes, lions or even cheetahs are spotted on these walks. Many travellers spend days doing the entire regimen of walks and become familiar with the animals' daily routines.

The armed guides have had extensive bush training and draw on their wealth of knowledge to answer questions and provide a running commentary about the birds, animals and vegetation.

For two or three nights around the full moon each month, Main Camp rangers lead a convoy of vehicles into the park for two hours to see what's brewing out there at night. Hitchhikers are normally welcome at such times – just ask the rangers or anyone with empty space in their vehicle.

Places to Stay & Eat Main Camp contains most park services, including ranger headquarters, a campground, pub, restaurant, shop, petrol station, cottages and lodges. The shop is open from 8 to 10 am, noon to 2 pm and 4 to 7 pm. Behind it, a small museum displays aspects of Hwange's natural history.

The camp site has a baffling policy of parking caravans on the grassy lawns and requiring tent campers to pitch their tents in the concrete-hard dirt in the parking spaces. Anyone caught setting up on the lawn is quickly shooed away.

Bear in mind that Hwange is Zimbabwe's most popular wildlife park and it gets more crowded every year. During South African school holidays, the campground begins to resemble a makeshift neighbourhood at the fringe of an overcrowded metropolis. Although it doesn't offer any guarantees, advance booking is eminently wise.

Ngwethla Loop

Although Ngwethla is accessible to any car via the Kennedy Pans, the scenically diverse Ngwethla loop drive requires a sturdy vehicle. The greatest concentrations of animals may be observed on the open savanna around Ngwethla picnic site. The Kennedy Pans are also magnificent, especially at dusk, when large numbers of elephants pack into the water to bathe and frolic, churning the pans into thick brown mud holes. The picnic sites at Ngwethla and Jambile are available for overnight camping. For details, see the discussion of Other Camps later in this section.

Sinamatella Camp

Sinamatella Camp sits atop a 50-metre mesa with a commanding 50-km view in all directions. It's the nicest of Hwange's three main camps, and is great for a few days appreciating its changing moods. There's a ranger office and museum display, a small craft shop, a kiosk selling basic supplies, petrol pumps and a restaurant and pub.

Wildlife around Sinamatella is profuse but without the abundance or variety of grazers and browsers seen around Main Camp. By day, buffaloes and antelopes are often seen in the grassy patch below camp, but at night, Sinamatella comes alive. Vicious little honey badgers skitter around the restaurant looking for hand-outs and even invade the chalets if given half a chance. Once you've bedded down, expect to be haunted by the contented roaring of lions and the disconcerting yowling of, hyena at the foot of the hill – along with a host of unidentified screeches, thumps, bumps and howls which will conspire to thwart sleep.

Accommodation at Sinamatella includes camping, chalets, cottages and lodges. Ranger-escorted walks are available during the day for groups of up to six people; a popular walk is cross-country to Mandavu Dam and back. Similar overnight treks with an armed game scout, also limited to six people, must be prearranged through the National Parks' central booking office.

Robins & Nantwich Camps

Robins and Nantwich camps, near the park's north-west corner, lie in prime lion, cheetah and hyena country. The campground at Robins has been described as 'rough' and is subject to frequent nocturnal invasion by lions and hyena. Even chalet guests are advised not to venture to the toilet at night and once you've heard the hyena whooping and yelping beneath your windows, the warning will be driven home.

Chalets include outdoor cooking facilities. Robins Camp also has a sparsely stocked grocery, the Hyaena Shop. The new Hyaena Restaurant (open for three meals daily) and Hyaena Bar (open 10.30 am to 10.30 pm) occupy the ground floor of the fire tower. As at Sinamatella, you can take guided day walks and overnight trips with armed game scouts.

Nantwich Camp, which lacks camping facilities, has three two-bedroom lodges, each accommodating up to six people, but there are no other facilities.

Hotels, Camps & Lodges

Camps and lodges, especially in the luxury range, are sprouting like mushrooms around Hwange National Park, but however numerous the choices, only Nyati Lodge is accessible to budget or even mid-range foreign travellers (for another budget option, see under Gwaai River earlier in this chapter). The following is a list of the latest count; if no address or phone number is given, find the name of the tour operator (given in brackets after the camp name) under Tours in the Zimbabwe Getting Around chapter.

Chokamella Camp (Landela Safaris) Set atop the bluffs overlooking the Chokamella River, this camp occupies a private game reserve just outside Hwange National Park. Access into the Ngwethla Loop area of the park is via the Nyantwe Gate. Accommodation in thatched chalets costs US$140 per person.

Detema Safari Lodge (☎ 256; fax 269) This pleasant lodge is on a private farm just outside the national park. It sits on a hilltop with commanding views over the surrounding countryside. Accommodation is in thatched one or two-bedroom chalets, or in elevated lodges.

Finot's Camp (Kalambeza Safaris) This luxury camp on the banks of the Gwaai River lies on a 30,000-hectare private game ranch, where they conduct game walks and night drives and they also run excursions into the national park. Accommodation in A-frame chalets costs US$64 per person, with meals. It's just off the main Bulawayo-Victoria Falls road and is accessible by ordinary vehicles. Bus travellers may be picked up from Gwaai River Hotel.

The Hide (☎ 707438; fax 723230), George Hotel, King George Rd, PO Box 5615, Avondale, Harare, is one of the very few lodges inside Hwange National Park. The atmosphere seems intended to evoke romantically rustic Hollywood images of Africa. This basic tented camp organises twice-daily game walks and drives with licensed guides, visiting a series of waterhole viewing hides. The surrounding bush is characterised by mopane, teak and acacia woodland. The accommodation isn't as plush as most other camps in its price range; the US$230 per person price includes meals, activities and a concept.

Hwange Safari Lodge (☎ 332), belongs to the Sun Hotel group and is the most accessible of Hwange's luxury accommodation. Set on the main road into Main Camp, Hwange Safari Lodge serves as the terminal for Ajay's Motorways. Amenities include a swimming pool and tennis and volleyball courts. For single/double rooms, foreigners pay US$125/182 and Zimbabwe residents pay US$48/70. Note that we have had several serious complaints about service and demeanour.

A buffet lunch is served for US$5, but non-guests must pay an additional US$1.50 'membership fee' even to go in for a meal. The patio overlooks the hotel's private pan, so diners are treated to a front row view of assorted locals lumbering up for a drink. Kudu, elands, impalas, waterbucks, sables, giraffes and zebras are common, and elephants and buffaloes visit occasionally.

At the lodge, on the corner of the lawn is a display with basic park and wildlife information and a craft shop where you can often watch the artists producing beautifully grained wooden bowls – not indigenous crafts but works of art, nevertheless.

Ivory Lodge (Ivory Safaris) Ivory Lodge sits in dense bush just outside the park; it's not far from Main Camp, on a private game ranch. It fronts up to Zingweni Vlei, where animals congregate to scratch for water. Accommodation, which is in elevated teak and thatch bungalows, costs US$180 per person.

Jabulisa Lodge, PO Box 23, Gwaai River (☎ 2101; fax 295, both in Dete) Jabulisa Lodge, the name of which is Sindebele for 'place of delight', is built around a converted colonial farmhouse dating to 1922. The commanding view from the low ridge takes in a vast expanse of countryside. For foreigners, accommodation in thatched chalets costs US$220 per person including meals, game drives in Hwange National Park, night drives on the estate, horse-riding and tours of the nearby crocodile farm and communal lands. Without the activities, it's just US$110 per person. Transfers from Gwaai River are US$10.

Jijima Safari Camp (Wild Horizons) Jijima is a luxury tented camp at the eastern boundary of Hwange National Park. The camp sits on a private ranch run by a family of professional guides. The high-season rate is US$200 per person, including meals and game drives. They have access to Hwange via Nyantwe Gate into the Ngwethla Loop area, where there's a good chance of observing big cats. No children under 14 are accepted.

Kanondo Tree Camp (Touch the Wild) Although Kanondo (☎ 273) advertises 'tree lodges', they're more like chalets on stilts, although some are actually built around or against trees. Each has a view over Kanondo Pan, which is one of the area's most popular watering holes. The Kanondo area is the home of Zimbabwe's 'Presidential Herd' of elephants, 300 individuals which are protected from culling and hunting by a decree from Robert Mugabe. Another novelty is the 'underground hide', a sunken viewing shelter beside the water hole. Rates are US$170 per person, including all meals and two game drives.

Kumuna Lodge Kumuna Lodge (☎ 2101; fax 295, both in Dete), PO Box 19, Gwaai River, is set beside a warm mineral spring 20 km outside the national park. In Batonka, the name means 'place of peace'. It occupies a large private estate with plenty of wildlife of its own, and the owners, Mr and Mrs De Vries, have 50 years worth of amazing bush stories. This is one of the few lodges which accommodates children. Rates, including all the activities listed under Jabulisa Lodge, are US$193 per person. With full board but no activities, they're US$97.

Linkwasha Wilderness Lodge (Nemba Safaris) Linkwasha is actually a private concession inside Hwange National Park. It lies in the remote wild area of the park (its southern four-fifths) where the landscapes differ greatly from those along the public road system. This tented camp provides a wilderness escape, and the chance to view wildlife on scenic open plains. It accommodates up to 12 people and costs US$250 per person.

Makalolo Camp (Touch the Wild) One of Hwange's most remote camps, this luxury tented camp sits beside the pan of the same name in the south-eastern part of the park. Wildlife viewing is both in vehicles and on foot with an armed professional guide. The daily rate is US$275 per person, including all meals and two game drives; children are not accepted.

Nyati Lodge (Gwaai Valley Safaris) This camp, the only budget lodge in the vicinity of Hwange National Park, offers accommodation in comfortable lodges on the nearby private game reserve, Hankano Ranch. Accommodation costs US$40 per person, including three family style meals with the management and guides. Self-catering is available for US$20. There's also a no-frills camp site available to participants on Gwaai Valley Safaris' Backpacker Special safaris. Nyati is a convenient spot for game drives into the park.

Sable Valley Lodge (Touch the Wild) Sable Valley Lodge overlooks a water hole in a forestry reserve just outside the park. The large luxury lodges, constructed of pink slate bricks and thatch, are scattered through a grove of teak trees around the water hole, and the restaurant and bar shelter appears to have been inspired by the Sydney Opera House. The whole thing is surrounded by an electrified fence to keep the wildlife at bay. In 1991, it hosted Queen Elizabeth and the Duke of Edinburgh. The cost is US$131/150 per person for half/full-board. A fully inclusive plan with two game drives is US$250.

Sikumi Tree Lodge (Touch the Wild) Yet again, don't be led to believe you'll be sleeping in the treetops; the thatched bungalows at Sikumi Tree Lodge are constructed on stilts just two metres off the ground. In addition to game drives in the national park and night drives on the private estate, you may also opt for game walks and visits to nearby African villages. Standard rates are the same as at Sable Valley Lodge; luxury suites cost US$300 per person, all inclusive. Children are welcome.

Simba Lodge (☎ 707438; fax 723230), PO Box 5615, Harare, lies 20 km off the Bulawayo-Victoria Falls road, 40 minutes from the Nyantwe Gate to Hwange National Park. It occupies a 600-hectare concession in the Gwaai Forest Reserve; the sandstone and thatch lodges sit at the edge of forest lands, overlooking an open grassy plain. Prices start at US$200 per person.

Other National Parks' Camps

Picnic Sites The enclosed public picnic sites at Shumba, Mandavu Dam, Masuma Dam, Ngwethla, Jambile, Kennedy Pan I and

The Presidential Elephants

Once upon a time, a herd of 22 elephants inhabited the vicinity of Hwange Safari Lodge. Without official protection, the herd was continuously being harrassed by humans, their animals and their vehicles, and many had fallen to the ravages of poaching. As a result, the intelligent beasts suffered what appeared to be psychological damage and lived a sorry and traumatised existence. They eventually resorted to raiding crops and menacing people, thereby bringing scorn upon themselves from the local human community.

When a private safari concern established Hwange Estate in 1972, a protected block of land outside Hwange National Park, hunting and poaching was stopped and the herd slowly began to recover. By the early 1990s, it had grown to 300 confident individuals who no longer lived in fear of humans.

In 1991, safari operator Alan Elliot approached President Robert Mugabe to suggest that the herd be accorded offical protection. The president responded by issuing a decree that this herd be forever protected, wherever it felt inclined to wander. It now enjoys what's more or less the pachyderm equivalent of royal status.

For more on the history of this privileged herd, see Alan Elliot's book *The Presidential Elephants of Zimbabwe*. It is available at Hwange Safari Lodge and elsewhere in Zimbabwe. ■

National Parks' Exclusive Camps Exclusive camps operated by the park service cater for groups of up to 12, including the use of cutlery and cooking facilities. Each camp has a resident guide who will take you walking for as long as you'd like during your stay. *Bumbusi Camp* near Sinamatella is the nicest of the lot but for holiday periods, it's spoken for over six months in advance, so book early.

Deka Camp, 25 km west of Robins Camp near the Botswana border, and *Lukosi*, in the Deka Safari Area near Mbala Camp just outside the park, offer nice amenities but there's not much wildlife around. Deka is accessible only by 4WD vehicle. Lukosi is open only during the non-hunting season between November and April. It's possible to walk within an eight km radius of Lukosi without a guide.

Getting There & Away

Air Air Zimbabwe flies to Hwange National Park from Harare via Kariba daily between 7.30 and 11 am, with a stop at Kariba every day except Wednesday. The flights then continue on to Victoria Falls. From Hwange to Harare, flights leave daily at 3.40 pm (Mondays at 3.05 pm), with a stop at Kariba en route. There are also daily flights to and from Victoria Falls.

UTC vehicles meet incoming flights and provide transfers to and from Hwange Safari Lodge or Main Camp for US$5 per person, with a minimum charge of six fares.

Bus If you're arriving on the Hwange Special Express bus from Bulawayo or Victoria Falls, get off at Safari Crossroads and hitch or walk the 11.5 km to Hwange Safari Lodge. A better option is Ajay's Motorways, which drops you at the Safari Lodge. From there, it's another five km walk or hitch to the Dete turn-off. You can't walk or hitch beyond the railway line so you must wait at the entrance for a lift into the park.

If you have more time, get off the Ajay's or Hwange Special Express bus east of Hwange town and try hitching along the

Detema Dam are made available to groups of up to eight people as exclusive camps. Lions are frequently seen in the area of Shumba (the name means 'lion') but the site itself isn't so appealing. Mandavu has a nice big expanse of water and Kennedy Pan I has hordes of elephants at night. The nice camping area at Ngwethla lies in an area of heavy wildlife concentrations.

My favourite site is Masuma Dam, where you can hole up in the hide overlooking the water and spend the night listening to belching hippos and trumpeting elephants and, if there's a moon, look on as endless parades of thirsty antelopes, zebras, giraffes and predators stop by for a drink. Unfortunately, during the drought of the early 1990s, Masuma Pan all but dried up and it still hasn't returned to its former splendour.

rough 40-km road into Sinamatella Camp. Expect long waits.

Train The train between Bulawayo and Victoria Falls passes Dete at 12.45 am eastbound and 1.30 am westbound. Refer to the Dete section earlier in this chapter for further information.

Getting Around

Car The park speed limit is 40 km/h, so don't try to see the whole park in a single day. Unless you're racing to reach your camp before closing time, there's no reason to rush, anyway. If you're booked into a camp, however, and don't turn up before the gates close, a search will be conducted and once you're located, you'll have to foot the bill for the rangers' time and efforts.

Petrol is sold to the public at Hwange Safari Lodge, Main Camp and Sinamatella Camp.

Hitching Officially, hitchhikers are not permitted inside the park. The rule is intended, of course, to prevent visitors being caught out among the lions and elephants without a vehicle. It is also in place to shield visitors with vehicles from the unpleasantness of having to refuse constant petitions for lifts when they'd rather enjoy a more solitary experience.

Having said that, it must be pointed out that park officials realise not everyone can afford to purchase or hire a vehicle and sometimes tolerate discreet or informal hitching outside the park entrances or around Main Camp.

Victoria Falls

The world-famous Victoria Falls, 1.7 km wide, drops between 90 and 107 metres into the Zambezi Gorge. An average of 550,000 cubic metres of water plummet over the edge every minute, but during the flood stage from March to May, up to five million cubic metres per minute pass over the falls. This is

what Mr Kodak had in mind when he was dreaming big. It's Zimbabwe's supreme contribution to the list of the world's great attractions, and miles and miles of film and videotape are gobbled through cameras every year here.

VICTORIA FALLS

Victoria Falls town was built on tourism and has now developed into an archetypal tourist trap. Although it's still a long way from the Ripley's-Believe-it-or-Not and wax museum scene of Canada's Niagara Falls, the kitsch curio shops, traditional dance shows, reptile parks, adrenaline sports, muzak marimba revues, buzzing and low-flying aircraft and zebra-striped tour buses all nurture the carnivalesque tourist jungle that has sprouted and taken root here.

Fortunately, the star attraction – Victoria Falls itself – is safely cordoned off by a real jungle of its own creation. To walk along the paths through the spray-generated rainforests that flank the gorge, you'd never suspect the existence of anything other than the monumental waterfall that's giving you a good soaking.

History

The original Victoria Falls town was Old Drift, established as a 'wild west' sort of trading settlement on the (now Zambian) riverbank shortly after David Livingstone's reports filtered back to White society elsewhere. In 1865 he wrote in purple-tinted and comma-laden prose:

The morning sun gilds these columns of watery smoke with all the glowing colours of double and treble rainbows. The evening sun, from a hot yellow sky, imparts a sulphurous hue and gives one the impression that the yawning gulf might resemble the mouth of the bottomless pit. No bird sits and sings in that grove of perpetual showers, or even builds its nest there...

The sunshine, elsewhere in this land so overpowering, never penetrates the deep gloom of that shade. In the presence of the strange Mosi-oa-Tunya, we can sympathise with those who, when the world was young, peopled the earth, air and river with beings not of mortal form. Sacred to what deity would be this awful chasm and that dark grove over which hovers an ever-abiding pillar of cloud?

The ancient Batoka chieftains used Kazuruka, now Garden Island, and Baoruka, the island further west, also on the lip of the falls, as sacred spots for worshipping the deity. It is no wonder that under the cloudy columns, and near the brilliant rainbows, with the ceaseless roar of the cataract, with the perpetual flow, as if pouring forth from the hand of the Almighty, their souls should be filled with reverential awe.

At the turn of the century, however, malaria began to take its toll and Old Drift was shifted to the site of present-day Livingstone, Zambia. The Zambezi Gorge was first bridged when the abortive Cape-to-Cairo railway came through between 1902 and 1904, and with the arrival of the railway came the first influx of tourists. The original Victoria Falls Hotel was constructed in 1906 and 66 years later, the growing village was granted town status.

Orientation

Most visitors who don't arrive by air chug into Victoria Falls by train. They alight at the colonial railway station which either issues them into the lawns and gardens of the Victoria Falls Hotel or along the tracks to the heart of town (inasmuch as the town has one). Most tourist-oriented businesses nestle inside arcades along or very near either Livingstone Way or Park Way (the intersection of these two streets is amusingly known as Wimpy Corner, after the fast-food outlet there). The bulk of Victoria Falls' population, however, is concentrated in Chinotimba township, down Pioneer Rd from the centre. Here you'll find lots of inexpensive local shops and a rollicking beer hall.

Information

The Victoria Falls Publicity Association (☎ 4202), adjacent to the Town Council Rest Camp & Caravan Park, distributes local advertising and sells town maps (US$1.30) and booklets about the falls area (US$2.50). It's open Monday to Friday from 8 am to 12.30 pm and 2 to 4 pm, and on Saturday from 8 am to noon. If you're interested in background information, pick up a copy of

---

Name Games

Humans have been living around Victoria Falls for hundreds of thousands of years. The first known name of the falls was Shongwe, given to it by the Tokaleya people who inhabited the area prior to the Nguni invasions. Later, the Ndebele changed the name to Amanza Thunquayo, or Water Rising as Smoke. The late-arriving Makalolo, a tribe of refugees from the Nguni invasions, changed it yet again, this time to Mosi-oa-Tunya or Smoke that Thunders. On 16 November 1855, Scottish missionary David Livingstone was brought to the falls by the Makalolo in a dugout canoe and, following the established procedure, promptly renamed them in honour of the queen.

During the Zimbabwean name games going on shortly after independence, Victoria Falls was not renamed 'Mosi-oa-Tunya' as it was pointed out that the country couldn't afford to sacrifice the familiarity of Livingstone's choice of names. They feared that by any other name, the tourism potential and income generated by Zimbabwe's monumental drip just wouldn't smell as sweet. ■

A Visitors Guide to Victoria Falls by Mrs M Newman (1987). It's full of information on local wildlife, including birds and vegetation, and also includes a historical summary.

Money The banks are lined up in front of the same car park as the post office and all charge the same 1% commission to change money. If you're caught out after hours, try Victoria Falls Hotel, which offers reasonable exchange rates and charges no commission. Avoid all street changers in Victoria Falls; otherwise, you'll either lose your money or wind up in trouble with the police.

Post & Telecommunications The post office in Victoria Falls is incredibly busy, and you'll often wait up to an hour just to buy postage stamps; fortunately, most hotel gift shops also sell stamps.

Film Film is most readily available at the immense Zambezi Productions photo shop in Sopers Arcade (where all those whitewater rafting photos and videos are

ZIMBABWE

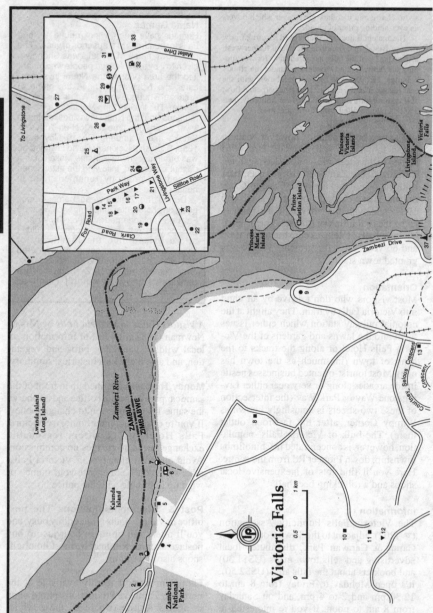

Victoria Falls

1 km

0.5

0

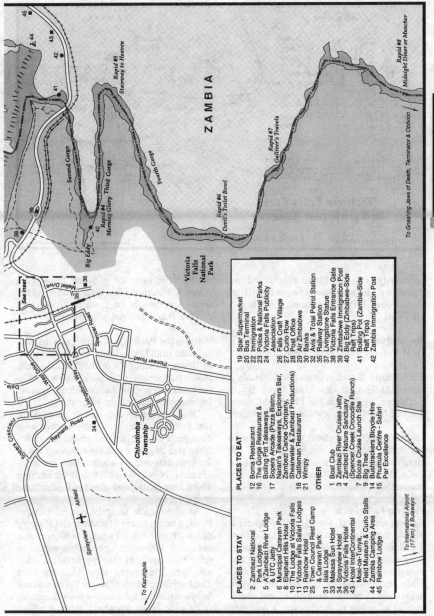

ZAMBIA

Rapid #5
Stairway to Heaven

Second Gorge

Rapid #4
40 April #4
Morning Glory Third Gorge

Fourth Gorge

Big Eddy

Rapid #6
Devil's Toilet Bowl

Rapid #7
Gulliver's Travels

Rapid #8
Midnight Diner or Muncher

To Gnashing Jaws of Death, Terminator & Oblivion

Victoria Falls National Park

See Inset

Mallet Drive

Spencer Road

Pioneer Road

Livingstone Way

West Drive

Dale

Speke's Crescent

Reynard Road

Chinotimba Township

Airfield

Sprayview

To Kazungula

To International Airport (17km) & Bulawayo

PLACES TO STAY

2 Zambezi National
   Park Lodges
5 A'Zambezi River Lodge
   & UTC Jetty
6 Municipal Caravan Park
8 Elephant Hills Hotel
10 The Lodge at Victoria Falls
11 Victoria Falls Safari Lodges
13 Rainbow Hotel
25 Town Council Rest Camp
   & Caravan Park
31 Ilala Lodge
33 Makasa Sun Hotel
34 Sprayview Hotel
36 Victoria Falls Hotel
43 Hotel InterContinental
   Mosi-oa-Tunya,
   Zambia Camping Area
44 Field Museum & Curio Stalls
45 Rainbow Lodge

PLACES TO EAT

12 Boma Restaurant
16 The Gorge Restaurant &
   Boiling Pot Takeaways
17 Sopers Arcade (Pizza Bistro,
   Naran's Takeaways, Explorers Bar,
   Zambezi Canoe Company,
   Shearwater & Zambezi Productions)
18 Cattleman Restaurant
21 Wimpy

OTHER

1 Boat Club
3 Zambezi River Cruises Jetty
4 Zambezi Nature Sanctuary
   (Spencer Creek Crocodile Ranch)
7 Booze Cruise Launch Site
9 Big Tree
14 Bushtrackers Bicycle Hire
15 Phumula Centre - Safari
   Par Excellence
19 Spar Supermarket
20 Bus Terminal
22 Immigration
23 Police & National Parks
   Victoria Falls Publicity
   Association
26 Falls Craft Village
27 Curio Row
28 Post Office
29 Air Zimbabwe
30 Banks
32 Avis & Total Petrol Station
35 Railway Station
37 Livingstone Statue
38 Victoria Falls Entrance Gate
39 Zimbabwe Immigration Post
40 Big Eddy (Zimbabwe-Side
   Raft Trips)
41 Boiling Pot (Zambia-Side
   Raft Trips)
42 Zambia Immigration Post

ZIMBABWE

Victoria Falls Park & Rainforest Reserve

produced) or at the Photo Fast just down Parkway. For a 36-exposure roll of Fujichrome 100, for example, you'll pay US$8.50.

Medical Services A recommended doctor is Dr H Vivian (☎ 4319) on West Drive.

Bookshops If you're desperate for reading material, go to the Upmarket Book Exchange, upstairs in the Phumula Centre. They also sell ethnic jewellery and clothing.

Laundry Victoria Falls doesn't yet have a laundrette (although one is planned), but laundry services are available at the Town Council Rest Camp & Caravan Park for very reasonable rates.

Victoria Falls Park

Before setting off for the falls, spend a minute thinking about water and the effects it will have on what you're carrying. Protect your camera equipment and wrap cash and valuables susceptible to sogging in plastic. (I made the mistake of carrying my airline tickets and even after hours hung out to dry, instead of going to Anchorage, I probably

could have boarded a plane to Ankara without detection.) It's also wise to either wear waterproofs or clothing that won't create a public scandal when soaked.

Visiting the Park You can approach the park entrance from Livingstone Way east of town or down the track from the Victoria Falls Hotel. Admission to the park is now US$20 for foreigners and the daily ticket can be used for multiple visits on the same day.

Once you reach the rim, a network of surfaced tracks – laid down to prevent tourist damage to the fragile rainforest ecosystem – takes you to a series of viewpoints. One of the most dramatic is Cataract View, the westernmost point, which requires climbing down a steep stairway into (and out of) the gorge.

Another track is aptly named Danger Point, where terraces of soaking and slippery moss-covered rocks and a sheer and unfenced 100-metre drop-off conspire to rattle your nerve as you approach the stunning and frightening view into the First Zambezi Gorge. From Danger Point, you can follow a side track for a view over the gracefully precarious Zambezi Bridge which

A Matter of Air, Mist & Light

The time of year and time of day when you visit will affect your experience of the Victoria Falls. The flow of water is greatest between April and June so these are the times for the misty views. When the wind is blowing, rainbows form over the gorge. During low water from September to November, you'll get the clearest views and photos with the most rock showing between segments of the falls. During midsummer, the humidity will be at its most stifling and the rains will be hard and frequent, making viewing a generally hit-or-miss proposition.

Sunrises and sunsets are the best from late October to December when the sun is in the south, humidity is rising, clouds are most dramatic and the river is still low enough not to obscure the view with spray. During the dry season, the best sunset view is normally from the viewpoints opposite main falls while sunrise is best from Cataract View. However, Cataract View is low in the gorge, so the morning sun won't be seen here until a good hour before it's already shining brightly elsewhere.

During the dry season, you may want to return to Cataract View in the mid-afternoon when the sun shines directly into the gorge and the refraction rainbow is strategically placed for an ideal photograph. For something really special, however, time your visit to coincide with the rising of the full moon. The park stays open later to allow you to witness the magical lunar rainbow over the falls.

Having said all that, it's important to point out that these are all just guidelines. Air, mist and light conditions could combine to offer magnificent surprises from any vantage point at any time of the year! ∎

---

connects Zimbabwe with Zambia. This is now a favourite vantage point for locals, who gather to watch the insane foreigners diving off the Zambezi Bridge on giant rubber bands.

Whilst walking through the rainforests, note the profusion of unusual species growing in this unique little enclave – ebony, ferns, fig trees and a variety of lianas and flowering plants. Also, watch for the bushbucks which may be seen browsing right up to the lip of the gorge.

Along the Zambezi

If you don't have a vehicle and can't afford a group tour, a free walk along the Zambezi above the falls is an excellent – and possibly even thrilling – alternative. The tracks don't enter Zambezi National Park, but the area is still packed with wildlife. Don't take this walk too lightly; you may see warthogs, crocodiles, hippos, a variety of antelopes and even elephants, buffaloes and lions.

Avoid walking too close to the shore – the crocs are thick along the riverbank and can appear from nowhere without warning. Although some silly travellers do swim in this stretch of the river, it's extremely

unwise. If you're not fazed by crocodiles and hippos, think about the bilharzia.

Livingstone Statue Most Zambezi walks begin at the Livingstone statue, which overlooks Cataract View at the upper end of the Victoria Falls Park track. Here you can gaze across the Zambezi as it steepens and gains momentum before disappearing over the edge. Thanks to a locked gate topped with barbed wire, to join the river walk, you have to go out via the main park gate.

The Big Tree As an attraction, the Big Tree is – well – a big tree, but as an excuse for a walk, it makes a fine destination. This corpulent arboreal character is a giant baobab or 'upside-down tree', so called because a distant ancestor reportedly offended some deity or another and in punishment, was uprooted, turned over and stuck back into the ground upside down. Although this specimen stands only about 25 metres high, from eye level, its 20-metre circumference makes it seem much larger.

The Big Tree served as a camp and a gathering site for early settlers and traders awaiting passage across the Zambezi to Old

The Zambezi Gorges

The geology behind the curiously formed gorges at Victoria Falls is fascinating. Since the Zambezi flows through alternating soft and resistant rock formations, the character of the river changes accordingly. Along the easy stretches, it follows a broad channel and the river becomes dotted with sandy islets carried and deposited by silty and slow-moving water.

Where the water encounters rough stretches, erosion rather than deposition is the primary force. In Zimbabwe's case, these resistant regions of basalt were laid down layer upon layer by volcanic eruptions during the Jurassic period. Subsequent even cooling of the layers caused it to crack and fissure and in one place, it opened up a gaping rift over 1700 metres wide. Over the following aeons, erosion continued and the entire area apparently did a brief stint underwater, as evidenced by the remains of aquatic creatures which have been discovered in the area.

Climatic changes (some undoubtedly caused by continental drift), however, subsequently caused the surface water to dry up, leaving two rivers flowing on either side of the basaltic plateau – the Matetsi to the north and the Zambezi to the south. Subsequent tectonic uplifting south of the Zambezi, however, shifted the river's course further and further north. At the point where it encountered the previously mentioned 250-metre-deep, 1700-metre-wide fissure, it plunged in and was forced to cut itself a new course through the difficult material – and eventually join up with the Matetsi. This original Victoria Falls was eight km downstream from the present falls. Weaknesses in the basalt perpendicular to the river's flow and two million years of erosion have allowed the river to cut through seven subsequent gorges, each further upstream from the previous one. The waterfall we see today is actually Victoria VIII! ■

Drift – and later to Livingstone – on the opposite shore.

Falls Craft Village

In this fortified mock-up of historical Zimbabwean lifestyles, you'll see a variety of ethnic huts, prefabricated in their area of origin and moved to the village. You can also watch craftspeople at work and consult with a nganga, who can let you in on your future – if you really want to know it. What they won't mention is that you're destined to exit the place through an immense curio shop. Guided tours are conducted at 9.30 am, and they stage a live traditional dance production from 7 to 8 pm nightly. The village is open from 8.30 am to 4.30 pm Monday to Saturday, and on Sunday from 9 am to 1 pm.

Curio Row & Snake Park

The area's first White settler, Percy Clark, opened the first in a long line of Victoria Falls curio shops in 1903, but the real boom arrived on the heels of the railway. One of the original places, *Soper's Curios*, has been in business since 1911. Outside its rustic shop is a pool where the original owner, Jack Soper, kept his commercial gimmick – a live crocodile. Not surprisingly, there's still a crocodile whiling away its days in the same

pool. Near the end of the street is the Victoria Falls Aquarium, with a range of Zimbabwean freshwater fish and crocodiles; the idea is to draw you into the curio shop which specialises in fish-inspired carvings, jewellery and clothing.

If you've always wanted to buy a copper cut-out in the shape of Zimbabwe, drilled through and installed with clock workings, etched with a giraffe-and-acacia design and mounted on a bit of anonymous wood, here's your chance. The kitsch value of the stuff sold in this curio shop cluster staggers the imagination. When you've finished browsing, you can check out the Zambezi Taxidermy Snake Park and pay US$1.50 to watch snakes being milked.

For real quality, however, go to the crafts halls at the end of the street, where local women display their creations and are happy to bargain over already competitive prices. Skilful bargainers can pick up great deals while contributing directly to the local economy.

Zambezi Nature Sanctuary (Spencer Creek Crocodile Ranch)

If you're impressed by all those photos of tourists cuddling up to crocodile hatchlings, here's the place for the hands-on experience.

With 5000 crocodiles of all sizes, the Zambezi Nature Sanctuary (formerly known as the Spencer Creek Crocodile Ranch) offers lots of crocs for your US$2 admission fee. They also screen informative videos about crocodile lifestyles and there's a crocodile museum, a tearoom, a cat enclosure, an aviary, a collection of insects, domestic animals and a curio shop.

It's open from 8 am to 5 pm daily except Christmas.

Activities

Victoria Falls is quickly becoming the biggest adrenaline capital-cum-tourist playground west of New Zealand. There are lots of operators and once you're in town, you won't be short of options. Despite the prices listed here, it's wise to shop around; you'll sometimes find great deals.

Flight of the Angels The name of this 10 to 15-minute buzz over the falls is derived from an overworked quote by an awe-struck David Livingstone, who, apparently seized with religious inspiration at the vision, wrote in his journal 'on sights as beautiful as this, angels in their flight must have gazed'. Most of today's angels are produced in Kansas by Piper Aircraft and the privilege of briefly joining them in their flight costs an appropriately celestial US$47 per person. Few earth-bound visitors relish seeing the planes buzzing over the falls, but those who've done the trip have invariably loved it.

Flights are operated by United Air (☎ 4530) at the Sprayview Aerodrome; you can book directly or through any Victoria Falls tour operator. They depart roughly every 15 minutes. A 30-minute version, including a buzz over the falls and a game flight over Zambezi National Park's Chundu Loop, costs US$60 per person.

Other scenic flights are organised by Southern Cross Aviation (☎ 4618) which runs 15-minute helicopter flights over the falls (US$53 per person), 30-minute flights up the Zambezi (US$90), 25-minute flights over the falls by Cessna (US$35) and a 40-minute Cessna flight along the Zambezi

Gorges (US$50). For something different, they fly by helicopter to a mid-river island for a two-hour champagne breakfast; it costs US$390 for up to four people.

Zambezi Raft Trips Although it's a splash out in more ways than one, don't miss the thrill of being swept and flung headlong down the angry Zambezi below the falls. White-water enthusiasts travel from all over the world to do just that (but bear in mind that resurfacing of the Batoka Dam project below the falls could someday put a permanent end to the rafting mania).

The rapids through the Zambezi Gorges are among the world's wildest – and safest, largely because of the deep water, steep canyon walls and lack of rocks mid-stream. The roughest rapids, which during low water are considered class IV and V (on the I to VI ratings scale), are negotiated by well-experienced oarspeople. People are always falling out of the rafts (if they manage to hold on, they're known as short swimmers; long swimmers are those who shoot the rapids without a raft) but the operators use the best safety gear available and have the situation well in hand. As a result, injuries are very rare. Bear in mind, however, that the river

---

Who Needs the Booze?

Several years ago, a group of Japanese businessmen in shiny shoes and three-piece suits reported at what they thought was the appointed spot for their pre-booked mid-morning 'booze cruise' on the Zambezi. After a detailed introductory chat in English – which none of them understood – they donned the proffered life jackets and helmets and were ushered into a bus and carried to the lip of the gorge. There they were instructed to follow an escort down a steep and narrow track to the water, where their boats would be waiting. The men, who spoke next to no English, followed instructions, then at the bottom, climbed aboard the waiting rubber rafts. After 15 wild and rollicking km of Zambezi abuse, the men, now soaked to the bone but visibly thrilled with the experience, reportedly enquired about when the booze would be served. ■

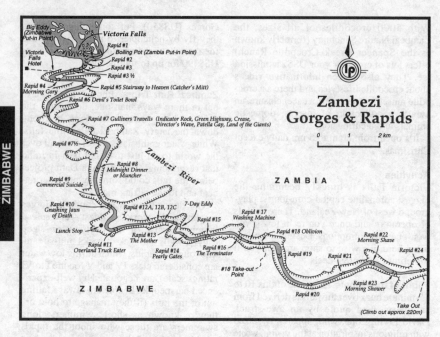

Zambezi Gorges & Rapids

Big Eddy (Zimbabwe Put-in Point)
Victoria Falls
Victoria Falls Hotel
Rapid #1
Boiling Pot (Zambia Put-in Point)
Rapid #2
Rapid #3
Rapid #3 ½
Rapid #4 Morning Gory
Rapid #5 Stairway to Heaven (Catcher's Mitt)
Rapid #6 Devil's Toilet Bowl
Rapid #7 Gullivers Travells (Indicator Rock, Green Highway, Crease, Director's Wave, Patella Gap, Land of the Giants)
Rapid #7½
Zambezi River
ZAMBIA
Rapid #8 Midnight Dinner or Muncher
Rapid #9 Commercial Suicide
Rapid #10 Gnashing Jaws of Death
Rapid #12A, 12B, 12C
7-Day Eddy
Rapid # 17 Washing Machine
Rapid #15
Lunch Stop
Rapid #13 The Mother
Rapid #14 Pearly Gates
Rapid #16 The Terminator
Rapid #18 Oblivion
Rapid #22 Morning Shave
Rapid #24
Rapid #11 Overland Truck Eater
#18 Take-out Point
Rapid #19
Rapid #21
Rapid #23 Morning Shower
ZIMBABWE
Rapid #20
Take Out (Climb out approx 220m)

0   1   2 km

god Nyaminyami normally demands some sort of offering from river travellers; don't take anything you're not prepared to lose.

The only other challenging element is the steep and slippery slog back up to the rim while your body is still jittery with adrenaline surges from the ride down. If you were so busy holding on that you missed the experience, the various Zimbabwean operators feature the day's runs on video at Ilala Lodge nightly at 7.30 pm, where you can also purchase videos and photo stills of your own run.

The main players are Safari Par Excellence (☎ 4224) in the Phumula Centre and Frontiers (☎ 4267) and Shearwater (☎ 4471), both in the arcade area. On the Zambian side, there's Sobek (☎ (260-3) 321432) on Katombora Rd in Livingstone, but they also have a small office on Parkway in Victoria Falls. For a half/full day's rafting, you're looking at US$80/100 on the Zimbabwe side and US$75/95 on the

Zambia side. Both Shearwater and Safari Par Excellence provide long-sleeved wetsuits, which temper the icy blast of spray on winter mornings.

High-water runs through rapids 11 to 18 (or 23), which are relatively mundane, can be done either from the Zimbabwean or Zambian side between 1 July and 15 August, though in low rainfall years they may begin as early as mid-May. Wilder low-water runs taking in the 22 winding km from rapids four to 18 (or 23) in Zimbabwe and rapids one to 18 (or 23) in Zambia operate from roughly 15 August to late December. The 'put-on' points for these are Big Eddy on the Zimbabwean side and the Boiling Pot on the Zambian shore. If you definitely want to continue to Rapid 23, make it clear when booking the trip; otherwise, they'll pull out at Rapid No 18 (known as Oblivion). All operators walk around Rapid No 9, which is affectionately nicknamed Commercial Suicide.

With Safari Par Excellence, you have the added option of overnighting at Camp Mukuni in Zambia before returning to Victoria Falls. You'll pay US$35 to sleep on the beach and US$45 for tented accommodation.

During low season, from January to July, Sobek runs trips further down, starting at Songwe Gorge, the site of the original Victoria Falls. Sobek also runs overnight trips, with a camp at Songwe Gorge, as well as rafting expeditions lasting from two to seven days. Frontiers and Safari Par Excellence offer similar trips on the Zimbabwe side. Three-day trips average US$250 per person, five days cost around US$500 and the seven-day trip through Batoka Gorge is US$1200, fully inclusive. This trip begins at Boiling Pot and heads downstream, taking in Chimamba Rapids, Moemba Falls and Batoka Gorge, and finishing up at the Matetsi River mouth.

For a unique perspective and a tamer option, the so-called Float of the Angels, operated by Safari Par Excellence, entails a breakfast raft tour along the base of the falls from Zambia's Boiling Pot. It costs US$50 per person.

River Cruises There is a variety of river booze cruises on the Zambezi above the falls, some of which include a stop on Kandahar Island in midstream. (Oddly enough, the African-sounding name of this island isn't African at all; it was named for Lord Roberts of Kandahar, whose title was in turn derived from the turn-of-the-century Battle of Kandahar, in Afghanistan.)

Some excursions, such as the Sundowner Cruise, include drinks in the price and are good value; others have a very expensive cash bar. You can choose between a champagne breakfast (6 to 8 am), a morning tea cruise (10 am to noon) a lunch cruise (12.30 to 2.30 pm) or an afternoon tea cruise (2 to 4 pm) for US$17. There's also an ornithologist's cruise from 2.30 to 4.30 pm which costs US$11; a no-frills morning backpackers' cruise for US$10; an afternoon champagne cruise from 4 to 6 pm for US$18;

a sunset cruise from 4 to 6.30 pm for US$16; and the most popular, a sundowner booze cruise from 5 to 6.30 pm for US$17. The boats don't stop anywhere and neither does the alcohol so things can get rowdy, but it's fun and the sunset may never seem more brilliant. A lighter variation on the Sundowner cruise opts for small boats and combines booze and birdwatching.

Boats leave from the jetties near A'Zambezi River Lodge. See Dabula Safaris, Zambezi Wilderness Safaris or Safari Par Excellence. Transport from hotels is included in the price, and leaves 30 minutes prior to cruise departures.

Livingstone Island Picnic Thanks to Tongabezi Lodge (in Zambia), you can enjoy a three-course champagne lunch at the 'world's most exclusive picnic spot' on Livingstone Island, that big chunk of rock that splits Victoria Falls into two bits. The picnic is open to anyone and does pick-ups from the Zimbabwean side of the falls. The price of US$65 includes car and boat transfers, a three-course meal (including alcohol) and park fees. They also arrange overnight camping trips on the island; these normally take place during the full moon to view the lunar rainbows over the falls. Book through Safari Par Excellence.

If you don't mind a bit of adrenaline with your meal, you can organise your own Livingstone Island picnic. When water levels are very low – as in late winter – you can actually pick your way to Livingstone Island along stepping stones from the Zambia side. This newly popular hike makes quite a spectacle for viewers on the Zimbabwe side, but it's not for the dizzy or faint-hearted.

Canoeing & Kayaking You may see photos of kayakers being tossed around in the Boiling Pot below the falls, but most Victoria Falls canoeing and kayaking tours take place above the falls (and fortunately stay there). It's a lot of fun to paddle around this wide, mostly smoothly flowing river, exploring its many islands and shooting its mini-rapids. If you want a relaxing time punctuated with the odd stretch of rolling water, walks around uninhabited river islands and lots of wildlife sightings, it's an ideal way to pass a couple of days.

The Zambezi Canoe Company offers several options, from a half-day dawdle around Kandahar Island to a three-day two-night camping tour, beginning above Katombora Rapids, near the Botswana border.

Kandahar Safaris runs half-day to four-day trips. Their initial put-in point is the same as Zambezi Canoe Company's, but they run the course at a more leisurely pace. The third option, Zambezi Odyssey (Safari Par Excellence) uses Klepper kayaks, rather than inflatables, but they offer only half-day and two-day options.

All three companies charge roughly the same rates. Morning trips (including breakfast) or afternoon trips (with tea) cost US$55. All-day trips cost US$90. Multi-day trips operate from 1 April to 15 October and cost US$135/365/495 for one/two/three overnights.

Microlighting Batoka Sky (☎ (260-3) 321830 or (260-3) 323672) organises microlight flights over the falls from the Livingstone airport on the Zambia side for US$55 for 15 minutes and US$95 for 30 minutes; the catch is that no photos are permitted. Book with the Sobek representative in Victoria Falls.

Bungee-Jumping A new option is bungee-jumping from the Zambezi Bridge, which costs US$90 per jump. Contrary to popular belief, the rescues aren't made in rubber rafts as they were when the concession first opened. Rather, dangling jumpers are actually retrieved and dragged back up to the bridge by a guy who must feel a bit like a yo-yo at the end of the day. Because of this, bungee-jumping can go on year round.

Fishing Trips For keen anglers, Dabula Safaris runs fishing trips on the Zambezi; the main prospects are yellow bream, tiger fish, squeakers and barbel (catfish). Two-hour trips, including drinks and all fishing tackle, cost US$15 per boat per hour, plus US$5 per person per hour. For all-day trips, you'll pay US$20 per boat plus US$5 per person for each hour.

Places to Stay – bottom end

The *Town Council Rest Camp & Caravan Park* (☎ 4210), smack in the centre of town on Livingstone Way, is spacious but still gets crowded with tents and overland trucks. Beware of gangs of thieving monkeys and baboons; like teenage thugs they make their rounds several times daily, dumping rubbish

---

Victoria Falls Hotel

The elegant Victoria Falls Hotel, which many travellers know for its lavish buffet breakfast, was the Falls' first. The earliest tourists to Victoria Falls had to arrive overland either on foot or in wagons, travelling for days along the Pandamatenga Trail from Botswana.

Once the railway arrived in 1904, tourism took a great leap forward. For the first year, visitors were required to bed down in railway carriages. As railway bridge workers and increasing numbers of tourists arrived, the need for a real hotel became evident and in 1905, work was begun on the first Victoria Falls Hotel, a wood and corrugated-iron structure perched between the railway station and the second Zambezi Gorge. Reports were that it wasn't very comfortable and in 1914, the rudimentary structure was replaced with a more permanent brick building. A trolley track was laid to transport tourists to the falls in carts pushed by servants. Once a hard-won destination only for the intrepid, Victoria Falls had now availed itself to wimpy tourism.

The current hotel is actually the product of several additions to the second early building but it still hangs together well. The equally appealing grounds are planted with green lawns, bougainvillea, frangipani, flamboyant, palms and other tropical finery. And don't forget to take a souvenir badge from your home town for the friendly doorman, who has amassed quite an amazing collection from all over the world. ■

bins and looting camps. Don't leave your tent unzipped. Otherwise, the campground is relatively well-guarded. Camping costs US$3 per person and two/three/four-person tents may be hired for US$4/5/6. Dorm beds are US$4.50, but security is slack and packs have disappeared. Chalets cost US$5.50 per person (minimum charge US$7), with use of bedding, a fridge, and pots and pans. Six-bed self-contained cottages cost US$5 per person (minimum US$12).

For more solitude, try the out-of-town camp site between A'Zambezi Lodge and the boat jetty, an enormous site catering mostly to caravans. Elephants wander through at night and by day, you can expect warthogs, baboons and antelopes. Camping prices are the same as in town, but there are no dorms or chalets.

For National Parks' accommodation, see Places to Stay under Zambezi National Park.

Places to Stay – middle

The only hotel within reach of budget travellers is the *Sprayview* (☎ 4344), just outside the town on Livingstone Way, with singles/doubles for US$33/44. The bar and disco are popular with travellers and the pool terrace is great for a cold beer.

Places to Stay – top end

All the hotels at this end of the Victoria Falls market charge three-tier rates, so foreigners have few alternatives.

The nicest of the lot architecturally – and the one with the least padding between the local and international rates – is the relatively new *Ilala Lodge* (☎ 4737; fax 4417), just downhill from the post office. Despite its central location, the natural décor, sunny terrace bar and restaurant, the green lawns and the nearby bushland provides just the atmosphere most people seem to want in Victoria Falls. For single/double rooms, foreigners pay US$90/140 and residents pay US$72/88.

If you have the money, the four-star *Victoria Falls Hotel* (☎ 4203, fax 4586) is a lovely, if fading old hotel. After you step off the train and pass through the Edwardian railway station, it provides a fitting climax to the grand colonial illusion. Never mind that it has been accused of resembling a mental institution; established in 1905, this stately colonial structure simply oozes atmosphere, and its setting above the Second Zambezi Gorge is nothing short of spectacular.

For single/double rooms, foreigners pay US$162/232, while locals pay the bargain rate of US$63/90. If you're after the height of luxury, lash out on the Presidential Suite, which will set you back only US$466.

The glitterati, sheikhs and gangsters haven't yet arrived in Victoria Falls, but the casino has. The *Makasa Sun Hotel* (☎ 4275), which contains one of Zimbabwe's four casinos, is a two-star hotel that was somehow awarded three stars. Still, the lobby sparkles and it's only from the outside that it looks like a government-funded high-rise housing project. Foreigners pay US$102/150 for singles/doubles while Zimbabwe residents pay US$40/58. Non-guests are charged a couple of dollars to use the pool. The one-armed bandits wake up at 10.30 am and the rest of the casino opens at 8 pm nightly. The bars, however, only remain open until 11 pm.

The three-star *Rainbow Hotel* (☎ 4585; fax 4536) is just a short walk from the centre. The architecture, which was apparently inspired by a Moghul palace somewhere in Rajasthan, seems a bit incongruous, but it is set in a quiet spot with green laws and gardens. Foreigners pay US$90/130 for single/double rooms and residents pay US$33/47.

Out of town opposite the crocodile ranch, the *A'Zambezi River Lodge* (☎ 4561) offers quiet three-star accommodation but it's quite a way from town and it would be useful to have a car for travelling back and forth. For foreigners, single/double rooms cost US$90/130; locals pay US$33/41. Out the back is a spacious lawn with a pool and terrace area where they serve up a buffet braai every evening; just beyond is the Zambezi.

Capping a nearby hill is the formidable-looking *Elephant Hills Hotel* (☎ 4793; fax 4655). It's clear that the architect had a good

ZIMBABWE

idea – to provide every room with a shaded thatched balcony and a view – but the result is ghastly. The standards of comfort are among the highest in Victoria Falls, but from a distance, the building itself could be mistaken for an immense grey-concrete prison fortress (complete with bars on some windows) or at best, a mound of stacked egg cartons. Many locals reckon it's the ugliest building in Zimbabwe, which probably makes it worth a look to judge for yourself. For single/double rooms – yes, with a thatched balcony and a view – foreigners pay US$162/232 and locals pay US$63/90. Elephant Hills runs a shuttle service between to and from the Makasa Sun, every hour on the half hour, from 8 am to 5 pm daily.

The newest addition to the Falls' hotel scene is *The Lodge at Victoria Falls* (☎ 708737; fax 733068, both in Harare). This immense but pleasantly designed series of hotel blocks (from a distance, it resembles a collection of Thai wats) has sunset views for everyone and does all it can to merit its five-star rating. They've tried to maintain an ecological theme, with recycled toilet paper and stationery, natural history reference books in every room, only indigenous bush species in the garden and periodic educational lectures on environmental issues. Since it was just opening at the time of writing, it's not yet possible to gauge its success. Surprisingly, the initial rack rate for foreigners is just US$100 per person, with bed and breakfast.

Self-catering units in the adjacent *Victoria Falls Safari Lodges* (☎ 4725; fax 4792) cost US$80/95 for two/three-bedroom lodges. Each lodge accommodates up to six people.

Places to Stay – Safari Lodges

Imbabala Safari Camp (☎ 4219), PO Box 110, Victoria Falls, is a luxury camp beside the Zambezi near Kazungula. The camp sits nestled in a dense forest with a view over the river banks, and is a popular fishing spot. The camp charges US$175 per person per day, including thatched chalet accommodation, meals, game drives, guides, boat trips and fishing tackle.

The nearby *Westwood Game Lodge* (☎ /fax 4614), PO Box 132, Victoria Falls, lies surrounded by trees on the Zambezi river bank. It accommodates only six guests at a time in three sandstone and thatch bungalows just metres from the river. Access is by air or 4WD only. Foreigners pay US$187 per person, including meals, transfers and wildlife-viewing activities.

Seven km from Victoria Falls is *Masuwe Lodge* (☎ 702634; fax 702546), PO Box 66293, Kopje, Harare, a newish Landela Safaris tented camp beside the Masuwe River west of the Bulawayo road. The name means 'place of soft stone' after a type of oxidised rock traditionally used for cosmetics. It occupies a 300-hectare private game ranch which abuts Zambezi National Park, so there's plenty of wildlife around. The light tents are set on raised wooden platforms and the dining area sits perched over the valley for the maximum views. Prices start at around US$200 per person with full board and activities.

Tongabezi Lodge (☎ (260-3) 323235; fax (260-3) 323224) sits on the Zambian bank of the Zambezi, roughly opposite Zambezi National Park's Chundu camp. The emphasis is on originality and luxury, and its central location makes it a favourite getaway spot for affluent Zimbabweans, Zambians and Namibians. Accommodation is either in luxury tents or in river-view bungalows, but every unit is imaginatively designed. For something really different, try the secluded open-air honeymoon suite, set atop a cliff with its own private garden, a sunken bathtub and a romantic four-poster bed.

If you have the cash and are looking for a real treat, give Tongabezi a try; no one ever dislikes it. Prices start at US$160 per person for the tented camp and climb to US$200 for the bungalows. Tongabezi also has a small associated camp, *Sindabezi*, on a tiny midriver island just downstream, and a mobile camp on Livingstone Island just above Victoria Falls.

Finally, there's *Chomunzi Camp* (☎ /fax 4453), a small and informal tented camp site in Zambezi National Park, which is run by

Dabula Safaris. For US$140 per person, you'll get all meals and two game walks per day.

Places to Eat

If you've had a hotel breakfast for six days running and are ready for something different, try *Naran's Takeaways* in the Sopers Arcade. They do a 'campers breakfast' including steak, bacon, egg, toast, chips and a glass of Mazoe orange for just US$2. For lunch and snacks, you can't beat their vegetarian specialities, including great curry and samosas. You can even get vegetarian curry sadza. Unfortunately, they close sometime between 4.30 and 6 pm, depending on afternoon business.

The *Wimpy* bar also fries up fast-food breakfasts and the rest of the day, serves its standard menu of burgers, chicken, chips and so on; you can eat for around US$2 per person.

In Sopers Arcade is the excellent *Pizza Bistro*, but it's probably the most popular eatery in town so you'll normally have to wait a while for a table – and they don't take bookings. (That makes for booming business at the Explorer's Bar next door.) On Parkway is another pizza joint, *Eatza Pizza*, which is much easier to get into. They even deliver pizzas to the campground across the road.

At the *Cattleman Restaurant*, in Phumula Centre, the speciality is beef, as the name would suggest. The *Gorge Restaurant* does 'backpacker specials' for less than US$1.50 and *Boiling Pot Takeaways* is handy for quick eats.

Alternatively, you can eat at one the hotels/lodges which offer buffet breakfasts, lunches and dinners. Some are veritable banquets, and you can eat your fill for a set price. The once popular buffet breakfast at Victoria Falls Hotel has now been placed off limits to backpackers and other outsiders. Fortunately, the one at *Ilala Lodge* is just as good and costs just US$3.50. Cheapest is the *Sprayview Motel* at US$2 for breakfast and US$3.50 for dinner.

More expensive is the highly recommended evening braai at the *Victoria Falls Hotel*, which costs US$8.50. If you have a real appetite at dinner time, this is a great way to smother it. Vegetarians can fill up on the table loads of salads, breads, casseroles and sweets while non-vegetarians have a choice of at least four braaied meats, sadza with various meat relishes and numerous hors d'oeuvres. You won't be able to move afterwards.

The buffets at *Elephant Hills Hotel* are also excellent (US$4 breakfast and US$6 lunch), as are the highly recommended US$2.30 buffet breakfast and the US$2 pub lunch at the *Ilala Lodge*. The rooftop bar at the *Makasa Sun Hotel* is enhanced by good views and free bar snacks at 6 pm nightly. The *A'Zambezi River Lodge* serves full meals and bar snacks all day on their pool terrace.

The recently opened *Boma Restaurant* (☎ 4725) at the Victoria Falls Safari Lodges has already received awards for its food. For US$8.50 you get a four-course African buffet (including both game dishes and traditional local cuisine), complete with an Ndebele choir performing in the background. It's a way out of town, but free pick up is available at the big hotels.

For an unusual dining experience, Dabula Safaris (☎ 4453) organises an outdoor *Bush Dinner* in a private wildlife reserve adjoining Zambezi National Park. The menu begins with a crocodile tail starter and runs through soup, sadza with venison relish and a dessert. All the while, I'd probably be envisioning reproachful eyes out in the bush... The price is US$30 per person, including transport and drinks.

For self-catering, the best all around shop is the relatively well-stocked Jay's Spar Supermarket. There's also a green grocer in Sopers Arcade and a decent butchery in Chinotimba township.

Entertainment

Beer and other drinks aren't as inexpensive as elsewhere in Zimbabwe, so don't be shocked when the Castle you had for US$0.35 in Harare costs double that in Victoria Falls.

Bars & Discos Until early evening, the beer hall in Chinotimba township is good for some local action. The big hotel bars offer toned-down live music, often pseudo-African 'banana boat' revues and insipid marimba muzak that resembles what you hear while waiting on hold. Beyond that and the Makasa Sun Casino, you're limited to just a couple of options.

Most travellers wind up at least once at the Sprayview Lodge disco which offers a good helping of reggae music as well as a lot of mundane local stuff nightly from 7.30 to 11 pm. Locals advise visitors to beware when walking into town from the Sprayview at night. Lions often wander into populated areas and chemically impaired disco ducks have been known to pass out and attract feline attention. A reader writes:

The Sprayview has a disco every night – very basic but good fun and a great place to meet locals. It's mainly Black people working in the tourist industry with a sprinkling of adventurous tourists and Finnish UNTAG people getting into the local 'hospitality.' They have reggae bands from Zambia, but the kids seem to prefer the American soul and disco on the tape machine. It's not *that* friendly – most of the people have jobs in which they have to smile all day at South African tourists who treat them badly, so a lot of them just want an evening away from tourists. But it's okay, and there are lots of others who want to talk, dance and whatever else might be on offer.

Andy Bollen, Australia

A favourite bar is Explorers in Sopers Arcade, which is popular with raft jockeys and overland truck drivers – as well as anyone who'd otherwise be stuck in a dark tent in the caravan park. Try their speciality drink, Toxic Sludge.

The Downtown Night Club (US$2.50 cover charge) in the basement of Ilala Lodge is frequented mainly by ex-pats, local tourism punters and backpackers. It's open nightly from 8 pm until late.

Falls Craft Village At night, the Falls Craft Village stages a traditional dancing performance at dusk (around 7 pm) for US$3.50. The dancing is reportedly very good, punctuated with such intriguing attractions as

ominous, myth-perpetuating drumming and even a circumcision ritual. Even if you don't attend, you're welcome to listen from almost anywhere in town.

Africa Spectacular *The* grand tourist show at the falls is Africa Spectacular, staged nightly at the Victoria Falls Hotel. Although the performers must have repeated their repertoire literally thousands of times and must be getting a bit weary of it all, they manage to convey a sense of enthusiasm. If not completely authentic, it does appeal as an entertaining introduction to traditional African dancing.

The show begins nightly at 7 pm in the pavilion behind the hotel and costs US$4 per person.

Sport It's probably stretching things to call it sport, but you can now have a go at Zambezi Survivor Splat Ball, described as 'a safe and fun alternative to real war'. Make bookings at Photo Fast on Parkway.

Getting There & Away

As the tourist hub of southern Africa, Victoria Falls, which sits at the intersection of four countries, is a crossroads for travellers from all walks of life. All tourist trails converge here, and nearly every visitor to Zimbabwe, Zambia, Namibia and Botswana is funnelled through at some stage. As a result, getting there and away is easy.

Air Air Zimbabwe flies at least twice daily between Victoria Falls and Harare; the flights at 7.15 am from Harare and 5.15 pm from Victoria Falls are nonstop. The others stop en route at both Hwange National Park and Kariba.

You'll also find international flights to Katima Mulilo, Namibia, and Maun, Botswana. The former, with Air Namibia, costs US$45, takes 25 minutes and provides a wonderful bird's eye view over the falls–a sort of incidental Flight of the Angels. In fact, some pilots kindly spend 10 minutes of the flight providing passengers with superb photo opportunities.

Bus The terminal for the Hwange Special Express (and other African buses) to Hwange town and Bulawayo is near the bottle return behind Sopers Arcade. The bus also stops on Pioneer Rd in Chinotimba township. There are normally about three buses daily, departing when full.

Ajay's Motorways departs from the Makasa Sun Hotel on Tuesday and Thursday at 7 am, stopping at Hwange Safari Lodge at 9.30 am and arriving in Bulawayo at 1.15 pm. On Sunday, the departure is at 8 am; scheduled stops are therefore one hour later. The fare between Victoria Falls and Hwange Safari Lodge is US$6.40; to Bulawayo, it's US$11. In the opposite direction, it departs from the Bulawayo Sun Hotel at 7 am on Monday, Wednesday and Friday.

The only public access to Kazungula and Kasane is the UTC or Dabula Safaris transfer buses, which leave every morning. UTC charges US$20 and Dabula charges US$30. The border crossing is straightforward. To book the UTC transfer, go to the UTC office in the post office complex, not the Hertz UTC office, which knows nothing about the bus. If you haven't booked, stand on the Bulawayo road, opposite Wimpy, and flag down the vehicle – it passes between 7.20 and 7.30 am.

If you're heading for Namibia, the Harare-Windhoek bus leaves from the Total petrol station in Victoria Falls on Wednesday at 7 am. The fare to Windhoek is US$75.

Train Until just a couple of years ago, the romantic highlight of a Zimbabwe trip was riding the steam train to Victoria Falls; now everything is diesel. The trains leave Bulawayo at 6.30 pm daily (passing Dete at 1.30 am) and from Victoria Falls at 7 pm daily (passing Dete at 12.45 am). The 1st/2nd-class fare is US$9/6. Economy class costs US$4. The former two have sleeper service while the latter has seats only.

A new development in 1995 was the addition of a twice-daily passenger service to Livingstone, Zambia, on the goods train over the Zambezi Bridge. Trains leave from Victoria Falls at 10 am and 5 pm daily and from Livingstone at 9 am and 3.30 pm. The trip takes 30 minutes and costs US$1.50 each way.

The booking office is open Monday to Friday from 7 am to noon and 2 to 4 pm. On weekends, it's open only in the morning.

Hitching The road between Bulawayo and Victoria Falls isn't exactly busy, but you'd have to be very unlucky not to find something. For Botswana, wait at the Kasane turn-off early in the morning and you'll almost certainly get a lift.

Getting Around
The push-trolley tracks that carried earlier visitors around Victoria Falls were long ago ripped up, but there are other options until one reaches Victoria Falls Park itself. There, everyone has to make it under their own steam.

To/From the Airport The Victoria Falls airport is 20 km out of town along the Bulawayo road. Air Zimbabwe and South African Airways run a free shuttle bus between the airport and town, which connects with all arriving and departing flights.

Taxi Midnight Taxis (☎ 4290), which isn't as dodgy as the name would imply, is the company serving the vicinity. The taxi stand is opposite the Total petrol station, behind the Wimpy Corner shopping centre.

Motorbike Anyone aged over 18 with a driving licence can hire a 50cc motor scooter from Scoot Hire (☎ 4402) in the Phumula Centre. You'll pay around US$25 per day, with insurance and unlimited km.

Bicycle You can hire mountain bikes at Bushtrackers, on the Parkway, for US$1.30 per hour, US$6.50 for eight hours and US$13 per 24-hour day. All rentals require a deposit of US$13. Their stock includes a lot of dud bikes, however, so check that they're in good working order before riding away.

ZIMBABWE

ZIMBABWE

VICTORIA FALLS – ZAMBIA SIDE

Most visitors either plough through Zambia as quickly as possible or venture only as far as Livingstone before retreating to Zimbabwe. That doesn't suggest the country has nothing to offer, however, and it's making a concerted push at attracting tourists. Unfortunately, multi-tier pricing all around means that accommodation, sightseeing and park and museum admissions are quite expensive.

The food riots and government paranoia of the early 1990s subsided with Zambia's recent transition to democracy, and the new Frederick Chilupa government has brought hope and optimism. However, violent crime is still a problem (especially in Lusaka) and foreigners are obvious targets. While it's still quite safe to visit the Zambian side of Victoria Falls – it is the country's major tourist attraction – things get tougher beyond Livingstone. Don't wear anything that could be construed as military dress (this advice holds all over Africa) and be wary when taking photographs. Photographing anything which could be considered sensitive – such as a bridge, powerline, public building, dam or a military installation – will invite problems.

The unit of currency in Zambia is the kwacha (ZKw) which has been trading at ZKw700 = US$1. There's no black market to speak of. Inflation is running at over 200% per annum, so only change what you need – the rate will be higher next week.

Crossing the Border

From the Zimbabwean town of Victoria Falls, it's an easy two-km walk over the Zambezi Bridge to Zambia. Most people make a day trip of it but some opt to continue into Livingstone, 11 km further on, and stay the night before returning to Zimbabwe. If you've hired a bike in Zimbabwe, there's no problem taking it over the border, but several cyclists have reported violent muggings along the road to Livingstone.

The Victoria Falls border crossing is open from 6 am to 8 pm. If you're just going over to Zambia for the day, get an early start because the queues can be long and you may not have much time left for sightseeing before you have to pass back through the whole mess in reverse. Searches are longest in the late morning and early afternoon.

Commonwealth citizens, and holders of Irish or Scandinavian passports don't require visas to enter Zambia, but everyone else does, whether they're entering for the day or a longer trip around the country. Visas currently cost US$10 and are issued on the spot – or more accurately, whenever the officials get around to it. Tour companies running day trips on the Zambian side normally take care of visa formalities for their participants.

Foreigners may export only Z$500 in Zimbabwean currency so if you're crossing for the day, either leave your money back at your hotel or deposit it with immigration officials at the border and collect it when you return. Any amount of Zimbabwean currency over Z$500 declared on your departure form (or discovered during a customs search) will be confiscated without reimbursement. However, departure forms are rarely scrutinised at this crossing.

Visiting the Falls

For visitors, the Zambian side of Victoria Falls provides an entirely separate experience than the Zimbabwean side. First of all, the view is different. In Zambia, you can sidle right up to the falling water, walk a steep track down to the base of the falls and follow spindly walkways perched over the abyss. What's more, the Zambian government has issued permits for several activities – among them microlighting, bungee-jumping and mid-river picnics – which have been refused by Zimbabwean officials. It's debatable whether or not these are good things, but the point is that Zambia presents a different face of the same falls.

From near the border post, a network of earthen or stone-paved tracks will lead you to and around the various Zambian viewpoints, and many visitors actually prefer the view on this side of the falls. Although they aren't as picture postcard perfect as those from Zimbabwe, they allow more close-up observation of the mesmerising water, and their more natural and less manicured surroundings create a more pristine atmosphere.

From the bridge, proceed up the hill through immigration and to the hotels, from which a jumble of tracks lead through the thick vegetation. A highlight is the track leading back along the customs fence, which affords a view over the Zambezi Bridge and into the main river gorges.

For close-up shots, nothing beats the Eastern Cataract. In one hair-raising spot, the very daring (and stupid) can crawl out a tree limb that hangs over the lip of the falls for an incredible view *straight down* the sheet of plummeting water. This isn't recommended, naturally, especially if you suffer from vertigo, but even on the bank, you can approach to within two metres of the big plunge itself.

In another place, the Knife Edge Point track issues onto a precarious footbridge, through swirling clouds of spray, and crosses to a cliff-girt island in the Zambezi River. If the water is low or the wind is favourable, you'll be treated to a magnificent and relatively close-up view of the falls, as well as the yawning abyss below the bridge. Otherwise, the view will be obliterated by drenching spray. Once you're good and wet, descend the steep track into the Boiling Pot for a view of the tortured river as it passes through a dynamic swirling maelstrom.

Around the Falls

Behind the curio stalls near the hotels on the Zambian side of the river is the small Field Museum, built on an archaeological site, with some displays from the excavation. The curio stalls themselves are good value, especially if you're paying in Zambian kwacha. There's an excellent selection of crafts, they're much cheaper than on the Zimbabwean side, and the people there are keen to barter; many travellers swap interesting foreign T-shirts. A reader had the following to say:

The garden is full of rich people doing black market deals with the waiters. There's a man whose only function is to walk around with a slingshot firing

pellets at the monkeys to keep them away from the tables. Outside there are people willing to sell just about everything they have for a loaf of bread, a bottle of cooking oil, a ball-point pen...You get the feeling that for a Ken Done T-shirt and an old TAA Junior Flyers badge, you could probably buy half of Zambia. There's a depressing story about an American who traded all his clothes for as much malachite as he could carry...

Andy Bollen

Mosi-oa-Tunya National Park

Mosi-oa-Tunya National Park, an insignificant little game park near the boat club north of the Maramba River, once had a few indigenous rhinos but they were all poached. They have been recently replaced by six white rhinos reintroduced from South Africa; these poor individuals are probably among the most vulnerable creatures on earth. If you go on your own, don't pay more than about US$0.50 for a walking safari.

Organised Tours

If you prefer an organised spin around the Zambian side, Savanna Touring Zimbabwe (☎ 4728 or 4493) offers a day trip taking in the Knife Edge bridge, Dambwa market, the National Museum in Livingstone, a boat trip through the Zambezi islands, a visit to the Maramba Cultural Centre and a trip to Mosi-oa-Tunya National Park to seek out the six reintroduced white rhinos.

If you just want to see Mosi-oa-Tunya National Park, the Hotel Intercontinental arranges quick tours for US$20.

The big hotels at the Falls also arrange evening booze cruises on the Zambezi, departing from the boat club. They're about the same price as those on the Zimbabwe side and non-hotel guests are welcome to participate.

For other possibilities on the Zambia side, including white-water rafting, microlighting and picnics on Livingstone Island, see Activities under Victoria Falls, Zimbabwe.

Places to Stay & Eat

The unattractive tent camp site is between the Hotel Intercontinental and the Rainbow Lodge and is administered by the latter.

Although it's in a good location, your belongings are not safe here and should be locked up in the hotel baggage room when you're away from your tent. Camping costs US$5 per night, which includes the use of hotel facilities since there are none at the camp site, but watch for hippos wandering out to graze on the hotel lawns.

The *Hotel Intercontinental Mosi-oa-Tunya* (☎ (260-3) 321121; fax (260-3) 321128) right beside the falls offers luxury for a whopping US$160 for a double room, payable only in foreign currency. Weekend buffets are fairly good value, costing around US$12 per person. Slightly more reasonable, the *Rainbow Lodge* (☎ (260-3) 322473) offers double accommodation in rondavels for US$40.

For meals, the *Rainbow Lodge* has a standard dining room. However, if money is no object, head for the *Hotel Intercontinental*, which has quite a fine dining room. On different nights, they do special theme meals: Chinese, Italian, Western, barbecue and so on.

For information about the popular Tongabezi Lodge, see under Safari Lodges in the discussion of the Zimbabwe side.

LIVINGSTONE (ZAMBIA)

Although it's not much to look at now, raggle-taggle Livingstone was once the object of nearly all tourist visits to Victoria Falls. Several years ago, however, when Zambia started down the road to economic and political chaos, the town was eclipsed by the noisy upstart across the river. Now that the political situation is improving, the Zambian side of the falls should appear on more and more itineraries.

The tourist office on Mosi-oa-Tunya Rd is good for information on happenings in Livingstone and can arrange hassle-free hotel bookings.

Railway Museum

The Railway Museum in Livingstone (technically known as the Zambezi Sawmills Locomotive Sheds National Monument) lies west of Mosi-oa-Tunya Rd as you enter town from the south. It was declared a national monument in 1976 to preserve the historic locomotive sheds, which fell into disuse in 1973.

The yards contain a charmingly motley collection of old engines and rolling stock while inside are lots of rail-related antiques as well as information and exhibits about general railway history. It's open daily from 8.30 am to 4.30 pm. Unfortunately, admission for foreigners is US$5 and unless you're a ravenous railway buff, it isn't worth it. However, if you're genuinely interested and can't pay that much, it's often possible to work out some sort of discount.

National Museum

The National Museum, adjacent to the tourist office, has an interesting collection of archaeological and anthropological relics including a copy of a Neanderthal skull estimated at over 100,000 years old. The original was uncovered near Kabwe, Zambia (north of Lusaka), during the colonial era and is now on display in the UK. There are also examples of ritual artefacts and Batonka material crafts, an African village mock-up, a collection of David Livingstone paraphernalia and a display of African maps dating back to 1690. Officially, the admission for foreigners is a whopping US$5.

Maramba Cultural Centre

Between Victoria Falls and Livingstone, about five km from the latter on the main road, is the Maramba Cultural Centre. On Saturday from 3 to 5 pm they stage traditional dance performances. Admission is a phenomenal US$0.03, and the performance is more authentic than Africa Spectacular on the Zimbabwean side.

Places to Stay

The *Red Cross Hostel* (☎ (260-3) 322473), Mokambo Rd, which is clean, friendly and costs US$10 for clean double rooms with washbasin is the best place in Livingstone.

ZIMBABWE

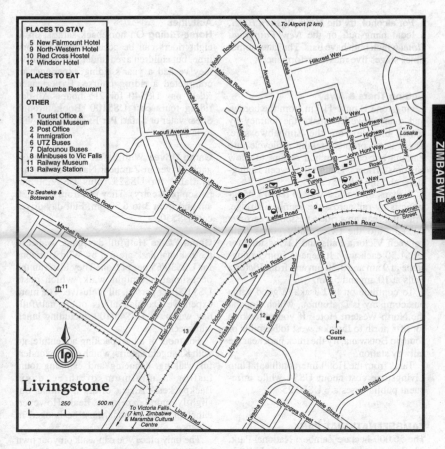

PLACES TO STAY

5 New Fairmount Hotel
9 North-Western Hotel
10 Red Cross Hostel
12 Windsor Hotel

PLACES TO EAT

3 Mukumba Restaurant

OTHER

1 Tourist Office &
  National Museum
2 Post Office
4 Immigration
6 UTZ Buses
7 Djafounou Buses
8 Minibuses to Vic Falls
11 Railway Museum
13 Railway Station

Livingstone

0   250   500 m

To Victoria Falls
(7 km), Zimbabwe
& Maramba Cultural
Centre

Similarly priced but much poorer value is the *Windsor Hotel*, on Edward Rd near the golf course about a 15-minute walk from the centre. It offers scruffy self-contained single/double rooms for US$13/17. There's a bar with cheap beer but no restaurant.

The *North-Western Hotel* (☎ (260-3) 320711), a deteriorating colonial structure on Zambesi St, has good double rooms for US$12. More up-market is the *New Fairmount Hotel* (☎ (260-3) 730726), Mosi-oa-Tunya Rd, which has self-contained rooms for US$45/55, but discounts of 15% are offered if business is slow. The New

Fairmount also has a low-key casino, which operates evenings.

Places to Eat

Eat Rite, opposite the post office, can be good for lunches. The best for evening meals is the *Mukumba Restaurant*, a block back from the main street. Although most of the attention focuses on the music videos from Zaïre, the food and atmosphere are quite acceptable. Otherwise, you can resort to the several greasy takeaway places along Mosi-oa-Tunya Rd.

For alcohol, try the *North-Western Hotel*, a local hang-out, or the *New Fairmount Hotel* which both have bars. The latter sometimes stages live music performances.

Getting There & Away

Livingstone is only 11 km from the border, and many travellers make the journey by rented bicycle from the Zimbabwe side. There is no problem taking a bicycle into Zambia but carry a rental receipt to show customs officers. Hitching between Livingstone and the falls is easy.

Perhaps the easiest way to reach Livingstone is by rail across the Zambezi Bridge. Travellers can now ride a passenger carriage tacked onto the twice daily goods train between Victoria Falls and Livingstone for US$1.50 each way. It departs from Livingstone at 9 am and 3.30 pm and from Victoria Falls at 10 am and 5 pm.

To continue on to Lusaka, a good value bus company is Djafounou, which stops at the North-Western Hotel. If you're looking for lifts north to Lusaka, west to Namibia or south to Botswana, try the truck park near the railway station.

Taxis from the Hotel Intercontinental into Livingstone cost about US$4 while infrequent public buses are US$0.25.

ZAMBEZI NATIONAL PARK

The 56,000-hectare Zambezi National Park, which is vaguely associated with Victoria Falls National Park, consists of 40 km of Zambezi River frontage and a spread of wildlife-rich inland mopane forest and savanna. Although the park is best known for its herds of sable antelopes, it also has elephants, zebras, giraffes, lions, buffaloes and many other types of antelopes.

The park office is open from 6 am to 6.30 pm. Just west of the park office is a cordoned-off area which was mined during the Second Chimurenga. This area is still riddled with unexploded mines and remains extremely dangerous, so heed the signs and keep out.

Activities

Horse-Riding On horseback safaris, up to eight riders can be accommodated at one time, but children aged under 12 must prove they've had a year's riding experience or completed a riding course. Experienced riders pay US$40 for 2½ hours. All-day riding tours cost US$100. Book through Shearwater or Safari Par Excellence in Victoria Falls.

Game Drives With Safari Par Excellence, game drives in Zambezi National Park are available for US$25 (plus US$2.50 per person park entry). They run from 6 to 9.30 am and from 3 to 6.30 pm. Full-day drives cost US$50.

Game Walks Half/full-day game walks in the national park are run by Wild Horizons for US$30/65 per person. They also run the occasional overnight walk, which costs US$100 per person, all inclusive. The more expensive Dabula Safaris offers half/full-day walks for US$45/100, including lunch and snacks.

For more of a backpacking adventure, go with Khangela Safaris, which offers wonderful walking, canoeing and camping tours lasting a minimum of three days. Backpackers' Africa offers a similar but slightly more expensive deal. However, either of these options must be booked in advance.

The only place you can walk on your own is between the riverbank picnic areas No 1 to No 25 near the park's eastern boundary.

Places to Stay

The National Parks' lodges, on the riverbank at the park entrance, each have two two-bed rooms, a living area and a veranda. They're comfortable but are booked up well in advance, so make arrangements at the Central Booking office in Harare.

There are also three fishing camps, *Mpala-Jena*, *Kandahar* and *Sansimba*, all beautifully located along the river, where you can fish for yellow bream and tiger fish. Each camp includes rudimentary shelters

ZIMBABWE

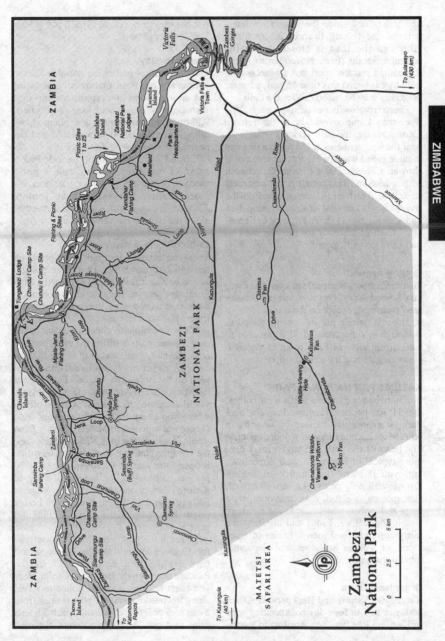

Zambezi
National Park

0   2.5   5 km

N

To Bulawayo
(430 km)

ZAMBIA

Victoria Falls
Victoria Falls Town
Zambezi Gorges

Lwanda Island

Kandahar Island

Zambezi National Park Lodges

Picnic Sites 1 to 25

Park Headquarters

Minefield

Kandahar Fishing Camp

Fishing & Picnic Sites

Tongabezi Lodge

Chundu I Camp Site
Chundu II Camp Site

Chundu Island

Mpala-Jena Fishing Camp

Sansimba Fishing Camp

Chundu Island

Zambezi River

Jena Loop

Mpala-Jena Spring

Sansimba (Bluff) Spring

Sansimba

Chamuzi Spring

Chamuzi Camp Site

Siamunungu Camp Site

Tsowa Island

To Katombora Rapids

ZAMBIA

Zambezi River

Chundu Drive

Zambezi Drive

Chundu Loop

Sansimba Loop

Chamuzi Loop

Siamunungu Drive

Chundu River
Mpala-Jena River
Matetsyanga River

Liunga River
Liunga Loop

Mpala Vlei
Sansimba Vlei
Chamuzi Vlei

Shimba Creek

Siamunungu Loop

ZAMBEZI

NATIONAL PARK

Hilne Loop

Kazungula Road

Kazungula

Chamabonda River

Chirema Pan

Chamabonda Drive

Kalankua Pan

Wildlife-Viewing Hide

Njoko Pan

Chamabonda Wildlife-Viewing Platform

Messége River

To Bulawayo (430 km)

To Kazungula (40 km)

MATETSI SAFARI AREA

and toilets and since the waters are international, no fishing licences are required. Although the road is closed during the summer months (from November to April) the camps remain open but are accessible only by canoe. At this time of year, advance bookings may be made in Victoria Falls.

There are also five exclusive camps. Visitors may camp overnight at the remote *Chamabonda Wildlife-Viewing Platform*, near the southern end of the park; amenities include piped water, a flush toilet and a cold shower. *Chundu 1* and *Chundu 2*, between Mpala-Jena and Sansimba, occupy a magical stretch of riverbank. *Chamunzi* lies on the riverbank 40 km west of the reception area and *Siamunungu* is seven km west of Chamunzi. Each of these camps may be used by parties of up to 12 people.

Getting Around

To tour Zambezi National Park on your own, you'll need a car; bicycles and motorbikes aren't allowed, except on the transit route to Kazungula, which passes through the park. Although it's discouraged, it is possible to walk from Victoria Falls town to the park entrance gate and try to find a lift.

KAZUMA PAN NATIONAL PARK

In Zimbabwe's extreme north-west corner, the 31,300-hectare Kazuma Pan National Park is an unusual enclave of savanna in otherwise teak and mopane-wooded country. The heart of the park is a large grassy pan, more typical of Botswana than Zimbabwe, and you'll have the chance of seeing Zimbabwe's only gemsboks, as well as such rare species as eland, roan antelopes, wild dogs and oribis, which are found nowhere else in Zimbabwe. Lions and cheetahs are fairly common, and many species of antelopes, as well as buffaloes and elephants, inhabit the pan area.

Organised Tours

Kalambeza Safaris and Backpackers Africa both run two to four-day backpacking trips in Kazuma Pan between April and December, but they're not cheap: you'll pay at least US$250 per person.

Places to Stay

Only two visitor parties are permitted in the park at any one time, mainly because facilities are limited to two primitive camp sites with only braai pits and long-drop toilets. Although improvements are planned, no other accommodation is available and the nearest services are at Victoria Falls.

Graced by a prominent baobab and a grove of teak trees, *Nsiza Camp* is just a shady spot at the edge of the grassland. It's more readily accessible than remote *Katsetsheti Camp*, which sits beside marshes along the river of the same name.

Getting There & Away

Everyone entering the park must pre-book through National Parks. Due to deep sand, access to Kazuma Pan is by 4WD only, even in the dry season. Because of road damage during the rainy season, the park is open only from March to December.

It's not possible to check in or out at the ranger headquarters inside the park; coming from the east, you must stop at the Matetsi Safari Area office. To get there, turn southwest off the Bulawayo-Victoria Falls road at the Matetsi Safari Area turn-off. After 25 km, you'll come to the Matetsi Ranger office, where you check in and pay relevant fees. (There's also access to Matetsi directly from Robins Camp in Hwange National Park – see the Hwange National Park map.) The office is open from 7 am to 12.30 pm and 2 to 4.30 pm on weekdays. For weekend entry to Kazuma Pan, phone (☎ 433526) in Victoria Falls or visit the office at Katombora Lodge (eight km downstream from Kazungula) prior to setting out.

To reach the park from Matetsi, continue for 12 more km to Tsabolisa Junction and turn right, then continue 27 km to Pandamatenga on the Botswana border. Here you must register with the police to travel along the border road; the post is open from 8 am to 5 pm, so you should reach Matetsi prior to 4 pm. At Pandamatenga, the road

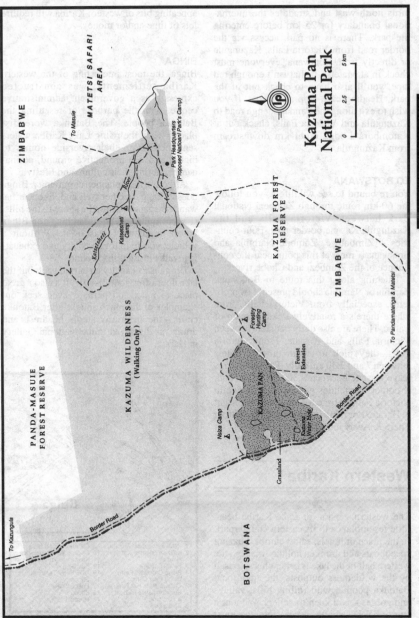

turns north-west and straddles the international boundary for 25 km before entering the park. There is no park access via the border road from Victoria Falls, Kazungula or directly from Botswana; everyone must check in at Matetsi. If that isn't enough red tape, you'll also have to check out of the park. Heading east, stop at Matetsi. If you wish to exit along the Pandamatenga road to Kazungula and Victoria Falls, check out at Katombora Lodge eight km downstream from Kazungula.

TO BOTSWANA

You're bound to see wildlife as you follow the 60-km route through Zambezi National Park between Victoria Falls and the Kazungula/Kasane border post. Four countries – Zimbabwe, Zambia, Namibia and Botswana – meet at this point near the confluence of the Zambezi and Chobe rivers.

Hitching along this route to Botswana, Zambia or Namibia should present few problems, especially from Victoria Falls, from where there's a relatively steady stream of traffic. There are also daily transfers between Victoria Falls and Kasane. From Victoria Falls, they pick up from the big hotels between 7 and 7.30 am daily. The return trips leave Kasane between 9.30 and 10 am and, if border formalities go smoothly, arrive in Victoria Falls in time for the afternoon flight to Harare. For more information, see Getting There & Away under Victoria Falls.

Western Kariba

The western version of Lake Kariba bears little resemblance to its eastern counterpart. In the place of hotels, safari camps, buzzing speedboats and drunken holiday-makers, the western half of the lake is better characterised by the wilderness outposts, the traditional Batonka people, wild rolling hills, valleys and gorges – and keen travellers. Without a sturdy 4WD vehicle, access into the most

appealing bits of western Kariba will require lots of time and/or money.

BINGA

Binga, the most interesting of the western Kariba settlements, was constructed expressly as a government administrative centre, with the purpose of resettling the Batonka people. The Batonka were displaced when the rising Lake Kariba waters sent them from their riverside homes to higher and less productive ground, permanently altering their culture and lifestyle.

Although it's a planned community, Binga doesn't hang together well and, like Kariba, wanders sparsely from the shore to the hills. (I spent quite a while searching for Binga before realising I was in it.) Without a vehicle, you're in for some dry and exhausting walks just getting around.

Binga isn't exactly an action spot, but the lake does offer good fishing. It's also a great place to relax and perhaps even seek out examples of the much sought-after Batonka crafts – the decorative stools, headrests and drums, as displayed in the National Gallery in Harare.

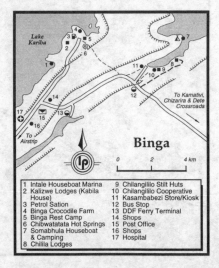

Binga

0   2   4 km

1 Intale Houseboat Marina
2 Kalizwe Lodges (Kabila House)
3 Petrol Sation
4 Binga Crocodile Farm
5 Binga Rest Camp
6 Chibwatatata Hot Springs
7 Somabhula Houseboat & Camping
8 Chilila Lodges
9 Chilangililo Stilt Huts
10 Chilangililo Cooperative
11 Kasambabezi Store/Kiosk
12 Bus Stop
13 DDF Ferry Terminal
14 Shops
15 Post Office
16 Shops
17 Hospital

ZIMBABWE

The Batonka

Until the tribe was permanently displaced by the rising Kariba waters in the late 1950s, few outsiders had ever heard of the Batonka (also called Batonga, or just Tonga) people of the Zambezi Valley. Nowadays, they command almost a cult following. Even the Colonial remnant, when speaking of someone who has, in their eyes, become inordinately liberal or countercultural in their thinking, is said to have 'run off to join the Tonkies'.

The Batonka are believed to have migrated to the Zambezi Valley from the area of Lake Malawi during the 15th or 16th century and settled in the Gwembe Valley area of present-day Zimbabwe and Zambia. The Tonga language, as it is called, is a more archaic dialect than Shona or Ndebele, both of which have undergone great changes through interaction with other groups. Although the Batonka came in contact with Portuguese traders and suffered occasional Ndebele mischief, they were naturally sheltered by the Zambezi Escarpment and were mostly left to go their own way.

During the colonial era and after Zimbabwean independence, however, their domain was split by superimposed international boundaries. Lake Kariba simply drove the wedge deeper and today, the government has tarred the road into their capital at Binga and is trying to absorb the Batonka into mainstream Zimbabwe by providing schools and medical services.

For the Batonka, as for the Rastafarians, smoking *mbanje*, or cannibis, has long been a way of life and only in this tiny enclave of Zimbabwe is the dreaded weed tolerated by the authorities. In reality, however, it's not so popular and any images travellers may have of a utopian Kathmandu-by-the-Lake are largely unjustified.

Although there are still a few red half-mast eyes around, the traditional Batonka culture appears to be sadly and permanently disappearing into history. The stereotypical image of the Batonka will invariably include an elderly woman smoking mbanje in a long gourd pipe. Thanks to some unusual and long moribund aesthetic values, her nose will have been pierced by a length of bone and her front teeth knocked out when she was a young girl. Today, however, it's unlikely you'll encounter such a person in Binga. ■

Crocodile Farm

At the end of the road, beyond the Bulawayo elite's dacha complex, is the Crocodile Farm, which is good for a brief look around. However, it doesn't really cater to visitors and probably isn't worth a visit unless you have a special interest. It's attended daily except Sunday.

Chibwatatata Hot Springs

Up the hill from the rest camp are Chibwatatata Hot Springs, the larger and hotter of which would more correctly be described as a fumarole. Long considered a 'power place' by the Batonka, in former times it served as a rain making site. The less violent hot spring nearby provides naturally heated water for the rest camp swimming pool. It's also used as a laundry and bath, and has become rather polluted.

Chilangililo Cooperative

The Chilangililo Cooperative project, a novel and successful tourism concept, is the brainchild of Dr Peta Jones, an anthropolo-gist in Binga. Her interests include promoting donkeys as transport and encouraging production of quality local crafts.

One arm of the project, Village Visits, came about when she noted many tourists to Zimbabwe were seeing plenty of wildlife, but missing opportunities for contact with the country's interesting cultures. The programme takes visitors on a boat ride to traditional Batonka kraals, where they have the chance to meet local people and sample traditional Batonka foods.

Because Village Visits is a genuine cultural experience and not a set up for mass tourism, you'll need to muster a group and book well in advance. Visitors are encouraged to relax, avoid the appearance of wealth and resist the temptation to dole out gifts to individuals (although donations to local projects are gratefully accepted). The price of an all-inclusive trip for 10 people is US$321, plus an additional US$100 fro the boat trip.

If you're in town for just a short while, you can still visit Qualitonga Crafts and purchase unique material arts – mostly wood carvings and basketry. For inexpensive overnights, guests can stay in Chilangililo stilt huts by the lake.

Ms Jones' office is a long but pleasant walk from the Binga Rest Camp. Otherwise, you will be able to contact her through the Kasambabezi Kiosk or the village librarian, Ms Rita White (☎ 237).

Places to Stay & Eat

For the cheapest and most interesting accommodation in Binga, go to the *Chilangililo Cooperative*, which has several stilt huts beside the lakeshore wetlands. With two very basic sleeping huts and a kitchen hut for cooking, it's ideal for self-sufficient backpackers. Hut accommodation costs US$4 per person.

The old stand-by is *Binga Rest Camp* (☎ 244), housed in the former District Commissioner's home. Here you can camp and use the pool facilities for US$3 per person. Rooms cost US$11/13 for singles/doubles; chalets are available for families. The attached restaurant serves very good fare, but it receives less patronage than the bar, which is *the* local gathering place. An alternative for camping is along the lakeshore near the Somabhula Houseboat.

A more up-market option, *Kulizwe Lodge* (locally called Butterfly Lodge), is actually an agglomeration of several private lodges. One which advertises itself separately from the others is *Kabila House* (☎ 67001; fax 76172), both in Bulawayo); it charges US$291/378 per day in low/high season for up to six people. The price includes use of the swimming pool, laundry services, cook, 4WD vehicle, driver, motorboat, cabin cruiser and a self-contained fishing raft. For accommodation only, without the amenities, you'll pay just US$32 per person. Meals are available if booked in advance. The other Kalizwe lodges accommodate four people and charge US$32 per lodge.

There's also another option, *Chilila Lodges* (☎ 72568; fax 76854, both in Bulawayo). These five traditional style self-catering lodges occupy a beautiful forested setting right beside a lovely harbour. However, they're a way out of town.

Getting There & Away

Vehicles were once rattled to bits on the tortuous washboard track to Binga from Dete Crossroads, but that road has now been replaced by a high-speed tarred road which is smooth as silk. Hitching isn't too difficult, but the DDF Binga ferry doesn't haul vehicles, so the ferry schedule won't offer much joy. You'll have the most luck hitching to Binga on Saturday mornings; leaving is easiest on Sunday afternoons.

One bus daily in either direction travels between Bulawayo and Siabuwa via Binga. If you want to reach Harare, you'll have to catch this bus eastbound and stay in desertified Siabuwa (camping only – there's no formal accommodation), and catch the bus leaving for Karoi and Harare the following morning.

The bus to Bulawayo leaves at 5 am from the market, beside the beer hall, so if you're staying at Binga Rest Camp, you'll need a good alarm clock and a torch to cover the five km to the bus stop. For Victoria Falls, get off this bus at Dete Crossroads and hitch or catch a westbound bus.

Informal fishing trips or boat trips to Mlibizi may be arranged privately from the boat harbour down the road opposite Binga Rest Camp. For information on the DDF ferries which serve Binga, see under Kariba in the Northern Zimbabwe chapter.

MLIBIZI

Unless they're fishing, most travellers spend just one night at Mlibizi, either arriving or connecting with the Kariba-bound lake ferry. At the ferry terminal is the mid-range *Mlibizi Zambezi Resort* (☎ 272), where you can stay in Mediterranean-style chalets for US$125 a double, or camp for US$2 per person. It also has a shop, bottle shop, restaurant and two swimming pools. Note that all water here must be boiled.

Further along is the more affordable *Mlibizi Hotel & Safari Camp* (☎ 271), which is beautifully set on a ridge. For a stone and thatch bungalow, you'll pay around US$75 a double. There's a restaurant, bar, children's playground, tennis courts and a swimming pool. To help you while away the time before the ferry arrives, they arrange boat trips through spectacular Devils Gorge upstream along the Zambezi.

Getting There & Away
For information on the Kariba ferries, see under Kariba in the Northern Zimbabwe chapter. In Victoria Falls, bookings may be made upstairs in the Zimbank Building.

To find a lift from Bulawayo or Victoria Falls, leave notices at hotels and camp sites, stating whether you'll share petrol costs and expenses. Transfer services are also available from Victoria Falls and Hwange National Park, but they average around US$80 for one to six people. If you have a large group, you can hire a UTC minibus for US$93 for the trip from Victoria Falls. A taxi costs around US$25 from Victoria Falls. Beware of unlicensed scam artists who quote reasonable prices; when it's time to leave, they demand double the agreed rate, knowing it would be difficult to find another option before the ferry leaves.

Hitchers should allow lots of time for the trip from Victoria Falls via Dete Crossroads. The friendly owner of the Crossroads petrol station may also be persuaded to take you to Mlibizi for US$7 (Z$50) per person, with a minimum charge of around US$20. Otherwise, catch the more or less daily Binga bus from Dete Crossroads and get off at the Mlibizi turn-off. From there, you can walk the final 15 km into Mlibizi, but carry lots of water. The ferries normally depart at around 9 am so you'll have to spend at least one night in Mlibizi.

Hitching from Mlibizi to Victoria Falls is more difficult because there's very little traffic and tourist vehicles arriving on the ferry are normally full.

DEKA DRUM
Another fishing resort, *Deka Drum* (☎ 250524, Hwange), idles beside the confluence of the Deka and Zambezi rivers, near the entrance to Devils Gorge. It's a beautiful spot where you can sit and fish the river to your heart's content. Camping costs US$2 per person and basic self-catering chalets are US$8 per person; the small on-site restaurant prepares meals and snacks. Petrol is available on site. Deka Drum lacks a ferry link; access is by road either from Victoria Falls or Hwange town, but there's no public transport.

CHIZARIRA NATIONAL PARK
The name of this remote and magnificent 192,000-hectare park is derived from the Batonka word *chijalila* which means 'closed off' or 'barrier', aptly describing its physical position. Look at a map of Zimbabwe and you won't find a spot further from the road system than the eastern boundary of this park.

Although access is difficult, Chizarira is Zimbabwe's most scenic park and until a couple of years ago, the dense bush made it one of the last great strongholds of the black rhino. During my most recent visit, however, only four black rhinos remained in Chizarira – the vast majority had been poached and the few survivors had been fitted with radio collars and transferred to Matusadona National Park where, in theory, they could be more readily monitored and guarded. It's quite conceivable that by the time you read this, not a single rhino will remain in Chizarira.

As far as the terrain is concerned, Chizarira is really three parks, each of which is distinct from the others and worlds away from the hot and dusty, goat-eaten baobab scrub of the Gwembe Valley communal lands below. In the north, cutting through the edges of the Zambezi Escarpment, are the magnificent green gorges of the Mucheni and Lwizilukulu (also spelt Ruziruhuru) rivers. Both drainages are readily accessible on foot from the Manzituba headquarters, but hikers must be accompanied by professional guides.

In the eastern part of the park, the Zambezi Escarpment is capped by the 1500-metre peak Tandezi. According to a Batonka folk tale, a large and volatile snake lies coiled upon its bald summit. (According to many Western visitors, Tandezi resembles a squashed hat.) Above the escarpment, the landscape changes to msasa-dotted upland plateau, prime wildlife country which was once a stronghold of the black rhino. The solitary summits of Chingolo and Gongoriba provide impressive vantage points and are worthy destinations for day hikes. Also

lovely are the soda springs at Mujima, south of Gongoriba.

South of the Sinamagoga Ridge, the land slopes gently down into the Busi Valley, which bears a strong resemblance to the Mana Pools river frontage, with almost identical riverine vegetation, including winterthorne acacia *(Acacia albida)*. It also has a similar density of wildlife – including everything from porcupines and warthogs to

The Power Struggle

At the time of Zimbabwean independence in 1980, the country's optimistic new leaders set about laying down plans to meet Zimbabwe's future power needs. Among other proposed ideas were plans to construct a new hydroelectric project on the Zambezi River by the year 2002, to supplement the output of Kariba Dam.

The initial proposal was for a new dam in the Mupata Gorge, between Mana Pools and the Mozambique border. However, the inevitable result would have been the flooding and destruction of the magnificent Mana Pools floodplain, and fortunately, environmental pressure groups (particularly the Zambezi Society) were able to bring the matter to worldwide attention. Mana Pools was subsequently placed on the World Heritage List, and in the end, the idea was scuppered.

Once the idea of a dam on the middle Zambezi had been abandoned, attention turned to the upper Zambezi, and specifically, Batoka Gorge, 54 km downstream from Victoria Falls. Conservationists weren't exactly happy with the prospect, but conceded that it was considerably more acceptable than the Mupata Gorge proposal, and plans were drawn up.

Initially, construction was set to begin in 1996, to be completed on schedule in 2002. However, a series of snags arose. Zambia, which was expected to pay half the expenses for the project, balked at the projected US$3 billion price tag and pulled out in early 1995. In any case, after heated disputes over Kariba, Zambians don't trust Zimbabwe to fairly allocate energy resources, anyway. Furthermore, Zambian villagers living along the riverbanks are determined not to leave their homes and fields, and have refused to accept the fate that befell the Batonka people when Kariba Dam came on line. Another drawback – albeit relatively minor in the overall scheme of things – would be the flooding of the Zambezi gorges and the loss of the whitewater rafting potential below Victoria Falls.

As opinions heated up, UNESCO called for an environmental-impact assessment of the project and conservation groups suggested a series of smaller and less imposing dams. In the end, the Batoka Gorge idea was set aside and alternatives were sought. One prospect was the development of recently discovered coal reserves at Sengwa, near Lake Kariba. Unfortunately, the Sengwa fields are estimated to hold only 35 years of reserves and a thermal-power plant there would produce an unacceptable level of carbon-dioxide emissions. Furthermore, the scale of mining required would severely alter an environmentally sensitive area for an admittedly meagre return.

Another possibility would be to tap into the power about to be generated by Mozambique's Cabora Bassa dam, which lay dormant through that country's years of civil war. However, Mozambique has already agreed to sell the power to South Africa, so any small surplus available to Zimbabwe would quickly diminish as South Africa's power needs increase.

Other more feasible possibilities would include power rationing, the development of Zimbabwe's immense solar potential, or plugging into the immense new Inga Barrage, currently being constructed on the Zaïre River. It's projected that Inga will have the capacity to power the entire African continent.

Whatever happens, the Zimbabwean government has determined that if no viable alternative is found, it will eventually go ahead with the Batoka Gorge project, but given the recent setbacks, it seems unlikely to happen anytime in the near future. ■

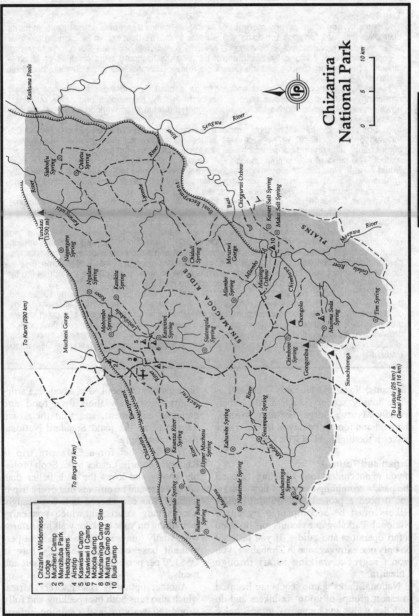

Chizarira
National Park

0   5   10 km

Legend

1. Chizarira Wilderness
   Lodge
2. Mucheni Camp
3. Manzituba Park
   Headquarters
4. Airstrip
5. Kaswiswi Camp
6. Kaswiswi II Camp
7. Mobola Camp
8. Muchaninga Camp Site
9. Mujima Camp Site
10. Busi Camp

The Tsetse Fly

The tsetse fly, one of the several scourges of Africa, resembles a common housefly except for its distinctive scissor-fold wings and its habit of sucking blood. It's best known for carrying the fatal cattle disease *trypanosomiasis* or *nagana*, which is occasionally passed along to humans as 'sleeping sickness'. Historically, the threat of this disease rendered large swathes of Africa – including the Zambezi Valley and the Okavango area – uninhabitable to pastoralists and their cattle.

Naturally, some conservationists count this as a blessing and indeed, many of Africa's remaining wilderness areas owe their existence to this fly. Developers and cattle ranchers, however, are naturally at odds with this assessment and have been working with local governments to eradicate the fly.

In Zimbabwe, the earliest national eradication attempts, which were developed in the 1960s, focused on the Zambezi Valley and were rather basic. The first plan involved very simple components: a tiny round boma, which was just large enough to hold one cow and one man on a stool. The concept was simple enough – whenever a tsetse fly landed on the cow, the man would swat it. Naturally, this optimistic programme, which hoped to keep zillions of potentially threatening flies at bay, met with limited success. You'll still see these bomas dotted around Chizarira National Park and other areas near the Zambezi.

The next proposed plan of attack was to build a fence along the base of the Zambezi Escarpment and shoot everything north of the fence. For some reason, this suggestion wasn't enthusiastically received and it was dropped before it got off the ground.

Inevitably, it was decided that the answer was aerial spraying of insecticides, and the environment was liberally misted with a cocktail of DDT, deltamethrin and endosulphan. In fact, this method is still used in Botswana's Okavango Delta and although it's clearly a threat to the delta's aquatic ecosystems, it conveys the unambiguous message that cattle come first in Botswana. (In fact, the Botswana government has gone so far as cutting trees to deprive the fly of shelter and killing buffaloes and kudu to wipe out its food supply.)

On a brighter note, the latest method of tsetse control – which began in the early 1970s and thankfully doesn't require drastic environmental sacrifice – appears to be the most effective. Strips of material impregnated with the hormone component in bovine breath are hung up up in known tsetse habitats. The flies don't realise – until it's too late – that these strips also contain a poison brewed up specifically for them. You'll often see these strips attached to metal frames throughout affected areas around northern Zimbabwe and north-western Botswana, including the Okavango Delta. ■

elephants, lions and leopards – as well as some lovely scenery, such as the otherworldly Mvurwi Gorge. For most visitors, the wild and remote beauty of the Busi area makes it the highlight of Chizarira.

Organised Tours

If you're not content four-wheeling it around the park's crumbling system of bush tracks, you'll need a professional walking guide. Hikers must be accompanied by either National Parks' game scouts or licensed safari operators and guides. If you lash out on only one extravagance in Zimbabwe, you won't regret a walking safari through Chizarira.

National Parks' game scouts are licensed to escort groups of up to six hikers and do both day walks and longer wilderness treks,

but trips must be booked in advance. Participants must carry their own food and camping equipment, and find their own transport into the park. Standard National Parks' rates apply.

Your best bet for a Chizarira trip is Khangela Safaris. Leader Mike Scott probably knows and loves the park better than anyone else and he ensures that every trip is unique. You can choose between straight backpacking safaris, in which you carry everything on your back, or walking safaris, where daily forays are made from semi-permanent base camps. The daily rate is US$120 per person, including transport and meals.

Another option is Backpackers Africa, which also runs both backpacking and fully supported walking and camping safaris lasting from five to 12 days. You can choose between the Lwizilukulu Gorge area in the northern sector or the more popular Busi Trail in the south. They also include the park as part of a 12-day circuit through Kazuma Pan, Hwange, Chizarira and Zambezi National Parks.

Places to Stay & Eat

Chizarira has no services, so all supplies – food, spares, camping equipment, fuel and so on – must be carried from outside. The nearest formal accommodation and restaurant is at *Chizarira Wilderness Lodge* (☎ 4637; fax 4417, Victoria Falls), near the bottom of the escarpment outside the park. Scenically situated on a bluff overlooking the communal lands, it's relatively convenient to the Manzituba area, where their guides lead game drives and day walks. However, it's too far for day trips to Busi and other remote areas of the park.

There are four main National Parks' exclusive camps in Chizarira, each of which may be occupied by only one party at a time and must be pre-booked in Harare.

The plushest is *Kaswiswi Camp* near the source of the Lwizilukulu River six km from Manzituba. It's a real wilderness compound with two raised sleeping huts, a cooking and dining area, hot showers and flush toilets. Kaswiswi is scenically unspectacular, buried as it is in dense scrub, but it's well placed for viewing the small herds of elephants and buffaloes that inhabit this area of the park.

On a ridge overlooking Mucheni Gorge are the two dramatically situated sites at *Mucheni Camp*, which also serves as a viewpoint and picnic site. It has long-drop toilets and a thatched picnic shelter.

The other northern area camp, *Mobola Camp*, lies beside the Mucheni River six km from the Manzituba offices. It sits beneath trees which serve as bat roosts and tents often suffer guano bombardment. There are no shelters, but it does have a concrete cooking bench, a table and pumped-in running water from the river, as well as flush toilets.

Busi Camp, which actually consists of two exclusive camp sites, lies 35 km down a

Rhino

rough 4WD track from Manzituba on the acacia-dotted flood plain of the Busi River. The main site has three shelters, two for sleeping and one for dining, as well as braai pits and cooking benches.

In addition, there's *Kaswiswi II*, an emergency camp near Kaswiswi, and two beautiful undeveloped camp sites, *Muchinanga* and *Mujima*. They're remote and little-known, even by park rangers, so you may have draw a blank trying to book them from Harare. These three camps are used mainly by safari operators on walking and backpacking safaris.

Water is available only at Mabolo and Kaswiswi camps, and at the Manzituba headquarters. At Busi, water must be obtained elephant-style by digging for it in the Busi riverbed.

Getting There & Away

Without a 4WD, resign yourself to joining a tour to visit Chizarira. The park just doesn't see enough visitors to make hitching even marginally feasible. (In fact, on my last visit, we had the park to ourselves, save for the day-trippers from Chizarira Safari Lodge and a solitary South African in a green microbus.) For drivers, petrol is sporadically available at Siabuwa. Failing that, you'll have to drive 90 km to Binga, so carry reserves.

On public transport, the nearest you will get is the park turn-off west of Siabuwa on the Karoi-Binga track. Park headquarters at Manzituba lies 24 km uphill from there, but walking past the mouth of Mucheni Gorge, which marks the park entrance, is not permitted.

If you're travelling this way, stop off at the Comednze Batonka crafts outlet near the corner of the Binga and Siabuwa roads. You'll find a wonderful variety of genuine Batonka crafts and material arts, including stools, headrests, drums and other traditional articles.

Getting Around
Both 4WD and high clearance are required to travel south of Manzituba and although the park is open year-round, heavy rains could render some areas inaccessible in the wet season.

Botswana

Facts about the Country

HISTORY

Early San & Bantu Groups

The original inhabitants of Botswana were San (Bushmen), who continue to inhabit the Kalahari regions of eastern Namibia and western Botswana. Their origins are unknown but they are believed to have occupied the area for at least 30,000 years. They were followed by the Khoi-Khoi (Hottentots), who probably originated from a San group cut off from the mainstream. Sheep remains and pottery in late Stone Age diggings provide evidence that they had eventually adopted a pastoral lifestyle.

Next arrived the agricultural and pastoral Bantu groups, who migrated from the north-western and eastern regions of the African continent – there is evidence that they originated in the area of present-day Cameroun – sometime during the 1st or 2nd century. It is likely, however, that this 'Bantu migration' bypassed or just skirted the edges of present-day Botswana, avoiding the harsh Kalahari sands and continuing on to the more amenable areas of the Transvaal and the Cape, where the newcomers inevitably encountered San and Khoi-Khoi people. Relations between the three societies appear to have been amicable and they apparently mixed freely – trading and intermarrying.

The Bantu peoples of southern Africa have been divided into groups by anthropologists, based on similarities in their languages and social structures. The earliest such group probably arrived in Botswana during the first centuries AD, settling along the Chobe River.

Another Bantu group, the Sotho-Tswana, consisted of three distinct tribal entities: the Northern Basotho, or Pedi, who settled in the Transvaal; the Southern Basotho of present-day Lesotho; and the Western Basotho, or Tswana, who migrated northward into present-day Botswana. The Kgalagadi, the first Setswana-speaking tribe to colonise Botswana, arrived from the Transvaal

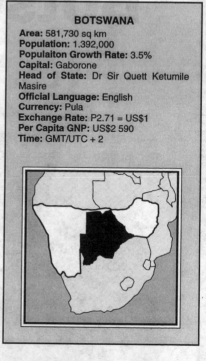

BOTSWANA

Area: 581,730 sq km
Population: 1.392,000
Populaiton Growth Rate: 3.5%
Capital: Gaborone
Head of State: Dr Sir Quett Ketumile Masire
Official Language: English
Currency: Pula
Exchange Rate: P2.71 = US$1
Per Capita GNP: US$2 590
Time: GMT/UTC + 2

around the 14th century and settled in the relatively arable and well-watered south-eastern strip of the country between present-day Francistown and Gaborone.

At that stage, north-eastern Botswana lay within Shona territory and was affiliated with the Torwa and later the Rozwi dynasties. (See History under Zimbabwe earlier in this book.) Indications, however, point to its earlier occupation, probably by the Leopard's Kopje people, who were based in the Khami area of south-western Zimbabwe. These Shona speakers, now known as the Babirwa, were later completely absorbed into the Tswana culture, adopting the Setswana language and customs.

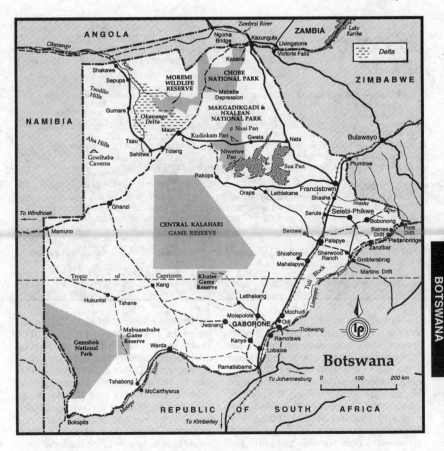

Between the 15th and 18th centuries the majority of the Bantu people in Botswana lived east of the Kalahari sands, but during the early 1700s peaceful fragmentation of tribal groups became the standard. Familial and power disputes were solved amicably, with the dissatisfied party gathering followers and tramping off to establish another domain elsewhere.

Fragmentation was an ideal solution to disputes as long as there remained an 'elsewhere' to set oneself up; in the case of the people living in south-eastern Botswana, it was to the vast expanses of country to the

west, areas previously inhabited only by the San and Khoi-Khoi. In the north-west, where the Lozi Empire dominated, it was to the Okavango Delta region and around the shores of Lake Ngami.

For Botswana history, perhaps the most significant of the Tswana splits was that of Kwena, Ngwaketse and Ngwato, the sons of a chief called Malope (or Masilo) whose domain took in the Boteti River area of central Botswana. When the three brothers quarrelled, Kwena went to Ditshegwane, Ngwaketse set himself up at Kanye in the far south-east and Ngwato settled at Serowe.

Botswana Itinerary

Low-Budget Tour Although there's no such thing as a low-budget tour in Botswana, the following suggestions will take you to places accessible on public transport, where camping options are available.

1. Kasane – camp at Chobe Safari Lodge and take river trips and game drives into Chobe National Park (two days)
2. Nata – camp at Nata Lodge and visit Nata Sanctuary (two days)
3. Gweta – camp at Gweta Rest Camp and take camping and wildlife-viewing tour to Nxhasin Pan
4. Maun & the Okavango Delta – camp at Audi Camp and take budget mokoro camping trip in the Eastern Delta (three to seven days)
5. Shakawe – camp at one of the riverside camps (two days)

Cultural & Historical Tour As with most trips through Botswana, this tour will require access to a 4WD vehicle and good desert wilderness driving skills. Other sites of interest not included in this itinerary are the Kgalagadi Village Cluster in the central Kalahari and Kubu Island on Sua Pan in north-eastern Botswana.

1. Gaborone – National Museum, Mochudi, Mokolodi Nature Reserve and a couple of the arts & crafts centres in Gaborone's hinterlands (two to three days)
2. Serowe (one day)
3. Nata – Nata Sanctuary (one day)

The Ngwato clan split further with a quarrel between Chief Khama I and his brother Tawana, who subsequently left Serowe and established his chiefdom in the area of Maun at the end of the 18th century. The three major modern-day Tswana groups can trace their ancestry to this three-way Tswana split.

Late in the 19th century, the nomadic and primarily pastoral Herero, faced with German aggression at home, began migrating eastward from Namibia and settling in the north-western extremes of Botswana.

The Zulu

By 1800, all suitable grazing lands around the fringes of the Kalahari had been settled by pastoralists and peaceful fragmentation was no longer a feasible solution to disputes. Furthermore, Europeans had arrived in the Cape and were expanding northward, creating an effective barrier against movement towards the south. By 1817, Kuruman, the first Christian mission in Tswana territory, had been founded by Robert Moffat .

In 1818 came an event which would alter the face of southern Africa. Shaka, the fierce

and determined new chief of the Zulu tribes, forced the amalgamation of all area tribes. Shaka set out with his ruthless fighting machine on a military rampage, conquering or destroying all tribes and settlements in his path. By 1830, Kwena, Ngwato and Lozi had fallen and Mzilikazi (see History in the Zimbabwe Facts About the Country chapter) had broken away and fled northward on a similar crusade with the Kumalo clan, which would later be known as the Ndebele.

Mzilikazi stormed his way across the Transvaal and Botswana, frequently sending raiding parties into the Tswana villages and scattering them north and westward. Some were dispersed as far as Ghanzi and the Tshane cluster of villages in the dead heart of the Kalahari. Ngwaketse was rousted out in the process and sent fleeing into the desert, finally settling near Lethlakeng.

The Missionaries

As a result of all the displacement and scattering, the Tswana people realised that fragmentation was no longer a feasible

4. Kasane & Kazungula (one day)
5. Chobe National Park (two days)
6. Moremi Wildlife Reserve (two days)
7. Maun & the Okavango Delta (three days)
8. Gcwihaba Caverns & the Aha Hills (three days)
9. Shakawe & the Tsodilo Hills (three days)

Wildlife Tour Botswana offers some of the world's finest wilderness wildlife viewing, with rich ecosystems and wide open spaces that will present the Africa you've always dreamed about. However, unless you're booked onto a comprehensive safari package, most of the following suggestions will require a 4WD vehicle.

1. Chobe National Park – both the riverfront and the Savuti area (three days)
2. Moremi Wildlife Reserve (three days)
3. Maun & the Okavango Delta – fly-in trip to the Inner Delta, with visits to Chiefs Island (five days)
4. Makgadikgadi & Nxai Pans National Park – with game drives through the Makgadikgadi Pans region and visits to Baines' Baobabs and Nxai Pan (three days)
5. Nata Sanctuary (one day)
6. Serowe & Khama Rhino Sanctuary (one day)
7. Gaborone & Mokolodi Nature Reserve (one day)
8. Khutse Game Reserve (two days)

BOTSWANA

option and that their divided nation would be particularly vulnerable to subsequent attacks. They began to regroup and developed a highly structured society. Each nation was ruled by a hereditary monarch and aristocracy whose economic power was based on tribute labour and the ownership of large herds of cattle. In each of the Tswana nations, the king's subjects lived either in the central town or in satellite villages. Each clan was allocated its own settlement, which fell under the control of village leaders. These leaders were responsible for distributing land and recruiting tribute labour for work in the monarch's fields and pastures. By the second half of the 19th century, some towns had grown to a considerable size. For example, by 1860, for example, the capital of the Ngwato clan at Shoshong had an estimated population of 30,000.

The orderliness and structure of the town-based society impressed the early Christian missionaries at Kuruman Mission. The prime mover behind the missionary effort was the dogmatic and uncompromising Robert Moffat, who was responsible for the first transliteration of the Tswana language into the Roman alphabet as well as the first translation of the Bible into written Tswana. Even after years in Africa, however, Moffat couldn't be distracted long enough to appreciate the continent's unique characteristics and problems, instead remaining uninterested in – and intolerant of – traditional cultures and beliefs.

In 1841 came the inquisitive and charismatic Dr David Livingstone who based himself at Kuruman and married Robert Moffat's daughter, Mary. With a scientific background, Dr Livingstone found it difficult to settle down to sedentary family and missionary life. Instead, he left the mission and staged a series of forays north to Lake Ngami and into the domain of the Lozi Empire. In the end, Livingstone's itchy feet got the better of him; he sent his family to England and struck out for parts unknown – to Victoria Falls and beyond. It is significant that before Livingstone left he was unjustly accused by the Boers of selling firearms to the Tswana and rallying local people against them. In a Boer attack on the Tswana,

Livingstone's Kuruman home was destroyed and his weapons stolen.

None of the missionaries converted great numbers of Tswana, but they did manage to advise the locals, sometimes wrongly, in their dealings with the Europeans that followed – explorers, naturalists, traders, miners and general rabble. The traders provided firearms and, in the name of commerce, sent the Tswana to gun down and practically exterminate the country's elephant, rhino and hippopotamus populations, especially around Lake Ngami. So great were the numbers killed that the European market for animal products was flooded, and prices could scarcely have justified the slaughter. At the same time, the Tswana, having been paid for the skins and ivory they bagged, were dragged into the European cash economy.

The Boers

While Mzilikazi was wreaking havoc on the Tswana and the missionaries were busy trying to Christianise them in the north-west, the Boers, feeling pressure from the British in the Cape, embarked on their Great Trek across the Vaal River. Confident that they had Heaven-sanctioned rights to any land they might choose to occupy in southern Africa, 20,000 Boers crossed the Vaal River into Tswana and Zulu territory and established themselves as though the lands were unclaimed and uninhabited (indeed some were, having been cleaned out earlier by Mzilikazi).

Each male farmer staked his claim by riding out an area of 3000 *morgen* (about 2400 hectares) and set up his farm. The remaining local people were either forced to move or were pressured into working as servants and farm hands.

When Mzilikazi came up against the Boers in 1837, the superior Boer firepower under the command of Hendrik Potgieter stalled his campaign and sent him fleeing north-eastward to settle in the Bulawayo area. Between 1844 and 1852, the Boers, bent upon establishing trade links with the Dutch and Portuguese, set up a series of fragmented republics which were independent of the British connection in the Cape.

At the Sand River Convention of 1852, Great Britain recognised the Transvaal's independence and the Boers immediately informed the Batswana that they were now subjects of the new South African Republic. Boer leader MW Pretorius notified the British that the Tswana were acquiring weapons from White traders and missionaries and preparing for war. Maintaining that this rendered his country unsafe for travellers, he closed off the road through the Transvaal. Pretorius' allegation was technically true: the Tswana were obtaining muzzle-loading rifles to bring down the big game they were busy decimating.

Meanwhile, the prominent Tswana leader of the Kwena clan, Sechele I, and Mosielele of the Kgatla clan decided to rebel against White rule, but the Boers came back with a vengeance, launching a destructive rampage in the Tswana communities. Incurring heavy human and territorial losses, the Tswana sent their leaders to petition the British for protection from the Boers. Great Britain, however, already had its hands full in southern Africa and was in no hurry to take on and support a country of dubious profitability. Instead, Britain offered only to act as arbitrator in the dispute. By 1877, however, animosity had escalated to such a dangerous level that the British finally conceded and annexed the Transvaal, launching the first Boer War. War continued until the Pretoria Convention of 1881, when the British withdrew from the Transvaal in exchange for Boer allegiance to the British Crown.

The Protectorate

With the British out of their way, the Boers looked northward into Tswana territory, pushing westward into the Molopo Basin of what had become known as Bechuanaland. They managed to subdue the towns of Taung and Mafeking (now Mafikeng) in 1882 and proclaimed them the republics of Stellaland and Goshen. The British viewed this encroachment as threatening to their 'road to the north' – the route into Rhodesia and its presumed mineral wealth.

Meanwhile, the Tswana lobbied for continued British protection from the Boers, as well as from a possible renewal of the Ndebele threat in the north-east. John Mackenzie, a close friend of the Christian Ngwato chief, Khama III of Shoshong, travelled to London and actively campaigned for British intervention to stop the erosion of Tswana territory by the expansionist Boers. Mackenzie was appointed Deputy Commissioner over the region, a post which was quickly and underhandedly taken over by Cecil Rhodes. Rhodes saw Mackenzie's opposition to Bechuanaland's' incorporation into the Cape Province as a threat to Rhodes' 'Cape to Cairo' scheme. (Rhodes dreamt of British domination of Africa from the Cape to Cairo, and planned to link the two with a railway line through the heart of the continent.) Cecil Rhodes also complained that Boer control was cutting off the labour supply from the north to his British South Africa Company (BSAC).

In 1885, Great Britain finally resigned itself to the inevitable. The area south of the Molopo River became the British Crown Colony of Bechuanaland, which was attached to the Cape Colony. At the same time, British jurisdiction and protection were extended to cover the newly created British Protectorate of Bechuanaland, which took in all lands north of the Cape Colony, south of 22°S latitude and east of 20°E longitude. This inadvertently divided Khama III's Ngwato territory in half, but Khama, grateful for the protection, chose to ignore the issue.

The rationale behind the protectorate was to prevent Boer expansionism to the north and west and stall encroachment by other European powers, particularly the Germans in German South West Africa (Namibia). Only secondarily was it to provide protection for the existing Tswana power structures. Unfortunately, the new 'protectors' remained blase about Bechuanaland and tried to transfer control to the Cape Colony which refused on the grounds that the expense would be too great.

Rhodes Loses Ground

A new threat to the Tswana chiefs' power base came in the form of Cecil Rhodes and his British South Africa Company, who remained keen to take control of the country. By 1894, the British had more or less agreed to allow him to do so.

Realising the implications of Rhodes' aspirations, three high-ranking Tswana chiefs, Bathoen, Khama III and Sebele, accompanied by a sympathetic missionary, W C Willoughby, sailed to England to appeal directly for continued British government control over Bechuanaland. Instead of taking action, Colonial Minister Joseph Chamberlain advised them to contact Rhodes directly and work things out among themselves. Chamberlain then conveniently forgot the matter and left on holiday.

Naturally, Rhodes was immovable, so they turned to the London Missionary Society (LMS), who in turn took the matter to the British public. Fearing that the BSAC would allow alcohol in Bechuanaland, the LMS and other Christian groups backed the devoutly Christian Khama and his entourage. The public in general felt that the Crown had more business administering the empire than did Cecil Rhodes, with his business of questionable integrity. When Chamberlain returned from holiday, public pressure had mounted to such a level that the government was forced to concede to the chiefs. Chamberlain agreed to continue British administration of Bechuanaland, ceding only a small strip of the south-east to the BSAC to allow construction of a railway line to Rhodesia.

In 1890, the strip between 22°S latitude and the Chobe and Zambezi rivers came under British control by agreement with the Germans. Rhodes was still scheming to gain control in the protectorate. Posing as an agent of Queen Victoria, he tricked the Tawana king, Sekgoma, into signing a treaty of 'friendship' with Britain, which incidentally granted the BSAC mineral extraction rights. This treaty, known as the Bosman Concession, was later disallowed by the British government. In 1896, the government persuaded Sekgoma to open the Ghanzi area to White settlement in exchange for the guarantee of Tawana sovereignty over the remainder of Ngamiland. Rhodes lost ground, but wasn't yet defeated.

Much to the embarrassment of the British government, in 1895, Rhodes' cohort Leander Starr Jameson launched an abortive private military foray into the Transvaal, aiming to rein it into some sort of southern African confederation. The Boers were not impressed and as a result Jameson was imprisoned and Rhodes was forced to give up his position as prime minister of the Cape Colony. This time, Rhodes was forced to admit defeat.

Colonial Years

Now that British rule had settled in, the chiefs more or less accepted that their tribal rites, traditions and lifestyles would be forever altered by the influences of Christianity and Western technology. The cash economy had been solidly emplaced and the Tswana had begun to actively participate. As a result, taxes were levied in the Bechuanaland Protectorate, and a capital was established at Mafeking (which was actually in South Africa, outside the Protectorate).

Each chief in the protectorate was granted a tribal 'reserve' in which he was given authority over all Black residents. The British assigned the chiefs, who still held some degree of autonomy over their tribes, to collect taxes, offering them a 10% commission on all moneys collected. Thus, everyone was effectively forced into the cash economy.

In 1899, Britain decided it was time for a consolidation of the southern African states and declared war on the Transvaal. The Boers were finally overcome in 1902, and in 1910 the Union of South Africa was created, comprising the Cape Colony, Natal, the Transvaal and the Orange Free State – with provisions for the future incorporation of Bechuanaland and Rhodesia.

By selling cattle, draught oxen and grain to the Europeans streaming north in search

of farming land and minerals, Bechuanaland enjoyed some degree of economic independence. However, any sense of security this may have offered didn't last long. The construction of the railway through Bechuanaland to Rhodesia (built at the rate of a mile a day!) and a serious outbreak of foot-and-mouth disease in the 1890s destroyed the transit trade.

By 1920, commercial maize farmers in South Africa and Rhodesia were producing grain in such quantities that Bechuanaland no longer had a market. Furthermore, in 1924 South Africa began pressing the Tswana chiefs to vote for Bechuanaland's amalgamation into the Union of South Africa. When they refused, economic sanctions were brought against the recalcitrant protectorate and its beef market dried up completely.

Economic vulnerability, combined with a series of drought years and the need to raise cash to pay British taxes, sent protectorate subjects migrating to South Africa for work on farms and in the mines. As much as 25% of Botswana's male population was abroad at any one time. This accelerated the breakdown of traditional land-use patterns and eroded the chiefs' powers, leaving the traditional leaders no longer in charge of the economy. Agriculture and domestic work were left in the hands of women, who remained at home. Some aristocrats and cattle barons turned the situation to their advantage by increasing their areas of cultivation and the size of their herds.

In 1923, Ngwato chief Khama III died at the age of 89 and was succeeded by his son Sekgoma, who died himself after serving only two years. The heir to the throne, four-year-old Seretse Khama, wasn't ready to rule over the largest of the Tswana chiefdoms, so his 21-year-old uncle, Tshekedi Khama, left his studies in South Africa to become regent over the Ngwato. This intelligent and competent leader was criticised by colonial authorities for his handling of local disputes according to tribal law. These included flogging Phineas McIntosh, a White resident of Serowe, for the rape of a local woman.

Tshekedi Khama was deposed by Resident Commissioner (well, not quite resident since he was based in Mafeking) Sir Charles Rey, but public opposition to the decision forced the chief's reinstatement.

Rey, who was keen to develop the territory in his charge, determined that no progress would be forthcoming as long as the people were governed by Tswana chiefs. He issued a proclamation turning the chiefs into local government officials answerable to colonial magistrates. So great was popular opposition to this decision – people feared it would lead to their incorporation into South Africa – that Rey was ousted from his job and his proclamation voided.

During WWII, 10,000 Tswana volunteered for the African Pioneer Corps to defend the British Empire. At the end of the war the heir to the Ngwato throne, Seretse Khama, went to study in England where he met and married Ruth Williams, an Englishwoman. (For more about this story, see the boxed aside under Serowe in the Eastern Botswana chapter.)

Tshekedi Khama was furious at the breach of tribal custom (although he was accused of exploiting the incident as a means to gain real power in his nephew's place) and the authorities in South Africa, still hoping to absorb Bechuanaland into the Union, were none too happy either. Seretse's chieftaincy was blocked by the British government and he was exiled from the protectorate to England. Bitterness continued until 1956, when Seretse Khama renounced his right to power in Ngwato, became reconciled with his uncle, and returned with his wife to Bechuanaland to serve as vice-chairman of the Ngwato Council.

Independence

The first signs of nationalist thinking among the Tswana occurred as early as the late 1940s, but during the 1950s and early 1960s, political changes were spreading across Africa and many former colonies were gaining their independence. As early as 1955 it was apparent that Britain was preparing to release its grip on Bechuanaland. University graduates returned from South Africa with political ideas, and although the country had no real economic base, the first Batswana political parties surfaced and started thinking about independence.

Following the Sharpeville Massacre in 1960, South African refugees Motsamai Mpho of the African National Congress (ANC) and Philip Matante, a Johannesburg preacher affiliated with the Pan-Africanist Congress, joined with K T Motsete, a teacher from Malawi, to form the Bechuanaland People's Party. Its immediate goal was independence for the protectorate.

In 1962, Seretse Khama and the Kanye farmer Quett Masire formed the more moderate Bechuanaland Democratic Party (BDP). They were soon joined by Chief Bathoen II of the Ngwaketse. The BDP formulated a schedule for independence, drawing on support from local chiefs and traditional Batswana. Their first acts were to successfully promote the transfer of the capital into the country, from Mafikeng to Gaborone, draft a new nonracial constitution and set up a countdown to independence. The British gratefully accepted their peaceful plan for a transfer of power, and when general elections were held in 1965, Seretse Khama was elected president. On 30 September 1966 the country, now called the Republic of Botswana, was peacefully granted its independence.

Sir Seretse Khama (he was knighted shortly after independence) was certainly no revolutionary. He guaranteed continued freehold over land held by White ranchers and adopted a strictly neutral stance (at least until near the end of his presidency) towards South Africa and Rhodesia. The reason, of course, was Botswana's economic dependence upon the giant to the south. He stood at the helm of one of the world's poorest nations and the wages of Batswana mine workers in South Africa formed an important part of the country's income. Furthermore, Botswana was heavily reliant upon South African food imports.

Nevertheless, Khama refused to exchange ambassadors with South Africa and offic-

BOTSWANA

ially disapproved of apartheid in international circles. He also courageously committed Botswana to the so-called 'Front Line' states of Zambia, Tanzania and Mozambique in opposing the Smith regime in Rhodesia and South African control in Namibia, but pragmatically refused to set up training camps for Zimbabwean liberation fighters. When Rhodesian armed forces carried out 'hot pursuit' raids into Botswana and bombed the Kazungula ferry to Zambia, Botswana's only frontier with a majority-ruled country, Botswana reacted by forming an army, the Botswana Defence Force.

Modern Developments

Economically, Botswana was catapulted into new realms with the discovery of diamonds near Orapa in 1967. The mining concession, which was given to De Beers, allowed Botswana 75% of the mining profits. Although most of the population remains in the low income bracket, this mineral wealth has provided the country with enormous foreign currency reserves (US$1.2 billion in 1987). In 1986, Botswana achieved the world's second highest rate of economic growth, and the pula remains Africa's strongest currency. In the early 1990s, the market for pula in neighbouring countries eclipsed that of even the South African rand, which declined steadily.

Sir Seretse Khama died in 1980, shortly after Zimbabwean independence, but his Botswana Democratic Party (BDP), formerly the Bechuanaland Democratic Party, still commands a substantial majority in the Botswana parliament. Sir Quett Ketumile Masire, who has served as president since then, continues to follow the path laid down by his predecessor, while the government generally follows cautiously pro-Western policies.

During the 1980s, South Africa accused Botswana of harbouring ANC members and other political refugees from South Africa's version of 'justice'. They retaliated in the form of two helicopter raids on Gaborone in 1986 in which several innocent civilians were killed (none of whom were affiliated with the ANC). One hopes that recent dramatic changes in South Africa will support more sane policies and eschew future violence and aggression.

Although economic dependence on South Africa is declining slightly, the two countries remain active trading partners and most of Botswana's food imports originate in South Africa. Currently, Botswana's biggest problems are unemployment, urban drift, and a rocketing birth rate – currently the third highest in the world – but thus far, economic growth has managed to keep apace.

Botswana remains a peaceful country the overall character of which is a positive force on the continent. In fact, it is one of just a handful of African countries – others include Namibia, Senegal, South Africa and Zambia – which enjoy scheduled popular elections and a democratic, multiparty, nonracial system of government.

There is, however, some urban support for the BDP's rival party, the Botswana National Front, which supports redistribution of wealth and an isolated artificial economy, either of which would dismantle Botswana's relatively stable affluence. Most of its support comes from unskilled migrants to urban areas who are the source of most of Gaborone's current unemployment problems. A growing complaint is the government's awarding of development contracts to overseas firms, which import their own workers.

Still, the recent electoral results would indicate that most people are content with the status quo; in the election of 15 October 1994, the BDP won a landslide victory for the sixth time, retaining the presidency and all but three of the 34 parliamentary seats.

GEOGRAPHY

With an area of 582,000 sq km, landlocked Botswana extends over 1100 km from north to south and 960 km from east to west. It's about the same size as Kenya or France and somewhat smaller than Texas. It's bounded on the south and south-east by South Africa, across the Limpopo and Molopo Rivers. In the north-east is Zimbabwe while Namibia

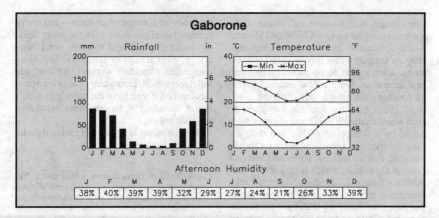

Gaborone

Rainfall / Temperature (Min / Max)

J	F	M	A	M	J	J	A	S	O	N	D
38%	40%	39%	39%	32%	29%	27%	24%	21%	26%	33%	39%

Afternoon Humidity

wraps around the western and northern frontiers. At Kazungula, four countries – Botswana, Zimbabwe, Zambia and Namibia–meet at a single point at midstream in the Zambezi River. Therefore, Botswana has a border crossing with Zambia, although the two countries don't actually share a common border.

Most of Botswana lies at an average elevation of 1000 metres. Much of the country consists of a vast and nearly level sand-filled basin characterised by scrub-covered savanna. In the north-west, the Okavango River flows in from Namibia and soaks into the sands, forming the 15,000 sq km of convoluted channels and islands that comprise the Okavango Delta. In the lower elevations of the north-east are the great salty clay deserts of the Makgadikgadi Pans. Covering nearly 85% of Botswana, including the entire central and south-western regions, is the Kalahari (Kgalagadi), a semi-arid expanse of wind-blown sand deposits and long sandy valleys (which sporadically serve as stream channels) and ridges stabilised by scrubby trees and bushes. The shifting dunes that comprise a traditional 'desert' are only found in the area of the Bokspits in the far south-west.

Although Botswana has no mountain ranges to speak of, the almost uniformly flat landscape is punctuated occasionally by low desert hills, especially along the south-

eastern boundary and in the far north-west. Botswana's highest point is 1491-metre Otse Mountain near Lobatse, but the three major peaks of the Tsodilo Hills, in the country's north-western corner, are more dramatic.

CLIMATE

Although it straddles the Tropic of Capricorn, Botswana experiences extremes in both temperature and weather. Botswana is primarily a dry country, but it does have a summer rainy season, which runs roughly from November to March. Afternoon showers and thunderstorms are the most frequent manifestations of *pula*, the commodity so precious that Botswana's currency was named for it.

In the winter, the period from late May to August, rain is rare anywhere in the country. Days are normally clear, warm and sunny and nights are cool to bitterly cold. In the Kalahari, subfreezing night-time temperatures are normal in June and July and, where there's enough humidity, frosts are common.

The in-between periods – April/early May and September/October – still tend to be dry, but the days are cooler than in summer and the nights are warmer than in winter.

NATIONAL PARKS & WILDLIFE RESERVES

Botswana's national parks are undoubtedly among Africa's wildest, characterised by open spaces where nature still reigns. Even the most popular parks – Chobe and Moremi – are dominated by wilderness. Although they do support a few private safari concessions, there's next to no infrastructure and few amenities. Only a few national parks' camp sites even have a long-drop loo.

In 1989, entrance fees for foreigners to Botswana's national parks and reserves were hiked by a whopping 600%, and they are now independent travellers' biggest thorn in the side. For all national parks and reserves (except Gemsbok, which is tied with South Africa's Kalahari Gemsbok National Park), foreigners pay US$18.50 (P50) per person per day, plus US$7.40 (P20) per person for camping. Children from eight to 15 years of age get a bit of a break at US$9.25 (P25) for entry and US$4 (P10) for camping. Botswana-registered vehicles (including aircraft) pay US$0.75 (P2) and foreign-registered vehicles cost, US$4 (P10).

Because the government discourages independent travel, organised tour participants pay only US$11 (P30) per person per day admission and US$3.70 (P10) to camp. Botswana residents pay US$3.70 (P10) per day entry and US$1.85 (P5) to camp and Botswana citizens pay US$0.75 (P2) entry and US$1.85 (P5) to camp.

The multiple-level pricing is not, as many people are inclined to believe, a product of economic disparity between Botswana and some foreign countries – residents of Zambia, Kenya and Cameroun would be charged the same rates as residents of Norway or Japan. Another myth is that the park fees are used to maintain the parks and pay staff. In fact, all revenue collected goes directly into the central treasury, and the parks themselves operate on a minimal shoestring budget.

Having said that, the rationale behind the high fees seems at least partially sound. The government hopes to extract maximum tourism revenue while minimising expenditure on infrastructure and limiting the negative effects of mass tourism. ('Just look at Kenya', they say.) However, since few Botswana citizens have long holidays – or the ready cash to spend on them – and many foreign travellers can't foot the entry fees, the national parks and reserves are essentially private playgrounds for tour companies, expatriate workers and overseas volunteers. Still, Botswana's parks are spectacular, and if you have the cash, you won't regret spending it to see these relatively unspoilt jewels.

The following is a listing of national parks and wildlife reserves:

Central Kalahari Game Reserve – This vast 52,000 sq km reserve, which is among the world's largest national parks, was once set aside exclusively for research and groups of nomadic San and Bakgalakgadi. Deception Valley in the north was the site of Mark & Delia Owens' brown hyena study in *Cry of the Kalahari*. It's now open to the public, but only the northern areas are reasonably accessible. The southern parts are still home to 800 traditional people.

Chobe National Park – This diverse and popular national park takes in a range of habitats, stretching from the lush elephant-rich Chobe riverfront to the mopane forests of Ngwezumba and wildlife-packed savannas around the ephemeral Savuti Marshes.

Khutse Game Reserve – Khutse, the nearest reserve to Gaborone, is still extremely wild and remote. It supports a variety of antelopes and predators and is a particularly good spot to see smaller creatures, like porcupines, bush squirrels and bat-eared foxes.

Gemsbok National Park – Accessible only from South Africa's Kalahari Gemsbok National Park, this immense roadless desert reserve is one of Africa's last great wilderness areas.

Mabuasehube Game Reserve – This remote desert reserve is a beautiful red wilderness of dunes. The six main waterholes attract gemsbok and other desert wildlife.

Makgadikgadi & Nxai Pans National Park – When the tarred Nata-Maun road came through, these two formerly separate but complementary reserves were combined. They're the scene of one of Africa's last great wildlife migrations. During the dry season, large herds gravitate toward the Makgadikgadi Pans section, but with the rains, they move north to the water-filled Nxai Pans.

Moremi Reserve – Taking in the north-eastern end of the Okavango Delta, Moremi is undoubtedly Botswana's most beautiful reserve, and it's home to an amazing variety of wildlife.

North-East Tuli Game Reserve – This odd park is comprised of large chunks of private land, which are operated as private game reserves allowing limited access. The largest is Mashatu Game Reserve followed by Tuli Game Reserve. Remaining bits of protected private land fall into the generic North-east Tuli Game Reserve.

GOVERNMENT

The Botswana government is one of Africa's success stories, a stable and functioning multiparty democracy which oversees the affairs of a peaceful and neutral state. Freedom of speech, press and religion are constitutionally guaranteed.

The constitution, which was drafted prior to independence in 1966, provides for three governmental divisions. The executive branch consists of the president, who is the head of state, as well as 11 cabinet ministers and three assistant ministers. The ministers are selected by the parliament while the president is elected by non-compulsory vote of all citizens over 21 years of age. The presidential term coincides with that of the National Assembly, which is described in the following paragraph.

The legislative branch is made up of the aforementioned parliament, which in turn is composed of the 41-seat National Assembly and the executive president. Assembly members are elected by voters every five years unless the body is dissolved by an interim popular election. Before acting on issues of land tenure, local government and traditional law, parliament must first consult the House of Chiefs, an eight-member advisory body made up of chiefs from Botswana's eight major tribes.

Judicial responsibilities are divided between the national and local governments with the *dikgotla* or town councils handling local civil and domestic disputes. Rural issues and services are overseen by district councils.

ECONOMY

Botswana's economy is one of the world's fastest growing. Aided by a stable political climate and vast natural resources, the pula is Africa's strongest currency, and Botswana's economic outlook is fairly good. In 1988, the GDP, for a population of one million, was nearly US$2 billion, with an average per capita income of over US$1600. By Western standards, it may not sound like much, but when you consider that most people exist at subsistence level and generate little income at all, it becomes apparent that urban dwellers working at professional and vocational levels aren't doing badly.

Since independence, Botswana has experienced the world's fastest-growing economic rate – between 11% and 13% annually. Even with the population growth taken into account, until 1992, the per capita growth rate was 8.5% annually. In addition, Botswana's external debts are not excessive and the government actually operates within its budget.

Mineral Resources

To some extent, Botswana's booming economy is a product of government stability, but it's also derived from a natural geologic wealth, which was created by terrestrial heat, pressure and time working on carbon deposits laid down some 300 million years ago. The diamond-bearing geologic formation in Botswana is known as the Karoo, a layer of sediments which underlies the entire Kalahari region. These deposits are natural intrusions known as kimberlite pipes, igneous dykes which have pushed through the Karoo rock and provided sufficient heat and pressure to form diamonds.

Botswana's diamond industry represents 40% of the country's GNP, 50% of its government revenue and 70% of its foreign exchange. It's overseen by the De Beers Botswana Mining Company Ltd (Debswana) which mines, sorts and markets the diamonds. The country's greatest known deposits lie around Jwaneng (the world's richest diamond mine), Orapa and Lethlakane. Between them, they produce a combined annual yield of over 13.2 million carats, and profits of over US$750 million (P2 billion).

Other mineral resources, although not as economically important as the shiny rocks,

The Buffalo Fence

If you've been stopped at a veterinary checkpoint in Botswana, or visited the Eastern Okavango Delta, you'll be familiar with the country's 3000 km of 1.5-metre-high 'buffalo fence', officially called the Veterinary Cordon Fence. It's not a single fence, but a series of high-tensile steel wire barriers which run cross-country through some of Botswana's wildest terrain. The fences were first erected in 1954 to segregate wild buffalo herds from domestic free-range cattle and thwart the spread of foot and mouth disease. However, no one has yet produced conclusive proof that the disease is passed from species to species.

The issue, however, isn't whether the fence works or not. The problem is that it not only prevents contact between wild and domestic bovine species, but also prevents other wild animals from migrating to water sources along age-old seasonal routes. While Botswana has set aside large areas for the protection of wildlife, these areas don't constitute independent ecological systems.

In fact, Botswana's wildebeest population has declined by 99% over the past decade and all remaining buffaloes and zebras are stranded north of the fences. Mark and Delia Owens, authors of the book *Cry of the Kalahari*), spent several years in the central Kalahari, and reported seeing tens of thousands of migrating wildebeests – as well as herds of zebras, giraffes and other animals – stopped short by the Kuke fence that stretches along the northern boundary of the Central Kalahari Game Reserve. Some became entangled in it, while others died of exhaustion searching for a way around it. The remainder were cut off from their seasonal grazing and watering places in the north and succumbed to thirst and starvation. The last great wildlife slaughter occurred during the drought of 1983, in which wildebeests heading for the Okavango waters were barred by the Kuke Fence. They turned east along the fence toward Lake Xau, only to find the lake already dried up, and thousands died.

Yet the fences have to some extent kept cattle out of the Okavango Delta, which is essential if Delta wildlife is to survive. However, the new 80-km long Northern Buffalo Fence north of the Delta, which is now being constructed, will open up a vast expanse of wildlife-rich – but as yet unprotected – territory in wildlife to cattle ranching. Safari operators wanted the fence set as far north as possible to protect the seasonally flooded Selinda Spillway; prospective cattle ranchers wanted it set as far south as possible, maximising new grazing lands; and local people didn't want it at all, for they were concerned it will act as a barrier to them as well as wildlife. The government sided with the ranchers; the fence opens 20% of the Okavango Delta to commercial ranching.

Because much of Botswana's cattle ranching industry is subsidised by the EU and the World Bank, and international guidelines require strict separation of domestic cattle and wild buffalo, it's unlikely that the fences – or the issues they raise – will go away. Although there have been credible proposals to create migration corridors between the fences, nothing has yet come of them. ∎

provide further foreign exchange income. Copper and nickel are mined in large quantities at two major deposits near Selebi-Phikwe (oddly enough, the town is named after the mines, which are called Selebi and Phikwe!).

Some gold is still mined around Francistown and limited amounts of coal are taken from eastern Botswana. The most recent large-scale project is the soda ash (sodium carbonate) and salt extraction plant recently brought into operation on Sua Pan. This has been set up as a joint Botswana-South Africa venture to diversify Botswana's current diamond-dependent economy. It will involve pumping over 16 million cubic metres of brine per year from 40 wells into 25 sq km of solar evaporation ponds. The expected annual yield is 300,000 tonnes of soda ash and 700,000 tonnes of sodium chloride.

Agriculture

Because of Botswana's large extent of desert, beyond cattle ranching, commercial agriculture doesn't play a major role in its economy. It is significant, however, that 80% of the country's population depends upon agriculture, to some extent.

Currently, Botswana's grasslands support over twice as many cattle as people, and since the 1950s, the national herd has grown from around 400,000 to three million. Nowadays, most of these cattle are controlled by just 5000 large-scale ranchers, who are propped up by World Bank loans. This is largely thanks to the ill-conceived Tribal Grazing Lands Policy adopted in 1975, whereby most communally owned lands were parcelled out to individual ranchers. About US$100 million worth of this beef is exported to the European Union (EU) annually under favourable trade agreements in which Botswana receives well above the market rates.

This encouragement to increase the number of cattle on the land has led to destructive overgrazing of large-scale ranching areas and made life very difficult for the remaining traditional pastoralists. Given the near desert conditions, most people on communal lands must depend on bore holes for their water supply. However, bore holes are few, and during dry years, some fail. At these times, people from far and wide cluster around productive bore holes, bringing with them their cattle and other herds and placing severe strain on the environment. Again, the overgrazed land suffers irreversible desertification and everyone loses.

In addition to herding cattle, sheep and goats, people grow maize, sorghum, beans, peanuts, cottonseed and other dry land crops on a subsistence scale. Larger cotton and citrus projects are evolving in the irrigated Tuli Block along the Limpopo River and dry land farming of sorghum and other crops is being tested at Pandamatenga near the Zimbabwe border.

POPULATION
Botswana has an estimated population of 1.4 million, about 60% of whom claim Tswana heritage. It currently has one of the world's highest birth rates – about 3.5% – and the average Batswana woman will bear five children. As a result of this high fertility rate, the Batswana are overwhelmingly youthful, with half the population under the age of 20. Since independence, the national average life expectancy has climbed from 49 to 69 years.

Botswana is also one of the world's most predominantly urban societies. Thanks to the adoption of Christianity and an essentially European form of central government, most traditional practices have been phased out and rural villages are shrinking as people migrate into urban areas for cash-yielding vocational and professional jobs.

The increasingly urban population is concentrated in the south-eastern strip of the country between Lobatse and Francistown. The small percentage of Europeans and Asians live mainly in larger cities, and such groups as the Herero, Mbukushu, Yei, San, Kalanga and Kgalagadi are distributed through the remote hinterlands of the west and north-west.

In Setswana, the predominant language, tribal groups are denoted by the addition of the prefix 'Ba' at the beginning of the word. Therefore, the Herero are sometimes referred to as 'Baherero' and the Kgalagadi as 'Bakgalagadi'. The San people are occasionally known as 'Basarwa', a Tswana word meaning 'people of the bush', or, more colloquially, 'Bushmen'. The Tswana themselves are known as Batswana, but any citizen of Botswana, regardless of colour, ancestry or tribal affiliation, is also referred to as Batswana.

PEOPLE
Tswana
The Tswana are divided into a number of lineages, the three most prominent having descended from the three sons of 14th century Tswana chief Malope: Ngwato, Kwena and Ngwaketse. The Ngwato are centred on the Serowe area, the Kwena west of Molepolole, and the Ngwaketse in the south-east. An early split in the Ngwato resulted in a fourth group, the Tawana, who are concentrated around Maun in the northwest. Another group, the Kgalagadi, is probably an offshoot of the Tswana that broke away sometime around the 15th century. Since then they've mixed with the San and other peoples to form a new group, generally considered separate from the Tswana.

A typical Tswana village is a large, sprawling and densely populated affair comprised mainly of pole and daga huts. The individual homes are normally arranged around some

BOTSWANA

BOTSWANA

commercial venture such as a food and bottle store, and a *kgotla*, a traditionally constructed community affairs hall.

Historically, the village chief lived at the village centre with the hierarchy of *wards* or family groupings arranged in concentric circles around him. Although he had councillors and advisers, the chief was considered the ultimate authority in all matters and the nearer one lived to him, the higher the family's community status.

Family units typically have three homes: one in the village, one at their fields and one at their cattle post, where village boys or San men look after the herds. As in many African societies, family wealth was once – and in some cases still is – measured by the number of cattle owned. Land, however, was not owned but rather held in a village trust and used by individual families, allocated at the discretion of the chief.

San

Much has been written about and attributed to the San (Bushmen) of the Kalahari. The San have probably inhabited southern Africa for at least 30,000 years but unfortunately, their tenure hasn't yielded many benefits. Although they're being catapulted into the modern world, most San are still regarded as second-class citizens in both Botswana and neighbouring Namibia. One of the most fascinating peoples on earth, they are now sadly resigned to the changes that have ended forever their historical existence, in which they enjoyed complete integration and harmony with their harsh desert domain.

The historical San had no collective name for themselves, but there's evidence that some referred to themselves as 'the harmless people' or in other self-deprecatory terms. The early Europeans in southern Africa knew them as 'Bushmen' and that name stuck for several centuries. The Tswana people generally refer to them by the rather derogatory name *Basarwa*, which essentially means 'people from the sticks'. The word 'San' originally referred to the language of one group of indigenous people in

San hunter

southern Africa (the entire language group was known as 'Khoisan', and included Khoi-Khoi dialects), but when the term 'Bushmen' fell from grace even as both racist and sexist, 'San' was adopted by Europeans to refer to several groups of non-Negroid peoples of southern Africa.

Although their characteristics and languages are distinct, all Khoisan languages share the dental and palatal clicks that have been adopted even by some Bantu groups, such as the Ndebele (see Language in the Zimbabwe Facts about the Country chapter). The San clicks are of three types: '!' is the palatal click made by pulling the tongue away from the roof of the mouth. 'X' or '/' is the lateral click, formed by pulling the tongue away from the upper right teeth. 'C' or '//' is a dental click, made when the tongue is pulled from the upper front teeth.

The traditional San were nomadic hunters and gatherers who travelled in small family bands. They had no chiefs or system of leadership and individualism was respected. Personal decisions were made individually and group decisions by the group. In fact, there was no pressure to conform to any predetermined ideals, and anyone with itchy feet could leave the group without placing stress on the whole. During times of plenty, groups could swell to as many as 120 people, while during hard times, when people had to spread out to survive, they diminished to family units of 10 or fewer people.

A thoroughly mobile society, the San followed the water, the game and the edible plants. They had no animals, no crops and no possessions. Everything needed for daily existence was carried with them. Women spent much of their time caring for children and gathering edible or water-yielding plants, while the men either hunted or helped with the food gathering.

One myth has it that the San are unable to distinguish colour because most San languages contain few colour-related words. In fact, the languages are more concerned with tangibles than abstracts. It's simply considered unnecessary to linguistically separate an object from its attributes. Similarly, there's no word for work, which is a fundamental facet of life.

Another myth is that the San people possess extremely keen senses of hearing, eyesight and direction. Although their awareness of surroundings certainly seems phenomenal to the technology-dependent world, anthropological studies have determined that it's been learned as a result of necessity rather than a physiological adaptation. It's generally agreed that anyone, given the right circumstances and healthy faculties, can develop a similar awareness.

Early San encounters with other groups were probably happy ones. It's generally believed that they peacefully coexisted, and perhaps even traded with early community-minded Bantu groups which moved in from the north. Eventually, however, the pressure of the Bantu numbers forced the San to take action. Some made themselves quite unpopular by purloining the Bantu herders' cattle. Others opted to attempt integration with the Black communities, but they almost invariably wound up as slaves. Still others abandoned their traditional hunting grounds and sought out unpopulated areas to continue their nomadic ways.

However, the choice of unpopulated areas was quickly diminishing. The Europeans who arrived at the Cape in the mid-17th century, however, saw the San and Khoi-Khoi as little more than wild animals and potential cattle raiders. The early Boers hatched an extermination campaign that lasted 200 years and killed as many as 200,000 people.

Of the remaining 55,000 or so individuals, approximately 60% live in Botswana, 35% in Namibia and the remainder are scattered through South Africa, Angola, Zimbabwe and Zambia. Of these, perhaps 2000 still live by hunting and gathering. The remainder work on farms and cattle posts or languish in squalid, handout-dependent and alcohol-plagued settlements centred on bore holes in western Botswana and north-eastern Namibia. Among many other Batswana and Namibians, their reputation as cattle rustlers and undesirables places them at the bottom of the human heap.

It would be pleasant to end this discussion on a more hopeful note, but the outlook for the San isn't good. The pattern, already in place among Australian Aborigines and Native Americans, is summed up in the San concept of life as a burden. Sadly, the Botswana government, which once allowed the San to use the Central Kalahari Game Reserve for traditional lifestyles, has begun allowing mineral exploration and started looking at the cattle ranching and tourism development potential of the vast reserve. Most San express the desire to join the Batswana mainstream, with access to land, education and health care, and the same rights and privileges as other citizens, but as yet, racism, prejudice and their own growing sense of worthlessness have thwarted any progress in that direction.

Kalanga

Most of the Kalanga people, who are related to the Shona, now live in western Zimbabwe, but they still comprise the second-largest group in sparsely populated Botswana. They are generally considered to be descendants of the people of the Rozwi Empire, who were responsible for building Great Zimbabwe and what are now the series of ruins centred on Bulawayo. The Rozwi were overcome and scattered by the Ndebele in the 1830s, spreading as far west as the Thamalakane River in northern Botswana and south to the Boteti River, where some were partially absorbed by the Ngwato branch of the Tswana.

Mbukushu & Yei

The Mbukushu, who now inhabit the Okavango Delta area of Ngamiland, were originally refugees from the Caprivi in north-eastern Namibia. They were forced to flee in the late 1700s after being dislodged by the forces of Chief Ngombela's Lozi Empire. The fleeing Mbukushu, in turn, displaced the Yei people, who occupied the Chobe and Linyanti Valleys of north-western Botswana.

The Mbukushu carried on to south-eastern Angola, just north of present-day Andara, Namibia. There, they encountered Portuguese and African traders who began purchasing Mbukushu commoners from the tribal leadership, to be used and resold as slaves. The local rain-making deity also had a taste for Mbukushu infants and many people decided it was in their best interest to move on. Essentially a riverine tribe, some of the Mbukushu headed down the Okavango to farm maize and sorghum in the Panhandle area of the Delta. Their running days were finally over and, having mixed with later-arriving Tawana, many remain in villages like Shakawe and Sepupa.

Meanwhile, the Yei scattered down the Panhandle, roaming as far south as Lake Ngami. Essentially a matrilineal society, they never settled in large groups and eventually melted into the islands and channels of the Okavango Delta where they travelled around the shallow waters by *mokoro*, or pole boat.

Like the Mbukushu, many Yei have now mixed with the Tawana, who arrived in the mid-1800s, although the connection wasn't

entirely voluntary. The Yei were conquered by the more powerful Tawana and forced into clientship, a sophisticated form of enslavement in which the clients' lot was similar to that of a serfs' in a fiefdom. Interestingly, the Yei (who were second-class citizens in Tawana society) themselves took clients among the San, who wound up at the bottom of the heap. Many Yei still inhabit the delta, depending mainly upon fishing and hunting.

Herero

Visitors to Maun and western Botswana will notice the colourfully dressed Herero women, attired in their full-length Victorian-style finery on even the most stifling days. The unusual dress, which is now a tribal trademark, was forced upon them by prudish German missionaries in the late 1800s.

The Herero people probably originated in eastern or central Africa and migrated across the Okavango River into north-eastern Namibia around the early 16th century. There, the group apparently split: the Ovambo settled down to farming along the Kunene and Okavango Rivers and the Herero moved south to the Central Plateau. Disputes with the Nama sent one contingent into the Kaokoveld of north-western Namibia (where they developed into the Himba). Subsequent disputes created another sub-group, the Mbanderu, which moved eastward and adopted a pastoral life-style in the western Kalahari.

The nomadic Herero never practised farming and were dependent upon their cattle, which took on a religious significance as the source of Herero life. The Hereros' dietary staple was *omaeru* or sour milk.

In 1884 the Germans took possession of South West Africa (Namibia) and summarily took over the Herero grazing lands in that country. While the Germans were engaged in a war with the Nama people, the Herero, hardened by their own years of war with the Nama, seized the chance to take revenge for injustices meted out by the colonials and attacked a German settlement, killing about 150 people. Predictably, the Germans came back with a vengeance and the remaining Herero were forced to abandon their herds and flee into Botswana.

The refugees settled among the Tawana and were initially subjugated to clientship, but eventually regained their herds and independence. Today they are among the wealthiest herders in Botswana and, now that Namibia is independent, many speak of returning to the 'old country' with which they still seem to feel strong kinship. The Botswana government, however, has stipulated that returnees to Namibia must do so permanently and without their animals or other personal assets which were acquired while in Botswana. So far, only a handful have made the move.

EDUCATION

Sadly, the colonial government almost entirely neglected matters of health and education of the Batswana, and five years after independence, literacy was still at less than 15%. Over the next 10 years, diamond funds became available and the government used them to step up its primary education programmes. By 1981, an amazing 84% of primary school-aged children (years one to seven) were attending classes and secondary and tertiary degrees were offered as well.

Approximately 97% of Botswana's primary school-aged children – both boys and girls – are attending school. Currently, however, only 33% of the population has access to a full secondary education. In rural areas, only seven to nine years of schooling are available locally.

The Brigades

The Brigades movement was founded in 1965 by Patrick van Rensburg, headmaster of the Swaneng Hill Secondary School in Serowe. It was designed as a means of providing vocational training in carpentry, horticulture, forestry, welding, construction and other subjects for early school-leavers. Brigades schools operate on an apprentice system whereby classroom and practical training are given concurrently.

The University of Botswana

On 1 January 1964, the University of Basutoland, Bechuanaland and Swaziland opened in Lesotho in answer to Black Africans' need for an alternative to a South African university education. After Lesotho nationalised the university campus in 1975, Batswana and Swazi students removed themselves to a new campus in Swaziland, the University of Botswana and Swaziland.

In 1980, the two divided into fully independent schools, and on 23 October 1982, the University of Botswana was founded at Gaborone. It now has a total enrolment of over 3000 full-time undergraduate students and 400 part-time students. Staff from all over the world are employed to assist with the institution's rapid growth and graduate programs are currently being developed.

ARTS
Architecture

A typical Tswana village is comprised mainly of pole and *daga* rondavels, known as *ntlo*. Some of these traditional homes are constructed from bricks *(dipolwane)* which are made from soil taken from termite mounds. The final product is then plastered with a mixture of termite mound soil and cow dung *(boloko)*. In places short of termite mounds, homes are built from woven sticks plastered with ordinary mud and cow dung.

The roof poles *(maotwana)* to support the thatching are taken from strong solid trees and lashed together with flexible branches. The thatching grass itself, called *motshikiri*, is then sewn onto these flexible branches. When it's finished, the thatch is coated with oil and ash to discourage infestation by termites. Barring weather-related problems, a good thatching job can last five to 15 years and a rondavel can last thirty years or more.

Often, the outside of the hut is then decorated with a paint made from a mixture of cow dung and different coloured soils. Most of these are lovely and can be quite fanciful.

Literature

Since the indigenous languages have only been written since the coming of the Chris-

BOTSWANA

tian missionaries, Botswana doesn't have much of a literary tradition. What survives of the ancient myths and praise poetry of the San, Tswana, Herero and other groups has been handed down orally and only recently written down.

Botswana's most famous modern literary figure was South African-born Bessie Head, who settled in Sir Seretse Khama's village of Serowe. Her writings, many of which are set in Serowe, reflect the harshness and the beauty of African village life and indeed of the physical attributes of Botswana itself. Her most widely read works include *Serowe – Village of the Rain Wind*, *When Rain Clouds Gather*, *Maru*, *A Question of Power*, *The Cardinals*, *A Bewitched Crossroad* and *The Collector of Treasures*; the last is an anthology of short stories. Bessie Head died in 1988.

Material Arts

The original Batswana artists were everyday people who managed to inject individuality, aesthetics and aspects of Batswana life into their utilitarian implements. Baskets, pottery, fabrics and tools were decorated with meaningful designs derived from tradition. Europeans introduced a new sort of art, some of which was integrated and adapted to local interpretation, particularly in weavings and tapestries. The result is some of the finest and most meticulously executed work in southern Africa.

Hoping to provide a cash income for rural Batswana, the Botswanacraft Marketing Company (☎ 312471, fax 313189) was set up by the government-run Botswana Development Corporation to identify the best of cottage creativity and purchase it for resale or export. The company has now been privatised and sells baskets and artwork from all over Africa, but still ensures that the bulk of the profit goes to the producer. In addition, it holds an annual basketry competition and awards bonuses for the highest quality work. For more information or a catalogue, write to Botswanacraft, PO Box 486, Gaborone.

Visitors to rural areas have the opportunity to purchase crafts directly from the produc-

ers. Alternatively, you can visit one of the several weavings and crafts cooperatives operating around the country. Whether you're buying or just appreciating the artesans' skill, you can't fail to be impressed at the quality of what's on offer.

Botswana Baskets Botswana baskets are the most lauded of the country's material arts. Interestingly, some of the most beautiful designs aren't indigenous, but were brought to north-western Botswana mainly by Angolan Mbukushu refugees in the last century.

Although the baskets are still used practically – for storage of seeds, grains and *bojalwa* mash for sorghum beer – the art has since been finely tuned and some of the work is incredibly exquisite, employing swirls and designs with such evocative names as Flight of the Swallow, Tears of the Giraffe, Urine Trail of the Bull, Knees of the Tortoise, Roof of the Rondavel, Forehead of the Zebra, Back of the Python and The Running Ostrich.

The baskets are made from fibrous shoots from the heart of the *mokolane* palm

Basket weaving

(Hyphaene petersiana), which are cut and boiled in natural earth-tone dyes. Dark brown comes from *motsentsila* roots and tree bark, pink and red are derived from a fungus which grows in sorghum husks, and blood, ochre, clay and cow dung are also used as dyes. These strips are wound around a base of coils made from vines or grass. From start to finish, a medium-sized basket may require two to three weeks to complete.

Generally, the finest and most expensive work comes from Ngamiland; more loosely woven but still beautiful Shashe baskets are produced mainly around Francistown.

Weavings Contemporary weavings – tapestries, rugs, bed covers and the like made from *karakul* wool – combine African themes with formats adopted from European art to produce work that appeals to both cultures. Most of the country's output is produced at two weaving cooperatives in south-eastern Botswana: the Lentswe-la-Odi Weavers in Odi village and the newer Tiro ya Diatla in Lobatse, where artists are given free reign to choose their own themes, colours and presentation. Some of the results are truly inspired.

Woodcarving Woodcarving has been used traditionally in the production of such practical items as tools, spoons, bowls and containers from the densely grained wood of the mopane tree. Artists are now utilising mopane wood to produce jewellery, as well as both realistic and fantastic figurines of animals and renditions of more modern innovations such as tractors and aeroplanes.

Pottery The original pottery used in Botswana was constructed from smoothed coils and fired slowly, leaving it porous. Therefore, evaporation through the pot worked as a sort of refrigeration system, keeping the liquid inside cool and drinkable on even the hottest days. Although today's productions are more modern in appearance, traditional patterns and designs are still used at pottery workshops around the country. The most accessible are Moratwa Pottery in Lobatse,

Hand made coil pottery

Thamaga Pottery in Thamaga and Pelegano Pottery in Gabane. The latter two lie in small villages west of Gaborone.

Other Material Arts The San of western Botswana are adept at creating seed-and-bead bracelets and necklaces and beaded leather bags and aprons. The beads were traditionally hand-made from ostrich eggshells, but nowadays plastic beads are the norm. It's just as well; the ostriches are happier, and some countries don't allow the import of ostrich egg products.

The Herero people, who emigrated to Botswana from Namibia, dress in a unique style introduced by German missionaries during the last century – the women habitually wear billowing Victorian-style skirts and the men, when traditionally dressed, wear a variation on the Scottish tartan kilt. The Herero women are skilled at making dolls dressed in Herero costume of fabric and natural materials. The dolls are much in demand and may be found around Maun and Ghanzi.

RELIGION

Botswana's early tribal religions were primarily cults in which ancestors directed family matters from their underworld

BOTSWANA

domain and were contactable only through the heads of family groups. Religious rites included the *bogwera* and *bojale*;or male and female initiation ceremonies, and the *gofethla pula* or rain-making rites. The supreme being and creator, who was incidental in the scheme of things, was known as Modimo.

Polygamy was practised. The head wife wasn't necessarily the first wife, but rather the one with whom an inheritance agreement had been made prior to marriage. A man's estate was inherited by the children of his head wife, while his cattle were typically transferred to that woman's family.

San folklore is rich with supernatural explanations of natural events that pervade many cultures. Their traditional religious beliefs are quite simple and not burdened with dogma or ritual. Their two supernatural beings represent good and evil, order and entropy. N!odima, the good, is the omnipotent creator who seems to have little time to meddle in the affairs of mortals. His opponent, Gcawama, is a mischievous trickster who spends his time trying to create disorder from the perfect natural organisation laid down by N!odima. Gcawama, unfortunately, seems to take a bothersome amount of interest in the lives of humans.

Like that of most Africans, the religion of the Herero was based upon ancestor worship. In their estimation the first ancestor, Mukuru, surpassed even Ndjambi, their supreme deity. So revered were the ancestors that Herero men set aside up to 200 head of cattle for their purposes. When a man died, his reserved beasts were sacrificed to keep the ancestors in a pleasant mood lest his family suffer.

When the first Christian missionaries arrived in the early 1800s, they brought with them an entirely new set of ideas which dislodged nearly all the Tswana traditions and practices, as well as those of many other tribes. They naturally forbade ancestor veneration and the rites associated with it, as well as polygamy, inheritance practices and the consumption of alcohol.

Christianity is currently the prevailing belief system in Botswana, with the largest number of Christians belonging to the United Congregational Church of Southern Africa. The Lutheran, Roman Catholic, Anglican and Methodist churches also have significant followings in the country.

LANGUAGE
English is the official language of Botswana and the medium of instruction from the fifth year of primary school on. The most common language, however, is Setswana, a Bantu language in the Sotho-Tswana group which is understood by over 90% of the population. It is the language of the dominant population group, the Tswana, and is used as a medium of instruction in early primary school. The second Bantu language is Sekalanga, a Shona derivative spoken by the Kalanga people who live around Francis-town.

Most of Botswana's population is of Tswana heritage, and the Tswana people are known as Batswana (although the word has also come to apply to any citizen of Botswana) just as the Yei people are known as Bayei. By the same token, a Tswana individual (or individual citizen of Botswana) is called Motswana. The language of the Tswana people is Setswana, while that of the Kalanga is Sekalanga and that of the English is naturally Seenglish! The land of the Tswana is, of course, Botswana.

Setswana is spelt more or less as it is pronounced, except the 'g' which is pronounced as 'h' or, more accurately, as a strongly aspirated 'g'. 'Th' is pronounced simply as a slightly aspirated 't'.

The greetings *dumêla rra* when speaking to men and *dumêla mma* when speaking to women are considered compliments and Batswana appreciate their liberal usage. When addressing a group, say *dumêlang*.

When accepting a gift or anything for which you're grateful, receive it with both hands or take hold of it with your right hand and hold your right arm with your left. Another useful phrase, which is normally placed at the end of a sentence or conversation is *go siame* meaning the equivalent of 'all right, no problem'.

The book *First Steps in Spoken Setswana* is useful; it's available from the Botswana Book Centre in Gaborone. The list of words and phrases below should get you started.

Useful Phrases	
Yes/No.	*Ee/Nnyaa.*
Do you speak...?	*A o bua Se?*
Where are you from? (birthplace)	*O tswa kae?*
I'm from Australia.	*Ke tswa kwa Australia.*
Where do you live?	*O nna kae?*
I live in Maun.	*Ke nna kwa Maun.*
Where are you going?	*O ya kae?*
What is your name?	*Leina la gago ke mang?*
My name is...	*Leina la me ke...*
Where is the way to...?	*Tsela...e kae?*
Where is the railwaystation/hotel?	*Seteseine/hotele se kai?*
Is it far?	*A go kgala?*
What would you like?	*O batla eng?*
I would like...	*Ke batla...*
Cheers.	*Pula.*

Greetings & Civilities	
Please.	*Tsweetswee.*
Thank you.	*Kea itumela.*
Hello. (to a woman/man)	*Dumêla mma/rra.*
Hello. (to a group)	*Dumêlang.*
Hello! (hailing someone from your door)	*Ko ko!*
Come on in!	*Tsena!*
How's it going?	*O kae?*
I'm fine. (informal)	*Ke teng.*
How are you? (lit. 'how did you wake up?')	*A o tsogile?*
Did you get up well?	*A o sa tsogile sentle?*
Yes, I woke up well.	*Ee, ke tsogile sentle.*
How are you? (afternoon)	*O tlhotse jang?*
I'm fine. (response)	*Ke tlhotse sentle.*
Goodbye. (to person leaving)	*Tsamayo sentle.*
Goodbye. (to person staying)	*Sala sentle.*
OK/all right/ no problem.	*Go siame*

Food & Drink	
bread	*borotho*
milk	*mashi*
meat	*nama*
food	*dijo*
mealies	*bogobe*
water	*metsi*

BOTSWANA

Facts for the Visitor

VISAS & EMBASSIES

Everyone entering Botswana must have a valid passport. For tourist visits, no visas are required by citizens of the following countries: Commonwealth countries (except Ghana, India, Mauritius, Nigeria and Sri Lanka), Austria, Belgium, Denmark, Finland, France, Germany, Greece, Iceland, Ireland (Eire), Israel, Italy, Liechtenstein, Luxembourg, Namibia, Netherlands, Norway, Pakistan, San Marino, South Africa, Sweden, Switzerland, USA, Uruguay and Western Samoa. Others may apply for visas through Botswana diplomatic missions, or a British High Commission where there is no Botswana representation. Alternatively, apply by post to the Immigration and Passport Control Officer (☎ 374545), off Khama Crescent, PO Box 942, Gaborone, Botswana. For lists of embassies and diplomatic missions see the asides on the following pages.

On entry, you'll be granted 30 days, which may be extended for up to a total of three months. You may be asked to show an onward airline ticket or sufficient funds for your intended stay.

If you wish to stay longer than three months for tourism purposes, apply to the Immigration Office (☎ 374545), PO Box 942, Gaborone, in advance of your trip. Otherwise, you're permitted to remain for a maximum of 90 days in any 12-month period. Renewable three year residence permits are generally available to those with skills in demand in Botswana. See the Work section later in this chapter.

DOCUMENTS

Travellers entering from a yellow fever infected area require a yellow fever vaccination certificate, but otherwise no vaccinations are required.

Visitors may drive using their home driving licence for up to six months (non-English licences must be accompanied by a certified English translation), after which they must apply for a Botswana licence. There's no driving test involved; just present your old licence and pick up the local one.

Those entering by vehicle need current vehicle registration papers from the vehicle's home country and evidence of third-party insurance from somewhere in the Southern African Customs Union (South Africa, Botswana, Namibia, Lesotho, Swaziland). Otherwise, drivers must purchase insurance at the border. All foreign vehicles are subject to a road safety levy of US$1.85 (P5) upon entry.

CUSTOMS

Botswana (and South Africa, Namibia, Swaziland and Lesotho) is a member of the Southern African Customs Union which allows unrestricted and uncontrolled carriage of items between them duty-free. Goods brought into Botswana from any other country are subject to normal Botswana duties unless they're to be re-exported.

Visitors may import up to 400 cigarettes, 50 cigars and 250 grams of tobacco duty-free. Extra petrol and South African alcohol are subject to duty, but otherwise, you can import up to two litres of wine and one litre of beer or spirits duty-free. Cameras, film and firearms must be declared upon entry but aren't subject to duty. All edible animal products, including untinned meat, milk and eggs, are confiscated at the border.

Special regulations apply to importing items such as unworked metals and precious stones, live plants, game trophies, pets and firearms. Information and applications for bringing in animals or birds are available from the Director of Veterinary Services, Private Bag 0032, Gaborone, Botswana.

MONEY

If you want to enjoy your visit, the first thing to remember about money in Botswana is to bring a lot of it; few of the most interesting

Botswana Diplomatic Missions

In countries where Botswana has no diplomatic representation, information and visas are available through the British High Commission.

EU (European Union)
Botswana Embassy & Mission to the EU, 189 Ave de Tervueren, 1150 Brussels, Belgium
UK
High Commission of the Republic of Botswana, 6 Stratford Place, London W1N 9AE
UN
Permanent Mission of the Republic of Botswana to the UN, 866 Second Ave, New York, New York 10017, USA

USA
Embassy of the Republic of Botswana, 3400 International Dr NW, Washington, DC 20008
Zambia
High Commission of the Republic of Botswana, 267 Haile Selassie Ave, PO Box 1910, Lusaka
Zimbabwe
High Commission of the Republic of Botswana, 22 Phillip Ave, Belgravia, Harare

sites are accessible to budget travellers. For a rough idea of what to expect, see Costs later in this chapter.

Travellers entering the country must declare their currency upon entry, and when departing, must estimate the amount of money spent in Botswana; this is to determine how much tourists are spending and ensure no one takes more money out than they brought in (which is a bad idea without a work permit).

Officially, foreigners may export up to US$185 (P500) in cash or up to US$370 (P1000) in foreign bank notes. Any more than that should be in travellers' cheques. You may hear of meticulous scrutiny, but in the many times I've entered Botswana, no one has ever asked to see either my declared currency or travellers' cheques.

Currency

Botswana's unit of currency is the pula, which is divided into 100 thebe. 'Pula' is also the national motto of Botswana and appears on the national coat of arms. That doesn't, however, mean that the Batswana are inordinately pre-occupied with money. Rather, 'pula' means 'rain', which is as precious as money in this largely desert country. Predictably, 'thebe' means 'raindrop'. Bank notes come in denominations of P1, 2, 5, 10, 20 and 50, and coins in denominations of 1t, 2t, 5t, 10t, 25t, 50t and P1.

Note that in some rural areas, someone may occasionally refer to the *pondo* (pound)

as a unit of currency. It hails from the colonial days of pounds, shillings and pence, and is normally valued at P2.

The pula is currently stronger and more in demand than even the South African rand. Generally, South African imports are priced the same in pula as they are in rand across the border, making shopping approximately 50% dearer in Botswana.

Exchange Rates

At the time of writing the pula was worth:

A$1	=	P1.94
US$	=	P2.71
UK£1	=	P4.33
¥100	=	P3.23
DM1	=	P1.93
SFr1	=	P2.35
FFr1	=	P0.55
NZ$1	=	P1.81
C$1	=	P1.97
SAfR1	=	P0.74
Z$	=	P0.32

Banking

Full banking services are available in the following places: Gaborone, Francistown, Mahalapye, Palapye, Selebi-Phikwe, Serowe, Jwaneng, Kanye, Maun, Mochudi, Ghanzi and Molepolole, and in Kasane on weekdays except Thursday. In major towns, banking hours are from 9 am to 2.30 pm on Monday, Tuesday, Thursday and Friday, from 8.15 am to noon on Wednesday, and

BOTSWANA

BOTSWANA

Foreign Embassies & Consulates in Botswana

The following is a list of foreign diplomatic missions in Botswana; all addresses are in Gaborone. As yet, South Africa has no representation in Botswana.

Angola
Angolan Embassy, 2715 Phala Crescent, Private Bag 111, Broadhurst (☎300204)

Denmark
Danish Consulate Royal, 142 Mengwe Close, PO Box 367 (☎353770)

EU
Delegation of the EU to Botswana, 68 North Ring Rd, POBox 1253, (☎314455)

France
French Embassy, 761 Robinson Rd, PO Box 1424 (☎353683)

Germany
Embassy of the Federal Republic of Germany, 3rd Floor, Professional House, Broadhurst, PO Box 315 (☎353143)

Namibia
Namibian Embassy, BCC Building, 1278 Lobatse Rd, PO Box 1586 (☎314227) note: Australians and New Zealanders can get Namibian visas in Maun through Okavango Tours & Safaris; they cost US$19 and take 24 hours to issue.

Netherlands
Netherlands Consulate, Haile Selassie Rd, PO Box 10055 (☎357224)

Sweden
Royal Swedish Embassy, Development House, The Mall, Private Bag 0017 (☎353912)

UK
British High Commission, Queens Road, The Mall, Private Bag 0023 (☎352841)

USA
US Embassy, Badiredi House, The Mall, PO Box 90, Gaborone (☎353982)

Zambia
Zambia High Commission, Zambia House, The Mall, PO Box 362 (☎351951)

Zimbabwe
Zimbabwe High Commission, Orapa Close, PO Box 1232 (☎314495)

from 8.15 to 10.45 am on Saturday. On Saturday, Barclays Bank at the Gaborone Sun Hotel is open 8.30 am to 2 pm. The Sir Seretse Khama International Airport branch is open for foreign exchange from 9.30 am to 5 pm weekdays. Barclays and Standard Chartered banks charge US$1.85 (P5) commission on travellers' cheques.

In remote towns and villages where there are no established banks, travelling banks are available at regular intervals, normally for an hour or two at the end of the month, after pay day. In Lethlakane, the bank arrives on the Debswana (De Beers of Botswana) payday, probably because all the town's income is generated by Debswana, anyway. In Shakawe and Gumare it comes on the government payday. Some villages have banking services once or twice weekly. For specific days and hours, which change periodically, enquire at branches in larger towns. These rural banking services may change foreign travellers' cheques but not cash.

To exchange money anywhere in the country at the end of the month, it's vital that you queue up early and set aside the entire morning for the task. The exchange process is excruciatingly slow, with lots of form-filling compounded by the sinuous queues of recently paid workers.

Credit Cards

Most major credit cards – especially Barclays' Visa – are accepted at tourist hotels and restaurants in the larger cities and towns, although you can't use them to buy petrol. You can use Barclays Visa to purchase Barclays US$ or UK£ sterling travellers' cheques with little or no commission taken. Credit card cash advances are available in Gaborone, Lobatse, Maun and Francistown through Barclays Bank or Standard Chartered Bank. In smaller towns, you can apply at the banks for credit card cash advances but authorisation can take hours or even days.

Cash transfers from foreign banks are most conveniently done through Barclays where it will be received by the Barclay

House Branch on Khama Crescent, Gaborone. If the money isn't sent through a Barclays branch overseas, allow seven to 10 working days for the process to sort itself out. All monies are converted to pula on receipt (with a commission plus a transfer fee deducted), and if you want to convert it into US$ or UK£ to purchase travellers' cheques, yet another commission is taken.

Costs

Botswana's tourism policy makes things difficult for shoestring travellers. Travelling cheaply, while not impossible as long as hitchhiking is permitted, will prove frustrating. If you can't afford a flight into the Okavango, a day or two at Moremi Reserve or Chobe National Park or a 4WD-trip through the Kalahari, you may want to think twice before visiting Botswana. For more information, see National Parks under Flora & Fauna in the Botswana Facts About the Country chapter.

Supermarket, fast-food and restaurant prices are comparable to those in Europe, North America and Australasia. Small local food halls are normally a cheap option but don't expect much variety beyond *bogobe* (sorghum porridge) and relish. Buses and trains aren't too expensive but they won't take you to the most interesting parts of the country. The cheapest vehicle hire is expensive by anyone's standards and to hire a 4WD is formidable.

Tipping

While tipping isn't exactly required, thanks to the official policy of promoting only up-market tourism, it's now expected in many tourist hotels and restaurants. However, it is recommended that you tip only for exceptional service. In most places a service charge is added as a matter of course, so if you feel the urge to augment that, about 10% should suffice. Taxi drivers generally aren't tipped.

WHEN TO GO

If you want to hit the back roads, enjoy wildlife viewing or explore the Okavango,

summer is not the best time. Prolonged rains may render sandy roads impassable and rivers uncrossable, and during periods of high water, Chobe National Park and Moremi Wildlife Reserve may be closed. Unless you are after flamingoes in the salt pans, the wildlife will be harder to spot anyway. Animals disperse when water is abundant, making it unnecessary to stick close to perennial water sources. Summer is also the time of the highest humidity and the most stifling heat; daytime temperatures of over 40°C aren't uncommon.

In the winter – late May to August – rain is not likely anywhere in the country. Days are normally clear, warm and sunny, and nights are cool to cold. Wildlife never wanders far from water sources so viewing is more predictable than in the summer. Bear in mind, however, that this is also the time of European, North American and South African school holidays. In general, June, early July and mid-to-late September are reasonably uncrowded times to visit. In Maun in August, however, you may get the impression that every tourist within a thousand mile radius is clamouring to get into the Okavango.

TOURIST OFFICES
Local Tourist Offices

The national tourism office in Gaborone (☎ 353024, fax 371539) is conveniently located on The Mall, the heart of all activity in the capital. It has maps, pamphlets and brochures and the staff are quite helpful with queries. The offices in Kasane (☎ 250327) and Maun (☎ 260492), opposite the airport, are less helpful.

BUSINESS HOURS & HOLIDAYS

Normal business hours are from around 8 am to 5 pm, often with a one or two hour lunchtime closure, normally from 1 to 2 or 3 pm. On Saturday shops open early and close at noon or 1 pm, while on Sunday there's scarcely a whisper of activity anywhere.

For banking hours, see under Money earlier in this chapter. In major towns, post offices are open from 8.15 am to 4 pm, closing for lunch from 12.45 to 2 pm. On Saturday they're open between 8 and 11 am. Government offices remain open from 7.30 am to 12.30 pm and 1.45 to 4.30 pm, Monday to Friday.

Bottle shops generally open mid-morning and close at precisely 7 pm. If you want to purchase alcohol after that hour, you must resort to hotel and restaurant bars.

Public Holidays

1 January
  New Year's Day
2 January
  Day after *New Year's Day*
March or April
  Good Friday, Easter Saturday, Sunday & Monday
April or May
  Ascension Day
July
  President's Day
  Day After President's Day
30 September
  Botswana Day
1 October
  Day After Botswana Day
25 December
  Christmas Day
26 December
  Boxing Day
27 December
  Day After Boxing Day

POST & TELECOMMUNICATIONS
Post
Although generally reliable, the post can be painfully slow. Allow weeks to a month for delivery to or from an overseas address. In major towns, post offices are open between 8.15 am and 4 pm, closing for lunch from 12.45 to 2 pm. Expect long slow-moving queues while the lackadaisical postal employees chat on the phone or among themselves between customers.

The best poste restante address is the GPO on the Mall in Gaborone, but it's not 100% efficient. If you are staying in Botswana for some time, get your name on the waiting list for a post box as soon as possible. Until something becomes available, which can take years, you'll have to rely on poste restante or receive mail via your employer's private bag.

To post or receive a parcel, go to the parcel office around the side of the GPO, fill out the relevant customs forms and/or pay duties. Parcels may be plastered with all the sticky tape you like, but in the end they must be tied up with string or they won't be accepted; bring matches to seal knots with the red wax provided. To pick up parcels, you must present your passport or other photo ID.

Aerogrammes, which are sold at post offices, or postcards are the least expensive to send, followed by 2nd-class airmail letters, which are designated by clipping the corners off the envelope.

Telephone
Reliable call boxes may be found around post offices in all major towns. Direct dialling is available to most locations within Botswana, but for international calls you'll have to use the operator and have pockets full of coins to slot into the box.

Gaborone and Francistown have good but slow telephone offices for international calling. The offices are only open during normal business hours, so if you're phoning Australia or North America you'll probably be dragging someone out of bed.

Few if any countries have reciprocal reverse charges agreements with Botswana, but time and charges information is available for private telephones immediately after you hang up if you request it when booking the call.

Botswana's country code is (267); there are no regional area codes, so when phoning Botswana from outside the country, you should dial (267) followed by the telephone number. When dialling an outside number from Botswana, the international access code is (00); this should be followed by the desired country code, area code and telephone number.

Fax
Fax services are now commonly used by businesses in Botswana. For the general public, the best place to send or receive faxes

is the Copy Centre on the second floor of Hardware House in Gaborone. For specifics see under Telecommunications in the Gaborone chapter.

LAUNDRY

Gaborone now has a self-service laundrette and there's a commercial drycleaning and laundry service at No Mathatha shopping centre in Gaborone, but that's the extent of it. Large hotels all offer laundry services, but at a premium, while in smaller villages you'll always find local women happy to fill the laundry gap for a few pula. Failing all that, you can wash by hand and take advantage of Botswana's desert climate, which dries clothing in record time.

BOOKS

The Botswana Book Centre on The Mall in Gaborone is one of the region's best-stocked bookshops, with lots of international literature as well as novels, reference books, school texts and souvenir publications. Botsalo Books in the Kagiso Centre, Broadhurst North Mall, is also quite good. For book exchange, see J&B Books upstairs at Broadhurst North Mall. There's also an excellent bookshop on The Mall in Selebi-Phikwe. Smaller and more limited selections are available at several bookshops in Francistown and Maun. Most tourist hotels also stock souvenir and coffee table books as well as limited selections of pulp novels.

Literature & Fiction

Apart from the recent writings of Bessie Head (listed under Literature in the Arts section of Botswana Facts About the Country) and the 19th and early 20th century works by Sol Plaatje, there's really very little Botswana literature to recommend. Perhaps it's because the country simply hasn't had the sort of tumultuous history that normally inspires the creative outpouring of social statement. It may pay to keep watch on the African literature shelves, however, in case something appears.

Nor is there much foreign fiction dealing with Botswana. For light reading, try Wilbur Smith's *The Sunbird*, two fanciful, well-told tales about the mythical 'Lost City of the Kalahari'.

Also entertaining is *A Story Like the Wind*, Sir Laurens van der Post's fictional treatment of a meeting between European and San cultures. The story continues in the sequel *A Far Off Place*. Both these books are published by Penguin and are available in paperback.

Nonfiction

Cry of the Kalahari by Mark & Delia Owen (Fontana-Collins, Glasgow, 1986). Entertaining and readable account of an American couple's seven years studying brown hyenas in Deception Valley in the Central Kalahari. This book is to Botswana what *The Snow Leopard* is to Nepal and *Gorillas in the Mist* is to Rwanda.

The Harmless People by Elizabeth Marshall Thomas (Africa South Paperbacks, David Philip, Cape Town, 1988). This hard-to-find book is a collection of informal and sensitive observations of the Kalahari San by an American woman living among them.

History of Botswana by T Tlou and Alec Campbell, MacMillan Botswana, Gaborone, 1984. This is the best history devoted exclusively to Botswana.

Kalahari – Life's Variety in Dune and Delta by Michael Main (Southern Book Publishers, Johannesburg, 1987). A study of the many faces of the Kalahari from its vegetation and wildlife to its geological and cultural history. Good colour photos and extra helpings of personality are thrown in to keep it moving along smoothly.

Lost World of the Kalahari by Laurens van der Post (Penguin, Harmondsworth, UK, 1962). This well-written work about the San of the Kalahari is an anthropological classic and is essential reading for those interested in their traditional lifestyles. The author's quest for an understanding of their religion and folklore is continued in his subsequent work, *Heart of the Hunter*.

A Marriage of Inconvenience: The Persecution of Seretse and Ruth Khama by Michael Dutfield (Unwin Hyman, London, 1990). This recommended account details the largely negative responses, both African and colonial, to the marriage of Ngwato heir Seretse Khama and Englishwoman Ruth Williams in the 1950s.

Monarch of All I Survey: Bechuanaland Diaries 1929-1937 by Sir Charles Rey (Botswana Society, Gaborone, 1988). These colourfully insightful diaries by the eight-year Resident Commissioner of Bechuanaland reveal the overall ho-hum attitude of the British towards the Protectorate.

BOTSWANA

Okavango – Jewel of the Kalahari by Karen Ross (BBC Books, London, 1987). Filled with stunning colour photos, this typically BBC publication expounds on the natural and cultural wonders of the Okavango Delta.

Serowe – Village of the Rain Wind by Bessie Head (Heinemann African Writers' Series, Oxford, 1981). This account of Serowe told by Bessie Head through interviews with its residents straddles the division between history and literature. It's marvellous reading for its insight into modern Botswana village life, especially for intending visitors to Serowe.

Shell Field Guide to the Common Trees of the Okavango Delta & Moremi Reserve by Veronica Roodt (Shell Oil). This excellent and detailed paperback includes scientific data on the Okavango vegetation, as well as legends about its trees. The informative descriptions are accompanied by useful paintings and drawings.

Starlings Laughing by June Vendall-Clark (Transworld Publishers, London, 1990). This memoir of 43 years in Africa describes the end of the colonial era in Southern Africa. The author spent many years in the Maun area before the tourist invasion and was instrumental in the creation of Moremi Reserve. Some of the hardships may be a bit exaggerated, but Ms Clark met a lot of characters and it's an interesting story.

Travel Guides

Guide to Botswana by Alec Campbell (Winchester Press, Gaborone, 1980). This thoroughly researched but long outdated guide is still the best source of background information on the land and people of Botswana.

Guide to Namibia & Botswana by Chris McIntyre & Simon Atkins (Bradt, Chalfont St Peter, UK, 1994). If you're the sort of traveller who carries two books, this is a worthy choice. The asides, written by various contributors, are particularly interesting and informative. Namibia gets first billing, but the coverage of Botswana is also good, and it contains especially detailed descriptions of luxury lodges around the country. The maps, however, are of very limited usefulness.

Namibia und Botswana by Karl-Günther Schneider & Bernd Weise (DuMont Büchverlag, Cologne, Germany, 1991). This German language book is full of information on the political and natural history, the arts and cultures and the sights of these two countries. The main topic is Namibia, with Botswana getting relatively light treatment.

Traveller's Guide to Botswana by Peter Comley & Salome Meyer (Pula Press, Gaborone, 1994). This full-colour publication is weak on cities and towns, but contains detail on wilderness areas and is great for exploration off the beaten track.

Visitors Guide to Botswana by Mike Main, John & Sandra Fowkes (Southern Book Publishers, Johannesburg, 1991). This book is excellent for travellers venturing into the never-never with their own vehicles, but otherwise, it's a bit short on practical and background information.

Wusten, Sumpfe und Savannen: Reise-Handbuch Botswana by Michael Iwanowski (Herausgeber Verlag u. Vertrieb, Ettenheim, Germany, 1992). This book contains concise history and background information but it's available only in German and is weak on coverage of the cities. Earlier editions were better.

Zimbabwe & Botswana – the Rough Guide by Tony Pinchuck & Barbara McRae (Penguin, London, 1993). If you're after lots of editorial and background information, this good all-round guide is where to find it.

Language

There are a couple of English-Setswana dictionaries as well as the useful *First Steps in Spoken Setswana*, available at the Botswana Book Centre in Gaborone. There's not much available in the way of English-Setswana phrasebooks; amusing but otherwise a complete waste of time is the *Setswana-English Phrasebook* by 19th century Molepolole missionary A J Wookey .

MAPS

The Department of Surveys and Lands in Gaborone publishes topographic sheets, city and town plans, aerial photographs, geological maps and Landsat images. Regional and national maps of various scales are available to the public for US$2 to US$4 per sheet from their office in Gaborone. For a catalogue, write to the Department of Surveys and Lands, Private Bag 0037, Gaborone. For Geological Mapping, contact The Director, Department of Geological Survey, Private Bag 14, Lobatse.

The best and most accurate overall map of the country is the 1:1,750,000 *Republic of Botswana* published by the Cartographic Department, Macmillan UK. It contains several good inset maps, including the tourist areas and central Gaborone.

Also useful is the *Shell Road Map* which shows major roads and includes insets of several tourist areas. It's available from Shell

Oil Botswana, Shell House, The Mall, Gaborone.

A similarly useful production is the *Botswana Mini-Map*, published by the Map House in South Africa and distributed by B&T Directories (☎ 371444, fax 373462), PO Box 1549, Gaborone. There are several editions of this map, which variously include insets of the National Parks and city plans of Gaborone. They cost US$2.50 and are sold in bookshops and hotels around the country. B&T Directories publishes the Botswana Map Pack, which contains town plans of Francistown, Selebi-Phikwe and Lobatse on one sheet. A second sheet is devoted to Gaborone and its suburbs.

MEDIA
Newspapers & Magazines
The government-owned *Daily News*, published by the Ministry of Information and Broadcasting, is distributed free in Gaborone and includes news pertaining to the Botswana government, as well as major national and international news. In addition, there are four weekly independent papers. The *Gazette*, which comes out on Thursday, and the *Botswana Guardian*, published on Friday and the *Midweek Sun*, published on Wednesday, take a middle-of-the-road political stance and are good for general national news. If you prefer something more politically vocal you should check out the loudly left-wing *Mmegi* (Reporter), published on Wednesday. Its relentless criticism of the Botswana government is a tribute to official tolerance for dissenting opinion.

Several South African dailies are also available and provide an array of voices and coverage. In the Gaborone Sun and the Botswana Book Centre in Gaborone you can often pick up the *International Herald Tribune*, but sometimes a week after it's published. In large hotels and bookshops in Gaborone, Francistown and Selebi-Phikwe, you'll find up-to-date editions of *Time* and *Newsweek*. The *New African*, an Africa-oriented news magazine, is more widely available.

To keep up with local events, pick up a free copy of the *Botswana Advertiser* in Gaborone or the *Northern Advertiser* in Francistown. They're both published weekly on Friday.

Air Botswana's in-flight magazine, *Marung*, includes a range of travel-related articles, as well as features on Batswana arts and culture. It's also available by subscription from Marung (☎ (27-11) 463 3350), PO Box 98034, Sloane Park 2152, South Africa.

Alternatively, there's the Gaborone magazine, *Hello Botswana*, which is supported by advertising and is distributed free. Articles deal mostly with local events, travel and business. For information on subscriptions, contact Hello Botswana, Desk Top Publishing & Office Services (☎ 374134; fax 357433), Private Bag 0053, Gaborone.

Radio & TV
Nationwide programming is provided by Radio Botswana, broadcasting in both English and Setswana. With a short-wave set, you'll be able to pick up the BBC World Service there. You can also pick up the Voice of America, the quirky American Armed Forces Radio, and Radio Australia.

Botswana has one television station, the Gaborone Broadcasting Corporation (GBC), which transmits nightly for a few hours beginning at 7 pm and provides an interesting blend of foreign programming – mostly British and American – and occasional local productions. It can be picked up only in the capital. In trendy Maun, you can pick up satellite television from various sources.

In addition, four South African stations are boosted in for Botswanan consumption. The clearest reception is on BOP-TV, which originates in Mafikeng. The other three come from Johannesburg and broadcast typically inane South African game shows, news programmes and sitcoms in English and Afrikaans on alternating evenings.

HEALTH
As a relatively wealthy country, Botswana enjoys high standards of health care, and in the large hospitals in Gaborone and Francistown, facilities are comparable to those you'd find in Europe. Dental services are

available in Gaborone and Francistown, and all the main towns, except Kasane, have reasonably well-stocked pharmacies.

Although the malaria risk in Botswana isn't great, prophylaxis is especially recommended for travel in the Tuli Block, the North -East and the Okavango Delta. For further information, see the overall Health section in the Regional Facts for the Visitor chapter.

DANGERS & ANNOYANCES

The greatest dangers in Botswana are posed by the natural elements combined with a lack of preparedness on the part of visitors. Some of these are covered under Dangers & Annoyances in the Regional Facts for the Visitor chapter. For guidelines on dealing with dangers presented by travel in remote areas, see the Getting Around chapter.

Police & Military

Although police and veterinary roadblocks, bureaucracy and bored officials may become tiresome, they're more a harmless inconvenience than anything else. Careful scrutiny is rare, but they may ask you to unpack your luggage – or your entire vehicle, should you have one – and go over your belongings with a fine-tooth comb. Rather than anything insidious, they're usually just looking for meat products.

The Botswana Defence Force (BDF), on the other hand, takes its duties quite seriously and is best not crossed. Avoid the State House in Gaborone at all times, but after dark don't even walk or drive past it. If you're using an old map, be sure to avoid the airstrip marked as the Gaborone airport. This is now a BDF base; after dark, even to drive down Notwane Rd is extremely risky. You'll undoubtedly hear tales – which are unfortunately true. Trespassers aren't asked any questions before it's made certain they never trespass again.

Theft

Although theft occurs, Botswana enjoys a very low crime rate compared to other African (and most Western) countries. Set aside a good block of time if you do have something stolen and have to report it to the police for insurance purposes.

WORK

Botswana is developing rapidly and the educational system can't seem to keep up with the growing demand for skilled professionals in several fields, so if you have a skill which is in demand, the country will probably welcome you with open arms.

Those with background, training and experience in a variety of professions – medical doctors, secondary school teachers, professors, engineers, computer professionals and so on – will have the best chances. At the present time there is no shortage of primary school teachers or nurses; but the situation may change, so if you're keen on staying, it wouldn't hurt to try anyway.

Most people want to remain around Gaborone or Francistown but if you are willing to work in the back of beyond your chances of finding work will probably improve considerably.

Those accepted will normally be granted a three-year renewable residency permit. Applications and information are available from the Immigration and Passport Control Officer (☎ 374545 Gaborone), off Khama Crescent, PO Box 942, Gaborone, Botswana. Applications must be submitted from outside the country.

Prospective residents of Gaborone should realise that the city is the world's fastest growing capital and experiences sporadic housing shortages. Construction can't keep up with demand and many expatriate professionals are being housed in pricey hotels at government or business expense while languishing on a long waiting list for long-term housing. At times, the system is being taxed beyond all reason.

International volunteer organisations – Danish, German, Swedish and Norwegian volunteers and the American Peace Corps – are very active in Botswana and may provide an alternative for those suitably disposed.

HIGHLIGHTS

Outside the cities, there's little that's artificial or pretentious about Botswana. What it lacks in diversity, it happily makes up for in inspiration. Although it's missing the diverse attractions found in neighbouring countries, its appeal lies in the pristine wildness of its empty spaces, the friendly unhurried pace of its rural villages and the stability and security provided by its generally peaceful nature. For me, the top attractions are:

Okavango Delta Botswana's watery number one tourist destination is one of Africa's highlights – a maze of channels and islands teeming with wildlife and inviting exploration. The magnificent pristine landscapes of Moremi Reserve in the eastern Delta support a full complement of African wildlife.

Chobe National Park Actually several parks in one, the game-rich and elephant-ravaged river front and the inland marshes and savannas make Botswana's most accessible game park the country's second most visited area.

Tsodilo Hills Brought to world attention by Laurens van der Post in *The Lost World of the Kalahari*, the remote Tsodilo Hills are an incredible gallery of ancient San paintings. They're not only the country's most impressive peaks, but also one of its best hiking areas.

Sua Pan The vast and featureless expanses of Sua Pan have been immortalised in the popular 1985 film *The Gods Must be Crazy* and in the more recent spectacular film *March of the Flame Birds*. Sua Pan is also the site of Botswana's newest economic diversification – the mining of soda ash on Sua Spit.

Tuli Block Lying along the Limpopo River, the private wildlife reserves and spectacular Old West scenery of the Tuli Block make it appealing for well-heeled – and wealthy – travellers.

Makgadikgadi & Nxai Pan National Park The beautiful and almost undeveloped grasslands and palms of Makgadikgadi provide habitat for most game species found in Botswana. The grassy expanses of Nxai Pan, an ancient lake bed, is used as a unique rainy season gathering place for migrating wildlife. Nearby, Baines' Baobabs offer an interesting stand of misanthropic trees.

Gcwihaba Caverns Remote and forgotten, the Gcwihaba Caverns, or Drotsky's Cave, in the heart of the Kalahari offer an entirely undeveloped underground experience, but only for the most adventurous...and those with a bit of luck or cash to arrange transport.

Serowe Sprawling Serowe, home of Sir Seretse Khama and his forebears, is said to be the largest village in sub-Saharan Africa, and the museum devoted to the history of the Khama clan is definitely worth a visit. The new Khama Rhino Sanctuary outside Serowe protects Botswana's last rhino.

The Kalahari Although several of the other Top 10 attractions are within the Kalahari, the land itself offers the opportunity to experience a spectacular solitude all its own. If possible, don't miss a starry night camping in its wild expanses. Botswana's aboriginal inhabitants, the San, maintain that at night in the Kalahari 'you can hear the stars in song.'

ACCOMMODATION
Camping

Several hotels and lodges provide camping areas with varying amenities for campers. Most offer showers as well as a cooking and washing area. Campers have access to hotel bars and restaurants but few of these are accessible to shopping areas without a vehicle. These camps average around US$6 per person per night.

The national parks offer camps are normally rudimentary. Foreigners, who pay US$18.50 (P50) just to *be* in the park, must shell out another US$7.50 (P20) to set up a tent and use the loos – if they exist. There are several reasonably comfortable camp sites with *braai* pits and flush toilets in Moremi Reserve and Chobe National Park, but the rest are basically just cleared spots in the dust. For your money, expect lots of wildlife activity in the night.

You can also camp away from official camp sites. There is no legal prohibition, and if you can get out of sight – as you can throughout most of Botswana – and are self-sufficient in food, water, transport, petrol and so on, you can set up camp just about anywhere, cook over an open fire and soak up the unbelievable Kalahari night skies, sounds and smells. This could well be Botswana's greatest appeal. However, if you're caught out near a village and can't escape local scrutiny, enquire after the local chief or visit the police station to request permission to camp and directions to a suitable site. Remember to carry out all rubbish

BOTSWANA

with you, and keep cooking fires to a minimum size.

Camps & Lodges

Most of Botswana's safari camps and lodges are found in Chobe National Park, the Tuli Block and the Moremi/Okavango Delta areas. They're difficult to generalise; some lie along the highways and others occupy remote wilderness areas. They range from tent sites to established tented camps, brick or reed-built chalets and luxury lodges – or any combination of these. Prices range from US$7.50 to camp at Oddball's in the Okavango to well over 100 times that at Abu's Camp, also in the Okavango Delta, which features circus elephant rides.

Most up-market camps are prebooked overseas in conjunction with an organised tour or through a local travel agency or company representative. The main exceptions are some down-market camps around Maun and Kasane, where travellers can turn up at any time.

Many lodges and camps, especially in the Okavango Delta, lie in remote areas. Access is normally arranged by the booking agency or tour organiser, and is included in the package price. Other camps are readily accessible from the road system and are open to anyone with a suitable vehicle.

Hotels

Hotels in Botswana are much like hotels anywhere. Every town has at least one and the larger centres offer several price ranges. However, you won't find anything as cheap as the bottom end in other African countries and the less expensive hotels in Botswana are likely to double as brothels.

Although the housing shortage in Gaborone is tapering off, some Gaborone hotels still provide interim housing for expatriate residents awaiting permanent accommodation. Therefore, room availability is erratic. For up-market accommodation, it's always wise to pre-book or you may have problems. In other price ranges, the pickings are better unless there's a special event on.

FOOD

While eating in Botswana isn't particularly exciting – there's no delectably refined national cuisine to knock your socks off – self-caterers will find the pickings among the best in Africa. The restaurants, however expensive, normally serve decent, if unimaginative, fare.

Snacks & Meals

Both takeaway and fast food outlets figure prominently in Botswana's cities and towns; cheap eating in Gaborone and Francistown revolves around quick chicken and burger fixes.

As for beef, just because it's one of Botswana's main export commodities doesn't mean you'll find a cheap, high quality supply. The best beef is exported, while a few choice cuts are reserved for up-market hotels and restaurants. The inexpensive meat served in local establishments is evidence that cattle are considered more as a sign of wealth than a food source – they aren't slaughtered until they're ready to drop dead anyway.

To my knowledge, there's only one health-food-cum-vegetarian restaurant in Botswana – The Kgotla in Gaborone. The normally pretentious hotel dining rooms and finer restaurants concentrate heavily on the beef end of the scale, although fish, lamb and chicken dishes are also served.

International cuisine is available only in Gaborone, where Chinese, Indian, French, Italian, Portuguese and other cuisines are represented. In smaller towns, however, expect little menu variation. Chicken, chips, beef and greasy fried snacks are the standards, as well as *mabele* or *bogobe* (sorghum porridge), served with some sort of meat relish. Beyond the staples, you may want to try *vetkoek* (an Afrikaans word which is pronounced as and means 'fat cake'). This variation on the doughnut is available nearly everywhere.

Self-Catering

To visitors entering Botswana from Zimbabwe and other points from the north, the quantity and variety of food available in some Botswana supermarkets may well seem amazing. You can buy anything from Marmite to taco shells, corn chips to freshly ground coffee, fresh prawns to grapefruit. If you've been haunted by food fantasies while travelling across Africa, Botswana is where they can be fulfilled.

The reason for the abundance is Botswana's long-standing trade links with South Africa. The only food items originating in Botswana are beef, mealies, bitter melons and groundnuts. In the right season, you'll also find citrus, mainly oranges, being cultivated in the Tuli Block.

Prices in Botswana supermarkets and bush shops are comparable to or slightly lower than those in North America, Australasia and Europe. Open markets aren't as prevalent as in Zimbabwe and other countries, but both Gaborone and Francistown do have informal markets. In Gaborone, the market sprawls beside the railway station and there's also a small impromptu produce market between Broadhurst North Mall and the BBS building. In Francistown, there's a small market building on Baines St just off Blue Jacket St, and lots of impromptu stalls clustered around the railway station.

Traditional Foods

Historically, men were responsible for tending the herds and subsisted primarily on meat and milk, while women were left to gather and eat wild fruits and vegetables. The Tswana staple was mainly beef, but each of the several Tswana groups had its own food taboos. No one ate fish or crocodile – the latter being the totem of the tribe as a whole – and other groups were forbidden to eat their individual totems. Some tribes relied upon different food staples: the Yei of the Okavango were dependent upon fish, the Kalanga ate mainly sorghum, millet and maize, while the Herero subsisted mostly on thickened, soured milk. Nowadays, *mabele* or *bogobe* (millet and sorghum porridge, respectively) form the centre of most Batswana meals, but these are rapidly being replaced by imported maize mealies, sometimes known by the Afrikaans name, *mielie pap*, or just *pap*.

Before South African imports reached the furthermost corners of the Kalahari, the desert was dishing up a diverse array of wild edibles to augment the staple foods. Although most of modern-day Botswana derives its food from agriculture or the supermarket, people in remote areas still supplement their diets with these items.

One of the most useful desert plants is the *morama*, an immense underground tuber, the pulp of which contains large quantities of water and serves mainly as a source of liquid for desert dwellers. Above ground, the morama grows leguminous pods which contain edible beans. Other desert delectables include *marula* fruit, wild plums, berries, tubers and roots, *tsama* melons, wild cucumbers, and honey.

There's also a type of edible fungus related to the European truffle but now known to marketing people as the Kalahari truffle. This San delicacy has now been discovered by outsiders, who think it may be well received in Western markets. The truffle's spores grow on the root of the woody *Grewia flava* bush, which has a small shrivelled berry locally used to make *kadi* wine. In Kalahari mythology, the truffles are thought to be the eggs of the lightning bird because the truffles' presence is revealed by rings of cracked soil around the bush after electrical storms.

The nutritious and protein-rich *mongongo* nut, similar to the cashew, is eaten raw or roasted, and has historically been a staple for some San groups.

People also gather wild animal products when available: for example, birds and their eggs, small mammals and reptiles and even ant eggs!

An interesting item you may encounter is the mopane worm, a caterpillar-like inhabitant of the mopane tree which may remind Australians of their own beloved witchetty grub. They're normally gutted and cooked in hot ash for about 15 minutes. Alternatively, they're boiled in salt water or dried in the sun

BOTSWANA

for several days to be later deep-fried in fat, roasted, or ground up and eaten raw.

Because of the scanty water supply, traditional crops are limited to *monoko* (ground nuts or peanuts), *mabele*, *digwana* (gourds), *magapu* (melons), *dinawa* (beans) and *mabelebele* (millet).

DRINKS

A range of 100% natural fruit juices from South Africa are sold in casks in supermarkets in the major cities and towns. You'll also find a variety of teas, coffees and sugary soft drinks.

Botswana's alcohol production is limited to beer; the three domestic options are Castle, Lion and Black Label. Otherwise, bottle shops are well stocked with imported beer, wine and spirits at prices comparable to those in Europe or North America. You may want to sample some of the superb red and white wines produced in the Cape which are available for very reasonable prices. Note that alcohol may not be sold before 10 am and that bottle stores close at 7 pm nightly and all day on Sundays.

Traditional drinks are plentiful. Several of the more popular ones are less than legal, including mokolane or palm wine, an extremely potent swill made from distilled palm sap. Another is *kgadi*, made from distilled brown sugar and berries or fungus; the flavour is enhanced with any of a variety of additives.

Legal home brews include the common *bojalwa*, an inexpensive, sprouted sorghum beer which is brewed commercially as Chibuku. Another serious drink is made from fermented marula fruit. Light and non-intoxicating *mageu* is made from mealies or sorghum mash. Another is *madila*, a thickened sour milk which is used as a relish or drunk (normally 'eaten' would be a more appropriate term) plain.

THINGS TO BUY

The standard of Botswana handicrafts is generally very high, particularly the beautifully decorative Botswana baskets which were originally produced in Ngamiland, the district which takes in all of north-western Botswana. If you think they're too inspired to use as bins, laundry hampers or magazine holders, they also make lovely decorations and you'll see fine examples of this in business establishments all around Botswana.

In Gaborone, they're sold at Botswanacraft on The Mall and at several other cooperatives, including an excellent one in the Naledi Industrial Site on Old Lobatse Rd, run by a school for disabled Batswana. A range of basketry is available in Maun curio shops, but in such Panhandle villages as Gumare, the Etshas or Shakawe, where you can buy directly from the artists and craftspeople, you'll pay less and contribute directly to the local economy.

In the remote western regions, beaded San jewellery and leatherwork are normally of excellent quality and you'll be deluged with offers. You'll find the famous leather aprons, ostrich eggshell beads (which may not be imported into some countries) and strands of seeds, nuts, beads and bits of carved wood. The genuine articles, however, will probably grow scarcer as tourism pushes further into the desert areas and demand for mass-produced items increases. They also make some concessions to tourists, making and selling the tiny bows and arrows which foreigners often associate with the San.

Beautiful weavings and textiles are also available. Although the most inspired pieces can be quite pricey, they'll probably cost a lot less than you'd pay at home and the handmade quality and individuality easily justify the expense. The best and least expensive work is normally found right at its source at weavings cooperatives around Gaborone and Francistown.

The Herero people in the north-west sell dolls representing Herero women in the four stages of life: pre-puberty, puberty, adulthood and old age. All but the last are normally dressed in the distinctive Herero women's dress, a Victorian-style crinoline which was introduced in Namibia by German missionaries. The old-age dolls are arrayed in traditional leather costumes, which were used prior to European contact. The Herero also produce milk jugs, which are carved from a single chunk of hardwood, and containers for storing cooking fat, which are made from wet bits of leather which have been moulded into shape.

If you're interested in Botswana's colourful and interesting stamps, most of which are wildlife-oriented, either visit the philatelic desk at the GPO in Gaborone, or write to Philatelic Bureau, Botswana Postal Services, PO Box 100, Gaborone.

For further information about Botswana's material crafts, refer to the discussion in the Arts section of the Botswana Facts about the Country chapter.

Export Permits

In theory, an export permit is required for any item made from animal products, including ostrich eggshells, game skins and feathers. If you purchase the item from a handicraft outlet, the items will have been registered upon acquisition but anything bought directly from locals must technically be registered with the Veterinary office.

Getting There & Away

AIR

In general, air travel to and from Botswana is more expensive than to neighbouring countries, and you'll normally find fares are cheaper to Harare, Windhoek or Johannesburg than to Gaborone.

Air Botswana and Air Zimbabwe fly nonstop between Harare and Gaborone twice weekly. Air Botswana flies nonstop between Lusaka and Gaborone on Monday and Friday.

Air Namibia serves both Windhoek airports – Eros in the city centre and Windhoek International 42 km east of the city. On Wednesday and Friday, they fly between Windhoek Eros and Maun, connecting with Air Botswana flights to and from Gaborone. This is a straightforward way to travel between Botswana and Namibia, with the cheapest fares at around US$150 one way. On Friday they operate a return flight between Maun and Katima Mulilo, Namibia.

South Africa and Botswana have good air links. Between them, Air Botswana and South African Airways connect Gaborone and Johannesburg twice daily with connections to and from Durban and Cape Town.

In Zimbabwe, the Air Botswana office (☎ 733836) is on the 5th Floor of the Southampton House, at the corner of 1st St and Union Ave. In Gaborone, the office is in the IGI Building on The Mall, and also serves as the agent for Air India, Air Mauritius, Air Zimbabwe, Lufthansa, Royal Swazi Airlines, South African Airways, SAS, Swissair, Air Tanzania, Air Malawi and KLM. The Zambia Airways office (☎ 312027) is at Zambia House on The Mall in Gaborone.

LAND
Border Crossings

Overland entry into Botswana is normally straightforward and if you respond respectfully to the officers and comply with instructions, you'll have few hassles. When entering Botswana overland, visitors must wipe all their shoes, even those packed away in luggage, in a disinfectant dip to prevent carrying foot and mouth disease into the country. Vehicles must also pass through a pit filled with the same disinfectant.

Border Opening Hours Border opening hours are subject to frequent changes so use these opening times as general guidelines only and check locally for the latest information before turning up at remote posts, especially on weekends. Some border posts are closed for lunch between 12.30 and 1.45 pm. The international airport immigration offices at Gaborone, Francistown, Kasane and Maun open whenever scheduled flights arrive or depart. (During the winter months, Namibia is one hour behind Botswana.)

To/From Namibia
    Mamuno/Buitepos; 6.30/7.30 am to 4/5 pm
    Ngoma Bridge; 8 am to 4 pm
    Mohembo/Shakawe; 6 am to 6 pm

To/From South Africa
    (note: Molopo River crossings close when water is high)
    Bokspits/Gemsbok (Molopo River); 8 am to 4 pm
    Bray (Molopo River); 8 am to 4 pm
    Martin's Drift/Groblersbrug (Limpopo River); 8 am to 6 pm
    McCarthysrus (Molopo River); 8 am to 4 pm
    Middelputs; 8 am to 4 pm
    Parr's Halt/Stockpoort (Limpopo River); 8 am to 4 pm
    Pioneer Gate-Lobatse/Skilpadsnek-Zeerust; 7 am to 8 pm
    Pitsane (Molopo River); 8 am to 4.30 pm
    Platjanbridge (Limpopo River); 8 am to 4 pm
    Pont Drift (Limpopo River); 8 am to 4 pm
    Ramatlhabama/Mmabatho (road & railway); 7 am to 8 pm
    Ramotswa; 8 am to 4 pm
    Saambou (Limpopo River); 8 am to 4 pm
    Sikwane/Derdepoort (Mochudi); 8 am to 4 pm
    Tlokweng (Gaborone); 7 am to 10 pm
    Werda (Molopo River); 8 am to 4 pm
    Zanzibar (Limpopo River); 8 am to 4 pm

BOTSWANA

To/From Zambia
Kazungula Ferry (Zambezi River); 6 am to 6 pm

To/From Zimbabwe
Kazungula Rd (Kasane/Victoria Falls); weekdays 6 am to 6 pm
Mpandamatenga/Pandamatenga; weekdays 6 am to 4 pm
Ramokgwebana/Plumtree (road & rail); 6 am to 6 pm

To/From Namibia

There are three land crossings between Botswana and Namibia: Ngoma Bridge between East Caprivi and Chobe National Park; Mohembo/Shakawe in the upper Okavango Panhandle; and Buitepos-Mamuno, west of Ghanzi in the Kalahari.

There's no public transport between Namibia and Botswana through any of the three land crossings (except the Harare–Windhoek bus, which passes through Ngoma Bridge en route), and the only one consistently open to non-4WD vehicles is Ngoma Bridge. Roads on the Namibian side of the Mohembo-Shakawe and the Buitepos-Mamuno crossings are good dust/gravel until the tar begins at Divundu and Gobabis, respectively. On the Botswana side, they deteriorate into rough tracks covered in places with mud or drifted sand, requiring 4WD and high clearance vehicles.

On the Botswana side, petrol is available at Kasane, Ghanzi, Etsha 6 and Maun. In Shakawe, it's sold by the Brigades from steel drums and costs nearly twice what it does elsewhere; enquire at their camp about five km upstream from the village.

Contrary to a rumour that won't die, there is no longer guerrilla activity in the Caprivi (although there are occasional cross-border raids by Angolan factions). All travel restrictions and permit requirements were dropped after Namibia gained its independence in 1990.

Bus The bus service from Harare, Zimbabwe to Windhoek, Namibia, passes through Kasane at around 8 am on Wednesday morning. The best place to wait is the Kazungula border post.

Hitching The easiest access for hitchhikers is Ngoma Bridge. The 54-km transit route through Chobe National Park is relatively well-travelled, and if you avoid the riverfront tourist drives you won't pay park fees. Once you've crossed into Namibia, the roads through the Caprivi Strip are relatively well-maintained. Since nearly everyone stops to refuel before heading towards Namibia (or in any direction), it may be better to wait for a lift at the petrol station near Chobe Safari Lodge rather than the Ngoma Bridge transit route turn-off near Kazungula. On the Botswana side, there's a shop and restaurant at the village of Charles Hill, five km east of the border crossing.

The hot, dry route between Ghanzi and Gobabis (Namibia) remains a 4WD route (thanks to one 200-metre stretch of very deep sand) and sees only a handful of vehicles daily. In Ghanzi, enquire about lifts at the Kalahari Arms hotel petrol station; naturally, most potential lifts depart early in the morning. Shared taxis are available as far as the border, from where you can continue along the smooth gravel road to Gobabis. Hitching on this route should improve with the completion of the Trans-Kalahari highway between Gaborone and Windhoek. If you're coming from Namibia and miss the border closing, inexpensive accommodation is available at the *East Gate Service Station & Rest Camp*, on the Namibian side of the border. On the Botswana side, there's a shop and restaurant at the village of Charles Hill, five km east of the border crossing.

To/From the Republic of South Africa

Most traffic between Botswana and South Africa passes through the crossing at Ramatlhabama/Mmabatho (open 7 am to 8 pm); the Tlokweng Gate less than 20 km from Gaborone (7 am to 10 pm); or the Lobatse/Zeerust (7 am to 8 pm) post further south. The numerous other posts service back roads across the Limpopo in the Tuli Block or across the Molopo in southern Botswana. These posts are open only from 8 am to 4 pm, with the exception of Pont Drift, which closes at 6 pm. Because of the Southern African Customs Union and the normally good attitude of Botswanan immigration officials, travellers entering Botswana from South Africa should encounter a minimum of fuss.

Bus An easy way to reach Johannesburg is by minibus; they leave when full from the main bus terminal in Gaborone and cost US$15 per person. To be assured of a departure, arrive at the terminal as early as possible. Similarly, minibus services leave Mafikeng for Lobatse at around 10 am and cost US$4.

Alternatively, Greyhound (☎ 372224) has a bus service from Gaborone to Johannesburg via Zeerust, departing at 8 am on Monday, Friday and Saturday from the Kudu Service Station Shell Garage on Queen's Rd. It arrives at Johannesburg's Rotunda bus terminal at 1.15 pm the same day. The fare is US$24. Coming from Johannesburg, it departs at 3 pm on the same days and arrives in Gaborone at 8.15 pm. For information in Johannesburg, phone ☎ (011) 333 2130.

Train There is currently no passenger rail service between Botswana and South Africa.

Hitching Hitching between South Africa and Gaborone is easy and straightforward if you stick to the Ramatlhabama, Tlokweng and Lobatse borders. Tlokweng is reportedly the most relaxed border crossing into South Africa, with few searches and well-disposed officials. Tlokweng is reportedly the most relaxed border crossing into South Africa, with minimal searches and generally well-disposed officials.

To/From Zambia
Apart from the air route, your only straight-through option between Zambia and Botswana is the ferry across the Zambezi at Kazungula.

Road & Ferry Travel between Botswana and Zambia is via the free Kazungula ferry across the Zambezi River. However you look at it, this ramshackle set up is an experience,

although perhaps not as interesting as it used to be. Once upon a time, a heavy truck had to speed on board the ferry and slam on the brakes in order to provide the ferry with enough momentum to break away from the shore. If the truck stopped a little long or a little short, the ferry was known to flip and the system would have to close down while everything was righted and cleaned up. Fortunately, it has now been renovated and is able to cast off under its own steam. The crossing is free for vehicles registered in Botswana, but those with foreign registration must pay; currently, the price is US$10 for cars and US$20 for pickups.

Without a vehicle, it's a quick, straightforward crossing. Under normal circumstances, the ferry operates from 6 am to 6 pm daily. In Kasane or on the Zambian shore, you can pick up trucks going through to Livingstone, Lusaka and points beyond. From there, you have the choice of buses and trains to Lusaka.

If the delays are too long, or if the ferry isn't operating, you can cross into Zimbabwe at Kazungula, hitchhike to Victoria Falls, and enter Zambia at Livingstone, but Zimbabwe Immigration may require an onward ticket. Naturally, all this applies in the opposite direction as well.

There's also a Tuesday and Thursday bus service between Gaborone and Lusaka, Zambia, which runs via Francistown, Nata, Kasane, Livingstone and the Kazungula ferry. Check at bus terminals for the best details you're likely to find. The fare between Gaborone and Lusaka is a reasonable US$60 each way.

To/From Zimbabwe
There are two well-used border crossings between Zimbabwe and Botswana: the road and rail link at Plumtree/Ramokgwebana and the Kazungula/Kasane border west of Victoria Falls. There's also a lesser-used back road crossing at Mpandamatenga-Pandamatenga near Kazuma Pan National Park in Zimbabwe and Kazuma Forest Reserve in north-eastern Botswana. If you're

driving, fuel is considerably cheaper on the Zimbabwe side.

Bus Buses are operated by Express Motorways (☎ 304470, Gaborone) from the African Mall and the Gaborone Sun Hotel in Gaborone to Francistown, Bulawayo and Harare on Tuesday and Saturday at 6 am. Although things are improving, you should still plan on lengthy delays at the border. Between Kasane and Victoria Falls, United Touring Company operates a transfer service for US$20.

The no-frills Bulawayo-based Zimbabwe Omnibus Company operates a direct service daily (except Sunday) between Francistown and Bulawayo. The trip takes from three to six hours, depending on the delay at the border. Mach Coach Lines, also in Bulawayo, offers a slightly posher service six days a week at 4 pm.

The Windhoek-Harare bus service passes Kasane sometime between 1.30 pm and 2 pm on Saturday. Since it uses the Chobe transit route, the best place to connect with it is at the Kazungula border post.

Train Trains run daily from Gaborone to Bulawayo, departing at 9 pm. You can choose between 1st and 2nd-class sleepers or economy-class seats. Security is dodgy in any case, but in economy class, people are packed in like cattle and belongings are at risk. These trains normally have a buffet car, but never leave your luggage unattended. Fares are US$30/45 in 1st/2nd class and US$10 in economy.

Sexes are separated in 1st and 2nd-class sleepers unless you book a whole compartment or pay a slight surcharge and reserve a two-person coupe. You must pay for everything bought in the buffet car in the currency of the country you are travelling through. That is, Zimbabwe dollars are not acceptable for purchases while the train is passing through Botswana. Because there isn't always a buffet car, you may want to stock up on food and drink before departure.

Customs and immigration formalities are handled on the train. For further information on this route, refer to the discussion under To/From Botswana in the Zimbabwe Getting There & Away chapter. Timetables are included in the Zimbabwe Getting Around chapter.

Hitching Hitching between Francistown and Bulawayo via the Plumtree border crossing is fairly easy. Mornings are best for hitching into Botswana, while most afternoon traffic is headed towards Bulawayo.

Wait at the Kazungula road turn-off about one km south-east of town for lifts from Victoria Falls to Kazungula/Kasane. From Kasane, the direct route to Maun across Chobe National Park should essentially be considered unhitchable. It's very rough 4WD terrain most of the way and although some people have been lucky, this is certainly the exception to the rule. Although it's laboriously roundabout, the route from Kasane to Maun via Nata will prove far quicker.

BOTSWANA

Getting Around

Botswana's surface public transport network can be summed up in a couple of words: very limited. Although the air services are relatively good, domestic Air Botswana routings and air charters are pricey and the country's small population means that only a few locations are regularly served. Botswana's single railway line offers slow but reliable service, and existent bus services are restricted by the highway system – only a handful of main routes are viable for bus traffic.

AIR

The national carrier, Air Botswana, operates scheduled domestic flights between larger communities around the country. They occasionally run air-fare package deals, especially between Maun and Gaborone, in conjunction with hotel accommodation and sightseeing, and sometimes offer half-price special fares for students aged from 12 to 25. Otherwise, the frequently changing prices are generally quite high, but you may get some relief with 14-day advance purchase.

Air Botswana has four flights weekly between Gaborone and Francistown (US$123), and daily flights between Gaborone and Maun (US$173). On Monday, Wednesday and Friday, you can fly between Francistown and Maun via Gaborone (US$120). Kasane is served from Francistown (US$110) on Monday and from Gaborone (US$193) and Maun (US$143) on Monday, Thursday and Saturday. Air Botswana often runs special weekend fares, such as a popular US$75 return ticket between Gaborone and Francistown, which is valid on Friday and Sunday.

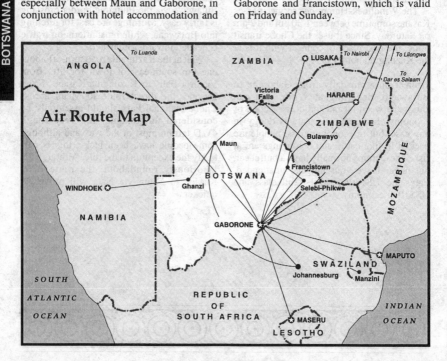

Air Botswana has offices at Blue Jacket Mall, PO Box 222, Francistown (☎ 212393; fax 213834); IGI Bldg, The Mall, PO Box 92, Gaborone (☎ 351921; fax 374802); and at Airport Rd, PO Box 191, Maun (☎ 660391; fax 660598). There are also Air Botswana offices in Kasane (☎ 650161) and Orapa (☎ 270250), Botswana.

Air Charters

Air charters provide the most viable access to remote tourist lodges and isolated villages. None are cheap, but if you book an organised trip through a travel agency or safari company (as opposed to chartering individually), you'll pay a set ticket price. Otherwise, you'll pay by the km for a *return* trip to your destination – even if you're just flying one way (charter companies justifiably charge for their return to home base once they've dropped you off).

Air charters are most commonly used to access lodges in the inner Okavango Delta and the Savuti area of Chobe National Park. If seats are available, you may be able to turn up just prior to departure and there is a possibility that you will pay less than when booking through an agency.

Naturally, the more remote your destination, the more expensive the air fare will be. Charter flights (agency-arranged) from Maun to the Inner Delta are currently around US$95 return. Kalahari Air concentrates on freight and business charters to isolated villages in central, western and south-western Botswana.

The average rate is around US$225 per hour for a five-passenger plane or US$1.20 per km, depending upon the company and the speed of the plane. Naturally the more passengers you have, the lower the price for each person will be. For example, flights between Kasane and Victoria Falls will work out to be around US$45 per person with five passengers and US$73 per person with just two people. Between Maun and Kasane, the charge for flights is US$600 for the whole plane or US$119 per person, with a minimum of five people.

The following is a list of major charter companies in Botswana:

Aer Kavango PO Box 169, Maun Airport, Maun (☎/fax 660393)

Delta Air PO Box 39, Maun (☎ 660044; fax 660589)

Elgon Air PO Box 448, Maun (☎ 660654; fax 660037)

Executive Air Private Bag SK-6, Sir Seretse Khama International Airport, Gaborone (☎ 375257; fax 375258)

Kalahari Air Services PO Box 41278, Broadhurst, Gaborone (☎ 351804; fax 312015)

Ngami Air PO Box 119, Maun (☎ 660530; fax 660593)

Northern Air PO Box 40, Maun (☎ 660385; fax 660379)

Okavango Air Services PO Box 54, Selebi-Phikwe (☎ 313308; fax 356949)

Quicksilver Enterprises (Chobe Air) PO Box 280, Kasane (☎ 650532; fax 650223)

Swamp Air Private Bag 13, Maun (☎ 660569; fax 660571)

BUS

Bus and minibus services operate mainly through the eastern part of the country. Schedules are erratic at best and buses normally run according to demand, departing when full. Intending passengers must haunt the bus terminals enquiring and waiting for something to happen, so it's best to turn up early in the morning. Many travellers find the procedure too time-consuming and, especially along the Lobatse-Francistown route, opt to hitchhike or take the slow but scheduled train.

The most frequently served bus routes follow the highway corridor between Ramatlhabama and Francistown, often doing only part of the route. Buses may connect Gaborone and Mahalapye six times a day, for example, but perhaps only three of these continue to Palapye and only two may go through to Francistown.

Other services operate between Francistown and Bulawayo (Zimbabwe); Serule and Selebi-Phikwe; Palapye, Serowe and Orapa; and Francistown, Nata and Kasane. Now that the Nata-Maun highway is graded and tarred, there are daily services with Mahube Express, as well as a marginally reliable daily connection between Maun and Shakawe.

There's no bus service through Chobe National Park between Kasane and Maun but safari companies offer three-day trips via Moremi starting at around US$220, excluding park fees (see the Okavango & North-western Botswana chapter). Between Kasane and Maun, a daily minibus runs via Nata, and between Kasane and Victoria Falls, UTC operates a pricey transfer service; book through any Kasane area hotel.

Major bus companies include Sesennye (☎ 212112) and Mahube Express (☎ 352660), both in Gaborone, which operate between Gaborone and Francistown. KB Transport (☎ 410202) in Mahalapye serves the Gaborone to Mahalapye route. Between Palapye and Selebi-Phikwe, the main operator is Loedza (☎ 810025) in Selebi-Phikwe.

TRAIN

Although it's slow, rail travel is a relaxing and effortless way to pass through the vast stretches of dusty and virtually featureless Botswana scrub. The railway line runs through the country between Ramokgwebana on the Zimbabwe border and Ramatlhabama on the South African border, but currently, service only extends as far south as Lobatse. The main stops are Gaborone, Mahalapye, Palapye, Serule and Francistown. There are also single-class commuter services between Gaborone, Pilane and Lobatse.

The timetable for the main route is included in the Zimbabwe Getting There & Away chapter. For more information, see To/From Zimbabwe in the Botswana Getting There & Away chapter, and To/From Botswana in the Zimbabwe Getting There & Away chapter.

Reservations

Information, reservations and tickets are available at the Gaborone station on weekdays from 7 am to 1 pm and 1.45 to 4.30 pm. In Francistown, the windows are open on weekdays from 8 am to noon and 1 to 4 pm.

For 1st and 2nd-class sleepers, advance bookings are essential.

Classes & Fares

By all accounts, the train is an inexpensive way to travel through Botswana, and in 1991 comfortable new carriages were purchased from South Africa. Economy class, which is rather crowded and uncomfortable, costs only US$8 from Gaborone to Francistown. In 2nd class six-passenger sleeper compartments, that trip costs US$25.50. In 1st-class carriages with four-passenger compartments, it's US$31.50. Bedding costs an additional US$2 per night in either 1st or 2nd-class. Other 1st/2nd/economy-class fares from Gaborone include Mahalapye (US$19/14/4), Palapye (US$23/19/6) and Ramokgwebana/Plumtree (US$41/30/10). The fare to Lobatse, which offers only economy class, is US$1.50.

CAR & MOTORBIKE

To get the most out of Botswana, you'll need a vehicle or plenty of time to wait for hitchhiking luck. A road journey in Botswana will fall into one of three categories: a high-speed rush along the excellent tarred road system; an uncertain rumble over typically poor secondary roads, or an expedition through the wildest terrains in a sturdy, high-clearance 4WD passenger vehicle or truck.

Conventional motorbikes perform excellently on the tarred roads and high-powered dirt bikes can be great fun on desert tracks, but in-between are roads where clouds of dust and sand kicked up by high-speed vehicles will make for a miserable experience on a motorbike. Note that motorbikes aren't permitted in national parks or reserves.

Roads

At the time of independence in 1966, Botswana's one and only tarred road extended for five km from Lobatse station to the High Court in Lobatse; it was completed in 1947 in preparation for the visit by King George VI.

Currently tarred sections include: Francistown to Orapa; Francistown to Ramok-

BOTSWANA

gwebana; Nata to Maun; Maun to Sepupa via Sehitwa, Gumare and Nxamseri; Mopipi to Rakops; Palapye to Orapa; Gaborone to Lethlakeng via Molepolole; Kazungula to Ramatlhabama via Nata, Francistown and Gaborone; Tshabong to Werda; Serule to Bobonong via Selebi and Phikwe; Lobatse to Jwaneng via Kanye; Martin's Drift to Selebi-Phikwe via Sherwood. There are also plans to complete a road from Rakops to connect with the Nata-Maun road.

Away from the increasing number of tarred km, where population centres are connected by nearly straight, dashed white lines, roads are often carved from shifting sand and vary in quality. Many are impassable without 4WD and some are difficult even with it. This partially explains why this country of vast distances lacks an extensive, reliable and organised public transport system. Even some stretches of the recently tarred road from Sehitwa to Sepupa in the north-west are often covered with sand drift.

Road Rules
As in neighbouring southern African countries, cars must drive on the left-hand side of the road. The national speed limit on tarred roads is 120 km/h, while through towns and villages it's normally posted lower. In the absence of a sign, assume a speed limit of 60 km/h through towns and villages. Seat belt use is compulsory, as is proof of no-fault insurance. If you have an accident causing injuries, it must be reported to authorities within 48 hours. If vehicles have sustained only minor damage and there are no injuries – and all parties agree – you can simply exchange names and addresses and sort it out later through the insurance companies. Note that anyone bringing in a vehicle registered outside Botswana must pay a road-safety levy of US$1.50 (P5) upon entry.

When driving through open areas, especially at night, be on the lookout for animals wandering onto the road. In theory, stock owners are responsible for keeping their charges off the roads, but of course it's best not to hit stock in the first place. If you do, in addition to your distress, the red tape involved in finding and filing a claim against the owner will probably come to nought and may backfire if the owner can prove driver negligence.

Leave a copy of your intended itinerary and estimated time of return with someone who will sound an alarm if you're not back or in touch at the specified time.

Bush Driving & Wilderness Travel
Botswana's maze of criss-crossing ruts and bush tracks can utterly confound drivers. They usher you into sandy villages from which tracks radiate in all directions, without a clue as to which leads where. Some provide access to remote cattle posts or small villages and then disappear, often to re-emerge somewhere on the other side of the post or village. Some tracks take you to larger roads or water sources. Still others merely disappear, leaving you stranded, with no way to turn but back the way you came.

Few bush roads appear on maps. The Department of Surveys & Lands has given up trying to keep track of these spontaneously created routes which are maintained only by use. Once they become too rutted, flooded or muddy to pass, a new route is created. Indicative of changing surface conditions, multiple parallel tracks split and join, cross, wander off and back and even disappear altogether on occasion.

The following helpful hints should at least get you started down the bush track to insanity (a pre-requisite for driving in the Botswana bush). For a comprehensive look at tested tips and techniques, as well as descriptions of many remote routes, refer to the *Visitors' Guide to Botswana* by Mike Main and John & Sandra Fowkes (Southern Book Publishers, Johannesburg, 1992), which is sold in bookshops and tourist shops around the country, as well as in overseas travel book and map shops.

- Take the best set of maps you can find. The Department of Surveys & Lands in Gaborone has reasonably accurate and up-to-date maps of remote areas. Tracks change frequently, however, so ask directions locally whenever possible.

BOTSWANA

- Carry a compass and take readings periodically to make sure you're still travelling in the right direction. Vehicular mechanisms create their own magnetic fields; to get an accurate reading, stand at least three metres from the vehicle.
- A minimum 150-litre reserve fuel tank is essential for off-road travel in central or western Botswana. Fuel is available consistently only in Maun, Ghanzi, Kang, Etsha 6 and over the borders in South Africa and Namibia.
- Carry at least five litres of water per person per day (allowing for delays and breakdowns when calculating the length of the trip). It will travel best in an indestructible metal container. Plastic may not stand up to the constant bumping the roads will mete out.
- Even if you're using relatively well-travelled routes, confirm that your 4WD and other vehicular mechanisms are functioning before setting off. Although the ingenuity of some villagers will astound you when it comes to gerry-rigging repairs, if you must have a particular spare and it isn't locally available (it almost never will be), you can spend lots of time and money awaiting a delivery from a larger centre.
- Travellers through the remotest never-never must be self-sufficient in everything, including vehicle spares, tools and the expertise to repair problems that may arise. The following items should be considered essential: a tow rope, torch, shovel, extra fan belt, vehicle fluids, spark plugs, baling wire, jumper leads, fuses, hoses, a good jack (and a wooden plank to act as a base in sand or salt), several spare tyres (or a tyre lever and a puncture repair kit) and a pump. A winch would also be an asset, but very few rental vehicles are so well equipped.
- Wrap tools and solid or heavy objects in blankets or other soft packing materials and place them in the bottom of the boot or truck bed. Food should be wrapped and packed tightly in solid unbreakable containers – cardboard boxes will disintegrate on back roads. Aluminium packing boxes are available in Gaborone for less than US$15. Once packed, the whole thing should be strapped down tightly. Keep plastic drink bottles, fragile snacks and poorly packaged items in the cab.
- A minimum camping kit will include a tent and a warm sleeping bag – Kalahari nights get very cold, especially in the winter. Camp beds are normally unnecessary – the soft Kalahari sand works adequately. For fire cooking, follow the locals' example and use a three-legged cast-iron *potjie* (most often pronounced 'POY-kee'), available throughout Botswana. A plastic basin and soap for washing up are essential to preserve water supplies. And don't forget a few pots and pans, eating implements, a tin opener and lots of waterproof matches.
- Sand tracks are more easily negotiated and less likely to bog vehicles in the cool mornings or evenings, when air spaces between sand grains are smaller. To further prevent bogging or stalling, move as quickly as possible and keep the revs up, but avoid sudden acceleration. Shift down in advance of deep sandy patches or the vehicle may stall and bog. When negotiating a straight course through rutted sand, allow the vehicle to wander along the path of least resistance. Anticipate corners and turn the wheel slightly earlier than you would on a solid surface – this will allow the vehicle to ski smoothly around – then accelerate gently out of the turn.
- Much Kalahari driving is through high grass and the seeds it scatters quickly foul radiators and cause vehicle overheating. If the temperature gauge begins to climb, stop and remove as much of the plant material from the grille as possible.
- Unbogging or driving on loose sand may be facilitated by lowering the air pressure in the tyres, thereby increasing their gripping area.
- When driving on the salt pans, keep to the tracks of vehicles that have gone before, or stick to within a couple of hundred metres of the pan's edge. The tempting flat, grey expanses easily become graveyards for vehicles which stick, sink and even break through into hidden subsurface cavities.
- For information about dealing with the animal hazards, see Dangers & Annoyances in the regional Facts for the Visitor chapter at the beginning of the book. For more about driving on the salt pans, see the aside, Driving on the Pans, in the North-Eastern Botswana chapter.

Car Hire

Hiring a vehicle – such as a 4WD – requires a large cash outlay, but will allow you the freedom to wander and explore the best the country has to offer. Best of all, it will allow you to visit the Kalahari, which is one of Africa's most pristine wilderness areas.

To hire a vehicle in Botswana, you must be at least 25 years of age and have a valid driving licence from your home country, which is valid for six months in Botswana. If it isn't in English, you must provide a certified translation.

Rental prices are high, and given the great distances involved, per km charges rack up very quickly. With all car hire, however, be wary of add-on charges and check the paperwork carefully. Also, thoroughly check the vehicle before accepting it, especially if you're taking a 4WD. Make sure the 4WD engages properly and that you understand how it works. Also check the vehicle fluids, brakes, battery and so on. The Kalahari is a harsh place to find out that the rental agency has overlooked something important.

Of Botswana's two car-hire firms, Avis and Holiday, the latter tends be cheaper and friendlier. As a general price guide, for a standard Toyota Corolla, Avis charges US$29 per day and US$0.29 per km, or US$60 per day with unlimited km and a minimum rental of six days. For a Toyota Hilux, you'll pay US$67 per day and US$0.58 per km or US$121 per day with unlimited km, with a minimum six-day rental period.

Holiday Car Hire, charges US$26 per day for the Corolla and US$0.26 per km, or US$52 per day unlimited km with a minimum rental period of six days. A Toyota Hilux 4WD vehicle, which includes a 150-litre reserve fuel tank, will cost US$50 per day and US$0.45 per km, or US$84 per day for unlimited km, with a minimum six-day rental. The head office in Francistown can also provide camping equipment.

The following is a list of the Avis and Holiday offices in Botswana:

Avis
  Sir Seretse Khama International Airport, PO Box 790, Gaborone (☎ 313093; fax 312205)
  Sheraton Hotel, Gaborone (☎ 312320)
  Francistown Airport, PO Box 222, Francistown (☎ 213901; fax 212867)
  Maun Airport, Maun (☎ 660039; fax 660258)
  PO Box 339, Kasane (☎ 650144; fax 650145)
Holiday Car Hire
  168 Queens Rd, The Mall, Gaborone (☎ 353970; fax 314894)
  Sir Seretse Khama International Airport, Gaborone (☎ 303255)
  VIP Travel, Blue Jacket St, PO Box 717, Francistown (☎ 214524; fax 214526)
  Francistown Airport, Francistown (☎ 215258)
  Chobe Safari Lodge, PO Box 197, Kasane (☎ 650226; fax 650129)
  Northern Air Bldg, opposite Maun Airport, Maun, Maun (☎ 660820; fax 660690)
  Syringa Lodge, PO Box 264, Selebi-Phikwe (☎ 810444; fax 810450)
  Shinga House, Main St, Serowe (☎/fax 430520)

Purchase
Unless you're spending some time in Botswana, it's probably not worth purchasing a vehicle there. Even used vehicles are extremely expensive and a 4WD, which you'll need to get around the most interesting parts of the country, will be out of the question for most people. A second-hand Botswana-standard Toyota Hilux, for example, starts at around US$20,000. A Land Rover would be considerably cheaper, but they're hard to find.

However, if you do buy a vehicle with hard currency and resell it in Botswana, you can remit the same amount of hard currency to your home country with no hassles. Just keep the papers and inform the bank in advance.

An alternative would be to buy a used vehicle in South Africa – it's fairly easy to find a used Land Rover in Johannesburg, for example – where prices are considerably lower, then return to South Africa and sell it when you're finished. You can't sell a South African vehicle in Botswana without paying heavy import duties.

BICYCLE
Botswana is largely flat but that's the only concession it makes to cyclists. Some travellers still take a bike in the hope of avoiding the uncertainties of hitching and public transport, but unless you are an experienced cyclist and are equipped for the extreme conditions, abandon any ideas you may have about a Botswana bicycle adventure.

Distances are great, horizons are vast; the climate and landscape are hot and dry; and even along major routes, water is scarce and villages are widely spaced. What's more, the sun is intense through the clear and semi-tropical desert air and prolonged exposure to the dry heat and burning ultraviolet rays will naturally be potentially hazardous.

On the tarred roads, which are mostly flat and straight, the national speed limit of 110 km/h doesn't prevent traffic cranking up the speed and when a semitrailer passes at 150 km/h, cyclists may unwittingly be blown off the road. To access areas off the beaten track,

BOTSWANA

bicycles are also unsuitable; and even experienced cyclists have pronounced most of the country's roads and tracks uncyclable. Along untarred roads, vehicles howl past in billowing clouds of sand and dust, and on lesser-used routes, you're likely to encounter deep drifted sand. Unless you're prepared to carry your bike and luggage over long, uninhabited distances, don't venture off main routes. Also bear in mind that neither bicycles nor motorbikes are permitted in Botswana's wildlife reserves.

Sorry to be so discouraging. If you have a go anyway, please let us know what you think!

HITCHING
Because public transport is somewhat erratic, many locals and travellers rely on hitchhiking as their primary means of getting around. On main routes, there should be no major problems.

The equivalent of a bus fare will frequently be requested in exchange for a lift. Ascertain a price or negotiate a fare before climbing aboard, however, to prevent uncomfortable situations at the end of the ride. The standard charge is one or two thebe per person per km, and drivers who do charge normally bring this up before prospective passengers climb aboard.

Hitching the back roads is another issue. If you're travelling between Lobatse and Ghanzi, through the Tuli Block or from Maun to Chobe, Moremi, Ghanzi or Namibia, carry camping equipment and enough food and water for several days of waiting. For trips even further afield, such as to the Makgadikgadi Pans or Gcwihaba Caverns, lifts must be arranged in advance. Your best chances of finding lifts to remote destinations are the lodges at Maun, as well as at Nata, Gweta, Shakawe and Ghanzi. For the Lobatse-Ghanzi trip, try the Botswana Meat Corporation in Lobatse.

From Kasane, the direct route to Maun across Chobe National Park is a very difficult and expensive hitch (park fees)! Although it's laboriously roundabout, the Kasane-Nata-Maun route is easier and far more practical. (Please see the hitching warning in the Zimbabwe Getting Around chapter.)

LOCAL TRANSPORT
Only Gaborone has a local public transport system and, sadly, it isn't really adequate for the city's growing population. Solidly packed little white minibuses, recognisable by their blue number plates, circulate according to set routes. The standard city route passes all the major shopping centres. Minibuses to outlying villages depart from the main bus terminal.

To/From the Airport
The only reliable transport between Gaborone, Francistown and Selebi-Phikwe and their respective airports are the minibuses operated by big hotels for their guests. If you're not a guest and there's space available, you can sometimes talk the driver into a lift, but a tip of at least several pula is expected. Taxis turn up at the airport only occasionally; if you need one, you'll normally have to phone.

Taxi
Although the collective public transport minibuses in Gaborone are known as 'taxis', conventional taxis are thin on the ground – even in Gaborone – so it's hardly worth searching for one on the street. Your best hope is to phone the taxi company and have them send one out. If you do find one, you'll have to negotiate a price with the driver. Licensed taxis are recognisable by their blue number plates.

TOURS
The Botswana government heartily promotes organised tours and offers tour discounts on national park entry fees. Most tours in Botswana focus on the Okavango Delta area, but you'll also find possibilities in Nata, Gweta, Shakawe and other places. Most package safari tours may be more economically arranged through Botswana companies than through overseas agents.

The following is a list of particulars for major operators referred to in the Botswana section of this book. For information about some individual tours, see the following regional chapters.

Bonaventures Botswana, PO Box 201, Maun (☎/fax 660502). This company handles booking for most camps in the Okavango Delta – but has no strong links with any of them – so it's a good place to pick up objective information.

Bush Camp Safaris, Baagi House, PO Box 487, Maun (☎/fax 660847). They organise transfers and mokoro trips around Ditshipi in the Okavango Delta and run mokoro camping safaris in the Chiefs Island area. They also do mobile safaris to other National Parks in Botswana.

Chobe Flyfishing Safaris, Andre Van Aardt, PO Box 206, Kasane (☎ 650414; fax 650223). As the name would imply, this company specialises in flyfishing expeditions along the Chobe River. The quarry includes pike, tigerfish and bream.

Crocodile Camp Safaris, PO Box 46, The Mall, Maun (☎/fax 660265). They mainly do high-priced tours around the Okavango Delta, Chobe National Park and the Kalahari, but also run trips into Zimbabwe and Namibia.

Desert & Delta Safaris, PO Box 32, Kasane (☎ 650340; fax 650280). Desert & Delta is affiliated with several up-market safari lodges in the Okavango Delta and Chobe National Park, including Camp Moremi, Camp Okavango and Chobe Game Lodge.

Gametrackers, PO Box 100, Maun (☎ 660351). Gametrackers operates several Okavango Delta and Chobe lodges, including Qhaaxwa, Khwai River Lodge, Xaxaba, San-ta-Wani, Allan's Camp and Savuti South. From overseas, contact their South African address: Gametrackers, Destination Africa (☎ (011) 884 2504; fax(011)8843159), PO Box 786432, Sandton 2146.

Game Trails Safaris, Private Bag 0062, Maun (☎ 660536). This informal operation runs budget mobile safaris through Moremi Reserve. Prices are around US$120 per day, including transport and driver only.

Go Wild Safaris, PO Box 56, Kasane (☎ 650468; fax 650223). This popular company based at Chobe Safari Lodge in Kasane operates the popular morning and evening game drives in Chobe National Park and cruises on the Chobe River, as well as mobile safaris in Chobe, Moremi and the Okavango Delta.

Gweta Rest Camp, PO Box 124, Gweta (☎ /fax 612220). In addition to day and overnight tours in the immediate vicinity – including excursions to their bush camp at Nxhasin Pan 25 km from Gweta – this reliable operation also organises customised safaris throughout Botswana.

Island Safaris, PO Box 116, Maun (☎ /fax 660300). This is the safari branch of Island Safari Lodge; it operates customised mobile safaris to Botswana national parks and reserves and mokoro and motorboat trips through the Okavango Delta. They're considered a budget option, but they're more expensive than their direct competitors.

Ker & Downey, PO Box 40, Maun (☎ 660211; fax 660379). Ker & Downey is Botswana's most exclusive and expensive luxury operator. Their camps include Abu's, Machaba, Pom Pom and Shinde Island, all in the Okavango Delta.

Merlin Services, Private Bag 0013, Maun (☎ 660351; fax 660471) Although they're not a tour operator, per se, Merlin Services acts as a booking agent for several Okavango camps and safari companies. They can also cobble together a full programme of excursions and activities around Botswana.

Okavango Explorations (Hartley's Safaris), Private Bag 0048, Maun (☎ /fax 660528). This company runs the luxury-class Xugana and Tsaro Camps in Moremi Reserve. From Xugana they operate mokoro trips and from Tsaro, a unique two-night walking safari along the beautiful Khwai River.

Okavango Tours & Safaris, PO Box 39, Maun (☎ 660220; fax 660589). This company's speciality is lodge-based tours in the Okavango Delta. They're also the agents for the popular budget camp, Oddball's, as well as Delta Camp and Xakanaxa Camp.

Okavango Wilderness Safaris, Private Bag 014, Maun (☎ 660086; fax 660632). A subsidiary of the same operation as Wilderness Safaris in Zimbabwe. They offer a range of expensive package safaris to the up-market Jedibe, Mombo and Tchau camps in the Okavango, as well as much cheaper 'participation' safaris which take in the points of interest between Maun and Victoria Falls.

Penstone Safaris, PO Box 330, Maun (☎ 660978; fax 660623). They run luxurious but reasonably-priced overland safaris around the highlights of Botswana, including all the national parks and reserves. They can even take you to Deception Pan in the Central Kalahari Game Reserve. Alternatively, you can opt for 'participation' safaris, in which you help with the chores for a substantial discount.

PhotoAfrica Safaris, PO Box 11, Kasane (☎ 650385; fax 650383). As the name would suggest, they specialise in photographic safaris, concentrating on the remote Linyanti Marshes area of northern Botswana, where they operate three wilderness luxury camps. They also organise customised mobile safaris in the area for US$47 per person per day on a self-catering basis.

BOTSWANA

Sitatunga Safaris, Private Bag 47, Maun (☎ /fax 660570). They run camping-based overland trips through the Okavango Delta, Moremi Reserve, Makgadikgadi Pans and Nxai Pan. They also operate Sitatunga Camp near Maun and run trips to and around Camp Okuti at Xakanaxa Lediba in the Moremi Wildlife Reserve.

Trans Okavango, Private Bag 033, Maun (☎ 660023; fax 660040). This company owns of Gunn's Camp in the Okavango Delta; the booking agent is Merlin Services (☎ 660635; fax 660571), Private Bag 013, Maun.

WALKING

Distances between towns are great in Botswana and the intervening spaces are typically empty and waterless. Outside the cities and towns, not even the local people will attempt to walk from place to place, so walking is not a practical way for you to get around in Botswana.

As for hiking and bushwalking, the best venues are the Tsodilo Hills in north-western Botswana and the low hills around Gaborone and Lobatse. In the Okavango Delta and Moremi Wildlife Reserve, guided walks are available through private lodges and safari companies.

Gaborone

Capital or not, Gaborone is little more than a sprawling village suffering from the growing pains and lack of colour or definition that accompany an abrupt transition from rural settlement to modern city. Although Gaborone has a few interesting sights, it is one of the continent's most expensive cities and isn't something to go out of one's way for. Having said that, urban planners may be drawn by curiosity or the desire to assess the extent of the disaster!

What went wrong – or more accurately, what *is going wrong* – with Gaborone is its lack of integration and its uncontainable sprawl. It's a bit like a nascent, microcosmic Los Angeles. Distances are long and uninteresting, and heavy traffic and lack of footpaths place pedestrians at risk. Beyond the Mall, which was an early attempt to provide the city with a heart, Gaborone has no central business district. Low-cost housing meshes with blocks of flats, shopping centres and industrial complexes. High-rise buildings sprout wherever there's a block of land to fit them and new suburbs materialise like mushrooms. Few visitors want to linger.

History

Archaeological evidence indicates that the site of Gaborone has been inhabited since the Middle Stone Age. Excavations below the Gaborone Dam in 1966 uncovered ancient tools and artefacts and, in fact, nearly every new building site has yielded similar finds.

The first modern settlement was built on the banks of the Ngotwane River, just a few km from the South African border, in 1884 by Kgosi (Chief) Gaborone of the Tlokwa clan. Unlike Harare, Gaborone was never intended to be a capital. Whites in the area came to know the place as 'Gaborone's village', which was inevitably abbreviated to Gaborones. The railway came through in 1897, passing just four km west of the orig-

inal village. Before long, a tiny settlement with a hotel and a few shops – known as Gaborones Station – appeared around the station.

In 1962, thanks to its proximity to water and the railway line, this otherwise unlikely spot was selected as the future capital of Botswana, which was confidently treading the road to independence. At the time, the seat of government was Mafikeng, South Africa, which had served as Bechuanaland's absentee capital through the Protectorate days. Construction of the new capital began in 1964, in order that the administration could be transplanted into the country.

The task of designing the new city, which was intended to accommodate a population of no more than 20,000, was assigned to the Department of Public Works. By 1990, however, the population had exceeded that figure by over 100,000 and it continues to grow at an astonishing rate. In fact, Gaborone is among the world's fastest growing cities and now has a population of over 150,000.

In 1968, the 's' was officially dropped from 'Gaborones', in honour of the original chief's real name. Now, most of the rest of

BOTSWANA

the word has been dropped, as well, and the place is affectionately known as just 'Gabs'.

Orientation

Gaborone lacks any definite central business district; urban action focuses on the city's dispersed shopping malls. The main one, imaginatively called The Mall, is a concrete slab between the town hall and the government complex of ministries and offices that are cradled in the sweep of Khama Crescent.

About five blocks south is the more down-to-earth shopping area known as the African Mall, which has several good restaurants and some inexpensive shops. Everything north of Nyerere Dr is known as Broadhurst, where there are several other shopping centres. The most prominent is Broadhurst North Mall (actually a complex of several shopping centres), which contains more up-market shops. Also in Broadhurst are the Old Spar (also known as Julius Nyerere) Shopping Centre and the Maru-a-Pula (commonly known as No Mathatha) Shopping Centre, both on Nyerere Dr. East of town, north of Tlokweng Rd, is the up-market Village Mall. The Metro Mall is in the Broadhurst Industrial Estate west of the Francistown road and the rapidly growing new suburb of Gaborone West also has its own Gaborone West Mall.

Information

The tourist office in The Mall is the only really helpful office in the country. It distributes a range of brochures and advertising, and is helpful with advice and accommodation bookings. National tourist information is also provided at the National Museum Information Centre. You may also want to pick up a copy of the weekly publication *Consumer Info Gaborone*, with TV and cinema listings, a calendar of events and useful advertising.

A reliable source of information on Botswana's conservation movement and visits to wilder areas of the country is the Kalahari Conservation Society (☎ 314259), PO Box859, Gaborone, in Botsalano House on The Mall. For information on visiting Botswana's national parks, contact the Department of Wildlife & National Parks (☎ 371405).

Money The best and quickest place to exchange cash or travellers' cheques is the Gaborone Sun branch of Barclays Bank. It's open Monday, Tuesday, Thursday and Friday from 8.30 am to 2 pm; on Wednesday from 8.30 am to 1.30 pm and on Saturday from 8.30 to 10.45 am. If you're changing money at any of the banks on The Mall, queue up as early as possible. The Zimbank and Barclays Bank on The Mall both close at noon on Wednesday, but Standard Chartered remains open until 3 pm.

Cash transfers should be directed to the Barclay House branch of Barclays Bank.

Post & Telecommunications The GPO on The Mall is open from 8.15 am to 1 pm and 2 to 4 pm Monday to Friday, and from 8.30 to 11.30 am on Saturday. Expect queues and generally lethargic service at any time of day.

There are phones outside the post office and the National Museum. For overseas calls, go to Botswana Telecom on Khama Cres; overseas calls average US$3.70 per minute. You can book calls to anywhere in the world, but allow plenty of time. The office is open Monday to Friday from 9.15 am to 1 pm and 2.15 to 4.30 pm and on Saturday from 8.15 to 11.30 am. No reverse charge calls are accepted.

To send or receive faxes, go to the Copy Shop (fax 359922), on the second floor of Hardware House, beside the Capitol Cinema on The Mall. Tell fax correspondents to mark faxes clearly with your name, as well as the name and telephone number of your accommodation.

Visa Extensions The Department of Immigration (☎ 374545), near the corner of State Dr and Khama Cres, handles visa extensions and enquiries.

Travel Agencies There are several travel agencies on The Mall, all about equally useful. The American Express representative is Manica Travel Services (☎ 352021; fax 305552) in Botsalano (Debswana) House.

Bookshops The Botswana Book Centre on The Mall is one of the continent's best-stocked bookshops. Of comparable quality is Botsalo Books in the Kagiso Centre (part of Broadhurst North Mall). Botsalo offer back issues of *Botswana Notes and Records*, a scholarly journal dealing with Botswana topics. For new, used or exchange books, see J&B Books beside the Kgotla Restaurant, upstairs at Broadhurst North Mall. Also at Broadhurst is Kingston's, a branch of the well-known Zimbabwean chain. Gift shops in the big hotels sell souvenir books and pulp novels.

If you have transport and have some time in Gaborone, try to find a copy of the booklet *Sites of Historic and Natural Interest in and Around Gaborone*, published by the National Museum in 1978. It describes many rock paintings, caves, abandoned mine workings and ruined villages in the area.

Libraries The University of Botswana library has a Botswana Room with books and periodicals dealing exclusively with Botswana and related topics. The Botswana National Library, just east of The Mall on Independence Ave, is open Monday to Friday from 9 am to 6 pm and on Saturday from 9 am to noon. On the same premises is a reference room with Botswana-related publications. Researchers of Botswana topics should try the National Museum library.

The British High Commission on The Mall has a comfortable reading room with British periodicals. At the American Library, also on The Mall, you can read the latest editions of *Time* and *Newsweek* and other US periodicals and newspapers. Alliance Francaise (☎ 351650), on Independence Ave near The Mall, screens French films and language courses and has a library of French-language books and periodicals.

Maps The maps in this book provide enough information for a casual visit, but several other publications are available. B&T Directories (☎ 371444, fax 373462), PO Box 1549, Gaborone, publishes a good overall town plan of Gaborone and its inner suburbs, complete with insets of main shopping centres. It comes in the US$3 Botswana Map Pack, which includes a map of the country and street plans of all large cities and towns.

Another excellent map, the *Gaborone City Centre Street Map*, is published by *Tru-Ads & Promotions*, but it's overpriced at US$5.

The 1:1,750,000 map *Republic of Botswana* (Macmillan UK) contains several good inset maps and includes a good map of The Mall area of Gaborone.

Some editions of the *Botswana Mini-Map*, published by Map Studio in South Africa, contain inset city plans of Gaborone. They're available at bookshops and hotel gift shops.

The Department of Surveys & Lands (☎ 352704), at the corner of Station Rd and the old Lobatse road, publishes a large-scale city plan in several sheets. It sells for US$4 per sheet, but unless you're surveying for a new building site, it's too bulky and contains more detail than you probably want or need.

Dangers & Annoyances The BDF Airport, which is marked on some old maps as Gaborone Airport, should be given a very wide berth. After dark, even to drive down Notwane Rd is risky. (See Dangers & Annoyances in the Botswana Facts for the Visitor chapter.)

Left Luggage There's a left-luggage service at the railway station but it's open at rather inconvenient hours: 8 am to 1 pm and 2 to 4 pm, on weekdays only. If you may need to pick up your things at any other times, think twice before depositing them.

Laundry You'll find automatic washing machines at Kofifi Laundrette on Allison Cres near the showgrounds. Drycleaning services are available beside Maru-a-Pula (No Mathatha) Shopping Centre in South Broadhurst. All the hotels also offer laundry services.

BOTSWANA

Film Although film is readily available in Gaborone, it's expensive and you'd be lucky to find a roll of good slide film. There's a one hour photo-processing service at Photolab on The Mall, but its quality varies.

Camping Equipment The best place for camping equipment, including butane cartridges, is Woolworths – unlike any Woolworths you've ever seen – in the Broadhurst Industrial Estate. A more conveniently located option is the appropriately named Explosions guns and ammo shop in the African Mall. Gaborone Hardware on The Mall also sells outdoor supplies.

Emergency Services The Princess Marina Hospital (☎ 353221), on North Ring Rd at Hospital Way two blocks east of The Mall, is equipped to handle standard medical treatments and emergencies. For anything serious, however, you'll probably have to go to Johannesburg.

The police (☎ 351161) are based on Botswana Rd opposite the Cresta President Hotel.

National Museum & Art Gallery

The museum complex in Gaborone, with its stuffed wildlife and cultural displays, is good for a morning looking at examples of Botswana's past and present. The displays of San crafts, material culture and hunting techniques thoroughly cover the desert dwellers and other ethnographic displays provide background on Botswana's diverse cultural groups. The desultory junk yard spreading through the museum grounds isn't the result of poor cleanup policies; it's intended to exhibit some of colonial Bechuanaland's early technology.

The small National Gallery is a repository for both traditional and modern African and European art. Most of the African art on display originates outside Botswana (a brilliant work is *Cops & Robbers* by Zimbabwean artist Obert Sithole), but some San artwork, revolving around the ostrich egg, is also given a place of honour. Besides the permanent collection, visiting exhibitions are staged and the museum also holds the annual Botswana baskets competition, for which entries are submitted from around the country.

The complex is on Independence Ave just north-east of The Mall. The museums are open Tuesday to Friday from 9 am to 6 pm, and on weekends and holidays (except Easter weekend, Christmas and Boxing Day) from 9 am to 5 pm. Admission is free. The museum shop sells artwork, crafts and books and is open Tuesday to Friday from 9 am to 4.30 pm. Occasional lectures and presentations are given at the museum lecture hall. The *Pitse-ya-Naga* ('zebra'), the prominent zebra-striped museum vehicle, transports museum exhibits for display in small villages around Botswana.

Orapa House

If you're spending awhile in Gaborone and don't mind lots of security-related red tape, muster a group of people and take a tour of Debswana's Orapa House at the southern end of Khama Cres. This is Botswana's Fort Knox, from where the country's diamond wealth is stored, sorted and exported.

Gaborone Game Reserve

On 1 March 1988, the Gaborone Game Reserve was opened to give the Gaborone public the opportunity to view Botswana's wildlife in a natural setting, just one km east of Broadhurst. Access is by vehicle only. The park offers mainly a variety of antelopes, although there's also a well-guarded male white rhino in a separate enclosure. Negotiations are currently underway with the Republic of South Africa to find a mate for this lonely soul.

The Reserve is open from 6.30 am to 6.30 pm daily and costs US$3.70 per person and US$2 per vehicle. Access is from Limpopo Dr; turn east on the back road just south of the Segoditshane River.

Activities

If you want to play cowboy in the scrubby bush north-west of Gaborone, Arne's Horse Safaris offers day trips and longer camping

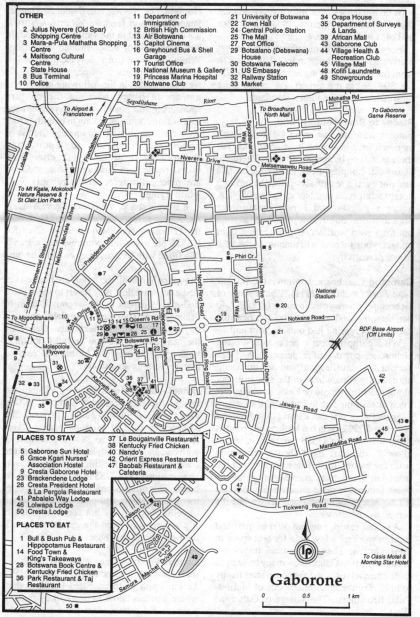

OTHER
2 Julius Nyerere (Old Spar) Shopping Centre
3 Mara-a-Pula Mathatha Shopping Centre
4 Maitisong Cultural Centre
7 State House
8 Bus Terminal
10 Police
11 Department of Immigration
12 British High Commission
13 Air Botswana
15 Capitol Cinema
16 Greyhound Bus & Shell Garage
17 Tourist Office
18 National Museum & Gallery
19 Princess Marina Hospital
20 Notwane Club
21 University of Botswana
22 Town Hall
24 Central Police Station
25 The Mall
27 Post Office
29 Botsalano (Debswana) House
30 Botswana Telecom
31 US Embassy
32 Railway Station
33 Market
34 Orapa House
35 Department of Surveys & Lands
39 African Mall
43 Gaborone Club
44 Village Health & Recreation Club
45 Village Mall
48 Kofifi Laundrette
49 Showgrounds

PLACES TO STAY
5 Gaborone Sun Hotel
6 Grace Kgari Nurses' Association Hostel
9 Cresta Gaborone Hotel
23 Brackendene Lodge
26 Cresta President Hotel & La Pergola Restaurant
41 Pabalelo Way Lodge
46 Lolwapa Lodge
50 Cresta Lodge

PLACES TO EAT
1 Bull & Bush Pub & Hippopotamus Restaurant
14 Food Town & King's Takeaways
28 Botswana Book Centre & Kentucky Fried Chicken
36 Park Restaurant & Taj Restaurant
37 Le Bougainville Restaurant
38 Kentucky Fried Chicken
40 Nando's
42 Orient Express Restaurant
47 Baobab Restaurant & Cafeteria

Gaborone

0   0.5   1 km

BOTSWANA

trips on horseback. For information, contact the Travelwise agency (☎ 303244; fax 303245) in Gaborone.

For something more offbeat, you can get a private pilot's licence in less than a month from the Kalahari Flying School (☎ 309775; fax 309776) at the airport. Prices are quite reasonable by international standards.

Places to Stay – bottom end

Finding accommodation in Gaborone isn't as much of a headache as it once was, but there is still no budget alternative. There are no official camping areas, no reliable hostels and not even a reasonably priced dump of a hotel to fall back on. Not even the YWCA accepts guests and foreign volunteer organisations don't accommodate anyone but their own workers. If you're on a tight budget, your success will amount to the sum of your creativity.

Camping The cheapest option is the *St Clair Lion Park* (☎ /fax 372711), 17 km south of Gaborone, where you can camp for US$7.40 per person – and at night you can hear the caged lions roaring just outside your tent.

Wild camping isn't permitted around Gaborone, but if you're desperate and can keep a low profile, you can set up a tent unofficially somewhere in the low hills out along the Molepolole or Lobatse roads; just hitch or take the bus to and from the city.

Sometimes you can camp at the *Mogotel Hotel* (☎ 372228) on the Molepolole road in Mogoditshane for US$8 per person, but to allow it, the staff must secure permission from the owner. It isn't safe to camp out the front, but in the dusty gravel area behind the hotel, security is more effective. The hotel is a long way from Gaborone centre but it's served by minibuses.

As a last resort, you can offer ex-pats and foreign workers a few pula for tent space in their garden. They understand travellers' predicaments in Gaborone – many have been there themselves – and are sometimes happy to help. Try the neighbourhoods of Maru-a-Pula, Broadhurst, The Village or Gaborone West.

Hostels The Norwegian, Swedish, Danish, PeaceCorps and German *Volunteer Hostels* are concentrated in the vicinity of The Mall, but they do not accommodate travellers. While the Peace Corps is typically immovable and accepts no one, other hostels welcome guests in the following order: volunteers in Botswana from the country sponsoring the hostel, volunteers from the sponsoring country working in neighbouring countries, families of volunteers, friends of volunteers, citizens of the sponsoring country, and finally, everyone else. Travellers' chances of finding accommodation are practically zero, so it probably isn't worth trying.

If there's space, the *Grace Kgari Nurses' Association Hostel*, at 2684 Phiri Cres near the Gaborone Sun, will take travellers for US$26 per night single/double, but it's usually filled with live-ins from outside the city.

Sleepers When all the hotels are booked up, desperate travellers may resort to the US$26 2nd-class sleepers in the overnight train to Francistown. They can visit Gaborone one day, Francistown the next, then Gaborone the next day... Once you've left Gaborone, however, you may not be all that excited about returning so quickly!

Hotels A distance out of town, but cheap and erratically accessible by minibus, is the *Mogotel Hotel* (☎ 372228), just off the Molepolole road in Mogoditshane village. Rooms cost US$18.50/28 a single/double, with bed and breakfast, and are just about the cheapest around. 'Resting rooms' (use your imagination) cost US$15 for a couple of hours. This place is now under new management and is clean and pleasant, but women travelling alone may not feel comfortable. It's a long way from the centre, so you'll have to rely on minibuses.

Lodges For a real treat, stay in the chalets at the *Mokolodi Nature Reserve* (☎ 353959), 12 km south of town. Sited beside a dam where animals come to drink, they make a perfect wild retreat from the bustle of the nearby city. Dormitory accommodation at the Mokolodi Environmental Education Centre costs US$12 per person while three/six-bed self-catering chalets rent for US$47/65 on weekdays and US$56/84 at weekends. The acclaimed outdoor restaurant at the reserve headquarters offers an alternative to self-catering. For more information, see under Mokolodi Nature Reserve later in this chapter.

Places to Stay – middle

B&Bs Gaborone's most pleasant recent development is the emergence of a trio of privately-run B & Bs. At *Lolwapa Lodge* (☎ 359061; after 10.30 pm, ☎ 351646), on Maakakgang Close near the Tlokweng Rd roundabout, single/double rooms with shared bath start at US$23/37, including breakfast. For en suite facilities, you'll pay US$34/52.

Pabelelo Way Lodge (☎ 351682) at Plot 838, Pabelelo Way near the African Mall is more formally organised and charges US$28/44.50 a single/double. To book, either phone or write to Pabelelo Way Lodge, PO Box 20661, Gaborone.

The cosy *Brackendene Lodge* (☎ /fax 312886), just three minutes' walk from The Mall, has single/double rooms with shared bath starting at US$30/37, including breakfast. Rooms with bath are US$34/40 and family lodges accommodating one or two children cost US$110. Each additional child (up to a total of four) costs an extra US$10. Meals are available on request. To book by post, write to Brackendene Lodge, PO Box 621, Gaborone.

Hotels Out on Tlokweng Rd, seven km from town, is the seedy *Morning Star Hotel* (☎ 352301; fax 356844). Indicative of the hotel's general disposition, the reception area is secured in a wire cage. Singles/doubles cost US$30/34, breakfast is US$6 and lunch or dinner is US$8. There's no public transport from the centre, but plenty of traffic makes hitching relatively easy.

Considerably better – but unfortunately sliding downhill – is the *Oasis Motel* (☎ 356396; fax 312968), also in Tlokweng, with singles/doubles for US$45/58 and chalets for US$58/67. However, there's no public transport.

Quite a bit nicer is the *Cresta Gaborone* (☎ 375200, fax 375201) north of the railway station. It fills the gap left by the historic but recently demolished Gaborone Hotel. In addition to a great bar and live music at weekends, it offers snacks and takeaway meals. Rooms with bath and TV cost US$43/56 for singles/doubles. This place is understandably popular so it's wise to pre-book. The central reservations number is ☎ 312431, fax 375376.

Places to Stay – top end

Considerably more expensive than it's companion hotel, the Cresta Gaborone, is *Cresta Lodge* (☎ 375375; fax 375376) on the south side of Samora Machel Dr near the old Lobatse road. Singles/doubles cost US$58/71; an English/continental breakfast is an additional US$8/6.50.

Once known for snobbishness, the *Gaborone Sun* (☎ 351111; fax 302555) on Nyerere Dr has happily been humbled by competition in its market range. It's frequently booked up by business travellers and residents awaiting permanent accommodation in Gaborone. In the old wing, singles/doubles cost US$76/99, while in the newer wing they're called 'luxury' rooms and cost US$90/115. An English/continental breakfast is an additional US$10/7. For other meals, both the Savuti Grill and Giovanni's Restaurant are frightfully expensive. If you're in town for a while, an annual membership fee of about US$32 allows access to the swimming pool and squash and tennis courts.

Right on The Mall, the *Cresta President* (☎ 353631, fax 351840) offers friendly, central accommodation. Standard single/double rooms cost US$63/82; executive suites are US$75/89. A buffet English/continental breakfast costs an additional US$8/6. The attached La Pergola terrace restaurant overlooking The Mall offers healthy European-style cuisine, including vegetable-rich

BOTSWANA

lunches, cappuccino and European cakes and pastries.

The immense *Sheraton Hotel* (☎ 312999; fax 312989), between Gaborone West and Mogoditshane, offers five-star international standards at surprisingly reasonable rates. For standard single/double rooms, they charge US$76/89; deluxe rooms are US$89/99.

Places to Eat
Snacks & Lunches For a cheap food fix, try the *Food Town* dining hall on The Mall, which is very popular with lunchtime crowds. A filling and adequate dose of stew or mealies and relish costs just US$1.50. Alternatively, try the market near the railway station for such offbeat lunch specialties as pickled spinach, goat, mopane worms or bojalwa (sorghum beer). Burgers, chips, snacks and the like are found at *King's Takeaways* on The Mall. It's a favourite office-workers' lunch spot so expect long queues at midday.

For familiar chicken snacks, you'll find *Kentucky Fried Chicken* outlets on The Mall and in the African Mall; lunches with chicken, mashed potatoes and coleslaw cost around US$3. Americans who prefer the Northern way of doing things may prefer *Chicago Fried Chicken*, with two locations. Also competing with the Colonel is *Nando's*, in the African Mall, specialising in Portuguese-style peri-peri chicken. Yet another quick chicken chain is *Roosters*, with outlets in the Kagiso Centre at Broadhurst North Mall and on the Lobatse road.

At No Mathatha Shopping Centre, the *Gourmet 2000 Dial-a-Meal* (☎ 313474) does walk-in or phone-in takeaway orders for pizza, burgers, pies and sweets from 11 am to 9 pm weekdays and until 10 pm on Friday and Saturday nights.

At the Cresta President Hotel, *La Pergola* on the terrace serves such wonderful lunch-time concoctions as spinach quiche, cream of asparagus soup and vegetable curries. At other times, you can linger over a rich and frothy cappuccino and crème éclairs while surveying the passing Mall scene below. In

the evenings, they do a variety of steak specials for a bargain US$5.

For an unexpected pleasure and an exhaustive menu of sweets and vegetarian options, try the *Kgotla* (☎ 356091) in the Broadhurst North Mall. It's open from 9 am to 9 pm daily. The salads, desserts, cappuccino and iced coffee are particularly appealing.

For tempting snacks, try one of Gaborone's two speciality bakeries. *Hot & Crusty* in Broadhurst North Mall sells great personal-size pizzas for US$2 as well as a variety of breads and sweets. *Sugar & Spicy* in the Old Spar Shopping Centre offers tarts, meat pies, pastries, cakes, gateaux, scones, biscuits, rolls and an assortment of other gooey and delectable sweets.

Dinners In the Oasis Motel is the up-market *Reflections* (☎ 356396) which features a wide choice of seafood. Your meal will be rounded off with a free glass of sherry and chocolates. Book in advance for this popular dinner spot.

The African Mall has several good options. Most popular is the folksy *Park Restaurant* (☎ 351456), which serves pub meals and full dinners, including fabulous pizzas, steak, chicken, crêpes, ribs, salads and other delights. It's open seven days a week from 11.30 am to 2.30 pm and 6 to 10.30 pm. The rebel theme is developed by a large Confederate flag, motorbike posters and a neon legend over the bar proclaiming 'Harley's – a Botswana Tradition'. There's live music on Friday and Saturday nights and the billiards table will keep you busy on other evenings.

Next door is the *Taj* (☎ 313569) which dishes up Indian, Mauritian and continental cuisine and excellent salads. Their buffet lunch, which costs US$8, is served seven days a week. The nearby *Mandarin* (☎ 375038) serves Chinese, Indian and Mauritian dishes. It's open daily and the 'executive lunch buffet' is a bargain at US$8. In the back streets near the African Mall is the Swiss-owned *Le Bougainville* (☎ 356693), an expensive haunt specialising in French and continental cuisine. On Wednesdays, the speciality is fresh mussels from South Africa.

Da Alfredo (☎ 313604) at Broadhurst North Mall specialises in seafood and Italian cuisine. It's open every day for lunch and dinner, and also does takeaways. The *Moghul* (☎ 375246), in the Julius Nyerere (Old Spar) Shopping Centre serves Indian and Pakistani fare; their popular Indian buffet lunch costs US$8. The well-acclaimed *Orient Express* (☎ 356287) in The Village is a pleasant and exclusive Chinese restaurant. In the Maru-a-Pula (No Mathatha) Shopping Centre is the popular *China Restaurant* (☎ 357254), open for lunch from noon to 2 pm and dinner from 6.30 to 11 pm.

Difficult to reach but a great choice for breakfast, lunch or dinner is the *Baobab Restaurant & Cafeteria* (☎ 352488), near the corner of Tlokweng Rd and Mobutu Dr, in the BNPC industrial complex. The cafeteria offers buffet-style meals for one price, specialising in traditional Tswana dishes, while the restaurant serves a reasonably priced range of salads, grills, pasta and game dishes. The entrance is on a back street off Independence Ave. It's open every day from 6.30 am until late.

If you prefer a British twist or a nice patio meal, visit the *Bull & Bush Pub* (☎ 375070) off Nelson Mandela Dr; look for the west-pointing sign reading 'Police Housing Bull & Bush'. Meals cost from US$7 to US$10 and on Thursday nights, they serve all-you-can-eat pizza. The Italian-oriented *Hippopotamus*, which is attached to the Bull & Bush, serves full dinners. Alternative European options include the *Swiss Chalet* (☎ 312247) on Tlokweng Rd, which serves both Swiss and Italian dishes, and *O Cheff* (☎ 308354), a Portuguese restaurant on Kenneth Kaunda Rd.

The main hotels all have formal dining rooms and more casual grill restaurants. *Chatters* (☎ 313234) at the Cresta Lodge is particularly recommended. The more expensive *Giovanni's* (☎ 351111) at the Gaborone Sun dishes up live entertainment along with their Italian and international fare. They cater mainly to business travellers on expense accounts or live-ins with government or private meal subsidies. In most hotel restaurants, menus are typically heavy on the beef dishes.

The outdoor restaurant at the *St Clair Lion Park* is open from 4 pm until late and serves mainly US and British cuisine, as well as impala venison and vegetarian options. Even better is the wonderful outdoor restaurant and bar at the *Mokolodi Nature Reserve* (☎ 353959). Game meat is sometimes available. In the evenings, diners don't pay admission to the reserve.

Self-Catering Gaborone doesn't have a traditional open market, but you will find a spreading expanse of impromptu stalls around the railway station and east of the Broadhurst North Mall. The best stocked supermarkets are the *Spar Markets* at the Julius Nyerere (Old Spar) Shopping Centre and the Broadhurst North Mall. Other options include the *Fairways* in the Station House Shopping Centre near the railway station, the *Corner Market* on The Mall and *Woolworths Market* at the Metro Shopping Centre.

At *Tony's* in the African Mall you can stock up on fruit and cheap fresh vegies for bargain prices, but you will need to muster a group to share them with; 50 oranges cost only US$2.50. Also in the African Mall is the cheapest butchery, the *Gaborone Meat Centre*, where you will also find Oriental groceries.

Entertainment
Theatre & Cinema The 450-seat theatre in the Maitisong Cultural Centre (☎ 371809) at Maru-a-Pula (Rain Cloud) Secondary School was opened in 1987 as a venue for cultural events. All productions are well attended, so book in advance. A schedule of coming events is posted on a bulletin board outside the centre, and listed in the *Botswana Advertiser*, published on Friday. All the more serious local theatre groups, including some excellent new African troupes, perform exclusively at Maitisong and every March,

BOTSWANA

they hold the fabulous nine-day Maitisong Performing Arts Festival. If you're in Gaborone at the time, don't miss it.

The local amateur troupe Capital Players (☎ 372120) is also good fun. Performances are held at the Memorable Order of Tin Hats (MOTHS) Hall just off the Molepolole road, although they also participate in the Maitisong Performing Arts Festival. For information on productions, check the *Botswana Advertiser* or write to Capital Players, PO Box 65, Gaborone.

Gaborone's only cinema, the Capitol on The Mall, provides predominantly escapist US entertainment and the Gaborone Film Society and Alliance Francaise frequently screen classic films. Refer to the *Botswana Advertiser* for information.

Casino The Gaborone Sun Hotel hosts Botswana's only casino, which boasts slots, blackjack and roulette. The games are open Monday to Friday from 7 pm until late and on weekends and public holidays (except Christmas and Good Friday) from 4 pm until closing, around 3 am or later. The slot machines open daily from 10 am to closing. You must be at least 18 years of age to gamble in Botswana.

Discos & Nightclubs A newish live music venue is the Diamond Club at the Oasis Motel in Tlokweng, which emphasises soul music. Their promotional flyer proclaims 'You have been there in your dreams – Now go there in reality. U ain't gonna miss out. Be there.' Are you convinced?

A long-standing hit with the more affluent sector of Gaborone youth is the popular Night Shift in the Broadhurst North Mall. The bar is upstairs and the rather trendy disco rocks below.

For African disco music and dancing, try the well-attended Platform beside the Casino in the Gaborone Sun Hotel. A very popular local dance spot is the Wadiba Night Club in Mogoditshane, beyond the BDF base. They specialise in Zaïrois kwasa-kwasa music. The best time to attend (believe it or not) is Sunday afternoon. Also in Mogoditshane is

the Club W, with a disco on Saturday nights. Admission is US$3.70.

In town, a strong favourite is Sinatra's (formerly known as Visions and Club 585) in the Maru-a-Pula (No Mathatha) Shopping Centre. They charge US$5.50 admission and smart dress is required. The disco operates from Thursday to Sunday nights. On Sunday, the theme is jazz.

Homesick British may appreciate the popular Bull & Bush Pub, which lolls in the boondocks off Nelson Mandela Dr. There's a cover charge on weekends. For good ol' boys and girls, Harley's bar at the Park Restaurant perfectly imitates a rebel watering hole in the USA, complete with Budweiser and Harley-Davidson decor.

Folk music performances are staged at 7.30 pm on the first Saturday of the month at the Gaborone Club on Okwa Rd in the Village.

Sports The club scene carries over into the athletic end of the spectrum, with clubs devoted to tennis, cycling, running, golf, squash, cricket, riding, yachting and so on. The best established all-purpose sports centre, The Gaborone Club (☎ 356333), and the Village Health & Recreation Club (☎ 300990), both in The Village, feature swimming, tennis, squash, rugby and bowls. Membership is required if you're living in Gaborone, but visitors are welcome if invited by a member.

The Gaborone Sun allows the use of its pool and squash and tennis courts for US$75 annually. The Notwane Club (☎ 352399) and the Gaborone Squash Racquets Centre (☎ 314620), both near the National Stadium on Notwane Rd, sell annual memberships for around US$100. Information about other participatory sports clubs is published weekly in the *Botswana Advertiser* and the *Consumer Info Gaborone*.

Things to Buy
The Botswanacraft Marketing Company (☎ 312471, fax 313189) on The Mall deals in a selection of material arts and crafts from all over the country. Among the offerings are

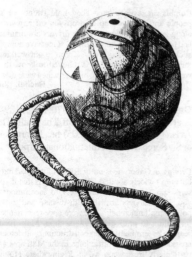

Drinking vessel and necklace made from
ostrich egg-shell, used by early San

San pouches, hunting bows and jewellery, as
well as both Ngamiland and Shashe baskets,
wooden animal carvings from the Francistown area, weavings from Odi, silkscreen
from Mochudi and pottery from the
Gaborone hinterlands. Although many of the
items on offer may be cheaper at the point of
origin, Botswanacraft does provide a
measure of quality control.

At Mokolodi Crafts, 12 km south of
Gaborone along the Lobatse road then three
km east, you'll find a selection of original
potato-printed fabrics, wall hangings,
ceramic and carved bone jewellery and
children's toys. It's open Monday to Saturday from 8 am to 4 pm.

The National Museum is also a good place
to find inexpensive Botswana baskets. For
other options, see under Gabane, Mochudi,
Odi and Thamaga in the Around Gaborone
section later in this chapter.

Getting There & Away
Air Air Botswana, British Airways, Zambia
Airways, Air Zimbabwe, Air Namibia, Air
Malawi, Air Tanzania, Kenya Airways and

South African Airways all serve Gaborone
from abroad, and Air Botswana operates
scheduled domestic flights to and from
Kasane, Maun and Francistown. The Sir
Seretse Khama International Airport is 14
km from the centre. The more central airport,
marked on older maps as Gaborone Airport,
belongs to the Botswana Defence Force and
should be given a wide berth.

Bus Intercity buses, as well as minibuses to
outlying villages, arrive and depart from the
new bus terminal over the Molepolole flyover from the town centre. Most buses
simply leave when full – few buses are
scheduled – so it's wise to arrive at the terminal in the morning. Minibuses to
Johannesburg leave when full from the main
terminal and cost US$15 per person. To be
assured of a departure, arrive at the terminal
as early in the morning as possible.

Greyhound's service from Gaborone to
Johannesburg (US$24 one way) runs at 8 am
on Monday, Friday and Saturday from the
Kudu Shell Garage on Queen's Rd. For more
international information, refer to the
Botswana Getting There & Away chapter.

The larger domestic buses plying the
tarred highways operate according to tentative timetables. Service is available
(although not always directly or when you'd
like to go) to Lobatse, Ramatlhabama,
Mahalapye, Palapye, Serowe, Selebi-
Phikwe, Francistown, Nata, Kasane and
Maun, with semi-reliable connections to
Shakawe. All bus trips to the north require
an overnight stop in Francistown. From
Gaborone to Francistown costs US$10 each
way. Mochudi is served more regularly and
the trip costs just US$1.50.

Train Gaborone has daily rail connections to
and from Bulawayo, Francistown and
Lobatse. The northbound train departs at 9
pm and you can choose between 1st, 2nd or
economy classes; 1st and 2nd class both have
sleepers. The fare to Bulawayo is US$30/45
in 1st/2nd class and US$10 in economy. To
Lobatse, there's only economy class, which

BOTSWANA

costs just US$1.50. Phone Botswana Railways (☎ 351401) for current information.

The big hotels send minibuses to the station to pick up arriving guests, so when you're pre-booking, remember to specify that you'll be arriving by train and would like to be met.

Hitching If you want to hitch to Francistown, take the Broadhurst 4 Combi and ask the driver to drop you at the standard hitching spot at the north end of town. There's no need to wave down vehicles – anyone who has space will stop for passengers. Expect to pay around US$6 per person.

Getting Around

Gaborone's local public transport system is scarcely adequate for the city's growing population and people have a real battle making their way between home and work.

To/From the Airport The only reliable transport between the airport and town are the courtesy minibuses operated by the top-end hotels for their guests. If there's space, non-guests can sometimes talk the driver into a lift, but expect to tip at least several pula. Bizarrely, taxis only rarely turn up at the airport, so they can scarcely be considered an option. If you do connect with a taxi, you'll pay anywhere from US$3 to US$12 per person for the 14-km trip to the centre. Alternatively, walk down the road a few hundred metres and try hitching a lift.

Minibus The crowded white minibuses, or combis, recognisable by their blue number plates, circulate along set routes and cost US$0.25 (70t). The standard city circuit passes all the major shopping centres. Minibuses to surrounding villages depart from the main bus terminal, but follow no real schedule; the best sources of information are the drivers or other prospective passengers.

Combis are everywhere. They hold twenty or so people and pick you up or drop you off anywhere along a set route. However, the drivers are maniacs and pull over anywhere, anytime – some have bumper stickers warning you of this. If you're out walking, they will honk at you. I was relieved to know they weren't flirting – just letting me know they were there.

Rachel, USA

Car Holiday Car Hire (☎ 353970; fax 314894) is at 168 Queen's Rd, just off The Mall. The Avis (☎ 313093; fax 312205) headquarters is at Sir Seretse Khama International Airport.

Driving in Gaborone is nutty. Rules of the road exist but aren't widely applied. The best thing is that if you screw up, other drivers are likely to accommodate you. Roundabouts are rife with dispute and traffic police aren't much help – we were once reprimanded for failing to gridlock an intersection. Main roads seem to be terminally under construction, and detours are poorly planned. Traffic jams in the Mall area are particularly frustrating; avoid driving there around lunchtime and after work. The Francistown and Lobatse roads are impenetrable on Fridays.

Rachel, USA

Taxi Although the public transport minibuses in Gaborone are known as 'taxis', Gaborone has very few conventional taxis (called 'special taxis'), so it's hardly worth searching for one. Not even the big hotels can easily get you a taxi. If you're intent on searching, taxis are recognisable by their blue number plates. Fares are left up to the whims of the drivers. It's better to just resign yourself to walking, using the minibuses, hiring a vehicle or hitching.

Around Gaborone

Once you've exhausted the slim pickings in town, head for the desert hinterlands, where there are several natural, historical and cultural attractions to keep you occupied.

MOCHUDI

The most interesting village in south-eastern Botswana, Mochudi was first settled by the Kwena in the mid-1500s, as evidenced by a

BOTSWANA

few remaining stone walls in the surrounding hills. In 1871 it was settled by the Kgatla people, who had been forced from their lands by northward-trekking Boers.

Phuthadikobo Museum

The Cape Dutch-style Phuthadikobo Museum, established in 1976, is one of Botswana's best, focusing on the history of Mochudi in particular and the Kgatla people in general. It sits atop sacred Phuthadikobo Hill, which was a ceremonial site and the domain of Kwanyape, the rain-making Gaboon viper. The 1936 Case tractor at the foot of the hill was once owned by Chief Isang Pilane; other vintage debris scattered about dates to the same decade.

The museum is housed in the first secondary school in Botswana, the Mochudi National School, which was founded in 1921 by Isang Pilane. All the townspeople, weary of the sectarian education provided by the Dutch Reformed Mission School, participated in its construction by contributing money or labour to the project. The museum leaflet states that all materials, including the 300,000 bricks used in the construction, were either hand-made in the village or paid for by Mochudi citizens and carried up the hill 'by means of head and hand'. The building was finally completed and the school opened in 1923.

The museum is open Monday to Friday from 8 am to 5 pm and on weekends from 2 to 5 pm. Admission is free but donations are gratefully accepted. During museum hours on weekdays, a screen-printing workshop operates in the courtyard. It was founded in 1980 by a German volunteer as a source of dressmaking fabric for local women and has now been turned into a successful commercial enterprise producing silkscreened curtains, wall hangings and clothing.

Other Sites

Once you've seen the museum, it's worth an hour or two appreciating the variety of designs in the town's mud-walled architecture. Particularly unusual are the odd double-walled rondavels, the *sefala* huts

(small granaries), and the several homes and walls decorated in dark-toned indigenous patterns. Also, look under eaves for the clay storage pots that are a Mochudi trademark.

At the foot of the museum hill is the village *kgotla*, a covered open-walled platform structure used as a meeting house and village court. If you're lucky enough to encounter a meeting in session, you're welcome to watch the proceedings, but visitors are discouraged from entering the structure.

Opposite the kgotla is the royal kraal, the burial site of Chief Lentswe Pilane I, who died in 1924 at the age of 89, and Chief Molefi Kgamanyane Pilane, who died in 1958. A number of other Kgatla chiefs are buried in the Royal graveyard beside the Dutch Reformed Mission church.

If you wish to learn even more about Mochudi, pick up a copy of the booklet *Guide to Mochudi*, produced and published by the Phuthadikobo Museum. For further information on the Kgatla, the book *A History of the Bakgata-Bagakgafêla* by I Schapera is sold for US$1.50 at the museum gift shop.

Places to Stay & Eat

There's no accommodation in Mochudi itself, but the *Sedibelo Hotel* on the Francistown road in Pilane, which has seen better days, offers very basic mid-range accommodation just six km away. Single or double rooms cost US$32. In the village are several basic restaurants: the *Good Hope*, the *Road & Rail* and the *Ranko*.

Getting There & Away

Buses to Mochudi depart from Gaborone when full, at least six or seven times daily, or you can take any northbound bus, get off at Pilane and hitch the remaining six km to Mochudi village. Alternatively, on weekdays, there's a commuter train to Pilane, departing from Gaborone at 5 am and 5.45 pm, and leaving Pilane at 6.30 am and 6.30 pm. On Saturday, it runs at 5 am southbound and 6.30 am northbound. The fare is US$0.30 each way.

BOTSWANA

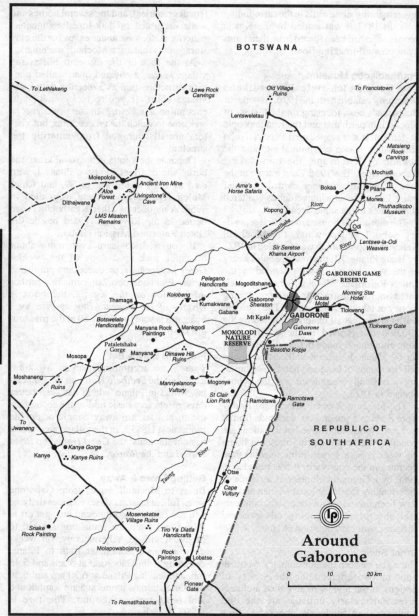

Around Gaborone

With your own vehicle, follow the Francistown road 35 km north of Gaborone and turn east at Pilane. After six km, turn left at the T-junction and then right just before the hospital into the historic centre of the village. The road ends with the kraal on your left and the *kgotla* on your right. From there, a track winds up Phuthadikobo Hill to the museum on its summit.

AROUND MOCHUDI
Matsieng Rock Carvings
Matsieng, a hole containing some footprint rock carvings, is believed by the Tswana to be a creation site. The footprints on the walls belonged to early humans who marched out of the hole followed by both wild and domestic animals. Matsieng lies about 700 metres east of the highway, and is accessible on a rough track which turns off eight km north of Pilane and three km north of the Lentswelatau turn-off.

ODI
The small village of Odi is best known for the Lentswe-la-Odi (Hills of Odi) weavers (☎ 312368). The cooperative was established in 1973 by Swedes Ulla and Peter Gowenius in an attempt to provide the village with an economic base. It has grown into Botswana's most renowned such cooperative and has been internationally acclaimed.

The wool, hand-spun and dyed over an open fire, is woven into spontaneous patterns invented by the individual artists. Most of these depict African wildlife and aspects of rural life in Botswana. The richly coloured products include handbags, table mats, bed covers, hats, jackets, tapestries and table-cloths which are all available at the workshop. They'll even weave custom pieces based on individual pictures, drawings or stories. The tapestries, oddly enough, are sold by the square yard, with apparently no judgments made about their comparative aesthetic values. Unfortunately, quality has apparently slipped in recent years, but that could change so it's still worth a visit.

The workshop is open to visitors from 8 am to 4 pm weekdays and 2 to 4.30 pm on Sunday. Coffee, tea, biscuits and *vetkoek* are served at the shop.

Getting There & Away
Follow the Francistown road 18 km north from Gaborone and turn east at the Odi sign post. From there it's five km to the railway line and the bridge over the Notwane River. The road takes a sharp left turn at the 'two hills of Odi', from where it's about 1500 metres through the village to the weaving cooperative.

By public transport, take any northbound bus or minibus from Gaborone and get off at the Odi turn-off. From there, either walk or hitch the remaining distance into the village.

WEST OF GABORONE
Gabane
The village of Gabane lies 12 km south-west of Mogoditshane, just a short drive from Gaborone. Its claim to fame is the renowned Pelegano Pottery, where you can buy a variety of hand-painted ceramics, some of which are lovely original creations. Popular items include masks, finely decorated bowls and charming animal figurines.

Manyana
With a vehicle, you can visit Manyana village, south-west of Gaborone, with some Zimbabwe-style rock paintings, a rarity in south-eastern Botswana. About 500 metres north of the village, on the road west of the river, is an eight-metre-high rock face. Opposite an overhang at its southern extreme are paintings of three giraffes, an elephant and several antelopes.

Molepolole
The tongue-twisting name of this hillside village (MO-lay-po-LO-lay), 52 km north-west of Gaborone, means 'Let him cancel it'. It's thought to be derived from the utterance of the chief in response to a spell placed upon the land where the village now stands. It was first inhabited by the Kgwatleng tribe in the 1500s, but they were displaced by the Kwena who stayed for nearly 100 years before abandoning it. A Kwena group returned to

Molepolole in the mid-1800s and have occupied the site ever since.

When you're there, have a look at the Scottish Livingstone Hospital, where students of two local schools have taken to covering the walls with painted murals.

Places to Stay & Eat Molepolole's only hotel is the *Mafenya-Tlala* (☎ 320394), which offers thatched chalet accommodation with private bath. In the hotel restaurant, you can opt for sit-down service or takeaways. There's also a bottle shop and a disco operates on weekends.

Getting There & Away From Gaborone, minibuses leave for Molepolole when full. In your own vehicle, take the Molepolole flyover across the railroad tracks and travel 52 km along the tarred highway to the village.

Around Molepolole

If you have lots of energy or a sturdy vehicle, the Molepolole area is good for a day of exploration. In the village itself, note the stone-walled enclosures constructed by the Kwena to divide the settlement into family groups.

One km west of the Scottish-run Livingstone Hospital in the village is a large and eerie forest of Marloth aloes *(Aloe marlothii)*. Legend has it that in 1850, the Boers trekked into Molepolole to punish Chief Sechele of the Kwena for befriending David Livingstone. Approaching stealthily on a dark night, they encountered the extraneous aloes and fled in fear, having mistaken them for ranks of Kwena warriors!

Six km along the Lethlakeng road from Molepolole, in the gullies immediately north-west of the airstrip, are large deposits of silica asbestos which resembles petrified wood. The site is officially protected and collecting of stones is forbidden.

From two to six km south of Molepolole, west of the road towards Thamaga, lies a trio of interesting sites. The first is an ancient trench excavation where the Kwena once mined iron. Two km beyond it is the entrance

to a hillside cave which David Livingstone visited despite a Kwena shaman's warning that to do so would bring about a speedy death. His survival supposedly prompted Chief Sechele's conversion to Christianity.

One km south of the cave is the ruin of the LMS mission which operated from 1866 to 1884 under Reverend Roger Price and his wife, Elizabeth, who was a daughter of Robert Moffat. West of the stream, below the ruin, is a high rock face from which the Kwena flung unauthorised witches and wizards.

Lowe Rock Carvings

You'll need a 4WD vehicle to visit the Lowe rock carvings, which depict some animal and human tracks as well as crude bovine figures. To get there, follow the Botlhapatlou track about 30 km north of Molepolole, turn right onto a side track and proceed five km to Kopong. From there, you must walk the remaining couple of km to Lowe.

Thamaga

Thamaga is best known as the home of Thamaga Pottery Workshop, which produces and sells original – if a bit kitsch – ceramic work, including dishes, ashtrays and other practical items. At Botswelelo Handicrafts, you can buy folding kgotla chairs; they're ornately carved from wood and the seats are woven from leather thongs. They're not too heavy and are relatively portable.

Fifteen km from Thamaga, off the road from Gaborone, is the ruin of Kolobeng, once the home and mission of David Livingstone in the 1840s. It was actually Botswana's first European-style settlement, and the site of the country's first Christian church. The only remnants are the decaying floor of Livingstone's home and several graves, including that of Livingstone's daughter. A museum is planned for the site.

THE LOBATSE ROAD
Mt Kgale & Basutho Kopje

The 'sleeping giant' peak overlooking Gaborone is easily climbed and affords the capital's best view. To get there, take any

Lobatse bus to the Kgale siding or hitch out along the new Lobatse road eight km from town to the satellite dish. Just a couple of hundred metres towards town, opposite the dish, is a concrete stile over a fence. Cross it, turn left, and follow the fence until it enters a shallow gully. From there a set of white-washed stones lead the way up the hillside to the summit.

Immediately east of the railway line, nine km south of Gaborone, lies Basotho Kopje, which was the site of a campaign of the Boer War in February 1900. The railway bridge was destroyed in the skirmish, and soon thereafter, a fortress of sorts was established by Rhodesian forces to protect the repaired bridge from further sabotage. Some graves and part of a stone wall are still visible. North of the hill is the original river ford, which was established by the Voortrekkers' oxen-drawn wagons in the 1830s.

Gaborone Dam

The Gaborone Dam, on the Notwane River, provides the capital's water supply and serves as a marginal recreational site. From the prominent satellite dish on the new Lobatse road, just south of Gaborone, it's three km down the old Lobatse road to the lake. Follow the tarred road until you reach a barricade and walk from there to where the road disappears beneath the water (this should explain the old/new Lobatse road dichotomy). There's good birdwatching here amid the drowned trees and bushes but swimming is not permitted. Watch out for crocodiles.

You'll need permission from the Water Utilities Corporation, which is on Luthuli Rd just south of the Khama Cres roundabout near the Gaborone railway station in order to access the dam wall. To reach the dam wall, head down Mobutu Dr and turn left at the Sanitas Nursery sign just north of the Cresta Lodge. The dam wall is five km along that road.

Mokolodi Nature Reserve

A rewarding wildlife excursion is to the 3000-hectare Mokolodi Nature Reserve

(☎ 353959; fax 313973), an educational centre 12 km south of Gaborone. Its main mission is wildlife education, with the secondary purposes of establishing nature reserves in south-eastern Botswana and protecting the country's endangered species. It also operates as a research facility, a breeding centre for rare and endangered species and a sanctuary for orphaned, injured or confiscated birds and animals.

Mokolodi is Botswana's only protected habitat for mountain reedbucks and both white rhinos and elephants have been reintroduced from South Africa. On this large and scenic reserve, you'll also see zebras, baboons, warthogs, hippos and a variety of antelopes, including gemsboks, kudu, impalas, waterbucks, klipspringers, steenboks, duikers and red hartebeest. Also present but harder to see are leopards, honey badgers, jackals, hyenas and civets. Guided two-hour game walks or drives cost US$5.50 per person.

Admission costs US$2 per car, plus US$2 per adult and US$1 per child. There are also comfortable chalets and a super restaurant. For details, see Places to Stay and Places to Eat under Gaborone. It's wise to pre-book accommodation and game drives.

To get there, take a Lobatse minibus 12 km south of Gaborone, then walk the final 1.5 km west to the reserve entrance.

St Clair Lion Park

If you don't mind seeing your lions in enclosures, the St Clair Lion Park may be of interest. There's a small zoo set up for children, horse rides around the attached wildlife area cost US$10 per hour and guided walks to a nearby stone-age site are available. It's also a good place to watch birds, and visitors are even given the opportunity to feed the vultures. The real emphasis, however, is on the off-road vehicle competitions which are held four times a year; they eventually aim to attract aficionados from all over the world.

St Clair is Gaborone's only camp and caravan site. For details, see Places to Stay and Places to Eat under Gaborone.

BOTSWANA

Otse

Otse ('OOT-see') village, a former manga-nese-mining and forestry village 45 km south of Gaborone, is best known for its vultury on Mannyelanong Hill, one of only two Cape vulture nesting sites in Botswana. The second site is at another Mannyelanong (meaning 'place where vultures shit') near the village of Mogonye, but it's less accessible. At Otse, you can easily approach the base and watch the ungainly birds wheeling around their nests above.

The vultury, which occupies the dramatic cliffs at the southern end of Otse's backdrop hill, once served as a nesting site for thousands of mating pairs. The numbers dropped to about 60 pairs in the late 1960s, but have been increasing since then. Coming from Gaborone, turn left into the village at the Shell petrol station then immediately bear right and follow the badly rutted road to the obvious track leading to the cliffs.

Just a short distance north along the western side of the same hill is Refuge Cave, a large fault in the cliff face 50 metres above the base. Pottery has been found inside and the cave was probably used as a hiding place during the Boer invasions of the 1870s.

LOBATSE

Despite its nice setting 68 km south of Gaborone, Lobatse is one of Botswana's dullest places, known mainly as the site of the national mental hospital and the country's largest abattoir. The original Lobatse was established by the Ngwaketse in the late 18th century. It served as the site of the High Court of Bechuanaland Protectorate when Mafikeng was the seat of government. Due to a lack of permanent water, it just missed out becoming the national capital when Gaborone was selected in the early 1960s.

Information

Few of Lobatse's visitors hail from beyond Gaborone, so there's little need for a bona fide tourist office. There is, however, a decent bookshop in Choppy's Cash & Carry complex.

Arts Cooperatives

Tiro Afrique Knitwear creates designer woollen knitwear from Accorda wool imported from New Zealand; the finished products are destined for France. They sell quality clothing for reasonable prices, and the women serve refreshments to visitors and accompany them around the work area.

The Tiro ya Diatla Weavers, opposite the Botswana Meat Commission, started out producing heavy and durable rugs of high quality karakul wool. They now weave artistic tapestries and clothing from the same materials and sell the finished product at factory prices. The weavers also conduct tours of the site.

Anglican Church

Lobatse's most beautiful structure is St Mark's Anglican Church, a thatch-roofed stone building which would be more at home in a damp, rural English village. When the church is open, visitors are welcome to have a look inside.

BMC Abattoir

Lobatse has been known as a meat town since 1934 when Imperial Cold Storage first opened. At independence in 1966, after the operation had closed, re-opened and changed hands several times, Imperial was taken over by the government and the Botswana Meat Corporation (BMC) was formed. They've been in charge ever since.

The Lobatse abattoir is the country's largest. For some unfathomable reason, BMC conducts tours of the operation. Even more unfathomable is the popularity of these tours. If you're looking for lots of gore, however, don't bother; the company proudly advertises that its dirty work is 'humanely' executed.

Places to Stay & Eat

If you're stuck in Lobatse while trying to hitch to Ghanzi or South Africa, the hills behind town provide suitable unofficial camp sites. The spartan Lobatse Hotel has now shut down, so you're limited to the up-market *Cresta Cumberland* (☎ 330281;

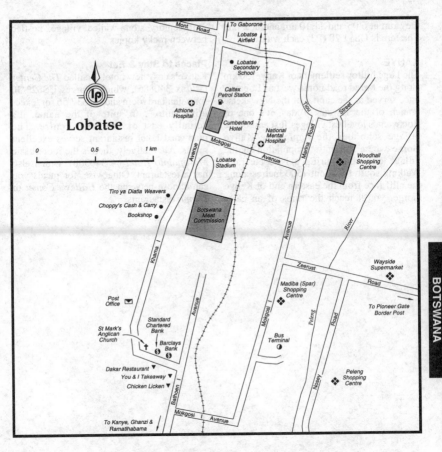

Lobatse

fax 332106) on the Gaborone road. Single/
double rooms with en suite baths cost
US$60/86 with breakfast while executive
suites are US$74/91. The dining room,
which is open to everyone, does buffet English breakfasts for US$8 and continental
breakfasts for US$6.50, while dinners in the
grill cost from US$10 to US$15.

A cheaper meal option is *El Shaddai Restaurant & Takeaway* in the Madiba (Spar)
Shopping Centre. You can't miss the building – it strongly resembles a Rubik's Cube.
They serve à la carte meals, pasta, pizzas,
steaks and seafood. In the main street is the

basic *Dakar Restaurant* and there are also a
couple of fast-food joints along the street
parallel to the railway line, including
Chicken Licken and the *You & I Takeaway*.
For self-catering, there's *Choppy's Cash &
Carry* or the *Spar* supermarket in the Madiba
Shopping Centre.

Getting There & Away

There are frequent buses from Gaborone to
Lobatse, departing from the main bus terminal. There's are also daily commuter trains
which depart from Gaborone at 6.05 and 10
am and 3.10 and 5.45 pm. From Lobatse,

they run at 6.05 and 11.10 am and at 2 pm.
The fare is US$1.20 (P3) each way.

KANYE

The large hilltop settlement of Kanye, 50 km
along the tarred road north-west of Lobatse,
once served as the capital of the Ngwaketse
branch of the Tswana. Today, it's one of
Botswana's loveliest villages.Just east of the
village school is the impressive Kanye
Gorge where the entire population of the
village once hid during a Ndebele raid.
Walking south for about 1500 metres along
the cliff face from the eastern end of Kanye
Gorge, you'll reach the ruins of an early
18th-century stone-walled village, nestled
between rocky kopjes.

Places to Stay & Eat

Kanye's cosy new hotel is called *The Center*
(☎ /fax 340885), which charges US$23/30
for a standard room and US$37/56 for 'exec-
utive suites'. In spite of the name, it's
actually east of the town centre. The
renowned hotel restaurant serves excellent
meals. Alternatively, there's the more basic
Marapalalo Hotel (☎ 340308), which also
has a restaurant. Otherwise, for meals you
can choose between the *Halley's Comet* or
Lempu restaurants.

Eastern Botswana

Although in the winter it bears a strong resemblance to a desert, the scrubland strip along the South African and much of the Zimbabwean border is the part of Botswana most amenable to agriculture, and therefore human habitation. It couldn't be called lush, but it still receives most of the country's rainfall and in the summer months, takes on a pleasantly green cloak.

FRANCISTOWN

Just as randomly organised as Gaborone, Francistown is without pretences; it may be a mining and industrial centre, but as far as many people are concerned, its *raison d'être* is retail and wholesale shopping. Although it's Botswana's second city, visitors should not expect much of Francistown. It does have a small museum, but apart from that, there's hardly a scrap of interest for tourists – no monuments, no interesting churches – not even a statue for the pigeons or a bit of kitsch architecture to liven the scene.

History

Francistown's history is its most interesting component. There is archaeological evidence in the form of stone tools and rock paintings that the Francistown area has been inhabited for at least 80,000 years by the San or their predecessors. Agricultural activity was introduced by Bantu groups around 200 AD. The area was later incorporated into the series of Shona states – the Torwa and the Rozwi – that controlled much of present-day Zimbabwe until the early 1800s. The Sekalanga language spoken in Francistown is a dialect of Shona rather than Setswana, and ruins in the north-east district are similar to those around Bulawayo rather than those of early Tswana settlements.

There is evidence that the Francistown area lay along early Swahili and Portuguese trade routes, and ancient gold workings in the vicinity date back to the Great Zimbabwe era, between the 12th and 15th centuries.

In the 1820s, the Ndebele stormed through, coming to rest near Bulawayo, and the Kalanga territory of north-eastern Botswana was subject to their influence and taxation. The first European to enter the area and visit Nyangabgwe (which was the nearest village to present-day Francistown) was missionary Robert Moffat.

Moffat was followed by geologist Karl Mauch, who changed the course of local history by discovering gold along the Tati River in 1867 and sparking off the first big gold rush in southern Africa. It drew prospectors from as far away as California and Australia. With little regard for the reaction of the Kalanga people who inhabited the area, an impromptu settlement sprang up on the Tati River to accommodate the incoming White population.

A contingency of Australians along with Englishman Daniel Francis arrived in 1869. Francis sunk a 20-metre shaft which turned out to be quite productive and established the basis for his mining operation, Tati Concessions, before pulling up stakes in 1870 and migrating to the newly discovered Kimber-

Eastern Botswana

0   25   50 km

ley diamond fields. He returned 10 years later, however, to negotiate mining rights with King Lobengula of the Ndebele (based in Bulawayo) and helped lay out the town which now bears his name.

Although gold is still mined in small quantities, the beginnings of Francistown's current industrial boom were set down in the late 1970s. To avoid closure under economic sanctions prior to Zimbabwean independence, many Rhodesian firms headed for Botswana and established themselves in Francistown, two hours drive from Bulawayo. The growth trend continues unabated;

expansion has occurred with little reason or planning and the town has now grown into the economic hub of eastern Botswana.

A new development is the go-ahead for the construction of Letsibogo Dam on the Motloutse River south of Francistown. Completion is scheduled for 1998 and will result in the relocation of several villages. The intent is to eventually build a water pipeline to Gaborone.

Orientation

Most of the shopping activity is concentrated in the few blocks between the railway line on the west, Khama St on the east, Selous Ave on the north and the Thapama Lodge on the south. The main drag, Blue Jacket St, was named after the Blue Jacket Gold Mine. The mine's name was in turn derived from the moniker bestowed upon the colourful Danish miner, Sam Andersen, who always wore a denim jacket.

Shopping malls are mushrooming, and three large new ones have appeared within the past couple of years. In addition to the oldest one, The Mall, there's now the Blue Jacket Mall, the multistorey Barclays Plaza Mall and the Blue Jacket Plaza – and there are more on the way. Wholesale outlets are concentrated in the industrial area west of the centre.

Beyond the central enclave, Francistown is mainly a dusty, desultory settlement, and its perimeter is characterised by Botswana's most squalid shanty towns. This is one of few places in this prosperous country where you'll see real poverty.

Information

As it lacks tourist attractions, Francistown doesn't bother with a tourist information office; queries may be directed to the Supa-Ngwao Museum. For listings of coming events and local advertising, see the free weekly papers *The Northern Advertiser* and the *Francistown News & Reviews*. Both come out on Friday.

Money Francistown's banks include the Standard Bank, on Haskins St opposite the railway station, and several others along Blue Jacket St. If you're changing money, join the queue early and plan on a good wait, especially around the end of the month. For foreign exchange transactions, you must wait in one queue to pick up the forms and another queue to make the transaction.

Post & Telecommunications The GPO is on Blue Jacket St. Make phone calls from the Teletswana Office on Lobengula Ave near Blue Jacket St. Hours are Monday to Friday from 7.45 am to 12.30 pm and 1.45 to 4 pm, and Saturday from 8 to 11 am.

Travel Agencies VIP Travel (☎ 213909), on the corner of Lobengula Ave and Blue Jacket St, is Francistown's largest agency and is a good bet for travel bookings. It can arrange lodging, transport or car hire and also handle international airline bookings with amazing efficiency. In the same office is the Francistown branch of Holiday Car Hire.

Laundry Automatic laundry service is available at the Polina Laundromat at the northern end of Blue Jacket St.

Bookshops Blue Jacket Mall has a fairly good branch of the Botswana Book Centre, Blue Jacket Plaza has Northern Botsalo Books and there's yet another bookshop, Chapter's, in Barclays Plaza Mall. The Francistown Stationers Bookshop on Haskins St, opposite the railway line, offers a limited selection of light novels and magazines. Glossy souvenir books on African topics are sold at BGI across the railway line from the centre.

Camping Equipment Your best bet for camping equipment is Ebrahim Store on Tainton Ave.

Left Luggage The left-luggage office at the railway station is open Monday to Friday from 4.45 am to 12.30 pm and from 2 to 9 pm and on Saturday from 4.45 to 10.30 am and 5 to 9 pm.

Emergency Services The newish Nyangabgwe Hospital lies a few hundred metres east of the roundabout near the Cresta Thapama Lodge. For emergency medical services dial (☎ 997). The Hana Pharmacy in Blue Jacket Plaza is the best-stocked. The police station (emergency ☎ 999) is on Haskins St, north of the central area.

Things to See & Do

Francistown isn't the most exciting of cities, but there is a new cultural and historical museum, the Supa-Ngwao, housed in the old Francistown Court House. It serves as the

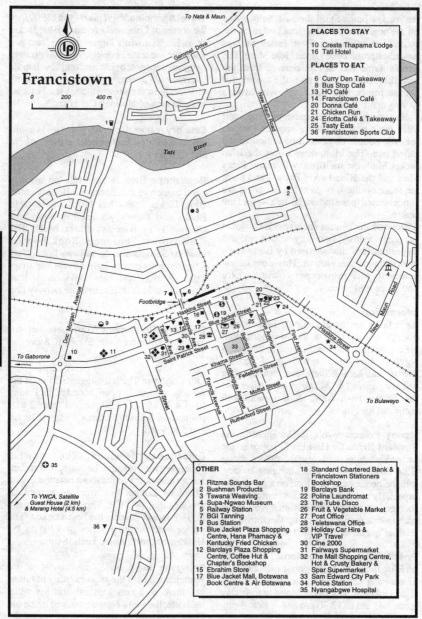

Francistown

0   200   400 m

To Nata & Maun

Gemmel Drive

New Maun Road

Tati River

Doc Morgan Avenue

Footbridge →

Haskins Street

Blue Jacket Street

Selous Avenue

First Avenue

Haskins Street

Blaine Street

Tainton Ave

Francis Ave

Saint Patrick Street

Khama Street

Dallnes Avenue

Lobengula Avenue

Feitelberg Street

Moffat Street

Guy Street

Francis Avenue

Rutherford Street

To Gaborone

To Bulawayo

*To YWCA, Satellite
Guest House (2 km)
& Marang Hotel (4.5 km)*

PLACES TO STAY

10 Cresta Thapama Lodge
16 Tati Hotel

PLACES TO EAT

6   Curry Den Takeaway
8   Bus Stop Café
13 HO Café
14 Francistown Café
20 Donna Café
21 Chicken Run
24 Eriotta Café & Takeaway
25 Tasty Eats
36 Francistown Sports Club

OTHER

1   Ritzma Sounds Bar
2   Bushman Products
3   Tswana Weaving
4   Supa-Ngwao Museum
5   Railway Station
7   BGI Tanning
9   Bus Station
11 Blue Jacket Plaza Shopping
    Centre, Hana Phamacy &
    Kentucky Fried Chicken
12 Barclays Plaza Shopping
    Centre, Coffee Hut &
    Chapter's Bookshop
15 Ebrahim Store
17 Blue Jacket Mall, Botswana
    Book Centre & Air Botswana

18 Standard Chartered Bank &
    Francistown Stationers
    Bookshop
19 Barclays Bank
22 Polina Laundromat
23 The Tube Disco
26 Fruit & Vegetable Market
27 Post Office
28 Teletswana Office
29 Holiday Car Hire &
    VIP Travel
30 Cine 2000
31 Fairways Supermarket
32 The Mall Shopping Centre,
    Hot & Crusty Bakery &
    Spar Supermarket
33 Sam Edward City Park
34 Police Station
35 Nyangabgwe Hospital

BOTSWANA

regional museum for north-eastern Botswana and also hosts visiting exhibits and events. In the small museum shop you can purchase maps, books and scholarly publications dealing with the region. It's open Tuesday to Saturday from 9 am to 1 pm and from 2 to 5 pm.

Also, while you're in town, keep an eye out for the self-proclaimed King of Botswana, who wears a black business suit and rides around on a bicycle which bears his flag.

Places to Stay

The best deal is the friendly and recently refurbished *Marang Hotel* (☎ 213991; fax 213991), five km from the centre on the old Gaborone road. You can camp on the secluded, grassy lawn on the bank of the Tati River for US$5 per person, including access to hotel facilities (hot showers, swimming pool, laundry facilities, etc).Comfortable rooms or rondavels on stilts cost US$65 a single or double. Booked guests – including campers – are treated to free pick up from town in a London taxi (for airport runs they charge US$3.70). If you're walking or hitching from the centre, turn left towards 'Matsiloje' at the Thapama Lodge roundabout.

The *YWCA* (☎ 213046) is also a good budget option. Again, head out along the Marang road, turn right onto Teemana Dr at the Botsalano Bar, past the Nyangabgwe Hospital, and continue 200 metres down the road – the YWCA is on the left. Dormitory accommodation costs US$15 and both men and women are welcome.

If you prefer the town centre, the tatty *Tati Hotel* (☎ 212255) on Lobengula Ave has singles/doubles with toilet and shower for US$19/21, but it's not recommended for lone women.

Out in the Satellite township is the *Satellite Guest House* (☎ 214665; fax 202115), a veritable tribute to pre-fab architecture surrounded by a walled compound. Single/double rooms cost US$41/56 and lunch and dinner are available during set hours. From the Cresta Thapama Lodge roundabout,

follow the Marang road for three km; turn left opposite the school for the deaf and continue about 250 metres.

Francistown's most up-market hotel is the recently expanded *Cresta Thapama Lodge* (☎ 213872; fax 213766) on the corner of Doc Morgan Ave and Blue Jacket St. It caters mostly to business travellers and is now planning a casino, which should be open by the time you read this. Singles/doubles with breakfast cost US$78/93.

Places to Eat

The English breakfasts at the *Marang Hotel* are quite good and in the evening, there's a salad bar and fixed menu for around US$10 per person. The buffet breakfast at the *CrestaThapama Lodge* costs US$8; for dinner you can try their Ivory Grill, which serves carvery and curry dishes. Light snacks are available at the pool terrace in the afternoon and the cocktail bar serves light meals and snacks.

The *Francistown Sports Club*, open daily except Monday, serves up tasty and inexpensive lunches and dinners, but visitors must pay US$2 for temporary membership. Takeaways are also available and members have access to the miniature golf course.

A new addition is the *Kentucky Fried Chicken* in the Blue Jacket Plaza. At the opposite end of the same street is *Chicken Run*, which of course also serves chicken, and across the street is 'strictly Halaal' *Tasty Eats*, with curries, rotis, grills and savoury snacks. For Greek-style meals, go to *Donna Café* on Selous Ave. Another basic sit-down restaurant is *Eriotta Café* on the corner of Haskins and Blue Jacket Sts.

There are also a number of cheap takeaway places on or near Haskins St, including several 'boozing and billiards' places like *Ma Kim's*, the *HO Café*, the *Bus Stop* and the *Francistown Café*. Across the railway line is the Indian-oriented *Curry Den Takeaways*. For a simple break with coffee, try the *Coffee Hut* in Barclays Plaza.

Besides four well-stocked supermarkets, Francistown has a small outdoor market and bus-terminal food stalls offering fruit, vege-

BOTSWANA

tables and light hot snacks. *Hot & Crusty Bakery* in The Mall bakes fresh bread and sweet treats. It's also a breakfast possibility.

Entertainment

For entertainment, you don't have many choices. The most popular dance spot is the Ritzma Sounds Bar out Doc Morgan Ave just beyond the Tati bridge. It's open for alcohol and fast food from 6 am to midnight, with jazz music and dancing in the evenings. On weekends, The Tube Disco on Blue Jacket St is popular with the younger crowd, but security is dodgy. The only cinema, Cine 2000, has one show (mainly reject films from the USA) nightly at 8 pm. Ma Kim's Café also has a lively and well-patronised bar.

The bar at the Marang Hotel is always crowded, while the pub at the Thapama Lodge attracts mainly business travellers. The Kudu Bar at the Tati Hotel has the same dodgy atmosphere as the hotel itself.

Things to Buy

BGI Tanning, across the pedestrian bridge over the railway line, concentrates on leather products and stuffed African wildlife (imagine buying a stuffed kudu – 'the ideal decorative piece as a reminder of your visit to Africa'). However, it's also a source for Shashe baskets, which are more loosely woven than their Ngamiland counterparts. Bushman Products (☎ 213821) on the New Maun road also sells leather products – handbags, wallets, carrying cases and cushions – as well as San crafts.

Tswana Weaving (☎ 214554) in the Tswelelo Industrial complex sells original design cotton rugs and tapestries which are hand-woven on site from karakul wool. It's open during shopping hours on weekdays and by telephone appointment on weekends.

Marothodi (☎ 213646) produces brilliant fabrics and clothing handprinted in wildlife motifs and traditional basketry patterns. The colours are fast and the designs beautiful and original. The shop is off the Gaborone road five km from the centre; head towards Gaborone and turn right on BML road. After 200 metres, look for the sign on your left.

Getting There & Away

Air The Air Botswana office (☎ 212393) is in the Blue Jacket Mall. You can fly from Francistown to Gaborone at least once daily; most flights depart between 8 am and 1 pm, but on Wednesday and Friday there's an evening flight at 6.15 pm.

Between Gaborone and Francistown, Air Botswana has one or two flights daily in the morning and an additional afternoon flight at 4 pm on Wednesday and Friday.

Bus Because it lies at the intersection of the Gaborone, Nata/Kasane, Bulawayo and Orapa roads, Francistown is a transportation hub, with bus service to Gaborone (US$10) several times daily and twice-daily service to Nata (US$3) and Maun (US$11). The bus terminal is wedged between the railway line and the small-frontage road connecting Haskins St to Doc Morgan St. The Mahube Express bus to Maun departs daily at 9.30 and 10.30 am.

For international connections, see the Botswana and Zimbabwe Getting There & Away chapters.

Train The daily trains between Bulawayo and Gaborone pass through Francistown at 9 pm southbound and 6.45 am northbound. The ticket office at the Haskins St train station is open on weekdays from 8 am to noon and 1 to 4 pm. For further timetable information, turn to the Zimbabwe Getting There & Away chapter.

Hitching To hitch to Maun, walk out to the airport turn-off to the tree where locals wait for lifts. Heading south, wait either at the roundabout near Thapama Lodge or further out the Gaborone road.

Getting Around

When driving in the town centre, be mindful of the one-way streets between Haskins St and Blue Jacket St.

As well as the ubiquitous minibuses, Francistown has a few taxis (☎ 212260) which resemble the minibuses and operate much like Zimbabwe's emergency taxis.

They're most easily found at the railway station. To the Marang Hotel costs US$0.40 (P1), while normal minibuses cost US$0.30 (70t). As in Gaborone, taxis and minibuses are recognisable by their blue number plates.

There's a branch of Holiday Car Hire (☎ 214524; fax 214526) at VIP travel, on the corner of Lobengula Ave and Blue Jacket St. Avis (☎ 213901; fax 212867) is based at Francistown Airport.

SELEBI-PHIKWE

Selebi-Phikwe is now Botswana's third largest community, but prior to 1967, it was nothing but a cattle post. In the early 1960s, the twin copper-nickel-cobalt deposits of Selebi and Phikwe, 14 km apart, were discovered and taken over by Bamangwato Concessions Ltd (BCL). Mining commenced in 1973 and the mines now output a combined annual total of 2.5 million tonnes.

Selebi-Phikwe has grown into a large company town, which shelters below a hill between the two mines. Fortunately, it's surrounded by small rock kopjes, scrubby savanna and low, rugged hills, and is therefore more scenically endowed than other eastern Botswana communities. It also has one of Botswana's few coherent and successful zoning plans and a concerted community effort adorns much of the business district in flowering trees and plants. It's actually a pleasant little town, but once you've had a stroll down The Mall, there's not much else to do. That could change, however, if they ever start up mine tours and allow visitors to gaze into the impressive Phikwe mine shaft.

Information

On The Mall, the heart of town, are the police, Teletswana, and post offices and a couple of eating places, as well as one of Botswana's finest bookshops. For a rundown of what's on at the many sports clubs, pick up a copy of the *Phikwe Bugle*, which is published on Friday.

Places to Stay & Eat

The pleasant *Bosele Hotel* (☎ 810675; fax 811083) on Tshekedi Rd near The Mall exists mostly for visitors on mining business. Singles/doubles cost US$70/90. It has a standard dining room which often puts on special braais and buffets for bargain prices. Booked guests may request to be picked up at the airport or bus stop.

If you don't mind being away from the centre, the *Syringa Lodge* (☎ 810444; fax 810450), on the corner of Independence and Airport Rds, makes a nice alternative. The attached *Red Lobster Restaurant* is the finest restaurant in town and there are also two bars. Singles/doubles with en suite facilities are US$69/84. With just a shower, they're slightly cheaper.

For meals on The Mall, you can choose between *Pioneer Restaurant & Takeaways*, *Southern Fried Chicken Takeaways* and *Copper & Nickel Takeaways* (the name honours the mine and has nothing to do with the food). Further east on Independence Ave is the *Old Spice Catering Restaurant & Takeaways*. The market immediately north of The Mall is a good source of cheap produce and hot snacks. For self-catering, go to the *Fairways Supermarket* and the *Louise Garden Fresh Fruit & Vegetables*, both on The Mall.

Getting There & Away

The only reason for non-business travellers to visit Selebi-Phikwe would be to find a lift into the Tuli Block, and for that it should serve well, since there's a bit of commercial traffic. Buses normally run between Selebi-Phikwe, Serule and Francistown once or twice daily.

Getting Around

Syringa Lodge has an office of Holiday Car Hire (☎ 810450).

LEPOKOLE HILLS

An extension of Zimbabwe's Matobo Hills, the Lepokole Hills lie about 25 km north-east of Bobonong village on a track passable by conventional vehicles. Drier and more desolate than their Zimbabwean counterparts, the Lepokole Hills still bear the characteristic domes and castle kopjes that reveal the

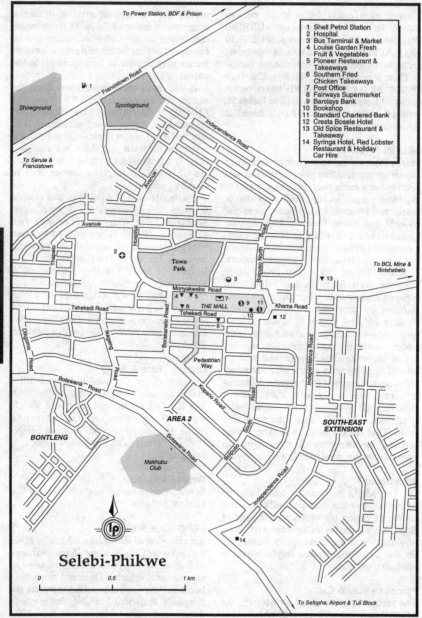

To Power Station, BDF & Prison

1 Shell Petrol Station
2 Hospital
3 Bus Terminal & Market
4 Louise Garden Fresh
  Fruit & Vegetables
5 Pioneer Restaurant &
  Takeaways
6 Southern Fried
  Chicken Takeaways
7 Post Office
8 Fairways Supermarket
9 Barclays Bank
10 Bookshop
11 Standard Chartered Bank
12 Cresta Bosele Hotel
13 Old Spice Restaurant &
   Takeaway
14 Syringa Hotel, Red Lobster
   Restaurant & Holiday
   Car Hire

Showground

Sportsground

Francistown Road

Independence Road

To Serule & Francistown

Avenue

Avenue

Thapelo

Hospital

Town Park

Bopuso North Road

To BCL Mine & Botshabelo

Monyakwebo Road

THE MALL

Khama Road

Tshekedi Road

Tshekedi Road

Borakanelo Road

Ikageng Road

Dikgomo Road

Botswana Road

Pedestrian Way

Kopano Road

AREA 2

BONTLENG

Makhubu Club

Botswana Road

Bopuso South Road

Independence Road

SOUTH-EAST EXTENSION

Selebi-Phikwe

0   0.5   1 km

To Sefophe, Airport & Tull Block

BOTSWANA

geologic relationship. The Lepokole Hills are also riddled with caves, gorges and overhangs decorated with paintings by the early San. The hills are, in fact, believed to be the final domain of the San people in eastern Botswana and are thought to hold religious significance for them.

Near the largest painted cave is a stone-walled ruin dating back to the Great Zimbabwe period, probably around the early 15th century. As in Matobo, wildlife is profuse. Commonly observed species include dassies, baboons, klipspringers and larger antelopes. Leopards are also present but are reclusive.

No transport or services are available in the hills and only very basic supplies are sold at Bobonong. Visitors wanting to camp or bushwalk must be self-sufficient in food and water and carry the appropriate topographic sheets.

TULI BLOCK

The Tuli Block is a swathe of freehold farmland extending 350 km along the northern bank of the Limpopo from Buffels Drift to Pont Drift, and reaching widths of 10 to 20 km. It was originally held by the Ngwato tribe, but shortly after the Bechuanaland Protectorate was established, it was ceded to the BSAC for a railway. The projected cost of bridging the many intermittent streams, however, rendered the project unfeasible. The land was instead opened to White settlement and the railway route was shifted north-west to its present location.

The Tuli Block's main attraction is the 90,000-hectare North-east Tuli Game Reserve. It takes in both the Mashatu and Tuli Game Reserves, which are open to the public, as well as several other private reserves. The two main reserves provide both a sampling of Botswana's wildlife and access to the country's most fabulous landscapes, savanna, rock kopjes, river bluffs, riverine forests and tidy villages.

Neither great nor greasy, the Limpopo may not exactly recall Kipling's *Just So Stories*, but under certain conditions, it could be described as 'grey-green'. Still, you're

welcome to search for fever trees; according to *Collins*, they're 'tall, mimasaceous swamp trees *Acacia xanthophloea*, of southern Africa, with fragrant yellow flowers'. Although the river has been dry for several years, you can experience the illusion of flow by crossing at Martin's Drift, where a dam wall creates a lovely green and tree-fringed reservoir in the riverbed.

Sherwood & Zanzibar

The two rustic and decomposing villages of Sherwood (Martin's Drift) and Zanzibar have little to offer apart from access to border crossings between Botswana and South Africa. Neither place has accommodation, but Sherwood Ranch, eight km from Martin's Drift border post (open 8 am to 6 pm), does have a basic shop, a bank, post office, petrol station and bottle store. Sherwood got a new lease of life with the opening of the tarred road from Selebi-Phikwe, but this was offset by the closure of the nearby Stevensford Game Ranch, 14 km to the east.

The 105-km road between Sherwood and Zanzibar is horrid, with very rough gravel and numerous dips through dry riverbeds. At Zanzibar, there's only a small shop and bottle shop. Between Zanzibar and Pont Drift are two insignificant border crossings, Saambou and Platjanbridge; both close at 4 pm. From near Baine's Drift, where there's a police checkpoint, you'll have a long-range view of South Africa's dramatic and squared-off Blaberg Range. The micro-climate and natural springs atop this lost world support jungle-like vegetation, including wild bananas and tropical fruit.

Pont Drift

Botswana's easternmost village, Pont Drift is mainly just a border crossing between Botswana and South Africa, with the requisite immigration and police posts. There's no bridge, however, so when the Limpopo is too deep to be forded, vehicles may not cross. Passengers are carried across the river on the rustic Pont Drift cableway, which costs US$4 per person.

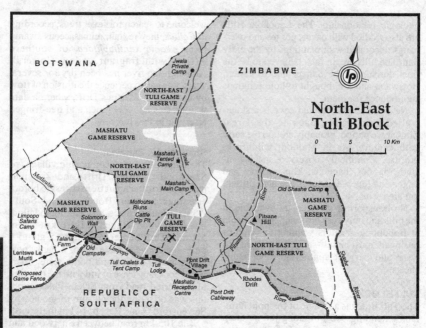

Immediately beyond the immigration post is the Mashatu Reserve office.

Motloutse Crossing

The sandy scar of the Motloutse ('large elephant') River enters the Limpopo about 27 km west of Pont Drift. The river rarely flows, but the deep sand necessitates using 4WD. Immediately east of the river, the road enters a small detached chunk of the Mashatu Game Reserve, with lovely landscapes and good opportunities for wildlife viewing.

As you plough through the riverbed, notice the prominent 30-metre-high dolerite (a coarse-grained granite-like basalt) dyke that slices across the landscape on either side of the vehicle track. This bizarre formation is known as Solomon's Wall and provides scope for exploration on foot (but stick to the western bank of the river only – the eastern bank is in Mashatu). Look for agates and crystals of quartzite in the riverbed.

It was once possible to camp in the prom-inent stand of riverine mashatu trees im-mediately west of the crossing (which belongs to Talana Farm), but thanks to an up-market coalition against budget travel-lers, it's now officially prohibited.

Mashatu Game Reserve

The 45,000-hectare Mashatu Game Reserve occupies an arrow of land between the Shashe and Limpopo rivers, which form the boundaries with Zimbabwe and South Africa. It's Africa's largest private game reserve and is an excellent place to view big cats, antelopes and large herd of elephants, as well as the stately mashatu trees for which the reserve is named. In a remote area near the Limpopo are the Motloutse ruins, a Great Zimbabwe-era stone village which belonged to the Kingdom of Mwene Mutapa.

Places to Stay No wild camping is permit-ted, and except for the small exclave immediately east of the Motloutse crossing, the reserve is open only to guests of the Mashatu lodges. Access is from the main Mashatu office near the cableway at Pont Drift.

Inside the reserve is the luxury-class *Mashatu Main Camp* (formerly *Majale Lodge* (☎ 845321). It's one of the country's most exclusive resorts, with a swimming pool and an air-conditioned conference centre for up to 44 people. The Gin Trap, a dugout bar, overlooks a floodlit waterhole. Further out in the bush is the *Mashatu Tent Camp* (formerly *Thakadu Tent Camp*), a 'rustic' but still luxurious alternative. Each tent is furnished like a hotel room and has en suite flush toilets and shower facilities. The tent camp also has a swimming pool.

Prices for Mashatu Main Camp are US$249/386 for a single/double chalet, while Mashatu Tent Camp is US$186/297. Rates include accommodation, meals, game drives and transfers from the Tuli Lodge airstrip or the Pont Drift cableway. For reservations and information, contact Mashatu Game Reserve (☎ (011) 789 2677; fax (011) 886 4382), Suite 4, Tulbaugh, 360 Oak Ave, Ferndale (PO Box 2575, Randburg 2125), South Africa.

Tuli Game Reserve

The Tuli Game Reserve takes in a 7500-hectare chunk seemingly bitten out of the Mashatu Game Reserve. The beautifully situated *Tuli Lodge* (☎ /fax 845303) occupies a green riverine oasis beside the Limpopo, which is approached through lovely red rock country resembling southern Utah in miniature. It's more down-to-earth and a bit more affordable than Mashatu. Tuli Lodge is known as the one-time sponsor of Gareth Patterson, heir to George & Joy Adamson's *Born Free* legacy. When George Adamson was murdered in Kenya in 1989, Patterson transferred the lion cubs to the relatively safe environment afforded by eastern Botswana.

Rooms at the shady main lodge cost US$176/298, or US$474/784 for a three-night package. Rates include accommodation, three meals, two game drives and one game walk.

Two km upriver, at the former Nokolodi Camp site, Tuli Lodge offers self-catering chalets for US$43 per person, including rondavel accommodation and one game drive. The site is dominated by an immense mashatu tree, which is thought to have been growing here for over a millennium. There's also a small tented camp with self-catering facilities for the same price; it accommodates up to eight people. Guests at both camps have access to all facilities at the main lodge: the restaurant, bar and swimming pool. Camping is no longer permitted.

For bookings, contact Tuli Lodge (☎ (011) 482 2634; fax (011) 482 2635), PO Box 32533, Braamfontein 2017, South Africa.

Landing at the private airstrip costs US$4 per seat in the plane (whether or not the seats are occupied), plus US$21 for customs fees.

Limpopo Safaris Camp

The open land immediately west of Mashatu Reserve is a 12,000-hectare Limpopo Safaris hunting concession, with an office at Lentswe le Muriti, west of the Motloutse River. Their rough and ready hunting camp, five km north of the main road (4WD only), is open to the public for US$30 per person, including very basic accommodation and game drives. However, there are no meals available.

On the concession, you can see kudu, impalas, blue wildebeests, bushbucks, duikers, steenboks, zebras, leopards and hyena, but since they've been subjected to hunting activities, they may be a bit more skittish than usual. There's now a proposal to build a game fence between this concession and Talana Farm and the Mashatu Game Reserve, to prevent animals from straying into the hunting area.

For information and bookings, contact Gerhard Pretorius, Limpopo Safaris (☎ (011) 7803374 or (011) 976 3674) in Johannesburg, South Africa.

Getting There & Away

Air Okavango Air (☎ 313308) has a return flight between Gaborone and the Pont Drift airstrip (which belongs to Tuli Lodge) every

Rhinos & Conservation

No large southern African animals are more endangered than the white and black rhinoceros, and as with the elephant, their rapidly dwindling numbers have raised cries of both alarm and outrage both locally and around the world. And with good reason. Over the past 25 years, nearly 70,000 black rhinos and uncounted white rhinos have been slaughtered by poachers, thanks mainly to the mistaken Asian belief that rhino horn has medicinal and aphrodisiac properties, and the Yemeni notion that all real men need a dagger made of rhino horn.

In traditional Chinese medicine, rhino horn has been used mainly as a fever reducing agent, and although it works to some extent, its efficacy is considerably less than that of aspirin or paracetamol. Attempts at promoting substitution of other products, such as water buffalo horn, have met with resistance from Chinese pharmacists, who claim that the 'delicate constitutions' of the typically sedentary modern Chinese wouldn't be able to absorb such 'rough' medicines.

The dramatic decline in rhino populations has caused prices for African rhino horn to rise to around US$5700 per kg on the Asian market (Asian horn is valued at a whopping US$52,000 per kg!) and the cycle grows more vicious. As a result, in several African and Asian countries, rhinos have been completely exterminated.

One can hardly blame the poachers – the risks may be great but they can earn as much from a single rhino horn – US$100 to US$350 – as from a lifetime of farming. The potential rewards are so great that although around 200 poachers have been shot and killed in Zimbabwe alone, many more have got away with the goods and poaching continues unabated. Determined conservation efforts in Zimbabwe, Botswana and Namibia have been unable to keep pace with the losses from poaching and most programmes are faring poorly. Many translocated animals die of stress. Radio collaring only reveals the location of dead animals and parks' patrols are daunted – and endangered – by the poachers' utter ruthlessness. There's also a lack of funding.

Dehorning programmes were once thought to be the answer, considering they'd render the animals commercially worthless. However, they've enjoyed only limited success (mainly in Namibia and South Africa, where poaching activity isn't as rampant as in other countries).

First of all, poachers will kill a rhino for the smallest stump of horn which may remain. Secondly, after a poacher has spent four or five days tracking a hornless rhino, it's shot so it won't have to be tracked again. Thirdly, far eastern dealers realise the rhino's extinction will render priceless the estimated five to 10 tonnes of horn they currently have stockpiled in Taiwan alone (currently worth US$35 to 70 million). Mainland China is estimated to have around nine tonnes, most of which are off-cuts from Yemen. To that end, they've ordered poachers to shoot every rhino they encounter, whether it has a horn or not. In September 1993, 90 rhinos were poached in Hwange National Park; of these, 84 had been dehorned. What's more, the horn grows back at a rate of around six cm annually.

As a result, the prognosis for the black rhino is not good; their numbers in Africa have declined from 65,000 in 1970 to perhaps 1500 today, and they're being poached much faster than they can reproduce. This scarcity of black rhinos has already been reflected in increased poaching of white rhinos in Zimbabwe, South Africa and Swaziland.

Zimbabwe It has been estimated that half the remaining numbers live in Zimbabwe, but most experts feel those figures are optimistic, and that a more realistic count would fall between 100 and 200. Three more are poached every week.

Currently, technology is being employed in the war on poaching. Black rhinos are being translocated from such risky areas as Chizarira National Park and moved to Intensive Protection Zones in Matobo, Hwange and Matusadona National Parks and the Chiping area of the Eastern Highlands. They're then fitted with microchip receivers, which are surgically implanted under the neck skin and linked up to a computer database that will set off a noisy alarm if a rhino stops moving or wanders into a high risk area. This system allows conservation officers to either move the rhino to safer ground or, in the case of a kill, apprehend the poachers before they can get away with the horn.

Sadly, when it comes to protecting rhinos, Zimbabwe has not had a good record. Officials like to cite low funding as an excuse, but officials so badly want to sell their stockpiled horn that any international move to squash the market has been vociferously opposed by the Zimbabwean government.

There's also conclusive evidence that national parks' people and high-level government officials are themselves in on the trade. In the late 1980s, the rhino population in Gonarezhou

National Park was wiped out by the Zimbabwean army. In 1992, four members of the central intelligence organisation were caught with two horns. In 1993, a government minister was convicted, along with six others, for illegal possession of two rhino horns. In two separate incidents, North Korean diplomats were discovered smuggling horns out of the country in diplomatic pouches. There's evidence that several Department of National Parks & Wildlife Management officials have been involved in both trade and multiple cover-ups. Planes and vehicles donated for anti-poaching patrols have been commandeered by high officials for their own use, and at least eight people who've had evidence against the officials, or dared to speak out, have been involved in some sort of fatal 'accident'. Others have been arrested on trumped up charges in order to discredit their claims.

Botswana In 1992, a survey in northern Botswana revealed that only nine white rhinos remained in the entire country. In response, the Khama Rhino Sanctuary was established near Serowe to provide high-security protection for the remaining individuals. However, while the sanctuary was being prepared, four of the rhinos were poached. The reserve now contains four individuals, while Mokolodi Reserve in south-eastern Botswana has brought in several white rhinos from South Africa. Unless the trade in rhino horn dies completely, it seems unlikely that Africa's wildest country will ever again have rhinos living in the wild.

Namibia Namibia currently has the third largest black rhino population in the world, and many of these live in the unprotected desert wilds of northern Damaraland. The rate of loss to poachers is approximately 5% annually, and growing. By the turn of the century, the desert rhinos of Damaraland may well have been wiped out.

Namibia was actually a pioneer in using dehorning to protect its rhinos, but sadly, dehorned female rhinos in Namibia have been unable to protect their young from attack by hyenas. During the drought of 1993, when other game was scarce, all calves of dehorned females were lost.

The non-governmental Save the Rhino Trust (☎ (061) 222281; fax (061) 223077), PO Box 22691, Windhoek, Namibia, has been formed to promote conservation education and public sponsorship of individual animals, and to provide area residents with alternative sources of income, which will hopefully allay the temptation to poach wildlife. A particular problem has been the town of Khorixas, which has an unemployment rate of 80%.

Most Damara people are aware of the need for rhino protection and keenly promote conservation of desert-dwelling rhinos, elephants, lions and other specially adapted sub-species, in the hope that increased tourism will provide funding for local community projects. Thus far, STR's most successful projects have been handicrafts sales in Khorixas and the locally-operated tourist camps which have been established at Khowarib, Ongongo and Twyfelfontein.

Solutions The most effective local answer, it seems, is to educate people living in rhino country about the value of wildlife and demonstrate that for their communities, rhinos are worth more alive than dead. Many people have advocated permitting limited high-priced hunting of rhinos in order to provide funding for both conservation and local communities. However, seeing some people killing the rhinos which others are committed to saving from extinction may send mixed signals to local subsistence farmers, who have little experience with outside economic practices.

On a global scale, everyone can help simply by attacking the rhino horn market. The worst offender, Taiwan, is a modern industrial nation whose economy depends heavily on exports. The US has already stopped the import of all wildlife products from Taiwan, but few conservationists think that goes far enough and advocate a full-blown boycott of all goods manufactured by (or in affiliation with) Taiwanese interests. Perhaps then the Taiwanese government would get serious about enforcing its own laws against trade in endangered species. If you're interested, the Environmental Investigation Agency in the UK (see Useful Organisations in the Regional Facts for the Visitor chapter) can provide a list of companies which may be targeted.

Other proposed solutions include commercial dehorning; after all, if the rhinos aren't slaughtered, the horn becomes a renewable resource (it grows back at six cm per year). To flood the market with legal horn would cause the collapse of the illicit trade because the huge amounts of cash currently involved would no longer figure. The counter argument runs that dehorning currently costs around US$1000 per animal, which would make it commercially unfeasible at a price low enough to cut out the illicit trade.

Sadly, all arguments may already be moot. ∎

Sunday. Flights are guaranteed if two or more people are interested. The fare is a very steep US$178 return.

Car & Motorbike Although some roads on the Botswana side are relatively well-graded gravel or dirt and are accessible to conventional vehicles, the most interesting areas require 4WD, particularly the Motloutse River crossing west of Pont Drift.

The easiest access from Gaborone is via tarred South African highways through one of the several Limpopo border crossings. However, if the Limpopo flows again and the river can't be forded, you'll have to leave the vehicle in South Africa and cross into Botswana on the cableway at Pont Drift. With advance notice, either game lodge will pick up guests from Pont Drift. Remember the border closes at 6 pm.

From the Gaborone-Francistown road, seven access routes lead into the Tuli Block: Artesia (just 53 km north of Gaborone); Dinokwe; Mahalapye (if you're coming from the north, there's a rough shortcut from Lose); 10 km south or 20 km north of Palapye; from Serule to Zanzibar via Selebi-Phikwe and the most travelled – and therefore easiest to hitch – the tarred road from Selebi-Phikwe to Sherwood via Sefophe.

Hitching Hitching is viable, but the byways are little-travelled so prepare for long waits. The only public transport is the occasional bus from Selebi-Phikwe to Bobonong and Molalatau. Sometimes it continues on as far as Mathathane, just 23 km from Platjanbridge. Service is erratic, so enquire at the bus terminal in Selebi-Phikwe.

PALAPYE

The original name of this town was Phalatswe, meaning 'many impalas' in Sekgalagadi or 'large impalas' in Setswana. The current spelling is the result of mistransliteration by early colonials. Palapye began life as a humble railway station and siding serving the old Ngwato capital.

When the Ngwato people shifted their capital to Serowe, 50 km west of Palapye, the town's economy shifted to agriculture, but when Botswana's largest coal reserves were discovered at Morupule in the desert west of town, mining proved more lucrative. There's now an immense coal-burning power plant at Morupule, which was opened in 1986. Palapye has therefore earned the nickname 'the Powerhouse of Botswana'.

Information

The commercial heart of town is the Engen Shopping Centre on the main highway, with a petrol station, a couple of takeaway places and the Crossroads Bookshop. Around the corner, 200 metres down the road into the village is a gallery selling local arts.

Old Phalatswe Church Ruin

If you have a vehicle, you can visit the site of the Old Phalatswe Church 20 km east of Palapye. It stands in the former Ngwato capital of Phalatswe, at the foot of the Tswapong Hills near present-day Malaka. After the Christian Ngwato King Khama III arrived with his people from Shoshong in 1889, Phalatswe was transformed virtually overnight from a spot in the desert into a settlement of 30,000 people. The simple 'Gothic'-style church, now in ruins, was completed in 1892 at a cost of P3000, funded by the people themselves.

When the Ngwato capital shifted to Serowe in 1902, King Khama sent a regiment to set fire to Phalatswe (the rail siding of Palapye was left intact), but the church remained standing. Since then, the weather has taken its toll and bits of the church have been conscripted for use on construction projects in Serowe. Today, only 1½ gables remain standing, but restoration work is now underway and Phalatswe is slated to become a national monument. While you're exploring, look out for the remaining poles of King Khama's kgotla and the stone remnants of other early Phalatswe buildings. Of course, Botswana law requires that everything be left intact.

Places to Stay & Eat

Palapye has two hotels. The up-market *Cresta Botsalo* (☎ 420245) on the Gaborone-Francistown road is used mostly by drivers on the dreary trip between Botswana's two largest cities. Rooms cost US$66/83, with bed and breakfast. Its dining room is probably the best restaurant in town and the hotel bar is predictably popular.

The friendly little *Palapye Hotel* (☎ 420277) lies opposite the railway station five km east of the highway. It may look a bit tatty from the outside, but it's quite viable and is good value at US$34/43 for single/double rooms with TV and breakfast. More basic rooms are available for as little as US$23/34.

In the prominent Engen Shopping Centre along the main highway are two options for a quick bite: *Chicken Licken*, which serves the ubiquitous chicken and chips, and *Tla Pitseng Takeaways*.

Getting There & Away

Buses along the main Gaborone-Francistown road pass through Palapye, as does the railway line. The bus fare to or from Gaborone is US$6.50. Travelling in either direction, the train arrives in the wee hours of the morning.

MAHALAPYE

Mahalapye has little to offer but spacious skies, distant horizons and a welcome break from the highway. Most drivers aim for Mahalapye like a speeding bullet, past the cacographical sign announcing the 'Tropic of Capricon', with the radio blaring, the pop tops open and dreams of a snack at Kaytee's – the truckies never miss this one – before facing the next stretch of open highway.

Although it's not much to look at, Mahalapye is actually one of Botswana's nicer small towns, with a friendly demeanour and shabby but relaxed appearance. With good reason, Mahalapye is frequently confused with Palapye, 69 km to the north. The original name, Mhalatswe (until mis-transliteration took its toll), was probably derived from the Sekgalagadi word for 'a large herd

of impalas'. Since Mahalapye is mainly a refuelling stop for both vehicles and travellers, there are lots of petrol stations, shops and takeaway places.

Shoshong

In the Shoshong Hills, 45 km west of Mahalapye, lie the stone-walled ruins of another Ngwato capital, which was inhabited prior to the Ngwato relocation to Phalatswe (Palapye). In the same area are ancient mine workings dating perhaps from as early as the 8th century.

The modern village of Shoshong, accessible from Mahalapye, is laid out according to the traditional Batswana plan, with both a primary and subsidiary kgotla. You can also see the remains of the Hermannsburg Mission and the LMS mission, both established in the mid-19th century.

Places to Stay & Eat

To reach the *Mahalapye Hotel* (☎ 410200) which, according to the Peace Corps was once known as the Chase-Me-Inn, turn east at the post office, left at the roundabout and continue until you see the hotel signpost, about 1.5 km further along. Single/double rooms cost US$45/52 without breakfast. Camping is permitted on the site for US$6 per person and a laundry service is available. A set English-style breakfast costs US$6. The dining room is also good for other meals and isn't too expensive.

Most travellers stop at *Kaytee's*, at the southern end of town, which serves up the best fare along the highway. The service is friendly and you can choose between takeaway and à la carte meals. The sign above the bar reads 'Kaytee's, the Pride of Botswana'. Other options include *Mr Rooster Golden Crisp Chicken*, the *Safari Restaurant*, the *Corner House Restaurant* and the *Chicago Takeaways Wagon*. For its size, Mahalapye also has a well-stocked supermarket.

Entertainment

At Madiba, four km west of Mahalapye, is a disco that for some reason operates only on

Thursday. On Friday the Railway Club screens films, but guests must be invited by a club member. It was started by Zimbabwe Railway employees when Zimbabwe ran the railway. Club membership, which includes access to the cinema as well as the basketball, tennis and squash courts, the swimming pool, ping-pong tables and the cheapest bar in Mahalapye, costs US$35 per family per year.

Getting There & Away

Getting to and from Mahalapye is the same as for Palapye, but with more frequent buses running between the former and Gaborone. The bus fare to or from Gaborone is US$5.

SEROWE

With a population of around 90,000, sprawling Serowe, the Ngwato capital, is the largest village in Botswana – and one of the largest in sub-Saharan Africa. It is the capital of Botswana's largest political district, the Central District, and has served as the Ngwato capital since King Khama III moved it from Phalatswe in 1902. Serowe, like Mochudi, is historically one of Botswana's most interesting villages. So taken by it was writer Bessie Head, a South African immigrant, that she immortalised it in her classic treatise *Serowe – Village of the Rain Wind* and used it as the setting for several other works.

Swaneng Hill Secondary School in Serowe was the source of the highly successful Botswana Brigades movement, which was established in 1965 and has brought vocational education to the most remote areas of the country. A detailed history of the Brigades Movement is found in *Serowe – Village of the Rain Wind*.

Khama III Memorial Museum

Over (or around) the mountain from The Mall is the Khama III Memorial Museum (☎ 430519). It was opened in October 1985 after a concerted effort by local citizens, including Leapeetswe Khama who donated

---

Sir Seretse Khama

When Ngwato chief Khama III died in 1923, he was succeeded by his son Sekgoma, who died only two years later. Because the heir to the throne, Seretse Khama, was only four years old, the job of regent went to his 21-year-old uncle, Tshekedi Khama, who left his studies in South Africa to return to Serowe.

An uproar in the Khama dynasty came in 1948 when Seretse Khama, heir to the Ngwato throne, met and married Englishwoman, Ruth Williams, while studying law in London. As a royal, Seretse was expected – and required – to take a wife from a Tswana royal family. Indignant at such a breach of tribal custom, Tshekedi Khama had his nephew stripped of his inheritance. He was exiled from Serowe by the Ngwato government, and from the Protectorate by the British, who assured him that he'd be better off in London than Bechuanaland.

Furthermore, Tshekedi Khama lost his regency when an overwhelming majority of the Ngwato population backed Seretse over his uncle, forcing Tshekedi Khama to gather his followers and settle elsewhere. Subsequent breakdowns in the Ngwato tribal structure prompted him to return in 1952 with a change of heart. Seretse was still being detained in the UK, however, and it wasn't until 1956, when he renounced his rights to the Ngwato throne, that he was permitted to return to Serowe with Ruth and take up residence. There, they began campaigning for Botswana's independence, which came 10 years later. As a result, Seretse Khama was knighted and became the country's first president, a post which he held until his death 14 years later.

In final reconciliation of past turmoil, Sir Seretse Khama was buried in the royal cemetery in Serowe. Seretse's son, Ian Khama, was given the title of Kgosi, 'chief' of the Ngwato and Ian's mother, Lady Ruth Khama, now holds the status of *Mohumagadi Mma Kgosi*, 'Honoured wife of the King and Mother of the Chief'.

For a thorough treatment of this amazing saga, which reads like a well-conceived novel, check out *A Marriage of Inconvenience – the Persecution of Seretse & Ruth Khama* by Michael Dutfield. For details, refer to the section on Books in the Botswana Facts for the Visitor chapter. ■

PETER PTSCHELINZEW

PETER PTSCHELINZEW

BOTSWANA
A: Village near Maun, Okavango Delta
B: Store in Okavango Delta

DEANNA SWANEY

DEANNA SWANEY

DEANNA SWANEY

A	
B	C

BOTSWANA
A: Tour group crossing a log bridge, Chief's Island, Okavango Delta
B: Okavango Delta
C: Island in the Okavango Delta

his home, the Red House, for the museum premises.

The museum outlines the history of the Khama family, both in and away from Serowe. Displays include the personal effects of King Khama III and his descendants, as well as artefacts illustrating the history of Serowe. There is also a growing natural history display, featuring a large collection of African insects and a display on snakes of the region.

It's open Monday to Friday from 8.30 am to 12.30 pm and 2 to 4.30 pm, and on Saturday from 11 am to 4 pm. Admission is free.

Royal Cemetery

Atop Thathaganyana Hill in the village centre are the ruins of an 11th-century village, which provide evidence of habitation long before the arrival of the Ngwato and the Khama dynasty in 1902. The royal graves lie atop the hill overlooking the kgotla, with the grave of Khama III marked by a bronze duiker, the Ngwato totem. Police consider this vantage point to be sensitive, and require visitors to climb with a police escort.

Khama Rhino Sanctuary

A new attraction currently being developed is the Khama Rhino Sanctuary, 20 km northwest of Serowe, which will serve as a safe house for Botswana's few remaining rhinos. There's currently a boma containing four rhinos, and once the perimeter fence is finished, the animals can be released into the reserve. There are also plans for a tented camp and a camp site.

In the early 1990s, the need for a well-protected rhino reserve was recognised and the reserve was established, on the initiative of Serowe residents, as a sanctuary for both white and black rhinos. The aim of the reserve is to protect Botswana's few remaining rhinos in a safe location away from the country's vulnerable borders.

Once the ball was rolling, it was decided to return the chosen 12,000 hectares to its natural condition, and to reintroduce all species endemic to central Botswana. Two

bore holes were made at Serowe Pan and local farmers were relocated with compensation. The reserve is to be patrolled by BDF trainees stationed in the nearby village of Paje. Although the land can accommodate up to 30 white and 30 black rhinos, a 1992 survey concluded that only nine rhinos, all white, remained in Botswana. Since that survey, four of the rhinos have been poached.

Currently, admission to the reserve is whatever donation you can afford; be assured that whatever you give goes to a good cause. For further information, contact Raymond & Norma Watson at the Dennis Service Station in Serowe (☎ 430232; fax 430992), PO Box 60, Serowe.

Places to Stay & Eat

The *Serowe Hotel* (☎ 430234) on the Palapye side of town has bright single/double rooms with shared facilities starting at US$45/52; they're cheaper without a phone. An English breakfast costs US$5 while a continental breakfast is only US$4.

The run-down *Tshwaragano Hotel* (☎ 430377), on the hillside above The Mall, has grimy single/double rooms for US$37/45. From the outside, at least, it wouldn't look half bad if it weren't for all the trash lying around – at the time of this research, the entrance to one room was graced by a broken toilet. Only eat at the restaurant if you have sterling patience. When you can get them, very basic meals cost US$3 to US$6. The attached bar, which runs surprisingly smoothly, is the heart of the village social scene.

The best option for meals is either the Serowe Hotel dining room or *Tshukudu (Rhino) Takeaways* at the Engen petrol station. You'll also find Indian and Chinese takeaway meals at the *Central Supermarket Restaurant* in The Mall.

Things to Buy

The uniquely intricate and easily recognisable Serowe woodcarving is produced at Marulamans on the fringes of Serowe. You can either visit the Serowe Woodcarvers

BOTSWANA

outlet near the Cash Bazaar in The Mall, or the workshop, which is a complicated trip from the centre. For directions, see the Roman Catholic mission, which sponsors the artists.

Getting There & Away

Getting to Serowe on public transport first entails getting to Palapye, then catching one of the several daily buses for the remaining 46 km into the village. Some of the buses continue on to Orapa while others just return to Palapye. Hitching the route from Palapye is straightforward since there's a fair amount of traffic to and from the Orapa diamond mine further up the road.

Drivers who are tempted to try the short-cut to Maun via Orapa and Rakops should note that the road effectively ends at Rakops and 4WD is necessary for the rugged trip through to the Nata-Maun road. This route isn't feasible for hitching.

Getting Around

There's a branch of Holiday Car Hire (☎/fax 430520) at Shinga House in the centre.

North-Eastern Botswana

With its several national parks and wildlife reserves, north-eastern Botswana holds a strong appeal for visitors. Although the newly amalgamated Makgadikgadi & Nxai Pan National Park offers an almost pristine vision of Africa, access is difficult and it lacks facilities, leaving Chobe National Park as the biggest drawcard. Indeed, many of Botswana's visitors get their only taste of the country on a one or two-day foray to the Chobe riverfront from nearby Victoria Falls in Zimbabwe.

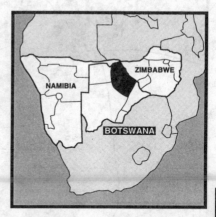

The Makgadikgadi Pans Region

Covering more than 12,000 sq km, Botswana's great salt pans, Sua (or Sowa) and Ntwetwe, collectively comprise the Makgadikgadi pans. (They shouldn't be confused, however, with the grassy national park of a similar name which encompasses only a small corner of Ntwetwe Pan.) It was on these pans that Tim Liversedge made his award-winning wildlife film *March of the Flame Birds*. On a different artistic level, the pans also provided a bleak backdrop for the scene from *The Gods Must be Crazy*, in which a tiny tractor towed a decrepit Land Rover across the blazing salt. What's more, the ancient ruins on Kubu Island in south-western Sua Pan were the inspiration for Wilbur Smith's fantasy novel, *The Sunbird*.

If you've never experienced a salt pan landscape, you'll discover it's like no other scene on earth. Especially during the sizzling heat of late winter days, the stark pans take on a disorienting and ethereal austerity. Heat mirages destroy all sense of the terrestrial, and imaginary lakes shimmer and disappear, ostriches fly and stones turn to mountains and float in mid-air.

Then, in September, the great herds of wildebeests, antelopes and zebras begin moving into the thirsty grasslands west of the pans to await the first rains. Hours after it falls, the pans become a perfect reflection of the sky, dissolving all sense of up or down, distance or direction. Although the water is short-lived, animals gravitate towards depressions which retain stores of water after the surface film has evaporated.

Then around December, the deluge begins. The fringing grasses turn green and the herds of wildlife migrate in to partake of the bounty. As if from nowhere, millions of flamingoes, pelicans, ducks, geese and other water birds arrive at the mouth of the Nata River in Sua Pan to build their nests along the shoreline, feeding on the algae and tiny crustaceans which have lain dormant in the salt awaiting the rains.

Geology

The Makgadikgadi pans are the residue of a great lake which once covered much of northern Botswana, fed by rivers carrying salts leached from the lake's catchment area. Ancient lakeshore terraces reveal that the water depth fluctuated as much as 33 metres and, at its greatest extent, the lake covered

BOTSWANA

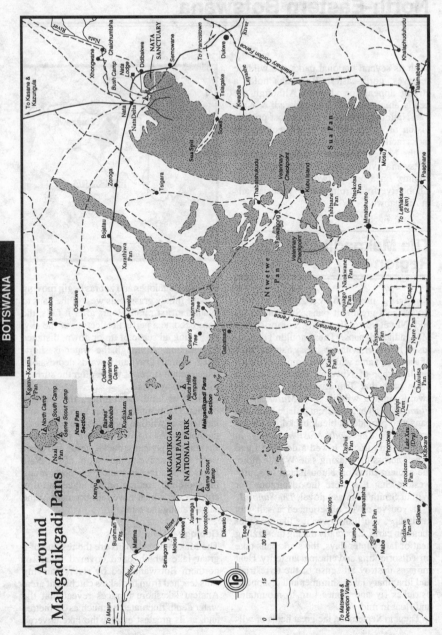

Around Makgadikgadi Pans

an area of 60,000 sq km. Since the basin had no outlet, the salts were concentrated on the lowest lying areas. Less than 10,000 years ago, climatic changes caused the lake to evaporate, but the salt deposits remained.

NATA

Although all the roads converging on this three-way junction are now tarred, Nata has somehow managed to remain a dust hole. Thanks to the distance between petrol stations, it serves mostly as an obligatory refuelling stop for anyone travelling between Kasane, Francistown and Maun. If you're counting, Nata lies 190 smooth km from Francistown, and 300 from both Kasane and Maun. Many travellers find themselves hitching through en route between these three centres, and most wind up at the Sua Pan Lodge, which offers inexpensive camping options. Nata now also has a resident vehicle mechanic, Peter Robson (☎ 611226).

Organised Tours

For groups of four to 10 people, Nata Lodge runs organised trips to the edge of Sua Pan and runs custom safaris onto the pans, to Makgadikgadi & Nxai Pan National Park, and even as far afield as Chobe and the Okavango.

Places to Stay & Eat

The action in Nata, such as it is, centres on *Sua Pan Lodge* (☎ /fax 611220) with its fuel pumps, water tap, bottle store, bar, restaurant, hotel, swimming pool (albeit dust-corrupted) and campground. Single/double rondavels with bath cost US$37/45 while camping is US$4 per person. A simple single rondavel without bath is just US$28. The camp site lies at the intersection of the three highways, just 50 metres from the public bar, so it's not the most tranquil of locations. Non-residents can use the pool for US$4 per person.

Friendly *Nata Lodge* (☎ /fax 611210), 10 km south-east of Nata on the Francistown road, has a much nicer campground. It's set in a green oasis of monkey thorn, marula and mokolane palms, and also boasts an excellent and affordable restaurant, an outdoor bar, a Shell petrol station and a cool swimming pool. Three-bed chalets cost US$63 and extra beds are US$8. Preset four-bed tents with bedding included cost US$37 – a good deal if in a group. Camping in your own tent or caravan costs US$4 per person, which includes use of the pool. A continental/English breakfast costs US$6/7 and three-course dinners are US$15. Hitching is easy both ways between the lodge and town.

Nata Lodge also has a remote self-catering *bush camp* on the normally dry and sandy bed of the Nata River; they like to promote it as 'a beach without water'. Up to 12 people are accommodated for a nightly rate of US$30 per person, which includes transfers from Nata Lodge and organised game walks and drives through the lovely desert landscape. Birdwatching is particularly rewarding here, especially in the rainy season. Pony-trekking is being considered.

For another nearby camping option, see Nata Sanctuary, under Sua Pan later in this section.

Getting There & Away

All buses travelling between Kasane, Francistown and Maun pass through Nata. Since the petrol station at the Sua Pan Lodge is a natural stop for everyone travelling through Nata, it's the best place to wait for a lift. Alternatively, you can perhaps arrange a lift around the bar at Nata Lodge. The Mahube Express bus for Maun passes between 10 and 11 am.

SUA PAN

Sua Pan is mostly a single sheet of salt-encrusted mud stretching across the lowest basin in north-eastern Botswana. *Sua* means 'salt' in the language of the San, who once mined the pan to sell salt to the Kalanga. Except during the driest years, flocks of water-loving birds gather during the wet season to nest at the delta where the Nata River flows into the northern end of Sua Pan. At this time of year, the entire expanse is often covered with a film of water only cm

---

Driving on the Pans

In addition to the directives on bush driving in the Botswana Getting Around chapter, prospective drivers on the salt pans should remember other standard rules. First, follow the tracks of other drivers (unless you see bits of vehicles poking above the surface, of course). If they've made it, chances are the way is dry. Second, stay aware of where you are at all times by using a map and compass. If you're driving through a complicated area near the edges of the pans, note any islands or landmarks you may encounter.

If you're unsure about whether the pan is dry, stick to the edges. If it has recently rained, however, don't venture onto the pans at all unless you're absolutely sure that both the salty surface and the clay beneath it are dry. Foul-smelling salt means a wet and potentially dangerous pan, very similar in appearance and character to wet concrete. When underlying clay becomes saturated, vehicles can break through the crust and become irretrievably bogged.

If you do get bogged and have a winch, anchor the spare wheel or the jack – anything to which the winch may be attached – by digging a hole and planting it firmly in the concrete-like pan surface. Hopefully, you'll be able to anchor it better than the pan has anchored the vehicle! ∎

---

deep, an eerie and surreal surface that reflects the sky and obliterates the horizon.

Nata Sanctuary

The 230-sq km Nata Sanctuary is a community project designed as a refuge for the wildlife on and around Sua Pan (45% of the reserve's land area is on the pan). The idea of a sanctuary was raised in 1988 by the Nata Conservation Committee. With the expertise of the Kalahari Conservation Society and funding from organisations around Botswana and elsewhere, it was realised four years later. Local people voluntarily relocated 3500 cattle onto adjacent rangeland and put in a network of dust roads.

Most of the wildlife is of the winged variety, and around 165 species have been recorded, from kingfishers and bee-eaters to eagles, bustards and ostriches. There are also numerous small birds native to both savanna and woodland. When the Nata River is flowing, this corner of Sua Pan becomes a watery paradise that attracts water birds from all around Africa, including teals, ducks and geese, as well as hosts of pelicans, spoonbills and both greater and lesser flamingoes.

Mammal species are restricted to a few antelope species – hartebeests, kudu, reedbucks, springboks and steenboks, and small African mammals, like springhares, jackals, foxes, monkeys and squirrels. Elands, gemsboks and zebras are also being reintroduced, and there are currently plans to engineer a permanent water hole, which will be filled with water pumped from the Nata riverbed.

In the dry season, you won't need 4WD, but high clearance is advisable. The entrance lies 20 km from Nata on the Francistown road. It's open for day visits from 7 am to 7 pm daily (special permission may be granted for early morning or late evening visits) and admission costs US$4 per person, including one night camping and use of braai facilities. Proceeds benefit the local community, which manages the sanctuary. At the entrance, women from surrounding villages sell handwoven Nata baskets.

Kubu Island

Near the south-western corner of Sua Pan lies the original desert island. But for one tenuous finger of grass, the alien-looking outcrop of Kubu Island and its ghostly baobabs lie surrounded by a sea of salt. The island, an ancient scrap of rock thrust up from beneath the salt, rises perhaps 20 metres above the flats and affords an expansive but nearly featureless view.

At one edge of the island is an ancient crescent-shaped stone enclosure of unknown age or origin, and a number of artefacts – pot shards, various stone tools and ostrich eggshell beads – have been discovered. Current estimates place the date of habitation anywhere from 500 to 1500 years ago. It may be difficult to imagine a time when the water supply was sufficient for human habitation, but it's also worth noting that the name of the island means 'hippopotamus' in Zulu-based languages. It's a mystery worthy of further investigation.

If the weather isn't too hot, Kubu Island makes an excellent otherworldly camp site, and it's worth experiencing its changing moods. It's an undeniably bizarre and magical place and you may have the sense of being a castaway on an alien planet.

Bear in mind that no water is available.

Getting There & Away Access to Kubu Island isn't entirely straightforward – lost beyond a maze of grassy islets and salty bays, the final approach crosses an open expanse of salt. However, tracks are becoming more obvious as increasing traffic carves them deeper and deeper. A 4WD vehicle and a reliable compass are essential.

One of the routes turns off the Nata-Maun road at an unsignposted route about 17 km west of Nata. After two km or so, you'll cross the old Nata-Maun road, but don't turn. As best you can, follow the convoluted tracks in a general southerly direction. In several places, the road ushers you into a cattle post and appears to stop. Don't despair – just look around in the bush for a track heading south.

After about 65 km, you'll reach the sparsely built village of Thabatshukudu, which occupies an unearthly landscape on a low ridge. The locals are accustomed to lost visitors enquiring about where Kubu Island is, and some can provide help.

Immediately south of Thabatshukudu, the route skirts the edge of a salt pan. After 15 km or so, it passes through a veterinary checkpoint; 1.5 km south of this barrier is the turn-off onto the northern route to Kubu Island. Here you turn south-eastward (left).

Alternatively, you can approach from the south. Turn north from the Francistown-Orapa road about 20 km east of Orapa along the road that passes between Sua and Ntwetwe pans. After 20 km, you'll reach the convoluted village of Mmatshumo. (Coming from Francistown, you can also reach Mmatshumo via the back road from Tlalamabele via Mosu.) Make sure you leave the village on the right track – there are several of them and the right way isn't obvious.

North of Mmatshumo, you'll have 14 km of alternating rough and sandy track before the route crosses an obvious line of trees perpendicular to the road. The trees mark a fault line and the presence of water in the underlying geological structure. After another six km, you'll reach the southern veterinary checkpoint; from this landmark, it's a further five km to the east (right) turning to Kubu Island, which is marked only by a small cairn.

Assuming you've found the proper turning from either direction, Kubu Island lies less than 20 km away. There should be at least vague vehicle tracks leading across the salt and tussocks of salt grass, and before long, the rocky 20-metre summit of the island should come into view. If you're not sure the pan is dry, stick to the roundabout route along the edge of the salt.

Ntwetwe Pan

Convoluted Ntwetwe Pan covers more area than its eastern counterpart, Sua Pan. It was once fed by the waters of the Boteti, but they were diverted at Mopipi Dam to provide water for the Orapa diamond mine. Since then, the pan has remained almost permanently dry. The western shore of Ntwetwe Pan is probably the most interesting landscape in the Makgadikgadi area, with mazes of rocky outcrops, dunes, islets, channels and spits.

Getting There & Away

Of the two big pans, Sua Pan is the more accessible, but to explore it at length, you need 4WD and a good map and compass, as well as lots of common sense and confidence in your driving and directional skills.

The pans have a mesmerising effect and emit a sense of unfettered freedom. Once I'd driven out onto the salt, all sense of direction, connection, reason and common sense appeared to dissolve. If you're like me, you'll be tempted to speed off with wild abandon into the white and empty distances – but restrain yourself. To do so could prove disastrous. Drive only in the tracks of vehicles that have gone before and keep to the edges of the pan.

There's no problem camping anywhere around the edges of the salt – indeed it's a haunting experience – but you must be self-sufficient in food, fuel, water and all other necessary supplies.

If you prefer leaving the driving to someone else, Nata Lodge (see under Nata) arranges custom mobile safaris into the pan. They're not cheap, but you will save the considerable time and expense of organising a private expedition. Alternatively, you can join one of the lodge's trips to the edge of Sua Pan for US$19 per person (with a minimum of four people).

Car & Motorbike Although the pans area is crisscrossed with mazes of tracks, safe routes are changeable and unreliable, so always seek local advice before venturing into remote areas. Three north-south networks of tracks connect the Nata-Maun road with the Francistown-Orapa road, one on either side of the pans and one down the strip between them (which passes within striking distance of Kubu Island). Taking any of these routes, however, amounts more to an expedition than a casual drive.

During the dry season, you can have a cursory look at Sua Pan from several places without 4WD. The easiest and quickest is in the previously described Nata Sanctuary. Another access route is via the signposted turn-off to Sua Spit, about a 10-minute drive north of the Dukwe buffalo fence. The spit, a long slender protrusion extending into the heart of Sua Pan, is the nexus of Botswana's lucrative soda ash industry. Security measures prevent public access to the plant, but private vehicles may proceed as far as Sua, on the pan's edge.

Hitching To find a lift, ask around Nata Lodge or Gweta Rest Camp and see who's going. Alternatively, hitch to Nata Sanctuary and walk; maps of the tracks are available at the entry gate.

GWETA

The village of Gweta, 100 km west of Nata, is a popular refuelling and travellers' rest stop. The name is onomatopoeic; like Kwe Kwe in Zimbabwe, it was derived from the croaking sound made by large bullfrogs *(Pyxicephalus adspersus)*. The frogs actually bury themselves in the sand until the rains provide sufficient water for them to emerge and mate.

Organised Tours

Gweta Rest Camp organises a variety of tours in the area, as well as customised safaris further afield. A popular destination is their affiliated tented camp at Nxhasin Pan, 25 km north of Gweta. It's super for birdwatching and is also frequented by elephants, lions, kudus, jackals and hyena, as well as other species. An overnight trip to the pan costs US$45 per person, including accommodation, dinner, breakfast and transfers from Gweta. They also run three-hour bird-watching and wildlife-viewing visits to Nxhasin Pan at 3 pm each day for just US$12 per person.

Alternatively, you can choose between a three-hour horse-riding trip for US$12 per person; an all-day 4WD spin through the salt pans for US$75; or a simple walking tour of Gweta village for just US$2 per person. Two-night package tours of the salt pans on four-wheel ATVs (all-terrain vehicles), including one night each in Gweta and Nxhasin Pan, cost US$149 per person.

Places to Stay & Eat

The focus of activity for visitors in the picturesque village is the friendly *Gweta Rest Camp* (☎ /fax 612220), which provides an affordable respite along the route between Nata and Maun – and the best hot showers in Botswana. At the popular rest camp restaurant and bar, you'll get inexpensive and well-prepared meals and snacks. Single/double thatched rondavels with shared bath are US$28/34; with a private bath, they are US$36/45. Camping costs US$4 per person. You'll find reasonably priced fuel at the cooperative near the back gate.

Getting There & Away

Gweta lies just off the main Nata-Maun road. You can take the Mahube Express bus from either Maun (US$5) or Francistown (US$6).

MAKGADIKGADI & NXAI PAN NATIONAL PARK

West of Gweta, the road slices through Makgadikgadi & Nxai Pan National Park. Because of their complementary natures regarding wildlife migrations, Makgadikgadi Pans Game Reserve and Nxai Pan National Park were established concurrently in early 1970s, in hopes of protecting the entire ecosystem. In 1992, when the new tarred highway went through, Nxai Pan National Park was extended south to the road to take in Baines' Baobabs, and the two parks are now administered as one entity: Makgadikgadi & Nxai Pan National Park.

Visitors to either section of the park are subject to the usual park fees (unless you're just transiting on the Nata-Maun road), which are payable at the Xumaga or Nxai Pan Game scout camps. To camp at any of the park camp sites, visitors pay the standard parks fees, regardless of amenities provided.

Makgadikgadi Pans Game Reserve Section

South of the Nata-Maun road is the Makgadikgadi Pans Game Reserve section of the park, a 3900-sq-km tract of pans, grasslands and beautiful savanna country. Wildlife is plentiful but since the reserve is unfenced, animals may wander in and out at will, and you won't see the artificially high numbers found at Chobe. During the winter dry season, animals concentrate around the Boteti River, but between February and April, huge herds of zebras and wildebeests migrate north to Nxai Pan and beyond, only returning to the Boteti when the rains cease in early May.

There is a range of antelopes, including impala, gemsboks, hartebeests and kudu, but they don't appear in large numbers except during the in-migrations in May and June. Lions and hyena are present (and heard nightly at Game Scout Camp), cheetahs are

Mokolane Palm

Dotted around the park are islands of mokolane palm (*Hyphaene petersiana*), from which comes vegetable ivory. (They're known in Zimbabwe as ilala palms and in Namibia as makalani palms.) This solid white nut carves beautifully and is used in jewellery and art, and the fronds are the main component in the beautiful Botswana baskets. The palm is also tapped for its sap, which is allowed to ferment or is distilled into a potent liquor known as palm wine. The Makgadikgadi specimens are officially protected from thirsty sap-tappers, but elsewhere, over-exploitation and increasing numbers of cattle, which nibble the young shoots, have brought the palm under serious threat. ■

sometimes observed and the Boteti River supports a healthy population of hippos. You'll also see a stunning array of birds, but owing to the lack of reliable water sources, elephants and buffaloes are missing. Only during extremely wet seasons does the occasional stray wander in.

Places to Stay The public camp site is at the *Game Scout Camp* near Xhumaga, on the park's western boundary. There's a loo and a sometimes operable cold shower, and drinking water is available but it's quite sulphurous. Wild camping is prohibited in the park; some people try it anyway, but it can be dangerous and penalties are stiff.

You'll also find two *wild camp sites* atop the two Njuca Hills, 20 km from the Game Scout Camp. Each has a pit toilet, but no water is available.

Getting There & Away All visitors need 4WD. The most straightforward access is via the well-worn but unsignposted route turning south from the Nata-Maun road, eight km east of the Phuduhudu access road. From there, it's 30-km of deep sands through beautiful stands of palms and vast savanna to the Game Scout Camp beside the Boteti.

Nxai Pan National Park Section

Thanks to its recent extension, the Nxai Pan National Park section, which once covered

BOTSWANA

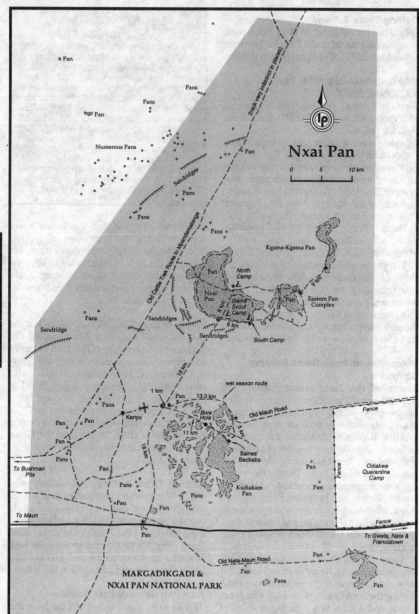

2100 sq km, now takes in over 4000 sq km. Nxai Pan itself is part of the same ancient lake bed as Sua and Ntwetwe pans, but it wasn't so low lying and when the lake evaporated, it escaped the encrustations of leached salts. However, Kudiakam Pan, in the park's southern area, is actually a complex of mini salt pans similar to Sua and Ntwetwe pans.

Nxai Pan is one of the few places in Botswana which are more interesting in the rainy season. Although your movements may be restricted by flooding around some pans, from February to April is the best season to see large herds of animals in Nxai's grassy pans. The numbers can be staggering; wildebeests, zebras and gemsboks appear in their thousands, along with large herds of other antelopes and giraffes. Lions, hyena and wild dogs come to take advantage of the varied menu and bat-eared foxes also emerge in force. At such times, Nxai Pan, which is specked with umbrella acacia trees, can resemble a wilder version of the Serengeti (without all the safari vehicles). During the dry, wildlife activity concentrates on the one artificially pumped water hole.

From the public camp site at South Camp, it's 15 km to the eastern pan complex, which is also rich in wildlife. Another nine km further on, you'll reach the southern end of Kgama-Kgama Pan, where King Khama III of the Ngwato once had a cattle post.

Baines' Baobabs Originally known as the Sleeping Sisters, this hardy clump of large baobabs was immortalised by artist and adventurer Thomas Baines on 22 May 1862, when he painted them for posterity. Baines, who was a resourceful self-taught naturalist, artist and cartographer, first came to Botswana in 1861, travelling with trader and naturalist John Chapman from Namibia to Victoria Falls. He had originally been a member of David Livingstone's expedition to the Zambezi, but was mistakenly accused of theft by Livingstone's brother and forced to leave the party. Livingstone later realised the mistake, but never admitted it and Baines remained the subject of British ridicule.

There's nothing out of the ordinary about this stately group of trees, but when the pan contains water their setting is especially lovely. A comparison with Baines' painting reveals that in well over 100 years, only one branch has disassociated itself.

When the new Nata-Maun road went through, Baines' Baobabs were incorporated into Makgadikgadi & Nxai Pan National Park. To visit them or to camp, you need a permit from either the Xumaga Game Scout Camp in the Makgadikgadi Pans Game Reserve section, or from the one at Nxai Pan headquarters. Bush camping is possible with a permit, but there are no facilities.

Places to Stay Visitors to Nxai Pan must be self-sufficient. From the Game Scout Camp, the North Camp public camp site lies eight km north across the pan (it may be inaccessible during the wet) and the South Camp is eight km east of the Game Scout Camp. South Camp has toilets and, most of the time, water. There's also an elevated viewing platform overlooking the pan. North Camp has toilets and a tap for water. Pay for camping permits at the Game Scout Camp.

Getting There & Away As with the Makgadikgadi Pans Game Reserve section, a 4WD vehicle is necessary to visit Nxai Pan. Turn north from the Nata-Maun road 170 km west of Francistown and continue along that track for about 35 km to the Game Scout Camp at the edge of Nxai Pan.

To reach Baines' Baobabs also requires 4WD. Take the same turn-off as you would for Nxai Pan, but drive only 18 km north of the Nata-Maun road and turn right. After one km, the road forks. During the wet season, you'll have to take the left fork which follows a longer route around Kudiakam Pan. After just over 13 km, take the right turning and follow that side track four km further to the baobabs. During the dry season, however, you should take the right fork and follow the 11-km shortcut across Kudiakam Pan to Baines' Baobabs.

Without your own vehicle, access to the park is either expensive or nigh impossible.

Mobile safaris into the park are most easily arranged through Maun travel agencies. Otherwise, you may be out of luck unless you can find the sort of golden lift that pervades the dreams of hitchhikers in Botswana.

ORAPA

Orapa's *raison d'être* is diamonds, and it's surrounded by several huge fences to keep the public at bay. To visit this self-contained community and have a look at the mines, you will need a permit from Debswana (☎ 351131; fax 352941), PO Box 329, Gaborone. Orapa is served by buses from both Francistown and Palapye.

LETHLAKANE

This rather aloof little diamond mining centre lies 40 km south-east of Orapa. Although the Lethlakane mine is smaller than its Orapa counterpart, the gem quality is generally better. The town itself is little more than a collection of workers' housing, government buildings and petrol stations, but the mountainous heaps of mine tailings are impressive.

For anyone passing through, a good place to eat is *Granny's Kitchen* at the Shell petrol station, which features such typically Botswanan fare as roast beef and Yorkshire pudding with port wine sauce – by candlelight. The sign out the front reads 'Book early to avoid disappointment'.

MPANDAMATENGA

This minor Zimbabwe-Botswana border crossing just off the Nata-Kasane road sits in the heart of sorghum and maize country between the Kazuma and Sibuyu Forest Reserves. The name comes from the Mpandamatenga Trail from central Botswana, a route used by early White hunters to transport ivory to the Zambezi River. There's little action in Mpandamatenga; even the Shell petrol station seems to be perpetually closed.

If you're entering Zimbabwe from this direction (the Zimbabwean village is spelt Pandamatenga but pronounced the same way), check in at the police station on the Zimbabwe side, which is open until 5 pm Monday to Friday. Immigration formalities may be handled at either Bulawayo or Victoria Falls. Note that you cannot visit Zimbabwe's Kazuma Pan National Park until you've checked in with Immigration, so this is not an alternative route to the park from Victoria Falls.

Chobe National Park

After a visit in the 1930s, the Resident Commissioner of Bechuanaland, Sir Charles Rey, proposed that Chobe be set aside as a game reserve, but nothing came of the proposal until 1960 when a small portion was placed under official protection. It wasn't until 1968, after Botswana's independence, that the present national park was created by the new government. Today the park encompasses 11,000 sq km and contains Botswana's most varied wildlife.

The riverfront strip along the northern tier, with its perennial water supply, naturally supports the greatest wildlife concentrations, but the lovely Savuti Marshes of the Mababe Depression in western Chobe also provide prime wildlife habitat and when they contain water, they support myriad water birds. Little-visited Ngwezumba, with its pans and mopane forests, is the park's third major region, and Chobe's north-western corner just grazes another magnificent ecosystem, the vast Linyanti Marshes. As yet, this region remains unprotected.

The northern park entrance lies eight km west of Kasane and is accessible to conventional vehicles. However, to proceed across the park or approach from Maun, you'll need high-clearance 4WD. Due to high water and deep mud, the Savuti area is normally inaccessible (and closed) from January to March.

KASANE & KAZUNGULA

Kasane was once the capital of the Makololo, who came to this area as refugees from the invading Ndebele. The Makololo conquered the incumbent Lozi tribe and were responsible

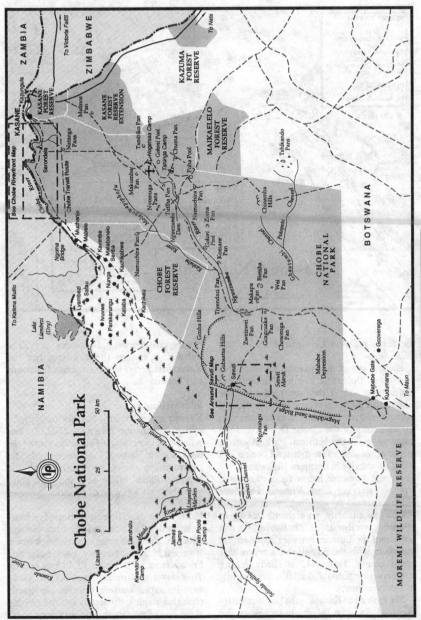

BOTSWANA

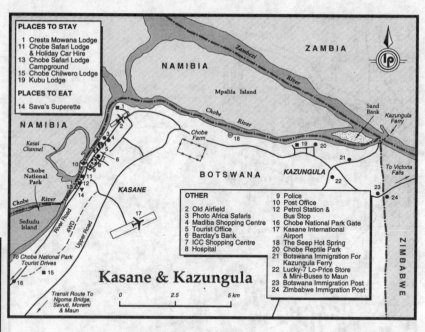

PLACES TO STAY

1 Cresta Mowana Lodge
11 Chobe Safari Lodge
   & Holiday Car Hire
13 Chobe Safari Lodge
   Campground
15 Chobe Chilwero Lodge
19 Kubu Lodge

PLACES TO EAT

14 Sava's Superette

OTHER

2 Old Airfield
3 Photo Africa Safaris
4 Madiba Shopping Centre
5 Tourist Office
6 Barclay's Bank
7 ICC Shopping Centre
8 Hospital
9 Police
10 Post Office
12 Petrol Station &
   Bus Stop
16 Chobe National Park Gate
17 Kasane International
   Airport
18 The Seep Hot Spring
20 Chobe Reptile Park
21 Botswana Immigration For
   Kazungula Ferry
22 Lucky-7 Lo-Price Store
   & Mini-Buses to Maun
23 Botswana Immigration Post
24 Zimbabwe Immigration Post

Kasane & Kazungula

for guiding David Livingstone to Victoria Falls.

Kasane sits at the meeting point of four countries – Botswana, Zambia, Namibia and Zimbabwe – and the confluence of the Chobe and Zambezi rivers. It's also the end of the tarred road and serves as the administrative centre of the Chobe District and the gateway to Chobe National Park. As such, this town of just a few thousand people is a focus of activity in northern Botswana.

Kasane, however, has no focus of its own. Visitors arriving from Victoria Falls are either charmed or appalled by its sense of African spontaneity, an element lacking in relatively well-ordered Zimbabwe. Strung out along the tarmac, it teases approaching travellers with the promise of a centre that never comes. However, its shady setting amid riverine woodland adds a strong positive dimension.

Six km east of Kasane is the tiny nonsettlement of Kazungula which serves as the

border post between Botswana and Zimbabwe. It's also the landing for the Kazungula Ferry, which connects Botswana and Zambia.

Information

Kasane has a friendly but not too helpful tourist information office (☎ 250327). You will find it in a cluster of caravans east of the bank. Chobe National Park information and rudimentary maps are available at the National Parks' office near the park entry gate about six km west of Kasane.

Money The main branch of Barklays Bank is housed in an odd-looking ultra-modern structure along the main road through town. It's open Monday, Tuesday, Wednesday and Friday from 8.15 am to 12.45 pm and on Thursday and Saturday from 8.15 to 10.45 am. To avoid wasting time in the queue changing money, especially around payday at the end of the month, you may want to try the Barklays sub-branch upstairs at the Cresta Mowana Lodge. It's open Monday and Thursday from 10 am to 2 pm; Tuesday, Wednesday and Friday from 10 am to 12.45 pm; and on Saturday from 8.30 to 10 am.

Post & Telecommunications The post office lies about 300 metres east of Chobe Safari Lodge. There are public telephones at the new airport, at the post office and in Kazungula village. Chobe Safari Lodge also books calls, but charges inordinate rates.

Immigration Since all local border posts now have immigration facilities, it's no longer necessary for arriving travellers to check into Botswana at the Kasane police station. The Immigration posts for Zimbabwe and Zambia are at the Victoria Falls road border and the Kazungula ferry, respectively. There's also a new post at the Ngoma Bridge border with Namibia.

Film & Photography You can buy a limited range of film at Savas Superette; for a better selection try the Cresta Mowana Hotel.

Things to See
The newish **Chobe Reptile Park**, in Kazungula downriver from Kubu Lodge, claims to be the proud owner of the world's largest captive crocodile (known as Nelson), among other things. Tours are conducted at 9 and 11 am and 2.30 and 4.30 pm daily. Admission is US$6 per person.

When you're in Kazungula, don't miss the two hollow **baobabs** at the Botswana Women's Prison; in past years, one was actually used as a cell and the other as a prison kitchen. This is considered a strategic site and photography is prohibited.

About two km west of Kubu Lodge, along the river, is **The Seep Hot Spring**, which bubbles out above the riverbank and is popular with local bathers. The water is thought to be rich in health-promoting minerals.

Activities
At the Cresta Mowana Lodge, you can participate in two-hour horse-riding trips at 6 and 9 am and 2 and 4 pm daily. The cost is US$19 per person.

Organised Tours
For information on organised trips and tours in Chobe National Park, see River Trips and Game Drives in the next section.

Places to Stay – bottom end
The most popular, convenient and inexpensive place to stay is the campground at *Chobe Safari Lodge* (☎ 250336), behind the petrol station in Kasane. The campground, which can get crowded and noisy, sits right on the river bank abutting the national park boundary. During 1994, it became extremely popular with hungry elephants from the national park. They often stayed around all night chomping and toppling trees, and became a perceived threat to campers who weren't familiar with elephants. During my last visit, one man sleeping in his vehicle was rattled awake by an elephant who stumbled against the vehicle; the car alarm went off and havoc ensued. A fence has now been built to keep the elephants at bay.

Tent or caravan camping costs P10 per person and there's plenty of space. It does get crowded, especially at weekends and holidays, but they just keep squeezing people in.

Places to Stay – middle
The most popular mid-range accommodation is the conveniently situated *Chobe Safari Lodge* (☎ 650336; fax 650437), which overlooks the river in the heart of Kasane. Basic single/double rondavels cost US$29/35; chalets with en suite facilities are US$50/58, a 'river-view suite' is US$54/65 and (as mentioned previously) camping costs US$6 per person. There's also a laundry service, bottle store, swimming pool, dining room and three bars of varying standards. Book in advance, especially for weekends and holidays.

Alternatively, there's *Kubu Lodge* (☎ 650312; fax 650412), eight km nearer the Zambia and Zimbabwe borders but a long way from Chobe. It lies about one km north of the main Kasane-Kazungula road.

Thatched Swiss-style chalets cost US$52/65 for single/double occupancy. Basic two-bed rondavels cost US$47 and camp sites near the riverbank are US$8 per person. They run transfers to or from the airport for US$8 per person.

Places to Stay – top end

For a taste of luxury, splash out at the wonderfully situated *Cresta Mowana Lodge* (☎ 312222; fax 374321). The hotel, which was designed by a Polish architect, is a lovely, delicate-looking structure that makes the most of the open air and the superb view. It's certainly Botswana's most beautiful building. The name means 'baobab' after the tree which dominates it.

During construction, lightening struck the hotel's namesake baobab and destroyed both the hotel and the tree; they were rebuilt and replaced, respectively.

Batswana artists were employed to paint murals to enliven communal areas, and the tasteful overall décor and close attention to detail work together to enhance the total picture. Each room has a river view and features its own unique designs, with handwoven rugs and hand-painted porcelain washbasins. For a single/double room with bed and breakfast, you'll pay US$109/188. Transfers from the airport are US$3.

An even more up-market option is the secluded *Chobe Chilwero Lodge* (☎ 250234) which sits on the hill about three km from the Chobe entrance gate. The name means 'the vista' and, appropriately, its thatched bungalow accommodation affords a fantastic view over the park and the river. Singles/doubles cost US$207/441 including accommodation, meals, laundry, park fees, game drives and river trips.

If you want to frivolously fling some big bucks, one of Botswana's pinnacles of luxury is the tasteful *Chobe Game Lodge* (☎ 650340; fax 650223), inside Chobe National Park. Overlooking the Chobe River and the plains of Namibia, you'll never be far from the nearest lion, elephant or hippopotamus. Richard Burton and Elizabeth Taylor spent one of their honeymoons in a plush suite, complete with a private swimming pool, which now costs a paltry US$560 per night. More down-to-earth accommodation is US$278/482 for singles/doubles, including park fees, three meals (a lavish buffet breakfast and lunch and a gourmet dinner prepared by renowned European chefs), all the game drives and river trips your heart may desire and meticulous attention to detail. If you forego the frills and opt for just bed and breakfast, single/double rooms are just US$110/175.

For information on Ichingo Camp, which lies on Mpalila Island on the Namibian bank of the Chobe River, see Around Katima Mulilo in the North-Eastern Namibia chapter.

Places to Eat

A buffet English breakfast at *Chobe Safari Lodge* costs US$6.50 and dinners are US$13 for respectable fare. The service may seem chilly, but the coffee is hot and delicious. At *Kubu Lodge* a buffet breakfast or lunch costs US$7.50 and dinners are US$15.

For self-catering, you're limited to the surprisingly well-stocked *Sava's Superette*, diagonally opposite the petrol station. It has a good variety of freeze-dried food and packaged groceries for trips into the bush. Between Kasane and Maun there are only a couple of sparsely stocked bush shops (and well-stocked bottle stores), so it's wise to load up here.

Getting There & Away

Air Air Botswana, with the help of Kasane's new international airport, connects the town to Maun, Gaborone and Victoria Falls. On Monday and Saturday, there are flights to and from Gaborone and Maun; on Thursday to and from Johannesburg and Maun. If you're coming from Gaborone, Air Botswana has recently introduced a 'Chobe Weekend Getaway' package for US$296, including return flights from Gaborone, four nights accommodation at Chobe Safari Lodge, two game drives and a river cruise.

Quicksilver Enterprises (☎ 640532; fax 650223), also called Chobe Air, operates charters from Kasane to Maun, as well as other northern Botswana destinations and Victoria Falls. Single-engine five-passenger planes charter for an average of US$0.75 per km; clients also pay for the plane's return to base, even if it's empty. The average charter rate for five passengers to Maun is US$600.

Bus In theory, two daily buses run between Kasane and Nata, departing from the petrol station sometime between 9 am and 1 pm, but they aren't terribly reliable. The trip takes all day and costs US$10. From the Lucky-7 Lo-Price Store (locally known as the Gumba shop) in Kazungula, there's a daily minibus which leaves for Francistown at 6 am. If you wish to be picked up elsewhere, book at the front desk of the Chobe Safari Lodge.

Between Kasane and Victoria Falls, UTC runs daily transfers for US$20 per person. They leave Victoria Falls at around 7.30 am; in Kasane, they pick up at the hotels between 9.30 and 10 am and then return to Victoria Falls. Under ideal conditions, the trip takes about two hours, including border formalities. The border post is open each day from 7 am to 8 pm.

There's also a weekly bus service between Harare, Zimbabwe and Windhoek, Namibia, which passes through Kasane. Westbound, it arrives at around 8 am on Wednesday morning and eastbound, on Saturday in the mid to late afternoon. The best place to wait is the Kazungula border post.

Car & Motorbike The Kazungula ferry crosses the Zambezi to and from Zambia from 6 am to 6 pm, but because trucks must cross one at a time, drivers should queue up early to minimise the waiting. The trip is free for vehicles registered in Botswana or Zambia. Others pay US$10 to cross with a car and US$20 for a pickup or other large vehicle. Foot passengers travel free of charge. For more information, see the Botswana Getting There & Away chapter.

Hitching Hitching normally proves more convenient than the bus for reaching Nata or Francistown. In the morning, when most people are starting out, hitchhikers have lots of company at the intersection of the Kasane-Kazungula road and the Kasane-Francistown road. You can sometimes increase your chances of a lift by hanging around the petrol station and chatting with drivers as they fill the tank. For lifts to Ngoma Bridge, where the bus runs only weekly, this normally proves relatively fruitful. If you're heading for Ngoma Bridge, ascertain whether your driver intends to travel via the transit route or the riverfront tourist drives. For the latter, you'll have to pay park fees.

Hitching from Kasane to Maun via Chobe National Park isn't really feasible. If you're looking for a through lift from Kasane, remember that most people travelling this scenic but horrid road make the most of it by spending a day or two in Chobe National Park and visiting Moremi Wildlife Reserve along the way. That means – you guessed it – park fees for every day you spend in a national park. The only way to avoid the expense is to hitch to Maun the long way around: through Nata.

Mobile Safaris For information on mobile safaris between Kasane and Maun via Chobe National Park, see under Maun in the Okavango & North-Western Botswana chapter.

Getting Around

Avis (☎ 650144; fax 650145) is based at Kubu Lodge and Holiday Car Hire (☎ 650226; fax 650129) is at Chobe Safari Lodge. For approximate rates, see the Botswana Getting Around chapter. Information on trips in Chobe National Park is provided under River Trips and Game Drives in the following Chobe Riverfront discussion.

CHOBE RIVERFRONT

If you're on a tight budget, a Chobe visit will probably entail a cruise or game drive along the riverfront. While these trips are reasonably priced, park fees must be added for each day or partial day spent in the park.

The most obvious feature of the riverfront

BOTSWANA

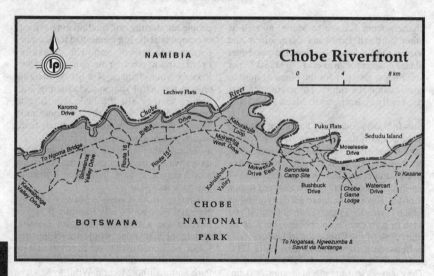

landscape is the damage done by the area's massive elephant herds (see boxed story on the following page) but there's more to the riverfront than decimated bush. You'll have an excellent chance of observing lions and cheetahs, and by day, the water is full of hippos which submerge at dawn and emerge at dusk. Buffaloes are present in their thousands, and amid the scrub live numerous giraffes and zebras.

Most antelope species endemic to Botswana are found here, including kudu, elands, roans, sables, wildebeests, tsessebes, bushbucks, impalas and waterbucks, among others. On rare occasions, you may also see grysboks and oribis. Along the marshy river floodplain, you'll often spot the two antelope trademarks of Chobe, the water-loving red lechwes and the rare pukus, of which perhaps 100 remain. This ruddy antelope has a face like a waterbuck, but has notched, inward-curving horns and the build of a small but stocky impala.

Other residents include jackals, warthogs, brown and spotted hyena, baboons, wild dogs, crocodiles and cape clawless otters, which are often seen playing in the river.

The variety and abundance of bird life in

this attractive zone of permanent water are also notable, from flashy lilac-breasted rollers and white-fronted bee-eaters right up to kori bustards, korhaans, secretary birds, vultures and marabou storks. In the water, you'll see African jacanas, snakebirds, gallinules, herons, ducks and more. Near the river, listen for the screaming fish eagles overhead as they practice their precision diving for fish in the river.

Activities

River Trips One of the best ways to enjoy the riverfront is to take a river trip offered by Kasane-area lodges, but since most cruises enter the park, you must pay park fees as well as the cruise price. The best time to cruise is late afternoon, when the hippos amble onto dry land and the riverfront fills with elephants heading down for a drink and a romp in the water.

Chobe Safari Lodge runs a three-hour afternoon 'booze cruise' up the river on the multi-level boat, the *Fish Eagle*. Lodge guests (including campers) pay US$12 per person while others pay US$17. The Cresta Mowana Lodge does three-hour afternoon booze cruises aboard its riverboat

Chobe's Elephants

As far as wildlife is concerned, the Chobe Riverfront is the park's most densely inhabited area, and here, it may seem the word 'wildlife' is synonymous with 'elephant'. An estimated 73,000 elephants inhabit Chobe National Park, and herds of up to 500 elephants wreak havoc along the riverfront, as evidenced by the trampled bush and the numbers of rammed, flattened, uprooted, toppled and dismembered trees that litter the landscape. It resembles the aftermath of war.

Until recently, the Botswana government maintained that the best course would be to let nature handle the problem. Hunting bans were imposed in the hope that the pressure on riverfront vegetation would decrease once elephants felt safe to migrate elsewhere. Unfortunately, the pachyderms have continued to multiply and refugees have migrated from neighbouring countries to this safe haven (across the Chobe River in Namibia, the wildlife has long since disappeared and one now sees only cattle on the opposite bank). In 1990, the Botswana government decided culling would begin the following year; as in Zimbabwe, entire herds rather than individual elephants were to be shot. These plans didn't go ahead, however, and the elephant population is still booming. ∎

Mmadikwena for US$17. Early morning breakfast cruises cost US$26.

Chobe Game Lodge runs an afternoon cruise on the *Mosi-oa-Tunya*, a pretty good replica of the *African Queen*, for US$17 per person. During the day, the game lodge runs river tours by small motorboat whenever someone wants to go. Non-guests of the lodge pay US$19 per person for the two-hour trip. The small boats are preferable to the larger ones because they accommodate smaller groups and can move in for good views of the animals without alarming or endangering them.

Game Drives Kubu Lodge and Chobe Game Lodge set out to ply the riverfront routes at 6.15 am and 4 pm; the trips last for 2½ hours. Both times of day are worthwhile, but if you take a morning game drive, you can also take an afternoon booze cruise and pay park fees

for only one day. For maximum economy, you can do both game drives as well as a small boat trip at midday. The two-hour game drives cost US$17.

Cresta Mowana Lodge offers a variation on the standard game drive, which lasts five hours and includes either a bush breakfast (US$26) or a champagne brunch (US$41).

Places to Stay

Serondela Camp, 10 km west of the park gate, is Chobe's most accessible camp site. According to game drivers, Serondela was once an inhabited village which was uprooted and shifted to Kasane when Chobe became a national park.

Serondela occupies a lovely spot and has toilets, cold water showers and incredible wildlife-viewing opportunities, but don't count on sound snoozing. Activity hums through the night and the incessant noises – many of them unclassified – may leave campers feeling vulnerable and unnerved. By day, campers are under constant surveillance by cheeky baboons, who long ago learnt that all the best pickings come from tents and backpacks.

Chobe Game Lodge, Kubu Lodge and Chobe Safari Lodge (Go Wild Safaris) run transfers to and from Serondela Camp in conjunction with morning and afternoon game drives, but this isn't considered an organised tour, so campers must pay the full park and camping fees. You can ask to be picked up the following day.

Getting There & Away

Northern Entrance The northern entrance of the park lies eight km west of Kasane and is accessible by conventional vehicle. However, to approach from Maun or proceed southward across the park requires a high-clearance 4WD vehicle. Due to high water, Savuti is normally closed (and inaccessible anyway) between January and March.

Transit Route Driving or hitching the transit route across the park to the Namibian Border at Ngoma Bridge is free, but it shouldn't be considered a cheap way of seeing the park.

BOTSWANA

Sedudu Island

While travelling along the river between Kasane and the Chobe park boundary, you will notice Sedudu Island, a flat, grassy mid-river island with a look-out platform and a Botswana flag planted on it. Old German maps placed this island in Namibia, English ones had it in Botswana. During the South African occupation of Namibia, the dispute heated up and international arbitration was called in to settle the matter. The experts determined that the deeper river channel passed to the north of the island, thus placing Sedudu Island on the Botswana side.

The Namibians, on the other hand, call the island Kasikile, and they reject the ruling that it belongs to Botswana, instead maintaining that the issue 'remains in limbo'. During the Namibian elections held at the time of independence, one emotional issue that cropped up in campaign platforms was the call for the repatriation of Namibia's 'stolen' territory. Even today, this issue comes up whenever a politician requires a common national cause to rally people together. ∎

The scenery is decidedly uninteresting along this straight, wide thoroughfare and most of the wildlife stays hidden in the trees. A good place to look for lifts is the petrol station in Kasane.

SAVUTI & THE MABABE DEPRESSION

The Mababe Depression (no, it's not the affliction caused by paying Botswana park fees), like the Makgadikgadi pans and Nxai Pan, is actually a remnant of the large lake that once covered much of northern Botswana. It takes in most of southern Chobe, including the Savuti region, the park's second most popular area.

The intensely flat, wildlife-packed expanses of Savuti are an obligatory stop for mobile safaris and overland trips between Kasane and Maun. Although there are a couple of tourist lodges, this country of typically harsh African colours and vistas has a distinctly empty feeling, and it won't disappoint anyone with the transport, cash and inclination to visit. The numbers of animals at Savuti, especially between November and May, can seem overwhelming at times. The place teems with elephants. Lions, wild dogs and hyenas prowl through immense herds of impala, wildebeests, buffaloes and zebras while other antelopes are present in numbers rarely seen elsewhere.

While Savuti is normally well-watered, dry years aren't uncommon and being so far from perennial water sources – the Chobe, Linyanti and Okavango rivers – drought threatens animals lured into the area in wetter years. Those capable of escaping to the river systems do so, but the majority, weakened by the elements, crowd into dwindling water holes and eventually succumb to hunger and thirst. Some creatures have little hope; for example, the bed of Savuti Marsh is littered with the shells of dessicated freshwater mussels. On the other hand, trees which keenly take root in and along intermittent watercourses during dry years may find themselves drowned or washed away during heavy flows.

Magwikhwe Sand Ridge

From the griddle-flat plains of the Mababe Depression, the Magwikhwe Sand ridge, just 20 metres high and 180 metres wide, seems a prominent feature. It extends for over 100 km across southern Chobe and is thought to have once formed a barrier beach on the western shoreline of northern Botswana's ancient great lake.

Gubaatsa & Gcoha Hills

The Gubaatsa Hills were once much higher, but with years of erosion, these negligible rocky outcrops have worn down to their present knobby shapes. Their north-eastern faces provide evidence of the constant battering of waves when the Mababe Depression was still underwater. Gobabis Hill, south of the Savuti gate near the Savuti Channel, bears several sets of 4000-year-old rock paintings, which are probably of San origin. There are some on the north end of the hill, near the base, but the best ones are about halfway to the summit and face east. Only in this area can you leave your vehicle and walk around; the paintings lie just a short walk from the road.

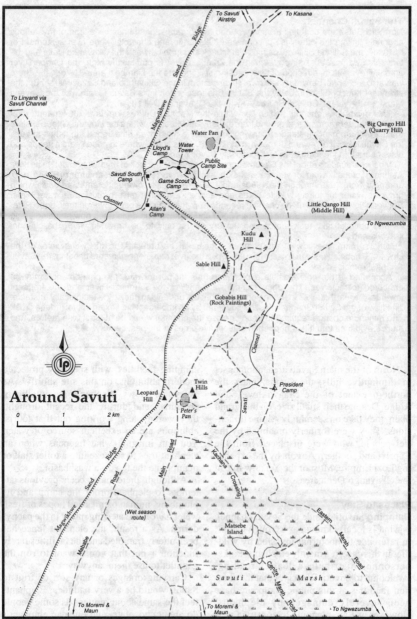

To Savuti Airstrip

To Kasane

Ridge

Sand

Magwikhwe

To Linyanti via
Savuti Channel

Big Qango Hill
(Quarry Hill) ▲

Water Pan

Lloyd's ■
Camp
Water
Tower
Public
Camp Site
Savuti South ■
Camp
Game Scout
Camp ▲

Little Qango Hill
(Middle Hill) ▲

Savuti

Channel

To Ngwezumba

■ Allan's
Camp

Kudu
Hill ▲

Sable Hill ▲

Around Savuti

Gobabis Hill
(Rock Paintings) ▲

Channel

BOTSWANA

0   1   2 km

Savuti

Leopard ▲
Hill

Twin
Hills ▲

President ▲
Camp

Peter's
Pan

Main

Road

Kachikau Crossing

Sand

Ridge

Road

(Wet season
route)

Eastern

Mababe

Matsebe
Island

Marsh

Road

Central

Marsh

Road

Savuti   Marsh

To Moremi &
Maun

To Moremi &
Maun

To Ngwezumba

The Savuti Channel

Northern Botswana contains a bounty of odd hydrographic phenomena – a land of mysterious channels linking the otherwise unconnected Okavango and Linyanti-Chobe river systems. For instance, the Selinda Spillway passes water back and forth between the Okavango Delta and the Linyanti Swamps. Just as odd, when the Zambezi river is particularly high, the Chobe River actually reverses its direction of flow, causing spillage into the Liambezi area. Historically, there was also a channel between the Khwai River system in the Okavango and Savuti Marsh. But the strangest item of all is probably the Savuti Channel, which links Savuti Marsh with the Linyanti Marsh and – via the Selinda Spillway – with the Okavango Delta itself.

This mysterious channel, which lies within the Mababe Depression, is a 100-km-long river which meanders across level ground from the Linyanti Marshes, where the Linyanti-Chobe system makes a sharp bend. Instead of carrying water to the main river, as all good tributaries should, the Savuti takes it away and dumps it in the desert. At its finish, where in good years it seeps and disappears into the sand, it waters the lovely Savuti Marsh.

Most confounding about the Savuti Channel, however, is the lack of rhyme or reason to its flow. At times it stops flowing for years at a stretch, as it did from 1888 to 1957, and from 1966 to 1967 and now, from 1979 through the 1980s and 1990s. When it's flowing, it creates an oasis which provides water for thirsty wildlife herds and acts as a magnet for a profusion of water birds. Between flows, the end of the channel recedes from the marshes back towards the Chobe River while at other times, the Savuti Marshes flood and expand. The dead trees now standing along its bed optimistically took root during the dry years, only to be drowned when the channel reawakened.

What's more, the flow of the channel appears to be unrelated to the water level of the Linyanti-Chobe river system itself. In 1925, when the river experienced record flooding, the Savuti Channel remained dry.

According to the only feasible explanation thus far put forward, the phenomenon may be attributed to tectonics. The ongoing northward shift of the Zambezi River and the frequent low-intensity earthquakes in the region reveal that the underlying geology is tectonically unstable. The flow of the Savuti Channel must be governed by an imperceptible flexing of the surface crust. The minimum change required to open or close the channel would be at least nine metres, and there's evidence that it has happened at least five times in the past century! ■

North of the main Savuti area, another set of diminutive hills, the Gcoha, mark the northern extent of the Magwikhwe Sand Ridge. Despite their small size, on this grand plain, they take on seemingly Alpine dimensions. They were formerly inhabited by the Yei people, who were displaced from the Caprivi and southern Angola by the expanding Lozi Empire. Most of the Yei now live in the Okavango Delta area.

Places to Stay

Camping Savuti, beside the Savuti channel, is what is locally known as a 'rough camp', in reference to nocturnal invasion by wildlife. In this case, it's mainly elephants. Parks' personnel distribute a leaflet reading: 'Welcome to Savuti. We regret that the ablution facilities at this public camp site have been severely damaged by elephants. However, we are planning to construct new camping facilities, with specially protected modern ablutions, on this site shortly'. As everyone knows, elephants are intelligent creatures, and during the recent drought, they weren't long working out that tourist ablutions are an excellent source of water. You can imagine what happens when an elephant tries to squeeze into a toilet stall or manipulate the tap on a washbasin.

Although there have been previous attempts to elephant-proof the camp and its plumbing, human picnics and hopes of fresh water have cultivated ingenuity in the pachyderms. As a result, the elephant fence has been utterly trampled and the facilities rarely function – not that you'd want to run the gauntlet to use them, anyway.

Carrying oranges or any sort of fruit to Savuti would be a very bad idea. Elephants feel the same about oranges as some people do about chocolate, and once an elephant's mind is set, there's little that can sway him or her. Make sure the boot of your vehicle is secure from tusky tin openers.

In the daylight, if anything is spilt, you can expect clouds of perky hornbills to move in and clean it up, but at night, extra caution is warranted. Savuti is also a haunt of hyena thugs and they get quite brazen when there's food at stake. They'll carry off anything that smells edible, so never leave empty tins or even dirty pots and pans lying around at night, and keep all your food safely packed inside a vehicle. At certain times, baboons also present a nuisance and must be actively kept at bay or you'll be cleaned out the minute your back is turned.

If you're still keen, book in at the Savuti entry gate south-east of the camp site.

Safari Lodges Just north-west of the public camp site are three private camps, all of which must be booked in advance.

The most interesting is *Lloyd's Camp* (☎ /fax 660351), PO Box 246, Maun, owned by Lloyd and June Wilmot. Lloyd emphasises that his camp must not be considered a 'luxury camp'. Lloyd's Camp is known for close encounters with wildlife – thanks mainly to its private water hole and viewing platform. It's also renowned for its excellent guides as well as its exotic cuisine, which reflects the efforts of a creative chef from Berkeley, California. Where else could you sample sausage, raisin and spinach pizza? Single/double high season rates are US$305/470, including accommodation, meals and activities. For lone travellers willing to share accommodation, the single rate is just US$235. Note that no credit cards are accepted.

Nearby *Allan's Camp,* operated by Gametrackers (☎ 660302; fax 660571) in Maun, likes to bill itself as a Botswana 'insiders' venue. Accommodation is in thatched A-frame chalets and the emphasis is on game drives, to complement Gametrackers' lodges in the Okavango Delta. Single/double rates are US$470/590, plus park fees. Its sister camp, *Savuti South* (☎ 260302), offers tented accommodation

also overlooking the Savuti Channel. Rates are the same as at Allan's Camp, except in November and December, when the price drops to US$168/ 210, but it's accessible to mobile operators only. Air transfers from Kasane to either Allan's Camp or Savuti South cost US$70 per person.

Getting There & Away
Under optimum conditions, you'll need four hours to drive from the northern entrance to Savuti. The more travelled route leads out of the national park south of Ngoma Bridge, and skirts the broad marshy area south of the Chobe-Linyanti river system. Up to this point, the road is good gravel, and passable to 2WD vehicles. At the village of Kachikau, however, the route turns south into the Chobe Forest Reserve and becomes little more than two parallel sand ruts requiring 4WD and high clearance.

After about 50 laborious km, it re-enters the park and continues a further 40 km to Savuti, which is also covered in deep sand. Except for the stretches through the small villages overlooking the river flats and in the immediate area of Savuti, it's not a very scenic trip.

In the dry season, the less popular route through Ngwezumba pans offers an alternative. Although it's passable with 4WD, the route is little-used and parks' personnel advise against it.

You can also approach from Maun and Moremi. Except for the first 100 km or so, the route is nearly all sand, and some sections, especially in the southernmost extension of Chobe National Park, are terribly slow going. There's no fuel anywhere along the route.

NGWEZUMBA DAM & PANS
Ngwezumba lies just over halfway between Serondela and Savuti by the alternative route. It's marked by an artificial dam and a series of clay pans set amid mopane forest. It doesn't get the overwhelming numbers of animals that occur along the riverfront or at Savuti, but the geography and vegetation

Game Drives – morning vs evening

The morning trips are generally better if you prefer a subtle, timeless sort of experience. The sweet, dusty smell of the morning bush combined with the last stirrings of night creatures; a normally hazy-red sunrise; the plodding of hippos into the river; and the emergence of the daytime shift remind one well of the cycles that govern the bush.

Evening drives, on the other hand, are generally more exciting. Things seem to happen on cue, and the low sun provides excellent photo opportunities. There will normally be so much wildlife (especially during the dry season) that one may soon become blasé. Big cats laze while skittish antelopes keep an eye on their intentions. Immense herds of elephants gather to drink, spray and play beside the river. Hippos plod onto the shore. Hundreds of buffaloes stand grazing on the dry grass and vultures pick at the remains of the unlucky while brilliantly coloured birds flit around in the late sun. ∎

support herds of buffaloes and elephants as well as reedbucks, gemsboks and roans.

You may also see the rare oribi in its favourite Botswana habitat. This unusual little antelope with spikey horns has circular black scent glands just below its ears and a sprig of black hair right at the end of its tail. It lives in groups of only four or five rather than in herds.

Places to Stay

Ngwezumba has two public camp sites. From the northern park entrance, it's 85 km to *Nogatsaa Camp*, a pleasant and secluded camp with cold showers and toilets – if the solar-powered pump is operational – and a hide overlooking Nogatsaa dam. There's also an airstrip which was built by the Botswana Defence Forces for use in their anti-poaching activities. (However, it's well away from the public campground and isn't a viable access.) As a result, it has become a bit of a BDF party venue and maintenance of the camp site hasn't been of a high standard.

Rudimentary *Tshinga* (also spelt Tjinga or Tchinga) *Camp*, 22 km away, has no facilities but a water tank with an erratic pump that requires some mechanical expertise to get started. Campers would be wise to bring their water supply from elsewhere. Essentially, the site is little more than a clear spot in the bush to pitch a tent; avoid camping near the pan lest you disturb the animals' routine.

Getting There & Away

The clay in the Ngwezumba area is popularly known as 'black cotton' soil which, when wet, becomes a bit like molasses and is impossible to negotiate, even with a 4WD.

From either the Chobe transit road (or Serondela Camp), the Ngwezumba route runs south past Nantanga pans to Nogatsaa. It then passes a series of pans to Ngwezumba Dam, where it turns west along the intermittent Ngwezumba River and makes for Savuti, 120 km away. By this route, it takes a full day to drive between Kasane and Savuti. To reach Tshinga from Nogatsaa, take the south-east turning about five km south-west of Nogatsaa.

LINYANTI MARSHES

West of Chobe, on the Botswana-Namibia border, lie the Linyanti Marshes. This lovely 900-sq-km region is reminiscent of the Okavango Delta, with similar vegetation, but it's actually just a broad flooded plain along the Linyanti River.

The Linyanti rises in southern Angola, where it's known as the Cuando. Once it crosses into Namibian territory, however, it becomes the Kwando, but across most of the Caprivi Strip, it's known as the Mashi. As soon as it hits the Linyanti Marshes and turns east, the name changes to the Linyanti, and further downstream, beyond the former Lake Liambezi, it changes yet again – this time to the Chobe.

The shallow Lake Liambezi, which once covered up to 10,000 hectares when full, has been completely dry since 1985 and much of the Namibian side has now been settled by people and their herds. Even wet years have failed to refill the lake, and it's now generally accepted that Lake Liambezi has disappeared for good. The lake's only hope, experts reckon, would be a dramatic flood on the Zambezi, which would create a large amount of backwash up the Chobe River. For more information, see the North-Eastern Namibia chapter.

Similarly, the Savuti Channel (which flows into or out of the Linyanti, depending upon the prevailing tectonic condition – see the aside under Savuti earlier in this chapter), no longer waters southern Chobe; since the channel last flowed in 1979, the Savuti Marshes have been dry. Another channel, known as the Selinda Spillway or Magwegqana Channel, connects the Okavango and Linyanti river systems and allows overflow to drain back and forth between them.

Further south and west, however, the marshes still enjoy a healthy supply of water, making them as much a wildlife paradise as the nearby Okavango Delta. On the Namibian side, these wetlands are protected by two recently established national parks, Mudumu and Mamili (see the Namibia section), but the Botswanan marshes are protected only by their remoteness, apart from seven km of frontage belonging to Chobe National Park. Most of the area, however, is open to controlled hunting, and has also been subjected to spates of cross-border poaching from Namibia. As a result, wildlife is often wary of humans.

Places to Stay

Your only options are the luxury tented camps, *Twin Pools*, *James Camp* and *Kwando Camp*, all operated by Photo Africa Safaris (☎ 630385; fax 650383). The office is opposite Madiba Shopping Centre in Kasane. These places are well off the beaten track, but the area is so fabulous that they promise to become much more popular in the coming years.

Twin Pools, the most southerly camp, overlooks two lovely pools along the Mashi/Kwando floodplain and hosts a large concentration of predators, particularly lions. Particularly appealing is the dining tent, which perches on the bluff with a view over the pools.

James Camp also sits beside the Mashi/Kwando floodplain and offers good chances of seeing red lechwe and the rare and reclusive sitatunga from the photographic barge.

Kwando Camp nestles in a wooded area on the southern bank of the Mashi/Kwando River. It's also amenable to sitatungas, and offers great fishing.

The daily single/double rates at Twin Pools and Kwando Camp are US$250/371, including accommodation, all meals, wildlife-viewing activities (game walks, drives and cruises in a double-deck pontoon boat) and laundry services. Children are accommodated at Twin Pools, but all eight beds must be occupied by a single party. At James Camp, which has only communal bathroom and toilet facilities, you wil pay US$234/337 for a single/double, including the same amenities and activities as the are available in the other camps.

Getting There & Away

With a 4WD vehicle, you can reach the area either along the river from Kasane or via the track along the Savuti Channel from Savuti to the James Camp turn-off from the road along the Selinda Spillway. Otherwise, you can take a Photo Africa air or overland transfer from Kasane. Charter flights to any of the camps cost US$460 each way for up to five passengers. Air transfers from Maun start at US$150 per person.

BOTSWANA

Okavango Delta & North-Western Botswana

The Okavango Delta, which sprawls like an open palm across most of north-western Botswana, serves as the magnet for most of the country's visitors, and they'll find hosts of lodges and tour companies scrambling to package it for them. The region's other attractions, however, are not so easily won. The remote Tsodilo Hills, a wilderness art gallery of rock paintings with the country's best bushwalking, provide unsettling evidence of dramatic cultural changes in the far deserts. More remote natural attractions include Gcwihaba Caverns and the Aha Hills, where the appeal lies in pervasive silence and solitude. These highlights are connected by broad spaces and scattered villages which represent Botswana at its scenic and cultural best.

Okavango Delta

The 1300-km-long Okavango, southern Africa's third-largest river, rises near the town of Nova Lisboa in central Angola, flows south-eastward across Namibia's Caprivi Strip, where it tumbles through the Popa Falls rapids before entering Botswana near Shakawe. There the river's annual 18.5 billion cubic metres of water begins to spread and sprawl as it's drunk up by the thirsty air and Kalahari sands. The Okavango is frequently described as 'the river which never finds the sea' but, unlike most abortive rivers doomed to die in burning desert salt pans, it disappears into a vast 15,000-sq-km maze of lagoons, channels and islands.

The Okavango Delta is the world's largest inland delta, covering an area the size of Switzerland or the US state of Massachusetts, and abounds with birdlife and other wildlife, including elephants, zebras, buffaloes, wildebeests, giraffes, hippos and kudu.

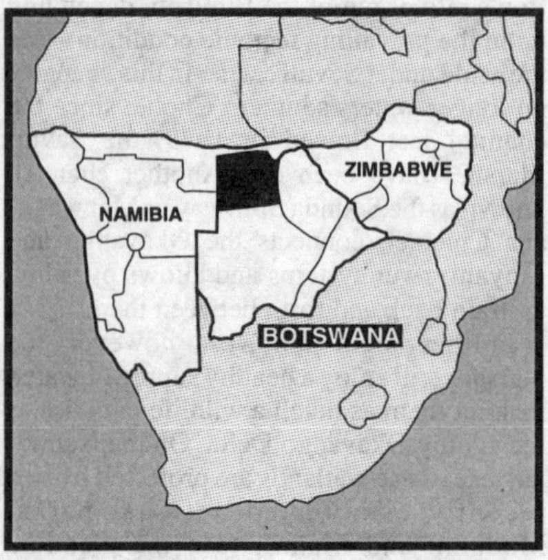

At its eastern fringes is Moremi Wildlife Reserve which also teems with wildlife. Its remarkable landscapes are considered by many to be the most scenic in any southern African reserve.

Although one occasionally encounters a travel-jaded cynic who claims the place is overrated, it's hard to resist the calming spell of this watery wilderness. It's an extraordinary environment of channels and islands that seems cut off from the modern world. If you can afford it, don't miss a trip into the Moremi wilderness or the Inner Delta.

While it's difficult to see the delta on a shoestring, mid-range budgets are accommodated. Most Okavango visits include at least some time travelling by *mokoro* (plural *mekoro)*, a shallow-draught dugout canoe hewn from ebony or sausage (*kigelia*) log, which is ideally suited to the shallow waters of the delta. The mekoro are poled from a standing position with a *ngashi* – a pole made from the *mogonono* tree *(Terminalia sericea)*. They accommodate three people, including the poler. Their precarious appearance belies their amazing stability.

Natural History of the Okavango Delta

Geology Around two million years ago, the Okavango River probably joined the Limpopo and reached the sea, but subsequent tectonic activity eventually diverted it into the Kalahari. Until a few thousand years ago, the water flowed into a great lake which covered the Makgadikgadi Pans, Nxai Pan, the Mababe Depression and Lake Ngami. However, silting, as well as the continuous imperceptible uplifting of the land to the east caused the lake to disappear and created the new basin which today stalls the river and seals its fate. Today, even during good flood years, only 2% to 3% of the annual in-flow finds its way into the Thamalakane River. From there, it's distributed to the Boteti which carries it toward the Makgadikgadi Pans, and the Nhabe, which takes it to Lake Ngami.

Today, the channels and boundaries of the delta itself are constantly shifting. Think of the whole system as a garden hose left running in a very large sandbox. In a normal flood year, the river will carry two million tonnes of Angolan and Namibian real estate – sand, leached nutrients and topsoil – to deposit it along the major channels. Carried off by termites for their nests or stirred, warped and shifted by low-level tectonic activity, it alters the channels and re-shapes the delta itself.

In the 1880s, for example, the Thaoge River, which once carried water to Lake Ngami, was blocked and ceased to flow. After a series of earthquakes in 1952-53, however, the Boro River, which passes through the heart of the delta, began flowing for the first time anyone can remember.

Seasonal Cycles In March or April, at the end of the rainy season along the Okavango headwaters in Angola, the river rises and rushes southward, entering Botswana at Shakawe, ploughing through and displacing the papyrus beds of the Okavango Panhandle. By early June, the water level has risen in the Inner Delta, drowning low islands and uprooting vegetation as it progresses south-east at about three km per day.

As it spreads out, however, it also evaporates and approximately 95% of the water that surged into the Panhandle is taken by the dry atmosphere; another 2% is lost in the sands. By July, a considerably weakened flood passes Maun, but by now, only 2-3% of the original in-flow remains to enter the Thamalakane River and be carried on by the Boteti and Nhabe. During poor flood years – and in the following year – the Boteti never rises above a trickle and the Nhabe remains dry, as it has for nearly 20 years.

This means that the Okavango water levels are at their lowest during the rainy season between November and March, when channels are constricted and water access to the most interesting areas is limited. In the Panhandle the flow peaks in April and May, while well-visited Chiefs Island and the Inner Delta are at optimum levels from late May to late June but are ideal for visits until late September. The Eastern Delta has the best chance of high water from late June to late July, but the increase in flow will probably be negligible this far along, especially during poor years. The best months to visit are July to September.

Further Reading If you're interested in cultures, wildlife, geology and complex cycles of the delta, the best readily available treatise is in the book *Kalahari – Life's Variety in Dune & Delta* by Michael Main (SouthernBook Publishers, Johannesburg, 1987). Another excellent book is *Okavango – Jewel of the Kalahari* by Karen Ross (BBC Books, London, 1987). For more on the arboreal side of things, pick up the excellent *Shell Field Guide to the Common Trees of the Okavango Delta & Moremi*, by Veronica Roodt (Shell Botswana, Gaborone). All three books are available in several Maun souvenir shops, and also in Gaborone bookshops.

The December 1990 edition of *National Geographic* also contains a very good article on the Okavango Delta and the recent issues affecting it.

Further discussion of the several population groups living in the Delta area – the Yei, Mbukushu and Herero – may be found in the Population & People section of the Botswana Facts about the Country chapter. ∎

BOTSWANA

Before you make the effort to reach Maun, it's worth considering that there's no practical way to see the Okavango Delta on an absolute shoestring. You'll almost certainly have to go through some sort of outfitter, be it a wilderness camp, travel agency, tour company or even a freelance boat owner. A bewildering number of options are available so it's wise to shop around before deciding which option fits your interests and budget.

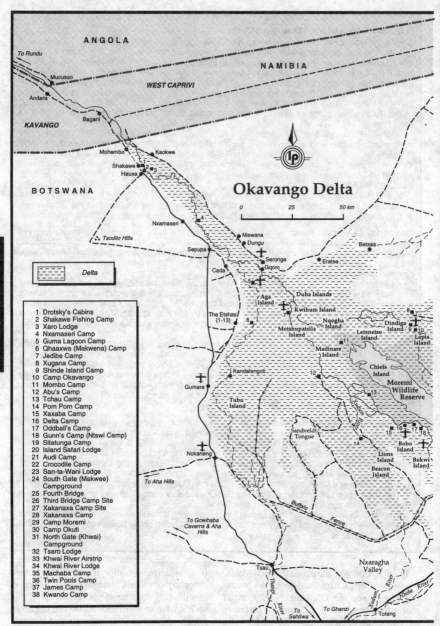

BOTSWANA

Okavango Delta

0   25   50 km

1   Drotsky's Cabins
2   Shakawe Fishing Camp
3   Xaro Lodge
4   Nxamaseri Camp
5   Guma Lagoon Camp
6   Qhaaxwa (Makwena) Camp
7   Jedibe Camp
8   Xugana Camp
9   Shinde Island Camp
10 Camp Okavango
11 Mombo Camp
12 Abu's Camp
13 Tchau Camp
14 Pom Pom Camp
15 Xaxaba Camp
16 Delta Camp
17 Oddball's Camp
18 Gunn's Camp (Ntswi Camp)
19 Sitatunga Camp
20 Island Safari Lodge
21 Audi Camp
22 Crocodile Camp
23 San-ta-Wani Lodge
24 South Gate (Makwee)
    Campground
25 Fourth Bridge
26 Third Bridge Camp Site
27 Xakanaxa Camp Site
28 Xakanaxa Camp
29 Camp Moremi
30 Camp Okuti
31 North Gate (Khwai)
    Campground
32 Tsaro Lodge
33 Khwai River Airstrip
34 Khwai River Lodge
35 Machaba Camp
36 Twin Pools Camp
37 James Camp
38 Kwando Camp

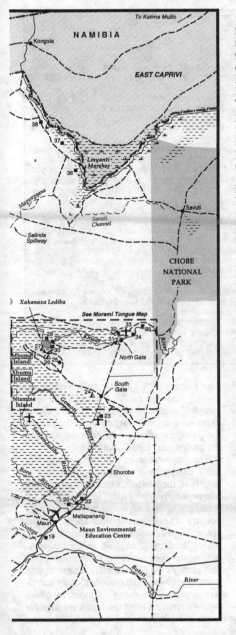

The most popular tourist destinations are found within Moremi Wildlife Reserve, the region of wetland bordered on the west by Chiefs Island – named after the Batswana chief Moremi – and on the east by the Moremi Peninsula (also named after Chief Moremi and sometimes called Moremi Tongue). This is where the wildlife and best-protected delta environments are located, but it's also the domain of park fees and up-market safari camps with awe-inspiring prices – and some of the lodge offerings are downright decadent.

On more or less the same level is the Inner Delta, the area west and north of Chiefs Island, where one finds the classic delta scenery. Accommodation is available in several price ranges, but you'll have to lash out on an airfare to get there. Some camps are up to an hour's flying time from Maun. If you're travelling by mokoro from the budget camps, ventures into Moremi Wildlife Reserve are optional; if you'd rather not pay park fees, instruct your poler to remain outside the reserve. There's still a bit of wildlife and most visitors encounter at least hippos and some antelopes.

The lowest-budget destination is the Eastern Delta which is accessible by a combination of 4WD vehicle, motorboat and mokoro. There aren't yet any controls on operations here – most are run by Maun area lodges – and the polers are normally unlicensed freelancers hoping to gain enough experience to move up to the bigger camps. If you're truly short of cash, however, the Eastern Delta can provide some idea of what the place is about. Prospective travellers to the Eastern Delta would do well to talk with travellers who have gone before and search out recommendations on operators, polers and the best areas to visit.

In the panhandle, the narrow finger that stretches north-westward from the main delta, a few fishing camps lie strung along the river, but they're accessible only by air or the long way around on the highway. It's a culturally interesting area, but most of the camps are geared for the fishing crowd and don't pretend to provide the classic delta

Flora & Fauna

While the profuse flora of the Okavango Delta is magnificent and even overwhelming, unless you're wealthy enough to spend part of your delta visit in Moremi Reserve, the wildlife will probably seem quite elusive. It's easy enough to deduce that such an abundance of water wouldn't be overlooked by the thirsty creatures of the Kalahari; but with a swampy surfeit of hiding places, they're simply not easily spotted. As one delta camp's brochure succinctly states 'If you see 10% of what sees you, you will have much to remember'.

The delta world is replete with interest. From mokoro level, visitors may get the idea that it's a papyrus-choked swamp dotted with palm islands. While that's not without some validity, the Okavango hydrography is more complex, with deeper and faster-flowing river channels and serene open areas of calmer water known as *madiba* (singular *lediba*), which are more or less permanent and remain largely free of vegetation.

The reeds and papyrus, however, are rife. They wave and clump and cluster along channels, blocking the mokoro-level view, but the slower-moving channels and even the madiba are festooned with the purple-bottomed leaves and pink and white blooms of water lilies. When roasted, their root stalks are delicious and even the flowers are edible. Polers will also tell you that one may snip the head off a lily and sip water through the stem, which acts as a natural filter against impurities.

On the palm islands, vegetation is diverse. In addition to the profuse hyphaene (mokolani) palms, you'll find savanna grasses, leadwood willows, marulas, strangler figs, acacia thorn, ebony and the whimsical sausage trees, with their long and unmistakable fruits (which yield an agent that has been proven effective against some forms of skin cancer). If you're visiting in January, you'll be able to sample the fruits of the African mangosteen and marula, while in July and August, the delicious ebony fruit ripens and falls to the ground. The beautiful mokolani palm ivory, which is used for carvings, ripens in September and is favoured by elephants who shake the trees to cause a rain of fruit.

The waters are home to small barbel fish, a mild and sweet-tasting fish for which locals lay nets or construct elaborate weir-like fish traps. Closer to the Panhandle, such marvellous fish as bream and fighting tiger fish provide the basis for local diets.

The delta's reptilian realm is dominated by the Nile crocodile, which lounges lazily along the island shorelines or lies quietly in the water, with only the eyes and snout breaking the surface. Although Okavango crocs are relatively small, you shouldn't swim at dawn or dusk. Ask a knowledgeable local before plunging into the (bilharzia-free) waters at any other time. Other

experience of mokoro trips and spectacular wildlife viewing. Panhandle camps are discussed in the North-Western Botswana section later in this chapter.

The best months to visit are July to September when water levels are high and the weather dry. For further recommendations on when to visit, see the aside entitled Natural History of the Okavango. Bear in mind that during parts of the rainy season, particularly from January to March when tourist numbers are low, some lodges close for a breather. Some remain open, however, so if you don't mind rain, stifling heat and humidity, this time of year will provide a unique experience with few other tourists.

Mokoro Trips

On most mokoro trips, travellers ride for several days with the same poler, breaking their journey with walks on palm islands and moving between established camps or wild camping along the way. The quality of the experience depends largely upon the skill of the poler, the meshing of personalities and the passengers' enthusiasm.

The importance of finding a competent poler cannot be overstated – your fate is largely in their hands, especially when they are negotiating labyrinthine waterways or leading you on bushwalks through wildlife country. The keenest polers speak at least some English; recognise and identify the plants, birds and animals along the way; explain the cultures of the delta inhabitants; and perhaps even teach clients how to fish using traditional methods. Ask other travellers around your camp or those in Maun who've returned from their mokoro trips for poler assessments and recommendations, reptiles of note include the immense leguaan or the carnivorous water monitors, that either swim through the shallows or bask on the sand. The amphibian world is represented by the tiny frogs which inhabit the reeds – and sometimes plop into your lap as you're poled by mokoro through reed thickets. Their resonant peeping is one of the delta's unforgettable sounds, while the tinkle-like croaks of bell frogs and the croaking of the larger and more sonorous bullfrogs provide a lovely evening chorus.

If your delta trip is normal, birds will probably provide the bulk of your wildlife viewing. To list but a few, you're bound to see African jacanas strutting across the lily pads while carmine bee-eaters, snakebirds, hoopoes, ibis, storks, egrets, parrots, shrikes, kingfishers, hornbills, great white herons and purple-and green-backed herons flit, squawk, fish, swim, dive, duck and perch along the way. Then there are the psychedelic pygmy geese (actually a well-disguised duck) and the brilliantly-plumed lilac-breasted roller, with its bright blue wings and green and lilac underside – and flashes of other colours which only appear in certain light. Watch also for birds of prey, like the Pel's fishing owl, the goshawk and the bateleur eagle and African fish eagle.

In addition to all the larger animals you'll find inside Moremi Reserve, the north-east corner of the delta is home to the rare and retiring sitatunga, a splay-hooved swamp antelope which is particularly adept at manoeuvering over soft, saturated mud and soggy, mashed vegetation. When frightened, it submerges like a hippo, leaving only its tiny nostrils above the surface. In order to lure it into firing range, local hunters set fire to clumps of papyrus which soon sprout new green shoots, an irresistible sitatunga delicacy.

Another antelope of the swamps is the red lechwe, of which there are an estimated 30,000, living mainly on the palm islands; it's most easily distinguished by its large rump. In shallow and still pools of the palm islands, you'll also see reedbucks wading and grazing on water plants. The islands are also inhabited by large herds of impalas.

One animal encountered throughout the delta is the hippopotamus. Hippos go mostly unnoticed during the day as they graze happily underwater, but in the evening, they move toward shore to graze on land. Around camps, you'll also encounter troops of typically thieving baboons.

The only large cat present outside Moremi Reserve is the leopard. It's normally nocturnal and quite shy, but the management of Oddball's Camp tells the tale of a leopard that killed an impala and in broad daylight dragged the carcass up the tree that overhangs their thatched bar! On the canine end of the spectrum, Moremi Reserve is home to 30% of the world's remaining Cape hunting dogs, which are also known as African wild dogs. ∎

BOTSWANA

and if you hear of a good poler, request their services.

If you're organising a budget mokoro trip in the Eastern Delta or from one of the budget lodges in the Inner Delta, enquire in advance whether you're expected to provide food for your poler. Even if they do bring their own supplies, many travellers who are wild camping prefer to share meals. That should be established with your poler before setting out on the trip. The polers normally provide a sack of mealies and cooking implements while travellers supply the relishes – tins of curries, stews and vegetables. If you have arranged with your poler to provide theri meals, the standard daily rations are 500 grams of mealie meal, 250 grams of white sugar, six tea bags and sufficient salt and powdered milk.

For information on individual trips, see the discussions of the Eastern Delta and the Inner Delta later in this chapter.

MAUN

Maun, the frontier town turned to tourism at the edge of the Okavango, has taken on the atmosphere of an exclusive club. With a bumper crop of characters from all sectors of Batswana society – as well as a fair few expatriates and immigrants from around the world – the prevailing 'us and them' attitude regarding tourists doesn't really rankle.

However, Maun's former distinction as an outpost in the back-of-beyond has now faded. Upon completion of the tarred road from Nata, Maun became accessible to everyone and since then, construction has run amok. Six-storey office buildings are now sprouting alongside beer-can-reinforced mud huts and the ubiquitous Toyota

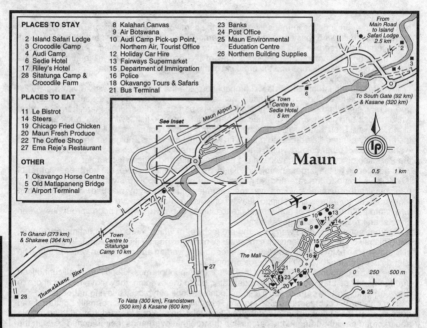

PLACES TO STAY
2 Island Safari Lodge
3 Crocodile Camp
4 Audi Camp
6 Sedie Hotel
17 Riley's Hotel
28 Sitatunga Camp &
    Crocodile Farm

PLACES TO EAT
11 Le Bistrot
14 Steers
19 Chicago Fried Chicken
20 Maun Fresh Produce
22 The Coffee Shop
27 Ema Reje's Restaurant

OTHER
1 Okavango Horse Centre
5 Old Matlapaneng Bridge
7 Airport Terminal

8 Kalahari Canvas
9 Air Botswana
10 Audi Camp Pick-up Point,
    Northern Air, Tourist Office
12 Holiday Car Hire
13 Fairways Supermarket
15 Department of Immigration
16 Police
18 Okavango Tours & Safaris
21 Bus Terminal

23 Banks
24 Post Office
25 Maun Environmental
    Education Centre
26 Northern Building Supplies

BOTSWANA

Hilux 4WDs share the roads with sedan touring cars from South Africa. With the large numbers of outsiders pouring in to participate in the boom, it's a safe bet that the old Maun is gone forever.

History

Maun (which rhymes with 'down') was originally called *Maung*, which was derived by adding the Setswana suffix for location to a corrupted form of the Yei word *kau*, meaning 'short reeds', thus yielding 'the place of short reeds'. The name was further slaughtered when the final 'g' was lost due to misspelling by early European visitors.

The village had its beginning in 1915 as the capital for the Tawana tribe. According to tradition, at Shoshong around 1795, King Mathiba of the Ngwato declared his son Khama I to be his successor rather than Tawana, who was the eldest son of his favourite wife and rightful heir to the throne. Tawana objected strongly to the arrange-

ment; fraternal relations were strained and the siblings eventually quarrelled. The dispute escalated to the point of warfare and polarised members of the tribe into different camps. Feeling betrayed by his family and people, Tawana gathered his followers and struck off north-west. Along the way, they conquered, enslaved, assimilated and intermarried with people of other groups. With their swollen numbers, they established themselves as the region's dominant force before coming to rest in the Kgwebe Hills, east of Lake Ngami.

Around 1824, the Tawana, which now included large numbers of Yei, Mbukushu and Gologa, as well as San slaves, resettled at Toteng on Lake Ngami. In 1883, however, they suffered devastating raids by King Lobengula's marauding Ndebele, who captured some Tawana people and foolishly drove them northward into the delta country. The Ndebele followed confidently, poised for a decisive second attack, but the Tawana,

CHRIS BARTON

DEANNA SWANEY

DEANNA SWANEY

BOTSWANA
A: Elephant ablutions, Chobe National Park
B: Hippo, Chobe National Park
C: Gcwihaba Caverns (Drotsky's Cave)

DEANNA SWANEY

DEANNA SWANEY

DEANNA SWANEY

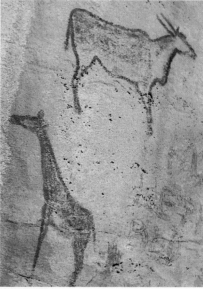
DEANNA SWANEY

BOTSWANA
A: Female Hill, Tsodilo Hills
C: San (Bushman) Paintings, Tsodilo Hills

B: Approaching Aha Hills
D: San (Bushman) Paintings, Tsodilo Hills

who were quite familiar with the delta, struck back with a vengeance and forced an Ndebele retreat. Defeated, the Ndebele returned to Bulawayo and the victorious Tawana returned home to Toteng.

In 1915, the Tawana capital was again moved, this time to Maun. The Tawana chief, now Kgosi Mathiba Moremi, still presides over the area's Tawana population. The present-day Tawana people share the town with other groups, including the distinctive Herero from Namibia and an equally distinctive and growing European population.

Orientation & Information

Like most towns in Botswana, Maun lacks a definite centre; it's strung out for several km along the tarred road that parallels the Thamalakane River. The only semblance of commercial concentration is found in the several shopping centres, while the de facto centre is the 'ambush' of tourism-oriented enterprises around the airport exit gate.

Tourist Office The tourist information office (☎ 660492), beside Northern Air at the airport entrance, is open from 7.30 am to 12.30 pm and 1.45 to 4.30 pm Monday to Friday. It isn't very helpful, but since you're probably heading for the delta, you'll have to shop around travel agencies anyway. The Matlapaneng lodges, particularly Audi Camp, can also answer questions and point you in the right direction.

Money On the Mall are branches of both Barclays Bank and Standard Chartered Bank.

Post The post office on the tarred road near The Mall is open from 8.15 am to 1 pm and 2.15 to 4 pm on weekdays and from 8.30 to 11.30 am on Saturday.

Immigration The immigration office is behind the Labour Office, on the south side of the road between Riley's Hotel and the airport road.

Travel Agencies & Safari Companies

Travel agencies and safari companies are Maun's mainstays and are responsible for Moremi and Inner Delta bookings. Each agency has affiliations with certain camps, however, so for information on the variety of accommodation available in the delta you'll have to visit several agencies. For Australians and New Zealanders, Okavango Tours & Safaris can arrange Namibian visas in 24 hours for US$19. Details about all safari and tour operators mentioned in this chapter are listed under Tours in the Botswana Getting Around chapter.

Film & Photography Hunter's World (☎ 660924) in The Mall provides a one-hour photo developing service for prints and T-6 processed transparencies.

Camping Equipment Lanterns, butane cartridges and minimal camping gear are available at Northern Building Supplies on the corner of the Nata-Maun road. You can hire camping and outdoor cooking equipment from Kalahari Canvas, just west of the airport, or Bush Camp Safaris in The Mall. Lightweight (3.6 kg) mountaineering tents cost US$6 and sleeping bags are US$2 per day. It's open Monday to Friday from 8 am to 1 pm and 2 to 5 pm and on Saturday from 8.30 am to 12.30 pm. Island Safari Lodge hires tents and sleeping bags to its safari clients and several inexpensive lodges in the delta also hire equipment on site.

Maun Environmental Education Centre

The 2.5-sq-km Maun Environmental Education Centre lies on the eastern bank of the Thamalakane River, directly opposite Riley's Hotel. Its main aim is to provide schoolchildren with an appreciation of the bush and its inhabitants, but everyone is welcome. From the office, you can pick up a brochure to guide you to the four walking trails and game hides where you can observe lechwes, wildebeests, impalas, giraffes, zebras, warthogs and other species. Foreigners pay US$3.70 admission, Botswana

BOTSWANA

Wasted Waters?
From the time of the first European colonists, settlers and developers have been eyeing the Okavango Delta as a source of water to transform north-western Botswana into lush green farmland. With more wilderness than they could handle, many early newcomers described the vast wetlands as 'wasted waters', apparently ignoring the fact that local people depended upon them for their livelihoods.

Nowadays, however, pressure from population growth, mining interests and increased tourism – particularly around Maun – are straining resources and placing the Okavango Delta at the crux of a heated debate between the Botswana government ranchers, engineers, developers, tour operators, rural people and conservationists.

At the heart of the latest controversy is the Botswana government's Southern Okavango Integrated Water Development Project, which was laid out in 1985. It called for the dredging of 42 km of the Boro River at the delta's eastern edge. In theory, the resulting decrease in water surface area would minimise evaporation and provide enough water to fill a series of small dams at the eastern edge of the delta. The scheme would provide a reservoir of water for Maun's growing needs, and would also be used to irrigate 10,000 hectares of planned farmland around Maun. Overflow would be diverted into the Boteti River for farmers further downstream. Unfortunately, the sandy soil and lush environment would require large amounts of chemical fertilisers and pesticides before it could be coaxed into large-scale agriculture.

However, no credible environmental impact study has been conducted and it was speculated that beneath the emotional arguments about Maun water shortages lay a hidden agenda. Since Lake Xau (about 200 km downstream, on the Boteti) dried up in the 1980s, the thirsty Debswana diamond mining operations at Orapa have had to depend upon bore-hole water. In the early 1990s, Orapa used 5 million cubic metres per year, and this figure is projected to double by the turn of the century. However, groundwater tables are dropping and at the increased usage rate, they'll be depleted by 2010.

In and around Maun, local people are divided over the plan. Safari operators don't want to see the delta's image tainted in any way, yet people involved in other service industries realise that increased development requires more water than is currently available. In addition to the Botswana government, other major proponents of the scheme include cattle ranchers, for whom any reduction of the delta would mean increased cattle range, and the Snowy Mountain Engineering Corporation, the engineering firm hired as consultants.

---

residents pay US$0.70 and citizens pay US$0.20. Remember to carry water.

To get there from town, cross the Thamalakane bridge on the Francistown road, turn left just east of the river, and continue on that road for two km to the Wildlife Training Centre.

Okavango Swamps Crocodile Farm

The crocodile farm (☎ 660570) at Sitatunga Camp, 12 km south of Maun on the Sehitwa road, is open to visitors free of charge. There are no guided tours, but you can pick up a hand-out which provides general information on crocodile farming and the lives and loves of Nile crocodiles.

Activities

If you fancy riding lessons or a day of horse-riding in the vicinity of Maun, or even a combined mokoro/horse trip north-west of Chiefs Island, see the Okavango Horse Centre (☎ 660449; fax 660493), down the side road near the new Matlapaneng bridge. For the longer safaris, the all-inclusive rate is US$182 per person per day. In April, May, August and September, the minimum length of these trips is four days. At other times, it's six days.

Alternatively, you can learn to fly over the swamps. The Kalahari Flying School (☎ 309775; fax 309776) offers reasonably priced flying instruction. Their intensive course prepares you for a private operators' licence in two to three weeks.

Organised Tours Several mobile safari companies also operate from Maun, and can organise trips around Makgadikgadi & Nxai Pans National Park, Moremi Wildlife

Traditional people, on the other hand, are almost universally opposed to the project. They maintain that the delta is their livelihood, and that any threat to the water is a threat to them. Small-scale local farmers fear that dredging could disrupt the flood cycle, which brings nutrients to their land. Some of the more militant factions have even pledged to resort to armed confrontation and sabotage should the dredging actually begin.

The conservationists, for their part, advocate that the delta be accorded World Heritage Status, which would make it eligible for international funding to protect it from development. They point out that the delta now brings in nearly US$50 million annually from tourism and any negative publicity regarding the delta would harm this profitable industry. (However, who could deny that tourism itself poses a threat to the delta and Botswana's 'high-cost, low volume' policy mainly attracts tourists who require such high-impact creature comforts as laundry facilities, hot showers, flush toilets, motorised tours and supplies which must be flown in from outside.) In reference to the Orapa connection, in 1991, Greenpeace attempted to organise an international boycott on Botswana diamonds under the slogan 'Diamonds are Death'. Some international consultants and aid agencies are so uneasy about being tied to the project that they've dropped it like a hot potato.

Conservationists operate on the premise that any change to the delta's natural hydrography will irreparably destabilise the unique ecosystem and lead to its eventual destruction. However, Alec Campbell, former director of Botswana's National Museum, believes the current dredging proposals should have little effect on the Okavango Delta as a whole. The real threats, he says, will be determined by projects upstream in Angola and Namibia, where the Okavango waters originate. If proposed dams are constructed and Botswana's tap is turned off, there could be 'catastrophic effects'.

In 1991, in response to these pressures, the government halted the dredging operation and approached the International Union for the Conservation of Nature and Natural Resources to formulate guidelines for a complete environmental impact study. In the end, officials agreed to explore alternative water plans while keeping the dredging issue open as a contingency plan if no other way is found to supply water for Maun's expanding population. What will happen is anyone's guess, but it's certain the dredging plan won't just disappear.

For further information on local opinion, contact the Tshomolero Okavango Conservation Trust (☎ (660060; fax 660059), Private Bag 0013, Maun. This trust is comprised mainly of Batswana in the Maun area whose livelihoods are directly threatened by the project. ■

BOTSWANA

Reserve and even right across Chobe to Kasane. They're not cheap, but they provide an alternative to hitching or resorting to the long detour through Nata. Furthermore, they'll allow you to see Third Bridge and the Moremi Tongue, as well as Savuti in Chobe National Park, with a minimum of effort and at the reduced park fees available to organised safari participants.

The least expensive are participatory safaris which require clients to help with cooking, washing up and erecting tents. Luxury-class versions cost upwards of US$200 per day including park fees, with the work done by camp staff.

Audi Camp runs recommended overland trips through Moremi Wildlife Reserve; these are the friendliest and most economical options you're likely to find. Sitatunga Safaris, based at Sitatunga Camp south of

Maun, offers mobile safaris to Moremi, Savuti and Nxai Pan for US$130 per person per day, plus park fees.

Island Safaris does custom mobile safaris to anywhere you want to go, including transport, 100 free km and a driver/guide, for US$186 per day for up to six people. Extra km are charged at US$0.50 per km. If you just want a quick taste of the delta, they do a one-day vehicle, motorboat and mokoro tour for US$50 per person, with a minimum of two people. All-day motorboat trips for up to six people cost US$130.

With Bush Camp Safaris, customised mobile safaris will cost US$112 per day for the vehicle only. Guides start at US$26 for up to five people per group and more for larger groups. All-inclusive safaris, with tented accommodation, transport, three meals and park fees, cost US$130 per person per day. Camping equipment is also available for hire.

Game Trails Safaris runs budget safaris through Moremi for US$121 per person per day, including only a 4WD vehicle, fuel and driver. Park and camping fees are extra, but you qualify for the lower organised tour rates. Powerboat trips through the delta cost US$112 per day.

Crocodile Camp Safaris also does mobile safaris to Moremi, Chobe and Kasane and beyond. Their 11-day Orient Express Safari takes in Xaxaba Lodge and a mokoro trip in the delta, a couple of days of wildlife-viewing in Moremi Wildlife Reserve and an overland excursion to Kasane via Savuti before finishing up at Victoria Falls. The price is US$2549 plus park fees.

If you're coming from Kasane trying to reach Maun, Go Wild Safaris at the Chobe Safari Lodge in Kasane offers six-day overland mini-safaris including the Chobe Riverfront, Savuti, Moremi, Maun and Gunn's Camp (Ntswi Camp) in the Okavango Delta. The price is US$955 per person, including transport, meals and camping gear.

For an unusual alternative, ask around Maun for Litten and Fleur of About Safaris – or look out for their one-of-a-kind vehicle, *On Dah Moon*. They do frequent runs between Maun and Victoria Falls, and their prices are quite reasonable, especially if you merely require a transit run. They also organise adventure safaris to all the far-flung places in Botswana. From September to November, they run 15 to 21-day canoe trips through the delta – under your own steam – for US$852/926 per person with a minimum of six people. In South Africa, you can contact them at About Safaris (☎ (03931) 44461; fax (03931) 7115), PO Box 1430, Manaba 4276.

Alternatively, check with the overland truck drivers who normally stay at Island Safari Lodge. Although most are heading in the opposite direction, some do go north and if they have space, you may be able to join a group for the standard rate of US$15 per day plus park fees.

Places to Stay

In Town The most up-market accommodation is *Riley's Hotel* (☎ 660204; fax 660580) which is comfortable, but falls outside the luxury range. Single/double rooms cost US$82/98 and suites are US$91/99. On Saturday, they organise a braai lunch which is open to anyone.

Alternatively, there's the *Sedie* (or Sedia) *Hotel* (☎ 660177; fax 660374) four km north of town. It charges US$47/56 for single/double air-conditioned rooms with bed, breakfast and transfers from the centre. Camping on the grounds costs US$3.70 per person. The nice cool pool is very welcoming and on weekends, they put on outdoor braais. On Friday and Saturday nights, a disco rumbles in the public bar until 4 am.

If you're on a tight budget and arrive in Maun too late to reach Matlapaneng, ask at the police station. Sometimes the friendly officers allow travellers to camp in their compound.

Matlapaneng Matlapaneng, eight km northeast of Maun along the Chobe road, is effectively a suburb and offers several affordable accommodation options. While you're there, have a look at the Old Matlapaneng Causeway, which is now a National Monument. From Maun, you can either hitch or phone the lodges to organise a transfer. For the lowdown on delta trips originating at the Matlapaneng lodges, see the Eastern Delta discussion later in this section.

The friendliest place is the riverside *Audi Camp* (☎ 660599; fax 660581) run by Jack & Eve Drew. Camping in your own tent costs US$3.70 per person; in a pre-erected two-person tent – with bedding – it's US$12 for two people. Breakfast is another US$3.70 and dinner costs US$7. With a bar, restaurant and swimming pool – and the most talked-about open-air showers in Botswana – it's an increasingly popular retreat. Another draw is the attached nine-hole golf course; 'dust fees' cost a bargain US$1 per person, including equipment hire. There may be the odd animal hazard, but you won't encounter any sand traps (the entire course is a bit of a sand trap). They also arrange boat hire, 4WD trips and mokoro trips. Free transfers from town depart from the Northern Air office at around 5 pm. Transfers from the camp to town run at around 8.30 am, in time to catch the bus to Francistown.

Next door is *Crocodile Camp* (☎ 660265; fax 660793) started by the crocodile hunter Bobby Wilmot. Its unappealing camp site, which is tucked inside a claustrophobic fenced enclosure away from the river, costs US$3.70 per person while pleasant chalets, which are probably the quietest digs around Maun, cost US$52/58 for singles/doubles. On Sunday afternoon, they hold a braai from noon to 3 pm for US$7 including drinks and braai packs. In the bar, Happy Hour runs from 6 to 10 pm (where but Maun would it last four hours). Transfers from town cost US$13 for up to eight passengers. They also hire canoes for paddling around in the Thamalakane River.

Island Safari Lodge (☎ 660300), four km off the Chobe road from the new Matlapaneng Bridge, is known for its rollicking social scene. If you relish your sleep, this may not be your best option, but it can be good fun and the river-view setting, complete with hippos, is lovely. Shady but rock-hard camp sites cost US$3.70 per person and chalets cost US$48/56. Transfers from Maun are free to chalet guests but campers pay US$12. There's a restaurant for chalet guests; campers and others must book well in advance or just eat at the bar (however, the US$6 buffet breakfast operates on a first-come-first-served basis.) There's a reasonably priced laundry service as well as do-it-yourself laundry sinks, but the campground facilities aren't well maintained. The shop in the reception area sells film, postcards and inexpensive Ngamiland baskets.

Other Camps For a quieter option, there's secluded *Sitatunga Camp* (☎ /fax 660570), 12 km south of town, which charges US$5 for camping, US$34 for a pre-erected tent and US$48 for a single or double self-cater-

ing chalet. There's a small shop as well, if you're not keen on the rough trip back into Maun for meals. Sitatunga Camp is adjacent to its well-signposted Crocodile Farm.

Further out is *Xyga Camp*, 35 km east of town along the Nata road. Double chalets cost US$37 and camping along a lovely papyrus-filled stretch of the Boteti River is US$4 per person. Boat hire for fishing or exploring the river is US$8/37 per hour/day.

Places to Eat
With the demise of the legendary Duck Inn, the local hang-out shifted to *Le Bistrot* (☎ 660718) in the BGI Shopping Centre, near the airport road turn-off. As their posters say, it has 'great food, charming company and nice pictures on the wall'. (The 'nice pictures' in question are prints of the Impressionists and French masters.) It does excellent meals, including a mean satay in peanut sauce, *Saté Ajam Soerabaja*, that is becoming the talk of the town, as well as a range of delicious and surprisingly inexpensive dishes from pasta, fish and prawns to lamb, burgers and steaks. Best of all, you can wash it down with a range of South African wines and top it off with some creative puddings followed by a choice of coffee concoctions.

In the mall opposite Le Bistrot is *Steers*, a South African fast-food chain serving burgers, chicken, chips, steaks and ice cream. Near Okavango Tours & Safaris you'll find *Chicago Fried Chicken*, serving up the omnipresent bird with equally ubiquitous chips. In The Mall, a good place for a snack is *The Coffee Shop* .

The *Island Safari Lodge* at Matlapaneng serves pizza, chicken and chips, meat pies and other inexpensive snacks at the bar, while their dining room offers full meals. Lunches and dinners cost US$8 to US$13 while breakfast will cost you US$6. *Crocodile Camp* charges US$7 for an English breakfast and US$10/15 for lunch and dinner, respectively.

Self-Catering The best-stocked supermarket is *Fairways* near Le Bistrot. If you're

BOTSWANA

flying into the delta, keep in mind you'll be allowed only 10 kg of baggage, including camping equipment, so go light on the food. In The Mall is a butchery selling reasonably priced biltong, which is lightweight and ideal for camping and mixing with tinned food on mokoro trips. Next door to Okavango Tours & Safaris is the green grocer *Maun Fresh Produce* with a varied selection of groceries, breads, and of course great fruit and vegetables.

Entertainment
The Maun entertainment scene focuses on Island Safari Lodge in Matlapaneng. It caters mostly to independent backpackers and organised groups travelling overland in trucks (neither of whom much approve of the other), but it's still good fun. In the thatched bar the booze normally starts flowing around 6 pm, and by 9 pm, participants are dancing, performing acrobatics, drinking upside-down margaritas (don't ask, just go see it – or try it – for yourself) and staging climbing competitions up the roof support pole. One of the nights I stayed there, the raging continued until dawn – half of one overland group missed their mokoro trip the following day and it's doubtful anyone in camp had a wink of sleep.

Alternatively, there's the Sports Bar above the furniture shop beside Barclays Bank. It's mostly just a drinking spot, but they also serve light pub meals. For a more local scene, check out the Friday and Saturday night disco at the public bar in the Sedie Hotel; it's good fun and rocks until 4 am.

Getting There & Away
Air The airport is a centre of Maun activity, especially with all the tourists, freight and safari operators buzzing back and forth between Maun and the myriad delta camps.

Air Botswana has daily flights between Maun and Gaborone (US$173), leaving between 2.30 and 3.30 pm. On Monday, Wednesday, Friday and Sunday, the Gaborone flights continue on to Francistown (US$120). On Wednesday and Sunday, you can also fly to Harare (US$170), via Victoria

Falls (US$120). Nonstop services to and from Johannesburg (US$123) and Windhoek (US$143) run three times weekly. The Windhoek services are divided between Air Botswana on Saturday and Air Namibia on Wednesday and Friday. Between Maun and Kasane (US$110), you can fly on Monday, Thursday and Saturday.

Most short-haul air travel is handled by air charter companies like Aer Kavango, Northern Air, Delta Air and Ngami Air. In addition to running flightseeing trips and transport into the delta camps, which are easily organised by travel agencies, they also wander further afield. For example, five or fewer people can fly to the Tsodilo Hills for around US$800 return. For more on air charter, see the Botswana Getting Around chapter.

Bus The bus terminal is at the north-eastern corner of The Mall. There are two daily Mahube Express buses to Francistown (US$11), departing at 7.30 and 8.30 am, and a notional daily bus to Shakawe, which leaves between 8.30 and 10.30 am.

Hitching Most travellers who've hitched to or from Maun have a story to tell about the experience, but everyone does arrive eventually. Most people are relegated to the back of a Hilux or other open truck. Heading east, a good hitching spot is Ema Reje Restaurant on the Nata road.

If you're hitching to or from Kasane, the cheapest and easiest option is to take the long route via Nata. The route north past Moremi and through Chobe National Park starts out nicely but rapidly deteriorates into a deep sand track requiring a good 4WD vehicle. Although hitching isn't impossible, you'd be wise to arrange a lift in Maun. Also, bear in mind that most drivers will be travelling via Moremi and you'll have to pay park fees for each day you spend in either park.

Mobile Safaris Another option to reach Kasane is with a mobile safari through Moremi and Chobe. They're not cheap, but they allow you to see some of the best of Botswana en route. For details, see Organised Tours earlier in this section.

Getting Around

Car Hire The Holiday Car Hire office is in the Northern Air building near the airport while Avis is down the road which parallels the airport tarmac. For rates, refer to the Botswana Getting Around chapter.

While you're off in the delta, you can lock up vehicles inside the Merlin Services compound for US$4 per day.

Bicycle Bicycles may be hired for US$1 per hour from Bush Camp Safaris on The Mall.

Hitching Hitching is normally easy between town and the Matlapaneng lodges. Transfers to Audi Camp and Sitatunga Camp are free, but Island Safari Lodge charges US$12 per party and Crocodile Camp charges US$13, which may be divided among up to eight passengers.

EASTERN DELTA

The area normally defined as the Eastern Delta takes in the wetlands between the southern boundary of Moremi Wildlife Reserve and the buffalo fence along the Boro and Santandadibe Rivers, north of Matlapaneng. If you can't manage the airfare into the Inner Delta, the Eastern Delta provides an accessible alternative.

Mokoro Trips

Some of the least expensive delta trips are organised by Maun lodges using freelance polers from Delta villages. Although these trips provide an affordable glimpse of the delta's fringes, few of the freelance polers in the Eastern Delta have completed courses in natural history and delta knowledge required for government certification. Because the poler normally sets the tone and the safety standards of a trip, it's wise to select one as carefully as possible.

That's not to say there aren't some good freelance polers out there, especially those who've grown up in the delta and learned its ways and moods from practical experience. Mostly it's just a matter of luck – some travellers have seen more wildlife or received better service from these operations than those paying more for an Inner Delta experience. Generally, the further north you travel, the better your chances of seeing wildlife.

The cheapest organised trips are arranged by Audi Camp, Sitatunga Camp, Island Safari Lodge, Bush Camp Safaris and the Community Development Corporation. They cost from US$13 (Community Development Corporation) to US$21 (Island Safari Lodge) per day for two people, plus a tip for the poler (say P5 to P10 per day) and a one-off transfer fee to the departure points above the buffalo fence on the Boro or Santandadibe Rivers. These start at US$25 per person with Audi Camp and climb to US$43 with Island Safari Lodge. In all cases, bring your own food and camping gear.

Bush Camp Safaris runs mokoro trips from Maun to Ditshipi Island, north of Chiefs Island, for US$19 per day for two people. The mokoro trips organised by the Community Development Corporation, represented by Ensign Agencies (☎ 660978; fax 60571), opposite Maun airport, are the cheapest of the lot, but their polers are generally inexperienced (once they have experience, they soon defect to the private lodges) and not everyone has been thrilled with this option.

Alternatively, you can forego the tour operators and lodges, except for transport to the buffalo fence, where you can hire your poler directly. Bear in mind that freelancers' rates don't include their meals, and clients must supply food for everyone.

The more adventurous can organise their own expedition – in Matlapaneng village, at the buffalo fence or in Maun – by seeking out mokoro owners who may be interested in doing trips. However, close scrutiny is in order – the delta is a convoluted complex of waterways and not everyone knows it as well as they'd have you believe.

BOTSWANA

Rates for Delta Lodges & Camps

All tourist lodges and camps around the Okavango Delta are superbly situated in scenic bush or on palm islands in lovely watery settings. Unless otherwise noted, the rates for all lodges and camps listed in this chapter include accommodation, meals and activities. The rates listed are high season rates, which are applicable from July to October. Low season rates average about 20% lower, but some lodges close during the lowest season, which falls between December and February.

All single rates in this chapter have been derived by adding the single supplement, which is often quite substantial, to the standard per person rate. In some cases, however, the supplement will be waived if a single traveller is willing to share twin accommodation with another person travelling alone, so be sure to ask when booking. To derive the single rate minus the supplement, simply divide the double rate by two. ∎

Motorboat Trips

If you're rushed, a motorboat trip may be your only opportunity to see the Delta. With a minimum of three people, Island Safari Lodge does day trips by motorboat around the Mporota Island area of the Eastern Delta for US$130 for up to six people.

For environmental reasons, however, motorboat trips aren't really encouraged. In the tranquillity of the Delta their buzzing engines sound like 747s and disturb wildlife, to say nothing of their effect on the relaxation factor. Furthermore, their wake creates ripples in the nearly still waters, disturbing and altering sand islands and delta vegetation, and there is a constant risk of engine fuel spilling into the water.

INNER DELTA

Roughly defined, the Inner Delta takes in the area west of Chiefs Island and between Moremi Wildlife Reserve and the base of the Okavango Panhandle. It contains lodges and camps catering to several budget ranges and provides some magnificent delta scenery and experiences. For convenience, this section also includes lodges and camps lying on the western shore of Chiefs Island along the boundaries of Moremi Wildlife Reserve.

Mokoro Trips

Mokoro trips through the Inner Delta are almost invariably arranged through the camps, each of which has its own pool of licensed (or trainee) guides/polers.

Most camps and polers assume you want to enter Moremi Wildlife Reserve and do so as a matter of course. If you do enter Moremi Wildlife Reserve you'll be charged the appropriate fee after your trip. If you'd rather avoid park and camping fees – they're reduced to P30 (US$12) and P10 (US$4), respectively, because mokoro trips qualify as organised tours – inform your poler at the outset and they will follow an alternative route. You won't see as much wildlife as in the reserve – and no elephants or lions – but the natural element is just as lovely and you'll normally see antelopes as well as baboons, warthogs, hippos and even the occasional leopard. Also, advise the poler if you'd like to break the trip with bushwalks around the palm islands.

The cheapest Inner Delta mokoro trips cost from US$19 to US$22 per person per day for the boat and poler. A mokoro normally accommodates the poler, two passengers and food and camping equipment. More up-market lodges run mokoro trips between established permanent camps and offer some degree of luxury; you won't need to carry your own equipment, but prices are considerably higher. The cheapest deal is with Gunn's Camp; their trips include a poler, self-prepared meals and cooking and camping equipment for US$93/130 per day for one/two people, without park fees.

Other Trips

For clients who aren't comfortable with the prospects of mokoro travel, up-market lodges run motorboat and pontoon trips and booze cruises (but see the comments on motorboats under Motorboat Trips above). Prices and offerings vary according to the lodge. For example, the relatively inexpensive Gunn's Camp runs powerboat trips for

US$75 per day. Maun travel agencies can fill you in on options but normally only provide information on their own lodges.

Camps – bottom end

Both inexpensive lodges lie just across the channel from Chief's Island and Moremi Wildlife Reserve, about 70 km from Maun. In theory, campers should carry food and other supplies from outside but because you're limited to 10 kg of baggage, your capacity for self-catering may be strained. Most people rely on camp meals and hire equipment from the camp shops. At either camp, mokoro trips cost US$30 per day, single or double.

Oddball's Palm Island Luxury Lodge (Okavango Tours & Safaris) Oddball's (☎ 660220; fax 660589), on Noga Island, is the Okavango's only real concession to backpackers. Don't be misled by the price, however. Like the more up-market lodges, it also enjoys a lovely setting and a friendly and relaxed atmosphere. (In case you haven't guessed, the 'Luxury Lodge' bit in the name is a facetious dig at its frightfully expensive neighbours.) Camping costs US$7.50 per person and it's backed up by a rustic bar, showers, Molly's Quickserv food shop, camping equipment rental and a couple of resident elephants (with a particular fondness for mokolani palms and campers' laundry). Alternatively, you can book the lovely 'honeymoon suite', five metres up in the treetops for US$80; it's an unforgettable place to spend a night. Breakfast, lunch and dinner cost US$3.50, US$4 and US$9.50, respectively, and delicious home-baked bread sells for US$1.50 per loaf (it's ideal on mokoro trips). Be sure to allow days for relaxation and bushwalking around the camp as well as time for your mokoro trip. Children are welcome. Air transfers cost US$93 return, and are arranged through Okavango Tours & Safaris in Maun.

Gunn's Camp (Trans Okavango) Gunn's Camp (☎ 660023; fax 660040) – also called *Ntswi Camp* – on palm-studded Ntswi Island is a bit more up-market than Oddball's. Here, camping costs US$7.40 per person; amenities include hot showers, flush loos, a barbecue area, a basic shop and a bar. 'Luxury tents' cost US$182/245 a single/double, including meals. Return flights from Maun cost US$93 per person, or you can fly one way for US$45 and travel by motorboat back to Maun for US$38. No-frills mokoro trips cost US$30 per day for two people. For more information, see under Mokoro Trips in this section.

Camps – middle & top end

Abu's Camp (Ker & Downey) This fairly recent addition to the Okavango scene is probably the most unique (and most expensive) camp in the delta. It was the brainchild of operator Randall Moore. In his book *Back to Africa*, he describes how he returned three African-born elephants, who were circus-trained in North America, to Botswana and put them to work in the safari business. The elephants, Abu, Bennie and Kathy (along with a clutch of orphaned elephant youngsters who follow them everywhere), are now the stars at Abu's Camp; the big draw for tourists is the novel opportunity to cruise around the African bush on the back of an African elephant. However, novelty doesn't come cheap, and the rate for a five-night stay at Abu's Camp, including meals and elephant rides, is US$4000 per person; that's US$800 per day or US$0.55 per minute. Think about it!

Delta Camp (Okavango Tours & Safaris) Near the southern end of Chiefs Island, near its sibling camp, Oddball's, is Delta Camp. It sits in a scenic, shady spot at the end of its own airstrip (complete with logs appropriately identified as the 'Domestic' and 'International' departure lounges). A real plus is the fact that owner Peter Sandenburgh prohibits powerboats entering the area, so the silence is preserved. All-inclusive catered mokoro trips and guided walks around the island are optional. The high-season rate of US$268/389 includes accommodation in single/double thatched chalets, three excellent meals, drinks and laundry.

Jedibe Camp (Okavango Wilderness) Accommodating 16 guests, Jedibe ('ostrich excrement') is the most remote camp in the Inner Delta. No motor vehicles are permitted and you're a long way from anywhere here, so the peace and seclusion factors will be nearly complete. Look for Pel's fishing owls, red lechwes and the rare sitatunga which are commonly seen in the area. Luxury mokoro trips, fishing, nature walks and pontoon cruises are available. Although air transfers from Maun are quite dear, Jedibe is surprisingly one of the more reasonably priced luxury camps at US$276/441 for a single/double.

Mombo Camp (Okavango Wilderness) Just off the north-west corner of Chiefs Island, Mombo Camp is one of the best for wildlife viewing. The area is especially known for its population of Cape hunting dogs and visitors have a good chance of observing these normally elusive animals. The camp accommodates 12 guests and offers mokoro trips, motor safaris and guided bushwalks. Single/double rates are US$276/441. Because Mombo Camp lies within Moremi Wildlife Reserve, park fees must be added to quoted rates.

BOTSWANA

Pom Pom Camp (Ker & Downey) This quite remote tented camp is accessible via air or bush track from the south-west end of the Delta. It's a particularly good area for birdwatching; other activities include game drives and short mokoro excursions. All meals and activities are included, but it's one of the more expensive Inner Delta camps at US$515/840 for a single/double.

Tchau Camp (Okavango Wilderness) Situated on Tchau Island inside Moremi Wildlife Reserve, Tchau Camp occupies a secluded spot near the northern end of Chiefs Island. There's no airstrip or vehicle access; you're brought in by boat up the Boro River from Xaxaba Camp, an hour away. Single/double rates are US$276/441. With a group of four or more people, they'll also arrange four-day semi-luxury camping trips by mokoro for the same price.

Xaxaba Camp (Gametrackers) This luxury camp beside a beautiful lagoon accommodates a maximum of 24 guests and offers gourmet food, a swimming pool and bar. The name means 'island of tall trees'. Mokoro trips are available as well as booze cruises, guided walks and birdwatching. Single/double accommodation in reed-constructed chalets costs US$470/590 and air transfers from Maun are US$70 per person.

MOREMI WILDLIFE RESERVE

Moremi Wildlife Reserve, encompassing over 3000 sq km, is the bit of the Okavango Delta officially cordoned off for the preservation of wildlife. It was set aside as a reserve in the 1960s when it became apparent that overhunting was decimating wildlife.

The park has a distinctly dual personality, with large areas of dry land rising between vast wetlands. The two most prominent dry features are Chiefs Island, deep in the Inner Delta, and the Moremi Peninsula or Moremi Tongue, comprising the north-eastern end of the reserve. While Chiefs Island is best reached by mokoro from Inner Delta safari camps, much of the Moremi Peninsula is accessible by 4WD vehicle. Habitats range from the mopane woodland and thorn scrub to dry savanna, riparian woodlands, grasslands, flood plains, marshes, permanent waterways, lagoons and islands.

Although Moremi has attracted lots of safari lodges, the only low-cost accommodation is in the previously described National Parks' camp sites: South Gate, Third Bridge, Xakanaxa Lediba and North Gate. The two

entry gates are open at 6 am to 6.30 pm from March to September and 5.30 am to 5.30 pm from October to February.

South Gate

The more southerly of Moremi's two road entrances is aptly known as South Gate, 84 km north of Maun. Here visitors pay park fees. Just inside the entry gate is a clean, developed camp site with showers and a shady picnic area.

Third Bridge

Moremi's most interesting camp site is Third Bridge, literally the third log bridge after entering the reserve at South Gate, 48 km away. The bridge, which crosses the Sekiri River, is rustically beautiful, but the area's main attractions are the sandy-bottomed pool of water beneath the bridge and the amount of wildlife (particularly lions) which uses the bridge as a thoroughfare. One could hardly imagine a more idyllic spot.

Contrary to official advice, nearly everyone swims at Third Bridge. If you can't be restrained, swim only in broad daylight, keeping close watch in the reeds – there are crocodiles – and don't camp on the bridge or sleep in the open, since there are many lions in the area. Camp sites are strung along the road on either end of the bridge. However, there are no facilities, so use common sense when cooking and performing ablutions. Burn your rubbish, bury solid waste well away from the water, use a basin when washing up and pour waste water into the sand.

Mboma Island

The grassy savanna of 100-sq-km Mboma Island – actually just a long extension of the Moremi Peninsula – contrasts sharply with surrounding landscapes. The sandy Mboma Island circuit route turns off two km or so west of Third Bridge and makes a pleasant side trip from the standard Moremi loop.

Xakanaxa Lediba

Around Xakanaxa Lediba are most of the private camps within Moremi Wildlife

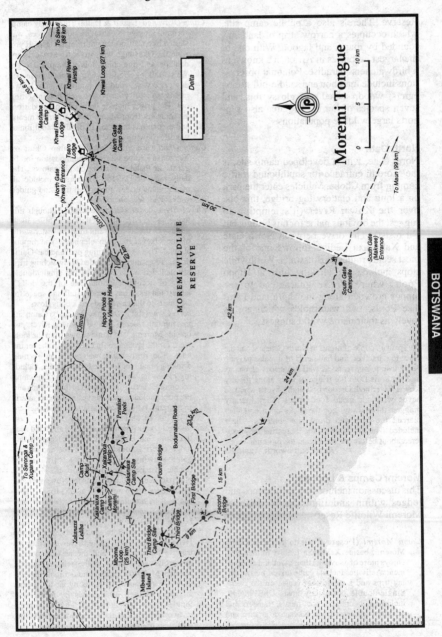

Moremi Tongue

Reserve. There's also a public camp site, which occupies a narrow strip of land surrounded by marsh and lagoon. With one of the largest heronries in Africa, it's known as a birdwatchers' paradise. Potential observations include marabou and saddle-bill storks; egrets; wood, sacred and glossy ibis; and seven species of heron. The area also supports large wildlife populations.

North Gate

North Gate, with a developed camp site, is the Moremi entrance for southbound traffic coming from Chobe. Vehicles enter the park on a long and clattery log bridge, this one over the Khwai River (it's tempting to suggest the obvious name for this bridge, but I'll resist). The drive between North Gate and Xakanaxa Lediba follows one of the most scenic routes in Botswana. Worthwhile stops include the viewing hide at Hippo Pools, where you're guaranteed to see hippos crowded along the shore, and Paradise Pools, two waterholes which are as lovely as their name would suggest.

We spent a couple of nights at North Gate and had the place to ourselves, and had herds of impalas passing very close to our tents, as well as curious elephants looking at us from the fringe of trees along the dry Khwai River bed. On our first night, hyena wreaked havoc with our metal food boxes. They literally dragged them away, got the locks open and then pierced the cans and drank the contents – beer included. The monkeys ate the margarine they scattered about before we were up in the morning.
Ann Shuttleworth, Australia

Moremi Camps & Lodges

This discussion includes top price camps and lodges within and immediately north of Moremi Wildlife Reserve.

Camp Moremi (Desert & Delta Safaris) Camp Moremi, beside Xakanaxa Lediba further east, enjoys more of a savanna than a wetland environment. Activities include game drives, birdwatching trips and a sundowner cruise on the Delta. Single/double occupancy costs US$398/640, including accommodation, meals, transfers and activities. Access is via Xakanaxa airstrip and 4WD vehicle.

Camp Okavango (Desert & Delta) This lovely camp, set amid sausage trees and jackalberry trees, was started by a Californian with elegant taste. If you want the Okavango with silver tea service, candelabras and fine china, this is the place to go. We're talking US$415/675 single/double per day price-wise, and the minimum stay is two nights, so stuff your wallet well before setting out. The prices include tented accommodation, air transfers from Maun, three gourmet meals, and meticulous attention to detail in addition to wildlife-viewing canoe trips.

Camp Okuti (Sitatunga Safaris) Camp Okuti on Xakanaxa Lediba offers accommodation for 14 guests in thatch-roofed brick bungalows. The daily rates of US$160 per person include all meals, game drives, motorboat trips and guided walks. Park fees are extra.

Khwai River Lodge (Gametrackers) Although this lodge, at the edge of the Okavango, allies itself more with dryland Moremi than the water world of the Okavango, both elephants and hippos abound. There's a swimming pool and bar. Game drives, foot safaris and guided birdwatching trips are included in the US$470/590 single/double price of accommodation. One of the delta's largest lodges, it has friendly staff and space for 24 guests in thatch-roofed brick bungalows.

Machaba Camp (Ker & Downey) Machaba Camp sits in a hunting reserve along the Khwai River, just outside Moremi. The name comes from the local word for the sycamore fig trees which shelter the tents. The surrounding waters are an evening drinking venue for hundreds of animals, including elephants, antelopes and zebras. The camp accommodates up to 10 guests in luxury tents and the price includes game drives and photo safaris in Moremi. All-inclusive single/double rates are US$515/840. Park fees are extra.

San-ta-Wani Lodge (Gametrackers) On an island near the South Gate of Moremi Wildlife Reserve, this lodge offers gourmet meals, a bar and superb game viewing and motorboat trips. Single/ double thatched bungalows cost US$470/590, plus park fees. In the off-season (November and December), it's more viable at US$168/210, but access is by mobile safari only.

Shinde Island Camp (Ker & Downey) This camp is beside a lagoon in a remote area of Moremi Wildlife Reserve. Between the savanna and the Delta, it offers 4WD game drives and mokoro trips to the heronries and the nesting sites of numerous water birds in the remote Moremi Madiba. Mokoro trips and photographic expeditions are available. Access is by air to Xugana airstrip and then 30 minutes by motorboat. Single/double rates are US$515/840 (minimum of two nights' stay) including accommodation, meals, air transfers from Maun and activities.

Tsaro Lodge (Okavango Explorations) Tsaro Lodge overlooks the Moremi flood plains, with their diversity of wildlife, near the Khwai River at the reserve's North Gate. There's 24-hour electricity and a bar and swimming pool. Meals and twice-daily game drives are included in the price of accommodation, but park fees are not. The real plus point of this camp is the two-night Tsaro Walking Trail, a wilderness camping and hiking trip which will take you on foot along the beautiful Khwai River to observe the profuse birdlife and wildlife. The single/double rates are US$259/371.

Xakanaxa Camp (Okavango Tours & Safaris) In the heart of Moremi, Xakanaxa is probably the best option if you want maximum wildlife-viewing and birdwatching. In a pleasant mix of delta and savanna, the area teems with elephants and other wildlife. It also contains three of the Delta's largest heronries – Xakanaxa, Gadikwe and Xobega Madiba lagoons. Accommodation is in luxury tents and the single/double price of US$297/445 includes meals, game drives, boat trips, fishing and birdwatching. Park fees will cost you extra.

Xugana Camp (Okavango Explorations) The area of Xugana Camp was originally inhabited by San hunters, and the name Xugana means 'kneel down to drink', in reference to the welcome sight of perennial water after a long hunt. The only access to this remotest of the Moremi area camps is by air. Accommodation is in luxury tents under big shady trees, and there's a bar, gourmet dining room and swimming pool to add to the overall wilderness opulence. Xugana Camp still gets considerable mileage out of the 1984 visit of Prince Charles. Single/double rates are US$259/371, not including transfers. If you want to set off on a camping trip by mokoro, you'll pay US$241/334 per day, plus park fees.

Getting There & Away

If you're booked into one of the delta camps, air, road or boat transport is normally arranged by the camp, but prices vary considerably. For wild camping, you'll have to join a mobile safari (see Organised Tours under Maun) or have access to a 4WD vehicle.

From Maun, go north-east on the new tarred road past Matlapaneng. North of Shorobe village, the road becomes good gravel, but at the tsetse camp, 10 km north of Shorobe, it deteriorates into sand. A further 13 km brings you to the Buffalo Fence; four km beyond that is the signposted Moremi turn-off.

From this westward turning, it's 20 km to the reserve entrance at South Gate. From South Gate to Third Bridge it's a two-hour, 48-km drive on a poor road through glorious, wildlife-rich country. It's only 25 km from Third Bridge to Xakanaxa Lediba and from there, about 60 km to the northern entrance at North Gate.

To hitch north from Maun wait at the lay-by north of the incongruous new roundabout (near the new Matlapaneng Crossing). Hitching is slow, but with an early start, you should at least reach the Moremi turnoff before dark. From the Moremi turn-off, getting into the park will be a matter of luck – be prepared to camp.

North-Western Botswana

North-western Botswana is best characterised as the meeting point between the Kalahari sands and the Okavango Delta. The Okavango Panhandle, which is distinct from the main body of the Delta, extends northwest to the Namibian border. Along it, people living in clusters of small fishing villages extract their livelihoods from the rich waters. The cosmopolitan society is made up of Mbukushu, Yei, Tswana, Herero, European, San and refugee Angolans peacefully sharing this quiet corner of the country.

Beyond the panhandle green belt, the Kalahari country sprawls westward towards the Namibian border, where access is difficult and distances seem great on the sandy roads. Until recently, it has remained isolated, but with the new tarred road almost completed between Maun and Shakawe – and soon to connect with the Namibian road system at Mohembo – things are changing.

For visitors, the region has a clutch of attractions. South-west of Maun is Lake Ngami, which figured prominently in the history and development of the region.

BOTSWANA

Under optimum conditions, it would be worth a visit, but it has been dry for many years and the bush has taken over. More interesting is the far western strip of the country, where you'll find Gcwihaba Caverns, the Aha Hills and a landscape dotted with lovely villages.

In Botswana's north-western corner, south of Shakawe, the Tsodilo Hills rise abruptly out of an otherwise featureless desert plain. Although the indigenous cultures have been considerably altered, the lonely outcrops still appear much as they did when Sir Laurens van der Post explored them and wrote his renowned works *Lost World of the Kalahari* and *Heart of the Hunter*. Currently, visitors are free to hike, climb, camp and soak in the mystery of what van der Post is frequently quoted as calling 'the Louvre of the desert'. With increasing accessibility, changes and tourist development are on the way.

Throughout Ngamiland, the district which takes in all of north-western Botswana, you'll have the opportunity to see and purchase the beautiful artwork typical of the area, especially the famous Ngamiland baskets. In western desert villages, you can purchase San material arts, including traditional weapons, leatherwork, wooden and seed necklaces and beaded jewellery.

A major problem, especially if you're doing lots of sand driving, is fuel. Although Shakawe has been granted a petrol station permit, as yet the only place to buy petrol is from the Brigades for roughly double the price in Maun. The most reliable source of petrol is the cooperative shop in Etsha 6 which has a supply whenever the truck has recently arrived. In an emergency you may be able to purchase a few litres at Shakawe Fishing Camp, south of Shakawe. Failing that, the nearest source is at Divundu, 40 km over the border in Namibia, but get hold of some South African rand or Namibian dollars beforehand. They do accept pula, but at the poor rate of 1:1.

LAKE NGAMI

The first people to see Lake Ngami and the surrounding Xautsha plain were probably 18th century Kwena hunters, but the area was first settled by the Tawana branch of the Ngwato in the late 18th century. In 1824, they established their tribal capital at Toteng, near the north-eastern end of the lake. (For more about the Tawana, refer to the history discussion in the Maun section.) When Dr David Livingstone arrived in 1849, Lake Ngami was a magnificent expanse of water, teeming with birdlife and inhabited by hippos and other large animals drawn to the water. He estimated its area at 810 sq km, although ancient lakeshores indicate that it once encompassed 1800 sq km.

Lake Ngami has no outflow and is filled only by Okavango overflow down the Nhabe River. When that happens, the water lures large flocks of flamingoes, ibis, pelicans, eagles, storks, terns, gulls, kingfishers, ducks and geese to its shallows to feed on crustaceans (which, during dry periods, lie dormant in the lakebed awaiting water). Soon after Livingstone had recorded the sight, the lake disappeared and reappeared for a brief period later in the 19th century. Its next appearance, in 1962, lasted for 20 years and the water covered only 250 sq km.

Since 1982, the lake has been dry, so don't be fooled by the blue swathe on Botswana maps or the lovely tourist-brochure photos of splashing pelicans and Egyptian geese. By the time you read this, Lake Ngami may be worth visiting, but at the moment it's just another nondescript spread of bush.

There's no accommodation in either Toteng or Sehitwa but you can camp anywhere away from the main road and villages.

Getting There & Away

There's no public transport to Lake Ngami, but if it does refill, it will probably attract a lot of fishing activity from Maun. The Maun-Shakawe bus passes through nearby Sehitwa. Sehitwa lies on the tarred road from Maun and hitching is fairly easy.

The main access route to Lake Ngami turns off the tarred road about two km north of Sehitwa. Don't let anyone tell you to look for a 'Fishing Camp' sign – it hasn't been there for years. Just look for the first prominent track turning off north-east of Sehitwa. Having said that, any track turning east from the tarred road north of Sehitwa will take you to the lakeshore.

GCWIHABA CAVERNS (DROTSKY'S CAVE)

In the !Kung language, the name of this decorated cavern system in the Gcwihaba Hills near the Namibian border means 'hyena's hole'. The caverns and their stalagmites and stalactites, which reach heights and lengths of up to 10 metres, were formed by water seeping through and dissolving the dolomite rock. The dripping water deposited minerals and built up the cavern decorations from the ceiling and floor.

The caverns probably weren't brought to European attention until the mid-1930s when the !Kung showed them to a Ghanzi farmer, Martinus Drotsky, and for years they were known as Drotsky's Cave. As with

many caves, there's a legend of buried treasure in Gcwihaba; the fabulously wealthy founder of Ghanzi, Hendrik Matthys van Zyl, is said to have stashed a portion of his considerable fortune somewhere in the cave in the late 1800s, but this is probably just wishful thinking.

Visiting the Caves

There are two entrances 300 metres apart (the route through, however, is more circuitous and hence, longer) and it's possible to make your way between them, but there are no guides, no lights and no indication of which route to take. Absolutely no natural light filters into the cave so you must carry several strong torches (and batteries) as well as emergency light sources, such as matches and cigarette lighters.

The easier passage begins from the lower entrance, which is hidden halfway up the hill from the end of the road. There, you'll enter

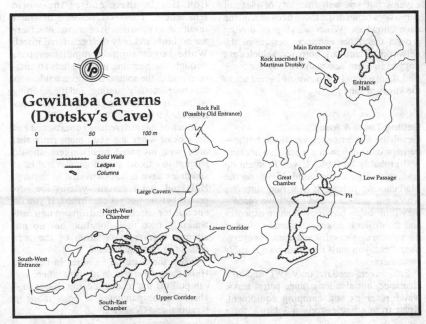

Gcwihaba Caverns (Drotsky's Cave)

0   50   100 m

Main Entrance

Rock inscribed to Martinus Drotsky

Entrance Hall

Rock Fall (Possibly Old Entrance)

Solid Walls
Ledges
Columns

Great Chamber

Low Passage

Large Cavern

Pit

North-West Chamber

Lower Corridor

South-West Entrance

South-East Chamber

Upper Corridor

a large chamber from which you'll proceed down an increasingly steep passageway. The only hairy bit of the trip is a short vertical climb down into a pit and then up the other side to a shelf, where there's a tight squeeze before you emerge into a large room. There was once a rope to facilitate the last couple of metres climb out of the pit, but latest reports indicate that it has been removed.

The remainder of the route, which is about one km long, passes through a series of large rooms and passages with lots of enticing side passages leading off into the blackness. About midway through the cavern, you may observe several species of bats that live there; the most common is the large Commerson's leaf-nosed bat. As you approach the other end of the cavern, you'll see light filtering in from the upper entrance, above a steep rubbly slope. Once you've been through the cave, it's pleasant to climb to the hilltop to see a sunset over the violet expanses of the Kalahari.

There are no water or facilities at the caverns but you will find lots of pleasant camp sites beneath the thorn trees around the cave entrances. When walking or driving around the upper entrance, beware of the networks of aardvark burrows; vehicles get bogged in them and walkers may suddenly find themselves face down or buried up to the knees in sand.

Getting There & Away

Gcwihaba Caverns sees very little traffic – perhaps one vehicle in a week – so hitching will probably be futile. If you're intent on finding a lift, ask around Maun or the Matlapaneng lodges. If you find someone who's going there – and they have space – they'll probably be happy to share expenses and the difficult driving. Ascertain whether the vehicle carries sufficient water for everyone; if not, you must take your own *durable* containers.

Self-drivers need not only 4WD and high clearance, but also long-range petrol tanks, water reserves and camping equipment. Apart from a bottle store in Sehitwa, there

are no facilities between Maun and Gcwihaba Caverns.

You'll have good tar road from Maun to the caverns turn-off, just under two km west of Tsau (it isn't signposted). The track is initially clear but deteriorates as you head over dunes, ruts and deep sand. After 86 km you'll reach the turning to Xhaba bore hole, which lies 27 km to the south. This road leads 55 km down the Gcwihabadum fossil valley to the caverns, which are set in the low and rocky Gcwihaba Hills. Alternatively, you can continue straight on. At 144 km from the Tsau turn-off, take the left turning down the Nxainxaidum fossil valley and follow this track for 27 km to the caverns.

AHA HILLS

Straddling the Botswana-Namibia border, the 700-million-year-old limestone and dolomite Aha Hills rise 300 metres from the flat, thorny scrub of the Kalahari sands. Although they're scenic enough, the attraction lies in their end-of-the-world remoteness. The total absence of water results in an eerie dearth of animal life; there are no birds and only the occasional insect. While larger animals sometimes pass through, the haunting night sounds so characteristic of the southern African wilderness are conspicuously missing, and the resulting stillness is as perfect as you're likely to experience anywhere.

Much of this area remains unexplored and the lack of water and good maps mean that only well-prepared bushwalkers should attempt to explore it on foot. Several large sinkholes have been discovered in the Aha Hills and major cavern systems are suspected but are not yet confirmed. If you do encounter such formations when out walking, note their location but do not attempt further exploration of the area without proper equipment.

While there are no facilities in the Aha Hills, there are a couple of spots where you can pull off the road and camp. Basic supplies may be purchased at bush shops in Nxainxai and Gcangwa.

Gcangwa

The friendly and charming village of Gcangwa, 25 difficult km north of the Aha Hills, is actually an agglomeration of separate Herero, San and Tawana communities. Each culture has its own distinct housing and dress. In Gcangwa, North American research teams have conducted extensive anthropological studies of the San culture and their work forms the basis for some of the most authoritative works on the subject.

Getting There & Away

There are two routes into the Aha Hills. One follows the track which passes the Gcwihaba Caverns turn-offs. The other turns west from the Maun-Shakawe road, just north of a small bridge near Nokaneng; from here, it's 190 km to the Aha Hills. Between Nokaneng and Gcangwa, this route is well travelled (that means at least one vehicle per day) and most of it is relatively easy driving. There are, however, three or four bad stretches through high and sandy dunes. Between Gcangwa and the Aha Hills, the way is rough and difficult, especially as it passes over domes of sharp, tyre-bursting rock.

Coming from Gcwihaba Caverns, the road up Nxainxaidum fossil valley is fairly good as far as the village of Nxainxai (spelt Caecae on some maps), 42 km from the caverns. In Nxainxai, there's a bore hole, but ask permission before drawing water. From there, it's 15 km through very deep and rutted sand to the Aha Hills. This bit will take at least an hour and is best negotiated in low 4WD.

GUMARE

Between Tsau and the village of Gumare, the tarred road is often covered with sand drift which acts like millions of ball bearings on the hard surface and makes for tedious driving. If you have the time, detour through the clean and pleasant village of Gumare, which merits a couple of hours' exploration. Services include a bakery and a couple of bush shops.

THE ETSHAS

In the late 1700s, Lozi aggressors forced the Mbukushu people from their homes along the Chobe and Linyanti valleys of north-eastern Namibia to the banks of the Okavango in southern Angola. The Mbukushu, in turn, displaced the peaceful Yei. Over the following decades their settlements spread slowly down the Okavango River into present-day Botswana.

The Mbukushu had a reputation for skilful rainmaking and this art, which originally required child sacrifice, was also adopted by some neighbouring tribes. Amazingly, there are well-substantiated reports that the tribal leadership was providing slaves for Portuguese traders as recently as the early 1900s.

In the late 1960s Angola was experiencing civil war, and many of the remaining Mbukushu people fled southward and were granted refugee status in Botswana. Initially they waited in Shakawe while a new settlement, Etsha, was completed for them. In the shift to Etsha in 1969, they naturally organised into 13 groups based on clan and social structure carried over from Angola, with each group settling a km or so from the next. To facilitate their accounting system, the government bestowed the villages with numerical names – Etsha 1 to Etsha 13 – and so they remain.

There's no accommodation at The Etshas. Apart from the prospect of buying fuel or supplies at the well-stocked bush shop at Etsha 6, there's not much reason to visit unless you're looking for original Mbukushu basketry. To accommodate the growing population, the government has constructed a new multi-million pula secondary school at The Etshas.

Getting There & Away

To get there, turn east off the tarred highway approximately 15 km north of Gumare. From there, it's 13 km to The Etshas.

SHAKAWE

Now that the tarred road has almost arrived, the desultory but picturesque village of Shakawe is awakening from its former status

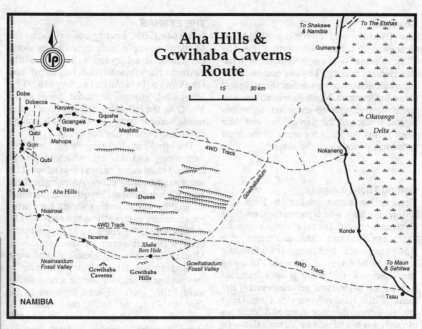

**Aha Hills &
Gcwihaba Caverns
Route**

as a sleepy little outpost on the Okavango. For travellers, Shakawe means a Botswana entry or exit stamp or a staging post for a visit to the Tsodilo Hills, 40 km away. For southern African holiday-makers, it's most often the start of a fishing trip in the Okavango Panhandle.

If you're heading for Namibia, try to exchange pula for Namibian dollars or South African rand at either Shakawe Fishing Camp or Wright's Trading Store.

Places to Stay & Eat
Activity in Shakawe centres on Wright's Trading Store, the new self-service supermarket and the bottle shop. In the compound opposite Wright's is *Mma Haidongo's Nice Bread Bakery* where you can buy home-baked bread for US$1 per loaf. The name of the *Ema Reje Liquor Restaurant* in the centre probably provides some clues about its character, but it does serve basic meals.

If you have transport, accommodation and meals are available at Drotsky's Cabins or the Shakawe Fishing Camp, five and eight km south of town, respectively. For details, see Okavango Panhandle in this chapter.

Getting There & Away
Bus Ostensibly, the bus between Shakawe and Maun runs daily and takes eight hours, but it leaves when full and there's no real schedule. Check for the bus at the police station and Wright's Trading Store; if it's parked in either place, it'll be heading for Maun after 9 am the following morning.

Car & Motorbike Drivers should note that the road from Shakawe north to Mohembo and the Namibian border is poor in places, but once you're through the fences separating the two countries, it's good gravel. Once inside Namibia, you'll have to stop at the gate of Mahango Game Reserve to secure an entry permit. Transit through the park is free, but to look around, you must pay park fees.

Just beyond the northern boundary of Mahango is Popa Falls, a series of cascades on the Okavango River, and a National Parks' camp site (see the Namibia section).

From Divundu, just north of Popa Falls, you may turn west at the T-junction towards Rundu and Windhoek or east towards Katima Mulilo, Kasane, Kazungula and Victoria Falls.

Although Shakawe has been granted permission for a petrol station, as yet, petrol is available – for US$0.70 per litre – only from The Brigades. It's sold from drums in a military-looking compound, north along the river beyond the secondary school.

OKAVANGO PANHANDLE

Distinct from the main body of the Okavango, the panhandle extends north-west to the Namibian border. This region is well contained by a 15-km-wide geologic fault through which the Okavango meanders until it's released into the main delta. Excess waters spread across the valley on either side to form vast reed beds and papyrus-choked lagoons. The local Mbukushu, Yei, Tswana, Herero and Angolans, whose livelihoods are largely dependent upon fishing with nets, lines and baskets, have built their villages in those places where the river's meanders flow past dry land and form proper riverbanks.

Panhandle Camps

Most of the panhandle camps fall within the middle price range and are geared mainly towards the sport-fishing crowd. Anglers can hope for a variety of species, especially tiger-fish, bream, pike and barbel. Your chances of catching tigerfish are promising except in July and August. Barbel run any time from mid-September to December.

Drotsky's Cabins (Merlin Services) Drotsky's Cabins (☎ 660978 or 660571; fax 660623 or 660351), a lovely and welcoming camp owned by Jan and Eileen Drotsky, lies beside a channel of the Okavango River about five km south of Shakawe. It's set amid a thick riverine forest with fabulous birdwatching opportunities and fine views across the reeds and papyrus. Prices for chalet accommodation fall within the middle-range, although inexpensive camp sites are sometimes available. Table d'hôte meals are available if booked in advance. Because this is the Drotsky's home, you'll be made to feel like a family guest; please behave as if you're visiting good friends and you won't find better hospitality anywhere in Botswana.

Guma Lagoon Camp (Merlin Services) The excellent-value Guma Lagoon Camp lies north-east of Etsha 13, on the Thaoge River at the base of the panhandle. It accommodates 10 guests in thatched-reed bungalows or tents, all with en suite facilities. The rate is US$128 per person, including accommodation, meals, drinks, boat trips and fuel, use of fishing tackle and day or overnight mokoro trips. Guma profiles itself as a family resort, and for longer stays special family rates are available on request. The focus is the excellent tiger and bream fishing available in the surrounding waters. The final 11 km from Etsha 13 may only be negotiated by 4WD vehicle, but the lodge can provide safe parking facilities and transfers at Etsha13.

Nxamaseri Camp (Gametrackers) The highest priced panhandle Camp, Nxamaseri provides luxury accommodation for the fishing crowd in five-star chalets. The highlights are birdwatching, horse-riding and fishing excursions. The camp lies about midway between Shakawe and Sepupa and is accessible by 4WD from either place, or by air from Maun to Shakawe and then by 4WD vehicle to the camp. For single/double chalets with en suite facilities, you'll pay US$275/363, including accommodation, meals and fishing tackle. Return air transfers from Maun cost US$167. Children are welcome.

Qhaaxwa (Makwena) Lodge (Gametrackers) At the base of the panhandle, Qhaaxwa Lodge lies east of The Etshas and resembles more the Inner Delta than any of the panhandle camps. The name means 'birthplace of the hippo', but the formidable-looking word apparently prompted someone to offer the name 'Makwena' as an alternative. You'll have good chances of seeing red lechwe and even sitatunga, as well as waterbirds and birds of prey. For US$295/590, you get single/double accommodation in reed chalets, meals, motorboat trips, fishing trips and birdwatching excursions. Their backpackers' rate of US$28 per person covers accommodation only; breakfast or lunch are US$10 and dinner is US$12. Transfers between The Etshas and the camp cost US$4 each way; trips to Mokoro Island are also US$4 and mokoro trips, which are organised directly with the polers, cost US$13 per day for two people. Motorboats are hired by the hour (US$23) or day (US$82).

Shakawe Fishing Camp (Travel Wild) Shakawe Fishing Camp (☎ 6608222; fax 660493) lies beside the Okavango River eight km south of Shakawe. This quirky camp lies in the northernmost part of the panhandle, easily accessible by 4WD vehicle from Shakawe or by a combination of air and motor vehicle from Maun to Shakawe airstrip. Amenities include a bar and swimming pool. In the riverside campground, you can pitch a tent and enjoy fishing and a lovely river view for US$3.50 per person. Chalets cost US$75 for up to four people; and pre-erected tents are US$56 for up to three people. Meals are available but quite expensive at US$12 for breakfast, US$15 for lunch and US$23 for dinner. A package plan including accommodation, meals, boating activities and transfers from the airstrip is US$158 per person. For US$150 per day plus US$1 per km, you can hire a vehicle to visit the Tsodilo Hills; don't laugh at the price until you've seen the road.

Xaro Lodge (Ensign Agencies) The luxury tented camp Xaro Lodge (☎ 660978) lies on the panhandle, just south of Shakawe Fishing Camp. Especially during the dry season, the sandy river banks serve as a nesting site for numerous species of water bird. Pel's fishing owl is also common here as are herons, fish eagles and several types of bee-eaters. All inclusive rates are US$145 per person. It's open from March to September and offers motorboat excursions, fishing, guided nature walks and add-on trips into the Tsodilo Hills. Access is by boat transfer only.

TSODILO HILLS

Whether or not you believe in the spirits that seem to gravitate towards ancient lands, the Tsodilo Hills cast a powerful spell. Like Australia's Ayers Rock, these lonely chunks of rock rise abruptly from a rippled, ocean-like expanse of desert and are imbued with myth, legend and spiritual significance for both the Makoko and Dzucwa San, as well as the recently arrived Mbukushu people. The Mbukushu believe that the gods lowered themselves and their cattle down a rope onto the Female Hill, while the San see the Tsodilo Hills as the site of the creation itself. These four masses of rock were the 'Slip-

pery Hills' of Sir Laurens van der Post, the place where his cameras inexplicably jammed, his tape recorders ceased to function and his party was attacked by swarms of bees three mornings running. When he learned from a local guide that two of his party had disturbed the spirits of Tsodilo by ignoring long-established protocol and killing a warthog while approaching the sacred hills, van der Post felt compelled to bury a note of apology beneath the remarkable panel of rock paintings that now bears his name.

The name 'Tsodilo' is derived from the Mbukushu word *sorile*, meaning 'sheer'. The several layers of superimposed rock paintings and a wealth of archaeological remnants suggest to researchers that the area has been inhabited by ancestors of the present-day San for up to 35,000 years. Bantu sites in the area date back as early as AD 500, and numerous flaked stone tools have been excavated. In addition, over 3500 individual outline-style paintings at over 350 sites have been discovered and catalogued, with more being found each year. Although no date can be fixed for most of the rock paintings, it's clear that some were produced fairly recently – after 700 AD. This assumption is derived from their degree of preservation and their depiction of cattle, which were introduced by Iron Age Bantu pastoralists around that time. Interestingly, on the summit of the Female Hill are the remains of two Iron Age village sites, Nqoma and Divuyu, which date from between the sixth and 11th centuries.

Orientation & Information
The Tsodilo Hills comprise four main chunks of rock: the Male, the Female, the Child and a hillock known as North Hill, which until recently remained nameless; one legend recounts that it was an argumentative wife of the Male Hill, who was sent away. Reaching both the Child Hill and North Hill requires effort, and only the Male and Female are frequently visited.

The highest hill, The Male, is a single peak rising a sheer 300 metres from its south-west base. The Female Hill, on the other hand, is

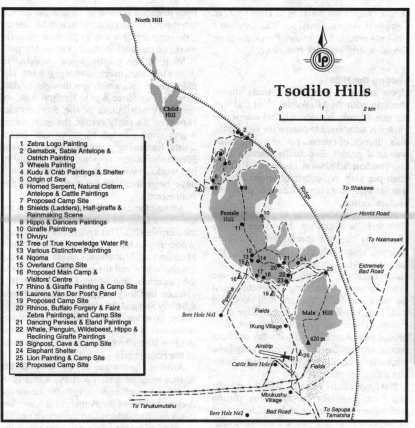

Tsodilo Hills

0   1   2 km

North Hill

Child Hill

1 Zebra Logo Painting
2 Gemsbok, Sable Antelope & Ostrich Painting
3 Wheels Painting
4 Kudu & Crab Paintings & Shelter
5 Origin of Sex
6 Horned Serpent, Natural Cistern, Antelope & Cattle Paintings
7 Proposed Camp Site
8 Shields (Ladders), Half-giraffe & Rainmaking Scene
9 Hippo & Dancers Paintings
10 Giraffe Paintings
11 Divuyu
12 Tree of True Knowledge Water Pit
13 Various Distinctive Paintings
14 Nqoma
15 Overland Camp Site
16 Proposed Main Camp & Visitors' Centre
17 Rhino & Giraffe Painting & Camp Site
18 Laurens Van Der Post's Panel
19 Proposed Camp Site
20 Rhinos, Buffalo Forgery & Faint Zebra Paintings, and Camp Site
21 Dancing Penises & Eland Paintings
22 Whale, Penguin, Wildebeest, Hippo & Reclining Giraffe Paintings
23 Signpost, Cave & Camp Site
24 Elephant Shelter
25 Lion Painting & Camp Site
26 Proposed Camp Site

Female Hill

Male Hill

Sand Ridge

To Shakawe

Horrid Road

To Nxamaseri

Extremely Bad Road

Pipeline

Bore Hole No1

Fields

!Kung Village

Airstrip

Cattle Bore Hole

Fields

420 m

Mbukushu Village

To Tshukumutsho

Bore Hole No2

Bad Road

To Sepupa & Tamatsha

BOTSWANA

an irregular series of valleys and summits where many of the most impressive rock paintings have been rendered. The cliffs and walls of both hills are streaked with vivid natural pastel colours – mauve, orange, yellow, turquoise and lavender – which actually appear artificial.

A few hundred metres west of the Male Hill is a decrepit !Kung San village, but don't expect to find the utopian San so esteemed by Laurens van der Post or so whimsically portrayed in *The Gods Must be Crazy*. Due to outside influences (including tourism), its dispossessed inhabitants are sadly preoccu-

pied with selling trinkets and awaiting handouts.

Further south is the Mbukushu village, which has flooded the surrounding countryside with its cattle – much to the dismay of the original San inhabitants, who hold the area sacred. Evidence suggests that the Mbukushu people have inhabited the area only since the early 1800s, despite their claims to a much longer tenure.

For further reading, you may want to refer to *Contested Images*, the scholarly work which is published by the University of Witwatersrand in Johannesburg, that contains a chapter on the Tsodilo Hills by Alec Campbell. Alternatively, see Tom Dowson's similarly erudite *Conference Proceedings on Southern African Rock Paintings*.

Visiting the Hills

Upon arrival in the hills, visitors should check in with the Mbukushu chief and sign his guest book. Incidentally, no one in the village is authorised to charge for visits to the hills (unless, of course, you're hiring someone as a guide). Eventually, there'll be a non-resident admission charge of P10 per adult per visit, regardless of length of stay. But it will be collected at the proposed visitors' centre.

Naturally, the best way to get around the Tsodilo Hills is to walk, but to see the site adequately requires several days, and even then you're unlikely to find many of the best paintings. Alternatively, you can hire a San guide from the !Kung Village. There are several people who are knowledgeable about the flora and fauna and are well versed in local lore, but there could be language difficulties. There are no set rates, but most groups pay around US$5 for a day of clambering around the hills. Alternatively, you can barter with things like sugar, rice, shoes, clothing or even batteries.

If it has recently rained, check the ephemeral rock pools for the tiny fairy shrimp which feed on the algae and residue settling to the bottom of these pools. The shrimp eggs are laid before the water actually dries up but don't hatch until they are first exposed to air and then again covered by water. Watch also for the brown geckos which skitter around the rocks; this particular species *Pachydactylus tsodiloensis*, occurs nowhere else in the world.

Rock Paintings Some researchers describe the Tsodilo Hills rock art as 'ordinary', but few visitors could agree. When measured on a modern scale, the minimalist representations of animals, people and geometric designs that dot the rock walls might be considered ingenious. While they may have

been intended as little more than doodles, it is tempting to envision an ancient Michelangelo straining upwards to produce masterly works on the walls of their 'Sistine Chapel'.

Most of the paintings are executed in ochres or whites using natural pigments. The older paintings, which are thought to date from the late Stone Age to the Iron Age, are generally attributed to the San people. However, it's fairly certain the most recent works were painted by 'copy-cat' Bantu artists. Interestingly, neither the San nor the Mbukushu accept responsibility for any of the works, maintaining that the paintings have been there longer than anyone can remember.

Among the most interesting paintings are the Zebra Logo on a small outcrop north of the Female Hill. This stylised equine figure is now used as the logo of Botswana National Museums & Monuments. Also interesting are the whale and the penguin paintings in the eastern hollow of the Female Hill. It is claimed that they suggest contact between the early San and the Namibian coast. Just as easily, however, they could be naive representations of a local bird and a fish from the shallow lake which once existed north-west of the Female Hill.

Around the corner to the west is the Rhinos painting which portrays a family of rhinos and a well-executed giraffe. Inside the deepest hollow of the Female Hill is another rhino painting, which also includes a buffalo 'forgery' of recent origin. Directly across the valley is one of the few Tsodilo paintings containing human figures; it depicts a dancing crowd of sexually excited male figures. Alec Campbell, the foremost expert on the hills and their paintings, has dubbed it the Dancing Penises.

If you're an adept scrambler, climb up to Laurens van der Post's Panel, which overlooks the track near the south-west corner of the Female Hill; it's accessed by a rather treacherous route from behind the panel. On the northern face of the Male Hill are two notable paintings: one portrays a solitary male lion and the other combines a well-realised gemsbok and a rhino.

Walks The current development plan for the Tsodilo Hills includes laying out of several walking circuits, which may be done either independently or with a guide. They'll take in the most interesting and renowned paintings and will also allow visitors to see the hills from many angles. Until these are established, there are several pleasant walks you can do on your own. Although most walks lead you between the various rock paintings around the base of the hills, there are other walks to keep you going for several days.

The summit of the Male Hill is accessible in under two hours by climbing up from the Lion painting at its base. It's rough and rocky for most of the way – and plagued by irritating false crests – but the summit view could well be the Kalahari's finest.

On the Female Hill, it's just a short (but hazardously rocky) climb up to Laurens van der Post's Panel. Further north, you can climb the steep trail from the established camp site to a small pit where dragonflies and butterflies flit around the slimy green puddle at the bottom. Near this site is the odd tree, described to Laurens van der Post as the *Tree of True Knowledge* by the San man who guided him to the site. According to his guide, the greatest spirit knelt beside this fetid little pool on the day he created the world. Unfortunately, it sometimes dries up into an unappealing mud hole. In the rocks beyond this pool are several 'hoofprints' in the rock; the Mbukushu believe they were made by the cattle which, along with the first humans, were lowered onto the hill by the god Ngambe.

On the other hand, the amazing natural cistern in the rock grotto near the north-west corner of the Female Hill has held water year round for as long as anyone can remember. The San believe that this natural tank is inhabited by a great serpent with twisted horns, and that visitors should warn the occupant of their approach by tossing a small rock into the water. This impressive feature is also flanked by several rock paintings.

Another worthwhile hike follows a fairly clear track up the prominent hollow in the eastern side of the Female Hill. As you proceed up the hollow, the track will gravitate towards the right wall. After a short climb to the summit, the route continues past several kopjes, which afford great long-distance views, then disappears into a broad grassy valley flanked by peaks. In this bizarre landscape, you may feel like you've been transported into an alternative universe.

Organised Tours

Several Maun travel agencies organise one-day air tours and charters to the Tsodilo Hills, but they allow only a few hours of sightseeing and cover only the major paintings, with no time for climbing or individual exploration. Return air charters from Maun cost US$298 per person with a minimum of two people, including wildlife-viewing over the Okavango Delta en route. If you can manage the cost, your best bet is to hire a vehicle from Shakawe Fishing Camp; see Getting There & Away in this section.

Places to Stay

There are still no shops or services in either the San or Mbukushu village, but you're free to camp anywhere around the bases of the hills. Water is available at the bore hole several hundred metres from the airstrip. The water is intended mainly for cattle and has a number of interesting flavours, none of which are particularly appetising, but when you're thirsty, it won't matter much. It's wise to purify the water before drinking it.

The current development plan for the Tsodilo Hills includes a visitors' centre, developed camp sites for up to 120 people, with toilets and showers, and guided walking tracks. All that has come about so far is a lot of bulldozing, but things should be well underway by the time you read this. It's a shame that the utter wildness of this magical place must be sacrificed to protect it, but that seems to be the way of the world (thanks in part to guidebook authors, no doubt).

The established camp site lies beside a prominent crevice on the western base of the Female Hill; this is normally the first site occupied by overland groups. There's also a site further south near the Rhino and Giraffe painting, and another near the southern tip of the Female Hill, in a sheltered but public space behind the 'Tsodilo Hills' sign. In a hollow around the eastern side of the Female Hill near the Rhinos and Buffalo painting is a lovely site amid shady trees. At the lion on the Male Hill there's also a fairly nice camp site; and it's not a bad spot to come home to after climbing the Male Hill.

Getting There & Away
Car & Motorbike If you fly into the Tsodilo Hills, you'll miss an excruciating but unforgettable drive. There are two main vehicle-access routes, one from the east which is signposted and turns off seven km south of Sepupa, and another from the northeast which turns off opposite the entrance to Shakawe Fishing Camp. (Before the new highway is completed, bear left at the fork immediately west of the turning and make your way over the highway construction to the point where the road continues.)

The southern route from near Sepupa is very poor; the first 22 km aren't bad, but at the cattle post, the road deteriorates as it surmounts a dune, and the final 15 km present an excruciating battle in low-ratio 4WD. The 41-km alternative route, however, would contend for the title of the Planet's Worst Drive; the sensation for vehicle passengers is akin to spending three to four hours on a bucking bronco. (According to the new development plan, this road is scheduled for closure which, given its notoriety, seems almost a shame.)

A third little-used access route turns west near Nxamaseri, about 20 km north of Sepupa. For much of the way, it passes through very deep sand, winding and twisting past abandoned villages and cattle posts, and squeezing through gaps in the trees barely wide enough for a vehicle to pass.

Shakawe Fishing Camp in Shakawe hires out 4WD vehicles for US$150 per day plus US$1 per km, including fuel, which isn't bad considering how much abuse the vehicle absorbs. Drivers should prepare for a challenge; if you'd rather not tackle the route yourself, a driver/guide can be provided with advance notice.

Hitching Although it's definitely not recommended, some travellers do try walking or hitching the 40 km from the main road, but the Kalahari is not to be taken lightly. Let someone know where you're going and be sure most of the weight you're carrying is water. To spend two days walking in the dry Kalahari heat, you'll need a *minimum* of eight litres of water per person, and perhaps more.

The Kalahari

Stretching across parts of seven countries – Botswana, Zambia, the Republic of South Africa, Zimbabwe, Namibia, Angola and Zaïre – the Kalahari sands form one of Africa's most prominent geographical features. It isn't a classic desert, but rather a vast deposit of sandy sediments. Unlike the Sahara, for example, it's covered with trees and scrub and crisscrossed by ephemeral rivers. During the summer the Kalahari may receive copious but unpredictable rainfall in the form of afternoon thunderstorms, and until recently – perhaps 100 years or so ago – there was permanent surface water. Springs and pools, and even marshes and reedbeds, were common, but overuse by humans and overgrazing have changed all that.

Visiting the Kalahari – or more accurately the Kgalakgadi, as it's known to the Tswana – isn't an easy prospect. Distances are vast, roads are rudimentary, transport is rare to nonexistent, facilities are few and the scant villages huddle around feeble bore holes. Currently, however, the road is being tarred between Gaborone and Ghanzi – and on into Namibia. When the project is complete, expect a dramatic change as the Kalahari opens up to development.

While the open skies and spaces of the Kalahari contribute to its undeniable appeal, there are few attractions to speak of and no real population centres. Elsewhere, the towns would be considered tiny outposts: the diamond-mining centre of Jwaneng on the ragged eastern edge of the region; and Ghanzi, the drowsy 'metropolis' of the western Kalahari, which is a transit stop between Botswana and Namibia. Further south is a destination of sorts, the Kalahari Village Cluster, a clump of tiny villages which comprise one of Botswana's most remote populations.

The four vast game reserves and national parks which dominate the map of western Botswana – Khutse, Central Kalahari, Mabuasehube and Gemsbok – have fabulous

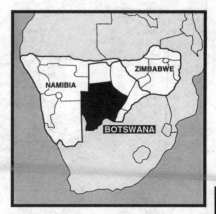

and unique environments but only sparse concentrations of wildlife. They're ideal for solitude and provide the chance to commune with the silence and open spaces, but if your main aim is to see animals, go to Chobe or Moremi.

Geology

The base of the Kalahari was created in the Triassic period when Africa was still part of the supercontinent of Gondwanaland. For 10 million years the continental rock surface was ground into deposits of sand and sediment now known as the Karoo. When Gondwanaland began breaking up, an outpouring of molten lava spread across the southern part of the African plate and covered the surface to depths of up to nine km. For the following 120 million years this lava also eroded and formed the near-level plateau that characterises most of southern Africa today.

Between 65 and two million years ago, the climate became more arid and continuing erosion caused sandy sedimentation, which was spread over vast areas by wind and ephemeral streams and was tossed about by increasing tectonic activity. To the north-east

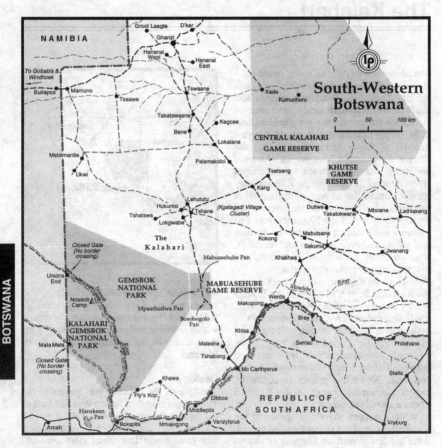

the Great Rift was forming, causing Africa to split apart. The rift, which ended in a maze of faults across Zimbabwe and northern Botswana, caused the land mass to stretch and resulted in an immense, shallow basin across the southern African plateau. Uplifting around the edges diverted rivers away from the basin while the sand deposits continued to shift and consolidate, settling finally into its lowermost parts.

In more recent times – between 25,000 and 10,000 years ago rainfall was much higher than it is now and the lowest parts of this basin were filled with the great lake

remnants of which include the Makgadikgadi pans, the Okavango Delta, the Mababe Depression and Lake Ngami. It was eventually lost to increasing aridity and tectonic uplifting.

LETHLAKENG

Practically in Gaborone's backyard, this easternmost Kalahari outpost is the gateway to the Khutse Game Reserve, which is the nearest wildlife reserve to the capital city. The Kwena name of the village means 'the place of reeds', and tradition recalls that it once bubbled with springs which attracted large numbers of elephants, rhinos and buffaloes.

Lethlakeng lies at the end of the tarred road, 116 km from Gaborone and 124 rough and sandy km from the Khutse gate.

KHUTSE GAME RESERVE

The relatively small (2600 sq km) Khutse Game Reserve is a popular weekend excursion destination for Gaborone dwellers. The name means 'where one kneels to drink'. Due to prolonged drought in recent years, Khutse lacks the concentrations of wildlife which can be expected in northern Botswana, but the solitude of the pans and savanna scrub can be almost complete. Expect to see a variety of antelopes – wildebeests, elands, duikers, steenboks, hartebeests, kudu, gemsboks and springboks – but not in large numbers. Also present are such predators as lions, leopards, brown and spotted hyena, jackals, caracals (which the San people believe to be the incarnation of the morning star) and even hunting dogs.

The parks literature also suggests that, especially around pans, visitors should watch out for such smaller creatures as ground squirrels, bush squirrels, hares (three species), bat-eared foxes, black-footed cats, pangolins, ant bears (aardvarks), aardwolves, porcupines and warthogs. Furthermore, the bird life is varied and profuse, and the hand-out suggests that if you leave fruit or sliced tsama melons (which resemble tennis balls and grow all over the Kalahari) near your camp, the moisture will attract numerous bird species, perhaps even ostriches. I haven't tested the advice but it sounds logical enough.

Places to Stay

Khutse has three camp sites but only Golalabodimo Pan, near the entry gate and the Game Scout Camp, has running water

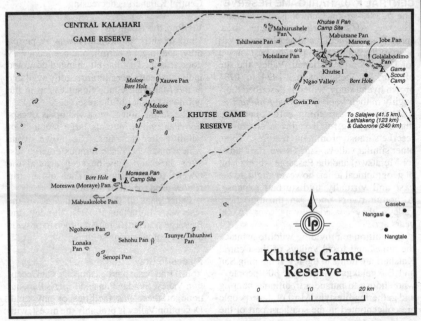

Khutse Game Reserve

and showers. However, the water tastes slightly saline, so you may want to bring drinking water from elsewhere. Fourteen km west from the entry gate, you reach Khutse II Pan, which has a rudimentary camp site. Much nicer is Moreswa Pan, but it lies 67 km beyond the gate, deep in the reserve.

Getting There & Away

Although sources claim that Khutse has been reached by conventional vehicles, 4WD is strongly recommended. The road between Lethlakeng and the park gate is quite sandy and a hardy vehicle will offer some sense of security in this remote area. Plan on at least five hours from Gaborone to the entry gate and carry all the fuel, food and water you'll need for the journey.

Hitchhikers should have relatively little difficulty finding lifts from Gaborone to Lethlakeng. Weekends are the best time to look for lifts into the reserve.

CENTRAL KALAHARI GAME RESERVE

The 52,000-sq-km Central Kalahari Game Reserve, Africa's largest protected area, sprawls across the flat and nearly featureless heart of the country. It's perhaps best known for Deception (or Letiahau) Valley, the site of Mark & Delia Owens' 1974 to 1981 brown hyena study, which is described thoroughly in their book *Cry of the Kalahari*.

Although it's nothing earth-shattering, this 80-km-long fossil valley is one of the reserve's most prominent features. Three other similar valleys – the Okwa, the Quoxo (or Meratswe) and the Passarge – bring a bit of geographical relief, however slight, to the vast and virtually undisturbed expanse. Although rivers once ran through these valleys, they ceased flowing over 16,000 years ago.

In addition to providing wildlife habitats, the dunes and fossil valleys of the Central Kalahari are home to the few remaining San and Bakgalakgadi – perhaps 800 people – who choose to pursue a traditional hunting and gathering lifestyle. Most of these people are concentrated in the southern part of the

reserve. Many now occupy nominally permanent villages.

For many San people, however, unemployment, landlessness, alcoholism and racism, among other social problems, have led to despair and abandonment of both the age-old ways – and the land – in favour of formal work elsewhere or a life of poverty on the fringes of existence. Botswana's non-racial policy of social integration ensures that no single group receives special government attention, so there are no public programmes for their specific problems.

In the Central Kalahari, other pressures on the San come from cattle ranchers, mineral exploration, some misguided conservation groups and, in the northern part of the reserve, tourism. If that isn't enough, the official government policy has been to encourage the San to leave the land, ostensibly for the protection of wildlife, but more probably to open it up for mineral exploitation and 'high-cost, low-volume' tourism. As a result, the number of traditional users in the Central Kalahari is decreasing.

Visiting the Reserve

Until recently, public entry was by permit only, and to get a permit, one needed a very good reason. That has all changed now, and individual entry permits are readily available at the Matswere Game Scout Camp in the north-east corner of the reserve.

The destination of most visitors is Deception Pan, which attracts large amounts of wildlife after the rains. The brown hyena which made the place famous emerge just after dark and may be seen around the Owens' former camp site. Their old airstrip is now used for safari traffic.

Other pans in the northern area of the reserve – Letiahau, Piper's, Sunday and Passarge – are artificially pumped to provide a supply of water for wildlife.

Places to Stay

You'll find basic public camp sites at Deception Valley, Sunday Pan and Piper's Pan, but none of these has facilities of any kind. Deception Valley is probably the nicest, with

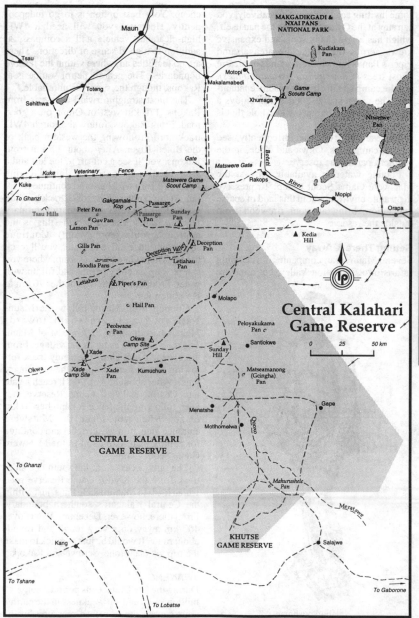

MAKGADIKGADI &
NXAI PANS
NATIONAL PARK

Kudiakam
Pan

Maun

Tsau

Motopi

Makalamabedi

Game
Scouts Camp

Xhumaga

Ntwetwe
Pan

Toteng

Sehithwa

Boteti

Kuke   Veterinary   Fence

Gate   Matswere Gate

Rakops   River

Kuke

To Ghanzi

Matswere Game
Scout Camp

Mopipi

Tsau Hills

Gakgamala
Kop   Passarge

Orapa

Peter Pan
Guv Pan

Passarge
Pan   Sunday
Pan

Lamon Pan

Kedia
Hill

Gills Pan

Deception Valley   Deception
Pan

Hoodia Pans

Letiahau
Pan

Letiahau

Piper's Pan

Central Kalahari
Game Reserve

Hail Pan

Molapo

Peolwane
Pan

Peloyakukama
Pan

0   25   50 km

Okwa Camp Site

Sunday
Hill

Santiokwe

BOTSWANA

Xade

Xade
Camp Site

Xade
Pan   Kumuchuru

Matseamanong
(Gcingha)
Pan

Okwa

Menatshe

Gape

Motlhomelwa

Quoxo

To Ghanzi

CENTRAL KALAHARI
GAME RESERVE

Mahurushele
Pan

Meratswe

Kang

KHUTSE
GAME RESERVE

Salajwe

To Tshane

To Lobatse

To Gaborone

some inviting acacia trees. Alternatively, you can stay at the Owens' camp on the pan itself, which has a few shady spots and expansive views across the flats. The area around Piper's Pan is known for its stands of bizarre ghost trees *(Commiphora pyracanthoides),* but the camp site itself isn't exactly enchanting. The camp site at Sunday Pan enjoys a good view over a pumped water hole that is popular with wildlife.

There are also two other infrequently used remote camp sites, Okwa and Xade, in the southern part of the reserve.

Potable water is available only at the Matswere Game Scout Camp. To preserve the fragile environment in this land of sparse vegetation, bring all your firewood from outside the reserve.

Getting There & Away

Several Maun safari companies run camping safaris into Deception Valley, but none are cheap. Your best option is to go independently. However, you will need a 4WD high-clearance vehicle and a compass, in addition to a good sense of direction. There are no facilities anywhere within the reserve boundaries. The nearest petrol source is at Rakops, though the supply is unreliable.

The most straightforward access is from Rakops, 170 km west of Orapa on a good road. From Rakops, follow the rough 4WD track north, following the western bank of the Boteti River. After about 2.5 km from Rakops, you'll see a cut-off to the left and a sign reading 'Central Kalahari Game Reserve'. Turn west here and continue for 60 km. At this point, you'll cross a track heading north along the reserve boundary veterinary fence towards Makalamabedi (this is the approach route from Maun). Continue straight ahead and five km later, you'll reach the Matswere Game Scout Camp, where you can pick up an entry permit and fill up with water. From this point, it's another 70 km to Deception Pan.

Coming from Maun, follow the Maun-Nata road and turn south towards Makalamabedi about 52 km east of Maun. The road is tarred as far as the village. From there, head south along the sandy track following the eastern side of the veterinary fence. After about 85 km, you'll reach a gate into Central Kalahari Game Reserve, but keep following the fence for another 20 km or so. When you reach the Matswere entrance gate, turn west (right) and continue for approximately five km to the Matswere Game Scout Camp.

The only access from the south is a side-track from the Khutse Game Reserve road which leads to Mahurushele Pans, just within the Central Kalahari's southern boundary. From there, however, Deception Pan is over 400 km away on a very rough and roundabout route. It would be just as quick to make the trip via Gaborone, Serowe and Rakops.

JWANENG

During the late Cretaceous period – some 85 million years ago – a weakness in the earth's crust caused the immense pressures in the

Kalahari bushman

BOTSWANA

mantle of the earth to build up against the carboniferous seams deep in the crust. Eventually molten rock was forced towards the surface, penetrating the overlying solid rock. With these intrusions – known in southern Africa as kimberlite pipes – came bits of carbon metamorphosed by pressure into the diamonds which now provide 85% of Botswana's export income.

The world's largest gem deposit was discovered at Jwaneng (then called Jwana – appropriately meaning 'mountain of small stones') in 1978. By 1981, the village of just a few huts had grown to a town of over 5500 people. The mine opened in 1982, and by the end of the decade the population of the Debswana-planned town had swelled to 14,000. The mine now produces nearly nine million carats annually and in a month, shifts and processes 480,000 metric tonnes of rock. Security is so tight that once a vehicle is allowed onto the mine site, it will never leave, lest it be used for smuggling diamonds.

Unlike Orapa, Jwaneng is an open town, and non-Debswana employees are permitted to settle and establish businesses. Tours of the mine may be arranged by appointment through Debswana (☎ 351131; fax 352941), Botsalano House, PO Box 329, Gaborone.

Places to Stay & Eat

For travellers heading north-west, Jwaneng has the last hotel and restaurant before Ghanzi. At the *Mokala Lodge* (☎ 380614), a cosy little place with pleasant gardens, singles/doubles cost US$58/78, with bed and breakfast. The hotel also has an à la carte restaurant and bar. For inexpensive snacks, ice cream and soft drinks, try *KRM Takeaways* in the Mall.

JWANENG TO GHANZI

The 650-km route between Jwaneng and the cattle town of Ghanzi follows the cattle route from the Ghanzi Block freehold ranches to the BMC abattoir in Lobatse. Although the overland cattle drovers have now yielded to the semitrailers, the occasional cattle drive still passes along the route. If you want to experience a taste of the Wild West, Botsw-

ana-style, get there before the road is tarred or it'll be too late.

At the moment, the route is a rough and tumble ride along miserable roads, but it's relatively well travelled and hitchhikers will eventually have success. The only place to fill up with petrol is Kang so if you're driving, carry a reserve tank. With a good 4WD vehicle, the journey takes from 11 to 14 hours, depending on conditions.

Travelling from Jwaneng to Ghanzi, opposing the cattle traffic, the tar ends at Jwaneng and launches onto a patience-wearing corrugated gravel surface to Sekoma, where the road to Tshabong and Bokspits branches south. West of this junction, you're ushered into rutted sand. After about 170 km of punishment, you'll enter the sandy but friendly and picturesque village of Kang. Here you'll find petrol – which is predictably expensive – and a friendly general store run by an Afrikaner couple. Everyone stops there so it's a good place to wait for a lift. There's also a garage, a bakery and a welding station run by the Brigades.

Turn south at Kang if you're heading for the Kgalagadi Village Cluster or Tshabong, which lies 360 km from Kang via the Mabuasehube Game Reserve. Otherwise, continue north-west towards Ghanzi; the road is characterised by deep sand for 150 km to the San village of Takatswaane, 125 km from Ghanzi.

KGALAGADI VILLAGE CLUSTER

The four villages of the Kgalagadi Village Cluster – Tshane, Hukuntsi, Lokgwabe and Lehututu – make up an unlikely population centre in the remotest Kalahari beginning 104 km west of Kang. The road into the villages travels through extremely deep sand, so 4WD will be essential. Although Hukuntsi does have blue-dyed petrol available for government vehicles, there is no fuel available to the public in any of the villages.

Hukuntsi

Hukuntsi, the largest of the villages, sprawls sparsely over a wide area. It has overtaken Lehututu, 12 km to the north, as the commercial centre of the cluster and serves as the government administration centre as well. Although the surrounding landscape is sandy and desolate, it has the most reliable bore hole in the area and there's a bush shop where you'll find a variety of supplies.

Tshane

In Tshane, 12 km east of Hukuntsi, take a look at the colonial police station which dates from the early 1900s. It's currently targeted for renovation by the National Museum. It overlooks Tshane Pan where, due to the shortage of water, cattle drink from hand-dug wells around its perimeter.

Lokgwabe

The other village, Lokgwabe, lies 11 km south-west of Hukuntsi. Its only claim to fame is that it was settled by Simon Cooper, who sought British protection in Bechuanaland after leading the 1904 Nama rebellion in German South West Africa (Namibia).

Tshatswa

About 60 km south-west of Hukuntsi is Tshatswa, a San village of 277 people. There's a serious water shortage in Tshatswa, so visitors should carry their own. The village bore hole yields only about 150 litres of saline water daily which must be condensed and desalinated before it's potable. The extracted salt is then sold to earn a bit of money for the village.

Along the route between Hukuntsi and Tshatswa you'll pass a lot of sparkling white salt pans and, as desolate as the area seems, there are significant populations of gemsboks, ostriches and hartebeests.

Places to Stay

The government hostel in Hukuntsi is only available to the public in an emergency, so visitors must either know someone to stay with in the villages or carry a tent. Before setting up camp, ask permission of the village chief and perhaps ask for suggestions of suitable sites where you won't disrupt village activities.

Getting There & Away

We're talking remote here. The Kgalagadi Village Cluster lies 104 km west of Kang and about 255 km north of Tshabong, neither of which are much to speak of in their own right. Without 4WD, the only chance of reaching this area would be to hitch to Kang and wait around the general store until a vehicle comes along. Finding a lift back will be an even greater challenge.

MABUASEHUBE GAME RESERVE

Remote Mabuasehube (or Mabuashegube) Game Reserve, a small 1800-sq-km appendage to Gemsbok National Park, focuses on three major pans and a number of minor ones. Each pan is flanked by beautiful red dunes up to 30 metres high on their southern and western edges and in the Segologa language, the name of the reserve appropriately means 'red earth'.

The largest and northernmost pan,

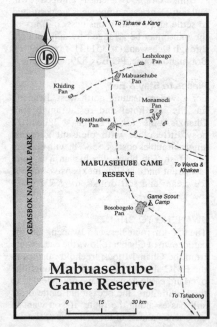

Mabuasehube Pan, is used as a salt lick by itinerant herds of elands and gemsboks. At its western end are wells artificially deepened by Gologa pastoralists for their cattle. The wells often hold water even when the rest of the pan is dry. Further south is the grassy Bosobogolo Pan, which has large herds of springboks and is also popular with such predators as lions, cheetahs, brown hyena and hunting dogs. There are also four other large pan complexes – Lesholoago, Monamodi, Khiding and Mpaathutlwa – and a number of smaller ones.

The reserve is best visited in late winter and early spring when herds of elands and gemsboks are migrating out of the Gemsbok National Park to the immediate west.

Places to Stay

There's a rudimentary camp site near the Game Scout Camp at Bosobogolo Pan. Although there are no facilities, if park personnel are there, you'll still pay standard fees. Water isn't always available at the Bosobogolo Pan bore hole, so carry all you require.

Getting There & Away

The roads into Mabuasehube are very bad and require a sturdy 4WD vehicle. There are three access routes. The one in the best condition – and the shortest if you're coming from the east – is the little-used route from the Khakea-Werda road. The west turning to Mabuasehube is just under two km north of the Moselebe River, about 50 km south of Khakea and 20 km north of Werda.

The most straightforward route is from Tshabong, the Kgalagadi District headquarters, which is reached via Jwaneng and Sekoma. However, it's quite a roundabout route unless you're coming from South Africa. The most difficult route runs via Kang and the Kgalagadi Village Cluster, and enters the reserve from the north.

On any of these routes, the thin to nonexistent traffic makes hitching a nonstarter. The area's extreme remoteness means that drivers need to be familiar with bush driving techniques and travellers must be self-sufficient in all respects.

The nearest reliable petrol pumps are at Kang, Ghanzi and Jwaneng, while Tshabong, 100 km south of the reserve, has a sporadic supply. Failing that, you'll have to cross into South Africa for fuel.

BOKSPITS

On the intermittent Molopo River in the extreme south-west corner of Botswana, the picturesque frontier settlement of Bokspits sits amid ruddy sand dunes. It's a centre of karakul wool production, but doesn't merit much of a side trip. Bokspits is accessible via South Africa or down the dry Molopo riverbed from McCarthysrus near Tshabong. There's no accommodation and most passing vehicles are merely crossing the border to or from South Africa, most likely on a visit to Kalahari Gemsbok National Park.

GEMSBOK NATIONAL PARK

In Botswana's remote south-west corner lies the immense 11,000-sq-km Gemsbok National Park. On the west, it abuts South Africa's Kalahari Gemsbok National Park and together, they make up one of the world's largest and most pristine wilderness regions. This is the one area of Botswana where you'll see the shifting sand dunes that many mistakenly believe to be typical of the Kalahari.

The gemsboks for which the park is named are best observed between March and early May when the rains have brought a splash of green to the overwhelmingly red landscape. At these times, springboks, elands and red hartebeests and blue wildebeests may also be seen in relatively large numbers, but during the rest of the year you may be lucky to see anything at all.

Since the Botswana side of the park isn't really accessible by road – it's reached by unofficially crossing the normally dry Nossob River from South Africa – Botswana park fees don't apply.

Places to Stay

There are two major large rest camps on the South African side of the Nossob River; see

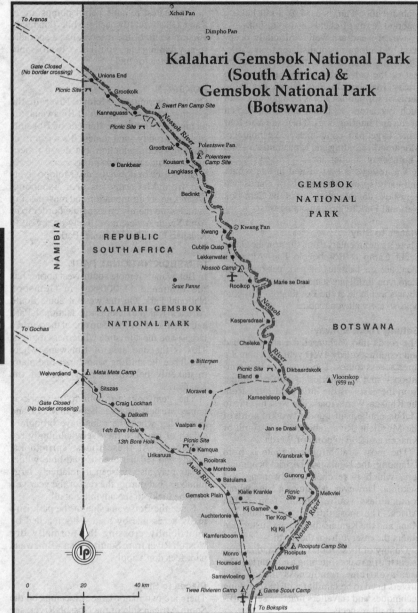

Xchoi Pan

Dimpho Pan

**Kalahari Gemsbok National Park
(South Africa) &
Gemsbok National Park
(Botswana)**

To Aranos

Gate Closed
(No border crossing)   Unions End

Picnic Site   Grootkolk

Swart Pan Camp Site

Kannaguass   Nossob River

Picnic Site

Grootbrak   Polentswe Pan

Dankbaar   Kousant   Polentswe
Camp Site

Langklass

Bedinkt

GEMSBOK
NATIONAL
PARK

NAMIBIA

REPUBLIC
SOUTH AFRICA   Kwang   Kwang Pan

Cubitje Quap
Lekkerwater

Nossob Camp

Sewe Panne   Rooikop   Marie se Draai

KALAHARI GEMSBOK
NATIONAL PARK   Nossob

To Gochas   Kaspersdraai   BOTSWANA

Cheleka   River

Bitterpan

Welverdiend   Mata Mata Camp   Picnic Site   Dikbaardskolk
Eland   Vloorskop
(959 m)

Gate Closed   Sitszas
(No border crossing)   Moravet   Kameelsleep
Craig Lockhart

Dalkeith

14th Bore Hole   Vaalpan   Jan se Draai
13th Bore Hole   Picnic Site
Urikaruus   Kamqua   Kransbrak

Rooibrak
Montrose   Gunong

Batulama

Gemsbok Plain   Kielie Krankie   Picnic   Melkvlei
Site
Kij Games

Auchterlonie   Tier Kop
Kij Kij

Kamfersboom   Nossob River

Monro   Rooiputs Camp Site
Houmoed   Rooiputs
Leeuwdril
Samevloeiing

0   20   40 km   Twee Rivieren Camp   Game Scout Camp

To Bokspits

under Kalahari Gemsbok National Park (South Africa), later in this chapter.

On the Botswana side, there's a camp site with cold showers and toilets at the Game Scout Camp on the Nossob River, opposite Twee Rivieren. There are also three undeveloped camp sites on the Botswana bank of the Nossob River; Rooiputs, 30 km north-east of Twee Rivieren; Polentswe Pan, 60 km north of Nossob; and Swart Pan, 30 km south-east of Unions End. If you're camping at Polentswe or Rooiputs, ask at the Game Scout Camp about water and firewood. All these sites are accessed from the South African bank of the Nossob River.

Getting There & Away

There is no access to Gemsbok National Park from elsewhere in Botswana; you'll have to cross into South Africa at Bokspits and use the gravel road along the Nossob River. The river forms the western boundary of both Botswana and the park; to reach the Botswana camps mentioned under Places to Stay, simply cross the river at the correct spot.

From Twee Rivieren, 53 km upriver from Bokspits, it's a further 160 km to Nossob Camp. From there, the route continues another 130 km to the locked gate at Unions End, where Botswana, Namibia and South Africa meet. There's no border crossing here; the nearest access to Namibia is via the Aoub River road, across the South African 'panhandle' from Twee Rivieren.

KALAHARI GEMSBOK NATIONAL PARK (SOUTH AFRICA)

South Africa's 10,000-sq-km Kalahari Gemsbok National Park is characterised by a semi-desert landscape of Kalahari dunes, camelthorn-dotted grasslands and the dry beds of the Auob and Nossob rivers. It lies in a wild and remote area of South Africa, wedged between Botswana and Namibia.

Most of the wildlife lives in the river valleys or around the pans, and because the park border is open to Botswana's Gemsbok National Park, animals aren't confined within Kalahari Gemsbok's park boundaries. Springboks and gemsboks are the most

Hyena

common, with the occasional herd of blue wildebeests. Elands inhabit the sandy dune areas and you might see red hartebeests around the northern end of the Nossob River. The park also has a full complement of predators, including lions, cheetahs, leopards, wild dogs, jackals and both brown and spotted hyena. There are also 238 bird species present; 44 of these are birds of prey.

Places to Stay & Eat

There are tourist rest camps at Twee Rivieren and Nossob, both on the Nossob River, and also at Mata Mata, where the Auob River crosses the Namibian border. Each camp has camp sites, caravan sites, self-catering chalets and cottages, and basic, inexpensive huts with communal cooking and ablutions facilities. Supplies are sold at all three rest camps, and Twee Rivieren has a restaurant, which is open from 6.30 am to 9 pm. Another Twee Rivieren highlight is the swimming pool for rest camp guests. Note that both the park and the rest camp gates close at dusk.

Accommodation in Kalahari Gemsbok National Park is operated by the South African National Parks Board. Bookings are necessary on weekends, public holidays and school holidays, and may be made by contacting the National Parks Board (☎ (012) 343 1991; fax (012) 343 0905), PO Box 787, Pretoria 0001, South Africa.

Getting There & Away
From Botswana, access is via Bokspits. Cross into South Africa and follow the road along the dry Nossob River. Park headquarters is at Twee Rivieren, 53 km from Bokspits. From there, it's 3½ hours to Nossob Camp, and 2½ hours to Mata Mata.

Note that there is no park entry or exit at Unions End, and the Mata Mata gate has also been closed due to over-use of the road as a quick transit route between Namibia and South Africa. The increased traffic apparently disturbed the wildlife. To enter Namibia, use the border crossing at Aroab/Rietfontein.

GHANZI
The name Ghanzi is derived from the San word for a one-stringed musical instrument with a gourd soundbox, and not, oddly enough, from the Setswana word *gantsi*, which means 'the flies' and would coincidentally be quite appropriate.

Ghanzi sits atop a 500-km-long limestone ridge that curves from Lake Ngami in the north-east to Windhoek, the capital of Namibia, in the west. Although it isn't visible from the ground, it contains great stores of artesian water which render agriculture and cattle ranching not only feasible but also profitable.

History
For such a small and remote place, Ghanzi has enjoyed quite a colourful history. Although a number of itinerant travellers passed through earlier, the man who made Ghanzi, Hendrik Matthys van Zyl, arrived in 1868. A ruthless character, this former Transvaal MP wandered the Botswana wilderness trading munitions, knocking over elephants, killing San people and gaining the respect of local Bantu chiefs. In 1874 he settled at Lake Ngami, and briefly usurped the leadership of dissident factions in Chief Moremi's Tawana

tribe. At one stage he avenged the San murder of a Boer, William Frederick Prinsloo, by luring 33 San people with tobacco and brandy and murdering them in cold blood.

By 1877, after a profitable trip to Cape Town, Van Zyl had returned to Ghanzi and established his residence. In his first year there, it's estimated that he shot over 400 elephants, which yielded at least four tonnes of ivory. With the proceeds, Van Zyl built himself a two-storey mansion with stained-glass windows, filled it with opulent imported furniture and lived the life of a maharajah in the Botswana wilderness. Rumours of his influence and generally disagreeable nature prevented many Boer Dorsland Trekkers from settling in the Ghanzi area.

The manner of Van Zyl's death is unknown; some tales have arisen, none of them very credible – some have him struck down by vengeful San and others by a wily San servant in his household. Another has him angering the Damara to the point of murder, while yet another credits the Khoi-Khoi. All that's certain is that after he died, his wife, three sons and daughter escaped to the Transvaal and were never heard from again.

Without Van Zyl, Ghanzi plodded into the late 19th century. That the town survived at all is probably due to Cecil Rhodes' designs on it as a foot in the Bechuanaland door of the British South Africa Company. Although the British takeover of the Ghanzi Block was ostensibly designed to thwart German aggression from Namibia, it was almost certainly for commercial rather than strategic reasons. After Rhodes fraudulently secured Tawana concessions to the land, he managed to divert a contingency of Voortrekkers into Ghanzi by offering free land and equipment and promoting it as a paradise on earth. Rhodes' commercial ambitions were stalled, however, by the Jameson raid, which was an unauthorised assumption of military power. This ill-conceived and abortive manoeuvre was intended to destabilise the Boer republics in the Transvaal and force their annexation to the Cape Colony. As a result,

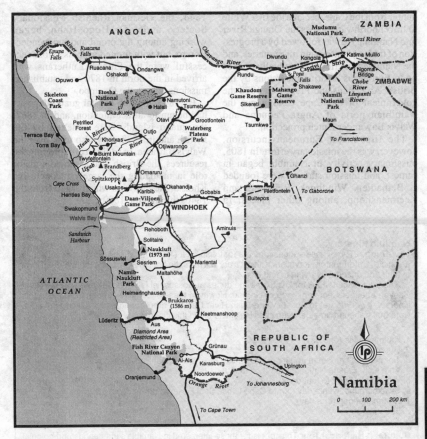

European Exploration

Against this background of tribal conflicts, the first European visitors, in the form of traders and missionaries, began shuffling into Namibia. Because Namibia has one of the world's most barren and inhospitable coastlines, it was largely ignored by the European maritime nations until relatively recently. The first European visitors were Portuguese mariners seeking a way to the Indies in the late 15th century. In 1486, Captain Diego Cão sailed as far south as Cape Cross, where he erected a limestone *padrão* (tribute to his royal patron, João II) to mark what for him was a big event. The cross was also to serve as a navigational aid for subsequent Portuguese explorers.

Bartolomeu Dias reached the site of present-day Lüderitz while en route around the Cape of Good Hope one year later on Christmas Day. On Diaz Point, just south of the modern town, there's another cross marking the event. During the early 1600s, Dutch sailors from the Cape colonies explored northward along the formidable desert coast of Namibia, but no formal settlements were established.

In 1750, Jacobus Coetse, a Dutch elephant

hunter from the Cape, became the first White to travel northward across the Orange River into Namibia. He was followed by a progression of traders, hunters and missionaries, and the Namibian interior was gradually opened up to Europeans. Fearing incursions by the British, Americans and French, in 1878 the government of the Cape Colony put the Namibian ports of Angra Pequena and Walvis Bay under Dutch protection.

The first major European incursion, however, was the missionary effort. In 1805, missionary activity in Namibia began in earnest, and mission stations were founded at Bethanien, Windhoek, Rehoboth and Keetmanshoop, among other places. In 1844, the German Rhenish Missionary Society, under Dr Hugo Hahn, began working among the proud and independent Herero, but with limited success. More successful were the Finnish Lutherans who arrived in the north in 1870 and established missions among the Ovambo.

By 1843, the rich coastal guano deposits had begun to attract attention, and in 1867, the guano islands were annexed by the British and in 1878, they also took over the Walvis Bay area. In addition to exploiting the resources, the British also assumed a major role in mediating the largely inconclusive Khoisan-Herero wars which raged from the 1840s through the 1880s.

Namibia Itinerary

Low-Budget Tour These suggestions are for those on a strict budget who don't have access to a vehicle. Unfortunately, travellers without a car will miss the best of Namibia without a great deal of time and uncertainty trying to find lifts.

The best place to look for lifts to see the dunes at Sossusvlei is Windhoek and for Fish River Canyon at either Keetmanshoop or Grünau. However, these sites haven't been included in this itinerary. If you do get to Sossusvlei or Fish River Canyon, drop out numbers seven and eight. Note that transport time between sites isn't included in this itinerary.

1. Katima Mulilo (one day)
2. Rundu (one day)
3. Tsumeb, visit museum and try to find lift into Etosha National Park (one day)
4. With luck, Etosha National Park (two to four days)
5. Windhoek (three to four days)
6. Swakopmund, with a day tour to Cape Cross Seal Reserve (three days)
7. Keetmanshoop (one day)
8. Lüderitz (one day)

Cultural & Historical Tour This tour is for those interested in Namibia's indigenous and colonial cultures and history. For these destinations, you'll need 2WD car. If you wish to visit Bushmanland or the Kaokoveld, which are arguably Namibia's most interesting cultural areas, you'll need both more time and at least one 4WD vehicle.

1. Windhoek (two days)
2. Swakopmund (two days)
3. Damaraland – Spitzkoppe, Brandberg & Twyfelfontein (three days)
4. Etosha National Park (two days)
5. Ovamboland – Ombalantu, Oshakati & Ondangwa (two days)
6. Kavango – Rundu (two days)
7. Caprivi – Katima Mulilo, Lizauli Village and Mudumu National Park (three days)

Natural History Tours Namibia has some of the world's most unusual flora, fauna and geology. Therefore, you'll have to pick and choose what you want to see. Generally, most visitors will want to divide the country into northern and southern sections. Both of these options will require access to a car.

Facts about the Country 555

The Colonial Era

In 1883, Adolf Lüderitz negotiated the purchase of Angra Pequena and its surroundings from Nama chief, Joseph Fredericks, then petitioned the German chancellor Otto von Bismarck to place what is now the Lüderitz area under German 'protection'.

The chancellor, already occupied with other tasks back in Europe, showed reluctance, preferring to leave the colonial scene to the British, French and Belgians. 'My map of Africa is here in Europe', he said. 'Here is Russia and here is France and here we are in the middle. That is my map of Africa.' But strong domestic lobbying – and the warning that Britain was eyeing the potential colony

for itself – forced him to concede and grant Lüderitz protectorate status. Years later, in the European powers' last-minute scramble for colonies, there arose territorial conflicts between Germany and Great Britain, and in response, Adolf Lüderitz persuaded the chancellor to annex the entire country.

Initially, however, German interests remained minimal, and between 1885 and 1890, the entire German colonial administration amounted to only three public administrators for the entire country, which was administered from the village of Otjimbingwe about 55 km south of present-day Karibib. Early German colonial interests were served through a colonial company,

Northern Namibia
1. Windhoek, with a visit to Daan Viljoen Game Park (two days)
2. Spitzkoppe via Otjihaenamparero Dinosaur Footprints and perhaps Ranch Ameib (two days)
3. Cape Cross Seal Reserve and Skeleton Coast Park (one day)
4. Damaraland – Twyfelfontein, Wondergat, Organ Pipes, Burnt Mountain, Petrified Forest (three days)
5. Palmwag (one day)
6. Etosha National Park (four days)
7. Tsumeb & Grootfontein – Lake Okjikoto, Hoba Meteorite & Tsumeb mining museum (one day)
8. Waterberg Plateau Park (two days)
9. Dordabis – Arnhem Cave (one day)

Southern Namibia
1. Windhoek, with a visit to Daan Viljoen Game Park (two days)
2. Brukkaros Crater (one day)
3. Keetmanshoop – Kokerboom Forest & Giant's Playground, Singing Rocks (two days)
4. Fish River Canyon & Ai-Ais, with day hike to bottom of canyon (three days)
5. Lüderitz – feral horses, Lüderitz Peninsula (two days)
6. Sesriem & Sossusvlei (two days)
7. Naukluft, with hike around Waterkloof or Olive Trail (two days)
8. Namib Desert Park – Kuiseb Canyon, Homeb & Welwitschia Drive (two or three days)
9. Walvis Bay, with day tour to Sandwich Harbour (one day)

Wildlife Tour If you've come to Namibia for the wildlife, you won't be disappointed. All of the following attractions will be accessible by 2WD. However, if you want to visit the Kaokoveld or Khaudom Game Reserve, you'll need more time and a convoy of at least two 4WD vehicles.

1. Windhoek, with a visit to Daan Viljoen Game Park (two days)
2. Waterberg Plateau Park (two days)
3. Etosha National Park (four days)
5. Mahango Game Reserve (two days)
4. Damaraland, including Palmwag Lodge (two days)
5. Cape Cross Seal Reserve (two hours)
6. Walvis Bay – bird paradise, lagoon, salt works and day tour to Sandwich Harbour (two days)
7. Sesriem & Sossusvlei (two days) ■

along the lines of the British East India Company in India prior to the Raj. However, this organisation was incapable of maintaining law and order.

Mainly due to renewed fighting between the Nama and the Herero in the 1880s, the German government dispatched Curt von François and 23 soldiers to restrict the supply of arms from British Walvis Bay in an attempt to restore order. Instead, however, a monster was created and by the early 1890s, the small peacekeeping regiment evolved into the more powerful and sinister organisation known as the Deutsche Schutztruppe. Forts were constructed in various places and unrest and opposition were put down.

At this stage, Namibia became a fully fledged German Protectorate, known as German South West Africa. The first German farmers arrived in 1892 to take up the land which was being expropriated on the Central Plateau, and were soon followed by merchants and other settlers. In the late 1890s, the Portuguese in Angola, the British in Bechuanaland and the Germans finally agreed on Namibia's boundaries.

Understandably, all this spawned bitterness in the local people, who resented the foreigners' laws, taxes and the takeover of water rights and theretofore communal lands. In 1904, the Nama, under their leader Hendrik Witbooi, launched a large-scale rebellion against the increasing colonial presence. Later that year, the Nama were joined by the Herero – an unlikely alliance, considering that incessant warring between them had been a major catalyst in the increased colonial involvement.

However, the rebellions were eventually suppressed by the Schutztruppe and when it was over, 75% of the Herero nation – and a large number of both Nama and German troops – had been wiped out. By 1910, the remaining Herero had fled eastward to the inhospitable country east of Windhoek – some as far as Botswana – where many died of hunger and starvation. Survivors were eventually shifted to their allocated 'homeland', the four-part Hereroland district in the barren western Kalahari.

Meanwhile, in the south, diamonds had been discovered at Grasplatz, east of Lüderitz, by a South African labourer, Zacharias Lewala. Despite the assessment of De Beers that the find probably wouldn't amount to much, prospectors flooded in to stake their claims. By 1910, the German authorities branded the entire area between Lüderitz and the Orange River a *sperrgebiet*, or 'forbidden area', chucked out the prospectors and granted exclusive rights to the Deutsche Diamanten Gesellschaft.

The colonial era lasted until WWI, by which time the German Reich had dismantled the Herero tribal structures and taken over all Khoi-Khoi and Herero lands. As more colonial immigrants arrived from Europe, the best lands were parcelled into an extensive network of White farms.

The Ovambo in the north were luckier and managed to avoid conquest until after the start of WWI, when they were overrun by Portuguese forces fighting on the side of the Allies. In 1914, at the beginning of WWI, Great Britain pressured South Africa into invading Namibia. The South Africans, under the command of South African Prime Minister Louis Botha and General Jan Smuts, gradually pushed northward, forcing the outnumbered German Schutztruppe to retreat. In May 1915, the Germans faced their final defeat at Khorab near Tsumeb and a week later, a South African administration was set up in Windhoek.

By 1920, many German farms had been sold to Afrikaans-speaking settlers and the German diamond mining-interests in the south were handed over to the South African based Consolidated Diamond Mines (CDM), which retains the concession to the present day.

The South African Occupation

Under the Treaty of Versailles in 1919, Germany was required to renounce all its colonial claims and in 1921, the League of Nations granted South Africa a formal mandate to administer Namibia as part of the Union, but not to prepare it for eventual independence. However, after a brief rebellion in 1924, the Basters at Rehoboth were granted some measure of autonomy and the following year, the territorial constitution was amended to permit the White population to set up a territorial legislature.

The mandate was renewed by the UN following WWII but South Africa was prepared to annex South West Africa as a full province in the Union and decided to scrap the terms of the mandate and rewrite the constitution. The International Court of Justice, however, determined that South Africa had overstepped its boundaries and ruled that the mandate would remain in force. The UN set up a Committee on South West Africa to enforce the original terms. In 1956, the UN decided that South African control must somehow be terminated.

Undeterred, the South African government tightened its grip on the territory, and in 1949, granted the White population parliamentary representation in Pretoria. The bulk of Namibia's viable farmland was parcelled into some 6000 farms for White settlers and the various ethnic groups were relegated to newly demarcated 'tribal homelands'. The official intent was ostensibly to 'channel economic development into predominantly poor rural areas', but it was all too obvious that it was, in fact, simply a convenient way of retaining the best lands for White settlement and agriculture.

As a result, there appeared a prominent line of demarcation between the rich, predominantly White areas in the central and southern parts of the country, and the poorer tribal areas to the north. Perhaps the only positive result of this effective imposition of tribal boundaries was the prevention of territorial squabbles between previously mobile groups now forced to live under the same political entity. Interestingly, this arrangement was retained until Namibian independence in 1990.

Independence

Through the 1950s, despite mounting pressure from the UN, South Africa refused to release its grip on Namibia. This intransigence was based on its fears of having yet another antagonistic government on its doorstep and of losing the income which it derived from the mining operations there. Namibia is rich in minerals such as uranium, copper, lead and zinc and is the world's foremost source of gem diamonds. These were all mined by South African and Western multinational companies under a generous taxation scheme which enabled them to export up to a third of their profits every year.

Forced labour had been the lot of most Namibians since the German annexation, and was one of the main factors which led to mass demonstrations and the increasingly nationalist sentiments in the late 1950s. Several political parties were formed and strikes were organised, not only among workers in Namibia but also among contract labourers working in South Africa. Among them was the Ovamboland People's Congress, founded in Cape Town under the leadership of Shafiishuna Samuel Nujoma and Adimba Herman Toivo ja Toivo.

In 1959, the party's name was changed to the Ovamboland People's Organisation and Sam Nujoma took the issue of South African occupation to the UN in New York. By 1960, his party had gathered the support of several others and merged to form the South West African People's Organisation, or SWAPO, with its headquarters in Dar es Salaam. Troops were sent to Egypt for military training and the organisation prepared for war.

In 1966, SWAPO took the issue of South African occupation to the International Court of Justice. The court upheld South Africa's right to govern South West Africa, but the UN General Assembly voted to terminate South Africa's mandate and replace it with a Council for South West Africa (renamed the Commission for Namibia in 1973) to administer the territory.

In response, on 26 August 1966, now called Namibia Day, SWAPO launched its campaign of guerrilla warfare at Omgulumubashe in Ovamboland. The following year, one of SWAPO's founders, Toivo ja Toivo, was convicted of terrorism and imprisoned in South Africa, where he would remain until 1984; Sam Nujoma

NAMIBIA

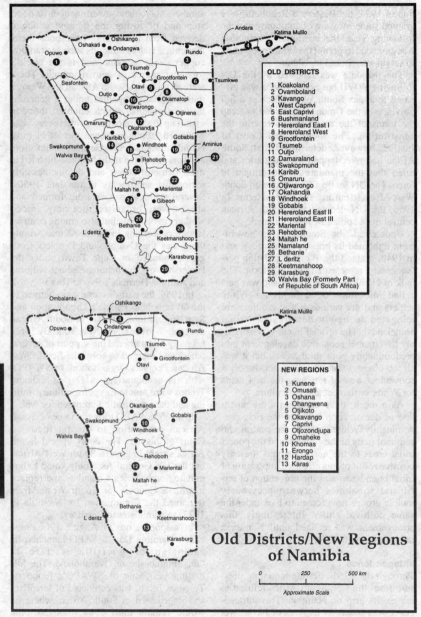

OLD DISTRICTS

1 Koakoland
2 Ovamboland
3 Kavango
4 West Caprivi
5 East Caprivi
6 Bushmanland
7 Hereroland East I
8 Hereroland West
9 Grootfontein
10 Tsumeb
11 Outjo
12 Damaraland
13 Swakopmund
14 Karibib
15 Omaruru
16 Otjiwarongo
17 Okahandja
18 Windhoek
19 Gobabis
20 Hereroland East II
21 Hereroland East III
22 Mariental
23 Rehoboth
24 Maltah he
25 Namaland
26 Bethanie
27 L deritz
28 Keetmanshoop
29 Karasburg
30 Walvis Bay (Formerly Part of Republic of South Africa)

NEW REGIONS

1 Kunene
2 Omusati
3 Oshana
4 Ohangwena
5 Otjikoto
6 Okavango
7 Caprivi
8 Otjozondjupa
9 Omaheke
10 Khomas
11 Erongo
12 Hardap
13 Karas

Old Districts/New Regions of Namibia

0   250   500 km

Approximate Scale

NAMIBIA

stayed in Tanzania. In 1972, the UN finally declared the South African occupation of South West Africa officially illegal and called for a withdrawal. UN secretary Kurt Waldheim proclaimed SWAPO the legitimate representative of the Namibian people.

In response, the South African government fired on demonstrators and arrested thousands of activists. While all this was going on, events were coming to a head in neighbouring Angola, culminating in its independence from Portugal in 1975, and the ascendancy of the Marxist-oriented Popular Movement for the Liberation of Angola (MPLA). This was anathema to South Africa which, in an attempt to smash the MPLA, launched an invasion of Angola in support of the UNITA (National Union for the Total Independence of Angola) forces, which controlled southern Angola at the time. The attempt failed and by March 1976, the troops had been withdrawn but incursions continued well into the 1980s.

Back in Namibia, in 1975, the Democratic Turnhalle Alliance (DTA, named after the site of its meetings) was officially established. Formed from a combination of ethnic parties and White political interests, it turned out to be a toothless debating chamber which spent much of its time in litigation with the South African government over its scope of responsibilities.

Meanwhile, in the late 1970s, the SWAPO ranks were split when two officials of the government in exile, Solomon Mifima and Andreas Shipanga, called for long overdue party elections. In response, party President Sam Nujoma had them imprisoned in Zambia, along with hundreds of their followers. Civil rights activists in Europe managed to have them freed, and they now head a minority party, SWAPO-D (the 'D' stands for Democrats).

In 1983, after the DTA had indicated it would accommodate SWAPO, it was dissolved and replaced by yet another administration, known as the Multi-Party Conference. This turned out to be even less successful than the DTA and quickly disappeared, allowing control of Namibia to pass

back to the South African-appointed administrator-general, Mr Justice Steyn, who was given power to rule by proclamation.

The failure of these attempts to set up an internal solution did not deter South Africa, which, until the estimated 19,000 Cuban troops were removed from neighbouring Angola, refused to negotiate on a programme supervised by the UN for Namibian independence. In response, SWAPO intensified its guerrilla campaign. As a result, movement in the north of the country became severely restricted.

In the end, however, it may not have been the activities of SWAPO alone or international sanctions which forced the South Africans to the negotiating table. The White Namibian population itself was growing tired of the war and the economy was suffering badly. South Africa's internal problems also had a significant effect. By 1985, the war was costing some R480 million (around US$250 million) per year and conscription was widespread. Mineral exports which once provided around 88% of the country's GDP had plummeted to just 27% by 1984. This was due mainly to falling world demand and depressed prices, but fraud and corruption were also factors.

By 1988, the stage was set for negotiations on the country's future. Under the watch of the UN, the USA and the former USSR, a deal was struck between Cuba, Angola, South Africa and SWAPO, which provided for withdrawal of Cuban troops from Angola and South African troops from Namibia. It also stipulated that the transition to Namibian independence would formally begin on 1 April 1989, and be followed by UN-monitored elections held in November 1989 on the basis of universal suffrage. Although minor score settling and unrest among some SWAPO troops threatened to derail the whole process, the plan went ahead. In September, Sam Nujoma returned from his 30-year exile and in the elections, SWAPO garnered a clear majority of the votes but the numbers were insufficient to give it the sole mandate to write the new constitution.

Following negotiations between the

NAMIBIA

various parties and international advisers, including the USA, France, Germany and the former USSR, a constitution was drafted. It provided incentive for cooperation between the executive and legislative bodies and included an impressive bill of rights: provisions for protection of the environment, rights of families and children, freedom of religion, speech and the press and a host of other things. It was adopted in February 1990 and independence was granted a month later, on 21 March, under the presidency of SWAPO leader, Sam Nujoma. His policies are based on a national reconciliation programme to heal the wounds left by 25 years of armed struggle and a reconstruction programme based on the retention of a mixed economy and partnership with the private sector.

So far, things have gone smoothly, and in the elections of December, 1994, President Sam Nujoma and his SWAPO party were re-elected with a 68% landslide victory over rival Mishake Muyongo and his Democratic Turnhalle Alliance party. Hopes for the future remain high.

GEOGRAPHY
Namibia is an arid country of great geographical variations. Broadly speaking, its topography can be divided into four main sections: the Namib Desert and Coastal Plains along the coast; the eastward sloping Central Plateau; the Kalahari sands along the Botswana and South African borders; and the densely wooded bushveld of the Kavango and Caprivi regions.

The Namib Desert, the world's oldest arid region, has been around for over 80 million years. It extends along the country's entire Atlantic coast and has an annual rainfall of between 15 and 100 mm. The Namib owes its existence to the cold Benguela Current, which flows northward from the Antarctic; warm onshore winds from the tropics blow over the cold seas and create a blanket of fog over the coast. This condensation provides moisture to sustain lichens and specialised plants that form the lowest echelons of the desert food chain and sustain the unique Namib flora and fauna that have adapted specifically to the hostile conditions.

Namib landscapes range from the mountainous red dunes in the south to the interior plains and flat-topped, steep-sided and isolated mountains – known as inselbergs – of the centre. The Skeleton Coast region in the north is known for bare scorched dunes.

Moving east from the desert, the altitude increases and the coastal dunes gradually give way to gravel plains. The width of these coastal plains varies from a few km in the northern Kaokoveld to almost 300 km at Lüderitz in the south. In Damaraland, the coastal plain is punctuated by dramatic mountains and inselbergs, some of volcanic origin. They're honeycombed with caves and rock shelters which provided homes for early humans. The Brandberg and Erongo mountains north of Karibib are both well-known examples.

The Namib Desert itself is scored by a number of rivers which rise in the Central Plateau, but seldom carry water. Some, like the ephemeral Tsauchab, once reached the sea but now end in calcrete pans. Others flow only during the summer rainy season, but at some former stage, they carried huge volumes of water and carved out dramatic canyons like the Fish and the Kuiseb.

East of the Coastal Plains, the terrain becomes more rugged and climbs steeply through rugged canyons to the savanna grasslands of the Central Plateau. This plateau is dissected by fossil river courses and is covered largely in thorn scrub. Still further east, the land slopes gently away to the sandy fossil valleys and dunes that characterise the western Kalahari.

The north-eastern band along the Angolan border, from Ovamboland through Kavango and Caprivi, is characterised by well-watered bushveld. It's bounded by the great rivers – the Kunene, Okavango, Kwando-Mashi-Linyanti-Chobe and Zambezi – which flow year-round and provide water for most of Namibia's human population.

Politically Namibia is now divided into 13 regions, which replace the old ethnically based regions which were demarcated by the colonial powers. However, it will be many years before Namibians become familiar with these new regions or refer to them in common usage. To avoid unnecessary confusion, I'm using the old names and divisions in this book, but will probably switch to the new ones in the next edition. To facilitate the changeover, refer to the maps in this section.

CLIMATE

Although it's predominantly a desert country, Namibia enjoys regional climatic variations corresponding to its geographical subdivisions. The most arid climate is found in the central Namib, which enjoys typically clear and windy weather. The region is cooled in the summer by cold onshore winds which are derived from the South Atlantic anticyclone pressure system.

The upwelling Benguela Current and onshore winds produce a steep temperature gradient between the sea and land. When the cold, moist sea breeze meets the dry desert heat, the result is instantaneous condensation and fog. In the desert, summer daytime temperatures climb to over 40°C, but they can fall to below freezing at night. Fog is common on the coast, generally developing during the night, and often lasts well into the morning up to 20 km inland.

In the winter, the Namib region is warmed by east winds which reach their peak between June and August. As they descend from the Central Plateau, they heat up and dry out. Especially around Swakopmund and Walvis Bay, they often create miserable conditions as they whip up clouds of swirling sand which block out the sun and penetrate everything with coarse grit.

On the Central Plateau the low humidity and gentle breeze of the winter months make for a pleasant and comfortable climate. During the summer both temperatures and humidity climb to uncomfortable levels. The area averages from 200 to 400 mm of precipitation annually, all of which falls in the summer. East of the Central Plateau, the rainfall decreases and along the Botswana and South African borders, one finds the near-desert conditions of the Kalahari.

Going north, however, rainfall steadily increases, reaching its maximum of over 600 mm per year along the Okavango River, which enjoys a sub-tropical climate. The northern and interior regions experience two rainy seasons. The 'little rains' fall between October and December, while the main stormy period occurs from January to April.

NATIONAL PARKS & WILDLIFE RESERVES

Despite its harsh climate, Namibia has some of the world's most magical landscapes and it boasts some of Africa's finest and most

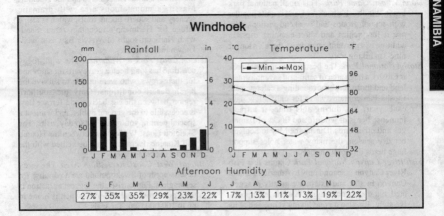

diverse national parks. The parks range from the open bush of the centre and north where wildlife is relatively plentiful, to the barren and inhospitable coastal strip with its huge sand dunes. Nevertheless, even here, many species have adapted to the rigours of the desert including elephant, giraffe, zebra and other large herbivores. Sadly, the lion population, which used to come down as far as the sea, has been wiped out by herders and poachers. In the extreme south is one of the natural wonders of the world – Fish River Canyon – which ranks as one of the most spectacular sights in Africa.

Access to most wildlife-oriented parks is limited to closed vehicles only – no bicycles or motorbikes are allowed – so visitors need a vehicle or a good lift. For most parks, 2WD is sufficient, but you need 4WD in some remote areas, such as the back roads in Namib-Naukluft Park. Hitchhikers aren't allowed in parks with big game unless they've secured a lift beforehand. Even in parks without dangerous animals, hitching is often not viable due to sparse traffic. The only alternative if you can't muster a group and hire a vehicle is to join a tour or wait around a petrol station near the park entrance and beg for a lift.

The following is a rundown of Namibia's major National Parks' units:

Daan Viljoen Game Park This small national park lies in Windhoek's backyard, and is quite popular with school groups and weekend visitors, who use it for picnics and short camping trips. In addition to a pleasant game drive, there's a longer nine-km hiking trail.

Etosha National Park The best known national park is Etosha, a huge area of semi-arid savanna grassland and thorn scrub surrounding a calcrete pan. Etosha Pan contains water for only a few days each year, but during this time, it attracts immense herds of wildlife and flocks of flamingos and other birds. During the May to September dry season, the many water holes support huge herds different animals.

Fish River Canyon National Park Claims that Fish River Canyon is second only to America's Grand Canyon in size and extent are greatly exaggerated, but there's no denying that it is an impressive sight. It's also a great hiking venue and at its southern end is the popular and relaxing hot springs resort of Ai-Ais.

Khaudom Game Reserve This surprising park in the western Kalahari is extremely difficult to access, but its wildlife-viewing opportunities are in the same league as Etosha's. The mostly forested landscape is crossed by a network of omiramba (singular omuramba), or fossil valleys.

Mahango Game Reserve This small park has suffered the ravages of poaching, but thanks to improved security, in the dry season it's an excellent place to see elephants. The nearby National Parks' rest camp at Popavalle (Popa Falls) provides pleasant accommodation.

Mamili National Park Mamili is a new and quite remote national park taking in the vast Linyanti Marshes along the Kwando-Mashi-Linyanti-Chobe River system. This area has often been referred to as a mini-Okavango Delta and indeed, the wetland landscape and the wildlife-viewing opportunities justify the comparison.

Mudumu National Park This new national park takes in the alluring wetlands of the Kwando-Mashi-Linyanti-Chobe river system, as well as surrounding wildlife areas. Although it has been ravaged by heavy poaching and destruction by cattle, it's certainly one of Namibia's loveliest landscapes and is an excellent bird-watching venue. It's also the home of Lianshulu Lodge, one of the country's best and most sensitive tourism operations.

Namib-Naukluft Park Namib-Naukluft, Namibia's largest national park, takes in much of the Namib Desert as well as the surrounding gravel plains and the dramatic Naukluft Massif. At Sossusvlei you can visit the archetypal Namib dunefield, where dunes rise over 300 metres above the plains. The remainder of the park is divided into the central Namib/Kuiseb area and the Naukluft Massif, a mountainous area with dramatic scenery and superb hiking trails, which is also a refuge for Hartmann's mountain zebra. Sandwich Harbour, south of Walvis Bay, is a well-known bird sanctuary.

Skeleton Coast Park & Wilderness The wild, foggy coastline has long been a graveyard for ships and for their crews, who were unable to survive the harsh desert conditions. Only the southern region, between the Ugab River and Terrace Bay, is accessible to the general public, and without a special permit, you're limited to day visits. The Skeleton Coast Wilderness between the Hoanib and Kunene rivers may only be visited with the official concessionaire.

National West Coast Recreation Area The grey deserts north of Swakopmund are a paradise for sea anglers. For tourists, the biggest attraction is the Cape Cross Seal Reserve, which is home to up to 100,000 Cape fur seals.

Waterberg Plateau Park This plateau area is used largely for the re-introduction of wildlife which is either endangered or no longer endemic to Namibia. Fabulous views, a comfortable rest camp and a series of game drives and walking tracks, including a four-day self-guided walk, provide the main draws.

West Caprivi Game Reserve Due to heavy poaching and an encroaching human population, the West Caprivi Game Reserve is almost devoid of wildlife.

Permits & Accommodation

All National Parks' and Rest Camps accommodation must be booked in advance through the Ministry of Environment & Tourism (MET) offices in Windhoek, Swakopmund or Lüderitz. Bookings may be made up to 18 months in advance. However, reservations for the Skeleton Coast Park and the Naukluft area of Namib-Naukluft National Park may only be handled in Windhoek. Entry permits for Namib-Naukluft Park are available after hours and on weekends from the Hans Kriess Garage and petrol station in Swakopmund and from the CWB Service Station in Walvis Bay. Transit permits for Skeleton Coast Park, which allow day passage between Ugabmund and Springbokwater, are sold at Okaukuejo Camp in Etosha National Park.

Park entry permits cost US$1.50 per car and US$1.50 per person and are payable on arrival at the park gate.

In Windhoek, park permits and accommodation reservations are handled by the MET. Reservations Office (☎ (061) 236975; fax (061) 224900), Private Bag 13267, Windhoek. The office is in the Oode Voorpost Building on the corner of John Meinert Strasse and Moltke Strasse.

If you pre-book by post or fax, be sure to specify the type of accommodation required, the number of adults and ages of the children and the dates you intend to stay (along with alternative dates, if possible). The confirmation and invoice will be sent by post; fees must be paid before the due date indicated on the form or the reservation will be cancelled.

Firewood gathering and open fires are prohibited in the national parks, but even outside the parks, wilderness hikers are strongly advised to carry a fuel stove and avoid lighting open fires, which can scar the landscape and may get out of control in the typically dry conditions. If you must gather your own firewood, note that it's illegal to use anything but mopane or acacia. If you're caught burning – or even carrying – any other sort of wood, you'll incur a large fine. That law is applicable even outside national parks.

Firewood – normally split camelthorn acacia – is available for reasonable prices (around US$2 per bundle) at national park rest camps, most private campgrounds and general stores around the country. It's ideal for car campers and eliminates the need to scrounge around the desert for a few dry twigs or destroy the surrounding bush for the sake of a braai. Carry a small hatchet to split the wood into kindling.

Hiking

For multi-day walks at Waterberg Plateau, the Naukluft Mountains, the Ugab River or Fish River Canyon, numbers are limited so book as far in advance as possible. You need a group of at least three people and once in Windhoek, you must procure a local doctor's certificate (not more than 40 days before the walk) stating that you're fit and healthy. Drs Rabie and Retief, on the corner of John Meinert Strasse and Stübel Strasse in Windhoek, charge around US$6 for the brief examination. If you have all day to wait, consultations are much cheaper at a government clinic. Pick up the forms at the MET office on the corner of John Meinert Strasse and Moltke Strasse.

As cumbersome as the booking system may seem, it does protect the environment from the numbers that would descend on the places should they be opened as a free-for-all.

GOVERNMENT

Namibia is an independent republic with a president who is elected by popular ballot for a maximum of two five-year terms. The legislative body, the National Assembly, is

NAMIBIA

comprised of 72 members, who are elected by the people as representatives of electoral districts around the country.

Any constitutional amendment requires a two-thirds majority vote of the national assembly. In the case of an irreconcilable dispute between the executive and legislative branches, the president has the power to dismiss the entire assembly. However, in such an event, the president must also stand for re-election.

The judiciary, which is independent of the executive and legislative branches, is presided over by a chief justice.

All national government functions are centred in the national capital, Windhoek. The country is divided into 13 regions, each with its own regional government, which in turn is subdivided into municipalities.

Since independence on 21 March 1990, Namibia has been governed by a SWAPO-dominated National Assembly which took 57% of the vote in the first national election. The principal opposition party, a moderate 11-party alliance known as the Democratic Turnhalle Alliance (DTA), took second place with 28% of the vote. The president, Sam Nujoma, a former SWAPO leader, is widely respected, and apart from some publicised incidents involving over-zealous bodyguards, the country's political future looks relatively optimistic.

Extremist minority parties, such as the Hersigte Nationale Party (HNP), which advocates apartheid, do still exist but are politically powerless. However, the Action Front for the Retention of the Turnhalle Principles (AKTUR), a White-dominated party to the right of the DTA, still retains some influence.

Unlike many newly independent African states, Namibia doesn't appear to be inclined toward political extremism, and despite its former Marxist affiliations, SWAPO takes pragmatic views regarding the domestic economy and international relations. Despite predictions of Armageddon by the large White minority, since independence, Namibia has remained stable and optimistic under the SWAPO-dominated government.

However, recent media and business allegations of corruption and less-than-ethical government practices probably shouldn't be swept under the rug.

ECONOMY

The Namibian economy is dominated by mining (diamonds and uranium), cattle and sheep herding, tourism and fishing, as well as subsistence-level agriculture. By African standards, Namibia is already a prosperous country. It does suffer some disadvantages – water shortages, lack of local fuel sources, vast distances and a widely scattered population – but its gross domestic product is twice the African average and its population remains small and diverse. Currently, over 80% of the food and manufactured goods must be imported from South Africa, creating an unhealthy degree of economic dependence. The development of the Namibian economy rests on its ability to attract foreign investment, and develop (via education and training) its own human resources to exploit the country's vast resource potential.

Mining

Namibia's mining income is the fourth largest in Africa and the 17th largest in the world, mainly thanks to both the world's richest diamond fields and its largest uranium mine. The diamonds are extracted mostly by strip mining the alluvial sand and gravel of the famed Sperrgebiet ('forbidden area') between Lüderitz and the Orange River. The major player is Consolidated Diamond Mines (CDM), one of Namibia's largest employers, which scours through 20 million tonnes of dirt a year, for a yield of 200 kg (one million carats) of diamonds. The Rössing uranium mine, near Swakopmund, produces more than 60 million tonnes of ore annually.

Of Namibia's other mineral deposits, which include lithium, germanium, silver, vanadium, tin, copper, lead, zinc and tantalum, 70% are extracted by the Tsumeb Corporation Ltd, which operates in the phenomenally rich environs of Tsumeb,

Grootfontein and Otavi in north-central Namibia. Other major mining areas include Uis, with rich deposits of tin; Rosh Pinah, near the Orange River, which produces zinc, lead and silver; and Karibib, with quartz, lithium and beryllium.

Herding & Agriculture

Around 16% of the Namibia's active labour force is involved in commercial herding, but over 70% of the people depend on agriculture to some extent. Most farmers are engaged in subsistence agriculture in the heavily populated communal areas of the north, particularly Ovamboland, Kavango and Caprivi. However, over 80% of the agricultural yield is derived from commercial herding in the central and southern parts of the country.

The industry is dominated by farmers of German or Afrikaner heritage who are involved in raising stock, especially beef cattle and sheep. This occupation is fraught with water shortages, but farms are generally well managed. The current trend is towards game ranching and many farmers now raise gemsboks, zebras and springboks for meat and hides – as well as tourism and hunting – and there is a growing ostrich-farming industry.

In the dry southern regions, the emphasis is on karakul sheep, which resemble scraggy goats, but are well suited to the conditions and produce high-quality meat and wool. Karakul wool once formed the basis of an expanding weaving industry and dominated the export market for luxury leather and skin goods, but in recent years, the bottom has dropped out of the market and it remains to be seen whether a recovery is on the cards.

There is also a small amount of commercial crop farming, mainly around Otavi, Grootfontein and Tsumeb, with maize as the principal crop. Thanks to irrigation from Hardap Dam, Mariental has a growing farming base and around Omaruru, citrus is the particular speciality.

Fishing

The Namibian coastal waters are considered some of the world's richest, mainly thanks to the cold offshore Benguela Current which flows northwards from the Antarctic. It's exceptionally rich in plankton, which accounts for the abundance of anchovy, pilchard, mackerel and other whitefish. But the limited offshore fishing rights have caused problems, and there is resentment that such countries as Spain and Russia have legal access to offshore fish stocks. Namibia has now declared a 200-nautical-mile exclusive economic zone in order to make Namibian fisheries competitive.

Each year, the waters off Lüderitz yield varying numbers of known as crayfish (rock lobsters), most for export to Japan in the form of frozen lobster meat. The fleet, which is comprised of 20 ships, operates from the Orange River mouth north to Hottentot Bay, 75 km north of Lüderitz. Strict seasons and size limits protect from overfishing. In all, the industry employs 1000 people.

The port of Lüderitz also produces and processes tinned fish, fishmeal and fish oil. However, the current decline in the fishing industry has meant that of the 11 fish-processing plants which were active in Walvis Bay and Lüderitz 20 years ago, fewer than half survive. Oysters are also cultivated and marketed around Swakopmund and Walvis Bay, and a new oyster farm has recently opened near Lüderitz.

Manufacturing

Currently, most manufactured goods must be imported from South Africa. Manufacturing comprises less than five percent of Namibia's gross national product, and most of this is made up of meat processing and goods and materials for the mining industry.

It is vital that Namibia develop this sector, but progress is thwarted by the high cost of raw materials, the lack of skills and training and a measure of political uncertainty. Currently, Namibia is desperately courting overseas investment for manufacturing projects, and to a large extent, their success will determine the country's economic future.

Tourism

Over the past few years, since independence,

NAMIBIA

Namibia has gone from a war-torn backwater known only to South African hunters, anglers and holiday-makers to a popular – not to mention chic and trendy – tourist destination for overseas visitors. Immediately following independence, the numbers of South African tourists dropped off sharply, then again began to climb. The country is also a big draw for German tourists, which isn't surprising since travel articles often describe the country as being 'more German than Germany.' That isn't exactly true, but in Windhoek, Swakopmund and Lüderitz, you'd be forgiven for making such an assumption.

As with Botswana, the official aim is to develop a high-cost, low-volume tourist base made up primarily of wealthy Europeans, Australasians and North Americans who have grown weary of the crime and the crowded national parks of East Africa. Unlike Botswana, however, everyone pays the same National Parks' entry fees which, although reasonable for the majority of tourists and wealthier locals, remain out of reach for most Namibians.

Retail
The expanding retail sector is flourishing, with a growing number of shopping venues in Windhoek and Swakopmund. Most people, however, depend upon small market and street-trading stalls. In Ovamboland and other parts of the north, supply and distribution of goods is handled by small *cuca* bush shops spaced intermittently along the main routes. The name is derived from the Angolan brew of the same name.

POPULATION & PEOPLE
Population
Namibia has an estimated population of 1,635,000, and one of the lowest population densities in Africa at 1.5 people per sq km. However, the annual growth rate of over 3% is one of the world's highest. Three quarters of Namibians live in rural areas but the uncontrolled drift to urban areas, particularly to Windhoek, in search of work or higher wages has resulted in increased homeless-

ness, unemployment and crime in the capital and in other cities and towns.

Namibia's population includes at least 11 major ethnic groups, ranging from pastoralists and hunter-gatherers to rural farmers and town-dwellers. Although this ethnic patina wears a heavy coating of colonial German and Afrikaner influence, since independence there have been efforts to emphasise the history and traditions of the individual groups.

People
Although it's difficult to make generalisations about people, the following descriptions briefly outline the history and distinctive characteristics of each major culture.

Ovambo The 650,000-strong Ovambo make up the largest population group and, not surprisingly, most of the ruling SWAPO party. The Ovambo live mainly in the north and are sub-divided into 12 distinct tribal groups. Four of these occupy the Kunene region of southern Angola, while the other eight form the main population group in Ovamboland. The most numerous group is the Kwanyama, which makes up 35% of Namibia's Ovambo population. The next largest groups are the Ndonga, with 30%, and the Kwambi, with 12%, while the remaining five groups each make up from 1 to 8% of the total.

Historically, each of these tribes was headed by an all-powerful hereditary king who had below him a council of head men. However, thanks to changes brought about by Christianity and both German and South African colonial influences, most of these tribes now operate under a council of chiefs or head men. Other changes have included a gradual shift from a predominantly matrilineal to a patrilineal system of inheritance.

The allocation of land is handled by the applicable chief or headman of each tribal group. Land may not be owned, sold or inherited and when a tenant dies, the authorities will decide whether it is passed in the same family or is allotted to someone else.

In rural areas of Ovamboland today, each

family has its own immaculate kraal or *eumbo*, which is very much like a small village enclosed within a stockade-like fence. Housing in these villages is in either round or square thatched huts, and there's always an area reserved for large round storage containers made of woven bark and chinked with mud. These hold mainly *mahango* or millet, which is used to make a delicious beer. In the centre of each eumbo is the family's *omulilo gwoshilongo* or 'sacred fire', a log of mopane which is kept burning around the clock. The eumbo is surrounded by the family lands, which are used for agriculture and grazing cattle.

Recently, large numbers of Ovambo have migrated southward to Windhoek or into the larger towns in the north to work as labourers, craftspeople and professionals.

Kavango The 120,000 Kavango people are divided into five distinct sub-groups – the Mbukushu, the Sambiyu, the Kwangari, the Mbunza and the Geiriku. Since the 1970s, their numbers have been swelling rapidly, thanks mainly to immigrants and refugees from warring Angola. As with other groups in northern Namibia, large numbers of Kavango, particularly young men, are migrating southward in search of employment on farms, in mines and around urban areas.

Most rural Kavango live on the level, wooded floodplains of the north-east, south of the Okavango River, where they make a living by fishing, herding livestock and subsistence farming of millet, maize and sorghum. They're also known as highly skilled woodcarvers and create some of the finest carvings available, which are sold along the Kavango roadsides and in tourist shops around the country. Although most carvers regard their work as merely a commercial endeavour, there are several competent artists.

Kavango society is organised along matrilineal succession which governs inheritance, marriage, politics and traditional religious rites. Politically, however, the tribe is governed by hereditary male chiefs, whose relatives and appointees, along with representatives from each clan, constitute the lower echelons of tribal government.

Herero Namibia's 100,000 Herero people, who are mainly herders, occupy several regions of the country and are divided into several sub-groups. The largest band includes the Tjimba and Ndamuranda groups in Kaokoland, the Maherero around Okahandja and the Zeraua, which is centred on Omaruru. The Himba of Kaokoland are also a Herero sub-group (see the separate discussion later in this section) and the third group, the Mbandero, occupies the colonially demarcated territory of Hereroland, around Gobabis in eastern Namibia.

From the early part of this century, the Herero have established various organisations, including chiefs' councils, to assert their nationalism, handle defence and oversee tribal affairs. One of these chiefs was Hosea Katjikururume Kutako, who became a national hero for his many direct petitions to the UN for help in securing Namibia's independence.

The Herero were originally part of the early southward Bantu migrations from Central Africa and their traditions assert that their origins were in the Great Rift Valley of East Africa. They arrived in present-day Namibia in the mid-1500s and after a 200-year sojourn in Kaokoland, they moved southward to occupy the Swakop Valley and the Central Plateau. Until the colonial period, they remained as semi-nomadic pastoralists in this relatively rich grassland, herding and grazing cattle and sheep.

However, bloody clashes with the northward migrating Nama and the German colonial troops and settlers led to violent uprisings. As a result, approximately 75% of the country's Herero population was wiped out and the remainder were dispersed around the country.

Large numbers of Herero also fled into neighbouring Botswana, where they settled down to a life of subsistence agriculture, growing grains and pulses and raising sheep, cattle and fowl. Now that Namibia is independent, many Herero would like to return to their roots, but the Botswanan government has made it clear that anyone who returns to Namibia must leave behind both their herds and their money. In some cases, families have been split; some family members have gone to Namibia while others have remained behind to look after the family wealth.

For most rural Herero in Namibia today, cattle remain the most prized possessions. Tribal hierarchy divides responsibilities for inheritance between *eendag* (matrilineal) and *oruzo* or (patrilineal) lines of descent, to which each person belongs. Mothers pass down material possessions, including cattle, while fathers handle religious and political instruction, rites and authority, and possessions which are considered sacred.

The characteristic Herero women's dress is derived from Victorian-era German missionaries who took exception to what they considered a lack of modesty among local women. It consists of an immaculate crinoline of enormous proportions worn over a series of petticoats, with a horn-shaped hat or headdress.

Himba The distinctive Himba (or Ovahimba – 'those who ask for things') of the Kaokoveld are actually descended from a group of Herero herders who were displaced by Nama warriors in the 1800s. They fled to the remote north-west and continued their semi-nomadic lifestyle, raising sheep, goats and some cattle.

The Himba still eschew the modern world, and the missionary 'modesty police' never managed to persuade Himba women not to go topless. As a result, Himba women maintain their lovely and distinctive traditional dress of multi-layered goat-leather mini-skirts and ochre-and-mud-encrusted iron, leather and shell jewellery. Their skin is also smeared with a mixture of butter, ash and ochre, ostensibly to keep it young-looking (it must work – even elderly Himba women have beautifully smooth skin) and plaster their plaited hair with the same mixture. The effect is truly stunning.

Damara The Damara, who number around 100,000, share a language group, but presumably no ethnic kinship, with the Nama people, with whom they've historically had major conflicts.

The Damara people have presented researchers with one of Africa's greatest anthropological mysteries: how did a group of hunter-gatherers of Bantu origin wind up in southern Africa speaking a Khoisan dialect? Their resemblance to some Bantu peoples of West Africa has led some anthropologists to believe they were among the first people to migrate into Namibia from the north. However it happened, it's tempting to conclude that the Damara have occupied the region far longer than their other Bantu neighbours, and perhaps that early trade with the Nama and San people caused them to adopt Khoisan as a lingua franca. Whether such a thing ever happened, however, is still a matter of speculation, and no conclusive evidence is available.

What is known is that prior to the 1870s, the Damara occupied much of central Namibia from around the site of Rehoboth westward to the Swakop and Kuiseb rivers and north to present-day Outjo and Khorixas. When the Herero and Nama began expanding their domains into traditional Damara lands, large numbers of Damara people were displaced, killed or captured and enslaved. Between the 1870s and the early 1900s, the Rhenish Missionary Society persuaded the Herero chiefs and colonial authorities to cede bits of territory to create a Damara homeland.

When Europeans first arrived in the region, the Damara were described as semi-nomadic gardeners, pastoralists and hunter-gatherers, who also maintained small-scale mining, smelting and trading operations. However, with colonial encouragement, they settled down to sedentary subsistence herding and agriculture. In the 1960s, the South African administration purchased for the Damara over 4.5 million hectares of marginal European-owned ranchland in the desolate expanses of present-day Damaraland. Unfortunately, the soil in this region is generally poor, most of the land is communally owned and it lacks the good grazing which prevails in central and southern Namibia. Most Damara work in urban areas and on European farms, and only a fraction of them (around 30,000) actually occupy Damaraland.

Europeans Namibia's 85,000 Europeans are mostly of German (20,000) and Afrikaner (65,000) heritage and are concentrated in the urban, central and southern Namibia. The first Europeans, in the form of Portuguese sailors, first arrived in the 15th century, but no one settled until 1760. After 1780 came the traders, hunters and missionaries. Today, they're involved mainly in ranching, commerce, manufacturing and administration. People of mixed European and African descent, sometimes known as Coloureds, number 52,000 and live mainly in Windhoek and other urban areas.

Caprivians In the extreme north-east, along the fertile Zambezi and Kwando riverbanks, live the 80,000 Caprivians, who are comprised of five separate tribal groups: the Lozi, Mafwe, Subia, Yei and Mbukushu. Most Caprivians derive their livelihood from fishing, subsistence farming and herding cattle.

Until the late 19th century, the Caprivi was under control of the Lozi kings and today, the lingua franca of the various Caprivian tribes is known as Rotse, which is a derivative of the Lozi language still spoken in parts of Zambia and Angola.

San For background information about the San culture, see Population & People in the Botswana Facts About the Country chapter and the section on Bushmanland in the North-eastern Namibia chapter.

The 37,000 San in Namibia were the region's earliest inhabitants, and still live in the north-eastern areas. They are divided into three groups: the Naro of the Gobabis area, the !Xukwe of Western Bushmanland, Kavango and Caprivi; and the Ju/hoansi (which is a sub-group of the Qgu or !Kung)

in eastern Bushmanland, particularly around the town of Tsumkwe. However, it has been over a decade since any Namibian San followed a traditional lifestyle, and many now work as servants and farm hands in Kavango and the Caprivi.

Nama Another Khoisan group is the Nama, who are variously known as the Bergdama, Oorlam, Khoi-Khoi or Hottentots. There are around 60,000 Nama people in Namibia. As with the San, most Nama people have a light skin colour, slight frame and small bones, but are on the average a bit taller. They normally have high cheekbones, flattish noses and beautiful almond-shaped eyes, narrowed by an Oriental-like fold of skin on the upper eyelid.

The Namas' origins were in the southern Cape, where they were known as Hottentots. However, during the early days of European settlement in the Cape, they were either exterminated or pushed northward by land-hungry Colonial farmers. They eventually came to rest in Namaqualand, around the Orange River, where they lived as semi-nomadic pastoralists until the mid-19th century, when their leader, Jan Jonker Afrikaner, led them to the area of present-day Windhoek.

On Namibia's Central Plateau, they came into conflict with the Herero, who already occupied that area, and the two groups launched themselves into a series of bloody wars and eventually, the German government confined them to a series of reserves.

Today, the Nama occupy the region colonially designated as Namaland, which stretches roughly from Mariental southward to Keetmanshoop. Many Nama people have adopted Western dress and Christianity and now work in towns or on commercial farms. They're especially known for their extraordinary musical and literary abilities; and their traditional music, folk tales, proverbs and praise poetry have been handed down through the generations to form a basis for their culture today.

Topnaar The Topnaar (or Aonin) people,

NAMIBIA

who are technically a branch of the Nama, mainly occupy the western central Namib Desert, in and around Walvis Bay. Unlike the Nama, however, which historically had a tradition of communal land ownership, the Topnaar passed their lands down through family lines.

Today, the Topnaar are perhaps Namibia's most marginalised group. Historically, they were utterly dependent upon the !nara melon, a thorny desert plant which derived its water by sending a tap root deep into the earth. This plant was the Topnaar's only source of income and the primary element in their diet, which was supplemented by hunting. Now, however, their hunting grounds are tied up in Namib-Naukluft Park – and therefore off limits to hunting – and the melon is under threat due to depleted water tables, which are being tapped to supply Walvis Bay's industrial needs.

As a result, many Topnaar have migrated into Walvis Bay and settled in the township of Narraville, from where they commute to fish-canning factories. Others live around the perimeter in cardboard boxes and make their living scrounging from garbage dumps. In the Topnaar community south-east of Walvis Bay, a primary school and hostel has been provided, but few students ever continue on to secondary school, which would require a move into Narraville.

Those that remain in the desert eke out a living growing !nara melons and raising stock, mainly goats.

Basters The 35,000 Basters are descended mainly from intermixing between the Nama (Hottentots) and Dutch farmers in the Cape Colony. From early on, they strongly professed Calvinist Christianity. In the late 1860s, when they came under pressure from the Boer settlers in the Cape, they fled north of the Orange River and established the settlement of Rehoboth. Although their name is derived from 'bastards', this fiercely independent group of people still uses it proudly because it stresses their mixed heritage. Most Basters still live around Rehoboth and either

follow an urban lifestyle or raise cattle, sheep and goats.

Tswana Namibia's 8000 Tswana make up the country's smallest ethnic group. They're related to the Tswana of South Africa and Botswana and live mainly in the eastern areas of the country, around Aminuis and Epukiro.

EDUCATION

During the German colonial era and the South African mandate, education for the masses took a low priority on the government agendas. As a result, there was a vast disparity between the educational performance of Whites, who normally paid to attend private schools, and other ethnic groups. Less than 75% of Namibian children were completing five years of schooling (to Standard 5), only 8% attended secondary school and under 1% went on for higher education or professional training. As a result, at the time of independence, there was a severe shortage of qualified teachers and educators received very poor salaries. Despite government-subsidised teacher-training colleges in both Ovamboland and Windhoek, there were very few Black Namibians with sufficient educational background to enter teacher training.

Nowadays, education is technically compulsory for all children. SWAPO policy has designated English as the official language of instruction. (However, in some primary schools, classes may also be conducted in Afrikaans or Bantu languages, and some private schools still stick with German.) In the first four years of independence, 832 classrooms were constructed, expatriate teachers were brought in, high-quality instructional materials were purchased and enrolment increased by 21%. Between 1991 and 1993, secondary-school pass rates jumped from 38 to 51%. Nearly 75% of the population has received, or is receiving, at least a primary school education.

Another primary emphasis is on the need to 'catch up' and achieve full literacy. To that end, the government has established over

700 literacy centres around the country to provide basic reading and writing instruction for children and adults alike.

Namibia has three institutes of higher education: the University of Namibia, which began instruction in March 1993, offers degree-level courses in arts, economics, education and medicine; the Technikon, a Polytechnic school, which emphasises career-orientated courses in business, agriculture, ecology and nursing and secretarial studies; and the College for Out-of-School Training which provides theoretical and practical courses in crafts and nursing.

Many Namibians leave the country to attend university in South Africa (at Stellenbosch, Witwatersrand or Cape Town) or study in Europe on UN or Commonwealth scholarships.

ARTS & CULTURE

Although Namibia is still developing a literary tradition, the musical, visual and architectural arts have now become established. The country also enjoys a wealth of amateur talent for the production of material arts, including carvings, basketry, taapestry, and simple but resourcefully designed and produced toys, clothing and household implements.

Music

Namibia's earliest musicians were the San, whose music probably emulated the sounds made by their animal neighbours and was sung to accompany dances and storytelling. The early Nama, who had a more developed musical technique, used drums, flutes and basic stringed instruments, also to accompany dances. Some of these were adopted and adapted by the later arriving Bantu peoples, who added marimbas, gourd rattles and animal horn trumpets to the range. Nowadays, drums, marimbas and rattles are still popular, and it isn't unusual to see dancers wearing belts of soft drink cans filled with pebbles to provide rhythmic accompaniment to their dance steps.

A prominent European contribution to Namibian music is the choir. Early in the colonial period, missionaries established religious choral groups among the local people, and both school and church choirs still perform regularly. Namibia's most renowned ensemble is the Cantare Audire Choir, which was started by Windhoek music teacher, Ernst von Biljon. It is composed of Namibians of all races and performs both African and European religious, classical and traditional compositions for audiences around the world. Naturally, the German colonists also introduced their traditional 'oom-pah-pah' bands, which feature mainly at Carnival and other German festivals.

Visual Arts

Most of Namibia's renowned modern painters and photographers are of European origin who concentrate largely on the country's colourful landscapes, bewitching light, native wildlife and more recently, its diverse peoples. Well-known names include François de Mecker, Axel Eriksson, Fritz Krampe and Adolph Jentsch. The well-known colonial landscape artists, Carl Ossman and Ernst Vollbehr, are both exhibited in Germany.

Non-European Namibians, who have concentrated mainly on three-dimensional and material arts, have recently begun to develop their own traditions. Township art, which develops sober themes in an expressive, colourful and generally lighthearted manner, first appeared in the townships of South Africa during the apartheid years. Over the past decade, it has taken hold in Namibia and is developing into a popular art form. Names to watch for include Tembo Masala and Joseph Madisia, among others.

Architecture

The most obvious architectural contribution in Namibia was made by the German colonial settlers, who attempted to re-create late 19th century Germany in Namibia. In deference to the warmer African climate, however, they added such features as shaded verandas, to provide cool outdoor living space. The best examples may be seen in Lüderitz, Sakopmund and Windhoek, but

German styles are also evident in other towns in central and southern Namibia.

The most ornate and monumental structures, including the railway station and old prison in Swakopmund, were done in what is known as *Wilhelminischer Stil*. Art Nouveau influences are most in evidence in Lüderitz and in Windhoek's Christuskirche.

RELIGION

At least 75% of Namibians profess Christianity and of these, German Lutheranism is the dominant sect. As a result of early missionary activity there is also a substantial Roman Catholic population, mainly in the central areas of the country and spread through isolated areas of the north, especially Kavango. Most Portuguese speakers are Roman Catholic. Most non-Christian Namibians live mainly in the northern areas of the country, and many people – particularly Himba, Herero and San – continue to follow old animist traditions. In general, most of these beliefs are characterised by veneration of ancestors, which aren't considered dead, but are believed to merely have taken on a new form. It's believed that they continue to interact with mortals, and serve as messengers between their descendants and the gods.

LANGUAGE
Indigenous Languages

As a first language, most Namibians speak either a Bantu language, which would include Ovambo, Herero and Caprivian languages, or a Khoisan language, which may be Khoi-Khoi (Nama), Damara, or a San dialect.

The Bantu language group includes eight dialects of Ovambo; Kwanyama and Ndonga are the official languages of Ovamboland. The Kavango group has four separate dialects – Kwangali, Mbunza, Sambiyu and Geiriku – of which Kwangali is the most widely used. In the Caprivi, the most widely spoken language is Rotsi (or Lozi), which originally came from Barotseland in Zambia. Herero people (not surprisingly) speak Herero, which is a rolling melodious language especially rich in colourful-sounding words. Most Namibian place names beginning with an 'O' – Okahandja, Omaruru, Otjiwarongo etc – are derived from the Herero language.

Khoisan dialects are characterised by 'click' elements which make them difficult to learn, and only a few foreigners ever get the hang of them. Clicks are made by compressing the tongue against different parts of the mouth to form different sounds. Names which include an exclamation point are of Khoisan origin and should be rendered as a sideways click sound, a bit like the sound one would make when encouraging a horse, but with a hollow element, similar to the sound made when pulling a cork from a bottle. The other three clicks are formed by quickly drawing the tongue away from the front teeth, which is represented as /; clicking a tutting disapproval, represented as //; and a sharp pop formed by drawing the tongue from the roof of the mouth, which is represented more or less as a vertical line with two crossbars.

The first English-Ju/hoansi dictionary (Ju/hoansi is the dialect spoken by most Namibian San) was compiled in 1992 by the late Patrick Dickens and published by Florida State University in the USA.

Many native Khoisan speakers also speak at least one Bantu and one European language, normally Afrikaans. The language of the Damara people, who are actually of Bantu origin, is also a Khoisan dialect.

European Languages

When the new constitution was drawn up at the time of independence, the official language of Namibia was designated as English. Although that may seem strange, considering that English is the native tongue of only about 2% of the population, it was decided that with English, all ethnic groups would be at equal disadvantage. Furthermore, it was recognised that the adoption of the language of international business would be appealing to both tourists and international investors.

NAMIBIA

Afrikaans, on the other hand, is also widely used, and although it's often dismissed as the language of apartheid, it's the first language of over 100,000 Namibians of diverse ethnic backgrounds, so it's unlikely to disappear anytime soon. Most Namibian Coloureds and Rehoboth Basters use Afrikaans as a first language; and only in the Caprivi is English actually preferred over Afrikaans as a lingua franca.

When written, this guttural dialect of Dutch which may appear intelligible to English speakers, but the spoken language is another matter. Although some rural Afrikaans speakers may be reluctant (or unable) to speak any other language, uniquely English speakers will have few communications problems.

German is also widely spoken, but is the first language of only about 2% of people. In the far north, around Rundu and Katima Mulilo, you'll also hear a lot of Portugese.

Afrikaans

Afrikaans is a phonetic language and words are generally pronounced as they are spelled, with the characteristic guttural emphasis and rolled 'r' of Germanic languages. The following pronunciation guide is not exhaustive, but it includes the more difficult sounds that differ from English.

a	like 'u' in 'pup'
e	like 'e' in 'hen'
i	like 'e' in 'angel'
o	like 'o' in fort, or 'oy' in 'boy'
u	like 'e' in 'angel', but with lips pouted
r	should be rolled
aai	like 'y' in 'why'
ae	like 'ah'
ee	like 'ee' in 'deer'
ei	like 'ay' in 'play'
oe	like 'oo' in 'loot'
oë	like 'oe' in 'doer'
ooi	like 'oi' in 'oil', preceded by w
oei	like 'ooey' in 'phooey', preceded by w
tj	like 'ch' in 'chunk'

Greetings & Civilities

Hello.	Hallo.
Good morning, sir.	Goeiemre, meneer. pronounced 'geemorreh'
Good afternoon, madam.	Goeiemiddag, mevrou.
Good evening, miss.	Goeienaand, juffrou.
Good night.	Goeienag.
Please.	Asselbief.
Thank you.	Dankie.
How are you?	Hoegaand?
Good thank you.	goed dankie.
pardon.	ekskuus.

Useful Words & Phrases

Yes.	Ja.
No.	Nee.
what?	wat?
how?	hoe?
how many/how much?	hoeveel?
when?	wanneer?
where?	waar?
emergency	nood
Do you speak English/Afrikaans?	praat u English/ u Afrikaans?
I only understand a little Afrikaans.	ek verstaan net 'n' bietjie Afrikaans.
Where are you from?	waarvandaan kom u?
from...	van...
Where do you live?	Waar woon u?
overseas	oorsese
What is your occupation?	Wat is jou beroep?
yes, no, maybe, sure	ja-nee
soon	nou-nou
Isn't that so?	n?
sons	seuns
daughters	dogsters
wife	vrou
husband	eggenoot
mother	ma
father	pa
sister	suster
brother	broer
nice/good/pleasant	lekker
bad	sleg
cheap	goedkoop
expensive	duur
party/rage	jol

NAMIBIA

Numbers

1	een
2	twee
3	drie
4	vier
5	vyf
6	ses
7	sewe
8	agt
9	nege
10	tien
11	elf
12	twaalf
13	dertien
14	veertien
15	vyftien
16	sestien
17	sewentien
18	agtien
19	negentien
20	twintig
21	een en twintig
30	dertig
40	veertig
50	vyftig
60	sestig
70	sewentig
80	tagtig
90	negentig
100	honderd
1000	duisend

Timetables

travel	reis
arrival	aankoms
departure	vertrek
to	na
from	van
today	vandag
tomorrow	mre
yesterday	gister
public holiday	openbare vakansiedag
daily	daagliks
single	enkel
return	retoer
ticket	kaartjie
am	vm
pm	nm

Days of the Week

Monday	Maandag, abbreviated to Ma
Tuesday	Dinsdag, Di
Wednesday	Woensdag, Wo
Thursday	Donderdag, Do
Friday	Vrydag, Vr
Saturday	Saterdag, Sa
Sunday	Sondag, So

Getting Around – Town

left	links
right	regs
exit	uitgang
on the corner	op die hoek
city	stad
city centre	middestad
town	dorp
avenue	laan
street	straat
road	pad verkeerslig
tourist bureau	toeristeburo
information	inligting
enquiries	navrae
rooms	kamers
office	kantoor
building	gebou
art gallery	kunsgalery
pharmacy/chemist	apteek
station	stasie
church	kerk
priest	dominee

Getting Around – Country

utility/pick-up	bakkie
river	rivier
mountain	berg
bay	baai
ford	drift
road	pad
point	punt
beach	strand
field, or plain	veld
marsh	vlei
caravan park	woonwapark
game reserve	wildtuin
hiking trail	wandelpad

Food & Drinks

vegetables	groente
fruit	vrugte
meat	vleis
farm sausage	boerewors
dried and salted meat	biltong
fish	vis
cheese	kaas
bread	brood
cup of coffee	koppie koffie
glass of milk	glas melk
wine	wyn
beer	bier
hotel bar	kroeg
barbecue	braaivleis or braai

NAMIBIA

Facts for the Visitor

VISAS & EMBASSIES

All tourists to Namibia require a valid passport issued by their home country, which is valid for at least six months after their intended departure from Namibia, in addition to an onward plane, bus or train ticket. Tourists are granted an initial 90 days, which may be extended by the Ministry of Home Affairs (☎ (061) 398 9111) on the corner of Kasino St and Independence Ave in Windhoek. The mailing address is Private Bag 13200, Windhoek. For the best results, it's wise to be there when they open at 8 am, submit your application in the 3rd floor offices (as opposed to those on the ground floor) and make an effort to be polite.

In early 1995, no visas were required by nationals of France, Germany, Austria, Italy, the UK, Ireland, the Netherlands, Belgium, Luxembourg, Switzerland, Liechtenstein, Austria, Switzerland, Russia and the CIS countries, Canada, the USA, Brazil, South Africa, Botswana, Zimbabwe, Zambia, Tanzania, Angola, Mozambique, Kenya, Japan, Singapore, or the Scandinavian countries.

All EU and Commonwealth countries should soon be included in the list of countries not requiring visas, and in mid-1995, the announcement was made that visa requirements were being dropped for Australians, New Zealanders, Spaniards and Portugese. There was no indication when the change would take effect, but your travel agent will have relevant details.

CUSTOMS

Any item from elsewhere in the Southern African Customs Union – Botswana, South Africa, Lesotho and Swaziland – may be imported duty free. From elsewhere, visitors can import duty free 400 cigarettes or 250 grams of tobacco, two litres of wine, one litre of spirits and 250 ml of eau de cologne. There are no limits on currency import, but entry and departure forms ask how much you intend to spend or have spent in the country.

Firearms require a temporary import permit and must be declared at the time of entry. For pets, you need a health certificate and full veterinary documentation. Bear in mind, however, that pets aren't permitted in national parks or reserves.

MONEY

For three years after independence, Namibia used the South African rand, but on 15 September 1993, the country issued its own currency. The Namibian dollar equals 100 cents and in Namibia, it's valued the same as the South African rand; in South Africa, however, it fetches only about R0.70. In Namibia, the rand remains legal tender at a rate of 1:1.

This can be confusing, given that there are three sets of coins and notes in use: old South African, new South African and Namibian. To complicate matters further, the three coins of the same denomination are all different sizes! It takes awhile to get the hang of it.

Namibian dollar notes come in denominations of N$10, 20, 50 and 100 and all bear portraits of Nama leader Hendrik Witbooi. Coins have a value of 5, 10, 20, and 50 cents and N$1 and N$5. South African notes are issued for R5, 10, 20, 50 and 100, and coins come in denominations of 1, 2, 5, 10, 20 and 50 cents, as well as R1 and R2. Namibia is currently trying to phase out the 1 and 2-cent coins by encouraging rounding of prices to the nearest 5 cents.

There is no limit on the amount of currency or travellers' cheques you can bring into Namibia. Major foreign currencies and travellers' cheques may be exchanged at any bank, but the latter normally fetch a better rate. When changing money, you can opt for either South African rand or Namibian dollars; if you'll need to change any leftover currency outside Namibia, the rand is a better choice.

Travellers' cheques may also be exchanged for US dollars cash – if the cash is

Namibian Diplomatic Missions

There are few Namibian embassies or high commissions around the world. If you have problems securing a visa, fax or send your passport details and state how long you want to stay to the Ministry of Home Affairs, Private Bag X13200, Windhoek (☎398 9111; fax 22 3817). Although visas may sometimes be issued on arrival at Windhoek International Airport, they are never issued at land borders. Namibia is diplomatically represented by the following missions:

Angola
Embassy of Namibia, Rua Rei Katyavala 6, PO Box 953, Luanda (☎ (244-2) 611966)

Belgium
Embassy of Namibia, Stephanie Square, Business Centre SA, 65 Ave Louise, 1050 Brussels (☎ (32-2) 535 7801; fax (32-2) 535 7766)

France
Embassy of Namibia, 224/226 rue du Faubourg, St-Antoine, Paris (☎ (33-1) 43 48 30 80; fax (33-1) 43 48 30 47)

Germany
Embassy of Namibia, Konstantinstrasse 25a, 5300 Bonn 2 (☎ (49-228) 359 091; fax (49-228) 359 051)

South Africa
Tulbagh Park, Eikendal Flat, Suite 2, 1243 Church St, Colbyn, PO Box 29806, Sunnyside, 0132 Pretoria (☎ (27-12) 342 3520; fax (27-12) 342 3565)

Sweden
Embassy of Namibia, Luntmakargatan 86-88, PO Box 26042, S-100 31 Stockholm (☎ (46-8) 612 7788; fax (46-8) 416 6655)

UK
Namibian High Commission, 34 South Molton St, London (☎ (44-171) 408 2333; fax (44-171) 409 7306)

USA
Embassy of Namibia, 1605 New Hampshire Ave NW, Washington, DC 20009 (☎ (1-202) 986 0540; fax (1-202) 986 0443)

Zambia
Namibian High Commission, 6968 Kabanga Rd and Addis Ababa Dr, Rhodes Park, Lusaka (☎ (260-1) 252 250; fax (260-1) 252 497)

Zimbabwe
Namibian High Commission, Lintas House, 46 Union Ave, Harare (☎/fax (263-4) 47930)

---

available – but the banks charge a 7% commission. There is no currency black market, so beware of street changers offering unrealistic rates; they could be passing counterfeit notes or setting you up for a robbery.

Exchange Rates

At the time of writing, the Namibian dollar had the following values against other currencies:

US$1	=	N$3.69
A$1	=	N$2.64
UK£1	=	N$5.89
¥100	=	N$4.39
DM1	=	N$2.63
SFr	=	N$3.20
FFr1	=	N$0.75
NZ$1	=	N$2.46
C$1	=	N$2.68
BotP1	=	N$1.36
Z1	=	N$0.43

Credit Cards

Credit cards are widely accepted in most shops, restaurants and hotels and credit card cash advances are available from BOB, First National Bank's automatic teller system. You'll find BOB in Windhoek, Gobabis, Rehoboth, Keetmanshoop, Lüderitz, Mariental, Swakopmund, Walvis Bay, Okahandja, Tsumeb, Grootfontein, Rundu, Otjiwarongo, Oranjemund, Oshakati and Ondangwa.

American Express is represented by Woker Travel Services (☎ 237946) on Peter Müller Strasse in Windhoek. Nedbank will issue cash against a personal cheque, but fees are high.

Costs

Thanks to a favourable exchange rate, Namibia remains a relatively inexpensive country to visit. You'll probably spend considerably more than in Zimbabwe, but less than in either Botswana or South Africa.

Foreign Embassies in Namibia
Since Namibia became independent, more and more countries are establishing diplomatic missions. All of the following addresses are in Windhoek.

Angola
Angola House, 3 Ausspann St, Ausspannplatz, Private Bag 12020 (☎227535; fax 221498)
Botswana
101 Nelson Mandela Rd, PO Box 20359 (☎221942; fax 236034)
Canada
111A Gloudina St, Ludwigsdorf, PO Box 2147 (☎222941; fax 224204)
France
1 Goethe St, PO Box 20484 (☎229021; fax 231436)
Germany
6th Floor Sanlam Centre, 154 Independence Ave, PO Box 231 (☎229217; fax 222981)
Italy
on the corner of Anna and Gevers Sts, Ludwigsdorf, PO Box 24065 (☎228602; fax 229860)
Kenya
5th Floor, Kenya House, 134 Robert Mugabe Ave, PO Box 2889 (☎226836; fax 221409)

Malawi
56 Bismarck St, Windhoek West, PO Box 23547 (☎221391; fax 227056)
South Africa
RSA House, on the corner of Jan Jonker and Nelson Mandela Dr, Klein Windhoek, PO Box 23100 (☎229765; fax 224140)
Spain
58 Bismarck St, Windhoek West, PO Box 21811 (☎223066; fax 223046)
UK
116A Robert Mugabe Ave, PO Box 22202 (☎223022; fax 228895)
USA
14 Lossen St, Ausspannplatz, Private Bag 12029 (☎221601; fax 229792)
Zambia
on the corner of Sam Nujoma and Republic Rd, PO Box 22882 (☎237610; fax 228162)
Zimbabwe
on the corner of Independence Ave and Grimm St, PO Box 23056 (☎228134; fax 226859)

If you're camping or staying in backpackers' hostels, cooking your own meals and hitching or using local minibuses, plan on spending a minimum of US$15 per day. Unfortunately, to get around the country on this sort of budget would prove both frustrating and time consuming, since the hitching isn't great and minibus routes are limited to main highways.

A plausible middle-range budget, which would include B&B or inexpensive hotel accommodation, public transport and at least one restaurant meal daily, would be around US$50 to US$80 per person (if accommodation costs are shared between two people).

In the upper range, the sky is the limit, but if you wish to stay at starred hotels, eat in restaurants exclusively and either take escorted tours or use 4WD, you're looking at a minimum of US$300 per person per day. It may be better value to pre-book a fly-drive or organised tour package overseas than to make arrangements on the spot.

In Namibia, the fly in the ointment is transport. To readily reach the most interesting parts of the country, you'll have to add car hire and petrol expenses. If you can muster a group of four people and share costs, you'll probably squeak by on an additional US$20 per day – that's assuming a daily average of around 200 km in a 2WD vehicle with the least expensive agency, including tax, insurance and unlimited mileage. If you prefer to hire a vehicle between only two people, again averaging 200 km per day with unlimited mileage, double that amount.

For a 4WD vehicle shared between two people, add yet another US$50 per person. The plus side of a 4WD is that many vehicles are equipped with camping gear, which would allow you to bring down the price of accommodation.

Bear in mind, however, if you hire the vehicle for a shorter period – normally fewer than seven days – most agencies charge an additional US$0.20 (N$0.75) per km, which must be added in.

Tipping
Tipping is expected only in up-market tourist establishments which don't already add a service charge as a matter of course. In any case, don't leave more than about 10% of the bill. Tipping is officially prohibited in national parks and reserves.

Bargaining
Bargaining is only acceptable when purchasing handicrafts and arts directly from the producer or artist, such as at roadside stalls. Quite often, however, the prices asked are quite low – and do represent fair market value – so bargaining is often unnecessary. The exception is crafts imported from Zimbabwe, which are generally sold for highly inflated prices due to the cost of transporting them from so far away. Shop prices aren't usually negotiable, although you may be able to wrangle discounts on very expensive curios or artwork.

Consumer Taxes
A general sales tax (GST) of 11% is applied to most purchases, including meals and accommodation, but it's not normally included in marked prices. Tourists buying such luxury items as leather and jewellery for export may be exempt from this tax if they can produce a valid passport and airline tickets.

WHEN TO GO
Most of Namibia enjoys a minimum of 300 days of sunshine a year, but generally, the winter climate is the most pleasant and it's probably best to avoid Namib-Naukluft and Etosha national parks in the extreme heat between December and March.

Daytime temperatures in the mountainous and semi-arid Central Plateau (including Windhoek) are a bit lower than in the rest of the country but the climate is generally pleasant most of the year. In the dry season from May to October, you can expect clear, warm and sunny days and cold clear nights, with temperatures often falling below freezing. Oranges and other fruits generally ripen between July and September.

There are two rainy seasons, the 'little rains' from October to December and the main rainy period from January to April. It's characterised by brief showers and occasional thunderstorms which clean the air and soak down the dust. January temperatures in Windhoek can soar to 40°C.

Low-lying areas in the eastern part of the country are generally much hotter than the Central Plateau and, except for Kavango and Caprivi, receive less rain. Between January and March, the rivers of the Caprivi often flood, making some roads either impassible or very tricky to negotiate.

Also, bear in mind that some resort areas, including Ai-Ais Hot Springs, close for part of the year. Others, such as Swakopmund, are always booked out over Christmas and Easter and during school holidays.

TOURIST OFFICES
Local Tourist Offices
Windhoek has both city and national tourist offices, as well as a private tourist office which will help plan your trip and make bookings. You'll also find tourist offices in municipal buildings in most towns, and there are small information bureaux in Karibib, Usakos, Omaruru, Okahandja and Gobabis, all of which are open during business hours.

Useful publications include the *SWA Namibia Accommodation Guide for Tourists* and Engen Oil's *Guidebook – Travel in Namibia*, published annually and available free from government tourist offices, or for around US$1.50 at private tourist offices and bookshops.

Overseas Representatives
The following Namibia Tourism addresses may be useful in planning your visit:

Namibia
> Namibia Tourism, Ground Floor, Continental Building, 272 Independence Ave, Private Bag 13346, Windhoek (☎ (061) 284 9111; fax (061) 221930)

Germany
> Namibia Verkehrsbüro, Im Atzelnest 3, Postfach 2041, W-6380 Bad Homburg 3 (☎ (06172) 406650; fax (06172) 406690)

South Africa

    Namibia Tourism, 200 Level, 209 Red Route, Carlton Centre, PO Box 11405, Johannesburg 2000 (☎ (011) 331 7055; fax (011) 331 2037)

    Namibia Tourism, Shell House, 4 Waterkant St, PO Box 739, Cape Town 8000 (☎ (021) 419 3190; fax (021) 215840)

UK

    Namibia Tourism, 6 Chandos St, London W1M 0LQ (☎ (0171) 636 2924; fax (0171) 636 2969)

USEFUL ORGANISATIONS

In Namibia's post-independence governmental reorganisation, the ministries for tourism and wildlife were combined into one entity, the Ministry of Environment & Tourism (MET). It now oversees all national parks, game parks and most government-owned resorts, and also dispenses information on wildlife and conservation. You'll find the main information and booking office on Independence Ave in Windhoek; the mailing address is Ministry of Environment & Tourism, Private Bag 13267, Windhoek (☎ (061) 36975 reservations, (061) 33875 information).

For information on road conditions, contact the Automobile Association of Namibia, 15 Carl List House, Independence Ave, PO Box 61, Windhoek 9000 (☎ (061) 224201; fax (061) 222446).

BUSINESS HOURS & HOLIDAYS
Business Hours

Normal business hours are Monday to Friday from 8 am to 1 pm and 2.30 to 5 pm. In the winter, when it's getting dark at 3.30 pm, some shops open at 7.30 am and close around 4 pm. Lunch hour closing is almost universal. Most city and town shops open on Saturday from 8 am to 1 pm.

Banks, government departments and information offices all keep to these hours, as do car hire firms and other businesses. Many petrol stations in cities and towns, and along well-travelled highways, open 24 hours a day, but in outlying areas, you'll have trouble getting fuel after hours or on Sunday. In towns, supermarkets generally remain open through lunchtime and on weekends, and small locally run convenience shops may remain open until late in the evening.

School & Public Holidays

Resort areas are busiest over both Namibian and South African school holidays. The dates vary, but Namibian holidays normally run from mid-December to mid-January, late April to early June, and the last week in August to the second week in September. Transvaal school holidays, which unleash half the population of Johannesburg, run from early December to mid-January, the last week in March and first two weeks of April, the first three weeks in July and two weeks in the middle of October. Holiday periods in the rest of South Africa will vary from these by about a week in either direction.

Banks and most shops are closed on the following public holidays. When a public holiday falls on a Sunday, the following day also becomes a holiday:

1 January
    New Year's Day
March/April
    Good Friday, Easter Sunday, Easter Monday
21 March
    Independence Day
April/May
    Ascension Day (occurs 40 days after Easter)
1 May
    Workers' Day
4 May
    Cassinga Day
25 May
    Africa Day
26 August
    Heroes' Day
10 December
    Human Rights Day
25 & 26 December
    Christmas, Family/Boxing Day

CULTURAL EVENTS

A big event to watch for is Maherero Day, towards the end of August, when the Red Flag Herero people gather in traditional dress at Okahandja for a memorial service to the chiefs killed in the Khoi-Khoi and German wars. It takes place on the weekend nearest 26 August. A similar event, also at Okahandja, is staged by the Mbanderu or

Green Flag Herero on the weekend nearest 11 June. On the weekend nearest 10 October, the White Flag Hereros gather in Omaruru to honour their chief Zeraua.

The Windhoek Karnival (WIKA) in late April or early May; the Küska (Küste Karnival) at Swakopmund in late August or early September; the Windhoek Agricultural Show in late September; and the Windhoek Oktoberfest in late October are all major social events, mainly among the European community.

Details on these events are provided in individual chapters.

POST & TELECOMMUNICATIONS
Post Offices
In major towns, post offices remain open during normal business hours; in resort areas, they open the same hours but offer limited services.

Domestic post generally moves slowly, and it can take up to six weeks for a letter to travel from Lüderitz to Katima Mulilo, for example. Overseas airmail is normally better, and is limited only by the time it takes an article to reach Windhoek.

Although postal rates are climbing, they aren't overly high, and for posting larger boxes overseas, surface mail is a real bargain.

All post offices sell current issues of Namibia's lovely pictorial and commemorative stamps. Upstairs in the Windhoek GPO is a special department for stamp enthusiasts.

Receiving Mail
Naturally, poste restante works best in Windhoek. Have correspondents print your surname clearly in block capitals, underline it and address it to you at Poste Restante, GPO, Windhoek, Namibia. As you'd expect, the further you are from Windhoek, the longer mail takes to arrive. Photo identification is required to collect mail.

American Express credit card or travellers' cheque customers may have post held for them by the Windhoek American Express representative, Woker Travel Services (☎ (061) 237946; fax (061) 225932) at

6 Peter Müller Strasse. Have post addressed to your name, American Express Client, PO Box 211, Windhoek, Namibia.

Telecommunications
The Namibian telephone service is relatively efficient. There are no telephone boxes in the streets, but you can make local or international calls from post office booths or private phones. Telecom Namibia has also introduced a new N$10 (US$3) phone card, which is available at post offices and some retail shops, but as yet, there are very few card phones available. The current international telephone rate is US$3.50 per minute to any foreign country. Most towns now have private fax bureaux where you can send and receive faxes.

Cellular phones are practically unknown and in very rural areas, most people who must communicate use short-wave radios. Some isolated locations use radio-telephones. Radio-telephone numbers are signified by the area code (0020) and are listed in the telephone directory, but calls to these phones must be booked through an operator.

Many remote bush locations subscribe to a message service operated by Walvis Bay Radio (☎ (0642) 3581); each subscriber has its own code number, and messages are passed on via radio.

There's only one slim telephone directory for the entire country but it conveniently lists most people's private and work addresses and has a separate section for government departments. The Yellow Pages also covers the whole country.

When phoning Namibia from abroad, dial the country code (264) followed by the telephone code without the leading zero, and then the desired number. To phone out of Namibia, first dial (09), then the desired country code, area code and number.

LAUNDRY
Even the smallest hotels have some sort of laundry service and most small towns have a laundry, but self-service laundrettes are scarce outside Windhoek and Swakopmund.

Washing facilities are often provided at government camp sites and resorts. Dry-cleaners are found in major towns and charge about US$2 per piece.

BOOKS

Thanks to its unique history, cultures and environments, Namibia is the subject of a growing number of books in English – as well as German and Afrikaans – and nearly all Namibian book shops have a special section dealing with Namibian and African topics. Many of these books, however, have only limited distribution in other countries; you'll have the most luck with specialist travel bookshops in the UK or USA.

Windhoek has several good bookshops, including two branches of the South African CNA chain. They sell everything from newspapers and magazines to dictionaries and journals. All bookshops have separate sections for works in Afrikaans, German and English. However, most are in English. Swakopmund is also a good place to look for books. In smaller towns, there's normally a selection of pulp paperbacks in the supermarket or general store.

History

Namibia – the Struggle for Liberation by Alfred T Moleah (Disa Press, 1983, Wilmington, USA) is an account of SWAPO's independence struggle which tells it like it was long before success was guaranteed.

If you're interested in desert survival, the *Sheltering Desert* by Henno Martin (Donker Publications, Craighall, South Africa, 1983) is the book to read. It recounts the story of German geologists Henno Martin and Hermann Korn, who spent two years in the Namib Desert to avoid internment by Allied forces during WWII. It contains excellent descriptions of the Namib ecology, though some parts are definitely not recommended for vegetarians.

You may also be interested in Sam Nujomo's autobiography *To Free Namibia: The Life of the First President of Namibia* (James Currey Pulishers, UK, 1995). Also, see *Namibia: The Nation after Independence*

Namibia Trunk Dialling Codes

When dialling a trunk call from within Namibia, be sure to include the first zero of the internal trunk code. Note that some rural areas have a farmline code instead of – or in addition to – a standard trunk dialling code. In this case, it's necessary to dial the code and verbally ask the exchange operator for the desired number. These are identified in the text where there are both standard and farmline codes. Some useful codes include:

Abenab, Horabe and Maroelaboom (06731)
Ameib (062242)
Aus, Grünau and Karasburg (06342)
Bethanie and Helmeringhausen (06362)
Divundu (067372)
Dordabis, Seeis and the Khomas Hochland (0628)
Gobabis (0688)
Gochas (06662)
Grootfontein (06731)
Henties Bay, Kalkfeld and Karabib (064)
Kamanjab and Hobatere (06552)
Katima Mulilo (0677)
Keetmanshoop (0631)
Khorixas (065712)
Kombat (067362)
Lüderitz (06331)
Maltehöhe (0663)
Mariental (0661)
Noordoewer (0637)
Okahandja and Gross Barmen (0621)
Omaruru (064)
Omitara (06202)
Onathinge (067568)
Ondangwa (06756)
Opuwo (06562)
Oranjemund (06332)
Oshakati (06751)
Otavi (06742)
Otjimbingwe (062252)
Otjiwarongo (0651)
Outjo (0654)
Radio Telephone Code (0020)
Rehoboth (0627)
Rundu (0671)
Solitaire (06638)
Stampriet (06652)
Swakopmund (064)
Tsumeb and Etosha National Park (0671; farmline 0678)
Uis (0629)
Usakos (066)
Walvis Bay (064)
Windhoek (061)
Witvlei (0683)

NAMIBIA

by D Sparks & D Green (Wesview Press, 1992) and *The Transition to Independence in Namibia* by L Cliffe, R Bush, J Lindsay, B Mokopakgodsi, D Pankhurst & B Tsie (Lynne Rienner Publishers, 1994) for a look at colonisation and independence.

Literature & Fiction

A literary tradition hasn't yet developed among Black Namibians, but it's certainly coming. If you're after stories set in Namibia, you're pretty much limited to pulp fiction, such as Wilbur Smith's highly entertaining *The Burning Shore* and Craig Thomas' *A Hooded Crow*.

Natural History Guides

Namib Flora: Swakopmund to the Giant Welwitschia via Goanikontes by Patricia Craven and Christine Marais (Gamsberg, Windhoek 1986) is an excellent little book which is ideal for plant identification around northern Namib-Naukluft Park.

The Namib – Natural History of an Ancient Desert by Mary Seely (Shell Guides Namibia, Windhoek, 1993) is a useful handbook written by the Director of the Desert Research Unit.

Other natural history guides which may be of interest include *Waterberg Flora – Footpaths in and around the Camp* by P Craven & C Marais (Gamsberg Press, Windhoek, 1989); *Waterberg Plateau Park* by Ilme Schneider (Shell Guides Namibia, Windhoek, 1993); *Welwitschia – Paradox of a Parched Paradise* by CH Bornman (Struik, Cape Town, 1978); *Animals of Etosha* by J du Preez (Shell Namibia, Windhoek, 1988); *The Birds of Daan Viljoen Park* by RAC Jensen & CF Clinning (Directorate of Nature Conservation, Windhoek, 1973); *The Birds of Etosha National Park* by RAC Jensen & CF Clinning (Directorate of Nature Conservation, Windhoek, 1983); and *Etosha – Life & Death on an African Plain* by M Reardon & M Reardon (Struik, Cape Town, 1984).

Travel Guides

Guide to Backpacking & Wilderness Trails by Willie & Sandra Olivier (Southern Book Publishers, Johannesburg, 1989) covers hiking and backpacking routes in South Africa and Namibia. Bizarrely, it's available only in a large format hardback edition.

As stated in the Botswana Books section, if you're the sort of traveller who carries two guidebooks, *Guide to Namibia & Botswana* by Chris McIntyre & Simon Atkins (Bradt Publications, Chalfont St Peter, UK, 1994) is a good choice. The maps aren't superb, but the text does provide enjoyable reading.

Guide to Namibian Game Parks by Willie & Sandra Olivier (Longman Namibia Ltd, Windhoek, 1993) has the lowdown on all the national parks, game reserves and other conservation areas in the country, with useful maps and advice on wildlife viewing.

Insight Guides Namibia edited by Johannes Haape (APA Insight, Singapore, 1993) is a full-colour book which contains lots of enticing photos and is highly worthwhile for trip planning and preparation, but the practical information is limited.

Namibia und Botswana by Karl-Günther Schneider & Bernd Weise (DuMont Büchverlag, K"ln, Germany, 1991) is a German-language book full of information on the political and natural history, the arts and cultures and the worthwhile sights. The Namibia section is particularly strong.

Spectrum Guide to Namibia by Camerapix (Struik, Cape Town, 1994) takes a similar format and angle as the Insight Guide, with lots of colour photos and background information. However, it was done by the same people as *Journey Through Namibia* and the same problems appear.

Visitors' Guide to Namibia by Willie & Sandra Olivier (Southern Book Publishers, Halfway House, South Africa, 2nd edition, 1994) is a concise little book which deals almost exclusively with fascinating background on natural history and sites of interest, but the practical information is limited and it contains little cultural background.

Other Publications

If you're looking for a collection of stunning photos, you could hardly beat *Journey*

Through Namibia by Mohamed Amin, Duncan Willetts & Tahir Shah (Camerapix, Nairobi, 1994), but the text does have some problems.

Kaokoveld – the Last Wilderness by Anthony Hall-Martin, J du P Bothma & Clive Walker (Southern Book Publishers, Johannesburg, 1988) is a compilation of beguiling photos, in coffee-table format, that will have you heading directly for north-western Namibia.

Although it's now quite dated, *National Atlas of South-West Africa*, by JH van der Merwe (University of Stellenbosch, 1983) still contains a wealth of useful information.

This is Namibia by Peter Joyce & Gerald Cubitt (Struik, Cape Town, 1992) is mainly a coffee-table book with a range of lovely photos and clear, concise text presenting a wealth of background information.

Skeleton Coast by Amy Schoeman (Macmillan South Africa, Johannesburg, 1984) is also worth a look.

MAPS

Government survey topo sheets and aerial photos are available from the Office of the Surveyor General (☎ 2852332 or 238110), Ministry of Justice, Private Bag 13267, Windhoek. The office is in the Justicia Building beside the GPO on Independence Ave in Windhoek. The 1:250,000 series maps cost US$2 each; the 1:50,000 maps are US$1.50.

The *Shell Namibia 1994* map is probably the best reference for navigation on remote routes, but it is difficult to discern which of these are passable to ordinary vehicles and which require 4WD, and the Caprivi is shown only as a small-scale inset. The map of Windhoek on the reverse side is the best you're likely to find. Shell has also published a good map of north-western Namibia entitled *Kaokoland-Kunene Region Tourist Map* which depicts all routes and tracks through this remote region. It's available at book-shops and tourist offices for US$2 to US$3.

Aesthetically, the Macmillan *Namibia Travellers' Map* at a scale of 1:2,400,000 is one of the nicest, with clear print and colour-graded altitude representation. However,

minor back routes aren't depicted and it does contain some notable mistakes. On the reverse side are decent maps of Windhoek, Swakopmund, Lüderitz, Walvis Bay, and Etosha and Namib-Naukluft national parks.

The MET produces an official *Republic of Namibia* 1:2,000,000 tourist map, which shows major routes and sites of tourist interest and will suffice for most trips around the country. It's updated more or less annually and is distributed free at tourist offices, hotels and travel agencies. The reverse side contains detailed maps of Windhoek and Swakopmund.

The Automobile Association Travel Service (☎ (061) 224201; fax (061) 222446) has produced the map *Namibia* at a scale of 1:2,500,000 which includes most back roads and settlements, although large swathes of the country, such as the Kaokoveld and Bushmanland are left blank. Quite useful is the town hierarchy, which is not determined by population but by availability of such services as accommodation, petrol and vehicle repairs. On the reverse side is a series of thumbnail town plans. The AA office is on the ground floor of the Carl List Building, on the corner of Peter Müller Strasse and Independence Ave. To pick up AA maps, however, you must prove membership in an official Automobile Association affiliate.

MEDIA
Newspapers & Magazines

Six of Namibia's seven main English-language newspapers are published in Windhoek: *The Windhoek Advertiser*, which is published from Monday to Thursday and on Saturday; the bi-weekly *Namibia Today*; *The Times of Namibia*, published weekdays; *The Namibian*, also published weekdays; the *Windhoek Observer*, published on Saturday; and the government-owned *New Era*. The seventh paper, *The Namib Times*, is published in Walvis Bay and is issued twice weekly. German-language newspapers include the *Allgemeine Zeitung*, published daily, and the *Namibia Nacrichten*, which comes out on Sunday.

The number of papers available is a direct

NAMIBIA

reflection of Namibia's free press policy, which allows all views to be heard. Unfortunately, no Namibian paper is known for its coverage of international events or mastery of journalism conventions. The readily available South African daily papers are better sources of world news and some European newspapers, including the London dailies, the *International Herald Tribune*, *Washington Post* and various large German papers, are available in Windhoek and Swakopmund, together with a full compliment of magazines and journals such as *Der Spiegel*, *The Economist*, *Time* and *Newsweek*.

The monthly publication *Namibia Review* is the best to read for national political, cultural and economic issues. It's available by subscription from Namibia Review (☎ (061) 222246; fax (061) 224937), Ministry of Information & Broadcasting, Private Bag 11334, Windhoek.

For lighter travel, culture and arts related articles and advertising, there's *Flamingo*, which is the in-flight magazine of Air Namibia. It's also available by subscription from Flamingo (☎ (27-11) 463 3350), PO Box 98034, Sloane Park 2152, South Africa. For information in Windhoek, phone Mr Cornel du Plessis whose contact number is available from Air Namibia.

Radio & TV

The Namibian Broadcasting Corporation (NBC) operates nine radio stations broadcasting on different wavebands in 12 languages. The national service broadcasts 24 hours a day, with news on the hour between 6 am and 1 pm on weekdays. On Saturday, there's news at 7, 8 and 11 am and 1, 6, 7, 9, 10 and 11 pm and midnight. On Sunday, the news broadcasts are at 8 and 11 am, 1, 7, 9, and 10 pm, and at midnight. German newscasts are also available.

NBC television broadcasts in English and Afrikaans from 5 to 11 pm weekdays and later on Friday and Saturday. On Sunday, they broadcast Christian programming from 11 am to 1 pm, then regular programming from 3 pm. News is broadcast at 8 pm nightly.

Only the larger hotels provide TV in rooms, but at some smaller places, it's an optional extra. In the big hotels, you can also tune into CNN.

WOMEN TRAVELLERS

Some Namibians dress conservatively, but in Windhoek and other urban areas, wearing shorts and sleeveless dresses or shirts is fine, and even in villages, Western dress is becoming more popular. However, if you're visiting former tribal areas or mission stations in the north, it's best to wear a knee-length skirt or loose-fitting trousers. Beach wear is okay in Swakopmund but it isn't really appropriate elsewhere.

Security-wise, solo female travellers should have few serious problems, but naturally, common sense is in order. By day, it's generally safe for a woman to walk around any of the towns, although in recent years, the number of rapes and muggings in Windhoek has increased. In Windhoek at night, always take a taxi if you're alone and don't walk through isolated areas alone at any time of day. In townships, seek local advice regarding dodgy areas to be avoided.

As for women hitching, Namibia is probably safer than Europe and considerably safer than North America. Although women should naturally try to hitch with a male companion – or at least in pairs – the greatest danger will be from drunken drivers.

DANGERS & ANNOYANCES

In Swakopmund, the Presidential Guard camps on the pavement near the president's summer palace when he is in residence. There have been a couple of incidents suggesting that the guards are trigger-happy, so it is wise to avoid them if possible.

En route to Lüderitz from the east, keep well clear of the Sperrgebiet, the prohibited diamond area. Well-armed patrols can be overly zealous and aren't interested in asking questions. immediately south of the A4 Lüderitz-Keetmanshoop road lies the off-limits area and it continues to just west of Aus, from where the Sperrgebiet boundary turns south towards the Orange River.

Except in central Windhoek and a couple of towns in the north, theft is not a serious problem anywhere in the country. However, Windhoek does have an increasing problem with petty theft and muggings, so it's sensible to try and avoid walking alone at night and conceal any valuables you must carry with you.

A particularly annoying problem is theft from camp sites – even those which are purportedly guarded. In Swakopmund, Grootfontein and to a lesser extent, Tsumeb, the public campgrounds are plagued by organised gangs of thieves. Anything left in a vehicle is at considerable risk, especially in Grootfontein, where tents are often robbed while their occupants sleep inside.

Kavango and Caprivi both have a serious mosquito problem so it is important to take all relevant antimalarial precautions. Bilharzia is present in the Kunene, Okavango, and Kwando-Mashi-Linyanti-Chobe river systems, and bathing is not recommended. The tsetse fly, present in East Caprivi, is especially active at dusk. All the northern rivers sustain large crocodile populations which pose a danger to swimmers, anglers and canoeists. There are also large numbers of hippos which will attack a boat even if unprovoked. To add a final cheerful note, leprosy is a relatively common disease in the north and Rundu has a large leper hospital.

WORK

The chances of a foreigner finding work in Namibia aren't terribly good, but having said that, some people are successful. The official policy is to accept only overseas investors starting up a business in the country or those who can provide skills and expertise not available locally. If you are offered a job, you (or better, your prospective employer) must secure a temporary residence permit from the Ministry of Home Affairs (☎ (061) 398 9111; fax (061) 223817), Private Bag 13200, Windhoek.

If you're interested in investing or starting a business in Namibia, direct enquiries to the Investment Centre, Ministry of Trade & Industry (☎ (061) 220241), Third Floor, Government Offices, Private Bag 13340, Windhoek.

Quite a number of overseas volunteer organisations – including the VSO and the Peace Corps as well as their German, Irish, Canadian, Australian and Scandinavian counterparts – have programmes in Namibia. However, none of these organisations allow volunteers to select their own postings, so your chances of winding up in Namibia will depend on the luck of the draw.

HIGHLIGHTS

Namibia is a large and sparsely populated country. Superimposed on a rich and diverse patina of African cultures is a modern and efficient infrastructure recalling the German and South African colonial legacies. The Teutonic angle adds a bizarre dimension: where else could you eat *sachertorte* on the edge of the desert, watching flamingoes overhead?

Etosha National Park A visit to Etosha National Park, the third largest in the world, is truly unique and memorable. The park surrounds a vast salt pan which occasionally holds water and attracts flocks of flamingoes. The surrounding bushveld is dotted with water holes where you can sit and watch the wildlife activity. Etosha has three rest camps of which the most striking is Namutoni, a whitewashed 'Beau Geste' German colonial fort.

The Namib No article about Namibia is complete without a photo of the brilliant waves of red and pink dunes which characterise the desert from which the country derives its name. For most visitors, the destination is the oasis of Sossusvlei, a desert pan which is surrounded by towering dunes and occasionally holds water. The northern part of the Namib is flatter and more stony, with isolated massifs protruding from the plains.

Fish River Canyon Fish River Canyon surely ranks as one of Africa's most spectacular natural wonders. Frequently compared to the Grand Canyon, it is an immense gorge, 161 km long, up to 27 km wide, and nearly 550 metres deep. At Ai-Ais, you can have a massage or beauty treatment, or luxuriate in hot mud springs.

Lüderitz The isolated and arid southern Namib is characterised by extraordinary pastel colours and the 'Little Bavaria' town of Lüderitz makes a good base for exploring it. Lüderitz is the northern anchor of the diamond-rich Sperrgebiet, and the nearby diamond ghost town of Kolmanskop is steadily being taken over by the dunes.

NAMIBIA

Caprivi National Parks & Game Reserves The Caprivi Strip, the corridor of land stretching eastward towards Zimbabwe and Zambia, has three small and remote national parks and game reserves – Mudumu, Mamili and Mahango – where you can experience a more verdant side of Namibia's character. Along the richly vegetated banks of the Okavango and Kwando-Mashi-Linyanti-Chobe rivers, you'll observe a range of wetland wildlife.

Waterberg Plateau Park This small national park is not only a lovely place to relax and enjoy the far-ranging views, it's also a repository for endangered African species, such as the white rhino. Visitors can either get around on foot or travel through the high plateau reserve on organised game drives.

Khaudom Game Reserve This wild and difficult-to-reach park in the north-east is an unexpected surprise. It's packed with every sort of wildlife found in Namibia and is so little visited that you're likely to have the whole place to yourself. Access is by 4WD only.

Swakopmund The coastal port of Swakopmund, with its long beach, provides more of a holiday atmosphere than Lüderitz. The language is German and it's packed with colonial architecture, little *konditorei* and beer gardens.

The Skeleton Coast & Damaraland The renowned Skeleton Coast, characterised by ethereal and fog-bound coastal scenery, has long been a graveyard for ships and their stranded crews. Don't miss the Cape Cross Seal Reserve, which is the best place to observe herds of Cape fur seals. The vast spaces of Damaraland provide habitat for a variety of desert species – outside any artificially protected reserve. Natural attractions include the imposing Spitzkoppe; the Brandberg massif with its many rock paintings; the rock engravings of Twyfelfontein; and the geologic wonders of the Petrified Forest and Burnt Mountain.

Windhoek Namibia's big smoke is a blend of German colonial and post-modernist 'birthday cake' architecture – much of the central area appears to be sweet and edible! All jumbled up among the bizarrely coloured high-rises and office blocks are splendid colonial buildings dating from the turn of the century. Overall, it's a clean and attractive capital city occupying a lovely setting amidst arid aloe-covered mountain ranges.

ACCOMMODATION
Namibia offers a range of accommodation for a range of budgets: hotels, rest camps, campgrounds/caravan parks, guest farms, backpackers' hostels, B&Bs, guesthouses and safari lodges. Hotels and most other establishments are graded using a star system; awards are based on regular inspections carried out by the Ministry of Environment & Tourism. Some establishments receive a T-grading, which indicates that they're primarily geared to foreign tourists. Hotels with restaurants also get a Y rating: YY means it only has a restaurant licence, while YYY indicates full licensing. An annual listing is available from tourist offices and travel agencies.

Accommodation and food are subject to a standard 11% general sales tax which is included in quoted prices. Because some hotels run special rates out of season, there's no harm in checking whether discounts are available.

To find advice or make bookings for guest farms and safari lodges, you may want to contact the central reservations agency, Lodge & Guest Farm Reservation Service (☎ 226979; fax 226999), PO Box 21783, Windhoek.

Camping
Most towns have campgrounds, which provide a green spot to pitch a tent or park a caravan. Camping prices are normally per site, with a maximum of eight people and two vehicles per site. Some campgrounds and caravan parks also have bungalows or rondavels as well as a pool, restaurant and shop. There's no central reservations system, but private and municipal campgrounds and caravan parks are rarely full, so you're unlikely to be turned away.

Camping in national parks is restricted to designated sites and bush camping on public land isn't permitted without special permission. MET enforces this rule strictly and it's certainly wise to keep on the better side of this organisation. For more information, see MET Rest Camps & Resorts later in this section. To camp on private or communal land, you'll need permission from the land owner or the nearest village, respectively.

Backpackers' Hostels
There are now several Hostelling International Hostels and private Backpackers'

Flamingo

Flamingoes flock in large numbers around the salts pans of Botswana and Namibia, and in pools along the Namibian coast, particularly around Walvis Bay and Sandwich Harbour. They're especially attracted by the proliferation of algae and crustaceans which thrive in the intermittent lakes of the Nata Delta in Botswana and Etosha Pan in Namibia. Flamingoes are excellent fliers and have been known to cover up to 500 km overnight.

Flamingoes have a complicated and sophisticated system for filtering the foodstuffs from highly alkaline – and toxic – soda lakes, seawater and brackish pans. Lesser flamingoes filter algae and diatoms from the water by sucking in and vigourously expelling water from its bill – which is held upside down in the water – several times per second. The minute particles are caught on fine hair-like protrusions which line the inside of the mandibles. The suction is created by the thick fleshy tongue which rests in a groove in the lower mandible and pumps back and forth like a piston. It has been estimated that a million lesser flamingoes can consume over 180 tonnes of algae and diatoms daily!

While lesser flamingoes obtain food by filtration, the greater flamingo is more a bottom feeder and supplements its algae diet with small molluscs, crustaceans and other organic particles from the mud. When feeding, it will rotate in a circle stamping its feet, apparently to scare out potential meals.

The greater and lesser flamingoes are best distinguished by their colouration. Greater flamingoes are white to light pink, and their beaks are whitish with a black tip. Lesser flamingoes are a deeper pink – often reddish – colour and have dark red beaks. ■

Hostels in Windhoek and Swakopmund, and more are planned, including a private hostel for Rundu in the near future. As with hostels anywhere, they provide dormitory accommodation and cooking facilities for very reasonable prices, ranging from US$6 to US$10 per person.

Hotels

The Namibian hotel-classification system rates everything from small guesthouses to four-star hotels.

One-star hotels must have private bathrooms or showers in at least one quarter of the rooms, and at least one communal bathroom or toilet for every eight other beds. They tend to be quite simple, but do provide clean, comfortable accommodation with adequate beds and towels. Rates range from around US$19 to US$25 (N$70 to N$90) for a double room, with bed and breakfast.

Hotels are most expensive in Windhoek, Swakopmund and Lüderitz. Most are locally owned and managed. They always have a small dining room and a bar, but few offer any frills, such as air conditioning.

To get a two-star rating, at least half the rooms must have private facilities and communal facilities for every seven other rooms. They must also have a heating system, a full-time head chef and 14-hour reception service. This is the most common hotel classification and takes in a wide range of establishments. Prices start at around US$27 (N$100) and climb right up to US$54 (N$200) a double at such places as The Strand in Swakopmund.

There are only a few three-star hotels, which must conform to minimum international standards: private bathrooms, heating, wall-to-wall carpets, a range of public rooms and lounges, 24-hour reception, room service and an à la carte restaurant. Double rates begin at around US54 (N$200).

Currently, there's one four-star hotel in the country – the Kalahari Arms in Windhoek – but more are planned. Essentially, to get a four-star rating, a hotel needs to be an air-conditioned palace with all the amenities of a three-star hotel plus a salon, valet service and range of ancillary services aimed at the business and diplomatic traveller.

Any hotel whose name includes the word 'Garni' means that it doesn't have a full dining room, but is only equipped to handle a simple breakfast.

Guest Farms

A growing number of private farms are also opening up to tourists, and provide insight into the rural White lifestyle. Many of these farms have also set aside large blocks of land as wildlife reserves and offer excellent wild-life-viewing. Other such farms serve only as hunting reserves.

Thanks to the recent drought, many private farms are turning to tourism to keep afloat, so it's difficult to keep track of them. The most outstanding ones are described in this book; for a complete listing see the booklet *Namibia – Accommodation Guide for Tourists*, which is available from most hotels and tourist offices around the country.

Guest farms have a rating system based on a scale of one to three stars. Generally more expensive than hotels, they seldom have more than half a dozen rooms and you need to book well in advance. The emphasis is on personal service and often, there's even a measure of quaint rural luxury.

In all cases, advance bookings are essential. When booking, ascertain that the farm isn't designated for hunting only (unless you're a hunter, of course). Some farms have a set 'hunting season' but are open for photography and wildlife viewing at other times of year.

It seems the biggest problem with guest farms is their preoccupation with keeping wild animals in zoo-like enclosures. This is curious, considering that most of these farms

are attached to game ranches which could only be called vast, with plenty of room for animals to run free. If enough visitors question the practice, perhaps guest farm owners will realise the majority of foreigners would prefer to see the animals in the wild.

MET National Parks Camps, Rest Camps & Resorts

You'll find excellent accommodation value at the Rest Camps and Resorts administered by the Ministry of Environment & Tourism. For details on booking, see National Parks Permits & Accommodation, under Flora & Fauna in the Namibia Facts About the Country chapter.

Camp sites in the National Parks' and Rest Camps all accommodate up to eight people and cost from US$3 for an undeveloped wilderness site up to US$7 for a site in a large rest camp, with access to a pool, shop, restaurant, kiosk and well-maintained ablutions blocks.

In addition, MET offers a range of other accommodation possibilities. All MET accommodation is self-catering, but most resorts have a restaurant and shop. Linen, towels and soap are normally provided, but guests must bring their own cutlery and cooking gear. National Parks' accommodation may be occupied from noon on the day of arrival to 10 am on the day of departure.

Prices are determined by the number of rooms, beds and the degree of luxury. For example, a four-bed flat with kitchen facilities, a toilet and a hot shower runs US$35; a four-bed hut with communal facilities and a cooking area is just US$21; two/five-bed bungalows with kitchens, toilets and showers cost US$16/33; and a 10-bed dormitory room is just US$16. The most expensive option is at Terrace Bay in the Skeleton Coast Park, where single/double accommodation, including all facilities and meals, costs US$44/68.

Namibian residents receive a 20% discount on park entrance fees (but not on vehicle or accommodation fees) at all MET sites. During school holidays, visitors are limited to three nights at each camp at Etosha National Park and 10 nights at all other camps. Pets aren't permitted in any of the rest camps, but kennels are available at the gates of Daan Viljoen, Von Bach Dam, Gross-Barmen, Ai-Ais and Hardap Dam. ■

Safari Lodges

As with other accommodation sectors in Namibia, a new crop of safari lodges is also sprouting around the country. A majority of these are set on large private ranches and offer luxurious standards of accommodation and superb international cuisine. As yet, Namibian safari lodges offer several advantages over their counterparts in Zimbabwe and Botswana. First of all, there's no multi-tier pricing, so foreigners and Namibians pay the same reasonable rates. A night in a lodge outside Etosha National Park, for example, will cost a third of what you'd pay for comparable accommodation in the Okavango Delta. What's more, prices are usually set per person, with no single supplement charges, so lone travellers aren't penalised.

FOOD
Traditional Cuisine

Each ethnic group within the country has its own pantry of preferred foods. For example, the staple for the Ovambo people of the north is mielie pap, which is merely the same corn-meal porridge enjoyed in Zimbabwe, Botswana and all around Africa. The second grain favoured in Ovamboland is mahango (millet), which is made into either a porridge or a soup. Both mielies and mahango are typically eaten with fish, goat, lamb or beef stew cooked in a potjie, a three-legged black pot. Pumpkins, peppers and onions also feature prominently in the Ovambo diet.

The spiny round !nara melons (Acanthosicyos horrida), which is a member of the cucumber family whose spiny bushes grow in places where it can tap subsurface water, is popular among the Nama people. They grow on vines along watercourses. The melon may be made into a naturally sweet cake, dried into flour or mashed and fermented to yield a sweet beer. The roots are said to have medicinal properties. It grows in the lower reaches of the Kuiseb.

The !nara (the exclamation mark is pronounced as a glottal click) figured prominently in the culture of the Nama people and each year during the harvest you can see donkey carts full of the spiky fruit being transported by the Nama back to camp to be dried and prepared for consumption. The seeds are then removed from the rind and dried for eating. The pulp is spread on the sand to make a kind of chewy cake which preserves well. The !nara seems to have been utilised in this way for tens of thousands of years, and the museum in Swakopmund has a full rundown on the plant's uses.

Historically, the Herero subsisted mainly from milk products such as curds and butter, and they still enjoy these staples to some extent, but nowadays, the Herero diet revolves around mielies, meat and locally grown black beans.

Although the San people are now adopting the diet of other Namibians, their traditional diet depended upon their wanderings and the cycle of the seasons. It consisted mainly of various desert plants – wild fruits, nuts, berries and tubers which ripened in turn – as well as birds' eggs (especially ostrich eggs – one of which can feed an entire clan), lizards, locusts and game hunted with small, poison-tipped arrows.

European Cuisine

Outside Windhoek and Swakopmund, you won't find many gourmet pretences in Namibia. Hotels all serve three meals, but menus are normally meat-orientated and aren't normally creative.

For a great treat, try one of the German-style konditorei where you can pig out on apfelstrüdel, sachertorte, Schwartzwälder kirschtorte and other delicious pastries and cakes. Gathemann's in Windhoek and Anton's in Swakopmund are national institutions, and Windhoek, Swakopmund, Lüderitz and other towns have pleasant cafes and small coffee shops. You may also want to try Afrikaner koeksesters and melktart. For after dinner, it's worth remembering Windhoek also produces delicious but expensive Springer liqueur chocolates.

Cooked breakfasts always include bacon and boerewors or 'farmer's sausage' (few people get through more than one of these), and don't be surprised to find something bizarre – curried kidneys for example –

NAMIBIA

alongside your eggs. Some people still eat beef for breakfast.

Small hotels normally provide a cooked breakfast with cereal and toast, and most big hotels include a buffet breakfast in the room price. In addition to the usual English breakfast constituents, they may also include such delights as kippers (smoked kingklip), porridge and a range of German breads, cold meat, cereal and fruit. If you take full advantage of what's on offer, you may not have to eat again for the rest of the day.

For lunch, one of the cheapest ways to go is a takeaway snack. Takeaway favourites include fish & chips, meat pies and sandwiches made in a German-style bread roll known as *brötchen* or 'little bread'.

Evening meals feature mainly meat – normally beef – and carnivores will enjoy the typically high-quality cuts served in restaurants. A huge fillet steak will set you back about US$8. Fish, almost always kingklip, is best eaten in Swakopmund or Lüderitz where there's a good chance of its being fresh. Chicken is most often prepared with a fiery hot peri-peri sauce.

Fruit & Vegetables

Namibia's small fruit and vegetable crops ripen during the winter season, roughly from May to September. At other times, fresh fruit and vegetables must be imported from South Africa and are quite expensive, so Namibians aren't great connoisseurs of fresh produce and vegetarianism hasn't really caught on. As a result, chips are the most popular potato incarnation and green vegetables are served sparingly and often from a tin or the deep freeze.

Among the most popular fresh vegetables are gems squash, a small and delicious green squash; pumpkin, and butternut squash; which resembles a gourd. Fruit is generally expensive, but in season the oranges are delicious. In the Kavango region, papayas are picked with a six-metre pole and a basket to catch them, and are served with a squeeze of lemon or lime.

For longer road trips, you can buy fruit in bulk at Windhoek supermarkets, at the open market in Tal Strasse or at one of the wholesalers in the North Windhoek Industrial Estate. In northern Namibia and occasionally elsewhere, fruit is often sold at roadside stalls.

Self-Catering

All major towns have at least one supermarket selling basic necessities. Because groceries become more expensive the further you move from Windhoek, it's wise to stock up with provisions before setting out on a tour of the country. Many places also have corner shops, often Portuguese owned, which sell everything from animal feed to spit-roasted chicken.

You'll find the best variety of meat and sausage, or *wors*, at the *slagtery* (butcher shop). Biltong (dried meat in strips or shavings), either beef or *wildsbiltong* (normally gemsbok or ostrich) comes in several shapes and sizes. There is also a variety of German salami and smoked meats, as well as an utterly solid 15-cm variety known as *landjäger*. It's normally gnawed like a bone, but it's cheap, tasty and lasts a long time.

Cheese is expensive and there's little variety; Edam is the most popular type. Campers may want to buy tinned fetta (goat's milk cheese), which last considerably longer than plastic-wrapped cheeses.

DRINKS
Nonalcoholic Drinks

Tap water is safe to drink but in some places, it may emerge rather salty and unpalatable, especially around the desert areas and Etosha. Bottled water is expensive and is available only in one-litre containers.

Packaged fruit juices provide an alternative; the best are the locally produced Ceres juices, which are 100% natural juice. Another popular brand from South Africa is Liquifruit. Both brands offer apricot, peach, mango-pineapple and combinations. Peach juice mixed with sparkling wine makes a refreshing cocktail. The cheapest are orange and guava juice.

Every takeaway place serves coffee and

tea – including an insipid herbal tea known as *rooibos* (red bush), which reputedly has therapeutic properties. Both Windhoek and Swakopmund have several particularly fine coffee shops.

Alcohol
You'll always find a pleasant place for a drink. All Namibian hotels have an attached bar, and some larger hotels feature a beer garden with table service. Many serve food as well as drink, but some open only in the evening. The bars in smaller, inexpensive hotels, however, are less sophisticated; and away from the cities and tourist lodges, you won't find cocktails or mixed drinks. Many cafés also serve wine and beer. On Sunday out of licensing hours, alcoholic drinks are available only at hotel bars.

Alcohol isn't sold in supermarkets, but must be bought from a *drankwinkel* (bottle store), which also sells ice. Standard opening hours are weekdays from 8 am to 6 pm and Saturday from 8.30 am to 1 pm.

Beer Namibia's dry heat makes an ideal environment for beer drinkers and the country's greatest producer of the amber fluid is Namibia Breweries (formerly Southwest Breweries). Certainly the most popular drop is Windhoek Lager, a light lager-style beer that is distinct and refreshing. It comes in standard lager strength, packaged in cans and bottles of varying sizes from a 375-ml *dumpi* (equivalent to the Australian stubby) to a 'large' 500-ml bottle. A dumpi costs from US$0.75 to US$1.25 in a beer garden; drankwinkels charge US$10 or so for a tray of 24 bottles. Namibia Breweries also produces the stronger and more bitter Windhoek Export, the slightly rough Windhoek Special and Windhoek Light, which has a 1.9% alcohol content, but is still quite agreeable. Guinness Extra Stout is also brewed under licence.

Windhoek's main competitor is Hansa, in Swakopmund, which produces both standard and export strength. In the far north, the preferred drop is Cuca, of Angolan origin, which has become so popular that it's also brewed in Swakopmund. South African beers like Lion, Castle and Black Label are widely available.

When you're camping in the wilderness, an excellent means of cooling a beer or soft drink without refrigeration is to soak a sock in water and place the cans or bottles inside and tie it from a branch – or even your side mirrors. The contents are cooled as heat is drawn away from the liquid to provide energy for evaporation – and it really works.

Wine You'll also find a range of typically excellent South African wines. Most bottle stores stock everything from 750-ml bottles to large one to five-litre boxes and economy-size one or two-litre jars. South African red wines definitely have the edge; among the best are the cabernet and pinot varieties grown in the Stellenbosch region of the Cape Province. Nederberg Winery produces particularly good wines, which are available in both 250 and 750-ml bottles.

Liqueur Namibia's speciality liqueur is Amarula Cream, which is distilled from the marula fruit. It tastes a bit like Bailey's Irish Cream – but arguably better – and is best chilled or served over ice.

Traditional Brews In the rural areas of Ovamboland, people socialise in tiny makeshift bars, enjoying such inexpensive local brews as *mahango* (millet beer); *mataku* (watermelon wine); *tambo* or *mushokolo* (a beer made from a type of small seed); and *walende*, which is distilled from the makalani palm and tastes similar to vodka. All of these confections but the walende are brewed in the morning and drunk the same day, and they're all dirt cheap – around US$0.10 per glass. Some, especially the mahango are excellent.

ENTERTAINMENT
Naturally, Namibia's entertainment capital is Windhoek, with a range of bars, discos and

Ngoma drums - made from the mutiti tree

night clubs to suit every taste. The capital also offers cinemas, theatre productions, concerts and sporting events. The beach resort of Swakopmund, with several discos and a lighthearted atmosphere, is a favourite with Namibia's more affluent youth.

In northern Namibia, the local social scene is dominated by the hundreds of cuca shops, bush bars, bottle stores and roadside discos and night clubs. At the bush bars, you can enjoy popular traditional alcoholic brews, such as *mahango* and *tambo*, along with a bit of relaxation and conversation. Especially in Ovamboland, both men and women participate in these sessions.

THINGS TO BUY

Potential souvenirs range from kitsch African curios and airport art to superb Ovambo basketry and Kavango woodcarvings. Most of the items sold along Post Street Mall in Windhoek are cheap curios imported from Zimbabwe; in Victoria Falls, you'll find the same things at a fraction of the price. Along the highway between Rundu and Grootfontein, numerous roadside stalls sell locally produced items, from woven mats and baskets to the appealing wooden aeroplanes and helicopters, which are a Kavango speciality.

In Rundu and other areas of the north-east, you'll find distinctive San material arts –

bows and arrows, ostrich-egg beads, leather pouches and jewellery made from seeds and nuts.

The pastel colours of the Namib provide inspiration for a number of local artists, and many galleries in Windhoek and Swakopmund specialise in local paintings and sculpture. Also, some lovely items are produced in conjunction with the karakul wool industry, such as rugs, wall hangings and textiles, which are often made to order. Windhoek is the centre of the up-market leather industry, and you'll find high-quality products, from belts and handbags to beautiful made-to-measure leather jackets. Beware, however, of items made from crocodile or other protected species, and note that those comfortable shoes known as *Swakopmunders* are made from kudu leather. Several shops have now stopped selling them.

Minerals and gemstones are also popular purchases, either in the raw form or cut and polished as jewellery, sculptures or carvings. Malachite, amethyst, chalcedony, aquamarine, tourmaline, jasper and rose quartz are among the most beautiful. Chess sets and other art objects are made from marble quarried near Karibib. A good spot to find an honest deal is the House of Gems near the corner of Stübel St and John Meinert Strasse in Windhoek.

For something different, you may want to look for an *ekipa*, a traditional medallion historically worn by Ovambo women as a sign of wealth and status. They were worn in strings hung from the waist and were originally made from ivory or hippopotamus tooth but later carved from bone, wood or vegetable ivory (the fruit of the makalani palm). Early ekipa were buried in urine soaked earth to achieve the necessary yellowed effect, and were decorated with geometric designs. They're available in a few speciality shops in Windhoek and Swakopmund.

Buying souvenirs made from protected wild species – cheetah, leopard, elephant or (heaven forbid) rhino – isn't necessary or ethically defensible. In Windhoek and other

NAMIBIA

places, you'll see lots of ivory pieces and jewellery for sale, but anything which is imported from manufacturers in Hong Kong is of highly dubious origin and should be avoided at all costs. The only legitimate stuff

is clearly marked as culled ivory from Namibian national parks. Still, it's better to avoid ivory altogether and stop fuelling the trade which makes poaching (and culling) profitable.

NAMIBIA

Getting There & Away

AIR

South African Airways (SAA) operates daily flights between Johannesburg, Cape Town and Windhoek's International Airport, which is about 42 km east of the city. Air Namibia has daily flights from Windhoek's in-town Eros Airport to and from Alexander Bay, which is the airport for Oranjemund. A single fare to Johannesburg or Cape Town costs around US$175.

Air Namibia also flies to Windhoek twice weekly from Harare, Lusaka, Maun and Gaborone.

LAND
Border Crossings

There are border-control posts between Namibia and Botswana at Ngoma Bridge (6 am to 7 pm), Buitepos/Mamuno (7 am to 5 pm), Mohembo/Mahango (6 am to 7 pm) and Mpalila Island/Kasane (7 am to 5 pm). The only border post between Namibia and Zambia is at Wenela/Sesheke (6 am to 7 pm), four km north of Katima Mulilo. You can cross between Namibia and Angola at Rundu/Calai (7 am to 5 pm), Oshikango/Namacunda (6 am to 7 pm) and Ruacana/Koaleck (6 am to 10 pm).

Road traffic between South Africa and Namibia crosses the border at Velloorsdrift-Onseepkans/Pofadder (6 am to 10 pm), Karasburg/Nonieput (6 am to 5 pm), Nakop/Ariamsvlei (24 hours), Hohlweg-Aroab/Rietfontein (7 am to 9 pm), Klein Menasse-Aroab/Rietfontein (7 am to 9 pm) or Noordoewer/Vioolsdrift (24 hours). This last option is on the main tarred road between Windhoek and Cape Town. There's no public access between Alexander Bay and Oranjemund without permission from the diamond company CDM; the border crossing is open from 6 am to 10 pm.

To/From Angola

There are three border crossings to Angola, at Ruacana, Oshikango and Rundu, but you'll need an Angolan visa permitting overland entry. Most tourists to Angola pick up their visas in Windhoek. The address of the Angolan consulate is Angola House (☎ 227535), 3 Auspann Strasse, Private Bag 12020, Windhoek.

At Ruacana Falls, you can enter the border area temporarily without a visa; just sign in at the border post.

To/From Botswana

A gravel road from Windhoek through Gobabis to Botswana crosses the border at Buitepos. On the Botswana side, it's currently only suitable for 4WD traffic, but the new tarred Trans-Kalahari Highway to Gaborone should be completed in the next couple of years, and there should be some sort of international public transport.

On the Namibian side, the *East Gate Service Station & Rest Camp* is a clean and friendly stop with inexpensive camp sites and bungalows. It's particularly handy for hitchers between Namibia and Botswana who are unable to find a lift or have missed the 5-pm border closing. By contrast, there's nothing on the Botswana side but a dusty spot at the border post where you can pitch a tent. Those coming from Namibia may want to wait for a lift on the Namibian side. That way, this place provides an option if you fail to find something before the border closes.

You can also cross between Namibia and Botswana via the Caprivi Strip, at either Ngoma Bridge or Mohembo (the Botswana side of the Mohembo crossing requires 4WD). Sparse traffic makes hitching unreliable, but you'll eventually get through. The new border crossing between Mpalila Island and Kasane is mainly for the benefit of tourist lodges on the island.

The Windhoek-Harare bus described under To/From Zimbabwe, later in this chapter, passes through Kasane, so it's also an option for reaching northern Botswana.

To/From South Africa

Bus A luxury Intercape Mainliner (☎ 227847) coach service from Windhoek to Capetown (US$90) or Johannesburg (US$92) runs twice weekly. In South Africa, book through their offices in Cape Town (☎ (021) 386 4400) or Johannesburg (☎ (011) 333 5231).

Alternatively, there's the more basic *P E Doyle Executive Liner & DD Minibus Services* (☎ (061) 214182 or 213459), which runs from Windhoek to Cape Town on Friday for US$50, including meals. The *Ekonoliner* bus (☎ (0642) 5935), which is based in Walvis Bay, also leaves for Cape Town on Friday, and returns on Sunday. Stand-by one-way tickets are US$52, with meals.

Train There's a US$26/62 economy/sleeper rail link between Windhoek and De Aar, South Africa, which passes through Ariamsvlei and Upington. The trip takes around 36 hours. At De Aar, you'll find convenient rail connections to both Johannesburg and Cape Town.

Car & Motorbike You can drive to Namibia along good tarred roads from South Africa, either from Cape Town in the south, crossing the border at Noordoewer; or from Johannesburg in the east, with a border crossing at Nakop. A major alternative route is the gravel road into south-eastern Namibia between Rietfontein and Aroab.

Hitching You can drive or hitch to Cape Town along good tarred roads, crossing the border at Noordoewer, or to Upington with a border crossing at Nakop. Hitching is easiest with trucks but most drivers want payment, so agree on a price before climbing aboard. The standard rate is around US$1.50

per 100 km, but they'll probably want more initially.

To/From Zambia

There is a border crossing between Namibia and Zambia at Wenela/Sesheke (open 6 am to 7 pm) about four km north of Katima Mulilo. The only other point of access is via the ferry at Kazungula but to get there you must use the Chobe National Park transit route via northern Botswana. From Livingstone, buses leave for Sesheke at 8 am and 2 pm each day; the trip takes around five hours over a horrible potholed road. From Sesheke to Livingstone, buses leave at around 7 am and 1 pm.

Zambia's UBZ Line has a Grootfontein-Lusaka bus service which runs weekly via Katima Mulilo and Livingstone. The fare to Livingstone will cost you US$35; to Lusaka, it's US$47. For information, phone the office (☎ 2222) in Grootfontein.

To/From Zimbabwe

There's no direct route between Namibia and Zimbabwe: to get there you must take the Chobe National Park transit route from Ngoma Bridge through northern Botswana to Kasane/Kazungula, and from there to Victoria Falls.

There's now a direct bus service between Windhoek and Harare, leaving the Wernhill Park Centre bus terminal in Windhoek on Friday at 7 am, calling in at Katima Mulilo on Saturday at 11 am, Victoria Falls (Zimbabwe) on Sunday at 7 am and arriving in Harare on Monday morning. The fare from Windhoek to Harare is US$92; to Victoria Falls it's US$75. Book at the Tourist Rendezvous Information Centre on Peter Müller Strasse.

NAMIBIA

Getting Around

AIR

Air Namibia services domestic routes out of Eros Airport in Windhoek, including flights to and from Tsumeb; Rundu and Katima Mulilo; Keetmanshoop; Lüderitz and Alexander Bay (South Africa); and Swakopmund and Oshakati.

Air Namibia Offices

Air Namibia has the following offices:

Central Reservations, Windhoek (☎ (061) 298 2552; fax (061) 221382)

Eros Airport, Windhoek (☎ (061) 238220; fax (061) 236460)

Gustav Voigts Centre, Independence Ave, Windhoek (☎ (061) 229630; fax (061) 228763)

International Airport, Windhoek (☎ (0626) 40315; fax (0626) 40367)

Katima Mulilo (☎ /fax (067352) 191)

Keetmanshoop (☎ (0631) 2337; fax (0631) 292290)

Lüderitz (☎ (06331) 2850; fax (06331) 2845)

Oshakati (☎ (06751) 20284; fax (06751) 21230)

Oranjemund (☎ (06332) 2764; fax (06332) 2225)

Rundu (☎ (067372) 854)

Swakopmund (☎ (0641) 4123; fax (0641) 2196)

Tsumeb (☎ (0671) 20520; fax (0671) 20821)

Walvis Bay (☎ (0642) 3102; fax (0642) 2928)

Air Charter

Namibia has a few air charter operations, but they tend to be expensive. One is Bay Air (☎ (0642) 4319) in Walvis Bay and another is Namibia Commercial Aviation (☎ (061) 223562) at Eros Airport in Windhoek. Typical return prices for up to five passengers would be US$1650 from Eros to Victoria Falls, US$1975 from Eros to Etosha and US$700 from Eros and Swakopmund.

BUS

Bus services in Namibia aren't extensive, but there are a couple of options. Luxury services are limited to the Intercape Mainliner, which has scheduled services between Windhoek, Cape Town and Johannesburg; they also serve Swakopmund, Walvis Bay and Tsumeb. On any of these services, you're

limited to two items of baggage, which can't exceed a total of 30 kg. Fares include meals.

There are also local minibuses which run up and down the B1 from Oshakati to Keetmanshoop. They depart from the corner of John Meinert and Mandume Ndomufayo Sts running from Windhoek to Swakopmund and Walvis Bay. Those heading south to Rehoboth, Mariental and Keetmanshoop leave from the large car park north of the Wernhill Park Centre; and those going north to Ovamboland and Kavango leave from the singles quarters in Katutura township. However, it would be unwise to turn up in Katutura with all your luggage; it's probably safer to wait on the bridge at the Independence Ave on-ramp to the Western Bypass.

Minibuses depart when full. Fares work out to around US$0.03 per km, and there's often an additional charge of US$2.70 (N$10) per large piece of luggage. There are additional services from Windhoek on Friday afternoons, especially on the route north to Ovamboland; coming from Ovamboland, extra services are added on Sunday afternoon.

The Trans-Namib Railways also operates buses between Keetmanshoop and Lüderitz and between Otjiwarongo and Outjo.

TRAIN

Trans-Namib Railways operates a reasonable rail network between most major towns but trains are slow – as one reader remarked, moving 'at the pace of an energetic donkey cart'. In addition, passenger and freight cars are mixed on the same train which tends to stop at every post.

On the other hand, because rail travel isn't a popular mode of transport, services are very rarely booked out. All trains carry economy and sleeper classes; sleepers offer four or six-bed compartments, while the very economical 3rd-class carriages have only seats. Book in advance if you want a sleeper; if there are no bookings, they don't bother to include the 1st-class carriage. Make advance bookings at any railway station or through the Windhoek Booking Office (☎ (061) 2982032). Tickets must be collected before 4 pm on the day of departure.

Windhoek is Namibia's rail hub, with service south to De Aar, South Africa (with easy connections to Cape Town and Johannesburg), and service north to Tsumeb, west to Swakopmund and Walvis Bay and east to Gobabis. Note that on weekends (Friday to Monday), fares are normally double what they are during the week. Some sample economy/sleeper fares are Windhoek to Keetmanshoop US$5/16 (weekdays) and US$11/33 (weekends); Gobabis US$5/13; Swakopmund US$3/9 (weekdays) and US$7/20 (weekends); Walvis Bay US$5/13 (weekdays) and US$10/29 (weekends); Tsumeb US$13/39; Upington (US$16/44); and De Aar US$26/62.

CAR & MOTORBIKE

By far the easiest way to get around Namibia is by road. There is an excellent system of tarred roads running the entire length of the country from the South African border at Nakop and Noordoewer to Divundu in the north-east and Ruacana in the north-west. As soon as construction is completed on the 200-km stretch between Divundu and Kongola in the Caprivi Strip, you'll be able to drive all the way from the South African border to Katima Mulilo on good tar.

Similarly, tarred spur roads connect the main north-south arteries to Gobabis, Lüderitz, Swakopmund and Walvis Bay. Towns and sites of interest around the rest of the country are normally accessible on good gravel roads. As a general rule, B and C-numbered highways are well maintained and passable to all vehicles. D-numbered roads may be a bit rougher, but are still normally (but not always) passable to 2WD vehicles. In the Kaokoveld, however, most D-numbered roads require 4WD.

Cars are required to drive on the left, as in the rest of southern Africa. There's a general speed limit of 120 km/h on open roads and 60 km/h in built-up areas. Drivers and passengers in the front seat must use seat belts. Petrol currently costs around US$0.45 (N$1.50) per litre.

Driving in Namibia theoretically requires an international driving licence, but in practice a valid driving licence from your own country is usually enough. Note that motorbikes aren't permitted in any of the national parks, with the exception of the main routes through Namib-Naukluft park.

Car Hire

Car hire is expensive, but if you have a group, it's the best and most straightforward way of seeing the country. Bear in mind that agencies are open only on weekdays during office hours. Remember that to the advertised daily rate and km charge, you'll need to add collision damage waiver, stamp duty and 10% general sales tax (GST). Because vehicles are in limited supply, book your car well in advance.

To drive a hire car into a neighbouring country, you'll need special paperwork. For South Africa, Botswana or elsewhere in the Southern African customs union, you need only the 'Blue Book', a sheet outlining the vehicle's particulars, such as the engine's serial number and the like. If you're continuing to Zimbabwe, ask for proof of insurance and all paperwork necessary to get a temporary export permit.

Note that some of the big car hire agencies will allow you to return vehicles to Cape Town for only the cost of the petrol; the catch is, you have only 24 hours to get there.

The least expensive companies would typically charge US$43 to US$55 per day with unlimited km (some have a minimum rental period) for a basic compact car. Most require a US$285 (N$1000) deposit and won't hire to anyone under the age of 25; most also hire 4WD vehicles. Note that it's normally cheaper to hire a car in South Africa and drive it over the border, but you'll need special permission from the car hire agency.

The best value 4WD hire is with Namib

NAMIBIA

Gravel Roads

Many main highways in Namibia are surfaced with unsealed gravel. Driving on gravel roads can be at best tricky and at worst treacherous. The following points may help:

- Keep your speed down to a maximum of 100 km/h.
- Follow ruts made by other vehicles.
- If the road is corrugated, gradually increase your speed until you find the correct speed – it'll be obvious when the rattling stops.
- Be especially careful on bends; if a curve is signposted, slow right down before attempting the turn.
- You don't meet other cars very often, but when you do, it's like dust clouds passing in the night. When a vehicle approaches from the opposite direction, reduce your speed and keep as far left as possible. On remote roads, it's customary to wave at the other driver as you pass.
- Keep your tyre pressure slightly lower than you would when driving on tarred roads.
- Try to avoid travelling at night when dust and distance create all sorts of confusing mirages.
- In rainy weather, gravel roads can turn to quagmires and desert washes may fill with water. If you're uncertain about the depth of the water in a wash, don't cross until it drains off.
- Be on the lookout for animals. Kudus, in particular pose problems at night and they don't move out of the way, often resulting in an unpleasant meeting.
- Avoid swerving sharply or braking suddenly on a gravel road or you risk losing control of the vehicle. If the rear wheels do go into a skid, steer gently into the direction of the skid until you regain control. If the front wheels skid, take a firm hand on the wheel and steer in the opposite direction of the skid.
- Dust permeates everything on gravel roads; wrap your food, clothing and camera equipment in dust-proof plastic or keep them in sealed containers.
- In dusty conditions, switch on your headlights so you can be more easily seen. Overtaking passing) can be extremely dangerous because your view ahead will normally be obscured by flying dust kicked up by the car ahead. Try to gain the attention of the driver in front of you by flashing your high beams, which will indicate that you want to overtake (this isn't considered obnoxious in Namibia). If someone behind you flashes their lights, move as far to the left as possible. If you can see that it's safe for them to overtake, flash your left turn indicator. ■

4x4, which charges as little as US$70 per day (minimum five days) with unlimited km. If you prefer a Land Rover, excellent deals are available from Swakop-Auto Rent in Swakopmund.

If you are paying by credit card, make sure you insist on a copy of the contract so you will know the charge for any excess km. If you pay a cash deposit and you are returning the car to the airport before you leave, make sure the deposit is repaid in a currency you can use outside the country and not a cheque for Namibian currency! Also, make sure it's absolutely clear what sort of repairs will be your responsibility; if at all possible, try to limit it to just tyres and windows. Otherwise, they may try to charge you for anything from wheel alignment to dust sitting on the back seat.

In the following list of car, camper and 4WD hire agencies, an asterisk denotes an inexpensive option:

Adventure 4 Hire PO Box 9544, Windhoek (☎ 226188; fax 224936)

Asco Car Hire, 10 Diehl St, Southern Industrial Area, Windhoek (☎ /fax (061) 232245)

Avis Car Hire, Hotel Safari, Jean St, PO Box 2057, Windhoek (☎ (061) 233166; fax (061) 223072)
10 Moltke Strasse, Swakopmund (☎ (0641) 2527; fax (0641) 5881)
Safari Centre, Jordaan St, Tsumeb (☎ (0671) 20520; fax (0671) 20821)
Rooikop Airport, Walvis Bay (☎ /fax (0642) 7527)

Bonanza Car Hire, Tal Total Service Station, Mandume Ndomufayo St, Windhoek (☎ (061) 240317; fax (061) 240318)
Dolphin Motors, 38 Kaiser Wilhelm Strasse, Swakopmund (☎ (0641) 4503; fax (0641) 5273)
Cash Service Station, on the corner of 13 Rd and 8th St, Walvis Bay (☎ /fax (0642) 5936)

Budget Car Hire, 72 Mandume Ndomufayo, Windhoek (☎ (061) 228720; fax (061) 227655) Roon St, PO Box 180, Swakopmund (☎ (0641) 4118; fax (0641) 4117)
  Suidwes Diensstasie, on the corner of 10th and 13th Sts, PO Box 1591, Walvis Bay (☎ (0642) 4624; fax (0642) 2931)

Camping Car Hire on the corner of Edison and Mandume Ndomufayo Sts, PO Box 5526, Windhoek (☎ (061) 237756; fax (061) 237757)

Cardboard Box Car Hire 15 Johan Albrecht St, Windhoek West (☎ 228994; fax 52128)

Champion Car Hire, PO Box 6221, Windhoek (☎ (061) 51306; fax (061) 51620)

Econo Car Hire Mezzanine Floor, Levinson Arcade, PO Box 2656, Windhoek (☎ (061) 236675; fax (061) 227841)

Imperial Car Hire, 43 Stübel St, Windhoek (☎ (061) 227103; fax (061) 222721)

Kessler 4x4 Hire, on the corner of Sam Nujoma and Mandume Ndomufayo, PO Box 20274, Windhoek (☎ (061) 233451; fax (061) 224551)

Namib 4x4 Hire, 90 Gobabis Rd, La Pardiz Centre, Windhoek (☎ (061) 220604; fax (061) 220605) 22 Kaiser Wilhelm Strasse, PO Box 4048, Swakopmund (☎ (0641) 4100; fax (0641) 5277)

Odyssey Car & Aircraft Hire, 36 Joule St, Southern Industrial Area, PO Box 20938, Windhoek (☎ (061) 223269; fax (061) 228911)

Okavango Car Hire, PO Box 854, Rundu (☎ (067372) 476)

Pegasus Car & Camper Hire, 88 Uhland St, Klein Windhoek, PO Box 21104, Windhoek (☎ /fax (061) 223423)

Punyu Car Hire, International Hotel, PO Box 247, Ondangwa (☎ (06756) 40313; fax (06756) 40177)

Rent-a-Safari Automobile, PO Box 2976, Windhoek (☎ (061) 235328; fax (061) 222741)

Swakop Auto Rent, PO Box 3991, Swakopmund (☎ /fax (0641) 61506)

Tempest Car Hire, 49 John Meinert St, Windhoek (☎ (061) 239163; fax (061) 230722)

Windhoek Engineering Microbus Hire, Parson St 36, PO Box 1038, Windhoek (☎ /fax (061) 21767)

Windhoek 4x4 Hire, Mr B Koudelka, Windhoek (☎ /fax (061) 240945)

Woodway Service Camper Hire, PO Box 11084, Windhoek (☎ (061) 222877; fax (061) 220335)

Zimmerman Garage Car Hire 5 Wright St, Southern Industrial Area, PO Box 2672, Windhoek (☎ (061) 237146).

HITCHING

Hitching opportunities in Namibia aren't bad, but hitching is illegal in national parks and there's little traffic on wide open highways, so expect long waits. On the other hand, it isn't unusual to get a lift of 1000 km in the same car. Lifts wanted and offered are advertised daily on Windhoek radio (☎ 291311) and at the Cardboard Box Backpackers' in Windhoek. At the Ministry of Wildlife, Conservation & Tourism Office, also in Windhoek, there's a noticeboard with share car hire and lifts offered and wanted etc. Truck drivers generally expect to be paid so agree on a price beforehand; the standard charge is US$1.50 per 100 km. Due to light traffic, hitching through the Caprivi is especially slow. (Please see the hitching warning in the Zimbabwe Getting Around chapter.)

LOCAL TRANSPORT
To/From the Airport

There is a regular bus service connecting the International Airport with Eros Airport and the Grab-a-Phone bus stop in the Windhoek city centre. Buses run to connect with both arriving and departing flights.

Taxis between the International Airport and Windhoek centre are quite expensive – around US$14 (R50) – and impractical when the bus is so convenient (unless you have three people to share a taxi). Taxis sometimes meet arriving flights at Eros Airport; if you don't find one, you'll have to call one from the telephone box.

Taxi

In Windhoek, the main taxi stand is at the Grab-a-Phone (☎ (061) 237070) bus stop, opposite the Kalahari Sands Hotel. It's better, however, to stop a taxi on the street (difficult), pick one up at the Wernhill Park Centre, or simply order one by telephone. This is especially true for anyone arriving at the Grab-a-Phone on the airport bus. The standard taxi fare within Windhoek is US$0.60 (N$2) to anywhere within the city, including Khomasdal and Katutura, but drivers will think up all sorts of add-on charges if they think you're an ignorant tourist. If you need a taxi in the wee hours of the night, it's best to book it beforehand.

Only in Windhoek are taxis an option – no place else is big enough to warrant extensive services. To get a taxi from a provincial airport or railway station, look for business cards attached to telephone boxes.

Local Buses

In Windhoek, there's a network of local buses connecting the city centre with outlying townships. They run according to no real schedule, but you'll naturally have most luck in the morning and late afternoon, when people are travelling to and from work. Your best bet is to start walking towards your destination and ask locals where to find a bus stop and how frequently the buses run.

ORGANISED TOURS

Even if you're one who spurns organised trips, there's a good case for joining a basic camping tour to such out-of-the-way and difficult-to-reach places as the Skeleton Coast, Damaraland, the Kaokoveld, the Kunene Valley, Ovamboland, Bushmanland and the wilder sections of the Namib Desert. If you are unable to muster a group for car hire, they also provide an alternative to hitching or battling with public transport to visit the more popular places. Many of them offer nothing but transport and camping options; participants do all the camp work and prepare their own meals.

Namibia has many reputable general and specialist operators; the following list includes some of the possibilities. Particularly interesting tours and prices are outlined in greater detail in relevant chapters:

Africa Adventure Safaris 72 Tal St, PO Box 20274, Windhoek (☎ 234720; fax 230001) Windhoek city tours, Daan Viljoen, Etosha and Sossusvlei. This is a good option for those with little time who wish to do a circuit around Namibia.

African Extravaganza Holstein St 9, Lafrenz Township, PO Box 22028, Windhoek (☎ (061) 63086; fax (061) 216356) This company mostly arranges ground tours around Namibia – as well as Zimbabwe and Botswana – for overseas agencies, but you may find good deals if there's space available.

Baobab Tours PO Box 24818, Windhoek (☎ (061) 232314; fax (061) 224017) Reasonably priced cultural and environmental camping tours, emphasising national parks and benefiting local communities

Beach Buggy Safaris Roon St, PO Box 4178, Swakopmund (☎ /fax 5377) Think of an unusual tourism angle and someone will cater for it. Beach Buggy Safaris runs daily, overnight and two to three day beach-buggy tours of Swakopmund's seemingly endless beaches and dunes.

Bona Safaris PO Box 804, Gobabis (☎ /fax (0681) 2988) Trips through Namibia's major sites as well as wilder corners of the country, like Bushmanland, Caprivi, Khaudom and South Africa's Kalahari Gemsbok National Park.

Canyon Tours 64 4th St, N Hoek, PO Box 375, Keetmanshoop (☎ 2095; after hours ☎ 2119) Canyon Tours does inexpensive day trips and longer trips to Fish River Canyon, Gallap Ost Karakul Farm, Lüderitz and the Kokerboomwoud.

Charly's Desert Tours 11 Kaiser Wilhelm Strasse, PO Box 1400, Swakopmund (☎ 4341; fax 4821) A variety of reasonably priced day tours around Swakopmund: rockhounding, Spitzkoppe, Welwitschia Dr, Cape Cross, Sandwich Harbour etc

Desert Adventure Safaris Namib Centre, Roon St, PO Box 1428, Swakopmund (☎ /fax 4072) This company runs inexpensive day tours around the Swakopmund area, Spitzkoppe and Cape Cross, as well as longer tours to Damaraland and the Kaokoveld. They also run the well-known Palmwag Lodge in Damaraland and the beautiful Serra Cafema Lodge on the Kunene, opposite Angola's mysterious-looking Serra Cafema Range, which lies just across the river.

Ermo Safaris PO Box 80205, Windhoek (☎ /fax 51975) – or dial 0020 and ask for Kamanjab 1312. This company, which is based at Ermo Safari Lodge near Etosha, runs multi-day camping safaris combining the Kaokoveld and Etosha National Park.

Farm Hilton W & A Fritsche, PO Box 20706, Windhoek (☎ (0628) 1111) This organisation, based on a farm in the Khomas Hochland, runs extensive horseback trips around the Hochland. For serious horse aficionados, they also organise a very popular 10-day riding and camping trip from the farm right across the Namib Desert to the sea at Swakopmund. This option must be booked well in advance.

Footprints The Cardboard Box, PO Box 9639, Eros, Windhoek (☎ /fax 249190) Recommended hiking, trekking and camping safaris, which focus on cultural contact (particularly in Kaokoland, Ovamboland and Bushmanland) and benefits to local communities. Especially appealing is their four-day trek along the Kunene River between Ruacana Falls and Swartbooi's Drift. These aren't luxury trips by any means, but they will provide unforgettable experiences.

Gloriosa Safaris PO Box 212, 215 7th St, Walvis Bay (☎ 6300; fax 2455) This long-established company specialises in day tours around the Walvis Bay area, as well as extended tours through the Namib-Naukluft Park, Damaraland and Etosha.

Gondwana Tours Canyon Hotel, PO Box 690, Keetmanshoop (☎/fax 3892) Gondwana Tours organises day trips to the Kokerboomwoud, Lüderitz, Fish River Canyon and other areas of southern Namibia.

Inshore Safaris, Casa Mia Hotel, PO Box 2444, Walvis Bay (☎ 2609; fax 2198) If you're visiting Walvis Bay, this is a good option for trips to Sandwich Harbour, the dunes, nature reserve and the Welwitschia Dr. They also do longer trips, including 10-day all-inclusive circuit tours of northern or southern Namibia for around US$1850.

Kaokohimba Safaris PO Box 11580, Windhoek (☎ /fax 222378) Kaokohimba offers 12 to 15-day cultural tours through the Kaokoveld and Damaraland, wildlife-viewing trips in Etosha National Park and hiking trips around northern Namibia.

Kolmanskop Tour Company PO Box 257, Lüderitz (☎ 2445; fax 2526) In addition to Kolmanskop tours, this company also runs trips to other recently opened parts of the Sperrgebiet (Diamond Area 1) such as Elizabeth Bay, Atlas Bay and the Bogenfels. Tours are available in English, German or Afrikaans.

Mola-Mola Safaris PO Box 34, Walvis Bay (☎ 3820; fax 7593) This generally water-oriented company runs half-day sightseeing trips by boat from Walvis Bay for US$38 per person; seabird-watching trips for US$55 per person; and full-day trips taking in Bird Island, Pelican Point and Sandwich Harbour, including a lunch featuring Walvis Bay oysters, is US$82.

Namibia Exquisit Safaris Roon Strasse 10, PO Box 4178, Swakopmund (☎ /fax 5377) German-oriented tours lasting one to 10 days, mainly through Damaraland, the Kaokoveld, the Namib Desert and the south

Namibia Pappot Safaris PO Box 130, Maltahöhe (☎ 42; fax 180) Unusual desert circuits around southern Namibia. The emphasis is on rugged driving trips for 4WD enthusiasts.

Namibia Photo Tours 8 Roon St, PO Box 442, Swakopmund (☎ /fax 4561) Photographic and fishing tours in and around Swakopmund. Day tours along the Welwitschia Dr or to Cape Cross cost US$36 per person; to the Spitzkoppe is US$38; and a sundowner on the dunes is US$23. Shark-fishing tours cost US$60 per angler. Longer trips may also be arranged.

Namibian Tourist Friend Eros Airport, Gus Uys Flying School, PO Box 11099, Windhoek (☎ /fax 233485) This unusual company offers four-hour city tours in small tuk-tuk-style vehicles for US$34 per person, but it specialises in expensive flying tours over Namibia's main sights. If you can muster five people, you can fly from Windhoek and enjoy a fly-in champagne breakfast at Sossusvlei for US$228 per person.

Namib Sky Adventure Safaris PO Box 197, Maltahöhe (☎ 5703) If you've always dreamed of looming over the dunes in a balloon, contact these people, who offer balloon flights over the Sesriem area of the Namib Desert. Especially appealing is the early morning flight, which departs before the sun comes up, when not a breath of wind is stirring. They're affiliated with the Namib Rand Guest Ranch.

Okakambe Trails PO Box 1591, Swakopmund (☎ 2319; fax 5874) This company does wilderness horseback tours around the Swakopmund area, including an overnight tour up the Swakop River to Goanikontes oasis. They also offer riding lessons.

Okashana Wilderness Tours PO Box 96, Okahandja (☎ (06221) 2802; fax (061) 31600) Multi-day cultural trips in the north, particularly the Kaokoveld, the Kunene region and Ovamboland. This is an opportunity to come in contact with traditional lifestyles in north-western Namibia.

Ondese Safaris PO Box 6196, Ausspannplatz, Windhoek (☎ (061) 220876; fax (061) 239700) Very expensive, all-inclusive tours around Namibia, also has trips into neighbouring countries

Oryx Tours 11 Van der Bijl St, Northern Industrial Area, PO Box 2058, Windhoek (☎ (061) 217454; fax (061) 63417) Day tours and longer trips through Namibia highlights, as well as trips to Kavango, Caprivi, Victoria Falls and the Okavango Delta. They take mainly overseas bookings, but can sometimes be booked locally.

Otjimburu Trails PO Box 5144, Windhoek (☎ 234359; fax 228461) Windhoek city tours and longer custom tours.

Otsa Safaris PO Box 140, Hotel Erongoblick, Karibib (☎ (062252) 9) German-oriented safaris around the country, with emphasis on the North-west and around Swakopmund.

Pasjona Safaris PO Box 24256, Windhoek (☎ /fax 223421) Northern and southern circuits of the major sites in Namibia. They cater mainly to German travellers.

Pleasure Flights Tours PO Box 537, Swakopmund (☎ 4500; fax 5325) Pleasure flights runs flightseeing tours all over Namibia, from the Skeleton Coast right down to Fish River Canyon. They're quite expensive and you need a group of five people to make it reasonable, but you can get a unique perspective from the air.

Rhino Tours, PO Box 4369, Swakopmund (☎ /fax 5757) Specialises in day trips around Swakopmund and longer safaris in the Namib Desert, the Skeleton Coast, Damaraland and the Kaokoveld, including Epupa Falls.

Skeleton Coast Fly-In Safaris PO Box 2195, Windhoek (☎ 224248; fax 225713) This company offers five-day trips taking in the Skeleton Coast, the Kunene River and Etosha National Park which cost US$2055 per person, including flights, accommodation and meals. A four-day tour which includes only the Skeleton Coast and the Kunene River region is US$1810 per person. All tours include a stop at Sossusvlei in the central Namib. Tours accommodate between four and 10 people.

Southern Cross Safaris 43 Independence Ave, PO Box 941, Windhoek (☎ 237567; fax 225387) Wilderness camping safaris through the wildest bits of Kaokoland and the Caprivi, and into Zimbabwe and Botswana

Sun Safaris Namibia PO Box 80226, Windhoek (☎ /fax 51069) Windhoek city tours, Swakopmund area and Etosha; they offer good rates on last-minute bookings

SWA Safaris 43 Independence Ave, PO Box 20373, Windhoek (☎ (061) 237567; fax (061) 225387)

Longer, mid-range tours around Namibia, from Etosha to Fish River Canyon

Trans-Namibia Tours Shop 28, Gustav Voigts Centre, 123 Independence Ave, PO Box 20028, Windhoek (☎ (061) 221549; fax (061) 2982033) Day tours, hiking tours and fly-in safaris around Namibia, as well as longer itineraries and self-drive tours. This company makes a point of being environmentally conscious. A highlight of theirs is the Fish Eagle Hiking Trail in southern Namibia, which costs US$700 per person, all inclusive.

Westcoast Angling Tours Otavi St 9; PO Box 545, Swakopmund (☎ 2377; fax 2532) As its name suggests, this company specialises in fishing tours. You can choose from deep-sea fishing to rock and surf angling from the beach. Anglers can even try for copper sharks, which may be caught from the beach.

Wilderness Safaris Namibia The Namib Travel Shop, PO Box 6850, Windhoek (☎ 225178; fax 239455) This company offers camping safaris, rock tours and Namib Desert tours, as well as fabulous rafting trips down the Kunene River.

Wildlife Tours PO Box 24374, Windhoek (☎ (061) 240817; fax (061) 240818) Ecology-based luxury tours with emphasis on walking, boating, canoeing, ballooning and mountain biking

Windhoek

Namibia's Central Highlands are dominated by its small, German-flavoured capital, Windhoek. Set at the geographical heart of Namibia, it serves as the major road and rail crossroads and the nerve centre of the country's business and commercial operations. It also boasts Namibia's main international airport.

At an elevation of 1660 metres and set among low hills, Windhoek enjoys dry-clean air and a healthy highland climate. The dryness and relatively high altitude also contribute to considerable temperature variations. Most of the annual 260 to 360 mm of precipitation falls in November and from January to April, resulting in lush gardens and spectacular flowers.

Windhoek has only 130,000 people, but Namibia's ethnic mix is reflected on its streets: you'll see the Ovambo, Herero and Damara people, together with Namas, the occasional San, 'Coloureds' and Europeans all hurrying along together.

History

Windhoek has only existed for just over a century, but its history is as colourful as its population. The original settlement, in what is now Klein Windhoek, was called Aigams or 'fire waters' by the Nama people and Otjomuise, the 'smoky place', by the Herero. Both names refer to the hot springs which provided a focus for early tribal attention and settlement. On a visit in 1836, British explorer and prospector Sir James Alexander took the liberty of renaming it Queen Adelaide's Bath, although it's fairly certain the monarch never did soak there. In 1840, Nama leader Jan Jonker Afrikaner and his followers arrived and again changed the name, this time to Winterhoek, after the Cape Province farm where he was born.

The modern name Windhoek, or 'windy corner', was corrupted from the original Winterhoek during the German colonial occupation. At that time, the town became

the headquarters for the German Schutztruppe under Major Curt von François. The Schutztruppe was ostensibly charged with brokering peace between the warring Herero and Nama. For over 10 years at the turn of the century, Windhoek served as the administrative capital of German South West Africa.

In 1902, a narrow-gauge railway was built to connect Windhoek to the coast at Swakopmund, and the city experienced a sudden spurt of growth. During this period it began to evolve into the business, commercial and administrative centre of Namibia, but the city wasn't officially founded until 1965. It's now home to all Namibia's government offices, as well as most of the country's commercial concerns.

Orientation

The city centre (but only the centre) is arranged in a straightforward grid pattern checked with green areas and characterised by a mix of German colonial structures and taffy-coloured modern buildings. It isn't what most people would expect of an African city, but it could be accurately described as both interesting and quite attractive.

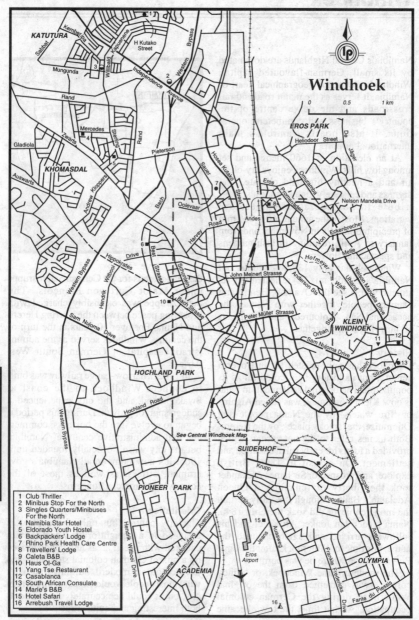

Windhoek

0   0.5   1 km

1 Club Thriller
2 Minibus Stop For the North
3 Singles Quarters/Minibuses
   For the North
4 Namibia Star Hotel
5 Eldorado Youth Hostel
6 Backpackers' Lodge
7 Rhino Park Health Care Centre
8 Travellers' Lodge
9 Caleta B&B
10 Haus Ol-Ga
11 Yang Tse Restaurant
12 Casablanca
13 South African Consulate
14 Marie's B&B
15 Hotel Safari
16 Arrebush Travel Lodge

KATUTURA

H Kutako
Street

KHOMASDAL

EROS PARK

Heliodoor Street

Nelson Mandela Drive

KLEIN
WINDHOEK

HOCHLAND PARK

See Central Windhoek Map

SUIDERHOF

PIONEER PARK

ACADEMIA

Eros
Airport

OLYMPIA

NAMIBIA

Central Windhoek is dominated by the lovely German Lutheran church, Christuskirche, which is visible from a considerable distance. Other prominent buildings include the Old Administration Building, appropriately nicknamed the Tintenpalast ('Ink Palace'), the Alte Feste – which was once a fort and now houses a museum – and three castles, which are now private homes.

The heart of Windhoek is Independence Ave which bisects the city and fronts up to most of the major shops and administrative offices. The tower of the Kalahari Sands hotel and associated Gustav Voigts Centre form an orientation point.

The heart of the shopping district is the Post Street pedestrian mall and nearby subsidiaries – Gustav Voigts Centre, Wernhill Park Centre and the more down-market Levinson Arcade. Verwoerd Park (or Zoo Park), beside the GPO, provides some welcome shade and a nice green spot to munch a takeaway meal.

The suburbs sprawl across the surrounding hills and provide impressive views, but just beyond the city limits, the wild country begins. Heading north along Independence Ave, you'll reach the industrial areas of North Windhoek.

Information

The Windhoek Information & Publicity Office (☎ 3912050; fax 3912091) on Post Street Mall is a friendly and worthwhile stop. Here you can pick up the reasonably useful quarterly publications, *What's On in Windhoek*, volumes one to four: *#1 Restaurants & Entertainment*, #2 Shopping Guide, *#3 Trails & Excursions* and *#4 Housing & Accommodation*. However, they contain mostly advertising. Nearly as friendly but less helpful is the Namibia Tourist Bureau on Independence Ave, which has information from around the country.

For transport bookings and information on private businesses, see the privately run Tourist Rendezvous Information Centre (☎ 221225; fax 224218) on Peter Müller Strasse near Stübel Strasse. They provide independent travel information, and can arrange and book safaris to anywhere in the country, including camping safaris in the Kaokoveld or rafting trips on the Orange River. They'll also book buses and minibuses and change money. Once that's done, you can have a cappuccino in their Rendezvous Coffee Shop.

The Ministry of Environment & Tourism (☎ 236975) was formerly known as the Directorate of Nature Conservation and later the Ministry of Wildlife, Conservation & Tourism, but is now just referred to as the MET. They have detailed information on the national parks and are the people to see for bookings for National Parks' camp sites, rondavels and lodges. The office is housed in the Oode Voorpost on the corner of John Meinert Strasse and Moltke Strasse. It's open Monday to Friday from 8 am to 1 pm for bookings and payment, and from 2 to 3 pm for bookings only.

Local papers, especially the *Windhoek Advertiser*, are a good source of information about current happenings. The Arts Association of Namibia (☎ (061) 231160) has up-to-date information about cultural events.

Money

All of Windhoek's major banks, most of which are concentrated along Independence Ave, will change money and should have no problem giving you South African rand. For VISA transactions, use First National Bank; their automatic teller system, known as BOB, will handle credit-card cash advances. Note that BOB (like everyone else) often runs short of money at weekends.

American Express is represented by Woker Travel Services (☎ 237946) on Peter Müller Strasse, but they don't change travellers' cheques.

Post & Telecommunications

The GPO is on Independence Ave, in the centre of town beside Verwoerd Park. For poste restante, go to counters four or five. There are telephone boxes in the lobby and just up the hill is the Telecommunications Office, where you make international calls and send or receive faxes from 8.30 am to 1 pm and 1.30 to 4.30

NAMIBIA

pm Monday to Friday and from 8.30 am to 12.30 pm on Saturday.

Another option for international or domestic phone calls (albeit an expensive one) is the convenient Grab-a-Phone on Independence Ave, which serves as the main bus terminal. You can also phone or send faxes at the Tourist Rendezvous Information Centre(☎ 221225; fax 224218) on Peter Müller Strasse near Stübel Strasse. Receiving faxes is free; to send an international fax to anywhere costs US$0.05 (N$0.17) per second.

Immigration For visa extensions and other immigration matters, as well as information on work permits, see the Ministry of Home Affairs (☎ 398 2036) near the corner of Independence Ave and Kasino St. It's open Monday to Friday from 8 am to 1 pm.

Medical Services In the telephone directory, physicians are listed under Medical and dentists under Dentists. Dr Rabie and Dr Retief (☎ 237213), whose offices are on the corner of John Meinert Strasse and Stübel Strasse, are recommended for consultations.

A useful and relatively inexpensive clinic is Rhino Park Health Care Centre, which will hopefully leave you feeling healthier than the average rhino. It's a 30-minute walk from the centre in Windhoek North. Alternatively, try the private hospital Medi-City (☎ 222687) on Heljudor St in Eros. They demand payment up front and aren't cheap, but the care and service are high quality. If your funds are tight and you have all day to wait, try the Windhoek State Hospital (☎ 3039111) or the government clinic on Robert Mugabe Ave near the corner of John Meinert Strasse.

Laundry There's a self-service laundrette near Ausspannplatz, opposite Tucker's Tavern.

Dangers & Annoyances Windhoek centre appears peaceful, but pickpocketing is still a problem. One ploy used by newspaper sellers is to shove the paper in your face; while you are reading the headlines, your pockets are being plundered by accomplices. Politeness can often defuse aggressive tendencies; if you do not want a newspaper, say something like 'No thanks, I have already read it'.

Although it's generally safe to walk anywhere around the city in the daytime, don't go out alone at night. The townships of Goreangab, Wanaheda, Hakahana and the southern areas of Katutura, where boredom and unemployment are serious problems, should be avoided at all times – unless you have a local contact and/or a specific reason to go there.

Travel Agencies Most travel agencies are clustered around the central area. The largest and most helpful is Trip Travel (☎ 236880). Also recommended is Woker Travel Services (☎ 237946) on Peter Müller Strasse, which represents American Express. There is also a branch of SAR Travel in the Gustav Voigts Centre (☎ 2982532). All of these provide travel information, as well as airline reservations and bookings for accommodation and tours.

Bookshops & Libraries Books, maps and stationery can be found at the two branches of CNA Bookshops in the Kalahari Sands (Gustav Voigts) Centre and Wernhill Park Centre. On Peter Müller Strasse is the German-run Der Bücherkellar, which has a selection of novels and literature in English and German. Uncle Spike's Book Exchange, on the corner of Garten Strasse and Tal Strasse, is an inexpensive place to stock up on reading material.

The Windhoek Public Library (☎ 224163) at 18 Lüderitz Strasse is open Monday to Friday from 9 am to 6 pm and on Saturday from 9 am to noon. Visitors can apply for temporary library cards.

Maps Pick up topographic sheets from the map section of the Surveyor General's office (☎ 2852332 or 238110). It's upstairs in the Ministry of Justice building, opposite the clock tower on Independence Ave.

Film & Photography A good range of film is available for reasonable prices at the Express Foto Photo Lab, downstairs in the Wernhill Park Centre.

Camping Equipment Camping equipment can be hired from Gav's Camping Hire (☎ 238745; fax 239015) at 49 John Meinert Strasse. You can hire dome tents for US$3 to US$5.50 per day; sleeping bags for US$11 for up to a week; and cool boxes, jerry cans, gas cookers (stoves) and eating/cooking utensils for less than US$1 per day each.

You can also purchase camping and cycling equipment, but virtually everything is from South Africa. The best places to look are Cymot's (☎ 234131) on Mandume Ndomufayo St and Gorelicks Camping Accessories (☎ 237700) at 119 Independence Ave. Limited camping gear is also available at Le Trip, downstairs in the Wernhill Park Centre.

Hendrik Verwoerd Park (Zoo Park)

Until 1962, Hendrik Verwoerd Park – also known as Zoo Park – served as the local zoo, but no longer. Today, you'll see a column, designed by Namibian sculptor Dörthe Berner, which commemorates a Stone-Age elephant hunt that took place on the spot some 5000 years ago. The remains of two elephants and several quartz tools used to cut up the carcasses were unearthed there in 1962. The fossils and tools were displayed *in situ* under glass until 1990, when they were found to be decaying and were transferred to the State Museum.

The Kriegerdenkmal (Soldier's) obelisk, topped by a golden imperial eagle, was dedicated in 1987 to the memory of Schutztruppe soldiers who died fighting the troops of chief Hendrik Witbooi in the Nama wars of 1893-94.

Christuskirche

One of Windhoek's most recognisable landmarks, the German Lutheran Christuskirche, stands on an island at the top of Peter Müller Strasse. It's an unusual building designed by Gottlieb Redecker in conflicting neo-Gothic and Art-Nouveau styles, and constructed of local sandstone. The cornerstone was laid in 1907. If you want to see the interior, pick up the key during business hours from the church office down the road on Peter Müller Strasse .

Alte Feste & the State Museum

The whitewashed ramparts of Alte Feste, Windhoek's oldest surviving building, date from 1890-92. It originally served as the headquarters of the Schutztruppe, who arrived in 1889 under the command of Major Curt von François. Minor alterations made in 1901 didn't affect the overall character. Today the building houses the Historical Section of the State Museum, which contains memorabilia and photos from the colonial period as well as some indigenous artefacts. The highlight, however, is the superb Independence display covering the history of the independence struggle. It's open weekdays from 8 am and 6 pm, and weekends from 10 am to noon and 3.30 to 6 pm. The building also houses a restaurant and pub.

The railway engines and coaches outside are from one of the country's first narrow-gauge trains. The bronze statue is known as the Reiterdenkmal, or Rider's Memorial, and commemorates Schutztruppe soldiers killed during the Herero-Nama wars of 1904-08. It was unveiled in 1912 on Kaiser Wilhelm II's birthday, 27 January.

The other half of the State Museum, known as the Owela Museum, is on Robert Mugabe Ave. Exhibits focus on Namibia's natural and cultural history. It's open the same hours as the historical section. Practically next door is the Windhoek Theatre, built in 1960 by the Arts Association. It's still Windhoek's major cultural centre.

Tintenpalast

The road leading east from the Reiterdenk-mal leads to the Tintenpalast, now the Parliament Building, which was designed by architect Gottlieb Redecker and built in 1912-13 as the administrative headquarters for German South West Africa. The name means 'ink palace', in honour of the large

NAMIBIA

amount of ink spent on the typically excessive paperwork generated there. It has also served as the nerve centre for all subsequent governments, including the present one. The building is remarkable mainly for its construction from indigenous materials. On weekdays – except when the assembly is in session – you can take a 45-minute tour of the building. Reserve a place by phoning (☎ 229251). The surrounding gardens were laid out in the 1930s, and include an olive grove and a bowling green.

Other Historical Buildings

Near the corner of Lüderitz St and Park St, take a look at the **old Magistrates' Court**. It was built in 1897-98 as quarters for Carl Ludwig, the state architect. However, he never used the house and it was eventually drafted into service as the Magistrates' Court. The verandah on the south side provided a shady sitting area for people waiting for their cases to be called. The building now houses the Namibia Conservatorium.

The building just opposite the Magistrates' Court dates from 1896. Prior to the construction of Christuskirche, it served as the Windhoek's German Lutheran church, but it currently houses a nursery school.

Heading down Park St from the Tintenpalast, you'll reach South West Africa House, now called the **State House**. The site was once graced by the residence of the German colonial governor, but it was razed in 1958 and replaced by the present building, which became the home of the South African administrator and from 1977, the administrator general. After independence, it became the official residence of the Namibian president. All that remains of the original building is a part of the old garden wall.

Diagonally opposite Christuskirche, also on Lüderitz Strasse, you will find the **Hauptkasse**. It was built in 1898-9 and became the revenue office of the German colonial administration. The building was extended in 1906 and 1909, and was later used as a school hostel. It now belongs to the Ministry of Agriculture.

A block from the Hauptkasse, on the corner of Neser Strasse and Peter Müller Strasse, is the **Ludwig von Estorff House**. It was built in 1891 as a mess for military engineers and was named after the former Schutztruppe commander who lived there, between campaigns, from 1902 to 1910. Over the years it has also served as a residence for senior military officers, a hostel and a trade school, and now houses the Windhoek Reference Library.

Heading south along Robert Mugabe Ave, you'll have a have a good view over the city, and the road is lined with interesting buildings. The first one on the right is the **Kaiserliche Realschule**, Windhoek's first German primary school, which dates from 1907-08. It opened in 1909 with 74 students, but over the next few years, enrolment increased and the building had to be enlarged. The curious turret with wooden slats, which was part of the original building, was designed to provide ventilation. It later became Windhoek's first German high school and after WWII, an English middle school. A plaque outside will remind you that Berlin is 11,000 km away.

Down the road is the **Officer's House**, built in 1905-6 by the Works division of the colonial administration to provide accommodation for senior officers. Although the house is closed to the public, you can visit the outbuildings, which include a six-horse stable and saddle room, both of which are now used as garages.

Around Werth Strasse, there are also some interesting buildings. The **Villa Migliarina** and **Villa Lanvers**, both of which are now private homes, were designed in 1907 by Otto Busch. A cylindrical tower on the Lanvers house gives it a castle-like appearance. Both homes are surrounded by lovely gardens, but they're not open to the public. Just up the stairs is Werth Lookout, which affords a good view over the central part of the city.

On the corner of Korner St and Robert Mugabe Ave you'll find the **Old Supreme Court**, a gabled brick structure which dates from 1908. It was used as a court from 1920 to 1930, at which time the legal system was changing from the German to the South African. Cases were heard according to whichever system seemed to be the most appropriate for the circumstances.

On Robert Mugabe Ave is the **Turnhalle**, also designed by Otto Busch. It was built in 1909 as a practice hall for the Windhoek Gymnastic Club, but in 1975, the building was modernised and turned into a conference hall. On 1 September 1975, it was the venue for the first Constitutional Conference on Independence for South West Africa, which subsequently – and more conveniently – came to be known as the Turnhalle Conference. During the 1980s, it was also the site of the political summits and debates which resulted in Namibian independence.

Around the corner on John Meinert Strasse are the **Officials' Houses**, which date from 1908. This block of six houses was originally built for government employees. Nearby, on the corner of John Meinert Strasse and Moltke Strasse, is the **Oode Voorpost**, a classic 1902 building which originally held the colonial surveyors' offices. Early government maps were stored in a fireproof archives. It was restored in 1988 and now houses the MET reservations office.

Southward along Independence Ave are three colonial-era buildings, all designed by architect Willi Sander. The one furthest south was built in 1902 as the **Kronprinz Hotel**. In 1920, Heinrich Gathemann bought it and converted it into a private business, to adjoin the **Gathemann House** next door, which he had built in 1913. The furthest north of the three is the **Erkrath Building**, which dates from 1910 and originally served as a private home and business.

Monuments

On the corner of Independence Ave and John Meinert Strasse is a **bronze kudu statue**. It honours the many kudus who succumbed to the rinderpest epidemic of 1896. Another prominent memorial is the **Ovambo Campaign Memorial** (described under the following Railway Station section) and the **Cross of Sacrifice** on Robert Mugabe Ave.

A **statue of Curt von François**, Windhoek's founder, stands outside the municipal buildings on Independence Ave.

Railway Station

Windhoek's lovely old Cape Dutch style railway station dates back to 1912 and was expanded in 1929 by the South African administration. Across the driveway from the entrance is the German steam locomotive, *Poor Old Joe*, which was shipped to Swakopmund in 1899 and reassembled for the run to Windhoek.

Upstairs in the railway station is the small but worthwhile Trans-Namib Museum, which outlines the history of transport in Namibia. It's open Monday to Friday from 9 am to noon and 2 to 4 pm. Admission is US$0.70.

At the entry to the station parking area is the Ovambo Campaign Memorial. It was erected in 1919 in commemoration of the 1917 British and South African campaign against the resistant chief Mandume, of the Kwanyama Ovambo people. When he ran out of firepower, the chief committed suicide rather than surrender.

St George's Anglican Cathedral

The Anglican Cathedral of St George, opposite the State Museum on Love Strasse, has the distinction of being the smallest cathedral in southern Africa. On the grounds of the nearby St George's Diocesan School is the oddly constructed Mansard Building. It was once a private home but now belongs to the school. It's remarkable chiefly for its Mansard roof – the only one in Namibia – which is totally unsuited to the desert climate.

Post Street Mall & Meteorite Exhibit

The throbbing heart of the Windhoek shopping district is the bizarrely colourful Post Street pedestrian mall, which might have been a set in the film *Dick Tracy*. It's lined with vendors selling curios, artwork, clothing and just about anything else that may be of interest to tourists.

In the centre of the mall is a prominent

display of 33 meteorites from the Gibeon meteor shower, which deposited at least 21 tonnes of mostly ferrous extraterrestrial boulders on the area of Gibeon, in southern Namibia. It's rare that so many meteorites fall simultaneously, and they're thought to have been remnants of an explosion in space, which stuck together as they were pulled in by the earth's gravitational field.

Between 1911 and 1913, soon after their discovery, they were brought to Windhoek for safekeeping. Over the years they were displayed in Verwoerd Park and at Alte Feste.

Private Castles
Just within walking distance of the city centre, not far from the Gobabis road, you'll see the three Windhoek 'castles' – Schwerinsburg (1913) on Schwerinsburg Strasse, Heinitzburg (1914) on Heinitzburg Strasse, and Sanderburg (1917) on Kastell Strasse. Schwerinsburg and Sanderburg are now private homes. Heinitzburg Castle (☎ 227044) is now open to the public as an art gallery. The European cemetery downhill from these castles is worth a brief look around.

South-West Brewery
Until recently, the home of Windhoek Lager was the old South-West Brewery building on Tal Strasse, where the company had produced Namibia's favourite liquid since 1902. The building is now home to the Warehouse, which is indisputably Windhoek's best night spot. The brewing operation has moved to the Northern Industrial Area out of Windhoek on the Okahandja road. For information on tours of the modern brewery, which are conducted Monday to Friday at 10 am and 2 pm, phone ☎ 238100.

Hofmeyer Walk
The Hofmeyer Walk walking track through Klein Windhoek Valley starts from either Sinclair St or Uhland St and heads south through the bushland to finish at the point where Orban Strasse becomes Anderson Strasse. The walk takes about an hour and

affords a panoramic view over the city and a close-up look at the *Aloe littoralis* aloes, which characterise the hillside vegetation. These cactus-like plants are at their best in winter, when their bright red flowers attract tiny sunbirds, mousebirds and bulbuls.

Katutura
Unlike its South African counterparts, the Black township of Katutura (Herero for 'we have no permanent place') is relatively safe by day if you stick to the northern areas or find a local who can act as a guide. Especially interesting are the colourful independence-theme murals along Independence Ave. A taxi from the centre to Katutura costs only US$0.75 (N$2).

Goreangab Dam
Goreangab Dam, nine km north-west of Windhoek, is a large artificial lake which is popular with water sports enthusiasts. Oddly enough, swimming and bathing aren't permitted, but boating and sailboarding are both allowed and it's a pleasant spot for picnics and braais. There's no public transport; you can get there only with a private vehicle.

Penduka
An excellent place to buy crafts – and a lovely excursion from town – is Penduka ('wake up'), a crafts cooperative set amid lovely hills about 15 km from the centre. Penduka works with over 300 women artists, representing the San, Herero, Himba, Damara, Nama and Ovambo traditions. There's also a tea room and scenic hiking trails, like the circular Baboon Trail. It's open from 8 am to 5 pm Monday to Saturday.

Organised Tours
For a Windhoek city tour, you have several options. Possibilities include Otjimburu Trails (☎ 234359; fax 228461); Sun Safaris Namibia (☎ /fax 233485), which offers good rates on late bookings; and Africa Adventure Safaris (☎ 234720; fax 230001) at 72 Mandume Ndomufayo St. All of these cover the main city sights in half or full-day tours; some also include an excursion to Daan

Viljoen Game Park. For something different, try the German-oriented Namibian Tourist Friend (☎/fax 233485). They offer four-hour city tours in a 'ricksha' (a tuk-tuk-style vehicle) for US$34 per person. The office is at the Gus Uys Flying School at Eros Airport.

Festivals

True to its partially Teutonic background, Windhoek stages its own Oktoberfest towards the end of October which lovers of the amber nectar should not miss. There's also the German-style Windhoek Karnival (or WIKA) which is held in late April and features a series of events and balls lasting about a week. In late September/early October, the city holds the Windhoek Agricultural, Commercial & Industrial Show. The venue is the Show Grounds south of the centre on Jan Jonker Strasse.

Places to Stay

Windhoek accommodation is relatively good value compared with Europe or North America. Prior to independence, the city boomed with South African visitors and it was often difficult to find accommodation. The boom has started anew, but now, hotels are just as likely to be occupied by visitors from Milan or Perth as from Cape Town or Pretoria. Finding a bed can be especially difficult during school holidays.

Places to Stay – bottom end

Camping The nearest camp site to town is at *Arebbusch Travel Lodge* (☎ 52255; fax 51670), PO Box 554, on the road south. Camping costs US$6 per person in a tent or caravan, double rooms with/without bath are US$29/35 and two/five-bed chalets with bath cost US$52/63. Amenities include a bar, shop, laundrette, swimming pool and trampoline. Taxis from the centre cost US$3.50 (N$12).

The most popular camp site is at *Daan Viljoen Game Park*, 18 km from the city; sites may be pre-booked at MET. For further information, see Around Windhoek, later in this chapter.

Alternatively, you can camp at *Harmony*

Seminar Centre, 15 km south of town and two km east on D1504, which charges US$3 per person. To get there, catch a south-bound minibus from the terminal north of Wernhill Park Centre, get off at the D1504 turn-off and walk the remaining distance.

A new camping option with basic dormitory accommodation is also planned for the *Penduka* crafts cooperative (☎/fax 264366), up in the hills 15 km north-west of Windhoek. It should be open by the time you read this. With hiking trails, a pleasant snack restaurant and great views, it promises to be a relaxing little get-away-from-it-all spot.

Hostels & Backpackers' Windhoek's favourite backpackers' hostel (and one of the friendliest places in all Namibia) is *The Cardboard Box* (☎ 228994; fax 52128) at 15 Johann Albrecht Strasse, on the corner of John Meinert Strasse, just 15 minutes' walk from the city centre. Dorm beds cost US$6, with use of cooking facilities and swimming pool; and breakfast, drinks and snacks are available. There's a noticeboard for lifts around the country and it's a great place to gather a group for car hire (Cardboard Box Car Hire is Namibia's cheapest) and trips to Sossusvlei, Etosha and elsewhere. The owner Aulden Harlech-Jones also organises airport transfers, Saturday evening sundowner trips to scenic spots around Windhoek, Sunday braais, and even night club excursions.

The friendly *Eldorado Youth Hostel* (☎ 213630; fax 214009), on the corner of Sterling and Austin St in Khomasdal, is a favourite with local business people and, although the location is a bit dodgy, security is good. Dormitory beds cost US$7 for Hostelling International members. Guests have access to the kitchen facilities and TV room. It's a long way from the centre but taxis cost just US$0.50 (N$2) – don't let them charge more.

The longest running hostel is the quirky *Backpackers' Lodge* (☎ 228355) at 25 Best Strasse. Dorm beds cost US$7 per person, but when this research was done most people had reservations about this place. It's also a real nuisance to be locked out from 10 am to 4 pm.

Another inexpensive option is *Travellers' Lodge* (☎ 236547) in Eros Park, which charges 'overseas guests' US$8 per person. If you stay three nights or longer, it's just US$7 per night. They offer free coffee and tea, kitchen facilities, bedding and a common TV room.

Bed & Breakfast A bit further from the centre – but fantastic value – is the friendly *Marie's Bed & Breakfast* (☎ 51787; fax 52128), 156 Diaz St, with large rooms for US$17/26 single/double, including breakfast; and dorm beds for US$7. In the dry season, they have a pre-erected tent where you can stay for US$4/6 with one/two people; in this case, breakfast costs an additional US$1.50. A flat for up to six people, with breakfast, costs US$36. Guests have access to the swimming pool, patio and barbecue, but otherwise, there are no cooking facilities. As president of the Namibian Bed & Breakfast Association, Marie can also provide guests with guidance on inexpensive accommodation around the country.

Another pleasant B&B is homely *Caleta* (☎ 226054) at 91 Nelson Mandela Dr, owned by June and Hans Bunke. They have two rooms, each with private facilities, starting at US$19/35 a single/double. Rates include breakfast served on the patio with a view of the nearby hills.

For more of a German atmosphere, there's *Haus Ol-Ga* (☎ 235852), at 91 Bach Strasse, PO Box 20926, Windhoek. The name is formed from the names of the owners – Gesa Oldach and Erno Gauerke. Single/double rooms cost US$19/30, with breakfast.

Hotel If you prefer hotel-style accommodation, somewhat cheaper than most – but three km from the centre in Khomasdal – is the *Namibia Star Hotel* (☎ 213205), with singles/doubles at US$15/23. The quality has recently improved, but due to its poor location and its reputation as a two-hour hotel, lone women should probably stay clear.

A bit more expensive is the Irish-owned *Tucker's Tavern* (☎ 223249; fax 227698), which is centrally located and serves as one of Windhoek's main overland truck stops. The hotel-style rooms are actually mid-range accommodation at US$39/56 for a single/double with breakfast and linen. At US$16 per person, without breakfast, it may not be a bad idea to forget the four-bed dormitory rooms. However, if you're into rugby, this is *the* place to be.

Places to Stay – middle

One of the cheapest mid-range hotels is the unusual *Hotel-Pension Handke* (☎ 234904; fax 225660) at 3 Rossini St, with 10 rooms at US$35/50 a single/double with breakfast. Larger rooms accommodating three or four people cost US$23 per person.

Further up-market is the friendly *Hotel Pension Cela* (☎ 226295; fax 226246) at 82 Bülow Strasse, which charges US$43/67 a single/double with breakfast. Rooms for three/four people cost US$84/104. Amenities include TVs, radio, telephones, ceiling fans and a swimming pool.

A motel-style place is *Hotel-Pension Moni* (☎ 228350; fax 227124) at 7 Rieks van der Walt Strasse, just south-east of the centre. Bright clean rooms with telephone, radio and mini-bar cost US$38/54 for a single/double.

The *Hotel-Pension Steiner* at 10 Wecke Strasse has double rooms for US$64 with breakfast. Rooms are spotless and have televisions and en suite facilities and guests can use the swimming pool, braai area and lounge. A similar place charging similar prices is *Hotel-Pension Uhland* (☎ 229859; fax 220688) at 147 Uhland St. There's a swimming pool and all rooms have private facilities.

On Johann Albrecht Strasse, you'll find the recommended *Villa Verdi* (☎ 221994; fax 222574). It's a unique sort of Mediterranean-African hybrid which charges US$57/95 for singles/doubles with en suite facilities, telephone and TV.

There are also several options along Independence Ave. The *Thüringer Hof* (☎ 220631; fax 232981), famous for its beer garden, has singles/doubles for US$65/95. The good-value *Continental Hotel* (☎ 237293; fax 231539), downhill from the GPO along Independence Ave, is also central and offers quality accommodation. Single/ double rooms with private facilities start at US$49/63, luxury suites are US$65/71, and singles with shared facilities cost US$27. All rooms include bed and breakfast.

The *Hotel Fürstenhof* (☎ 237380; fax 228751) is a large and impersonal sort of place, but it offers fairly good value. Single/ double rooms with shower or bath cost US$53/79. Luxury rooms aren't all that much more, at US$57/87 for a single/double. All room rates include breakfast.

If you have a vehicle, you can opt for Mr Hans Vonderstein's simple but charming *Aris Hotel* (☎ 236006), in Aris, 27 km south of the city along the Rehoboth road. Single/double rooms cost US$25/38, with use of the swimming pool and braai area. There's also a bar and à la carte restaurant.

Places to Stay – top end

The immense *Hotel Safari* (☎ 238560; fax 235652), near Eros Airport, three km from the centre, has pleasant gardens, a shady beer garden, a large pool and a golf course next door. Single/double rooms cost US$70/85 which includes a huge self-service buffet breakfast. It's probably the most pleasant of the top-end hotels.

At the top end of the market is Namibia's only four-star hotel, the *Kalahari Sands* (☎ 222300; fax 222260), at 129 Independence Ave, PO Box 2254, right in the heart of the city. It's Namibia's only international standard hotel, with 187 rooms all with TV, telephone, mini-bar and coffee machine. Note, however, that the quality of service does vary. Standard single/double rooms cost US$99/116 and deluxe rooms are US$122/137. An English or continental breakfast costs an additional US$7/9.

If you don't mind supporting the luxury hotel constructed specifically for the Miss Universe pageant in Windhoek, there's

always the *Watersworld Hotel*, the new blue building near Eros Airport. It's a Las Vegas-style water-theme hotel – complete with fountains, green lawns and rainforests – which may seem a bit incongruous here in the middle of the desert.

Guest Farms

For map locations of these farms, see the North Central Namibia map in the following chapter.

The German-style *Gästefarm Elisenheim* (☎ /fax 64429), PO Box 3016, Windhoek, is owned by Andreas and Christina Werner and lies 15 km from the city in the Eros Mountains. It has nine double rooms with private facilities, a pool and wildlife viewing on the surrounding ranch. Single/double rooms cost US$34/54; a full breakfast costs US$7 and other meals are an additional US$10 each. It's closed from 15 December to 31 January. To get there, take the Okahandja road and get off at the Brakwater interchange. Follow the D1473 until it curves to the north; turn east at the first opportunity and follow this road up to the guest farm. Transfers from Windhoek cost US$6 per trip, divided between all passengers; from the airport, they're US$41.

Another popular guest farm is the cattle and game ranch *Düsternbrook* (☎ 232572; fax 234758). Full board accommodation costs US$49 per person. It's set in a pleasant scenic area and offers a range of activities. As with many Namibian guest farms, however, animals are kept in enclosures. In this case, it's leopards and on Sunday, visitors pay US$8.50 to feed them. Game drives are US$8.50 and horse-riding costs the same per hour. To reach the farm, follow the B1 for 30 km north towards Okahandja and turn west onto the D1499. From there, it's 18 km to the farm.

Places to Eat

The best takeaway food in Windhoek is from *Steenbras*, on Bahnhof Strasse near Independence Ave, which serves great fish, chickenburgers and spicy chips, all of which are memorably delicious. Another good

Central Windhoek

0   150   300 m

PLACES TO STAY		6	Kenya Embassy & Grand China Restaurant	40	Minibuses to the south
4	Hotel-Pension Uhland	7	Werth Lookout	41	Wernhill Park Centre
13	Hotel Thüringerhof & Restaurant	8	Villa Migliarina	43	Tourist Rendezvous Information Centre
19	The Cardboard Box	9	Villa Lanvers	44	Old Magistrates Court
20	Villa Verdi	10	Turnhalle	45	Hendrik Verwoerd
21	Hotel-Pension Cela	11	MET- Ministry of		Park (Zoo Park)
22	Hotel-Pension Handke		Environment & Tourism	46	Old German Lutheran
23	Hotel Fürstenhof		(Oode Voorpost)		Church
30	Continental Hotel	12	Robert Mugabe Clinic	47	Hauptkasse
56	Kalahari Sands Hotel	15	Paradise Alley	48	Christuskirche
57	Hotel-Pension Steiner	16	Ovambo Campaign	49	Tintenpalast
66	Tucker's Tavern		Memorial	50	Alte Feste & State
71	Hotel-Pension Moni	17	Railway Station		Museum
		18	Minibuses to	51	Kaiserliche
PLACES TO EAT			Swakopmund &		Realschule
			Walvis Bay	52	Ludwig von Estorff
3	Roxy's	24	Minibuses for the south		House (Windhoek
14	Steenbras Takeaways	25	Gav's Camping Hire		Reference Library)
35	Central Café	26	Roman Catholic	53	Grab-a-Phone
36	Grand Canyon Spur		Cathedral & Catholic		Bus Terminal
	Steakhouse		Hospital	54	Woker Travel
42	Le Bistrot	27	Drs Rabie & Retief		Services
58	Kentucky Fried Chicken	28	Model 7-Day Store	55	De Bücherkellar
59	Wecke & Voights	29	Namibia Tourist Bureau		bookshop
63	Sardinia's	31	Ministry of Home	60	Officers' House
64	King Pies		Affairs (Immigration)	61	Namibia Crafts Centre
70	Gourmet's Inn	32	Officials' Houses	62	The Warehouse
		33	St George's Anglican	65	Laundrette
OTHER			Cathedral	67	Ausspannplatz
		34	State (Owela) Museum	68	The Weaver's Nest
1	Hospital	37	South-West Africa	69	Rockafella's
2	Joe's Beer Garden		House (State House)	72	Sanderburg Castle
5	Old Supreme Court	38	Post Office	73	Heinitzburg Castle
	(Obergericht)	39	Windhoek Information &	74	Schwerinsburg Castle
			Publicity Office		

option is *King Pies* on the corner of Independence Ave and Garten Strasse, which serves a variety of filled meat and vegetable pies. For quick snack meals, try the convenient *City Treff* in Post St Mall. If you are after the familiar and the mundane, Windhoek has a *Kentucky Fried Chicken* on Mandume Ndomufayo St, near Sam Nujoma Dr.

The *Grand Canyon Spur Steakhouse*, on Independence Ave near the GPO, has a good-value varied menu, plus you can eat on the balcony overlooking the street. Don't miss the fabulous salad bar and the chocolate brownies.

Le Bistro, a bit of a fish bowl on Post St Mall, is known for its breakfasts, pizza, salads and gyros. They serve breakfast from 7 to 11 am; for a 'health breakfast' or a continental breakfast, you'll pay US$2.50 and a full English breakfast costs US$3. The

recommended restaurant in the *Alte Feste* serves good value German-Namibian lunches and dinners, and in the afternoon, it's pleasant for a coffee and snack break.

Also pleasant is the laid-back *Central Café* in the Levinson Arcade; it's great for meals or just coffee, and is open from Tuesday to Saturday for lunch and dinner. On Monday, it's open for lunch only, and on Sunday from 8 am to midnight. The place gets extremely busy at lunchtime, but there's a takeaway window selling filled brötchen and other fast snacks. Less appealing is *Café Schneider*, which is in the same arcade, practically opposite the Central Café. For a slightly more expensive lunch, try the recommended *Manhattan's*, above Bülow St in the Post Street Mall.

Other alternatives for coffee, meals and snacks are *Wecke & Voigts* department store

NAMIBIA

coffee bar in the Gustav Voigts Centre and the *Rendezvous Coffee Bar* in the Tourist Rendezvous Information Centre on the corner of Peter Müller Strasse and Stübel Strasse. They serve decent brewed coffee, as well as cappuccino and espresso.

Mike's Kitchen, in Wernhill Park Centre, is a sort of yuppified family restaurant serving the standards: salads, steaks, burgers and chips. For a treat, splash out for a meal at *Gathemann's*, in a lovely and prominent colonial building on Independence Ave, which has great German-style food in pleasant surroundings. It offers wonderful terrace dining on local specialities, including the best snails in garlic butter in all Namibia; expect to pay around US$15 per person for a meal. In the morning and afternoon, they serve rich European-style gateaux and pastries, and downstairs, there's a nice sandwich takeaway.

For Italian cuisine, there's *Sardinia's*, on Independence Ave near Sam Nujoma Dr; by day, they serve up delicious gelato. An even better option is *Roxy's*, near the corner of Independence Ave and Uhland St, which serves takeaways, pub meals and the best pizzas in Windhoek. They have table service and live music in the evening.

A good beer garden and great-value lunch spot is the *Jägerstübe* at the Thüringer Hof Hotel, with German-style cuisine. Apart from Windhoek Lager, they offer an all-you-can-eat buffet of cold cuts, cheese, salad and hot dishes. It serves meals from noon to 2 pm and 7 to 10.30 pm. However, the adjoining beer garden is a haunt of prostitutes.

The best Chinese food is at *Yang Tse* on Sam Nujoma Dr near the petrol stations in Klein Windhoek. An alternative is the *Grand China Restaurant*, at the Kenyan Embassy on Korner St. For Korean cuisine, try *Seoul House* restaurant near Ausspannplatz, which serves lunch and dinner.

Spanish cuisine is the speciality at *Viva España* (☎ 222300), a restaurant and tapas bar in the Kalahari Sands Hotel. It's open Monday to Friday from noon to 2 pm and then 7 to 10 pm, and on Saturday from 7 to 10 pm only. For an authentic Spanish meal

for two, with wine, plan on spending around US$40.

The fully licensed *Marco Polo* (☎ 230141), on Post St Mall, serves top-quality Italian meals and pizza, but the portions tend to be small. Each morning, they have a champagne breakfast for US$6. It's housed in the Kaiserkrone Centre, one of Windhoek's earliest buildings, which dates back to 1927; it was originally a hotel and social centre. Also up-market is *Gert's Klause*, a quiet German-style dining establishment in the arcade south of Post St Mall.

If you really want to splash out, try the *Gourmet's Inn*, on Jan Jonker Strasse near Centaurus, which is a standard haunt of ambassadors, government ministers, dignitaries, VIPs and general power trippers. Reservations are essential and not easy to get – and the prices reflect the exclusivity.

There is an excellent hotel restaurant at the *Hotel Fürstenhof* (☎ 237380), off the beaten track on Hosea Kutako St. It's low key, but serves elegant French cuisine with flair. You'll pay US$10 to US$20 for a gourmet meal with wine.

If you are more interested in quantity than finesse, try the US$8 good-value all-you-can-eat dinner buffet at the *Hotel Safari*.

Self-Catering Self-caterers will find a grocery-shopping paradise in Windhoek. The big names are *Woolworths* in the Wernhill Park Centre, and the cheap and cheerful *OK Supermarket* in the Gustav Voigts Centre, or the nearby *Wecke & Voigts*. Wecke & Voigts is a small, expensive department store specialising in things Germanic and it has an excellent food department and delicatessen in the basement. They make good bread and cakes and prepare custom-made sandwiches and brötchen. They also have a wide selection of local smoked meats and biltong.

If price is a major issue and you don't mind sacrificing selection, try the always crowded *Model 7-Day Store* on lower Independence Ave, towards the intersection with John Meinert Strasse. The *Mini-Mark* out in Klein Windhoek is larger than it sounds and is open from 7 am to midnight seven days a week.

On weekdays, there's a small market on Mandume Ndomufayo St, selling mainly fruit, vegetables, baskets and woodcarvings.

Entertainment

Pubs, Discos & Night Clubs There are also some super night spots in Windhoek. Without doubt, the best is The Warehouse Theatre, in the old South-West Breweries building on Tal Strasse. This is probably the only truly integrated club in southern Africa – thanks mainly to its enlightened owner. It's open almost every night. It emphasises superb live music and theatre productions – both African and European – more than dancing, but most people get up and dance anyway and it's friendly, secure and lots of fun. The cover charge depends on the act, but it averages around US$3 and is worth every cent. This place is reason enough to spend a few days in Windhoek.

In the black township of Katutura is the wonderful Club Thriller, which imposes a cover charge of US$2.50. Once you're past the weapons search at the door, the atmosphere is very upbeat and surprisingly secure. Foreigners receive only a minimum of hassle – most people are there to simply party and have fun – but it's still not wise to carry valuables. Peripherals include a snack bar, braais and pool tables. However, don't attempt to walk around Katutura at night – always take a taxi, which costs just US$0.50 from town.

If you prefer something less animated, a good spot is Tucker's Tavern (an Irish-style pub) on Independence Ave. For good mellow vibes, go to Joe's Beer Garden, on Independence Ave between Luther and Uhland Sts. It's a favourite place to drink and meet people. Next door is Roxy's, with live music and fabulous pizza. A bit less of a sure thing is the tiny Club Taj Pomodzi in Katutura, which specialises in kwasa-kwasa music from Zaïre and charges a US$2.75 cover charge. This is your best option for an intimate taste of Windhoek's African scene. However, it's lost in the back streets of Katutura so without a taxi and some local help, it's hard to find (you shouldn't attempt to go there at night without either of these).

Another recommended option is the Casablanca on Sam Nujoma Dr, which serves up meals and good live music with no cover charge. Look out for the Windhoek Mini-Weekend on Wednesday, when everyone in the place gets blotto. Other possibilities include Manhattan's which is small and cosy, but has irregular opening hours; the historical but rather right-wing Alte Feste Pub, in the fort of the same name (open Monday to Saturday from noon to midnight); Paradise Alley, mainly a coloured club with ultra-violet lights and yuppie-club atmosphere; Club Latino in Khomasdal, a more aggro version of Paradise Alley; and the recently re-opened Rockafella's.

Cinema & Theatre Windhoek has an excellent cinema, Kine 300, on Nelson Mandela Dr and there's also the Windhoek Drive-In Cinema near Eros Airport. The Franco/Namibian Cultural Centre (☎ 225672) at 1 Mahler St, on the corner of Sam Nujoma Dr, shows French films and other international cinema productions, and also hosts visiting art and theatre exhibitions.

There are occasional theatre productions at the Academy and concerts by the Windhoek Conservatorium. The Kalahari Sands Hotel has cabaret evenings and there are productions at the National Theatre of Namibia on Robert Mugabe Ave. The Warehouse in the old South-West Brewery has jazz and light music concerts, as well as serious dramatic performances; for more information, see Pubs, Discos & Night Clubs earlier in this section.

Sjordes, lunchtime music and theatre productions, are sometimes held at the Space Theatre in the colonial maternity home, Elisabeth House, over the railway line from the centre on Storch St.

Lectures The State Museum in the Alte Feste hosts visiting exhibits and runs a programme of evening lectures, films and slide shows. Enquire at the desk.

NAMIBIA

Sports Windhoek offers some excellent sporting facilities. There's a fine municipal swimming pool at the south end of town near the corner of Jan Jonker Strasse and Centaurus Strasse. The local chapter of Hash House Harriers (☎ 224550) meets on Sunday at 4.30 pm.

Things to Buy

Windhoek is the shopping capital of Namibia, and you'll find everything from camping equipment to leatherwork and most shops can arrange shipping. The leather shops may appear slightly intimidating because of the security precautions, but they're good for inexpensive, high-quality belts and purses. Prices vary; ostrich leather from local farms is the most expensive, while a belt made of locally farmed buffalo hide costs US$22 and will last forever. Handbags start at US$110 and briefcases are double that. A good inexpensive place to buy high-quality leather shoes is Lederwaren in the Northern Industrial Area. Quality karakul wool products are available at The Weaver's Nest on Nachtigal St near Ausspannplatz, and other shops around town.

Windhoek also has a thriving jewellery industry, based upon locally mined gold, minerals and gemstones. These are sold in specialist shops, where artesans work to order and their original designs can be pleasantly unique. Some of the best work is with malachite and tiger-eye agates. For raw minerals and gemstones, the best place to find a good deal – and an interesting lesson on gems and mineralogy – is the House of Gems near the corner of Stübel Strasse and John Meinert Strasse in Windhoek. Owner Sid Pieters is Namibia's foremost expert on the subject and in 1974, along the Namib coast, he uncovered 45 crystals of jeremejevite, a type of sea-blue tourmaline, which is the rarest gem on earth. His discovery was one of only two bits ever found; the first was unearthed in Siberia in the mid-19th century.

If you're interested in San arts and crafts and aren't venturing into the Kalahari, have a look at the shop Bushman Art Gallery at 187 Independence Ave. Even if you're not buying, it's worth a look for the variety and beauty of what's available. The shop also specialises in Himba material arts.

On the first and third Saturday of each month there's a street market on Independence Ave which offers a good opportunity to meet local people and purchase handicrafts. In the old South West Breweries building at 40 Tal Strasse is the Namibia Crafts Centre (☎ 222236), which sells an amazing variety of stuff. It's open Monday to Friday from 8 am to 5 pm and on Saturday from 8 am to 1 pm.

Naturally, the city has a full complement of curio shops selling kitsch souvenirs, T-shirts, mass-produced art and woodcarvings. A few sell more original – and more expensive items – but in the case of anything which resembles an artefact, ask the provenance and be sure you don't need an export/import permit. If the dealer is authorised to sell antiquities, they'll have a special licence; before you buy anything exotic and expensive, it's worth checking with the police.

Handicrafts stalls and sales people are a common sight on Windhoek's streets. The stuff in Post Street Mall is mostly brought in by the truck load from Zimbabwe and only

Traditional wooden spoon

a small percentage of it is really worthwhile. A better option would be the Herero dolls, which are sold outside the Kalahari Sands Hotel, or the baskets and woodcarvings sold around Verwoerd Park. If you'll be touring around the country, save your money for the cheaper and better quality products which may be purchased directly from artists or craftspeople – or from cooperative crafts shops which have sprung up in many places.

See also Penduka, an out-of-town crafts cooperative, which is discussed earlier in the Windhoek section.

Getting There & Away

Air Air Namibia has daily flights between Windhoek's International Airport, Cape Town and Johannesburg. There is also a twice-weekly service to and from London and Frankfurt; and several airlines offer service to and from Gaborone, Maun, Harare, Lusaka and Victoria Falls. Domestic Air Namibia flights connect Eros Airport with Katima Mulilo, Keetmanshoop, Lüderitz, Oshakati, Rundu, Swakopmund and Tsumeb.

The major airline offices in Windhoek include:

Aeroflot, Carl List Building, on the corner of Independence Ave & Peter Müller Strasse, PO Box 6604, Ausspannplatz (☎ 229120)
Air France, Sanlam Centre, 4th Floor, 154 Independence Ave, PO Box 20975, Windhoek (☎ (061) 227688; fax (061) 232944)
Air Namibia, Ground Floor, Gustav Voigts Centre (☎ 229630; fax 228763)
LTU, 141 Stübel Strasse (☎ 238205; fax 222350)
Lufthansa, Third Floor, Sanlam Centre, 154 Independence Ave, PO Box 3161 (☎ 226662; fax 227923)
South African Airways, Carl List Building, on the corner of Independence Ave & Peter Müller Strasse, PO Box 902 (☎ 237670 and 231118)
Zambia Airways, 55 Independence Ave, PO Box 2933 (☎ 223623; fax 223439)

Bus The Intercape Mainliner luxury coach service runs bi-weekly between Windhoek and Cape Town (US$90) and Johannesburg (US$92), via Upington (US$54). En route, they stop in (fares are from Windhoek):

Rehoboth (US$18), Mariental (US$22), Keetmanshoop (US$30) and Grünau (US$36). Intercape Mainliner also connects Windhoek and Walvis Bay (US$25) via Swakopmund (US$25); and Windhoek and Tsumeb (US$37) via Okahandja (US$14), Otjiwarongo (US$19) and Otavi (US$25).

More convenient and much cheaper are the local minibuses, which depart when full and work out to about US$0.03 per km. For example, the fare to Oshakati in Ovamboland would be around US$16. For Swakopmund and Walvis Bay, they leave from the corner of John Meinert Strasse and Mandume Ndomufayo St. To either town, you'll pay US$11. For the route south to Rehoboth, Mariental and Keetmanshoop, the terminal is the large car park north of the Wernhill Park Centre. Those going north to Ovamboland and Kavango depart from the market near the dodgy Singles Quarters area of Katutura township. An alternative to risking your luggage would be to wait at the Western Bypass on-ramp from the northern end of Independence Ave. The best time to travel is on Friday afternoon, when services are most frequent.

Between Windhoek, Ondangwa and Oshakati, there's also the yellow SWAPO express bus. It leaves the Singles' Quarters bus terminal in Katutura on Friday at 5 pm and leaves Oshakati on Sunday afternoon. Northern terminals are the BP station in Ondangwa and the market bus station in Oshakati. Tickets cost just US$11 from Windhoek to Oshakati, but be sure to book as early as possible on Friday morning.

If you're heading for Swakopmund or Walvis Bay, a convenient service is Dolphin Express (☎ 221225), which does daily runs between Windhoek and the coast for US$14 one-way. Reserve or purchase tickets at the Tourist Rendezvous Information Centre on Peter Müller Strasse. Another company is Cheetah Liner (☎ 227935), which charges the same rates. Phone for reservations.

There's also a slow bus between Windhoek and Harare, Zimbabwe, which leaves the terminal north of Wernhill Park Centre on Friday at 7 am. It stops at Katima Mulilo

NAMIBIA

Vultures

Latin names: *Neophron percnopterus* (Egyptian vulture), *Neophron monarchus* (hooded vulture), *Trigonoceps occipitalis* (white-headed vulture), *Pseudogyps africanus* (white-backed vulture).

Along with hawks and eagles, vultures belong to the Accipitridae family. Many different species are represented in southern Afri-ca, but the most common are the Egyptian, hooded, white-backed and white-headed varieties. All vultures prefer savanna country with high animal concentrations, and are found in large numbers in Hwange, Chobe, Moremi, Mana Pools, Chizarira and Etosha, but are present in all the smaller parks, as well.

The largest birds have three-metre wing spans and can weigh up to five kg. Vultures are fairly inefficient fliers and must rely on rising hot-air thermals to ascend and glide. For this reason you won't see them in the air until well into the morning when the updraughts have started.

They feed almost exclusively by scavenging and fortunately for them, have no sense of smell. This means, however, that they must depend totally on their superb eyesight to locate food. Once a kill has been spotted, a vulture will descend rapidly and await its turn at the carcass. Of course, other vultures will follow the first down-wards, and before long, vultures are winging in from as far as 50 km away.

They're are very efficient feeders and a large flock of vultures – they often congregate in mobs of up to 100 – can strip an antelope to the bone in half an hour. However, they're no good at ripping into a completely intact carcass. Due to their poor flying ability, they're unable to get off the ground with a full belly, so after a good gorging, they retreat from the carcass until the meal is digested. ■

on Saturday at 11 am, leaves Victoria Falls (Zimbabwe) on Sunday at 7 am and arrives in Harare on Monday morning. To Harare costs US$92 and to Victoria Falls it's US$75. Pre-book through the Tourist Rendezvous Information Centre on Peter Müller Strasse.

Train There's a weekly international service, on the *Suidwester*, which runs on Wednesday from Windhoek to De Aar, South Africa (US$26/62 in economy/sleeper class), where you'll find easy connections to both Cape Town and Johannesburg. It returns from De Aar to Windhoek on Friday. This train may be used to travel between Windhoek and Rehoboth, Mariental, Keetmanshoop and Karasburg. The fare from Windhoek to any Namibian destination is US$9/25 in economy/sleeper class. There's also a weekly local train between Windhoek and

Keetmanshoop, which heads south on Friday and north on Sunday. Weekday fares from Windhoek are as follows: Rehoboth (US$2/5); Mariental (US$4/10); Keetmanshoop (US$11/33). These fares double on weekends.

On the northern sector, the line connects Windhoek with Tsumeb via Okahandja and Otjiwarongo, where the routes split and one branch goes to Otavi and Tsumeb; another goes to Otavi and Grootfontein; and a connecting railways bus heads for Outjo. Both northbound and southbound services run on Friday and Sunday.

The other main lines connect Windhoek with Swakopmund and Walvis Bay via Okahandja on Tuesday, Friday and Sunday; and Windhoek with Gobabis on Tuesday, Thursday and Sunday, on a very slow overnight run. From Keetmanshoop to Lüderitz,

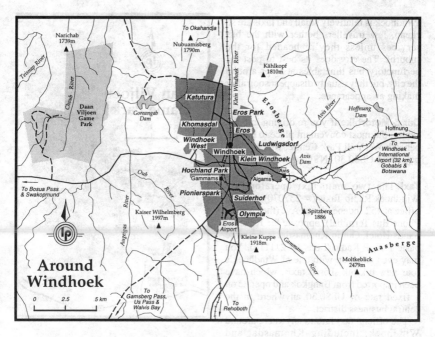

Around Windhoek

0   2.5   5 km

the train has been substituted with a bus service operated by the railways on Friday and Sunday westbound and Saturday and Sunday eastbound.

The railway station ticket and booking office is open from 7.30 am to 4 pm Monday to Friday.

Car & Motorbike Windhoek is literally the crossroads of Namibia – the point where the main north-south route (the B1) and east-west routes (B2 & B6) cross. All approaches to the city are spectacularly scenic, passing over beautiful desert hills. Roads are clearly signposted and there's a western bypass which allows you to avoid the town centre. See the Namibia Getting Around chapter for a list of car hire firms.

Hitching It's easier to hitch to and from Windhoek than anywhere else in the country. There is a lot of traffic on the major roads and you should be able to reach the capital relatively easily from any direction.

Getting Around

To/From the Airport There's an airport shuttle bus which operates between the Windhoek International Airport, 42 km from town, and the Grab-a-Phone Bus Terminal on Independence Ave; Eros Airport (for domestic flights); and the nearby Hotel Safari.

These buses connect with all arriving and departing flights and cost US$5.50 (N$20) per person between the airport and town. Bus schedules are posted on the wall at Grab-a-Phone. As a general rule, the buses leave the airport one hour after the arrival of an international flight and depart from Grab-a-Phone two hours and 10 minutes prior to international departures.

Bus City buses around the Windhoek area charge US$0.15 (N$0.50) per ride. Because

Windhoek is relatively small and taxis are so cheap, few travellers bother with the bus services unless they're headed for the suburbs. The city does its best to post the perfunctory bus timetables at stops around the city, but they usually disappear soon after making an appearance.

Car & Motorbike If you're driving into the centre, the most convenient place to park is beneath Werhhill Park Centre, where you'll pay about US$0.30 (N$1) per hour.

Taxi The two main taxi operators are Windhoek Radio Taxis (☎ 237070), with an office at 452 Independence Ave (the Grab-a-Phone Bus Terminal), opposite the Kalahari Sands Hotel. Out in Khomasdal is the more basic F & P Radio Taxis (☎ 211116). You may even catch up with one of Windhoek's four new tuk-tuk shared taxis, which have been imported from Bangkok and operate on a fixed rate of US$0.30 anywhere in the central business district.

The official taxi fare to anywhere around Windhoek, including Khomasdal and Katutura, is US$0.60 (N$2). Taxis caught at the Grab-a-Phone often charge several times the official rate, and may also try to charge extra if you have luggage. A better option would be the taxi stop north of the Wernhill Park Centre. Alternatively, you can phone for a taxi or flag one down, but there aren't many taxis, so the latter may prove difficult.

Around Windhoek

DAAN VILJOEN GAME PARK

The beautiful Daan Viljoen Game Park sits in the Khomas Hochland about 25 km west of Windhoek. Because there are no dangerous animals, you can walk to your heart's content through lovely desert-like hills and valleys. Wildlife is profuse and you'll almost certainly see gemsboks, kudu, mountain zebras, springboks and hartebeests. It's also the best place in Namibia to see elands.

Daan Viljoen is also known for its diversity of birds, with over 200 species recorded. Among them are the rare green-backed heron and pin-tailed whydah. The park office sells a bird-identification booklet. The dam is stocked with barbel, kurper and black bass; anglers need a fishing licence.

The park's hills are covered with open thorn-scrub vegetation which allows excellent wildlife viewing on foot, and two walking tracks have been laid out. The shorter and easier one, the three-km return Wag 'n Bietjie (Wait-a-Bit) Track, follows a dry riverbed from near the park office to Stengel Dam and back. The longer Rooibos Trail, a nine-km circuit walk, crosses hills and ridges and affords great views back to Windhoek in the distance.

Places to Stay & Eat

As it's popular with Windhoek residents, visitors should pre-book accommodation, camp sites and picnic sites at MET in Windhoek. The park is open to day visitors from sunrise to 6 pm year-round, and there's a restaurant which is open from 7.30 to 9 am, noon to 2 pm and 7 to 10 pm. There's also a kiosk for drinks and refreshments and a swimming pool. Day admission is US$1.50 per person.

The rest camp curls around one side of Augeigas Dam. Camping costs US$7 for up to eight people, or you can stay in two-bed rondavels for US$23 double, with breakfast.

Getting There & Away

There's no public transport to Daan Viljoen and traffic is sparse, so hitching may prove problematic, but persistent hitchers will find something. Several tour companies include Daan Viljoen in their Windhoek city tours (see Organised Tours under Windhoek).

With your own vehicle, follow the C28 west from Windhoek. Daan Viljoen is clearly signposted about 18 km from the city. Although you're welcome to walk in the park, no motorbikes are permitted.

North Central Namibia

Although the area east of Damaraland, south of Etosha and north and east of Windhoek is often ignored by visitors, it's replete with historical sites and some lovely natural landscapes. Having said that, almost everything along the tourist trail in North Central Namibia is aimed at ushering visitors into Namibia's most popular destination, Etosha National Park which, as one of the world's preeminent wildlife areas, is a requisite visit.

The region also holds other attractions, such as the hot-spring resort of Gross Barmen, the Von Bach Dam angling reserve and such small and picturesque communities as Okahandja, Tsumeb and Grootfontein. You certainly won't be disappointed with Waterberg Plateau Park, a lovely island in the sky and a repository for reintroduced and endangered species. The Erongo Mountains, with their prehistoric cave paintings, form a dramatic backdrop along the route between Windhoek and Swakopmund. Gobabis, in the karakul sheep-breeding area east of Windhoek, is the main settlement of the Namibian Kalahari. Further north, the economy is carried by rich ranching country and two major mining districts.

OKAHANDJA

Okahandja lies less than an hour north of Windhoek and functions mainly as a highway service centre and crossroads between the main north-south route (the B1) and the Swakopmund road. Okahandja is the administrative centre for the Herero people, who invaded this formerly Nama homeland in the early 1800s and sparked off a series of wars between the two groups.

A town museum is currently planned for the old German fort (which is currently closed to the public). If you're interested in the progress, phone ☎ 2700.

History

The first German missionary to visit the region was Heinrich Shmelen, who arrived in 1827, but a mission wasn't actually planned until Heinrich Kleinschmidt and Carl Hahn arrived in 1843. The mission was finally founded six years later by Friedrich Kolbe, but due to strife between the Herero and the Nama – under their highly charged leader, Jan Jonker Afrikaner – the effort lasted only a few months.

Over the next year, animosity between the Nama and Herero escalated and on 23 August 1850, over 700 Herero under the command of chief Kahitjenne were massacred at the hands of the Nama forces in the Battle of Moordkoppie. Half the victims were men and the other half children and women, whose bodies were dismembered for the copper bangles worn on their arms and legs. The scene of this tragedy is Moordkoppie, a small rocky hill just east of the B1, between Okahandja and the Gross Barmen turn-off.

Cemeteries

At the southern end of Church St is Friedenskirche, the Rhenish mission church, which was consecrated in 1876. In the churchyard, you can see the graves of several

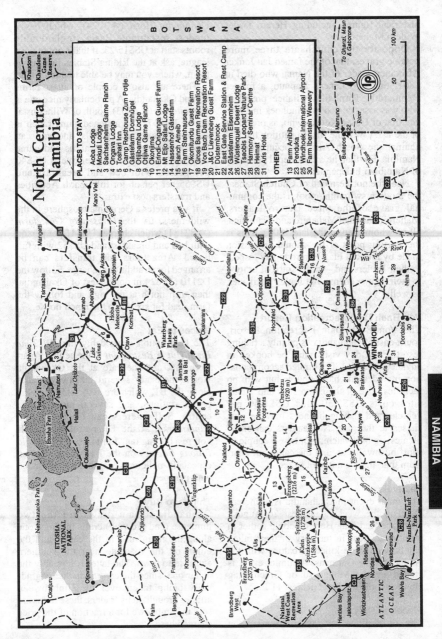

North Central Namibia

PLACES TO STAY

1 Aoba Lodge
2 Mokuti Lodge
3 Sachsenheim Game Ranch
4 Ongava Lodge
5 Toshari Inn
6 Camp Resthouse Zum Potjie
7 Gästefarm Domhügel
8 Otjibamba Lodge
9 Otjiwa Game Ranch
10 Okonjima
11 Erindi-Onganga Guest Farm
12 Mt Etjo Safari Lodge
14 Hassenhof Gästefarm
15 Ranch Ameib
16 Farm Steinhausen
17 Okonjundu Guest Farm
18 Gross Barmen Recreation Resort
19 Von Bach Dam Recreation Resort
20 J&C Lievenberg Guest Farm
21 Düsternbrook
22 East Gate Service Station & Rest Camp
24 Gästefarm Elisemheim
26 Wüstenquell Desert Lodge
27 Tsaobis Leopard Nature Park
28 Harmony Seminar Centre
29 Heimat
31 Aris Hotel

OTHER

13 Farm Anibib
23 Finkeldei
25 Hosea Kutako International Airport
30 Farm Ibenstein Weavery

historical figures, including Herero leader Willem Maherero.

Opposite the church are three more notable graves: that of the famed Jan Jonker Afrikaner, leader of the Nama, who died in 1861; that of Clemens Kapuuo, a former Democratic Turnhalle Alliance president who was assassinated in Windhoek in 1978; and that of Hosea Kutako who, as president of the DTA, was the first to petition the UN against the South African occupation of Namibia. For that, he's considered the father of Namibian Independence.

Near the northern end of Church St, near the modern swimming pool, is the communal grave of the three Herero leaders, Maherero, Samuel Maherero and Tjamuaha, all of whom died in the late 1800s. This is the starting point of the annual procession made by the Red Flag Herero to pay respect to their leaders and – in the spirit of unity – to their former enemy, Jan Jonker Afrikaner, as well.

Von Bach Dam Recreation Resort

The Von Bach Dam Recreation Resort, south-east of Okahandja, is mainly a fishing resort. Even day visits must be booked in advance (☎ 2475). The limited accommodation includes one basic double hut with no facilities. Use of the camp sites and picnic sites costs US$5.50 plus US$1.50 per vehicle, and fishing licences may be purchased at the gate. Non-anglers can enjoy picnics, go birdwatching or take a couple of short bushwalks around the camp but apart from that, there's not a lot to see.

Festivals

The main event in Okahandja is Maherero Day, on the weekend nearest 26 August, when the Red Flag Herero people gather in traditional dress in memory of their fallen chiefs, who were killed in battles with the Nama and the Germans. A similar event is staged by the Mbanderu or Green Flag Herero on the weekend nearest 11 June.

Places to Stay

The only place to stay in town is the *Okahandja Hotel* (☎ 3024), which has a modest restaurant. Basic single/double rooms start at US$15/23. If that's out of your league, ask at the Riding Stables just out of town, where you may be able to pitch a tent.

There are also a couple of guest farms around Okahandja. A particularly nice one is *Okomitundu* (☎ 6403), south of Wilhelmstal on the D1967. The attached game ranch is set amid scenic, rocky hills, and you can choose between walking safaris and game drives. It's relatively inexpensive at US$40 per person with bed and breakfast and US$55 per person for full board. Activities and transfers cost extra.

If you prefer a German atmosphere in the wilderness, try the *Haasenhof Gästefarm* (☎ 82131) which charges US$41 per person with bed and breakfast and US$52 with full board. Area tours and transfers can be arranged for an additional charge. Follow the D2110 for 62 km north-west of Okahandja, then turn north at the sign and follow the farm road for six km to the ranch house.

Places to Eat

The best option is probably the *'Ol Time Pizza Hut & Restaurant* in the centre. Apart from that and the café at the Okahandja Hotel, there are several takeaway places along the B1, which are associated with the petrol stations, and several more in the centre. Self-caterers can try the *Sentra Supermarket* at the BP petrol station. If you're a biltong fan, don't miss the *Namibia Biltong Factory* on the B1, which sells an especially delicious beef biltong seasoned with peri peri.

Things to Buy

Okahandja's main draws are the two immense (and growing) crafts markets, one along the main road in the centre and the other, on the roadside near the southern entrance to town. The latter is arguably the better one, since the central market is gradually being taken over by Zimbabwean articles brought in by traders; these items are sold in Zimbabwe for a fraction of the price charged here.

Getting There & Away

Okahandja is only 70 km north of Windhoek on the main B1, which provides easy driving. It is served by the main train service from Windhoek to Tsumeb, and Windhoek to Swakopmund. Northbound, trains pass at 10.30 pm on Friday and Sunday and at 7.30 pm on Tuesday and Thursday. Southbound, they pass at 3.25 am on Tuesday, Wednesday, Friday and Saturday. Westbound to Swakopmund and Walvis Bay, they pass at 9.30 pm daily except Saturday. Coming from Swakopmund, towards Windhoek, they pass at 4.40 am daily except Sunday.

It is also on the Mainliner bus route from Windhoek to Tsumeb. The bus leaves Windhoek on Thursday at 7 am, arriving in Okahandja at 7.55 am; on Sunday it leaves Windhoek at 2 pm, arriving in Okahandja at 2.55 pm. The fare is US$4. There is a return bus to Windhoek leaving on Monday at noon and on Friday at 7 pm.

GROSS BARMEN

Gross Barmen, 26 km south-west of Okahandja, once served as a mission station, but is now Namibia's most popular hot-spring resort. The resort has mineral baths, a 39°C hot pool indoors and an outdoor swimming pool with naturally warm water. There's also a shop, restaurant and tennis courts, and it feels like a cross between an oasis and a health farm, with lots of German-Namibians wandering around in dressing gowns.

It makes a decent stopover en route to the north or west, or a relaxing base for a couple of days, but it's nothing to go too far out of your way for. Naturally, most people come for the swimming and soaking in the hot water, but there are some nice walks around the dam and surrounding hillsides. For birdwatchers, a path has been cut through the reedbeds to a series of benches where you can wait and see what flies in.

Admission is US$1.50 per person and US$1.50 per vehicle; use of the mineral spring and warm water baths costs an additional US$0.50. There are two sessions per day: 8 am to 1 pm and 2 to 6 pm.

Places to Stay & Eat

Camp sites and picnic sites cost US$6 for up to eight people; their popularity means that even day visits must be booked in advance (☎ 2091). Pleasant self-contained double rooms or bungalows cost US$16, while bungalows with five beds cost US$35.

There's also a shop, bar, restaurant and petrol station on the site. At the restaurant, hard-core carnivores can cash in all their newly acquired health chips and order huge slab-like T-bone steaks and inexpensive Windhoek Draught beer.

Getting There & Away

There's no public transport to Gross Barmen, but on weekends, it shouldn't be difficult to hitch from the highway turn-off south of Okahandja.

KARIBIB

The small ranching town of Karibib began life as a station on the narrow gauge Windhoek–Swakopmund line. Early rail service travelled only by day so Karibib, which was halfway between Swakopmund and Windhoek, became an ideal overnight stop for travellers and, at one stage during the colonial period, it had six hotels.

Today, Karibib is known mainly as the site of the Navachab gold mine, which was discovered about five km south-west of town in 1985. Consolidated Diamond Mines in consortium with the Anglo-American Corporation developed the mine and it was in operation by November 1989. The mine now produces over 700,000 tonnes of ore annually, at a relatively low yield of three grams of gold per tonne.

Karibib is also known for its high-quality Palisandro marble (aragonite) quarries. These quarries currently yield over 1200 tonnes of marble annually. They're processed at the nearby marble works, which is imaginatively called *Marmorwerke* ('marble works' in German).

Information

The tourist information office in the Wolfgang Henckert Tourist Centre (☎ 28; fax

230), on the main street, can provide helpful information. This is also the place to enquire about tours of the Navachab gold mine, which are conducted twice monthly, as well as organised visits to the Palisandro marble quarry.

Historical Buildings

Most of the buildings along Karibib's main street are of some historical significance. Among them are the old railway station, which dates from 1900; the Rösemann & Kronewitter Building, built in 1900 as the headquarters of an early German trading firm; the Haus Woll, which was built of granite in the first decade of this century; and the Christuskirche, built in 1910. It was the first church in the country to be partially constructed of marble.

Places to Stay & Eat

The *Hotel Pension Erongoblick* (☎ 9; fax 95) is housed in a converted boarding school, but has been well refurbished and has almost completely shed its former institutional atmosphere. With a great pool and a reasonably priced restaurant, it's a very good mid-range option starting at US$14/28 for single/double rooms with shared bath and US$22/33 with private bath. All rates include bed and breakfast. For US$9 per person, they'll arrange 2½ hour sundowner tours to the private Karibib game ranch.

The more expensive *Hotel Stroblhof* (☎ 81; fax 240) at the eastern end of town has air-conditioned single/double rooms for US$25/40. Amenities include a restaurant and swimming pool.

Places to Eat

For meals, you'll have little choice beyond the two hotel restaurants and the *Karibib Bakery*, a small café/bakery on the main road through town. The building which houses this bakery was constructed in 1913 as one of the first hotels in Karibib.

Things to Buy

You can buy gemstones at several outlets in the town, including the Wolfgang Henckert Tourist Centre, which specialises in Karibib tourmalines, as well as quality local arts and handicrafts. At the Karibib Webschule, you'll find hand-woven articles made of karakul wool.

Getting There & Away

Karibib is accessible by any bus service between Windhoek and Swakopmund (See Getting There & Away under Windhoek). The Intercape Mainliner bus stops at the Hotel Stroblhof. The journey from Windhoek costs US$19 and takes about 2½ hours.

You can also travel by rail *from* Windhoek or Swakopmund daily except Saturday and *to* either city in the wee hours daily except Sunday. The train passes Karibib eastbound at 2.05 am and westbound at 12.40 am. The economy/sleeper class fares from Windhoek are US$3/9 from Monday to Thursday and US$7/19 over the weekend.

OTJIMBINGWE

One would never suspect that the lost and forgotten village of Otjimbingwe, 55 km south of Karibib on the D1953, was once the administrative capital of German South West Africa. The Herero name means 'place of refreshment', for the freshwater spring near the confluence of the Omusema and Swakop rivers. The availability of water and the fact that it lay midway along the wagon route between Windhoek and Walvis Bay led Reichs Kommissar Heinrich Göring to declare it the capital in the early 1880s.

History

Otjimbingwe was originally founded by Johannes Rath in 1849, as a Rhenish mission (the church, however, wasn't built until 1867). After the discovery of copper in the mid-1850s, the Walvis Bay Mining Company set up operations in Otjimbingwe and the quiet little mission station developed into a rollicking, Wild West-style mining town. Because of its position midway between Windhoek and the port at Walvis Bay, in the early 1880s, it was declared the administrative seat of German South West

Africa and in 1888, became the site of the country's first post office. When the capital was transferred to Windhoek in 1890, however, Otjimbingwe began to decline, and when it was bypassed by the Windhoek-Swakopmund railway in the early 1900s, its fate was sealed.

Historical Buildings

If you do make it to Otjimbingwe, have a look at the Rhenish church; the historic WBM trading store; the wind-driven generator used to power the Hälbich wagon factory; and the 1872 powder magazine, which was intended as a first line of defence against attack by the Nama.

Tsaobis Leopard Nature Park

This private park, which occupies 35 sq km of rugged rocky country, lies along the southern bank of the Swakop River. It was here in 1889 that Major Curt von François constructed a fortified barracks for the Schutztruppe. In 1969, it was established as a leopard sanctuary and is now home to leopards and a variety of other animals, particularly antelopes and mountain zebras, as well as wild dogs and cheetahs. Other animals are kept in enclosures.

It's a scenically super spot for hiking and the pleasant rest camp provides comfortable accommodation, but without a vehicle, access is nigh impossible. It lies 35 km or so west of Otjimbingwe, west of the junction of the C32 and the D1976.

Places to Stay

A good accommodation option is the rest camp at the *Tsaobis Leopard Nature Park* (☎ 1304), 35 km west of Otjimbingwe, which features two-bed self-catering bungalows starting at US$35 for a double. If arranged in advance, full board is available for an additional US$15 to US$20 per person.

The luxurious guest farm of *J&C Lievenberg* (☎ 3112), along the Swakop River between Otjimbingwe and Gross Barmen, offers full board accommodation starting at US$85 per person; bed and breakfast is a bit cheaper. Facilities include a tennis court and driving range.

USAKOS

Usakos ('grasp by the heel') originally developed as a station on the narrow-gauge railway that linked the port of Walvis Bay with the mines of the Golden Triangle. In the first decade of this century, its central location was deemed ideal for the site of the country's first railway workshops. Usakos held the distinction of Namibia's railway capital until 1960, when narrow gauge was replaced by standard gauge, steam-powered locomotives gave way to diesel engines and the works yard was shifted to Windhoek.

Locomotive No 40

In honour of Usakos' railway past, Locomotive No 40 still stands proudly in front of the railway station. It was one of three Henschel heavy-duty locomotives built in 1912 by the firm of Henschel & Son in Kassel, Germany. Its counterpart, Locomotive No 41, occupies a similar position at the station in Otjiwarongo.

Places to Stay & Eat

Usakos' only accommodation is the clean but austere *Usakos Hotel* (☎ 259), which has single/double rooms with bed and breakfast for US$19/35.

In the heart of the never never, 70 km south-west of Usakos on the D1914, you'll find the friendly *Wüstenquell Desert Lodge* (☎ 1312; fax 277). It actually sits at the fringe of the Namib Desert and in fact, the name is German for 'desert spring'. At US$30 per person, it's modestly priced for bed and breakfast. A room with full board costs US$45 per person. Otherwise, you can camp for US$5 per person; camping equipment can be provided. Farm tours will take you through the unusual rock formations and to an abandoned colonial railway station dating back to 1900.

Getting There & Away

Usakos lies on all the bus and minibus routes – and of course the railway line – between

Windhoek, Swakopmund and Walvis Bay. Eastbound trains pass at 12.40 am and westbound at 1.55 am, daily except Saturday. The fare to Windhoek, Swakopmund or Walvis Bay is US$3/8.50 in economy/sleeper class.

ERONGO MOUNTAINS

The Erongo Mountains, which are volcanic in origin, rise as a 2320-metre high massif north of Karibib and Usakos. After the original period of vulcanism some 150 million years ago, the volcano collapsed in on its magma chamber, allowing the basin to fill up with slowly cooling igneous material. The result was a hard granitic core which withstood the erosion that washed away all the surrounding material. The result is the Erongo Massif.

The range is best known for its caves and rock paintings, particularly the 50-metre deep Phillips Cave on the Ameib game ranch, which contains the famous White Elephant painting. Super-imposed on this pale pachyderm is a large hump-backed antelope (an eland?) and around it are depictions of other animals, including ostriches and giraffes. The Ameib paintings were brought to world attention in the book *Phillips Cave*, by the Eurocentric prehistorian Abbé Breuil, but his speculations about Mediterranean origins have now been discounted.

Phillips Cave lies three km off the road and is open to day visitors to Ameib ranch. It can be reached on foot in about 45 minutes. After seeing the paintings, you can stop at Ameib's picnic site, which shelters near several large outcrops of stacked boulders. One notable formation of rounded boulders is known as the Bull's Party, as it somewhat resembles a circle of gossiping bovines. Another oft-photographed formation resembles a Herero woman in traditional dress, standing with two children. Day visits to the paintings and picnic site cost US$2 per person.

North of the Ameib ranch, the D1935 skirts the Erongo Mountains before heading north into Damaraland. Alternatively, you can head east towards Omaruru on the D1937. This route virtually encircles the

Erongo Massif, and provides access to minor 4WD roads leading into the heart of the mountains. These roads will take you to some of the range's best bushwalking.

Places to Stay

Ranch Ameib (☎ 1111), whose name means 'green hill', occupies a superb setting beneath the Erongo foothills. It began life in 1864 as a Rhenish mission station and now operates as a luxurious guest farm and camp site. In fact, a stay there can be a bit like stepping into German Namibian history, but as with many guest farms, in addition to its game ranch, where animals roam free, it also maintains a zoo-like compound in which they're caged.

Accommodation in the historic farmhouse, complete with historic furnishings, is US$67 per person with full board and use of the appealing swimming pool. If you're booked into the farmhouse, they'll pick you up from Usakos, but campers must pay US$8 per trip for the transfer.

Camp sites cost US$7 per person, including use of braais, toilets and hot showers, and double pre-erected tents are US$17, but no caravans are allowed. Breakfast costs US$4, lunch is US$8 and substantial dinners are US$10.

OMARURU

Although it's not much to look at, Omaruru's dry dusty setting beside the shady Omaruru riverbed lends it a sort of Australian Outback feel. The name Omaruru means 'bitter thickmilk' in Herero and refers to the milk produced by cattle which have grazed on bitterbush *(Pechuelloeschae leubnitziae)*. In dry periods, this hardy plant remains green and appealing long after other vegetation has become insipid.

History

The town began as a trading post and Rhenish mission station in 1870, and it was here that the New Testament and the liturgies were first translated into Oshaherero (the language of the Herero people). Like so many Central Namibian towns, during the

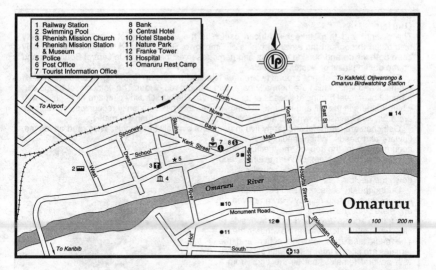

1 Railway Station
2 Swimming Pool
3 Rhenish Mission Church
4 Rhenish Mission Station
  & Museum
5 Police
6 Post Office
7 Tourist Information Office
8 Bank
9 Central Hotel
10 Hotel Staebe
11 Nature Park
12 Franke Tower
13 Hospital
14 Omaruru Rest Camp

Omaruru

colonial occupation later in the century, it inevitably became a German garrison town and as such, was a scene of local resistance.

In January 1904, the town was attacked by Herero forces under chief Manassa. German Captain Victor Franke, who had been engaged in an uprising in southern Namibia, petitioned the then Governor Leutwein for permission to march north and relieve the besieged town. After a 20-day 900-km march, he arrived in Omaruru and led the cavalry charge which defeated the attack. For his efforts, he received the highest German military honours and in 1908, grateful German residents of Omaruru erected the Franke Tower in his honour.

Information

The tourist office (☎ 277), in the municipal building on the main street, is open Monday to Friday, 8 am to 1 pm and 2.15 to 5 pm.

Franke Tower

Captain Franke's tower, which was declared a national monument in 1963, now contains a historical plaque and also affords a decent view over the town. It's normally kept

locked, but if you want to climb it, ask for a key at either the Central Hotel or the Hotel Staebe.

Rhenish Mission Museum

The Rhenish mission station, which was constructed in 1872 by Gottlieb Viehe, now houses the town museum. Displays include 19th-century household and farming implements, an old drinks dispenser and lots of historical photographs. Opposite is the cemetery where Herero chief Wilhelm Zeraua and several early German residents are buried. To visit, pick up the museum keys from the tourist office, opposite the Central Hotel in the main street. Admission is free.

Omaruru Birdwatching Station

Perhaps the best reason to visit Omaruru is to enjoy a birdwatching picnic or braai at the Omaruru Birdwatching Station (☎ 2802). It's set beside a water hole on the Omaruru River, four km from town, and features a birdwatching hide which allows the best possible views of the area's rich avifauna. To get there, head one km out on the Kalkfeld road (C33) and turn east on the D2329.

NAMIBIA

Ostrich

The distinct and unmistakeable African ostrich is the world's largest living bird. It's widely distributed throughout the savanna plains of Zimbabwe, Botswana and Namibia, and is widely seen both inside and outside of parks and game reserves, particularly in central Botswana and on the desert plains of western Namibia.

The adult ostrich stands around two metres high and weighs up to 150 kg. In breeding males, the neck and legs, which are normally bare, turn a bright red colour. The ostrich's long legs can propel it over level ground at speeds of up to 50 km/h. The black bushy plumage highlighted with white feathers in the tail and redundant wings makes the males instantly recognisable. Females are a uniform greyish brown and are slightly smaller and lighter than the males.

Ostriches are territorial and rarely live in groups of over six individuals. They feed on leaves, flowers and seeds. When feeding, the food is accumulated in the top of the neck. It then passes down to the stomach in large lumps, and it can be amusing to watch these actually sliding down the neck.

During the dry season, males put on quite an impressive courtship display. Having driven off any male rivals, he trots up to the female with tail erect, then squats down and rocks from side to side, while alternately waving his wings in the air. The neck also gets into the action and the females are clearly impressed. Males may mate with several females, but all the eggs from a given male's mates wind up on the same nest. Therefore, nests may contain as many as 30 eggs. By day, the eggs are incubated by the head female (the first one he mated with); by night, the male takes over nest duties. His other mates have nothing further to do with the eggs or chicks. ■

Anibib Farm

On the farm Anibib (☎ 1711), just off the D2315, you can visit one of the largest collections of ancient rock paintings in Namibia. This particular gallery is known especially for the depictions of both humans and animals, which are represented in a variety of positions and involved in various activities. The farmers run two guided tours daily for groups of six or fewer people; pre-bookings are essential.

Festivals

Each year on the weekend nearest 10 October, the White Flag Herero people hold a procession from the Ozonde residential suburb to the graveyard opposite the mission house, where their chief Wilhelm Zeraua was buried after his defeat in the German-Herero wars.

Places to Stay

The leafy *Omaruru Rest Camp* (☎ 109; fax 309) charges US$3 per site and US$0.50 per person. Basic two/three-bed bungalows rent for US$19/12, while self-catering chalets cost US$22 for four people. A miniature golf course is now in the works.

The low-slung, German-run *Hotel Staebe* (☎ 35; fax 339), occupying a pleasant leafy setting across the river from the centre, charges US$32/44 for a single/double room with breakfast.

The smaller and more spartan *Central Hotel* (☎ 30) is – as its name would suggest – in the town centre. Single/double rooms cost US$22/28 without breakfast.

Omaruru lies in the heart of guest-farm country, and there are several places to choose from. One recommended option is the hospitable *Erindi-Onganga Guest Farm*

(☎ 1202), which lies six km off the D2351, approximately 75 km north-west of Omaruru. Single/double rooms with private facilities and full board cost US$44/55.

Places to Eat

On the main street through town, you'll find the cosy *White House Café & Milk Bar*, housed in a historic building dating from 1907. In addition to the obligatory German bakery goods, they serve 'farmhouse' breakfasts, lunches and snacks. It's open daily from 8 am to 7 pm. For takeaways, freshly baked bread and ice cream, visit the *Mini-Markt*, also on the main street.

Both hotels also have attached restaurants; the wholesome German-style meals at the *Hotel Staebe* are especially recommended. Since Omaruru is in a major fruit-growing area, inexpensive citrus fruit is sold along the roadside from July to September.

Getting There & Away

Omaruru lies 280 km from Windhoek, but there's no public transport. For those with their own vehicle, the well-maintained C33, which passes through Omaruru, provides the quickest route between Swakopmund and Etosha.

Trains running from Windhoek to Tsumeb stop in Omaruru at 4.15 am on Saturday and Monday, and at 1.18 am on Wednesday and Friday. From Tsumeb to Windhoek, they stop at 9.15 pm on Monday, Tuesday, Thursday and Friday. The weekday economy/sleeper class fare from Windhoek is US$4.20/12; on weekends, it's US$8.50/25.

KALKFELD

Although there's nothing to the tiny town of Kalkfeld itself, a worthwhile excursion will take you to the Etjo sandstone impressions of a 25-metre saurian wander that took place 170 million years ago. Around 200 million years ago, Namibia was covered in a shallow sea, which gradually filled in with wind-blown sand and eroded silt. The footprints were made in what was then soft clay by a three-toed dinosaur that walked on its hind

legs – probably a forerunner of modern-day birds.

The tracks are 29 km from Kalkfeld on the challengingly named Otjihaenamaparero farm, just off route D2414. The site was declared a national monument in 1951, but visitors must still obtain permission of the farmer before entering. There's no place to stay in Kalkfeld, but the site makes a viable day visit from Otjiwarongo or the nearby Mt Etjo Safari Lodge.

Places to Stay

The only accommodation is the popular and luxurious *Mt Etjo Safari Lodge* (☎ 1602; fax 1644), PO Box 81, Kalkfeld, set in the heart of the private nature reserve owned by conservationist Jan Oelofse. The name Etjo means 'place of refuge', and its place in history was sealed in April 1989 with the signing of the Mt Etjo Peace Agreement, which ended the bush war and set the stage for Namibian independence the following March. Single/double rooms with en suite facilities cost US$68/124, including full board and game drives. Add a king-size bed and private veranda and they're US$75/137. For an opulent luxury flat, you'll pay US$260. Transfers are extra.

OUTJO

The small but attractive town of Outjo, which is decked in bougainvilleas for much of the year, was established in 1880 by trader Tom Lambert. It was rather a latecomer by local standards and unlike many other towns in the area, it never served as a mission station. In the mid-1890s, it did a stint as a German garrison town, but it didn't see enough trouble to earn itself much of a place in history.

Today, Outjo's environs boast citrus groves and, as with most of central Namibia, concentrate mainly on cattle-ranching. For visitors, the town best serves as a jumping-off point for trips into the Okaukuejo area of Etosha National Park.

Naulila Monument

The Naulila Monument commemorates

NAMIBIA

German officials and soldiers who were massacred by the Portuguese on 19 October 1914 near Fort Naulila on the Kunene River in Angola. It also commemorates the soldiers killed on 18 December 1914, under Major Franke, who was sent to avenge the earlier losses.

Franke House

One of Outjo's first buildings, the Franke House – originally called the Kliphuis or 'stone house' – was constructed in 1899 under orders of Major von Estorff as a residence for himself and subsequent German commanders. It was later occupied by Major Victor Franke, who lent it his name. The building now houses the Outjo Museum, which contains exhibits outlining the town's political and natural history.

It's open Monday to Friday from 10 am to 12.30 pm and 3 to 5 pm. At other times, pick up a key at the tourist office on the main road through town. Admission is free.

Windmill Tower

Out on the C39, east of Outjo, you'll see the old stone windmill tower which rises 9.5 metres beside the Etosha Hotel. It was constructed in 1900 to provide fresh water to supply the hospital and the German soldiers and their horses.

Places to Stay & Eat

Outjo's *Municipal Camp Site* (☎ 13) charges US$3 per site plus US$0.30 per person. Basic self-catering bungalows which sleep two/four people cost US$10/17.

Outjo's top hotel, the *Hotel Onduri* (☎ 14; fax 166), has single/double rooms with private facilities for US$29/40 without breakfast. As you'd probably guess, it caters mostly for tourists en route to Etosha. The pleasant courtyard contains some particularly fragrant citrus trees. The smaller *Hotel Etosha* (☎ 26), along the road towards Otavi, charges US$37/45 for single/double rooms.

Places to Eat

Both hotel restaurants and bars serve up meals and snacks. On the main street, diagonally opposite the tourist office, you'll find the super little *Café-Bäckerei*, which serves good basic meals – mainly the likes of chicken, wienerschnitzel and burgers – and the bread and sweet treats are famous throughout the region.

Getting There & Away

The only public transport serving Outjo is the thrice-weekly railways bus to and from Otjiwarongo. It leaves Outjo on Monday at 7.30 am and on Wednesday and Friday at 1 pm. The trip takes an hour and costs US$2 each way.

For hitchhikers, Outjo is a logical terminal for trips through Etosha National Park as Andersson Gate, near Okaukuejo Camp, lies just 105 tarred km away along the C38.

In addition to using the main C38 road, which connects Otjiwarongo with Etosha, you can reach Outjo via a short cut which turns off 10 km north of Kalkfeld (on the C33 from Karibib). From Damaraland, the best route to follow is the recently tarred C39, which crosses the Fransfontein Mountains from Khorixas. Hitching is likely to be slow on any of these routes, including the C38.

OTJIWARONGO

Otjiwarongo, whose Herero name means 'the pleasant place', has a population of 8500 and is a mainly agricultural and ranching centre. It's also the crossroads of northern Namibia, at the point where the roads between Windhoek, Swakopmund, Outjo/Etosha and the Golden Triangle converge. In September and early October, it positively explodes with the vivid colours of blooming jacaranda and bougainvillea. It's also the staging point for trips into the wonderful Waterberg Plateau Park.

In 1891, after a treaty was signed between missionaries and the Herero chief Kambazembi, a Rhenish mission station was established. A German military garrison followed in 1904, and when a narrow-gauge railway from Swakopmund to the Otavi and Tsumeb mines came on line in 1906, the town of Otjiwarongo was officially founded.

Information

The tourist office is in the municipal offices, which are signposted from the main road. Tourist information is also provided at the Hamburger Hof Hotel.

Locomotive Number 41

Train buffs will want to have a look at Locomotive No 41, which stands in front of the railway station. It was manufactured by the Henschel company of Kassel, Germany, in 1912 and was brought to Namibia to haul ore between the Tsumeb mines and the port at Swakopmund. It was retired from service in 1960 when the 0.6-metre narrow gauge was replaced with a 1.067-metre gauge.

Crocodile Ranch

One unusual attraction is Namibia's first crocodile ranch, open daily from 9 am and 6 pm. It's beside the caravan park, a short walk from the town centre, and is signposted from the main road. Guided tours are available and there's a café serving snacks and light meals.

Places to Stay

The municipal camp site at Otjiwarongo (☎ 2231; fax 2098) is conveniently located beside the crocodile ranch, allowing campers to take advantage of the café there. The charge is US$6 per site plus US$0.80 per person.

Another inexpensive option is the *Rent-a-Room* (☎ 2517), diagonally opposite the Hamburger Hof Hotel. For basic single/double accommodation with shared facilities, they charge US$17/26.

The nicer of Otjiwarongo's two hotels is the *Hamburger Hof* (☎ 2520; fax 3607) which is not, as it's name may suggest, any sort of fast-food outlet. Single/double budget rooms cost US$21/26, while rooms with television are US$30/45. A continental/ English breakfast costs an additional US$3/6.

The smaller *Hotel Brumme* (☎ 2420), which has been closed for renovations for some years now, last charged US$25/35 for single/double rooms with en suite facilities.

It should be re-opened by the time you read this.

Out of Town Less than one km west of the B1, three km south of Otjiwarongo, is *Otjibamba Lodge* (☎ 3133; fax 3206), which is a sort of low key resort offering an alternative to the in-town digs. Accommodation in pleasant little chalets costs US$37/46 for a single/double with breakfast. Facilities include a restaurant, bar, pool and nine-hole golf course.

On the B1, 30 km south of town, is the *Otjiwa Game Ranch Rest Camp* (☎ /fax 11002), with bungalows for one/three people costing US$29/40 and an eight-person bungalow for US$65. Meal areas are available for an extra charge. The main attraction is the wildlife viewing on this private ranch.

If you can spare a bit of cash, a real highlight of the Otjiwarongo area is *Okonjima* (☎ 18212 farmline; fax 4382), or 'place of baboons', which is technically a guest farm but in reality, more like a safari lodge. Run by conservationists Wayne and Lise Hanssen, it's one of Namibia's most pleasant and unique accommodation options. If you can manage it, don't miss the opportunity to stay at least a night or two. Accommodation is in double bungalows which cost US$60 per person including three excellent home-cooked meals, game walks and game drives. Horse-riding must be booked in advance and costs extra.

A big appeal of Okonjima is birdwatching from the three observation hides, and according to the brochure, over 200 species have been identified on the ranch, including the Damara rockrunner, Monteiro's Hornbill and Hartlaub's francolin. Other highlights are the Bushman Trail, an excursion which explains and demonstrates the traditional San lifestyle in Namibia, and the Bantu Trail, which compares the San traditions with those of their Bantu neighbours.

The real attraction, however, is the owners' affection for and interest in cheetahs and other wild cats, and they've established a cheetah and leopard rehabilitation centre, where problem cats are taught not to ravage

NAMIBIA

cattle. They've also set up an organisation, Africat, to protect all native wild cats under threat from humans. In addition to their rehab cases, they also keep two tame pet cheetahs, Caesar and Chinga, who behave like overgrown kitty cats and get on well with guests. Two other recent additions are Chui, who was hit by a car, and Schmoosi, who is too habituated to humans to be released into the wild. You may also catch sight of a baboon named Elvis and a warthog named Scratch. Because of the large cats, no children under the age of 12 are allowed at the farm.

For more information on their efforts with the large cats, you should contact Africat directly. The address is included under Useful Organisations in the regional Facts for the Visitor chapter.

To reach Okonjima, follow the B1 for 49 km south of Otjiwarongo and turn west onto the D2515, just beyond the sign reading 'Okahandja 130 km'. Follow this road for 15 km and turn left onto the farm road for the final 10 km to the farm.

Places to Eat
Both hotels have bars and restaurants serving meals and snacks, and the cafeteria and snack bar at the crocodile farm serves basic light meals. The main street through Otjiwarongo has the usual range of takeaway facilities. An excellent bakery in the centre is *Carstensen's*.

Getting There & Away
The Intercape Mainliner bus leaves the Grab-a-Phone terminal in Windhoek for Tsumeb on Monday, Wednesday, Friday and Sunday at 7 am, passing Otjiwarongo at 9.30 am. From Tsumeb, it departs at 1 pm on Monday, Wednesday, Friday and Sunday; and passes Otjiwarongo at 3 pm. The fare from either Windhoek or Tsumeb is US$19.

All minibuses travelling between Windhoek and Ovamboland also pass through Otjiwarongo; they stop at the Engen petrol station. (When approaching the town from the south, watch for the twin peaks of the Omatako – Herero for 'buttocks' – west

of the road.) There's also an occasional minibus service to Okakarara, which can drop you within reasonable striking distance (25 km) of Waterberg Plateau Park.

Rail service from Windhoek to Tsumeb departs at 9 pm on Friday and Sunday (arriving in Otjiwarongo at 7.33 am) and at 6 pm on Tuesday and Thursday (chugging into Otjiwarongo at 4.25 am). Southbound, it departs from Tsumeb on Monday, Tuesday, Thursday and Friday at 11.30 am and arrives in Otjiwarongo at 3.39 pm.

Between Otjiwarongo and Outjo, you can take the railways bus; it leaves Otjiwarongo on Monday at 8.30 am, Wednesday at 4.30 pm and Friday at 5 pm.

WATERBERG PLATEAU PARK
The Waterberg Plateau Park takes in a 50-km long and 16-km wide Etjo sandstone plateau, which looms 150 metres above the plain. As its name would suggest, around this sheer-sided Lost World is an abundance of freshwater springs, thanks mainly to the natural aquifer created by layers of sandstone underlain by mudstone. Rainwater is absorbed by the sandstone and percolates down through the strata until it reaches the south-west tilting mudstone; it flows down the slope to emerge in springs at the base of the cliffs. As a result, the area supports a relatively lush mosaic of trees and scrub savanna, and an abundance of wildlife.

The park is also known as a repository for rare and threatened species, including sable and roan antelopes and both white and black rhinos. You may also see wild dogs, tsessebe, buffaloes, cheetahs and lesser bushbabies, among more frequently observed animals. It's also one of the best places on the continent to see leopards.

Waterberg has more than 200 bird species including the black eagle and the rare Ruppell's parrot, rockrunners and both Bradfield's and Monteiro's hornbills.

History
In 1873, a Rhenish mission station was established at Waterberg, but it was destroyed in 1880 during the Herero-Nama

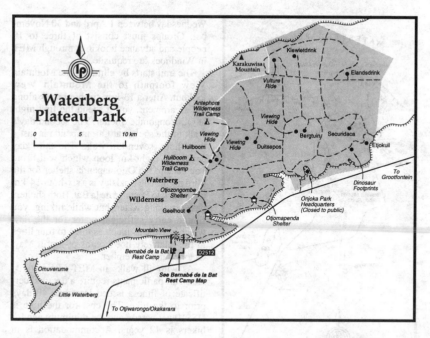

Waterberg Plateau Park

0   5   10 km

wars. In 1904, it was the site of the decisive Battle of the Waterberg between the German colonial forces and the Herero resistance. Thanks to superior communications, the Germans prevailed.

Every year on the weekend nearest 11 August, the local Herero people, the Scouts, the MOTHs, and the Alte Kamaraden (the German legion) commemorate the confrontation. It takes place at the memorial in the cemetery near the resort office. If you wish to attend, sober dress is appropriate.

Information

Tourist information is available at the warden's office in the Bernabé de la Bat Rest Camp. The camp is open year round from 8 am to 1 pm and from 2 pm to sunset. Admission to the park is US$1.50 per person plus US$1.50 per vehicle.

For background reading, see the booklet *Waterberg Flora: Footpaths in & Around the Camp* by Craven & Marais, which costs

US$8 at the camp shop. Alternatively, pick up a copy of the Shell guide *Waterberg Plateau Park* by Ilme Schneider, which is sold in many bookshops and rest camps in the country.

Bernabé de la Bat Walking Tracks

Around the main rest camp, which is built of lovely local pink sandstone, are nine short walking tracks, including one up to the rim of the plateau at Mountain View. They're good for a day or two of easy walking and slow appreciation of the natural elements. However, watch out for snakes, which like to sun themselves on rocks and even on the tracks themselves. No reservations are required.

Okarukuvisa Vulture Sanctuary

In Okarukuvisa Mountains on the plateau's western edge is the only Cape vultury in Namibia. The species was nearly wiped out after a crash in the 1950s, caused mainly by

NAMIBIA

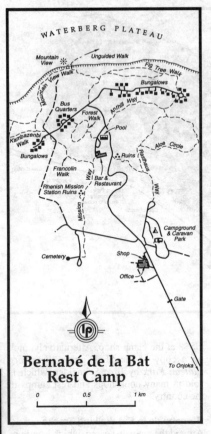

WATERBERG PLATEAU

Mountain View

Unguided Walk

Fig Tree Walk

Mountain View Walk

Bungalows

Bus Quarters

Anthill Way

Forest Walk

Pool

Kambazenbi Walk

Aloe Circle

Bungalows

Rasthaus Way

Ruins

Francolin Walk

Way

Bar & Restaurant

Rhenish Mission Station Ruins

Mission Way

Campground & Caravan Park

Cemetery

Shop

Office

Gate

Bernabé de la Bat Rest Camp

To Onjoka

0   0.5   1 km

Wednesday between 1 April and 30 November. Groups must consist of three to 10 people and advance bookings through MET in Windhoek are requisite.

The trail starts by climbing the Mountain View footpath to the Mountain View lookout. After a 13-km, six-hour walk along the escarpment, you'll spend the first night at Otjozongombe Shelter. The second day's walk to the shelter at Otjomapenda is just a three-hour, seven-km walk. The third day entails an eight-km loop which will bring you back to the Otjomapenda shelter for the third night. The final day is a six-hour 14-km walk back to Bernabé de la Bat. Both shelters have drinking water, but while hiking, you should carry sufficient water for the day, which may be as much as three to four litres in the relatively hot months of April, May, October and November.

As with all walks in MET-administered areas, all participants require a doctors' certificate of fitness issued less than 40 days prior to the hike. The cost for the hike is US$10 per person and the minimum age for hikers is 12 years. Accommodation is in basic shelters, so you won't need a tent, but you must otherwise be self-sufficient, with your own food and sleeping bag. If you don't have a group and can't make a reservation, MET may be able to put you in touch with booked groups which may have space remaining.

Organised Tours

Because visitors aren't permitted to explore the park in their own vehicles and tourist numbers are restricted, MET also arranges twice-daily game drives around the plateau in open 4WD vehicles. The morning drive runs from 8 to 11.30 am and the afternoon drive from 3 to 6.30 pm. Along the way, you can watch wildlife from strategically placed hides. The price is US$14 per person.

There's also the guided Waterberg Wilderness Trail, which is open to hikers every second, third and fourth weekend of the month, from April to November. Groups of six to eight people per trip are accompanied by armed guides. These walks, which must

insecticides sprayed on surrounding farms. MET is now making efforts to increase their numbers, and one tactic has been the establishment of a 'vulture restaurant' near the northern edge of the plateau, which provides the birds with a regular menu of kudu and gemsbok carcasses. Visitors can watch the vultures chomping away every Wednesday morning.

Unguided Hiking Trail

Four-day, 42-km unguided hikes around the roughly figure-eight track through the southern area of the park start at 9 am every

be pre-booked through MET, cost US$25 per person. Participants must be reasonably fit and have their own food and sleeping bags. Accommodation is in simple huts along the route.

The walk begins at 4 pm on Thursday from the Onjoka wildlife administration centre and ends early Sunday afternoon. Groups are driven onto the plateau, from where the walk commences; there's no set route and the itinerary is left to the whims of the guide, although the general interests and fitness of the group will be taken into consideration.

Places to Stay & Eat

The centre of action in the Waterberg is the *Bernabé de la Bat Rest Camp*, which was completed in 1989. Tent and caravan sites cost US$7 for up to eight people, with two vehicles and one caravan or tent. For three/four-bed self-catering bungalows,

you'll pay US$25/36. More basic bus quarters, with toilet and showers but no cooking facilities, cost US$25 for a double.

The camp restaurant is open for meals from 7 to 8.30 am, noon to 1.30 pm and 7 to 9 pm. The bar opens from noon to 2 pm and from 6 to 10 pm. There is also a shop selling staples and during daylight hours, a kiosk sells snacks whenever the restaurant is closed. Other facilities include braai pits, a petrol station and springwater-filled swimming pool. The pool is especially nice, built of russet-coloured sandstone which reflects the hues of the surrounding hills.

Getting There & Away

There is no scheduled public transport to Waterberg, so most travellers without vehicles attempt to hitch. You can take a train, bus or minibus to Otjiwarongo and, if you have plenty of cash, get a taxi from there, but it may cost as much as US$22 each way. Note

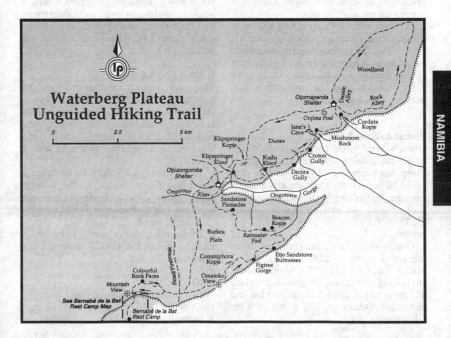

that bicycles and motorbikes aren't permitted in the park.

If you have a good vehicle and a bit of time, the D2512 between Waterberg and Grootfontein is a particularly scenic route.

OTAVI

Between Otjiwarongo and Tsumeb the B1 passes Otavi, not far from the mountains of the same name. It was originally a German garrison town whose natural springs were used to irrigate the surrounding land for the cultivation of wheat. The town grew after the railway was established in 1906 and became a major copper-mining centre linked to Swakopmund via a narrow-gauge railway.

Two km north of Otavi lies the Khorab Memorial, which was erected in 1920. It commemorates the German troops who surrendered to the South African Army under General Louis Botha on 9 July 1915. To get there, follow the road past the hotel, cross the railway line and turn right along the signposted track.

In recent history, Otavi is best known as the site of the 'Otavi ape' discovery. In 1991, French and US palaeontologists uncovered the jawbone of a prehistoric ape-like creature *(Otavipithecus namibiensis)*, which may offer insights into the prehistoric link between apes and humans.

Places to Stay & Eat

Otavi's very basic campground (☎ 22), beside the municipal offices, has 10 grassy camp sites costing US$3 per site plus US$0.50 per person. There are also six self-catering bungalows each with four beds, shower/toilet and cooking facilities costing US$8 per bungalow plus US$0.50 per person.

Otavi's single hotel, imaginatively called the *Otavi Hotel* (☎ 229; fax 73), has 11 rooms costing US$21/27 a single/double, including breakfast. Nonresidents are welcome to patronise the attached bar and restaurant. Otherwise, you're left with the takeaways.

Getting There & Away

All buses and minibuses between Windhoek, Tsumeb and Oshakati pass through Otavi.

HOBA METEORITE

On the farm Hoba, 25 km north-east of Otavi, the world's largest meteorite was discovered in 1920 by hunter Jacobus Brits. No one knows when the Hoba meteorite fell to earth (it's thought to have been around 80,000 years ago), but since it weighs in at around 54,000 kg, it must have made a hell of a thump. It's cuboid in shape – which is rare for meteorites – suggesting that it broke up during impact and that perhaps more bits are awaiting discovery. Analysis has revealed that it's composed of 82% iron, 16% nickel, and 0.8% cobalt, along with traces of other metals.

In 1955, after souvenir hunters began hacking off bits to take home, the site was declared a national monument, and a conservation project was launched with funds from the Rössing Foundation. There's now a visitors' information board and a short nature trail through the nearby bush, as well as a shady picnic site. Admission is US$1 per person.

Getting There & Away

There are frequent minibus services, but unfortunately, you can't catch a return bus on the same day and there's no accommodation in Kombat. Neither is there any public transport to Hoba, but you may be able to find a taxi from Otavi or Grootfontein for around US$14 (N$50).

To get there by car, follow the B8 between Otavi and Grootfontein. At the Kombat copper mines, about 25 km from Otavi, turn north towards the Farm Hoba and follow the 'Meteoriet' signs.

To reach the nearby abandoned mines at Ghaub, follow the D3022 from the B1, signposted 'Ghaub'.

GROOTFONTEIN

With a pronounced colonial feel, Grootfontein (which in Afrikaans means 'big spring') is characterised mainly by an 'upright and

PETER PTSCHELINZEW

CHRIS BARTON

CHRIS BARTON

NAMIBIA
A: Railway Station, Swakopmund
B: Kolmanskop ghost town
C: Diwsib Castle in the Namib Desert

DEANNA SWANEY

DEANNA SWANEY

NAMIBIA
A: Fish River Canyon
B: Dunes at Sossusvlei

respectable' ambience. Many of its buildings are constructed of local limestone and it boasts avenues of jacaranda trees which bloom in September. Today Grootfontein is the centre of Namibia's major cattle farming area and is a pleasant enough market centre.

History

Historically, it was the spring which attracted the earliest travellers to Grootfontein. It was later used by European settlers who first arrived around the 1880s. In 1885, the Dorsland trekkers set up the short-lived Republic of Upingtonia. By 1887, the settlement was gone, but because of the area's mineral wealth, six years later Grootfontein became the headquarters for the German South West Africa Company. In 1896, the German Schutztruppe constructed a fort and Grootfontein became a garrison town. More historical details are provided under individual sites of interest later in this section.

Information

Grootfontein's helpful tourist information office is at the end of the municipal building, just off the main Rundu road, past the Meteor Hotel.

Grootfontein Spring

The Herero knew this area as *Otjivanda tjongue*, or 'leopard's hill', but the current name, which means 'large spring' in Afrikaans, came from the Nama name *Geiaus*, which means the same thing. This reliable source of water attracted both people and wildlife for thousands of years, and also became a halt for European hunters as early as the 1860s.

Later, it attracted the area's first European settlers. In 1855, 40 families of Dorsland ('thirstland') trekkers arrived from Angola to settle on this land, which had been purchased by their leader, Will Jordan, from the Ovambo chief Kambonde. It was proclaimed the 'Republic of Upingtonia', which lasted only two years. In 1893, Grootfontein became the headquarters of the South West Africa Company, attracting still more Afrikaner settlers.

The spring from which the town takes its name and the adjacent Tree Park, which was planted by the South West Africa Company, can still be seen near the swimming pool on the northern end of town.

German Fort & Museum

In 1896, a contingent of Schutztruppe soldiers were posted to Grootfontein and, using local labour, they constructed a fort between Upingtonia and Eriksson Sts. It was enlarged several times in the early 1900s and in 1922, a large limestone extension was added. Later, until 1968, it served as a boarding school but then it fell into disuse. It was only a last minute public appeal that saved the building from demolition, and in 1974, it was restored to house the municipal museum. This display outlines the area's mineral wealth, early industries and colonial history and includes collections of minerals, domestic items, old cameras and typewriters, and a restored carpentry and blacksmith's shop.

The museum is open Tuesday and Friday from 4 to 6 pm and on Wednesday from 9 to 11 am. At other times, phone Mr Menge (☎ 2061) to have it unlocked.

Cemetery

In the town cemetery, just off the main Rundu road, are the graves of several Schutztruppe soldiers who died around the turn of the century.

Dragon's Breath Cave

If you're ticking off superlatives, how about this? Dragon's Breath Cave 46 km from Grootfontein holds the world's largest known underground lake. This fabulous two-hectare subterranean reservoir occupies an immense chamber 60 metres below the surface. Its waters are crystal clear and with sufficient light, allow 100 metres visibility. The name is derived from the spontaneous condensation caused by warm, moist outside air forcing its way into the cool chamber.

Visiting the lake isn't straightforward by any means, and it's currently closed to casual visitors. In any case, it would require more than a little stamina; you must first descend four metres on ropes and a hanging ladder, then crawl 15 metres down an underground slope before sliding seven more metres onto a ledge. At this point, there's a frightening 18-metre descent to another ledge, which affords a view through the dome-shaped ceiling of the lake chamber. The final 25 vertical metres to the lake and its small beach must be negotiated using ropes.

Places to Stay

The *Olea Municipal Camp & Caravan Park* (☎ 2930), beside the swimming pool, costs US$5 for a camp site plus US$1.50 per vehicle and US$1 per person. Four-bed chalets cost US$22, plus US$3.50 for bedding. For a luxury self-catering chalet, you'll pay US$42/50 for a single/double, or US$58/66 for one accommodating three/four people.

Campers should especially note that there's a serious security problem at this camp site. Don't leave anything in your tent or vehicle while you're away and bring everything inside at night. Don't even leave bags near the door of the tent, as several readers have reported thefts from tents while they were sleeping inside.

Grootfontein also has two hotels. The friendly *Meteor Hotel* (☎ 2078; fax 3072) on Kaiser Wilhelm St has singles/doubles at US$29/52, with breakfast. The integrated bar is fun and offers a pleasant whiff of fresh air. The smaller and more spartan *Nord Hotel* (☎ /fax 2049), off the main road, has 11 rooms and charges US$20 per person.

For an out-of-town option, there's *Gästefarm Dornhügel* (☎ 8164; fax 3349, Abenab), 42 km from Grootfontein, along the C44 towards Tsumkwe. Rooms with breakfast and dinner cost US$36 per person; with three meals, they're US$40. Game drives cost an additional US$7 per person.

Places to Eat

For the finest dining in Grootfontein, hit the restaurant at the Meteor Hotel, which specialises in seafood. Both hotels also have bars, and there's a small restaurant beside the campground. For coffee, sweet treats and light meals throughout the day, try *Bäckerei*

Steinbach, a bakery and coffee shop which is open from 7 am to 6 pm. Don't miss the chocolate-covered bananas. For a splurge, try *Le Club*. Takeaway meals are available at the Shell petrol station and the Sentra supermarket.

Getting There & Away

Given its size and importance, it seems odd that Grootfontein no longer lies on either the railway line or the Intercape Mainliner route. However, hitching is relatively good – it's best to wait at the petrol stations. There are minibuses which make the run between Grootfontein, Kombat, Otavi and Tsumeb.

Getting Around

Grootfontein has only a limited local taxi service. The Meteor Hotel is the local agent for Imperial Car Hire.

TSUMEB

Tsumeb lies at the apex of the 'Golden Triangle' of roads linking it with Otavi and Grootfontein. The name is derived from the melding of the San word *tsoumsoub*, 'to dig in loose ground', and the Herero word *otjisume*, or 'place of frogs'. To fathom the latter rendition, however, requires some imagination. The Tsumeb area isn't really known for its frog population; it's just that the red, brown, green and grey streaks created by minerals resembled dried scum (in Afrikaans, *paddaslyk* or frog spawn) that had been scooped out of a water hole and splattered on the rocks. Still, both the frogs and the digging equipment appear on the town's crest.

The prosperity of this mining town is based on copper ore and associated minerals (lead, silver, germanium and cadmium) around a volcanic pipe. In fact, it's currently the biggest lead-producing mine in Africa and the fifth largest in the world. Of the 184 minerals that have been discovered here, 10 are found nowhere else in the world. Collectors of minerals justifiably rank Tsumeb as one of the greatest natural wonders on earth, and the finest specimens have found their way into museum collections around the

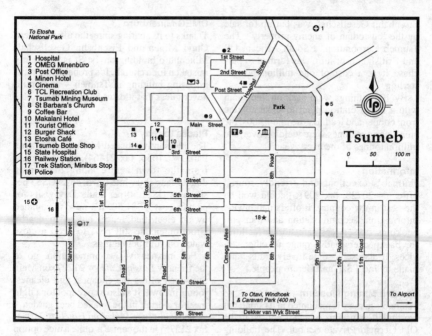

To Etosha
National Park

1 Hospital
2 OMEG Minenbüro
3 Post Office
4 Minen Hotel
5 Cinema
6 TCL Recreation Club
7 Tsumeb Mining Museum
8 St Barbara's Church
9 Coffee Bar
10 Makalani Hotel
11 Tourist Office
12 Burger Shack
13 Etosha Café
14 Tsumeb Bottle Shop
15 State Hospital
16 Railway Station
17 Trek Station, Minibus Stop
18 Police

1st Street
2nd Street
Post Street
Hospital Street
Park
5
6

Tsumeb

0   50   100 m

Main Street
8 7

12
13
11 10
14
3rd Street

4th Street
5th Street
6th Street

15
16

17

7th Street

8th Street

9th Street

1st Road
3rd Road
8th Road

Bahnhof Street
2nd Road
4th Road
5th Road
6th Road
Omega Allee
8th Road
9th Road
10th Road
11th Road

18

To Otavi, Windhoek
& Caravan Park (400 m)

To Airport

Dekker van Wyk Street

NAMIBIA

globe. The most complete collection is displayed in the Natural History Museum at the Smithsonian Institution in Washington, DC, but you'll also see a fine assembly of minerals and historical data at the small town museum in Tsumeb itself.

History

The discovery of numerous prehistoric mine sites in the area takes Tsumeb's mining history back to the Iron Age. The first European to be shown its riches was Sir Francis Galton, who passed through on a trip to the north in 1851. However, no serious European interest was taken for over 40 years. On 12 January 1893, a British surveyor, Matthew Rogers, working for the South West Africa Company of London was shown the extraordinarily colourful volcanic pipe there. In his report, Rogers exclaimed of the outcrop: 'In the whole of my experience, I have never seen such a sight as was presented before my view at Tsumeb, and I doubt very much that I shall ever see such another in any other locality.'

As a result, active exploration – with an eye towards exploitation – began in 1900. Early on, the German operations company, Otavi Minen-und Eisenbahn Gesellschaft, determined that the extent of the deposits merited a railway, and in November 1903, they signed a contract with the South West Africa Company to construct the 560-km narrow-gauge railway to the coast at Swakopmund. The project was interrupted by the German-Herero wars, but the railroad was finally completed in August 1906.

The mining operations came on line in 1907 and by the start of WWI, they were producing 75,000 tonnes of ore annually. Although the war brought everything to a standstill, production was resumed in 1921 and by 1930, the annual output peaked at 236,000 tonnes of ore. WWII again interrupted production and in 1946 after Germany lost the war, the Otavi Minen-und

Eisenbahn Gesellschaft was put up for sale by the 'custodian of enemy property'. The Tsumeb Corporation, a South African, US and British consortium, was formed to purchase it at a cost of one million pounds sterling.

By 1948, things were back on line again with a new flotation plant to separate zinc from copper and lead. By the mid-1960s, the area's various mines were yielding over one million tonnes of ore every year.

Information

Tsumeb's excellent and friendly tourist office (☎ 20728; fax 20916) could well be the best in the country. It offers nationwide information, accommodation and transport bookings, fax services, safe-storage facilities for backpackers and a range of other services. It also sells some lovely crafts hand made by local San and Herero people.

Tsumeb Mining Museum

Tsumeb's history is recounted in its small but worthwhile museum, which is housed in the Old German Private School. The building itself, which dates from 1915, served for two brief periods as a school and also did a stint as a hospital for German troops.

In addition to its outstanding mineral displays, mining machinery and ethnic exhibits, the museum holds lots of militaria, including weapons recovered from Lake Otjikoto. This was part of a dump of military materials, including German and South African field guns, cannons and vehicles, which were abandoned by German troops prior to their surrender to the South Africans in 1915. Entry costs US$1.50 and it's open from 9 am to noon and from 3 to 6 pm weekdays and 3 to 6 pm Saturday.

St Barbara's Church

Tsumeb's distinctive Roman Catholic church was consecrated in 1914 and dedicated to St Barbara, the patron saint of mineworkers. It contains some fine colonial murals and an odd tower, which makes it look less like a church than a municipal building in some small German backwater.

OMEG Minenbüro

Thanks to its soaring spire, the ultra-modern Otavi Minen-und Eisenbahn Gesellschaft Minenbüro building on 1st St is frequently mistaken for a church. It's probably the most imposing building in Tsumeb – and you'd never guess that it dates back to 1907!

Places to Stay

The pleasantly situated Municipal Caravan Park (☎ 21056; fax 21464), about one km from the town centre along the lonely double-lane entry into town, costs US$3 per site plus US$1.50 per adult. Day visits for picnics cost US$1.50. It's now surrounded by an electrified fence, but as in nearby Grootfontein, it still pays to keep a close watch on your belongings.

For inexpensive accommodation, go to the friendly Etosha Café (☎ 21207) on Main St, which offers the cheapest and cleanest rooms in town. It's also a cosy spot for a light meal or a drink in the relaxed beer garden.

The mid-range Makalani Hotel (☎ 21051; fax 21575) in the centre is quite a nice option at US$41/51 for single/double rooms with breakfast, TV and phone. The restaurant does good European-style buffet lunches for just US$3. For drinking, there are two attached bars: the lively Golden Nugget Bar and the more subdued private bar known as Pierre's Pub.

At the Minen Hotel (☎ 21071; fax 21750), air-conditioned single/double courtyard rooms with shower cost US$33/41; with bath and toilet they're US$37/49. The hotel's greatest asset is probably its nice leafy setting, near the end of a lovely avenue of jacaranda trees.

On the highway about 60 km south of Tsumeb is the Camp Resthouse Zum Potjie, which is set in a nice hilly area. It offers a restaurant and basic lodge accommodation.

Further from town is the very appealing Sachsenheim Game Ranch (☎ 13521 farmline; fax 21891), on a game ranch owned by Gerd and Babi Sachse. It lies just off the B1, 80 km north-west of Tsumeb and 30 km from the Von Lindequist Gate of Etosha National

Park. You can choose between rooms for US$21 per person with breakfast or camping for US$3 per person plus US$4 per vehicle.

Places to Eat

For a light snack or coffee in a homely atmosphere, go to the friendly *Etosha Café* (☎ 21207). A decent place for quick meals is *Burger Shack*, which opens from 8.30 am to 2 pm and 6 to 11 pm Monday to Saturday. A booming local disco rages on Friday and Saturday nights, and the pizza is recommended.

A good inexpensive cafeteria is the *TCL Recreation Club* by the cinema. It's for members only, but visitors can pick up a temporary membership card from the tourist information office.

You'll also find several smaller places, such as the takeaways at the petrol stations and the *Coffee Bar* on Main St near the park.

Things to Buy

Tsumeb has several shops specialising in minerals and ores (such as azurite) for collectors. They also deal in carvings, curios and jewellery made from local minerals. The shop in the tourist office is very good value.

Getting There & Away

Air Namibia serves Tsumeb four times weekly from Eros Airport in Windhoek. After stopping, the flight continues on to Rundu and Katima Mulilo before returning to Windhoek by the reverse route.

Intercape Mainliner buses from Tsumeb to Windhoek depart from the Minen Hotel on Monday, Wednesday, Friday and Sunday at 1 pm and arrive in Windhoek at 5.30 pm. They depart from Windhoek for Tsumeb on Monday, Wednesday, Friday and Saturday at 7 am and arrive at 11.30 am. The fare is US$27 each way; the tourist office serves as the booking agent. Minibuses to and from Windhoek and Oshakati stop at the Trek petrol station (look for the fibreglass zebra); most pass through around midday.

When the rail service to and from Wind-hoek is functioning, slow trains depart from Tsumeb on Monday, Tuesday, Thursday and Friday at 11.30 am and arrive in Windhoek at 5.06 am the following morning. From Windhoek, they leave on Friday and Sunday at 9 pm, arriving at 2.42 pm the following day; and on Tuesday and Thursday at 6 pm, arriving in Tsumeb at 9.25 am the following day. From Tuesday to Thursday, the economy/sleeper class fares are US$6/18; from Friday to Sunday, they're double that.

As the main jumping-off point for trips to Namutoni in Etosha National Park, Tsumeb does see quite a few hopeful hitchers. Despite the park's popularity, however, there isn't as much traffic as one might expect, and hitching can be slow.

Getting Around

There's an office of Avis Car Hire (☎ 20520) at the Safari Centre on Jordaan St.

AROUND TSUMEB
Lake Otjikoto

Lake Otjikoto ('deep hole' in Herero) lies about 24 km north-west of Tsumeb, just off the B1. In May 1851, explorers Charles Andersson and Francis Galton stumbled across this unusual lake, which fills the remnant of a limestone cavern whose roof collapsed, leaving an enormous sinkhole measuring 100 by 150 metres. Galton measured the depth of the lake at 55 metres, although some locals maintain that it's bottomless. Also interesting is the fact that Lake Otjikoto and nearby Lake Guinas are the only natural lakes in Namibia.

In 1915, during WWI, the retreating Germans dumped weaponry and ammunition into Lake Otjikoto to prevent the equipment falling into South African hands. It's rumoured that they jettisoned five cannons, 10 cannon bases, three Gatling guns and 300 to 400 wagonloads of ammunition. Some of this stuff was later recovered by a joint effort from the South African Army, the Tsumeb Corporation and Windhoek State Museum. Most of the artefacts were salvaged in 1916 – at great cost and effort – but that wasn't the end of it. In 1970, divers discovered an intact Krupp ammunition wagon at 41 metres, which is now on display at the State Museum in Windhoek. In 1977 and 1983, two more ammunition carriers were salvaged from the lake. Subsequent finds include another cannon, captured from South African forces early this century; it has now been restored and is on display in the Tsumeb Museum.

Lake Otjikoto and nearby Lake Guinas are the only known habitats of the unusual mouth-breeding cichlid fish *(Pseudocrenilabrus philander)*, which appear in a variety of brilliant colours, from dark green to bright red, yellow and blue. Biologists believe this may be related to the absence of predators, which made it unnecessary for the fish to develop camouflage. It's thought that the first cichlids were a species of tilapia (bream) washed into the lake by ancient floods.

Although Lake Otjikoto was once a free roadside stop, an enterprising local has now put in toilets and a curio shop, and surrounded it with a chain-link fence. Admission is now US$0.25. The lake itself is now lost amid a bit of clutter, but it's still worth a stop, if for nothing else but to read the sign painted on the curio shop.

Qualified divers who'd like to dive in Lake Otjikoto, which still contains remnants of the Germans' big equipment jettison, can contact Theo Schoeman of the Windhoek Underwater Club (☎ (061) 238320).

Lake Guinas

South-west of Lake Otjikoto is a geologically similar lake, Lake Guinas, which is used to irrigate surrounding farmland. It's considerably smaller and less touristy than its counterpart and is also twice as deep, less cluttered and costs nothing to visit.

However, it's not as readily accessible, so you'll need a vehicle. To get there, drive 27 km north-west of Tsumeb on the B1 and turn south-west on the D3043. After about 20 km, turn south-east onto the D3031. The lake is five km further along.

Etosha National Park

Etosha National Park is undoubtedly one of the world's greatest wildlife-viewing venues, and few visitors to Namibia will want to miss it. This vast park takes in over 20,000 sq km and protects 114 species of mammal, as well as 340 bird species, 16 reptile and amphibian, one fish and countless insect species.

The park's name, which means 'great white place of dry water', is taken from the vast white and greenish-coloured Etosha Pan. However, it's the surrounding woodlands and grasslands which provide habitats for the area's diverse animal and vegetable communities.

Etosha Pan is an immense, flat, saline desert covering over 5000 sq km which originated 12 million years ago as a shallow lake fed by the waters of the Kunene River. Over the intervening period, climatic and tectonic changes lowered the water level and created the brackish salt pan, which only occasionally holds water. In good rainfall years, this vast shallow depression is fed by incoming channels (known as *oshanas*, which are dry river channels, and *omiramba*, fossil river valleys which may flow underground). These include the oshanas Ekuma and Oshigambo in the north and the omuramba Ovambo *(omuramba* is the singular of omiramba) in the east. For a few days each year, Etosha Pan becomes a shallow lagoon teeming with flamingoes and white pelicans.

History

The first Europeans to see the wonders of Etosha were the traders and explorers John Andersson and Francis Galton, who arrived by wagon at what is now Namutoni in 1851. They were followed in 1876 by an American trader, G McKeirnan, who observed: 'All the menageries in the world turned loose would not compare to the sight I saw that day'.

However, Etosha didn't attract the interest of tourists and conservationists until after the turn of the century, when the governor of

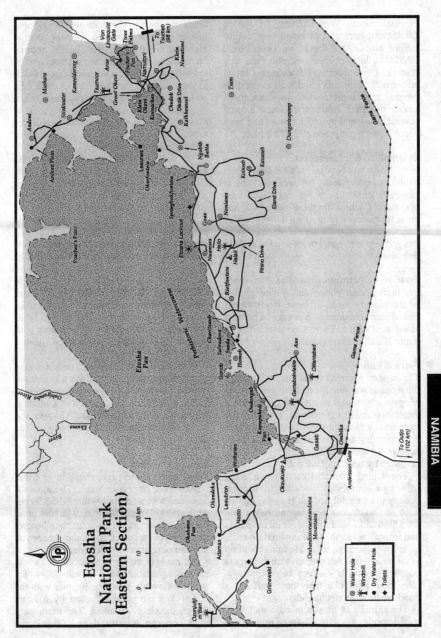

Etosha National Park (Eastern Section)

Water Hole
Windmill
Dry Water Hole
Toilets

NAMIBIA

German South West Africa, Dr F von Lindequist, became concerned over diminishing animal numbers and proclaimed 99,526 sq km, including Etosha Pan, as a reserve. There were no fences at this stage, so animals could still wander off along their normal migration routes. In subsequent years, the park boundaries were altered several times, and by 1970, Etosha had been pared down to its present 23,175 sq km.

Orientation & Information

Only the eastern two thirds of Etosha is open to the general public; the western third is reserved exclusively for organised-tour operators. Each of the three rest camps has an information centre open during office hours, and the staff at either of the main gates can sell you a map and point you in the right direction.

Post & Telecommunications Namutoni has both a coin phone and a card phone, which may be used to make international calls. From Okaukuejo, calls must be booked at the post office. There's no post office at either Halali or Namutoni.

Flora & Fauna

The most widespread vegetation in Etosha is the mopane woodland which fringes the pan. Mopane constitutes about 80% of the park's vegetation and from December to March, the trees wear a pleasant green coat. This sparse bush country also includes umbrella-thorn acacias *(Acacia torilis)* and other trees favoured by browsing animals.

The weird baobab-like *moringa* trees *(Moringa ovalifolia)*, peculiar to Etosha, occupy the area dubbed the Haunted Forest, west of Okaukuejo. San legend has it that after God had found a home for all the plants and animals on earth, he discovered a bundle of leftover moringa trees. He flung them up in the air and they fell to earth with their roots pointing skywards – and so they remain. Of late, these particular trees have suffered a good measure of elephant damage.

The animals of Etosha include such protected species as the black-faced impala and

black rhinoceros. There are also large populations of more common animals such as elephants, giraffes, Burchell's zebras, Hartmann's (mountain) zebras, springboks, red hartebeests, blue wildebeests, gemsboks, elands, kudu, roan antelopes, ostriches, jackals, hyenas, lions and a few cheetahs and leopards. Most visitors see a majority of these species during their visit. Good places to wait for predators are the water holes at Rietfontein and Kalkheuwel

The wildlife densities vary naturally, with the local ecology. As its name would suggest, Oliphantsbad (near Okaukuejo), is a good place to see elephants. For rhinos, however, you couldn't do better than the floodlit water hole at Okaukuejo. The further east you go in the park, the more wildebeests, kudu and impalas join the springboks and gemsboks. The Namutoni area, which receives 443 mm of precipitation annually (compared with 412 mm at Okaukuejo), is the best place to see the black-faced impala and the Damara dik-dik, Africa's smallest antelope. In addition to its large mammals, Etosha has some interesting smaller creatures, including both yellow and slender mongooses, honey badgers and leguaans.

Birdlife is also profuse. Yellow-billed hornbills are common, and on the ground, look for the huge kori bustard, which weighs 15 kg and seldom flies, as well as korhaans, marabou storks, white-backed vultures and many other species. You're also certain to see many birds of prey.

Visiting the Park

When entering the park, check in at either Namutoni or Andersson gates. There, you'll be issued with a permit costing US$2.50 per adult and US$3 per vehicle, which is good for your entire stay. This must then be presented at your reserved rest camp, where you pay camping or accommodation fees.

All roads in the eastern section of Etosha are easily passable to a 2WD vehicle, but for wildlife viewing, you'll be happier with the higher vantage point afforded by a Land Rover, bakkie or minibus. The main park road between Namutoni and Okaukuejo follows the edge of the Pan, providing super views of the white saline desert. Driving isn't permitted on the pan itself, but there is a good network of gravel roads around the surrounding savanna grassland and mopane woodland. Because of the huge area, crowds aren't yet much of a problem.

The park's speed limit is set at 60 km/h to protect plants and animals from the dust. If you have any belongings that won't tolerate a heavy dusting, pack them away in plastic. Car-cleaning services are available at any of the rest camps for a small fee.

In the dry winter season, wildlife clusters around water holes, while in the hot wet summer months, they disperse and spend the days sheltering under trees and bushes. Summer temperatures can reach as high as 44°C, which isn't fun when you're confined to a vehicle. However, because this is the calving season, you may be treated to the sight of tiny zebra calves and fragile infant springboks.

The best time for game drives is at first light and late in the evening. The three rest camps have 'sightings' books of what has been seen recently and where. If you're out and about in the afternoon, even in the dry season, look carefully for animals resting beneath the trees.

Places to Stay

Although Etosha may be visited on a day trip, it would be impossible to see much of the park in less than three days. Most visitors opt for at least a couple of nights at one of its three rest camps (Namutoni, Halali and Okaukuejo) which are spaced approximately 70 km apart. Each camp has its own character, so it's worth visiting more than one.

Each camp has a restaurant, bar, shop, petrol station and kiosk. The restaurants serve meals from 7 to 8.30 am, noon to 1.30 pm and 6 to 8.30 pm every day. For a special treat, especially at Namutoni, try the last thing you'd expect to find at Etosha: snails in garlic butter. The kiosks are open between restaurant hours – but avoid the ice cream, which appears to have been melted and refrozen several times. On weekdays and

Saturday, the rest camp shops open from 7 to 9 am, 11.30 am to 1.30 pm and 5 to 7 pm. On Sunday, hours are from 7 to 8 am, 11.30 to 1.30 pm and 5.30 to 6.30 pm.

Camping & Self-Catering Inside the park, you have a choice of either camping or self-catering. All three main camps are open year-round and each has a shop, restaurant, snack kiosk, picnic sites, a petrol station, swimming pool and firewood. All camp sites cost US$7 for up to eight people. A fourth camp will eventually be constructed at the Galton (Otjovasandu) Gate in the western end of the park, but as yet, budget restrictions have meant indefinite postponement of the project. So far, it serves mainly as a camp for conservation researchers.

Self-catering accommodation includes linen, towels, soap and kitchen facilities, but guests must provide their own cooking equipment. You must arrive in the rest camps before sunset and can only leave after sunrise; specific times are posted on the gates. If you arrive back later, you'll be locked out. If this happens, all it takes is a blast on your car horn to be let back in, but you can expect a lecture on the evils of staying out late and a black mark on your park permit.

Okaukuejo Okaukuejo (pronounced 'o-ka-KUI-yo') Camp, the site of the Etosha Research Station, has a pleasant pool and restaurant, and a floodlit water hole with strategically placed viewing benches. You'll have a better chance of seeing rhinos here than any place else in the park, particularly between 8 and 10 pm. Another popular visitor activity is the sunset photo frenzy from the top of the circular stone tower which is Okaukuejo's landmark. From the top you can see all the way to the distant range known as the Ondundozonananandana Mountains; try saying that after three pints of Windhoek Lager (or even before)!

The self-catering accommodation is lovely, but the campground is a bit of a dust hole and is probably the least appealing of the three. Self-catering bungalows at

Okaukuejo accommodate two/three/four people for US$19/25/29. All have a kitchen, braai pit, and bathroom and toilet facilities. 'Luxury' self-catering bungalows with four beds are US$36 and double 'bus quarters', rooms with a bath but no kitchen, cost US$25.

The visitors' centre at Okaukuejo outlines ongoing research at the park; one display identifies various examples of animal scat with their perpetrators. There's also a restored lookout tower which provides a panorama over the camp and surrounding park. The restaurant and pool areas (three small pools and a nice bar) are open for breakfast, lunch and dinner, and also serve drinks. There's also a shop, a snack kiosk and picnic sites.

Halali Halali, in the centre of the park, lies in a unique area with several incongruous dolomite outcrops. It takes its name from a German term referring to the ritual blowing of a horn to signal the end of a hunt, and the horn now serves as the camp's motif. The short Tsumasa track will take you to the view from the summit of Tsumasa Kopje, the hill nearest the rest camp. A floodlit water hole extends wildlife viewing into the night, and provides opportunities to observe nocturnal creatures.

Halali has similar facilities to Okaukuejo but the self-catering accommodation, which shelters beneath mopane trees, is slightly cheaper. Double bus quarters cost US$25 and self-contained double bungalows cost US$33, while a four-bed bungalow with a fridge and communal facilities costs US$15. Alternatively, you can opt for a pre-erected four-bed tent for US$10. Camping is the usual US$7 per site.

Namutoni The most popular and best-kept of the camps is Namutoni, with an obtrusive whitewashed German fort rising in its midst. Namutoni originally served as an outpost for German troops, and in 1899 the German cavalry built a fort from which to control the Ovambo people. In the battle of 28 January 1904, seven German soldiers unsuccessfully

attempted to defend the fort against 500 Ovambo warriors. The structure was renovated in 1906 and pressed into service as a police station. In 1956, it was restored to its original specifications and two years later, was opened as tourist accommodation.

There's a great view from the tower and ramparts, and every evening, a crowd gathers to watch the sunset from this appealing vantage point. However, if you can't arrive early to stake out a viewing spot, don't bother. Each night, there's a twee little sunset ceremony, accompanied by a bugle call, when the flag on the fort is lowered. In the morning, a similar ritual drags you out of your bed or sleeping bag.

Beside the fort is a lovely freshwater limestone spring, filled with reedbeds and attendant frogs. As a water hole, however, it's under-utilised by wildlife so the viewing benches and floodlights afford a nice place to eat lunch and views of a pleasant riparian scene, but surprisingly few thirsty animals.

The spacious Namutoni campground is quite pleasant, but it does experience frequent midnight raids by marauding jackals, so keep everything edible safely under lock and key.

At Namutoni, put your shoes into your tent. Jackals try to steal anything they find lying around at night, especially shoes. Looking out of my tent one night, I saw at least five jackal faces in the near surroundings.
Rainer Feil, Germany

Sites for up to eight people with two caravans and one tent cost US$7. Namutoni also offers a range of other accommodation, including two/three-bed rooms in the walls of the fort with communal facilities for US$9/14. Doubles with bath and self-catering facilities are US$25. Namutoni also has double bus quarters for US$25. Huge four-bed mobile homes, which shelter beneath hot tin roofs, each provide accommodation for four people and cost just US$19.

Safari Lodges The luxurious *Mokuti Lodge* (☎ 13084) lies just two km down a side road which turns south at Von Lindequist Gate. It generally serves as a base for up-market tour operations and for those who consider the rest camps too spartan. With nearly 100 rooms plus a pool and private game reserve, it's certainly accommodating. However, the buildings cut a low profile and they're widely spread, so it gives the illusion of being much smaller. Prices start at around US$80 per person for accommodation and half board; it's almost worth the price for the restaurant alone, which is known far and wide as a real winner. Game drives into the park cost an additional US$35 per person.

For amusement value, don't miss Mokuti's resident snake collection; serpentine demonstrations are presented every afternoon – and all the players were captured right around Mokuti. Now isn't that a comforting thought!

The friendly *Aoba Lodge* (☎ 13503), PO Box 469, Tsumeb, set on a 70-sq km private ranch, accommodates up to 20 people in comfortable thatched bungalows. Rates start at US$65 per person, including dinner, bed and breakfast. Game drives into Etosha cost extra.

South of the Andersson Gate, 27 km from Etosha, is the *Toshari Inn* (☎ 3602; fax 182, Outjo), a modestly priced safari-style place with 16 rooms, all with facilities en suite, but no pool. Room rates start at US$35/48 for a single/double room with breakfast. For full board, you'll pay US$52/90.

More up-market is the posh *Ongava Lodge* (☎ 3422, Outjo), which sits on its own wildlife reserve just three km south of the Andersson Gate, beside the Ondundozonanandana Mountains. The Herero name of the lodge means 'black rhino'. In addition to the main lodge, which has luxury accommodation and a shady swimming pool, there's also a tented bush camp, which provides a slightly more rustic experience. A novel feature at Ongava is the so-called Himba Camp, a series of beehive huts in a bush area of the wildlife reserve. Facilities are comfortable but quite basic, and meals are cooked African style in a potjie. Guests are able to learn bush survival techniques and receive information on local ecology; wildlife viewing is either on foot or horseback.

The tented camp and Himba Camp are the less expensive options, at around US$70 per person, including meals and wildlife-viewing activities. To stay at the main lodge costs US$165 per person, including accommodation in stone and thatch chalets, meals and game drives. Horseback trips cost an additional US$33.

Places to Eat

Each rest camp has a restaurant open for all main meals, plus a bar, a kiosk for cool drinks and snacks and a shop selling basic supplies as well as film, a few books and souvenirs.

Getting There & Away

Tsumeb has the nearest commercial airport to Etosha. It's also possible to take a bus or train to Tsumeb, but thereafter, Etosha-bound travellers must either join a tour or hire a car as there is no scheduled public transport into the park.

There are two main entry gates: Von Lindequist (Namutoni) Gate west of Tsumeb and Andersson (Okaukuejo) Gate, north of Outjo. Coming from Windhoek or Swakopmund, you must first get to Otjiwarongo. There, you can decide whether to head for the eastern or western ends of the park. For travellers coming from the Caprivi, Tsumeb will be your best option. Avis Rent-a-Car has a branch in Tsumeb, but book well in advance.

You might be able to hitch to Etosha; try petrol stations at any of the surrounding towns, especially Outjo or Tsumeb, but there could be complications:

It's possible to hitch out of Etosha; just ask at your camp the night before and someone will normally give you a lift. However, the gate officials hate hitchers and since the driver of the car you hitched in with kept your entry papers, you'll have no papers to present when you leave the park. Entry papers include information on the number of people in each vehicle, so the discrepancy caused by hitchers using different vehicles upsets them. However, kind words will usually solve the problem.

Sharon Freed, Australia

If you hitch, you will probably also cause problems for the driver you rode in with; when it's time to leave, some of their original party will appear to have vanished! To alleviate this problem for both yourself and your drivers, when entering the park, explain that you need a separate entry permit for your own records. However, it's probably unwise to reveal that you're hitchhiking.

At the Okaukuejo office, you can pick up transit permits to drive through Skeleton Coast park from Springbokwater to Ugabmund, but not to visit Torra Bay or Terrace Bay (however, in December and January, transit visitors may pop into Torra Bay to pick up petrol). You must reach Springbokwater before 1 pm and exit at Ugabmund by 3 pm.

Getting Around

Pedestrians, bicycles, motorbikes and hitching are prohibited in the park, so you'll need a private vehicle to get around on your own. If you have an open bakkie, the back must be screened off. Pets and firearms are prohibited and outside rest camps, visitors are confined to their vehicles. Functional toilets are marked on the map in this book.

Although hitching is prohibited per se, from Okaukuejo or Namutoni, you may be able to find lifts with delivery and maintenance workers who regularly travel between the camps.

East of Windhoek

GOBABIS

Gobabis is the administrative centre for the Tswana people and lies only 120 km from the Botswana border at Buitepos. The name is Khoi-Khoi for 'the place of strife', although a slight misspelling ('Goabbis') would render it 'place of elephants', which most locals prefer.

It's also the heart of a major cattle and sheep-farming region, and is the service centre for more than 800 surrounding farms. As you'd expect, it also supports huge dairy and beef-processing plants. It's said there was once a traffic light in Gobabis, but when it turned green, the cows ate it. Don't believe it – during the rainy season between January and April, the area can appear relatively lush.

Despite all that, Gobabis isn't much to look at. The only historic building is the old military hospital, the Lazarett, which once served as a town museum. It's not officially open, but if you want a look around, ask for a key at the library.

History

Gobabis came into existence in 1856, when a Rhenish mission station was established on the site. An 1865 attempt by the head missionary to broker a peace agreement between the squabbling Damara and the Khoi-Khoi, however, resulted in his expulsion from the area – and the temporary fall of the mission. Missionary work was reactivated in 1876, only to again be shut down by a renewal of hostilities. When they tired of fighting each other, the two groups turned around and started a rebellion against the German occupation. Things got so out of hand that in 1895, Major Leutwein ordered German troops to quell the disturbances; this resulted

---

Squatting with Intent

Travellers around the ranchlands of eastern Namibia are likely to see small rows of decrepit shacks lined up along the roadsides. They're far more basic than anything you'll see elsewhere in Namibia, but they aren't a sign of abject poverty in the region. They simply indicate that the adjacent farm is slated for government takeover and redistribution.

The people who build these shacks, most of whom live in Windhoek, are merely taking advantage of an opportunity. If they can prove occupation of the land in question, they'll jump to the head of the queue when it comes time to hand out parcels. You'll notice that the 'inhabitants' of these shacks are mostly children and grandmothers; in fact, they're simply 'minding the store' while the working-age folks get on with their daily business back home in Windhoek. ∎

in the construction of a fort which was later destroyed.

Places to Stay & Eat

The nicer of Gobabis' two hotels is the *Gobabis Hotel* (☎ 2568; fax 2703) with single/double rooms for US$24/33 and family rooms for US$46. The hotel swimming pool, bar, restaurant and weekend disco amount to at least 80% of Gobabis' action. The *Central Hotel* (☎ 2094; fax 2092) on Voortrekkerstrasse is less appealing but cheaper at US$19/25 for a single/double room. It also has a bar and attached restaurant.

The *Witvlei Hotel* (☎ 4), in nearby Witvlei east of Gobabis, is quite cheap, but the emphasis is more on the bar than the accommodation, and few patrons want to stay the entire night.

For a glimpse into German and Afrikaner farm life in Namibia, visit one of the several area guest farms. Among the nicest of these farms is *Farm Steinhausen* (☎ 3240) which charges US$35/70 for single/double accommodation with breakfast. It's in the Omitara telephone exchange. To get there from Gobabis, head about three km back towards Windhoek on the B6 and turn north on the C30. From there, it's 117 km to Steinhausen.

Perhaps your best option is the working farm *Heimat* (☎ 3622), PO Box 11186, Klein-Windhoek, owned by Rainer and Marianne Seifart. Here you're guaranteed to gain a perspective on ranching in Namibia. For a room with home-cooked meals included, you'll pay US$34 per person, but camping is also available. The farm is actually at the settlement of Nina; to get there from Windhoek, continue 40 km east to the international airport and turn south on the D1808; after 58 km, you'll reach a T-junction. Turn left and continue 37 km to Nina. Return transfers to Windhoek cost US$27 per trip; to book, dial the Dordabis code (0628) and ask the exchange operator for Nina, 3622.

Getting There & Away

Gobabis is easily accessible along the tarred B6 from Windhoek, but many D-numbered back roads through Hereroland require 4WD. The only public transport is by rail. Trains run from Windhoek on Tuesday, Thursday and Sunday and from Gobabis on Monday, Wednesday and Friday. They leave in either direction at 10 pm and arrive at 5.45 am. Economy/sleeper class costs US$4/13.

AROUND GOBABIS
Dordabis & the Karakul Weaveries

The area between Gobabis and Dordabis is the heart of Namibia's karakul country, and there are a number of farms raising the sheep and several weaveries. The most visited of these is the Farm Ibenstein, four km down the C15 from Dordabis. Here, visitors can learn about the spinning, dyeing and weaving processes – and purchase the finished products. It's open Monday to Friday from 8 am to 12.30 pm and 2.30 to 5.30 pm, and on Saturday from 8 am to noon. You can also arrange to visit the two other weaveries, Dorka Teppiche and Kiripotib, both of which are within a few km of Dordabis.

Dordabis is more easily reached from Windhoek than from Gobabis. Head east from Windhoek on the B6 and turn right onto the C23, 20 km east of town. Dordabis lies 66 km down this road.

Arnhem Cave

Arnhem Cave, at 2800 metres the longest cave system in Namibia, was discovered by farmer DN Bekker in 1930 and was originally used as a source of bat guano. It was formed in a layer of limestone and dolomite, sandwiched between quartzite and shale, in the rippled series of synclines and anticlines known as the Arnhem Hills. Because the cave is dry, there are few stalagmites or stalactites, but it is home to five species of bat: the giant leaf-nosed bat *(Hipposideros commersoni)*, leaf-nosed bat *(Hipposideros caffer)*, long-fingered bat *(Miniopterus schrelbersi)*, horseshoe bat *(Rhinolophus denti)* and Egyptian slit-faced bat *(Nycteris thebalca)*. The cave is also inhabited by a variety of insects, worms, shrews and shrimp

NAMIBIA

The cave lies on a private farm south of the international airport. If you wish to visit, contact Mr J Bekker (☎ 1430) in Dordabis. To get there, turn south just east of the airport on the D1458, towards Nina. After 66 km, turn north-east on the D1506 and continue for 11 km to the T-junction. There, turn south on the D1808. The farm is six km down this road.

Admission costs US$3 per person, and the hire of helmets and torches is US$2. Camping and braai facilities are available and meals may be booked in advance.

BUITEPOS

The non-community of Buitepos is essentially just a wide spot in the desert at the Namibia/Botswana border – little more than a petrol station and customs and immigration post.

Places to Stay

At Buitepos, on the Namibian side of the border, the *East Gate Service Station & Rest Camp* rises out of the desert like a mirage. It's run by a young couple who pull out all stops to create a bizarre but welcoming oasis. One would never expect to find anything like this here in the back of beyond – and the toilets are more than remarkable. Camping costs US$3 per person and a bungalow for three people is US$27. It's a particularly handy option for hitchhikers between Namibia and Botswana.

Getting There & Away

To get there, follow the B6 extension east from Gobabis; watch the signs, as the route detours several times. The road is relatively good gravel as far as the border, but to continue on to Ghanzi and Maun in Botswana, you'll need 4WD and high clearance.

North-Eastern Namibia

Windhoek may be Namibia's capital, but Ovamboland, Kavango and the Caprivi, with the country's highest population density, form its indigenous and cultural heartland. Sometimes referred to as the Land of Rivers, these three varied regions are bounded by the Kunene and Okavango rivers along the Angolan border, and in the east by the Zambezi and the Kwando/Mashi/Linyanti/Chobe systems.

This north-eastern region is geographically quite distinct from the rest of Namibia; it has the country's highest rainfall and most of its people live in small settlements on or near the Okavango River, which flows eastwards to feed the swamps of the Okavango Delta and forms part of Namibia's border with Angola.

Adjoining Bushmanland, a wild and sparsely populated region of scrub and acacia forest, along the northern fringes of the Kalahari, forms a desert barrier between north-eastern Namibia and north-western Botswana.

Until Namibian independence, travellers needed permits to travel in the region north of Grootfontein. Happily, these formalities have now been abandoned and outsiders can travel freely through the 'common' lands.

Although peace in the region has made life happier for the locals, the withdrawal of the military, the end of the conflict-inspired economic boom and an influx of Angolan refugees – as well as illegal immigrants – has resulted in declining transport services and health care.

During an outbreak of intestinal disease which happened during 1990 and 1991, a health emergency was declared.

Also the on-and-off war in Angola means that travel in the region still carries a slight risk, particularly if you want to go to the Caprivi Strip.

However, most cross-border forays that happen these days are merely for the purpose of robbery and they are not politically inspired incidents.

Ovamboland

As its name would suggest, Ovamboland is the homeland of the Ovambo people, which is Namibia's largest population group. Most members of the eight Ovambo clans pursue subsistence agricultural lifestyles, growing their own crops and raising cattle and goats. Visitors will be impressed by the clean and well-kept nature of Ovamboland, which gives the overall impression of a healthy and prosperous society.

During the war for independence, Ovamboland was the home base and primary support area for SWAPO. As a result, the villages of Ombalantu, Oshakati and Ondangwa were pressed into service as bases and supply centres for the occupying army. After the South Africans left, these new commercial centres began to attract a growing number of entrepreneurial people, many of whom are setting up small businesses. In addition, the government is currently pumping relatively large quantities of cash into Ovamboland, to be manifest in the form of housing projects, electricity

NAMIBIA

The Red Line

Between Grootfontein and Rundu, and between Tsumeb and Ondangwa, the B1 and B8 cross the 'Red Line', a veterinary control fence separating the commercial cattle ranches of the south from the communal subsistence lands to the north. This fence bars the north-south movement of animals as a precaution against foot-and-mouth disease and rinderpest, and animals bred north of this line may not be sold to the south or exported to overseas markets.

As a result, the Red Line also marks the effective boundary between the First and Third Worlds. The landscape south of the line is characterised by a dry scrubby bushveld of vast ranches which are home to no one but cattle and a few scattered ranchers. However, north of the 'Animal Disease Control Checkpoint' travellers enter a landscape of dense bush, baobab trees, mopane scrub and small kraals, where people and animals wander along the road and the air is filled with smoke from cooking fires and bush-clearing operations. ■

lines, roads, irrigation, agriculture, health care, schools, telephone services, irrigation and so on.

The Ovamboland landscape is characterised by flat, sandy plains dotted with makalani palms, patches of savanna and mopane forest. It experiences a semidesert climate with generally cool nights and hot days; summer daytime temperatures can climb to over 40° C.

Most of Ovamboland's population is concentrated around the area known as Oshana country, after the web of ephemeral natural watercourses – or oshanas – of the Culevai drainage system, which supply most of the region's water needs. They're filled during periods of heavy rainfall or *efundja*, and because they're underlain by solid rock, they hold underground water through the remainder of the year. Some kraals and villages receive their water from bore holes, but the main water supply runs through the prominent canal/aqueduct which follows the C46. The water is particularly important for growing *omavo*, or water onion, which is a local staple.

Ovamboland is known for its high-quality basketry and canework, which is sold at roadside stalls or the maker's home for a fraction of the price you'd pay in Windhoek. Favourite shapes include rounded baskets with lids in every size up to a metre in diameter, and shallow woven plates and bowls. Designs are simple and graceful, usually incorporating a brown geometric pattern woven into the pale yellow reed.

OSHAKATI

Oshakati, the capital of Ovamboland, may be a friendly and bustling hive of activity, but the commercial centre is little more than a long strip of development along the highway – an African version of an interstate motorway town in the US West.

There is nothing essential to see or do in Oshakati, but you will want to spend an hour or so wandering around the large covered market, which produces a range of (mostly unpleasant) smells. Here you'll find everything from clothing and baskets to mopane worms and glasses of freshly brewed tambo.

Information

If you're just passing through, note that the toilets at the Caltex station are impeccably clean. For changing money, there are branches of both Barclays and Standard Chartered Bank in the commercial centre. You can buy Fuji and Agfa slide and print film at the Agfa Oshakati Photo Shop, on the south side of the street about 600 metres west of the market.

Oshakati has three hospitals: the 800-bed government hospital, the Onandjokwe Lutheran Hospital and the Oshikuku Roman Catholic Hospital. If you need a hospital and have a choice, opt for either of the church-run places.

Places to Stay

The best place to stay is probably the *International Guest House* which charges US$27/35 for a single/double room with air-conditioning. Alternatively, there are the *Oshandira Hotel & Restaurant* and the *Continental #1 Guest House*, which charge essentially the same rates as the International. The *Santorini Inn* on the main road charges US$27/34 for a single/double with en suite facilities, air-conditioning, and an excellent restaurant.

Perhaps a better option is the Catholic mission, *Okatenda*, five km from Oshakati. For US$10 per person, you'll have accommodation in a spotless room with a good breakfast. Taxis from the centre cost US$0.75 per person.

Camping near Oshakati or any town or village in Ovamboland isn't recommended; locals don't appreciate it and there's always a risk of robbery. If you're caught out, ask for local advice on where you can safely pitch a tent without causing disruption.

Places to Eat

A good option is the *Club Oshandira*, which serves breakfast, lunch and dinner. There's an (apparently nameless) grilled-chicken restaurant on the highway east of town, as well as several appealing general-purpose restaurants along the commercial-access road on the north side of the main highway.

Entertainment

Oshakati offers plenty of scope for getting into the local entertainment scene. Two good places to begin are Club Put More Fire and Moby Jack, both of which normally feature live bands.

Getting There & Away

Oshakati's airport is 35 km away at Ondangwa. Air Namibia (☎ 20284; fax 21230) flies to and from Windhoek's Eros Airport, via Tsumeb and Mokuti (Etosha National Park), on Tuesday and Thursday.

Reaching Oskahaki – and travelling around Ovamboland in general – are straightforward. The C46 and B1 are both tarred and in very good condition, but away from these routes, road maintenance is poor and in many places, you'll need 4WD, especially during the rainy season. Fuel is available at Ombalantu, Oshakati and Ondangwa.

From the market bus terminal in Oshakati,

Bosnian Brews in Ovamboland?

Bars, night clubs and bottle stores along the highways of Ovamboland bear wonderfully colourful names, such as Clinic Happy Bar, Hot Box, Melody Shop, Salon for Sure, Club Jet Style, Hot Line, California City Style, Come Together Good Life, Bar We Like and even the philosophical The System or USA No Money No Life. One bottle store is called simply Botol Store. However, what sort of atmosphere could one expect in a bar called Sarajevo? It's currently one of the most popular names, appearing three times (in various spellings) in the vicinity of Oshakati! ∎

---

white minibuses serve various portions of the route between Ruacana and Oshivelo. Most, however, operate between Oshakati and Ondangwa. There's also service to Windhoek (via Tsumeb) several times daily, with extra departures on Sunday afternoon. Minibuses leave when full, so arrive as early as possible. Coming from Windhoek, they leave the singles quarters in Katutura township several times daily, with extra departures on Friday afternoon.

The big yellow SWAPO bus between Oshakati and Windhoek leaves the bus terminal in Katutura on Friday afternoon at 5 pm and from the market in Oshakati on Sunday afternoon. The fare is just US$11 – as opposed to US$16 on the minibuses. It often runs during the week as well, but you must go to the market early in the morning to book a seat.

ONDANGWA

The second largest town in Ovamboland, Ondangwa has huge warehouses which provide stock for the more than 6000 tiny cuca shops which serve Ovamboland's rural inhabitants. The name 'cuca' comes from the popular Angolan beer which is still served there.

Olukonda

At Olukonda village, 13 km south-east of Ondangwa on the D3606, is a collection of historic Finnish mission buildings. The first mission house, Nakambale House, was built in the late 1870s by Finnish missionary Martti Rauttanen – locally known as Nakambale – and is the oldest building in northern Namibia. In 1889, Reverend Rauttanen also constructed the area's first church. When a new church was constructed in 1972, however, the old building began to deteriorate and it wasn't renovated until 1991, with funds and expertise from the Finnish government. Martti Rauttanen and his family, along with the local chief Ellifas, are buried in the churchyard.

Lake Oponono

Lost in the maze of routes and tracks south of Ondangwa lies Lake Oponono, which is a large area of wetlands fed by the Culevai oshanas. After rains, the region attracts an amazing variety of birdlife, including saddlebill storks, crowned cranes, flamingoes and pelicans. The edge of the lake lies 27 km south of Ondangwa.

Places to Stay & Eat

You'll find a bar, restaurant and cheap accommodation at the *ABC Trading Centre* (☎ 40121) which, as its name would suggest, also sells just about everything from A to Z. It's actually in Oluno, which is effectively a suburb of Ondangwa. A similar operation is *Punyu Wholesalers* (☎ 40313; fax 40177) in the nearby Onethindi suburb, which also offers basic travellers' accommodation for US$26/30 for a single/double; it also has a 4WD hire. At Oniipa, about five km east of Ondangwa, is the inexpensive *Elcin Guesthouse*.

Things to Buy

If you want something both typical and useful, check out the household goods market in front of the Desert Inn Pub near the eastern end of town. You'll find a range of useful doo-dads from wooden kitchen utensils to some amazing wire mousetraps.

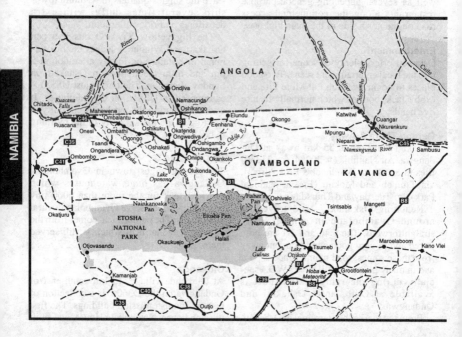

Getting There & Away

For information on air services, see Getting There & Away under Oshakati. All the minibus services between Oshakati and Windhoek stop at the BP petrol station in Ondangwa. The Sunday afternoon SWAPO bus is the cheapest way to get to Windhoek, but by the time it reaches Ondangwa, you'll have little chance of getting a seat.

OMBALANTU

This hot and dusty little place could well be one of the most typically 'African' of Namibia's commercial towns, but the place itself is nothing to go out of your way for. The main attraction is the old South African army base, where a chapel-cum-coffee shop was set up inside an enormous baobab tree. A sign on the wall reads *Die Koffiekamer Koelte*, which roughly translates as 'The Coffee Chamber Cult'.

The base entrance lies on the road about 350 metres south of the petrol station. Before you go in, respectfully ask permission at the police station behind the small market there. The officers are quite friendly and normally have no objections.

RUACANA

The tiny town of Ruacana, which lies on the Kunene River, takes its name from the Herero *orua hakahana*, which means 'the rapids'. The town was purpose-built to provide worker housing and services for the 320-megawatt underground Ruacana Hydroelectric Project, which now supplies over half of Namibia's power needs. As such, it has a more ordered feel than other population centres in Ovamboland. During the bush war, it also served as a base of the South African Defence Forces.

At Ruacana, the Kunene River splits into several channels before plunging over a staircase of escarpments and through a two-

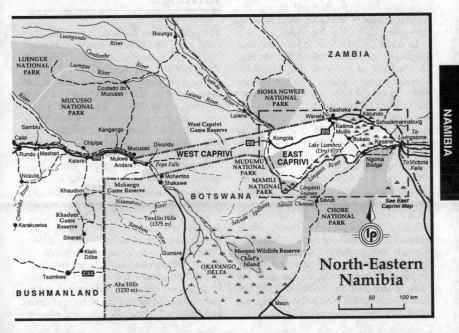

North-Eastern Namibia

km long gorge of its own making. In 1926, thanks to boundary disputes in the early part of this century, it was decided that the upper Kunene would fall into Angolan territory, while below the falls, the boundary would follow the main channel to the Atlantic Ocean.

Heading west into the Kaokoveld, Ruacana is the last petrol station before the Atlantic Ocean, so be sure you're carrying enough petrol to either get to Opuwo or back to Ruacana.

Ruacana Falls

The dramatic 85-metre high Ruacana Falls were once a great natural wonder, but that changed with the construction of Angola's Calueque Dam, 50 km upstream. The river is also controlled by an intake weir one km above the falls, which was built to usher water through the hydroelectric plant. As a result, the falls are in operation only during the very wettest seasons, when the power stations are sated and excess water is released over both the dam and the weir. For the best chance of seeing the water flowing, time your visit for March or April.

To reach the falls – or at least the place where they should be – follow the river road 15 km west of town to the Namibian-Angolan border crossing over the Kunene River. To see the falls, visitors must temporarily exit Namibia by signing the immigration officers' register. From there, you can descend the 488 steps to the old power station in the gorge.

Places to Stay & Eat

Five km west of Ruacana falls is the Hippo Point camp site, which is free and affords a great river view, but has no facilities.

One option in Ruacana town is the *SWAWEK Singles' Quarters Hostel*, where you may be able to find a room (although it's normally full) for US$17 per person, or set up a tent out the back. It's also a possibility for meals. Alternatively, try the *Ruacana Club*, where you can camp and use the toilets, but only on Wednesday, Friday and Saturday.

Getting There & Away

A good place to look for a lift to Ruacana Falls or elsewhere is the bar at the SWAWEK Singles' Quarters Hostel, which is the watering hole of choice for foreign social workers. Minibuses to and from Oshakati and Ondangwa arrive and depart at the petrol station, but you won't find anything after the early afternoon.

When Etosha's planned Otjovasondu Camp comes on line, the C35 from Kamanjab will probably be tarred. At the moment, however, the easiest access to Ruacana is via the C46 from Oshakati. The route is occasionally served by local minibuses.

West of Ruacana Falls, the roads fade into 4WD tracks leading into the remote Baynes Mountains and the Zebraberg. For more information, see the North-Western Namibia chapter.

Kavango

The gently rolling Kavango region is a typically green and heavily wooded corner of Namibia. It's dominated by the Okavango River and its broad floodplains. Along the banks, you'll see millions of butterflies, many as yet unclassified, as well as a large crocodile population. People cultivate maize, sorghum, millet and green vegetables along the bank, and supplement their diet with fish caught in woven funnel-shaped fish traps. The men also practice spearfishing from the riverbanks or from dugout canoes known as *watu* or *mekoro* (singular *mokoro*).

The region is also home to the Mbarakweno San people, but, they remain largely subservient to local Mbukushu, Sambiyu and other Caprivi tribal groups, and their services are 'inherited' within families.

The Kavango area was settled in colonial days by German Roman Catholic missionaries, and the church still sponsors missions, hospitals and clinics in Nyangana, Sambiu and Andara. Several of the mission stations and hospitals along the Okavango River welcome travellers. The one at Andara has a particularly interesting statue of Christ.

RUNDU

Rundu occupies a lovely setting on the bluffs above the Okavango River. It's a great spot for fishing and birdwatching along the river, but don't expect round the clock excitement.

It's worth checking out the Mbangura Woodcarvers' Cooperative, which is part of a government development scheme; you can buy traditional drums as well as some lovely handmade furniture there.

There's also a small zoo at Ekongoro Youth Camp, two km north-east of town, which is set amid pleasant tropical gardens. It's guarded by tame lions, which prance around behaving like watchdogs. Admission is US$0.85.

There are currently plans for a Kavango Museum in Rundu (a building has already been constructed) but as yet, nothing has

Rundu

1 Sarasungu Lodge
2 Zoo
3 Kavango River Lodge
4 Post Office
5 Police
6 Casa Mourisca
7 Ministry of Environment & Tourism Office
8 Hospital
9 Rundu Service Centre: Shell Petrol Station, Convenience Store & Hunter's Tavern

come of them. However, 30 km east of Rundu at Sambiu is a Roman Catholic mission museum (☎ 1111), which contains exhibits of traditional crafts and woodcarvings from southern Angola and Kavango. It's best to phone in advance to arrange an opening.

Places to Stay

The most central accommodation is the *Rundu Service Centre* (☎ 787), beside the Hunter's Tavern at the Shell petrol station. Standard single/double rooms cost US$29/44; rooms for three/four people are US$57/65. At a pinch, you can camp here for US$6 per person, but Sarasungu Lodge by the river has more pleasant camp sites.

Rundu is also slated to receive a backpackers' hostel in the near future. For the latest information, check with the Cardboard Box backpackers' in Windhoek or phone Ms Margaret Monanango (☎ 119, after hours ☎ 553) in Rundu. Another cheap alternative is the *ROC Club*, near the Kavango River Lodge at the end of town, which served as a hostel for the South African army during the war. Single rooms cost US$14.

Kavango River Lodge (☎ 244; fax 13), with the best view in town – especially at sunset – perches above the river about a km west of Rundu centre. Basic single/double self-catering bungalows, with air-conditioning and breakfast supplies, start at US$40/50; ask for one with a veranda. Family units accommodating up to four people cost US$55. All guests have access to the tennis courts, and there are plans to add a swimming pool and buy some canoes for paddling on the river.

A super alternative is the friendly German/Portuguese-run *Sarasungu River Lodge* (☎ 161; fax (061) 220694), in a shady riverside setting about four km from the centre. Camping costs just US$5 per person and the six lovely single/double bungalows, made from natural materials, are US$43/66, with breakfast. It's a magical setting and you can hire canoes or mountain bikes and take guided walks. Amenities include hot showers, a very pleasant restaurant specialising in pizza, a cool veranda and a new swimming pool. If you speak with Ines or Eduardo in advance, they'll pick you up from the Shell petrol station on the main road.

The next place downstream is the *Kaisosi Safari Lodge* (☎/fax 265). This rather stark riverside camp offers single/double bungalows for US$33/45; four-bed rooms are US$60, plus US$6 for each additional person. If there's a vacancy, request an upstairs room, which will provide a lovely river view. Camping costs US$3 per tent or caravan plus US$3 per person. For a full breakfast they charge US$4; river raft cruises cost US$7 per person per hour. For transfers to and from Rundu, you'll pay US$8.50 per trip; to or from the airport, it's US$14.

Beside the river about 20 km east of Rundu and four km off the river road, is the new Afrikaner-run *Kayangoma Lodge* (☎ 221646; fax 230706, both in Windhoek), PO Box 50150, Windhoek. I was told that it's named after a local chief, whose name means 'the man without front teeth.' On my last visit, the details weren't yet sorted out, but it appears the emphasis is to be on water activities: canoeing (US$4 per hour), river trips by pontoon or motorboat (US$9 per hour), as well as water skiing and a floating bar. Single/double bungalows with shared facilities are US$30/41; with bath they're US$36/46. Four/six-bed bungalows with shared facilities cost US$65/95. The à la carte restaurant highlights traditional dishes. Transfers from town are free.

Just a short distance further east, 21 km from Rundu, is the pleasantly informal *Mayana Lodge* (☎ 888). It's set in a leafy grove beside the Okavango River and affords excellent sunrise views. Four-bed bungalows with shared facilities cost just US$15, while 12-bed dormitories cost just US$27, plus US$3 for each additional person. It's an excellent and friendly option, and the à la carte restaurant is worth writing home about. To pre-book, write to Juan van Heerden (☎ (067362) 157), PO Box 144, Kombat.

Places to Eat

For an unexpected pleasure in Rundu, eat at the *Casa Mourisca*, which serves excellent Portuguese specialities. It's open Monday, Wednesday, Thursday and Friday from 10 am to 2 pm and 5 pm to midnight; on Saturday from 5 pm to midnight; and Sunday from 10 am to 2 pm and 5 to 10 pm.

An alternative is the *Hunter's Tavern* at the Shell petrol station on the B8 at the turn-off to Rundu centre. It serves breakfast, lunch and dinner seven days a week. At the *ROC Club*, near the Kavango River Lodge, you can also get decent fast burgers or fish and chips.

Self-caterers will appreciate the well-stocked supermarket in the centre and the almost excessive convenience store at the Shell petrol station – as well as the surprising variety of smaller shops and stalls. Between July and September, you'll be treated to fresh paw paw straight from the trees.

Things to Buy

Thanks to the relative abundance of wood, the Kavango people are known for their woodcarving skills and produce what is arguably the finest work in Namibia. Animal figures, masks, wooden mugs for beer, walking sticks and boxes are carved in a local light hardwood known as *dolfhout* (wild teak) and make excellent souvenirs. The best carvings can be difficult to find, but some very nice pieces are conveniently sold at stands along the B8 towards Grootfontein. One well-known stand specialises in toy trucks, aeroplanes and helicopters, which have become particularly popular. Don't fret if these stands aren't attended; as soon as a vehicle pulls up, someone will materialise.

The San people living in the Rundu area also come into town offering craftwork for sale (generally sets of bows, arrows and quivers) and often hang around the Shell petrol station. They also sell ostrich-eggshell beads strung into attractive necklaces and jewellery. If you prefer the casual tropical look, pick up one of the local palm-leaf hats, which appear to be a cross between a coolie hat and a Panama.

Getting There & Away

Air Namibia flies between Windhoek's Eros Airport and Rundu and Katima Mulilo, via Tsumeb, two or three times weekly.

Bus transport between Rundu, Windhoek and Katima Mulilo is provided by the Egoli Liner minibus, which stops at the Shell petrol station. For information, ask at the Shell or phone ☎ 53 in Katima Mulilo or ☎ 3345 in Okahandja.

Although the B8 doesn't carry a lot of traffic, hitching isn't too difficult between Grootfontein and Rundu. However, travelling east from Rundu to Katima Mulilo is a bit more challenging. If you wish to follow the beautiful river road towards Mashari, plan on long waits and a series of short lifts.

With an Angola visa, you can take the international ferry to Calai, on the Angolan bank of the Okavango.

Getting Around

Okavango Car Hire (☎ 476), PO Box 854, Rundu, operates occasionally, but rates are higher than in Windhoek and elsewhere. They also rent camping equipment.

KHAUDOM GAME RESERVE

The wild and undeveloped Khaudom Game Reserve, which covers 384,000 hectares on the borders of Bushmanland, is like nowhere else in Africa. Along the sand tracks, which meander through pristine bush, you'll see roan antelopes, wild dogs, elephants, zebras and almost everything else you'd encounter at Etosha, but in an unspoiled and un-touristed context.

The park is crossed by a series of omiramba, fossil river valleys which generally run parallel to the east-west-oriented Kalahari sand dunes. Because the roads can be so poor, the best time to visit is during the dry winter months, from June to October. During the wetter summer, however, the birdlife is profuse.

Places to Stay

Within the Khaudom Game Reserve are two camps, Khaudom and Sikereti (yes, it does mean cigarette); basic four-bed bungalows at

either camp cost US$10; camp sites for up to eight people are US$6. Accommodation must be pre-booked at Windhoek, Rundu or Katima Mulilo.

Getting There & Away

Although access is difficult, you're unlikely to regret the effort it will take to reach Khaudom. During the dry, the deep sand roads are excruciating but during the rainy season, they deteriorate into mudslicks. MET requires prospective visitors to travel in a convoy of at least two self-sufficient 4WD vehicles, equipped with food and water for three days. Caravans, trailers and motorbikes are prohibited.

From the north, you can enter Khaudom along the sandy track from Katere on the B8, which is signposted 'Khaudom', about 120 km east of Rundu. After 45 km, you'll reach the omuramba Cwiba, where you should turn east (left) into the park.

Alternatively, you can enter from the

south, via Tsumkwe and Sikereti. From Tsumkwe, it's 20 km to Groote Dobe, and another 15 km from there to the Dorslandboom turn-off (see Baobabs under Bushmanland, later in this chapter). From this turn-off, it's about 25 km north to Sikereti Camp.

The Caprivi

Namibia's spindly north-eastern appendage, the Caprivi Strip, is a typically unexceptional landscape typified by expanses of broadleaf forests – mainly mopane and terminalia. In fact, the land is so flat that the difference between the highest and lowest points in the entire Caprivi Strip, which measures nearly 500 km in length, is a trifling 39 metres. Throughout the Caprivi are traces of the parallel sand dunes, known as *shonas*, which are found all over the Kalahari and are remnants from the days when the climate here was much drier.

Most modern Caprivians live alongside the Kwando/Mashi/Linyanti/Chobe, Okavango and Zambezi and rivers. The region's original inhabitants were subsistence farmers who cultivated the banks of the Zambezi and Kwando rivers. The Caprivi is also home to substantial San populations, but none still follow their original nomadic hunter-gatherer lifestyles.

Minor roads in the Caprivi are in poor condition and apart from a couple of roadside cuca shops, there are no facilities along the so-called Golden Highway between Divundu and Kongola. Petrol is available only at Rundu, Divundu, Kongola, Linyanti and Katima Mulilo.

For many independent travellers, the Caprivi's relatively good roads provide an easy hitching route between Zimbabwe, Botswana and the main body of Namibia. However, visitors who spend more time – and have either a bit of cash or lots of patience – will find such hidden gems as Mudumu and Mamili national parks, Lizauli Traditional Village, the West Caprivi Triangle and the pleasantly African town of Katima Mulilo.

History

Until the end of the 19th century, the area that is now the Caprivi Strip was known as Itenge and was under the rule of the Lozi (or Barotse) kings. Although modern Caprivians are mainly from the Mafwe, Subia, Bayei and Mbukushu tribes, Lozi is still the lingua franca of the region and is used as a medium of instruction in primary schools.

The Caprivi's odd geographical shape carries with it an interesting bit of history. In the late 1800s, this strip of land was administered as part of the British protectorate of Bechuanaland (now Botswana). However, in 1890, Germany laid claim to the British-administered island of Zanzibar, off the coast of German East Africa (now Tanzania), and Britain objected. In July 1890, the Berlin Conference was called to settle the dispute.

In the end, Queen Victoria acquired Zanzibar, and land along the eastern boundary of German South West Africa was appended to Bechuanaland. Germany was granted Heligoland (an island in the North Sea) and the strip of territory which subsequently became known as the Caprivi Strip, after German chancellor General Count Georg Leo von Caprivi di Caprara di Montecuccoli.

The German motivation behind the swap was to acquire a strip of land linking German South West Africa with the Zambezi River, thus providing easy access to Tanganyika and ultimately, the Indian Ocean. Unfortunately for the Germans, the British colonisation of Rhodesia stopped them well upstream of Victoria Falls, which proved a considerable barrier to navigation on the Zambezi.

Although the Caprivi Strip was absorbed into German South West Africa in 1890, it didn't exactly make world news, and it was nearly 20 years before some of the region's inhabitants fully realised they were under German control. In October 1908, however, Herr Hauptmann Streitwolf was dispatched from Windhoek to serve as the Caprivi's first

'Imperial Resident' and the German administration took hold in earnest.

The local Lozi people reacted by rounding up all the cattle they could muster – including those belonging to rival tribes – and driving them out of the area. The cattle were eventually returned to their rightful owners, but the Lozi themselves opted to remain in neighbouring Zambia and Angola rather than submit to German rule.

On 4 August 1914, Britain declared war on Germany and just over a month later, the German administrative seat at Schuckmannsburg was attacked from the British base at Sesheke across the river and seized by the British police.

Note that an alternative – and apocryphal – tale recounts that in September 1914, German governor Von Frankenburg was having tea with the English resident administrator across the river in Northern Rhodesia (now Zambia) when a servant brought a message from the British authorities in Livingstone. After reading the message, the British official declared his guest a prisoner of war, thus taking Schuckmannsburg with negligible effort. Whatever the case, the seizure of Schuckmannsburg amounted to the first Allied occupation of enemy territory of WWI.

During the British occupation, the Caprivi was governed as part of Bechuanaland but it received little attention and became known as a lawless frontier area. When the administration was handed over to South Africa in 1935, the British moved their headquarters to Katima Mulilo. Seventh-Day Adventist missionaries set up a mission; merchants arrived; and in 1939, the idiosyncratic magistrate, Major Lyle French W Trollope was posted to Katima Mulilo and he remained so long that he came to be regarded as local royalty.

MAHANGO GAME RESERVE & POPA FALLS
Although it's technically part of the Kavango Region, the attractive area immediately west of the Okavango River actually lies in the Caprivi Strip. The main attractions for visitors are the mildly interesting Popa Falls and the wildlife-rich Mahango Game Reserve.

Mahango Game Reserve
This small (25,400 hectare) but surprisingly diverse park occupies a broad flood plain north of the Botswana border and west of the Okavango River. The reserve is known for its huge concentrations of thirsty elephants which invade this riverine region during the dry season. Mahango is actually the only wildlife park in Namibia where visitors are permitted to walk on their own; winter is the best time for seeing wildlife and staying safely visible.

With a 2WD vehicle, you can either zip through the park on the transit route or follow the scenic loop drive past Kwetche picnic site, east of the main road. With 4WD, you can also explore the 20-km Circular Drive, a loop track which follows the omiramba Thinderevu and Mahango and gets you into the best wildlife-viewing country. It's particularly nice to stop beside the river in the afternoon and watch the elephants swimming and drinking between the hippos and crocodiles.

There are no camp sites or other overnight facilities in the reserve; the nearest MET accommodation is at Popa Falls, 15 km north of Mahango.

Divundu
As far as anyone can tell, Divundu is merely a creation of the highway junction; the real population centres are the neighbouring villages of Mukwe, Andara and Bagani. For travellers, Divundu itself is little more than a 24-hour petrol station, but along the road south lie several pleasant river lodges, the popular Popa Falls Rest Camp and the Mahango Game Reserve. To the north lies Angola, to the south Botswana and to the east, the long and desolate gravel route across the West Caprivi Game Reserve.

Thanks to its proximity to Angola, this area is at marginal risk from cross-border insurgency, and during my most recent visit, three local teenagers were killed in a UNITA-orchestrated robbery attempt. If

NAMIBIA

Mahango Game Reserve & Popa Falls

0   5   10 km

you're spending any time here, it's worth keeping an ear to the ground.

Popa Falls

Near the village of Bagani, the Okavango River plunges down a broad series of cascades misleadingly known as Popa Falls. They're nothing to get too excited about, although periods of low water do expose a drop of four metres. They do, however, provide an excuse for a particularly amenable MET rest camp. Birdwatchers especially will appreciate the incredible range of avian life in the area.

Day admission costs US$1.50 per person and US$1.50 per vehicle; camp sites with braai pits are US$6 for up to eight people; and four-bed chalets are US$23. A small store on site sells basics: tinned food, beer, candles and mosquito coils.

Places to Stay & Eat

If you don't want to stay at Popa Falls, you have a couple of other options. A rather quaint place is the locally owned *Ngepi Camp Site*, which lies four km down a 4WD track from the main road (there are plans to make this road passable to 2WD). The name means 'how are you' in Mbukushu – and the emphasis seems to be on the bar – but the green, riverside location is great. Camp sites cost US$6 per site plus US$1.50 per person and US$1.50 per vehicle. Canoes for paddling around on the river cost US$3 per day.

Behind the Bagani Malaria Control Research Centre you'll find the German-run *Suclabo Lodge* (☎ 6222), PO Box 894, Rundu. It's set high on a bluff overlooking the Okavango River, 500 metres upstream from Popa Falls, and is blessed with a splendid view. Just one km off the main road, it's readily accessible to 2WD vehicles. Bungalows with shared facilities cost US$21 per person, including breakfast; with private shower and toilet, they're US$36. Boat trips on the river cost US$9 per hour and game drives in Mahango Reserve are US$10 per person. Note, however, that non-Germans may feel a bit disoriented.

The best place to stay is probably *Ndhovu Lodge* (☎ 259), PO Box 894, Rundu, run by Roy and Lynne Vincent. This tented camp sits in a lovely position beside the wide Okavango and enjoys a pleasant and homely atmosphere. Watch out, however, for their friendly but overly enthusiastic dogs! Comfortable single/double accommodation costs US$46/82 with breakfast. Other meals are served communally in the large thatched restaurant and bar. Wildlife-viewing trips by boat cost US$6 per person; game drives in Mahango Game Reserve are US$11 per person. To book by fax, contact their Windhoek agent, Ondese Safaris (fax (061) 239700).

Getting There & Away

With a 2WD vehicle, you can drive from Andara through Mahango Game Reserve to the Botswana border, but the deep sandy stretch from the border to Shakawe – the last bit of the Maun road remaining to be tarred – still requires 4WD.

If you're just transiting the park – and you don't leave the main road to take the scenic route or the circular route – you won't need an entry permit. To drive around the loop drives, you'll pay US$1.50 per vehicle plus US$1.50 per person.

WEST CAPRIVI GAME RESERVE

The gravelled road from Rundu to Katima Mulilo passes through the West Caprivi Game Reserve which, due to heavy poaching and encroaching population, is now almost barren of wildlife. Most of the reserve is actually scheduled to become an official resettlement area in the near future, but the sections immediately west of the Kwando River and east of the Okavango River may retain protected status.

Travellers through the reserve must still pass through MET control points at Divundu in the west and Kongola in the east.

West Caprivi Triangle

The West Caprivi Triangle, a wedge of unprotected land bounded on the north by Angola, the south by Botswana, the west by the West Caprivi Game Reserve and the east by the Kwando River, is actually the richest wildlife area in the Caprivi Strip. Because hunting, bush clearing and human settlement are currently on the increase, calls are being made for official protection either as a new reserve or perhaps even an extension of Mudumu National Park.

The easiest access is via the road south along the western bank of the Kwando River, near Kongola. However, the best wildlife viewing is north of the main road, towards the Angolan border.

Places to Stay

The only camp site is at Nambwa, 23 km south of Kongola in the West Caprivi Triangle, but it lacks any sort of facilities. Advance bookings may be made through MET in Katima Mulilo, Rundu or Windhoek. To get there, follow the 4WD track south along the western bank of the Kwando River. When you arrive, pick up your permit at the Susuwe ranger station, which lies north of the highway on the west bank of the river.

KATIMA MULILO

Out on a limb at the end of the Caprivi Strip lies Katima Mulilo, Namibia's most remote outpost. The Lozi name means 'to quench the fire', probably in reference to the fact that burning embers carried by travellers were frequently extinguished by the river crossing at the Mbova Rapids. It's a pleasant town with lush vegetation and enormous trees, and was once known for the elephants that marched through town. Nowadays, apart from the hippos and crocodiles in the Zambezi River, little wildlife remains.

Katima Mulilo is as far from Windhoek as you can get in Namibia – over 1200 km – and feels more like Zambia than the rest of Namibia (okay, it's true, Zambia is only four km away). The riverine vegetation, with its huge lush trees, tropical birds and monkeys, makes for pleasant – if hot – walks.

Information

There's no tourist office in Katima Mulilo, but the MET office (☎ 27; fax 341), Private Bag 1020, on the Ngoma Bridge road just east of town, can provide information and camping permits for Mudumu and Mamili national parks, and the West Caprivi Game Reserve.

Money The Bank of Windhoek sits beside the main square cum car park and changes cash and travellers' cheques at a typically tropical speed. They rarely have South African rand, so you'll have to accept Namibian dollars. It's open Monday to Friday from 9 am to 12.45 pm and 2 to 3.30 pm.

Post & Telecommunications The public telephone is in front of the post office, also in the main square. Calls must still be booked through the operator, but Katima Mulilo is scheduled to receive direct dialling in the near future. The post office is open Monday to Friday from 8 am to 1 pm and 2 to 5 pm, except on the second and third Wednesday of the month, when it opens at 9 am.

NAMIBIA

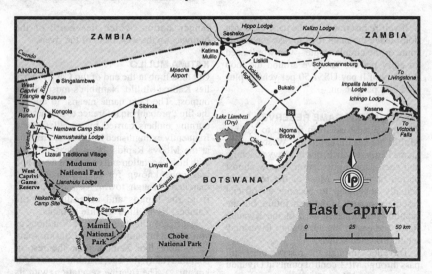

Medical Services Katima Mulilo has a well equipped hospital (☎ 12), as well as several VSO doctors and a chemist (☎ 203).

Vehicle Repairs For vehicle repairs and parts, a good honest place is the friendly Katima Spares.

Caprivi Arts Centre
The Caprivi Arts Centre is a good place to look for curios and material crafts, such as wood carvings of elephants and hippos, baskets, bowls, weavings, kitchen implements, knives, traditional weapons, and so on. There's a good range available and some of the work is of superior quality.

Festivals
The Caprivi Cultural Festival is held in Katima Mulilo around the end of September.

Places to Stay
A decent place to stay is the relaxed *Hippo Lodge* (☎ 685), six km downstream from the town centre. Camping costs US$3 per person and rooms are US$46/57 for a single/double. The restaurant meals are better than you'd expect, and the experience is further enhanced by the sunset views over the river and the riveting frog chorus after dark. Phone and they'll pick you up from town. A word of warning: if you're canoeing or wandering along this stretch of riverbank, watch out for the notorious Musanga Hippo, a real masked marauder who has been responsible for several deaths.

Alternatively, there's the pre-fab *Guinea Fowl Inn* (☎ 349; fax 285) by the river near the police station, which charges US$6 per person for camping and US$25/35 single/double for rooms without private facilities. For single/double rooms with bath and toilet, you'll pay US$29/41. The manager, Fred, is a friendly and interesting individual, but elephant lovers may not feel particularly comfortable here. You'll find it beside the river behind the police station; just follow the painted guinea fowl signs.

The most up-market option is the *Zambezi Lodge* (☎ 203), where self-catering bungalows cost US$54/62 for singles/doubles. Family rooms are US$85 for two adults and two children, and camping amidst flowery garden surroundings costs US$3 per person plus US$1.50 per vehicle. Breakfast is an additional US$4. Amenities include a pool, restaurant and floating bar on the Zambezi, as well as a nine-hole golf course out the front. Ask about cruises aboard the *Zambezi Queen* riverboat.

All three of the previously mentioned lodges hire out canoes for exploring the river for around US$7 per day, but steer well clear of hippos and avoid the temptation to pop over to Zambia. Surreptitious border crossing is illegal and the canoe is likely to be impounded by Zambian officials, which won't go down well with lodge owners back in Namibia.

Further downstream is *Kalizo Lodge*, which offers a real wilderness getaway. It's known for its excellent fishing and birdwatching opportunities, but is only accessible by 4WD. Camping costs US$6 per person and pre-erected tents are US$14 per person. Single/double accommodation in thatched bungalows, including full board and return transfers from Katima Mulilo or Mpacha airport, is US$62/102 and a special three-night package costs US$419/671 for a single/double. Transfers for campers from Katima Mulilo cost US$44 per trip. Fishing equipment is available for US$7 per day. Book through Kalizo Fishing & Photographic Safaris (☎ 203; fax (27-011) 764 4606), PO Box 195, Wilgeheuwel, Roodepoort 1736, South Africa.

Places to Eat

The best place to eat is the *Lyambai Restaurant & Takeaways*, near the Pep store in the shopping centre, which is open for lunch. There's also *Coimbra Restaurant & Takeaways*, just a block away. As the name might suggest, it specialises in Portuguese-African food. Their outdoor tables are particularly good for whiling away a typically hot and sticky afternoon over a pint or two of lager.

If you're headed towards the Zambezi Lodge, look out for the takeaway housed in an enormous beer can, which sits near the military base just outside the town centre.

For a more formal dining experience, try the restaurant at the *Zambezi Lodge*, which serves decent hot lunches and very good

dinners. The restaurant at the *Guinea Fowl Inn* specialises in pizza.

The *Katima Mulilo Yacht Club* has a licensed restaurant, but it is expensive. Petrol stations have limited facilities where you can get sandwiches, pies and beverages.

There's a supermarket in the shopping centre, near the Lyambai Restaurant, and Katima Mulilo also has a thriving open-air market near the Caprivi Arts Centre, which is active every day, and another less formal market in the shopping-centre car park. They're good places to look for traditional foods.

Things to Buy

Your best bet for curios is the Caprivi Art Centre, but along the road to Kongola, you'll pass several roadside stands selling the wood-and-soapstone elephant carvings for which the Caprivi is famous.

Getting There & Away

Air Air Namibia flies from Windhoek (Eros Airport) to Katima Mulilo's Mpacha Airport (18 km south-west of town) two or three times weekly via Tsumeb and Rundu. On Friday it flies in either direction between Katima Mulilo and Maun in Botswana.

On Monday, Wednesday and Friday around midday, Air Namibia flies to Victoria Falls and back. The flight affords super views of the falls and the pilots often oblige passengers with a gratis 'Flight of the Angels' along the way. The one-way fare is US$45.

Bus Katima Mulilo is served by the Egoli Liner minibus (☎ 53), which connects it with Rundu and Windhoek several times weekly. It stops at the Shell petrol station, which can provide schedule information.

The big blue bus service operating between Windhoek and Harare leaves Windhoek on Friday morning and passes through Katima Mulilo en route to Victoria Falls and Harare on Saturday at 11 am, to arrive in Harare on Monday morning. Coming from Harare, it leaves at 7 am on Tuesday, arrives in Victoria Falls at 7 am on

Wednesday and puffs into Katima Mulilo around five hours later, before continuing to Windhoek. From Katima Mulilo to Harare, the fare is US$50; to Victoria Falls, it's US$20. Buses depart from the market square, near the bank.

There's also a local bus service between Katima Mulilo and Ngoma Bridge, which departs from the main shopping centre in Katima Mulilo, but it runs according to no fixed schedule. It costs US$3 each way.

Car & Motorbike The Trans-Caprivi route, commonly known as the Golden Highway, is now tarred except for the 210-km stretch of gravel between Divundu and Kongola, which is scheduled to be tarred by the end of 1997. In the dry season, it's passable to 2WD vehicles, but there are some rough patches which may come as a bit of a surprise when you're cruising along at 100 km/h, so take it easy. Minor untarred roads in the region are typically in very poor condition.

Hitching Between Rundu and Katima Mulilo, hitching is more difficult, especially along the lonesome stretch between Divundu and Kongola. If you're stuck in either of these places, it's best to wait at either the petrol stations or the control gates into the West Caprivi Game Reserve. Some roads become impassable during the November to March rainy season, when the rivers are in flood.

Coming from Botswana, you can reach Katima Mulilo via the Ngoma Bridge border crossing, which is open daily from 6 am to 7 pm. It's relatively well used, particularly by travellers going through to Zimbabwe, making hitching possible between Kasane and Ngoma Bridge along the 54-km transit route through the Chobe National Park. If you avoid the Chobe riverfront tourist drives on the Botswana side, you won't have to pay the hefty national park fee. The only public transport along the route is the previously mentioned Windhoek-Harare bus.

The Zambian border crossing at Wenela is only four km from Katima Mulilo. If you just wish to visit Zambia for the day, there's a

bustling market in Sesheke, the Zambian border town opposite Wenela. From there you'll have little difficulty hitching or finding public transport to Livingstone (a five-hour trip on a horrid road) and beyond; buses leave at around 7 am and 1 pm daily.

AROUND KATIMA MULILO
Schuckmannsburg

Schuckmannsburg, on the Zambezi River 40 km east of Katima Mulilo, was named for the governor of German South West Africa. It was founded in 1909 as the administrative capital of the Caprivi by Imperial Resident Herr Hauptmann Streitwolf. However, at the outbreak of WWII, it was the first enemy territory to be taken by the Allies (see History at the beginning of this Caprivi section). When the South African administration took over the Caprivi in 1935, the administrative centre of the Caprivi was shifted to Katima Mulilo and Schuckmannsburg languished.

Today, Schuckmannsburg is reached only with difficulty along a 4WD track. However, all that remains is a clinic, a police post and several huts and unless you're a history buff, it's hardly worth the effort of getting there. If you want to have a go, follow the C87 (the Ngoma Bridge road) to Bukalo, 27 km south-east of Katima Mulilo, and turn north-east on the D3509. From the junction, it's 47 rough km to Schuckmannsburg.

Mpalila Island

Mpalila Island, driven like a wedge between Botswana and Zambia, sits at the outermost edge of Namibia; and a sandbank at its eastern end actually reaches out and touches the western point of Zimbabwe. On a map, it resembles Michelangelo's *Creation of Adam* on the ceiling of the Sistine Chapel (check it out). In addition to that gratuitous distinction, it's also the site of a couple of new safari lodges, which are designed to be within easy reach of both Chobe National Park in Botswana and Zimbabwe's attraction supreme, Victoria Falls.

Places to Stay The *Impalila Island Lodge* is affiliated with Kalizo Lodge further upstream (see Places to Stay under Katima Mulilo) and is available only as a package tour in conjunction with a stay at Kalizo. Six-day tours taking in two nights at Kalizo Lodge, boat transfers to and from Impalila Island Lodge, two nights on the island – plus wildlife-viewing cruises, mokoro trips, game drives and bushwalks – costs US$584 per person. The price includes accommodation, full board and all transfers and activities.

Also on Mpalila Island, is the luxury tented camp, *Ichingo Camp* (☎ (267) 650143; fax (267) 660040), Private Bag 33, Maun, Botswana, which lies opposite Kasane, Botswana. It's run by the same people who operate Gunn's Camp in the Okavango Delta. The easiest access is by boat from Kasane, Botswana, although you can also opt for an air charter to the Mpalila Island airstrip from Maun, Botswana, or Victoria Falls, in Zimbabwe. Single/double rates are US$178/245, including accommodation, meals and activities: Chobe river cruises, game drives in Botswana's Chobe National Park and fishing in the Chobe and Zambezi rivers. You'd never know you were in Namibia!

Lake Liambezi

As recently as 1958, there was no Lake Liambezi. In that year, however, the Zambezi floods reached record levels and the backwash up the Chobe River poured over the high ground between Ngoma Bridge and Katima Mulilo and created a new lake which acted as a magnet for waterbirds.

In 1985, however, low rainfall restricted the backflow and the lake dried up and disappeared. Over the following two years, fires raged across the dead reedbeds, turning the lakebed into a blackened dust hole. It's thought that overhunting of hippos actually contributed to the process; without the hippos to flatten tracks through the reeds, the river channels became overgrown with vegetation and restricted inflow from the Chobe.

Access is along 4WD tracks from the Katima Mulilo-Ngoma Bridge road.

MUDUMU NATIONAL PARK

Up to the late 1980s, Mudumu was a hunting concession gone mad, and over the years, the wildlife was severely depleted both by trophy hunters and the local people. In 1989, however, Mudumu National Park and neighbouring Mamili National Park were officially proclaimed in a last-ditch resort to rescue the area from environmental devastation.

Sadly, there are still problems. One of the greatest stems from the Caprivians' traditional belief that burning the bush will bring good rains in the coming year. As a result, much of the Mudumu area is characterised by scorched earth.

Before uncontrolled hunting and burning took its toll on the environment, this was Namibia's richest wildlife habitat, teeming with elephants, rhinos, giraffes, zebras, buffaloes, hippos, crocodiles, Cape clawless otters, waterbucks, elands, roans, wildebeests, impalas, tsessebes, sables, lechwes, sitatunga and the extremely rare puku, as well as a range of predators: lions, cheetahs, leopards, wild dogs, hyenas and so on. With official protection as a national park, some of Mudumu's former wildlife wealth is beginning to return, but it will take many years of wise policy-making and community awareness before it approaches its former glory.

Lizauli Traditional Village

As the wildlife population of Mudumu National Park increases, so do confrontations and conflicts of interest between the animals and local human communities. As has happened in many other places around Africa, elephants raid crops, hippos cause serious injuries to people, and lions and crocodiles take cattle and other stock. Naturally, the locals question the motives of those who would protect wildlife at their expense, and animals often fall victim to the bitterness of disgruntled communities which realise no economic benefits from national parks, wildlife or tourism. As a result, no one wins.

In the hope of linking wildlife conservation and sustainable use of natural resources

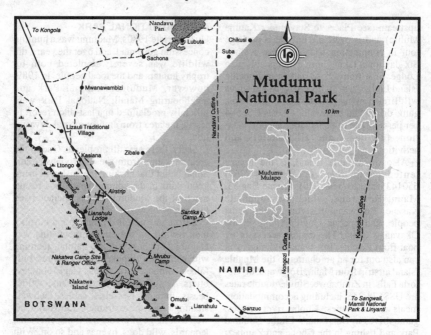

around Mudumu with economic development in the local community, Grant Burton and Marie Holstensen at Lianshulu Lodge – along with MET, the private sector and the Linyanti Tribal Authority – have helped the neighbouring community of Lizauli set up the Lizauli Traditional Village. Here lodge guests and other Mudumu visitors can visit and learn about traditional Caprivian lifestyles. The informal tours are interesting, entertaining and educational, and provide insight into the local diet, fishing and farming methods, village politics, music, games, traditional medicine, basket and tool-making and so on. In addition, Mudumu game scouts are recruited from Lizauli and other local villages, and charged with the task of providing community conservation education and checking poaching problems.

Tours cost US$5.50 per person. Afterwards, visitors are free to buy locally produced handicrafts (I picked up a hippo caller – an ingenious device used to prevent hippos raiding the crops!), and the prices are fair and there's no sales pressure. This is truly one of the best-run local efforts I've seen in Africa, and it's worth going out of your way for. Best of all, supporting such projects is probably the most effective way to improve the economies of surrounding villages and to help restore Mudumu to some of its former splendour.

The village lies 38 km down the D3511, south of the Kongola petrol station.

Places to Stay

My vote for the best and most beautiful lodge in all Namibia goes to *Lianshulu Lodge* (Walvis Bay Radio ☎ (0642) 3581, code 277; fax 486), PO Box 142, Katima Mulilo, a private concession inside Mudumu National Park. It's run by Marie Holstensen and Grant Burton, who were instrumental in setting up the Lizauli Traditional Village, and they do their best to ensure that every

CHRIS BARTON

PETER PTSCHELINZEW

DEANNA SWANEY

CHRIS BARTON

A	B
C	D

NAMIBIA
A: Kokerboom with a Social Weavers' nest
C: Ubusis Canyon, Naukluft Mountains

B: Cape Cross Seal Colony
D: Road between Lüderitz and Aus

PETER PTSCHELINZEW

DEANNA SWANEY

NAMIBIA
A: Shipwreck, Skeleton Coast
B: Flamingoes, Gosse Bucht, near Lüderitz

business decision is influenced by environmental concerns and local sensibilities. The result is a well-run lodge in a magical setting. And don't worry about communication – 10 languages are spoken here!

Activities include game drives around the national park, cruises in the double-decker pontoon *Jacana* and boat trips on the Kwando River to see colonies of carmine bee-eaters which nest in the river bluffs, as well as 400 other bird species and more wildlife than you may expect in this recovering area. We saw a herd of over 100 elephants along the riverbank. With advance warning, they can also organise trips into Mamili National Park. During the evening meal, hippos emerge to graze on the lawn; and diners are serenaded by an enchanting wetland chorus of insects, birds and frogs, including the unusual *tink-tink* of bell frogs.

Accommodation is in comfortable A-frame bungalows with en suite facilities; they're built of indigenous materials purchased from local communities. The meals, which are among the best in the country, have an emphasis on chicken, fish and vegetarian dishes. If you book from inside Namibia, you'll pay US$81/110 for single/double accommodation, including full board. With nature drives, walks and cruises, the price is US$109/163. These prices include a bed-night levy of N$5 (US$1.50), which goes directly to support local community projects and as compensation for locals whose crops or livestock have been damaged by wildlife. In addition, all lodge staff are employed from the local community.

Return transfers from Katima Mulilo cost US$41 per person. To get there with your vehicle, follow the D3511 for 52 km south of the petrol station at Kongola, then turn west onto the signposted track to Lianshulu. The lodge lies five km down this track, which may be negotiated with caution in a 2WD vehicle.

Between Mudumu and Kongola is another accommodation option, *Namushasha Lodge* (☎/fax 240375), PO Box 21182, Windhoek, which sits on a bluff above the Kwando River. It lies outside Mudumu National Park,

but is fairly accessible to the park by boat or vehicle. It's quite popular with Namibian tourists and enjoys a faithful weekend clientele from Katima Mulilo. A full package, including accommodation, breakfast, dinner, a one-hour game drive and a one-hour boat trip costs US$76 per person. For accommodation only, you'll pay US$44; half board is US$9 per day; boat trips average US$6 per hour and game drives cost US$40 per trip.

Mudumu's only official camp site is at *Nakatwa*, beside the Game Scout Camp seven km south-east of Lianshulu Lodge. It's essentially little more than a beautiful place to picnic or pitch a tent, with lovely views over extensive wetlands, but it lacks facilities of any kind. Camping was free at the time of writing, but a nominal fee may be implemented in the future.

There are also two other camps, *Santika (Sitwe)* and *Mvubu*, which were formerly run by Touch Africa Safaris; it's unknown whether they'll come back on line in the future.

MAMILI NATIONAL PARK

Wild and little-visited, Mamili National Park is Namibia's equivalent of the Okavango Delta, a watery wonderland of wildlife-rich islands, river channels and delightful wetlands. The largely forested islands brim with stands of sycamore figs, jackalberry, leadwood and sausage trees, and are fringed by reed and papyrus-choked marshes and open vleis.

Although poaching has taken its toll, Mamili still has enough wildlife to impress anyone – mainly such semi-aquatic species as hippos, crocodiles, puku, red lechwes, sitatunga and otters. You'll also see elephants, buffaloes, warthogs, giraffes and predators, which mostly inhabit the two largish islands of Lupala and Nkasa. Mamili's crowning glory, however, is its birdlife; the park is a rich paradise for birdwatchers, with over 430 species already identified.

As with parts of the Okavango Delta, the

dry season is actually the period of highest water levels, so unless you're travelling by boat, the best time to visit is probably from September to early November.

Places to Stay

Accommodation is limited to five undeveloped wilderness camp sites: in the eastern area of the park are *Lyadura* and *Nzalu*, and in the west, *Muumba*, *Shibumu* and *Sishika*. Camping permits are available from MET in Katima Mulilo or Windhoek.

On the Botswanan bank of the Kwando River are three comfortable up-market lodges: *Twin Pools*, *James Camp* and *Kwando Camp*. For details see under Linyanti Marshes in the North-Eastern Botswana chapter.

Getting There & Away

Access to Mamili is by 4WD track from Malengalenga, which lies north-east of the park, or from Sangwali village, which is due north. With advance notice, Lianshulu Lodge in nearby Mudumu National Park can organise tours through Mamili.

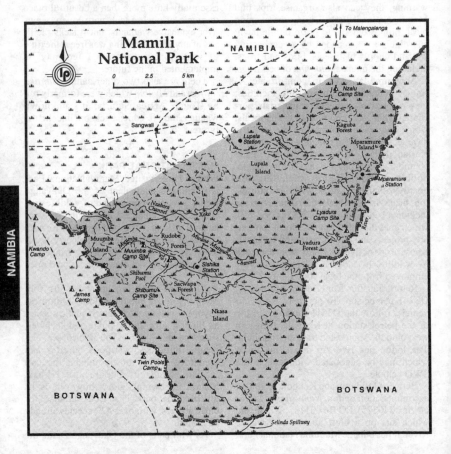

NAMIBIA

Mamili National Park

0   2.5   5 km

To Malengalenga

NAMIBIA

Nzalu Camp Site

Sangwali

Lupala Station

Gesika Channel

Kaguba Forest

Mparamure Island

Lupala Island

Mparamure Station

Nzahara Channel

Chorombe Channel

Koko Channel

Lyadura Camp Site

Lianshulu-Ikongo River

Muumba Island

Muumba Channel

Rudobe Forest

Mavina Mutswim Channel

Lyadura Forest

Linyanti

Kwando Camp

Muumba Camp Site

Sishika Station

Shibumu Pool

Sacwapa Forest

Shibumu Camp Site

James Camp

Mamili River

Nkasa Island

Twin Pools Camp

BOTSWANA

BOTSWANA

Selinda Spillway

Bushmanland

Mainly because it provides an alternative route into the Caprivi via Kavango's Khaudom Game Reserve, Bushmanland is opening up to visitors. This lovely and remote area is the home of the San people, who actually belong to the Ju/hoansi band, a subgroup of the !Kung. Although among Westerners the San have achieved legendary status as a self-sufficient hunting and gathering society, it has been well over a decade since anyone in Namibia followed a traditional San lifestyle.

History

For thousands of years, the San pursued their traditional hunting and gathering lifestyle in their harsh Kalahari home with little outside influence, but during the present century, there have been plenty of changes in this part of the world.

However, from 1970, when Bushmanland was established as a San homeland, and the time of Namibian independence in 1990, their territory shrank from 33,300 sq km to 9700 sq km and 11 of their 15 bore holes were expropriated. As a result, the Ju/hoansi were concentrated into a smaller area than they required to survive traditionally. This forced many of them to abandon their traditional lands (called *n!oresi* – 'homeland' or the 'lands where one's heart is') to either work on farms, where they were regarded as little more than slaves, or to migrate into Tsumkwe, where they were confronted with Western influences. Inevitably, the result in both cases was rampant disease, prostitution, alcoholism, domestic violence, malnutrition and other social problems associated with poverty and dispossession.

During the war for Namibian independence, their *n!ore* (singular form of n!oresi) was commandeered for use as a South African military base and 150 San men were attracted by the unimaginably high wages offered by the South African and territorial defence forces. They formed a Bushman

San (bushman)

Battalion, known as Battalion 31, to fight the SWAPO rebels in Angola and far northern Namibia. As a result, the Western concept of a salaried wage was introduced into a non-cash economy. It also introduced the concept of war and all its attendant horrors to a people who had historically preferred to move on than face conflict with any group. Having said that, some of their ancestors had seen plenty of horrors, as the San were historically pressed into service as executioners in the kraals of Ovambo chiefs.

In 1980, however, two expatriate filmmakers, US John Marshall and his British colleague, Claire Marshall, arrived to see what they could do to help the plight of the San. Over the next 10 years, they drilled bore holes, established 35 villages and formed the Ju/hoansi Bushmen Development Foundation, which encouraged the San to return to their traditional lands and take up farming of dry land crops and raising cattle. This fostered the formation of another organisation, the Nyae Nyae Farmers' Cooperative Organisation, to oversee production and assist in decisions affecting the farmers' interests.

Traditional San Life

We know a great deal about the traditional life of the San because they are one of the most heavily studied peoples in the history of anthropology. An important stimulus for this research was the idea that they were one of the world's last original hunting and gathering peoples. Scholars treated them as if they had lived in complete isolation, and this belief soon took hold among the general public. In fact, however, they have interacted and traded with other peoples for centuries.

Historically, the San have generally lived as hunter-gatherers or 'foragers'. The women were skilled at finding the fruits, nuts and roots which provided most of the daily diet. The meat which was hunted by the men – mostly various species of antelope – was a treat and was the most valued food. Some researches have suggested that the San lived in a state of 'primitive affluence'. That is, they had to work only a short time each day to satisfy all their basic needs. At certain times and locations, this might have been true, but during some seasons and conditions, life could be harsh, for their desert environment was above all very unpredictable.

Mostly, the San lived in nomadic bands of 25 to 35 people. Each group comprised of several families. They had their own land division system; bands had well-defined territories which could measure up to 1000 sq km. During part of the year, the whole band camped together at a water hole; then in the wet season, they'd scatter over the country. They had no political hierarchy or chiefs, and decisions were reached by group consensus; both men and women had a say.

However, not all the San lived by hunting and gathering alone. In the early 19th century, the San were responsible for one of the most extensive pre-colonial trade networks which extended across the Kalahari...

The San people today are landless and unequivocally impoverished. However, some are finding new lifestyles: learning to farm and keeping small numbers of cattle and goats on what land remains for them, but many still hunt when they have the opportunity. A group of such farmers in Namibia have joined to form the Nyae Nyae Farmers' Cooperative (NNFC), which is supported by the Ju/hoansi Bushmen Development Foundation in Namibia.

In 1991, at the Namibian National Land Conference, the Minister for Land stated that the San system of land-holding would be recognised by the government.

In the past, the flexibility of their society helped the San people to evade conquest and control. But at the same time, it made it exceedingly difficult for them to organise themselves to form pressure groups and claim and defend their rights. But now, through organisations such as NNFC in Namibia and The First People of the Kalahari in Botswana, some things, at least, are improving. The first signs of hope were the two regional conferences on Development for Africa's San Peoples' (in 1992 and 1993), in which San delegations from both Namibia and Botswana were present and made their needs known.

Survival International

Unfortunately, over the past several years, the development foundation has suffered a number of ideological conflicts among its expatriate staff. The main points of contention appear to be over the introduction of cattle (which was originally a cornerstone of the development foundation) and tourism. Some purists feel that both are big trouble, while the more pragmatic ones believe that both can play a role in rescuing the San from what appears to be a hopeless situation.

EASTERN BUSHMANLAND

The largely flat landscape of eastern Bushmanland is characterised by scrubby vegetation. In areas which receive more water, however, such as the meandering omiramba, you'll find stands of camelthorn, red umbrella thorn and blackthorn acacia.

Despite official reassurances that cattle, agriculture and traditional gathering would be accommodated, attempts to create a game reserve in eastern Bushmanland have met with local resistance. However, even without official protection, the region supports a rich natural ecosystem. During the dry season, herds of antelopes and other wildlife congregate around the Panveld south of Tsumkwe, but when the rains come, they fan out to the west and north-west.

Tsumkwe

As the 'administrative capital' of Bushmanland, Tsumkwe is the only settlement of any

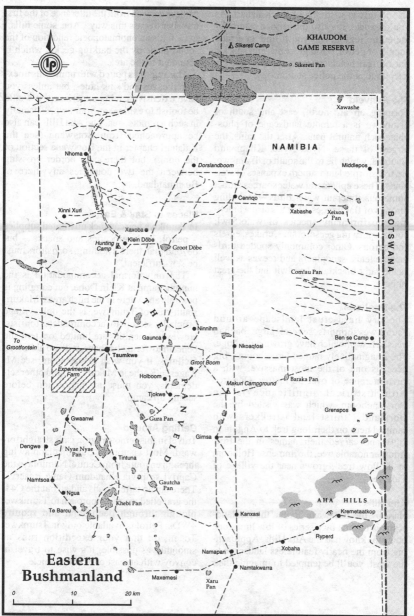

KHAUDOM GAME RESERVE

Sikereti Camp

Sikereti Pan

Xawashe

NAMIBIA

Nhoma

Dorslandboom

Middlepos

BOTSWANA

Cennqo

Xinni Xuri

Xabashe

Xeixoa Pan

Xaxoba

Klein Döbe

Hunting Camp

Groot Döbe

Com!au Pan

T H E

Ninnihm

To Grootfontein

Gaunca

Nkoaq!osi

Ben se Camp

Tsumkwe

P A N

Groot Boom

Experimental Farm

Holboom

Tjokwe

Makuri Campground

Baraka Pan

V E L D

Gura Pan

Grenspos

Gwaanwi

Gimsa

Dengwe

Nyae Nyae Pan

Tintuna

Namtsoa

Gautcha Pan

AHA HILLS

Ngua

Khebi Pan

Kremetaatkop

Te Barcu

Kanxasi

Ryperd

Xobaha

Eastern Bushmanland

Namapan

Namtakwarra

Maxemesi

Xaru Pan

0   10   20 km

NAMIBIA

size in this vast stretch of the Kalahari. As you'd expect, it's also the service centre for the entire region, and you'll find an erratic supply of petrol, basic groceries and snacks, but no real hotels or restaurants. There's a telephone at the police station.

The Panveld

Forming an arc north, east and south of Tsumkwe is a remote landscape of phosphate-rich natural pans. After the rains, the largest of these, Nyae Nyae, Khebi and Gautcha, which lie to the south of Tsumkwe, are transformed into superb expanses of wetlands. These ephemeral water sources attract numerous itinerant water birds – including throngs of flamingoes – but it's also a breeding site for many species of waterfowl: ducks, spurwing geese, cranes, crakes, egrets and herons. Other commonly spotted birds include teals, sandpipers and reeves as well as the rarer blacktailed godwit and the great snipe.

The Baobabs

The dry hard-crust landscape around Tsumkwe supports several large baobab trees, a few of which have grown quite huge. The imaginatively named Grootboom ('big tree') is one of the most massive, with a circumference of over 30 metres. One tree with historical significance is the Dorslandboom, which was visited by the Dorsland ('thirst land') trekkers who camped here on their long trek to Angola in 1891 and carved their names in the tree. Another notable tree, the immense Holboom or 'hollow tree', grows near the village of Tjokwe.

Aha Hills

Hard by the Botswana border, the flat landscape is broken by a series of low limestone outcrops known as the Aha Hills. Approaching from the nearly featureless landscape to the west, you'll be tempted to imagine their name is derived from the utterance of the first traveller to pass this way: 'Aha, some hills.' In fact, it's an onomatopoeic rendition of the sound made by the barking gecko, which is abundant in the area.

This region is potted with numerous unexplored caves and sink holes, but unless you have extensive caving experience, it would be foolish to explore on your own, especially in such a remote area. The Aha Hills can also be approached from Botswana (see the Kalahari chapter in the Botswana section of the book), but there's no border crossing between the two countries anywhere in Bushmanland.

Places to Stay & Eat

In Tsumkwe you can pick up limited supplies – petrol, basic groceries and snacks – but beyond that, there's nothing, so visitors must be self-sufficient.

The only formal accommodation is the hunting camp at Klein Dobe, but camping is possible anywhere in the bush areas. Makuri, south-east of Tsumkwe, is the only village officially set up to accommodate tourists. However, amenities are limited to a tent site beneath towering baobabs, with no ablutions facilities. If you wish to stay there, see Mr Kageshe/Kashe in Makuri. Around other settlements, you must ask permission before setting up camp.

Getting Around

Travel in this remote region isn't straightforward. Most visitors to Bushmanland swing through en route from Central Namibia to the Caprivi strip via Khaudom Game Reserve. There are no tarred roads and all but the C44, the gravelled western approach to Tsumkwe, plough through deep sand and require 4WDs. Petrol is available only in Tsumkwe. To ensure that your expedition runs as smoothly as possible, it's wise to travel in convoy with at least one other vehicle.

North-Western Namibia

For many armchair travellers, Namibia is synonymous with the Skeleton Coast, a mysterious desert coast dotted with the corpses of ships run aground in a sinister fog. This romantic – and surprisingly accurate – image is largely perpetuated by the travel industry; just try to find a travel brochure about Namibia that doesn't include the obligatory photo of a shipwreck being engulfed by icy breakers and thick fog. If this is what you want to see, you'll find it in north-western Namibia.

This largely desolate north-western corner of the country also takes in the regions of Damaraland and Kaokoland, which enjoy some of the country's most unusual natural features and fascinating cultures, including the enigmatic Himba. One of the least accessible parts of the country, it presents substantial rewards for those with the time, patience and cash to get there.

Away from the coast, petrol is available only at Uis, Khorixas, Palmwag, Kamanjab and Opuwo. Hitching can be extremely difficult and you're unlikely to reach any of the natural sites of interest using your thumb alone – at least not without a great deal of luck.

Damaraland

The territory between the Skeleton Coast and Namibia's Central Plateau has traditionally been known as Damaraland, after the Damara people who make up much of its population. Damaraland forms a hilly transitional zone between the arid Skeleton Coast and the scrubby plateau areas further east. Moving inland from the coast, the terrain gradually rises from the flat terraces and coastal dunes into the foothills. The rivers which flow through the northern Namib (the Uniab, Huab, Ugab and Omaruru) have their headwaters in these hills.

With lots of space and a negligible population, Damaraland has a host of natural attractions, including Namibia's highest mountain, Königstein (King's Stone), which rises to 2573 metres in the Brandberg massif. The Brandberg, along with Twyfelfontein and the Spitzkoppe area, are repositories of some of Namibia's best-known prehistoric rock paintings and engravings.

SPITZKOPPE

The 1728-metre Spitzkoppe (which means 'pointed hill'), one of Namibia's most recognisable landmarks, rises mirage-like above the dusty pro-Namib plains of southern Damaraland. Its dramatic shape has inspired its nickname, the Matterhorn of Africa, but the similarities between this desert granite inselberg and the glaciated Swiss alp begin and end at their sharp peaks. The Spitzkoppe is actually the remnant of an ancient volcano, formed in the same way as the nearby Brandberg and Erongo mountains. The Spitzkoppe was first climbed in 1946, but is now quite a popular climb with both local and foreign mountaineers.

Just east of the Spitzkoppe – sometimes called the Gross Spitzkoppe, is a small

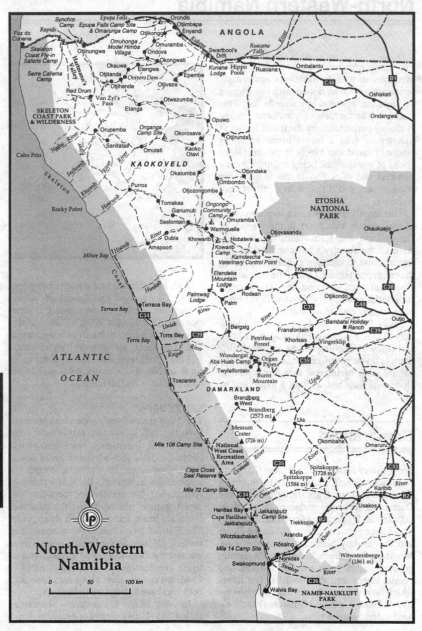

North-Western Namibia

massif known as the Pondok Mountains. In 1896, the German South West Africa Company established a farm at the south-eastern base of this rocky jumble and constructed a dam to provide irrigation water. Just east of this dam, a wire cable will assist you up to a smooth granite slope to a large vegetated hollow known as Bushman's Paradise. Beneath an overhang at one end of this hollow you'll find a badly vandalised panel of ancient San paintings.

Although the Spitzkoppe was transferred from the Damara Administration to the MET in 1986, there are currently no entry fees and no official restrictions on visiting the area. If it seems incredible that such a terrific place could have escaped bureaucracy, don't worry; it's now under consideration for protection as a MET conservation area. The official designation is probably inevitable – and requisite if the feature is to survive the ravages of tourism – but the overpowering sense of lonely wonder it once inspired is likely to be sacrificed.

Places to Stay

There's now a community-based campground which should halt the damage that was being caused by uncontrolled camping around the base of the mountain. The proceeds from this project are shared with the nearby village of Gross Spitzkoppe. Facilities include a reception office, ablutions and braai facilities, but water must still be trucked in. Sites cost around US$6. Local guides are available and the community is also building a curio shop.

Getting There & Away

There's no public transport to the Spitzkoppe, but if you have sufficient food and water for several days, you can get off any Windhoek-Swakopmund bus at the junction of the B2 and D1918 and hope to find a lift to within walking distance of the mountain, 30 km away.

The peak is so imposing that the route will probably be clear. If you're driving from the B2, turn north-west onto the D1918 towards Henties Bay and after 15 km, turn north onto

the D3116, which passes the mountain 15 km farther on. Coming from Uis, just head south on the D1930 from east of town. After 90 km (with great views of the mountain all the way) turn right on the D3116, which leads the final few km to the Spitzkoppe. This trip can be done with 2WD, but if it has been raining, the roads around the mountain itself aren't passable.

Alternatively, if you don't mind just a quick visit, you can take a day tour from one of several companies in Swakopmund (see Organised Tours under Swakopmund in the central Namib Desert chapter).

THE BRANDBERG

The Brandberg, the 'fire mountain', is named for the effect created by the setting sun on its western face, which causes the granite massif to resemble a burning slag heap glowing red. The Brandberg summit, Königstein, is Namibia's highest peak at 2573 metres.

The climb to the peak isn't exactly a technical operation, but it does require a great deal of agility and patience to clamber over the many boulders and rock faces that block the Tsisab and Numas ravines. However,

Euphorbia Euphoria

The several species of the prominent cactus-like euphorbia grow all over southern Africa, from the highlands of Zimbabwe where they reach tree-size *(Euphorbia ingens)* to the gravel plains of Damaraland, Namibia, where there's a variety known as *melkbos* or milkbush *(Euphorbia damarana)*, so called for its milky sap. Although euphorbia are poisonous to humans, they're regularly eaten by monkeys and baboons and for black rhinos, they're a real treat. In fact, they've been dubbed 'black rhino's ice cream'.

Euphorbia have also been useful to humans. The ancient San boiled them down and used them in their rock paintings, and locals still use them for fishing. When placed in the water, the sticky substance clogs the gills of fish and suffocates them. ■

those seeking a technical rock-climbing venue will find plenty of scope here.

Tsisab Ravine

The most popular reason to visit the Brandberg is the gallery of rock paintings in the Tsisab ('leopard') Ravine, which were first discovered in 1918 by the German surveyor Dr Reinhard Maack on a descent from Königstein.

The best known site is Maack's Shelter, which contains the famous painting of the *White Lady of the Brandberg*. The figure, which isn't necessarily a lady, stands about 40-cm high and carries what appears to be half an ostrich egg mounted on a stick (like a stem-glass) in one hand and in the other, a bow and several arrows. The figure's hair is light-coloured and straight – distinctly un-African – and the body is painted white from the chest down. It appears to be central in a bizarre hunting procession which includes several women, one of whom has skewered a small animal – an antelope with gemsbok horns and striped legs – and what may be a shaman, who appears to be holding a bunch of carrots in his left hand and a stick in his right hand, which he's using to prod the white figure.

The first assessment of the painting was

done by Abbé Henri Breuil in 1948, who speculated on Egyptian or Cretan origins for the work, based on similar ancient art he'd noted around the Mediterranean. However, this fanciful idea has now been discounted and it's generally accepted that the painting is of indigenous origin. The *White Lady* hasn't been reliably dated, but may be as much as 16,000 years old.

From the car park, it's a 45-minute walk up a scenic and well-defined track to Maack's Shelter. Along the way, watch for baboons, klipspringers and mountain zebras and carry plenty of water. Further up the ravine are many other shelters and overhangs which also contain ancient paintings. As you climb higher, the terrain grows more difficult and, in places, the route becomes a harrowing scramble over house-sized boulders.

Getting There & Away Access to Tsisab Ravine is 15 km north of Uis on the D2369, where a track marked 'Witvrou' turns off and leads 26 km to the Tsisab car park. There are no facilities at the site but there is an attendant who'll guard your vehicle for a tip.

Numas Ravine

Slicing through the western face of the Brandberg is the Numas Ravine, another treasure house of ancient paintings. However, they're not easily found and, without a guide, your hunt for ancient art may end up being more of a pleasant stroll through a dramatic ravine. For most people the destination lies about a half-hour up the ravine where, on a rock facing the southern bank of the riverbed, you'll find paintings of a snake, a giraffe and an antelope. Another half-hour up the ravine you'll reach an oasis-like freshwater spring, with several more paintings in the immediate surroundings.

Places to Stay There are unofficial camp sites at the parking areas near the mouth of both the Numas and Tsisab ravines, but neither has water or facilities. Despite the barrel at the parking area, there isn't any rubbish collection, so please carry away all your leftovers.

Lichen Fields

Neither plants nor animals, lichen actually consists of two components – an algae and a fungus – and perhaps provide nature's most perfect example of symbiosis between two living things. Both algae and fungi are cryptogams, which mean that they lack the sex organs necessary to produce flowers and seeds, and are therefore unable to reproduce as plants do.

There is a wide variety of lichen. Perhaps the most familiar are the *crustose* varieties that form orange, black, brown or pale green ring patterns on rocks, but there are also *foliose* lichen, which are free-standing. The gravel plains of the Namib support the world's most extensive fields of these foliose lichen, which provide stability for the loose soil in this land of little vegetation. These fields are composed mostly of stationary grey *(Parmelia hypomelaena)* lichen and free-blowing black *(Xanthomaculina convoluta)* lichen, but there's also a rarer orange variety *(Teleschistes capensis)*, an especially bushy variety which grows up to 10 cm high.

By day the lichen fields very much resemble thickets of dead shrivelled shrubs, but with the addition of water, the magic appears. On nights of heavy fog, the dull grey and black fields uncurl and burst into blue, green and orange 'bloom'. It's the fungus component that provides the lichen's root system and physical rigidity, absorbs the water droplets and draws limited nutrients from the soil. At the first light of dawn, however, before the sun burns off the fog and sucks out the moisture, the algae kicks in with its contribution: using the water droplets, light and carbon dioxide to photosynthesise carbohydrates for both itself and the fungus.

Lichens are also incredibly fragile and slow-growing, and the slightest disturbance can crush them. Once that happens, it may take 40 or 50 years before any regeneration is apparent. Most of the damage is now caused by thoughtless off-road driving. In some places scars made by vehicles remain visible from as far back as the German era.

The best places to observe the Namib lichens are south-west of Messum Crater, in scattered areas along the salt road between Swakopmund and Terrace Bay, and near the beginning of the Welwitschia Dr. ■

Getting There & Away Numas Ravine is accessible from the D2342. From the westward turning 14 km south of Uis, continue along this road for 55 km, where you'll see a rough track turning eastward. After about 10 km, you'll reach a fork; the 4WD track on the right will lead you to the Numas Ravine car park.

Messum Crater

One of Damaraland's most remote and difficult-to-reach natural attractions is the mysterious-looking Messum Crater, a secluded volcanic feature in the Gobobose Mountains, west of the Brandberg. In the lost world inside this vast crater, which is over 20 km in diameter, there's little chance of encountering another human being.

Messum is most easily accessed from the D2342 west of the Brandberg, but don't attempt this route without the relevant topo sheets (available from the Surveyor General in Windhoek). Follow the 4WD track leading west along the Messum River for about 30 km, where you'll enter the immense crater through a gap in the rim. Here the road track turns south towards a kopje rising from the centre of the crater, where there are several possible camp sites.

From here you must decide whether to return the same way or head south, through the West Coast National Recreation Area, to the coast. If you opt for the latter, stick to the track to avoid damage to the fragile lichens which carpet the plains.

UIS

This company town revolves entirely around the tin mine which dominates its economy. Services include a convenience supermarket and a petrol station that's open from dawn to dusk daily except on Sunday, when it has shorter opening hours.

Places to Stay & Eat

The alternative to camping at the Brandberg is the *Brandberg Rest Camp* in Uis (☎ /fax 235), which enjoys an unobstructed view of a heap of tin-mine tailings. Camping costs US$4 per person. Single/double units cost

NAMIBIA

US$17/29, but there are also flats for four people costing US$41 and bungalows accommodating six people for US$49. The camp also has an attached restaurant.

KHORIXAS

As the administrative capital of Damaraland, decrepit Khorixas is a possible base for exploring the area's natural features. However, there's absolutely nothing to see or do in the town itself and the general atmosphere isn't particularly pleasant, so few travellers linger. If you're not in need of creature comforts, you'd be better off at Aba-Huab Camp near Twyfelfontein, farther west.

Information

Tourist information is available in the municipal buildings. The bank opens only on weekday mornings. If you're around in May, you might like to check dates for the annual arts festival that's held here.

Places to Stay & Eat

The convenient *Khorixas Rest Camp* (☎ 196) lies three km north-west of town, off the Torra Bay road. Camping costs US$6 per vehicle plus US$6 per person. There are also 40 fully furnished single/double bungalows for US$43/57. Facilities include a restaurant, braai area, swimming pool and general shop. The organised evening barbecue is a great place to meet people.

The rest camp restaurant is virtually the only eatery in Khorixas, unless you count the petrol station takeaways. The *Makro Shop* ostensibly sells provisions for self-catering, but the pickings can get quite slim. One reader reported finding nothing but marmite and pitted olives.

Things to Buy

A good place to stop in Khorixas is the Khorixas Community Craft Centre, which is a self-help cooperative designed to provide an outlet for local artists and craftspeople.

Getting There & Away

As with the rest of Damaraland, there's no public transport to Khorixas, and the natural wonders in its hinterland are accessible only by private vehicle or very undependable hitching. Note that the petrol station in Khorixas is equally undependable, and can be without petrol for several days at a stretch.

PETRIFIED FOREST

Heading west of Khorixas, the Petrified Forest is the first main site of interest. This open veld is scattered with petrified tree trunks up to 30 metres in length with a circumference of up to six metres. In some, details of the bark and wood are plainly visible. The age of these chunks is estimated as being up to 260 million years. Because of the lack of root or branch remnants, it's thought that the fossilised tree trunks were actually transported to the site in a large flood.

About 50 individual trees are visible, some half buried in the surrounding sandstone. In some cases they're so perfectly petrified in silica – complete with bark and tree rings – that it's difficult to believe they're fossilised. The original trees belonged to an ancient group of cone-bearing plants known as *gymnospermae*, which include such modern plants as conifers, cycads and even welwitschias.

In 1950, after souvenir hunters had already begun to take their toll on the Petrified Forest, the site was declared a national monument. It's strictly forbidden to carry off even the smallest scrap of petrified wood. Visitors are now escorted around an organised circuit and admission is US$1.50, but you may also want to offer the guide a small tip, say N$2 (US$0.50). There's a large thatched picnic shelter and a small curio shop selling mainly local crystals and gems.

Getting There & Away

The Petrified Forest, signposted 'Versteende Woud', lies 40 km west of Khorixas on the C39. Beyond the gate, follow the footpath forking to the left.

If you're coming from Khorixas, watch for the prominent sandstone formation known as 'The Ship', which is visible just south of the C39, 52 km west of Khorixas.

TWYFELFONTEIN

The main attraction at Twyfelfontein ('doubtful spring') is its large gallery of rock art, one of the most extensive in Africa. The original name of this water source in the Aba-Huab Valley was Uri-Ais, or 'jumping spring', but in 1947, it was renamed by European settler Mr D Levin, who deemed its daily output of one cubic metre of water insufficient to sustain life in the harsh environment.

Rock Engravings

Unlike most prehistoric art sites in southern Africa, the bulk of the Twyfelfontein works aren't paintings but engravings, or petroglyphs, which were executed by cutting through the hard patina covering the local sandstone. In time, this skin reformed over the engravings thus protecting them from erosion. Most of the work probably dates back to the Early Stone Age, making them at least 6000 years old, and is probably the work of San hunters. From differentiations in colour and weathering, researchers have identified at least six distinct phases of engravings. Some of them, however, are clearly the work of 'copy-cat' artists, and were carved as recently as the 19th century.

Although animal tracks and geometric designs are both represented in the various phases, there are very few human figures. Most of the engravings depict animals, some of which are no longer found this far south: elephants, rhinos, giraffes and lions. One engraving of a sea lion indicates contact with the coast over 100 km away. Another one portrays a lion with pawprints in place of feet and a distinctively angular tail.

Although the farm was declared a national monument in 1952, it had no formal protection until 1986, when it was handed over to the MET as a natural reserve. Because of this delay many of the petroglyphs have been extensively damaged by vandals, and some engravings have been removed altogether.

Twyfelfontein has at least 2500 engravings, but visitors are only permitted to follow the two loop trails past the eight most striking sites, which takes under two hours. If you have a particular interest, it may be possible to get permission to explore further. Guides, which are technically compulsory, may be hired at the entrance. Admission costs US$0.50 plus a negotiable fee for the guide – plan on spending about N$5 (US$1.50) per group for the one to two-hour tour.

Wondergat

Wondergat is an enormous sinkhole affording impressive – and rather daunting – views into the subterranean world. To get there, turn west off the D3254 four km north of the junction with the D2612. From there, it's about 500 metres to Wondergat.

Places to Stay

The nearby *Aba-Huab Camp*, which is self-described as 'simple, rustic and natural', charges US$3 per person. Thanks to the expert management of Mr Elias Xoageb, many travellers rate this peaceful site among Namibia's finest. Camping is in small open-sided A-frame shelters; in the winter months, you'll even get hot showers. Hot and cold drinks and basic groceries are sold on site, and local meals are available with advance notice, but otherwise, campers must be self-sufficient. The camp lies beside the Aba-Huab River, just north of the fork between Twyfelfontein and Burnt Mountain.

Getting There & Away

There's no public transport anywhere in the area and there's little traffic along the access routes, so you'll probably need a vehicle to reach Twyfelfontein. From Khorixas, follow the C39 for 73 km west of Khorixas and turn south on the D3254 and continue for 15 km to a fork. Here, you should bear right; after 11 km, you'll reach the site.

BURNT MOUNTAIN & ORGAN PIPES

Just south-east of Twyfelfontein is the barren 12-km-long volcanic ridge known as Burnt Mountain, which appears to have been literally exposed to fire. Virtually nothing grows in this eerie panorama of desolation, but at sunrise and sunset, the vividly coloured rocks light up in a spectacular burst of colour. Imagine Ayers Rock in central Australia without the tour buses!

Burnt Mountain lies at the end of the D3254, 10 km from Twyfelfontein.

Heading towards Burnt Mountain on the D3254, you can stop at the parking area on the east side of the road, three km south of the Twyfelfontein turn-off. From there, follow the path down into the small gorge, where you'll see a 100-metre stretch of unusual four-metre dolerite (coarse-grained basalt) columns known as the Organ Pipes.

KAMANJAB

Kamanjab functions as a minor service centre for northern Damaraland and the southern Kaokoveld. Although it sits amid some lovely remote countryside, as a town it's quite unspectacular. A superior series of rock engravings may be seen on the Peet Alberts Kopjes, on the farm Kamanjab, 10 km east along the road to Outjo. On the road north, it has the last supermarket and petrol station before Opuwo or Sesfontein. The bank, however, only opens once a month, so unless you're habitually lucky, don't plan on changing money.

The road north to Hobatere and Ruacana has a good gravel surface and is normally passable to 2WD vehicles. About 10 km north of Hobatere, the road crosses the Red Line veterinary cordon fence, where the ranching changes from commercial to subsistence. North of the fence, the vegetation has suffered the ravages of millions of munching goats, and erosion has already begun to take its toll on the semi-denuded landscape.

Places to Stay

There's no accommodation in Kamanjab itself, but 86 km north (just 'over the fence' from Etosha's proposed Otjovasandu Camp) is *Hobatere* (☎ 2022), a private game ranch and lodge operated by Steve and Louise Braine. The name means 'you'll find it here' and – depending what 'it' is – seems to hold

a lot of promise. The vast ranch, which is a palette of stunning desert scenery, is reminiscent of places in Kenya's Great Rift Valley. It provides great habitat for mountain zebras as well as black-faced impalas and Damara dik-diks, and the wildlife viewing is generally good.

Accommodation is in widely dispersed cottages which cost US$65 per person with full board. Game drives cost an additional US$25 per vehicle per hour and game walks are US$6 per hour per group. To reach Hobatere, drive 70 km north of Kamanjab along the Ruacana road and turn west at the signposted Hobatere gate. From there, it's 16 km to the lodge.

VINGERKLIP

The unusual feature, Vingerklip (also known as Kalk-Kegel), lies on the Bertram farm 75 km from Khorixas. This towering finger of limestone, which rises 35 metres above its rubbly base, is an erosional remnant of a limestone plateau that was formed over 15 million years ago. Most impressive is the large cave in its base, which makes it appear even more precariously balanced. It was first climbed in 1970 by American Tom Choate.

Places to Stay

The *Bambatsi Holiday Ranch* (☎ (06542) 1104), with nine rooms, a pool and a tennis court, lies near the junction of the C39 and the D2743, 54 km east of Khorixas and 21 km north of Vingerklip. Accommodation and full board costs US$48 per person. As with all guest farms, bookings are essential. The surrounding landscape is rather wild, and characterised by a high desert expanse of mopane forest.

Getting There & Away

To reach the Vingerklip, head 54 km east of Khorixas on the C39 and turn south on the D2743. The Bertram farm lies 21 km south on this road and the Vingerklip – as should be obvious at this stage – rises about one km west of the farm.

PALMWAG

Few travellers through the stark red hills and plains from the coast expect to find anything like the desert oasis of Palmwag. The region's bizarre landscapes can boggle the mind, especially the areas covered with a meticulously and evenly distributed layer of almost uniformly sized stones. How this came about is anyone's guess.

The Palmwag region takes in two wildlife concessions: Palmwag Lodge in the south and west and Etendeka Mountain Lodge in the north and east. If you wish to explore the back tracks of this area, the lodges can arrange excellent game drives through their respective concessions.

Places to Stay

The beautifully situated and slightly aloof lodge and camp site, *Palmwag Lodge*, is run by Desert Adventure Safaris (☎ 4459), PO Box 339, Swakopmund. It nuzzles up against an unexpectedly green marsh and the air is so clear you'll swear it has never seen a carbon monoxide molecule. The human watering hole has a front-row view of its elephantine counterpart, fringed by makalani palms, and provides a welcome respite on a typically hot, dry and lazy afternoon. Even black rhinos have been known to drop by.

Accommodation in simple reed bungalows costs US$44 per person, with full board. Camp sites with access to luscious showers are US$6 per site plus US$6 per person. For guests there's a restaurant, bar, swimming pool, shop and laundry service, and the petrol station can repair punctures.

To explore the concession area on your own, pick up a permit and directions at the Palmwag reception office. Otherwise, you can go on an organised trip with Desert Adventure Safaris. The most popular destination is the wildlife-rich Van Zylsgat Gorge on the Uniab River.

The alternative is the nearby tented camp, *Etendeka Mountain Lodge*, run by Barbara and Dennis Liebenberg. It lies on the plains east of Palmwag, beneath the western foothills of the truncated Grootberg mountains.

Although it's rather basic, Etendeka is more expensive than Palmwag and must be booked in advance through the Namib Travel Shop (☎ 226174; fax 239455 in Windhoek). If you're driving, they'll meet you at the entrance and shuttle you to the camp in their own vehicles. A real highlight is the three-day, four-night hiking trips around the concession, with overnight stops in trail camps along the way. Accommodation, including meals, game walks and game drives, costs US$70 per person.

Things to Buy

A great souvenir (and a way to support initiative in this region of almost total unemployment) would be a pendant made from *uinidi* or 'vegetable ivory', the nut of the makalani palm. They're carved with animal designs, mounted on a thong and sold informally by local teens for N$5 each (less than US$1.50).

Getting There & Away

Palmwag lies just off the D3706, 157 km north-west of Khorixas and 105 km south of Sesfontein. Coming from the south, you'll cross the Red Line one km south of the lodge.

SESFONTEIN

Sesfontein ('six springs'), the northernmost outpost of Damaraland, is almost entirely encircled by Kaokoland. In 1896, after an outbreak of rinderpest, the German colonial government established a control post run by the military. A barracks was added in 1901 and four years later, it was converted into a full fort and military base. This arrangement lasted until 1909 when, due to the lack of any sort of military urgency, the base was requisitioned by a police unit, which used it until the outbreak of WWI.

The fort was restored in 1987 by the Damara Administration, but to look at the building today, you'd never know it. The historic graveyard nearby is also interesting. Once you've seen that, climb the hill behind the hospital for an overview of the dusty and rather threadbare town.

Sesfontein has some small shops selling

the staples, but as yet, there's no petrol station. If you need a place to camp, ask at the police station.

Warmquelle

Politically, Warmquelle is part of the Kaokoveld. However, because Warmquelle lies on the Palmwag-Sesfontein road, it's more closely affiliated with Damaraland. The town was named after the warm springs along the Hoanib River, which seep out of the artesian system less than one km east of the D3706.

The springs were purchased in 1900 by Dr C Schletwein, as part of a farm which he used to grow vegetables for the German troops stationed at nearby Sesfontein. In the early 1920s, the property was sold to the government as part of a reserve for the Topnaar Khoi-Khoi people.

To reach the springs, turn east at the turn-off to the primary school and follow this road around to the left for about 600 metres. The springs are OK for swimming – but you'll probably attract a bit of local attention.

Places to Stay

The Sesfontein region now supports two public rest camps, which were established jointly by the MET, the Save the Rhino Trust in Khorixas and the Natal Branch of the Wildlife Society of Southern Africa. They're now administered by local communities, which directly benefit from the proceeds.

The small *Ongongo Community Camp* (the name means 'beautiful little place') lies six km up the Italian-built irrigation aqueduct from Warmquelle. This lovely desert oasis features the paradisiacal Blinkwater waterfall and natural pool, which are the products of an incongruous natural tufa formation. Watch for the turtles which live in the small rock pool there. Camping in your own tent or in very basic huts costs US$3.50 per site or hut, but you may have to hunt a while to find someone to check you in. No other facilities are available so bring a sleeping bag and some sort of ground cover – the days may be sweltering but it's cold at night.

Further south is *Khowarib Camp*, run by

Mr Eliu Ganuseb, about three km east of Khowarib village on the D3706. It occupies a bluff overlooking a series of water holes in the canyon of the Hoanib River. Camping in rustic A-frame shelters costs US$3 per person, camping on the floor of a beehive-shaped chalet is US$10 for two people, and very simple two-bed chalets cost US$14. Camping in such enigmatically named tent sites as *Laughing Dove Camp* or *Waterfall Camp* costs from US$7 to US$21 per site plus US$3 per person. Toilets are of the long-drop variety and hot showers come in buckets. Given the lack of facilities, it seems a bit expensive, but the setting is admittedly very nice. For a diversion, you can also take hiking or donkey-cart trips with local guides for a reasonable US$10 per day. A small curio shop sells genuine but generally unremarkable local crafts.

There's no shop or restaurant at either of these sites, although Khowarib village does have a bush shop.

The Kaokoveld

You'll often hear the Kaokoveld described as 'Africa's last great wilderness'. Even if that isn't exactly accurate, this faraway corner of the country certainly is wilderness and perhaps represents Namibia at its most primaeval. This vast repository of desert mountains and fascinating indigenous cultures and communities is crossed only by rugged, unsignposted 4WD tracks, and is refreshingly short of tourist facilities.

Being so far removed from the mainstream, even the wildlife of the Kaokoveld has specially adapted to local conditions. The most renowned, of course, is the desert elephant, of which only about 35 remain. This unique animal is able to survive in harsh dry conditions that would be devastating to any other elephant. This factor, along with its especially long legs, has led taxonomists to consider the Kaokoveld elephants a separate sub-species. In addition to the elephants, small numbers of black rhinos still survive, as well as gemsboks, kudu, springboks, ostriches, giraffes and mountain zebras.

As you'd expect, travelling here isn't easy, and the classic Kaokoveld loop route requires at least five days of driving. Parts of Kaokoveld are hard going for even the most robust 4WD. You'll encounter little traffic beyond Opuwo, and the only settlements are small villages without services of any kind. Your best guide for exploring the region is the new *Kaokoland-Kunene Region Tourist Map*, produced by Shell.

Although the Kaokoveld technically takes in parts of Damaraland as well as the colonially demarcated region of Kaokoland, for the purpose of this discussion, 'Kaokoveld' and 'Kaokoland' are used interchangeably.

Here are a few words of Oshaherero which may be useful in your travels around the Kaokoveld:

Hello	*Moro*
How are you?	*Muwepe nduka?*
Fine, thanks	*Nawa*
Yes	*Eh*
No	*Eee*
Good bye	*Kana ranawa*

OPUWO

Although it's the 'capital' of the Kaokoveld, Opuwo is little more than a dusty collection of concrete commercial buildings ringed by traditional rondavels and Himba huts.

You'll see many Himba and Herero people around Opuwo, but lots of insensitive tourists have passed this way and the locals no longer appreciate having cameras waved in their faces (and who would?). In Opuwo, the going rate for a 'people shot' these days is N$2 (US$0.60). Don't be tempted to snap a photo anyway; camera confrontations have come to blows here. Please respect local wishes and either pay or put the camera away.

Places to Stay

Your best accommodation option is probably the Catholic Mission, which charges just US$14 per person for a clean and secure room. There's also a new stone guesthouse behind the petrol station which accommodates only one party and charges US$41 for up to five people. However, its proximity to both the petrol station and the drankwinkel may affect your sleep.

There are also two seedy guesthouses, which are used mainly by itinerants and traders and aren't recommended for foreign women. They charge from US$4 to US$6 per person; ask at the curio shop for contact details.

There's no official camping in Opuwo, but the owner of the wholesale shop may let you camp in his garden for around N$5 (US$1.50). If all else fails, see the friendly gents at the police station, who sometimes allow camping on their green lawn.

Places to Eat

The Opuwo equivalent of culinary delights are available at the bakery beside the petrol station. There you'll find doughnuts, pastries, bread and delicious sausage rolls.

Beside the curio shop is a sparsely stocked supermarket, but if you're stocking up for an expedition, you're better off using the *Groothandel* supermarket, uphill around the corner, and the nearby drankwinkel, which sells both soft drinks and alcohol.

Things to Buy

Opuwo's main attraction is the brightly painted self-help curio shop, which was started by a Christian group and now sells locally produced arts and crafts on consignment. With a few exceptions, most of the items on sale are used by the locals themselves, and you'll find all sorts of Himba adornments smeared with ochre: conch-shell pendants, wrist bands, chest pieces and even headdresses worn by Himba brides. There's also a range of original jewellery, appliquéd pillowslips and Himba and Herero dolls, drums and wooden carvings. The shop is open Monday to Friday from 8.30 am to 1 pm and 2.30 to 5.30 pm, and on Saturday from 8.30 am to 12.30 pm.

For something even more unusual, see the friendly women at the small material shop beside the drankwinkel. They'll be happy to sell you the material for a traditional Herero

NAMIBIA

hat – and will show you how to shape it into the usual bi-corned form. The normal charge is N$25 (US$7) per hat.

Getting There & Away

There's no public transport of any kind into or around Kaokoland. You'll have the most luck hitching into Opuwo from the township two km from Ruacana; at least a couple of vehicles leave every day. Because most of the traffic travels via Ruacana or Oshakati, it's considerably more difficult to hitch to or from the south. In any case, unless you're visiting someone or launching an expedition into the wilds, you may wonder why you bothered coming to Opuwo anyway.

WESTERN KAOKOVELD

West of Ruacana and Opuwo lies the Kaokoveld of travellers' dreams: stark and rugged desert mountains, vast landscapes, sparse scrubby vegetation, drought-resistant wildlife, and nomadic bands of Himba people and their tiny settlements of beehive huts. This region, which is contiguous with the Skeleton Coast Park & Wilderness, is currently under consideration for protection as the Kaokoland Conservation Area.

A trip through Namibia's wild and remote north-western corner will be an unforgettable experience, but when dealing with such harsh country, careful preparation is in order. Access to the nethermost corners of the western Kaokoveld is via a network of extremely rugged 4WD tracks laid down by the South African army during the bush war. The only maintenance these tracks receive is from the wheels of passing vehicles.

Travelling in the Kaokoveld

Before contemplating an independently organised trip into the Kaokoveld, consider that the region west of Opuwo has no hotels, shops, showers, hospitals, or vehicle spares or repairs. If that makes you uncomfortable, either book an all-inclusive tour with a safari operator or stick with other areas of Namibia.

If you're undaunted, then careful preparation is in order. For any trip west of Ruacana or Opuwo, or north of Sesfontein, you'll need a robust 4WD vehicle, plenty of time and sufficient supplies to see you through the entire journey. This includes water, since there are few bore holes and natural supplies are unreliable. You're also advised to take a guide who knows the region and travel in a convoy of at least two vehicles, lest something go wrong. You'll need to carry two spare tyres for each vehicle, a tyre iron, a good puncture-repair kit and a range of vehicle spares, as well as twice as much petrol as the distances would lead you to believe necessary. For navigation, carry a compass and/or Global Positioning System and the best maps you can find. The topo sheet to buy is the 1:500,000 *Opuwo 1711*, but the aforementioned Shell map will work just as well.

In the drier winter months, the poor condition of the routes can limit progress to five km/h, but in the summer, streams and mud can stop a vehicle in its tracks. For example, you'll need a *minimum* of five days for the standard Kaokoveld circuit, and that's not considering all the arresting scenery that will hold you up voluntarily.

Because the landscape and the flora are delicate and vulnerable, keep to the obvious vehicle tracks. In this dry climate, damage caused by off-road driving may be visible for hundreds of years to come.

If you're extremely keen, it's also possible to hike through the 120 km of enchanting river scenery between Ruacana and Epupa Falls in six days. You're never far from water, but there are lots of crocodiles and even in the winter, the heat can be oppressive and draining. Some people make a point of going during the full moon and walking at least part of the way at night. Then there's the problem of finding a way back from Epupa Falls...

The Western Kaokoveld Circuit

The Kunene The route begins at Ruacana in Ovamboland and heads west along the Kunene River to Swartbooi's Drift, where there's a monument commemorating the Dorsland Trekkers and a small tourist camp. If you have time, follow the road towards the

A Dam in Himba Country

'Now let's talk about the water. All the Himba were born here, beside the river. The river does a good job. When the cows drink this water, they become fat, much more than if they drink any other water. The green grass will always grow near the river. The cows who live far from the river will die. Beside the river grow tall trees, and the vegetables that we eat. This is how the river feeds us. This is the work of the river.'

These are the words of Hikomenune Kapika, a headman of the Himba people, who occupy the region of north-western Namibia and south-western Angola. One of the most self-sufficient peoples in Africa, they have evolved a system of pastoral land use which has enabled them to remain independent and even prosperous in spite of drought and war. For this reason, they've also been able to continue following their traditional lifestyles, with very little outside influence.

As with so many things, however, their traditions are under threat. The Namibian and Angolan governments are planning a hydroelectric dam on the Kunene River, which will flood 290 sq km of Himba territory. This will displace from 4000 to 5000 people on the Namibian side alone, and will affect thousands more. In addition, the resulting reservoir will cover many of the Himba's ancestral burial grounds, which are of considerable religious significance because traditional Himba people greatly honour their dead and consult the ancestral spirits before making major decisions. If that's not enough, the proposed dam would destroy Epupa Falls, which is one of the region's most beautiful natural features.

The dam is still in the planning stages – a two-year feasibility study was undertaken in 1995 – but one wonders whether the project is truly essential to Namibia's energy needs. Other projects would achieve the same end, and even the World Bank has questioned the cost-effectiveness of a dam on the Kunene.

Supporters of the dam claim that the Himba accept it, but those who fully understand the implications of the dam are angry at the prospect. As Hikomenue Kapika has said 'We refuse this dam. The river is our hope, our life. We refuse this dam – it's our death.' Something to think about.

Survival International

sodalite mine, which turns off a few km east of Swartbooi's Drift. The mine doesn't allow visitors, but you'll find plenty of blue sodalites lying along the road.

From Swartbooi's Drift, it's another 93 km to Epupa Falls. Even in dry weather, the entire trip to Epupa Falls from Ruacana averages 12 hours, so get a very early start. Alternatively, you can opt for the easier but less scenic route to Epupa Falls via Opuwo.

Epupa Falls Along the Kunene River, about 135 km downstream from Ruacana, lies the dynamic series of cascades known as Epupa Falls. The name *epupa* is a Herero word for the spume created by the falling water. Here, the river fans out into multiple channels and is dispersed into a series of parallel ravines. The river drops a total of 60 metres over a distance of about 1.5 km and at one point, reaches a total width of 500 metres. The greatest single drop, which is commonly identified as *the* Epupa Falls, is about 37 metres. It falls into a dark cleft and resembles a mini-Victoria Falls.

If you want to see the falls, you'd best go soon, as it's slated to become the site of a hydroelectric scheme which will dam the Kunene and flood the land up to three km upstream of the falls (see the aside, A Dam in Himba Country). In addition to supplying Namibia's power requirements, it will also produce excess power for export to neighbouring countries. The best time to visit is in April and May, when the river is in peak flow, but unless you fly in, access is tricky.

There are several sheltered spots to swim around the falls. The pools just above the lip make fabulous natural jacuzzis, but downstream, the crocodiles and hippos may present problems. You'll be the safest in eddies surrounded by rapidly racing water.

The North-West Corner From Epupa Falls, the circuit turns south towards Okongwati, where there's a basic bottle store. At Omuhonga village, 12 km north-west of Okongwati, locals have established a showcase 'traditional Himba kraal' for the benefit of tourists.

From Okongwati, the route heads west over the beautifully dramatic – and treacherously steep – Van Zyl's Pass into the Otjinjange Valley (the upper part of the valley is known as Marienflüss).

If you wish to explore the Otjinjange or Hartmann's valleys, which lead down to the Kunene River, allow extra time. The Otjinjange route ends at Synchro Camp on the Kunene, which is owned by Kaokohimba Safaris. The Hartmann's track ends at Skeleton Coast Fly-In Safaris' Camp beside the Kunene. The camp is open only to their safari participants.

Back to Opuwo You now have a choice of the two routes – the eastern or western routes – south to Orupembe. Along the way you can camp at the village camp site in Onganga. From there, it's a long 186-km track eastward to Opuwo via Kaoko Otavi. It's worth a stop at Kaoko Otavi to see the ruin of the church built by the Dorsland Trekkers in the late 1870s. Although it was declared a national monument in 1951, the building is now little more than a heap of rubble.

Organised Tours
Quite a few operators are recognising the Kaokoveld as an enigmatic destination, and

are offering many package trips through the region. In addition to Ermo Safaris (outlined under Places to Stay, later in this section), which has a permanent camp at Epupa Falls, a recommended company is Footprints Safaris (☎ 249190; fax 248000), PO Box 2639, Windhoek. As well as cultural tours through the Kaokoveld, they offer four-day adventure hiking trips along the Kunene River between Ruacana and Swartbooi's Drift.

Another great option is white-water rafting on the Kunene River, which is organised by Wilderness Safaris Namibia. These trips cover the fabulous 120-km stretch from Ruacana Falls to Epupa Falls. However, trips must be coordinated in conjunction with the rise and fall of the river dictated by the Ruacana hydroelectric scheme. The trips take a total of 10 days, five of which are spent on the river itself. The rest of the time is spent at Etosha National Park and the Waterberg Plateau. The all-inclusive tour costs US$1650 per person.

You can also get to the Kunene with Skeleton Coast Fly-In Safaris, which offers trips around the Kunene River, and into Hartmann's Valley and the upper Hoarusib Valley. Five-day fly-in trips taking in the lower Skeleton Coast, the Kunene River, Hartmann's Valley and Etosha National Park cost US$2055, including flights, meals and accommodation. A four-day tour which takes in the Skeleton Coast and the Kunene River region is US$1810 per person. These tours also include a fleeting stop at Sossusvlei in the central Namib Desert.

Desert Adventure Safaris in Swakopmund organises fly-in or wild 4WD tours between its own Palmwag Lodge in Damaraland and the delightfully located Serra Cafema Camp on the Kunene. If you're going to spend the money on this sort of adventure, I'd recommend the 4WD option, which will take you across 400 km of Namibia's wildest country. It may be gruelling at times, but you'll have a good feel for the harshness of this seemingly unearthly terrain.

For details about these and other companies operating in this region, see Organised

Tours in the Namibia Getting Around chapter.

Places to Stay

Apart from the aforementioned places in Opuwo and several camps along the river, there's no formal accommodation anywhere in the Kaokoveld, so travellers must be equipped for camping.

Camping Camping in the Kaokoveld does require a special awareness of the environment and local people. Avoid setting up camp in a riverbed, however shady and inviting it may appear. Large animals often use riverbeds as thoroughfares and even when there's not a cloud in the sky, flash floods can roar down them with alarming strength and speed.

Because naturally occurring water sources are vital to local people, stock and wildlife, please don't use clear streams, springs or water holes for washing yourself or your gear. Similarly, avoid camping near springs or water holes lest you frighten the animals and inadvertently prevent them drinking.

Visitors must also ask permission before entering or setting up camp anywhere near a settlement or camp, particularly as you may inadvertently cross one of the sacred burial lines. Also, be sure to ask before taking photos. Most rural Himba people, especially those who've had little contact with tourists, will be willing models. Some, however, may ask for payment, generally in the form of sweets, tobacco, sugar, mielies or soft drinks. In the interest of protecting teeth that may never meet a dentist, it's probably best to stick with mielies. Alternatively, you could offer some fruit, which is hard to come by locally.

There is an organised camp site with flush toilets at Epupa Falls, which is maintained by local Himba people. Camping is free, but you're advised to make a small donation to the caretaker for the upkeep of the site.

Note that no camping is permitted in the Hartmann's or Otjinjange (Marienflüss) valleys. The only official camp site open to casual tourists is *Synchro Camp*, owned by

Kaokohimba Safaris, east of the Otjinjange River mouth. For information and bookings, contact Kaokohimba Safaris in Windhoek.

Swartbooi's Drift East of Swartbooi's Drift, along the Kunene 45 km west of Ruacana Falls, a Portuguese-Namibian man called Pete has set up *Kunene Lodge*. This small camp has several basic bungalows and space to pitch a tent. He also runs inexpensive boat trips on the river. He eventually intends to expand his camp into a fully fledged tourist lodge, with a restaurant and swimming pool. Seek out the latest information in Ruacana.

Safari Lodges The only formal accommodation in this corner of Namibia is *Omarunga Camp*. This small tented camp lies in a grove of makalani palms beside the Kunene River just a stone's throw from Epupa Falls. In addition to the sense of peace and solitude that will envelop you here, the area's attractions include super rockhounding, birdwatching and amateur archaeology (naturally, leave everything as you find it). You can also arrange leisurely float trips on the Kunene River.

Rates are around US$115 per person, but that includes accommodation, meals and activities. Advance booking is essential: contact Ermo Safaris (☎/fax 51975), Top Travel, PO Box 80205, Windhoek. Most clients actually fly in on pre-booked Ermo Safaris packages taking in Etosha and other local attractions, but hardier types can drive in themselves. In a very long day, you can reach Omarunga from Ruacana along the very rough 180-km road along the river. An easier and considerably quicker alternative is the 270-km southern route from Opuwo via Okongwati.

Desert Adventure Safaris in Swakopmund operates *Serra Cafema Camp* at the mouth of the Hartmann's Valley, named for the striking range of mountains across the reed-lined Kunene River in Angola. Access is limited to clients of Desert Adventure Safaris.

Getting There & Away

Few travellers have the luxury of two 4WD high-clearance vehicles, so for them, the easiest way to travel through the Kaokoveld is with an organised camping safari. There aren't any cheap options, but mid-range travellers are catered for by companies who offer 'participation' safaris. The operator provides transport, drivers, guides and equipment; but clients erect their own tents, take turns preparing meals and help with packing and loading of the vehicles. A few overland companies also run trips through the Kaokoveld these days; if they have space, you should have no trouble signing on for a reasonable rate, especially at Opuwo.

Otherwise, all I can suggest is that you wait around the petrol stations in Ruacana or Opuwo and talk to expeditions passing through. If someone has space, you may be able to wangle a lift. Cooks, vehicle mechanics and doctors may well have the best chance of convincing someone they're indispensable.

Skeleton Coast

The term 'Skeleton Coast' properly refers to the stretch of coastline between the mouths of the Ugab and Kunene rivers. However, it's often used as a blanket term for the entire desert coast of Namibia, even as far south as Lüderitz. For the purposes of this discussion, however, it includes the National West Coast Recreation Area north of Swakopmund and the Skeleton Coast Park, which stretches from the Ugab River northward to the Kunene River on the Angolan border.

The Skeleton Coast parks take in nearly two million hectares of gravel plains and sand dunes to form one of the world's most inhospitable waterless areas. The name is derived from the treacherous nature of the coast, which has long been a graveyard for unwary ships and their crews. Once sailors were washed ashore in this desert wilderness, survival was out of the question. Shrouded in misty fog for much of the year, this barren stretch of coastline still exudes a mystical quality.

NATIONAL WEST COAST RECREATION AREA

The National West Coast Recreation Area, a 200-km-long and 25-km-wide strip from Swakopmund to the Ugab River, makes up the southern end of the Skeleton Coast. You don't require a permit to visit this area and the road is easily passable to 2WD vehicles.

This stretch of the coast is extremely popular with White anglers, who come from as far away as Zimbabwe and South Africa to try their hand with such salt-water species as galjoen, steenbras, kabeljou and blacktail. Along the shore between Swakopmund and the Ugab River, you'll see hundreds of concrete buildings, spaced at intervals of about 100 metres. These aren't coastal bunkers guarding against offshore attack, but are merely toilet blocks set up for use by anglers camping and caravanning along the coast.

There's a fog nearly every morning, caused by onshore winds blowing over the cold Benguela Current, but the sun remains intense and can burn badly, even through the fog.

Along the roadsides, you may spot clusters of broad-leafed plants, which are unusual in such desert areas. Chances are, they're wild tobacco plants, which are native to the Americas. No one knows how they arrived on this desolate coast, but it's speculated that the seeds were transported along with hay for the horses during the German-Khoi-Khoi wars. Botanists are currently removing the wild tobacco to learn what effect it has had on indigenous species.

Henties Bay

At the village of Henties Bay, 80 km north of Swakopmund, the relatively reliable Omaruru River issues into the Atlantic. Because it's a rich feeding ground for offshore fish, Henties Bay serves as a fishing resort for keen anglers from all over southern Africa. The town was named after Hentie van der Merwe, who visited the sweetwater spring here in 1929. Today, it's comprised

A Tern for the Worse

Around 90% of the world population of the tiny Damara tern *(Sterna balaenarum)*, of which there are just 2000 breeding pairs worldwide, breeds exclusively along the open shores and sandy bays of the Namib coast from South Africa to Angola. Adult Damara terns, which have a grey back and wings, a black head and white breast, measure just 22 cm long and more closely resemble swallows than they do other tern species, and are also considerably more agile. In their natural environment, they feed offshore in small groups on shrimp and larval fishes.

Damara terns nest on gravelly flats well away from other more prominently marked birds lest they attract the attentions of jackals, hyenas or other predators. They usually hatch only a single chick each year. However, because of their small size, the terns cannot carry food to predator-free islands to feed their chick. Instead, they must remain near their food source.

When alarmed they try to divert the threat by flying off screaming; their nest and egg or chick are usually sufficiently well-camouflaged to escape detection. However, if their breeding place is in any way disturbed, the parent tern abandons the nest and sacrifices the egg or chick to the elements. The following year, it seeks out a new nesting site, but more often than not, it discovers that potential alternatives are already overpopulated by other species, which it instinctively spurns.

Over the past few seasons, this has been a problem along the Namib coast, due mainly to the proliferation of off-road driving along the shoreline between Swakopmund and Terrace Bay. For several years now, the terns have failed to breed successfully and as a result, they'll probably be extinct within 20 years. ■

mainly of holiday homes and is also a popular place to refuel and organise provisions for fishing trips up the coast. Non-fishing travellers can choose between the C35, which turns inland through Damaraland towards Uis and Khorixas, or the coastal salt road, which continues north to the Cape Cross Seal Reserve.

Cape Cross Seal Reserve

Cape Cross is known mainly as a breeding reserve for thousands of Cape fur seals (see the aside). Although many leaflets and signs state that the Cape Cross Seal Reserve is closed on Friday, it's now open daily from 10 am to 5 pm – including Friday – the year round. Admission costs US$1.50 per person plus US$1.50 per vehicle. There's no accommodation, but beside the seal slaughterhouse is a basic snack bar with public toilets. Note that no pets or motorbikes are permitted inside the reserve and visitors may not cross the low barrier between the seal-viewing area and the rocks where the colony lounges.

In 1486, the Portuguese explorer Diego Cão, the first European to set foot in Namibia, planted a two-metre-high, 360-kg padrão (a tribute to João II) at Cape Cross in honour of King John I of Portugal. In 1893,

however, a German sailor, Captain Becker of the boat *Falke*, removed the cross and hauled it off to Germany. In 1894, Kaiser Wilhelm II ordered a replica made with the original inscriptions in Latin and Portuguese and a commemorative inscription in German. There's also a second cross which is made of dolerite and which was erected in 1980 on the site of Cão's original cross.

There is also a pattern of concrete circles containing information on the area's history. They're laid out in the form of the Southern Cross, the constellation which guided the course of Diego Cão's original expedition.

Places to Stay & Eat

Along the salt road up the coast from Swakopmund, you'll find several bleak little beach camp sites set up mainly for sea anglers: *Mile 4* (see under Swakopmund in The Central Namib Desert chapter), *Mile 14*, *Jakkalsputz*, *Mile 72* and *Mile 108*. Basic sites at any of these places costs US$3 per person and US$0.50 for a hot shower. Mile 72 and Mile 108 each have a petrol station which is open until 6 pm; and during Namibian school holidays, they also have kiosks selling basic supplies. At other times, it may be possible to buy fish from anglers along the beach, but you're still advised to be self-

NAMIBIA

Cape Fur Seals

Cape Cross has the best-known breeding colony of Cape fur seals *(Arctocephalus pusillus)* along the Namib Coast. This appealing species isn't a true seal at all, but an eared seal, which is actually a species of sea lion. Fur seals have a thick layer of short fur beneath the coarser guard hairs which remain dry and trap air for insulation, so the animals can maintain an internal body temperature of 37°C and spend long periods in cold waters. At Cape Cross, a large colony of these seals take advantage of the rich concentrations of fish in the cold Benguela Current.

Male Cape fur seals average less than 200 kg, but during the breeding season, they take on a particularly thick accumulation of blubber and balloon up to 360 kg or more. Females are smaller, averaging 75 kg, and give birth to a single, blue-eyed pup in late November or early December. About 90% of the colony's pups are born within just over a month.

Pups begin to suckle less than an hour after birth, but are soon left in communal nurseries while their mothers leave to forage for food. When mothers return to the colony, they identify their own pup by a combination of scent and call.

The pups moult at four to five months of age, turning from a dark grey to olive brown. Mortality rates in the colony are high, and up to a quarter of the pups fail to survive their first year, but the bulk of mortalities occur during the first week after birth. The main predators are brown hyenas *(Hyaena brunnea)* and black-backed jackals *(Canis mesomelas)*, which account for 25% of the pup deaths. Those which do survive may remain with their mother for up to a year.

Cape fur seals eat about 8% of their body weight each day and the colonies along the western coast of southern Africa consume more than a million tonnes of fish and other marine life (mainly shoaling fish, such as pilchards, and cephalopods, like squid and octapi) each year. That's about 300,000 tonnes more than is taken by the fishing industries of Namibia and South Africa put together. Naturally, this has been a source of conflict between seals, anglers and commercial fishing enterprises.

The inevitable knee-jerk reaction was artificial reduction of the seal populations. Historically, the seal slaughter was a free for all, but in recent years, management programmes have been

---

sufficient. Water is sold for US$0.05 per litre.

Supplies are available only at Henties Bay, which also has several places to stay. The primary one is *Hotel De Duine* (☎/fax 1), PO Box 1, Henties Bay. *De Duine* charges US$21/30 a single/double without bath and US$25/36 with a bath.

Another option is the basic *Die Oord Holiday Cottages* (☎ 239), PO Box 82, Henties Bay. Self-catering cottages accommodating three/five/six people cost US$20/25/30. Bring your own towels and toilet paper.

Finally, there are the *Eagle Shopping Centre Flats* (☎ 32; fax 299), which have televisions and are set up for self-catering. They accommodate up to four people and cost US$35.

For meals, the best place in Henties Bay is probably the *Spitzkoppe Restaurant & Pub* (☎ 394), which specialises in seafood (what else?). It boasts Namibia's longest bar and a painstakingly collected display of rare bottles.

SKELETON COAST PARK

At Ugabmund, 110 km along the salt road north of Cape Cross, the road passes through the skull-and-crossbones entry gate to the Skeleton Coast Park. The southern region of this park marks the southernmost habitat for large animals along the Namib Desert coast. North of the Ugab, you have a realistic chance of seeing populations of desert elephant, rhino, giraffe and lion, all of which have adapted remarkably to the harsh desert environment. In order to preserve this natural diversity and control tourism, MET is currently discussing the possibility of creating a Kaokoland Conservation Area, which would take in the wild western half of the Kaokoveld and double the size of the protected areas in north-western Namibia.

Only the southern zone of the park (that is, south of the Hoanib River) is open to individual travellers, but everyone requires a permit. These cost US$2.50 per person plus US$3 per vehicle and require you to spend at least one night at either Torra Bay (open only in December and January) or Terrace

implemented to prevent the colony from growing. However, because marine predators other than seals also compete with humans for the same fish, a reduction in the seal population causes a proliferation of these predators and the number of fish available to the fishing industry remains the same.

Still, the 'culling' continues. Currently, the programme is managed by a private company, Sea Lion Products, which operates a slaughterhouse beside the snack bar. Here, the animals are turned into high-quality skins and a sort of protein sludge to be used as cattle feed. The culling season runs from 1 August to 15 November. The company is clearly quite sensitive about its position here, and although you're welcome to have a look around (if your stomach can take it), photography is forbidden.

Nature also takes its toll on the colony. As recently as 1993, the Cape fur seals at Cape Cross numbered 250,000, but an outbreak of red tide (an algae whose growth is spurred by high levels of toxins and/or low oxygen levels in the water) in 1994, which caused the shoals of fish to remain further out to sea, has had a drastic effect on the seal population. By mid-1994, the Skeleton Coast was littered with the bodies of both pups and adults that had succumbed to starvation and it was estimated that the population had decreased to less than 25,000. The red tide appears to run on a 30-year cycle, so it's expected that the fish will return soon and things will probably be almost back to normal by the time you read this.

On a more sinister note, however, it has been recently revealed that the seals are also going to supply ground seal penises, which are mistakenly believed to have aphrodisiac properties and fetch over US$2000/kg on clandestine Far Eastern markets. This seems especially worrying when you consider the government has recently announced a massive cull which would bring the total seal population down to around half a million 'for management purposes', and has somehow determined that 300,000 seals have to go. Biologists, however, are concerned that the figures are premature, given the fact that no one yet knows how many seals actually survived the red tide of 1994. ■

Bay. If you're heading for either camp, you must pass the Ugabmund gate before 3 pm and or the Springbokwater gate before 5 pm.

No day visits are allowed, but transit permits allowing you to drive on the road between the Ugabmund and Springbokwater gates are available for US$2.50 per person and US$3 per vehicle at the MET offices in Windhoek and Swakopmund, Okaukuejo Camp in Etosha National Park and at the Springbokwater and Ugabmund check-points. You must enter through one gate before 1 pm and exit through the other before 3 pm the same day. Transit permits can't be used to visit Torra Bay or Terrace Bay, but in December and January, transit travellers may pop into Torra Bay to refuel.

Ugab River Hiking Route

The 50-km hiking trail along the Ugab River may be walked on the second and fourth Tuesday of each month. This guided hike, which accommodates groups of six to eight people, begins at 9 am from Ugabmund and ends on Thursday afternoon. It's wise to spend the Monday night at the Mile 108 camp (40 km south of Ugabmund) which allows you to reach the start before 9 am. The hike costs US$25 per person and must be booked in advance through the MET office in Windhoek. As usual, you'll need a doctor's certificate of fitness issued less than 40 days before the hike. Hikers must provide and carry their own food and camping equipment.

The route begins by crossing the coastal plain, then climbs into the hills and follows a double loop through some interesting fields of lichen and past caves, natural springs and unusual geological formations. Along the way, look out for lions, hyena, gemsboks and other antelopes.

Torra Bay

The camp site at Torra Bay is open only during December and January, to coincide with Namibian school holidays. Tent or caravan sites cost US$3 for up to eight people plus one tent or caravan. Petrol, water, firewood and basic supplies are avail-

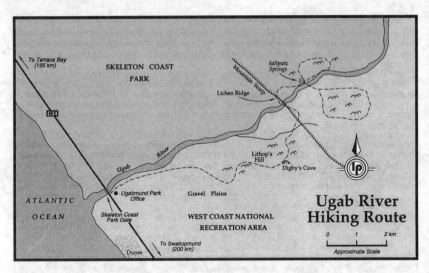

**Ugab River
Hiking Route**

able only in December and January. Campers at Torra Bay may use the restaurant at Terrace Bay.

Just behind Torra Bay is a textbook field of barchan dunes. It's the southernmost extension of the incredible dunefield which stretches all the way to the Curoca River in Angola.

Terrace Bay

Terrace Bay, 49 km north of Torra Bay, is considerably more luxurious than its counterpart and is open year-round. Like all the Skeleton Coast sites it is mainly set up to cater to the needs of surf anglers and there's nothing of particular interest in the area apart from the line of dunes to the north and the sparse but interesting desert coastal vegetation. The only wildlife you may encounter this near the coast will be black-backed jackals and brown hyena.

Single/double accommodation at Terrace Bay costs US$44/73, including accommodation with en suite facilities and hot showers, three meals and – of course – space in the freezer for the day's catch. The site has a restaurant, shop and petrol station.

Getting There & Away

The West Coast National Recreation Area and the southern half of the Skeleton Coast Park is accessed via the very amenable salt road which heads north from Swakopmund and ends 70 km north of Terrace Bay. Distances along the road are measured in miles from Swakopmund. The road is good but the bleak landscape, cold sea winds, fogs and frequent sandstorms don't make it very conducive to hitchhikers.

You can also reach the park via the C39 gravel road which links Khorixas with Torra Bay. Note that no motorbikes are permitted anywhere in the Skeleton Coast park.

SKELETON COAST WILDERNESS

The Skeleton Coast Wilderness, between the Hoanib and Kunene rivers, makes up the northern two thirds of the Skeleton Coast Park. This wild coastline is what the Skeleton Coast is all about. Seemingly endless stretches of foggy beach are punctuated by eerie and rusting shipwrecks, dolphins are often seen jumping offshore, and on beach walks you'll hear the cries of kelp gulls and gannets. In fact, it seems amazing that this desolate landscape could support much life at all, but, in fact, 64 bird species have been counted here. About a quarter of these are wading birds – including sandpipers, turnstones and plovers – migrating between the northern and southern hemispheres.

The most commonly visited sites of interest lie around Sarusas (which has historically been a commercial source of amethyst-bearing geodes), and include the coastal dunes, the Cabo Frio seal colony, the Clay Castles in Hoarusib Canyon and the Roaring Sands (so-called because the sound made by millions of sand grains rolling down the dune face approximates the lower ranges of a string bass).

A lone park ranger lives at Möwe Bay and sends daily weather reports by radio. He also maintains a small museum of shipwreck detritus and newspaper clippings recounting the stories of Skeleton Coast shipwreck survivors.

History
In the early 1960s, Windhoek-based lawyer Louw Shoemann began bringing business clients to this region. He thereby became involved in a consortium to construct a harbour at Möwe Bay, near the southern end of the present-day Skeleton Coast Wilderness. In 1969, however, the South African government dropped the project. It was around this time that Shoemann met an American named Dick Logan, who helped him to appreciate the magic of this unique region by contrasting its wildness to the thoughtless development that had tragically degraded the deserts of the US South-west.

In 1971, as part of its discredited homelands policy, South Africa declared the region a protected reserve and, five years later, agreed to allow limited tourism. The concession was put up for bid and Shoemann was the only one to tender. He set up Skeleton Coast Fly-In Safaris, and for the next 18 years, led small group tours through the area's natural wonders, practicing real ecotourism long before it became a buzzword.

In 1993, however, the concession was mysteriously transferred to the exclusive German tour company, Olympia Reisen. After a hotly contested court case, the transfer of the concession was declared null and void, but in an appeal, that decision was overturned and Skeleton Coast Fly-In Safaris lost its access to the region for at least 10 years. Sadly, however, Louw Shoemann passed away during the dispute and when it was over, the family was forced to alter the company's itineraries to include only the main Skeleton Coast Park, the Kunene region and areas further inland.

Olympia Reisen is currently going ahead with new tourism development projects inside the park.

Getting There & Away
The Skeleton Coast Wilderness is closed to individual travellers and access is only with organised fly-in safaris operated by the official concessionaire.

The Central Namib

Unlike the Kalahari, which is relatively well-vegetated, most of the Namib Desert gives an impression of utter barrenness. Stretching over 2000 km along the south-western African coast from the Oliphants River in South Africa to San Nicolau in southern Angola, its attractions are numerous and diverse. In the local Nama language, the name 'namib' rather prosaically means 'vast dry plain', but nowhere else on earth do such desolate landscapes reflect so many distinctive moods and characters. Around every bend is another photo and you won't tire of the surprises this region has to offer.

A number of watercourses, which are more like linear oases, slice through the gravel and sands to the sea. Some flow regularly, but others contain water only during exceptionally rainy periods. However, these riverbeds conduct sufficient subsurface water to support stands of green trees along their courses.

Much of the Namib's surface is covered by enormous linear sand dunes, which roll back from the sea towards the inland gravel plains. Heading north, the dunes stop abruptly at the Kuiseb River, where they give way to flat, arid gravel plains interrupted by isolated ranges and hills known as *inselbergs*. The dunes may seem lifeless but they actually support a complex ecosystem capable of extracting moisture from the frequent fogs (see the aside entitled Dune Life. These fogs are caused by the condensation which occurs when cold moist onshore winds, influenced mainly by the South Atlantic's Benguela Current, meet with the dry heat rising from the desert sands. They build up overnight and burn off during the heat of the day.

On these gravel plains live ostriches, gemsboks, springboks, zebras, ground squirrels, mongooses and small numbers of other animals, such as black-backed jackals, bat-eared foxes, caracals and aardwolves. After good rains, seeds germinate and the seem-

ingly barren gravel transforms into a meadow of waist-length grass teeming with wildlife. Unfortunately, the rains have been weak for several years now, but you'll still encounter small herds of zebras, ostriches, kudu and gemsboks.

The entire Namib area harbours ancient archaeological sites, providing evidence and artefacts of the hunting and gathering people who have occupied the region for perhaps as many as 750,000 years. The coastline is dotted with ancient middens of shells and fishbones which belonged to what the locals call the *strandlopers* ('beach walkers'), who were probably early Khoi-Khoi or San people. Inland, watch for ancient stone circles and rock paintings created by early San hunters.

KHOMAS HOCHLAND

The rugged upland region known as the Khomas Hochland creates a transition zone between the gravelly plains of the Namib Desert and the high central plateau where Windhoek is situated.

From Windhoek, three mountain routes lead westward through the Khomas Hochland, crossing the Bosua, Us and Gamsberg passes. These are the most interesting and dramatically scenic access routes into the Namib Desert.

Allow six to seven hours to drive any of these routes. The Gamsberg is the most popular and scenic of the three, but they're all quite steep in places and are therefore best travelled from east to west. There's no petrol or services available on any of the routes, so have an supply of everything you'll need.

Bosua Pass

The northernmost of the three routes is Bosua Pass, which provides the shortest – but not necessarily the quickest – route between Windhoek and Swakopmund. As the road descends onto the Namib Desert plains, this gravel road, which is one of Namibia's steepest routes, reaches a gradient of 1:5 or 20% slope so it isn't suitable for trailers.

To get started, follow the C39 west past Daan Viljoen Game Park. The highland area around the Matchless Mine, west of the park, is a rich copper-producing area, and in the 17th and 18th centuries indigenous people maintained small-scale smelting operations. This idea was taken up by the European colonists, who established the Walfisch Bay Mining Company in 1856. Production lasted only until 1860, and except for a brief active period in 1902, it didn't open again until the 1960s. It was run by the Tsumeb Corporation until it was closed in 1983.

Along the road westward, it's worth a quick stop at Neuheusis to see the derelict two-storey mansion known as Liebig Haus. It was built in 1908 as the home and head-quarters for the farm manager of an Anglo-German Farming Consortium. When it was occupied, this colonial dwelling was the very picture of opulence, and even sported a lavish fountain in the salon. It's now completely dilapidated but it may eventually be renovated and turned into a hotel.

Near the settlement of Karanab, 15 km west of Neuheusis, are the ruins of Fort Von François and its stables. The fort was named after Major Curt von François, who established a series of military posts to guard the

Windhoek-Swakopmund road. This one had an ignominious end as a drying-out station for German military alcoholics.

Us Pass

On the scenic Us Pass route, the D1982 follows the shortest distance between Windhoek and Walvis Bay. It isn't as steep as the Bosua Pass, reaching a gradient of only 1:10 or 10%, but the road condition can be quite poor, especially after rain. To get there, follow the C26 south-west from Windhoek; after 38 km, turn north-west on the D1982, which is signposted 'Walvis Bay via Us Pass'.

Gamsberg Pass

The gravel C36 from Windhoek to Walvis Bay drops off the edge of the Central Plateau at the Gamsberg Pass, which reaches an altitude of 2334 metres at the top of the Gamsberg range. On a clear day, you'll have a wonderful view across the Namib Desert, but most of the time the vista is concealed by dust. The name of the pass is a combined Khoisan and German construction meaning 'obscured range', after the flat-topped, 2347-metre Gamsberg Peak, which blocks the view southward. The mountain is capped with an erosion-resistant layer of sandstone.

The western side of the pass is steep and normally requires a downshift into second gear on the way up or down, but it isn't nearly as treacherous as some would have you believe. Don't be put off or you'll miss some lovely scenery.

Places to Stay

Along the Gamsberg Route, 65 km south-west of Windhoek, is the *Farm Hilton* (☎ (0628) 1111), a basic camp which revolves around horse-riding; transfers are available from Windhoek. Guests are taken on riding excursions around the farm or on three to five-day horseback camping safaris. If you're a real horse fan, you can even opt for a 10-day ride from the farm to the sea at Swakopmund. This option isn't cheap at nearly US$1700 per person, all inclusive, but it's booked up at least six months in advance.

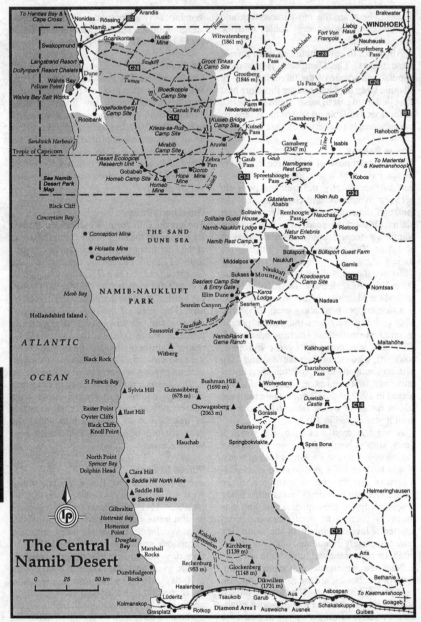

The Central Namib Desert

On the Us Pass Route, 72 km east of its junction with the C14, is the *Farm Niedersachsen* (☎ (0628) 1102), PO Box 3636, Windhoek, run by Barbara and Klaus Ahlert. Although it's registered as a hunting farm, it also welcomes non-hunting guests. On the farm is one of the desert hideouts used by Henno Martin and Hermann Korn during WWII. Accommodation in double rooms, including all meals, costs US$49 per person. They also organise 4WD excursions through the surrounding desert country.

SWAKOPMUND

With palm-lined streets, seaside promenades and some fine hotels, Swakopmund holds the title of Namibia's biggest holiday destination. Thanks to its pleasant summer climate and decent beaches, the town is popular with surfers, anglers and beach lovers from all over southern Africa. Best of all, however, it's quite a friendly place and you need not be loaded down with cash; it generally welcomes backpackers and midrange travellers with the sort of hospitality normally reserved for up-market tourists.

Swakopmund does like to bill itself as a beachfront paradise, and perhaps that's why tourist authorities never let you in on the origin of its name, which is a real winner. Of course in German, it's simply 'mouth of the Swakop River', but when you get to the bottom of the matter, the word *swakop* is a variation on the Nama words *tsoa xoub*, which literally translates as 'bottom excrement'. It was inspired by the appearance of the sea around the river mouth during times of particularly high water.

For better or worse, Swakopmund feels overwhelmingly German – indeed, some have said that it's more German than Germany. There are plenty of flower gardens and half-timbered houses as well as other colonial-era structures and if not for the wind-blown sand and the palm trees, Swakopmund wouldn't look out of place on the North Sea coast of Germany. Many German-Namibians own holiday homes or beachfront cottages in Swakopmund, and the town draws throngs of German-speaking tourists from overseas, who feel right at home. This Teutonic atmosphere contributes to the town's pervasive *Gemütlichkeit* (distinctively German appreciation of comfort and hospitality).

Swakopmund gets extremely busy around the Namibian school holidays in December and January, when temperatures average around 25°C, but during the cooler winter months, the mercury stays at around 15°C and there are few tourists about.

Thanks to its mild temperatures and negligible rainfall, Swakopmund statistically enjoys a superb climate. However, there is a bit of grit in the oyster; when an easterly wind blows, the town gets a good sand-blasting, and during the winter, cold sea fog often produces a dreary atmosphere and an almost perpetual drizzle. This fog rolls up to 30 km inland, and provides moisture for desert-dwelling plants and animals, including 80 species of lichen.

History

Swakopmund came into existence in early 1892 and after nearby Walvis Bay was annexed by the British-controlled Cape Colony, it remained as German South West Africa's only viable harbour. As a result, it rose to greater prominence than its relatively poor harbour conditions would have otherwise warranted. Early passengers had to be landed in small dories, but after the pier was constructed, passengers were winched over from the ships in basket-like cages. An example of these unusual contraptions is now on display in the town museum.

Construction began on the first building, now known as the Alte Kaserne ('the old barracks') in September 1892. By the following year, it housed 120 Schutztruppe soldiers, and ordinary settlers were arriving to put down roots. The first civilian homes in Swakopmund were prefabricated in Germany and transported south by ship.

As a port town, Swakopmund became the leading import-export funnel for the entire territory, and as a result, it attracted numerous government agencies and transport companies. During WWI, when South West

NAMIBIA

Swakopmund

0   250   500 m

Swakop River

To Walvis Bay

Africa was taken over by South Africa, Swakopmund lost its primary status as a port (Walvis Bay had a much better harbour) and fell into the role of holiday resort. The harbour subsequently silted up and became a bathing beach. As a result, Swakopmund is a generally pleasant place while Walvis Bay, its counterpart, remains a largely colourless port city with none of the interesting colonial architecture of its neighbour to the north.

Today, a major source of employment is the immense Rössing Corporation mine, which operates the world's largest opencast uranium mine just east of the town.

However, Swakopmund's economy is based on tourism. Although the bizarre weather – particularly in the winter – can throw a spanner into tourists' plans, Swakopmund's main appeal for holiday-makers lies in its beach frontage and the abundance of colonial architecture.

Information
The helpful Namib Information Centre (☎ 2224; fax 5101), in the Woermannhaus, is open Monday to Friday from 8.30 am to 1 pm and 2 to 5 pm; and on Saturday from 9 to 11 am. You may want to pick up the

pamphlet *What's On at the Coast*, which is published annually. Unfortunately, it seems to exist exclusively for its advertisers – no one else gets a mention – and it's actually of limited usefulness.

Also helpful and friendly is the MET office (☎ 4576) a block away on Brücken Strasse. It sells Namib-Naukluft Park permits and books private camp sites (US$3) in the park. It also distributes the Engen Namibia guide free of charge. The office is open Monday to Friday, 7.30 am to 1 pm and 2 to 4.30 pm. After hours and on weekends, you can pick up park entry permits from the Hans Kriess Garage on the corner of Kaiser Wilhelm Strasse and Breite Strasse.

Money Swakopmund has branches of all major banks, including Standard, First National and Swabank. They're open Monday to Friday from 9 am to 3.30 pm and on Saturday from 8 to 11 am.

Post & Telecommunications The GPO, on Garnison Strasse, has a public telephone for international calls. You can send or receive faxes at the public fax office (☎ 2720) in the GPO. There's also a private fax office (☎ 5872; fax 5874) at 55 Kaiser Wilhelm Strasse. It's open Monday to Friday from 8.30 am to 1 pm.

The Hotel-Pension Rapmund has a public telephone which accepts telephone cards.

Bookshops & Libraries Swakopmund has a couple of good bookshops, probably thanks to its reputation as a holiday town. For a range of local titles, as well as novels in German and English, see the Swakopmunder Büchhandlung on Kaiser Wilhelm Strasse. For something more esoteric, particularly books on art and local history, see The Muschel Book & Art Shop at 32 Breite Strasse. On the corner of Moltke Strasse and Brücken Strasse is a secondhand shop which has a back room full of used books in English, German and Afrikaans for less than US$1 each.

If you're researching any Namibian or African topic, hole up in the Sam Cohen

NAMIBIA

Library, near the Otavi Bahnhof (Otavi Railway Station). It contains the town archives, including newspapers dating from 1898, as well as 6000 books, at least 2000 of which deal with specifically African topics.

Laundry The Swakopmund Laundrette (☎ 2135) is at 15 Swakop Strasse, opposite Hansa Brewery on the same plot as the Rest Camp. They have plenty of diversions upstairs in their Le Club Casino & Joy World to occupy customers while their clothes are holed up in the machines. The casino is open from 7 pm every night; and free blackjack, poker and roulette lessons are given from 7 to 8 pm.

Firewood If you're heading north up the Skeleton Coast, or into Damaraland or the Namib Desert, you can buy firewood for US$2.25 per 15-kg bundle at the Swakopmund Laundrette. After hours, you can buy firewood from the Hans Kriess Garage on the corner of Kaiser Wilhelm Strasse and Breite Strasse.

Dangers & Annoyances When the president is in residence at the State House, a unit of the Presidential Guard camps out on the pavement, and several unpleasant incidents have suggested they may be a bit jumpy. If the president is in town, it may be best to avoid the area.

Historic Buildings & Structures

Swakopmund simply brims with interesting historic buildings and if you like traditional German architecture you'll stay occupied for quite a while. If you wish to learn more about the town's colonial history and sites, pick up a copy of the book *Swakopmund – A Chronicle of the Town's People, Places and Progress*, which is available at the museum and in local bookshops.

The Jetty In 1905, the need for a decent cargo and passenger-landing site led Swakopmund's founders to construct the original wooden pier. Over the following years, however, it was attacked by both

woodworm and the battering of the high seas, and in 1911 construction was begun on an iron jetty which would extend over half a km into the sea. However, when the South African forces occupied Swakopmund and the port was no longer necessary, the project became superfluous. The dangerous old wooden pier was removed in 1916 and the work on the new pier was discontinued while it was still less than 300 metres long. The unfinished iron jetty took a battering from the elements and had to be closed in 1985 for safety purposes. The following year, however, a public appeal raised a quarter of a million rand to restore the structure.

The Mole The seawall, designed by architect FW Ortloff in 1899, was intended to enhance Swakopmund's naturally poor harbour facilities and create a mooring harbour for large cargo vessels. Unfortunately, Mr Ortloff was unfamiliar with the Benguela Current, which swept northward along the coast, carrying with it a great load of sand from the deserts to the south. Within 4½ years, the entrance to the harbour had been closed off by a sand bank and two years later, the harbour itself had been invaded by sand and was turned into a sheltered beach which is now known as Palm Beach. The Mole is now used as a mooring place for pleasure boats.

Lighthouse The lighthouse, an endearing Swakopmund landmark, was originally constructed in 1902 with a height of 11 metres. An additional 10 metres was added in 1910.

Alte Kaserne This imposing fort-like structure was designed and built in 1906 by the railway company, which had got Swakopmund's economic ball rolling by completing the pier two years earlier. It now serves as Swakopmund's Hostelling International hostel.

Marine Memorial Often known by its German name, Marine Denkmal, this memorial was commissioned by the Marine Infantry in Kiel, Germany, in 1907 and was designed by sculptor AM Wolff of Berlin. It commemorates the German First Marine Expedition Corps, which helped to put down the Herero uprisings of 1904. As a national historical monument, it will of course continue to stand, but one does wonder how long before the Herero erect a memorial of their own.

Kaiserliches Bezirksgericht (State House) This rather imposing building, which originally served as the District Magistrate's Court, was designed by Carl Schmidt in 1901 and constructed the following year. It was extended in 1905 and a tower was added in 1945. After WWI, the building was modified to serve as an official holiday home of the territorial administrator. In keeping with that tradition, it's now the official Swakopmund residence of the executive president.

Altes Amtsgericht Designed by Otto Ertl, this gabled building was constructed in 1908 as a private school. However, when the funds ran out, the government took over the project and requisitioned it as a magistrate's court. In the 1960s, it functioned as a school dormitory, and now houses municipal offices. Just so no one can doubt its identity, the words *Altes Amtsgericht* are painted across the front of the building.

Railway Station (Bahnhof) The ornate railway station or Bahnhof was built in 1901 and declared a national monument in 1972. It was originally constructed as the terminus for the Kaiserliche Eisenbahn Verwaltung (Imperial Railway Authority) railway, which connected Swakopmund with Windhoek. In 1910, when this state railway was closed down, the building assumed the role as main station for the narrow-gauge mine railway between Swakopmund and Otavi. The building has now been renovated as part of an opulent hotel.

Old Franciscan Hospital The old Franciscan hospital, known as the St Antonius Gebaude, was designed by colonial architect Otto Ertl and built in 1907. It functioned as a hospital until 1987. You'll find it on Post Strasse, one block east of the old post office.

Litfass-Saule Named for Berlin printer Litfass, who came up with the idea of advertising pillars in 1855, the Litfass advertising pillars were a common source of information and advertising for the citizens of early Swakopmund. The only remaining example sits on the corner of Post Strasse and Breite Strasse.

Hohenzollern Building The excessively Baroque-style Hohenzollern Building, on the corner of Moltke Strasse and Brücken Strasse, is probably Swakopmund's most imposing and unusual structure. It dates back to 1906 and from its appearance, you can probably guess that it was originally intended as a hotel. Its rather outlandish décor is crowned by a fibreglass cast of Atlas supporting the world, which replaced the rather precariously placed cement version which graced the roof prior to renovations in 1988.

German Evangelical Lutheran Church The neo-Baroque Evangelical Lutheran Church on Otavi Strasse was designed by architect Otto Ertl. The building was constructed in 1910-11 to house the Lutheran congregation organised in 1906 by Dr Heinrich Vedder. It was consecrated on 7 January 1912.

Old German School Opposite the Lutheran Church is the building which houses the former government and municipal secondary schools. The Baroque-style building's design is the product of a 1912 competition which was won by Emil Krause. The building was completed in 1913.

Deutsche-Afrika Bank Building This pleasant-looking neo-Classical building near the corner of Woermann Strasse and Moltke Strasse has served as a bank since 1909 when it opened as the branch office of the Deutsche–Afrika Bank.

Hotel Kaiserhof The former Hotel Kaiserhof, on the corner of Kaiser Wilhelm Strasse and Moltke Strasse, was originally constructed as a two-storey building in 1905. It was destroyed in a fire nine years later and was rebuilt as a single-storey building.

Prinzessin Rupprecht Heim This pleasant single-storey structure, built in 1902, is one of Swakopmund's earliest buildings. Its first function was as the Lazarett or military hospital, but in 1914 it was transferred to the Bavarian Womens' Red Cross, which named it for their patron, Princess Rupprecht, wife of the Bavarian Crown Prince. The idea was to allow convalescents to benefit from the healthy effects of the sea breeze. Until recently, one wing was used as a maternity ward (the tourist literature claims it was closed due to a storks' strike) and is now a private guesthouse.

Woermannhaus Especially picturesque is Woermannhaus, which was once a hostel for merchant sailors. When seen from the shore, the delightfully archetypal German structure stands out above all surrounding buildings and you'd be forgiven for assuming that it's the town hall. In fact, it's currently occupied by the town library and tourist office.

The building was designed by Friedrich Höft and was constructed in 1905 as the main offices of the Damara & Namaqua Trading Company. In 1909 it was taken over by the Woermann & Brock Trading Company, which supplied the building's current name. In the 1920s, it served as a school dormitory and fell into disrepair, but was declared a national monument and restored in 1976.

The prominent tower, known as the Damara Tower, once served as a water tower and a landmark for ships at sea, and traders arriving by ox-wagon from the interior. It now contains the small Swakopmund Military Museum and affords a splendid panorama over the town. The tower and museum are open during the same hours as the Namib i Information Centre, where you can pick up a key.

Old German Homes On the corner of Otavi Strasse and Kaiser Wilhelm Strasse is Villa Wille, the 1911 home of an early colonial builder Karl Hermann Wille. The two-storey design, complete with an ornamented tower, is particularly appealing. A block north, on the corner of Post Strasse and Otavi Strasse is the 1910 home and surgery of Dr Schwietering, who was the town's doctor. The nice colonial home next door on Post Strasse is also worth a look.

Along Bismarck Strasse, just south of Brücken Strasse, is a line of simple and unimposing colonial homes and flats, including the MC Human Flats, a block of flats dating from 1902.

At the western end of Post Strasse is the old Lüdwig Schröder Haus, which was constructed in 1903 for an employee of the Woermann Shipping Lines as an extension of Woermann Lines' headquarters. The following year, a further house, which was to double as company offices, was constructed around the corner on Moltke Strasse. It was designed by architect Friedrich Höft and dubbed Altona Haus.

Alte Gefängnis (Old Prison) The impressive Alte Gefängnis was designed by architect Heinrich Bause and dates back to 1909. If you didn't know this building was a prison, you'd swear it was either an early eastern German railway station or a German health-spa hotel. In fact, the main building was used only for staff housing, while the prisoners occupied less opulent quarters to one side. Note that it still serves as a prison and is considered a sensitive structure, so photography is not permitted.

OMEG Haus The colonial company, Otavi Minen-und Eisenbahn-Gesellschaft, oversaw the exceptionally rich mines around Otavi and Tsumeb in north-central Namibia. Because there was a connection to the coast by a narrow-gauge railway in the early 1900s, the company also maintained an office in Swakopmund. Until 1910, the OMEG house on Kaiser Wilhelm Strasse served as a warehouse. Next door is the Otavi

Bahnhof, the railway station for the narrow-gauge line to Tsumeb. There are plans to turn it into a transport museum.

Beaches

Swakopmund is *the* beach resort in Namibia, but don't expect too much. Even in the summer, the seas are cold and the air temperature rarely climbs above 22°C, making it more like the Isle of Wight or Santa Cruz (California) than the Kenya coast. The most popular bathing beach is near the lighthouse. North of town, however, you can stroll along miles of deserted beaches, which stretch away towards the Skeleton Coast. In the lagoon at the mouth of the Swakop River, you can watch a range of water birds – ducks, flamingoes, pelicans, cormorants, gulls and waders.

In town, seaside amenities include a formal promenade, a pier, tropical gardens, minigolf and a heated swimming pool (open from 8 to 10 am and 2.30 to 7 pm).

Dunes

Just across the Swakop River is a large area of sand dunes which are accessible on foot from the town centre. They make a nice excursion for a couple of hours, especially for those without a vehicle.

Swakopmund Museum

If an ill wind blows up, don't fret. The superb Swakopmund Museum at the foot of the lighthouse is a great place to hole up for a couple of hours. Displays include exhibits on Namibia's history and ethnology, including information on local flora & fauna.

Especially good is the display on the !nara melon, which was vital to the country's early Khoi-Khoi inhabitants. It also contains a well-executed reconstruction of early colonial home interiors, including the shop of the apothecary Emil Kiewittand, and an informative display on the Rössing Mine. For military buffs, it's a treasure house. Note especially the stifling uniforms worn by the Camel Corps and the room of Shell furniture (so called because it was homemade from

petrol and paraffin tins during the depression of the 1930s).

The museum occupies the site of the old harbour warehouse which was destroyed in 1914 by a 'lucky' shot from a British warship. It's open from 10 am to 12.30 pm and from 3 to 5.30 pm; admission is US$1.20 (students pay half-price).

Hansa Brewery

If you're a beer fan – and you think that German-style lager is the bee's knees – then you'll certainly want to visit the Hansa Brewery (☎ 5021) at 9 Rhode Allee, which is the source of Swakopmund's favourite amber nectar. If you want to arrange a tour and sample the product, make arrangements by telephone as far in advance as possible.

Activities

Swimming in the sea is best done in the lee of the Mole, although even in summer, the water is never warmer than 20°C. You'll probably be happier at the municipal swimming pool, which is open Monday to Friday from 8 to 10 am and 5 to 7 pm, Saturday until noon and 5 to 7 pm; and Sunday from 5 to 7 pm. The best surfing is at Nordstrand or 'Thick Lip' near Vineta Point.

The Rössmund Golf Club (☎ 5644) accommodates anyone hankering after 18 holes of desert golf. The course lies five km east of Swakopmund on the main road. You can hire equipment on site. It's open daily except Monday.

Festivals

Swakopmund stages a number of mainly German-oriented local events, including a Reitturnier (gymkhana) in January and the Swakopmund Karnival in August. The latter is an extremely festive affair sustained by copious consumption of Hansa, the town's own German brew. Events include a parade of whimsically decorated floats and a traditional masked ball.

Organised Tours

Several prominent safari operators offer day sightseeing tours and overnight trips. Among

NAMIBIA

The Dune Community

Despite their barren appearance, the Namib dunes actually support a unique ecosystem. Nowhere else on earth does life exist in such harsh conditions, but here it manages, thanks mainly to grass seed and bits of plant matter deposited by the wind and the moisture carried in by fog.

Even a short walk on the dunes will reveal traces of this well adapted community. The sand provides shelter for a range of small creatures. By day, the surface temperatures may reach 70°C, but below, the spaces between sand particles are considerable and therefore, air circulates freely below the surface, providing a cool shelter. In the chill of a desert night, the sand retains some of the warmth absorbed during the day and provides a warm place to burrow. When alarmed, most creatures can also use the sand as an effective hiding place.

The best places to observe dune life are Sossusvlei and the dunes south of Homeb, on the Kuiseb River. Early in the morning, look at the tracks to see what has transpired during the night; it's easy to distinguish the trails of various dune-dwelling beetles, lizards, snakes, spiders and scorpions.

Much of the dune community is comprised of beetles, which are attracted by the vegetable material on the dune slipfaces, and the Namib supports 200 species of the *tenebrionid* family alone. However, they're only visible when the dune surface is warm. At other times, they take shelter beneath the surface by 'swimming' into the sand.

The fog-basking tenebrionid beetle *(Onomachris unguicularis)*, which is locally known as a *toktokkie*, has a particularly interesting way of drinking. By day, these beetles scuttle over the dunes, surviving on the plant detritus on the slipfaces, but at night, they bury themselves in the sand. They derive moisture by condensing fog on their bodies. On foggy mornings, toktokkies line up on the dunes, lower their heads, raise their posteriors in the air, and slide the water droplets down the carapace into the mouth. They can consume up to 40% of their body weight in water in a single morning.

The large dancing spider known as the 'White Lady of the Namib' *(Orchestrella longpipes* – it could be a character in a children's novel!) lives in tunnels constructed beneath the dune surface. To prevent these tunnels from collapsing, these tunnels are lined with spider silk as they are excavated. This enormous spider can easily make a meal of creatures as large as palmato geckos.

The dunes are also home to the lovable golden mole *(Eremitalpa granti)*, a yellowish-coloured carnivore which spends most of its day buried in the dune. It was first discovered in 1837, but wasn't again sighted until 1963. The golden mole, which lacks both eyes and ears, doesn't burrow like other moles, but simply swims through the sand. Although it's rarely spotted, look carefully around tufts of grass or hummocks for the large rounded snout, which often protrudes above the surface. At night, it emerges and roams hundreds of metres over the dune faces foraging for beetle larvae and other insects.

The shovel-snouted lizard *(Aporosaura anchitae)* uses a unique method of regulating its body

the most popular are Charly's Desert Tours at 11 Kaiser Wilhelm Strasse; Namibia Photo Tours at Roon Strasse 8; Rhino Tours on Garnison Strasse; and Desert Adventure Safaris on Roon Strasse.

These companies offer mostly a similar range of options, but some charge slightly less than others, operate different tours on different days and have different minimum group sizes. If one tour isn't running, they often share clients with the other companies to make up the requisite number of people, so your chances of a departure on the day you want to go are fairly good.

Half-day options (all prices are average per person) include Cape Cross (US$41);

geology tours around Rössing Mine (US$31); and Welwitschia Drive (US$31). Full day trips run to Sandwich Harbour (US$63); the Spitzkoppe (US$44); the Kuiseb Delta and Walvis Bay Lagoon, with a visit to a Nama settlement (US$52); a geology and botany tour (US$52) and Welwitschia Drive (US$41); Swakopmund city tours, visiting historical buildings (US$11); and Walvis Bay sightseeing (US$20). Namibia Photo Tours also offers 'Sundowner' tours on the dunes or at sea (US$22), beach braais (US$29) and shark fishing trips (US$60). Rhino Tours visits the Brandberg (US$55).

For flightseeing trips over the salt works,

temperature while tearing across the scorching sand. This lizard can tolerate body temperatures of up to 44°C, but surface temperatures on the dunes can climb as high as 70°C. To prevent overheating, the lizard does a 'thermal dance', raising its tail and two legs at a time off the hot surface of the sand. When threatened, the lizard instantaneously submerges itself in the sand.

Another unique creature is the rather appealing little palmato gecko *(Palmatogecko rangei)*, also known as the web-footed gecko after its unusual feet, which act as scoops for burrowing in the sand. This translucent nocturnal gecko has a pinkish brown colouration on the back and a white belly. It grows to a length of 10 cm and has enormous eyes, which are used for hunting at night. It's often photographed using its long tongue to clear its eyes of dust and sand. The tongue is also used to collect condensed fog droplets from the head and snout. Other gecko species present in the dunes include the barking gecko *(Ptenopus garrulus)* and the large-headed gecko *(Chondrodactylus anguilifer)*.

Another dune lizard is the bizarre and fearsome looking Namaqua chameleon *(Chamaeleo namaquensis)*, which grows up to 25 cm in length, and is unmistakable due to the fringe of brownish bumps along its spine. When alarmed, it emits an ominous hiss and exposes its enormous yellow-coloured mouth and sticky tongue, which can spell the end for up to 200 large beetles every day. Like all chameleons, its eyes operate independently in their cone-shaped sockets, allowing the chameleon to look in several directions at once.

The small, buff-coloured Namib sidewinding adder *(Bitis peringueyi)* is perfectly camouflaged on the dune surface. It grows to a length of just 25 cm and navigates by gracefully manoeuvring sideways through the shifting sands. Because the eyes are on top of the head, the snake can bury itself almost completely in the sand and still see what's happening above the surface. When its unsuspecting prey happens along – normally a gecko or lizard – the adder uses its venom to immobilise the creature before devouring it. Although it is also poisonous to humans, the venom is so mild that it rarely causes more than an irritation.

The three species of Namib sand snakes *(Psammophis sp.)* are longer, slinkier and faster-moving than the adders, but hunt the same prey. These metre-long back-fanged snakes grab the prey and chew on it until it's immobilised by the venom, then swallow it whole. As with the adders, they're well camouflaged for life in the sand, ranging from off-white to pale grey in colour. The back is marked with pale stripes or a pattern of dots.

Several varieties of Namib skinks *(Typhlosaurus s.p)* are commonly mistaken for snakes. Because they propel themselves by swimming in the sand, their limbs are either small and vestigial or missing altogether, and their eyes, ears and nostrils are tiny and therefore well-protected from sand particles. At the tip of the nose is a 'rostral scale', which acts like a bulldozer blade to clear the sand ahead and allow the skink to progress. Skinks spend most of their time burrowing beneath the surface, but at night, emerge on the dune slipfaces to forage. In the morning, you'll often see their telltale tracks. ∎

NAMIBIA

the Brandberg, the Namib Desert and the Skeleton Coast and even further afield, you can charter a plane from Pleasure Flights (☎ 4500; fax 5325), which has an office on Kaiser Wilhelm Strasse. These trips are not cheap, but you will get an unusual perspective on the rather ethereal landscapes in this part of the world. For one hour around Swakopmund, Welwitschia Drive and Sandwich Harbour, you'll pay US$44 per person with five passengers. A day tour around southern Namibia, including Fish River Canyon and the Sperrgebiet, costs US$320 per person, again with five passengers.

If you'd enjoy buzzing up and down the beach and the dunes, see Beach Buggy Safaris (☎ 5377) on Roon Strasse; they also organise overnight camping tours.

Westcoast Angling Tours (☎ 2377; fax 2532) organises deep-sea fishing trips for snoek and yellowtail, as well as rock and surf angling from the beach. From November to May, the main game is copper sharks, which can weigh up to 180 kg. All Westcoast Angling Tours cost US$48 per person per day, including equipment. If you're into this sort of thing, you won't find a more unusual venue.

Horsepeople are accommodated by Okakambe Trails (☎ /fax 2799), which runs overnight wilderness horseback trips along the Swakop River to the oasis of Goanikontes on the Welwitschia Drive. A two-hour ride, which costs US$17 per person, will take you down the Swakop River, through a dune field and back to town on the beach. Full-day rides from Goanikontes along the river back to town cost US$41 per person, including lunch at the golf club. Return trips from Swakopmund to Goanikontes, with a night camping at the oasis, are US$68 per person, including meals.

Finally, if you want a fairly idiosyncratic tour through historic Swakopmund – and you speak German – telephone Ms A Flamm-Schneeweiss (☎ 61647) or contact her through the Namib i Information Centre.

For contact details on any of these tour companies, see Tours in the Namibia Getting Around chapter.

Places to Stay
During the school holidays from October to March (and especially December and January) Swakopmund accommodation books up well in advance, so either come prepared to camp or make accommodation bookings as early as possible.

Places to Stay – bottom end
The bleak *Mile 4 Caravan Park* (☎ 61871; fax 62901), on the beach four km along the salt road towards Henties Bay, has 400 camp sites for US$3 per tent plus US$2 per person and a one-time fee of US$3 per vehicle. It's exposed to the wind, sand and drizzle – and security can be a problem – but it's one of the most unusual camp sites you'll ever see.

Day use costs US$1.50 per person and electric hook-ups are available for US$1.50, which isn't a bad idea for caravan campers since generators can be run only between 6.30 and 8 pm. Small bungalows are available for US$11, whilst a self-catering cottage costs US$41. Either of these options must be booked three months in advance, except for December, which requires a year's advance booking. There's no restaurant or kiosk, but during December school holidays, an itinerant restaurant known as the Grub Tub sets up on site and serves snack meals.

Another option is the *Swakopmund Rest Camp* (☎ 2807), Private Bag 5017, which has four-bed A-frame huts for US$32; basic two-bed 'fishermen's shacks' for US$12; four-bed 'fishermen's cabins' for US$19; and six-bed huts for US$34. A fully self-contained 'VIP bungalow' accommodating six people, complete with a television, kitchen and bath facilities, costs US$58. All guests have access to barbecue facilities. The huts fill up quickly at weekends and school holidays, so advance booking is wise. No animals or motorbikes are allowed.

Swakopmund Rest Camp is still good value, especiallly for a 'fishermen's shack' sleeping two people. This is what you'd expect of a fishermen's shack, nothing fancy, but a place where you can relax and conserve energy by sitting on the loo, brushing your teeth and having a shower all at the same time.
Philippa Woodward, UK

There's also a newish *Hostelling International Hostel* (☎ 4164) in the Alte Kaserne (Old Barracks) on Lazarett Strasse. Guests have use of the kitchen and laundry facilities. Policies are still being sorted out, but so far, the approach has been appropriately military and mature adults may feel cramped. Dorm rates are US$7/7.50 for HI members/non-members; private double rooms cost US$13. Note the amazing German-style paintings that adorn the walls, including the crests of the German Federal States which existed during the colonial era.

The cheapest and best inexpensive option is *Jay Jay's Restaurant & Hotel* (☎ 2909), on Brücken Strasse, which offers simple single/double rooms at US$8/16 and dorm beds for US$7. It's clean and well located just half a block from the sea. There's a basic restaurant downstairs and the bar, which is a centre of local action, can get quite lively.

Next up the scale in price – but not as clean – is the rather stark *Hotel Schutze* (☎ /fax 2718), which charges US$14 for a single with communal facilities and US$17/30 for a single/double with private facilities. The purpose of this establishment appears to be linked to its relationship with the attached Ho-Yin's Pub, so women on their own may want to stay clear. Still the restaurant does serve excellent German-style meals; look for the menu written on a blackboard outside.

At 81 Seeadler Strasse is a friendly and inexpensive B&B run by *Mrs Viviane Schultz* (☎ 61683). She charges US$11/20 for single/double occupancy. To book by post, write to PO Box 3182, Swakopmund.

For something a bit more unusual, try *Villa Anna* (☎ 2371), which is housed in the cloisters of an old convent at 1 Breite Strasse. It's run by Mrs Joost and costs US$7 per person.

Places to Stay – middle

The pleasant *Pension Dig-by-See* (☎ 4130; fax 4170) (commonly known as just Digby's) at 4 Brücken Strasse, PO Box 1580, has singles/doubles at US$19/32 with bed and a large and varied breakfast. Rooms for three/four people are US$17 per person, with breakfast, and self-catering holiday flats cost US$60. All rooms have a bath, shower, toilet and TV.

The *Pension Prinzessin-Rupprecht-Heim* (☎ 2231; fax 2019), housed in the former colonial hospital, has a lovely garden and charges US$29/46 for a single/double room with private facilities, including breakfast. Small single rooms with shared facilities are US$13 and family flats cost US$44 with two people, plus US$13 for each extra person up to four people.

Moving up in price, a very friendly option near the lighthouse is *Hotel-Pension Rapmund* (☎ 2035; fax 4524), PO Box 425. They charge US$33/51 for a single/double with breakfast and you won't feel more welcome anywhere in Swakopmund.

As its name suggests, the *Deutsches Haus* (☎ 4896; fax 4861), PO Box 13, at Lüderitz Strasse 13, oozes with German atmosphere and it's meticulously clean, but the ambience isn't exactly warm and cosy (maybe it's the post and street address). Single/double rooms here cost US$30/46 with bed and breakfast. A three-bed room is US$60. Use of the garage costs an additional US$2.50 per day and TV is an extra US$3.

The *Hotel-Pension d'Avignon* (☎ 5821; fax 5542) on Brücken Strasse is politely accommodating but I found the atmosphere rather stuffy. It caters mainly to German tourists and others may feel a bit out of their element. For single/double rooms with private facilities, including breakfast, they charge US$28/42.

Another adequate middle-range place is the renovated *Atlanta Hotel* (☎ 2360; fax 5649), centrally located at 6 Roon Strasse. Single/double rooms cost US$25/39 and family rooms for up to four people are US$44, all with breakfast. All rooms have private facilities and telephones, and televisions can be added on request for an additional US$3 per day.

In a similar range is *Hotel Grüner Kranz* (☎ 2039; fax 5016). For a single/double room with television and en suite facilities, they charge US$27/44. Suites cost US$33/55. For breakfast, you'll pay an additional US$4. This place attempts to fill the all-night party niche for the younger set, so the atmosphere is quite lively, with a rollicking disco on the 1st floor. There's also a lounge showing several videos every night.

At the top end of the middle range is the *Hotel Europa Hof* (☎ 5898; fax 2391), which looks like a Bavarian chalet, complete with colourful flower boxes and various European flags flying from the first floor windows. Single/double rooms will cost you US$44/63; garage parking is an extra US$6 per day.

A popular spot near the sea with a good view of the lighthouse is *Hotel Schweizerhaus* (☎ 2419; fax 5850), which is probably better known as the hotel attached to Café Anton. Standard single/double rooms cost US$37/67, while luxury rooms with a balcony are US$46/73 and deluxe rooms, also with balconies, cost US$52/82.

If you prefer to restrict your noise to sea sounds, go to *Alte Brücke Holiday Resort* (☎ /fax 4918), near the river mouth, south of town. Luxury-standard self-catering bungalows cost US$41 for double occupancy. With three/four adults sharing, they're US$53/67. Family units accommodating up to two adults and two children cost US$53.

Another less formal holiday-flat option is

that of *K & E Wojtas* (☎ 2402) at 4 Windhuker Strasse. They have two self-catering flats which they rent for US$8 per person, with a minimum charge of US$28.

Places to Stay – top end

The central *Hansa Hotel* (☎ 311; fax 2732), which bills itself as 'luxury in the desert', is Swakopmund's most upmarket place to stay and makes much of the fact that it has hosted the likes of Aristotle Onassis, Sir Laurens van der Post, Eartha Kitt, Oliver Reed and Ernest Borgnine. Standard single/double rooms start at US$49/71, but they're generally quite drab for the price. You'd be better off paying for a standard room with a balcony and garden view, which will cost US$61/88. Uniquely furnished luxury suites with individual décor cost US$75/102.

However, the Hansa's top-of-the-range standing may soon be usurped by the posh four-star hotel which is currently being installed in the renovated historic railway station. It will also be considerably more expensive.

On the main beach behind the Mole is the two-star *Strand Hotel* (☎ 315; fax 4942), which isn't housed in the most prepossessing of buildings, but still enjoys a good sea view. Singles/doubles with bed and a large breakfast cost US$57/76.

Also nicely situated is the relatively homey *Hotel Garni Adler* (☎ 5045; fax 4206) at 3 Strand Strasse. The building resembles a modern house lost somewhere in German suburbia. Standard single rooms cost from US$43 to US$50; doubles are US$70. Single/double rooms with a sea view cost US$59/81. Studio flats cost US$88/135. All room rates include breakfast. You'll pay an additional US$3 for the use of the garage or a television. Saunas cost US$6.

Places to Eat

As befits a seaside resort, Swakopmund has a variety of eating establishments, from simple takeaways right up to four-star restaurants. For inexpensive but excellent takeaways, try *La Paloma Takeaways*, on Breite Strasse south of Kaiser Wilhelm Strasse. This established place doubles as the minibus terminal. Near the corner of Moltke Strasse and Woermann Strasse is an inexpensive and highly recommended German takeaway outlet, the *Wurst Bude*. If you prefer something less exciting, the *Kentucky Fried Chicken* (☎ 5687) at 13 Roon Strasse stays open until 10 pm.

Another no-frills option – albeit loaded with atmosphere – is the locally popular and very down-to-earth *Fagin's* (☎ 2360), an inexpensive pub and bistro attached to the Atlanta Hotel. The atmosphere is reminiscent of a US truck stop or an Australian roadhouse, complete with jocular staff and faithful clientele.

A recommended favourite is the superb and inexpensive *Napolitana Pizzeria & Mediterranean Restaurant* (☎ 2773) at 33 Breite Strasse. The name says it all (or at least part of it – the menu is graced with a drawing of a Venetian canal). They're open Monday to Sunday from 10 am to 2 pm and 5.30 to 10 pm. Don't miss the excellent and icy German-style draught lager. Best of all, they'll deliver pizzas until 9.30 pm for US$0.75 to anywhere in town or US$1.10 to Vineta, including Mile 4 Caravan Park.

A good alternative for pizza is *Ron's Hideaway*, near the corner of Roon Strasse and Brücken Strasse; at the back is a public bar.

If you're really hungry in the morning, you'll find substantial breakfasts for US$3 at the *Strand Hotel* (☎ 315) on the Mole. They're also recommended for other meals, which are served German style and must be accompanied by draught Hansa lager. The *Swakopmund Bistro* (☎ 2333) does excellent and imaginative pub lunches and dinners, including a variety of salads, vegetarian specialities, crêpes, gyros, steaks and seafood specials. It's open nightly until 10 pm.

There are several smaller restaurants specialising in seafood, including the upmarket *Erichs* (☎ 5141) on Post Strasse, which is open for lunch and dinner. It specialises in fish and steak dishes, and does a mean Tiroler knödelsuppe. Similarly upmarket is *The Ol' Steamer* (☎ 4806) on

Moltke Strasse, which was named in honour of the poor old *Martin Luther* steam engine languishing just outside Swakopmund. It has a super salad bar and serves steak and fish in a charming atmosphere. It's closed on Sunday.

Another decent choice for fish is *The Tug*, which is housed in the beached tugboat *Danie Hugo* near the jetty at the shore end of Brücken Strasse. Perhaps the most prestigious option for fish, however, is the *Admiral's Restaurant*, which is on the beach near the Strand Hotel.

The *Western Saloon* (☎ 5395), a cowboy-theme place at Moltke Strasse 8, is known for its oysters and many different seafood and steak dishes. Although supply glitches do occur, fish is normally served fresh from the sea. It's open Monday to Saturday from 5.30 to 9.30 pm and on Sunday from 6 to 9 pm. Another place for steak is the *Wagon Wheel*, on Moltke Strasse north of Kaiser Wilhelm Strasse. For excellent barbecued ribs, as well as steak and seafood, go to the rather up-market *De Kelder* (☎ 2433) in the Klimas Building at 10 Moltke Strasse. It's open daily except Monday for lunch and dinner, and after eating you can try your hand at the attached Desert Dunes Casino.

For German specialities (this is Swakopmund, after all) try the mid-range *Bayern Stubchen* on Garnison Strasse. The down-to-earth restaurant at *Jay Jay's*, on Brücken Strasse, serves up hearty and inexpensive boerekos, or Afrikaner fare.

Then there's the rather pretentious *Café Anton* (☎ 2419) in the Hotel Schweizerhaus, whose patio and superb (albeit expensive and skimpy) coffee, apfelstrüdel, kugelhupf, mohnkuchen, linzertorte and a host of other Deutsche delights are almost legendary. It's best for an afternoon snack in the sunshine. Other German-style konditorei include the *Seebad Cafe* on Kaiser Wilhelm Strasse, which has a good takeaway bakery and confectioners, and the *Hansa Bäckerei & Cafe Treff*, further along the same street.

The best pub meals are found at *Kücki's Pub* (☎ 2407), which is actually one of the best restaurants in Namibia. Most of their meals are reasonably priced, but if you have a good stash of cash, don't miss their amazing seafood platter.

At the Sentra Supermarket, near the corner of Moltke Strasse and Kaiser Wilhelm Strasse, you can pick up groceries or have a snack at the coffee bar, which is even open on Sunday morning.

Entertainment

Scandal's Nightclub, which emphasises local music and disco dancing, is popular with the adult crowd; it's open from 8 pm until 4 am nightly. The younger set generally prefers The Stage Night Club disco, upstairs in Hotel Grüner Kranz. There's also a quiet private bar on the opposite side of the hotel.

For a slightly anachronistic experience, visit the Bacchus Taverna, a rather pedestrian pub in the row of historic flats opposite the Europa Hof Hotel. The bar at Jay-Jay's stays open until the wee hours and is popular with locals. Another favourite and down-to-earth watering hole for locals and visitors alike is Fagin's Pub, near the Atlanta Hotel on Roon Strasse. The Atlanta Cinema next door shows one film nightly at 8 pm.

Things to Buy

At Swakop River Angoras, you can buy quality clothing made of angora rabbit hair and learn about the spinning, dyeing and weaving processes. It's open daily from 10 am to 5 pm.

Similarly, you can visit the Karakulia outlet in the First National Development Corporation (ENOK) Centre, near the old prison on the corner of Mittel Strasse and the Nordring. It produces and sells hand-woven rugs, carpets and wall-hangings made of karakul wool. This is also a good place to pick up other quality souvenirs, including local art, minerals and gems. The art shop attached to the Hotel-Pension Rapmund sells some pleasant light-hearted paintings.

Swakopmund is known for its hardwearing kudu leather shoes called 'Swakopmunders' which are sold at the Swakopmund Tannery at 7 Leutwein Strasse. The tannery also sell handbags,

NAMIBIA

sandals, belts and all manner of leather goodsatexcellentprices.

There are a number of shops and small art galleries which specialise in prints and paintings of the area, ranging from classic watercolours to modern surrealistic African art. A small gallery called Reflections near Cafe Anton often has exhibits of local artists' work. There are a number of African souvenir and curio shops and several quite expensive jewellers, most of whom use local gems and semiprecious stones. Pieces may be commissioned and you can often watch the goldsmith at work. The T-shirt factory shop on Woermann Strasse prints and sells its own unique designs.

Getting There & Away

There's a choice of air, rail or road transport between Swakopmund and other places in central Namibia.

Air Air Namibia flies from Windhoek's Eros Airport to Swakopmund at 9.30 am on Tuesday, Thursday, Friday and Sunday. From Swakopmund to Windhoek, it flies on Monday, Wednesday, Friday and Sunday. You can also fly to or from Lüderitz, Oranjemund and Cape Town four times weekly.

Bus Inexpensive minibuses to Windhoek and Walvis Bay leave in the morning from La Paloma Takeaways. On the way to Walvis Bay, you can also flag them down on the corner of Breite Strasse and Rhode Allee.

Between Swakopmund/Walvis Bay and Windhoek, there's also the Dolphin Express (☎ (0642) 4118) five times weekly; and the daily Cheetah Liner buses (☎ 62454), which costs US$15 each way. Between Windhoek and Swakopmund/Walvis Bay, the more luxurious Intercape Mainliner runs four times weekly and costs US$25 each way. Any of these buses, including the minibuses, can be prebooked through Trip Travel (☎ 4013; fax 2114) at 11 Post Strasse.

Train Swakopmund is also accessible by overnight train from Windhoek. The service

departs from Windhoek at 8 pm daily except Saturday and arrives in Swakopmund at 5.05 am, then continues on to Walvis Bay. In the opposite direction, it leaves Walvis Bay at 6.35 pm Monday to Saturday, stops in Swakopmund at 7.57 pm, and then continues on to Windhoek arriving at 6.21 am the following day. This train can also be used to reach Usakos and Karibib. The fare between Windhoek and Swakopmund in economy/sleeper class is US$3/9 from Monday to Thursday and US$7/19 from Friday to Sunday.

Hitching Hitching is possible but, especially if you're headed for the Namib Desert or Skeleton Coast, conditions can be rough and hitchhikers risk heat stroke, sandblasting and hypothermia – sometimes all in the same day! Come prepared.

Getting Around

Taxis run to and from the airport but Swakopmund is so compact that it's easy to walk anywhere within the town. Most of the big car-hire agencies in Windhoek also have branches in Swakopmund. For a list of addresses, see the Namibia Getting Around chapter.

AROUND SWAKOPMUND
The *Martin Luther*

In the desert, four km east of Swakopmund, you'll pass a lonely and forlorn little steam locomotive. The 14,000-kg machine was imported to Namibia from Halberstadt, Germany, in 1896 to replace the ox-wagons which were used to transport freight between Swakopmund and the interior. However, its inauguration into service was delayed by the outbreak of the Nama-Herero wars, during which it languished in Walvis Bay. In the interim, unfortunately, the locomotive engineer had returned to Germany without having revealed the secret of its operation.

A US prospector eventually got the engine running, but it consumed enormous quantities of water, which simply weren't available. In fact, it took three months just to move it from Walvis Bay to Swakopmund. The engine survived just a couple of short trips before grinding to a halt within sight of Swakopmund. When it became apparent that this particular technology wasn't making life any easier for anyone, it was abandoned where it stood and dubbed the *Martin Luther*, in reference to the great reformer's famous words to the Diet of Reichstag in 1521: 'Here I stand. May God help me, I cannot do otherwise'. It was restored in 1975 and declared a national monument.

Burg Hotel Nonidas

The interesting Burg Hotel Nonidas (☎ 4544) lies on the main road about 10 km east of Swakopmund and, as its German name would imply, is built in the form of a castle. The current structure was built over the top of an early 1890s customs and police post. All that remains of the original building is the hotel bar area, which is full of historical photos and artefacts. It operated as a hotel until 1993, but hasn't offered accommodation for a couple of years. However, it does intend to reopen eventually.

Camel Farm

If you want to play Lawrence of Arabia in the Namib Desert, visit the Camel Farm (☎ 363), 15 km east of Swakopmund on the B2. Camel rides cost US$7 for 40 minutes. It's open from 3 to 5 pm. To book a camel and arrange transport from town, ring and ask for Ms Elke Elb.

Rössing Mine

Rössing Uranium Mine (☎ 2046), 55 km east of Swakopmund, is the world's largest opencast uranium mine and certainly merits a visit. Uranium was first discovered in the 1920s by Peter Louw, who attempted to set up operations there but without any luck. In 1965, the concession was transferred to Rio Tinto Zinc. After comprehensive surveys, it was determined that the formation was about three km long and one km wide. Ore extraction came on line in 1970 but didn't reach

capacity for another eight years. Today, the scale of operations is staggering and at full capacity the mine produces about one million tonnes of ore per week.

Rössing (an affiliate of Rio Tinto Zinc) is currently the major player in the Swakopmund economy and employs 2500 people. The company has set up the Rössing Foundation to provide an educational and training centre in Arandis, north-east of Rössing, and to construct and support medical facilities and housing for its workers in Swakopmund. They've also promised that once the mine plays out and is decommissioned, they'll undertake a massive clean-up project to make the site as amenable as possible. However, you may want to temper your enthusiasm about their environmental commitments until something is actually forthcoming.

Mine tours, which last 4½ hours, depart from Café Anton on Friday at 8 am and cost US$3 per person, including transport; all proceeds go to the museum. Book the previous day at the museum.

Trekkopje

The military cemetery at Trekkopje lies about 112 km east of Swakopmund and one km north of the B2. In January 1915, after Swakopmund was occupied by the South African forces, the Germans retreated and set about damaging both the Otavi and State railway lines to cut off supplies to the city. However, the South Africans had already begun replacing the old narrow-gauge track with a standard gauge, and at Trekkopje, the construction crew met the German forces. When the Germans attacked the camp on 26 April 1915, the South Africans defended themselves with guns mounted on armoured vehicles and easily prevailed.

The soldiers of both sides who were killed in the battle are buried in the Trekkopje cemetery. It lies immediately north of the railway line, near the old railway station.

Welwitschia Drive

If you have a vehicle – or enough cash to take an organised tour from Swakopmund – a

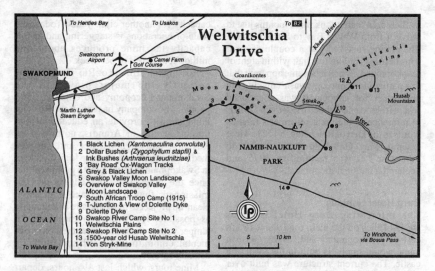

Welwitschia Drive

To Henties Bay
To Usakos
To B2

Swakopmund Airport
Camel Farm
Golf Course

SWAKOPMUND

Goanikontes

Moon Landscape

Khan River

Welwitschia Plains

12
11
13

Husab Mountains

'Martin Luther' Steam Engine

3
4
6
5
2
1

Swakop

10

9
8
7

ALANTIC

OCEAN

1 Black Lichen (Xantomaculina convoluta)
2 Dollar Bushes (Zygophyllum stapfii) &
   Ink Bushes (Arthraerua leudnitziae)
3 'Bay Road' Ox-Wagon Tracks
4 Grey & Black Lichen
5 Swakop Valley Moon Landscape
6 Overview of Swakop Valley
   Moon Landscape
7 South African Troop Camp (1915)
8 T-Junction & View of Dolerite Dyke
9 Dolerite Dyke
10 Swakop River Camp Site No 1
11 Welwitschia Plains
12 Swakop River Camp Site No 2
13 1500-year old Husab Welwitschia
14 Von Stryk-Mine

NAMIB-NAUKLUFT

PARK

River

14

To Walvis Bay

0   5   10 km

To Windhoek via Bosua Pass

worthwhile excursion is the Welwitschia Drive, which turns off the Bosua Pass route east of Swakopmund. Although this loop is actually inside Namib-Naukluft Park, it's most often visited as a day trip from Swakopmund and is therefore included in this section.

At the MET office in Swakopmund, you can pick up an entry permit and leaflet describing the drive, with numbered references to points of interest. The entire drive takes about hours but allow more time. The numbers in brackets refer to numbered sites of interest or 'beacons' along the route.

A highlight of the drive is the fields of grey and black lichen (1) which cover the ground. They almost appear to be small dead bushes. If you saw the BBC production *The Private Life of Plants*, it was in this area that David Attenborough encountered these delightful examples of plant-animal symbiosis (see the aside 'Welwitschias'), which magically burst into life and 'bloom' with the addition of fog droplets. If you visit during a heavy fog this will be obvious, but during dry periods try pouring a few drops of water on them and see what happens.

Another interesting stop is the old

Baaiweg (3), the ox-wagon track which was historically used to move supplies between the coast and central Namibia. It's still visible because the lichen that were destroyed when it was built have been growing back at a rate of only one mm per year, which hasn't been enough to obscure the track. Later in the main loop you'll see further evidence of the ecological impact humans can have on delicate landscapes in the form of a camp site (7) used by South African troops for a few days in 1915. These people were clearly *not* minimum-impact campers!

Further east is the Moon Landscape (4), a vista across the eroded hills and valleys carved by the Swakop River. At this point, you may want to take a quick 12-km return side trip north to the farm and green oasis of Goanikontes, which dates from 1848, long before Swakopmund was even a gleam in an early colonial's eye. It lies beside the Swakop River amid fabulous desert mountains and it makes a nice green spot for a picnic. There are also several shady camp sites and basic bungalows are available for very reasonable prices.

A few km beyond the South African camp site, the route turns north towards Welwitschia Plains. After turning, you'll approach a prominent black dolerite dyke (9) splitting a ridgetop. This was created when molten igneous material forced its way up through a crack in the overlying granite and cooled.

On the short side trip from the main loop, you'll reach the Welwitschia Plains (11), a site of several ancient welwitschia plants (see the aside). These unique plants are recognisable by their two long and leathery leaves which are normally torn into a tangle of windblown strips. Some welwitschias have lived as long as 2000 years. They grow in several locations on the gravel plains of the Namib Desert, but most of these places are kept quiet in order to prevent vandalism and theft of the unusual plants. However, the superb specimens on the Welwitschia Plains are open for viewing by tourists. The large plant known as the Husab welwitschia (12) is estimated to be at least 1500 years old.

Places to Stay Along the side trip to Welwitschia Plains, at the Swakop River crossing, there's a National Parks' camp site which is available to one party of up to eight people at a time. It must be prebooked through MET in Windhoek or Swakopmund.

Salt Works
The salt works north of Mile 4 Caravan Park are certainly worth a visit or a viewing from

---

Welwitschias

Among Namibia's many botanical curiosities, the extraordinary *Welwitschia mirabilis*, which exists only on the gravel plains of the northern Namib Desert from the Kuiseb River to southern Angola, is probably the strangest of all. It was first noted by science in 1859, when Austrian botanist and medical doctor, Friedrich Welwitsch, stumbled upon a large specimen east of Swakopmund. He suggested it be named *tumboa*, which was one of the local names for the plant, but the discovery was considered to be so important that it was named for him instead. More recently, the Afrikaners have dubbed it *tweeblaarkanniedood* or 'two-leaf can't die'.

Welwitschias reach their greatest concentrations on the Welwitschia Plains east of Swakopmund, near the confluence of the Khan and Swakop rivers, where they're the dominant plant species. Although these plants are real ugly ducklings of the vegetable world, they've adapted well to their harsh habitat. It was once thought that the plant had a tap root down through clay pipes to access the watertable 100 metres or more beneath the surface. In fact, the root is never more than three metres long and it's now generally accepted that although the plant gets some water from underground sources, most of its moisture is derived from condensed fog. Pores in the leaves trap moisture and longer leaves actually water the plant's own roots by channelling droplets onto the surrounding sand.

Despite their dishevelled appearance, welwitschias actually have only two long and leathery leaves, which grow from opposite sides of the corklike stem. Over the years, these leaves are darkened in the sun and torn by the wind into tattered strips, causing the plant to resemble a giant wilted lettuce.

Strangely, welwitschias are considered to be trees and are related to conifers, specifically pines, but they also share some characteristics of flowering plants and club mosses. Females bear the larger greenish-yellow to brown cones, which contain the plant's seeds, while the males have more cones, but they're smaller and salmon-coloured. They're a dioeceous species, meaning that male and female plants are distinct, but their exact method of pollination remains in question. It's thought that the large sticky pollen grains are carried by insects, specifically wasps.

Welwitschias have a slow rate of growth, and it's believed that the largest ones, whose tangled masses of leaf strips can measure up to two metres across, may have been growing for up to 2000 years. However, most mid-sized plants are less than 1000 years old. The plants don't even flower until they've been growing for at least 20 years. This longevity is probably only possible because they contain some compounds which are unpalatable to grazing animals, although black rhinos have been known to enjoy the odd plant. The plants' most prominent inhabitant is the yellow and black pyrrhocorid bug *(Probergrothius sexpunctatis)*, which lives by sucking sap from the plant. It's commonly called the push-me-pull-you bug, due to its almost continuous back to back mating. ∎

NAMIBIA

the air. Originally, this area was just one of many low salty depressions along the desert coast north of Swakopmund. In 1933, the Klein family began extracting salt from the pan. After 20 years the salt ran out. They then excavated a series of shallow evaporation pans for the concentration and extraction of salt. Now, water is pumped into the pans directly from the sea, and the onshore breeze provides an ideal catalyst for evaporation.

Water is moved through the several pans over a period of 12 to 18 months. Minerals in the water are concentrated by evaporation and eventually salt crystals develop. Due to the variety of algae present during the various stages of desalination, each pond takes on a different brilliant colour – purple, red, orange, yellow and even a greenish hue. From aloft, the complex takes on the appearance of a colourful stained-glass window.

Because the ponds provide a sheltered environment and concentrations of small fish, they teem with flamingoes, avocets, sandpipers, teals, grebes, gulls, cormorants, terns and many other birds. The Kleins have now registered the site as a private nature reserve. They've also erected a large wooden platform – an artificial island – which is used by cormorants as a breeding site. After the breeding season ends, scrapers are sent onto the platform to collect the resulting deposits of guano. Another peripheral enterprise is the Richwater Oyster Company, which was established in 1985 when 500,000 oysters were brought from the island of Guernsey. The oyster farm occupies the first pan reached by the newly pumped seawater.

Tours of the salt works and the oyster farm run daily from Monday to Friday at 4.45 pm and last 1½ hours. To book to a tour, either visit or phone the salt-works offices (☎ 2611) in Swakopmund during business hours. After hours, phone ☎ 4015. You can also arrange guided birdwatching tours of the site.

WALVIS BAY
Walvis Bay (pronounced *VAHL-fis*) may be architecturally uninspiring, but it makes an interesting possible day excursion from Swakopmund, 30 km to the north. It does have a sort of otherworldly charm (which may elude some visitors), but until recently, its principal claim to fame was a clutch of fish canneries and its status as the only decent port between Lüderitz and Luanda. The superb natural harbour is created by the sandspit Pelican Point which forms a natural breakwater.

Today, Walvis Bay remains a busy port with 40,000 residents, a tanker berth, a dry dock and facilities to load and unload container ships. It also supports a salt works and a fish-processing industry. However, due to decline in fish stocks several years ago, the late 1980s saw a rash of factory closings and high unemployment. Strict controls have now stabilised the industry and it appears to be on the upswing. In an effort to diversify the economy by attracting tourists and conventioneers, a massive 10-year waterfront tourism development project is currently in the planning stages.

History
Portuguese navigator Bartolomeu Dias sailed into Walvis Bay in his ship, the *São Cristóvão*, on 8 December 1487 and named it Bahia de Santa Maria da Conceição and later, Bahia das Baleias or 'Bay of the Whales'. Due to a lack of fresh water, however, the excellent natural harbour lay forgotten for the next 300 years. From 1784, American whalers began operating in the area, calling it simply Whale Bay.

Word got out that rich pickings were to be had and on 23 January 1793 the Dutch vessel *Meermin* from the Cape arrived to annex the bay and translate its name into Dutch: Walvisbaai. This sparked off a 200-year game of political football with the 1124-sq-km enclave.

In 1795, when the Cape Colony was taken over by the British, Captain Alexander of the fleet went north and claimed Walvis Bay for Britain, as a means of ensuring safe passage for vessels around the Cape. In 1878, after it had become apparent that Germany had its eye on the area, Walvis Bay was formally annexed by Britain and six years later it

Walvis Bay

ATLANTIC OCEAN

WALVIS BAY

Lagoon

To Swakopmund & Langstrand

To Dune 7, Solitaire & Sesriem

To Lagoon, Salt Works & Sandwich Harbour

PLACES TO STAY	PLACES TO EAT	OTHER
1 Casa Mia Hotel	5 Harbour Café	3 Post Office
2 Golden Fish Guesthouse	8 Kentucky Fried Chicken	6 Port
4 Mermaid Hotel	14 Willie Probst Café/Bakery	7 Railway Station
10 Suidwes Holiday Flats	15 The Steakhouse	9 Viggo-Lund Bookshop
& Suidwes Diensstasie	16 Lalainya's	11 Police
18 Hotel Atlantic	17 Crazy Mama's	12 Walvis Bay Public Library
19 Flamingo Hotel		& Museum
20 Esplanade Municipal Camp		13 Tourist Office
& Caravan Park		21 Rhenish Mission Church
24 Esplanade Park Bungalows		22 Hospital
		23 Bird Paradise

NAMIBIA

became an official part of the Cape Colony. In 1910, it was annexed to the Union of South Africa, while the rest of South West Africa remained under German control. However, when the Germans were defeated after WWI, South Africa was given the United Nations mandate to administer South West Africa and the Walvis Bay enclave was transferred to the mandate. This stood until 1977, when South Africa unilaterally decided to return it to the Cape Province. Naturally, the United Nations wasn't impressed by this unauthorised act of aggression and insisted that the enclave be returned

to the mandate immediately, but South Africa refused to bow.

When Namibia achieved its independence in 1990, its new constitution included Walvis Bay as part of its territory, but the South Africans stubbornly held their grip. Given the strategic value of the natural harbour plus the salt works (which produce 90% of South Africa's salt, amounting to 400,000 tonnes annually), the offshore guano platforms and the potential fishing wealth, the issue of control over Walvis Bay became a matter of great importance for Namibia.

In 1992, as it became apparent that the

days of the White South African government were numbered, the two countries agreed that South Africa would remove its customs and immigration posts and the two countries would jointly administer the enclave. Over the following year, negotiations continued over what would be done in the long term. Finally, facing growing domestic troubles and their first democratic elections, South Africa gave in. At midnight on 28 February 1994 the South African flag was lowered for the last time, and in the first minutes of 1 March the Namibian flag was raised. As an indication of how quickly the transition occurred, almost immediately the old Cape Province – Walvis Bay CWB number plates were being replaced with Namibian NWB numbers.

Orientation

Walvis Bay is fairly small and compact, and is laid out in a grid pattern, so it would be difficult to become disoriented. There's a bizarre system of street naming. The streets, from 1st to 14th run north-east to south-west. The roads, from 1st to 18th, run north-west to south-east. Needless to say, this can be confusing.

Information

The helpful tourist office is found on the main floor of the monumental Civic Centre. It's open weekdays from 8 am to 1 pm and 2 to 5 pm. On Friday, it closes at 4.30 pm. While you're there, ask to see the carved wooden panels on the wall in the next room.

If you haven't already picked up a Namib-Naukluft Park permit in Windhoek or Swakopmund, they're available at the Suidwes Diensstasie (Total service station) and the CWB service station.

Post & Telecommunications The post office on 7th Rd also has public telephone boxes and fax services.

Emergency Services Emergency services include the police (☎ 2055), ambulance service (☎ 5443), hospital (☎ 3441), fire

!Nara Melons

Historically, human existence in the Namib has been made possible by an unusual spiny plant called the !nara melon *(Acanthosicyos horrida)*. It was first described taxonomically by the same Freidrich Welwitsch who gave his name to the welwitschia.

Although the !nara melon lives and grows in the desert – and lacks leaves, to prevent water loss through transpiration – the !nara is not a desert plant because its moisture is taken from the groundwater table via a long tap root. Its lack of leaves also protects it from grazing animals, although ostiches do nip off its tender growing shoots.

Like the welwitschia, the male and female sex organs in the !nara melon exist in separate plants. Male plants flower through-out the year, but it's the female plant which each summer produces the 15-cm melon that provides a favourite meal for jackals, insects and humans. Indeed, it remains a primary food of the Topnaar Khoi-Khoi people and has also become a local commercial enterprise. Each year at harvest time, the Topnaar erect camps around the Kuiseb Delta for collection of the fruits. Although melons can be eaten raw, most people prefer to dry them for later use, or prepare, package and ship them to urban markets. ■

brigade (☎ 3117) and sea-rescue service (☎ 2064).

Bookshop You shouldn't expect too much from the Viggo-Lund Booksellers & Stationers on 7th St, but it is good for picking up reading material.

Walvis Bay Museum

If you have a spare half hour, visit the town museum, which is housed in the library. It concentrates mostly on the history and maritime background of Walvis Bay, but there are also archaeological exhibits, a mineral collection and a rundown on the natural history of the Namib Desert and the Atlantic Coast. It's open weekdays from 9 am to noon and 3 to 6 pm. Admission is free.

Rhenish Mission Church

The Rhenish Mission Church on 5th Rd, the oldest remaining building in Walvis Bay, was prefabricated in Hamburg, Germany, and reconstructed beside the harbour in 1880. Services were first held the following year. Because of machinery sprawl in the harbour area, it was relocated to its present site earlier this century. It functioned as a church until 1966.

Bird Island

On the road to or from Swakopmund, look out to sea about 10 km north of Walvis Bay and you'll see the huge wooden platform known as Bird Island. It was built to provide a roost and nesting site for seabirds and a source of guano for fertiliser. The annual yield is around 1000 tonnes and the smell is memorable.

The Port

With permission from the Public Relations Officer of the Portnet (☎ 8320; fax 8390) or from the Railway Police at the end of 13th Rd, you can visit the fishing harbour and commercial port and see the heavy machinery that keeps Namibia's import-export business ticking. It's actually more interesting than it sounds. Take your passport.

Dune 7

Dune 7 is in the bleak expanses just off the C14 eight km east of town. Locals like to use it as a slope for sand boarding and skiing. There's a popular picnic site with several shady palm trees tucked away in the lee of the dune. Note that there's no water available at the site.

Nature Reserves

Three diverse Walvis Bay wetland areas – the lagoon, the Bird Paradise at the sewage works and the salt works – together form the single most important coastal wetland for migratory birds in southern Africa, and up to 150,000 transient avian visitors stop by each year.

Lagoon The 45,000-hectare lagoon, a shallow and sheltered offshore area south-west of town and west of the Kuiseb Mouth, attracts a range of coastal water birds. These

are mainly flamingoes, but you may also see chestnut banded plovers and curlew sandpipers, as well as other migrants and waders. It's also a permanent home of the rare Damara tern. In fact, this one wetland system supports fully half the flamingo population of southern Africa.

Salt Works South-west of the lagoon is the Walvis Bay salt works. As with the similar operation in Swakopmund, these pans concentrate salt from seawater with the aid of evaporation. The 3500-hectare salt pan complex currently supplies over 90% of South Africa's salt. For a tour, make an appointment by phoning ☎ 2376.

Bird Paradise Immediately east of town at the municipal sewage purification works is the bird sanctuary known as Bird Paradise, which affords good birdwatching along a short nature route. It consists of a series of shallow artificial pools, fringed by reeds, with an observation tower to facilitate viewing. It lies a half-km east of town, off the C14 towards Rooikop airport.

Rooibank

At the extreme south-eastern corner of the former Walvis Bay enclave is Rooibank, which is named for a cluster of red granite outcrops along the northern bank of the Kuiseb River. This area is known mostly as the site of one of Namibia's few Topnaar Khoi-Khoi settlements. When you're in the area, notice the unusual vegetation, which includes the fleshy succulent dollar bush (*Zygophyllum stapffii*) and the !nara bush (*Acanthosicyos horrida*), a leafless and unprepossessing plant that bears the spiky !nara melons which are still a food staple for the Topnaar Khoi-Khoi people. They grow a long tap root to derive moisture from underground sources and thereby provide a monitoring system for underground water tables: when plants are healthy, so is the water supply.

East of Rooibank, 1.5 km upstream towards Scheppmansdorp, is a marked three-km walking track which will take you along the sandy riverbed to some picturesque dunes. At Scheppmansdorp itself is a monument marking the site of an old church built by the missionary Scheppman in 1846.

Organised Tours

Gloriosa Safaris, at 215 7th St, organises local day trips as well as longer camping trips around the country. Another popular company is Inshore Safaris which offers half/full-day tours of the town, the Swakop River and Welwitschia Drive for US$30/35 per person, with a minimum of four people. Half-day 4WD tours to the bird lagoon at Sandwich Harbour (see the Namib-Naukluft Park in the following section) cost US$44 per person.

The water-oriented Mola-Mola Safaris operates half-day boat trips from Walvis Bay for US$38 per person and seabird-watching trips for US$55 per person. Full-day trips taking in Bird Island, Pelican Point and Sandwich Harbour, including lunch featuring Walvis Bay oysters, costs US$82. All trips depart from the yacht club.

Festivals

The annual Walvis Bay Arts & Crafts Festival (WAC), which is held from mid to late December, features a host of arts events. You can learn silk-painting, glass-etching, porcelain-painting, dyeing, batik and make pottery and stained glass, among other things. Competitions include sandcastle construction, (appropriate in Walvis Bay), chess, mural-painting and pavement art.

Places to Stay

The Walvis Bay area has two campgrounds. The friendly *Esplanade Municipal Camp & Caravan Park* (☎ 6145; fax 4528) near the Esplanade in town charges US$5 per camp site plus US$0.50 per person. There are several special backpackers' camp sites, complete with a kitchen area for self-catering. Campers also have access to the tennis courts.

The other-worldly *Langstrand Resort* (☎ 5981) lies 15 km north of town and also charges US$5 per camp site plus US$0.50

per person. It also has two/four-bed bungalows costing US$17/29. This place looks like an archetypal desert mirage, especially in a fog or sandstorm. The restaurant has a good reputation and you can stay busy poking around tide pools and swimming in the pool and from the specially constructed jetty. Also in Langstrand is the mid-range *Guesthouse Levo* (☎ 7555) belonging to Mr & Mrs Lieppert.

A cheap but especially seedy choice would be the *Mermaid Hotel* (☎ 6212; fax 6656) on 6th St. For the entire night, they charge US$21/25 for a single/double room, but they'd probably be just as happy renting it for two hours or so. Be sure to specify that you want the quietest and safest room available.

Inexpensive hotel accommodation can be found at the *Golden Fish Guesthouse* (☎ 2775; fax 2455). Doubles with/without shower cost US$19/17 without breakfast. The *Flamingo Hotel* (☎ 5975; fax 4097) isn't bad either at US$35/46 for a single/double with breakfast, but it does have a noisy off-licence academically named The Boozerama. The more up-market but good-value *Hotel Atlantic* (☎ 3811; fax 5063) is on 7th St between 10th and 11th Rds. Single/double rooms cost US$36/47 with bed and breakfast.

The most up-market hotel in Walvis Bay is the friendly *Casa Mia* (☎ 5975; fax 6596), which charges US$55/70 for a single/double room. Single/double suites are US$79/92. This recently refurbished place does its best to provide all the comforts of home. The restaurant is worthwhile even if you're not staying there and the bars provide a comfortable venue for drinks.

At the Suidwes Diensstasie (the Total service station), on the corner of 13th Rd and 10th St, is the *Suidwes Holiday Flats* (☎ 2260; fax 2931), where you can rent a self-contained flat for US$29 a double.

Another decent self-catering option is *Esplanade Park Bungalows* (☎ 5981) which has five/seven-bed bungalows for US$34/48 during the holiday season and slightly less off season. This is a great option for groups.

You'll find it near the seawall west of the town centre. The similar *Lagoon Chalets* (☎ 7151; fax 7469) south-west of town offer six-bed two-bedroom chalets for US$41, six-bed one-bedroom chalets for US$36 and eight-bed three-bedroom chalets for US$46. All units are self-catering.

A new self-catering place is the *Dolfyn-park Resort Chalets* about 12 km north of town, which has a swimming pool and water park. Four/six-bed self-catering chalets cost US$34/41.

Places to Eat

If you're looking for a reason to visit Walvis Bay, *Crazy Mama's* is it. This place can't be recommended highly enough. The service and atmosphere are great; the prices are right and they serve fabulous pizzas, salads and vegetarian options, among other things.

The Steakhouse (☎ 5490) serves tasty food – steaks, fish, crayfish and Walvis Bay oysters – at excellent prices. They also do fabulous bar lunches which are popular with the local office crowd. You'll also enjoy the recommended *Willie Probst Café/Bakery* and the *Harbour Café*. If you prefer something more mundane, there's the old stand-by, *Kentucky Fried Chicken*.

The posh *Lalainya's* (☎ 2574) on 7th St serves up-market dinners, including an excellent seafood platter. There's also a smart banquet hall for catered events.

If you're after fresh fish to cook yourself, see the Sea Pride Food Services (☎ 7661). It sells the catch of the day, as well as Lüderitz lobster tails, Alaskan smoked salmon and other frozen or processed seafood products through its wholesale shop on the corner of 13th Rd and 6th St. It's open Monday to Friday from 8.30 am to 1 pm and 2 to 5.30 pm, and on Saturday from 8 am to 1 pm.

Entertainment

When you first see Walvis Bay, you'll probably wonder whether entertainment is even feasible; people seem too lethargic to care one way or another. However, there actually are a couple of things to do at night – and that's in addition to uncorking a bottle of booze or downing a six-pack of lager in one sitting.

The Plaza Cinema not only shows films, but also has a lively bar and dance floor. For more rollicking local entertainment and dancing, visit the Palace disco in the Narraville township, east of the town centre. The Casa Mia Hotel actually has two bars: the Nautilus Karaoke Bar and the more intimate Captain Simon's.

Getting There & Away

Air The airport for Walvis Bay is at Rooikop ('red hill'), 10 km east of town on the C14. Air Namibia flies between Walvis Bay and Windhoek on Monday, Tuesday and Sunday, although it's easy enough to get there on the more frequent flights to Swakopmund. On Wednesday and Sunday, you can fly direct to or from Cape Town.

Bus There are both express coaches and trains between Windhoek and Walvis Bay via Swakopmund. The Intercape Mainliner bus runs on Monday, Wednesday, Friday and

Barred owl

NAMIBIA

Sunday to and from Windhoek and Swakopmund. The fare to Windhoek is US$25; to discourage anyone taking such a short hop, the fare to Swakopmund, 30 km away, is US$13. The bus stops at the Flamingo Hotel & Casino.

Dolphin Express (☎ 4118) operates daily bus services between Windhoek and Walvis Bay for US$15 per person.

There's also a private bus connecting Walvis Bay with Mariental, leaving Mariental on Monday and Walvis Bay on Tuesday. Because it drops supplies at various farms and bush shops along the way, the trip takes most of the day. Routes alternate between Büllsport and Sesriem. See the folks at Suidwes Diensstasie (Total service station).

Train Rail service from Windhoek to Walvis Bay runs via Swakopmund. Trains depart from Windhoek at 8 pm daily except Saturday, passing Swakopmund at 5.45 am the following morning and arriving in Walvis Bay at 7.05 am. They leave Walvis Bay at 6.35 pm on the same days and pass Swakopmund at 7.57 pm. The economy/sleeper-class fares between Windhoek and Walvis Bay are US$5/13 on Monday to Thursday and US$10/28 on Friday and Sunday.

In the winter, rail service between Swakopmund and Walvis Bay is often plagued by windblown sand which covers the tracks and undermines their foundations and crossties. This isn't a new problem – five km east of town on the C14, you'll see an embankment which has interred a section of narrow-gauge track from the last century. In front of the railway station are the remains of the *Hope*, an old locomotive which once ran on the original narrow-gauge railway. Both were abandoned after the line was repeatedly buried beneath 10-metre sand drifts. The *Hope* is now a national monument and stands in front of the railway station on Sixth St.

Getting Around

Dolphin Express minibuses operate around town and to other parts of the former enclave.

The Budget and Kessler Car Hire offices are at the Suidwes Diensstasie (the Total service station), on the corner of 10th St and 13th Rd. See Car Hire in the Namibia Getting Around chapter.

Namib-Naukluft Park

The Namib-Naukluft Park, Namibia's largest wildlife conservation area, is also one of the world's largest national parks. The present park boundaries were established in 1978 by merging the Namib Desert Park and the Naukluft Mountain Zebra Park with parts of Diamond Area 1 and bits of surrounding government land. Today, it takes in over 23,000 sq km of desert and semi-desert, including the diverse habitats of the Namib Desert Park between the Kuiseb and Swakop rivers, the Naukluft (formerly the Naukluft Mountain Zebra Park), the high dunefield at Sossusvlei and the bird lagoon at Sandwich Harbour.

The Namib Desert is one of the oldest and driest deserts in the world. As with the Atacama in northern Chile, it is the result of a cold current – in this case, the Benguela Current – sweeping north from Antarctica, which captures and condenses humid air which would otherwise be blown ashore.

The core area is a sea of sand, made up mainly of apricot-coloured dunes interspersed with dry pans. The best-known of these is Sossusvlei, a dusty pan surrounded by 300-metre dunes. On those rare occasions when the Tsauchab River is flowing,

---

Sandwiched Treasure

Local legend has it that over 200 years ago, a ship carrying a cargo of gold, precious stones and ivory intended as a gift from Lord Clive to the Moghul emperor was stranded at Sandwich Harbour en route to India. It's believed that the cargo, which was valued at 6 million pounds sterling, lies somewhere beneath the towering dunes. However, not a trace of it has yet been found – and not for a lack of searching. ∎

Sossusvlei fills with water and attracts gemsboks, springboks, ostriches and a variety of aquatic birds.

Heading north from Sossusvlei, the dunes end abruptly at the Kuiseb River. Here, the Namib assumes a completely different character: a landscape of endless grey-white gravel plains with isolated kopjes. It supports gemsboks, springboks and mountain zebras as well as the bizarre welwitschia plants whose only source of moisture is dew and fog. Historically, this region was also home to desert elephants and black rhinos, but these are now gone and attempts to reintroduce them have met with failure.

The eastern extreme of the park contains the Naukluft Mountains, characterised by a high plateau bounded by gorges, caves and springs cutting deeply into the dolomite formations. It's a lovely trekking area, with one-day, four-day and eight-day circuits through the range.

Fortunately for travellers, most of the main park roads are accessible to 2WD, but minor roads are often in poor condition and only marginally passable. Services are few, so for travel off the main routes, come equipped with food, water, a tent, sleeping bag, spare fuel and two spare tyres. If you do break down on a minor road, it's better to stay with your car than try to walk for help. Distances are great and eventually someone will come along. A fair number of hitchhikers are managing to get around, but hitching isn't a particularly good idea, and you'll need to be self-sufficient for several days – just in case your luck is running low.

For the purposes of this discussion, the park has been divided into four units: Sandwich Harbour, a wetland reserve on the coast south of Walvis Bay; the Namib Desert Park, which includes the northern end of the park and takes in the central Namib Desert; Naukluft Park, which includes the Naukluft Massif and surroundings; and Sesriem/ Sossusvlei, which provides easy access to the park's vast sea of dunes.

Travellers don't require permits to merely drive through the park along the main routes (the C28, the C14, the D1982 or the D1998) but you will need a permit to drive other roads and to use the picnic sites or visit any sites of interest off the main routes, including Sandwich Harbour and Welwitschia Drive (see under Around Swakopmund earlier in this chapter).

Permits may be picked up for US$1.50 per person at the MET office in Swakopmund or at Sesriem, Hardap Dam (see the Southern Namibia chapter) and at several after hours petrol stations in Swakopmund and Walvis Bay (see Information under those towns).

All camp sites must be prebooked through the MET offices in Windhoek or Swakopmund. Camping fees are payable when the park permit is issued. Note that permits for entry and hikes in the Sesriem/Sossusvlei and Naukluft sections of the park must be booked in Windhoek.

SANDWICH HARBOUR

Sandwich Harbour, 50 km south of Walvis Bay, historically served as a commercial fishing and trading port, and indeed, the name may be derived from an English whaler, the *Sandwich*, which operated here in the mid-1780s. It's thought that the captain of this ship produced the first map of this coastline. (However, the name could also be a corruption of the German word *sandfische*, a type of shark which is commonly found there.)

Although it seems a total wilderness nowadays, Sandwich Harbour has historically hosted a range of enterprises, from fish processing, shark-oil extraction, sealing and guano collection. In the late 1800s, believe it or not, the southern end of the lagoon was the site of an extensive abbatoir. Some enlightened soul had apparently decided to drive cattle over the dunes to the harbour, where they'd be slaughtered and exported by ship. All that remains of these enterprises is a hut from the guano-collection era (early to mid-1900s), a rusting barge, a graveyard and a couple of wooden beams from the abbatoir complex.

The inlet has silted up considerably since those days and is no longer used commer-

NAMIBIA

cially, but the northern end of this lovely lagoon provides an ideal environment for an extraordinary proliferation of birdlife. Sandwich Harbour itself extends another eight km south of the wetland area. For the best overview, struggle up one of the enormous dunes which flank the lagoon.

The site is open between 6 am and 8 pm every day of the year. There are no facilities for visitors, not even a camp site. Permits are available in Windhoek, Swakopmund and Walvis Bay (see Information under each of those towns).

The Wetlands

Anichab, at the northern end of the reserve, lies 3.5 km south of the angling concession car park. This area is characterised by a series of wetland pools filled from both the sea and the Anichab freshwater springs (which are probably created by water percolating through the dunefield from the Kuiseb River, 40 km to the north). The name of these springs comes from the area's early Nama inhabitants, for whom the word *anichab* meant simply 'spring water'. These reed-filled pools provide both sustenance and nesting sites for an astonishing variety of waterbirds. In all, over 100 species have been recorded at Sandwich Harbour and the bird population averages 150,000.

Under normal conditions, the Anichab springs reduce the salinity of the wetland area and make it amenable to salt-tolerant freshwater bird species. Over the past decade, however, the sand has encroached on the southern part of the lagoon, causing the sandspit which protects the wetlands to recede. This in turn has widened the area open to the sea, and the increased wave action has built a beach along the eastern shore of the lagoon. With more sediment pouring in, the lagoon has become shallower and saltier, and the northern sandspit sheltering the lagoon has moved inland. As a result, the reed pools are silting up and many of the terrestrial birds and wading birds have gone. It's speculated that over the next several decades, the lagoon may disappear.

Getting There & Away

Sandwich Harbour is accessible only with a sturdy 4WD high-clearance vehicle. Head south from Walvis Bay and take the left fork after five km. When the road splits, bear left again and continue across the salt works and the marshy Kuiseb Delta (which isn't like any delta you've ever seen before – this region belonged to the former South African Nature Reserve which occupied the southern third of the Walvis Bay enclave). After 15 km, you'll reach the checkpoint into the Namib-Naukluft Park, where you must show your permit.

For the final 20 km, you can either continue straight ahead along the sandy beach route (you'll have to time your journey at low tide) or bear left past the control post and follow the tracks further inland. However, at several points, you'll have to negotiate tedious stretches through high dunes, so you'd be wise to have a shovel, tow rope and a couple of planks handy for unbogging exercises. Vehicles aren't permitted beyond the car park at the southern limit of the angling concession, which lies 3.5 km north of MET's Anichab hut.

From Walvis Bay, half-day tours may be arranged through Inshore Safaris at the Casa Mia Hotel. You'll pay US$175 for up to four people and US$44 per person thereafter.

NAMIB DESERT PARK

The most accessible area of the Namib, the Namib Desert Park, lies between the canyons of the Kuiseb River in the south and the Swakop River in the north. Although it does include a small area of linear dunes, it's characterised mainly by broad gravel plains punctuated by abrupt and imposing ranges of hills, some of which appear to have been moulded from chocolate or caramel! Beyond that, there's only an occasional inselberg (a small granite kopje), thorn tree or ostrich to provide a sense of depth.

For information on Welwitschia Drive, which is inside the park but is most often visited as a day trip from Swakopmund, see Around Swakopmund earlier in this chapter.

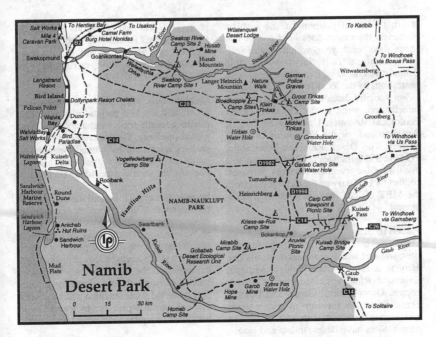

Kuiseb Canyon

The dramatic Kuiseb Canyon lies on the Gamsberg Route west of the Khomas Hochland. For much of the year, the ephemeral Kuiseb River is little more than a broad sandy riverbed. It may flow for just two or three weeks a year, but even then, the surface stream never reaches the sea. In a good year, it may reach Gobabeb, but further west, the water seeps into the sand. At Rooibank, drinking water for Walvis Bay is pumped from this subterranean supply.

Although this region doesn't support an abundance of large animals by any stretch of the imagination, there is wildlife about. The Kuiseb Canyon supports families of chacma baboons, which are often seen along the road. Dassies enjoy basking on the kopjes, and the canyon is also home to klipspringers and even leopards. Spotted hyenas are often heard at night and jackals make a good living from the herds of springbok on the plains above.

It was in the Kuiseb Canyon that geologists Henno Martin and Hermann Korn went into hiding for three years during WWII, as recounted in Henmo Martin's book *The Sheltering Desert*. The upper reaches of the canyon are uninhabited, but further down, where the valley broadens out, several Topnaar Khoi-Khoi villages lie scattered along the north bank.

Desert Ecological Research Unit

Gobabeb or the 'place of figs', off the main route west of Homeb, is the site of the Desert Ecological Research Unit of the Desert Research Foundation of Namibia, which was established by South African researcher Dr Charles Koch in 1963. This complex of laboratories, research facilities and a weather station appropriately sits at the transition point between the Namib's three distinct ecosystems: the gravel plains, the dune sea and the Kuiseb Valley.

Although it enjoys an inspiring location,

NAMIBIA

it isn't normally open to the public. However, the centre does hold one or two 'open days' each year, which feature self-guided nature trails, lectures and field demonstrations, as well as educational demonstrations by the local Topnaar community.

For specific dates of open days or other information, write to the Director, Desert Ecological Research Unit, PO Box 1592, Swakopmund, or the Friends of Gobabeb Society, The Desert Research Foundation, PO Box 37, Windhoek. If you're interested in visiting for scientific research purposes, contact Dr Hu Berry on the radio phone from the MET offices in Windhoek or Swakopmund.

Places to Stay

The central Namib area has eight basic camp sites, some of which accommodate only one party at a time: Kuiseb Bridge, Mirabib, Kriess-se-Rus, Vogelfederberg, Bloedkoppie, Groot Tinkas, Ganab and Homeb. These sites also function as picnic areas which may be used with just a day-use permit. Sites have tables, toilets and braais, but no washing facilities. None of the sites has a reliable water supply (though some do have brackish water suitable for cooking), so it's wise to bring all the water you'll be needing.

Use of any of these sites is by advance booking only, which must be done at MET in Windhoek or Swakopmund. Camping fees are payable when your park permit is issued.

Kuiseb Bridge This shady double camp site, which lies at the Kuiseb River crossing along the C14, is merely a convenient place to break up a trip between Windhoek and Walvis Bay. The location is scenic enough, but the dust and noise from passing vehicles makes it less appealing than other area sites. There are pleasant short walks into the canyon, but during heavy rains in the mountains, the site can be flooded; so during the summer months, keep tabs on the weather.

Kriess-se-Rus This rather ordinary camp site lies beside a streambed on the gravel plains, 107 km east of Walvis Bay on the Gamsberg Pass Route. It is shaded but isn't terribly prepossessing and is best used simply as a convenient stop en route between Windhoek and Walvis Bay.

Mirabib This very pleasant site, which accommodates two parties, is comfortably placed beneath rock overhangs in a large granite inselberg. There's evidence that these shelters were used by nomadic peoples as many as 9000 years ago, and also by nomadic shepherds in the 4th or 5th century.

Vogelfederberg This small inselberg about two km south of the C14 makes a convenient overnight camp within easy striking distance of Walvis Bay, 51 km away, but it's more popular as a picnic site or a place for a short walk. It's worth having a look at the intermittent pools on the top, which are home to a species of brine shrimp whose eggs hatch only when the pools are filled with rainwater. The only shade is provided by a small overhang with two picnic tables and braai pits.

Bloedkoppie The beautiful camp sites at the large inselberg, Bloedkoppie, or 'blood hill', are among the most popular sites in the park. If you're coming from Swakopmund, they lie 55 km north-east of the C28, along a signposted track. The northern sites are readily accessible to 2WD vehicles, but they're often plagued by the worst sort of yobs who drink themselves silly and make life miserable for everyone else. The southern sites are quieter and more secluded, but are reached only by 4WD. The surrounding area offers some very pleasant walking, and at Klein Tinkas, about five km east of Bloedkoppie, you'll see the ruins of a colonial police station and the graves of two German police officers dating back to 1895.

Groot Tinkas The camp site at Groot Tinkas, 15 km east of Bloedkoppie, must be accessed with 4WD and rarely sees much traffic, so if you want a secluded spot to camp in the Namib this is a good choice. The site enjoys a lovely setting beneath ebony trees and the surroundings are super for nature walks. During rainy periods, the brackish water in the nearby dam attracts varied birdlife.

Ganab The dusty and exposed camp site at Ganab sits beside a shallow streambed on the gravel plains. It's shaded by hardy acacia trees and a nearby bore hole provides water for antelopes.

Homeb The scenic camp site at Homeb, which accommodates several parties, lies upstream from the most accessible set of dunes in the central Namib, which make a pleasant destination for a short walk. Although the Kuiseb floods rarely make it this far west, it's clear that the river has prevented these dunes from encroaching on the gravel plains which spread out from the northern bank. Residents of the nearby Topnaar Khoi-Khoi village dig wells in the riverbed to access water flowing beneath the surface, and one of their dietary staples is the !nara melon, which takes its moisture through a long tap root which reaches the water table. This hidden water also supports a good stand of trees, including camelthorn acacia, ebony and figs along the banks. You have a good chance of seeing steenboks, gemsboks and baboons which also take advantage of the water. It's also used by chickens, dogs, goats and donkeys from the nearby village.

We've had several reports of campers being hassled for gifts of money and alcohol by the villagers. While it's certainly pleasant to meet local people, please avoid the temptation to play Santa Claus or snap photos indiscriminately, or you may affect community values and render impossible any chance of real communication between the locals and future visitors.

Swakop River The lovely and shady Swakop River camp sites lie – not surprisingly – on the banks of the Swakop River, in the far northern reaches of the park. The southern one has five camp sites and is the better of the two, with lots of greenery – camelthorn, anaboom and tamarisk trees –

while the northern one, beside a plain of welwitschias, is utterly flat and treeless. The only shade is beneath an odd sunken picnic site.

The sites are accessible via Welwitschia Drive, along the side route towards Welwitschia Plains, and therefore sees a fair amount of passing tourist traffic. For more information about this area, see under Around Swakopmund earlier in this chapter.

Getting There & Away

The only public transport through this part of the park is a weekly bus connecting Mariental with Walvis Bay, via Maltahöhe and Solitaire. The westbound trip is on Monday and the eastbound on Tuesday. It alternates between the Büllsport and Sesriem routes. Naturally, you'd do a lot better with a vehicle.

NAUKLUFT PARK

The Naukluft Park was originally set aside in 1964 as the Naukluft Mountain Zebra Park as a reserve for Hartmann's mountain zebra, but it's now a highland appendage of the Namib-Naukluft Park. The Naukluft Massif, which rises steeply from the gravel plains of the central Namib, is mainly a high-plateau area cut around the edges by a complex of steep gorges. Indeed, the park's name is Afrikaans for 'narrow gorge'. The Tsondab, Tsams and Tsauchab rivers all rise in the massif; and the relative availability of water makes it ideal habitat for mountain zebras, kudu, leopards, springboks and klip-springers.

History

In the early 1890s, the Naukluft was the site of heated battle between the German colonial forces and the Witbooi Namas. The Nama resistance to German rule was led by the gifted military strategist Hendrik Witbooi, who refused to bow to the colonial power. In January 1893, a contingency of Schutztruppe soldiers under Major Curt von François were posted near Oniab, north of the Naukluft, and managed to force Witbooi and his followers to flee their settlement at

Hoornkrans. Von François was transferred in March 1894 and replaced by Major Theodore Leutwein, who began a serious campaign against the Nama forces in the Naukluft Mountains. At the end of that same month, German cavalryman Richard Kramers was killed in a skirmish near what is now the Hiker's Haven hut in the Naukluft Valley (his grave may still be seen there).

The Germans had originally estimated they could defeat the Nama within three days, but their unfamiliarity with the territory and the essentials of guerrilla warfare slowed them down considerably. However, by late August, they'd captured the Nama camp at Oniab and Witbooi and his forces retreated into the mountains. The Germans followed with their cannon and other firepower (you can still see portions of the old cannon route), chasing the Nama across the plateau.

After heavy losses, Witbooi approached the Germans with a conditional surrender, which stipulated that he would accept German sovereignty over the country and permit them to set up a military post at Gibeon if he could retain his chieftaincy and the Nama could retain their lands and weapons. Leutwein accepted and the Battle of the Naukluft was over.

Hiking Routes

Most visitors to the Naukluft section of the park come to hike one of two day walks, the Waterkloof Trail or the Olive Trail. These day hikes are open to anyone and need not be booked, but if you wish to camp at the Naukluft camp site, be sure to reserve a site as far in advance as possible.

There are also two longer hikes – a four-day and an eight-day loop – with more restrictions attached. Due to uncomfortably hot summer temperatures and potentially heavy rains, the hikes are available only from 1 March to 31 October on the first and third Sunday and Wednesday of each month. The price of US$10 per person includes accommodation at the Hikers' Haven hut near park headquarters on the day before and after the hike, as well as camping at basic trail shelters

along the way (with the exception of Ubusis Canyon, which has a fully fledged mountain hut). Groups must be comprised of at least three and not more than 12 people and as with all official National Parks' hikes, each member of the group needs a doctors' medical certificate issued less than 40 days before the hike.

Waterkloof Trail This lovely 17-km loop takes about seven hours to complete and is followed in a counter-clockwise direction. It begins at the Koedoesrus camp site, about two km west of the park headquarters. For this trip, you'll need to carry two to three litres of water per person.

The trail begins by climbing up the Naukluft River past a weir, up a tufa waterfall and past a series of pools which offer cool and refreshing swimming. About one km beyond the last pool, the trail turns west, away from the Naukluft River and up a tributary. From there to the half-way point, the route traverses increasingly open plateau country.

Shortly after the half-way mark, it climbs steeply to a broad ridge which, at 1910 metres above sea level, is the highest point on the route. From here you'll have fabulous desert views in both directions before you begin a long and steep ascent into the Gororosib Valley. As you descend along the valley, you'll pass several inviting pools, filled with reeds and tadpoles; and climb down an especially impressive tufa waterfall before meeting up with the Naukluft River.

Leopard

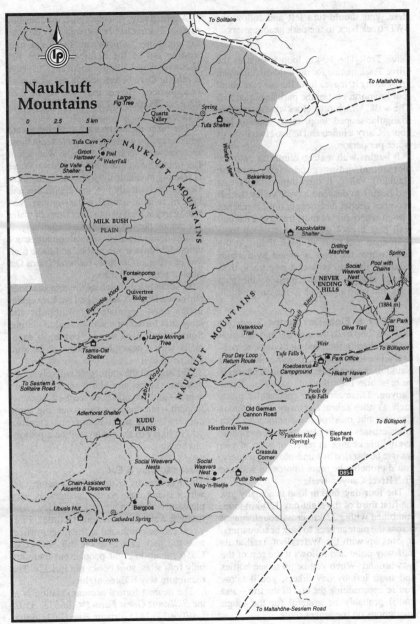

Naukluft Mountains

0   2.5   5 km

To Solitaire

To Maltahöhe

Large Fig Tree

Quartz Valley

Spring

Tufa Shelter

Tufa Cave

Groot Hartseer

Pool WaterFall

Die Valle Shelter

World's View

Bakenkop

N A U K L U F T   M O U N T A I N S

MILK BUSH PLAIN

Kapokvlakte Shelter

Drilling Machine

Spring

Social Weavers' Nest

Pool with Chains

Fonteinpomp

Quivertree Ridge

Euphorbia Kloof

NEVER ENDING HILLS

(1884 m)

Car Park

Olive Trail

To Büllsport

Large Moringa Tree

Waterkloof Trail

Naukluft River

Tsams-Ost Shelter

N A U K L U F T   M O U N T A I N S

Zebra Kloof

Four Day Loop Return Route

Tufa Falls

Weir

Park Office

To Büllsport

Koedoesrus Campground

Hikers' Haven Hut

To Sesriem & Solitaire Road

Adlerhorst Shelter

KUDU PLAINS

Old German Cannon Road

Heartbreak Pass

Pools & Tufa Falls

Fontein Kloof (Spring)

Elephant Skin Path

Social Weavers' Nests

Social Weavers' Nest

Crassula Corner

Putte Shelter

D854

Chain-Assisted Ascents & Descents

Wag-'n-Bietjie

Ubusis Hut

Bergpos

Cathedral Spring

Ubusis Canyon

To Maltahöhe-Sesriem Road

NAMIBIA

Here, you should turn left and follow the 4WD track back to the park headquarters.

Olive Trail The 10-km loop known as the Olive Trail, named for the wild olives which grow along it, leaves from the car park about four km north-east of the park headquarters. The walk, which runs clockwise around the triangular-shaped loop, takes four to five hours. Carry a lunch and at least two litres of water per person.

It begins with a steep climb up onto the plateau, affording good views into the Naukluft Valley. It then turns sharply east and begins to descend a river valley, which becomes deeper and steeper until it reaches a point where hikers must traverse a canyon wall past a pool using chains which have been anchored there to assist them. At the point where the river is joined by a major tributary, the trail crosses a jeep track, then swings sharply south, returns to the jeep track and follows it back to the car park.

Four-Day & Eight-Day Loops There are also two loop trails through the massif which can be hiked in four and eight days, respectively. For some people, myself included, the Naukluft is a magical place, but its charm is more subtle than that of, say, Fish River Canyon. There are some spectacular parts, such as the Zebra Highway and Ubusis Canyon; but most of the distance on both loops crosses desert plateau, with comparatively little change in relief. In short, if you want to be dazzled by mind-blowing scenery, you'd probably be more impressed with the Fish River Canyon walk.

The four-day, 60-km loop is actually just the first third of the eight-day 120-km loop, combined with a 22-km cross-country jaunt across the plateau back to park headquarters. It joins up with the Waterkloof Trail at its half-way point and follows it the rest of the way around. When you begin to see bottles and trash left by day hikers, you'll know you're approaching the end of the trip – and you'll probably be grateful for the tough restrictions on the longer route.

Alternatively, you can finish the four-day route at Tsams Ost Shelter, mid-way through the eight-day loop, where there's a road leading out to the Sesriem-Solitaire Rd. However, you will have to arrange to leave a vehicle there before setting off from park headquarters. Hikers may not begin their hike at Tsams Ost under any circumstances.

The hikes themselves are straightforward and marked by white footprints (except those sections which coincide with the Waterkloof Loop, in which case, they're yellow). Water is reliably available only at overnight stops. Due to the typically hot, dry conditions and lack of reliable natural water sources, you must carry at least two to three litres of water per person per day – and use it sparingly. If you're doing the eight-day circuit and can't carry eight days worth of food and stove fuel, you can drop off a supply cache at Tsams Ost Shelter prior to the hike.

In some places, such as the requisite side trip down Ubusis Canyon and back up again, hikers must negotiate dry waterfalls and steep tufa formations with the aid of chains. Some people find this off-putting – especially with a heavy backpack – so be sure you're up to it.

Throughout the route, you're likely to see baboons, kudus and Hartmann's mountain zebras – and you may even see the occasional leopard – but this is certainly not 'big game country'. The most dangerous creature you're likely to encounter will be a poisonous snake.

Places to Stay & Eat
The Koedoesrus (Kudu's Rest) camp site, which is not open to day visitors, is very pleasantly situated in a deep valley, with running water and ablutions facilities. Firewood can be purchased at the ranger office, near the park gate over the hill. Sites cost US$6 for up to eight people, but there are only four sites, so it books out quickly. The maximum stay is three nights.

The nearest formal accommodation is at the *Büllsport Guest Farm* (☎ (06632) 3302; fax (06632) 141), Private Bag 1003, Malta-

The Namib Dunes

The magnificent Namib dunefields, which take on mythical proportions in tourist literature, stretch from the Orange to Kuiseb rivers in the south (this area is known as the 'dune sea') and from Torra Bay in the Skeleton Coast Park to the Angola's Curoca River in the north. They're composed of colourful quartz sand, and come in hues which vary from cream to orange, red and violet.

Unlike the Kalahari dunes, those of the Namib are dynamic. Over time, the wind shifts them and even sculpts them into a variety of distinctive shapes. The top portion of the dune which faces the direction of migration is known as the slipface. Here the sand spills from the crest and slips down. Various bits of plant and animal detritus also collect here and provide a meagre food source of dune-dwelling creatures. It's here that the majority of dune life is concentrated.

Along the eastern area of the dune sea, including around Sossusvlei, the dunes are classified as parabolic or multi-cyclic and are the result of variable wind patterns. These are the most stable dunes in the Namib and therefore, are also the most vegetated.

Near the coast south of Walvis Bay, the formations are known as transverse dunes, which are long linear dunes lying perpendicular to the prevailing southwesterly winds. Therefore, their slipfaces are oriented towards the north and north-east.

Between these two types of dunes – for example around Homeb in the Central Namib – are the prominent linear or *seif* dunes, which are enormous northwest-southeast oriented sand ripples. They reach heights of 100 metres and are spaced about one km apart and show up plainly on satellite photographs of the area. They're formed by seasonal winds; during the prevailing southerly winds of summer, the slipfaces lie on the north-eastern face. In the winter, the wind blows in the opposite direction and slip-faces build up on the south-western dune faces.

In areas where individual dunes are exposed to winds from all directions, a formation known as a star dune appears. These dunes have multiple ridges and when seen from above may appear to have a star shape. Considerably smaller are the tiny hump dunes, which build up around vegetation – mainly near water sources – and reach only two to three metres in height.

Around the southern portion of the Skeleton Coast Park and south of Lüderitz, barchan dunes prevail. These are the most highly mobile dunes of all, and are created by unidirectional winds. As they shift, these dunes take on a crescent shape, with the horns of the crescent aimed in the direction of migration. It is barchan dunes which are slowly devouring the ghost town of Kolkmanskop near Lüderitz. They're also the so-called 'roaring dunes' for the rumbling sound they make as sand grains spill over the slipface. On particularly large dunes, or in especially warm weather, the roar is at its loudest. ■

höhe, run by Ernst and Johanna Sauber. There's a certain charm in this rather austere setting below the Naukluft Massif, and the surrounding farm holds several attractions which can be reached on foot or a 4WD excursion. These include a ruined colonial police station and such natural attractions as the Bogenfels arch and mountain pools. Rooms cost US$38 per person for bed and breakfast or US$51 per person with full board. The property also has its own shop and petrol station.

Getting There & Away

The Naukluft section of the park is most easily accessed along the C24 from Rehoboth and the C14 north from Gamis (or the less travelled short-cut along the D1206 from Rietoog). From Sesriem, 103 km away, the nearest access is via the dip-ridden D854.

The Mariental-Walvis Bay bus passes Büllsport, which will put you within reasonable – but not easy – hitching distance of the park entrance.

SESRIEM & SOSSUSVLEI

The name Sesriem means 'six thongs', which was the number of joined leather ox-wagon thongs necessary to draw water from the bottom of the gorge.

Both Sesriem Canyon and Sossusvlei are open year-round between sunrise and sunset. If you want to see the sunrise over Sossusvlei – as most people do – you'll have to stay at the Sesriem campground. Otherwise, you won't be allowed through the gate early enough to reach Sossusvlei in time.

Sesriem Canyon

Four km south of Sesriem is 30-metre deep Sesriem Canyon. Here the Tsauchab River, which rises high in the Naukluft Massif, has carved a km-long gorge through the 15-million-year-old deposits of sand and gravel conglomerate. The canyon makes a pleasant and interesting walk from the parking area upstream to its narrow head and downstream to its broad lower reaches. After rains, the canyon often contains lovely pools suitable for swimming.

Elim Dune

This oft-visited red dune, 1.5 km from the Sesriem camp site, can be reached in a 2WD vehicle, but also makes a decent morning or afternoon walk. It lies on the former Elim Farm, which now lies within the Namib-Naukluft Park.

Dune 45

The most accessible of the large red dunes along the route between Sesriem and Sossusvlei is Dune 45, so called because it's 45 km from Sesriem. It rises over 150 metres above the surrounding plains and is flanked by several scraggly but picturesque trees, which will provide your photos with foreground interest.

Sossusvlei

The area around Sossusvlei is the most accessible part of the 300-km-long and nearly 150-km-wide sand sea that covers over 32,000 sq km of western Namibia. This vast expanse of dunes stretches from the Khoichab River in the south to the Kuiseb River in the north, and is reputed to contain some of the world's highest and most picturesque dunes.

It's likely that this sand originated in the Kalahari between three and five million years ago. It was washed down the Orange River and out to sea, where it was swept northward with the Benguela Current to be deposited along the coast.

Sossusvlei itself is a huge ephemeral pan set amid red sand dunes which tower as much as 200 metres above the valley floor and over 300 metres over the underlying strata. At any time of year, you may observe gemsboks and ostriches roaming over the sand, but if you visit during the summer months, you may be treated to a rare occasion when the pan actually contains water. This happens only when the Tsauchab River has gathered enough volume and momentum to drive its waters right across the thirsty plains into the sand sea. When it has, you'll be treated to a rather ethereal vision: red dunes reflected in a still pool, enhanced by a variety of birdlife, including flamingoes.

Although it's very hard going, the best way to get a feel for this sea of sand is to climb one of the dunes and have a look around. When you realise that this sandy sprawl extends 75 to 150 km in all directions, you'll have some idea how vast it is.

Activities

It probably wouldn't occur to most people to visit Namibia for skiing, but French skier Eric Lon wasn't put off and dune skiing made its debut at Sossusvlei. Sand-skiing is done on flexible nordic skis using a shoe-like boot fastened only at the toe. The bottom of the skis are fitted which allows a good grip on the uphill climb – the increased surface area makes skiing up a dune far easier than walking – and a slicker surface for skiing down.

After teaching sand skiing in both Algeria and Tunisia, Eric set his sights on Sossusvlei and has now taught the new sport to several Namibians. Although nothing commercial

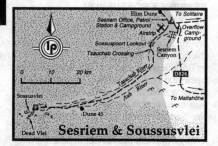

Sesriem & Soussusvlei

has yet been set up, he'd eventually like to establish a skiing operation for tourists. If you're interested, you can write to him at 2 Rue JB Baudin, 83000 Toulon, France.

Organised Tours

Most lodges and guesthouses in the area run day tours to Sossusvlei, and prices are generally proportional to the amount you're paying for accommodation. See Places to Stay later in this discussion. Alternatively, a good value way to do a day trip is to take the tour from the Maltahöhe Hotel in Maltahöhe. For details see the Southern Namibia chapter.

Places to Stay

Sesriem Sesriem is the most convenient campground to Sossusvlei. Sites must be booked in Windhoek and cost US$6, but arrive before sunset or they'll allot your site to someone else on a stand-by basis. Those who were unable to book a site in Windhoek can get in on this nightly lottery. Failing that – or if you arrive late – you'll be relegated to the emergency overflow area outside the gate. It also costs US$6 but isn't nearly as nice as the main camp and there are no braai pits or ablutions facilities. Toilets are available only when the petrol station is open.

Unfortunately, the lovely camp site has recently acquired an unsightly backdrop in the form of new luxury hotel, *Karos Lodge* (☎ (27-11) 643 8052; fax (27-11) 643 4343, both numbers in Johannesburg). This curiously conceived entity bears a strong resemblance to what happens when two fighting children topple a stack of coloured blocks. One doesn't necessarily object to a tourist-class hotel at Sesriem, but why wasn't it placed a bit further from the campground. Single/double accommodation in small cuboid bungalows costs US$123/176 with dinner, bed and breakfast. To book from Namibia, contact Trip Travel in Windhoek (☎ 236880; fax 225430).

Around Sesriem If you're not camping, an inexpensive and relatively convenient option is the ultra-friendly *Solitaire Guest House* (☎ 3230), Private Bag 1009, Maltahöhe, which is at the petrol station in Solitaire, 65 km north of Sesriem. This pleasantly anachronous place could have provided the inspiration for the film *Baghdad Café*. Dusty camp sites or floor space to roll out a sleeping bag cost US$1.50 and rooms are US$6. At the attached restaurant, you're limited to whatever they're cooking that day, but the food is always good.

The *Namib Rest Camp* (☎ (06632) 3211), PO Box 1075, Swakopmund, run by Pieter and Ella Vosges, lies on the Dieprivier Farm 16 km south of Solitaire, and just west of the C36. It's actually a bit more plush than its name would imply, and you will appreciate the swimming pool. Accommodation in two/four-bed self-catering bungalows costs US$39/49 without meals. Half/full board for either type of bungalow is US$34/45 per person. The rest camp also runs reasonably priced excursions to Sesriem and Sossusvlei. An interesting attraction on the farm itself is the unusual violet-coloured Tsondab sandstone formation, which is actually an exposed section of an active dunefield that was solidified by moisture some 20 million years ago. In fact, this formation underlies most of the Namib Sand Sea, including the dunes around Sossusvlei.

Over the road and a bit farther south is the relatively posh *Namib-Naukluft Lodge* (☎ (06632) 3203), PO Box 22028, Windhoek. Accommodation in double rooms cost US$65 per person with full board. In self-catering bungalows, it's US$50 per person with breakfast. Road or air transfers from Windhoek are available for a fairly substantial extra charge. For bookings, contact African Extravaganza (☎ 63082; fax 215356) in Windhoek.

The nearby *Gästefarm Ababis* (☎ 3340), PO Box 1004, Maltahöhe, run by Meike and Klaus Würriehausen, lies just south of the C14, 15 km south-east of Solitaire. This working farm raises mainly cattle, sheep and ostriches, but there's also a fair amount of wildlife on the property and the farmers run

NAMIBIA

game drives and also organise vulture-feeding sessions. Accommodation with full board costs US$50 per person.

An excellent option – and an attraction in its own right – is the *Namibgrens Rest Camp* (☎ (0628) 1322), PO Box 21587, Windhoek, which is run by Mr JJ Rabie. This beautiful game farm, which is known for its hiking trails, occupies a scenic position on the Spreetshoogte Pass (Namibia's steepest road, with a hair-raising 1:4 slope) north-east of Solitaire. The hiking routes form a ragged figure eight, allowing hikes of one to three days; accommodation is in basic huts where the loops cross. Along the way are bore holes where hikers can fill their water bottles, while earth dams provide water for wildlife. Non-hikers can take the soft option and tour the farm by vehicle for US$7 per person. Single/double accommodation in the spacious old farmhouse costs US$23/41, including bed, breakfast and use of kitchen facilities. If you're not cooking, lunch and dinner cost US$8 and US$10, respectively.

South of Sesriem and west of the Maltahöhe road is the 140,000-hectare *Namib Rand Game Ranch* (☎ (06632) 5230), the largest privately owned property in southern Africa. Accommodation ranges from camping to fully catered packages at Mwisho luxury tented camp, but most people come for the unique – and rather expensive – early morning balloon flights over the dune sea. Full-board accommodation costs US$65 per person and the balloon flights are US$135 per person per hour. For bookings, contact their Windhoek agent. The Namib Travel Shop (☎ 236720; fax 220102), PO Box 5048, Windhoek.

A new option now being set up is *Natur Erlebnis Ranch* at Farm Rustenberg, which lies on the D1261, the Remhoogte Pass road, near the C14 junction. It's planned as a basic backpackers' resort, and when it opens it will provide basic accommodation for just US$6. Meals and horse-riding will cost an additional US$6, and twice-weekly transfers from Windhoek will cost US$9 per person. They also intend to run horseback safaris, day trips to Sossusvlei and longer trips around Namibia for very reasonable prices. For information on the progress of the project, phone Stefan Rust (☎ (0628) 1221) in Seeis or Heidi Rust (☎ (061) 41299) in Windhoek.

Places to Eat
Apart from the various accommodation options and the shop/restaurant at Solitaire, your only option is the small shop at the Sesriem office, which sells little more than crisps and cold drinks.

Getting There & Away
You reach Sesriem via a signposted turn-off from the Maltahöhe-Solitaire road (C36). The only public transport is a weekly bus that runs from Mariental to Walvis Bay on Monday and returns on Tuesday. The catch is that it only travels via Sesriem every second week; on other weeks, it runs via Büllsport.

The 65-km road south-west from Sesriem is good gravel to within four km of Sossusvlei; from there, the road traverses deep sand and requires 4WD. Most visitors with lesser vehicles just park at the end of the gravel and walk the remaining distance, which takes about an hour and is actually quite pleasant if you're not pressed for time.

When you reach Sossusvlei, you may experience a sense of *déjà vu*. Nearly every photo story ever written about Namibia includes a photo of Sossusvlei which features in numerous films and advertisements worldwide. As with the Skeleton Coast, it's a national icon.

Southern Namibia

Southern Namibia takes in everything from Rehoboth south to the South African Border, east to the Botswanan border and west to the diamond coast. Geographically, southern Namibia encompasses the rich cattle country of Namaland, the semidesert of the Kalahari borders, the forbidden wilderness of the southern Namib as well as the sensational Fish River Canyon, which lies near the South African border.

Undoubtedly, this massive gorge is one of Africa's most captivating natural features and merits a couple of days' visit. At Ai-Ais resort, beside the river at the canyon's southern end, you can camp, hike and relish the hot springs while soaking up the sun and the fabulous scenery. At Hobas, on the rim at the canyon's northern end, you'll have fabulous views into the depths.

Most visitors to Fish River are safari groups, hikers or southern African holiday-makers. There are no luxury-class hotels, so most package-tour groups just fly in for a view over the rim of the canyon and leave the same day.

Further north you will find Hardap Dam Recreation Resort. The resort makes a convenient central place to stay. In its surprisingly good wildlife reserve, visitors may wander at will. Other major attractions include the Duwisib Castle, the Kokerboom Forest, Brukkaros Crater and the bizarre Bavarian-style town of Lüderitz, which is brim full of colonial architecture.

Strung along the B1 corridor are the three small but significant Namibian towns of Rehoboth, Mariental and Keetmanshoop. These towns are connected by rail, bus and road links. Unfortunately – as elsewhere in Namibia – the sites of greatest interest and appeal in these towns can not be reached by public transport. To visit Fish River Canyon, for example, you will need to have a vehicle, endure typically long waits hitching, or join an organised tour from Keetmanshoop or elsewhere in Namibia.

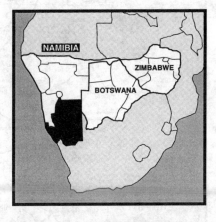

The Central Plateau

The Central Plateau of southern Namibia is characterised by truly wide open country. The region's widely spaced towns, which are generally uninspiring in their own right, and function mainly as commercial and market centres. This is the country's richest karakul sheep and cattle ranching area, and around Mariental some citrus fruit and market vegetables are grown under irrigation.

The region is bisected by Namibia's main north-south route, the B1, which stretches from Windhoek southward across the Central Plateau towards the South African border. The road is so good, however, that for most drivers, southern Namibia is nothing but an endless broken white line stretching away towards a receding horizon; in short, a paradise for leadfoot drivers and cruise-control potatoes. Too bad, because the Central Plateau's hinterlands are well off the worn route and with time and a vehicle, you'll find plenty of scope for exploration and you're unlikely to encounter more than a handful of other tourists.

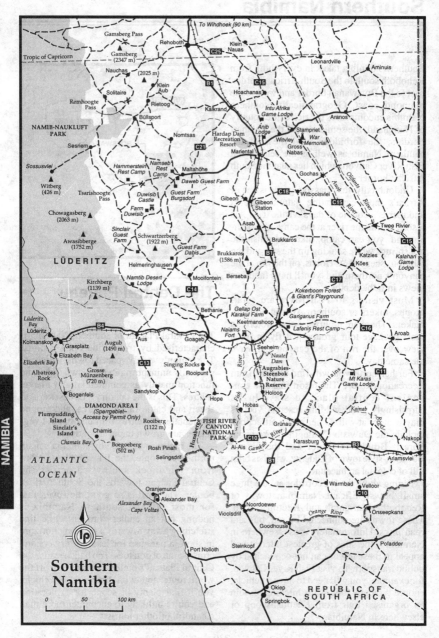

Southern
Namibia

0   50   100 km

REHOBOTH

The small town of Rehoboth lies on the B1 85 km south of Windhoek and just a stone's throw north of the Tropic of Capricorn. In general, it feels more animated than most other Namibian towns south of the Red Line, and the streets are normally thronged with people and activity.

The area's first inhabitants were the Nama, who were displaced by the Herero in the middle of the 19th century. The settlement of Rehoboth originally developed around a Rhenish mission station, which was founded in 1844 by Heinrich Kleinschmidt. He named Rehoboth after the biblical place of wide open spaces.

Although the mission was abandoned in 1864, it was revived in the early 1870s by the Basters, an ethnic group of mixed Khoi-Khoi/Afrikaner origin, who had migrated north from the Cape under their leader Hermanus van Wyk. They'd originally intended to settle around the Orange River, but when the Cape government began demanding proof of land ownership in the mid-1860s, they headed north yet again and set down stakes in Rehoboth. To stay, they were required to pay an annual tribute of one horse each to the Nama, the Afrikaners and the Herero.

The Rehoboth Basters remain proud of both their heritage and their name, which literally means 'bastards'. Never mind that the word is used as an insult elsewhere – for them, it emphasises a proud ancestry.

Rehoboth Museum

For a bit of insight into the Baster heritage, visit the Rehoboth Museum (☎ 2954), beside the post office. It's housed in the 1903 residence of the settlement's first colonial postmaster. It outlines the area's natural and cultural history and includes a photo exhibit of the period from 1893 to 1896. The photos depict the early mission station, which was rebuilt by the Basters under their leader Hermanus van Wyk.

Outside is a garden of local plants and examples of historic homes and transport. There's also an archaeological annexe at an Iron Age site 10 km from town which can be visited by prior arrangement.

The museum is open Monday to Friday from 10 am to noon and 2 to 4 pm, and on Saturday to noon. Admission for residents of Rehoboth is US$0.25, while others pay US$1.50.

Reho Spa

The Reho Spa complex surrounds a thermal spring and an elaborate spa complex complete with a 39°C thermal pool, bungalows and a camp site (see Places to Stay below). The early Nama knew it as 'aris' – meaning 'smoke' – after the steam which rose from the hot spring. Accommodation must be pre-booked, but the spa is open to day visitors without bookings from 7 am to 6 pm. Admission costs US$1.50 per person plus US$0.50 per person for use of the hot baths.

Oanab Dam

The 2.7-sq-km Oanab Dam, 10 km west of Rehoboth, was completed in 1990 to make the most use of the district's water supply. The route is well signposted from the B1. At the overlook, which affords an impressive view of the dam, you'll find a picnic site and small exhibit outlining the dam's history and construction. Several short walking tracks have also been laid out.

Places to Stay

Most visitors to Rehoboth take advantage of the hot water at *Reho Spa Recreation Resort* (☎ 2774), which lies down a gravel road less than one km off the main street. The turn-off is near the church. You have a choice of self-catering accommodation, from a one-room five-bed bungalow or a one-bedroom four-bed model for US$19 to a two-bedroom four-bed bungalow for US$36. Camp sites for up to eight people cost US$4. Facilities include a cafeteria, swimming pool and thermal bath.

The seedy *Rio Monte Hotel* (☎ 2161), near the railway station, has minimal facilities and charges US$18/21 for a single/double room.

Places to Eat

The *Reho Spa* restaurant serves cheap and adequate food. In the town centre are *Sigi's à la Carte Restaurant* and the basic but locally popular *Dolphin Fish & Chips*.

Getting There & Away

Rehoboth is 85 km south of Windhoek on the B1. If you're hitching from Windhoek, bear in mind that a taxi from the town centre to a good hitching spot south of Windhoek will cost US$3.50, while minibuses from the bus terminal near Wernhill Park Centre cost just US$2 per person. They leave when full, which is approximately every 20 minutes.

The Intercape Mainliner bus between Windhoek and Cape Town stops in Rehoboth. It's also a stop on the main railway line between Windhoek, Keetmanshoop and De Aar, South Africa.

MARIENTAL

Mariental is a small administrative and commercial centre in the heart of the karakul ranching district, and is also the site of various new agricultural endeavours, including large-scale irrigation and ostrich farming. It also remains the largest stronghold of the Nama people, who are mainly of Khoi-Khoi descent. It makes a convenient place for travellers to stop for a night, but don't expect any action at all; Mariental is one of the most lethargic and lifeless places I've ever seen.

History

The original Nama name was *Zaragaebia*, meaning 'dusty', but the current name, which means 'Maria's valley', was bestowed on the original farm by the area's first White farmer, Hermann Brandt, in honour of his wife Anna Maria Mahler. Brandt had purchased land from the Nama chief Hendrik Witbooi in 1890.

From 1903 to 1907, this area saw a great deal of action as the colonial and Nama forces engaged in battle after battle and quite a few German civilians fell victim to guerrilla raids. After the railway came through in 1912, local residents petitioned for village status, but their hopes were dashed by the German surrender to the South African Defence Force in 1915. It wasn't until 1920, when Namibia's first Dutch Reformed church was built there, that Mariental officially came into existence.

Information

Believe it or not, Mariental does have a tourist information office. It's at the town hall, just off Michael van Niekerk St about one km from the town centre.

Places to Stay

The nearest camp site to Mariental is at Hardap Dam (see later in this section). The *Sandberg Hotel* (☎ /fax 2291), not far from the northern turn-off from the B1, has basic singles/doubles for US$29/45. For rooms with three/four beds, you'll pay US$50/60. There's also has a restaurant and bar. I found the management to be friendly and helpful, but there have been complaints.

A block further down Main St is the new *Mariental Hotel* (☎ 856), which provides a more plush option. Single/double accommodation costs US$35/46.

The cheapest accommodation is the pleasant *Guglhupf Café* (☎ 718) which costs US$25/35 a single/double. It has a swimming pool, and the attached café serves excellent steaks and beef dishes.

Midway between Mariental and Stampriet, three km north of the C20, is *Anib Lodge* (☎ 12421), PO Box 800, Mariental, run by Anka and Claus Schultz. This reasonably priced guest farm, which bills itself as 'your nest on the edge of the Kalahari' offers comfortable accommodation with private facilities, a swimming pool and good birdwatching opportunities in a secluded setting. Bed and breakfast costs US$32 per person; full board is US$43.

Slightly further afield on a large game ranch is the posh *Intu Afrika Game Lodge* (☎ 4274; fax 4921, both in Walvis Bay), PO Box 652, Walvis Bay. Single/double rooms cost US$103/168 and chalets are US$114 per person. All prices include accommodation, full board and game drives around the ranch. It lies on the farm Onze Rust, along the D1268 about 44 km north of the C20. In a novel move, they're currently attempting to settle five San families on the reserve, to pursue their hunting and gathering lifestyle and educate tourists about the traditional San way of life.

Places to Eat

For meals, there isn't much to choose from. Apart from the hotel and guesthouse restaurants, there are only a couple of basic takeaways where tourists will definitely attract local attention. Try *Bambi's Takeaways* beside the Engen petrol station, near the Sandberg Hotel.

Getting There & Away

Bus The Intercape Mainliner stops at the Engen petrol station at 9.45 pm on Monday, Wednesday, Friday and Sunday southbound; and 3.45 am on Tuesday, Thursday, Saturday and Sunday northbound. The fare to or from Windhoek is US$22 and to or from Keetmanshoop, US$18. There are also daily minibuses running between Windhoek and Keetmanshoop.

There's also a private bus between Mariental and Walvis Bay which leaves every Monday and drops off supplies to remote farms and stores along the way. It stops in Maltahöhe and Solitaire, sometimes travelling via Büllsport and sometimes via Sesriem.

Train The southbound rail services from Windhoek to Keetmanshoop and De Aar (South Africa) pass Mariental at 5.04 pm Wednesday (for De Aar) and daily except Sunday at 12.37 am (for Keetmanshoop only). Northbound, the Keetmanshoop train passes at 11.10 pm daily except Saturday and the De Aar train passes at 3.34 am Saturday. The economy/sleeper-class Windhoek fare is US$4/10 from Monday to Thursday and US$8/22 from Friday to Sunday. For Keetmanshoop, subtract about 30% of those fares.

HARDAP DAM RECREATION RESORT & GAME PARK

If there is a reason to visit Mariental, it's Hardap Dam, which lies 15 km north of town. The idea of siting a dam on the upper Fish River was discussed as far back as 1897 by a German professor, but the idea waited 63 years for construction to begin. The dam wall is 39 metres high and holds back a lake 25 sq km in area. The name is a Nama word meaning 'nipple', after the conical hills topped by dolerite knobs which are typical of the area.

The big attraction for most local holiday-makers is the lake itself, which breaks up the arid plateau landscape and provides a venue for anglers after carp, barbel, mudfish and blue karpers. Fishing licences are available at the park office, which is open from sunrise to 1 pm and 2 pm to sunset. It also has an information centre and an aquarium full of bored fish from the lake – unfortunately, there are no labels identifying the species. There is also a research establishment where MET is studying the feasibility of fish breeding and commercial exploitation.

Entry permits cost US$1.50 per person and US$1.50 per car, and entitle you to unlimited use of the splendid swimming pool and picnic sites. Despite the name 'Recreation Resort', swimming in the lake is not allowed. You can pick up a map from the park office, but the map in this book will probably be sufficient.

Visitor Centre

One of Hardap's most appealing features is its unobtrusive visitor centre, perched on a crag overlooking the dam. However, the setting it overlooks is one of little vegetation, sombre colours and unsettlingly low water levels, so the place has a rather austere feel.

Hardap Dam Game Park

The 80 km of gravel roads west of the dam will take you through the 25,000-hectare Hardap Dam Game Park, which harbours antelopes, zebras, birds and small animals. Because there are few dangerous animals,

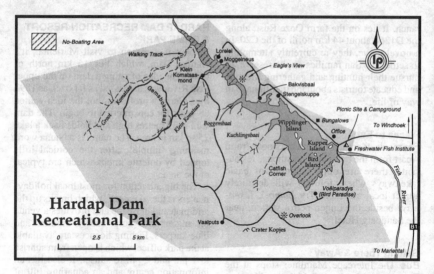

Hardap Dam
Recreational Park

you can walk wherever you like. In the northern end of the reserve is a 15-km loop walk, with a short cut across the middle which makes it into a nine-km loop. However, it's not well marked, so pay close attention to where you're going.

The vegetation is a combination of flat shrub savanna plains with stands of camelthorn, wild green-hair trees and buffalo thorn. You're bound to see kudu, gemsboks, springboks, ostriches and mountain zebras, and might even catch sight of an eland or red hartebeest. On the rocky kopjes, you're likely to see dassies and perhaps klipspringers. At the northern end of the park live three black rhinos, which were translocated from Damaraland in 1990. The terrain is also ideal for cheetahs, and indeed, there was once a large cheetah population at Hardap Dam. However, the rich pickings caused a cheetah explosion. The antelope population couldn't take the strain, so MET relocated all the cheetahs to other parks (which seems a bit drastic – they could have left a few).

The reserve also provides habitat for over 260 bird species and the reservoir area is now home to prolific birdlife: flamingoes, fish eagles, pelicans, spoonbills, Goliath herons and many varieties of migrants and bush dwellers. However, you may want to ignore the sign reading 'Voëlparadys' (Bird Paradise), which indicates a stand of dead camelthorn trees where a colony of white-breasted cormorants took up residence immediately after the dam filled up in 1963. When the water levels receded, the birds lost interest and went off in search of a new paradise.

Places to Stay & Eat

Camping at Hardap Dam costs US$7 per site, and two/five-bed bungalows cost US$17/35. There's also a bland 10-bed dormitory bungalow which costs US$17 for the whole thing and some adjacent two-bed rooms for just US$10. Other amenities include a shop, restaurant, kiosk, swimming pool and petrol station. The restaurant, which is built on a terrace overlooking the lake, certainly has a wonderful view, as does the pool, which sits on a cliff top.

You'll find picnic areas at the rest camp, at Lorelei near the north-western end of the lake and at Crater Hills, near the southern boundary of the wildlife reserve.

Getting There & Away

The Hardap Dam turn-off from the B1 is signposted 15 km north of Mariental. From there, it's six km to the entrance gate. There's no public transport to the site, but you could conceivably get off the Intercape Mainliner bus or minibus at the B1 turn-off and walk the final six km to the resort; just take plenty of water. Between sunrise and sunset, you can walk anywhere in the reserve, but camping is allowed only at the rest camp.

STAMPRIET & GOCHAS

The small settlement of Stampriet, accessed via an east turning 10 km north of Mariental, lies in the heart of a fruit and vegetable growing area. The numerous springs in the area also attract an inordinate amount of birdlife to this otherwise desert area.

At the farm Gross Nabas, about 25 km south of Stampriet on the C15, a monument commemorates a battle fought from 2 to 4 January 1905 between colonial forces led by Lieutenant von Burgsdorff and the Nama resistance under Hendrik Witbooi. The Germans were defeated with heavy losses.

The small town of Gochas (Nama for 'many candle-thorn trees') lies beside the Auob River 53 km further south, and is also of historical interest. South-west of the village on the C18, towards Witbooisvlei, are two more war monuments. These commemorate battles on 3 and 5 January 1905, which took place on the farm Haruchas (☎ 1121) between the German troops of General Stuhlmann and the Nama under Simon Koper. Phone in advance if you want to have a look around. In Gochas itself is a cemetery containing the graves of numerous German soldiers killed in these and other turn-of-the-century battles and skirmishes with the Nama resistance.

Places to Stay & Eat

The only accommodation in the area is the basic *Gochas Hotel* (☎ 44), which also has an equally basic restaurant – and of course a bar. Single/double rooms cost U$20/37.

On the Sandheuwel Game Ranch 170 km south-east of Gochas, is the up-market *Kalahari Game Lodge* (☎ (06662) 3112), PO Box 22, Koës, which is set beside the dry bed of the Auob River. Accommodation is in A-frame chalets with en suite facilities, and there's a restaurant, general shop, bottle store, curio shop, swimming pool and petrol station – all surrounded by the Kalahari dunes. Because it lies right on the South African border opposite Mata Mata camp in Kalahari Gemsbok National Park, the wildlife viewing on this protected ranch is similar to that in the park. Unfortunately, the Mata Mata border gate is now closed, so to reach the national park drivers must take the long way 'round the barn through Aroab and Twee Rivieren.

GIBEON

The former Rhenish mission station of Gibeon, 91 km south of Mariental and nine km west of the B1, was founded by missionary Knauer beside the spring Gorego-re-abes ('where zebras drink') 1863. The mission was named for the biblical character mentioned in the Old Testament book of Joshua.

In 1894, a German garrison was established in Gibeon on orders from Major Theodore Leutwein. While a fort was under construction, the troops were housed in the mission church.

There was a brief attempt at diamond exploration in the early 1900s, but because of a particularly fierce battle which took place there on 27 April 1915, Gibeon's name will always be associated with the Germans' loss of Southern Namibia to the South African Defence Forces. You can see the results of this battle by visiting the graveyard beside the Gibeon railway station, which lies immediately east of the B1 and 10 km east of the settlement of Gibeon.

Today, Gibeon is also known as the source of the meteorites which grace the Post Street Mall in Windhoek. These 33 fragments of space rock – along with at least 44 more, which have been found within a 2500-sq km area around Gibeon – fell to earth in a single meteor shower sometime in the dim and distant past. Those found so far are at least 90% iron.

MUKUROB

Once a dramatically balanced stone pinnacle, Mukurob collapsed on 8 December 1988, shortly after seismic waves from the big Armenian earthquake of 7 December registered in Windhoek, and is now just another fallen attraction. However, even the 1994 edition of the official government map, *The Republic of Namibia*, still bears a picture of it prior to the big collapse.

The Nama name of this heap of rubble means 'look at the neck', probably in reference to the spindly pedestal on which it once rested. Afrikaners called it the Vingerklip, or Finger Rock, and Anglo-Namibians knew it as the Finger of God. When the rock came crashing down, White Namibians saw the event as a sign of divine discontent with the idea of Namibian independence. Blacks countered with the question of why God would have been holding up a single finger *until* the prospect of Namibian independence!

What is left of the Mukurob, which is just a 1.5-metre-wide neck of rock on a pedestal, once supported the 12-metre-high, 500 tonne rock head, bits of which still lie nearby. The feature was actually a remnant of a sandstone formation which was shot through with vertical intrusions of softer rock material. When that material eroded away, most of the remaining sandstone blocks collapsed, but this particular one remained balanced there for at least 50,000 years.

Getting There & Away

To reach Mukurob, turn east onto the D1066 from the B1 about two km south of Asab. After 12 km, turn right on the D620 and continue another 10 km to the site.

BRUKKAROS

The extinct two-km wide volcanic crater, Brukkaros, can be plainly seen from the B1 between Mariental and Keetmanshoop. The name is thought to be a combination of the Afrikaans words *broek* or 'trousers' and *karos* or 'leather apron', in deference to the mountain's Nama name, Geitsigubeb, which means the same thing. It stems from the feature's resemblance to a traditional article of clothing worn by Nama women.

From the car park there's a path which was laid out in the 1930s when the Smithsonian Institute developed a sunspot-research post on the crater's western rim to take advantage of the phenomenally clear air. From the car park, it's a 3.5-km half-hour walk to the crater's southern edge. At that point, the path enters the crater and heads up to the abandoned research station. To get there will take another 1½ hours.

Camping is permitted anywhere around the crater and the clear night skies make for a magical experience, but there's no water available so bring all you'll need.

History

Brukkaros was formed some 80 million years ago when a magma pipe came into contact with groundwater around one km below the earth's surface. The superheated water vaporised and expanded, causing the surface to swell into a bulge 10 km across and nearly 500 metres high. This left space for more magma to intrude, which in turn heated more water and caused further swelling. It reached the stage where something had to give – and something did. The resulting explosion caused the surface material and all the water to collapse into the magma pipe, causing another explosion. This set off a series of subsequent explosions which ejected material from deep in the earth and deposited it around the gaping crater, forming a rim.

Before long, a lake and a number of attendant hot springs formed in the crater itself. Subsequent erosion washed the rim into the crater lake, while the springs carried quartz deposits and other minerals to the surface, providing an adhesive cement which solidified the volcanically displaced sediments. Over the following millions of years, erosion removed all the surrounding material, leaving the 650-metre-high resistant plug we see today.

Getting There & Away

From Tses, 80 km north of Keetmanshoop,

you'll see Brukkaros rising about 35 km west of the B1. To get there, follow the C98 west for 40 km and then turn north on the D3904. From there it's 18 km to the car park.

KEETMANSHOOP

Keetmanshoop, with 15,000 people, is the main crossroads of southern Namibia and a centre for the karakul wool industry. It has more petrol stations per capita than any other town in Namibia, which may provide some hints about its main function for travellers.

History

Keetmanshoop was originally a Nama settlement on the banks of the Swartmodder River, with the evocative name of Nugoaes, meaning 'black mud' (as does the Afrikaans word Swartmodder). The present town was founded in April 1866 by Reverend John Schröder of the Rhenish Mission Society and named after the German industrialist and philanthropist Johann Keetmann, who provided funds for the mission.

Schröder's successor, Reverend Thomas Fenchel, constructed the town's first mission station and church and stayed on for 33 years. This church was swept away by muddy black floodwaters in 1890 and five years later, a new one was built. In 1950, it ceased to function as a church and became a hang-out for squatters, who proceeded to vandalise the building. After 10 years of abuse, it was renovated and now houses the town museum. In the same year, Keetmanshoop became the site of a brewery and ice house.

Information

The Southern Tourist Forum information office (☎ 3316; fax 3813) in the municipal building is open Monday to Friday from 7.30 am to 12.30 pm and 2 to 5 pm. On Saturday, it's open from 9 to 11 am. They also sell a

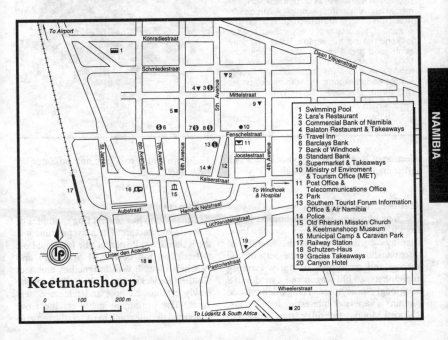

1 Swimming Pool
2 Lara's Restaurant
3 Commercial Bank of Namibia
4 Balaton Restaurant & Takeaways
5 Travel Inn
6 Barclays Bank
7 Bank of Windhoek
8 Standard Bank
9 Supermarket & Takeaways
10 Ministry of Enviroment
   & Tourism Office (MET)
11 Post Office &
   Telecommunications Office
12 Park
13 Southern Tourist Forum Information
   Office & Air Namibia
14 Police
15 Old Rhenish Mission Church
   & Keetmanshoop Museum
16 Municipal Camp & Caravan Park
17 Railway Station
18 Schutzen-Haus
19 Gracias Takeaways
20 Canyon Hotel

Keetmanshoop

0   100   200 m

NAMIBIA

Karakul Sheep

Around the southern and eastern borders of Namibia, you'll undoubtedly notice the karakul sheep, scraggy and uninspiring goat-like creatures which have come to be known as Namibia's 'black gold'. The hardy karakul sheep, which was first bred for its pelts in central Asia, is able to survive in harsh arid conditions.

The first karakul sheep – two rams and 10 ewes – were imported to German South West Africa in 1907, and two years, later, a further 22 rams and 252 ewes arrived. By the start of WWI, their success at breeding in the new country was well illustrated by sheer numbers: the country had a total of 350 rams and nearly 850 ewes, as well as over 20,000 mixed breed sheep. After the war, a breeding and experimental station was established and it was found that the presence of karakul sheep actually improved land quality. Their grazing habits stimulated the growth of new plants and other plant material trodden into the ground by their hooves helped to prevent surface erosion of the soil.

By the early 1990s, 2500 breeders were producing five million pelts annually and the national breeding herd numbered well over a million purebreds. However, numbers are unstable due to intermittent drought conditions, which cause herd sizes to drastically diminish and during the dry spell of the past several years, the numbers have plummeted.

Most karakul sheep are black, but there are also grey, white, brown and spotted individuals. Today the industry is centered on Keetmanshoop, Maltehöhe and Dordabis. Some of the sheep go for mutton, and the wool is the basis for Namibia's thriving textile industry, but it's the karakul pelts which are renowned. Although the central Asian republics and Afghanistan produce larger quantities, the quality of the Namibian pelts is reckoned to be the world's finest and they fetch good prices on the triennual pelt auctions held in Frankfurt. Namibian karakul forms the basis for the country's luxury leather-goods exports and is marketed under the name *Swakara* (South West African Karakul). ■

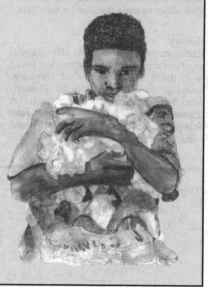

selection of Keetmanshoop postcards, which will someday be collectors' items.

Keetmanshoop Museum

The free museum, which is housed in the 1895 Rhenish mission church, merits a look. Displays concentrate on the history of Keetmanshoop and there are lots of old photos and examples of early farming implements, an old wagon and a model of a traditional Nama home. The garden outside contains a variety of interesting local plants. It's open Monday to Friday from 7.30 am to 12.30 pm and 2 to 5 pm; and on Saturday from 9 to 11 am.

Old Post Office

Keetmanshoop has several fine examples of colonial architecture. The most prominent is the Kaiserliches Postampt (the Imperial Post Office), on the corner of 5th Laan and Fenchelstrasse. It was designed by architect Gottlieb Redecker and built in 1910 for the newly established post and telegraph services. The prominent gable on the front supported the telegraph mast and the remainder of the building housed postal officials, who at that stage still made deliveries by camel. It now houses Air Namibia and the tourist information office.

Organised Tours

Mr Wynand Erasmus of Canyon Tours (☎ 2095; after hours ☎ 2119) organises day tours to Fish River Canyon (Hobas) for US$52 per person, including lunch. He also does excursions to Gallap Ost Karakul Farm, Lüderitz, Ai-Ais and the Kokerboomwoud. You're welcome to phone any time. He currently intends to set up a budget hostel for backpackers; phone and check on the progress of this plan.

Gondwana Tours at the Canyon Hotel also organises guided tours around southern Namibia, but they charge considerably more.

Places to Stay

The large bougainvillea-decked *Municipal Camp & Caravan Park* charges US$1.50 per vehicle, US$2 for a caravan and US$1.50 per person. The coin-operated laundry will probably be a welcome sight, but you must bring your own washing powder.

There's also the plush new *Lafenis Rest Camp*, five km south along the road to South Africa. Fully equipped two/four-bed bungalows cost US$28/43. Guests have use of the laundry and hot showers, and they also offer a swimming pool, horse-riding and mini-golf.

Whatever the tourist office may say, you can also stay at the Kokerboomwoud on the *Gariganus Farm* (☎ (0638) 11302 or 11303) run by Coenie Nolte. Camping costs US$3 per person and single/double rooms cost US$25/38.

Other inexpensive accommodation is available through the Community Development Project run by Mrs Esau (☎ 3454) at Gate 12, Schmeide St, PO Box 1381, Keetmanshoop. Dormitory beds cost US$7 and rooms are US$14 per person. For bed and breakfast accommodation, there's Mr & Mrs Gessert (☎ 8832 or 3892) at 138 13th Ave, PO Box 680, Keetmanshoop. They

have six rooms, all with private facilities, for US$25/41 for a single/double.

There are also two hotels. The adequate *Travel Inn* (☎ 3344; fax 2138) on 6th Ave has single/double air-con rooms for US$41/57, including breakfast and a free carwash. Budget single rooms cost US$28 and family rooms for up to four people are US$77. Among the amenities are a restaurant, beer garden, laundry and fax service.

The *Canyon Hotel* (☎ 3892; fax 3714), which is a bit nicer and more popular, has rooms from US$46/72. The affiliated tour company, Gondwana Tours, organises day trips to the Kokerboomwoud, Lüderitz and Fish River Canyon.

The *Schutzen-Haus*, 200 metres south of the Municipal Camp & Caravan Park, has simple double rooms with shower and toilet for US$30.

Places to Eat

Good meals are available at *Lara's Restaurant*, a popular place with strange décor – which plays equally strange music – on the corner of 5th Ave and Schmeide St. You'll also find basic meals at the *Schutzen-Haus*, a German-style pub and restaurant 200 metres south of the Municipal camp site. The bar portion boasts an unusual billiards table and there's also informal accommodation. Another good place is the Hungarian-oriented *Balaton Restaurant & Takeaways* (☎ 2539), which is open for breakfast, lunch and dinner.

For coffee or snacks, the coffee shop at the Canyon Hotel stays open from 9 am to 7 pm. The hotel restaurant is open daily from 6.30 to 9 am, 12.30 to 2 pm and 7 to 10 pm. The restaurant at the Travel Inn is generally more expensive, but not any better quality.

On the corner of 4th Ave and Mittel St there's a supermarket and takeaway that's open late. Another decent takeaway outlet is *Gracias Takeaways* on Pastorie St.

Entertainment

Keetmanshoop isn't a thriving entertainment centre, but there is a 50-metre swimming pool on Konradie St at the north-west end of

NAMIBIA

town. It's open weekdays from 10 am to 7 pm.

Getting There & Away

Air Keetmanshoop's J G van der Wath Airport lies north-west of town on the D609. Air Namibia flies from Windhoek to Cape Town via Keetmanshoop on Monday, Thursday and Saturday morning. On Monday and Thursday, they return to Keetmanshoop in the afternoon and continue back to Windhoek. The one-way fare between Keetmanshoop and Windhoek is around US$100.

Bus The Intercape Mainliner bus between Windhoek and Cape Town passes through Keetmanshoop at midnight on Monday, Wednesday, Friday and Sunday night southbound and at 1.45 am on Tuesday, Thursday, Saturday and Sunday northbound. The fare to or from Windhoek is US$30; the bus stops at the Du Toit BP petrol station in Keetmanshoop. Minibuses also do the run between Windhoek and Keetmanshoop; they leave when full from the terminal north of the Wernhill Park Centre in Windhoek.

Train Trains run daily except Saturday between Windhoek and Keetmanshoop, departing at 6.30 pm in either direction and arriving between 5 and 6 am the following day. The trains between Windhoek and De Aar, South Africa, also pass through Keetmanshoop. They leave Windhoek on Wednesday at 11 am and arrive in Keetmanshoop at 9.46 pm. From Keetmanshoop, they leave on Friday at 10.17 pm and arrive in Windhoek at 10.10 am the following day. The economy/sleeper-class fares in either direction are US$5/15 from Monday to Wednesday and US$11/33 on Friday and Sunday.

Hitching Hitching is fairly easy on the B1 between Keetmanshoop and Windhoek or Grünau but there's less traffic between Keetmanshoop and Lüderitz. Hitchers bound for Fish River Canyon will have the most luck on the route to Ai-Ais, which turns west 30 km south of Grünau.

AROUND KEETMANSHOOP
Kokerboom Forest & Giant's Playground

Namibia's largest stand of the kokerbooms or quivertrees *(Aloe dichotoma)* (see below) lies at Kokerboomwoud, on the Gariganus Farm, 14 km north-east of town. Day admission and access to the picnic facilities is US$3 per vehicle plus US$1.50 per person.

Entry to the Kokerboomwoud also permits access to the Giant's Playground, a bizarre natural rock garden five km away. The odd black formations were created by igneous intrusions into overlying sediments around 170 million years ago. When the surrounding sediments eroded away, all that remained was the more resistant *ysterklip* or 'iron rock' (which contained no iron at all – only basalt).

Camping and accommodation are available at Gariganus Farm; see Places to Stay under Keetmanshoop.

Gellap Ost Karakul Farm

The 13,700-hectare Gellap Ost Karakul Farm (☎ 11503) was first established in the 1930s as an experimental farm for improving the quality of karakul wool. Unlike other

---

Kokerbooms

Kokerbooms *(Aloe dichotoma)* or 'quiver trees' are widespread throughout southern Namibia and north-western South Africa. They are in fact aloes and can grow to heights of eight metres. The name is derived from the lightweight branches, which were formerly used as quivers by San hunters. They removed the branches' fibrous heart, leaving a strong, hollow tube.

Slow-growing kokerbooms grow mainly on rocky plains or slopes, storing water in their succulent leaves and fibrous trunk and branches. Water loss through transpiration is prevented by a waxy coating on the leaves and branches. In June and July, their yellow blooms appear, lending bright spots of colour to the desert. ■

wool, which is sheared from the sheep, the karakul wool is taken from newborn lambs in the form of pelts, which of course requires the lambs to be slaughtered. When prices are low, the lambs are sold for mutton.

The farm is open to the public by prior telephone arrangement Monday to Friday from 10 am to noon. To get there, follow the D609 north-west from Keetmanshoop towards the airport and after 15 km turn left at the signposted turning to the farm.

Naute Dam

This large dam on the Löwen River, surrounded by low truncated hills, attracts large numbers of birds and is scheduled to eventually become an official recreation area and wildlife reserve. As yet, it's used mainly as a picnic site, although informal camping is permitted on the southern shore. To get there, drive 30 km west of Keetmanshoop on the B4 and turn south on the D545. After about 20 km, you'll see the dam.

Naiams Fort

About 13 km west of Seeheim (the B4 road junction for access to the northern end of Fish River Canyon) is the farm Naiams, where there's a signpost indicating a 15-minute walk down to the remains of a 1906 German fort. The purpose of the fort was to prevent Nama attacks on travellers and freight using the Lüderitz route.

Singing Rocks

On the farm Rooipunt 50 km south of the B2 is one of Namibia's strangest national monuments. The main attraction is the Singing Rock, a large flat black rock with artificial white holes drilled into it. When it's struck sharply with a stone, it produces different notes, like a marimba. Nobody knows who made it, but it's thought to have been fashioned specifically for use as a musical instrument. The farm also has some magnificent rock engravings.

From the railway station at Goageb (106 km west of Keetmanshoop) turn south on the D459 and continue for 50 km to the farm Rooipunt. To arrange a visit to the Singing Rock and the ancient engravings, which are difficult to find without help, phone the farmer, Mr de Vries (☎ (06362) 81). There's a small charge but it's worth it, and Mr de Vries is full of interesting stories about the area.

BETHANIE

Bethanie, which is one of the oldest settlements in Namibia, was founded in 1814 by the London Missionary Society. Oddly enough, the first missionary posted there, Reverend Heinrich Schmelen, wasn't English but German. Apparently London had experienced a staffing crisis and recruited missionaries trained in Berlin. The settlement was first called Klipfontein ('rock spring' in Afrikaans), but was later renamed Bethanien (later Anglicised to Bethanie) after the suburb of Jerusalem.

After seven years of operation, the mission was abandoned when tribal squabbling rendered it unviable. Schmelen attempted to revive the mission several times, but he was thwarted by drought and in 1828 he left. Twelve years later, Bethanie was handed over to the Rhenish Missionary Society.

Things to See

Schmelen's original 1914 mission station, now known as Schmelenhaus, occupied a one-storey cottage. It was burned when he left Bethanie in 1828, but was rebuilt in 1842 by the first Rhenish missionary, Reverend Hans Knudsen. The building now sits on the grounds of the Evangelical Lutheran Church and houses a museum outlining the history of the mission in old photographs. It's normally left unlocked during the day, but otherwise, there'll be a notice on the door telling you where to pick up a key.

Other historical buildings include another former church, which was built in 1859 by missionary Hermann Kreft. It once had two towers, but they started to collapse and were removed. Earlier in this century it served as a school, but is now becoming dilapidated. It's currently scheduled for renovation, complete with the original towers.

NAMIBIA

Also, take a quick look at the 1883 home of Captain Joseph Fredericks, the Nama chief who signed a treaty with the representatives of Adolf Lüderitz on 1 May 1883 for the sale of Angra Pequena, which is now Lüderitz. In this house in October of the following year, Captain Fredericks and the German Consul General, Dr Friedrich Nachtigal, signed a treaty of German protection over the entire territory.

Places to Stay & Eat
The basic *Bethanie Hotel* (☎ 13) has six rooms and charges US$21/34. You can also eat there. Barring that, you can stay at the enigmatically named *Bethanie Outfitters & Motors* (☎ 7, after hours 2; fax 87), which has camping for US$7 per vehicle up to five people. Room accommodation costs US$17/21 for a single/double with bed and breakfast.

Getting There & Away
Bethanie lies on the C14 about 30 km north of the B4. The turn-off is signposted 140 km west of Keetmanshoop. There's no public transport.

DUWISIB CASTLE
Duwisib Castle, a curious baroque structure about 70 km south of Maltahöhe, was built in 1909 by Baron Captain Hans-Heinrich von Wolf. Von Wolf, who came from Dresden and served in the German-Nama war, was descended from Saxon nobility. After the war, he returned to Dresden and married Jayta Humprhies, the daughter of the US consul, and together, they returned to German South West Africa. At this stage, Von Wolf commissioned architect Willie Sander to design a home that would reflect his commitment to the German military cause and closely resemble the Schutztruppe forts of Namutoni, Gibeon and Windhoek.

Although the stone came from a nearby quarry, much of the raw material for the home was imported from Germany, and it required 20 ox-wagons to transport it across the 640 km of desert from Lüderitz. Artesans and masons were hired from as far away as Ireland, Denmark, Sweden and Italy. The result was a U-shaped castle with 22 rooms, suitably fortified and decorated with family portraits and military paraphernalia. Rather than windows, most rooms have only embrasures, emphasising Von Wolf's apparent obsession with security.

In August 1914, the Von Wolfs sailed for England in search of stud horses for their stables, but when WWI broke out, their ship was diverted to Rio de Janeiro. Jayta, who was an US citizen, successfully found a passage on a Dutch ship to Holland, but her German husband had to travel as a stowaway. Eventually, they reached Germany, where Von Wolf rejoined the army. In 1916, however, he was killed at the Battle of the Somme in France and Jayta settled in Switzerland and sold the castle to a Swedish family, which in turn sold it to a company called Duwisib Pty Ltd in 1937.

Duwisib Castle and the surrounding 50 hectares were transferred to the state in the late 1970s. The castle was opened to the public in 1991 and now houses an impressive collection of 18th and 19th-century antiques and armour. It's open 8 am to 1 pm and 2 to 5 pm daily. Admission costs US$1.50 and official guided tours are available.

Places to Stay
You can camp at the MET camp sites on the castle grounds for US$6 per site. Each site accommodates up to eight people.

At *Farm Duwisib* (☎ 5304), near the castle, you'll find a shop, takeway restaurant, swimming pool, picnic sites and camp sites with basic facilities. Self-catering bungalows accommodating two/four people cost US$23/39. Camping costs US$6 per site.

Getting There & Away
There's no public transport to remote Duwisib Castle. Coming from Helmeringhausen, drive north on the C14 for 62 km and turn north-west onto the D831. After 27 km, turn west on the D826 and continue for 15 km to the castle.

MALTAHÖHE

Maltahöhe, in the heart of a karakul ranching area, has little to recommend it except an excellent little hotel. Thanks to its convenient location along the back route between Lüderitz and Namib-Naukluft Park, the surrounding area supports a growing number of guest farms and private rest camps.

The town's name means 'Malta's heights', in honour of Malta von Burgsdorff, the wife of Lieutenant von Burgsdorff. The lieutenant was made commander (or *bezirksamt*) of the Gibeon district after the German-Nama war. The only sites of interest today are graveyards. The one just east of town contains many graves of Schutztruppe soldiers killed in the wars between the colonial forces and Hendrik Witbooi. At the farm Nomtsas, 55 km north of Maltahöhe, are the graves of the family and neighbours of Ernst Hermann, who were killed in 1904 by Hendrik Witbooi's rebels.

Places to Stay & Eat

The unguarded camp site in Maltahöhe is quite run-down and should be used only in an emergency. The toilets are especially bad.

The friendly and comfortable *Maltahöhe Hotel* (☎ 13; fax 133), PO Box 20, Maltahöhe, run by Manfred and Gerda Schreiner, has single/double accommodation for US$19/27. It has restaurant and bar, which are open in the evening, and the owner organises inexpensive day trips to Sossusvlei in his 4WD. In 1991, it won Namibia's Hotel of the Year award.

Two km south of Maltahöhe on the C14 you'll find the pleasant *Daweb Guest Farm* (☎ 1840; fax 66), run by Rolf and Rosemarie Kirsten; the Nama name means 'tamarisk'. Singles/doubles with private facilities in the lovely Cape Dutch-style farmhouse costs US$30 per person with bed and breakfast and US$40 with full board. Guests will have the opportunity to gain insight into the Namibian cattle-ranching business, or they can organise guided walking and 4WD expeditions through the surrounding countryside.

For something a bit unusual, you can opt for the *Namseb Rest Camp* (☎ 166; fax 157),

PO Box 76, Maltahöhe, on a private game ranch run by ostrich farmers Jan and Piens Bruwer. It lies at the edge of the Schwarzrand Range, down a back road about five km north-west of Maltahöhe, and is an excellent place to get the scoop on ostrich farming. The accommodation is set on a rise, affording a good view. Singles/doubles cost US$23/34 and double chalets are US$45. Meals are available in the restaurant and yes, they do serve ostrich.

The family oriented *Guest Farm Burgsdorf* (☎ 1330; fax 141), 25 km south of Maltahöhe, is a working cattle and goat ranch run by Walter and Lindi Kirsten. There are several archaeological sites on the farm and the diverse landscape offers plenty of scope for walks and drives. They charge US$41 per person for bed and breakfast and US$55 with full board. Tours to Duwisib Castle, Sesriem and Sossusvlei are available with advance notice.

Midway between Maltahöhe and Sesriem, one km east of the C36, is the *Hammerstein Rest Camp* (☎ 5111), run by Anton and Gerty Porteus. It has several two/four-bed self-catering units for US$33/46. With full board, the price is US$41 per person.

Getting There & Away

The private bus between Mariental and Walvis Bay passes through Maltahöhe on Monday westbound and Tuesday eastbound. It sometimes travels through Büllsport and sometimes via Sesriem.

HELMERINGHAUSEN

The tiny settlement of Helmeringhausen is little more than a homestead, hotel and petrol station, which has been the property of the Hester family since 1919.

Agricultural Museum

The highlight here is the idiosyncratic Agricultural Museum, which was established in 1984 by the Helmeringhausen Farming Association. At first, it appears to be a pile of discarded junk, but on closer inspection, becomes quite interesting. It displays old furniture and farming implements – wagons,

NAMIBIA

farm machinery, tools and so on – collected from farms all around the area. You can also see an antique fire engine from Lüderitz. The museum is open daily and admission is free. Pick up a key from the hotel next door.

Mooifontein

At the end of the 19th century, nearby Mooifontein ('beautiful spring'), 21 km south-east of Helmeringhausen, was the site of a German garrison. The current farmhouse is a rebuilt version of the original barracks, which was prefabricated in Germany in 1899 and transferred to this site beside the Konkiep River. You can also visit the interesting semi-circular cemetery for German soldiers who died during the German-Nama war, which lasted from 1903 to 1907.

Places to Stay

The friendly *Helmeringhausen Hotel* (☎ 7), PO Box 21, Helmeringhausen, run by Heinz and Altna Vollertson, has bed and breakfast for US$21 per person. Full board costs US$30 per person. The food is excellent, the beer is always cold and they keep a well-stocked cellar. However, anyone who's fond of game meat may feel uncomfortable in the restaurant, which is full of accusing stuffed animal heads, including a giraffe that still has half its neck. They also run day tours to the graveyard at Mooifontein and to nearby rock paintings.

The two-star *Sinclair Guest Farm* (☎ 6503), PO Box 19, Helmeringhausen, run by Gunther and Hannelore Hoffmann, lies 65 km west of Helmeringhausen on the D407. The surrounding property was originally purchased from a Nama chief by two Scottish settlers in the 1870s, because they wanted access to the copper which the Nama had been mining for centuries. Legend has it that the price was two wheelbarrows full of brandy. Later, they set up a farm and sold it to the grandparents of the present owners. Guests can now enjoy organised walks, drives and excursions to the ancient copper workings three km from the farmhouse. The five rooms cost a very reasonable US$41 per person, with full board.

A few km north-west of town, seven km off the C14, is the *Guest Farm Dabis* (☎ 6820), PO Box 15, Helmeringhausen, on a karakul farm run by Jo and Heidi Gaugler. Accommodation is in basic but comfortable rooms which cost US$60/105 for a single/double with full board and all activities. Dinner, bed and breakfast costs just US$48/82. Meals include home-baked bread and eggs, meat and vegetables produced on the farm. The activities feature hiking, wildlife viewing, sunset drives and instruction on the day to day workings of a karakul farm. The ruddy landscape around the ranch is quite fascinating.

The South Coast

The South Coast area includes the town of Lüderitz, which is rich in colonial architecture, the Sperrgebiet (forbidden Diamond Area) and the rest of the southern Namib Desert.

AUS

Aus, whose curious name means 'out' in German, is a tidy and tranquil little place 125 km east of Lüderitz. After the Germans surrendered to the South African forces at Otavi on 9 July 1915, Aus became one of two internment camps for German military personnel. Military police and officers were sent to Okanjanje in the north and the non-commissioned officers went to Aus.

Soon, Aus was home to 1552 prisoners and 600 South African guards, who were housed in tents and living in poor conditions and suffering from the extreme desert temperatures. As a result, the ever resourceful inmates turned to brickmaking and constructed their own houses, then sold the excess bricks to the guards for 10 shillings per 1000. The houses weren't opulent by any means – roofs were tiled with unrolled food tins – but they did provide some protection from the elements. The prisoners also built several wood stoves, and eventually the

South Africans sunk bore holes to provide water and built barracks for the guards.

After the Treaty of Versailles, the camp was dismantled and by May 1919 it was closed. Virtually nothing remains today, although some attempt has been made to reconstruct one of the brick houses. The site lies four km east of the village, down a gravel road, then right; there's now a national monument plaque commemorating the camp.

If you're interested in knowing more about this unusual setup – and you can decipher Afrikaans – the book *Aus 1915-1919* contains a map and covers the history and background information. You can pick up a copy at the bookshop in Lüderitz.

Places to Stay

Part of the appeal of rustic-looking Aus is the friendly and quaint *Bahnhof Hotel* (☎ 44),

where comfortable single/double rooms, which have the same musty fuel oil smell as your grandparents' living room, cost US$17/27. Larger rooms with en suite facilities are US$20/35. There's also a good bar and restaurant.

Beneath the grand and desolate Tirasberge Mountains north of Aus is the *Namib Desert Lodge* (☎ 6640), PO Box 19, Aus, a German-oriented guest farm run by Renate and Walter Theile. The landscape is truly astounding – there's nothing else like it in Namibia. Singles/doubles with full board is reasonable at US$40 per person. Take the C13 north for 55 km, then turn west on the D707 and continue for 60 km to the farm.

Getting There & Away

If you've come as far as Aus, chances are you're headed for Lüderitz, and the railways

---

Feral Desert Horses

On the desert plains west of Aus live the world's only wild desert-dwelling horses. There are several theories about the origins of these eccentric equines. Some theorise that they are descended from German Schutztruppe cavalry horses abandoned during the South African invasion in 1915. Others claim that they were brought in by Nama raiders moving north from beyond the Orange River. Another tale asserts that they're descended from a load of shipwrecked horses en route from Europe to Australia. Others maintain they're descended from the stud stock of Baron Captain Hans-Heinrich von Wolf, the owner of Duwisib Castle, who set off for Germany in search of more horses but was killed in battle in France and never returned to Namibia.

These horses, whose boney and scruffy appearance belies their probable high-bred ancestry and apparent adaptation to the harsh conditions, are protected inside Diamond Area One and in years of good rains, they grow fat and their numbers increase. At present, the population fluctuates between 150 and 160, but there have never been more than 280 individuals. Their only source of water is Gorub Pan, which is fed by an artificial bore hole.

If not for the efforts of CD security officer Jan Coetzer, they would probably have been wiped out long ago. He recognised that they were clearly horses of high breeding and managed to secure funding to install the bore hole at Garub. At one stage, MET considered taming the horses for use on patrols in Etosha National Park, but nothing ever came of it. There have also been calls to exterminate them, by individuals citing possible damage to the desert environment or disruptions of gemsbok herds. So far, however, their potential for tourism has swept aside all counter arguments and in Europe, various wildlife organisations have organised fund-raising drives to benefit the horses, so at the moment, anyway, their future appears to be secure.

The horses may also be valuable for scientific purposes. The region is so dry that the horses are relatively free of diseases and parasites, and having been isolated for so long, they're unlikely to have any immunity to disease, making them ideal for immunity studies. Because they urinate less and are smaller than their supposed ancestors, they're able to go without water for up to five days. These adaptations may be valuable in helping science understand how animals cope with changing climatic conditions.

There's now a hide and a water hole where people can view the horses, as well as a small informative display. It lies 100 km east of Lüderitz about 1.5 km north of the highway. ■

bus between Keetmanshoop and Lüderitz will stop in Aus.

The landscape of the southern Namib west of Aus is quite distinct from the flat gravel plains of the north. The pastel-coloured Awasib and Uri-Hauchab ranges rise from a greenish-grey plain though a mist of wind-blown sand and dust, and the effect is somewhere between mesmerising and ethe-real. When driving through this area, be on the lookout for feral desert horses (see the aside), which may be descended from the stud animals bred by Baron von Wolf of Duwisib Castle in the early 1900s.

LÜDERITZ

Lüderitz is a surreal colonial relic – a Bavar-ian village huddling on the barren, windswept coast of the Namib Desert, seem-ingly untouched by the 20th century. The present town has everything you'd expect of a small German town, from delicatessens to coffee shops and Lutheran churches. Here, the South Atlantic is icy but clean, and is home to seals, penguins and other marine life. The desolate beaches are also home to flamingoes and ostriches.

The picturesque port of Lüderitz supports a fleet of crayfish (rock-lobster) boats, which are active during the season from November to April. Other industries include the harvest of seaweed and seagrass, which are mainly exported to Japan, and experimental oyster, mussel and prawn farms.

History

On Christmas Day in 1487, Portuguese nav-igator Bartolomeu Dias and his fleet of three ships sailed down the coast he called the Areias do Inferno ('sands of hell') into Lüderitz Bay, which he named Angra das Voltas ('bay of the turnabouts'), because he could only enter the bay by tacking cau-tiously into the wind. (Later, the bay came to be known – somewhat less creatively – as Angra Pequena, or 'little bay'.) Here he shel-tered from the weather for five days. In July 1488, he returned north from the Cape of Good Hope and, according to Portuguese

seafaring custom, erected a stone cross at Diaz Point near the entrance to the bay.

Apart from a brief Dutch East India Company attempt at trade with the Nama in 1677, it was over 300 years before anything else happened at Lüderitz. In 1793, however, faced with possible rival interest in the area, the Dutch governor of the Cape sent Captain Duminy in his ship *Meermin* to annex Angra Pequena and its surrounding islands.

Over the next half century, whalers began operating in the area and the offshore islands became a rich source of guano. Between 1844 and 1848, over 20 metres of guano were scraped off the most productive islands, amounting to hundreds of thousands of tonnes. The rich pickings attracted more guano collectors than the islands could support and inevitably, clashes occurred.

In the mid-1800s, the British administra-tion in the Cape sent Captain Alexander in his ship, the *Star*, to annex Angra Pequena and all the guano islands for Britain's Cape Colony.

On 9 April 1883, Heinrich Vogelsang, under orders of Bremen merchant Adolf Lüderitz, entered into a treaty with Nama chief Joseph Fredericks. The treaty gave Vogelsang rights to the land within a five-mile radius of Angra Pequena in exchange for £100 sterling and 60 rifles; for an addi-tional £500 and another 60 rifles, he got a 20-mile-wide coastal strip from the Orange River to the 26th parallel.

Later that year, Adolf Lüderitz himself arrived in the area and on his recommenda-tion, on 24 April 1884, the German chancellor Otto von Bismarck designated South West Africa a protectorate of the German Empire. In October 1886, on the verge of bankruptcy, Adolf Lüderitz sailed south to the Orange River in search of busi-ness prospects, but on the way back, he went missing at sea and was never seen again.

In 1904, during the German-Nama war, Lüderitz was used as a prisoner of war camp and two years later the railway line was completed to Keetmanshoop. On 1 November 1909, after the discovery of diamonds in the desert (see following section) had brought

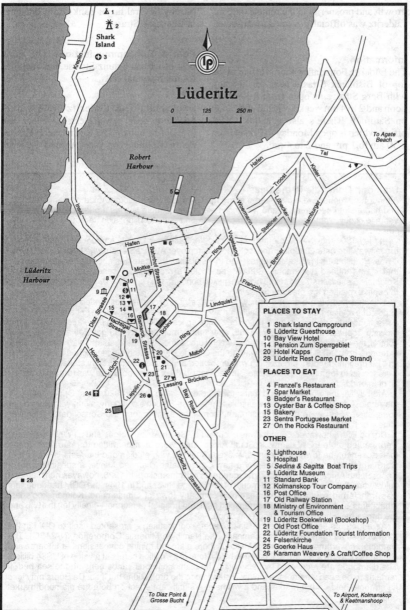

Lüderitz

0   125   250 m

Robert Harbour

Lüderitz Harbour

To Agate Beach

To Diaz Point & Grosse Bucht

To Airport, Kolmanskop & Keetmanshoop

PLACES TO STAY

1   Shark Island Campground
6   Lüderitz Guesthouse
10 Bay View Hotel
14 Pension Zum Sperrgebiet
20 Hotel Kapps
28 Lüderitz Rest Camp (The Strand)

PLACES TO EAT

4   Franzel's Restaurant
7   Spar Market
8   Badger's Restaurant
13 Oyster Bar & Coffee Shop
15 Bakery
23 Sentra Portuguese Market
27 On the Rocks Restaurant

OTHER

2   Lighthouse
3   Hospital
5   *Sedina & Sagitta* Boat Trips
9   Lüderitz Museum
11 Standard Bank
12 Kolmanskop Tour Company
16 Post Office
17 Old Railway Station
18 Ministry of Environment
    & Tourism Office
19 Lüderitz Boekwinkel (Bookshop)
21 Old Post Office
22 Lüderitz Foundation Tourist Information
24 Felsenkirche
25 Goerke Haus
26 Karaman Weavery & Craft/Coffee Shop

NAMIBIA

growth and prosperity to the remote outpost, Lüderitz was officially granted town status.

Information

The Lüderitz Foundation tourist office, at the top of Bismarck Strasse near the junction with Berg Strasse, is open from 8.30 am to noon and 2 to 4 pm weekdays, and until noon on Saturday. There's also a helpful MET office, which is open Monday to Friday from 7.30 am to 1 pm and 2 to 4 pm.

Money Several major banks have branches in Bismarck Strasse.

Post & Telecommunications The main post office, on Schinz Strasse, has facilities for international calls.

Bookshops The Lüderitz Boekwinkel bookshop sells newspapers, jewellery and even a few books. The Kolmanskop Cafeteria in Kolmanskop (see Around Lüderitz

Diamond Dementia in the Desert

Although diamonds were discovered along the Orange River in South Africa as early as 1866, and had also turned up on guano workings taken from offshore islands around Lüderitz, it didn't seem to occur to anyone that the desert sands around Lüderitz might also harbour a bit of crystal carbon.

In May 1908, however, Coloured railway worker Zacharias Lewala found a shiny stone along the railway line near Grasplatz and took it to his employer August Stauch, who knew exactly what it was. Stauch took immediate interest and to his elation, the state geologist Dr Range confirmed that it was indeed a diamond. Stauch applied for a prospecting licence from the Deutsche Koloniale Gesellschaft and set up his own mining concern, the Deutsche Diamanten Gesellschaft, to begin exploiting the presumed wealth.

This sparked off a diamond frenzy, and hordes of prospectors descended upon Lüderitz in hopes of exploiting the fabulous wealth that lay buried in the sands, awaiting to be uncovered. As a result, Lüderitz was soon rolling in money, and service facilities sprang up to accommodate the growing population. In September 1908, after the diamond mania had got well and truly out of control, the German government intervened and proclaimed the Sperrgebiet. This 'forbidden area' extended from 26° S latitude southward to the Orange River mouth, and stretched inland for 100 km. Future independent prospecting was prohibited and those who'd already staked their claims were forced to form mining companies. In February 1909, a Diamond Board was formed to broker all diamond sales.

After WWI, the world diamond market was so depressed that in 1920, Ernst Oppenheimer of the Anglo-American Corporation was able to purchase Stauch's company, along with eight other companies which were still producing, and combined them to form the Consolidated Diamond Mines, or CDM.

During WWI, however, Lüderitz was occupied by South African forces and all White residents were hauled off to POW camps in South Africa. They were later permitted to return, but during their absence, the town had been ransacked. After the war, all diamond interests in the former German territory were taken over by a new Consolidated Diamond Mines, a subsidiary of De Beers South Africa, which set up its headquarters at Kolmanskop. In 1928, however, rich diamond fields were discovered around the mouth of the Orange River and in 1944, the CDM headquarters was transferred south to the purpose-built company town of Oranjemund. Kolmanskop's last inhabitants – which included some transport staff and hospital personnel – finally left in 1956 and the dunes have been encroaching ever since.

As a footnote, in 1994, a new business facet – competition – presented itself to CDM in the form of a small British-Canadian company, the Namibian Minerals Corporation (NAMCO). The Namibian government awarded NAMCO offshore diamond mining concessions at Lüderitz and Hottentots Bay, which were estimated to hold a total of 27 million carats at a value of US$4 billion. The diamonds are recovered by vacuuming the diamondiferous sands beneath the sea bed. It remains to be seen whether the yield will stand up to the projections but if so, De Beers may lose its strangle-hold on the market and it will have a significant effect on both the diamond market and prices. ■

NAMIBIA

later in this section) offers a selection of old German hardback novels as well as modern German pulp fiction.

Dangers & Annoyances Be sure to stay well clear of the Diamond Area 1 or Sperrgebiet ('forbidden area'). The northern boundary is formed by the B4 and extends nearly as far east as Aus. It's patrolled by some fairly ruthless characters, and tresspassers will be prosecuted.

Felsenkirche
The prominent Evangelical Lutheran church, Felsenkirche, dominates Lüderitz from high on Diamond Hill behind the town. Lüderitz petitioned for a church as early as 1906, and thanks to the German-Nama war, the railway and the discovery of diamonds, by 1909 the town's population was sufficient to bear the costs. The church was designed by Albert Bause, who implemented the Victorian influences he'd seen in the Cape. With assistance from private donors in Germany, construction began in late 1911 and was completed the following year. The brilliant stained-glass panel over the altar was donated by Kaiser Wilhelm II himself and the Bible was a gift from his wife.

You can visit Felsenkirche on Monday to Saturday from 6 to 7 pm (from 5 to 6 pm in winter). This is the best time to see the late sun shining directly through the extraordinary stained-glass work over the altar. Every evening a long and hearty spiel on the history of the church and the town is delivered in German to a large audience. If you wish to see it at any other time, make arrangements by phoning Mr Schröder (☎ 2381). Booklets and postcards are sold near the entrance.

Lüderitz Museum
The Lüderitz Museum (☎ 2582) on Diaz Strasse contains information on Lüderitz' history, including information on natural history, local indigenous groups, Bartolomeu Dias and the diamond-mining industry. It's open Monday to Friday from 3.30 to 5 pm, or at other times by phoning (☎ 2312). Admission is US$1.

Colonial Architecture
Lüderitz is chock-a-block with colonial buildings and every view reveals something interesting. The curiously intriguing architecture, which mixes German Imperial and Art-Nouveau styles, makes this already bizarre little town appear even more otherworldly.

Goerke Haus Lieutenant Hans Goerke arrived in Swakopmund with the Schutztruppe in 1904 and was later posted to Lüderitz, where he served as a manager of a diamond company. His home, which was designed by architect Otto Ertl and constructed on Diamond Hill between 1909 and 1910, was one of the town's most extravagant.

Goerke left for Germany in 1912 and eight years later, his home was purchased by the newly formed Consolidated Diamond Mines to house their chief engineer. When the CDM headquarters was transferred to Oranjemund in 1944, the house was sold to the government and used to house the resident Lüderitz magistrate. In 1981, however, the magistrate was shifted to Keetmanshoop and the house so desperately needed repair that it was sold back to CDM for a token sum of R10 on condition that it be renovated.

They did an admirable job and today, this truly amazing blend of Art-Nouveau elements and period furnishings is open to the public as a window into the more garish side of Lüderitz' past. It can be visited Monday to Friday from 2 to 3 pm and on Saturday from noon to 1 pm.

Railway Station The imposing Lüderitz railway station stands on the corner of Bahnhof Strasse and Bismarck Strasse. The original Lüderitz station building was completed in 1907 – along with the railway line itself – but with the discovery of diamonds, the facilities quickly became swamped. To handle the increased traffic, a new building was commissioned in 1912. It was designed by state architect Lohse and completed two years later.

Old Post Office The interesting old post office was originally designed by railway commissioner Oswald Reinhardt, but before the building was constructed his successor added a first floor and a tower. Construction was completed in 1908; the building now houses the Ministry of Environment & Tourism.

Activities
A most unusual activity is to dig for the lovely crystals of calcium sulphate and gypsum known as sand roses, which develop when moisture seeps into the sand and causes it to adhere and crystalise into flowery shapes. MET issues digging permits which are valid for a two-hour dig and good for up to three sand roses or a total weight of 1.5 kg. You can't use any hard tools lest you damage other buried specimens. Diggers must be accompanied by an official from MET.

Believe it or not, there's a golf course about five km outside the town, near the airport. However, it isn't exactly green and there is no shortage of sand traps. It's open daily for golf, but the clubhouse opens only on Wednesday and Friday evening after 6 pm, and all day on Saturday.

Organised Tours
Sailing trips to the Cape fur-seal sanctuary at Diaz Point leave the harbour jetty daily, weather permitting. The trips last two to three hours and cost US$10. If the seas are calm, you can also include the penguin sanctuary on Halifax Island for an additional US$5 per person. You can choose between the schooner *Sedina* (☎ 2919) or the single-masted yacht *Sagitta* (☎ 2170). Be sure to take warm gear. Trips may be booked through Diaz Souvenirs in the centre.

Town tours, trips to Agate Beach and Diaz Point and other excursions are offered by Lüderitzbucht Safaris & Tours. The affiliated Kolmanskop Tour Company organises trips to several areas of the Sperrgebiet. In addition to Kolmanskop, you can visit Elizabeth Bay, the Cape fur-seal colony at Atlas Bay and the Bogenfels. Because CDM permits are required, you need to book at least 24-

hours in advance through their office near Pension Zum Sperrgebiet.

Places to Stay
Lüderitz' beautifully situated but aggravatingly exposed and windy *Shark Island Campground* is connected to the mainland by a causeway one km north from town. Camping costs US$7 per site.

Alternatively, there's the *Lüderitz Rest Camp* (☎ 3351; fax 2869), formerly known as The Strand. Basic bungalows with shared facilities start at US$10/19 a single/double; with a fridge and shower they're US$17/27; and with fridge, shower and toilet they cost US$19/33. The excellent restaurant serves good salads and a variety of seafood dishes, particularly crayfish. It's not cheap, but is still decent value for what you get.

The friendly *Lüderitz Guesthouse* (☎ 3347), housed in a colonial building near the harbour, has homey German-style rooms with shared facilities starting at US$22 per person, including use of kitchen facilities. A self-catering flat costs US$16 per person, with a minimum of three people.

The *Pension Zum Sperrgebiet* (☎ 2856; fax 2976) is. as anachronistic as the town itself. It has singles/doubles with private facilities for US$30/55. This place is a particular favourite of German tourists. A buffet breakfast in the retro dining room costs US$4.50.

The two main hotels in Lüderitz are still owned by descendants of the original Lüderitz family. The *Bay View* (☎ 312288) complex has 30 rooms opening from shady courtyards; there's also a pool. Cool and airy single/double rooms cost US$37/56. Rooms with three beds are US$67. Nearby is the affiliated *Hotel Kapps* (☎ 12701), which is smaller and charges US$32/44 for a single/double room. This is the town's oldest hotel.

Places to Eat
Many people opt for the hotel and guesthouse restaurants. If there has been a good catch that day, the affiliated hotels, *Bay View* and *Kapps*, both serve decent seafood dishes; specialities include crayfish, local

oysters and kingklip. Otherwise, you get frozen fish. The Bay View has two eateries: *Ray's Café* on the main floor and the *Bahnhof Ocean View Bar/Restaurant* upstairs.

You also have several other options. The *Oyster Bar* on Bismarck Strasse serves a range of light meals and snacks. Even if you're not into shellfish, they also serve breakfast from 9 am as well as takeaway food. For lunch, my favourite is the recommended *Badger's Restaurant* which serves great burgers, soup, salad and other light meals.

On the Rocks (☎ 3110) beside the Shell petrol station specialises in seafood and beef dishes, and serves the cheapest and best crayfish in town. It's open daily from 7 pm. At the stark north end of town is the good-value *Franzel's Restaurant*, which is quite popular with local patrons; it specialises in seafood, but also serves lamb and game from the owners' farm near Bethanie.

For self-catering, there's a *Spar Market*, and also the *Sentra Portuguese Market* at the top of Bismarck Strasse.

Entertainment
Bizarrely, the Hotel Kapps skittle alley remains segregated: it's open to women on Monday evenings and to men on Tuesday and Thursday.

Things to Buy
The Karaman Weavery at the top of Bismarck Strasse is certainly worth a visit. They produce high-quality rugs and garments, which are woven in desert pastel colours with Namibian flora & fauna as favoured designs. The weavery employs local artesans and is happy to take special orders and post them worldwide. Visitors are welcome Monday to Friday from 8 am to 1 pm and 2 to 7 pm, and on Saturday to noon.

Karaman also has an attached coffee and crafts shop selling locally woven items, artwork and curios; as well as art cards, wooden toys, wire cars and bicycles, and knitted socks made from wool that has been spun and dyed by hand. It's open Monday to Friday 8 am to 5 pm and Saturday to 1 pm.

Diaz Souvenirs in the town centre has the usual range of kitsch curios and T-shirts.

Getting There & Away
Air Air Namibia flies between Windhoek, Swakopmund and Lüderitz on Monday, Wednesday, Friday and Sunday. They also fly from Windhoek to Cape Town, via Lüderitz and Alexander Bay, on Tuesday, Thursday, Friday and Sunday. These flights return to Windhoek by the same route on Monday, Wednesday, Friday and Sunday.

Bus Although there's no longer a passenger train running between Keetmanshoop and Lüderitz, the Trans-Namib railways does operate a passenger bus. From Keetmanshoop, it departs on Friday at 6 pm and Sunday at 2 pm, and returns from Lüderitz on Saturday at 6 am and Sunday at 7 pm. The trip costs US$8 each way.

Car & Motorbike Lüderitz is definitely worth the 300-km trip from Keetmanshoop, which is now all tarred. Between Aus and the coast, the road crosses the desolate southern Namib; to the south lies the forbidden territory of Diamond Area 1.

When the wind is blowing – which is all the time – the final 10 km into Lüderitz may be partially blocked by the barchan dunefield which seems bent upon crossing the road. The drifts can pile quite high before the road crews get to work on it, and conditions do get hazardous, especially if it's foggy.

If you're considering a dune buggy trip from Lüderitz through the Namib Desert to Sossusvlei, it's worth noting that a permit to do so takes at least 1½ years to process and you need a very good reason to want one. So far, just about the only people allowed through have been tourist office film crews making promotional videos to be shown abroad. (It may seem odd to promote tourism in Namibia with scenes of places off limits to tourists, but who am I to question their methods?) At last notice, British travel writer Benedict Allen was also planning such a trip – which will actually continue all the way to

NAMIBIA

the Angolan border – and he intends to write an account of the experience.

Getting Around
There's limited taxi service between the airport and the town centre.

AROUND LÜDERITZ
Kolmanskop
A popular excursion from Lüderitz is to the ghost town of Kolmanskop, which was once a substantial diamond-mining town. It was named for an early Afrikaner trekker Jani

Kolman, whose ox-wagon became bogged in the sand there. The town once boasted a casino, skittle alley and theatre with fine acoustics, but the slump in diamond sales after WWI and the discovery of richer deposits at Oranjemund ended its heyday and by 1956 it was deserted. Several buildings have been restored, but many have already been invaded by the dunes and the ghost-town atmosphere remains.

Information Permits to visit Kolmanskop are sold for US$3 per person at the

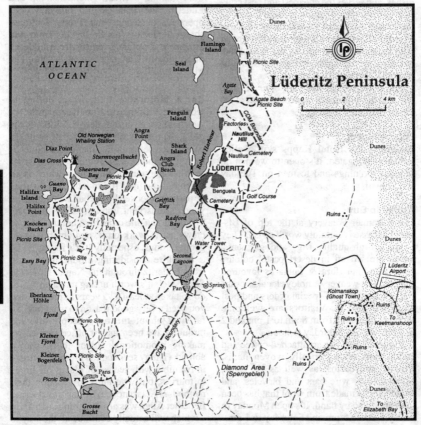

Kolmanskop Tour Company agency, beside Pension Zum Sperrgebiet in Lüderitz. Tours are conducted in English and German from Monday to Saturday at 9.30 am and 2 pm. Visitors must provide their own transport from town. If you wish to photograph the town at other times of day, you can purchase a special 'sunrise to sunset' permit for US$6 per person.

Before and after your tour, you're welcome to look around the impressive museum near the entrance, which contains relics and information on Namibia's diamond-mining history. Also impressive is the large display on Oranjemund, the boom town to the south which supplanted Kolmanskop as the CDM headquarters and turned it into a ghost town.

The Kolmanskop tea room serves unimpressive cakes and chicory coffee (which seems unfathomable for a German-Namibian enterprise) all morning until noon.

Elizabeth Bay

In 1986, CDM again began prospecting in the northern area of the Sperrgebiet and found heavy concentrations of diamonds in the area of Elizabeth Bay, 30 km south of Kolmanskop. Although the supply of diamonds, which was estimated at a total of 2.5 million carats, wasn't expected to last more than 10 years, CDM decided to install a full-scale operation. However, because it was so near Lüderitz, they opted not to build on-site housing, but rather to provide workers with daily transport from town.

Half-day tours to Elizabeth Bay are available from Kolmanskop Tour Company in Lüderitz. Prices start at US$20 per person and also take in Kolmanskop and the Atlas Bay Cape fur-seal colony. The company also runs tours as far south as Bogenfels, which has only recently been opened to the public.

Bogenfels

A third of the way down the Forbidden Coast between Lüderitz and Oranjemund is the 55-metre natural sea arch known as Bogenfels ('bow rock'). The only access to this remote and amazing region is with the Kolmanskop Tour Company in Lüderitz. Bogenfels tours also take in the mining ghost town of Pomona, the Maerchental Valley, the Bogenfels ghost town and a large cave near the arch itself. Tours cost US$65 per person, including lunch and permits.

Radford Bay

Radford Bay was named for David Radford, the first European settler to live there. As there was no water, he survived by collecting the dews created by the heavy coastal fog. The oyster farm in Radford Bay south of town is open for tours Monday to Friday from 10 am to noon.

Sturmvogelbucht

This picturesque and relatively calm bay has a lovely beach and is viable for swimming, but the water temperature would only be amenable to a polar bear. A Norwegian whaling station was sited there in 1914, but it's now little more than a rusty ruin. The salty pan just inland from Sturmvogelbucht actually appears to be iced over, and is worth a quick stop.

Jackass Penguin

The jackass penguin or Cape penguin, which is common along the southern Namibian coast, lives in colonies on the many rocky offshore islets. Penguins' wings have evolved into flippers which are used for rapid underwater locomotion and its endearing stocky appearance belies its ability to manoeuvre gracefully through the water. The skin is insulated against the chill water by a layer of air trapped beneath the feathers. Penguins also have supraorbital glands which excrete salts, allowing them to take their liquids from salt water.

Like Australia's fairy penguins, jackass penguins breed twice annually. They produce an average of three eggs per season, but egg mortality is fairly high. The penguins' main enemies are Cape fur seals, which inhabit the same coastline. ■

NAMIBIA

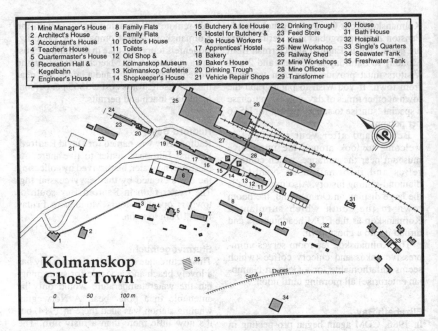

1 Mine Manager's House	8 Family Flats	15 Butchery & Ice House	22 Drinking Trough	30 House
2 Architect's House	9 Family Flats	16 Hostel for Butchery &	23 Feed Store	31 Bath House
3 Accountant's House	10 Doctor's House	Ice House Workers	24 Kraal	32 Hospital
4 Teacher's House	11 Toilets	17 Apprentices' Hostel	25 New Workshop	33 Single's Quarters
5 Quartermaster's House	12 Old Shop &	18 Bakery	26 Railway Shed	34 Seawater Tank
6 Recreation Hall &	Kolmanskop Museum	19 Baker's House	27 Mine Workshops	35 Freshwater Tank
Kegelbahn	13 Kolmanskop Cafeteria	20 Drinking Trough	28 Mine Offices	
7 Engineer's House	14 Shopkeeper's House	21 Vehicle Repair Shops	29 Transformer	

Kolmanskop Ghost Town

0   50   100 m

Sand Dunes

Diaz Point

At Diaz Point, 22 km south of Lüderitz, is a lovely classic lighthouse and a replica of a cross erected in July 1488 by Portuguese navigator Bartolomeu Dias on his return voyage from the Cape of Good Hope. Remaining bits of the original cross have been dispersed as far as Lisbon, Berlin and Cape Town.

Dress for windy and chilly weather. From the point, there's a view to the nearby sea-lion colony and jackass penguins are often seen frolicking, diving and surfing off the rocks. You can also observe cormorants, flamingoes, wading birds and even the occasional school of dolphins.

Grosse Bucht

The 'big bay', Grosse Bucht, at the southern end of the Lüderitz Peninsula, is another wild and scenic beach. This normally cold, windy spot is favoured by flocks of flamingoes, which feed in the tidal pools. It's also the site

of a small but picturesque shipwreck on the beach. Just a few km up the coast is Klein Bogenfels, a small rock arch beside the sea. On the rare occasions when the wind isn't blowing a gale, it makes a pleasant picnic spot.

Agate Bay

North of Lüderitz a similar road leads to the wonderful beach at Agate Bay, which is made of tailings from diamond workings. There aren't many agates these days, but you will find a fine sand consisting partially of tiny grey mica chips.

ORANJEMUND

Oranjemund, inside the Sperrgebiet at the mouth of the Orange River, owes its existence to diamonds. So great was its wealth that in 1944, it supplanted Kolmanskop as the Consolidated Diamond Mines headquarters.

With a population of 8000, Oranjemund is now an archetypal company town, with 100% employment, subsidised housing and free medical care for workers and their families. Despite its desert location, the company manages to maintain a golf course and large areas of green parkland. In fact, CDM now accounts for approximately 90% of the Namibian government's tax revenue, which probably goes a long way toward explaining why CDM is still protected from competition and the Sperrgebiet continues to exist.

All visitors to Oranjemund must have a permit from CDM and as yet, there's no real tourism. Applications must be made at least a month in advance of your intended visit and should be accompanied by a police affadavit stating that you've never been convicted of a serious crime. Permits are normally issued only to those who have business in the town.

So strict is the security here that broken-down equipment used in the mining operations may never leave the site, lest it be used to smuggle diamonds outside the fence. Despite the heavy security, a fair number of stolen diamonds still manage to find their way onto the illicit market. Thieves come up with some ingenious methods of smuggling the diamonds over the security fence, including using pigeons, discarded rubbish and even tunnels.

Sperrgebiet Museum
If you do have reason to visit, don't miss the Sperrgebiet Museum (☎ 2183), which contains exhibits and relics from the various Sperrgebiet ghost towns, as well as background on natural history – particularly fossils, diamonds and minerals.

Getting There & Away
Oranjemund's airport is across the river in Alexander Bay in South Africa, and the town's only road access is also via Alexander Bay. Air Namibia has four flights weekly to and from Lüderitz, Swakopmund and Windhoek.

The Far South

Set in the angle between South Africa's two most remote quarters, Namaqualand and the Kalahari, the bleak southern tip of Namibia exudes a sense of isolation from whichever direction you approach. Travelling along the highway, the desert plains stretch to the horizon in all directions and seem to carry on endlessly. You can imagine, then, how surprising it will be to suddenly encounter the startling and spellbinding Fish River Canyon, which forms an enormous gash across the desert landscape.

GRÜNAU
For most travellers, Grünau is either the first petrol station north of the border area or a place to settle in while awaiting a lift to Ai-Ais, Fish River Canyon or points beyond.

Grünau is a stop that time has passed. There was a hand-cranked phone in my hotel room, the dinner was whatever delicious thing the cook decided to cook, the street was unpaved and the rooms were amazingly good value. Here I was offered two lifts. As a bonus, the one I went with decided to drive around the African township in Karasburg.
Wayne Lidlehoover, USA

Augrabies-Steenbok Nature Reserve
This forgotten nature reserve north-west of Grünau was created to protect not only steenbok, but also Hartmann's mountain zebras, gemsbok and klipspringers. Camping is allowed but apart from basic toilets, there are no facilities. To get there, follow the C12 for 59 km north-west of Grünau, then turn west and continue for another 10 km to the reserve. There's no admission charge.

Places to Stay
The inexpensive *Hotel Grünau* (☎ (0020) 1), down a side road at least a km from the petrol station, is a bit seedy, but generally acceptable. Single/double rooms cost US$16/23. The petrol station on the main road has a shop, snack bar and takeaway outlet.

NAMIBIA

FISH RIVER CANYON NATIONAL PARK

Nowhere else in Africa is there anything like Fish River Canyon. The Fish River, which joins the Orange River about 70 km south of the canyon, has been gouging out this gorge for thousands of years and the result couldn't be improved upon. It's also enormous – 160 km in length, up to 27 km wide and the dramatic inner canyon reaches a depth of 550 metres. But these figures convey little of the breathtaking vistas which open up from the various vantage points. Although tourist literature likes to claim it's the world's second largest canyon – after Arizona's Grand Canyon – it's in fact well down the list. However, that doesn't make it any less awe-inspiring.

The river normally flows between March and April. During the early part of the season, from April to June, chances are the Fish River will be just a small stream and later in the tourist season little more than a chain of remnant pools along the canyon floor.

The two main areas of activity are Hobas, near the northern end of the canyon, and Ai-Ais Hot Springs resort, in the south. Both of these places are administered by MET; all accommodation should be prebooked in Windhoek.

History

The early San had a legend that the wildly twisting Fish River Canyon was gouged out by a frantically scrambling snake named Koutein Kooru as he was pursued into the desert by hunters.

The geological story is only a bit different. Fish River Canyon is actually two canyons, one inside the other, which were formed in entirely different ways.

It's thought that the original sedimentary layers of shale, sandstone and loose igneous material around Fish River Canyon were laid down nearly two billion years ago and were later metamorphosed by heat and pressure into more solid materials, such as gneiss. Just under a billion years ago, cracks in the formation admitted intrusions of igneous material, which cooled to form the dolerite

dykes (which are now exposed and readily visible in the inner canyon).

The surface was then eroded into a basin and covered by a shallow sea, which eventually filled up with sediment – sandstone, conglomerate, quartzite, limestone and shale – washed down from surrounding exposed lands. Around 500 million years ago, a period of tectonic activity along crustal fault caused these layers to rift and to tilt at a 45° angle. These forces opened up a wide gap in the earth's crust and formed a large canyon. This was what we now regard as the outer canyon, the bottom of which was the first level of terraces we now see approximately 170 metres below the east rim and 380 metres below the west rim. This newly created valley naturally became a watercourse (the Fish River, in fact) which began eroding a meandering path along the valley floor and eventually gouged out what is now the 270-metre deep inner canyon.

Hobas

The Hobas Information Centre, at the northern end of the park, is open daily from 7.30 am to noon and 2 to 5 pm. It's also the check-in point for the five-day hike through the canyon. Cool drinks are available but not much else.

From Hobas, it's 10 km along the gravel road to Hikers' Viewpoint, a picnic site with tables, braai pits and toilets. Here you'll find the start of the walking track to Ai-Ais and just around the corner is a good overview of the northern part of the canyon. Main Viewpoint, a few km further south, is probably the best – and most photographed – overall view of the canyon. Both these northern viewpoints take in the particularly sharp river bend known as Hell's Corner.

Admission costs US$1.50 per person and US$1.50 per vehicle, whether you're there on a day visit, doing the hike or spending several days in Hobas campground. This permit is also good for Ai-Ais.

Places to Stay & Eat Camp sites cost US$7 at the pleasant well-shaded Hobas campground, 10 km from the main viewpoints near the northern end of the canyon. Facilities are clean and there's also a kiosk and swimming pool. There's no restaurant or petrol station.

Fish River Hiking Trail

The four to five-day hike from Hobas to Ai-Ais is Namibia's most popular long-distance walk – and with good reason. The magical 85-km route, which follows the sandy bed of the river course (although in May and June, it actually does flow), begins at the main northern lookout point and ends at the hot-spring resort of Ai-Ais.

Due to possible flash flooding and extreme heat in the summer months, the route is open only from 1 May to 30 September. Although groups of between 3 and 40 people are allowed through every day of the season, this is a very popular hike so it's wise to book well in advance. The permit costs US$10 per person but you must arrange your own transport and accommodation in Hobas and Ai-Ais. Hikers must also sign an indemnity form releasing MET from any responsibility and as usual you'll need a doctors' medical certificate stating that you're fit and able to complete the hike.

During the hiking season, the typically warm, clear weather alleviates the need to carry a tent, but you must take a sleeping bag and all the food you'll need. Before setting out from Hobas, check on the availability of water in the river. In August and September, the final 15 km of the walk can be completely dry and you'll need a couple of two-litre water bottles to get through this hot, dry and sandy stretch. Large plastic soft drink bottles normally work just fine.

The Route From Hobas, it's 10 km to Hikers' Viewpoint, which is the start of the hike. No transport is provided, so without a vehicle, you'll either have to find a lift or walk.

The first section, which takes you from the canyon rim down to the river, is quite steep but very scenic. Once at the bottom you'll have a choice of fabulous sandy camp sites beside cool, green river pools.

Fish River Canyon

0   5   10 km

Fish River
Hell's Corner
Hikers' Viewpoint
Car Park
Main Viewpoint
To Grünau & Seeheim
Dolerite Dykes
Hobas
Sulphur Springs Viewpoint
Sulphur Springs Trail
Sulphur (Palm) Springs
Table Mountain
To Ai-Ais
South Viewpoint
Rock Pinnacle
Bushy Corner
Kooigoedhoogte Pass
Short Cut
Three Sisters Rocks
Kanebis River Track
Short Cut
Kanebis Bend
Thilo von Trotha's Grave
Four Finger Rock
Emergency Exit
Fish
Kraal
Fool's Gold Corner
To Orange River
Ai-Ais
To Grünau

NAMIBIA

After 13 km of rather rough and exhausting walking along the east bank, over fields of large boulders and patches of deep river sand, you'll see the day track coming in from Sulphur Springs Viewpoint. If you're completely exhausted at this stage and simply can't hack it, this track can be used as an emergency exit route. If it's any encouragement, however, take comfort in the fact that the going does get easier as you move downstream, so it's probably better to head two more km downstream to Sulphur Springs; set up camp and see how you feel in the morning.

Sulphur Springs, which is more commonly called Palm Springs, is an excellent camp site with thermal sulphur pools (like something out of paradise) to soak your aching muscles. The springs, which have a stable temperature of 57°C, gush up from the underworld at an amazing 30 litres per second and contain not only sulphur, but also natural chloride and fluoride.

Legend has it that during WWI, two escaped German prisoners of war hid out at Palm Springs to escape internment. One was apparently suffering from asthma and the other from skin cancer, but thanks to the spring's healing powers, both were cured. It's said that the palm trees growing there sprung up from date pits discarded by these two. This site is also accessible on a day walk down from the Palm Springs viewpoint and unfortunately is normally quite crowded – and also fouled by the picnic trash they tend to leave behind.

The next segment of the route consists mostly of deep sand, pebbles and gravel. You'll have to cross the river several times to take the most direct route through the inside of the river bends. Fifteen km beyond Palm Springs, you'll reach the formation known as Table Mountain and another 15 km on is the first short cut, which cuts off an area of dense thorn scrub known as Bushy Corner. Around the next river bend, just upstream from the Three Sisters formation, is a longer short cut past Kanebis Bend up to Kooigoedhoogte Pass. At the top, you'll have a superb view of Four Finger Rock, an impressive rock tower consisting of four thick pinnacles that resembles more a cow's udder than a set of fingers. If you see a billboard here reading 'Cold Drinks 7 km', you're not hallucinating; read on.

After descending to the river, you'll cross to the west bank and start climbing over yet another short cut (although you can also opt to follow the river bend). At the southern end of this pass, on the west bank of the river, you'll see the grave of Lieutenant Thilo von Trother, who was killed on this spot during a 1905 confrontation between the Germans and the Nama.

The final 25 km into Ai-Ais, which can be completed in a long day, follows a relatively easy but still sandy and rocky route. South of the soldier's grave, the canyon widens out and becomes drier, there are fewer bends, and river pools grow less and less frequent. At the end of the winter, the final 15 km are normally completely dry, so you'll have to carry all your water for this segment. Five km south of Von Trother's grave you'll see the object of the billboard you passed back at Four Finger Rock. During the hiking season, an enterprising local normally operates a kiosk where hikers can buy staples, cool drinks and hot dogs. It's not 100% reliable, but when it is open, few hikers can pass it up.

Day Walks If the entire canyon hiking route seems too daunting, there are several day hikes from near the northern end. You can begin at either the Sulphur Springs or Hikers' Viewpoints and descend nearly 500 metres to the bottom of the canyon for a picnic and a swim before returning the same way.

Alternatively, you can follow the bottom of the canyon between the two viewpoints, but this will require a good early start. Bear in mind that unless you have two vehicles, you may have to walk at least 10 km back to Hobas from your ending point. Note also that any of these options will require a 500-metre ascent out of the canyon during the hottest part of the day.

Ai-Ais Hot Spring Resort
For many travellers, Ai-Ais (Nama for 'scalding hot') serves as both the staging and ending point for their canyon hike. This pleasant hot-spring oasis lies beneath towering peaks at the southern end of Fish River Canyon and is popular with Namibians and South Africans who come to soak up the natural thermal baths which originate beneath the riverbed.

Although the 60°C springs have probably been known by the San for thousands of years, the legend goes that they were 'discovered' by a nomadic Nama shepherd rounding up stray sheep. They're rich in

Ostrich

chloride, fluoride and sulphur, and are reputedly salubrious for anyone suffering from rheumatism or nervous disorders. The hot water is piped to a series of baths, jacuzzis and an outdoor swimming pool.

A pleasant diversion is the short rocky hike up to the peak which rises above the opposite bank. It affords a superb view of Ai-Ais itself and you'll even see the four pinnacles of Four Finger Rock rising far to the north. The return trip takes about two hours.

Due to the risk of flooding, Ai-Ais is closed from 31 October to the second Friday in March. In fact, in early 1972, a year after the resort opened, the entire complex (save one building which sat on higher ground) was utterly destroyed by the Fish River's worst flood in recorded history. In early 1988, it was again flooded and required a three-month clean up.

The site is geared mainly towards Namibian and South African holiday-makers, so foreign backpackers may feel a bit out of their element, but the setting is pleasant enough. Admission costs US$1.50 per person and US$1.50 per vehicle. This permit is also good for visits to Hobas. Day visitors are welcome between sunrise and 11 pm.

Places to Stay & Eat Amenities at Ai-Ais include a shop, restaurant, petrol station, tennis courts, post office and, of course, a swimming pool and spa and mineral bath facilities (US$0.50 per session). Camping costs US$7 per site for up to eight people, with ablutions blocks, braai pits and use of all resort facilities. Accommodation is in bungalows, caravans and tents; all equipped with beds and bedding. Flats accommodating four people cost US$35 while basic four-bed bungalows are US$22. Again, accommodation should be prebooked at the MET office in Windhoek.

The restaurant is open from 7 to 8.30 am, noon to 1.30 pm and 6 to 8.30 pm. The attached shop sells basic supplies.

Getting There & Away
There's no public transport to either Hobas or Ai-Ais, but from mid-March to 31 October, hitchers should eventually be successful. Thanks to South African holiday traffic, the best-travelled route – and therefore the easiest to hitch – is to Ai-Ais via the turn-off 30 km south of Grünau. Once in Ai-Ais, nearly all the holiday-makers head for the viewpoints at the canyon's northern end, so it shouldn't be too difficult to find lifts from Ai-Ais to Hobas and the Hikers' Viewpoint trailhead.

From Seeheim on the tarred Keetmanshoop-Lüderitz road, the C12 turns south, signposted for Visrivierafgronde (Fish River Canyon). It passes the Augrabies Steenbok Nature Reserve and after 87 km, reaches Holoog, where the D601 turns south-west; after 31 km is the west turning for the final 18 km to Hobas. This route is

NAMIBIA

relatively little-travelled and we've had reports from people who've waited four days for a lift from Seeheim, so be prepared and don't set off from Seeheim the day before your hiking permit begins!

ORANGE RIVER

The Orange River has its headwaters in the Drakensberg Mountains of Natal, South Africa, and forms much of the boundary between Namibia and South Africa. It was named not for its muddy colour, but for Prince William V of Orange, who was the Dutch monarch in the late 1770s.

Most people come to this region for river trips, but if you prefer the equine route, Mr Korbus Johnson, who lives on a farm near the mouth of the Fish River, runs multi-day horse-riding and camping trips between Ai-Ais and the Orange River. Prices are negotiable. Mr Johnson is rather difficult to get hold of, so you'll probably have to track him down through the Ai-Ais Hot Springs Resort. (See under Fish River Canyon National Park earlier in this section.)

River Trips

Several South African companies now offer Orange River canoeing and easy rafting trips from Noordoewer to Selingsdrif. Part of the route follows the river boundary between Namibia's Fish River Canyon National Park and South Africa's Richtersveld National Park. Trips are normally done in stages and last from three to six days, although two-day weekend trips can be arranged with advance notice. These aren't treacherous trips – nowhere is the water rougher than class II – and the appeal lies in the opportunity to experience this wild and otherwise almost inaccessible canyon country.

In order, the stages are Noordoewer to Aussenkehr; Aussenkehr to the Fish River mouth; Fish River mouth to Nama Canyon; and Nama Canyon to Selingsdrif. Some companies also do a five-day stage from Pella Mission to Goodhouse, further upstream. Generally, canoe trips are slightly more expensive than raft trips. To give you some idea of prices, a four/six-day canoe trip

will cost US$190/250, while the raft trips are around US$165/220.

The following operators currently run trips:

Felix Unite 1 Griegmar House, Main Rd, PO Box 96, Kenilworth 7745, South Africa (☎ (27-21) 762 6935; fax (27-21) 761 9259) Offers a range of canoe trips on the Orange River, as well as other South African rivers and also hires canoes. If you wish to organise your own canoe trip, Felix Unite hires a two-person canoe package, including canoes, paddles, life vests and cool boxes for US$28 per day. A guide costs an additional US$39 per day.

Orange River Adventures 5 Matapan Rd, Rondebosch 7700, South Africa (☎ /fax (27-21) 685 4474) Offers five-day canoe trips between Noordoewer and Fish River mouth.

The River Rafters (☎ (27-21) 725094) This informal rafting operation runs four, five and six-day raft trips year-round. They're the least expensive available at US$96 for a self-catered six-day trip. Add meals and it's US$160.

River Runners, PO Box 583, Constantia 7848, South Africa (☎ (27-21) 762 2350; fax (27-21) 761 1373) This friendly company runs both canoeing and rafting trips on the Orange River. It comes highly recommended.

Southern Africa Adventure Centre 48a Strand St, Cape Town, South Africa (☎ (27-21) 419 1704; fax (27-21) 419 1703) This isn't an operator per se, but rather an adventure-travel agency which sells an amazing range of thrill-oriented trips, including Orange River runs, in both South Africa and Namibia.

South African River Adventures PO Box 4722, Cape Town 8000, South Africa (☎ /fax (27-21) 685 1569) This company runs raft trips on the Orange and other South African rivers, and is one of the least expensive.

Places to Stay

The *Camel Lodge* (☎ (0020) 13; fax (0020) 43) in Noordoewer has single/double rooms for US$23/36.

KARASBURG

Although it's Southern Namibia's third largest town, Karasburg is little more than a service centre along the main route between Namibia and Johannesburg. The name means 'rocky mountains', after the nearby Karas Mountain range. The Nama people, however, still call it Kalkfontein ('limestone springs') Suid. It has a good supermarket, a bank, several petrol stations and two hotels.

Warmbad

The area's main site of interest is the historic mission, fort and spa village of Warmbad, 36 km south of Karasburg. (The name is German for 'warm bath', in case you hadn't worked that out.) Warmbad, which was Namibia's first mission station, was founded in 1805 by missionary Edward Cook. The ruins of the old spa building are currently being restored as a national monument and a museum is planned for the portals and gatehouse of the old fort (now the police station).

Places to Stay & Eat

Both of Karasburg's hotels, the *Kalkfontein* (☎ /fax 172) and the *Van Riebeeck* (☎ /fax 23), are under the same management. The former has a restaurant and charges US$30/42 for a single/double room. The latter costs US$27/39.

Near the junction of the D259 and the C26, 119 km north of Karasburg, you'll find the up-market *Mt Karas Game Lodge* (☎ (06352) 3212), owned by David and Anna Fourie. It enjoys sensational views of the impressive Karas Mountains and lies within easy reach of several historical sites, including the Stansvlakte monument; the Baron von Schauroth castle; various graves from the German-Nama war; and examples of ancient San painting. Amenities include a swimming pool, shop, petrol station, kitchen facilities and braai pits, as well as wildlife-viewing and bird-watching opportunities, and an 11-km hiking, trail.

NAMIBIA

Glossary

ANC – African National Congress

apartheid – 'separate development of the races'; a political system in which people are officially segregated according to race

assegais – Ndebele spears

ATVs – all terrain vehicles

barchan dunes – migrating crescent-shaped sand dunes

Basarwa – Batswana name for the San people

BDF – Botswana Defence Forces

bilharzia – disease caused by blood flukes which are passed on by freshwater snails

biltong – normally anonymous dried meat which can be anything from beef to kudu or ostrich, is usually delicious and makes a great snack

BMC – Botswana Meat Corporation

boerewors – a spicy Afrikaner sausage

bogobe – sorghum porridge, a staple food in Botswana

bojalwa – sorghum beer drunk in Botswana; brewed commercially as Chibuku

boomslang – a dangerous snake which measures up to two metres and likes to hang out in trees

braai – a barbecue which normally includes lots of meat grilled on a braai stand or pit.

BSAC – British South Africa Company

CDM – Consolidated Diamond Mines

chibuku – the 'beer of good cheer'. The alcoholic drink of the Zimbabwean masses. It's also drunk in Botswana and parts of Namibia.

chikuva – small platforms placed behind Shona huts for offerings to ancestral spirits

cuca shops – small bush shops of northern Namibia; named for a brand of Angolan beer normally sold there

daga hut – in Zimbabwe, a traditional African round house

dikgotla – traditional Batswana town council

dolfhout – Afrikaans name for wild teak

drankwinkel – literally 'drink shop'; Namibian or South African off-licence

drift – a river ford

dumpi – a 375 ml beer; Namibian equivalent of an Australian stubby

dwala – bald, knob-like domes of slickrock

efundja – period of heavy rainfall in northern Namibia

ekipa – a traditional medallion historically worn by Ovambo women as a sign of wealth and status

ESAP – Economic Structural Adjustment Programme

eumbo – immaculate Ovambo kraal; very much like a small village enclosed within a pale fence

euphorbia – a variety of cactus-like succulents which are found in southern Africa

FRELIMO – Frente pela Liberacão de Moçambique or Mozambique Liberation Front

Gemütlichkeit – a distinctively German appreciation of comfort and hospitality

gudza – tree bark used by the Shona for making blankets, mats and clothing; it's made soft and pliable by chewing on it

guti – drizzly mists which occur in Zimbabwe's Eastern Highlands

ilala – Zimbabwean name for the *Hyphaene petersiana* palm. It's a source of thatching material, vegetable ivory and palm wine.

induna – early Ndebele military captain; also translated as 'chief'

inselbergs – isolated ranges and hills; common in the Namib desert

jesse – dense, thorny scrub, normally impenetrable to humans

kapenta – *Limnothrissa mioda*, an anchovy-like fish caught in Lake Kariba and favoured by Zimbabweans

karakul – variety of Central Asian sheep which produce high-grade wool and pelts; raised in Namibia and parts of Botswana

kgotla – traditionally constructed Batswana community affairs hall, used for meetings of the dikgotla, or town council

Khoisan – language grouping taking in all southern African indigenous languages, including San and Khoi-Khoi (or Nama), as well as the language of the Damara (a Bantu people who speak a Khoi-Khoi dialect)

kimberlite pipe – geologic term for a type of igneous intrusion, in which extreme heat and pressure has turned coal into diamonds

kloof – a ravine or small valley

kokerboom – quiver tree, which grows mainly in southern Namibia

Konditorei – German pastry shops, which are found in larger Namibian towns

kopje – small hill, often just a pile of boulders on an otherwise flat plain

kraal – either an enclosure for livestock or a fortified village of daga huts

location – Namibia name for township

LMS – London Missionary Society

mabele – Setswana for sorghum; used to make bogobe, which is a dietary staple

madiba – serene open areas of still water in the Okavango Delta; singular lediba

mahango – millet; a staple of the Ovambo diet and used for brewing a favourite alcoholic beverage of the same name

makalani – Ovambo name for the Hyphaene petersiana palm

marimba – African xylophone, made from strips of resonant wood with various-sized gourds for sound boxes

mbanje – Zimbabwean name for cannabis

mbira – thumb piano; it consists of 22 to 24 narrow iron keys mounted in rows on a wooden sound board. The player plucks the ends of the keys with the thumbs.

MET – Ministry of Environment & Tourism

mfecane – an exodus or forced migration by several southern African tribes in the face of Zulu aggression

mhondoro – literally 'lion'; a Shona spirit which can influence natural conditions and bring fortune or disaster on a community. When a problem such as a plague or drought strikes, these are the spirits who must be consulted.

midzimu – spirits of Shona ancestors

mielie pap – Afrikaans name for maize meal porridge, known in Zimbabwe as *sadza*

miombo – dry open woodland, comprised mostly of acacia and/or mopane or similar bushveld vegetation

mokolane – Batswana name for the *Hyphaene petersiana* palm

mokoro – dugout canoe used in the Okavango Delta; it is propelled by a poler who stands in the stern (plural: mekoro)

mombo – a powerful chief or king in precolonial Zimbabwe

morgen – unit of land measurement used by early Boer farmers; about 1.25 hectares

mukwa – a rich-grained wood used in Zimbabwean carvings and others crafts

mujejeje – 'stone bells'; natural rock formations, caused by exfoliation, which produce melodic tones when struck

musika – Shona township market and bus terminal

mutasa – a Manyika dynastic title established in the 16th century

Mwari – supreme being in traditional Shona religion

!nara – a type of melon which grows in the Namib desert; a dietary staple of the Topnaar Khoi-Khoi people

n!oresi – traditional San lands; 'lands where one's heart is'

nxum – San 'life force'

omaeru – soured milk; a dietary staple of the Herero people

omiramba – fossil river channels in northern Namibia and north-western Botswana (singular: omiramba)

omulilo gwoshilongo – 'sacred fire' which serves as a shrine in each Ovambo eumbo; a log of mopane which is kept burning around the clock

oshana – dry river channel in northern Namibia and north-western Botswana

padrão – tribute to a royal patron, erected by early Portuguese navigators along the African coast

pondo – 'pound', occasionally used in Botswana to refer to two pula

pula – 'rain' in Setswana; the Botswanan unit of currency

pungwe – 'from darkness to light'; during the Second Chimurenga all-night celebrations of nationalistic unity between villagers and guerrillas. Now, any sort of event which begins in the evening and carries on through the night.

RENAMO – *Resistência Nacional de Moçambique* or MNR, Mozambique National Resistance

renkini – Ndebele township market and bus terminal

rondavel – a round, African-style hut.

rooibos – literally 'red bush' in Afrikaans; an insipid herbal tea which reputedly has therapeutic qualities

sadza – Zimbabwean name for maize meal porridge

sefala huts – traditional Batswana granaries

seif dunes – prominent linear sand dunes, as found in the central Namib Desert

shebeen – an illegal drinking establishment cum brothel

skokiaan – a dangerous and illegal grain-based swill spiked with whatever's lying around. It's no longer popular

Sperrgebiet – 'forbidden area'; alluvial diamond region of south-western Namibia

SWAKARA – South-West Africa Karakul

tenebrionid – a collection of beetle species which inhabit the Namib desert

toktokkie – Afrikaans name for a particular fog-basking tenebrionid beetle, Onomachris unguicularis

township – high-density black residential area outside a central city or town

trypanosomiasis – 'sleeping sickness'; disease passed on by the bite of the tsetse fly; known in Zimbabwe as nagana

tsama – a bitter desert melon historically eaten by San people; also eaten by stock

tsotsis – thieves

UNITA – Uniãopela Independência Total de Angola

UTC – Universal Time Coordinate (formerly GMT)

veld – open grassland, normally in plateau regions. One variation, 'bushveld', has the grassland replaced with thorn scrub.

vetkoek – literally 'fat cake'; a type of doughnut eaten in Botswana and other places with Afrikaner influences

vlei – any low open landscape, sometimes marshy

watu – Kavango dugout canoe, used on rivers and in wetlands of north-eastern Namibia

wag 'n bietjie – Afrikaans name for the buffalo thorn tree; literally 'wait-a-bit'

welwitschia – *Welwitschia mirabilis*, an unusual plant which grows in the Namib Desert. Thought to be related to coniferous trees.

ZANLA – Zimbabwe African National Liberation Army

ZANU – Zimbabwe African National Union

ZAPU – Zimbabwe African Peoples' Union

zhii – 'vengeful annihilation of the enemy'; a cry of solidarity among Black Zimbabweans against the colonial power in the late 1950s

ZIPRA – Zimbabwe Peoples' Revolutionary Army

ZUM – Zimbabwe Unity Movement

Index

ABBREVIATIONS

Ang	– Angola	GP	– Game Park
Bot	– Botswana	GR	– Game Reserve
Nam	– Namibia	NP	– National Park
SA	– South Africa	NR	– Nature Reserve
Zam	– Zambia	WR	– Wildlife Reserve
Zim	– Zimbabwe	WS	– Wildlife Sanctuary

MAPS

TEXT

Map references are in **bold** type.

WILDLIFE RESERVES & NATIONAL PARKS

784 Index

Thanks

Thanks to those travellers who took the time and trouble to write to us about their experiences in Zimbabwe, Botswana and Namibia. Writers (apologies if we've misspelt your name) to whom thanks must go include:

Timothy Abbott (USA), G Addams, Mark Azavedo (UK), David Banfield (Aus), James W, Bannister (C), John Batcheller (USA), Reto Beeli (CH), Dean & Emily Benbow (UK), Rhuari Bennett (UK), Harry Bennie, Peter Bessell (Aus), Christine Bill (Irl), B Binder, Tyler Bjornson (C), Karl Bolton, Stephane Borella (CH), Eric Brand, Tom & Sue Bright (Aus), Valerie Broom (UK), Tony Broughton, E A Bruce, Andrew Bryceson (UK), Joost Butenop (D), Dandemutande Calender (USA), Natalie Campbell, Rebecca Carron (UK), Scott Ciener (USA), Marg & Michael Clark (Aus), Mrs M Coetzee, Robert Colgrave, Mrs M O'Connell-Jones, Peter Connolly (UK), Christina Cordoza (USA), M F Correia (C), Juliet Cragg, Nick & Lucy Crawley, John Cross (USA), Myrtle Davis (UK), Brian de Gras (UK), Virginia de Ronde (C), Juiliana Dooley (USA), Mark Doro (Aus), J Dube, Angela Engler (S), Rainer Feil (D), Paul Ferguson (Aus), R K G Fonteijn (Nl), Linda Foss, Annalisa Francese (I), Celia Fraser (UK), Sharon Freed (Aus), M Fry, Thomas Gerber (CH), E Goslinga (Nl), Yves Gourves (Fra), Guido Govoni (I), J Grinelley (Aus), Deborah Guner (UK), Dr Michal Harel (Isr), Marie Harlech-Jones, Vic Hatt (Aus), Miss Hayes (UK), J L High, Viv & Kent Holman (Aus), Marie Holstenson, Nick Hone, Mrs & Mr C Horn, Peter Horsfall (UK), Peter Howard (UK), Andrew Howard, Clarissa Hughes, Mrs C Huston (UK), John van Galen Jansen (Nl), Scott Jenkinson (Aus), Ian Johnson (Aus), Peta Jones, Sian Jones (UK), W Joseph, Karyn Kaplan (USA), Denis Kearney, M King (UK), Amy Kingston (UK), James Knight (UK), Kristina Knudsen (Dk), Jon Krog (Dk), Marie Laforest, Dr A Lane (UK), Stephen Lees (Aus), Sonya Lejeune, Vittorio de Leonardis (I), Susan Loucks (USA), Renette Louw, Eleanor Lowe, Anna Lundh (S), Maurice Luttman (Aus), Flemming Lyrdal (S), Beverley Mackie (NZ), Keith Mallinson (UK), Rachel Marcus (UK), Toshiyuki Marutani (J), Elizabeth Masson, C McIntyre, SR McCombie (UK), Peter McIntyre, R J Miles, Dennis J Mitchell (USA), Leonardo Mormandi (It), Alastair Mowson (UK), T Moyo, P Murphy, Ndevashiya Natangwe, Susy Neehouse (Aus), Sheila O'Donohue (Ire), Trevor Parry, Mrs Margie Pearce, Andrew Phillips (UK), Mr Pincus (Aus), Jordan Pollinger, Michael Polster (USA), Caroline Porter (UK), Bram Posthumus (Nl), R Potasznik (USA), James Redmond (C), Dave Reid (UK), Patricia Renny (UK), Mark Ritchie (Aus), Andrea Robbins (USA), C W Roberts, John Robertson (Aus), Drifters Roger, Christina Rood (USA), Edward Rother (USA), Mr & Mrs W Rowell (UK), Ruwa, Graziella Sassoe (I), Andree Schlater (D), Gerda Schreiner, Schreurs (Nl), Luc Selleslagh (B), Mark Seltzer (C), Fanuel Shava, Miss A Sheppard (UK), Ann Shuttleworth (Aus), Keith & Liz Somerville (UK), Eleftheria Soulia (G), A & F Spowart Taylor (UK), Maud Steeman (Nl), Kate Stewart (Aus), T W Stoker, Valerie Stone (USA), Kristin Storey (C), Diane Strebbent (USA), T R Twizell (UK), Anne Uren, Jan van de Graaff (Aus), Joep van de Laar (Nl), C Van der Hedst (NZ), Connie Van Der Hught (NZ), Marc van Doornewaard (Nl), Greg van Druten (Nl), G A Van Loo (Nl), Frank van Rensburg, Stella van Zuijlen (Nl), Michael Ward, Simon EJ Warren (UK), Mrs M C Washaya, Catherine Webster (UK), Martin Weinstein (USA), Petra Peters Wendisch (D), Kate Wheater (UK), Richard Wilcox (J), Alex Wilkinson (UK), Judith Williams (NZ), Kate Worster.

Aus – Australia, C – Canada, CH – Switzerland, D – Germany, Dk – Denmark, F – France, Hun – Hungary, I – Italy, Ire – Ireland, Isr – Israel, J – Japan, Nl – Netherlands, NZ – New Zealand, S – Sweden, Taiw – Taiwan, UK – United Kingdom, USA – United States of America

LONELY PLANET PHRASEBOOKS

LONELY PLANET PHRASEBOOKS

Nepali phrasebook — Listen for the gems

Ethiopian Amharic phrasebook — Speak your own words

Latin American Spanish phrasebook — Ask your own questions

Building bridges,
Breaking barriers,
Beyond babble-on

Ukrainian phrasebook — Master of your own image

Greek phrasebook

Vietnamese phrasebook

- handy pocket-sized books
- easy to understand Pronunciation chapter
- clear and comprehensive Grammar chapter
- romanisation alongside script to allow ease of pronunciation
- script throughout so users can point to phrases
- extensive vocabulary sections, words and phrases for every situations
- full of cultural information and tips for the traveller

'...vital for a real DIY spirit and attitude in language learning' – Backpacker

'the phrasebooks have good cultural backgrounders and offer solid advice for challenging situations in remote locations' – San Francisco Examiner

'...they are unbeatable for their coverage of the world's more obscure languages' – The Geographical Magazine

---

Arabic (Egyptian)
Arabic (Moroccan)
Australia
  Australian English, Aboriginal and Torres Strait languages
Baltic States
  Estonian, Latvian, Lithuanian
Bengali
Burmese
Brazilian
Cantonese
Central Europe
  Czech, French, German, Hungarian, Italian and Slovak
Eastern Europe
  Bulgarian, Czech, Hungarian, Polish, Romanian and Slovak
Egyptian Arabic
Ethiopian (Amharic)
Fijian
Greek
Hindi/Urdu

Indonesian
Japanese
Korean
Lao
Latin American Spanish
Malay
Mandarin
Mediterranean Europe
  Albanian, Croatian, Greek, Italian, Macedonian, Maltese, Serbian, Slovene
Mongolian
Moroccan Arabic
Nepali
Papua New Guinea
Pilipino (Tagalog)
Quechua
Russian
Scandinavian Europe
  Danish, Finnish, Icelandic, Norwegian and Swedish

South-East Asia
  Burmese, Indonesian, Khmer, Lao, Malay, Tagalog (Pilipino), Thai and Vietnamese
Sri Lanka
Swahili
Thai
Thai Hill Tribes
Tibetan
Turkish
Ukrainian
USA
  US English, Vernacular Talk, Native American languages and Hawaiian
Vietnamese
Western Europe
  Basque, Catalan, Dutch, French, German, Irish, Italian, Portuguese, Scottish Gaelic, Spanish (Castilian) and Welsh

---

LONELY PLANET JOURNEYS

JOURNEYS is a unique collection of travel writing – published by the company that understands travel better than anyone else. It is a series for anyone who has ever experienced – or dreamed of – the magical moment when they encountered a strange culture or saw a place for the first time. They are tales to read while you're planning a trip, while you're on the road or while you're in an armchair, in front of a fire.

JOURNEYS books catch the spirit of a place, illuminate a culture, recount a crazy adventure, or introduce a fascinating way of life. They always entertain, and always enrich the experience of travel.

THE RAINBIRD
A Central African Journey
Jan Brokken
translated by Sam Garrett

The Rainbird is a classic travel story. Following in the footsteps of famous Europeans such as Albert Schweitzer and H.M. Stanley, Jan Brokken journeyed to Gabon in central Africa. A kaleidoscope of adventures and anecdotes, *The Rainbird* brilliantly chronicles the encounter between Africa and Europe as it was acted out on a side-street of history. It is also the compelling, immensely readable account of the author's own travels in one of the most remote and mysterious regions of Africa.

Jan Brokken is one of Holland's best known writers. In addition to travel narratives and literary journalism, he has published several novels and short stories. Many of his works are set in Africa, where he has travelled widely.

SONGS TO AN AFRICAN SUNSET
A Zimbabwean Story
Sekai Nzenza-Shand

Songs to an African Sunset braids vividly personal stories into an intimate picture of contemporary Zimbabwe. Returning to her family's village after many years in the West, Sekai Nzenza-Shand discovers a world where ancestor worship, polygamy and witchcraft still govern the rhythms of daily life – and where drought, deforestation and AIDS have wrought devastating changes. With insight and affection, she explores a culture torn between respect for the old ways and the irresistible pull of the new.

Sekai Nzenza-Shand was born in Zimbabwe and has lived in England and Australia. Her first novel, *Zimbabwean Woman: My Own Story*, was published in London in 1988 and her fiction has been included in the short story collections *Daughters of Africa* and *Images of the West*. Sekai currently lives in Zimbabwe.

This project has been assisted by the Commonwealth Government through the Australia Council, its arts funding and advisory body.

LONELY PLANET TRAVEL ATLASES

Lonely Planet has long been famous for the number and quality of its guidebook maps. Now we've gone one step further and in conjunction with Steinhart Katzir Publishers produced a handy companion series: Lonely Planet travel atlases – maps of a country produced in book form.

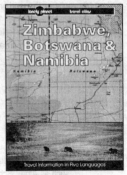

Unlike other maps, which look good but lead travellers astray, our travel atlases have been researched on the road by Lonely Planet's experienced team of writers. All details are carefully checked to ensure the atlas corresponds with the equivalent Lonely Planet guidebook.

The handy atlas format means no holes, wrinkles, torn sections or constant folding and unfolding. These atlases can survive long periods on the road, unlike cumbersome fold-out maps. The comprehensive index ensures easy reference.

- full-colour throughout
- maps researched and checked by Lonely Planet authors
- place names correspond with Lonely Planet guidebooks
  – no confusing spelling differences
- legend and travelling information in English, French, German, Japanese and Spanish
- size: 230 x 160 mm

Available now:
Chile & Easter Island • Egypt • India & Bangladesh • Israel & the Palestinian Territories •Jordan, Syria & Lebanon • Kenya • Laos • Portugal • South Africa, Lesotho & Swaziland • Thailand • Turkey • Vietnam • Zimbabwe, Botswana & Namibia

LONELY PLANET TV SERIES & VIDEOS

Lonely Planet travel guides have been brought to life on television screens around the world. Like our guides, the programmes are based on the joy of independent travel, and look honestly at some of the most exciting, picturesque and frustrating places in the world. Each show is presented by one of three travellers from Australia, England or the USA and combines an innovative mixture of video, Super-8 film, atmospheric soundscapes and original music.

Videos of each episode – containing additional footage not shown on television – are available from good book and video shops, but the availability of individual videos varies with regional screening schedules.

Video destinations include:
Alaska • American Rockies • Australia – The South-East • Baja California & the Copper Canyon • Brazil • Central Asia • Chile & Easter Island • Corsica, Sicily & Sardinia – The Mediterranean Islands • East Africa (Tanzania & Zanzibar) • Ecuador & the Galapagos Islands • Greenland & Iceland • Indonesia • Israel & the Sinai Desert • Jamaica • Japan • La Ruta Maya • Morocco • New York • North India • Pacific Islands (Fiji, Solomon Islands & Vanuatu) • South India • South West China • Turkey • Vietnam • West Africa • Zimbabwe, Botswana & Namibia

The Lonely Planet TV series is produced by:
Pilot Productions
The Old Studio
18 Middle Row
London W10 5AT UK

For video availability and ordering information contact your nearest Lonely Planet office.

Music from the TV series is available on CD & cassette.

LONELY PLANET PRODUCTS

Lonely Planet is known worldwide for publishing practical, reliable and no-nonsense travel information in our guides and on our web site. The Lonely Planet list covers just about every accessible part of the world. Currently there are eight series: *travel guides*, *shoestring guides*, *walking guides*, *city guides*, *phrasebooks*, *audio packs*, *travel atlases* and *Journeys* – a unique collection of travel writing.

EUROPE

Amsterdam • Austria • Baltic States phrasebook • Britain • Central Europe on a shoestring • Central Europe phrasebook • Czech & Slovak Republics • Denmark • Dublin • Eastern Europe on a shoestring • Eastern Europe phrasebook • Estonia, Latvia & Lithuania • Finland • France • Greece • Greek phrasebook • Hungary • Iceland, Greenland & the Faroe Islands • Ireland • Italy • Mediterranean Europe on a shoestring • Mediterranean Europe phrasebook • Paris • Poland • Portugal • Portugal travel atlas • Prague • Russia, Ukraine & Belarus • Russian phrasebook • Scandinavian & Baltic Europe on a shoestring • Scandinavian Europe phrasebook • Slovenia • Spain • Spanish phrasebook • St Petersburg • Switzerland • Trekking in Greece • Trekking in Spain • Ukrainian phrasebook • Vienna • Walking in Britain • Walking in Switzerland • Western Europe on a shoestring • Western Europe phrasebook

NORTH AMERICA

Alaska • Backpacking in Alaska • Baja California • California & Nevada • Canada • Florida • Hawaii • Honolulu • Los Angeles • Mexico • Miami • New England • New Orleans • New York, New Jersey & Pennsylvania • Pacific Northwest USA • Rocky Mountain States • San Francisco • Southwest USA • USA phrasebook • Washington, DC & the Capital Region

CENTRAL AMERICA & THE CARIBBEAN

Bermuda • Central America on a shoestring • Costa Rica • Cuba • Eastern Caribbean • Guatemala, Belize & Yucatán: La Ruta Maya • Jamaica

SOUTH AMERICA

Argentina, Uruguay & Paraguay • Bolivia • Brazil • Brazilian phrasebook • Buenos Aires • Chile & Easter Island • Chile & Easter Island travel atlas • Colombia • Ecuador & the Galápagos Islands • Latin American Spanish phrasebook • Peru • Quechua phrasebook • Rio de Janeiro • South America on a shoestring • Trekking in the Patagonian Andes • Venezuela

Travel Literature: Full Circle: A South American Journey

ANTARCTICA

Antarctica

ISLANDS OF THE INDIAN OCEAN

Madagascar & Comoros • Maldives• Mauritius, Réunion & Seychelles

AFRICA

Africa on a shoestring • Arabic (Moroccan) phrasebook • • Cape Town • Central Africa • East Africa • Egypt • Egypt travel atlas• Ethiopian (Amharic) phrasebook • Kenya • Kenya travel atlas • Malawi, Mozambique & Zambia • Morocco • North Africa • South Africa, Lesotho & Swaziland • South Africa, Lesotho & Swaziland travel atlas • Swahili phrasebook • Trekking in East Africa • West Africa • Zimbabwe, Botswana & Namibia • Zimbabwe, Botswana & Namibia travel atlas

Travel Literature: The Rainbird: A Central African Journey • Songs to an African Sunset: A Zimbabwean Story